an evening of **Pride & Inspiration**

In loving memory of an unforgettable man
Ernie Markel
In commemoration of his Yartzeit
With love from his grandchildren
Russell, Ivy, Harper and Aidan Herman

May 13, 2014 - 13 Iyar 5774

Bread and Fire

Jewish Women Find God
in the Everyday

Bread and Fire

Jewish Women Find God in the Everyday

edited by Rivkah Slonim
consulting editor: Liz Rosenberg

URIM PUBLICATIONS
Jerusalem • New York

Bread and Fire: Jewish Women Find God in the Everyday

Edited by Rivkah Slonim, consulting editor: Liz Rosenberg

Layout design by Satya Levine

Printed at Hemed Press, Israel. First Edition.

ISBN-13: 978-965-524-002-3

ISBN-10: 965-524-002-9

Urim Publications

P.O. Box 52287, Jerusalem 91521 Israel

Lambda Publishers Inc.

3709 13th Avenue Brooklyn, New York 11218 U.S.A.

Tel: 718-972-5449 Fax: 718-972-6307, mh@ejudaica.com

www.UrimPublications.com

Contents

II. HOME AND FAMILY

III. COMMUNITY AND BEYOND

It is not by bread alone that man lives,
but by all that comes out of God's mouth.

– Deuteronomy 8:3

In loving memory of my grandparents,

Rabbi Schneur Zalman and Rebbetzin Chava Gurary,

with love and gratitude for the bread
and fire they gave me.

Acknowledgments

It has been said that an anthology is a labor of love; it takes passion and a deep kind of engagement with the subject matter. That said, it takes a great amount of assistance and cooperation as well. It is my pleasure to thank the many people who have assisted me in significant ways with this project.

Firstly, I thank the thousands of women – some who have become acquaintances and even friends but most of whom remain nameless – whom I have met over my years of travel and public speaking on the subject of women and Judaism. Their incisive questions and comments served as the catalyst for this collection and continue to fuel my interest in this important subject. In the same vein I thank my students, especially the women who, over the years, have come through the doors of our Chabad House. In our discussions and heated arguments about the role of women in Jewish life they forced me to consider these issue in wholly new ways, prodding me to move more deeply into my studies. Truly they were my most effective teachers.

I thank each one of the contributors to this volume. Their voices make this a book that speaks to the mind, heart and soul in a deep and meaningful way.

For her unstinting assistance and support with this project from its inception, I thank my dear friend Michla Schanowitz. She gave me encouragement, astute advice and practical help whenever I sought it and for this I am deeply grateful. I thank Susan Handelman for her sincere encouragement from the very beginning and for the many connections she so generously offered me. To Chana Silberstein goes my appreciation for her wise advice and specifically for her assistance with this book's title.

For their careful reading of and insightful comments on my introduction I thank Shaindel Muller, Michla Schanowitz, Rabbi Immanuel Schochet and Gila Shaw, to whom I also extend special appreciation for her feedback on the project as a whole and her input regarding the side bars and the order of the essays. I thank Yanki Tauber for his trailblazing work in rendering kabbalistic and Chassidic concepts accessible to the modern reader (particularly regarding the masculine and feminine). I have drawn deeply from his work and am sure it has found its way into my introduction. Special thanks go to Dr. Tamar Frankiel for her scrupulous attention to each word and subtlety and for drawing my attention to the date of the Seneca Conference and its confluence with important changes in the spiritual arena. For their careful proofreading of the manuscript I thank my friends Ann Brillant and Marlene Serkin. Special thanks to artist Karla Waller, whose original art graces the book cover and title page of each essay, and to Sara Esther Crispe, editor of the award-winning JewishWoman.org, for connecting us.

On the home front, I thank my parents, Rabbi Menachem Nochum and Mrs. Esther Sternberg, tireless champions of their children's work and accomplishments and an infinite source of strength and support to us all; my parents-in-law, Rabbi Zeev Dov and Rebbetzin Gitel Leah Slonim, who while far from us geographically are always close at heart; my sisters and sisters-in-law, my brothers and brothers-in-law, each of whom has enriched my life enormously; my paternal grandparents, Rabbi Mordechai and Rebbetzin Gitel Sternberg, *aleihem ha-sholom,* and my maternal grandparents, Rabbi Schneur Zalman and Rebbetzin Chava Gurary, *aleihem ha-sholom.* My grandparents are the roots of our large and far-flung family; we benefit from their strength and nurturing every day.

From the depth of my heart I thank my husband Rabbi Aaron Slonim, my anchor in this project as in every facet of our lives together. It is due to his wisdom, love and generous support that I have been able to follow my dreams and live such a blessed and rich existence. To our beloved children – Levi, Chany, Yehudah, Shmuly, Chaya Mushkah, Yisroel, Mendel, Motty and Schneur Zalman – goes my appreciation for their tolerance of Mommy's projects and the interest and moral support they constantly display. I pray that Aaron and I merit to raise them to Torah, to Chupah and to good deeds together, in good health and happiness. And to a special member of our family, Carol, goes my thanks for everything – we can't do it without you!

Acharona acharona chaviva – the last, our sages have taught, is the most beloved. In closing, I extend my deepest gratitude to my friend and teacher, Liz Rosenberg, the advisory editor of this volume. Liz, an award-winning author and poet and much-sought-after teacher of creative writing, brought spectacular God-given talent and years of hard-earned experience to this work. Beyond that she brought a spiritual sensitivity and deep understanding of human nature and the complexity of our lives to every contribution to this collection. I thank her deeply for the many gifts she has given me: her time, love, encouragement, and the many, many lessons in writing and in life that she has taught me. I pray that Hashem bless her and her beautiful family with all good.

80 CR

I am profoundly humbled, yet privileged and deeply grateful, to number myself among the Chassidim of the Rebbe, Rabbi Menachem M. Schneerson, of blessed memory. It is his wisdom and inspiration that are at the heart and soul of my life. His singular teachings on the subject of Jewish womanhood and his radically forward-thinking posture on this subject may have done more to advance the cause of Jewish women than anything else over the last few decades but remain, for many, an as-yet-undiscovered gift. I hope that this volume contributes in some small measure to the fulfillment of his vision: a world in which women and men raise their voices and maximize their gifts in the service of the Almighty.

In this vein, I give thanks to the Ribbono Shel Olam, the Master of our Universe, for the opportunity to complete this project on Zos Chanukah, the last day of Chanukah, 5765. May Chanukah's lesson – the victory of light over might, spirit over matter – illuminate our lives' paths always.

Preface

This is a book about the lives of Jewish women: their struggles and dreams, their aspirations, failings and triumphs within the arena of their spiritual endeavors.

The women who share their lives in this volume span a wide range of age, educational background, religious orientation and profession. Each in her own way reveals God as the anchoring force in their disparate lives: in the birthing room and in the boardroom, in the kitchen and while scrubbing down for surgery, in Jerusalem and Southern India. Each of them helps us find the sacred within the apparently mundane.

Some of us have traveled far – literally and figuratively – from our roots, in a quest for meaning. Today we are retracing our steps, hungry to form an authentic relationship with our Creator. I believe that we may finally be ready to take an honest look and find that what is ancient can also be new and surprisingly relevant: Judaism is first and always a home-based religion; a faith that builds far more upon our personal commitments than upon even the most elaborate communal institutions.

We all have moments of existential reflection. We might question why we are here. We might doubt our ability to make a difference, or despair of connecting to our inner self and to God.

Many of us spend a lot of time in search of the inner "I." But our moments of truth often come at those times when we lose ourselves within something larger, be it family or community. Those feelings of mystical connection to God come when we least expect them, triggered often, it seems, by the most unlikely, even prosaic, events. From deep within rises a surprisingly strong response. If we listen, we might hear ourselves echo that primal, supra-rational declaration wrenched from our ancestors' souls at Sinai: *Na'aseh* – we will do!

Bread and Fire addresses these questions: What can it mean to be a Jewish woman today? Does the Jewish tradition offer ways in which a contemporary woman can bring spirituality and meaning to her life? How and where does one begin in a practical way?

This collection offers teachings and ruminations, reassurance and fortitude, as we come face to face with women moving forward in the ancient quest to find God in the everyday.

Perspective

Before I knew the word feminism, it knew me. I had been raised in a home and community with many strong influences. The men and women who served as my role models were powerful figures – equally so – and if being a girl was an impediment, I never knew it. I felt supported, important and fulfilled. As a young child, I would have been shocked to hear that people were actually treated as inferior because of their gender or to learn of women who hated being women. Yet I had been raised in a strictly observant Jewish home, the kind often described as ultra-Orthodox or fanatic. If women were happy within that patriarchal construct, went the cliché, they could best be compared to slaves smiling in the sun. Why the divergence between my experience and this perception?

I remember a Friday morning some fifteen years ago when I was a young wife and mother visiting with my parents and grandparents, who live next door to each other in a row of Brooklyn homes in New York City. I had been grappling with the intersection of women and observance within traditional Jewish law. I had studied the classic sources and sought new texts in search of answers. I was mostly at peace with tradition, but a part of me was agitated. Why were women excused from certain obligations and actually barred from others? I knew that women were exempt from many time-bound mitzvot in order to allow them the freedom to raise their families. I also knew that some of the differences in gendered roles were rooted in modesty, a value that I deeply appreciate, and still other differences were connected to spiritual journeys women need not undertake since in a certain sense they were already there. That was all the larger picture. But when I looked at the individual details, when I encountered certain situations, I worried: did women somehow end up with the short end of the stick? Were we being cheated out of important opportunities in our religious lives and expression?

I still remember the feeling of righteous indignation that filled me and spilled over as I ran into my grandparents' kitchen that Friday morning, determined to discuss these issues with my learned grandfather. I wanted answers and I wanted them right away. Instead, I was arrested by a scene so pure that I can still feel its power today.

In one corner, my grandfather, wrapped in his *tallit* and *tefillin*, was completing his morning prayers; in the other, my grandmother was concentrating on her prayers as she fulfilled the Biblical commandment of *challah*, taking a portion of one's dough and designating it as sacred unto God. I felt like a trespasser on holy ground. They were both completely immersed in conversation with God: intimate conversation, loving conversation, in a place where little else mattered. In that moment, my perfectly valid questions concerning equal access for women within Judaism seemed somehow unworthy. If it was truly service of God I was after, if what I honestly craved was that connection, then I had found my answer in the devotions that filled the room. My grandparents' love of and sense of connection to God was just as palpable as their deep love for each other. Neither one of them was thinking about self-actualization or equal opportunity. Yet they had achieved it.

My questions did not vanish into thin air. Much like that carnival game in which shooting down one duck causes another to pop up in its stead, there are and always will be more issues to address. Such is the nature of a world still unperfected, fragmented, and awaiting redemption. It begs for explanation and cries out for rectification. But now I ask my questions with less arrogance and a little more honesty. I understand that finding the proper context – the larger framework – for our queries may just be the biggest challenge of all.

My personal experience might be explained through a combination of socialization and my ignorance of a wider world filled with different realities. But why are so many women raised in secular homes and egalitarian societies drawn to a traditional way of life so widely described as sexist? Why do so many Jewish women, regardless of their background, find deep meaning and resonance in observances that were pronounced archaic and meaningless decades ago?

I believe that finding answers to these questions necessitates our stepping across a border to a different place. *Bread and Fire* is a collection of writings by women who write about their day-to-day lives as Jews. It is not a book about "women's issues." It does not address questions such as why according to *halakha*, Jewish law, women can't complete the *minyan* (the quorum of ten men necessary for public prayer), why they are not called up for an *aliya* to the Torah, or even why men recite that famous blessing in the morning thanking God that they were not created women. I am an avid student of these issues. But even more urgent, it seems to me, is an exploration of the larger system of actions and beliefs we call Judaism, against or within which these important issues are set. It is within this larger context, the landscape of spiritual experiences that fill the lives of Jewish women – many of them far from the public eye – that we can understand these issues properly.

I hope *Bread and Fire* grants readers access to this new territory, a uniquely Jewish land where previous assumptions are challenged, held up to a new light.

Seen through the lens of Western societal values where the inalienable rights of an individual are sacred and equal access and opportunity are the means towards that end, religion – which is by definition autocratic as opposed to democratic – may well be termed sexist. Compared to society in general, where the struggle for power and control – often between men and women – looms large, Judaism appears out of step. But that perception ignores a crucial difference between Western, or modern, life and Jewish life. Jewish life is not about rights or power or access. In Jewish life the point of departure and return is not the self; it is God. Judaism is neither patriarchal nor matriarchal – it is covenantal.

℘ ℆

In the time before time, before space, before limitations, God had a desire. The masters of Kabbalah and Hasidism expound upon the midrashic teaching that God craved a "dwelling place below." Unlike the celestial sphere in which He alone defined reality, this dwelling place would allow room for a multi-faceted, complex existence that offered ongoing need and opportunity for choice. And so, in a process that the Kabbalah terms *tzimtzum*, God contracted or withdrew His infinite light to create a physical space that skillfully masks its creator. This space has come to be known as the world. It is instructive that in the Holy Tongue, the word for world is *olam*, which is etymologically rooted in the word *he'elem*, which means "shrouded" or "obscured."

Into this new space God placed the Adam creature, a wholly original design with the ability to choose – or reject – its creator. Its being spoke of conflict and choice. Created as it was of two ingredients, earth and the Godly spirit, the human being would simultaneously and constantly be pulled towards heaven and earth.

Only humankind could fulfill God's ultimate desire: namely, that a being seemingly independent from its creator would choose to live in service of its maker. This being could infuse the material world with Godliness. Judaism teaches that God created everything from nothing; a popular Chassidic adage adds that humanity's job is to create nothing from everything – that is, to peer behind the curtain of pluralistic existence and reveal the unifying reality. Our job is to see through and beyond the façade of multiplicity, to perceive the Godly spark inherent in all matter and restore creation's essential, eternal One-ness.

There is a name for this process: *mitzvot*. Widely understood to mean "good deeds," *mitzvot* are more correctly defined as bridges or connections; the connecting points between the infinite God and the finite people He created.

How can God "need" humanity? This is indeed a central conundrum in Judaism. But God desires humankind's voluntary embrace. The fulfillment of mitzvot – those between humanity and God and those between person and person – is the fruition of His desire, the reason for creation.

Central to Jewish philosophy is the idea of *bechira chofshit*, freedom to choose. But the choice is more limited than we might suspect.

As the Talmud succinctly puts it: *Hakol bidei shomayim chutz me-yirat shomayim* – all is in the hands of Heaven except for the fear of Heaven. Almost everything about our lives is predestined: the family into which we will be born, our gender, our genetic makeup, our intellectual capacity, our talents, etc. Our personal choices may effect "detours," but the ultimate ends are predestined. The only area of true choice is in our moral decisions: we can embrace God or we can spurn Him. Judaism teaches that everything else, including our Jewish identity, is determined.

Modernity posits the self as an autonomous being with endless choices and infinite possibilities. There is no single imperative. Human beings can do as they choose, shedding one prospect for another like an old coat. These possibilities include, of course, one's religious orientation or lack of it. From the perspective of tradition, however, one's identity as a Jew is the most essential definition of the self. The term *Jew* is not an adjective but a noun. It cannot be replaced or discarded. It is not something we choose; it chooses us eternally. When we say "I am a Jew," we refer not to our bodies but to our souls. Accordingly, every Jew, by birth or by choice, is locked into a covenant with God. We are left only to choose the degree to which we will actively engage ourselves in this arrangement. The covenant is the single most enduring feature of Jewish life.

It is here that we encounter another pivotal distinction between Western life and Jewish life. As moderns, we are raised to revere the inalienable rights of the individual. We cherish our rights and zealously guard against their erosion. Many have argued that the notions of respect and sensitivity for each individual are rooted in the Jewish tradition. While this may be true, the foundation of the Jewish religion is the concept of obligation. The Torah legislates the individual obligations of man, woman, parent, child, spouse, teacher, healer, and the communal obligations of society towards its creator, towards the environment and towards itself, especially its more vulnerable segments. It is a radically different paradigm, and within it a person's quest for individual rights often yields to the more pressing question of one's duties and commitments to the community. The fulfillment of obligations is one's most important responsibility and greatest privilege.

Unquestionably, women have equal obligation and opportunity in realizing God's plan for the universe. Just as clearly, they have their own strengths, modes of expression, and areas of concentration.

One of the basic tasks of feminism is to combat the premise that women are less important or worthy than men. Society does not do much to foster a woman's sense of worth. On the contrary, it often seems that a woman can prove her worth only in so far as she is able to prove herself to be "like a man." But a woman who is certain that her position and function was ordained by God, that her overtures in that direction are cherished by her creator, recognizes her femininity as a strength, is certain of her worth, and can use her powers to the full.

Chief among the world's dichotomies is the presence of male and female. Shortly after creation of the first Adam creature – a dimorphic being comprised of both male and female characteristics – God declared His intention to change that model: *lo tov heyot adam levado*, said God. "It is not good for a human being to be alone." No longer would Adam be a self-contained entity. Separating woman from man created an opposing force, a different type of human being with distinct energies and contributions. Only by recognizing and respecting these differences and allowing them to develop could humankind actualize God's vision of a dwelling place below.

God's separation of woman from man is a mirror image of His own "partition." The decision to enter into a relationship with humankind meant that the male and female aspects of the Godhead would be divided. The feminine, the *Shechina*, God's immanence, would be separated from the masculine, *Kudsha Brich Hu*, God's transcendent quality. We would relate to and feel comforted by the God within, by the closeness of the Divine presence as it hovers, and we would be awed by, and sometimes wrestle with, the God above and beyond us.

In creating a space in which human beings could operate autonomously, God opened up a space that can be described as "free" or "empty." Humankind's role is to reinstate this original light, and not surprisingly, Kabbalah and Hasidic philosophy teach that this exercise requires a binary approach.

The infinite light that was banished at creation must be re-imported from beyond the circumscribed space known as *olam*. Through the fulfillment of mitzvot, we draw upon this original, primordial light and bring it back into our arena. Simultaneously, we engage in mitzvot that uncover the Godly light that remained always within this world. When we speak of *tzimtzum*, we do not mean that God allowed for a space bereft of His light but rather that it was cloaked, beyond our perception.

It is possible to understand this duality as related to male and female modes of spiritual service. The male trajectory is often linked with conquest and reconfiguration, moving things from one domain to another. The female modality is more aligned with the inner dimension, with nourishing and nurturing, cultivating that which exists. He contributes the sperm; she, an ovum generated deep within her body, and the womb, the space in which the child will grow, together with the nutrients, fluid and oxygen necessary to its development. It is quiet and not always appreciated work, this powerful state of active passivity.

To succeed in our life's work as individuals we must harmonize our masculine and feminine characteristics. To fulfill humankind's essential mission we must understand, value and utilize the contributions of both male and female.

For thousands of years, it has been a man's world, a world saturated with male energy. Although throughout history women have made immense physical and spiritual contributions without which the world could not be sustained, the male force has been more highly valued. The spiritual source for this is easy to trace. The creation of this world can be understood as a state of being in which God takes on a more feminine, passive mode, waiting for mankind to fulfill its mandate, to rise towards God. Likewise, the six days of the week are a time for work – harnessing and transforming the world's resources and energies. Kabbalistically, we understand this to be a male modality. Little wonder, then, that it is primarily the more outward expressions of physical and spiritual service that were, and continue to be, appreciated and publicly extolled.

According to Jewish tradition the world can exist in its present form for six thousand years, after which time the Messianic era must commence. Tradition teaches that like the Sabbath that comes after six days of labor, the Redemption that follows six millennia of spiritual toil will be a time of receptivity. God's light, which was previously contracted, shrouded and obscured, will manifest. Creation will be exposed for the thin veneer it is and humankind will arch upwards towards its Creator, aware of and at peace with our source. Unleashed during this era will be the female energy referred to in Kabbalistic terminology as *Malkhut*, sovereignty.

One of the greatest social changes to sweep the world, including the Jewish world, has been the rise of the feminine consciousness. The women's movement of the last century and a half is surely an expression of a celestial truth. It is no coincidence that the event recognized as the beginning of the women's movement – the Seneca Falls convention of 1848 – occurred shortly after the era designated by the *Zohar*, the seminal book of Jewish mysticism, as that of a new "flood" – not a physical flood, as in Noah's time, but the opening of a floodgate of secular and spiritual knowledge. From this time, the approach of the Messianic era intensifies in all realms and, as we move closer, the dormant feminine powers struggle to be free.

In a painful irony, however, the rightful assertion of a woman's place and worth has often taken the form of woman imitating man. We cannot afford this loss. What this world needs most is not more men or doubled male energy but rather the full-bodied contributions of women. *Zakhar u-nekeva bara otam* – male and female did He create them.

₱₱

The big surprise, the wild card in the feminist movement, is how after all these years and seismic shifts in our social landscape, so much remains the same. Women still light Shabbat and holiday candles, bake *challah,* raise children, visit the sick, comfort the afflicted and help bury the dead. It is humbling to learn through our new-found interest in women's history that our generation did not discover or invent spirituality and that our grandmothers' religion offers such a warm and rich homecoming.

Bread and Fire presents readers with an intimate, panoramic view of Jewish women engaged in an effort to embrace God, an effort that goes back to the beginning of time. It offers teachings, inspiration and practical advice for our own labors. It offers insight into the birth pangs of the feminine energies that are trying to emerge now, the sparks that will become a new light for all humanity in the Messianic era.

The three sections of this collection – Self, Home and Family, and Community and Beyond – speak to three central arenas of spiritual service. In an apt reflection of Hillel's dictum, "If I am not for myself, who will be for me? And if I am only for myself, what am I?" (*Avot* 1:14), there is significant overlap between the sections. Again and again women's lives show themselves inextricably woven of these three strands.

Some of the voices have a calm strength. These women's spiritual lives appear to be of a seamless cloth. In others, however, we hear conflict and ongoing search. Serving God and their own needs – not to mention those of family and community – often has them locked in a struggle. Some of the voices are steeped in the fine points of Torah knowledge, while for others, Jewish learning is a journey newly embarked upon.

In all these voices we hear a reverence for something larger than the self. We recognize a tempo of discipline. We identify that same determination and strength displayed by our foremothers spanning the generations.

I believe these writings speak to a deep desire; a need we have to connect to that which has eternal value, and through this endeavor, to leave this world a better place than we found it. In the end, we all want to have a grandchild who might run in, unannounced, to our kitchen one Friday morning, to find not only bread but a fire that will sustain them.

For further reading:

Schneider, Sarah. *Kabbalistic Writings on the Nature of Masculine and Feminine.* Lanham, MD: 2001
    Available by contacting the author directly at smlvoice@netvision.net.il.
Frankiel, Tamar. *The Gift of Kabbalah.* Woodstock, Vermont: 2001.
Schochet, Jacob Immanuel. *Mystical Concepts in Chassidism.* Brooklyn, NY: 1979.

Self

A sound! My beloved knocks! He said; "Open your heart to Me, My sister, My love, My dove, My perfection…"

Song of Songs 5:2

Introduction

What is the self if not the soul, striving valiantly and ceaselessly to be at peace with – to fulfill the wishes of – its creator? But the soul's vessel and partner in this task, the human personality, has its own drives and agenda and is most often oblivious to the wishes of its creator. Although the world offers unparalleled opportunity for spiritual endeavor, its material, corporeal face pushes for physical gratification above all. The animal soul within is locked in endless pursuit of the tangible and readily available. The Godly soul agitates and exercises, striving mightily to be heard above the static. Accosted as we are, within and without, by energies and drives that run contrary to God's wishes, it is small wonder that our religious devotions are often the culmination of a prolonged battle to put God's will above our own.

It is taught that when the Written Law was compiled into what we now refer to as the Tanakh, a great controversy erupted. The majority of sages felt that *Shir ha-Shirim*, the Song of Songs, was too sexually explicit to be included in sacred scripture. Indeed, that portion of the Jewish scriptures is a love story richly described in all its physical dimensions.

Rabbi Akiva alone dissented. He taught that the Song of Songs was the holiest book in the canon, a powerful metaphor for the love shared by God and the Jewish people. The Song of Songs teaches that our archetypal relationship with God was never meant to be platonic; played out in the abstract, theoretical, metaphysical realm alone. On the contrary, Judaism is very much an organic religion, a nexus of the body and soul; lips on lips, flesh on flesh. Judaism means allowing God into every aspect of our lives, an all-pervasive experience. It means rising upward and opening ourselves to accept God into our lives even when it is not easy.

This section showcases women locked in this struggle with the self. These women are real. They want to pray with deeper intent. They want to forgive those who have wronged them and be more careful of how they speak of others. They want to channel their sexuality properly, to dress with dignity and modesty. One battles her addiction to food, another grapples with the male gender attributed to God. One woman in the process of committing to *kashrut* wrestles with the demands of her children who clamor for fast food, while another shares her battle with house-cleaning for Passover and the spiritual insights she has gleaned from the process. Yet another woman rises above the pain and primal urges of childbirth to find a point of connection to the Divine.

These women want to lay claim to their traditions and add their link to the chain of Jewish women who preceded them. They want to bring their power as Jews and as women to full bloom.

With conviction and iron will they work to uncover their essential selves. In the minutiae of their everyday lives, they strive to bring their souls to the fore. In the final analysis, it is this struggle that defines the religious experience: sublimating – or ideally, rechanneling – our egos, our desires, our agendas so that they become aligned with the fulfillment of God's desires.

Where is God's dwelling? Wherever human beings let Him in.

R. Menachem Mendel of Kotzk

Connecting Up

Rachel Naomi Remen, MD

Consecrating the Ordinary

Soon after I moved to California from New York, I planted a vegetable garden. I had never seen fresh vegetables except in a supermarket, and the first year I found an endless fascination in this tiny garden. I especially loved the lettuce which I had planted tightly in a square whose edges I harvested for dinner every night. One evening, I had gone out to pick the salad as usual and ran a hand lightly over the crisp green square of lettuce leaves, marveling at its vitality, almost as if it were bubbling up out of the ground. Suddenly words from my childhood came back to me, words that I had heard countless times over the dinner tables of aunts and uncles and knew by heart, words that I heard now for the first time:

Blessed art Thou O Lord, King of the Universe who bringest forth bread from the earth.

Far from being the usual meaningless mumble, these words suddenly were a potent description of something real, a statement about grace and the mystery of life itself. Up until then I had taken this blessing as a theory or a hypothesis, someone's idea of how things worked. I had no idea that these familiar words were simply a description of something true. I had never witnessed them happening in the world before.

I had done ritual the way I had done life. Automatically. Life can become habit, something done without thinking. Living life in this way does not awaken us. Yet any of our daily habits can awaken us. All of life can become ritual. When it does, our experience of life changes radically and the ordinary becomes

---

* Excerpted from her book *Kitchen Table Wisdom: Stories That Heal.*

consecrated. Ritual doesn't make mystery happen. It helps us see and experience something which is already real. It does not create the sacred, it only describes what is there and has always been there, deeply hidden in the obvious.

Connecting Up

Perhaps the wisdom lies not in the constant struggle to bring the sacred into daily life but in the recognition that there may be no daily life, that life is committed and whole and, despite appearances, we are always on sacred ground. In the midst of daily living ritual can become a way of remembering this.

A young patient, newly recovered from surgery, told me this story of preparing food to celebrate the holiday of Passover for her Orthodox Jewish sweetheart and forty of their friends. One of the basic beliefs of Judaism is that the home is sacred ground, a place of religious ceremony and ritual. Many of these rituals involve eating, and range from the simplicity of the washing of hands and the blessing of Sabbath wine and bread to the enormous complexity of the Passover dinner. My patient, who was Jewish by background, was raised by people who had lapsed in their observance of the religion and she had never participated in the preparation of the Passover dinner before. Her young man, however, had celebrated the holiday yearly since infancy and had helped his mother make the same preparations year after year. He knew them by heart and he taught her.

The kosher law prohibits eating milk products with meat products. She was surprised to discover that a traditional Jewish kitchen has four complete sets of dishes, pots, silverware, and cooking tools. One set is used daily for food containing milk, and a complete second set is for foods that contain meat. These dishes are never commingled and her friend had two dishwashers and two sinks in his kitchen. In addition to these two sets of dishes there are two more sets, one for milk and the other for meat, which are used only at the time of Passover. Tradition decrees that at this time the daily dishes and utensils are put away in cabinets that are both separate and sealed shut and the holiday dishes are then brought out to prepare the Passover dinner. It is a formidable undertaking.

All this almost overwhelmed her. "Rachel," she said, "you have never seen so many dishes, pots, knives and forks, and pancake turners. It all seemed really pointless to me, but it was so terribly important to Herbert and I was terrified of making a mistake and ruining things for him. But a really strange thing happened. Sometime in the middle of setting up things, I was standing by myself in the kitchen with my arms filled with the everyday milk dishes, looking around me desperately for some shelf room to be able to seal them away. Every shelf was full. I remember thinking, 'Where am I going to put these daily milk dishes?' and suddenly I was not alone. I had a very real sense of the presence of the many women who had ever asked themselves this very ordinary question, thousands and thousands of them, some young, some old, in tents, in villages, in cities. Women holding dishes made of clay and wood and tin, women dressed in medieval clothing, in skins, in crudely woven fabrics and styles I had never seen. Among them were my own grandmothers who had lived and died in Warsaw before I was born.

"In that same instant I also knew that if the human race continued there would be women dressed in fabrics I could not even imagine, holding dishes made of materials not yet invented, who would be standing in their kitchens facing this same problem. Women who had not yet been born. They were there too. In the blink of an eye, alone in Herbert's kitchen, I was in the company of women across more than five thousand years. And too, at that very moment all over the world there were women asking themselves this very question in every human language, 'Where do I put these daily milk dishes?' And I was among them, too.

"Well, Rachel, I almost dropped the dishes, I was so surprised. And it is hard to put it into words, but this was not just an idea, it was more like a happening. I had this vast perspective. I knew myself to be a thread in a great tapestry woven by women in the name of God since the beginning. You would think this would make you feel small, but it didn't. I was a single thread, but I belonged, something I had never experienced before. For a few seconds I had a glimpse of something larger, not only of who I am but Whose I am. It only lasted for a second, but I can remember it very clearly. I feel changed by it."

Judaism considers food a visible manifestation of the covenant between man and God. There is a special way to prepare the food as well as special dishes on which to eat specific sorts of food; special blessings to be said over the food and over the cooking. In the life of a woman who prepares food in this way and maintains the kosher kitchen with all its ritual complexity, God can become almost as tangible as the stove.

What If God Blinks?

When I was small, God was still discussed in the public schools. I remember one assembly in which our principal, a fundamentalist, delivered a fire-and-brimstone kind of sermon to the entire grammar school. She read a passage from the Bible to us and told us it was important that we kneel and pray three times a day because we needed to remind God that we were there. Thinking back, she may not have said this in so many words, but this is what I took away. You prayed because you had to make Him look at you. If God turned His face from you, she told the hushed assembly of children, you would wither up and die, like an autumn leaf. And this part I am sure of, she actually held up a large dried and withered leaf. Even as a five-year-old it seemed to me that God had a lot of other things on His mind besides me. And in between the times that I was praying, He might blink and then what would become of me? I remember the fear, the enormous terror. What if God blinks? I became so obsessed with this question, so fearful, I was unable to sleep.

My parents were young socialists who considered religion to be "the opiate of the masses," and my grandfather, who was a rabbi, was my only connection to a reality larger than social well-being and the class struggle. When I was this small, I actually thought of God as a friend of his, like the men who came over to smoke cigars and play gin rummy in our kitchen with my father.

As these fears were not something I could discuss with my parents, I had to wait until my grandfather visited. It was probably only a few days, but I remember the waiting. I don't think you can feel such anguish and aloneness as an adult. You have to be very young.

When I finally got my grandfather to myself I told him what had happened. Shaking, I asked him the fearful question: "What if God blinks?" and at last my terror overwhelmed me and I leaned against his shoulder and began to cry. My grandfather stroked my hair to comfort me. Despite his gentleness he seemed distressed and even angry.

But in his usual calm way, he answered my question with some questions of his own. "Nashume-le," he said (and by the way, for years I thought that my grandfather's name for me meant "Little Naomi" – it actually means "Little Soul"), "if you woke up in the night in your room, would you know if your mother and father had gone out and left you alone in the house?" Still crying, I nodded yes. "How would you know that?" he asked. "Would you see them and look at them?" I shook my head no.

"Would you hear them?"

"No."

"Could you touch them?"

By then I had stopped crying and I remember puzzling over his questions because it seemed obvious to me that I would simply know that I wasn't alone in the house. I told him this and he nodded, pleased. "Good! Good! That's how God knows you're there. He doesn't need to look at you to know that you are there. He just knows. In just the same way you know that God is there. You just know that He is there and you're not alone in the house."

God's presence in the house is an inner experience that never changes. It's a relationship that's there all the time, even when we're not paying attention to it.

Perhaps the Infinite holds us to itself in the same way the earth does. Like gravity, if it ever stopped we would know it instantly. But it never does.

This inner knowing is a way in which I orient myself, an unfailing point of reference. Its effect on my life is as profound, as deep as gravity's influence on my body. More than anything else, my sense of not being alone in the house has been what has allowed me to accompany people as they meet with pain, illness, and sometimes death.

For further reading:

Remen, Rachel Naomi, MD. *Kitchen Table Wisdom: Stories That Heal*. New York: 1996.

Twerski, Abraham J., MD. *I'd Like to Call for Help, But I Don't Know the Number: The Search for Spirituality in Everyday Life*. New York, NY: 1996.

When the King Was Alive

When the king was alive,
the glory of the princess
was within
in the house.
Now the house is in shambles.
When the king was alive
there was modesty,
there was celebration.
When the king was alive,
The Sabbath was roses;
now it's a wound.
When the king was alive,
the heart's thoughts were birds
flying about in the evening,
waiting for evening's rest.
Now my roots are exposed
and people trample them.

Zelda,
Translated from the Hebrew by Marcia Falk

A Little Bit Innocent?

Wendy Shalit

My father is an economist, of the Chicago-school variety, so my earliest memories concern Coase's theorem, Stigler's laws, and the importance of buying and selling rights to pollute. Other children played in bundles of blankets and were scared of monsters; I played with imaginary bundles of competing currencies which would float, but really be more stable, and had nightmares that the Federal Reserve Board would ruin the business cycle. The fact that I was a girl never really came up. It was like having blue eyes, just a fact about me. On occasion, I would experience being a girl as a kind of special bonus: it meant getting to be a cheerleader and later, being taken to the prom. It would never

---

* Edited excerpts from *A Return to Modesty: Discovering the Lost Virtue*.

even have occurred to me that my participation in these so-called "feminine" activities meant that I was somehow being oppressed, or that such activities precluded my thinking or doing anything else I wanted. When I returned home from the prom, after all, I could discuss anything I chose with my father. To be sure, I had heard of those who claimed that being a woman was not all fun and games, but those people were called feminists, and as every budding conservative knows, feminists exaggerate. Indeed, that is how you could tell that they were feminists: because they were the ones exaggerating all the time.

Don't ask me how I was so sure of this, or what this had to do with any other part of my ideology. As anyone who has ever had an ideology knows, you do not ask; you just look for confirmation for a set of beliefs. That's what it means to have an ideology.

But life can have a rude way of intruding on theory. Sometimes you have to change your mind when things turn out to be more complicated than you initially thought. Coase's theorem may still be true but it also assumes zero transaction costs, and sometimes, you discover in life, there can be extremely high transaction costs.

Perhaps you can imagine my surprise, growing up as I did, to come to college and discover that in fact the feminists were not exaggerating. All around me, at the gym and in my classes, I saw stick-like women suffering from anorexia. Who could not feel for them? Or I would hop out to get a bagel at night and see a student I knew – who must have weighed all of 70 pounds – walk into our corner campus hangout, Colonial Pizza. Oh, good, I would think, she's finally going to eat. I would smile and try to give off see-isn't-eating-fun vibes. No, in fact she hadn't come to eat. Instead she mumbled weakly, looking like she was about to faint: "Do you have any Diet Mountain Dew, please? I'm so tired.... I have a paper, and I can't stay up because I'm so, so tired.... I have a paper... and it's due tomorrow... any Diet Mountain Dew?" Then in the dining halls I would observe women eating sometimes ten times as much as I and then suddenly cutting off our conversation. Suddenly, um they had to go, suddenly, um they couldn't talk anymore. Until that moment I hadn't actually realized that some women really did make themselves throw up after bingeing.

The bursting of my ideological bubble was complete when I began hearing stories of women raped, stories filled with much too much detail and sadness to be invented.

The feminists were not exaggerating. The feminists were right.

But what was going to happen to young women if the feminists were right? Was there a way out of this morass? I really couldn't see any.

Then I started to hear about the mysterious modestyniks.

A modestynik (pronounced mod'-da-stee-nik) is my word for a modern single young woman raised in a secular home, who had hitherto seemed perfectly normal but who, inexplicably and without any prior notice, starts wearing long skirts and issuing spontaneous announcements that she is now *shomer negiah*, which means that she isn't going to have physical contact with men before marriage, and is now dressing according to the standards of Jewish modesty. She is the type of woman who, when you hear about how she is living her life, might cause you to exclaim: "Yikes! What's her problem?!" Hence, among those who do not know her, she is usually known as an abusenik ("o-byuz'-nik"), a woman you know has been abused, even though she insists she hasn't been. Otherwise, you figure, why would she be so weird?

I first heard about these modestyniks from grandparents' pictures and hushed voices in the backseats of cars. In my freshman year I became friends with an elderly couple who had retired in our college town. It turned out that they knew my grandpa and grandma from way back, so I saw a lot of them between classes, when I would hear many funny stories about my grandparents. One night after dinner they brought out some pictures of one of their granddaughters, and this turned out to be my formal introduction to the modestyniks. She and her husband were Orthodox Jews, they explained. Then they offered me the first picture – of the granddaughter with her then-fiancé.

What a curious picture. Although the blissfully betrothed were grinning very widely, unlike most engaged couples they didn't have their arms around each other. Here were a young, beautiful brunette and a tall and handsome man standing extremely close together, but they weren't touching each other at all. Indeed, if you looked at the picture closely, you could trace a thin blue line of sky between the two of them. How strange, I thought: If they didn't really like each other, then why in the world did they get married?

Fortunately my friends spoke up. "See," said the grandfather, pointing at the photo, "they observe the laws of *tzniut*." I said, "God bless you!" He said, "No, I didn't sneeze: *tzniut* means modesty. They observe the Jewish laws of sexual modesty."

"Oh," I said, a bit offended. For I was Jewish and I certainly didn't know about there being any Jewish modesty laws. I was a bit of a know-it-all, but about Judaism, I figured my parents were Jewish, I was Jewish, and I could recite a few blessings, if pressed. I even insisted on becoming bat mitzvah in a ceremony at the Reform temple my parents belonged to, so there were official people who had actually seen me be Jewish once, and they had already given me their seal of authenticity. But no one had ever told me about any modesty laws.

The second picture was of the wedding. This time the young couple weren't looking at the camera but at each other. Specifically, he was gazing down at her and she up at him. Now they were embracing each other very tightly. Upon seeing this particular picture, I felt tears float up to my eyes. I hoped the next photo would arrive soon enough to distract me, but unfortunately it didn't quite, and I was left blubbering for an excruciating eight seconds. "I don't know why I'm crying. I'm so embarrassed! I don't even know your granddaughter!" Somebody handed me a tissue, and then I was ready for the third and final picture.

In this one the granddaughter was on the beach holding a little baby boy – only now her *modestynik* smile was twinkling under the brim of a black straw hat. "That's for the head covering," her grandma piped up proudly over my shoulder. "A married woman cannot leave her hair uncovered."

That's how I learned that there are different stages in the life cycle of a modestynik. No Touching, Touching, then Hat. Okay, I figured, I could remember that. I made a mental picture, like that second-grade diagram which helps you remember how a caterpillar becomes a butterfly, and then I knew that I would never forget it. No Touching, Touching, Hat. Got it.

Once I learned how to identify one *modestynik*, I started to see them all over the place. It seemed every Jewish family had one. And even if a person didn't happen to have a *modestynik* in his or her family, then at least they knew of one- and more often than not, two or three.

All around me I started to hear, and read, about young women who were observing Jewish modesty law, not touching their boyfriends and suddenly sporting hats. And all with the same blue line of sky between them and their fiancés. All with the same *modestynik* twinkle at the end. It was like an epidemic.

I was fascinated. First, because although I had certainly been touching my boyfriends, I wasn't – how I wish there were a more elusive way of putting this – having sexual intercourse with them. Though boyfriends would occasionally grumble about my "hangups," l never gave much thought to what I would come to know as my sexual repression. I just assumed it was my peculiar problem, something to be sorted through privately, something of which one is ashamed. When I began to hear about these women, though, I started to think that maybe my "problem," such as it was, was not a problem at all but about something else entirely, something that could even be valued. Could I have been a *modestynik* all along and not known it?

Alas, I had to conclude that no, I couldn't be. I certainly wasn't shy or quiet, and that's what modesty really means, right? The whole women-should-be-seen-and-not-heard philosophy? That's what I associated it with. Furthermore, I didn't have any hats back in my dorm room. There were only two non-weather-related hats I had ever owned: a purple cone hat, from when I went trick-or-treating as a purple crayon, and a black cap with horns from when I sang the part of a little devil in a Lukas Foss opera. Somehow I didn't think those hats would count with whoever was in charge of the modestyniks.

Nevertheless I was still fascinated, particularly with the way others would react to them. People around me were saying that these modestyniks were really abuseniks: This one was "obviously very troubled," and that one seemed to have a "creepy" relationship with her father. Or the more poetic version, whispered in a sorrowful tone: "She is turning herself into the kind of woman her father could never touch." Or "Maybe she just had a Bad Experience." Either way, whatever her problem is, "Why doesn't the poor girl just get some counseling already, and then she won't take it all so seriously?"

Now that I knew what was really going on with these modestyniks, I started to worry about them. All these women, and all sexually abused by their fathers! But that's also when I began to get suspicious. If all modestyniks were really abuseniks, I asked myself, then why were they so twinkly? Why did they seem so contented? Why were their wedding pictures so viscerally and mysteriously moving?

During the spring of my senior year at Williams, in our main student center there was a display called "The Clothesline Project." It was a string of T-shirts designed by women on campus who had been victims of sexual harassment, stalking, or rape. "I HATE You!" announced one shirt, in thick black lettering. "NO doesn't mean try again in 5 minutes!" read another one, in a red banner. At the end of the clothesline, in plain blue lettering: "How could you TAKE that which she did not wish to GIVE?" The shirt next to it read, "Don't touch me again!" and, beside that: "Why does this keep happening to me? When will this end?"

I was struck, reading these T-shirts, with how polarized the debate about sex is today. Just like on the national level, there were the college Republicans who stopped to snicker and then moved on, tittering about "those crazy feminists," and then there were those who lingered, shook their heads in dismay, and could be heard whispering about the patriarchy.

I want to offer a new response. First, I want to invite conservatives to take the claims of the feminists seriously. That is, all of their claims, from the date-rape figures to anorexia to the shyness of teenage girls, even the number of women who say they feel "objectified" by the male gaze. I want them to stop saying that this or that study was flawed; or that young women are exaggerating; or that it has been proven that at this or that university such-and-such a charge was made up. Because ultimately, it seems to me, it doesn't really matter if one study is flawed or if one charge is false. When it comes down to it, the same vague yet unmistakable problem is still with us. A lot of young women are trying to tell us that they are very unhappy: unhappy with their bodies, with their sexual encounters, with the way men treat them on the street – unhappy with their lives. I want conservatives really to listen to these women, to stop saying boys will be boys, and to take what these women are saying seriously.

As for the feminists, I want to invite them to consider whether the cause of all this unhappiness might be something other than the patriarchy. For here is the paradox: at Williams, as on so many other modern college campuses, where there was such a concentration of unhappy women, everything was as nonsexist as could be. We had "Women's Pride Week," we had "Bisexual Visibility Week," we were all living in coed dorms, many of us even used coed bathrooms. We were as far from patriarchal rules as we could get. So if we were supposed to be living in nonsexist paradise, then why were many of us this miserable?

A friend of mine had an affair with her professor when she was twenty-one. She was in his class at the time and madly in love with him; he had no intention of doing anything other than using and summarily disposing of her. She was a virgin before the affair. As she related the story to me, ten years after it happened, I was struck, not that what had happened had deeply upset her, but that she felt she had to apologize for the fact that it had deeply upset her: "And, well, and it didn't mean the same thing to him, and um… this is going to sound really cheesy but, um… I mean, for God's sake, he took my virginity!" As she struggled to find the words to explain what had happened to her, it occurred to me that in an age where our virginity is supposed to mean nothing, and where male honor is also supposed to mean nothing, we literally cannot explain what has happened to us. We can no longer talk in terms of someone, say, defiling a virgin, so instead we punish the virgin for having any feelings at all. Nevertheless, although our ideology can expunge words from our vocabulary, the feelings remain and still cry out for someone to make sense of them.

Today modesty is commonly associated with sexual repression, with pretending that you don't want sex though you really do. But this is a misunderstanding, a cultural myth spun by a society which vastly underrates sexual sublimation. If you stop and think about it, you realize that without sublimation, we would have very few footnotes and probably none of the greatest works of Western art. Moreover, leaving aside the whole question of utility, when you haven't yet learned to separate your physical desires from your hopes and natural wonder at everything, the world is, in a very real sense, enchanted. Every conversation, every mundane act is imbued with potential because everything is colored with erotic meaning. Today, this stage in one's life – when everything seems significant and you want to get it all "exactly right" – is thought to be childish, but is it really? Maybe instead of learning to overcome repression, we should be prolonging it.

Many children these days know far too much too soon, and as a result they end up, in some fundamental way, not knowing – stunted and cut off from all they could be.

What, then, will become of this generation? Is all lost for us? Should we give up and get depressed? I think, on the contrary, that we have a lot to be optimistic about.

The most obvious connotation of sexual modesty is, of course, innocence. Because of the onslaught on childhood today, because of the intrusion of sex educators and condoms and obscene lyrics into our earliest days, or because of parents who have abandoned their kids, many of us feel as if we never had a chance to be young. Sexual modesty is a virtue for us and, I predict, will become a virtue for increasing numbers of us because it's a way of affirming our essential innocence. It's a way of saying, At least maybe all this is not my fault. It may be a mess, but maybe I didn't do it, and what's more, maybe with my own life I can start anew.

Sometimes we would prefer not to have learned about AIDS in kindergarten. You may think that because of Freud, or because of MTV, our virginity doesn't mean anything, but some of us actually think Freud was wrong. And sometimes MTV might surprise you. One of the most popular videos for months, after all, was called "A Return to Innocence." Sometimes it comes as a relief to think when everyone else is telling me how provocative I am, or have to be, or how many men I have to have – maybe, at least in my own life, before God, I could be just a little bit innocent?

For further reading:

Shalit, Wendy. *A Return to Modesty: Discovering the Lost Virtue*. New York: 1999.

Manolson, Gila. *Outside/Inside: A Fresh Look at Tzniut*. Southfield, MI: 1997.

Friedman, Manis. *Doesn't Anyone Blush Anymore?* Minneapolis, MN: 1996.

It is customary to put a few coins in a charity box before lighting Shabbat candles. The correct time to light the candles is 18 minutes before sunset every Friday.

First light the candles. Then spread your hands out around the candles drawing your hands inward in a circular motion three times to indicate acceptance of the sanctity of Shabbat. You then cover your eyes and recite the following blessing:

Ba-ruch a-tah A-do-noi Elo-hai-nu me-lech ha-o-lom a-sher kid-sha-nu b'mitz-vo-tav v'tzi-va-nu le-had-lik ner shel shab-bat ko-desh.

Blessed are You, God our Lord, King of the universe, who has hallowed us through His commandments, and has commanded us to kindle the lights of the holy Shabbat.

The time of lighting is considered especially propitious for praying to God for health and happiness. Many women offer their own personal prayers at this time.

Uncover your eyes and behold the Shabbat lights.

Shabbat: A Love Story

Alys R. Yablon

I am what they call a workaholic. Perhaps that is because I am at the beginning stages of my professional life. More likely, it is an integral part of my nature. As a student I pulled more all-nighters than I care to remember. And now, as a book editor for a Manhattan publishing company, it is rare for me to leave the office without a manuscript or a proposal stuffed into my bag, a little something to do before drifting off to sleep. If it weren't for Shabbat, I don't think I'd ever stop.

Living in Manhattan, the city that never sleeps, encourages my hectic inclinations. Day and night sirens blare, people shout, buses make their way endlessly up and down Broadway. And every Friday, two hours before the sun sets, I leave behind whatever it is I am working on at the moment and rush like a crazy woman (fitting right in) to my Upper West Side apartment, where I set timers, boil soup, make last-minute phone calls and set the table. My roommates and I yell down the hall to one another: "You done in the shower yet?"; "Can you help me with the urn?"; "Did so and so drop by with the wine?" And then, just when the frenzy reaches an unbearable pitch and we are all moving at top speeds, the pace slows, and in a single moment everything stops completely. We light our candles, and a hush falls over us. It is Shabbat, the Sabbath, the day we look forward to all week long.

We walk to shul curiously unaffected by the same honking cars and screaming kids and pushing and shoving, the same business as usual of the city that surrounds us all week. But we move through it on Shabbat in a new way. People have an aura about them that you can spot a block away, before you can reasonably expect to recognize a tallit bag or a yarmulke; an unspoken sense of unity and belonging is in the air that is unlike anything I experience in the other aspects of my life. Shabbat, it seems to me, is the time during which Jews are most connected to God, and by extension, to one another.

Solomon's Song of Songs, often recited on Fridays just as the Sabbath begins, is thought of as a love song between the Jewish people and God as personified by a human love story, suggesting that the way in which we conduct our interpersonal relationships informs the way we relate to God, and vice versa.

The kabbalists wrote that there are four verses that one should recite on the eve of Shabbat if one is unable to say the whole song. The first verse illustrates the theme of privacy and private communication:

Israel in exile, to God: "Communicate Your innermost wisdom to me again in loving closeness, for Your friendship is dearer than all earthly delights." (1:2)

During the week our focus is almost entirely external. We have jobs to do, errands to run, commitments to fulfill. By the end of the day we are lucky to have a few moments to talk to our friends and family and those moments are usually used to recap the many goings-on of the day. But when the pace slows for Shabbat, we have time to pray slowly and reflect on our inner selves. It is the time when I am prohibited from marking up manuscripts, making endless phone calls, stopping at any number of stores to purchase any number of items. I catch up with friends, talk about what's really going on in our lives, go for long walks and read books that require sitting still; it is a time when we can be together as a community and function as a whole, rather than as many separate beings running in different directions.

In the second verse, God projects the future ingathering of the exiles at the time of the Messiah, a larger-scale version of coming home and achieving meaningful communication. There might be a hint here of a feminine, maternal tone, like that of a mother calling her children home:

God to Israel: "Awake from the North and come from the South! Like the winds let my exiles return to my garden, let their fragrant goodness flow in Jerusalem." (4:16)

This image of God eliciting a homecoming intimates the Shechina, God's feminine side, which is especially present on Shabbat. The verse also portrays Shabbat as an island of time, literally (the end of days when a new era of timelessness will exist) and figuratively (enclosing yourself in your home for Shabbat with no deadlines, phones, cars, etc. – a time for self imposed serenity).

Once we are in communicative mode, and are gathered home, we are told to reflect not only on ourselves but on Torah, as the third verse says:

God to Israel "If you know not where to graze, O fairest of nations, follow the footsteps of the sheep, your forefathers, who braced a straight, unswerving path after my Torah. Then you can graze your tender kids even among the dwellings of foreign shepherds." (1:8)

Religious Jews are expected to be in a constant state of Torah reflection. Of course, this is not always reasonable for those of us who live and work in the modern world. For us, for me, Shabbat is the best time to return to that ideal frame of mind. We actually hear the Torah being read from its scroll in shul, listen to words of Torah in the form of rabbis' sermons, learn with peers and (once we are parents) our children.

The last of the broad themes illustrated in the fourth excerpt is recognizing and achieving a state of spiritual awareness:

God to Israel: "To your Tabernacle Dedication, my sister, O bride, I came as if to my garden. I gathered my myrrh with my spice from your princely incense: I accepted your unbidden as well as your bidden offerings to me: I drank your libations pure as milk. Eat, my beloved priests! Drink and become God-intoxicated, O friends!" (5:1)

Here God invites us not only to follow the specific commandments of sacrifice that applied in the days of the Temple, but reminds us that in our day, without a Temple, meaningful prayer and other mitzvot take the place of physical offerings. Women have three such mitzvot specific to their gender: challah, Shabbat candles and the laws of family purity. On Shabbat these mitzvot take on a larger meaning as the time in which a woman's actions and prayers are the most powerful, the time in which her feminine spirituality is most aligned with God's.

෴ ෴

I remember when I first became fascinated by Shabbat. It was in the kindergarten classroom of the Jewish day school I attended. Every Friday one boy would get to be the "Shabbos abba" and say the kiddush over the wine, and one girl would get to be the "Shabbos ima" and say the blessing over the candles. I couldn't wait for it to be my turn to say the bracha and "be the ima." At the tender age of five, I wanted to be a mother and perform the mitzvah of lighting the candles. When I started to observe shabbat for real, I learned that many women have the custom of lighting one candle before they are married, two after the fact, and then additional candles for each child they have. This enables a woman to create a physical reminder of the extensions of herself and to give each of them, the individuals comprising her most intimate and precious world, a blessing of her own.

The candles, and the mitzvah of lighting them, have been a very significant part of my Shabbat experience. A single woman lighting candles enables herself to achieve emotive eloquence on her own merit. If the candle represents the body, and the flame represents the soul (reaching upward, defying gravity, toward heaven), this act of lighting the candles unifies the two and helps a woman to become a whole person, which is a necessary prerequisite to joining her life with another and creating a family.

A prayer some women say after they light their candles includes the hope that with this mitzvah, they will merit the light of Torah, which includes children who will delight in the Torah. It is in the personal – the unified force of the husband and wife (home, family) that we as a people truly appreciate the meaning of Shabbat in physical, loving individual relationships and come to love God more completely. It has always made sense to me that by lighting candles and being truly aware of why I lit them, I was bringing myself closer to accomplishing my goal of becoming the "Shabbos ima" every week.

It was the keen sense of community that first drew me to Orthodoxy as a teenager. At the beginning, it was all about fitting in, finding a place, and feeling at one with a higher cause. The first time I experienced a real Shabbat, complete with singing, dancing, Friday night dinner, and the simple joy of conversation, I knew that it was to become a central focus of my life. I had fallen in love and ran headlong into observance – because it was right, because it was good, not because I had thought of the practicality of the life change. The focus was so intensely internal, in fact, that the daily hardships of observance (weaning myself of non-kosher food, Saturday morning television, an extra day to do my homework) never seemed burdensome. What was more important was learning the seemingly endless number of laws governing what you were and were not permitted to do on Shabbat, and finding my own place in the small Orthodox community of Harrisburg, Pennsylvania, where I was growing up.

I took pride in explaining to myself, my family, and my secular high school friends why I did certain things, what they meant to me, and why I planned to continue doing them. Shabbat was my version of a boyfriend in a rock band, with earrings, yet. Other people's reactions (often baffled, frustrated, negative to say the least) kept me going and helped me to strengthen my own faith. Teenagers love what is difficult, what is different. Having to explain myself so many times to so many people solidified my faith, and with every explanation this lifestyle made more and more sense.

As I left home for college and moved from a small Jewish community to a sizeable one (Montreal), and then to a huge one after that (New York City), the hardships were gradually removed, the balance shifted, and being observant became easy. I was living on my own terms, with people who practiced Judaism in similar ways, in cities that offered me readily-available kosher food and Jewish culture. Once there was nothing left to fight against, nothing left to justify, I had to reestablish my reasons for belief, and focus on the true meaning of my observance. Shabbat then became my "island in time," my oasis from work and city life. But I am coming to realize as the years pass by that an island is more than an isolated space, it is a space that is enclosed on all sides, like a home or a domain. The essence of Shabbat as I know it is the home, it is whatever I make of it within my own four walls. It is at the same time a communal day and a very personal, private experience. It is like a marriage. It is as though my earring-laden boyfriend has donned a suit and tie and walked with me to shul.

In traditional Orthodox marriages, a husband and wife are supposed to separate from one another, to refrain from sexual intimacy, during a woman's menstrual cycle and for seven days thereafter. When that time has passed, the wife immerses in the mikveh, the ritual bath, and is reunited with her husband. A rich, complex and beautiful system, it allows a couple the time to miss one another, to learn how to communicate effectively, and (biologically) to raise the chances of conceiving children together.

Family purity laws are, in a sense, similar to the laws of Shabbat: there are numerous restrictions, and most of them are difficult separation, self-control, repression. But in actuality, what these laws create is the ultimate, ever-new love. When a couple reunites after their time of physical separation, they experience a gladness that elevates their physical love to a Godly plane. Regular physical separation helps to ensure that couples do not take their intimacy for granted, and that they continue to develop their essential friendship and partnership.

Shabbat is also kept from us for regular periods of time. For six days we go about our business, and then finally we come to the day of rest. This separation, like the separation a husband and wife experience, allows us to enter the Sabbath with a sense of newness and excitement every Friday night. All week long I will be apart from my beloved, the Shabbat, and when I light candles, I will again be with my most intimate confidante and companion. I will go to shul, and sing the

Lecha Dodi, feeling again the energy I so fell in love with years ago. The melody will rise to the heavens, muffling the sound of honking cars and blaring sirens. And at the part of the prayer where we turn around as a congregation to welcome the Schechina, the Sabbath bride, I will bow, close my eyes, and believe that one day I will be a bride, a renewed lover, and a Shabbos ima, and I will sing from my heart:

Bo'ee b'shalom, ateret ba'ala,	Enter in peace, O crown of her husband,
Gam b'simcha u'v'tzahala	Even in gladness and good cheer
Tokh emunei am segulah:	Among the faithful of the treasured nation:
Bo'ee, kallah; bo'ee, kallah	Come, bride; come, bride.

For further reading:

Grunfeld, I. *The Sabbath.* New York: 1998.
Palatnik, Lori. *Friday Night and Beyond: The Shabbat Experience Step by Step.* Lanham, MD: 1994.
Steinsaltz, Adin. *The Miracle of the Seventh Day.* San Francisco, CA: 2003.

*May it be Your will, Lord our God and God of our
fathers, that just as I remove the chametz from my
house and from my possessions, so shall you remove
all extraneous forces, purge the spirit of impurity
from the earth, eradicate our evil inclination from
within us and grant us a heart of flesh to serve You
in truth....*

*From the prayer said as the chametz is burned
on the morning before Passover begins.*

Siddur Tehilat Hashem

Cleaning with Meaning

Sherri Mandell

Recently, a friend opened my silverware drawer and said: "I haven't seen a
drawer that looks this bad since college."

"Listen," I said. "There's a reason."

She gave me a skeptical look.

"I am cleaning challenged," I said. "It's a disability, especially when you've
got four kids and a messy husband."

It's not that I don't like order. I just have a hard time creating it. I'm not the
kind of mother or housewife who spends her time ordering and cleaning. I'd
rather write. Or even better, lie on the couch and read a novel.

I am prone to laziness and self-indulgence, neither of them great weapons in
the war against dirt. And space management is not my strength either: in
elementary school when I was tested for spatial relations, I scored in the eighth
percentile. All in all, I fail domestic engineering.

When I have a cleaning lady, I look to her as a God.

On those rare days when I do clean, and the house is for a moment perched
on the edge of order, it's like I'm on a ship sailing on tranquil Caribbean seas.
Then, as my kids and I and my husband go about our ordinary routine, it's as if
I'm watching the sky darken, hearing the first murmuring of thunder. And when
the inevitable storm of crumbs and dirt and chaos begins to descend, I feel the

terror and disappointment of a pilot watching her ship smash onto an unforgiving shore.

And yet, despite the difficulty of keeping a clean home, I think it's important to clean for Passover – with my husband and my kids. Not that I wouldn't rather go on a Passover cruise, mind you, and forget about the whole thing. But Passover allows me to dwell in the nexus between order and chaos, central themes in my life.

Think of it. Passover is the holiday of freedom. Passover commemorates the most dramatic moments of the Jewish people. Imagine yourself, for a moment, a Jew in Egypt. You are told to mark your door lintels with blood so that God will know not to kill your first born. You leave Egypt in the middle of the night and walk for seven days until you come to the Red Sea. Then when you think it's over for you, with the Egyptian chariots bearing down and no place to run but into the sea, the waters part and you walk on through. And what do we do to prepare for the holiday that marks this awesome event?

We clean.

Passover comes to redefine cleaning. Our work is so mundane: scrubbing, dusting, sweeping. We work, burdened with an incredible amount of self-inflicted labor, as stressful as moving house or painting all the rooms. Jewish law tells us to remove all bread and crumbs from our midst. Passover comes to tell us that no matter how high we have risen in this world, we have to bend to clean. In bowing, we begin to acknowledge our humility. Like the Jews of Egypt, who when the chips were down, had to be saved through Divine intervention, when all is said and done, we are dependent on others and dependent on God.

Cleaning itself is not the point. Cleaning itself can be a futile exercise in control, an unsuccessful means of dealing with chaos, of keeping the beasts at bay. Look what happened in *Four Letters of Love*, a wonderful novel set in Ireland. When Nicholas's father runs off to paint, his mother, in fear of how the family will survive without money, cleans: "Then the house was set, poised for a moment on that precipice of perfect cleanliness, and my mother would be almost happy – standing there in the fragile instant of stillness before the next particle of dust arose and softly fell." To combat her sadness and impending madness, she cleans. And then she kills herself.

Cleaning is a paradox: it contains within itself the seeds of its own destruction. But cleaning for Passover can be an exercise in spiritual growth. Passover cleaning comes to clean us out from the inside and teach us: we are not in charge. During that moment right before Passover, we perch on the achievement of order for a short while, search for all of the crumbs in our home with a candle and make a blessing. For this moment I've gotten rid of all of the dirt. I've imposed order on the world.

But we are not the ones who create order in this world. God is the ultimate cleaner, the one who gives and takes away. He returns you to dust and lets the dust return to earth. He sends down the rain to clean, the wind to blow the dirt away.

So we are ultimately humbled in our cleaning. In fact: we clean and clean and then comes the holiday of matzah which is one of the messiest things you can eat: one bite and those crumbs are all over.

The freedom of Passover is in recognizing that God is in control, right here in our homes, in our cleaning and our cooking and in our sitting around the table discussing an event that happened thousands of years ago.

The beauty of Passover is that we can reach God by dwelling in the domestic details, in the everyday ordinary world around us. For a short time each year, cleaning holds a place of honor; it becomes a means of spiritual growth. It reminds us that even something as insignificant as a crumb can be infused with holiness.

So this Seder night I'm going to invite my friend over to inspect my silverware drawers and when she exclaims how clean and orderly they appear I'll smile and say: "It just goes to show you – there is a God in this world."

For further reading:

Twerski, Abraham J., MD. *From Bondage to Freedom: The Passover Haggadah*, with a commentary illuminating the liberation of spirit. Suffern, NY: 1995.

We Are What We Say

Sarah Shapiro

When I as a teenager was searching for truth as only an assimilated Jewish teenager can, one of the New Age disciplines I dipped into for a while was a system of self-study based on the teachings of a nineteenth-century Russian mystic by the name of Gurdjieff. Gurdjieff's goal had been for people to "wake up" and become fully conscious human beings rather than live out their lives as robots.

I joined a self-study group whose leader (a psychologist who was Jewish, too, of course, as were most of the other members) took as his central premise this contemporary spin on the Gurdjieff principle: Human beings live with the unconscious feeling of being the worst in the world.

And what behavior is it that most hinders an individual's psychological and spiritual awakening? What ensures that his mind will stay securely behind bars, in the prison of his unrecognized bad feelings about self? Indulging in the pervasive human impulse to put other people down.

To me at nineteen, put-downs didn't seem like such a big deal, and I found it odd to have such emphasis placed on eliminating something that, to my mind, was just a natural part of life. Nonetheless, as a diligent and earnest young seeker, I took it upon myself to adhere to the rules, and the chief rule was: Don't let a put-down pass your lips.

Months went by, and something interesting began to happen. This single abstention, inadequate as my sporadic practice of it proved to be, increasingly had the effect of casting a disconcerting light onto all sorts of feelings within that had previously been hidden from my view. It seemed that this one gesture of self-restraint, that of denying myself the luxury of imposing my negativity upon others, was indeed, automatically, getting me in touch with the much deadlier negativity that my mind was directing my own way. Stopping my lips from speaking against others threw me back onto my own self, again and again, and with increasing clarity I came upon a core of emptiness, a sense of painful wanting... of unbearable inferiority, weakness, fear, neediness.

Terrible feelings, frightening. I wondered sometimes if I was making it all up in order to conform to the group. I wondered if my experience was being influenced by the dogma. But one thing I could not deny: It was easier to criticize someone else than to take a look at myself. "Looking" at myself, in fact, was an amorphous business altogether, like gazing for one's reflection in a murky pond, whereas I had no problem at all spotting the faults of others. And recognizing someone else's failings involved a certain unacknowledged pleasure. What was this pleasure? Why did putting the other one down give me an unarticulated, half-conscious sense of being one up, as if I were one on end of some kind of invisible seesaw?

Let's say, for example, that there was a sharp, critical voice within castigating me for laziness. But the volume would be turned down low enough to allow me to go my merry way, and I'd cope with its muffled diatribe by dulling myself to its ongoing remarks. If, however, someone else came along who appeared to me as lazy, the same critical voice would instantly become audible.

Did it burn me up, so-and-so's selfishness? Or that one's insincerity? This one's small-mindedness, or irresponsibility, or vanity? Or the other one's lack of vanity? My critical responses were sure-fire indicators that I had come upon some weakness or bad feeling of my own of which I was unaware. By restraining that impulse to speak ill of others, the desire to criticize could be used, instead, as a sort of perpetually activated Geiger counter, one that could guide me through unexplored regions towards long-buried radioactive feelings about myself.

Gradually I started to see how it works: Let the put-down cross your lips and presto, you've got a moment's reprieve from your own self.

80 03

Not much time passed before God in His wisdom plucked me up out of the sunny West Coast and, to my surprise, set me down – where else? – in Orthodox Brooklyn.

The cultural milieu could not have been more different, except, to my mind, in one noticeable respect. Just as put-downs had been strictly forbidden during my memorable stint at the self-study group, whose forty or so members had waged a lonely, uphill battle against the socially accepted, casual denigration of one's fellows – here was an entire community that made *shemiras halashon* (literally: guarding one's tongue) a pivotal, community-wide, institutionalized aspect of religious observance. The Torah, apparently, had forbidden gossip, slander, and derogatory speech quite some time ago, at Mount Sinai, actually well before the advent of California's Human Potential Movement.

A book published just about the time I arrived in New York, *Guard Your Tongue* by Rabbi Zelig Pliskin, set forth for the English-speaking public Judaism's laws governing this area of behavior. I learned that since human nature is such that we're all experts at rationalization and self-justification, good will is insufficient. The commitment to refrain from put-downs has to be buttressed by a subtle, comprehensive network of laws, which apply to all the infinitely varied situations that arise in daily life.

The nuances were intriguing. Sometimes, divulging negative information can be essential, for instance, when it comes to a prospective marriage partner or a business deal. Under other circumstances, saying something positive about someone is the *wrong* thing to do – for example, when it's likely to arouse a listener's jealousy or skepticism.

I was taken aback by such savvy psychological realism in an ancient tradition which, tribally speaking, I could claim as my very own.

Aside from its vastly more comprehensive scope, however, there was an essential difference between what I'd learned in the self-study group, and Judaism's concept and practice of this discipline. As understood in this observant Jewish community, the focus of *shemiras halashon* was not *me and my enlightenment*. At the center was God.

What I came to see in Brooklyn was that as legitimate, noble and desirable a goal it may be to foster personal growth by guarding one's speech, *shemiras halashon* goes beyond any particular individual's quest for personal liberation. To the extent that my mundane daily speech is morally sensitive, in private or in public, to that extent will it promote not only my own psychological well-being but the well-being of the group. In fact, it has an effect on the world beyond my reach, and to indiscernible worlds beyond human perception.

I learned that the seemingly insignificant little words I utter have infinite significance in the eyes of our Creator. Refraining from putting people down, and from putting oneself down, is an aspect of our purpose here in the world: to arrive at the recognition that each and every one of us is a miraculous piece of Divine handiwork. To insult or disparage one of His creations is to disturb our own relationship with God.

Decades passed. It's been years since I was picked up out of that community in Brooklyn and replanted once again, in Jerusalem, where the ancient traditions are far more deeply rooted than the tall old pine tree out my window. But I'm still surrounded, as I was back then, by Jews of all ages who are conscious of the obligation to guard their speech. It's an environment in which, generally speaking, the idealism in this regard is as fervent and sincere as was mine, when, as an innocent teenager, I first started looking for truth.

ℰℐ ℭℛ

There's a simple question which we can ask ourselves when in doubt as to whether a particular remark would be permitted: *Would the person I'm talking about be pleased or displeased were I saying it in his presence?* With a guideline as obvious and straightforward as that, why should it be necessary to review the laws of proper speech on a regular basis?

Another way of asking the same question is: why were we created with a feeling of weakness at our core?

That is indeed a mystery of the human soul. But the good news is this: If we felt complete rather than lacking, perfect rather than inadequate and at fault, we wouldn't sense any need for something greater than ourselves. And if we didn't have to resist the temptation to build ourselves up by diminishing our fellows, we'd live without this recurrent opportunity to create our own characters daily. The identifying characteristic of our species is our ability to speak, so it's no coincidence that only to the extent that we refine our use of it can we develop our intrinsic human dignity.

Once we start curbing that inexplicable impulse to put people down, we find ourselves less often in the company of imbeciles, lowlifes, ingrates, and sadists, and more frequently, much to our surprise, surrounded by fallible, vulnerable, striving human beings who resemble – how uncanny – none other than you and me.

For further reading:
Telushkin, Joseph. *Words That Hurt, Words That Heal: How to Choose Words Wisely and Well.* New York, NY: 1996.

Jewish thought pays little attention to inner tranquility and peace of mind. The feeling of "Behold, I've arrived" could well undermine the capacity to continue, suggesting as it does that the infinite can be reached in a finite number of steps. In fact, the very concept of the Divine as infinite implies an activity that is endless, of which one must never grow weary. At every rung of his ascent, the penitent, like any person who follows the way of God, perceives mainly the remoteness. Only in looking back can one obtain some idea of the distance already covered, of the degree of progress.

From The Thirteen Petalled Rose
by Adin Steinsaltz

Seasons of the Soul

Elizabeth Ehrlich

September

Work and house and errands and physical fitness and activities and things. The expediencies of every day. This cannot be all there is.

Something more is calling. It is of the past, it embodies tradition, yet tradition is only the vehicle. It is of the heart, but it is more than diffuse sentiment. Some of it dimly remembered, yet remembered for a reason.

It is a coherent way of life and the taste of home. It is a way to teach the children right and wrong, consciousness, history, and appreciation of all we have. It connects them to their grandparents and mine.

It is an ancient religion. It beckons, and half the time I am not even sure why. Its rituals tantalize and will not be denied.

What is the lure of ritual when passionate belief is hardly ever to be found, when fulfillment of ritual is a matter of choice? It is more than preservation of an empty vessel. It is the conviction, deep and unspoken, that ritual, the vessel,

---

* Excerpted from *Miriam's Kitchen*.

contains a precious substance, though I cannot name it. My ignorance is my problem, not that of the vessel.

Why do I, having long ignored the rituals, yearn in their direction? Some of its caretakers have been those I loved best and respected most. I cannot forget them. I start from there.

October

A new year in the Jewish calendar. I pause to consider it. I give myself this year to this calendar, to see where it takes me. I have been so mixed in my own mind.

Not so much a brand-new beginning as intensifying. We have been lighting candles at least some Friday nights for some years, though self-consciously. The children like it. So do I. What is the meaning of the lights? Weekday darkness, Sabbath illumination. The world out there, the spirit in here. Lights of the city versus lights of home.

Recently we light candles more often. Every Friday, more or less. We aim the week in their direction. Subtly, the week incorporates their shape. Friday evening becomes a time to gather, a family island, a quietness in the week's flutter and noise. We are staying home most Saturdays, venturing to synagogue now and again, a family together.

The candles, at first, were purely of the past, a way to bring tradition tangibly home. It was a nice way to remember, to gather those scattered Friday nights of candles strewn over childhood's inconsistent terrain. A token of memory, and also of history, the collective remembrance far beyond memory's reach.

Now the rhythm is itself compelling. Sabbath is becoming a gift to us, one we are choosing and wrapping ourselves and then opening with a kind of astonished surprise. I can't say precisely when it happened. All I know is this: Saturday morning cartoons, errands, and bill-paying once were the standard. Now such mornings seem empty, barren, a cheat.

We will try for a Sabbath more often, think about holidays in advance. But I remain cautious. I long drew from observant households a metaphor never written in the Book: the symbolic sacrifice not of Isaac but the Mother. The mother who bends the course of life to have everything ready for that Friday night, who brings in the Sabbath but never rests.

And always, I have feared my own obsessions. I fear losing myself and then discovering my location is a point of no return.

The Sabbath, one of Ten Commandments. As important as not murdering, as ancient as the knowledge that envy can tear the heart out of human life. Are the Rules still rules to live by, for those such as me, raised to pick and choose, raised without God? Does the peace of Sabbath pertain, without the Divine to enforce it? I have never been much interested in whether God is, or is not. I have not believed it matters, either way.

Piety aside, I cherish the cultural forms. I don't like to see them fade away. But I don't know if regret contains meaning, in this great wide universe of ours. There are so many sources of wistful regret to choose from, so many different clocks to mark time.

For the moment I will try Sabbath, and stop all our clocks, step out of time. I will light the candles and watch them burn, and think about it. So far with no sense of obligation, no sense of commandment. I will recite prayers, but to What or to Whom?

November

I teeter on some intermediate balancing point. On one side there is kashrut, on the other, citizenship in the regular world. My balancing point is the kosher meat I bring home for cooking, the segregation of milk from meat in one meal, the picky selection from restaurant menus: no bacon, no prosciutto, no pork.

The pivoting plank, unstable, leans to the kosher end. I who loved shellfish have caused their extinction within my house. It happened in stages. I lost the taste for it when pregnant, or when jostled by pollution scares. We began to feel scruples about preparing shrimp at home, when our ecumenical pots would be called on to serve my observant in-laws. My husband requested we desist for their comfort level, and increasingly, I understood, for his.

Our scruples escalated as the children grew. Dining out as a family, I found myself avoiding mollusks, crustaceans, not out of pure conviction, but in the interests of consistency. Eventually, the shifting standards – here shrimp, there none – made me seasick. I began to slip away from the appetite of it, the idea of shrimp and mussels and squid.

I am not sure that I want this. I always have wanted the world. So I teeter, I worry, but I don't turn away. Because it is the tradition of my grandparents and those who went before. Because I'm not sure I can bear to finally cut the string connecting those lives to those of my children. Because I don't want hamburgers with milk shakes at my table.

I am trying to balance the claims of the mind and the soul with the belly's blind, indulgent appetites. I am trying to respect the life of the calf that I eat. I will imbibe of its mother's milk, but at some other meal. Still I do not say I can possibly meet the detail evolved by generations of rabbis. I don't know if I can truly scour myself and begin afresh. I don't know if I really wish to. Purge the ambivalence, the daring U turns, what is left after all?

Keeping kosher has this value: I daily reaffirm identity, purpose, and rhythm. Separateness is intrinsic to that, separation from the world outside as well as within the meal. Yet I do not enjoy setting myself apart. I fear a statement of difference in a world that needs to see itself as one.

December

Let me just see if I can do it. I mean we've been moving in that direction. We're on the way to getting there. Our ingredients are kosher, our intentions are kosher. The wooden bowls and spoons are separate, those very porous implements of wood.

I'll divide up my dishes. I have a lot of dishes. I'll say blue are dairy and white are for meat. We'll have a trial run.

I'll need a few sponges, a pot, a pan. No big deal. I remember enough from the olden days. Miriam will tell me the rest.

Gradualism is the answer. This is going to be easy. We're practically there, more than halfway there. Sixty percent kosher, I'd say.

January

Does anyone draw a January list without a diet or exercise goal, without aspiring to self-perfection? As the secular calendar turns, I, too, plan on fitness, on household organization, on wisely budgeted resources and time. Most calendar years begin tired or hung-over or a bit physically overindulged. These conditions are incentives to forswear excess and attempt a fresh, more disciplined routine. In contrast to the old, flawed me, I will create a person whose achievements engender pride, whose willpower will be evident from without and can be judged by all who care to notice.

My thoughts in autumn, the start of the ancient lunar year, tend differently. After a week of introspection and a day of fasting, I am more worried about the pitfalls of envy or gossip or indifference than about a few excess pounds. Of my success or failure in that sphere, no one at the gym will know.

Beginning the autumn new year, I do not turn my mind to willpower, but to the acceptance of obligations. It is not a matter of resolutions, but of opening one's eyes to the same old requirements that were there all along. They are always there, notice them or not, accept them or not. Choose them or not, they are inevitable, yours. The rabbis of old, I have read, believed that even outright renunciation doesn't change your internal essence. Lapse, turn hostile, disconnect, convert, be named pope, what have you – you are still inescapably of the people.

It is January. So, sculpt a shapely muscle.

Grandmother's religion waits.

February

We're not there. We're miles from kosher. I sorted my dishes, pots, and implements for a trial run, assigned drawers and cupboards. Some of these items can't properly be kashered, or bear associations that taint them. Throw them in the drawer and pretend. Pretend I will use that barbecue fork to stir pasta with meat sauce from now on, because I've committed the pasta stirrer for dairy. Pretend the cheese grater never grated Parmesan.

Must I live without real Parmesan?

Don't have enough things. Washing up is a nightmare. Pareve things should be washed separately. Dishwasher half-full of the wrong kind. Meat and dairy sponges stacked together. Quick dinner leaves dairy plates; sink is full of previous meal's meat dishes. Silverware jumbled together in the dish drainer. Spatulas and graters in the wrong drawers, contaminated, pulled out by someone and used the wrong way.

Do I have to stand there clearing the decks after each meal? Washing, drying, putting away, supervising, being preoccupied? Does this force me into a little sphere, the kitchen?

I'm only interested in the symbolism, so what if things get mixed up? I sort them out... but it's not the same anymore, the object carries a projected burden, projected by me, if not by actual molecules.

March

I resist assimilation, but that is a negative identity, not a positive one.

I recover the communal-cultural-fork tradition, but this is not a lasting recipe.

I embrace the values, but values can be taught without ritual.

I follow the ritual, but at a distance.

Shall I set myself toward something more? Commitment? Study? Belief? Where does the road lead?

The impossible existence of these questions, after thousands of wandering years, renders them insistent. I can't drop them. If I don't answer the questions, my children may.

Questions are not such a bad way of life. Maybe questions are the point of it all.

April

I've been ignoring it, with a mixture of advance regret and resistance. What's hard is that it rolls around every year. Every year to excavate, clean, change over, cook, return to normalcy. Renewing, uplifting, etc., etc. But definitely exhausting. I can either write about it or do it, but not both. I'm not doing Passover this year.

I'll wipe down the counter and use paper plates. I'll buy a box of matzo. It doesn't have to be a big production. I'll simplify.

We'll have a simple Seder. I'll buy a few bags of groceries, the basics – that's it. Five boxes of matzos, a box of matzo meal, a couple of cans of macaroons, soup nuts, a dozen eggs, odds and ends. Parsley. Everyday plates.

We must have a Seder. Miriam will do some cooking at home, and we'll hold the dinner at my house. I told her to keep it simple and she sort of shrugged. "We have to eat something," she remarked.

I can't put Miriam's Passover cooking on an everyday plate. What was I thinking? I have scruples.

I suppose I will unearth the Passover dishes, gingerly balancing as I creak down the attic steps. The boxes won't be properly labeled: I won't be sure which are dishes, which pots and gadgets, so I will take down all of them.

I will need a place to put the Passover dishes, so I will empty a cabinet, just one, pack up the everyday dishes and move them downstairs. I'll wipe out the shelves and line them with paper. I have to wash the Passover dishes, so I will *kasher* the dishwasher, by running an empty machine through a boiling hot cycle. Then I will load the Passover dishes.

I can't let Miriam stand on her feet and cook everything. I'll have to cook something. I guess I should unpack the Passover pots. I will take just the minimum – a couple of mixing bowls, and a big soup pot, and another pot for matzo balls. I'll need a few pans, for roasting chickens and potatoes. Chickens are already in the freezer.

I'll need a few more things at the store. Seder plate, symbolic foods. Horseradish root, greens, roasted shankbone.

Oh, no, I forgot to order a shankbone when I bought the chicken, every lamb shank in New York State must be spoken for by now.

Roasted egg on the Seder plate. You boil it then hold it over the burner with tongs to brown it. Eggs in salt water for the Seder meal: Better get an extra dozen eggs.

I enjoy making haroses, the heap of chopped fruits, nuts, and wine that stands for the mortar used by Hebrew slave in Egypt – that to me is Passover. Put walnuts, sugar, apples, sweet wine on the list.

Passover wine to drink. Grape juice for the kids. Add beverages to the list.

Soup. I've been to the butcher for broilers but forgot the pullets for the soup. Have to go back anyway for the shankbone. Call for that shankbone RIGHT NOW.

Must watch Miriam make egg noodles this year.

I'll have to do the utensils. If we're using the Passover pots, we'll need turners and slotted spoons and soup ladles and silverware and chicken shears and a grapefruit knife and a strainer and a chopper and a good knife. I'll need to Passoverize a few everyday utensils.

Pickles.

Dried fruit for compote.

Fresh fruit. It wouldn't be Passover without grapefruits, oranges, strawberries, and bananas.

Why would I want any life to live other than a Passover week with my family?

I'll buy a few fresh packages of salt and pepper, coffee, tea, ginger, paprika. I guess I'll sell the spices, the whiskeys and liqueurs, that a Jew is not supposed to own on Passover. I know it's a legal charade; authorizing the rabbi to sell the items, too expensive to give or throw away, to a non-Jew, and then arranging to buy it all back.

Where is that legal form from the rabbi?

I will need a new bag of sugar and new cinnamon for the bubelekh – matzo meal pancakes – and for the matzo brei. Take out a Passover frying pan. Can't use everyday oil in a Passover pan. Add oil to the list. And – yes, another dozen eggs. For my children, I'll make bubelekh for breakfast.

I should make the stove kosher for Passover, burn out the oven to clean it, take off the stove knobs and soak them, sear burners in their own flame. I should move out the stove and see what's underneath. Under the refrigerator, and under the sink.

I'm not going to put Passover things down on this counter, where I've been slicing bagels for fifty-one weeks. I'll just scrub and cover it. I'll pack away the toaster over, as long as I've done all of this.

I might as well invite a few more people to the Seder. The floors, the corners, crumbs everywhere! Hand me the mop, that bucket, that rag!

We're finishing up the hametz, leavened foods banned during Pesach. Eating the last crusts of bread, the last frozen bagels, the Greek spinach triangles and crescent rolls. We're having rice crackers for breakfast and soba noodles for lunch. We're baking chocolate chip cookies to use up the flour. We're making corn bread, five days before Pesach.

Enough, already. I will bag up theses packages of pasta and rice, and give them away to the soup kitchen, the one at the Methodist church.

Add it to the list: Church.

I will make Pesach.

May

Here are the things I have to give up.

Lobsters in New England, oysters sensually slithering down my throat, the French butcher. I give up calamari on Christmas Eve with a favorite friend, a traditional meal that links her to her Italian grandparents, and thus connects me to my friend's childhood. I sacrifice bacon at my aunt's house, crisped and greaseless beside a home-baked corn muffin, forgo Western omelets at diners I once loved to frequent.

I give up being able to eat comfortably anywhere, able to make casual assumptions. It is like being an immigrant, maybe; never quite feeling at home.

Once I knew I was a certain kind of Jew and I was comfortable in that identity. My heritage was Jewish, I was culturally a Jew. My cultural memories were Jewish. But I was Jewish and American, and the identification with my hybrid roots was also strong. I strove to be pure hybrid.

Ten years ago in my life, I would have found it unthinkable to divide my activities and concerns into the secular and the Jewish. Now I do, almost reflexively. I think about shaping everyday life according to principles not of my devising. Now I don't know what kind of Jew I am and what I am becoming. I only know that my two grandmothers had sixteen grandchildren between them, none of whom so far are raising children in a kosher home. I need to do something about this.

In striving to give my children their history, I take risks. Establishing their differentness may strain their sense of belonging to this American society. Connection to their tradition may lead to dissociation: a paradox. Plug in here, disconnect there.

What if one of my children says to me, someday, "There is nothing here for me"?

Those words imagined chill me. It is Israel that lures them, and I shiver at the distance. My grandchildren will not speak my language. They will not grow up in my backyard, or share the reference points I take for granted.

My mother loved this American ground, twisted her Polish/Lithuanian/Canadian self into knots to become a citizen. I call to my children in advance, shaking out a sack of Americana: Bill of Rights, blues, Walt Whitman, heartland, rustbelt, New York. Will all of this be like a melting ice cube to the vibrating heat of the identity we are forging?

I remember how strong the drive can be to connect somewhere but get away from here, when you are twenty years old. I feel as powerless to hold things together as we all finally are. The generations scatter, those who have gone turn to dust.

The traditions of our foreparents will lead my children away from me. But is this not as it should be? I should be giving my children the wherewithal to surpass me, to live life in a different way, to understand more, to go farther, to be responsible but also free.

I am building a floor under my children. I must live on it, too.

June

I've finally gone out and bought a set of dairy dishes to replace my blue odds and ends, and I've put together a white meat set. It feels good. I look at the stacks of dishes on their shelves, at the cutlery in their drawers, at soup ladles in two plastic colors, each a code for a different phase of life's appetites. Meat and dairy. There is a difference, in the essence and in my kitchen. This gives me a tidy, settled feeling. I look at these dishes and feel happy.

I still need a dairy soup pot and a few meat saucepans. I could use a matched set of dairy tableware instead of the odd lots I have commandeered. Generally, though, I feel content with this, fortunate and whole, but not complacent; aware that equilibrium is dynamic. A sense of balance this has given me.

"You are what you eat." In a society of excess, this is true. Consumption by choice is different from consumption out of need. I make choices based on my view of myself on the planet, and in the end I become the expression of those choices. Should I adorn my home with rare woods harvested from a shrinking rain forest? I can have almost anything on my plate. But should jets fly, barges course, trucks lumber, should oil wells pump and atoms split, so I can eat fruits out of season and swim in a distant sea? How important are the words "I want"?

It is inconvenient, this kosher keeping. I drive my hungry children past the fast-food outlets, I do not drive through to emerge with a Styrofoam box of fried chicken. I lose convenience and time, and time is precious wealth. I have to explain it to my children, sometimes firmly, sometimes faltering and evasive. Once my son, five years old, cried: He wanted to stop for fried chicken.

I was evasive. "Well..." I said. I wanted to minimize the appeal without banging shut the door. Maybe we should try it one day; maybe he would go with a friend. I was not yet ready, and still am not ready, to sit stolidly behind the wheel of my station wagon and say, firmly and finally as we pass the chicken place, "We don't eat that. It is treyf." I don't want to engender revulsion and disgust. What others eat should not be scorned.

But it was unkosher chicken, not fed or killed or examined according to Jewish law, and then it was maybe dipped in milk and fried in I don't know what, and served with macaroni and cheese and a roll with butter and string beans with bacon bits and a complimentary ice cream for dessert. Solid food not to be scorned, but not what I wanted to allow, just then, even just this once.

Here is the difference between those returning to tradition (me) and those securely rooted but not absolutist in life. My husband could have taken the kids and said to the teenager behind the counter, "Chicken, please, and fries, and Coke – no bacon or butter or ice cream." Good enough, shoyn, already.

My husband wasn't there. I was piloting our boat through the shifting tides of subjectivity. What we did instead was this. We came home and fixed dinner, the children helped or had to wait longer, and at last we ate, looking at one another around our own kitchen table. I knew what went into our bodies that evening, and I could feel good about it. Not such a loss, perhaps.

But we also cemented one more brick into the rising edifice of our life as a family. We eat at home, mostly, and less and less often dine out. We don't make spur-of-the-moment food decisions. We pick and choose and have a certain consciousness about it. We don't have a fast-food life.

Exploring Kashrut is my way of bundling up all the broken twigs that belong together. I can tie up my past, and transmit to my children something that, if not unbroken, is patched and coherent. They will receive the tradition. It is something to leave behind, perhaps – that will be their choice, later – but also something on which to build.

July

I want to create a home of rightness and wholeness, to establish the percussion beat of work and Sabbath, Sabbath and work. I want to infuse the minutiae of everyday life with something more – meaning or history or awe – and to experience it without too much sentimentality or irony.

Then on the other hand, I know, I now know for a fact, that this sort of thing must become a priority mission for someone in the household, and that person would have to be me.

Let me explain. If you are going to light candles on Friday night and have it feel like Sabbath, the house should be clean on Friday afternoon and the table dressed and the meal cooked by sundown. It's a satisfying feeling to have made ready, to have cleared away the detritus of a whole workaday week, sure it is. But then Friday is going to be about cleaning and cooking.

I can't cook on Friday, I'm working on Friday. I can cook on Thursday night after the children are in bed if I'm not too tired, or I can cook at five in the morning on Friday. My husband could cook, but he can't cook. If I have the money, I'll have the house cleaned.

I have to shop before cooking, and when will I do it? I will shop on Thursday evening, if I have the strength. Or my husband could shop, if I made up the list on Wednesday.

Friday's meal is not all I must plan for. To have a traditional Sabbath of rest, in which you neither drive, shop, light fires, nor do anything that resembles work, Saturday's meals should be prepared ahead. One could begin cooking Saturday dinner after sunset if it is not summer when days are long, but all the ingredients should be in the house by then. Or one could go out for pizza. We will go out for pizza, post-Sabbath.

What else must be done? We all should be home and our bodies bathed by the onset of Friday sundown. That is 4:32 or so on those winter afternoons when sudden dark falls early. It's a forgone conclusion that much of the year I will fail to hew to rabbinic timetables. If you're late lighting candles, the rabbis say, you'd better not light at all. You'd be lighting a fire forbidden on Sabbath.

I will deem Sabbath begun when mother is ready. Or I will light candles on time, and bask in their light, surrounded by clutter. I'll welcome the Sabbath and bathe children later. Or maybe they'll go to bed dirty. We'll have our imperfect Sabbath, our soupcon of grace and peace.

Then there is Sunday. Sunday's plans may need preparations, cash transactions. I cannot achieve spiritual refreshment from the material world, and still pop out to the A&P on Saturday afternoon. I must think about Sunday on Friday.

There may be a birthday party Sunday with a present to buy. We mean to plant tulips and fix a faucet, but the garden center is closed on Sunday and so is the hardware store.

I or my someone must buy things on Friday, but Friday I'm cooking – no, working. Thursday night I am grocery shopping. On Wednesday, then, the Sunday errands somehow must be done.

And then comes the week. A child needs a library book Monday at school. The library is open late only on Thursday. I could go to the library Thursday night, and get the groceries on Wednesday. Will the avocado hold up from Wednesday to Sunday? We promised guacamole for a neighbor's Sunday brunch.

Sunday is our day for going and doing, for children's sports and family activities, all the myriad house chores must get done during the week. Even our cleaning is done Friday, and even though we no longer mend and sew and iron and bake, there is still yard work and laundry and reorganizing a set and fixing a door handle and paying bills – all those tasks that the rest of the world does on

Saturday. When to do these things? Some of it can't get done. Or the family runs on overdrive. Or else it all falls on the wife.

The Sabbath is a gift: you give over twenty-four hours to contemplation, rest, and praise. It is regenerating. It punctuates the temporal world, or, as the sages explained it, provides a glimpse of the world to come. Also, it is a good deed to make love on the Sabbath.

Not that I believe in a world to come. But a roasted chicken on Friday night after candles are lit and lights are turned low and blessings are said, in a clean house, is for the moment, paradise enough. So I will roast a chicken Monday and freeze it, then on Friday defrost and reheat. Or order in. Like a mad escapee from an unknown century, I explain myself to myself, hoping for the right answer.

August

It's nice to live in a world of bright diversity, with many forms and colors from which to choose in designing a life. It is enjoyable to select from among the many manifestations of many traditions: Chinese New Year tonight, gospel music tomorrow, a Passover Seder. But the wellspring must be authentic, or else it is just a museum. Someone, many someones, must keep the sources alive.

We want to pick and choose from the great shopping mall of expedient culture: a certain sandwich to feed a hungry nostalgia, particular communal values when we need them, ritual expertise at times of joy or stress. But when one decides, after all, to celebrate a son's bar mitzvah, the synagogue and all the trappings must be there, maintained by a community. The old kosher bakery will close without regular shoppers. With no passionate discussants, the valued argumentative traditions of Jewish study will fade away into irrelevance.

Without commitment, the sources will die. The forms we love to have the choice to return to will wither and disappear, or worse yet, become hollow shells, cultural theme parks. Someone, many someones, have kept the forms alive and vital, have kept the choices available to me. They may have been skeptical; they must have had moments when their preferences were elsewhere.

It is my turn now.

September

The stories were remembered for a reason. Family stories, they were told and retold because they contained essential truths. Life and ourselves were in those stories, whether they were flattering or not, straightforward or opaque, legend or history. They showed us, in one way or another, how to live.

Religion is a story that tells us how to live. The pious scholars believe everything is in the Torah, if you know where to look. I don't know if everything is in it, but a lot is in it. I want to know more of that.

Drawn to ritual, I may perhaps draw nearer to meaning. First principles are becoming interwoven in the fabric of daily life. I like this dimension, this reminder, this presence of something timeless, as my own clock ticks. Random, sparkling, incredible, the world can hold both reason and awe.

I can relinquish, perhaps, the physical things of the past, if I believe that their essence continues through time. I can go on with everyday life in the company of ancient values, insights, questions, and doubts.

After all the millennia, I give my doubts another year.

For further reading:

Ehrlich, Elizabeth. *Miriam's Kitchen: A Memoir*. New York, NY: 1997.

Grunfeld, Isidore. *The Sabbath*. Nanuet, NY: 1998.

Palatnik, Lori. *Friday Night and Beyond: The Shabbat Experience Step by Step*. Northvale, NJ: 1994.

Steinsaltz, Adin. *Teshuvah: A Guide for the Newly Observant Jew*. Northvale, NJ: 1996.

Stern, Fruma, Yehudis Cohen and Deborah Bell. *Body and Soul: A Handbook for Kosher Living*. New York, NY: 1989.

Steinsaltz, Adin. *The Miracle of the Seventh Day*. Hoboken, NJ: 2003.

One Hundred Thirty-Three

ICU

My heart calls You, Holy One,
My heart bottom, bone marrow,
Flesh of soul of being,
Calls You to my questioning.

My heart calls in suddenness
Of my distress, and the mute days
When I praise forgetting and compliance,
Choice surrendered.

My heart calls You in the wakeful times:
Surfacing, succumbing. You are there,
Sustaining my momentary consciousness,
Reminding me to praise You in this place.

Ancient words remind me. Newly learned,
I clutch them tightly, syllable and tone.
You hover in their echo, Holy One,
Supporting my courage and my hope.

                    Debbie Perlman

How I Spent my Summer Vacation
Debbie Perlman

In early July 1996, two weeks before Tisha B'Av, the day commemorating the destruction of the first and second Temples, my summer cold accelerated to pneumonia, complicated by an accumulation of fluid below my left lung. My maneuvers became a daily struggle toward recovery.

I have been physically disabled and oxygen-dependent for many years, the result of radiation treatments and chemotherapy that spared my life in my twenties and thirties. I face these aftereffects with thanks that I am alive, with adjustments and compromises that let me live.

My body badly handled the challenge of pneumonia. When I awoke several days later in the intensive care unit, I found that time lost to me had been busy for my caretakers.

At the age of 27, I was diagnosed with Hodgkin's disease, a form of lymphatic cancer. I remembered the hospital rabbi who came to visit me shortly after. His pale, embarrassed face swam before me as I sat weeping with the terror of my news. Making his rounds, he stood just inside the doorway, but offered no ancient comfort words. He had no ritual, no prayer book, no laying on of hands. I had no words to comfort myself but "God, oh God."

Through the subsequent years of surgery and chemotherapy, radiation treatments, side effects and recurrence, I struggled to accommodate to the strange tasks of daily living necessitated by illness. I was busy with a growing baby, distracted by the need to surrender control when I was hospitalized again and again.

A bright moment in these days came when we brought our then three-year-old daughter to our newly joined congregation to be named. Our rabbi suggested we find verses of Psalm 119 to spell out her Hebrew name, Chava Gevurah, to read during the ceremony.

I had always felt the need for prayer and for ritual, but lacking all but the most rudimentary knowledge, I was stymied until I began my own Jewish education. Those classes fed my mind and spirit and led me to begin to compose my own psalms, prayer poems.

In the hospital, as I found myself fighting pain and confusion, I was drawn again and again to a recently assimilated piece of text: the last stanza of King David's Psalm 150.

Praise God with resounding cymbals!
Praise God with clanging cymbals!
Let every soul that has breath praise God!
Hallelujah!

The festival melody for the psalm played in my head as I was wheeled to a special procedures room to have a tracheotomy performed. It would return as I became more alert and able to move around. Its cadences helped me regulate my breathing as I exercised.

I was discharged, only to be readmitted to the hospital two weeks later. More of the same. More fluid in my chest. More clogged bronchi. More pneumonia. Another period of lost days where, sedated and mute, I tried to communicate through scribbled notes. It is hard to carry on conversations like this; it's impossible to kibbitz, to joke, to schmooze. And the term of this second contest shook my faith – a new struggle in the now familiar land of ventilators, triple lumen lines and beeping machines. It was the Hebrew month of Elul. It was the time of reflection and preparation for the Days of Awe. And I was still fighting to breathe on my own.

One Hundred Thirty Four
Struggle

I am gasping beneath this waterfall of illness,
Frozen limbs straining,
Lungs pushing against the crash,
Heart crying out in rapid beat.

Gasping, Sacred Healer, frantic
To whisper Your name,
To grasp blessing and power
And raise it above me in shelter.

Torrents overwhelm me,
They drown me in foaming water.
My hand moves, reaching,
Rising to protect my face.

Turn to me, Holy One!
Turn back the blasting water;
Turn back the pain and sadness,
The shuddering of chances lost.

Turn to me, Sacred Healer!
Multiply my tiny motions;
Bring my passage
To dry land.

Then I was home again. Physically stronger, I could walk a bit. But I was readmitted the afternoon before Rosh Hashanah. Weeping and frightened, a chest tube was inserted to drain the reaccumulated fluid. Then, on the second day of Rosh Hashana, unrousable, I crashed. I was rushed to the I.C.U., to the terrifying waking sleep, to muteness and total dependence.

Months before Yom Kippur, the solemn and awesome day of atonement, I had written a psalm. I needed to defy the reality of these weeks of illness.

One Hundred Thirty Five
Kol Nidre

Ruler of the Universe!
At our season of renewal,
We are turning, bending,
Viewing front and back.

Ruler of the Universe!
At our season of revival,
We are uncovering, revealing,
Sweeping out.

Ruler of blessing,
We lean upon the Gate
Testing the hinges,
Rubbing sharp edges.

Ruler of mercy,
We test our souls,
Rubbing fresh cloth over sorrow,
Binding away disappointment.

Called, called to the Gate,
We jostle, then quiet,
As memory and hope
Soothe us.

Standing, striving,
We empty our hearts' longing
Before You, Holy One,
Source of life.

The Ten days of Repentance between Rosh Hashana and Yom Kippur had moved me from a general medical floor to the intensive care unit and on the afternoon of Yom Kippur, back to my room. Everyone was familiar to me this time. I was greeted with kindness and dismay as once again I went through the process of shedding I.V. lines and tubes, of moving from assisted to independent breathing. I regained my voice. The gaping hole of the tracheotomy became smaller. Physical therapy resumed. I could not break a fast I had not observed.

All those days incarcerated! For the first time in many years, we did not build our sukkah, the fragile outdoor booth that commemorates the Jews' years of wandering. On the Sunday in Sukkot, a kind young couple bearing lulav and etrog to hospitalized Jews gave me back a piece of holiness as I stood by the bed in my purple robe and shook it all directions.

The doctors planned my discharge for the afternoon of Simchat Torah, the closing festival of the autumn holiday cycle. I looked forward to attending the celebration at my synagogue, to watching the dancing with the Torah scrolls.

I was released two days later.

One Hundred Thirty Six
Home Again

Strengthen me, Holy One, on my walk from illness;
Even as you gave courage
As the children fled from Egypt,
Open the sea to my steps

Like a Hebrew slave,
I have sojourned in pain;
Under whips of illness and despair,
I have shed my tears of bitterness.

Show me again the path of freedom,
Speeding toward a Promised Land
Of wholeness and health,
Creating my completeness for Your sake.

Bring me up through recovery,
Through remedies and therapies,
To an altered yet acceptable life,
Again, rejoicing in the commonplace.

Then will my songs fill this recovered shore,
Where my mind will dance for joy
At my deliverance,
Singing Your praises, Holy One, singing new songs.

For further reading:

Perlman, Debbie. *Flames to Heaven: New Psalms for Healing and Praise*. Wilmette, IL: 1998.
Lamm, Maurice *The Power of Hope: The One Essential of Life and Love*. New York, NY: 1995.
Kirzner, Yitzchok. *Making Sense of Suffering: A Jewish Approach*. Brooklyn, NY: 2002.

Those who pray even when in pain are rewarded doubly.

Rashi on Berakhot *63a*

At the time when someone is in pain, what does the Almighty say?
He says, "Woe to My aching head, woe to My aching limb."

Talmud, Hagigah *15b*

Expecting Miracles

Chana Weisberg

From the interview with Rabbanit Hadassah Saphir:

We're talking about different things women feel in their pregnancies and during birth, so you know, for me it's been a long learning experience the whole time. I certainly didn't conclude with the same feeling I had when I first started, although the intensity was there from the very beginning. There's one experience, I think it was just after getting married. I went to Yad Vashem [Israel's Holocaust Museum] and I walked out with a feeling that I'm going to bring down as many neshamot [souls] as I can, that that's the only answer that there is. There's no answer, but that's what I can do now, and that was my decision. That's how I walked out, and that's how I continued for thirty years. That was my starting point as a mother and my feeling was always that the dead were giving life (*ha-metim natenu et ha-hayyim*). In other words, I saw that God had sent me into this world with the mission to bring life.

It was only recently, a year or two ago, that I had more time to talk with my father about what he went through during the Shoah, and his long escape. In speaking with my father, the way he described what kept him going through this

---

* Edited excerpts from *Expecting Miracles: Finding Meaning and Spirituality in Pregnancy through Judaism.*

whole thing was that he knew that he had to live and he thought that he was the last Jew left in the whole world. He was able to do all of these amazing things because he knew that he just had to continue. So now, after speaking with him, I realize that my feeling at Yad Vashem so many years ago is a continuation of my father's sense of mission in his own life.

So I decided that I was going to help bring down all the neshamot I could, although bringing this down to the reality was not easy, and that took me a long time. In other words, to keep this lofty idea in my mind while going through all of the difficulties of pregnancies and births and, more than that, while dealing with all of the physical tasks in the household and with children – that took a longer time. The point, the idea, the light was there, but to translate it into a day to day message was this thirty year venture.

Through most of my pregnancies I wasn't aware of how to understand pregnancy as a religious experience. I loved learning Torah then, and I still love learning, and when I have any free time that's what I'll do. So, for example, it was hard for me then, even with all this great idea of bringing down souls, not to have any time to learn. If you're into just learning Torah and doing mitzvot, and you're not aware that you're doing this all as a woman, then you can look at a lot of the things that happen in our lives as mothers and wives as taking away from precious time for Torah study. And that's what I was challenged with for my first years of early motherhood, and there was no one who could really answer my questions.

I came to a deeper understanding of women's experience through a switch fifteen years ago, at the midpoint of my life, when I began learning more *penimiyut ha-Torah,* learning the deeper teachings of the Torah, that shed new light on all of the verses and the commentaries in the Bible that I had been learning and teaching before. I also gave up the idea that women's Torah learning should follow the model of the type of learning that men do. I found that the perspective I gained from this new way of approaching things was able to change a lot of the experiences I had during the day – the great experiences and the small experiences, and it provided me with a new way of looking at the daily chores of being a woman, as well as my pregnancies and births. I think that was one of the great turning points in my life.

I can even remember when this change happened and during which pregnancy because it related to a certain new teaching I learned from Hasidic philosophy. Rebbe Nahman of Breslov teaches that you should try to remember as far back as you can. That was the first thing the Ba'al Shem Tov would ask a child, "What's the first thing you remember?" So, of course, for the child to remember way, way back, his mother first has to remember very, very far back. Rebbe Nahman would ask "Can you remember when the apple fell off the branch of the tree?" which is the birth. And "Can you remember back even further, when the seed was first planted, and when the thought of planting the seed first came up?" So those are all important parts of the description of how a soul comes down. I can remember deciding I was going to remember the answers to these questions from now on, for myself and for my children. It was an active decision on my part.

At this point in my life there is nothing that I learn in Torah which I do not translate or integrate into being a Jewish mother – being a Jewish woman. I think that's what learning is for. That's the difference between women's learning and men's learning. As women we must at some soon point take the kind of removed learning which men do and bring it down into the reality. It was nice to learn and it still is nice to learn, but I will go so far as to say that it's not necessary to be a Torah-learning woman to have great spiritual Divine experiences. You just have to have a little bit of insight and perception. The Torah will come from inside you.

I apply what I am teaching and learning about women in the Bible or Hasidic philosophy to my understanding of the pregnancy, or the birth, or in the name I gave a child. This was mostly simple stuff, for example, how I would carry myself during pregnancy. Everyone knows that sometimes this is an issue, especially if you're getting very big, or are not feeling your best physically or emotionally. So the moment that I understood and internalized this idea that the soul inside of me is like a living sefer Torah [Torah scroll], and that the fetus is learning Torah inside me all the time, all of a sudden when I walked it was with a lot of happiness. Of course, not every day was like this, but in general it did help.

Or the teaching that every Jewish woman walks with pride because she knows she's giving birth to Moshiach [the Messiah], in a certain sense, because every Jewish soul has its point of Moshiach inside it. All of these thoughts could transform much of the difficulty involved in the pregnancy and take me to another place.

I was always thinking about very practical ways of using some of these little things I learned, not even talking about the great experience of birth itself, but just for the little moments in a long pregnancy, of using little sparks of Torah that I heard or collected on the way to change the everyday of pregnancy. Another thing I learned was about not just waiting and counting towards the end, like during the long ninth month that never ends, but being able to count each day that has passed with happiness, reminding ourselves that the pregnancy itself is great joy, and that's not always an easy thing. Every day I could actually feel, and I taught this in my classes, that either you have a sefer Torah in you or you are holding a baby. I didn't live my first pregnancy like that, but during difficult times this way of thinking suddenly enabled me to appreciate not just the final moment, but every healthy, happy day.

When you're learning Torah, or involved in prayer or another mitzvah, you are coming closer to Hashem. But in the birth itself, Hashem is right there – you don't need to search. You're not even caught up in yourself, which is what keeps us from doing all of the mitzvot the way we should, since we're still thinking about how we're doing it and if I'm doing it right or if someone else thinks I'm doing it OK. But when you're in a birth, you're not involved in the physical or spiritual niceties of how you're doing. You are completely involved in the birth itself. This is the most important thing in the world that has to be done right now and you're going to do it.

After the birth, and at all other times, you're striving for that same place. But it's never as direct as it is in the moment of birth, but when you know that moment you can take it with you for your whole life. But you first must know that moment. And then you can approach prayer and the Torah and mitzvot with the same intensity. The easiest way to learn this is through a birth. You can learn it from giving birth, or you can even learn it if you have witnessed another woman giving birth. If, for some reason, by Divine providence, a woman does not become a mother, then she's given the ability to do the other mitzvot of Torah, and prayer and good deeds, with that same kind of intensity of a woman who has given birth.

I never used any drugs during my births. I think that most of my pregnancies and births were pretty regular even though by the books some were more and some were less. People do use all kinds of drugs and pain relievers. I could never decide for anyone else. For my daughters and daughters-in-law, I never say anything. When I was a young woman, the world wasn't using so much of this stuff. It wasn't so safe then, and there weren't so many possibilities. The world's different now. So I'm not going to tell people what to do.

I'm grateful, though, for all the experiences that I went through. In other words, I wouldn't trade in one moment of even any of the longer painful births. That's the difference of before and after! Now I can feel the sweetness of every moment of those difficult births. I can taste what it will be like in the future when Hashem will show us and explain to us all of the tzarot [troubles] of the Jewish people, of all the exiles. And this is because I can now say that if I were given the choice again, I would still go through every birth naturally and not use anything. Because now afterwards, particularly afterwards, I'm grateful for every moment, even every painful moment that there was.

A lot of times, even in the pregnancy or the labor I would connect the experience with the birth of the Jewish people and the birth of Moshiach. The words in Hebrew are all the same, you can't not connect between them. *Hevlei*

Mashiah, the "birth pangs" that precede the coming of the Messiah, are *hevlei ledah,* the pain of childbirth. They're all the same words, they're all amazingly the same. And this feeling during the transition where it will never end, it's just this point in the birth when you can't handle it. You don't know where to go with the pain. And it seems like it will never end. And that's the state of Am Yisrael, the Jewish people, many times. We've been in a state of transition for a very long time.

When transition ends, you have this knowledge that the birth will take place. It should be soon now. This is a teaching also of the Baal Shem Tov, that everything that happens to a person in his lifetime can teach him about the state of the Shechina [Divine Presence] or the state of the Jewish people. It's a simple and powerful teaching.

I can remember the most difficult birth was one where labor started, my waters broke, then all of a sudden the labor pains stopped and I waited. And then there was this other place of just waiting, and wanting the pain to come. I suddenly knew that the most difficult place is where you don't feel anything at all – where you're just nowhere. Feeling the pain means you're part of the process, you're in the labor, assured of the redemption. I can remember yearning for the contractions to come as a sign for what will take place finally, and understanding the message to the Jewish people of what that place means.

This birth represented what a person goes through – where you're not sensitive to what's going on, where you don't feel the pain of the situation. You sense that there's something wrong, and you need to feel the pain in order to know what to pray for, in order to combat what's taking place. If you don't feel anything, then nothing is going to happen. We see this so often nowadays in the Jewish people, that we know something is wrong, but we are out of touch. We can't find where the pain is. But it can be sweet at that moment when you feel the pain, in that moment the redemption can take place. We all think that the birth is going to take a long time, but sometimes all of a sudden it happens just like that. But you just have to be connected and be sensitive to what's going on and feel for a moment the pain, and then that's enough. The birth can take place already.

During that birth, after all those hours, I hadn't taken anything, I hadn't really slept, I just had no strength. And I was grateful that the labor was finally beginning and I was in labor, but I just had no physical strength to give birth. I always did breathing, like most women do, but I was at that point already where I had been learning more Hasidic philosophy, and I had also learned verses and meditations to go along with the breathing, so in the less intense stages of labor, I would use them. I would breathe verses and I would breathe Hebrew letters. This is a well-known technique now, accompanying breathing exercises with Jewish meditation. This is something you can do in less intense stages of labor.

When you're in intense labor, you just have to be there. There's just nothing else you can do except that itself. The idea is, at the intense part of labor, you're in the essence of the matter. You don't have to say any verses anymore. You just do it. You're it and you're doing it and there's nothing else.

At that point, the birth was finally progressing, but not too quickly. I still had time. So all of a sudden this verse came to me from the Prophets, *"Ba'u vanim ad mashber, ve-koah ayn Ie-ledah"* – the children have come to the final stage of labor, and there is no strength to give birth (Isaiah 37:3). The verse is talking about the Jewish people while they were besieged by the King of Assyria, and King Hizkiyahu recites this verse in his prayer to Hashem. So during the birth, this verse came to me and it stuck, and I could only hold onto this verse. And I'm saying, "Yes, right, I know that place now. That's right where I am. And how will I get out of it?"

Now, this is a Biblical verse that I had studied many times over the years but before this birth I learned about it in Kabbalistic teachings, which added a new dimension. In Kabbalah, when you see that you are "ayn," that you have no strength of your own, then you can know the *"Ayn ha-Eloki,"* which is a name for God, that He is the source of all strength. God is the *Ayn ha-Eloki* which really gives sustenance to all that exists.

So all of a sudden I realized, very far into this long transition, that the verse that had been with me all this time was saying that I couldn't give birth. I said, I need another verse, I'm not going to give birth with this verse. I needed to get to some other place, to get out of this fatigue. But I didn't get another verse. That verse kept on coming, but then all of a sudden I got this other meaning, this "ah, no, no, not ayn. It doesn't mean there's no strength, it means the strength for the birth is not coming from you. Really, you have no strength, so where will the strength come from? From the *ayn,* from the *Ayn ha-Eloki,* because now only God can do it." So then the verse changed around – that the strength of *Ayn* will give birth. That was something of a revelation, it just came all of a sudden, and immediately I gave birth.

It was in the births after that one that I came to understand that always the key to birth is in the hands of God. The most intense feeling is when you have this feeling, that everything is from God and at the same time you have to actively participate in a birth. You're supposed to push, you're supposed to do, but you know it's all from God.

Then the next birth was a regular birth. I can't even tell you, I don't remember anything about it. And I was just into the birth itself. Just doing. And then I realized, I had this understanding that God is with you not only when you have these great highs. That last birth that I described to you now was a very high moment. If someone's going to hear this she's going to say, "Oh, this spiritual lady." But the next birth was so regular and I was so simple in it. Just simply doing, just giving birth. And I was so grateful to be simply giving birth, with no verses, just a normal, regular length, and I was giving birth in a regular, normal way. There was plenty of breathing, but there was no great test.

But I can remember being so very grateful just to be having a simple birth and because of the last time I knew that God was there too. I had realized that God is with you in the simple moments, that it's not more or less a revelation of Heaven. I learned that I don't always have to look for these great highs, spiritual wild moments, but I simply had to know that God was with me all the time. That understanding also allowed me to remember all the births before that, that had just passed over me, and I could remember them in a different way, and see that God was there very clearly, directly and simply all the time. That's the biggest lesson. You don't need some big revelation of verses and letters, as long as you know that it's all from God.

For further reading:

Weisberg, Chana. *Expecting Miracles: Finding Meaning and Spirituality in Pregnancy through Judaism.* Jerusalem: 2004.

Finkelstein, Boruch, and Michal Finkelstein, R.N. *Be-Sha'ah Tovah – Nine Wonderful Months: The Jewish Woman's Clinical and Halachic Guide to Pregnancy and Childbirth.* Nanuet, NY: 1993.

How to begin

suspend tautologies you live by
release chords of association
hear a different music
abandon yourself to strange rhythms
seek fire

let rising fever direct you
let eyes drag magnets
to the proximity of heat
when you stumble against the edge
of a deep precipice

jump into flames
easily as into cleansing water
hold your breath
until all the stories
of your old houses

go to ashes to ashes
stay
burn
to embers that glow
with memory of other fires

emerge
altered
if you recognize yourself
by the slightest thread
begin again

    Judy Belsky

Studying Prayerfully

Sarah Yehudit (Susan) Schneider

Avi, Adoni, Dodi, My father, my master, my friend, my beloved.

I enter into this study in order to draw close to You – for the sake of holy service and the fulfillment of Your will for me and for all of Israel and for this entire planet. Please assist my efforts and guide my understandings.

Let me internalize Your Torah to the depth of my being so that I become transformed by Your will and its truths.

Let neither myself nor anyone else come into stumbling as a result of this study.

Gal einai ve-abita niflaot mi-toratekha.[1] *Open my eyes that I may behold wonders from Your Torah.*

This is a prayer I wrote many years ago, when I first began studying Torah. I continue to say this prayer every day before I begin learning, and I say it with my students before I begin teaching. To better understand this prayer and its deep roots, we must first put on a wide-angle lens and examine some of the broad and archetypal themes that are raised by the biblical story of Chana,[2] the quintessential role model of Jewish prayer. In particular, we want to look at the fact that Chana, a woman, had such an enormous impact on the way we, as Jews, pray. And secondly, we want to explore why it is that her watershed prayer was, significantly, a prayer for a child.

There is perhaps no other instance of a woman having such a profound, direct and acknowledged impact on Jewish practice.[3] And it is not just prayer in general that we learn from Chana... it is our Amida, the silent prayer, the prayer that is the very essence of Jewish prayer. All other Jewish liturgy is either building up to or winding down from the Amida. The Talmud and Midrashim list many essential features of this prayer that are modeled after Chana's prayer, including the fact that it is a whispered prayer, and even the fact that it comprises eighteen blessings.[4]

I believe that HaShem chose Chana to bring all this down, not just because she possessed exceptional personal qualities, but because it was appropriate, and even necessary, that our collective prayer bear the imprint of a woman.

It is certainly true that in chassidut and kabbalah, prayer is considered a feminine mode of service, and study, a more masculine one. The conventions of

---

[1] Psalms 119:18.

[2] The story of Chana, the mother of the prophet and judge Samuel, is told in the first two chapters of the book of Samuel. She was childless for many years. The Bible describes her pilgrimage to the Tabernacle at Shilo, where she poured out her anguished prayer inaudibly, with only her lips moving, vowing to dedicate any son born to her to the Tabernacle, where he would dedicate his life to the service of God. Chana subsequently gave birth to Samuel and the Bible recounts her glorious prayer of thanksgiving.

[3] Kama hilchita gavrivata ika le-mishma mei-hanei kra'ei de-Hanna, Tractate Berakhot 31a.

[4] *Yalkut Shimoni,* 1 Shmuel.

gender here echo the physical differences between men and women. Bestowing is a masculine role, receiving is a feminine one.

The prayer we are discussing here is a prayer of request (as opposed to prayer of praise and thanksgiving). This is the actual mitzvah of prayer, which Ramban defines as the obligation "to entreat HaShem for all that we lack."[5] Only when prayer comes from a place of lack and longing does it attain the status of mitzvah and the unique opportunity for closeness with HaShem that such longing provides.

Rabbi Tsadok HaKohen[6] explains that prayer (unlike study) cannot happen without God in the picture. Prompted by lack, a person turns to HaShem and asks that his or her deficiency be removed. In this sense prayer is feminine, for in prayer we are not only receptive, we are begging to be filled. A master of prayer knows the secret of turning lack into an empty-space-of-longing that has enough vacuum power to pull its answer down from the heavens. This was Chana's expertise. Conversely, says Rabbi Tsadok, study can happen, at least theoretically, without ever touching a place of lack. Study is empowering, and the acquisition of knowledge enables one to feel they can control their reality because of what they now know about the laws of nature (both human and physical). Knowledge is a good thing, but it is also why, in study, there is the danger of forgetting that one needs HaShem.

Nevertheless, traditionally, study is more valued than prayer. Numerous sources suggest this hierarchy. Rabbis are even rebuked for drawing out their prayer: *Manichin chayei olam v'oskim b'chayei sha'a?*[7] – They forsake eternal life [i.e., study] to occupy themselves with temporal life [i.e. prayer]? The idea is that study expands consciousness, which is an eternal acquisition for the soul. Once a mind opens there is no turning back. And the truths and wisdom a soul absorbs in the course of its life pass straight through the pearly gates. They are not touched by the body's demise.

Conversely, the "good life" that we pray for – health, livelihood and even peace – are earthbound concerns. They improve our quality of life in *this* world, but don't join us in the next, as the Zohar testifies, anything heavier than a mustard seed gets left behind.[8]

So the Talmud questions the wisdom of taking time that could be used for study, with its *eternal* fruits, and using it instead for what, by Talmudic

---

[5] Ramban, *Sefer ha-Mitzvot*, Positive Commandment #5: *Shulhan Arukh* 98:3.

[6] R. Tzadok HaCohen, *Tzidkat ha-Tzadik*, Essay 211.

[7] Tractate *Shabbat* 10a.

[8] Zohar II, 197a.

standards, is simply a glorified form of immediate gratification.

Rebbe Nachman explains, however, that there are two kinds of prayer.[9] One *is* lower than study, and secondary to it, for precisely the reasons explained. Yet there is another kind of prayer, he says, that is equal to study and actually, perhaps, even higher than it. In this prayer, one asks for help in translating study into practice. One prays to be transformed by the Torah one learns, to turn its teachings into deeds, to embody its truths. This kind of prayer, says Rebbe Nachman, goes beyond study, fulfilling the Talmudic maxim, "The real goal is not study but action."[10] Higher prayer is the secret of turning study into action.

I wrote the prayer that I share above because as I began to go deeply into the study of Jewish text I felt a gap between what I was able to absorb with my head and what I could integrate into my heart. I always saw my learning as a spiritual path, so this gap was quite painful for me. I felt the only way I could have any fighting chance of solving this dilemma was to study prayerfully, to bring HaShem into the picture because HaShem can do anything.

I say this prayer every day before I study because I believe it aids me in translating my studies into my life. One could say that in higher prayer one is seeking to become pregnant with the lights of study, which also include the lessons of daily life, as the Talmud clearly states, *ein emet ela Torah*[11] – There is no truth except Torah. Whenever one discovers truth, one acquires a spark of Torah.

In the higher prayer that Rebbe Nachman speaks of one is asking to birth the Torah he or she is learning into the world as a physical deed. For what does it mean to bring forth child? It means that a soul, a bundle of lights, comes into a body. Similarly the lights of Torah, when embodied as behavior, are thus born into the world. And so, it is no coincidence that Chana's archetypal prayer was a prayer for child, for that is the essence of higher prayer, the longing to bring light down into body, both literally, as child, and metaphorically, as rectified behavior.

Now this can also, perhaps, help to explain the halachic difference in the way Torah study has traditionally applied to men and women. Professor Susan Handelman[12] explores this difference in an essay she wrote based on a discussion by the Lubavitcher Rebbe in *Likutei Sichot* where the Rebbe states that it is possible that there might be no difference in what, or how much men and women

---

[9] R. Natan Steinholtz, *Likutei Halachot,* Orah Hayyim, Rosh Hodesh 5.

[10] *Pirkei Avot* 1:17: *Ki lo ha-midrash hu ha-ikar ela ha-ma'ase.*

[11] Jerusalem Talmud, *Rosh ha-Shannah* 18a.

[12] Handelman, Susan. "Women and the Study of Torah in the Thought of the Lubavitcher Rebbe." In *Jewish Legal Writings by Women,* edited by Micah Halpern and Chana Safrai, 143–178. Jerusalem: 1998.

learn. The only difference might be in the source of their obligation. Men are obligated to study *lishma*, for its own sake, because of the mitzvah itself. Women are also obligated to study, but only to the extent that it is required to complement their practice. For some women this might mean the study of the bare minimum of practical halacha, whereas others might find that their obligations to love and fear HaShem, and the mitzvah to believe in His oneness, require a constant exploration of text and tradition.

By defining women's obligation to study in more practical terms, it is perhaps acknowledging their greater drive and/or capacity to make their learning practical, to translate it into life and deed. In other words, to become pregnant with their study.

Now everything has its up-side and down-side. As a female teacher of women I can certainly say that I see this and appreciate it, and yet sometimes feel frustrated by my students' need for every idea to be turned into practical Torah within a class period. There is little patience for teachings that can't impregnate immediately. And yet, on the other hand, on the other side of the mechitza, there are too many learned minds that have little ability to connect their knowledge with their actions. There's not enough pregnancy happening there.

And so, addressing this problem, Rabbi Tsadok emphasizes the need for their interinclusion. *Lah garsi ela haycha de-matzli*[13]*... lah havah matzlayna, ela haycha de-garesna*[14] – "I don't learn except where I pray... I don't pray except where I learn." Study must be prayerful, and must be accompanied by an explicit plea to absorb truth and be changed by it. And conversely, the prayerful yearning to grow and transform requires the fortification of study. For learning, says Rabbi Tsadok, stretches one's capacity to bear the discomfort of not-yet-answered prayer, and increases one's tolerance for the delayed gratification of not-easily-integrated teachings.

For this we must thank Chana, the mistress of higher prayer, who gave voice to our yearning to birth holy lights into the world.

For further reading:
Elper, Ora Wiskind, and Susan Handelman, eds. *Torah of the Mothers: Contemporary Jewish Women Read Classical Jewish Texts*. Jerusalem: 2002.
Kaplan, Aryeh. *A Call to the Infinite*. New York, NY: 1986.
Schochet, Jacob Immanuel. *Deep Calling unto Deep*. New York, NY: 1995.

---

[13] Tractate *Megillah* 29a.
[14] Tractate *Berakhot* 8a.

If you only knew the power of the psalms and what they accomplish in the Heavenly Realms, you would say them all the time. You should know that the Psalms breach all barriers and rise successively higher without any interference, and prostrate themselves before the Master of the Universe, and produce their effect with kindness and mercy.

Rabbi Menachem Mendel, third Rebbe of Lubavitch, known as the Tzemach Tzedek

The Voice of Jehillim

Varda Branfman

During my first months in Jerusalem, I soaked up information about everything related to Judaism, from the kosher species of birds and animals, to the order of the sacrificial offerings in the Temple, to the proper observance of the Sabbath. I did nothing but attend classes, read books, and engage in discussions.

From the outside, I may have looked like a person drowning who grabs for the nearest solid, buoyant material, whatever it happens to be. Some friends and family explained it as a need for structure and purpose, or even a temporary lapse of reason. In reality, I was peeling off the layers of my American cultural identity until I was left with the essence of what I had been all along, a Jew. I knew it was permanent. Having found essence, why would I ever want to paste back on the peel?

I had an excellent Hebrew teacher when I was a child of ten, and I was lucky that I still remembered how to read. Besides some other rudimentary knowledge, I was a beginner in a sea of information that just kept getting deeper.

One of the pieces of information that I gathered along the way was the custom of saying the psalm (from the collection of one hundred and fifty psalms recorded by King David) that corresponds to the number of years of a person's life. For instance, at the age of twenty-nine, I was living my thirtieth year of life, and the psalm of that entire year was Chapter 30.

I vaguely remembered the Psalms having cropped up here and there, mostly in a Christian context. In fact, I had never associated them with anything Jewish, and had erroneously believed they had been written in High English by some medieval cleric.

Now I set out to reclaim them as my own. I learned that most of the Psalms were composed by King David at different times in his life – times of explosive joy and devastating sorrow, times of his betrayal by those closest to him, and times of his elevation to royalty.

The word "Psalms" had the ring of posturing, as if one had to adopt a position of reverence and supplication that created a distance from one's real feelings. But King David's words, as I read them now, carried the weight of his suffering and his deepest longing. His pleading was raw and immediate. His delight was rapture. His tranquility was healing.

I had just bought a translation of Tehillim with the Hebrew on one side of the page and the English translation facing it, and I straightaway looked up my Tehillim for that year.

"Hashem, my God, I cried out to You and You healed me. Hashem, You have raised up my soul from the lower world, You have preserved me from my descent to the pit.... You have changed for me my lament into dancing, You undid my sackcloth and girded me with gladness. So that my soul might sing to You and not be still, Hashem my God, forever will I thank You."

Here was an expression of the gratitude that had been welling up in my own heart. I did feel that I had been pulled out from a pit just as I was nearing the point of no return. Suddenly, everything changed. I found my soul, and that soul wanted to sing out and never again be silent.

I said the chapter of Tehillim over and over again in the English translation that whole year, and I continued to be amazed at how perfectly it spoke about the turn of events in my life. Just months before, I had been living as a stranger to my own soul. Now, I often felt like jumping up and breaking out in a spontaneous dance to express the shock of my sudden happiness.

"For You have delivered my soul from death, my eyes from tears, my feet from stumbling." (116:8)

Ten years later, I am sitting in a synagogue in the Zichron Moshe section of Jerusalem. The women's section is packed, and the same downstairs by the men. Over time, I have warmed up to the original language of Tehillim, so I can even read the Hebrew words with a bit of understanding.

We are saying the words of Tehillim together, from the beginning to the end, all 150 chapters. It takes us about two hours. This doesn't allow for lingering over the meaning of each word. The recitation is in unison and at a brisk pace.

I look at the women sitting beside me and in the rows around me, their books of Tehillim open in front of them. Most of these women grew up in

Jerusalem and never set foot outside of Israel. Many of them know only a few English words. Did they ever hear of Bob Dylan or *The Little Prince?*

Doubtful.

Are we saying the same Tehillim?

It occurs to me that the words of Tehillim are expansive enough to contain all of us: our vital statistics, our youth, our old age, number of children, times that we were broken and had to rebuild our lives. The words of Tehillim are a common denominator, words of the Jewish soul.

Though I lag behind, the rhythm of my words joins the greater rhythm. We stand with King David as he pleads with Hashem. We are pleading for our lives. It's the eve of the Gulf War, and we have been targeted for Iraqi Scud missiles. For three consecutive days, the Jerusalem community gathers in neighborhood shuls to say Tehillim.

"Shelter me in the shadow of Your wings…."

"I am poured out like water, and all my bones became disjointed; my heart is like wax, melted within my innards. My strength is dried up like baked clay, and my tongue cleaves to my palate; in the dust of death You set me down. For dogs have surrounded me; a pack of evildoers has enclosed me, like a lion's prey are my hands and my feet. I can count all my bones – they look on and gloat over me…."

"Favor me, O God, favor me, for in You has my soul taken refuge; and in the shadow of Your wings I shall take refuge until the devastation shall pass…."

We are doing what Jews have done throughout history when faced with danger.

Say Tehillim and do what needs to be done.

Essentially, we are always saying Tehillim. We say Tehillim when we pray for the return of health, for the easy birthing of our babies, for their wholeness and health. We say Tehillim when we hit the inevitable snags in raising our children, and then again when we feel they are ready to begin life with their own soulmates. Tehillim on the Sabbath and on holidays, at the start of each new month. We say Tehillim as we voyage on the bus, as we anxiously sit in a waiting room for our appointment, as we wait at the lawyer's to sign the lease on the new apartment.

One day, when our taxi took a shortcut through an Arab settlement and the traffic pinned us in a narrow street, there was absolutely nothing I could do during those tense few minutes. I looked over to my nine-year-old daughter, and she was whispering the words of Tehillim.

We don't need an excuse to say Tehillim. The children say Tehillim in school at the beginning of their lessons. When the country is threatened by drought and everyone anxiously awaits the winter rains, the school children say more Tehillim.

One of our e-mail messages from Baltimore alerts us to say Tehillim for a newborn whose life is in danger. We are not acquainted with the family and have never heard of the baby's rare genetic disease, but we make a point to memorize his Hebrew name and the Hebrew name of his mother.

We relay the name to friends in Jerusalem and abroad. An ever-widening network of Tehillim goes up, people who are not relatives and not even distant acquaintances wonder daily about the baby's progress and feel cheered by the news of his weight gain and gradual improvement.

Tehillim and the Western Wall are a powerful combination. This Wall is the last standing remnant of the Holy Temple. We have been in exile so long that we can hardly comprehend what it will feel like to experience the open revelation of God's presence when the Temple is rebuilt. At the Wall, we can feel the palpable nearness of the Shechinah, God's Holy Presence, and can believe in a time when God will dwell openly in the world.

The ledges between the stones of the Wall are crammed with scraps of paper where we've scribbled our prayers for health, for a livelihood, for finding a life's partner, for the blessing of children. These papers get pushed deeper into stone with subsequent waves of visitors to the Wall and their offerings of paper prayers. These tiny folded papers testify to our belief that this Wall has a special interface with God, and these paper prayers reinforce what He has already read in our hearts. The Wall receives the pressure of our hands, the imprint of our lips, and hears the voice of our Tehillim.

Every day, there are hundreds of women gathered at the Wall saying Tehillim, and on the afternoon before the Sabbath and the first day of the new month, the plaza in front of the Wall is packed. Shavuos is the yarhzeit of King David, and thousands of Jews stream to the Western Wall from all corners of Jerusalem. Not everyone can even glimpse the Wall because of the sea of people, but all feel its proximity. Throughout the night, the silent thunder is Tehillim.

Over the years, our books of Tehillim begin to take on the shape of our hands. They are much more than books we loved to read, that opened new horizons to us. These words we never leave behind, because they never finally serve their purpose. The Tehillim are infinitely timely, timeless, and inscrutable. The words grow as we grow. They bridge this world to the next.

In the last three months of my mother's life, I say more Tehillim than I have said in fifteen years. She is semi-conscious, and I sit beside her bed as the Tehillim pour out. The doctors suspect that she can't hear or see, but I sing to her the old Yiddish songs that my grandmother sang. I speak to her directly to settle old accounts, ask her forgiveness, tell how much I love her, ask her to pray for me and my family.

When I open up the Tehillim, then I sense my soul speaking to her soul in a time and place beyond the reality of the hospital bed. I'm shaking inside, but my voice is steady.

The words of Tehillim are absorbed through her permeable skin. They are the last words I speak to my mother before she leaves this world.

Tehillim is a continuous thread that runs through our lives, our good fortune and our losses. It's our response to the twists and turns in our journey. If we can hold on to this weaving thread, then the whole emerges as scenes in one tapestry.

The thread of Tehillim doesn't stop its weaving motion in this world. When we say Tehillim here, it is also weaving there. Our Sages tell us that if we could know what the saying of Tehillim accomplishes both in this World and the worlds beyond, we would be saying Tehillim at every possible opportunity.

At a certain point in time, the book of Tehillim was divided into seven parts for each day of the week, as well as thirty divisions according to the days of the month. In this way, a person can say a portion of Tehillim daily and expect to complete the whole book periodically. There are a number of individuals in Jerusalem who manage to say the whole Tehillim each day by rising in the middle of the night and finishing before morning prayers.

I know a group of twenty-four women who gather each Wednesday for a short break during the day. With each woman say saying five or six chapters of Tehillim, they manage to complete the whole book of Tehillim in the space of about 10 minutes, and then they go on their way.

Remarkable how Tehillim can regenerate the spirit from the disabling effects of regret, loneliness, and angry recriminations. The Tehillim slowly fill in the missing parts. How can these words, which are not even mine, comfort me and set me on my feet? How can words more than two thousand years old give me strength to face the challenges of life?

These words have no ownership. They belong to us all; they have been taken out of the particular and into the universal. It doesn't matter who we are, how old we are, married or single, abandoned or surrounded by our generations. Whoever we are and whatever is happening to us, the words are there to express our grief and our happiness, and especially our longing for wholeness.

Even before we begin to say them, the act of taking the Tehillim down from the shelf returns us to the calm at the center of the storm. By saying these words, we climb into a lifeboat that carries us beyond this moment, beyond peril, beyond our finite lives.

"Were I to take up wings of dawn, were I to dwell in the distant west – there, too, Your hand would guide me, and Your right hand would sustain me."

For further reading:

Branfman, Varda. *I Remembered in the Night Your Name.* Jerusalem: 2001. Available from the author at info@carobspring.com or www.carobspring.com.

Iskowitz, Yaakov Yosef. *Tehillim Eis Ratzon: An Integrated English Translation of the Psalms and a Guide to Saying Tehillim for the Sick.* Jerusalem: 2004

Schwartz, Avraham Tzvi. *Hearts on Fire: Inspirational Thoughts on Verses from Tehillim and Insights into the Life of King David.* Jerusalem: 2004.

Zakutinsky, Rivkah. *Techinas: A Voice from the Heart. A Collection of Jewish Women's Prayers.* Brooklyn, NY: 1992.

The dignity of God lies in hiddenness.

Proverbs 25:2

"It has been told to you, O man, what is good and what the Lord requires of you, but to do justly, and to love mercy, and to walk modestly with your God."

Micah 6:8

"… in what is wondrous to you do not probe; in what is hidden from you do not explore; understand deeply what is permitted to you, but you have no business attending to hidden things."

Talmud, Hagiga 13a

 *How a Daughter of the Enlightenment Ends Up in a Sheitel*

Jan Feldman

A sheitel (Yiddish for wig) is an object of both beauty and controversy. Perhaps more than any other mitzvah that a woman performs, covering the hair best exemplifies the attitude of self-negation as exemplified by the Jews' spontaneous affirmation to God at Sinai, "We will do and we will hear" – maybe especially for the newly observant woman like me.

Most of my contemporaries knew that traditionally, Jewish women had covered their hair after marriage. But sheitels were, in our view, part of the mythology about Jewish life that included the notorious sheet with the hole. We heard stories about Jewish girls having to shave their heads on their wedding day in order to escape the sinister attentions of Christian overlords. It never occurred to us that a bride might willingly cut and cover her hair in the fulfillment of a mitzvah rather than reluctantly, in order to avoid some horror.

It is reported that some of our male forebears tossed their tefillin over the ship's rail as they entered New York Harbor in celebration of their "liberation" from the shtetl. Similarly, we conjectured, some women may have taken the opportunity to jettison their sheitels and scarves. The first sympathetic portrayal I saw of a sheitel-wearing young immigrant woman in the nostalgic Yiddish-language film, *Hester Street*, ended with her being persuaded to discard her sheitel, and with it, her "greener" status, thereby becoming a real American.

This image was not challenged by the photograph of my great-grandmother, Chaya Leiba, for whom I am named. In it she sat dour, stolid and somber. The photograph was taken in America, but you would never have known it from her pose and attire. She sat on a velvet-covered horsehair chair, and we joked that her sheitel was horsehair as well. It was voluminous, stiff and combed straight back from her forehead, creating a visible line. Nothing about it suggested human hair.

My great-grandmother never adjusted to life in her new country and remained the paradigmatic "greener." She was remote and distant in her demeanor, as if her personality was a metaphor for her geographical origins. She was, in our lives, incomprehensible, as she was uncomprehending. My grandmother and her sisters did not wear wigs and only covered their heads to bless the Shabbos candles or when they went to shul. By my generation, the very idea of a sheitel seemed as antiquated as the black-and-white photo of Chaya Leiba.

Understandably, the sheitel represented for us a gendered institution, imposed upon women by a human, specifically male power structure as a daily reminder of women's uncleanness, inferiority, and "otherness." It was a reminder of the ugliness and superstition of shtetl life where women were doubly oppressed. The sheitel was necessary to keep non-Jewish men at bay and to protect Jewish men from temptation. What a message for Jewish girls like me! Nothing suggested that the sheitel had some other rationale in Jewish law and custom that transcended the specific context of shtetl life.

This view was not only prevalent among my peers, but understandable in light of the fact that few of our elder women relatives could explain the custom in the "rational" terms that we girls demanded. Most of these women had strict Jewish training, but not a real Jewish education. Small wonder that we could not understand the sheitel in terms of a mitzvah and concluded that it was a symbol of women's subjugation created and perpetuated by men in their attempts to diminish or circumscribe the sexual power of women.

Moreover, why would the sheitel endure in a world where sociologists predicted, and demographers graphed the decline toward disappearance of Judaism, and indeed of religion in general? But belying the pundits' predictions, Judaism has not vanished. If anything, religion is experiencing a national resurgence. Judaism is back. So is the sheitel. Even among sectors of the observant community that had hitherto considered complete covering of the hair not to be mandatory, more young wives are adopting sheitels. And it isn't your Bubbe's sheitel, either!

Nothing symbolized more potently both to me and to my relations and friends my return to Yiddishkeit than did covering my hair. After all, covering one's hair suddenly one day is read by all as not just a positive embrace of Judaism, but also a clear rejection of one's former values. And there is no hiding the fact. It is absolutely visible and palpable. Of all of the observances that I took upon myself and my children, covering my hair seemed to be the most dramatic repudiation of my prior life and, therefore raised the most question, if not outright hostility, among my less observant peers. And there was no explaining it away in terms of vanity; after all, my own luxuriant hair had always been considered an asset unmatched by a succession until recently, of, well, less-than-flattering sheitels.

Here are several questions that have been posed to me, and I am guessing, at some time, to most of us.

Why would a feminist, a true daughter of the Enlightenment, subject herself to a gendered and antiquated custom?

Why treat hair as erotic at all? And if a man responds to a woman's hair as erotic, isn't that his problem? And shouldn't he just learn to deal with it?

If a wig is intended to conceal a woman's beauty, shouldn't she wear an ugly wig, or better yet, a shmatta or scarf? Why is it that some woman wear wigs that are, in fact, nicer and more attractive than their own hair?

And why restrict covering of the hair to married women? Why not do like the Moslems or the Amish and require *all* females to cover their hair?

References to covering the hair, from which the obligation was derived, are to be found in numerous places, including the Torah (Parshas Nasso), Zohar (III, 126 a), various tractates of both the Babylonian and Jerusalem Talmud, the *Shulhan Arukh, Tosefta,* Psalms, anecdotes and commentaries of the sages. The covered versus uncovered head has been a persistent marker of proper behavior on the part of a Jewish woman even though the various references to head coverings provide access into other debates of interest in their own right.

Sheitel or Shmatta?

While there remain differing opinions concerning the best possible way for a woman to cover her hair, according to the Lubavitcher Rebbe, Rabbi Menachem M. Schneerson, it is actually preferable to wear a wig rather than a scarf or alternative covering (*Beautiful Within: Modesty in Conduct and Dress as Taught by the Lubavitcher Rebbe*). He explained this in the context of the Jewish woman's quest for tznius (modesty), kedusha (sanctity) and taharah (purity), citing the verse from Tehillim 45:14 (psalms) which says, "The entire glory of the king's daughter is within." From Devarim 23:15, "Your camp shall be holy, that He not see in you any immorality and turn away from you," it is derived that the contemporary equivalent of the "camp" is the home and community. Moreover, the woman's inner spiritual quest is aided by and reflected in her clothing and demeanor, of which covering the hair is a part.

The Rebbe stressed that hair covering was not just a lapsed custom but an actual law (*Shulhan Arukh*, Orah Hayyim, chapter 75) binding in all times and places regardless of prevailing custom. The Rebbe emphasized that wearing a sheitel was an important aspect of tsnius and worked many years to make it a norm of the community. He preferred the sheitel to other forms of covering for several practical reasons. A sheitel stays in place and covers all of the hair. A scarf or tichel is liable to slip and reveal hair and a hat is customarily removed indoors, making a woman likely to remove it accidentally by force of habit.

In addition, he stressed the positive support for covering one's hair in terms of blessings as opposed to prohibitions. The Talmudic story is related about Kimchis, who attributed her manifold blessings, including the elevation to the High Priesthood of her seven sons, to the fact that "the rafters of her roof had never seen the plaits of her hair" (Tractate *Yoma* 47a). The Rebbe often quoted the teaching of the Zohar (III, 126a: *Mishnah Brurah*), where covering the hair is asserted to bring down blessings upon the woman and her family. When the wife covers her hair, "they shall be blessed with all blessings, blessings of above and blessings of below, with wealth, with children and grandchildren." "Her children will be superior... her husband will be blessed with spiritual and material blessings, with wealth, children and children's children."

"Nakedness": the erotic and distracting nature of a married woman's hair

If a wig is an acceptable and, according to some, the preferred covering, then what is it about the woman's own hair that is problematic? Why is a married woman's hair considered alluring or distracting to her husband and to men other than her husband?

And why, if uncovered hair is considered "nakedness" and arouses erotic thoughts, don't Jews insist that all girls, as well as women, cover their hair? Why not follow the Moslems, who mandate hijab for all females? After all, the rules of tsnius begin to apply to Jewish girls at the age of three and certainly to bnos mitzvah at twelve. Yet it is derived from *Tur* and *Shulhan Arukh* that besulos (virgins) are not obligated to cover their hair, since the act of "uncovering the hair of the woman" clearly refers to married women, even women who are elderly or who have been divorced or widowed. This suggests that there is a special, almost mystical change in the quality of a woman's hair after marriage that renders it erotic and distracting. After marriage, a woman has changed her status, and this is reflected subtly in her hair. All human hair (a man's beard, for instance) possesses special properties. In the case of the wife, her hair is inextricably connected to her beauty and sensuality and takes on changes imperceptibly wrought by her initiation into married life and intimacy. These changes are irreversible regardless of any subsequent changes in her married status.

A sheitel, whether made of another woman's hair or even her own, is considered halachically acceptable. Once separated from its "living source," the hair has no special qualities. Being cut and made into a sheitel neutralizes the sensuality of living human hair. Therefore, it becomes clear why it is a mistaken notion to assume that a woman is obligated to wear a sheitel to conceal her beauty. On the contrary, a woman is permitted, even encouraged, to feel and look attractive. If her sheitel happens to be nicer than her own hair, so be it. The purpose of the sheitel is not to conceal a woman's beauty; rather, it is to conceal that special and beautiful change that takes place within a woman after marriage. After marriage, a woman has an increased need for modesty, which the sheitel serves.

That the Rebbe not only preferred the wearing of sheitels to scarves and snoods meant that there was no reason to feel vain for acquiring a good-quality, flattering sheitel. On the contrary, the Rebbe reportedly enjoined husbands, if they had the means, to allow their wives to buy a suitably beautiful sheitel. Finally, the requirement that a woman wear her sheitel throughout her life lends validation to her sense of continuing femininity (as opposed to the general culture which treats older women as asexual and no longer womanly).

Personal Reflections: My Journey from Hair to Shmatta to Sheitel

So how, indeed, did an emancipated child of the Enlightenment like me come to adopt a sheitel? Every ba'al teshuvah starts out on the path toward greater observance of the mitzvot for reasons and in ways that are personal, though not unique. The path they traverse must necessarily be similar though the order and interval of adoption may vary. Eventually, they take on the 'big ticket' mitzvot: Shabbos, kashrut, and family purity. This accords with the Chabad approach of adding mitzvah upon mitzvah. We are not required to make the all-or-nothing decision to adopt full observance in one grand gesture. My guess is that would be too dramatic a leap for most people. We want to test the waters and feel that we will have a greater likelihood of success if we climb from level to level gradually. We may even fear that taking on too much too quickly will lead to frustration and then, God forbid, a "flash-in-the-pan" effect where we adopt all and then reject all. This is better known in common parlance as "biting off more than one can chew."

Accordingly, I began to take on mitzvot sequentially in a way that appeared rational, at least to me though, perhaps irrational to others. For instance, I began to observe the laws of family purity and mikveh first, since we were building a family, then kashrut, and finally, became shomer Shabbos. Preceding all of this was a lengthy "latent" period during which my children were enrolled in Chabad camps and preschools and during which we davened in a Chabad shul but did not feel ready to dramatically change our lives. It wasn't that I was resistant to the idea; on the contrary. But in a place like Burlington, Vermont, where there are no Jewish schools and only a handful of observant families, not to mention the fact that we lived a good nine miles from shul; it all seemed impossible.

I realized that trying to completely revamp my children's lives without a dramatic scene shift would have been nearly impossible. You can't just wake up one morning and announce that what was permitted is suddenly forbidden. This constitutes what children understand on an intuitive level to be an imposition of *ex post facto* law. My opening came during my sabbatical year. This allowed me to take up a visiting professorship at McGill University in Montreal, where I moved to the Westbury Avenue neighborhood of Snowden. In this area, which is heavily populated by religiously observant Jewish families, it became utterly natural for us to build on the initial steps toward observance that we had already taken in Vermont.

In Montreal I immediately began to cover my hair so as not to embarrass my children when I went into their schools. This was all well and good for the academic year. I was willing to go to work every day in a shmattah or tichel. I remember acquiring my first snoods from a local out-of-the home purveyor. There were enough women in tichels and snoods in the neighborhood so that I did not feel strange. The Metro platforms and my office were more of a challenge, but my little oppositional streak reared up and I stood firm in the face of stares. Anyway, Montreal was delightfully full of women in hijabs and various head coverings. The moment of truth came in the spring as my son's bar mitzvah approached. It was he who suggested that it might be nice if I didn't attend with a shmattah on my head. And ironically, just in case I still didn't believe in Divine providence, my son's bar mitzvah portion was Nasso, the portion of the Torah which contains the verse upon which the mitzvah of hair covering is based. I had to decide what to do. In all the planning, I had really not given any thought to my hair.

Then began the consultations with friends and finally the decision to purchase a sheitel. With my coterie in tow, I went to the sheitel macher, tried on a few numbers, and settled on a human-hair (low-end) sheitel. Reassuringly, when I first wore it out on the street, the neighborhood girls would call across the street, "I like your sheitel." I had passed muster!

The real moment of truth came as I prepared for reentry into our "natural habitat" in Vermont. I had to decide whether I would revert to my old ways or become the only professor on campus in a sheitel. I decided to stick with the sheitel on the premise that one should not take a step backwards – no retreat! Moreover, I reasoned, if I wanted my children to continue in their observance, it would send a bad message if I dropped the part of observance that was most challenging or inconvenient for me. If my boys were willing to continue to wear kippot and tzizit, making themselves visible as Jews, I should be willing to do the same.

Of course there were awkward moments. One particularly poignant one came while I was stopped at a red light. The woman in the next lane, wearing a scarf, obviously undergoing chemotherapy, looked over and gave me a warm nod of sympathy and solidarity, assuming that my headscarf meant the same as hers. I felt really sheepish. Wearing a sheitel saved me this sort of encounter, but posed its own dilemmas. My children named my sheitel "Tina" after Tina Turner. The realization that my sheitel brought to mind a talented but notoriously immodest R&B singer was not comforting. I concluded, as do many first-time sheitel buyers, that I had made a mistake. Deciding that Tina was too curly, I went in the opposite direction and, needing to economize, bought a very cheap, completely straight sheitel from a novelty store in Montreal for about twenty dollars. My children immediately dubbed this bargain-basement wig "Vashti" after the evil and ugly Persian queen whom Esther replaced in the Purim story. Need I say more? Vashti found her way instantly into the costume basket. It was that or become a nest for the gerbils. Recently, at the suggestion – should I say insistence – of a dear friend, we went together to Crown Heights to a bona-fide sheitel-macher. That was a whole story in itself. But now, I am happy to report, I have a sheitel with which I am truly satisfied. I must have hit the jackpot, because this sheitel has not earned itself a name from my children.

Every woman I know has her sheitel "mistakes" in the back of the closet. She also has some funny anecdote involving flying sheitels – wind, ice, capsizing canoes, etc. Mine happened in a pet store and involved a three-foot iguana getting its claws deeply entangled in Tina (don't ask). Extricating the iguana without removing the sheitel was quite a project. And this story was topped last week when the newspaper reported a woman bringing a roller coaster in New York to a screeching halt when her sheitel fell into the mechanism.

On the positive side, I see that most women do adjust to wearing a sheitel. While some young brides may harbor a touch of regret at cutting their gorgeous locks, it is possible these days to match one's own hair closely, as did my redheaded friend. Donning a sheitel is such a rite of passage that I think most brides do it with very little regret and with a lot of pride and encouragement from women friends and relatives. When I have spoken to women about their feelings and experiences I have been struck by several themes that commonly arise. First and most important, of course, is the sense of *kabbalas ol,* or willingly taking on the yoke of Torah. As is often noted, the simplest explanation is often the best. In this case, the fact that Hashem has commanded it is sufficient and decisive for the observant, married Jewish woman. Whether it is personally considered convenient or inconvenient would simply not enter in to an observant woman's thinking on the subject. Other justifications, or lack of them, would be quite beside the point.

The mothers that I know have a strong conviction that wearing a sheitel will bring blessings upon the family. Several references, especially the words of the Zohar concerning the woman who carefully covers her hair – "shall be blessed with all blessings, blessings of above and blessings of below" – attest to the beneficial impact on the family of the woman's covering her hair.

Another frequent and least anticipated theme had to do with dignity, not just tsnius. The idea was repeatedly expressed that a sheitel was like a crown, making its wearer feel like a queen. The very untouchability and immobility of the sheitel was a sort of armor for modesty and regality. This stunningly countered the claim that wearing a sheitel somehow reflected the submissiveness and inferiority of women. On the contrary, the sheitel symbolized to the women I met, their status and power. They controlled the "how, what, where and when" of being seen by others. The sheitel, like all attributes of modesty in dress and conduct, allows a woman control in each situation. The sheitel, understood in this context, is a power equalizer for women.

And so for me, donning a sheitel represented the seriousness of my commitment to Hashem. That ever-so-slight but constant awareness of the sheitel is a reminder for me in much the same way that tzitzit must be for boys and men.

If wearing a sheitel means that I sometimes have to explain its significance to my friends, family, colleagues and students, so be it. One of the most satisfying outcomes of adopting a sheitel in a largely secular environment like a campus is that it has created many an opening for my Jewish female students. I have been delighted to find that so many of my students who seemed to be committed secularists were just waiting for a role model to give them a sense that one could combine Jewish observance with a life in the world. Do I miss the sensation of the wind lifting my hair off my neck on a hilltop in Vermont? Well....

Wearing a sheitel or hair covering is, in the contemporary, secular world, fraught with meaning by both those who cover and those who do not. It is infused with ideological symbolism, in addition to the obvious religious rationale. Covering the hair signifies boundary-maintenance, a component of identity, resistance to the larger culture and its values, as well as respect for halachah. The sheitel will continue to be a symbol of beauty and controversy, but mostly, it will continue to be a source of blessing.

For further reading:

Schreiber, Lynne. *Hide and Seek: Jewish Women and Hair Covering.* Brooklyn, NY: 2003.

Manolson, Gila. *Outside/Inside: A Fresh Look at Tzniut. Jerusalem*: 1997.

"Passover Seder" is an oxymoron: The word Pesach (Passover) means to leap, to bypass the normal order, whereas Seder means order and organization! The Seder is an order that allows us to transcend order… The fifteen Seder steps represent fifteen keys to open doors freeing us from our confinements.

Rabbi Simon Jacobson, from his article,
"Passover's 15-Step Program"

Dayenu – It's Enough for Us: My Passover Guide for Spiritual Sanity

Elana Friedman

Metaphors for the Haggada

C'mon, when are we going to eat?!"

Some families tolerate the Haggada as a necessary but boring delay before the Passover meal. The whole thing gives everyone at the table a bad case of fidgets. More appreciative families read the Haggada as a commemoration of the past, like an old souvenir. It provides a sense of family history.

But the Haggada wasn't written as a souvenir of the past. It's more like street theater, a drama springing up in our own living room. It undermines distinctions between the characters and the audience, between the script and reality. One minute we read about the bread of ancient Egypt, the next minute we are eating it. We tell the story to our children by reading several descriptions inside the book itself of recounting this story to four children. Is this about history or about us? This question lies behind any good street theater.

"In every generation a person is required to look at himself as if he himself escaped from Egypt." (The Haggada)

The real work of the Haggada lies in helping us escape out of her own personal slavery each year. The Haggada has within it the blueprint and healing of every exile in Jewish history. It has the pain and healing of any exile within the individual life of any Jew who will ever sit down to a seder.

Ultimately, the Passover ceremony resembles a DNA molecule. An untutored onlooker sees only a double helix. The educated observer understands that this particular pattern is a biological program for millions of biological systems in the body. It carries a powerful instruction kit for the entire organism. This same power is packed into the Haggada.

Finding Our Own Map

The first year I celebrated Passover in Jerusalem, I unexpectedly caught a glimpse of this power inside one page of the Haggada, the song "Dayenu" (It's Enough for Us). To the naked eye (or ear), "Dayenu" is a sweet learning song. For readers who get lost in the tangles of the full text of the Haggada, it simply restates the basic story of how the Jews left Egypt. It also wakes up tired children very nicely. In fact, we regard it with so much universal affection that it usually gets included even when the entire Seder has been reduced to ten minutes of edited highlights.

But like the Haggada as a whole, this little children's song is as concentrated as a cell of DNA. It contains the pattern of each of our exiles and redemptions. The fifteen little verses unfold into a complex instruction kit for spiritual development.

The opening problem in our song is Egypt. In Hebrew, Egypt (Mitzrayim) translates as "double narrowness." We open our song in that narrow, hopelessly stuck part of life where we have become compressed, suppressed, and trapped.

The fifteen verses of "Dayenu" map a fifteen-step stairway out of Egypt's narrow trap. Fifteen is the number of days it takes the moon to move from complete darkness to complete fullness. Fifteen is the number of stairs from the outside courtyard into the inner court of the Holy Temple. The Levites would sing their fifteen "psalms of rising" on those stairs. Fifteen is the number of phases or steps we pass through as we rise from negative to positive. It is the number of metamorphosis.

The lubricating factor between the steps is the chorus of "Dayenu," which translates as "enough." In the Ashkenazic melody, the chorus is "Enough, it would be enough for us. Enough, it would be enough for us. Enough, it would be enough for us. Enough for us, enough for us."

In other words, just this much is enough. Today with its minor achievements and tiny commonplace pleasures is enough.

The cornerstone of development is feeling satisfied with what is already here and already now.

A small marital difficulty negotiated into peace can be a cause for celebration. We don't have to heal the entire marriage into sturdiness and vibrancy before we allow the first sigh of contentment.

The excitement of travel begins with locking our front door, not with arriving at the halfway point of our itinerary. If we don't extract satisfaction from each segment of the journey, we will either fail to arrive at the goal, or we will reach it completely unaffected by the traveling.

In short, "Dayenu" must nest upon each level of growth before the next level can be hatched.

My Own Understanding

I think about each verse of Dayenu both generally and personally. Most years, I have used the fifteen verses to look at my most intense personal slavery: compulsive food bingeing and junk novel reading. As I have bonded these addictions together, I will call this problem eating/reading from here on.

Egypt: How to Develop a Problem

Before this metamorphosis is the story of coming down into Egypt, into slavery, in the first place. How did we get into this mess?

It starts innocently enough. Historically, Jacob sent his sons down to Egypt to buy grain during a severe famine. As the famine continued and the story unrolled, he was invited to move his extended family into an Egyptian suburb for temporary refuge.

Jacob's family settled in and grew from an extended family of seventy to a large population. One generation passed, then another. A new Pharaoh came into power, or maybe the old one changed his mind. He began a new volunteer labor tax that hardened into outright slavery, then deteriorated into deliberate abuse. The noose tightened.

In personal terms, we each come to our own Egypt to help us through a temporary time of inner hunger. We've just come to visit, not to put down roots.

Then, before we get around to leaving our refuge, its generous hospitality changes to iron-fisted oppression. Suddenly we realize our pet pleasures have grown into cruel inescapable traps. They have devoured our lives. The guests are now slaves. Over the years, this oppression only gets harsher. Those who have gone through this will recognize the description. In one area or another, we have all experienced the fall from seeking refuge to being buried alive.

At this point the song, "Dayenu" (it is enough) comes to lead us step by step out of the grave.

In my story, I began with reading. No one ever suggested it could be addictive when I was a child. Reading was interesting, informative, great for getting adult approval, seductive, and hypnotizing. Books were a refuge from family fights and confusions, from troubles with friends, from sports, and from the empty spaces in the day. On a family vacation, rife with family complications, I added candy to my reading and also began reading mysteries. It was like switching from beer to heroin. The trance was exponentially deeper, mesmerizing enough to block out the intense family dynamics cooked up while we were all inside a car for hours and hours, for weeks on end.

The eating brought more and more dieting, which brought more and more eating. Psychologists didn't know yet that either dieting or eating could be addictive. By the time I was nineteen, my pet pleasure had buried me.

Just Getting Out

"If He had only brought us out of Egypt but had not executed judgments on the Egyptians, [just bringing us out of Egypt] would have been enough for us."

It is enough just to escape out of our disastrous circumstances. "Forget about how I got here or where I'm going next. Just get me out of this!"

Once we are stuck inside the doubled narrowness of slavery, we won't get out by natural means. A shift of tide, a change of season, or even a few more years of emotional maturity won't do the job. We cannot even free ourselves by deliberate effort. Our struggles, our rebellions, our endless well-laid plans: none of it can get us out. Inside slavery, we lose our power of choice. We start out each morning promising ourselves that today will be different, but somewhere along the way the new plan collapses. Often, struggling to get out only digs us in deeper. The more we fight, the faster the destructive cycle spins.

For example, increasing the number of corrections only increases the number of mistakes. Stricter dieting creates wilder binges. Extra religious restrictions spin off into new transgressions. More threats bring more rebellions.

Only something from outside the system can dissolve the system. We cannot free ourselves from inside. God has to break through with His mighty hand and pull us out. When He finally does, dayenu. We are not going to ask for anything more.

In my Egypt, eating/reading narrowed my life several times over. In its most intense form, I was so caught up in it that food and weight were the first things I thought of each morning. Worry about how I looked entered into every relationship, and worry over what I had last eaten cast a shadow over every task. Then there were the hours I lost every day in eating/reading. It took up more of my schedule than a job. That was all the first layer of narrowing.

What created the "double narrowness" of Egypt was that each attempt I made to control my eating actually increased my bingeing. I used to joke that I ended up gaining a pound for every day I was on a new diet, but it wasn't very funny to live that way. The more I struggled against the problem, the deeper into the hole I went. Each dieting solution only tightened the vise of craziness.

Just Judging the Egyptians

"If He had executed judgments on them, but not on their gods, it [just executing the judgments on *them*] would have been enough for us."

Rescue is only temporary without awareness. To stay free, we must pass judgment on our Egypt. We must hold an inner trial, examine our slavery carefully, and firmly condemn the tyranny. It's not enough to say "I can't stand it." We each have to go on to say, "This is a bad place for me and always will be."

Without this judgment, the harmfulness of Egypt stays fogged over by confusion. Then, the next time there is a famine (an inner hunger) we'll probably jump into Egypt again and repeat the cycle. "How can it hurt to travel to Egypt for just this one last famine?" soon becomes "I can't believe I'm back here again!"

Once we realize that any return to Egypt will always hurt, we're out of Egypt in a different way.

It took years for me to become thoroughly convinced that every part of my Egypt was harmful. The first thing I understood was that dieting only tightened the noose, and always would. It was an intensifier, not a solution. It took longer to realize that both sweets and junk reading were slave masters, not helpers. I traveled back to Egypt hundreds of times as I learned to name my oppressors.

Judging Their Gods

"If He had made judgments on their gods, but had not killed their firstborn, [judging their gods] would have been enough for us."

One purpose of the ten plagues God sent to the Egyptians was the undermining of their idolatrous system of worship. For instance, the Nile, which irrigated the entire country, was worshipped as a god. So the first plague turned the water in the Nile into blood.

It is not complete freedom just to know Egypt is a destructive place for us. We have to get beneath the surface and find the false gods, the destructive beliefs and inaccurate assumptions that underlie our slavery. Otherwise those beliefs will recreate similar conditions tomorrow or a year from now. If we don't want to end up back in the same picture, we have to throw away the old framework.

"If I worry, I'll be better prepared if something goes wrong."

"It's better to solve problems by myself."

"Maybe they secretly think I'm obnoxious and aren't telling me."

If we subscribe to belief systems that encourage inner slavery, we stay slaves, no matter how often God pulls us into freedom.

The Hebrew word for "gods" can also mean "judges." When God judges the gods/judges of Egypt, He is showing how the belief system that irrigates Egypt is a set of false judgments. The way that we have judged things is off kilter. We have to change our whole way of thinking about the world.

Leaving Egypt is leaving a destructive system. Judging its judges is going one step deeper, one layer more abstract. It is emerging out of the destructive meta-system of Egypt. It is eliminating the false perspectives saturating the culture. Dayenu. We don't need to ask for more.

One of the core false gods inside my eating disorder was a burning dissatisfaction with myself and my life. Nothing I did registered on my contentment scale. No accomplishment pulled my self-evaluation even as high as neutral. Little that I ate registered as enjoyment either. I was too busy reading to notice. Life was always a black hole because nothing I saw or did was anything but an insufficiency. I was too anxious, desperate, and distracted to notice any abundance.

I could only move out of this desperation by condemning this negative judge. I lowered the threshold of demands enough to register my efforts and attainments. I needed to learn to count small pleasures, minuscule shifts, and pocket-sized completions in order to slow this storm of despair, and eventually pull out of it.

Another core false god in my pantheon was one many women will recognize – the consumer society ideal woman's body. During the years I was eating/reading the most, the ideal size was a size 7. Now it is a size 4 or 2. At the risk of stating the obvious, this media standard condemns any scars, wrinkles, stretch marks, or sags. It demands youth (if not actual pubescence), a flat stomach, even features, firm muscles, and extreme willingness. This false god measures women on a one to ten scale, as well as by pounds. Any shortcoming translates into a lack of sexuality and/or womanhood.

Without debunking this false judge, I could find no exit from my slavery.

Destroying the First-Born

"If He had killed their first-born, but had not given us their wealth, [just killing their firstborn] would have been enough for us."

The last plague, the heaviest blow, struck the Egyptians the night before the Jews escaped. The first-born sons of every Egyptian family, from the highest official down to servants and prisoners, died that night. As every household in Egypt mourned, Pharaoh capitulated and let the Jews leave Egypt.

The first-born bring a society into the next generation. They traditionally inherit their ancestral land as well as the wealth and power base of the past generation. Later these first-born pass the power on to the next generation. Until this chain is eliminated, the society of Egypt will continue.

In personal terns, damaging habits have an enduring inertia. They resist change. Our original needs may have evaporated, but the old way of doing things keeps going on, decade after decade. Even after we don't believe in our original premise any more, even if we've forgotten the original premise, even after we can't stand our situation any more, our destructive patterns go on.

An all-out attack won't work for long, no matter which method we use: frogs, boils, lice, even three days of darkness. Once Pharaoh's heart was hardened, the Jews couldn't smash their way out. The only way to stop Egypt in its tracks was by eliminating each and every first-born.

Inner slavery, too, can only be halted by the determined hunt for any and every element that carries the process of slavery forward. Issues as over-riding as pessimism or as petty as an uncomfortable shoe style must be examined. Every household of Egypt had to be neutralized, from Pharaoh's palace to the most minor servant's quarters. Only then did the trap spring open for a massive exodus.

Pharaoh was considered a god in Egypt, so the first-born son of Pharaoh in my own story was an offspring of the false god of endless dissatisfaction. I discovered that the thought "You really wasted your day (week/year/life), Elana" was always a precursor to a binge. This was such a frequent comment that it was almost an inner theme song. I had to uproot it as much as possible. I've learned to recognize it as an express elevator back to Egypt.

Some of the firstborn of more minor "officials" included comparing my body to other people's bodies, comparing my life to other people's lives, any sort of diet including health diets or psychologists' eat-what-you-want diets, perfectionism, trying to teach myself by scathing self-criticism, and mean jokes about myself.

Sons of peons and prisoners include weighing myself, storing small-size clothes that I might fit into someday, keeping novels in the house, buying sweets for Purim gifts, reading about diets in magazines, and talking about diets or weight loss with family or friends. This list could go on, of course.

Some of these firstborn were really killed off over the years. Others have been weakened or confined.

Giving Us Their Wealth

"If He had given us their wealth, but had not split the sea for us, [just giving us their wealth] would have been enough for us."

What is this talking about? Exodus 12:36–37 says: "They requested silver and gold articles and clothing from the Egyptians. And God gave the people grace in the eyes of the Egyptians and they complied with the requests, and they drained Egypt of its wealth."

These two lines explain that the Jews left Egypt with valuables they wouldn't have had if they hadn't gone into Egypt in the first place. These valuables address the bitter question asked by anyone who has escaped from personal darkness: "Why did I have to go through all that in the first place?" What sort of cold and unempathic God deliberately sends us into anguish and then pulls us out again, over and over? Why bother? It would be better to never live at all and skip the painful melodrama."

This picture changes if we come out of each trouble wealthier than we went in. If we are deeper, more patient, more skilled, more than we were before, then the blessing of freedom is not stale, but remarkably profitable.

This is the concept of hidden sparks in a nutshell. When God created the world, He had billions of sparks of spiritual light inside "shells" of materiality. These sparks, like sweet walnuts encased in walnut shells, are waiting for us to find these hidden sweetmeats. The secret agenda behind descending into Egyptian slavery, into places of great personal darkness, is finding and freeing those trapped sparks of spiritual light.

God has not locked us into a meaningless, gray cycle of struggle and relief, struggle and relief. He has sent us on a voyage of exploration and discovery, boldly going into dark spaces where no one has gone before. We go to bring back riches (riches in ourselves, in the world, even in God Himself) that would have otherwise remained hidden and unknown.

This is what a recovering alcoholic refers to when he tells his self-help group, "I am a grateful alcoholic." He does not mean the addiction was an entertaining pleasure-trip. He means that after he left his Egypt, after he left drinking behind, he found his hands were filled with riches. He held a much deeper understanding of the world and of his place in it.

The secret of going down to Egypt is that we'll find something there that we can't get by remaining safely in our own land.

This is true historically. The Jews have been collecting treasures during their exiles that they never could have acquired if the nation hadn't been traumatized and scattered. Hanukkah exists only because the Greeks placed their idol in the Holy Temple. The *Guide to the Perplexed* was written only because the Moslem world of Maimonides was so interested in Aristotle. Our Sabbath melodies sound like Russian drinking songs, Viennese waltzes, or American folk songs. The second day of festivals, Rabbenu Gershon's edict on monogamy, the fairy tales of Rebbe Nachman... none of them would have come into being without our exiles. We have collected music, cuisines, languages, clothing styles, philosophical concerns, and methods of commentary from our many temporary places of refuge. "Jewish" has become, by now, a collage of cultural "sparks."

This principle also works existentially. There is something to be gained from the dramas of life. Our souls couldn't have found these sparks over centuries of searching by remaining outside the corrupt, confusing world and basking in eternity. We will return home richer than we left. That is enough.

In my private exodus, I also carried out a treasure house of sparks. Here are just a few:

I learned a lot about patience, about the exploration necessary for good problem-solving, about reaching out to others for help, and about creating habits and rituals that support sanity.

I'm forced to work on my relationship with God and with myself every morning just to keep from bingeing. Being forced like this to do something I want very much to do is a gift. Over time, I was pushed through the long, difficult work of finding God's gentleness and caring. I also got through the even longer and more difficult work of finding out how to treat myself with gentleness and caring. I found out about God's sense of humor, something I now enjoy frequently.

I now believe that God deliberately creates flaws in every human being. I now believe that mistakes are a normal part of each day, not a sure sign of incompetence and hopelessness. I know something about apologizing and fixing mistakes, skills I couldn't learn when I regarded mistakes as frightening disasters.

I've finally become mostly immune to the siren songs of the latest miracle diet and of magazine model bodies. I've become less open to the instant solutions advertised for almost every problem on almost every corner. I've become uninterested in the smoothed-out, touched-up pictures of reality offered by the cheerleaders in every community, including the religious communities.

I've found a lot of Torah on eating. I've collected this and taught classes in it. My experiences also deepened my understanding of Hassidic teachings on how falling is a preparation for rising, how stumbling is a preparation for real comprehension, and how an individual's weakness is an inherent part of that individual's spiritual task in the world. (Those who have read these teachings will recognize them.)

This list names only some of the riches that I brought out of Egypt. The longer the darkness, the greater the light.

Splitting the Sea

"If He had divided the sea for us and not brought us through it on dry land, [just dividing the sea for us] would have been enough."

What is the scene here?

Three days after the Jews left Egypt, Pharaoh changed his mind about letting them go and chased after them with his army. The Jews were trapped, dead-ended at the edge of the Red Sea, when they saw the soldiers and chariots coming around the bend. They panicked, reproaching Moses. "Weren't there enough graves in Egypt, that you had to take us into the wilderness to die?" So God came to their rescue by splitting the sea into walls of water, allowing the Jews to walk along the newly exposed, amazingly dry sea-bottom.

The commentaries explain that as the sea split, they had a deep and massive visionary experience of God.

The first barrier we meet after coming out of Egypt is the sea. Poets, psychologists, and literary analysts have long spoken of deep water as the uncontrolled, irrational part of a human being. The wild rising and falling of ocean waves resemble the waves of emotion. Dark and dangerous ocean currents are like the currents of the unconscious.

Psalm 107 captures the panic of trying to navigate in these murky and overwhelming waters when it describes those

> who go down to the sea in ships,
> who do business on great waters…
> they mount up to the heavens,
> they descend to the depths.
> They would melt away because of trouble.
> They reel to and fro
> and stagger like a drunkard.
> All their wisdom is exhausted.

Egypt had none of these stormy waters. The original attraction of Egypt was, after all, that it provided a refuge. This solution creates its own problems, though. Each time we descend into our narrow refuge to avoid pain, our capacity to face the world weakens. Meanwhile, we are only avoiding the original pains, not eliminating them. The inner hungers we seek refuge from, the storms we can't confront, and the uncomfortable perceptions we deny all remain just outside of the Egyptian boundary, waiting to overwhelm us.

When we finally emerge from slavery, we face that sea head-on. We find every bit of mess we didn't deal with. It looks hopeless. We'll be swept away by the waves and currents. Either that, or Pharaoh will take us back to the false "security" of Egypt. The whole escapade becomes an unmitigated disaster, so we might as well turn back.

Then God splits the sea. It's a kindness and a miracle. It's illogical. But it happens. For a short time, every one of us leaving Egypt gets an emotional reprieve, a honeymoon of clarity. The overwhelming becomes negligible, ambiguity and confusion evaporate, and our path is clear.

Once the sea is removed, a second kindness occurs. We see the landscape that is usually underneath the waters. That most concealed contour of reality is unexpectedly revealed. As the commentary describes it: during the splitting of the sea, even the simplest maidservants and unborn babies could see more of God than Ezekiel saw in prophecy.

Suddenly we see how the land lies, how the world fits together. It's a very limited period of enhanced perception and extraordinary understanding. God gives this honeymoon of clarity as an unearned gift at the very beginning of a journey. This "beginner's high" never lasts. In a short time the walls of water will crash back into place, and the hidden landscape will disappear again. At best, this experience may be a preview, a taste of the way we will understand the world far in the future, at the end of our journey. Still, for this hour, a miraculous clarity has emerged, and we can go forward again. That is enough.

Eating/reading took me out of the world as thoroughly as an anesthetic. Someone could call my name and I wouldn't hear. Whatever frightening stress sent me into a binge disappeared... until I tried to stop eating and reading. Moreover, as someone coming out a movie theater is half blinded by ordinary light, any time I emerged from my eating/reading cave, I found the ups and downs of a normal day overwhelming.

When I actually got out of my Egypt, I was too amazed to notice any of this. I remember my surprise after every breakthrough. "Oh, my goodness! You mean this barrier is actually going to give way? I thought this would *never* happen for me."

Walking On Dry Land

"If He had led us through it on dry land and had not drowned our oppressors in it, [leading us through the sea on dry land] would have been enough for us."

When we walk on dry land, our "feet are on the ground." A visionary perception without grounding only means our heads are in the clouds. Prophetic understanding is exciting, but it is not actually helpful unless it is accompanied by some practicality. When we explore our spiritual insights while the dishes, and finally bugs, mass in our sink, it is a sign of delusion, not mystical understanding. If we contemplate the ultimate unity of all mankind, yet argue with our partners over who contributes more, we are becoming distorted, not wise.

The miraculous, temporary removal of the overwhelming waters allows each of us to face the situations of our lives realistically. Which logistics need to get done first? What shouldn't be worked on at all right now? What are the demands and limits of daily living?

Instead of being swept out to sea, we are walking along the hard ground, one step at a time. This alone is enough.

This is my weak area. (Notice how short this section was.) Even as a young child, before I could read anything more complicated than a first grade reader, I was a space cadet. It took me a long time to understand that practical skills were friends, and not weapons of the enemy. I now collect advice from people talented at logistics. I immerse myself in systems that connect spiritual work to washing the dishes and filing systems. After decades, I can report that dry land works. Cleaning, organizing, facing bureaucracies, and making to-do lists actually strengthen my sanity and inner life, instead of undermining them. Unbelievable.

Sinking Our Oppressors

"If He had drowned our enemies in it, and had not supplied our needs in the wilderness for forty years, [just drowning our enemies in the sea] would have been enough for us."

Egypt doesn't want to let us go so easily. Even after we break out of our darkness, renounce its "protection" and abandon its gods, it chases after us. It tries to pull us back. The heaviness of slavery has its own field of gravity. We can take off as often as we want, but we'll fall back in every time… until we break out of that gravitational force.

That hour when the Egyptian army sinks into the sea is the hour we break through the gravitational field of Egypt. It has no more power to pull us back against our will. How does this breakthrough occur? It occurs because the waters of the sea return to their place.

The first phase after escaping an Egypt is often living on a pink cloud. In the next phase. the waves of problems and intense emotions return to their normal places. That trap of Egypt was, after all, a sort of protection, an anaesthetic numbing its captives. As that anesthetic dissipates, the original inner famines and covered-over pain rises back to the surface.

What destroys the power of the Egyptian army? Its destruction occurs when a former numbed slave becomes willing to feel those overwhelming reactions and face difficult situations without anesthetic or avoidance. We don't run back to the denial of Egypt, but endure reality. At that point the Egyptian soldiers no longer have a way to compel us to return to numbed slavery. The Egyptian's power to pull us back is dissolved in the stormy sea and that is enough.

Whenever I had to make a transition, like coming into work or coming back home, I ate and read. After an upsetting phone call, I ate and read. After almost any interaction with one particular relative, I ate and read. Before, during, and after large social gatherings, I ate and read. I often ate and read to avoid a social occasion entirely. I didn't realize these situations always set me off. I'd been much too panicked over my overeating and my weight to identify common precipitating factors. I'd also been too involved in eating/reading to have time to develop tools for handling my problems.

Exodus required looking beyond the anesthetic of eating/reading in order to find the upset that caused me to want to be unconscious. Noticing these events, naming them, and talking about them became a path to freedom. I could learn alternative reactions. I could invent tailor-made rituals to keep me conscious. Sometimes I could find a way to avoid the trigger situation completely. Other times I could figure out a way to protect myself when I knew a tense occasion was coming around.

The longer I work at this, the more aware and creative I become. My old automatic responses become less and less overwhelming. They have less and less power to drag me back to Egypt.

Providing Our Needs in the Wilderness

"If He had provided for our needs in the wilderness for forty years and had not fed us the manna, [providing for our needs in the wilderness] would have been enough for us."

The beginning of any metamorphosis is electric with hope. For a moment we were higher than prophets, capable, and joyous. But this beginner's high was just a foretaste, a promise of what we will be like at the end of a long process of transformation. In actuality, we are at the beginning of a long, hard trek in the desert. We are at the beginning of the learning road now, and learning is neither continual excitement nor a sense of wholeness. On the contrary, it is a frustrating series of mistakes, failures, and disappointments. Most of all, it is unbelievably slow.

Learning is practicing scales on a musical instrument, memorizing grammatical conjugations, practicing basic living skills over and over and over.

In order to get through this long, dry process, we need continual support. In the external wilderness, the wandering Jews suffered from hunger, thirst, rebellions, plagues, and enemy armies. Wanderers in the internal wilderness suffer from loneliness, ingratitude, discouragement, boredom, self-righteousness, and negativity. Without continual support, we would collapse on our way. We are not yet wise enough to fulfill our needs. We're not even wise enough to recognize our needs. But one way or another, God keeps us going. We don't know how to get from where we are to where we are traveling to, but He leads us on, journey by journey. And that is enough.

I can't say this strongly enough. Once I was bound up in my Egypt, there was no way I could get untangled by myself. The same thing is true for my forty-year trek in the wilderness. This is a lifelong process for me, with three steps forward and two steps back. Sometimes I go five steps back. I need a lot of handholding and many helpful techniques to keep on going.

I've relied on therapists, fellow travelers, books, visualizations, prayer, endless conversations, and whole networks of creative reminders. Each morning I make a credit list of things I accomplished the day before to forestall the deadly words, "You really wasted your day, Elana." I read over my own highest priorities each day so that I remember that the purpose of my life is not to die a size 9. I try to keep a journal most days, which is often more frustrating and more effective than any other daily task. In addition, I have filled a little book with inspiring articles, prayers, and wise sentences. I carry it around with me all the time, including to synagogue, including (or maybe especially) on Yom Kippur. I sometimes meditate, and often talk to other people with similar problems.

The landscape changes *so* slowly and there are *so* many setbacks. But the alternative to hiking onward is returning back to where I started, and that would be a return to torture.

Feeding Us Manna

"If He had fed us manna and had not given us the Sabbath, [feeding us with manna] would have been enough for us."

Soon after they went through the splitting of the sea, the Jews began to complain about hunger. God announced, "I will rain bread from heaven upon you. The people will go out and gather enough for each day." And so it happened. The manna came down invisibly each night, leaving the earth covered each morning with thin, tiny flakes about the size of coriander seeds. No matter how much the Jews collected, they all came home with exactly one day's portion of manna: no more, no less. Those people who tried to store some of their manna for the next day found it had become putrid and wormy overnight. The almost imperceptible manna had to be gathered one day at a time. Still, for forty years those flakes sustained the people's bodies and fed their hearts.

Each day has its own subtle, small sources of sustenance lying on the ground, the smallest, thinnest pieces of happiness. We have to learn to notice them and gather them in. These simple, almost imperceptible moments can sustain us and flavor our lives.

Finding these short moments of joy, collecting them, and nurturing ourselves with them is a rare, yet absolutely necessary art. We gather the breath of a sleeping child, the flavor of a pear, the warm side of the sidewalk in winter. Each day just enough manna falls to sustain us. It's not substantial the way a loaf of bread or meat is, but it can keep us going.

According to the commentary, the righteous people found their measure of manna just by their tents. The less righteous had to wander further afield. When we are especially tuned in, we find all the small moments we need right at hand. The more out of tune we are, the harder we have to look, and the further from home we have to travel.

No one, though, could store away yesterday's small satisfactions to avoid gathering them again today. If we don't continue to gather these flakes each and every day, our small moments will turn rancid and wormy. There is no alternative but to open our clenched hands and trust that we will find new manna in the morning. Nor can we let our attention drift off for a week or two. Each day requires its own harvest of gratitudes.

Until now, the stairway of "dayenu" has been climbing out of negativity, slavery, and darkness. With the arrival of manna, there is a radical shift. Now the stairway starts climbing into light. Before this verse, we were moving, step by step, out of our own deaths. Now we begin moving into our lives.

The first step is learning to value the small happiness, to sustain ourselves with the tiny, almost invisible gifts that lie around us on the ground. Developing that one art is enough.

Personally, I had to start learning about gratitude from ground up. I knew a great deal about complaining about discomfort. I knew how to angrily yank at my imperfections. I knew how to worry over lacks that could appear tomorrow. But I had no idea how to stop to enjoy a small, ordinary moment. I didn't know it was possible or appropriate to be grateful; for joy which might not recur. I didn't know it was permitted to count a partial success. I had to train myself by making lists of things to be grateful for each day. I needed to verbalize enjoyment. It took years to figure out how to sincerely give myself credit for imperfect work. But as I leaned, the whole tenor of my life shifted from flailing around in dangerous waters to a sense of support. I moved from deeply cranky to slightly pleased.

I'd only meant to make things better by keeping my eye so open to what needed fixing. But instead I had emotionally starved myself. As I learned to gather those tiny flakes of joy, my life became lighter and more nurturing. I found minuscule slices of holiness everywhere.

I have to keep practicing this skill every day. I still do those gratitude lists, after almost two decades. I still stop to notice tiny beauties. I still work at appreciating others and still sweat over appreciating myself. I understand now that if I want to see the world as "and it was good" the way God does, I have to gather that good in flakes the size of coriander seeds.

Giving Us the Sabbath

"If He had given us the Sabbath, but had not brought us near to Mount Sinai, [giving us the Sabbath] would have been enough for us."

On most mornings, the Jews went out to gather one *omer* (about two and a half quarts) of manna. On Friday, they received a double portion, two omers, which lasted through to Sunday morning. What was this day of not going out and gathering about?

The best way to understand the layout of a neighborhood is to walk away from it, to go up a nearby hillside and look down at the way the houses and streets are arranged. The best way to understand the winding, knotted streets of our daily lives is to move away a bit, to look at the design from a slightly higher viewpoint.

This is the relationship of the Sabbath to the week. The many limitations of Sabbath observance remove us from earning a living, paying bills, making telephone calls, running errands, buying and selling. The Sabbath pulls us off the whole merry-go-round of daily hassle. It allows us to let go of endlessly gathering and unwind.

At the same time, the traditions of the day quietly offer a series of opportunities to tune into deeper currents of life, to the "layout of the neighborhood." Our existence, the complexity and beauty of reality, the satisfaction of friends and family, or the possibility of a relationship to God: all the larger roots that disappear under the pressure of bills, laundry, and business meetings.

The Sabbath allows us enough space and distance to breathe a sigh of relief and take notice. The Sabbath hints to us that the world is not just a problematic, knotted ball of yarn, but a fairly amazing piece of artwork. As with any piece of art, it is not only an aesthetic experience, but also a communication from its creator.

Egypt narrowed our experience. The world became a restrictive sarcophagus. The process of redemption is described in a psalm: "Out of my narrowness I called to God, and He answered me from His wide place." By the time we receive the Sabbath, our confinement has been shattered. We can stand on a hill and see the stretch of the horizon. (Enough.)

At the very beginning, anxious concern about whether I binged and what I weighed took up more than half my waking day. Over time, those issues became less and less the center of my existence. Eventually the sarcophagus shattered, and there were whole days I didn't worry over these narrow issues at all. Larger, more beautiful themes began to show upon my wider horizon.

For half an hour, I may remember that life is about relationship instead of about what I look like, or how successful I am. The ever present fact that I am alive and in this world occasionally moves out of invisibility. I take less and less for granted and find more and more occasions for wonder.

I still live in a very mundane reality, but sometimes the focusing lens slips into place for a time. "Do they like me?" becomes "How can I help out?" "Did I accomplish anything?" gives way to "Is the world a little better for my being here, or a little worse?" There still are weeks when the size of a budget looms larger than life itself. But there are more and more moments when it becomes clear that life is a limited engagement, when money no longer looks like the core issue, when the whole world becomes a labyrinth which eventually leads me to God.

These glimpses are the heart of my journey out of Egypt, the hub of my wheel. I now find my way back after periods of getting lost on the periphery.

Bringing Us Close to Mount Sinai

"If He had brought us before Mount Sinai, and had not given us the Torah, [bringing us to Mount Sinai] would have been enough for us."

"They departed (verb in plural form) from Refidim and they came (verb in plural form) to the wilderness of Sinai. They camped (verb in plural form) in the wilderness, and Israel camped (verb in singular form) there before the mountain."

"'Camped' (verb in singular form) as one person and with one mind" – from Rashi's commentary

At Mount Sinai, we first experienced ourselves as a unified community, as a "we." We also experienced God in a new way. He spoke to us. He didn't just appear. He became someone to know.

We saw God at the splitting of the sea, but we didn't know who we were or who He was. Our knowledge of God was undifferentiated, the way a small baby knows its mother. The infant has no language yet to conceptualize the difference between self and other. It is too young to distinguish clearly between its own subjective sense of itself as a baby being held and the mother's objective lap. In a similar way, we experienced an undifferentiated, preverbal meeting with God at the Red Sea. Our vision of God had no object constancy, as psychologists say. Neither our sense of ourselves nor our sense of God remained steady and persistent. So our high evaporated.

Coming to Mount Sinai means coming into a more mature spirituality. It involves two separate entities, a beloved community and a beloved Creator, coming together to form a committed relationship. In psychology, this growing sense of oneself and one's partner as separate and real beings is called developing boundaries. "Set a boundary for the people and tell them to be careful not to go up the mountain or to touch it" (Exodus 19). The description of Mount Sinai mentions boundaries three times. We weren't supposed to get too close to the mountain or to God. The point was not to merge with Him but rather to stand apart, facing each other.

At Mount Sinai we found our singularity and God's singularity, which allowed a relationship that could last over time.

In my earliest eating disorder years, I was a fog. I hadn't yet crystallized into a solid self. Without firm borders or a sense of direction, I was continually disoriented. I couldn't begin to figure out how the world worked, and tried without success to navigate by maps other people had charted for themselves.

As my center coalesced, I discovered an inner compass of my own. Instead of wandering in confusion, I began to chart a map of my own; my own desires, my own point of view, my own metaphors. My body became a Geiger counter. Instead of signaling where the radioactivity lay, my body signaled where meaning and importance lay. *This* book. The person who just walked in – who is she? *That* sentence was the most important thing I've heard all month.

This ability pulled relationships to a new level. I was less afraid. I could choose friendships with more fervor. I was more direct. I could place my map next to a friend's map to compare and share. I could hold my own better in an emotional squall. I could even help others hear their own Geiger counters more clearly.

The other change was the way I related to God. Before, I'd imagined God as a great Teacher trying to give us directions. I'm slowly beginning to think of God as someone who wants to reveal Himself, who wants to have a friendship (so to speak) with human beings. Until I was more than a fog, I couldn't relate to God as more than a transcendental foghorn.

Giving the Torah to Us

"If He had given us the Torah and had not brought us into the land of Israel, [just giving us the Torah] would be enough for us."

Torah is the private lovers' language which God and the Jews use to speak to each other, to explore each other. It is filled with little secrets, with the history of our relationship, with God's desires of us, and with our desires of Him. Torah is the form of our mutual commitment. It is also our place of rendezvous with Him, both as individuals and as a community.

The Torah is like a pocket version of Mount Sinai that we take with us everywhere. Eventually the "where" of Mount Sinai was forgotten, but the facing each other that happened on that mountain continues. The more we study the Torah that was received there, the more we can meet God's singularity and our own. Since the Torah is said to be the blueprint of creation, the more Torah we uncover and study, the more we understand the universe.

What looks like a bundle of coiled-up parchment and black ink is actually a form of concentrated intimacy. We only have to learn how to take off the cover and dilute the contents appropriately. Perhaps this work, more than any other, is what finally, permanently prevents us from falling back into the tight limitations of Egypt. Once God gives us this language of intimacy, our relationship only gets deeper. "Turn it, turn it, for everything is in it." (Pirkei Avot, chapter 5) This coiled-up rendezvous is the epitome of enough.

Some of my non-religious friends and relatives worry that Torah is too limiting. I've had the opposite experience.

Metaphor one: A microscope or a telescope limits our view to a small eyehole. Inside the small circle, layers and layers of reality are exposed that I otherwise wouldn't expect.

Metaphor two: A skilled gardener sees a limited area of dirt, the same square every day. It's insignificant compared to what a hiker sees in just an hour. But the gardener's work goes deep. That parcel of soil and the gardener together create something amazing. That garden reveals both the gardener's potential and the earth's potential.

The limited Torah unwraps into vast spirals of transformation for millions of individual Jews in hundred of places.

I am also learning to think of my eating disorder as my patch of soil. It's only one of many issues, and one that certainly reduces and limits me. Yet it has that same unfolding quality. The more I work with it, the more layers of reality are exposed, the more I see of God's hand in the world. The more I work with it, the more amazing the garden becomes.

Over the years, I've cultivated my own individual way of speaking to God, my own special prayers, my own confessional list to enrich my Yom Kippur, and many of my own private customs. As can happen with gardens, the soil gets more fertile over the years, and so do I.

Bringing Us to the Land of Israel

"If He had brought us into the land of Israel, but had not built us the Holy Temple, [bringing us into the land of Israel] would have been enough for us."

Spiritual studies may bring meaning, but they don't always help us manage in the "real world." There is a gap between inner life and down-to-earth practicality. Annoying ants can invade the kitchen even on the holy Sabbath. A sense that people are made in the image of God will not protect us from horrendous bureaucratic entanglements. The demands of politics, of logistics, and of physical reality can seem diametrically opposed to the demands of creativity or emotional balance. These different realities occupy the same lifetime with disturbing dissonance. It's like perpetually listening to the orchestra tuning up before the performance. There is no harmony or pattern at all.

The major subjective symptom of our exile is this lack of harmony between the inside and the outside. Moving from your internal reality to the external reality, or vice versa, requires an awkward, unsatisfying translation into a foreign language. "Gathering the exiles into the Land of Israel" means emerging from this experience of mismatch. This land is not inherently and disturbingly foreign, but carefully tailored by the Master of the Universe. This does not mean that there are no ants in the kitchen, no bureaucratic knots, no tear-your-hair-out frustrations. But the Land of Israel, challenges included, is somehow holy. Ideally, its demands and pitfalls are *not* diametrically opposed to spiritual life. They are complementary. When there is disharmony, it doesn't disintegrate into cacophony.

Entering Israel is entering a synergy between the internal and external worlds. The logistical, physical reality works better with the application of Torah. Our spiritual connection deepens as we struggle with the down-to-earth problems. The cycle of prayers and holidays fits the weather patterns. The complex agricultural laws change a person's sense of eating and of economic security. The haunting desert wilderness, the lack of water sources, the abundance of olive and almond trees, the layers of old communities... all give a physical immediacy to "theoretical" religious concepts.

To a certain extent, "coming into Israel" is a personal metamorphosis that can occur in our lives regardless of our immediate geographical location. It is harnessing together the external landscape and the inner landscape. When these forces are working together, our wagon moves much more quickly and smoothly. Exile is a mismatch between these forces; it pulls our wagon apart. "Entering Israel" is the discovery that the practical and the existential, that daily life and ultimate values, are not two completely separate species, but different varieties of the same species. They can be harnessed together. They can even be mated. The dialectic can be fruitful and creative.

Once I inhabited two ends of a spectrum. On the high end, I was bright, creative, visionary, and sufficiently competent. On the lower end of the spectrum was a huddled, frightened compulsive eater/reader, overwhelmed, socially inept, and not a little self-destructive. These ends of the spectrum never conversed. Each found the very existence of the other a mind-boggling contradiction.

In time I discovered that not only were they both who I am, but that I am the entire spectrum of different levels of functioning that runs between them. The trick is to use all of the sections to live in the world including how high I am with how low I am, how sublime the world is with how ugly it is. The more I include, the more synergy there is between the "contradictions." Struggling through a difficult or inspiring commentary is related to getting through Purim without bingeing. Not only are they related, they elaborate and enhance each other.

Building the Holy Temple

Our song in the Haggada does not go on to a sixteenth verse. It doesn't ever say, "If He had only built a Holy Temple, it would have been enough for us." That part of the process has not yet been completed. It still waits in the wings.

To understand the Holy Temple, we need to recall any small experiences we may have had of the Divine Presence appearing "at home" in the world. In exile, the needs of down-to-earth reality and the needs of our deepest inner selves are antagonistic, endlessly sabotaging each other. Coming into Israel embodies the end of the war. The inner and outer realities finally work together as partners. The holy Temple raises the ante from partnership to intimate friendship. God comfortably settles in among the cedar walls and woven curtains. The exacting measurements, the physical metals, stones, plants, and animal skins required for the building all offer God a warm hospitality. This will not be war, not even a careful compromise. This will be a warm, mutual embrace between measurement and the immeasurable. It will be an embrace between the weekday logistical world of laundry, lists, and overdrafts and the Sabbath world of appreciation and acceptance.

The Holy Temple embodies that level of experience where the secret, existential twinges inside of us express themselves easily in the world. Picture the way Monet delighted in the sunlight landing on his garden pond. That delight eagerly moved into the paint of his palette. The sense of light and the pigments were not enemies. They were not even partners. They were the warmest of mutually fulfilling companions.

A meal will not be an annoying but necessary interference in the day's meaningful activities, nor will it be a bingeing escape from the conflicts of reality. The body will enjoy the flavors and nutrients. The emotional child will feel nurtured. The soul will sense the blessings poured from God's open hand onto the table. Each meal will be an interweaving of gratitude, health, and pleasure. Each meal will be a dance with God.

In the Holy Temple, the layers of the world are actually beautifully tailored to each other. What a relief and a surprise to find that life works. We won't have to struggle to make the pieces fit. In the present world of the destroyed Holy Temple, we can only have tastes of how it's supposed to fit together. We can only believe that these tastes are not freak accidents, but intimations of what God was yearning for as He planned the world.

The final redemption will not be an escape out of present reality, but an emergence of what this reality was always truly about. That will be finally and utterly enough.

For further reading:

Twerski, Abraham J., MD. *From Bondage to Freedom: The Passover Haggadah.* With a commentary illuminating the liberation of spirit. Suffern, NY: 1995.

Idem. *Life's Too Short!: Pull the Plug on Self-Defeating Behavior and Turn on the Power of Self-Esteem.* New York: 1995.

Idem. *Self-Improvement? I'm Jewish!* Suffern, NY: 1996.

Wherever intimacy as a mitzvah is found – there the Shechina dwells.

Zohar, *Vayishlah 176a*

My Life as a Nun

Gila Berkowitz

When I was a girl of about eight or nine, I created a new concept in world religion: the observant Jewish nun. The order was unabashedly modeled on the Roman Catholic sisterhood. Naturally, there would be some changes. The ugly "Golda" shoes would have to go, to be substituted by ballet slippers, while the starched wimples and wools of those pre-Vatican II habits would be replaced by silky fabrics in either lilac or turquoise – the sisters would decide by majority vote. And, of course, there would be no Christian stuff, just plain God.

The nuns' regimen would be highly regulated. Long days of prayer and the study of holy books would be gently punctuated by peaceful walks in the convent's herb gardens. Most important, our world was to be entirely devoid of those pests – boys.

In my fantasy, nuns were free of all mundane responsibility; they were liberated from the shackles of work and worry. They had no obligations to family. They didn't even have to waste time deciding what to wear in the morning. There was only one thing they had to do, to rise steadily in spirituality until they reached an apex of holiness.

You'd think any observant Jew would have enough piety, with a constant set of religious obligations and a bulging calendar of sacred days. But I yearned for a distinctly maidenly way to be holy. And a pre-adolescent with troubling stirrings of sexuality could safely bury them in the convent gardens.

Deep down I always understood that my Jewish nunnery was a fantasy. My parents, and most of the adults I knew, were Holocaust survivors. To remain single and childless would add the ultimate insult to the ultimate injury. But even so, the nun's life remained a secret ideal.

The first real nun I met sat on a stool in a subway station, completely motionless, with a bowl in her hand. She did not implore passersby for contributions, neither in word nor glance. She never thanked anyone who put a coin in the bowl. She did not pray or read or converse with anyone. I was shocked. Surely this was one of the greatest wastes of human potential that I could imagine. What holiness could make up for this absence of human intercourse, the missed opportunity to smile, to thank, or to be an example of piety in prayer?

Later, I grew friendly with a veteran nun, Sister Abraham of the Ethiopian Church in Jerusalem, a tiny, impoverished sect, where she was the only nun among the monks, the only white woman among Africans, and a clergywoman with a keen interest in the scholarly. The Ethiopians went out of their way to provide Sister Abraham with living quarters and research facilities, and her teaching salary helped their finances considerably. Mostly, she was on her own.

At first, despite Sister Abraham's really homely habit, all black and boxy, I found her situation enviable. But when she revealed the spiritual side of her life, my own Jewish background began to assert itself. Sister Abraham showed me her tales about hermits and saints of the Holy Land in the first few centuries of Christianity. The stories were oddly familiar from Jewish and other folklore, but the *moral* of each story seemed absent. Missing was what is called in Yiddish the *chop,* the crux or point of the legend.

An example: an anchorite enters his cave for increasingly long periods of time. Each time, his fellow monks marvel at his survival without food or water. Finally, he is absent for forty days and nights. The monks enter the cave but they do not find him, either dead or alive. He has vanished, leaving only his crucifix and his shepherd's crook. He has gone directly to heaven, they proclaim.

In this story, saintliness is a personal trait, leading to personal spiritual fulfillment. In a Jewish story, whether told in Hebrew, Yiddish or English, saintliness is nearly always an act of community: of charity to another, perfumed further by compassion, respect, and modesty. In both cases, believers accept and declare the supernatural, but in the Jewish tales, great human acts startle us more than miracles.

Another factor of Christian holiness is chastity. This for me lay at the heart of the nuns' mystique. While chastity *before* marriage is highly desirable in Judaism, the state of virginity itself is no ideal.

At the heart of the idealization of chastity lies a fear of the power of sexuality. This power is not ignored in Judaism, but neither is it demonized. Sex, like everything else, can be good or evil. Kedusha, holiness, swings both ways sexually. *Kiddushin* is the word for marriage, while the word *kedesha,* from the same root, means a pagan temple prostitute. To extract the holiness of sexuality, it must dwell in marriage and be guarded by many laws and commandments.

These rules promote and strengthen the bonds between one man and one woman. From this, it is hoped, connections grow in concentric circles, to family, to community, to the world. Holiness grows outward from a single divine bond between two people.

It will come as a surprise to many Jews, even quite learned ones, that among the six hundred thirteen commandments – the mitzvot – is a distinct call to men not only to engage in the marital act, but to bring one's wife to sexual satisfaction. This is the mitzvah of *onah*. It is derived from the statement in Exodus 21:10: "He may not diminish his wife's allowance, her clothes, or her conjugal rights." That is, a husband is explicitly required to supply necessities and clothes generously for his wife, and give her ample sexual pleasure.

Later, in Deuteronomy 23:18 we learn that a man who marries must "rejoice" with his bride for a full year and may not be drafted into the army. (This does not apply during wars of defense.)

Whatever their feelings about woman's place in society, the rabbis of the Talmud and their successors unanimously championed her right to satisfaction in bed. Sexual happiness is the one absolute obligation of a husband to his wife. A woman's sexual obligations are more vague. A woman may sue for lack of sexual services – including work that keeps her husband away from home for excessive periods – while a man usually has to prove malice on the part of a sexually indifferent wife.

Orgasm is an important measure of a woman's satisfaction, and the rabbis ruled that a man must do whatever his wife requires to achieve it. They stress the need for verbal as well as physical foreplay. A man should be available whenever his wife is in the mood, but must never press her to comply with his own. The Talmud and later rabbis do recognize that achieving female orgasm requires some skill in lovemaking on the part of the couple, but there is an assumption that female orgasm is as natural and inevitable as that of the male.

Sex is not a privilege for the young, pretty, and pliable. It is not a reward to be bestowed for wearing a certain brand of lipstick or ironing shirts to a crisp finish. It is the inalienable right of every married woman.

Why is there a mitzvah of onah? To build Jewish homes on solid foundations of love? For procreation? These are surely good reasons, but they are covered by other mitzvot. The mitzvah to love one's neighbor as oneself applies to no one more than to a spouse. To be fruitful and multiply is to imitate God's way in the act of creation. But the mitzvah of onah applies to pregnant and post-menopausal women as much as to fertile ones.

Sex, like all actions, is transformed by mitzvah into a form of spiritual expression. It is one of the rare instances where complete union with another can be achieved, ideally becoming a metaphor of divine Oneness. The great Talmudic sage Rabbi Akiva declared the Song of Songs, a sensual, explicit metaphor for the love between God and Israel, the holiest book in the Bible.

For this transformation to take place, all the factors must be in order. Man and woman must be sanctified to each other in marriage. Spiritual elevation cannot be achieved in an adulterous, incestuous, or homosexual relationship, nor in the frivolous coupling of the unmarried. Unmarried cohabitation is a dead zone of sexuality in the Jewish context; if man and woman cannot pledge commitment to each other, what can they possibly pledge to God? Men and women might ask themselves, "If this person isn't good enough to marry, why is s/he good enough to sleep with?"

The spiritual goals of Jewish sexuality do not exist in a vacuum. They are part of a broad philosophy of the integration of body and soul, the material and the spiritual, the earthly and the heavenly. Judaism insists that it is action that leads to belief and good values.

The Torah's warnings against sexual misconduct are terrifying. The prohibition against sleeping with a menstruant woman is cheek-by-jowl with the prohibition of human sacrifice! But the aim throughout is to emphasize that intercourse is a spiritually elevating act. Millennia before modern law, halachic law considered marital rape a crime and a sin. Even when force is not involved, coitus is forbidden if one partner is angry with the other, when the woman is asleep or unconscious, or when either spouse is drunk.

The most important fence guarding Jewish sexuality is *tzniut,* modesty. The word smacks of coyness and prudery but nothing could be further from this essential Jewish value, whose object is to enhance human dignity. The breaching of modesty shatters the divine union of woman and man and God.

In dress, Judaism requires not dowdiness or unattractiveness but a sense of dignity and respect for one's own body, which, male or female, is the image of God. Women are advised not to treat themselves as male playthings. Wearing suggestive, teasing clothing is a desperate and doomed attempt to wheedle favors from those in power. Those in power – men as well as women – almost always dress with dignity and modesty. Consider a head of state, a corporate CEO, and so on. Jewish observance demands no less of each man and woman.

Because of modesty, the secrets of Jewish sexuality have been kept hidden from outsiders. The mystery has had many guessing. In pre-modern times many gentiles saw the endurance of so many Jewish marriages as evidence that the Jews had some special sexual power and this was a source of both awe and anti-Semitism.

Does the Jewish ideal of sexuality stand a chance in this world? Squeezed between the convent of virginity and the overwhelming crush of sensuousness on all sides, Judaism reaffirms its own values: spirituality expressed through the everyday world by everyday people.

I have cast off the wimple and veil of my imagined Jewish nunnery. I traded them in long ago for the yoke of mortgages and tuitions and responsibility to my people.

It's no herb garden, this place I live in. Work, family, religion – I often wonder where the stop button is on this treadmill. But here, outside the garden, there is also conversation and laughter, and love and joyful sex with my husband. There is pride and joy in our children and family and people, and an irrepressible hope for humanity.

For further reading:

Friedman, Manis. *Doesn't Anyone Blush Anymore?* Minneapolis, MN: 1996.
Bulka, Reuven. *Jewish Marriage: A Halakhic Ethic.* Jersey City, NJ: 1986.

Sometimes, when [you feel that you are] unable to pray, do not believe that you are definitely unable to pray that day. Strengthen yourself all the more and the awe [of God] will come upon you ever more.

This is comparable to a king who sets out to wage war and disguises himself. Those who are wise recognize him by his mannerisms. Those who are less wise recognize the king by noting the place with extraordinary guarding: surely that is the place of the king.

Thus it is when you are unable to pray with kavanah. You must know that there is additional guarding all around the King. The king is there, but you are unable to approach Him because of the special protection surrounding Him. Thus fortify yourself with awe, great strength and additional kavanah, so that you will be able to come close and pray before God.

From Tzava'at ha-Rivash, The Testament of Rabbi Israel Baal Shem Tov, *translated into the English by Rabbi J. Immanuel Schochet*

Between Woman and God

Ruchama King Feuerman

When I was fifteen, in the midst of all kinds of turmoil and upheavals, I made a decision to pray not only on Mondays through Fridays, when the girls' yeshiva high school I attended was in session, but at home, on the weekends. This was a great leap in my spiritual development: to pray because I chose to, not merely to appease teachers and rabbis. But I could not fully claim my decision – my own sincerity embarrassed me. It almost felt like a betrayal of/to my peers and family: Cool Rocky (as I was known then) was turning up the heat on her piety. Didn't I already keep Shabbat and kosher? Wasn't I already *frum*, pious? Who was I to stand out and be more religious than anyone else? So on weekends or at friends' sleepovers, I'd hide and pray in the basement, like some ancient persecuted Marrano, to avoid detection.

Eventually I became comfortable enough with the act of prayer so that I could whip out my prayer book and pray in phone booths, parks, libraries and, when I moved to Israel, bus stations and restaurants. Once, after finishing an impromptu afternoon *mincha* on a city sidewalk, I looked up to discover I had prayed next to a go-go club. Did I love praying? I think I approached it like flossing teeth, with great resistance, but once I got past the first two teeth, I actually found myself close to enjoying the process. Afterwards I always felt clean and virtuous.

But I wanted more. I wanted to raise prayer above the rote mumblings of my elementary school days. I wanted to experience the passion of *dveykus*, cleaving to God. My apartment in Jerusalem was near a forest and except for the rainy season I often was able to pray outdoors. This made a huge difference. I got an inkling of what Rebbe Nachman of Breslov meant when he wrote about including the outdoors in your prayers. It was almost impossible not to view the swaying blades of grass as bowing in acknowledgement of God's supreme being. Then through singing powerful tunes to different sections I found I could elevate the prayers to a different realm. A tune wasn't merely nice background music, but provided nuances of meanings that brought me to tears. And then, if a particularly phrase struck me, I could always stop and repeat it, savor it, meditate over and over, the phrase becoming part of my understanding of life. Finally, studying more about the texts, either the simple meaning or more mystical aspects, always enriched my experience of prayer. And then the shuls themselves – they're gems. Something about Israel makes it the ideal place for transcendence.

So yes, I did have some amazing davenning times, sensations of God that were shockingly visceral, what one might call spiritual experiences. I still remember them, and there is no greater joy. But such experiences were rare. My regular morning davenning sessions in my rented Jerusalem apartment were something else. Most of the time the act of praying resembled moving along a swift river, carried here and there, catching stray bits of inspiring scenery, but nothing to steady me, nothing to take hold and transform me. Often I was bored and distracted. When I opened my siddur to pray, lists would assail me: the ingredients I needed to buy for dinner that night, the number of guys I'd gone out with whose name started with "Y," phone calls I needed to make, appointments I needed to go to. Life clearly began in earnest after I put down the siddur, not before. The Sages wrote that one shouldn't approach one's prayers as if they were a burden, but that's how I usually went about it.

The truth was, I was angry at God. I was furious at God for my single status. I had accompanied too many roommates to the chuppah. What about me? I didn't understand what God wanted from me – greater devotion, acrobatic acts, jumps through flaming hoops? What would satisfy this God of mine? Hadn't I given enough?

I had a friend who had been dating longer and was even more discouraged than I was. "What's God running, some torture chamber here? Does He enjoy sitting back, listening to people plead and beg, and maybe then, maybe, maybe He'll change His mind?" She shook her head. "I can't pray to a God like that."

I tried to argue with her. "You're frustrated with your own limited conception of God. You've adopted a shallow understanding of God and prayer, and then you've attacked that. Hardly a rebuttal."

"So, what's your understanding?" she challenged me.

Hm. "The point of prayer," I began, "isn't to nudge God to the point where He says, 'Enough already. I give in. Here's the job, man, house you want. Whatever. Just stop kvetching.' No." I dug my finger into the coffee table for emphasis. "The point is, the act of prayer changes you, elevates and refines and even changes the kind of things you ask for. And God then responds to a changed you."

"Very nice," she said. "Wish it would happen to me."

Well, I tried. The truth is, I was speaking to myself as much as to her. I didn't understand why God didn't answer me, or worse, why He'd said no. Even beyond that I wondered if prayer really elevated me at all. I had tried so hard, prayed at the Kotel forty days in a row, taken myself to Rabbi Shimon Bar Yochai's grave every Rosh ha-Shana, spread myself flat on the ground and cried out, "Whatever you want me to do, God, I'll do, I'll do. Just give me a sign. Don't be subtle." Now I felt let down, exhausted, angry, the same struggling Jew I'd always been, no better.

I moved back to the States, and one day I realized a week had gone by and I hadn't prayed. I decided to make it formal – I stopped. It seemed lots of religious women – married with children – didn't pray. The lack of prayer in their lives didn't stop them from leading vibrant, spiritual, religiously committed lives. I could do the same without sacrificing any piety.

The prayerless years began. I loved the sensation of freedom, the unburdened feeling in the morning of spending it the way I wanted. Instead of focusing on a siddur first thing in the morning, I could linger over a magazine or newspaper at breakfast. There were so many other religious rituals in my life – learning Torah, the blessings over food and countless other blessings throughout the day – that I hardly noticed a difference in the quality of my religious life. I just didn't pray. As a fifteen-year-old, I had chosen to pray; now, as a thirty-year-old, I chose not to.

Wonderful things followed. I got an MFA. My career crystallized. I got engaged and married to a wonderful man with a satisfying blend of irony, irreverence, and holiness, qualities I had been seeking for many years to the bafflement of matchmakers with whom I'd spoken. I had children, threw myself into being a wife and mother. All was well.

And yet there were many Shabbats where my mind wandered during Kiddush, where the singing and Torah thoughts and guests around me all felt ho-hum. Hollow. I was happy when the meal was over and I could cuddle up with a magazine or novel. Every now and then I'd waken from my malaise and wonder: where was the passion, the joy, the transcendence of it all? Where did it all go? At times I felt like an impostor, someone impersonating the external responses of a religious Jew. In shul I imagined the rabbi pointing a finger at me: "Seize her!"

People told me, "You're not a single anymore. Things are different now. You've got children to raise. That alone can knock the stuffing out of you." True. Also, I was no longer in Israel. Living in Brooklyn, no matter how many yeshivas, shuls and kosher stores dotted the streets, could not compare to the ecstasy of living in Jerusalem. Perhaps I had just grown up. My twenties were a kind of spiritual Disneyland. What I was experiencing now was a different life. I re-adjusted my expectations.

One day I got a phone call from an old Jerusalem friend with whom I hadn't spoken in years. We caught up on a number of topics. I mentioned there was a psychotherapist I was seeing about once a month and how much the relationship had enriched my life. "You're seeing a therapist?" she said. "Is there something wrong?"

"No." I was a little taken aback at her question. It seemed archaic. Everyone I knew saw a therapist. "Nothing wrong. Just for general life-enhancement. There's always issues that need to be worked out." I stopped. "Well, what do you do for skilled support and guidance through life's murky waters?"

"I – well…" she gave an embarrassed laugh, "I pray."

Her words startled me. "And that really helps?"

"I get what I need. Yeah, it really helps."

I let out a sigh, a long one. Those two words – "I pray" – filled me with an intense nostalgia. I remembered when prayer was the only thing that got me through anguished times, when it was the only steady nurturance I could count on, when my relationship with God absolutely sustained me. I choked up. We spoke a little more and then I had to get off the phone.

The next afternoon I tentatively picked up a siddur and started to pray mincha. It was gentle and pleasant to pray again, nothing earth-shattering. But I paid attention to the after-effect. I faced the rest of the day more solidly planted and assured. "Centered," I guess, is what they call such a feeling. A tinge of cosmic loneliness lessened a bit. I was lonely for God, I realized. I had felt cut off.

The next day I forgot to pray, and after that, too.

A year passed. One day my four-year-old daughter commented, "Daddy davens and learns Torah. And Ima reads magazines."

I gave her a sharp look. I coughed. "Avigayil, uh, what about that Chumash class I go to?"

"That's not davenning," she scoffed.

Oh, there was no fooling that one. She was a handful. I remember when she was three and I took her to shul on Simchat Torah. She asked then, "How come the women aren't dancing with the Torahs?"

I reached into my bag of answers, the things I had told myself in my twenties, and said, "The men hold the Torahs as if they're babies. The women hold the babies as if they're Torahs." She smiled and nodded. That answer satisfied her at three and me at twenty-three. But what would I tell her when she was thirteen? How would I keep up with my spiritually precocious daughter if I wasn't even davenning myself? And what image was I was reflecting back to her of Jewish women?

I started looking back on those years without prayer, to put my finger on the quality and mood of it, what those years had been like. I worried more. It used to be that the first words of print I saw in the morning were from the siddur. Now I looked at the headlines. It's good to be aware. I believe this. If Jews are specially charged to be involved in *tikkun olam*, repairing what's wrong with the world, how can I repair if I'm oblivious? I read and worried: about contaminated water, contaminated air, nitrates in hot dogs and salami, about race relations and poverty, about children being turned into slaves and human shields in Third World countries, about the decadence and dullness of American mass culture, and of course about Israel, the bombs, the people, the conflicts between the religious and secular, slanted media coverage, Saddam Hussein and Islamic fundamentalism. These are real concerns. Boy, did I worry. But what did I do? Did I join Greenpeace, become an Israel activist? Help out at a soup kitchen, teach a Torah class? No, I just worried, but I did nothing to help out.

It hadn't always been that way. Since I was seventeen years old, I had volunteered at children's hospitals, mental institutions, after-school programs for the disabled and troubled. I was part of a community chesed hotline where someone could call me at a moment's notice to wash a poor overwrought mother's floor. Then all my volunteer work had stopped. Why? When? About the time that I had stopped praying. My davenning had been fueling my acts of giving and I hadn't even known.

Other aspects stood out about those prayerless years. They had been effective, strong years for me. I had accomplished much, but there was no question that my deep sense of God's abiding concern had diminished. With that, some of the zest had leaked out of life. Then it crept up on me, how prayer had affected me. Even in the boring tiresome moments, the day-in day-out of it all, some kind of spiritual chiropractic had been taking place, an inner alignment that set me straight and steady for the entire day. On some osmosis level I was absorbing that God runs the world, not me. I could relax and stop worrying. If God was in charge, then the universe wasn't a hopeless place where an act of kindness would get lost in the world's bedlam. The words of prayer let me know I was more than a lone woman trying to put together a decent life. I had a mission, I was part of God's plan of tikkun olam. He was interested in me. He loved me. And sometimes, I allowed He even liked me, and enjoyed my personality quirks.

I used to call my morning sessions meaningless if they didn't produce a high. It seemed so many plodding prayers had to be undergone in order to produce one great amazing experience. But are these peak experiences the raison d'etre of prayer? Was my precious high the point of it all? In this way, I had turned prayer into a Chinese laundromat – to service me and make sure my needs for depth and meaning and intense experience were ministered to consistently and effectively. Wasn't it supposed to be the other way around?

I once read in a Hassidic book that a person prays many dutiful plodding prayers that pile up, one on top of the other, forming a tottering tower, and finally one strong prayer comes along and is able to leap over to the other side – to the place of complete connection with God. And when this last prayer makes its leap, it pulls all the former plodding prayers along with it to the other side.

I don't mean to glorify the idea of boredom, but I think it has its place and uses. I see the importance of boredom in my own children's development. Their ability to endure a certain amount of boredom goes hand in hand with their ability to imagine and innovate. If they didn't have the down time, they'd lose that skill of looking inside themselves to create. What is boredom anyway if not time and space, a chance to hang out with yourself – or your soul – and see what comes up? Often a spiritual idea can be outside a person's reach, hovering over, above and beyond. It's that boring time in prayers, that alone-with-yourself, facing-yourself time, where the idea that's out there can enter you, profoundly. *Lehitpallel*, the word for prayer, is a reflexive verb that literally means an act of self-regard, even judgment.

Moreover, boredom grounds a person in what he or she truly believes. A person's willingness to confront boredom means that this experience just isn't about her high. She's in it for the long haul. The prayer enters the level of a true spiritual discipline. Just as marriage is the institution that keeps a couple together as they fall in and out of love, so too prayer is the anchor and stronghold as we fall in and out of love with Torah and God. After all, what does it mean if spirituality turns into a side-show that goes on and on or else must lose all its adherents?

And yet, I have a Self. And if I pickle too long in a vat of boredom, my Self will dry out and die. Surely, God doesn't only want my automaton obedience. After all, it's the Self that I bring to worship Him that makes me want to pray in the first place. I am not just a cog in the prayer machine! God wants Me, and therefore my needs – be it for more inspiring tunes in the synagogue, more meaningful sermons and creative participation – must have some place in the act and place of worship. But how much and how far should the Self go?

Certainly, in religion there's an ongoing struggle between the Self and God: Who gets star billing? In certain circles the Self is annihilated in the service of God, and in other circles the Self is worshipped to the point that God is insignificant, even an annoyance. There's got to be some balance here.

From the way I'm talking, you'd think I'd arrived at my goal of integrating prayer into my life. I'm still struggling. The desire is there, but the will, the will. It's not easy to reacquire a spiritual discipline in the throes of raising a family. Still, I look to my family for inspiration. I don't want them growing up thinking women don't pray, that it's just a man thing. How absurd, when so many prayers and the laws of prayers are based on the practices of biblical women.

I grab an afternoon mincha here, a morning shacharis there. Often I'm harried and distracted, rushing to finish before getting interrupted by the kids. But now I notice the after-effects, the subtle sensations that accompany prayer. This time I won't be so dismissive and obtuse. What I feel is a quiet, bone-deep settledness, an equanimity, as the verse says, "Shiviti Hashem le-negdi tamid." It translates to, "I have placed God before me always," but it can also mean, "Through my relationship to God I achieve equanimity." Shiviti comes from "shaveh," equal. God balances me out.

I still get frustrated and angry at God. But instead of going numb on Him, I try to tell Him when that happens. I like the prayer in the Shemoneh Esreh, "Blessed is God who listens." Not "who gives you whatever you ask for." But He listens, takes note. And I, in turn, am learning to listen for His answers.

A friend taught me how to say the Shema in sign language. 'Shema' – to hear, is easy. A hand touching the ear. 'Yisrael' is two hands forming a V, like a book, as in the People of the Book. 'Hashem' is one arm gracefully extended outward and upward. 'Our God,' is touching the heart, and 'One' is one straight finger. Sometimes I sing the Shema to my children this way, using all the gestures. First we sing the words and make the appropriate signs. Then we hum and sign the Shema. Then we neither hum nor sing, but simply sign. The tune and words echo in our ears just the same. We do this over and over. The children are entranced and so am I. It's as if we're dancing with the words, ingesting them into ours innards, dancing with God. Afterwards there's a little moment of quiet. We look at each other and burst out laughing. We've all just had a spiritual experience and we need to diminish some of the intensity.

"Those who seek God will not lack good." I am always struck by this verse from the grace after meals. Even though you're in a state of seeking, yearning – a state of unfulfilled desire as it were, you're not lacking. The yearning itself has a richness and fullness.

I think I'm learning to get comfortable with yearning again. Yearning and not getting answers – or at least the answers I want. That's probably why I stopped praying in the first place. I thought all that yearning was depleting me and getting me nowhere – in either the spiritual or practical realms of my life. But looking back, those years of intense longing were years of completion and inner formation. The yearning for God engraves itself upon a person. It creates a character, a self, a soul, a will for goodness. After all, where does all the longing for God go? What happens to it? Is it like all the random thoughts that stray through our minds, or does it have some separate existence? I imagine all those intense feelings we have for God being contained, somehow, in a vessel, and that vessel always stays inside us. As the psalmist, King David, wrote, "I am prayer." We long, we yearn, we pray, and then in turn we become a prayer. Transformed. An expression of beauty and holiness to God. That's what I like to think.

For further reading:

Kaplan, Aryeh. *A Call to the Infinite.* Brooklyn, NY: 1986.

Mindel, Nissan. *My Prayer.* Brooklyn, NY: 1978.

Steinsaltz, Adin. *A Guide to Jewish Prayer.* New York, NY: 2000.

Zakutinsky, Rivkah. *Techinas: A Voice from the Heart. A Collection of Jewish Women's Prayers.* Brooklyn, NY: 1992.

Blessing upon immersion in the mikveh:

After entering the mikveh and immersing once, the following blessing is recited:

Ba-ruch a-tah A-do-noi Elo-hai-nu me-lech ha-o-lom a-sher kid-sha-nu be-mitz-vo-tav v'tzi-va-nu al ha-tevilah.

Blessed are You, Lord our God, King of the Universe, Who has sanctified us with His commandments and has commanded us concerning immersion.

After immersing once again, many women also say the following:

May it be your will, Lord, Our God, and God of our fathers, that the Holy Temple be rebuilt speedily in our days, and that you grant us a portion in Your Torah.

Directly before, during, and after immersion in the mikveh is a very auspicious time for a woman to offer her private prayers to God.

Sacred Spaces

Emily Benedek

Ella Bedonie's mother, Bessie Hatathlie, a traditional Navajo woman, was bothered by something she saw while visiting her daughter in college. "How can you have a bathroom inside your home?" she asked Ella, who then lived in married-student housing at Northern Arizona University. "The home is a sacred place and you should not go to the bathroom in it."

This remark amused me, then startled me. For Navajos, the hogan – their traditional igloo-shaped one-room house – is sacred not only because it is the place where they raise their children, but also the place into which they usher in their gods. Religious ceremonies are held in the hogan, every piece of which—the

---

* Edited excerpts from *Through the Unknown, Remembered Gate.*

entrance poles, the doorway, the ceiling-has religious significance and is built, the Navajos believe, as the gods built their own homes.

I was moved by Bessie's idea of the home as sanctuary, and I couldn't let go of the idea of a place in which the divine is expected. Although modern society has been desacralized to a great extent, there are still numerous remnants that reveal the primordial importance of the experience of the sacred. For example, the doors of synagogues or churches – whose majesty and grandeur can affect even the nonreligious – mark boundaries between the sacred and the profane. The demarcation itself is important, as in the doorways of homes or other buildings that are marked, if not by imposing architecture, then at least by gargoyles or signs (such as the mezuzah on a Jewish home) to invoke divine protection. There are also behaviors characteristic of passing across thresholds: a bow, a touch or shake of a hand, a prostration, traces of notice paid to the spirit guardians of the door. Our celebrations connected with the laying of the cornerstone of a new building are related to ancient practices of blood sacrifices made to animate new constructions.

Thinking about sacred spaces, my thoughts wandered to the strange sunken shower in my grandmother's house. Off a downstairs bathroom in this elegant Georgian home in Boston was a mikveh, or ritual bath, used by Orthodox Jewish men and women. Behind a door that at first glance appeared to be a closet, about twenty steps led into a deep, white-tiled shower stall.

As children, my sister and I dreamed of filling the mikveh with water and swimming in it; we could have done somersaults and never touched bottom. But we were not allowed. Even though my grandmother had never used this ritual bath (it had been built by the previous owners), there was a non-negotiable rule that this room was not to be used for fun and games.

For forty years, the mikveh went unused. The green paint above the tiles faded and flaked; moisture spots grew until they were the size of balloons. The tiles on the steps became loose. But every time I visited my grandmother, from my earliest childhood until the house was sold, I opened the door and looked in. I didn't know why I was compelled to inhale the familiar mustiness, let the mysterious feelings wash over me. Sometimes I closed the door behind me and called out; I heard the echo of my own voice.

I knew that a woman dipped in the mikveh to restore ritual purity at some point after the completion of her menstrual cycle and before physically rejoining her husband. And I knew that some religious men dipped in the mikveh before the Sabbath. But it wasn't until I returned to New York that I learned more about this ritual from my friend Ruchama. First, she cleaned herself thoroughly between her toes, under every nail, behind her ears, in the holes of her pierced ears. She even removed her nail polish. In the course of this methodical cleaning, she had an opportunity to think about the last month, to take an accounting of things, to observe changes. As she inspected her hands, arms, and legs, memories of the last month's joys and pains, desires and failures, came to mind. The scrutiny of her body offered an opportunity for the examination of her soul, and the body's cleansing offered her a parallel opportunity to renew her spiritual intentions.

There was excitement and anticipation involved as well, as her trip to the mikveh marked the end of the two-week period in which observant husbands and wives refrain from touching each other and sleep in separate beds. Married women say that when they return to their husbands after the mikveh, they feel like brides once again, full of hope and expectation, and that this mandated separation serves to keep excitement alive in a long marriage. Of course, it is in the time just after immersion that the woman's fertility is highest and conception most likely; it is part of the sacred marriage bond that children begin to grow after a time the mother has prepared herself for a meeting with the divine.

It also occurred to me, as I glanced into the changing rooms and saw piles of fluffy white towels, Q-tips, and other cosmetic items, that although this was a private ablution, the women here were sharing a ritual not only with their forebears – mothers and grandmothers – but also with the entire fabric of religiously observant women. Bessie Hatathlie had a puberty rite as a girl, during which time she was "molded" into a woman in the pattern that First Woman was molded at the beginning of time by Changing Woman, a Navajo god. Her daughters and granddaughters had similar rites, during which they were given instruction by one of their elder female relatives. What rituals did I have? Graduating from college? A daily run? A book tour? In my family, like many other families of modern, assimilated Jews, ritual is considered primitive, a throwback. Further, some people find the custom of the mikveh offensive; the idea that a menstruating woman is unclean seems primitive to us. Although I had never dipped in a ritual bath at the time I last saw my grandmother's mikveh (traditionally, it is used only by married women), I rather liked the idea of it. I don't think of it as cleansing impurity, but rather as an opportunity to prepare oneself for a meeting with the divine, a meeting with oneself.

Ritual, something you do over and over, links you with those who came before; you understand it and them a bit more each time. Modern life has eliminated ritual in favor of ideas or symbols. When we were growing up, our holy place was no longer the synagogue or the mikveh, but the university. Learning was sacred for us, but I could see it lacked one great thing: the animating presence of the "other" – the divine. There is no question that people need and seek out rituals. They calm us, they gratify us, they may repeat old stories, both pleasant and unpleasant, while we indulge in the unconscious wish of altering their endings. Rituals anchor us, help us recalibrate our internal compasses. I think religious rituals serve a similar purpose. They make belief manifest in one's daily life, for isn't ritual the active repetition of our sacred stories?

I was never sure if the mikveh in my grandmother's house was real, that is, built according to the laws set forth in the Torah, as I never knew those rules until recently. I learned that the chamber could not be filled with tap water alone; the contents were required to circulate with rainwater collected in another chamber. But I remembered a shower faucet in the wall of the sunken room. Could it just have been a fancy shower?

My grandmother was ill by the time I returned to her house to examine the room closely. I opened the door and walked down the mikveh's steps, unhappily dislodging some tiles from the drying grout. At the very bottom, I peered at the wall: there was indeed a crude hole that twisted into a cement passage. Now what was behind there? I hurried up the steps and across the hall, down the stairway to the finished basement, then into the cellar and toward the laundry room, to the place I calculated to be beneath the mikveh. There I found a tall cement-block wall. I dragged over a chair, grabbed hold of the top of the wall and pulled myself over it. Inside, beneath me, like an open sarcophagus, was a concrete cistern. A network of pipes leading out the side of the house suggested that rainwater may have been collected in the backyard and piped in here, where it could then flow through the wall into the mikveh.

Hanging over the top of the raw cement-block wall, looking into the smooth, ancient lines of the cistern, I wondered why it had been blocked off. No one could go in to clean it this way or fix the pipes. Had my grandparents done it when they moved in as a sign that this was a ritual they had outgrown? Or, conversely, had their predecessors walled it up when they learned the new owners would not use it? Was there some effort made to protect the insides of this sacred chamber from uncomprehending or hostile eyes?

I climbed back upstairs, imagining the former lady of the house taking a trip down the elegant upstairs stairway, all clean from her bath, and then down the steps of the mikveh. Who was she? Did she have children who had been conceived after those trips? When I got back to my grandmother's room, I told her I had been looking at the mikveh and her eyes lit up. Though she had been quite unresponsive for days, she smiled. I wondered why that place excited her, that place she never used.

I realized what I had been searching for every time I closed that mikveh door and listened for my own echo. It wasn't myself I was trying to hear, but rather the splashes and steps of that woman making room for the sacred, performing a ritual that connected her with generations of women before her. I was waiting to hear her voice, their voices, so I could learn what they believed, and even more, what they did. I had no one who could teach me or show me.

The echoes of that place perhaps had something to do with why my grandmother protected it, kept it from frivolous use. Something important happened there, a ritual that held a piece of our imaginations, though it no longer had a place in our lives. Like Marranos – Spanish Jews who converted to Catholicism, yet hundreds of years later still observed secret customs they didn't understand, such as lighting candles on the eve of the Sabbath – my grandmother, in her own benign way, honored a tradition whose purpose she no longer understood.

My grandmother died not long afterward, and her house was sold. Even though I have mementos of her here with me, I was sad to learn that the new owners planned to demolish that mysterious chamber off the downstairs bathroom and turn it into a closet. To them it was a meaningless remnant, a puzzling mechanism of a foreign culture, as bewildering as indoor plumbing was to Bessie Hatathlie. And so, by rights, it should be for me too. But it is not. I feel a tender wound when I think of that primitive cement cistern, still as a sleeping baby, cracked into pieces, the pipes sold for their copper.

The mikveh is an intimate symbol of faith, the chamber where a woman goes, alone, to prepare herself for the conception of a child, the cardinal act of a small tribe. Jews have built mikvehs for two thousand years wherever they have lived, from Jerusalem to Berlin to the ancient fortress of Masada, while under Roman siege. Ritual immersion is such an important rite that in traditional communities the mikveh is built before the synagogue. Some Soviet Jews, prevented from public worship, built secret mikvehs at great personal risk, in solemn testimony to the unbroken faith that links the generations one to another.

Before my marriage to Jonathan, and after several weeks spent learning the rules of *taharat ha-mishpahah,* or family purity, from Ruchama, I take the subway to Brooklyn, and Ruchama accompanies me to the mikveh. It is plain brick on the outside, modest, indistinguishable from any other building, but inside, it is grand, inviting, spanking new, resembling a Roman bath with sandy-colored square stone walls and vaulted archways. I have already done my preparations at home, bathing for an hour, rubbing away callus and dead skin from my feet, knees, and elbows, trimming my nails. I have brushed and flossed my teeth, washed my hair and poked straight earrings with alcohol through the holes in my pierced ears. I have soaked and scrubbed and wiped every part of my body. And I have removed anything that could keep the waters from completely enveloping me – rings, earrings, dirt.

I am ushered into a beautiful bathroom with sparkling tub, mirrors, and shiny stone walls. I take a quick shower just to get wet, and comb my hair until all strands are lying in the same direction. I step into a white terrycloth robe, and after going through the checklist, I ring the buzzer to call the mikveh lady. A young religious woman in a blond sheitel comes to inspect me. She looks over my hands and feet and spots a tiny speck of clear nail polish. She rubs it off with a cotton ball and a bit of nail-polish remover, touches me with great gentleness, gives me a tender smile, and leads me to another chamber, in which is an angular pool reached by several steps and a stainless steel railing. The woman lifts the robe off my shoulders and I step down the stairs. My body feels very light and free as I step into the water. When I reach the bottom, I turn and look at her for instructions. "Dip in the water, making sure to get your head and all your hair under, and don't cross your legs," she says. "Then stand up." I do so, and she smiles and says, "Kosher!" Then she asks me to recite the brachah written on a chart on the wall. It is printed in Hebrew and English transliteration. I read it aloud, and she motions me to dunk again. The water is pleasantly cool and clear. I come up, blowing bubbles out of my nose, tipping back my head to let the water run off. One more dip, she tells me, and I linger for a few extra seconds underwater thinking to myself a few hopes I have for my marriage. I imagine the words going straight to God through the special water. When I step out, my wet hair plastered to my skull, I am beaming like a little girl.

When I rejoin Ruchama in the waiting room, there is a party of women with baskets of food wrapped in bright cellophane. Ruchama tells me it is a Sephardic custom for family to greet the bride-to-be with nuts and fruits and other delicacies when she emerges from the mikveh. I am moved by the sweetness of this practice, and I imagine my grandmother Lillian here, giggling in childlike delight, as she often did at the sight of something new. Perhaps she would have handed me some almonds that she had roasted and salted, or some of her famous fruit compote, in celebration of the first time she had seen a woman emerge from the mikveh.

After my first dip in Brooklyn, I find my way to the mikveh on the Upper West Side of Manhattan. The building is not as grand, but the mikveh lady is Hungarian and has an accent like my father's mother, whose Hebrew name I now know was Hannah. She wears a housecoat and a blond wig and is warm and chatty. The place is homey and easygoing. In every shower is a reminder about breast self-examinations, and tucked discreetly in the corner of the mirrors are numbers for women's shelters and abuse counselors. I feel the place is eminently woman-centered, woman-embracing. Although I am not accustomed to finding myself in such places, I feel comfortable here.

In addition to counting the days for determining when I should dip in the mikveh, I am checking other signs to predict when I might be ovulating, because Jonathan and I would like to have a baby. My trip here tonight marks the intersection of the two methods, ancient and modern, religious and secular. I feel happy and calm, and I have come to love the opportunity for a luxurious bath, which I take at home. (The claw-footed tub in our turn-of-the-century apartment is outrageously long-in fact, as long as I am tall.) Lying in it, completely submerged save an oval around the top of my face, the sounds of pipes echoing in my ears full of water, I think of women in Temple times preparing for the mikveh, scrubbing the sand out of their skin and luxuriating in warm water, probably for the only time they will do so in the month. I imagine them in public baths, pouring water from large pitchers for each other. I find the process of sitting in the hot water for one whole hour an almost obscene luxury, one that affords me time for all kinds of imaginative wandering.

I know I am ovulating today. I imagine an egg inching its way down a Fallopian tube and I try to send good feelings and intentions its way. I know that the word "mikveh" means "hope." I am about to dunk in the rainwater pool, a deliberate act of purification and renewal with which I hope to set a new life off on its fabulous journey toward becoming a human. I would like the baby that might grow from that egg to be full of the knowledge of his or her mother's kavannah, or intention, that it have a successful journey sanctified by the richness of the tradition that its mother is discovering. I hope that the baby will grow to become an adult who knows the animating power of belief.

On Passover, every Jew is commanded to imagine that he or she was present at the exodus from Egypt. None of the slaves who left Egypt actually made it to the Promised Land, so their astonishing act of rebellion and self-determination benefited not them, but the generations to follow. One seder night, Yisroel Feuerman offered a more mystical interpretation, suggesting that we are commanded to imagine ourselves present at the Exodus because we were present in the hopes of our forebears at that time. Our forefathers and foremothers wandered in the desert for forty years to secure freedom for us, souls they could only imagine. And so, I imagine a soul preparing to inhabit the tiny egg making its way through my body. I hope that that person who may emerge will one day assume his or her place among the six hundred thousand and come to love the remarkable tradition they offered up to the world. I hope he or she will learn to read and speak Hebrew, and therefore have full access to the mysteries of the original texts.

The mikveh lady looks at my hands and feet and turns me around and lifts up my hair to check the back of my neck. I think it's funny she should check these areas, as if I were a worker in the fields. "OK," she says, and lifts the terry robe from my shoulders and holds it in front of her eyes while I step down into the warm water. I dunk and she says "Kosher," and I recite the blessing and dunk twice more. When I am done, I feel like staying in the water and doing somersaults, swimming around slowly underwater like a fish. After hesitating for a moment, I climb back out and up the stairs to the robe the mikveh lady holds out for me. I put on my clothes (one is not supposed to wash off the mikveh water right away), dry my hair, and step out into the cold December air.

The next day I have an intuition that I have become pregnant when I realize I have been humming "Hineh Mah Tov" all morning. "How good it is when brothers and sisters dwell together in harmony," reads the translation at B'nai Jeshurun. My hunch is correct. On September 24, 1998, between Rosh Hashanah and Yom Kippur, Hannah Shira was born, the spitting image of her father, who came up with her pretty name.

I return to the mikveh a few months after Hannah Shira is born and tell the mikveh lady of my great good fortune in getting pregnant quickly and having an easy delivery and a beautiful healthy baby. She looks at me and smiles. "I am not surprised," she says in her charming Hungarian accent. "The water here, it is very good."

For further reading:
Abramov, Tehilla. *The Secret of Jewish Femininity*. Jerusalem: 1988.
Kaplan, Aryeh. *Waters of Eden: The Mystery of the Mikveh*. New York, NY: 1985.
Slonim, Rivkah. *Total Immersion: A Mikveh Anthology*. Jerusalem: 2006.
For a global mikveh directory, visit www.mikveh.org.

Liberation

I love Brahms, Beethoven and Bach, Sibelius,
O'Neill and Pinter:
Whitman, Wolfe and Eakins.
I love my cooking, mink and silver,
my jewels, bed and home.

But most of all, I love Thee.
Thou warmest my heart when it's lonely.
To study Thy Law, delights my soul:
And I feel part of Eternity.
A mother Thou hast made me,
Children Thou hast given me –

And roses, mimosa and the sea,
Brahms, Beethoven and Bach

I love Thee, I love Thee, I love Thee.

Esther Sheldon

The Holy Room

Francesca Lunzer Kritz

It's nice when new memories bring out old ones. Even better if they are fond memories, remembered warmly. That's how I felt several weeks ago as my daughter, almost eleven, and I sat in the bet midrash, the beautiful chapel and study hall, of our synagogue. Approaching the year of her bat mitzvah, Dina and I are looking through books of Jewish law to choose what we will settle on to study together for her bat mitzvah.

In this bet midrash, beautifully appointed and named for quiet benefactors, we glanced at titles and chose one for this particular afternoon on the laws of blessings. We sat together with light streaming through stained-glass windows, recently installed in memory of a friend, a young mother, and talked about the laws. To our surprise, we learned some new things such as the appropriate blessings before eating pizza (what blessing to make depends on how many slices you will be eating). And as we sat together, I found myself transported back to another, similar, room where I had studied more than twenty years before.

Soon after the High Holidays one year, Rabbi Haskel Lookstein, rabbi of the Kehillath Jeshurun Synagogue in Manhattan, announced that Rabbi Herschel Schachter, a renowned Torah Scholar and eminent rabbi at Yeshiva University, would be giving a weekly Talmud class open to the full congregation.

This would be a rare opportunity but not one I could easily take advantage of. Years after finishing formal Torah study in elementary school, high school and college, my days were now filled with a new job as a cub reporter at *Forbes Magazine*. Exciting, challenging and not a small bit foreign to a girl who had grown up in a sheltered, observant community, the job was hardly nine-to-five.

Most days, in fact, rookie reporters not only wrote their own stories, but also fact-checked other articles in the magazine. You didn't work every night, but you couldn't choose your nights either – reporters were plucked as needed and stayed until the job was done. Burning the midnight oil was common. But since I needed to leave before sundown each Friday, I struck a deal with my editor. I would work every Monday through Thursday taking on an overload as needed in exchange for sailing out the door in time to light candles on Friday afternoons.

We all kept to our ends of the bargain and I made it home, out of breath most weeks, for Shabbat. But I worked so many late nights that friends knew they could usually find me at the office close to midnight, and I once even suggested to a blind date that we each buy a sandwich and talk on the phone for fifteen minutes while we ate instead of taking the time to go out.

Getting to a class every Monday night, especially in a week when the magazine was going to press, would often mean going back to the office afterwards or, certainly, taking work with me to start once I got home after ten o'clock.

Nonetheless, I began heading uptown each week, in time to be in my seat at eight when Rabbi Schachter would begin his class. While many women came in the first few weeks, most Monday nights into the course would find me the only woman in the group. But I was undeterred. My work day was everything I had dreamed it would be – travel, interviews with business and government leaders, and – icing on the cake – my byline in a national magazine. But that work week was also bereft of anything Jewish and certainly anything spiritual. And so this brief respite in a room full of books where Torah was being taught was a weekly reminder of who I was at the root. This was my *zeman kavua*, my set-aside time for study that Jewish law prescribes.

This class, I am sure, was very different from Rabbi Schachter's daily class at the rabbinical school where the men would first prepare the difficult arguments. We had it easy. No preparation was required for the class. The rabbi would expertly go through the opinions and then tell us the final decision – kindly soliciting our thoughts, but always helping us along as we struggled to lay out the argument and find the correct conclusion.

While we may have missed out on what many see as the compelling aspect of learning Talmud, figuring out the issues that troubled the commentaries and led them to their questions and answers, my goals were different. I had little time to prepare; what I wanted from the weekly class was to be *asuk ba-davar* – involved in the matter. I wanted to be in that room, hear this learned man, soak up the words and atmosphere so that it would hold me until the next Monday. My typical work week in between might find me checking some deceased CEO's will, flying to a city where even the potato chips had lard or, more than once, being stuck in a hotel room for Shabbat far from my family and any synagogue.

While the full hour-and-a-half-class was an oasis in my work week, by far my favorite part of Rabbi Schachter's class was only about three hundred seconds long. Five minutes before the class ended, the Rabbi would close his volume of the Talmud and slowly open a Chumash, portraying with his hands and fingers the holiness of the book he was touching, as he turned the pages to reach the upcoming week's Torah portion. While the rabbi read from the page, he seemed to pluck the words from his heart. Rabbi Schachter would read a few sentences that he found central to a theme in the Torah portion, then thumb through the Chumash to a seemingly different concept, and effortlessly connect the two. Week after week he'd connect the sentences, starting as disjointed and ending in harmony until, for me, the weeks all came together, a joining of chaotic, disconnected weeks held together by these Mondays of Torah.

Of the five *masechtot* or tractates I studied with the class, my favorite was *Menahot*, the laws of writing a Torah, mezuza or megilla scroll. The details were so intricate. There were rules for writing each letter, more rules for erasing a letter written incorrectly, and intricate steps required before writing God's name. What was necessary to begin and complete the task was so elegant and methodical, so different from my work days which might include an early meeting in New York, and a late flight to Atlanta, all on a moment's notice.

By contrast, the class was measured holiness. Listening, searching, studying, learning, these were my goals each week. But I got an added bonus I hadn't expected. Rabbi Schachter would take a moment or two every so often during the class to find an exact passage in the Talmud. As he quickly scanned the page, his face simultaneously intense and joyful as he dove inside the words, I would savor the quiet, the spiritual silence of a room devoted to nothing but prayer and study. Sometimes, especially during the most hectic weeks, my mind would stray to my future. Some day, I hoped, there'd be the chance to do everything – to write, to raise a family and to find a husband who would be my study partner and help me teach our children. Where would my path take me? I wondered. Would my husband one day find spiritual power in this room as well?

Five years after joining the class, I was offered a senior reporter's post in Boston. I thought the move away from New York, and away from Rabbi Schachter's Talmud class, would be temporary. But a year later a new job offer in Washington, D.C. changed everything and found me in a new synagogue and a new house of study.

On my second Shabbat in Washington as I entered the Georgetown Synagogue's bet midrash, a man with a smile that still leaves me tingling when our eyes meet across a room welcomed me to the synagogue. Over the next few weeks we would say hello after Shabbat services, study during the week, hear havdala together, all in that room.

Our wedding, just six months after we met, was held at the synagogue where Rabbi Schachter taught his class. And while our friends and families think we were joined before God in the Synagogue sanctuary late on a brilliant Sunday morning, our true joining came hours earlier, when Neil decided to start his day early and came to the congregation for morning services held in the bet midrash where I had studied all those years.

My heart and soul visit that bet midrash frequently. I remember passages, quiet moments, and the energy of Torah study that propels me now to study with a chavruta, study partner, with my husband, once a month with other couples, with my children and with our congregation. Actual visits are seldom, but recently I was in the neighborhood on my mother's yahrzeit. As I hurried to the minyan to say kaddish, sadness was pushed away by her voice, from phone calls so long ago each Monday night when she would check in to hear about the week's discussion.

The room, its spirit, opportunity and poetry all came back to me again as Dina and I sat in our synagogue's bet midrash, linked with every other house of study by the people who sit down to pray, study and contemplate. It is where Dina and I will study the books of her past and the lessons of her future. My fondest wish for Dina, and for her brother and their children, is that every room of study they enter will bring them the same respite and renewal of the houses of study where their parents have studied, and which continue to infuse us with spiritual power.

For further reading:

Elper, Ora Wiskind, and Susan Handelman, eds. *Torah of the Mothers: Contemporary Jewish Women Read Classical Jewish Texts*. Jerusalem: 2002.

Zolty, Shoshana Pantel. *And All Your Children Shall Be Learned: Women and the Study of Torah in Jewish Law and History*. Lanham, MD: 1993.

Converse with God, and consider carefully what is your purpose in life. Delve into yourself, and beg God to help you find Him...

If you set aside a time each day to converse with God, you will be worthy of finding Him. You may do this for days and years with no apparent effect, but in the end you will reach your goal.

Rabbi Nachman of Breslov, Sichot HaRan 68

Speaking to God

Tamar Frankiel

Questioning the Language of Prayer

Prayer is a great mitzvah, "to serve God with the heart." Yet it is also a great mystery, at least to many women of our era. Not only do we wonder, as Jews have for ages, how to approach God, what we are really doing when we pray, what we should say and what effect it has. As modern women, we often find an additional source of questioning or even alienation. When we pick up our traditional prayer book, the beloved *siddur* from which our grandmothers prayed, we find that we seem to be speaking to a male God. We have asked: can we relate to such a figure? Are we trapped in anthropomorphisms that are no longer relevant? What do these words mean?

Apparently this was not a major issue for most women before our times. Certainly, the rabbinic tradition had stated that God was beyond gender, so presumably someone had thought of the question. But it was not the same kind of issue that it is for us. The gift of feminism – and it is truly a gift – is the way it has encouraged us as women to come to consciousness, to raise our awareness of so many things that used to be unconscious or taken for granted. We have been awakened and asked to take a new look at what our grandmothers and great-grandmothers simply accepted as the way things are.

That they accepted does not mean they were incapable of questioning or that they were forced into silence. Perhaps they lived and breathed a greater sense of gratitude to those who came before. Perhaps, linked in a network of female and male relatives, they felt the support of tradition as a key to always-tenuous survival. But our world is quite different. Taught to search and to challenge received wisdom, freed from the constraints of ghettos and extended families at the same time as we nostalgically yearn for their support, we ask many questions. Moreover, as vistas of education have opened up a larger world to us, we find ourselves facing a public world created largely by men. We have discovered, often to our dismay, that virtually everything in that world reflects male preferences, men's power, masculine perceptions of reality.

So we come to the Torah and prayer book and find that here, too, God seems to be male. We wonder: is this, "the Lord our God," the shadow behind the "patriarchy," the power behind the dominance of males that we see everywhere in the world? Especially when we recognize the injury and pain that men have inflicted on women, on our bodies and on our self-respect, we ask, as do all sufferers: did "their" God do this?

In the face of this profound questioning of received traditions in general and masculine reality in particular, what has happened in the past twenty years is remarkable. Our love of Judaism, our love of God has been so great that we refused to accept such an interpretation of God. We pointed out that the God of our *imahot* and *avot*, the matriarchs and patriarchs from Sara and Avraham onward, honors women equally with men and cherishes family life as the incubator of holiness. We insisted, with the rabbis of the Talmud, that women are crucial to the redemption of the world. We held, with Rashi, that the Torah was given to women first. We undertook learning and teaching with renewed vigor. As a result, women have played an enormous part in the renewal of Jewish life. Like our mothers in ancient Egypt who kept the nation going through slavery, we refused to believe that even the devastation inflicted on us in Europe meant the death of the Jewish nation, or that the attractions of the secular world would destroy us through assimilation. Shoulder to shoulder with the men, we have resurrected our nation once again, like the moon turning to full – may this fullness never cease.

Yet, after all this, as we now try to raise our daughters with the pride and accomplishment of Jewish womanhood, how do we speak the prayers? What can we think, what do we feel as we pick up one of the gilded little books crammed with tiny letters from decades ago or the modem linear translation that helps us move, however haltingly, through our prayers in the holy tongue?

Some have argued that after all this, we can no longer speak this language, that we cannot call out to God as King, Father, Judge, Master. We must rewrite the prayers. Talk of our Source, not our Creator. Assert our participation in the creative process – we bless, not just You, for we will not be subjugated or diminished again. Speak of our mothers, not merely our fathers; and remember the goddesses, not only the Lord our God, for women need models of strength, compassion, and creativity.

I have often wondered why, from the beginning, I had so little sympathy with most of these efforts. Perhaps, I thought, it was because I came to learning Hebrew so late, and I was not sensitive to all the gendered language. But, as Israelis have pointed out to me, people who speak languages where all nouns and pronouns are gendered actually notice genders less – if a table is masculine and a door is feminine, the pronoun "he" doesn't always imply something sexual. Perhaps, then, I was so brainwashed to think of God as a male that I could not transcend my childhood perceptions. But as I began to think about what I was really feeling and imagining as I said these prayers, I decided that my limited imagination was not the source of the problem I had with rewriting the prayers. I could follow along and imagine my God with either "masculine" or "feminine" characteristics.

I learned, too, that the sages had explained long ago that God reveals a different face to every person. We say in our prayers, "God of Abraham, God of Isaac, God of Jacob" (and not "God of Abraham, Isaac, and Jacob") to acknowledge that God appeared differently to each one. Could I imagine extending the list to God of Sara, God of Rivka, and so on? Of course. Could I address God in feminine terms? Certainly. Our private prayers are our way of speaking to God in our own language. Yet I found myself, more and more, addressing God simply as *Ribbono shel olam*, "Master of the Universe."

The Divine Marriage of God and Israel

Still, I could not dismiss the problem. The God who is beyond all attributes still is portrayed in attributes. We know God through the Divine self-revelations in history. The Torah named them: merciful, gracious, compassionate, slow to anger, abundant in kindness and truth, preserving kindness for thousands of generations, ever-forgiving. The sages had their own names for God: *Ha-Kadosh Baruch Hu* – the Holy One, blessed be He; *Ha-Rahaman* – the Compassionate One, *die Ebishter* – the One Above, *Ha-Borei* – the Creator, *HaShem* – the Name. Awesome names, and yet often spoken with a touch of affection, of intimacy. The mystics named the Divine attributes too: wisdom, understanding, knowledge, lovingkindness, strength, harmony, perseverance, glory, beauty, foundation, kingship. Were these gender-bound attributes? It didn't seem so to me. On the contrary, it seemed as though the naming of God was deliberately stretching to go beyond gender. Except for *Avinu Malkenu* (our Father, our King), which is prominent in the High Holy Day prayers, most of the traditional language about God emphasized love, power and awe much more than gender.

Yet I had to admit that there remains a strong sense of gender in the way that our tradition conceived of the relationship of the people to God. The more I studied mysticism, the more I saw how pervasive that imagery was. The mystics tell us, following images used by the Prophets, that we can best understand our relationship to God by imagining God as male and the Jewish people as female. The *Shir ha-Shirim* ("Song of Songs"), which accompanies the Pesach celebration and in some communities is sung every Friday night, represents God and Israel as two lovers, and Rabbi Akiva regarded this book as the "holy of holies" of all the Writings. The mystics conceived the sequence of the pilgrimage holidays as stages in the relationship between God and Israel: Pesach is the first commitment of the two lovers – the engagement, so to speak – Shavuot is the sealing of the wedding contract, with the Tablets of the Law as our ketubbah, and Sukkot is the consummation of the marriage. In a related set of images, all Israel together is the crown of the Shabbat Queen, an aspect of the immanent Divine Presence known as *Shekhinah*, who unites with her "husband," the transcendent aspect of God, on Friday night. These images are too potent to be dismissed. They say to us that the relation between God and ourselves is a dynamic model that we can best understand by analogy to the human relationship between a man and a woman. Yet this is not always comfortable to women. Many feminists have dismissed the mystical tradition because of its strong interest in the sexual model, not to mention its tendency to view the masculine in a more positive light than the feminine. Some writers have sharply criticized the whole Jewish model of the Divine/human marriage. (We are speaking here only of imagery, not of critiques of the actual laws of marriage and divorce, which are beyond our purview in this essay.) [1]

I find the rejection of that model rather curious. A variety of questions can be raised, of course, about the actual application of the Divine/human marriage model in specific writings. But when women turn away from this gendered view of the Divine-human relationship, I suspect it reflects a failure of imagination, an inability to empathize with the particular poesis of the prophets and mystics. And, if indeed our imagination fails at this point, we must ask why. Is it a failure of our society, particularly the widespread weakening of marriage and family ties in our times? Do we fail to grasp the meaning of marriage? Surely we have too

---

[1] For example, the feminist theologian Rosemary Radford Ruether attacked the image found in some prophetic writings that accuses Israel of being the harlot while God acts like a petty, jealous husband. See "Sexism and God-Language" in *Weaving the Visions*, edited by Judith Plaskow and Carol Christ, 152. New York: 1989. However, the prophetic critique of Israel's behavior would have no point unless the bond between God and Israel as "husband" and "wife" were extraordinarily deep.

often idealized it as romance, like the teenagers Romeo and Juliet; and recently it has been fashionable to criticize it as an instrument of patriarchal oppression, where the husband "owns" and dominates the wife. Perhaps the turn away from that imagery reflects the grief and disappointment of so many women of our time in their relationships with husbands and fathers, as we have struggled to be authentically ourselves and still be loved and accepted in relationships.

But such criticism fails to understand the depth and richness of the husband/wife experience as it has been expressed in Judaism. The powerful ancient image of the *hieros gamos* or sacred marriage was certainly understood by the audiences whom the prophets addressed. Judaism brought this image into the home, insisting on the sacredness of marriage for the ordinary person. It insisted on the notion of fidelity as applicable not only to our spouses but also to our contract with the One God, Creator and Ruler of the universe. And, especially in the hands of the mystics, Judaism asked us to deepen our understanding of the marriage relationship, particularly in its sexual dimensions, as the ultimate model for God's love. If we want to move more deeply into the prayers, we must take this quite seriously.

We can barely grasp this. Yet it holds the secret of the apparently patriarchal language of the Bible and the siddur. In our days, when one of our most pressing cultural questions is what it means to be female or male, this language turns us back to our fundamental relationship to God. A woman discovering herself as woman first questions God: Why do You appear as male? She questions the authors of Tanach and the rabbis of the Talmud: Why did you write about "Him" as like you and not like us? But we must push the question to a deeper level: What do masculine and feminine really mean? How do they come together in a total picture of the Divine?

Love – Not Gender – Is the Foundation

Let's assume, for the sake of exploration, that we cannot easily define masculine and feminine appropriately because the terms have been so heavily overlaid with cultural constructions. Whether one looks at traditional Jewish ideas, ideas from other societies, or secular psychological theories, they could all be treated as cultural creations. The only clear thing we can say is that masculine and feminine, while they may refer to different dimensions of human experience, are intimately interrelated. They are part of an integral whole, which is epitomized in the (sexual) act of love. This certainly is not the only kind of love, or the only kind of sexual act, but it is an archetypal and culturally universal point of departure.

In this context, masculine and feminine can only be understood in the context of the positive and intimate and passionate response of two entities for one another, which we call love. We cannot define masculine as one thing and feminine as another, and then bring them together to construct our understanding of love. Rather, love comes first, and the genders emerge from it.

This is suggested by the teachings of the Ramchal, Rabbi Moshe Chaim Luzzatto, who taught that God desired to bestow goodness on another, and so created the world. There arose in the Endless One, the *Ein Sof*, a desire to give – this is Love – and then followed the creation of an (apparently) separate entity, the human being, who could be the object of that love. Love is the beginning, and then comes the separation of lover and beloved. Shir Ha-Shirim starts with the phrase, "the song of songs of Shlomo (Solomon)." The name Shlomo has the same root as "peace," shalom, or "completeness," shalem. The song of all songs is of union and completion. The poem then describes the union, separation, union of the two lovers, representing God and Israel. In other words, God is completely one, a perfect Unity. Yet God is also Love, and love demands separation or differentiation as well as unity. Thus God created the universe in order that there would be Two-in-Love. At the same time, since everything came from God, there is an ultimate Unity. The duality between God and universe, Lover and Loved, is only apparent. We do not understand this very well because we tend to imagine creation along the lines of manufacture. When we make something, such as a ceramic vessel, it becomes separate from us. Divine creations, however, are different. They are still connected to, indeed a part of, God.[2]

Here is another way to think about this. Remember that the Divine creative force is described first of all as speech: "God said, 'Let there be – '" and things came into existence. Speech is a miracle of vibrations combined into interpretable sounds. Vibrations do not truly separate from their source. We hear the notes of a flute when its vibrations strike our eardrums, but the reed is also still vibrating. The vibration created by the flutist and the one heard by our ears are intimately

---

[2] Rabbi Schneur Zalman of Liadi explains this in the *Tanya*, using the analogy of speech rather than manufacture:

> When a man utters a word, the breath emitted in speaking is something that can be sensed and perceived as a thing apart, separated from its source.... But with the Holy One, blessed be He, His speech is not, Heaven forfend, separated from His blessed Self, for this is nothing outside of Him.... Truly... are the "speech" and "thought" of the Holy One, blessed be He, absolutely united with His blessed essence and being, even after His blessed "speech" has already become materialized in the creation of the worlds, just as it was united with Him ere the worlds were created.

See *Likutei Amarim* (Brooklyn: 1981), Chapter 21, 87, 89.

and lastingly connected. Similarly, the created universe is always and intimately connected to its Creator.

The Torah tells us that God, after creating the universe, said it was good. The first thing that was "not good" was that Adam was created as a single entity; the first human was alone (Genesis 2:18). How odd! Would it not be better, in order to be truly in the image of the One God, for humanity to be a singular being? But God recognized that just as God had come to know separation within the Divine – by virtue of having created a universe – so Adam would have to know that too. Otherwise, Adam would be only the object of (Divine) love, and would never know what it was to love, to be love. Thus masculine and feminine were separated within Adam. The duality of God and universe was replicated in the duality of man and woman. But they are intertwined, like the double strands of DNA, each bound to the other. Or, to use the metaphor of vibration, they resonate with one another like harmonizing parts. The longing of male and female for one another is a hint, a constant reminder, that God and the world are bound to, and longing for, one another.

The Hidden and the Revealed

I am suggesting that if we want to grasp the deeper mystery of prayer, its language and metaphors beyond the accidents of grammar, we have to ask a more profound question: What is the relationship between God and the world? Typically, if we ask what that relationship is, we think of the duality of Creator and created. We are taught, in accordance with classical (originally Greek) thinking, that God is infinite and omnipotent, creation is finite and limited. This creates a conflict for us. Judaism insists that God is all-loving, all-merciful, but also that humans are responsible and responsive. But in the Greek model, we hardly think of creation loving God at all. Perhaps humans can weakly return God's mercy and love.

I am objecting to this definition, this way of separating and distinguishing Creator and created. There is a distinction to be sure, but it is not best represented by a hierarchy of power such as "all-powerful vs. weak." This kind of dichotomy reflects a kind of logical slippage, a mistake of applying terms to the wrong levels of existence. When we use words such as "omnipotent" we are referring to the Divine Unity, the essential nature of God. But from the perspective of God-after-Creation, so to speak, this is not the case; the Lord of the universe is not literally omnipotent because He has given us the power to go against His will. Another way of putting it is that God has defined the rules of the game so that we humans can genuinely participate – which means refusing to exercise Divine omnipotence. God will play on our terms, so to speak, by limiting

Divine power and knowledge. Most importantly, these abstractions have led us to forget the most fundamental ground of all: Creation has its source in Love. And if the source is love, how can there be such a hierarchy of power? True loving is mutual. As the Maharal pointed out, love can only be between equals or near-equals.[3] Even inanimate things, we learn from *Tehillim* (Psalms), express praises to God as their response to the acts of creation. Our tradition insists that God created humans as beings who could appreciate and reciprocate, not as robots that were mere recipients. We are co-creators with God; God needs us as we need God. Likewise, man and woman were created as equally able to give and receive; the description of woman as *ezer ke-negdo* (Genesis 2: 18) suggests a "helper parallel to him."

So what is the difference between God-after-creation and the world, understood as the created universe, if they are intertwined? I will formulate it like this: God is hidden, the world is manifest. (Kabbalistically, God is *Keter* – Crown; the world is *Malkhut* – Manifestation.) There may be other differences as well, for example in quantity of energy or clarity of focus. But this is the principal difference relevant for understanding gender: the hidden and the manifest. There is no hierarchy here, only a difference of perspective. There is a hidden love and a manifest love, Divine love and human love.

The hidden love is concealed precisely because it is so great that it cannot be contained in the physical world. Mystical teachings tell us that God had to conceal His Divine Light to make a world. The classic formulation, as taught by the great mystic known as the Arizal (Isaac Luria, sixteenth century), is that God contracted His Infinite being in order to make a space for the universe, and then allowed one beam of Divine Light to enter that space. From that came all creation. There were stages in which the "vessels" which contained the light shattered because even then, the light was too great. Now, each created entity is, so to speak, a piece of a broken vessel in which a spark of Divine Light and Love is concealed.

The manifest love is what we humans can show forth, to God and to the rest of creation. When we do this, the original potential of the created "vessel" –

---

[3] Rabbi Norman Lamm discusses this point in his survey of the views of the MaHaRaL (Rabbi Yehudah Loew of Prague, c. 1512–1609): "We are commanded to fear and honor but never to love father, mother, or teacher. The reason is self-evident: love is only possible between equals or near-equals, not between those who are essentially unequal." See *The Shema: Spirituality and Law in Judaism* (Philadelphia: 1998), 91. He speaks also of the "abyss" that separates God and humanity, then points out that it is when our human existence (the vessel) is dissolved that we can truly love God. While the epitome of this is the death of the martyr, as in the famous example of Rabbi Akiva, it is also approachable in *devekut* achieved through prayer.

ourselves or some other entity – shines through in a way that the world can bear it. Love and Light are apparent. That is, indeed, why God depends on us and needs us. For God to reveal the Light unilaterally would shatter the vessel, and defeat the purpose of having a partner to work with in Love.

The Snake in the Garden

In order to apply this to understanding gendered language in the prayers, let us go back to the story of Adam and Chava, to look more closely at how these first gendered beings were defined.

Adam, before separation into genders, was earth (*adamah*). The ancient sources tell us that Adam was a glorious likeness of God (*a-dam*, "I will be like") and he could see from one end of the world to another. As such he was manifest love, Divine Light revealed in an actual form. But this light could not be fully revealed unless Adam could also love, because love is the active expression of the Divine light, the creative potential. Only when masculine and feminine were separated within Adam could this occur. Names appeared that reflected this interdependence; his gendered name is *ish*, while his partner was called *ishah*. In the mystery of the unconscious realm, while he was asleep, she was created. It is notable that this process occurred in such a way that it was hidden from Adam. In our physical realm as well, the male's role in the production of new life is hidden – one can see who is the mother of a child, but not with certainty the father. The masculine side of loving and giving is concealed.

As woman, Chava was the manifestation of man's need: Just as God needs humanity, so the man needed a "helper." This word is so often taken in such a simplistic way that we must emphasize it is actually a matter for deep contemplation. God needed a partner to love, so the universe was created, culminating in human beings who could be conscious partners. Likewise, man needed a partner because it is impossible to manifest the essence of one's own light without another. One needs to love and be loved. Chava thus was created to be the receiver of Adam's love, so that his inner light could become active.

Yet, at the same time, Chava also had to be a being capable of love. This is expressed in her other name "mother-of-life" (*chai*). The secret of nourishing the seed into growth and full humanity was hidden in the mother, but it would be much more obvious than with the man. The feminine as mother-love is clear and manifest to the whole world.

It is important also to remember that God realized he had to create a partner with free will and full responsibility. If freedom were not complete, love could not be equally exchanged. Similarly with male and female: Chava was created equal to Adam in freedom and responsibility. Between the two of them and with

God's help, more beings would come into the world with ability to love freely and responsibly.

This idyllic partnership was not to last, however. The Torah tells us that the first human beings questioned whether through their own relationship they could achieve the purpose of human existence. They came to doubt that just by being male and female, giving and receiving, they were living in the Divine image. This doubt came through the serpent, who in ancient times represented wisdom, and in the biblical account is presented as the "most cunning" of animals.

What was its wisdom? The snake knew the secret of the concealed and the revealed. As the animal best known for shedding its skin, it represented the exterior (manifest) hiding the interior (the concealed). The Tree of Knowledge of Good and Evil also had some of that quality. "Knowledge" here is *da'at*, which means the awareness that comes from intimate union; in Hasidic thought it is the quality by which one "binds" oneself to a spiritual concept. The tree could be called the Tree of the Unification of Good and Evil. All the other food of the garden had been pronounced "good." This tree had fruit that was "good to eat, pleasant to look at and desirable" (Genesis 3:6) – i.e., externally good, but mixed or hidden within it was evil. The evil was the potential for separation from God.

The snake presented this knowledge to Chava: by eating of the tree, "You will be like gods, knowing (united with) good and evil." Chava thought that this would be a higher service – human beings could even bring evil into the service of God. They could unite even that tiny portion of creation, hidden within the tree, that was potentially separated from God. In that way, she and Adam would be able to return even more love to God and achieve their fullest potential.[4]

The World As We Know It

Reality as we know it came into existence at this point. We cannot really conceive of how it could have been different, because we live totally within the banishment from the Garden that is called Exile (*galut*). What we can say is that after the banishment, humans were given specific work to do – namely, to develop the love in our hearts and minds that will enable us to make manifest the Divine Light within creation. It is said that, in the messianic era, the true

---

[4] Some commentators argue that Adam and Chava would indeed have been able to do this if they had waited until after they had experienced the majestic holiness of Shabbat – because on Shabbat, the hidden and revealed (transcendent and immanent) aspects of God are united, as mentioned above.

achievement of humanity will be revealed, and we will see what a great thing it was to overcome the darkness of this world.

Yet this task was much more difficult than Adam and Chava could realize at the time. They forgot their original divine spark. Instead of harmonizing with one another and responding to God with love, they became preoccupied with the intensity of physical separateness. When the Torah reports that they "saw that they were naked," it is telling us that the physical became overwhelming. When they realized they would have to leave the Garden of Eden, they faced another separation, a division of labor. Adam tilled the ground, so that it would eventually give forth food, and Chava bore and raised children, each one taking a long time to mature. In that work they forgot that their job was to transmit God's love to creation, and instead became concerned about achievement. Immersed in "doing," – doing their jobs – they forgot about "being" – being in Love.

We should note that Adam and Eve were not "cursed." The Torah specifically says that the serpent was cursed, as well as the ground that Adam would have to till, but not Adam and Chava themselves. They were given different spheres of work. God understood that Chava could develop her ability to love by spending long years raising children (the most accurate interpretation of the oracular saying does not refer to painful labor, but length of pregnancy and childrearing). By nurturing and bringing out the inner potential of each child, she would model what it is to evoke the Light within, to make the hidden love manifest. That her "desire would be for her husband" suggests also that she would help bring forth his more hidden inner light – but she might, in the process, forget her own.

Adam had to work with the intractable soil, to make it produce food for his wife and their offspring. (When the text says to Chava that she would want a husband and he would be her master, it was also understood that the master had to provide for all those dependent upon him.) His challenge was to crack through the husks that prevented the light of the material world from shining forth. The danger was that he would be so immersed in material reality that he would forget that mission.

Adam gave himself to work in the material world, and Chava gave herself to the children. In the process, they lost their original unity, their quality of being Two-in-Love, reflecting God's image. Their egos became invested in their different projects. As this division hardened into social reality over generations, masculine and feminine came to be defined as separate spheres in society, and a hierarchy of power emerged. Men produced wealth, women produced children; men needed children to produce more wealth, so they came to deal in women. Masculine became identified with worldly activity, feminine with confined passivity. That is the way things have often been in this world. Sometimes, the whole human species has come close to losing track of our true mission, to reveal Divine Light through love. The Torah records the achievements of a few – Enoch, Noach, Avraham and Sara and their descendants – who kept the world alive with that awareness.

Yet the Torah also suggests that women often found it easier to reconnect to the Divine Source. Whether we speak of Sarah and the other matriarchs or the ordinary women who refused to contribute their jewelry to make the golden calf, women were strong in their spirituality. Perhaps this was because they were closer to children, because their job was to nurture the light in each child. When our tradition says that women are "more spiritual" than men, it may simply mean that it is easier for women to see the Light and to bring it out in others. Clearly, this is not a universal trait in all women, nor is it exclusive to one gender; thus Jewish practice is designed to nurture sensitivity, inwardness, and compassion in men as well as women.

Archetypes of Masculine and Feminine

But now let us return to the language of prayer. Prayer is full of metaphor, rooted in the archetypal. Adam's world was that of working the soil, cracking the husks and shells of material reality, enabling matter to be assimilated by beings of spirit. It is easy to ignore the presence of love in this process, so we would say that the Divine Light is more deeply concealed. In addition, the work distances man from the circle of hearth and home (again speaking archetypally), so his Light is removed, separated. The masculine thus represents the hidden. Chava is given the task of seeing the light in other beings and helping to reveal it, a long and sometimes arduous process, but one in which the work of love is obvious. Feminine love and light is more directly manifest in human activity. The masculine as the hidden and the feminine as the manifest love are symbolized in Shir Ha-Shirim. The relation between male and female here is portrayed as a union of equal but different partners, not one of domination and servitude. The male figure in the poem, allegorically symbolizing God, disappears, while the woman seeks Him out.

THE WOMAN: Upon my bed at night I sought the one I love. I will rise now and roam about the city; through the streets and through the squares I will seek the one I love. (3:1–2)

THE WOMAN: Hark! The sound of my beloved knocking!

THE MAN: Open to me, my sister, my love, my dove, my perfect one....

THE WOMAN: My beloved reached out.... I rose to open.... I opened for my beloved, but my beloved had turned and gone.... I adjure you, O daughters of

Jerusalem, if you find my beloved, what shall you tell him? That I am sick with love! (5:2–8)

"Tell him!" Here, feminine love calls forth the creative powers of the masculine. This understanding is certainly not free from cultural presuppositions, but it has the advantage of moving beyond a literal reading of the text as dictating male and female "roles." We can re-imagine what we usually call the masculine and feminine along these lines, in order to create a different sense of the language of our prayers. When we as the Community of Israel speak to God as "He," we call forth the hidden powers. "Tell Him!" We ask through our speech, our prayers – which must be spoken aloud, not just thought – that the hidden love and light become manifest. This is the essence of that crucial part of Jewish prayer called blessing. Blessing, "*Baruch ata*," is the unique signature of Jewish prayer.[5] It is not a plea or supplication, nor only a thanksgiving, properly speaking. Rather, it is an evocation. One who blesses can see or sense the hidden reality, the concealed light, within what is being blessed, names it, and calls it forth. Blessing amplifies and magnifies so that the hidden spark can be seen, so that it is manifest in the world. When we call out in prayer, we are asking that God be manifest, that Love emerge more fully into being. When we as part of a worshipping community say *Baruch ata*, we are saying: as a "woman," I seek the one I love! Let the hidden creative power be manifest in goodness! Love, show yourself!

Being Completely Loved

We can learn still more about the nature of the relationship between God as "masculine" and the Jewish people as "feminine" by looking at another, universal dimension – namely the physical act of love between man and woman. We learn from our mystical tradition that the biological is a metaphor for the spiritual. Everything in physical life teaches us something about spirit. And certainly, the physical experiences of men and women in love are quite different.

But it turns out that this is an aspect difficult for us as women to understand, partly because of women's historic experience of the masculine. Collectively, we as women have sometimes – too frequently – experienced the masculine as

---

[5] The power of blessing was promised to Abraham and then bestowed upon him by Melchizedek, also known as Shem, the son of Noach who was the priest of Shalem (the region of Jerusalem) and had preserved this power through the centuries since the flood. This eventually was formulated into the Priestly Blessing, for one person to bless another, and into the blessings of our prayer services, kiddush, havdalah, etc., for blessing God. For a discussion of blessing, see Tamar Frankiel and Judy Greenfeld, *Entering the Temple of Dreams* (Woodstock, VT: 2000), Chapter 5, on the Priestly Blessing.

possessive and objectifying, denying our full humanity. When we call forth the love of the male, what will we receive? Will we be loved, or merely possessed? Will we be loved, or will we be treated in some way that denies our full humanity?

Above, we said that man's role in the production of new life is hidden. The role of love in toiling among thorns and thistles is even more hidden. And, according to the testimony of many men and women, the role of love in the act of making-love is also frequently hidden, on the male side especially. For a man, from what seems a purely physical pleasure comes the seed of life, whether he consciously loves his partner or not. In an appropriate relationship, the woman must at least lend her body to the experience, which women frequently describe as giving of themselves in love. The act of lovemaking can in turn lead to pregnancy, initiating many, sometimes difficult physical changes over a long period of time, as well as emotional changes that may make her feel more deeply connected to her husband. After the birth of a child, she experiences a bonding that deepens her ability to love. Mother-love has become an archetype because, as we noted above, hers is a work of love that is obvious to all. Men who can truly appreciate women are in awe of her physical self-sacrifice and her depth of attachment.

How different their experiences are! A man, in the act of the most intimate love, expends himself completely, giving over the essence of his being in one brief, explosive moment to another being. On a physical level, his is an act of complete love – so much that it is often hard for men to admit the depth of the experience, and they frequently keep it unemotional. Perhaps it is even deeper than emotion.[6] Women, noticing this, often believe that men's love is shallow, for it is nothing like the emotion-filled love they shower over months and years on their children and their husbands. But this love can be complete and profound, and occasionally a husband will allow a wife to know how completely he loves her. She can only be in awe, for her giving of herself, in all her acts of sacrifice, is not like this.

The love that sometimes comes upon us in our relationship to God is like the archetypal masculine. That is, the metaphor of it is man's physical love for woman – sudden, complete, deep, unbelievably powerful. This is the hidden

---

[6] This is suggested by the fact that kabbalistically, the sefirah Yesod is the primary energetic source of male sexuality, and Yesod combines and channels all the energies from Keter through Hod. It includes but also goes beyond ordinary emotion.

On the basis of our earlier discussion it should be clear that we are speaking archetypally, not of a specifically male ability among humans to manifest this love. Women also have a "masculine side" in love as in all other attributes.

light that we may call forth in prayer and find it manifest upon us unforeseen. Divine love certainly comes in daily miracles, but there it is filtered through the physical world like womanly love. There is another kind of experiencing of love, knowing that you are so completely and fully and unconditionally loved that you wonder how this could ever be contained in an earthly form.

We may run from this love. Like an abused child who cannot suffer an intimate touch, we as women often fear to evoke too much passion from men. In our religious lives, we also may guard ourselves from evoking the love of God, from asserting our ability to call forth Love. So we have frequently chosen to take a meeker role, quietly asking God for sustenance and protection and health, for our children and ourselves. Or, in the awkward movement of religious feminists some years ago, we take authority into our own hands, gently but firmly letting God know who is blessing Whom. But "your desire shall be for your husband." The yearning does not go away. Deep within, we want to know that complete love, which will remind us of our true divinity.

To love and yearn, to call forth love and receive it. Surely, at this point, the meaning of gender defined in specific "roles" disappears. Devekut, the clinging of lover and Beloved, Lover and beloved one to another, each feeling completely loved and loving, receiving and giving, transcends the labels of male and female. Only in the moment of return to ourselves do we again attain embodiment and describe the experience in such terms. But we can remember, and know that we have been shown our true selves. We can experience ourselves totally affirmed as God's partners in creation.

So we return to the question: why do we call on the name of God in male language? We want above all that the most hidden love will be revealed, the love that bursts forth in a complete revelation of essence. This love dissolves Twoness without denying it, allowing us to taste of unity. This is part of the deeper truth that our mystical tradition understood. The love that comes forth in these experiences, those moments of prayer where we grasp the deeper essence of ourselves-with-God, is not like the love we are granted on a day-to-day basis, the support of our families and communities, the shared experience. That "everyday" kind of love is the beauty of the feminine, manifest through the Shekhinah, which is the feminine presence of God in the world. "She" expresses divinity through the acts of kindness and support of the Jewish people, as in "All Israel are responsible for one another." This is the beauty of the feminine, of revealed love, and is indeed the way that love can become substantial in our world.

The other aspect of love, the hidden love represented by the masculine, is the creative force that tells us, in our deepest being, that we are completely and perfectly loved, as we are. We need to know this love, and to carry it with us every day. Sometimes too we will experience it from another person, one who loves us so deeply. We may even have the blessing of receiving such love in a physical way. But it is always and eternally available to us in our relationship with God. This is what we are seeking in prayer.

And this blessing, this knowing is essential for women. To love the world, to give birth and nurture the coming generations into a fuller life, we must have great strength, love, and compassion. For this to become our inner, daily reality, we must come to know how fully we are loved, and this can happen through the work of prayer. When we open the siddur, we can watch the letters dance toward us with a hint of that light, that love telling us who we truly are. The letters and words can become the containers that receive our yearning, and allow us to open our hearts, for a moment, to know this truth.

For further reading:

Frankiel, Tamar. *The Gift of Kabbalah*. Woodstock, VT: 2001.

Schneider, Sarah. *Kabbalistic Writings on the Nature of Masculine and Feminine*. Lanham, MD: 2001.
    Available by contacting the author directly at smlvoice@netvision.net.il.

Arouse your concentration and remove all disturbing thoughts from your mind, so that when you pray, your thoughts will be pure.

If you were speaking to an earthly king, who is here today and tomorrow in the grave, you would be careful with your words, concentrating on each one lest you say something wrong. When you pray, you are speaking before the King of Kings, the Blessed Holy One. You must concentrate all the more....

Tur, *Orach Chaim* 98

A Sanctuary within a Sanctuary

Roxane Peyser

First, I am not a Torah scholar. Second, I am not a Torah scholar. I am a Jewish woman, a modern woman, a wife, a mother, and – occupationally – a lawyer. I am a knee-jerk moderate and philosophical pragmatist. I believe in equal economic, political, and social opportunities for women as a general proposition. I believe in privacy and try to remain consistent in my views on privacy-related issues.

As a woman, I believe in limiting membership in certain groups, such as Hadassah and any sisterhood group, to only women. Similarly, I believe in preserving the privacy of private acts and, therefore, separation of bathroom facilities. (I refer specifically to the "bathroom" here as it was used as a red flag by those most strenuously opposing equal rights for women in the 1970s. The argument was that equal rights would lead to coed bathrooms. The argument was, of course, not a red flag but a red herring – i.e., a ploy used to distract attention from the real issues.)

Those of us women who believe in all of the above can reconcile the ostensible contradiction between economic and political equality on the one hand and bathroom discrimination on the other. The distinction is based on the simple fact that men and women are different. (And those of us who have children of both sexes know that such differences are determined, in large part, well before the child's entry into whatever environmental circumstances he or she is born into.)

Unfortunately, throughout both our secular and Jewish history, we have seen women who have been treated unjustly, unfairly, unlawfully, unwisely and disrespectfully. In some instances, these treatments have been the result of a corrupt system – either in the home or outside of it – or have resulted in facilitating such a systematic maltreatment. But "unjust," "unfair," and "unwise" are not definitions for "unequal."

Some women feel deeply that the *mehitza* is a symbol of degradation, that its presence in the synagogue represents something that is unjust, unfair, unlawful, unwise and/or disrespectful. I submit that if the *mehitza* were not an ancient man-made invention, it could be a modern woman-made invention.

I remember a fairly recent episode where I attended services at my old Temple in New York, a very large, liberal synagogue. I ran into a friend of mine whose daughter is a strikingly beautiful blonde young woman of twenty. She cringed as she watched her daughter walk through the sanctuary to take a seat next to her father. "Roxane," she said, "I can't stand the way some of these men – married men, too! – eye my daughter. It's revolting and it's disrespectful."

I'm no Bo Derek, but there is everything natural about a man looking at any woman entering a room, coming towards or going away from him. I rather like the fact that the *mehitza* aids in reducing such inspections during services. Those who attend services usually go to pray. Perhaps that's being too presumptuous. I guess I know that for some, synagogue attendance has less to do with religious reasons and more to do with social or political ones, or both. The point is that when I go, I am trying to focus on the genuineness of the moment, which, for me, means to pray to God without distractions, or with as few as possible.

Before I joined an Orthodox shul, I would sit next to my husband and find myself unable to control the distraction of having him next to me. Whether it was holding hands or whispering about something – anything – unrelated to the purpose of prayer, there was a very real distraction.

Recently I was reminded of something I learned in a geocultural course while an undergraduate. It has to do with the role a house of worship plays in various religions. I was reminded that in Christianity, the church is the center of the community; it is where Christians must go to in order to speak with God. In contrast, it is not the synagogue but the home that is the center of Jewish life. And, incidentally, one may speak with God anywhere.

I submit to the reader that perhaps some of us have forgotten that in Jewish life, there is no higher place than the home. Since women have been charged by Jewish law with general responsibility for the care and peace of the home, this would not, in my mind, logically lead to the conclusion that women are therefore inferior to men. And consider further that being charged with such responsibility does not necessarily mean to the exclusion of the other gender.

I submit the because the home is not only central but paramount in Jewish life, the role of women in traditional Judaism is not "separate but equal." Instead, the role of women is separate and equal. Which brings us back to the issue of the *mehitza*.

Was it invented to subjugate women? To treat them as inferior? To imprison them?* Personally, I feel liberated. To elaborate further, I will rely on a more subjective source. Rabbi Joseph Telushkin states in his book, *Jewish Literacy*, "It [the *mehitza*] seems... to have been a response to human nature. God is abstract, and it is an effort for people to focus on an abstract Deity while praying. For me, and I think for many other men, it is a natural reaction to look around when a group of women is present and let one's gaze rest on a pretty woman. Indeed, people usually dress up before going to synagogue in an effort to look attractive. In the 'battle' between an intangible God and a tangible member of the opposite sex, Jewish law assumed that the tangible is more likely to win. Hence, physical separation can help bring about spiritual concentration for both sexes."

I have to believe in this notion simply because I know that had it not been the invention of certain men some centuries ago, it likely would have been the invention of certain modern, self-described feminists today.

I propose that the *mehitza*, considered not in a vacuum, but in context – as set in and against the conditions a discussed in this writing – offers women a sanctuary within a sanctuary.

For further reading:
Kaplan, Aryeh. *A Call to the Infinite*. New York, NY: 1986.
Meiselman, Moshe. *Jewish Woman in Jewish Law*. New York, NY: 1978.
Goodman, Marina. *Why Should I Stand behind the Mechitza....* New York, NY: 2004.

---

* The issue of how to configure or situate the mehitza appropriately so that it enhances a woman's prayer experience and does not detract from it is a very important subject that is outside the scope of this article. Mehitzas that have been less than comfortable for women have been due in large measure to sociological and/or pragmatic reasons, that have shifted over the past decades. The specific type of mehitza (of which there are many) should not be confused with the essential concept.

Sabbath Candles

Bella Chagall

The table, like a white dream palace, stands so calm, it might be awaiting something. Suddenly the fringes of the tablecloth begin to flutter. From somewhere a distant noise reaches me. I hear the shutters of the shop falling. The unrolling metal screeches. Thank God, the shop is closed at last! I make out the voices of the employees, hastening home. "Go now, leave everything! You might miss your streetcar!" This is Mother speeding the cashier, who lives at the edge of the town and is in the habit of lingering in the shop longer than anyone else.

Now Father comes in. I stand waiting for him as for a guest. "Bashke, don't you know where I can find a clean collar and a pair of cuffs?" he asks.

"Here, Father, they're on the dressing table."

Father passes by the mirror, turns away his head; he has seen his face in the mirror.

"What a nuisance! Why are the buttonholes ironed in so tightly that there's no way of pushing a button through?" Father sweats and chokes as he puts on his fresh collar.

"Father, do you want me to ask Sasha for another collar?"

"Who has time for that? We must soon go to shul."

Sasha brings in the samovar, lights the lamp. The polished samovar boils and bubbles like a locomotive. The hanging lamp spatters fire. It is now warm and light all around. Father sits at the table quietly taking sweet tea with jam.

The last to leave the shop is Mother. She tries all the doors once more to see that they are locked. Now I hear her pattering steps. Now she shuts the metal

---

* From *Burning Lights*.

door of the rear shop. Now her dress rustles. Now her soft shoes slip into the dining room. In the doorway she halts for a moment: the white table with the silver candlesticks dazzles her eyes. At once she begins to hurry. She quickly washes her face and hands, puts on a clean lace collar that she always wears on this night, and approaches the candlesticks like a new mother. With a match in her hand she lights one candle after another. All seven candles begin to quiver. The flames blaze into Mother's face. As though an enchantment were falling upon her, she lowers her eyes. Slowly, three times in succession, she encircles the candles with both her arms; she seems to be taking them into her heart. And with the candles her weekday worries melt away.

She blesses the candles. She whispers quiet benedictions through her fingers and they add heat to the flames. Mother's hands over the candles shine like the tablets of the Decalogue over the Holy Ark.

I push closer to her. I want to get behind her blessing hands myself. I seek her face. I want to look into her eyes. They are concealed behind her spread-out fingers.

I light my little candle by Mother's candle. Like her, I raise my hands and through them, as through a gate, I murmur into my little candle flame the words of benediction that I catch from my mother.

My candle, just lighted, is already dripping. My hands circle it to stop its tears.

I hear Mother in her benedictions mention now one name, now another. She names Father, the children, her own father and mother. Now my name too has fallen into the flames of the candles. My throat becomes hot.

"May the Highest One give them his blessing!" concludes mother, dropping her hands at last.

"Amen," I say in a choking voice, behind my fingers.

"Good Shabbes!" mother calls out loudly. Her face, all open, looks purified. I think that it has absorbed the illumination of the Sabbath candles.

For further reading:

Grunfeld, Isidore. *The Sabbath.* New York: 1998.
Palatnik, Lori. *Friday Night and Beyond: The Shabbat Experience Step by Step.* Lanham, MD: 1994.
Steinsaltz, Adin. *The Miracle of the Seventh Day.* San Francisco, CA: 2003.

"Separate the first portion of your kneading as a dough offering… in future generations, give the first of your kneading as an elevated gift to God."

Numbers 15:20–21

Challah is separated after the dough is kneaded before it has been divided and shaped into loaves. Before the piece of dough is separated, the following blessing is said:
Ba-ruch a-tah A-do-noi elo-hai-nu me-lech ha-o-lom a-sher kid-sha-nu b'mitz-vo-tav v'tzi-va-nu l'haf-rish cha-lah.

Blessed are You, Lord our God, King of the Universe, Who has sanctified us with His commandments and commanded us to separate Challah.

Then remove a small piece, approximately one ounce, from the dough. Today, since we cannot give the Challah to the kohanim and we may not eat it ourselves, the prevailing custom is to burn this piece.

Baking Lessons: A Six-Braided Meditation

Tzivia Emmer

I. "Establish for us the work of our hands." (Psalms 90:17)

I'm looking at a snapshot taken of a woman wearing a denim apron, somewhat blurred as it shows her hands as they roll a mass of dough on a large wooden board. You can't see the face very well but it doesn't matter; it's the hands that count.

They're my hands, and my husband took the picture soon after we were married, an homage to the Jewish earth mother image I presented: hands deep in dough, face and clothing smudged with flour, baking challah for Shabbat. I learned to bake bread in a country bakery back when everyone I knew was either getting back to the land and nature or seeking God, or both. It seemed to me there was something magical or even spiritual in the transformation of flour, water and air – earth, water, air and fire becoming bread, the staff of life. A few years later, married and newly Torah-observant, I found myself again standing in front of a large stainless steel bowl, my hands deep in flour and water as I mixed dough the old-fashioned way in order to make challah for Shabbat, as on the day of the photograph.

But the truth is that I'm not at all domestic, earth-mother image notwithstanding. Although I come from a line of strong, competent women (described by a friend of mine as salt of the earth), I knew early on that I was not one of them. I never learned or absorbed the rhythms of household routine, the constants of effort over time that add up to a seemingly effortless control over one's environment. From my grandmother I did learn that to produce the best results you must use the best ingredients, and although she could not read or write English, no storekeeper ever got the better of her. Once, I made an 8mm movie of my grandmother as she rolled dough and chopped nuts and raisins for her strudel that had once been a must at every family simcha. Her powerful hands moved with the speed and sureness of years, the ingrained memory of flour and dough and sugar and honey with a wisdom that resided in the hands themselves.

She could never give a recipe. I once tried to follow her steps: I watched as she mixed each ingredient, noting measurements as she took a pinch of this, a cup of that. It didn't work, so I made the pictures. In those days, anyway, pictures were probably more important to me than things themselves.

That may be why I came to like the very grounded, physical feeling that comes with making bread by hand and why, years later, I mixed and kneaded and shaped the dough for challah as if rolling all my hopes for the future into a braided loaf for the Shabbos table. My grandmother, I felt, would have been proud.

II. "Make for Me a sanctuary and I will dwell among them."(Exodus 25:8)

A scene: I'm standing in the main synagogue of 770 Eastern Parkway, Lubavitch headquarters, on one of the occasions when the Rebbe, Rabbi Menachem M. Schneerson, would give a talk especially for women. The large hall is packed from wall to wall with women and girls sitting or standing, listening intently. The Rebbe is speaking in Yiddish and I am trying to listen both to his voice and to a simultaneous translation delivered via a small transistor radio at my ear.

The radio squawks. I pick up some words and sentences in Yiddish that I can understand as a result of my intensive efforts to learn the language of my grandmother. The Rebbe is speaking about the fundamental part women play in making the world a dwelling place for God. As the *akeres habayis,* mainstay of the home, women were the elite vanguard force in what might be called Operation Redemption the ultimate purpose of all creation.

I'm paraphrasing widely, of course. And in my recollection of that *sicha* (talk), many of the Rebbe's discourses that I've heard or learned about all run together, so that I don't know exactly what year this was. But I do remember clearly how I felt as I looked around me.

Everyone was concentrating very intently, some taking notes, some swaying slightly. I remember thinking that the Rebbe was, in effect, placing Jewish women – us – at the very spiritual center of the universe. God had said, "Make for Me a sanctuary and I will dwell within them." Within them specifically. In other words, within the sanctuaries in microcosm that were each Jewish home. The transformative power of women, specifically as the *akeres habayis,* he was saying, is instrumental in making the world a place where God is revealed.

And I remember looking around and wondering whether anyone besides me felt at all overawed or daunted by what the Rebbe was telling us was our mission. An earlier, vaguely feminist version of myself may have objected on the grounds that so singular a role was confining and arbitrary. But now I only wondered if I was up to the task. My home may be a microcosm of the universe and the arena in which mitzvot create a dwelling for God in the lower worlds, as Jewish mysticism teaches, but it is also the place where laundry has to be put away, dishes washed, babies tended, children disciplined, meals cooked, floors vacuumed. Other women, I was sure, had perfect homes, children who always said their brochos (blessings), and harmonious Shabbat tables. I felt at times that I could barely get through a day of simple tasks. Yet collectively and individually, the Rebbe was telling us, we were bringing the world to that culminating state called *geulah,* redemption, with the coming of Moshiach (the Messiah).

There was at that time a song by the popular Jewish singer Mordechai ben David about building the Holy Temple "brick by brick... doing mitzvos, adding precious stones...." Mitzvah by mitzvah, we would add to the edifice of God's dwelling in the world and thus bring the messianic age and the grand finale, the purpose of it all. There was a song, too, about a cup filled with tears that would finally run over. Beyond my little domestic challenges lay the sweep of history. How many bricks would it take? How many Jewish tears and how much suffering?

And how were women like me going to accomplish it? Somehow, if the Rebbe was telling us this, it had to be that he was simultaneously giving us the strength and his blessing to accomplish the task. His faith in the women of our generation was unbounded. With that thought, I resolved to simply do my best.

III. "If a man brings home wheat, does he chew it? If [he brings home] flax, does he wear it? Does [his wife] not, then, bring light to his eyes and put him on his feet?" (*Yevamot* 63a)

It is said that women make the raw materials of the world fit for use and bring ideas down to earth "to weave abstract values and spiritual principles into the palpable fabric of the home," as author Malka Touger writes in her introduction to the book *A Partner in the Dynamic of Creation*.

Accepting it as so, one day I asked, "What does this mean?" That is, what does it mean to me? Words can weave a gossamer web of fine feeling over the things we do, and sometimes they can slip away just as easily as they can inspire. The words had become abstractions and even as I understood them in principle I found that I could no longer grasp their meaning.

The Talmud says women naturally have the ability to make bread from wheat, cloth from flax. I sensed this the first time I mixed raw flour and water into dough. Raw spiritual potential, however great the energy inherent in it, cannot satisfy God's desire for a transformed physical world, and transformation is the sphere of women.

For this women were given an extra measure of binah, the mind function that develops and expands the point called chochma. Binah branches into details, words, paragraphs, elements, galaxies. Binah chops and dices and makes a stew.

Binah reaches into the heart of an idea and lays it out, makes it visible. Binah can spin and weave and mill and grind until the raw materials of the world are fit for humankind. Then it must start anew and make it fit for God.

At the same time binah needs something to connect to. The finest weaving needs a finished garment; dough must become bread.

IV. "Separate the first portion of your kneading as a dough offering.... In future generations, give the first of your kneading as an elevated gift to God." (Numbers 15:30)

As the years went by I would make challah sporadically. One of the nice things about baking is being able to do the mitzvah of taking challah separating a piece of dough which, if we lived in the time of the Holy Temple, would have been given to the kohen, the priest. But in burning it I'm still, today, dedicating a portion of my world for holiness. On one such occasion I said the blessing and put a small piece of dough into the hot oven and then forgot about it. Suddenly, the slightly acrid smell of burning dough hit my nostrils as it spread through the kitchen and to the other rooms of the house.

Whether it was a trick of perception or a gift of understanding from above, I connected the spreading smell of burnt dough with the idea that giving away a part of something actually changes what is left behind as well. But suddenly I knew, or felt I knew, how it was that a home becomes a sanctuary through the act of performing mitzvot. Not symbolically as a sign or a reminder but in actuality, as tangibly real as the molecules of scorched challah permeating the room.

In geometry class years back I had learned that the whole is equal to the sum of its parts. No, I thought, Euclid was wrong: not only was the whole not equal to the sum of its parts, but a part can be more than the whole. The piece of dough, no bigger than a baby's fist, had the power to elevate the remaining dough that it was taken from, as well as the bread that came from it, and the entire household.

God's math is different from ours. I saw that the Bais Hamikdosh would not have to be built brick by brick, adding one mitzvah after another in the way one constructs a building. It's not about construction after all, it's about transformation.

There are other examples. In the Tanya, Rabbi Schneur Zalman writes that money given away for tzedaka, charity, transforms the part that one keeps and "carries the other... parts with it up to God, to provide a dwelling for Him, blessed be He" (Chapter 34), and with it all the time and energy by which the income was earned.

In the Bais Hamikdosh the offering of "one-tenth of a measure of fine meal mingled with oil" had the power to elevate all plant life; [the sacrifice of] one animal, all beasts. So the whole world could be brought to holiness through the power of subtraction, not laborious addition: taking away just one part of many and dedicating it to a Godly purpose.

V. "All that's left is to open our eyes and see." (The Lubavitcher Rebbe, Autumn 1991)

I would like to be able to say that my observations led to a new ability to glide through my domestic chores with the effortless knowledge that my actions can transform my home into an abode for God – a sanctuary in microcosm. That's not quite what happened, but a shift in perception is still something in itself. For me it was an opening to see unequivocally that effects are not proportional to their cause and that the whole idea of "part" and "whole" or the notion of quantifying the value of our efforts is meaningless.

If we really had to build God's dwelling place in the lower worlds brick by brick, I think we would have grown discouraged a long time ago. I tell myself that the same is true in personal life and that any single moment can be the opening or gateway to a perception of holiness in the world. The Rebbe eventually told us that if we were to open our eyes we would see that geulah, the redemption, is already here. It wasn't easy to understand, and most of us puzzled long over what the Rebbe meant. On some level, though, it became clear that perceiving could be an act of transformation, and that transformation, unlike construction, can happen in an instant.

Even Mordechai ben David, after meeting the Rebbe, recorded a song that had as its joyous refrain the single word "Moshiach" repeated over and over – no bricks, no tears. That song didn't need to be understood or dissected or analyzed; it sailed clear over all our calculations and made a tiny shift in Jewish perception that itself brought us closer to being able to share in the dream of geulah.

VI. "Every year [on Rosh ha-Shanah] there descends and radiates a new and renewed light that never yet shone." (*Tanya, Iggeres ha-Kodesh,* Chapter 14.)

A scene: it is nearly Yom Tov. In all these years I have not yet mastered the mystery of the calendar, the startling progression by which the month of Tishrei follows Elul each year and brings with it Rosh ha-Shanah, Yom Kippur, Sukkos and Simchas Torah. It always takes me by surprise and leaves me wondering why I haven't stored up challahs and cakes and chicken soup in the freezer.

But this year I've spent long, sunny mornings through the summer writing this essay and meditating upon the deeper meaning of dough becoming bread, and I decide at last to bake challah because Rosh ha-Shanah is the time when challah is dipped in honey for a "sweet year." Fresh flour, white and whole wheat, yeast and honey have to be bought. The stainless steel bowl comes down from atop the kitchen cabinet and the wooden board and heavy-duty mixer come out of retirement. At last all the ingredients sit on the counter, and with trepidation, almost reverently, I begin.

Slowly the dough takes shape, becoming smooth and round and elastic. I remove the piece called challah, my offering to the kohen. I begin to roll out shapes – a single strand for each loaf because the custom is to bake round challahs for Rosh ha-Shanah. I divide the dough into six and coil each one into a spiral like the cycle of time that repeats and yet advances each year to a new and higher level. As Jewish women have always done, I link the simple domestic task to my hopes for the new year.

Finally the loaves are ready for the oven, each one culminating in a curl of dough on top, pointing upward.

For further reading:

Aiken, Lisa. *To Be a Jewish Woman*. Lanham, MD: 1992.

Frankiel, Tamar. *The Voice of Sarah: Feminine Spirituality and Traditional Judaism*. New York: 1990.

Freeman, Tzvi. *Bringing Heaven Down to Earth: 365 Meditations from the Wisdom of the Rebbe*. New York: 2002.

Lubavitch Women's Organization. *Spice and Spirit: The Complete Kosher Jewish Cookbook*. Brooklyn, NY: 1990.

Schneerson, Menahem Mendel. *A Partner in the Dynamics of Creation: Womanhood in the Teachings of the Lubavitcher Rebbe*. Brooklyn, NY: 1994.

You cannot blame yourself, never mind persecute yourself for how you feel. But you can rejoice in the battle of controlling and sublimating those feelings. Every small victory within yourself is a major triumph over the darkness of this world. Indeed, this is why this darkness was placed within you. In order that you may transform it into great light.

Meditation No. 97 from Bringing Heaven Down to Earth: 365 Meditations of the Rebbe *by Rabbi Tzvi Freeman.*

Prayer before Retiring at Night

Chaya Rivkah Schiloni

Master of the Universe! I hereby forgive anyone who has angered or vexed me, or sinned against me either physically or financially, against my honor or anything else that is mine, whether accidentally or intentionally, inadvertently or deliberately by speech or by deed, in this incarnation or in any other, any Israelite; may no person be punished on my account.

The first time I read these words they had a sea-change impact.

The protocol of this prayer demanded that I not go to sleep at night with a grudge in my heart or revenge on my mind. The recognition that I felt for the personal importance of these words didn't mean that I lay in bed each night with accusations on my mind. Rather the subtleties of the words seemed to me to ask that at the close of the day, the stuff accumulated throughout it should be discarded, whether I was consciously aware of stewing over wrongs or not. To say the words with integrity I also had to examine the stuff of a lifetime.

This was much more difficult than it seemed. As I began to pray nightly, I did an inventory of myself and found that as I peeled away layers of my psyche, there were some longings for retribution I couldn't release. I found that while most prayers, such as the Amidah and the Shema, were verbal ladders to God, this prayer led me deep within myself. I searched and found myself lacking.

I had only learned a few of the 613 mitzvot when I first began to develop this davening practice. They were some of the positive mitzvot: charity, keeping Shabbat and kashrut. Yet the mitzvah "Do not cherish hatred within your heart"

(Leviticus19:17) stalked me silently, months before I read it in print. This commandment implies that we should not shy away from honest confrontation and discussion, we shouldn't poison our world with loathing. It was the bedtime prayer itself that initiated me into the practice of this mitzvah in a very (to me) surprising way.

I had had, by any accounting, a childhood that came up short of even the basics. My family life was violent, confusing and painful. My mother left to make a new start for herself, leaving my brother and me behind. When she moved she severed all contact with us, as did the rest of her family. A few years later, my father remarried and did the same. I had spent most of my life frightened and lost, my existence felt fuzzy and vague. I tried to conjure a reality for myself based on external achievement.

Several weeks after committing to davening at night, but before learning of the mitzvah to dispense with hatred, I received a card from my maternal grandmother, from whom I had been estranged for more than a decade. My initial response was to write a short, polite note in the same impersonal tone as her note.

Years before, instead of speaking to my grandmother directly about the cursory nature of our relationship, I had said nothing. Our relationship had remained shallow and peripheral to both our lives. We spoke on the phone a few times a year, and generally discussed her social life and my work. I wasn't invited to holidays, weddings, or bar mitzvahs. I tried once to tell her how isolated I felt. I started talking without carefully framing my words, without kindness, and she ended the phone conversation and our relationship.

Now I was urged by a good friend to write to my grandmother honestly, to tell her how her previous refusal to speak to me had compounded the grief I had endured for so long. He urged me to write candidly, and endorsed the old cliché "You have nothing to lose." Finally, after ten years, here was my chance to write the truth I couldn't speak. I was older and braver. I had been regretting the skin-deep way I davened.

I hereby forgive anyone who has angered or vexed me or sinned against me.... I wrote and rewrote and finally sent the most honest letter I had ever written to her.

Later on in the bedtime prayers I read nightly that God takes my soul while I sleep, purifies and cleanses it, watches over it and returns it to me in the morning. It seemed to me not only an act of humanity to let go of any grudges I may feel, but also an act of piety and respect. How could I hand over my soul to God in the sullied state it was in? In order for me to appear before God with any integrity I felt I must immerse myself in the true spirit of the prayer, and pray that not even God punish the wrongdoers.

The forgiveness was of a different nature then I had been taught in modern American culture. It was a purging, a letting go, a cleansing. It was an unconditional acceptance of reality and justice. I didn't have to even see good in the people that harmed me. I had to believe that what was done was done and wishing for revenge, no matter how subtle, was injury to my soul and an insult to God.

May no person be punished on my account.... Perhaps this was my chance to begin davening with true intent.

For more than twenty-five years, instead of letting go I had nurtured my grief until I had created a knot of pain within that became a permanent part of my make-up. My kindnesses to others in no way negated the fact that I walked around with the ache of aversion for my family within my heart. I realized by merely putting the words on paper that my desire for rectification was leaving. The answer was in my pen, in words, in this opening and forgiving. Suddenly it seemed obvious to me that my family members and I couldn't connect because of their shame, their suffering. A new emotion began to blossom in place of the hatred: compassion.

My grandmother and I still write at cross purposes, at different depths. But we're writing. Somehow my words have released me. Instead of drowning in my own sorrow, I recognize what must be hers.

... whether accidentally or intentionally, inadvertently or deliberately... Perhaps she wasn't able to see herself or me clearly. Perhaps her coldness was her suit of armor, deflecting wounds I couldn't imagine.

If we don't feel heard, we must look harder, for we can hear ourselves and, more importantly God hears us, utterly. Through this examining, telling and hearing He heals and grants peace. We must be the ones to ask for forgiveness through the act of dispensing it. This mitzvah holds up a mirror so that we can see even the hidden parts of ourselves through God's eye.

When I learn and commit to a mitzvah I don't assume that I already understand and practice it correctly. For me each new pathway I am taught requires constant application to sustain and develop my connection to God.

Davening leads me (sometimes indirectly) to awareness of the mitzvot. The prayer before retiring at night ends with the sentence *Blessed are You, Lord, Who in His glory gives light to the whole world.*

I stand at my window and say words I have now said many times. Sometimes I just say them. But sometimes the light from my window or my bedside lamp seems to fall more brightly on a passage or a page, and at such moments I have learned to look within.

For further reading:

Frankiel, Tamar. *Entering the Temple of Dreams: Jewish Prayers, Movements and Meditations for the End of the Day*. Woodstock, VT: 2000.

Twerski, Abraham J. *Successful Relationships at Home, at Work and with Friends*. Brooklyn, NY: 2003.

Schochet, Jacob Immanuel. *Deep Calling unto Deep*. Brooklyn, NY: 1995.

Home and Family

Said R. Yossi: I never called my wife my wife, but my home.

Talmud, *Shabbat* 118b

Introduction

Women have long been synonymous with home and family, and the more things change the more they stay the same. As ever more women work outside of the home, and men take on additional domestic duties, it is still women who strive to make a home out of a house, and by and large put more effort into its smooth functioning. Though the term "mothering" has given way to the politically correct "parenting," it is still women who are pregnant, birthing and lactating and it is the mother, in most cases, who remains the single most important influence in her children's lives. It is also daughters (sometimes daughters-in-law) who most often care for their ailing and aging parents and escort them through their twilight hours in this world.

For women, life is primarily about relationships; about the sometimes exhilarating, often difficult and even painful but necessary fusing of our varied roles. We are mothers and daughters, professionals and friends, teachers and students and always welders as we smelt and solder in our effort to hold it all together.

Jewish life, too, is all about relationships; about the synergy of body and soul, the material and the spiritual. God's ultimate wish is for the mundane to be elevated, transformed into the sublime; for matter to become spirit.

After their exodus from Egypt, the Jews traveled towards Sinai, received the revelation and prepared for their entrance into the Promised Land, the climax of their journey from slavery to freedom. Just as they were about to enter, however, they sent scouts to spy the land. Upon hearing of the land's vastness and the strength of its inhabitants, the men refused to enter the land, preferring instead to stay in the desert. In response, God declared that indeed they would not enter the Promised Land. Only after forty years, after this generation of men passed from this world, would their wives – who loved the land and wanted to enter it – and their children enter the land of milk and honey.

The men's refusal to enter the land is conventionally understood to be rooted in their fear of the nations that inhabited it. However, Rabbi Menachem M. Schneerson, the Lubavitcher Rebbe, offered a new perspective. He taught that it was not the physical war and conquest that they feared; after all, God had promised to fight for them as he had before. Rather, they feared that entrance into the land would mean the end of an era. For the duration of the time they had spent in the desert, all their physical needs had been taken care of in a miraculous fashion. They ate the manna that rained down from the sky and drank the water that sprang forth from Miriam's Well. This allowed them a great luxury: to be busy exclusively with the study of God's Torah and other spiritual pursuits. Entering the Land meant a new reality: daily involvement in the physical, material facets of life. They feared that amid the plowing and harvesting they would lose their connection with the Divine; that they would be dragged down and become mired in earthiness. On the other hand, the women did not fear entering the land. On the contrary, they yearned for it. They understood the physical, corporeal aspects of life to be not a hindrance but fertile ground in which Godliness blossoms.

The Jewish home is for each one of us a promised land, the ultimate nexus of body and soul – material and spiritual – and the Jewish woman its high priestess, its anchor.

In this section we meet women who open their hearts and speak their minds on making a home and caring for family. They give eloquent voice to the discovery of holiness within the material; of infinity captured within finitude. But they do not gloss over the challenges. More than one speaks to the conflict between raising healthy families and pursuing their own careers. New mothers share their joy (and bewilderment); daughters share the pain of their parents' waning lives. One describes her elation at her son's *brit* while another portrays her struggle with infertility. One shares her loss of a child, another an uplifting life lesson learned from her Down Syndrome son. One offers a meditation on raising her children properly, while another speaks of what happens when her child becomes religiously observant and wants to raise her!

Our work in the arena of home and family is arguably the one in which success is most difficult to achieve. Its demands are incessant and always subject to change. We sometimes have difficulty liking the people we love. Often, we don't feel appreciated. We need to remind ourselves of the significance of home and family in our lives, its value and inherent sanctity. The women writing in this section help us honor the manna hidden within the bread of our daily lives.

How Long Does It Take?

how long does it take to write a poem?
between births that punctuate ten years?
between dinners?
lunches don't count
between drafts of dreams
before breakfast
when you wake up starved
for words
for words that will
fill out your flesh
cradle your bones
glisten
on your throat
a strand of pearls
hear the clasp
click
shut
before the baby cries

Judy Belsky

Life Lessons

Deena Yellin

In the beginning, I brought my baby home from the hospital and promptly burst into tears. In only a few hours with my newborn, I had discovered the dark secret about bringing a child into the world that nobody ever talks about. That it requires us to surrender a large part of ourselves to motherhood. It sidelines our ambitions and forces us to make the compromises we never thought we'd have to make. Suddenly, we find ourselves abandoning our hobbies, interests, even dreams for the sake of a virtual stranger who doesn't seem to appreciate us enough.

I suddenly realized that my son was not going to allow me to sleep, eat, read or accomplish any errands or work. He only wanted me to hold him, feed him and give him every ounce of my fading energy. I mourned the many pleasures lost: peace and quiet, sleeping late, reading novels, an orderly home and eating out at restaurants.

I stopped playing guitar, canceled my karate class membership and no longer had time for swimming. Mostly, I thought about how I had always wanted to do something with my life but that all I was doing now was changing diapers and heating up baby formula.

The arrival of my son changed everything at once. I knew I didn't want to relinquish my status as a professional after all my years of training. I didn't want to waste my education or betray the feminist ideals I had picked up from my idols, Betty Friedan and Gloria Steinem. But I also wanted to be a good mother and spend time with my child. On my drive into work, I listened to Dr. Laura berating working mothers and preaching motherhood as the world's most important job and my eyes filled with tears.

When I cut down my hours from five to four days, I thought I had reached the perfect compromise. But I still felt I couldn't win. At the office I felt guilty and wished I were home with my child. When I was home, I felt guilty about the pile of work on my desk. Then there were the twinges of jealousy when other colleagues gained promotions or published books. When my friends from graduate school, who had landed jobs with prominent newspapers, asked how work was going, I just sighed.

During my late night nursing sessions, I watched reruns of Murphy Brown on television and marveled at how she leaped from the delivery room after giving birth back to her demanding full-time career as a television news reporter. She had enough energy to chase hot stories, interview the President and romance a boyfriend, all while keeping her house immaculate, her wardrobe up to date and her hair and makeup perfect.

Once my son was born, his toys took over and I was no longer in control of the clutter. At restaurants, my husband and I could no longer enjoy conversation over a leisurely meal. Instead, we followed my son around as he strolled to other tables, chatted with waiters, sang to patrons and, every once in a while, pulled something off their plates. My dry-cleaning bills skyrocketed and I no longer wore white, a magnet for stains. Sleeping late, reading novels or peace and quiet became memories of a very distant past.

But when I find myself grousing about all that I have sacrificed since my son's birth, I remind myself of all that I have gained. While he has wreaked havoc on career, hobbies and home, he has also reminded me that I am in this world to live life.

In my existence Before Child (B.C.), for example, I ushered in new days by hitting the snooze bar. Nowadays, or A.C., just an hour or two after sunrise, my son pitter-patters over to my bedside ordering me to get up and play. To him, it is impossible to remain in bed when a new day beckons. Every sunrise offers a new opportunity for exploration. Armed for adventure with his knapsack and sippy cup, the possibilities are limitless.

I remember when I used to embrace news days with such enthusiasm. But then I grew old and jaded. I crossed days off calendars with abandon, ushering in mornings by lingering rather than leaping out of bed. Yet all my son's optimism got me thinking: If a toddler can be this excited about all the unforeseen potential of a new day, maybe there are possibilities for me too.

B.C., I hurried through routine errands at a marathon pace, oblivious to everything around me. But with Yehudah in tow, even the quickest trip to the bank or the grocery has been transformed. Each chore is akin to a spiritual journey to be savored. Along the way, he looks intently at bugs and birds. He marvels at airplanes passing overhead and turns strangers into friends with wide smiles and heartfelt greetings. Even grouchy clerks at the post office warm up when he grins at them through the glass partition.

Traipsing through the neighborhood at my son's heels, I have discovered all the things I had neglected to notice; that a car lumbering down the street is a miracle in motion and that, if examined closely, even a spider is beautiful. But my son did more than point out the magic in everyday life. He also pushed me onto the proper path.

At first, I thought I would steer him in the direction that suited my ideals: I stocked up on Harvard sweatshirts, classical music tapes and educational videos. I read aloud to him from the New York Times and made sure he could identify all the major politicians. The first time he smiled at a photo of Al Gore, I cheered.

But since then, I am the one who has gained the education. My proudest moments came not when he talked, walked or identified his colors but when he did good. He shared a favorite toy with a friend, showed compassion for an animal and tried to convince a stranger's baby to stop crying.

Now I know with certainty that what I want for him most is not genius, athletic prowess or fame. My greatest dream for him is goodness. I discovered that such qualities must be cultivated through hard work by the parents. My husband and I are keenly aware that we now have to watch our behavior and words to make sure we are setting a good example. How horrified I was when my son greeted a friend with a four-letter word I had accidentally uttered when I stubbed my toe. Now that my words are being monitored more closely than a closed-circuit TV, I am more careful to avoid curse words or nasty things about other people. There is no telling what he may repeat or to whom.

Recognizing that our son's experiences today may be forever embedded into his consciousness, we have also altered our religious routines A.C. On Shabbat, he reminds me that the day of rest is a gift that bond our family and community together.

Suddenly, I am paying more attention to my Sabbath preparations. I polish my candlesticks until they gleam and the aroma of freshly baked challah fills our home on Friday afternoons. My husband and I no longer breeze through the rituals. Instead, we sing *zemiros*, Shabbos songs aloud and clap our hands. When my son dances to the *zemiros*, my husband and I join him.

My Saturday morning routine has changed as well. Instead of curling up with a novel and showing up in shul fashionably late, I arrive earlier. I have no choice, since my son hurries me there with cries of "Kiss the Torah!" Even if his primary motivation is to visit our synagogue's candy man, who sits near my husband, I must give him credit; all my parents' prodding never got me to service so early.

He worships in his own style, opting to stand when congregants sit and sit when they stand. When the cantor sings, he sings along with his own tune. He swaggers up to the ark to kiss the Torah, gazing at it with all the awe generally reserved for *Teletubbies*.

His spirit has nourished us and he has unwittingly pushed us into better observance. He has awakened in us the need to experience life in a deeper, more vivid way. By showing the world to us through his eyes, he has given us a new sense of awe for the world.

All of this comes just in time for me to realize that my cuddly baby has disappeared and is being replaced by an independent toddler. I suddenly feel the time marching on and wish I could slow it down just enough to enjoy his youth a little longer.

Already, he is less clingy and more anxious to play with friends. I am attempting to savor my moments with him as a child, memorizing his funny lines and capturing his antics with cameras. Soon, there will be fewer kisses planted on my face and fewer bedtime stories and songs.

Before I know it will come his bar mitzvah, college graduation and someday, marriage. The peace and quiet I had craved when he was born will return all too quickly.

In my life BC, I had grandiose dreams about what I would accomplish by age forty. I envisioned groundbreaking books, shocking discoveries and travel to war zones to cover the news. Now I am coming to grips with all the goals that will never come to fruition. As a mother, writer and volunteer in my community, I will probably never solve an international crisis or cure a disease. The Pulitzer Prize committee has shown no interest in calling me and I have given up hope of becoming the next Barbara Walters.

The tension I feel between wanting to be a success in the home as well as the workplace is a battle that will rage within me for the rest of my life. I am grateful to those before me who pioneered the way so that women like me can beam with pride at the accomplishments of Ruth Bader Ginsburg, Cynthia Ozick and, most recently, the governor of Massachusetts, among countless others who juggled parenthood and high-powered careers.

In my life AC, I have become older and wiser. I take comfort in knowing there are small steps we can take to change the world. We can plant a tree. We can forge lasting friendships. We can elicit laughter and create beautiful memories. We can usher in each new day with a sense of excitement and awe. And we can teach our children goodness. They are our greatest gift, after all, to future generations.

This is the message I want to pass on to my son. It was a lesson that took me three years to learn, but I learned it well. I had an excellent teacher.

For further reading:

Mogel, Wendy. *The Blessing of a Skinned Knee: Using Jewish Teachings to Raise Self-Reliant Children.* New York, NY: 2001.

Shapiro, Sarah. *Growing with My Children: A Jewish Mother's Diary.* Jerusalem: 1990.

The Soul Is No Flat Terrain

The soul is no flat terrain,
no rough diamond
but a jagged shard
cutting roughly
into the tissue of our life.
It tears skins of ease
and leaves you less at home
in body's house. The soul
is a dark haired lady
with worker's hands
kneading the stale dough of habit
over and over till it springs back,
the staff of life again.
The soul is a carpenter
who plans the new extension off the porch
to stretch the walls that hem us in
until the light dances alike
on grass and kitchen floor.

Vera Schwarcz

A Woman of Velcro

Ellen Golub

Mama, Mama, Mama! There was magic in the word," wrote Henry Roth in his magnificent novel, *Call It Sleep.* On my instruction, my students would diligently copy this line into their notes.

"And don't forget *Portnoy's Complaint*," I'd lecture, "where little Alexander Portnoy thought all of his teachers were his mother in disguise. In the Book of Numbers, The Hebrew God even speaks of himself as having conceived the people of Israel, carrying them in his bosom like a suckling child. So where does it all come from, this Jewish literary obsession with mothers?"

Two decades ago, it was an academic question I posed to my students. I had, as they say, a reading knowledge of the material. But it has taken me years – hundreds of Shabbatot and four children – to resolve the deeper meaning of this question and to answer it, as a Jewish mother myself, from my heart.

When I gave birth to my daughter twenty-two years ago, I had a Ph.D. and a teaching job at an Ivy League university. With abundant day care and a willing husband, I carved my professional career into the schedule of our home. We divided chores on a fifty-fifty split. During the six years preceding my tenure decision, I would spend every spare moment either writing my book or teaching.

My husband Steve was on the same academic treadmill in a different department, so he knew the drill: whoever cooks doesn't clean up, and the reverse. During fall semester I'd teach on Tuesdays and Thursdays while he was home on Mondays, Wednesdays, and Fridays. Spring semester: the reverse. There was little time built in for slippage or sloth. "Life is short," the writer Grace Paley once told me, "and literature is so long."

But even as my egalitarian marriage marched to the beat, my baby was not with the program. She kept odd hours and wanted my attention during unscripted moments. Colic, teething, and bedtime threatened my tenure. Worse yet, I was in love. I would fall asleep with her at my side and awaken mesmerized by the sound of her cooing. Steve continued to read and write his way through her infancy. But I was besotted with her. Jubilant. Dazzled. Intoxicated. Obsessed. Smitten.

I had grown up alone, the surviving child in a very small family. But for Frannie, I wanted more. "She needs a sister," I told her father.

"And you need to finish your book," he would remind me. I agreed. I swore to myself that I would not let mere motherhood come between me and tenure. But truthfully, the book felt like a rag doll next to my very real baby. The baby gurgled and laughed and said, "Mama." The book sulked and dragged. To whom would *you* listen?

So I gave birth to Alex, a hearty green-eyed boy. And I fell in love all over again. "Next time it will be a sister," I promised my daughter, the little Jewish feminist-in-training. But the next time it was Yoni, with dancing blue eyes, another guy in need of a bris.

"Where's my sister!?" my little daughter pouted when she saw my third child wrapped in a blue hospital blanket.

"Where's your book?" my tenured husband reminded me, meaning: are you really willing to give it all up?

"Where is justice?" I balked. Increasingly, it was my labor that was fueling this family, my Velcro that bound it together. Meanwhile, I was hindered in my work by troubled pregnancies, nursing, and the amorphous mitzvah of mothering. Inevitably, I fell behind in my career. My husband spent increasingly more time working outside the home, compensating for my waning income.

I still worked, but I had given up on the big prize: tenure at an Ivy. When I gave birth to Zoë, my fourth and the promised sister, I had a job teaching journalism at the local state college. Steve was already completing his second book, still in the field he trained in. "The women's movement lied to women," said my friend, Bill. "It told them they could have it all." Bill and Steve had it all. In my spare time, if I had any, I would have killed them both.

Mine is not all a tale of tenure interruptus. After Zoë was born, Steve and I experienced an amazing sense of completeness and symmetry. In a generation plagued by late marriages and infertility, we had succeeded in producing an enviable *mishpocha*: four children, two girls and two boys – and a Hebrew day school bill greater than our combined salaries. (Riddle: What do committed Jewish families use for birth control? Answer: Day school.)

Steve was now writing his third book and had a prestigious publisher. He lectured internationally and went on national TV. I scrambled between the college and the kids and wrote short pieces during nap times, for the local Jewish paper. I was frustrated. I hadn't given up on my professional ambitions, but I found myself sufficiently enamored of my four DNA masterpieces that I couldn't bear to leave them. Between ear infections and birthday parties, piano lessons and Little League, they gradually absorbed the time I had set aside for my professional projects.

Truth be told, the responsibility of raising our four Jewish children engaged and inspired me. I feminized classic Jewish texts giving women voices and roles (You've heard of Moshe and Tzipora Rabbeinu – the Rabbeinus; Aishet and Noach, the charming pair of the flood generation....). I told the tale of the Exodus as if it happened last month to our family, planting us in the middle of Egypt ("And Pharaoh made Auntie Lottie wash the palace floors on her bad knees!") and raised Purim to a joy more exquisite than Halloween.

On the walls of our house, I painted Hebrew letters and in my children's ears, while rocking them to sleep, I crooned Bialik poems. Though I still pined after my intellectual ambitions, I enjoyed life as a Jewish holiday – in play dough, paint, rubber stamps, craft glue, song, and verse. Each day became a fresh opportunity to weave Frannie, Alex, Yoni, and Zoë into the thread of the *tallit*.

You'd think that with the joy of raising Jewish children, the painful loss of my academic career would have subsided. But it continued to sadden me. Perhaps it was that I drifted through Jewish bookstores most Fridays on the way to buying groceries. There were my former colleagues' books. Even more incredible to me were the books written by my graduate students. I felt like I had fallen out of time.

Which is why I hated Shabbat: it pinned me to the wall and demanded my *eyshes hayilness* relentlessly. Cooking, cleaning, preparing, inviting guests.... "Why should I be the one to be doing this?" I would demand of my husband. "I should be sitting in front of some Jewish text reading and interpreting." If there was one thing I detested about my life, it was the *challah*-baking, meal-making, Shabbat-welcoming function that Orthodoxy thought I was born to. My *yetzer ha-me* – my selfish inclination – was wildly out of control.

With difficulty, I had renounced my future for the four *zisse Yiddishe neshumes* that I loved. But Shabbat! It was just insult heaped on injury. It was over the edge. Too much to ask of me. Even as a guest in other people's homes, I saw Jewish women enmeshed in all the things feminism supposedly had freed me from: cooking, cleaning, baking, preparing, and the dreaded cleaning up.

Shabbat – or rather my expected role in it – infuriated me. "Let me get this straight," I would tirade each week, "If I had a bris, I wouldn't have to be doing all this, would I?"

Steve understood. He felt guilty that his twelve-hour workdays kept him from his share of the domestic dross. "Don't do it, then," he said emphatically. "We can live without Shabbat."

"'More than the Jewish people have kept Shabbat, Shabbat has kept the Jewish people,'" I quoted. "But I'm so domesticated, I can't even remember where I read that."

"We'll order pizza," Steve volunteered. "Just take some time for your own work. You can have all day Friday to work on your own stuff."

I did. I stopped making Shabbat dinner. I took the time to read and think. I stopped inviting other Jewish families. We ordered out: pizza, subs, Chinese. Then we started going out to eat, because it was easier. We stopped lighting candles, because it was unsafe to leave them burning. Eating *treif* in a fast-food restaurant wasn't conducive to discussing the *parsha*, so we skipped that. Eventually, Steve and I found ourselves wandering aimlessly through the mall on Friday nights, pushing a carriage and dragging our kids through meaningless aisles of material goods.

We didn't much look like the chosen people. We certainly didn't feel like the chosen people. "Let somebody else make Shabbat, if it's so important," I told my friends and anyone who would listen. "It's just not my job."

I am still convinced, in the abstract at least, that preparing for Shabbat should not be a woman's role. If you were looking for an inconvenient, oppressive, time-bound mitzvah to avoid, this one would more than suffice. But turning my children into mall rats on Friday nights was not my idea of maintaining their spiritual health, either.

After months of watching our Jewish identity melt into secular anonymity, materialism, and randomness, my thinking began to change. I missed the Jewish experience. I missed feeling centered in time. I missed Shabbat.

I began thinking that if I did not make Shabbat dinner for my children, then who would? And if they did not have *erev* Shabbat in their lives, what would they become? And if I didn't start now, then when? I remembered the *midrash* wherein *HaShem* sends an angel to look into the windows of Jewish homes every Friday night, to see whether the table is set and the children are washed. Is every Jew observing Shabbat? If the angel reports, "Yes," *HaShem* will send *Mashiach*. If no, we remain in limbo another week.

Who was I to be the obstruction to *Mashiach*? Because I desperately wanted to raise Jewish children, because I knew that Shabbat was an essential ingredient in that recipe, and because I missed the celebration so terribly, I finally took it upon myself to restore Shabbat to our home. I began cooking again, began inviting families over on Friday nights, began racing toward that deadline of three stars to get everything accomplished. I gave up my personal day to work and think not because it was morally right or fair or even appropriate. I just wanted my children to have this gift and I realized I was the only one who was able to give it to them. Like the story goes in all the popular ballads, "I did it for love."

These days, my Shabbat table is bursting with grandparents, family, and friends – we almost never have enough chairs. The kids keep reminding me to take the *challah* out of the oven in time; but as I multi-task, I fall into my grandmother's recipe for toast. "Tell me how much you want it scraped." Martha Stewart I'm not.

But as we sing *kiddush*, I close my eyes and picture the births of each of my four babies. I remember that Shabbat is the birthday of the world and I am grateful for the planet, for the Torah, and for the love of my husband. I am especially grateful for the great blessing bestowed upon me to raise a Jewish family.

Sometimes, the journey you're on is not the one you planned. You become a mother instead of an Ivy League professor. You cook instead of read, you illuminate a room instead of a library. You sit simply in your vineyard, water your plants and watch the grapes grow. You open your door to the spiritual, learning as you go, that being female is far more complex and rewarding than you had imagined – and that "Mama," indeed, is a magical word.

For further reading:

Jacobson, Simon. *Toward a Meaningful Life: The Wisdom of the Rebbe Menachem Mendel Schneerson*. New York, NY: 1995.

Steinsaltz, Adin. *Simple Words: Thinking about What Really Matters in Life*. New Jersey: 1999.

If I Could Recycle Tears

...Must I trust the Craftsman of
a diamond's sparkle,
who crushes coal, a jewel to make?
Or spend vain years, my life rewrite,
its course in vain to recreate?

Yes! I shall trust the Craftsman of
my sigh's desire,
to crush my soul, a Jewel to make.
Yes! Trust the Craftsman of
my sigh's desire,
and light from coal anticipate!

From the poem by Arlene Geist Sidelsky

Being There, New Millennium Style: Infertility Redefined
Shulamis Yehudis Gutfreund

Recently, an editor friend of mine asked me to write an essay on "Infertility as a Pathway to Serve God." Or, in more simple terms, how the struggles to have children have enhanced and refined my relationship with God.

I would have liked to oblige her, but I can't seem to do it. The topic is so vast for me that it's hard to get perspective. In many ways, the effort to have children is not a part of my life; it *is* my life. True, I do other things – I'm a wife and homemaker, I'm a daughter, I teach in a high school, I write, and I run a small yeshiva for women in my home. Yet, perhaps because I experience success in these other activities, they're like part-time jobs as opposed to the full-time job of seeking to have children. When I'm not doing those other activities, I'm not necessarily thinking about them. But my mind never stops churning – innovating, developing new strategies, cross-examining myself – in my constant quest to have children.

In my moments of objectivity – those few times I allow myself to retreat from the battlefield and view the fray from a distance – I have noticed there are a few notable benefits to this struggle. Judaism teaches that there are three partners in the creation of a child – the father, the mother, and God. And so it is with infertility as well. I'm part of a three-member team and I never feel I'm alone. Although my husband probably doesn't feel the pain to the same extent that I do, he's my partner in every development. Our struggles have clearly brought us closer. Some of the most romantic moments of my life have been those when he's used all his ingenuity to console me. And some of the most bonding moments have been those when we've had to laugh ourselves through the indignities of infertility treatment or jump hand in hand over obstacles we didn't think we could surmount.

So, too, I've gotten much closer to God. I've grown to trust God more, not less, in this nearly six-year ordeal. It has drained me and built me in a way few other challenges in life have. Although I deal with endless medical professionals, I wrestle only with God. I can be angry or briefly disappointed in medical professionals, but those emotions are truly fleeting because I know Who my real doctor is, and I know success and failure are in His hands only.

And yet, for the most part, I'm far too consumed by this exhausting campaign to wax philosophical about it.

I know some mothers envy me because they think I have all the free time in the world. That's because they can't imagine the hours this challenge consumes. It may even rival motherhood. Not a day goes by without a kaleidoscopic array of activity – physical, spiritual and psychological. The mileage on my car stems largely from trips to doctor's offices and clinics, and my checkbook register is packed with payments for therapies insurance won't cover. To date, I've been under the care of four different reproductive endocrinologists (fertility M.D.s) and consulted nearly half a dozen more, spanning the world. The list of alternative health-care professionals we've seen dwarfs this number by far.

During the years, we've taken on dozens of projects to improve our chances of conceiving; at any one time we can be occupied in several. These projects range from the sublime (intense prayer) to the humorous (gulping down a finely-ground ruby – a revered Jewish folk remedy) to the time-consuming (becoming macrobiotic for a year and a half) to encounters with energy healers and psychics that pierced the Twilight Zone of how far we were willing to go.

Currently, I have only one thing left that I'm trying. Don't get me wrong. The wheels are still turning and the brain is still churning hours every day on possible bold new avenues of effort, including new drugs and even moving to a new home (Judaism says that fortune is bound to place and moving one's home can change one's fortune). But this "other" effort is definitely the last frontier in many ways.

Here it is: For the past few months, I've flirted with the thought of what life would be like if I gave up trying. It would certainly liberate huge sections of time.

I would also have to redefine myself. I would become a completely different person necessarily, because I would no longer be doing the same things or thinking the same thoughts. When the thought of giving up first occurred to me, it was tantalizing, even a little exciting. Why? Because I would be out of the "box" I've been struggling within for nearly six years. Life would be radically new.

There was only one small problem with this idea. I would be a new person, but I would have to cut out such an essential part of me I'm not sure what would be left after the operation. I decided I couldn't go that far. I couldn't give up on having children.

And yet, at the same time, I realized that something had to give. The time was up; I had to get out of this box of repeated efforts and repeated failures to be a mother. And, although I couldn't speak for Him, I felt that God also wanted me to be out of the box. It's no way to live.

And so, this week, I tore down the walls of my box. Gingerly, I stepped over the rubble – my self-image as a childless woman who is trying unsuccessfully to become a mother – and left it behind forever. I couldn't hold up under that identity one minute longer. In its place, I began to search for something deeper. Something more genuine, more true to who I am.

In an interesting moment a few days ago, I asked myself who indeed I am. Blushing, I replied: "I am the mother of quite a nice family, thank God. I just don't know who they are yet." Then a few seconds later, I shocked myself with an addition: "I am the mother of quite a *large* family, thank God," I said. "I just don't know who they are yet." When I said it, it reverberated down to my toes.

Only God can give a couple success in having children – whether by natural means, by drugs or by adoption. None of these things are in our hands. But our self-concept is. We can choose to define ourselves by what life's circumstances say about us, or we can choose to define ourselves by something different – by who we are in essence.

Earlier today, the Jewish holiday of Tisha b'Av, I read the Book of Job. Job is a righteous man whom God tests by sending him terrible afflictions. Some of Job's friends try to comfort him by suggesting that the afflictions are proof that Job is not who he says he is; that he must have sinned, and therefore, if he repents, his afflictions will end. And yet, even as his afflictions multiply, Job won't relent about who he is. He maintains that he was and is a righteous man. And God ends up verifying it.

There's a craziness and yet also a deep sanity in not letting life define us but instead, digging down to the quintessence of our beings and defining ourselves only by that.

A rabbi I know, a *chassid* of the Lubavitcher Rebbe, gave an intriguing speech at a party following his daughter's wedding. He said the following: The way a person defines himself is critical. If a person "tries" to become something, he may end up trying for the rest of his life. If the person, however, declares that he is already that which he'd like to be, the external circumstances to match that internal identity are much more likely to develop.

This rabbi should know. Several years ago, both he and a friend of his left New York to become emissaries of the Lubavitcher Rebbe and teach Judaism in outlying areas. With almost no knowledge of Russian, the rabbi and his family went off to a small, remote town in Russia. The friend, also a rabbi, went off to a far easier post in the United States.

As they departed to their respective towns, the friend said to others, "I'm going to try to be an emissary. " The rabbi who was heading off to Russia heard those words and knew his path had to be different. He told people, "I *am* an emissary of the Rebbe." As he explained it, "I knew that if I were going to try to be an emissary, for sure I would be a goner. I would never make it." Within a few years and with stunningly few resources, he managed to revive Judaism in the Russian town. He also weathered hardships that few would be able to master. The friend gave up after a few years and took on a different occupation.

How did the rabbi get this wisdom? I don't know. Perhaps it was from his teacher, the Lubavitcher Rebbe, who insisted that Jews around the world remember who they are in essence and not in external circumstances. As the Rebbe explained, Jews don't belong in the situations we find ourselves today. We are at the tail end of a two-thousand-year-long estrangement from our homeland (Israel as it once was, in all its glory), from Judaism, and from the essence of our identities, an estrangement so real that we no longer see it as estrangement. It is simply our reality.

But we are different creatures. We belong in a different setting than what we see. And part of the way to get there, to the *geulah* – the redemption of the Jewish people from exile, an illusory state of alienation from God — is to devour every piece of information we can get about the *geulah* so that we can begin to live it, even now. In other words, to change our identities from exile-Jews to *geulah*-Jews.

In showing me how to get to *geulah*, the Rebbe switched on a light for me. Praying for what we want, whether it's *geulah* or a more private desire, is essential, but it's not enough. Even increasing in our *mitzvot*, those magic channels that draw God's blessings into our lives, is not enough. As long as our goal remains a dream or a far-fetched reality to us, we've missed the boat. *Be there already*, the Rebbe taught us. Imagine it. Live it. Breathe it. See it.

In my own personal situation, is my new commitment to "be there already" as a mother just the latest and most subtle in my strategies to convince God to give us children? In part, of course it is. But it's also more. If it's just a strategy (and no more), then in the face of failure, I'll abandon it as I have countless other techniques. But if it's what I truly believe it to be, my essence, then I will cling to it through thick and thin because it's me.

Already, on a daily basis, my life has changed. If a distraction pops up, I announce to myself: "I can't afford to waste time on that. I'm the mother of a large family, thank God!" Or, if something disconcerting happens, I push it aside more easily, saying: "I can't let that worry me! I'm the mother of a large family, thank God!" And, when disappointment shows its face, I say, "I can't afford the time to mope! I'm the mother of a large family!"

Without a doubt, those who define themselves by external reality only will certainly cluck their tongues in pity at my words. "Deep denial," they may say. "Driven off the deep end by the unending pain." "Lost in a world of wishful thinking." (I mutter these criticisms to myself on a regular basis.)

But, if I may say so, I think God at His post is smiling. Why? Because God likes courage. "Trying" to be something requires courage, without a doubt. But believing we are something which life's circumstances have not yet confirmed requires far more. As women, we're willing to gamble our fortunes and even our health far more readily than we are willing to gamble our hearts.

From this week on, my heart is a different heart. It's a mother's heart, a mother anxiously waiting for her children to come home.

With deep gratitude to Rabbis Yitzchok Lipszyc and Manis Friedman for their inspiration.

Boston, Massachusetts, August 2000

For further reading:

Finkelstein, Baruch, and Michal Finkelstein. *The Third Key: A Jewish Couple's Guide to Fertility.* Jerusalem, Israel: 2005.

Grazi, Richard V. *Overcoming Infertility: A Guide for Jewish Couples.* New Milford, CT: 2005.

Kirzner, Yitzchok. *Making Sense of Suffering: A Jewish Approach.* Brooklyn, NY: 2002.

Gross, Mindy. *How Long the Night: A Triumph of Healing and Self-Discovery.* Jerusalem: 1991.

"A home," wrote Solomon the Wise, "is built with wisdom." And not with a hammer. Because wisdom is the glue of beauty. Wisdom, meaning the ability to step back and see all of the picture, the past and, most important, the future to which all this leads. To see the truth inside each thing. Without wisdom, there are only fragments. With wisdom, there is a whole. And there is peace between all the parts of that whole.

From the Rebbe Rashab, Sefer Hasichot 5704, *as quoted by Rabbi Tzvi Freeman in* Men, Women and Kabbalah: Wisdom and Guidance from the Masters

The Wisdom of Spinning

Leah Perl Shollar

I used to wonder: why is it that buildings fall down but never self-assemble? Why is it that dust accumulates on pictures on the wall, but never moves itself out of the house? In short – why won't a sock that made its way onto the living room sofa eventually make its way into the dresser drawer of its wearer?

To some extent, this question goes beyond the undoing of my housework to bear directly on the larger question of chaos in the world and what we are supposed to do with it. When my house is really out of control, I find the one clean spot and sit and gather myself. Staring into the other rooms exploding messily every which way, the Chassidic aphorism pops into mind: "In a place where there is order and cleanliness, there is holiness and purity." Oy vey! Where does that leave me? But wait! Is the goal having arrived at the destination? Or – is the goal the planning, the preparations, the struggle to make it happen? I meditate on this: "In a place where there is order and cleanliness, there is holiness and purity." Rabbi Pinchas ben Yair goes beyond this with his amazing statement that "diligence leads to cleanliness, cleanliness leads to purity, purity leads to separateness, separateness leads to holiness, holiness leads to humility, humility leads to dread of sin, dread of sin leads to piety, piety leads to the Holy Spirit, the Holy Spirit leads to the resurrection of the dead. And the resurrection of the dead will come with Elijah the Prophet, may he be remembered for good, Amen."[1] So, cleanliness is a stepping stone to boost us up to the next level and each successive level leads us upward to the coming of Moshiach. Thus, cleanliness is not a goal in itself, but the means through which we advance toward our goal. It is one of the tools we have in our battle against evil and chaos. On one erev Shabbos, Rabbi Yisrael Meir Kagan[2] found his daughter scrubbing the floor with great fervor. "Better to expend this passion scrubbing your soul to prepare for Shabbos," he said. True, it is a mitzvah to clean the house in anticipation of Shabbos, but we must see it as a tool for enhancing our display of honor and love for Shabbos and as a step toward bringing holiness and purity into our homes. Once, Rav Zeira saw people eating oatmeal with bread. He said, "The Babylonians are fools. They eat bread with bread!"[3] When we work so that we can eat and eat so that we can work, we are eating bread with bread. People whose self-identity derives from their job ('I am' a lawyer, etc.,) do the same. "Do not be like the horse or mule that has no understanding, whose mouth must hold the bit and bridle."[4] A person who sees herself always in physical terms 'dwells' in her physicality like a horse or mule who pulls a load because their rider tells them to. They work toward no master plan or vision.[5] We must not let this happen with our role as homemakers.

Who oversees this cleaning of inner and outer home? A look at the world around us shows that in nearly every culture and society it is women. In English this might be called a homemaker, in German a *hausfrau*, but in the Holy Language of Hebrew, a woman is the "akeret ha-bayit" – the mainstay of the home. She is so called, Kabbala teaches, because she is *ikar ha-bayit*, the essence of the home. "She has the unique emotional nature necessary... to shape the personalities of the members of her household."[6]

When my grandfather would see the teen me helping out at home, he'd say approvingly "I see you're getting to be a real *baalebuste*." Immediately I saw a Russian peasant type with a kerchief on her head scrubbing the floor with worn hands. Not my ideal. I wanted his praise, but didn't see myself and "baalebuste"

---

[1] Mishnah *Sotah*, Chapter 9, Mishnah 15.

[2] Popularly known by the title of his most famous work, *Chafetz Chaim*.

[3] *Betza* 16.

[4] Psalms 32:9.

[5] Rabbi Meir Leibush ben Yechiel Michel.

[6] Letter of Rabbi Menachem Mendel Schneerson to N'Shei U'Bnos Chabad Convention, 28 Iyar 5751.

in the same sentence. Because my understanding was limited and external, I didn't see the beauty in his compliment.

Later, like many newlyweds, I accepted and rejected various patterns I saw at home. Feeling that "daughter knows best," I had the idea that my husband and I were going to establish an egalitarian household. We would share everything – cooking, cleaning, laundry. With the addition of children, life became more complex, and suddenly I found that I was doing most of the cooking, cleaning and laundry (surprise!) while he was toiling away to support this grand enterprise. As time went on I realized that in that first flush of utopianism I had given away my personal sphere. I had bereft myself of a realm in life where I could say what "went" and when – even though most of these decisions concerned myself primarily (should we build shelves in the laundry room? buy stroller A or B?). I resolved to change this.

It started with a pot. Its handle had fallen off a long time ago and I had no idea it which dusty recesses it lurked – if it still lurked at all. My husband, in one of his periodic frenzied attempts to control the clutter in our life, threw it out. When I noticed its absence, I was furious.

"You went into my kitchen and threw something out without asking me?!"

He was baffled and amused by my vehemence. "It had no handle. It was dangerous. And anyway, what do you mean, 'my' kitchen?"

I was astonished at his ignorance. "You don't know that this is my kitchen?"

He laughed. "Do I get to claim a room in the house as 'mine'?"

I stormed off to more sympathetic ears – my sister-in-law and my husband's grandmother. My sister-in-law clucked sympathetically. My husband's grandmother laughed. "We all know it's your kitchen, even if he doesn't admit it."

What was I so upset about, anyway? Why did the tossing of the pot set off some alarm? What line had been crossed? Why did I feel that my role as the akeret ha-bayit had been challenged?

Input the word "homemaker" into any internet search engine and you'll find: "Make Your Own Baby Wipes!," "Sixty Uses for Table Salt," "131 Ways Vinegar Can Change Your Life!" Glance at "homemaking" magazines in the supermarket checkout line; they're a schizophrenic potpourri of highly caloric dessert recipes, super-fast diets, the "must-have" cosmetic of the season, and pop-psychology "love me as I am" articles. On the other end of the spectrum are magazines written by people for whom making their own swag curtains or soap is the ultimate in *gemütlichkeit*. Is this the sum total of homemaking?

The world around us is externally focused. Value is assigned to what can be seen: physical beauty, power, money, fame. The intangible and internal is undervalued, even denigrated. Thus, this interpretation of homemaking focuses on external trappings, robbing it of its intrinsic meaning. No one wants to dedicate their heart, soul, and life to learning how to fold napkins into swans. But what changes in a Jewish home that invests the external with significance?

What is a Jewish home? A young couple marries, and we wish them *mazal tov* – and that they should merit to build a "Faithful home in Israel, an everlasting structure." Two mortals are supposed to establish something eternal; a fine expectation for Abraham and Sarah, progenitors of the Jewish people. But how can two regular kids create a home that will live on after them?

The American Heritage Dictionary defines home as: "A place where one lives; a residence; a dwelling place together with the family or social unit that occupies it; a household; an environment offering security and happiness; a valued place regarded as a refuge or place of origin; the place, such as a country or town, where one was born or has lived for a long period; the native habitat, as of a plant or animal; the place where something is discovered, founded, developed, or promoted; a source; a headquarters or home base."

A Jewish home is all of these things and one more. Our homes are to be established on the model of God's Home – The Holy Temple. The keruvim – cherubs, male and female forms adorned the cover of the Ark with the Tablets in the Holy of Holies. They symbolize that when a marriage is built on the foundations of Torah, that home becomes a miniature Holy Temple.[7] In the Holy Temple the *kohanim*, the priests, prepared a special bread, showbread, for the table, lit the golden Menorah, and adhered to strict levels of spiritual purity. In our homes we are the priests. We separate *challa* from our dough, light our candles to usher in Shabbat and holidays, and follow the laws of family purity. These mitzvos serve as shorthand for the homemaking we do every day – to prepare food and drink for our families, give spiritual and moral guidance to our husbands and children, and participate in bringing holiness to the world through creating and drawing down souls.

The Temple derived from the Tabernacle. The Tabernacle was built to mirror the Tent of Sarah our Matriarch. Sarah's son, Isaac, married Rebecca. "He brought her to his mother's tent, married her, loved her, and was comforted for the loss of his mother."[8] The Ba'al HaTurim[9] points out that the word "ha-ohela – to the tent," appears eight times in the Torah, teaching us that God's Shechina[10]

---

[7] Rashi on Numbers 7:89.

[8] Genesis 24:67.

[9] Ibid., Rabbi Yaakov ben Asher.

[10] God's Presence, described in feminine form.

rests in eight places.[11] Thus, Sarah's tent is the model for all homes, God's and ours. Based on a Kabbalistic understanding[12] of the verse "make for Me a mikdash and I will dwell within them," we can add a ninth place where the Shechina dwells: in addition to the macro-Temple, there is the micro-Temple – our homes and hearts.

What was it about Rebecca that comforted Isaac for the loss of his mother Sarah? While Sarah lived, three constant miracles occurred in her home. Her candles remained burning from one Friday evening to the next, her dough was blessed in that it did not diminish even though it was used, and a cloud rested upon her tent to signify the Presence of the Divine.[13] When Sarah died, these miracles ceased. After her death Abraham certainly lit the Sabbath candles and prepared dough for bread, yet these miracles did not return until Rebecca stepped into Sarah's place.

These three miracles set the pattern for the actions of the priest in the macro-Temple and for the woman in her micro-Temple. They also appear in another familiar context, the "Shalom Aleichem" hymn sung at home on Friday night. "Rabbi Yossi Bar Yehudah says: Two ministering angels accompany a person on Friday night from the synagogue to his home, one good and one evil. If, when he comes to his home, he finds the candles lit,[14] the table set,[15] and the beds prepared,[16] the good angel says, "May it be His will that it should be this way next Shabbat." The evil angel answers "amen" against his will. But if the house is unprepared, then the evil angel says, "May it be His will that it should be this way next Shabbat," and the good angel answers "amen" against his will."[17] This underscores the centrality of the home. If a home brings God into every room then it is tied to something eternal, becoming a home that will endure forever. Our current crisis of intermarriage and assimilation is a symptom of the problem that we lack a sufficient number of Jewish homes. Without Jewish homes there is no Judaism. Even a tsunami of synagogues, temples and Jewish community centers can never replace the fundamental power and crucial necessity of the Jewish home.

---

[11] The Tabernacle, Gilgal, Shiloh, Nov, Giv'on, the First Temple, the Second Temple, and the future Third Temple.

[12] Rabbi Moshe Alsheich; Exodus 25:8. See also Or HaChaim there.

[13] Genesis 24:67.

[14] Signifying the mitzvah of lighting Shabbat and Yom Tov candles.

[15] Signifying the mitzvah of setting aside challah.

[16] Signifying the mitzvah of Family Purity.

[17] *Shabbat* 119b.

The candles that Sarah and Rebecca lit remained burning from erev Shabbos to erev Shabbos, foreshadowing the miracle of Chanukah. The Jews find oil enough for one day, but it lasts eight. The difference between the two miracles is that our Matriarchs had only to light their candles once a week, while the Menorah was lit every day. The Talmud says "Ner beito v'ner chanukah, ner beito kodem" – if one has only enough money to purchase oil for Shabbat lights or Chanukah lights, Shabbat takes precedence. The word used in the Talmud to refer to Shabbat lights is "beito" – his house. The home is the primary locus of Judaism and model for the Tabernacle and Temple.[18]

The connection between Abraham and Sarah and the Tabernacle goes deeper. Genesis 21:33 states that Abraham and Sarah planted an 'eishel' in Beersheba so that guests would have a shady place to rest. The Talmud says that this tree was later cut down and hewed into the "beriach ha-tichon," the central beam that supported and united the structure of the Tabernacle. God's Home was literally built upon the home of Abraham and Sarah, on a solid platform of love and giving. This same "beriach ha-tichon" holds up our homes. That is what makes a Jewish home an eternal structure. Women hold up the emotional "beriach ha-tichon" of family life. Studies show that widowers cope less well than widows. Researchers attribute this to the loss of their emotional center. Women often have close emotive relationships with other females, but for most males, their emotional centers are their wives.[19] Judaism noted this phenomenon generations ago, when Rabbi Yose said: "I never call my wife 'wife,' but 'home.'"[20]

Sadly, modern society has made a joke of the Jewish woman[21] and her unfettered giving. Too many think that giving equals weakness, having no self-

---

[18] *Likutei Sichos*, vol. 15, 183.

[19] *Soc Psychiatry Psychiatr Epidemiol.* July 1999 34 (7):391–398: Sex differences in depression after widowhood. Do men suffer more? van Grootheest DS, Beekman AT, Broese van Groenou MI, Deeg DJ. (Department of Psychiatry, Vrije Universiteit Amsterdam, The Netherlands) PMID: 10477960 [PubMed – indexed for MEDLINE]
Am J Public Health. 1996 Aug; 86(8 Pt 1):1087–1093. Mortality after the death of a spouse: rates and causes of death in a large Finnish cohort. Martikainen P, Valkonen T. Department of Sociology, University of Helsinki, Finland. PMID: 8712266 [PubMed – indexed for MEDLINE]
There are numerous other studies which find similar results.

[20] *Shabbat* 118b.

[21] Jewish Mother jokes, J.A.P. jokes. For example: One day a Jewish mother and her eight-year-old daughter were walking along the beach, just at the water's edge. Suddenly, a gigantic wave flashed up on the beach, sweeping the little girl out to sea. "Oh, God,"

respect. But doing kindnesses for others is in our spiritual genealogy. Instead of debasing us into a *schmatte*[22] it allows us to rise to the level of *imitatio Dei*. One of my fondest memories of my paternal grandparents is watching Bubbe prepare breakfast for Zayde. He sat at the table; she set a bowl in front of him and poured in cornflakes and milk. Bubbe was no milquetoast, and Zayde had made his way alone from Bessarabia to the United States as a young orphan – he was certainly capable of preparing his own cold cereal! Bubbe poured Zayde's cereal because it gave her pleasure to do so and because she was the akeret ha-bayit.

Somehow even mother-love has gotten a bad name. And yet its power is inescapable. When my nonagenarian grandmother entered a nursing home because of Alzheimer's, she was heavily sedated. In half-sleep, she cried out for "Mamme" – mother-love knows no limits. A Yiddish expression succinctly states: *Fatherless – a half-orphan; motherless – a complete orphan.*

In Genesis we read of Eliezer's journey to find a wife for Isaac. When Rebecca is chosen she runs "to tell her mother." Rashi comments,[23] "A girl only tells things of this nature to her mother." A generation later, when Rebecca's son Jacob meets Rachel, she runs to tell her *father*. This prompts Rashi to conclude that Rachel's mother had died. Otherwise she would have shared this news with her mother first.[24] We read of our mother Rachel who cries for her children in exile, inducing God to vow that her children will come home.[25] Rabbi Yosef Yitzchak Schneerson[26] expounds on mothers teaching their children to read Hebrew. It is traditional to begin with reading "kometz alef – oh."[27] This same combination of kometz alef – oh is the beginning of the word *anochi*, "I am," the first word of the Ten Commandments. The Ten Commandments encompass all of the Torah. When a mother rocks and sings to her child "kometz alef – oh" (or any other Torah song), it is said that the subconscious of the child absorbs all of

---

lamented the mother, turning her face toward heaven and shaking her fist. "This was my only baby. I can't have more children. She is the love and joy of my life. I have cherished every day that she's been with me. Give her back to me and I'll go to the synagogue every day for the rest of my life!" Suddenly, another gigantic wave flashed up and deposited the girl back on the sand. The mother looked up to heaven and said, "She had on a hat!"

[22] A rag, a nobody.

[23] Genesis 24:28.

[24] Genesis 29:12.

[25] Jeremiah 31:15.

[26] Also known as the "Frierdiker Rebbe," the sixth Lubavitcher Rebbe.

[27] The vowel, the letter, and the two combined.

Torah, from the alef of "Anochi" through Torah thoughts not yet drawn down to this world.[28]

Why are women so connected with giving? Most people assume that because you love someone, you give to them. In fact, it's just the opposite! Giving engenders love. Studies show that when people hurt others, after the fact they dislike them. Conversely, when a person does good to another, they like them. This amazing concept is seen in the Hebrew word for love – *ahava*. It comes from the root-word *hav*, meaning "to give." Consider the mitzvah of *tzedaka*. We think that because there are poor people, God commanded us to give. Rabbi Yerucham Levovitz of Mir says it's just the opposite! Because we need to learn what it is to be a giving person, God created some people in need. Maimonides discusses various levels of giving charity. Some think it's better to give a lot to one cause than a little to many causes; Maimonides disagrees. Since giving *tzedaka* teaches us to be giving people, it is better to give repeatedly and frequently, even if the individual amount is less. Compassion and caring are a central beam that holds up mankind's home – our world.[29]

Noam Elimelech[30] comments that the first verse in Genesis "Bereishis – in the beginning," that this word can also be read "bishvil reishis – for the sake of reishis, beginnings or firsts" the world was created. He lists three things that are called reishis: the Jewish people, Torah, and the first fruits. Each of these can be correlated to three pillars that hold up the world:[31] Torah learning, prayer and acts of kindness. Each of these pillars of service of God can be symbolized by one particular letter of the alef-beit. Torah[32] is symbolized by the alef – meaning first or head. Prayer is symbolized by the *bet*, meaning house, because of the service of the "*bet* hamikdash – the Holy Temple." Acts of kindness are symbolized by the *gimmel*, which means to tend to others. This made me wonder if one reason that women are exempt from prayer with a quorum is because a woman is already involved in the "service of the bet" and halacha dictates that one who is in the midst of performing one positive mitzvah is exempt from doing another.

This facility for empathy, emotion, and nurturing is innate to women. When God created Chava (Eve), It says "va-yiven – And He built woman."[33] Va-yiven is also a cognate of the word "bina," showing that God instilled within woman an

---

[28] *Likutei Sichos,* volume 15, pg. 183.

[29] *Pirkei Avot* 5:3.

[30] Rabbi Elimelech of Lizhensk.

[31] *Pirkei Avot* 1:2.

[32] And God, since Torah is an expression of God.

[33] Genesis 2:23.

extra measure of bina, understanding. The word "built" also reminds us that women are like buildings in that they are narrower on top than on the bottom so that they can safely carry a child. For women, giving and nurturing are "built-ins," not "add-ons." Furthermore, being built from an internal part of Adam[34] made Chava and all women after her more internal creations than man. As it states in Psalms: "All the glory of the princess is *penima* – within"[35] the internal sphere of emotions and feelings. Studies show that women talk more than men, and their conversations more often concern feelings and emotions.[36][37][38]

A survey of Scriptures reveals a fascinating connection between wisdom and building a home. The very first verse in Genesis states "B'reishis – In the beginning, God created the heavens and the earth." Rabbi Yonasan ben Uziel translates the word "reishis" to mean "wisdom." Thus, "using wisdom God created the heavens and the earth." The word "using" (the B of "b'reishis") is spelled with the letter *bet* in Hebrew. The meaning of the word *bet* is *bayit* – house. Humankind's house, the world, was built with wisdom.

"Wisdom has built her home; she hewed out her seven pillars. She has prepared her meat and mixed her wine; she also set her table. She sent out her servants to call to the high places of the city.... 'Come and eat of my bread and drink of the wine I mixed....'"[39]

The classical commentators agree that Wisdom, personified here as a woman, refers to God. This passage describes the creation of the world (i.e., the preparing of the food and drink), the sending of Adam and Chava to populate the world and a call to the souls above to descend (the servants calling to the high places). Once in this world, God implores mankind "Eat of my bread." This is the Torah. The Talmud says that sharing bread with another draws us together – this is the greatness of bread.[40]

---

[34] Variously described as Adam's side, rib. Other commentators state that the primordial human being was a multi-drogynous creature, containing male and female back to back.

[35] Psalms 45:14.

[36] *Kiddushin* 49b.

[37] *Emotional Intelligence* by Daniel Goleman points out that MRI scans show that women decipher emotions from facial expressions more sensitively than men do.

[38] A study by Shlomo Argamon at the Illinois Institute of Technology in Chicago developed a program that can determine the gender of an author. Women tend to use terms that apply to personal relationships more frequently than men do.

[39] Proverbs 9:1, 3, 5.

[40] *Sanhedrin* 103b.

Kabbalistically, the seven pillars of wisdom's home, above, symbolize the seven emotive attributes of God and mankind, known as "middot": chessed, gevurah, tiferet, netzach, hod, yesod, malchut.[41]

The verse above can also refer to the donning of tefillin. The arm and head tefillin represent feminine and masculine energies respectively. They also symbolize the two main facets of Torah life – doing and learning. The 'feminine' tefillin is the arm tefillin of action, worn next to the heart, to show the expression of emotion through action. The coils of the arm tefillin are wrapped seven times – the seven pillars. They represent the manifestation of God within nature, as seen in the seven days of creation, the seven-day week, the Sabbatical year, and so forth.[42] The boxes of the tefillin which contain the Torah verses are called "batim" – houses in Hebrew. Thus, the "house" holds the wisdom of Torah. Kabbala explains that what a man achieves through donning tefillin, a woman does through "strapping on" her home.[43] A man utilizes the physical construction of leather, parchment, ink and sinews, to attach himself to the wisdom of the "house." A woman likewise employs various physical elements of life to create and unite with her home.

The story of the Hebrew midwives in Egypt may shed light on the connection between building a home and wisdom. When a new Pharaoh rises to power and feels threatened by the Jews in his nation, he devises a plan to destroy them. "Come, let us deal *wisely* with them, lest they multiply..."[44] His "wise" plan is to enslave the Jews and cause them to die out. When that backfires[45] he calls upon the head midwives of the Jews and tells them that they must kill all baby boys at birth.[46] "But the midwives *feared God* and did not as the king of Egypt commanded them, but made the baby boys live."[47] The text further states "Because the midwives feared God, God made houses for them." [48] We have a

---

[41] Loosely translated as: giving, withholding, synthesis, victory, awe, foundation, and kingship. A fuller explanation of these terms is outside the focus of this essay. For a comprehensive treatment of these and related concepts see *Mystical Concepts in Chassidism* by Jacob Immanuel Schochet (Brooklyn, NY: 1979). An easy-to-understand explanation of these terms can be found at www.aish.com by clicking on the link to "Kabbala 101."

[42] *Tefillin: The Inside Story* by Rabbi Moshe Shlomo Emanuel.

[43] *Tefillin*, Rabbi Aryeh Kaplan.

[44] Exodus 1:10.

[45] The more they afflict the Jews, the more numerous the Jews become. (Exodus 1:12)

[46] Exodus 1:16.

[47] Exodus 1:17.

[48] Exodus 1:21.

king who misuses wisdom to destroy the House of Israel and God-fearing midwives who thwart his plans. Their fear of God is the basis of their wisdom, as it says "The beginning of wisdom is fear of God."[49] Through their wisdom they built the House of Israel. And they were rewarded by God with houses of their own. Rabbi Shlomo Yitzchaki [50] elucidates: "houses" means dynasties of Kohanim, Levites, and kings. These three categories of Jews fulfill their roles in Temple times. Thus, the reward for their self sacrifice in building many micro-temples is that they are part of the building of the macro-Temple of the future.[51]

The chapters of Exodus concerning the building of the Tabernacle deepen the connection between wisdom and building a home. God tells Moses: "See, I have called by name Bezalel... and I have filled him with... *wisdom, understanding, and knowledge*, and all types of creative work."[52] "And in the hearts of all who are *wise-hearted* I have put *wisdom* that they may make all that I have commanded."[53] Proverbs echoes these verses: "With *wisdom* a home will be built, and with *understanding* it will be established. And with *knowledge* its rooms are filled...."[54] These three intellectual powers of God and mankind, *wisdom (chochma)*, *understanding (tevuna/bina) and knowledge (da'at)*, can loosely be described as idea, development, and implementation. Thus, to "build a home" and furnish and decorate its "interior" requires the active involvement of all of one's intellectual powers. This is bolstered by the verse from Proverbs "God with *wisdom* founded the earth, established with *understanding* the heavens. By His *knowledge* the depths were cracked open, and the skies dripped down dew."[55]

The portions of the book of 1 Kings that describe Solomon's building of the Temple reinforce this. "And God gave *wisdom* to Solomon, and much *understanding*, and expansiveness of heart like the sands of the seashore. And Solomon's wisdom exceeded that of all of the people of the East, and all the wisdom of Egypt. For he was wiser than all men...."[56] [57] When Solomon is ready

---

[49] Psalms 110:10.

[50] Popularly known as Rashi.

[51] *Midrash HaGadol* gives a fascinating interpretation to the phrase "vayaas lahem batim," that G-d made the midwives into beams of a house. So at one and the same time they serve to hold and support a "safe house" for the entire nation and for themselves – an apt description of wife/motherhood!

[52] Exodus 31:1–3, see likewise 35:31, 36:1–2.

[53] Exodus 31:6, see likewise 35:10, 35:35, 36:4, 8.

[54] Proverbs 24:3.

[55] Proverbs 3:19.

[56] Kings I, 5:9–10.

to begin construction of the Temple, he sends for Chiram, who is described as being "filled with *wisdom* and *understanding* and skill...."[58] When the construction is completed, Solomon leads the dedication ceremony with a prayer. He wonders how God will dwell in this house if even the heavens are not able to contain God's presence, but goes on to say that if this house is one where people seek to draw closer to God, then all the people of the world will know that "Your Name is called upon this house which I have built."[59] The wisest of all men has given us a prescription for making our homes ones where God will dwell.

"The wise amongst women builds her home, but the foolish one *with her [own] hands* tears it down."[60] A wise woman builds her home through her supervision of everything that comes into the home whether it is a physical item, an attitude, or a spiritual perspective. She understands that building a home takes wisdom, intelligence, and close examination. A foolish woman destroys her home through lack of supervision over her household because she does not understand or value her crucial importance and influence.[61] The phrase *"with her [own] hands"* suggests the verse from Exodus concerning the building of the Tabernacle:[62] "Every wise-hearted woman *spun with her hands*; and they brought the spun yarn of turquoise, purple, and scarlet wool, and the linen."[63] This is followed by another verse concerning spinning and wisdom: "All the women whose hearts stirred them up with wisdom *spun the goat* [hair]."[64] Spinning is mentioned only twice[65] in all of Scripture, and both times in connection with chochma – wisdom.[66] What is the wisdom of spinning, and how does it connect to building a home? Spinning involves many steps. The animal must be shorn, the fleece carded to separate the hairs, then sorted into shorter hairs and longer

---

[57] Solomon is also known by the name Isi'el. This is explained to mean "God is with me, so I am able," (*Ishei HaTanach*, Rabbi Yishai Chasida), a good message for us to remember. Lev Eliahu (Rabbi Eliahu Lopian) says that the name Isi'el means that he understood how to combine the letters of the Hebrew alphabet – a spiritual ability that finds an echo in the physical act of spinning.

[58] Kings I, 7:13–14.

[59] Kings I, 8:27, 43 – intervening verses have been paraphrased.

[60] Proverbs 14:1.

[61] Rabbi Levi ben Gershom.

[62] Mesorah, Proverbs 14:1.

[63] Exodus, 35:25 – referring to the inner covering of the Tabernacle.

[64] Exodus 35:26 – referring to the outermost covering of the Tabernacle.

[65] Proverbs does mention spinning implements – distaff and spindle – in chapter 31, popularly known as "Eishet Chayil."

[66] Twice in Exodus (ibid); the third time in Proverbs 31:19.

ones, each with their own purpose. Then the threads are spun into yarn using a spindle or wheel. This is the wisdom of building a home: we take natural materials, clean them, separate them into individual fibers, and then bind them back together to make thread – something greater than the sum of its parts. Spun wool is magnitudinally greater than hundreds of threads laid side by side.[67]

When the Torah was given, the Jews responded "na'aseh venishma" – we will do and we will learn. The Sefat Emet says that na'aseh – the doing of God's will – is the building of a Jewish home. Learning Torah is important, but implementing God's will is the main thrust of Jewish life. Pirkei Avos 1:17 says, "Learning is not the *ikar*, the main thing; doing is."[68] Our nature as builders is innate – just as the womb builds a structure to nurture life, so too we can build our homes to nurture our families, carrying out this privilege of "na'aseh," expressing our womanly wisdom and understanding.

Homemaking is "101 Uses for Vinegar" and the "Best Brownie Recipe"; it is scrubbing the stain on the toddler's pants and sweeping the floor for the nth time that day while listening to your preteen daughter discuss her latest class politics, and spinning all of this into whole cloth. That is chochma. A Jewish home is sacred space and we are in the service of the Almighty. While we are linking our clean floors, healthful meals and emotional nurturing we are also making a home on a cosmic level.

---

[67] Yet the women mentioned in the second verse went one step further. They "spun the goat," washing and spinning the wool on the animal's back (*Shabbat* 99). Once the tapestry was complete, they cut it off (Rabbi Shlomo Yitzchaki, Exodus 35:26). What purpose is there in all this trouble when they could simply shear the animal first? Anything that is excised from its life source is susceptible to spiritual impurity, including wool. By spinning on the backs of goats, these women ensured that the spiritual purity of the tapestries was of the highest standard. If so, why was this not done with everything associated with the Tabernacle? What was so important about the second set of tapestries that this extra step was taken? This set was the outermost covering of the Tabernacle. It was the essential piece which held the Tabernacle together and made it a tent. Without the outer covering, the Tabernacle could not be a place of habitation for God, but would remain simply a collection of individual items. This facility for uniting disparate items into one whole, for making a home, is the quintessence of womanhood. Thus the women showed extra care and wisdom in ensuring that the item which united the parts, making a home for God, was of the highest spiritual status. (Rav Samson Raphael Hirsch: *Commentary on the Torah*: II, 677–678).

[68] Interesting that the *ikar* is *maaseh* (action), just as the *akeret habayit* is involved with the *naaseh!*

So, why is it that buildings fall down, but never self-assemble? Why won't that sock eventually make its way into the dresser drawer? Kabbalistic teachings confirm the hunch that chaos in the home relates to chaos in the world. Before God created our world, He created the world of *tohu* – chaos. Tohu was a world overflowing with Godly energy but had few containers to hold this abundance of energy. Because the containers were stuffed beyond capacity, they shattered, and the Godly energy fell in a shower of sparks. In Kabbala this is called shevirat hakelim, the shattering of the vessels. After this, God created the Universe in which we live. This world is called *tikkun* – correction. The world of tikkun is the exact opposite of tohu in that we have an abundance of external 'shells' in which to store Godly energy – but there is quantitatively less Godly energy. Our job in the world of tikkun is to dig through the ruins of the broken vessels of tohu to find the great lights buried there and then to store them in our large, empty vessels. According to Kabbalistic thought,[69] wisdom derives its power from the dazzling chaos of tohu that existed *right before creation*. Wisdom is the ability to take disparate strands of knowledge and abilities and to spin them together into one whole. Our struggle is to *combine* the power of tohu with the containment and focus of tikkun. Kabbala explains[70] that chaos and brokenness are the prerequisites for a situation in which wisdom has application. Without that, there is no possibility for wisdom to exercise its talents.

So, my exertions to corral the itinerant socks, to move the dust off the family photos and out of the house – essentially, to direct the energy and power in my home toward a Godly purpose, mirrors our efforts to do the same in God's Home, the universe as a whole. Perhaps this is one reason why Kabbalistic teachings refer to God as the *akeret ha-bayit*, "the mainstay of the home" of the Universe. God too is engaged in a struggle to keep His Home from being wrecked by His sometimes thoughtless and scattered children.

When our efforts are for the purpose of drawing Godliness into our homes, they rise above the mundane. In the Talmud, the sage Resh Lakish says that without the acceptance of the Torah by the Jewish people, God would return all of existence to its primordial state of chaos – tohu. The vessels in which we store Godly energy are the commandments. By our active involvement in carrying them out, we bring order to chaos and firmly establish our homes and the Home of God.

Exodus begins with the building of individual homes and concludes with the construction and erection of the Tabernacle. "A man from the house of Levi took

---

[69] *Derech HaShem* by Rabbi Moses Chaim Luzzato.

[70] Ginsburgh, Yitzchak. *The Alef Bet.*

as a wife the daughter of a Levite. The woman conceived and bore a son and saw that he was good."[71] Moses's birth filled his parents' home with light; just so, each individual family and home have the power to bring much light to the world. Through building these small temples,[72] we act to assemble and establish our great Temple, may it be speedily in our days.

For further reading:

Frankiel, Tamar. *The Voice of Sarah: Feminine Spirituality and Traditional Judaism.* New York: 1990.

Aiken, Lisa. *To Be a Jewish Woman. Lanham,* MD: 1992.

Freeman, Tzvi. *The Book of Purpose: Meditations My Rebbe Taught Me, volume 1.* New York, NY: 2004.

---

[71] Exodus 2:1–2.

[72] "Moshiach's coming will be hastened by our gifts to tzedaka and by making tzedaka a fundamental part of our being. In this context, it is worthwhile to mention the importance of having a tzedaka pushka placed in the kitchen and for a woman to give to tzedaka before she begins to cook. Needless to say, this is in addition to giving a portion, and indeed a choice portion, of the food she prepares to the poor." Excerpt of a letter from Rabbi Menachem Mendel Schneerson OBM to N'Shei U'Bnos Chabad Convention, 28 Iyar, 5751.

My Grandmother's Candlesticks

Yocheved Reich

In this story, the author gives voice to the true life experiences of her former students in
Be'er Hagolah, a school for Russian immigrants in Brooklyn, NY.

I didn't know why we had to come to America. It was hard to understand why
my parents, comfortably ensconced in the security of the Workers' Paradise,
wanted to subject their family to a land of filthy streets, juvenile delinquency,
and unbridled freedom. For material gain, some would say. Free enterprise!
Capitalist initiative! I doubted it.

Living above a fish store and under train tracks was not my idea of luxury.
My parents who worked long hours as cooks trying to put bread on their own
table after long days of putting bread on someone else's, were not your typical
tycoons. As for me, I was pressed into baby-sitting for my younger brother while

my parents were at work and other girls went to the movies. I thus viewed myself as an accomplice to my parents' decision to desert the shores of happiness. Free enterprise? More enterprise than free, is how I felt about it. What was for free?

There were always some kind souls willing to attribute our motives for immigration to noble causes. We had come to America to "identify as Jews," they would say, to "flee religious persecution." Well, I for one was never persecuted. More importantly, I was never religious.

Which brings me to the matter of my grandmother's candlesticks. When she was alive they were useless appendages to her dinner table on Friday nights. I was vaguely aware that they signified some quaint religious observance. I didn't know exactly why they were there. My parents didn't either, and I wonder whether my grandmother herself remembered. It's not that in the Russian atmosphere of stifled religious observance I was afraid to ask; I simply didn't care. Lighting candles on Friday night was just one of those antiquated practices I thought my grandmother had, like brushing her teeth with salt water instead of toothpaste and drinking warm milk before retiring at night.

I was therefore surprised to find that some of the precious space allotted to us for baggage was for these candlesticks. They were fashioned of tin, blackened by age, and on their value alone they would never have merited a trip around the room, let alone half way around the world. Mother, however, was firmly decided that they were to come with us. "These were Babushka's candlesticks," was all she would say, and the matter was put to rest.

We did have a few precious valuables that accompanied us on our trip as secret stowaways. One by one, these earrings, necklaces, bracelets and rings disappeared in the form of bribes to the various border officials. In search of illegal valuables, these officials would slice open our bars of soap, squeeze our toothpaste out of the tubes and, with equal aplomb, pocket the jewelry we offered in exchange for a coveted stamp on our visas.

By the time we reached Berst, our point of departure, we were left with barely more than our clothing, my grandmother's candlesticks, and a few personal items of worth. One of these was my grandmother's wedding ring which she had given to me before her passing. I had loved my grandmother and cherished this ring as my most precious possession. I wore it on a length of thread suspended under my dress, hidden from greedy eyes.

As we neared the last check point, I held my breath. The customs officer was a woman of the shrewdest kind, and by the benefit of my experience in similar encounters, I knew nothing would escape her notice. She soon gestured to my mother, in almost imperceptible manner, that she wanted the candlesticks. I breathed a sigh of relief. Let her take both tin candlesticks. It seemed it was taking my parents an interminably long time to give the official the candlesticks. Why didn't they just hand them over? My father turned to face me and the little hairs on the back of my neck froze to attention. Something was wrong. *Give her the ring*, my father whispered between clenched teeth. My palms broke out in sweat. There was no time for thought, no space for question. An impatient official was a dangerous official. If I hesitated a moment my father would have to rip the ring from my neck himself to protect us all. Slowly I detached the ring and joined my family as we filed past the checkpoint.

The joy of freedom was lost on me. I was crushed and enraged. The guard had not specifically asked for my ring; she would have been satisfied with the candlesticks. It was my mother adamantly refusing to surrender the candlesticks, who had offered my ring instead. I hurled words at my parents with furious force. Why, I demanded to know, were a meaningless pair of tin Sabbath candlesticks worth more to us than the ring my grandmother had worn on the happiest day of her life? What sudden interest did we have in an empty tradition that my family had discounted long ago? We should have buried the candlesticks with my grandmother, I raged, along with all the rest of the archaic customs practiced by our primitive forbearers. My father had no words, and my mother had no answer, for on a conscious level they agreed with me. All my mother could say was, "These are Babushka's candlesticks." At the time I vaguely understood what subconscious feelings my mother had not been able to articulate. She wanted these candlesticks because they represented a link to the past; the passkey to a heritage of which she was not wholly ashamed. This made me uncomfortable, for it was a feeling inconsistent with our politics and ideas. The inconsistency was frightening. It seemed to me that my parents, paragons of intelligent rationale, had fallen prey to maudlin sentimentality. What strange things were happening to us as we embarked for America?

Once we were settled, my parents were of the opinion that a Jewish child should be sent to a Jewish school, and so I was enrolled in a yeshiva for teenage Russian immigrant girls like myself. I favored this idea because after all, I was proud of being a Jew. To me being Jewish was a simple matter, a matter of birth. It never occurred to me that being Jewish involved a system of practices and beliefs. I was totally unprepared for the onslaught of shocking facts presented in the yeshiva: God is omniscient and all-powerful. He is here whether or not you believe in Him. He gives reward and punishment. He is aware of all events and thoughts, past, present and future.

As the months passed, my parents would dismiss these fantastic fantasies that I brought home with an educated wave of the latest issue of the Russian-language newspaper. But, they were quick to assure me, as Jews, they did believe in God! Try as I might, however, I could not get them to give me a definitive statement of what and who, exactly, they thought God to be. Then there was the disturbing matter of the chain. My teacher claimed that Jews were links in a chain of tradition handed down from one generation to the next. I had always been taught that as intelligent, modern products of Soviet society, we were eons ahead of our ancient and primitive ancestors. Now I was expected to believe that instead of the proud Soviet, I was really a disadvantaged Jew because the Jewish chain of tradition had been broken by the Communists. I was far less educated than my pious forefathers had been. The whole issue was unsettling for despite my automatic defenses, I found myself interested in the yeshiva teachings. The "Shabbos party" each week aggravated my discomfort.

To our class of teenage girls, the novelty of the "Shabbos party" was a welcome break from schoolwork. It was entertaining enough until the teacher introduced the Shabbos candlesticks. At first sight of them my stomach churned. I couldn't help it. The association with the disturbing incident of my grandmother's candlesticks was bitter. My ring, which had meant a great deal to me, had been sacrificed for a pair of candlesticks which meant nothing. The uneasiness I had felt at the time resurfaced in a new conflict. If these candlesticks weren't meaningless, I reasoned bitterly, but brought peace, light, security as my teacher now claimed, why had my mother discarded the custom? And if they were so meaningless that she had never used them, why had she insisted upon keeping them? If the ideas I was learning here in the yeshiva were as meaningless as my parents claimed, why was I here at all? What was the "Jewishness" of which I was so proud? And if these ideas weren't so meaningless but important enough for me to change my life, why didn't I believe in them? I was confused, sickened, and overwhelmed at the certainty that eventually I would have to cast my lot with one side or the other of the argument. I would either accept what Judaism claimed had always been my own or turn my back and walk away. And how could I turn my back on being Jewish? As sure as my shadow, it would follow me forever.

I brought my frustration home with me. I observed that my parents and other Russian Jews did have certain practices they adhered to: The Yizkor prayer on the holidays, sounding the shofar on Rosh ha-Shanah, eating matzah on Pesach. I saw that they observed these few customs not as a result of any intelligent process of selection but because these had somehow eluded the filter of Soviet orientation. Could it be that whole generation of Jews, including myself, had been victims of ignorance imposed on us by Communist design? I realized that my grandmother's candlesticks had died a slow death. Smothered by years of anti-religious laws, snuffed out by ignorance, the spirit and flame of the candlesticks had been extinguished, leaving only the scarred tin and the shell of an ancient practice. Was I then, too, to submit? No matter how long it would take me, I would reinstate my link to a long gone past. I would breathe new life into my grandmother's candlesticks.

At this time my relationship with my parents was undergoing a perceptible change. They had hardly believed that the freedom for which they had longed would infiltrate their home in this unforeseen manner. They saw, to their consternation, that I was quick to take advantage of America's new freedom of thought and expression and increasingly, our views on various subjects began to widen in different directions. They saw their friends' children experimenting with behavior, clothes and fads popular on the streets but unacceptable to traditional Russian parents. More and more, they heard their friends lament their helplessness in exacting standards of behavior from their children in America's permissive climate. In short, they were losing the control that most Russian parents took for granted. My parents began watching me closely, sharply searching for the first signs of what they called "degeneration."

My parents had nothing to fear from me in that direction. I might have been tempted to experiment with the drugs of our neighbors' children, but I was off on a direction of my own. After months of concentrated reading which I had solicited from my teacher, the internal ferment of my convictions was coming to a boil. All this time, I had kept my thoughts to myself, zealously guarding my social status among my classmates. In classroom discussions of Jewish philosophy I had hedged, never committed myself, never daring to expose my sympathy with the teacher's views. I have never performed any mitzvah on my own, never participated in a school-sponsored Jewish event, never accepted any well intentioned invitation for Shabbos. But I could no longer live in my world of thoughts. I had to commit myself with some action. However slight that action might be in the great scale of things, to me it would be a dramatic step. Just where it would lead me, I was unwilling to admit. I only knew that it had to be done. I was curious and excited to see how I would feel. The time had come, I decided, for me to light the Shabbos candles in my grandmother's candlesticks.

The first part of the week passed uneventfully. Friday dawned, and only I perceived that the world trembled with the rising of the sun. My parents could never be expected to understand or even sympathize; they would interpret this one act as my having been converted to a fanatical "pesati." They would be shocked and horrified. I therefore concentrated on myself and my surroundings. As the day waned, I arranged my room in quiet order. I showered, dressed and reached for the package hidden under my bed. During the week I had surreptitiously gathered its contents: candles, matches and my grandmother's candlesticks. Furtively I made my way through the house to the one room where I would not be discovered. I thrust my package inside, and locked myself in the bathroom. I didn't know that it's improper to perform a mitzvah in the bathroom. In my mind, I was performing the ultimate service to God, in the most sheltered place I knew. I set up the candlesticks on the edge of the sink, lit the candles and in the quiet, dim light, covered my face. Suddenly, there was knocking on the bathroom door. The knocking was my father's. I ignored it, desperately trying to reenter that uplifted chamber of holiness in my mind where I had been for those last few seconds. The knocking grew louder, accompanied by warnings, threats and shouts. We had only one bathroom in this house, what right had I to monopolize it? I had worked myself up to this moment, and now I was shaken, in the sweat of violent anticlimax. Taking hold of myself, I answered that I would be out in a minute. Frantically I doused the candles and hid them with the candlesticks in the water tank. A delicate wisp of smoke still curled behind me as I unlatched the lock and with crimson face, edged past my father. His face was dark and as he moved into the bathroom I heard him sniff.

The tears had not yet started when I was summoned back to the bathroom by my father's stentorian voice and my mother's anguished cry. They had found the evidence, they charged; it was no use denying it. I had been smoking cigarettes in the bathroom, idiot that I was. What else had I been doing? What other things had I been hiding from them? Had they brought me to America to bring disgrace on the family?

My cries of innocence were to no avail. It was only after I showed them the candlesticks in the water tank that there was complete silence. My father shrugged, shook his head, and muttering to himself, left the bathroom. My mother, her eyes moist with relief, looked away in embarrassment. She rescued the candlesticks, rinsed them in the sink and after a minute's hesitation, handed them back to me.

Months passed. On Friday nights, my father still shrugs, and my mother looks away. But my candles are lit, placed prominently on the dining room table, and the tin of my grandmother's candlesticks shine like silver. I have many conflicts that must be resolved, many doubts that must be laid to rest. These days I am asking many questions, and questioning many answers. My teachers encourage me and give me strength when I am down. On Friday nights, when I cover my face to say the blessing over the candles, I am temporarily overwhelmed by darkness, and once again aware of the darkness of ignorance. I am heartened, however, that for me, illumination lies only as far as my grandmother's candlesticks, and the lights that glow beyond my covered eyes.

For further reading:

Lubavitch Women's Organization *A Candle of My Own: Thoughts on Shabbos Candles by Girls Who Light Them*. New York: 1979.

Branover, Herman. *Return: The Spiritual Odyssey of a Soviet Scientist*. Jerusalem: 1982.

Chazan, Aaron. *Deep in the Russian Night*. New York, NY: 1990.

The Holy One, Blessed be He, said to Moses, "Go speak to the daughters of Israel [and ask them] whether they wish to receive the Torah." Why were the women asked first? Because the way of the men is to follow the opinion of women.

Pirkei de-Rabbi Eliezer, *chapter 41*

A Personal Retrospective on Women and Jewish Learning

Esther Shkop

(Some names and particulars have been modified to protect the privacy of the author's family.)

In her review of Shoshana Pantel Zolty's important book about the history of Jewish women's education and their study of Torah,[1] Dr. Sylvia Barack Fishman[2] notes the "critical evidence of the widespread nature of literacy among Jewish women in many societies" and points out that the "intellectual roles accorded Jewish women in traditional Jewish societies were often far more extensive than might appear."

While there is substantial evidence that Jewish women throughout the ages were far more learned in Jewish lore and law than most of our contemporaries, there is a sense that for centuries the erudite woman, proficient in original texts, was more the exception than the rule. Even if the numbers of female Jewish scholars throughout history were large, the fact remains that formal education and schooling for the majority of Jewish women was not a priority of communal life. Consequently, reviewing the same book, Malke Bina[3] comments, "I thank

---

[1] *And All Your Children Shall Be Learned: Women and the Study of Torah in Jewish Law and History* (Northvale, NJ: 1993).

[2] Assistant Professor of Contemporary Jewish Life, Near Eastern and Judaic Studies at Brandeis University.

[3] Founder and director of MaTaN, the Women's Institute of Torah Studies in Jerusalem, Israel.

God every day that I was born in the middle of the twentieth century and not in earlier periods when so little Jewish learning was available to members of the female sex."

In reading these disparate views, I was struck by how deeply they resounded with the conflicting messages I myself had received from the women in my family. I had grown up in the presence of the two extremes, and came to know first-hand the Old World women who exemplified the two opposite sides of the coin.

My parents emigrated from Israel to America in the 1950s in search of medical treatment for my baby sister, who had been crippled by polio. Although I attended an American public school, my Jewish education was based in the home and augmented by several European immigrants who taught Talmud Torah at our local synagogue. As a daughter of Chassidic parents, fluent in Yiddish and with some proficiency in Hebrew, I was among the rare children who identified with and appreciated the scholarship and piety of these teachers, who were primarily refugees or survivors of the Holocaust. Most of my American classmates were put off by their thickly accented English and freely expressed contempt for the "old-fashioned" instruction. As a "greenhorn" myself, I was fascinated by the lessons; and my teachers – hungering for a receptive ear – favored me with focused attention. One teacher in particular stands out in my memory. He had escaped Germany in the late 1930s and had taught at the Rabbi Shimshon Raphael Hirsch *Hochschule* in Frankfurt, of which he spoke with pained longing. He taught me to read Rashi script and how to analyze a verse of Torah, and excitedly urged me to ask questions and voice my ideas. Consequently, I developed skills and knowledge in Torah studies far exceeding those of most students in the synagogue afternoon *cheder*. Nevertheless, these achievements paled to nothingness in the light of the women and girls I would meet later in Israel.

My father was worried that we would become too Americanized and that my Jewish education was inadequate. He resolved to send me to study in Jerusalem and live with my grandparents in Mea Shearim. Despite a traditional upbringing and a mode of dress and behavior that made me blatantly different from most of my peers, I had unwittingly absorbed many of the mannerisms and ideas of 1960s America. Thus the transition to my grandparents' small apartment in the heart of the Old Yishuv of Jerusalem was jarring. Even as I struggled to overcome the culture shock, I was intrigued and enchanted by my grandmothers.

My paternal Babbe Fraidel was a firebrand, witty and sharp-tongued, who rushed from task to task and spoke a mile a minute. Her speech was peppered with sharp humor, sweetened with Biblical quotations and salted with *yeshivish* (Aramaic) expressions. Her sons and husband admired her wisdom and were enamored with her loquacious charm. Babbe Fraidel regaled me with stories about her mother, for whom I'm named, whose erudition in Talmudic texts was legendary.

As an only child, my great-grandmother – Babbe Esther Malka[4] – became the heiress and transmitter of her father's scholarship and social honor. She had acquired her learning from her father, the rabbi of Hebron, whom she served as secretary and reader since he was blinded in his mid-thirties by diabetes. Apparently, she brought a quickness and fierce intelligence to these tasks. My father had described how she tested him and his brothers on their weekly learning of both written Law and *Gemara* while serving them home-baked rolls and *café au lait*. Esther Malka was renowned in Old Jerusalem and she expected her seven daughters and three sons to live up to their legacy. Her mother-in-law, who was also famous for great wit and wisdom, had purportedly hand-picked her for her only son. The two of them were instrumental in founding the first Jewish asylum for the insane in Jerusalem, as well as a mutual-aid society for pregnant women in which members assisted one another before, during and after childbirth. The family joke was that the two of them were more successful with the girls than with the boys.

Her daughter, my Babbe Fraidel, who was no less extraordinary, proved a vivacious guide into the ways and lore of Old Jerusalem, as I tripped after her as she literally dashed from one task to another. She awoke me at dawn on my first day in Israel and urged me to join her in baking – explaining that any woman worth her salt can finish her household duties between morning prayers and ten o'clock, before the sun gets too hot. I then rushed to keep up with her as she moved from stall to stall in the marketplace, haggling with the merchants who jocularly called her by name, exchanging news with her fellow shoppers, inquiring about their children and husbands. She knew everyone, and everyone knew her.

On the other hand, my maternal grandmother, Babbe Gittel, long widowed and silently prayerful, was soft-spoken, slow-moving and warm, but not nearly as much fun. It took several years before I understood and revered the hours she spent in prayer and study. Using Yiddish translations, she was knowledgeable in Midrashic literature, the entire *Tanakh,* and had a thorough understanding of halakhic literature. Her learning was acquired primarily in her later years, when she filled her lonesome hours with holy books. She rarely offered an opinion and never jumped into a Shabbos table argument. But when asked (on rare and

---

[4] She actually was born on Purim, and she took on the name and persona of the heroine, Queen Esther, Malka meaning "queen" in Hebrew.

usually sad occasions) by a granddaughter – whose tearful eyes reflected a sincere desire for her wisdom – she revealed a hidden life of the mind, heart, and spirit.

Babbe Gittel and I became close only when I matured enough to care. Then and only then did she open her cabinets and share her treasures with me. She showed me the unfinished *Tallis* bag she had been embroidering for my grandfather when he had died suddenly of a massive heart attack. She showed me his books and his paintings (deep, dark secrets), her wedding portraits, all hidden among the starched and ironed linens. And she told me her story and her thoughts. By then I was married and had a baby daughter, and we talked in the dusk of *seudah shlishit* when I paid my weekly visit.

Both of my grandmothers, who were reared in Old Jerusalem, attributed their education to three years of formal tutelage under one or another nameless "rebbetzins" who were assigned to teach the young girls aged six to nine. Their curriculum consisted of learning the mechanics of reading and writing in Hebrew and Yiddish, as well as the rudiments of arithmetic. The former language was reserved for prayer, while Yiddish became the mode of oral and written expression. Once they had mastered the *siddur* and could translate the prayers, the little girls were taught the Pentateuch and some commentaries through the Yiddish translations, and were introduced to the major stories of the early prophets and some selections from the *haftarot*. They were then escorted through some moral and midrashic essays (in Yiddish, of course). Teachings about keeping a kosher home, observance of Shabbos and holidays, social and ethical behavior as well as cooking, sewing and housekeeping were left to their mothers and other female relatives.

Once her basic literacy was assured, a young girl in turn-of-the-century Jerusalem could rely on her own curiosity and access to books for the continuation of her Torah studies. Secular literature was generally *verboten.* If the women in one's family were more knowledgeable, and more affluent, that girl was encouraged to use her spare time for reading. Reading aloud and singing in unison was common as the women sat in the late afternoons sewing and embroidering.

Since my Babbe Fraidel was never much good with a needle she read and sang, and was allowed by her relatively well-to-do parents to continue her formal schooling through the age of twelve. She read newspapers regularly and seemed to have a good grasp of geography and general history. She often spoke about the fall of the Ottoman empire and the struggles of the Yishuv during World War I, and explained all the political intricacies behind the fall of the Austro-Hungarian Empire and the rise of the British Empire. She was proud of her command of Arabic and Ladino and "showed off" how much English she still remembered.

On the other hand, Babbe Gittel's parents were much poorer, and she began to work in the family grocery store by the age of ten, where she learned the fine art of dealing with customers, keeping accounts and negotiating prices. Nevertheless, she had learned not only the lore but also the passion of *Yiddishkeit*.

Years later I read Rabbi Joseph B. Soloveitchik's eulogy of the Rebbetzin of Talne in which he noted that, historically, mothers were entrusted with the transmission of their own *mesorah*, distinct from the tradition of the fathers. In describing what he had learned from the "Torah of Your Mother,"[5] Rabbi Soloveichik recalls:

> Most of all I learned that Judaism expresses itself not only in formal compliance with the law but also in a living experience. She taught me that there is a flavor, a scent and warmth to mitzvot. I learned from her the most important thing in life – to feel the presence of the Almighty... Without her teachings... I would have grown up a soulless being, dry and insensitive.[6]

I too learned from the quiet and unassuming Babbe Gittel to feel the presence of the Divine, and to palpably experience Holiness.

I was regaled with stories about the family heroines from both sides of the family tree. Babbe Rochel Leah was renowned in Old Jerusalem for her piety and mysticism. Her wisdom and mastery of holy texts were legendary and famous rabbis, both Sephardi and Ashkenazi, would rise "in honor of her Torah." She prayed daily at the Kotel and her blessings were sought by men and women alike, as were her secret methods for exorcising an "evil eye" and diagnosing the cause of "night terrors." My grand-aunt Chana Devorah was not only renowned for her smart mouth but also for her courage and resourcefulness as she scrambled for ways to bring in some money when the family suffered business downturns as a result of a worldwide depression. My father adored her and called her the *"eizene kop."*[7] My mother's great grandmother, Chaye Yuta, sensed the hour of her death and called for a *minyan* to surround her bed with whom she could recite the *viduy* and to whose prayers she could, respond "Amen. Blessed is the name of the Almighty" for the last time, after which she turned her face to the

---

[5] Based on the verse in Proverbs: "Heed, my son, the mussar (translated variously as "the discipline" or "the transmitted lore") of your father, and do not abandon the Torah of your mother." (Proverbs 1:8)

[6] Soloveitchik, Joseph B. "A Tribute to the Rebbetzin of Talne." *Tradition* 17:2 (Spring 1978), 73–83.

[7] Yiddish expression, literally "an iron head," meaning extraordinary intelligence.

wall and returned her soul to its Maker. In similar fashion, I heard the praises of female relatives who could debate a Talmudic point with the men in the family and who could recite chapters of Scripture by heart, interjecting Biblical verses and Rabbinic phrases and idioms into appropriate junctures of conversation.

This vision of women's life and education in Old Jerusalem is consistent with Baskin's findings that while most girls were "taught housekeeping skills and religious laws connected to domestic rituals, food preparation and marital relations," it was only the exceptional women, "generally daughters of elite families [who] received far more thorough training in traditional texts and commentaries, and some of these... supervised the instruction and prayers of other, less fortunate women."[8]

Apparently, a substantial number of the women in our family were among the more fortunate, given the liberty to study and to express their thoughts and feelings within the family circle. Clearly, as with men, the more gifted and tenacious shone more brightly. In any event, by the nature of the family's bubbe maises,[9] it was clear that intelligence and eloquence were admirable traits in women as in men, even if the formal and communal structures favored the latter over the former.

But even with the brightest women, such was not always the case.

My paternal grandfather, the Zaide, grew up as the youngest in a middle-class Chassidic family in Poland. Like his brothers, he was given an intensive yeshiva education that was supplemented by private lessons. My great-grandfather, a well-to-do businessman and the scion of a scholarly family, hired private tutors and established the curriculum for his seven sons, and oversaw their achievements. They studied foreign languages including Polish, Russian and German as well as Biblical Hebrew – including formal grammar and composition – Aramaic and Yiddish. Once having mastered both speech and reading in these languages, they also learned to read and write in the Queen's English. They studied mathematics, including algebra and geometry. And – most unusual – they all studied music – learning to read and write musical notes. In addition to classic Talmudic study, with *Rishonim* and *Acharonim*, all of the sons were required to study a chapter of *Tanakh* every day.

At the behest of the Gerrer Rebbe, of whom he was a fervent follower, Zaide was sent to study in Israel in 1924, where he ultimately settled and married. His

---

[8] Judith R. Baskin (ed.), *Jewish Women in Historical Perspective*. Detroit, MI: 1991, 20.

[9] Yiddish term that means, literally, "granny tales." It is sometimes used pejoratively to refer to family legends known more for superstition and hyperbole than for their veracity. In truth, bubbe maises are often the repository of great wisdom and little-known facts.

parents and unmarried brothers and sisters followed him in 1936. Those who did not leave Poland then perished in the ensuing Holocaust. Thus, when I came to know my Zaide, he was not only a *talmid chacham* – he was a walking, breathing biblical concordance, with extraordinary memory and perfect recall. My Zaide's brothers, three of whom lived in Jerusalem, were also renowned for their learning, though my grandfather and his eldest brother were deemed the most gifted among them.

For all of his learning and his remarkable writing, my grandfather earned his meager livelihood in manual labor. This income was supplemented by earnings gleaned from long hours in the night, editing Torah writings of prominent scholars and *Roshei Yeshiva,* preparing them for publication. In his younger days he'd dreamed of founding a yeshiva that would formalize the rich education he had received in his father's home, but those dreams were crushed by financial insolvency as well as communal distrust or indifference. Though my grandfather and his brothers earned my reverence, I was always more fascinated by his mysterious and distant sisters, whom I met for the first time when I was sixteen years old.

My first encounter with my great-aunts was disconcerting. I was taken aback to find them so "modern," living the life of secular Tel Aviv, delighting in theater and café society. Two had never married, and one married well beyond child-bearing age. She met a Holocaust survivor, a deeply religious artist, with whom she made an observant home in fashionable northwest London. Of the two single great-aunts, I bonded with Doda Rivka for her zany sense of humor and patience with my endless questions. She was always curious about my thoughts and studies, and closely followed my progress.

Doda Rivka adored my grandfather, her baby brother, and got vicarious *nachas* from his large brood. But she felt out of place in pious Jerusalem, and even when she visited on holidays or simchas she usually avoided going to shul with the family. I did not know if she was a non-believer and was too timid to pry. Nonetheless, we struck up a friendship and she seemed drawn to me as the *Amerikaner.* We maintained contact, and when thrown together at a family get-together she would whisper comments – sometimes disparaging and mocking, followed by a deep sardonic laugh. Such was her response when a young nephew responded to her rambunctious greeting with a blushing face and downcast eyes. Sometimes she waxed reverent and nostalgic, and her voice would close over the unshed tears, particularly as one of the elders gave a *devar Torah* or reminisced over a childhood memory from the *alter heim.* She was a curious "old bird" and a very affectionate and endearing one, with her mink stole and feathered hats.

When I became engaged to my husband a few years later, she demanded that I bring him for a visit to her apartment in Tel Aviv so that she could check him out. As we drank tea in her salon she praised me to my fiancé, expressing her delight that I had completed my university degree in English literature and philosophy, and added her astonishment that I had remained *frum* and would be marrying a *talmid chacham*. Then, in a lower voice – as if sharing a secret – she explained that she would never marry someone of whom her father would disapprove but would never consent to be matched to the Chassidic young men who were her contemporaries in Lodz. "Most of them were not like my brothers," she explained. "They were narrow-minded and didn't understand a life of culture." When I asked her if she did not appreciate their Torah learning, she turned to me, answering in a tight voice, "How can you appreciate what you do not know or understand?" Her eyes flashed angrily as she punctuated her words with a slap on the table.

After an awkward silence, she began speaking again, with a more gentle and sad tone. She bemoaned the lack of formal Jewish education for women in Poland, and the apparent indifference of her dear, revered *Tata'she*[10] to his daughters' schooling. The same man whose breadth of vision and knowledge had fostered my Zaide's remarkable education had not given his daughters' learning a second thought! Though Doda Rivka would never speak ill of her adored father, her tone of voice echoed with pain that was still palpable.

Her words were reminiscent of Sarah Schenirer's[11] recollections of the life of Jewish girls in Poland of the 1920s:

> … as we pass through the Elul days the trains which run to the little *shtetlekh* where the Rebbes live are crowded. Thousands of *Hasidim* are on their way to spend the *Yamim Nora'im* with the *Rebbe*. Every day sees new crowds of old men and young men in hasidic garb, eager to secure a place on the train, eager to spend the holiest days in the year in the atmosphere of their Rebbe, to be able to extract from it as much holiness as possible. Father and sons travel… thus they are drawn to Ger, to Belz, to Alexander, to Bobow….

---

[10] An affectionate term common in Polish Yiddish which is equivalent to "Daddy," which is a contraction of "Father, may he live long."

[11] The visionary founder of the Bais Yaakov Movement, the first rabbinically-approved religious day school system originated in Poland in 1918 which has since made formal religious education de rigueur for Orthodox girls.

And we stay at home, the wives, the daughters, and the little ones. We have an empty *Yom Tov*. It is bare of Jewish intellectual content. The women have never learned anything about the spiritual content that is concentrated within a Jewish festival. The mother goes to the synagogue, but the services echo faintly into the fenced and boarded-off women's galleries. There is much crying by the elderly women. The young girls look at them as though they belong to a different century. Youth and the desire to live a full life shoot up violently in the strong-willed young personalities. Outside the synagogue, the young girls stand chattering; they walk away....

They leave behind them the wailing of an older generation... further and further away from synagogue they go....[12]

In a similar vein, Doda Rivka described her sense of alienation from the world of her father and brothers. She and her sisters would never dream of hurting their father, yet they were deeply hurt by their sense of exclusion.

The lively conversation around the Shabbos table was dominated by the boys and included concepts and language of which the daughters knew nothing. They sat silently as if they were strangers, hungrily wishing to understand and participate. Though they had been taught to read the Hebrew text of the prayer book and could read Yiddish well enough to understand the adjacent translation, the girls were more inclined to read modern Yiddish literature that mocked the ways of their father – the ways which seemed to ignore their very presence.

By law they were required to attend a public school, and being bright they managed to gain admission to the *gymnasia*, while their religious education and spiritual development were largely ignored. At school their developing intellects were applied to the study of Polish culture and secular knowledge and their academic advancement was encouraged. No such attention was devoted to the study of sacred texts or the understanding of religious thought or observance. In the absence of a full spiritual life and lured by the culture and literature of the secular, gentile world in which they participated during the week, Doda Rivka and her sisters began to live a double life, trapped between two worlds.

She whispered to me, "As you know, the *Tata'she* and my brothers came home late on Friday nights."[13] After candle-lighting, the sisters would sneak off

---

[12] Sarah Schenirer as recounted by her young colleague Judith Grunfeld-Rosenbaum in "Sarah Schenirer" in *Jewish Leaders* 1750–1940, edited by Leo Jung, 410–411, Jerusalem: 1953, 1964.

with their friends (Jews and gentiles alike, boys and girls) to the theaters or dance halls. "But we were always home in time for *kiddush*, and no one was the wiser." And then, in a sad tone, she added, "He always asked us if we had *davened* and reminded us every *Shabbes* afternoon not to forget to eat *seuda shlishit*, the third Shabbos meal, as he left for the *shtibel* for mincha. How blind could they be?!"

Such conversations with Doda Rivka gave me a glimpse into the life of women in Eastern Europe before the introduction of Jewish day schools for girls. I knew that women had always been creative in injecting meaning into the mundane and had been entrusted with transmitting not only the traditions but also the religious feelings that constitute the lifeblood of Jewish survival. But how could they do so when they were permeated with the competing noise and values of an alien culture, particularly when that culture seemed more inviting to women than the one to which they belonged by birth?

Oddly enough, even in Western European communities with overwhelming rates of assimilation, many women – without benefit of extensive formal Jewish education – still carried on traditions and maintained a living relationship with their faith. Perhaps this is the reason why many rabbinic and lay leaders seemed sanguine to the threat looming over the continuity of the Jewish people, both physical and spiritual. Women seemed to be fulfilling their roles as guardians of the faith extremely well, perhaps too well. In her study of Jewish women in Imperial Germany, Marion A. Kaplan found that even among more secular, urban and bourgeois Jews – those who had long since ceased observing dietary rules or the Sabbath, "it was frequently the women in the family who were the last bastions regarding enforcement of dietary laws and other traditions."[14]

Sigmund Freud's son, whose father persuaded his mother to drop all religious practice and who was raised without any instruction of Jewish ritual or faith, nevertheless recalled his grandmother's religiosity. "On Saturdays we used to hear her singing Jewish prayers in a small but firm melodious voice."[15] Freud's grandchildren would have no such recollections.

It seems that women's resistance to the complete abandonment of their religious heritage was surely contingent upon their acquaintance – through study or memory – with Yiddishkeit as an experiential reality if not an intellectual one.

---

[13] It was, and often still is, customary in the shtiblech to spend an hour between Kabbalat Shabbat and Maariv learning. Fathers and sons would frequently spend the time reviewing the Torah portion that would be read communally on the following morning, or going over the week's lessons in yeshiva.

[14] Op cit. in Baskin, *Jewish Women in Historical Perspective*, 207.

[15] As quoted by David Averbach, *Commentary*, June 1980, 37.

Such was the commitment of Doda Rivka – she felt bound to a covenant and to a father and mother who were living symbols of it. She would remain single and alone, distant but not lost, rather than breach that sacred commitment.

It is surely accurate that throughout Europe, as in the United States, the Jewish family was "the most prominent institution involved in ethno-religious identity formation and the transmission of... norms and values."[16] However, with the advent of public schooling and infusion of competing and alien norms and values into the society, women could no longer serve as the last bastion against cultural eradication. Thus, once the "golden chain" had been broken, the home and its women could no longer serve as reliable transmitters of Torah.

Even where observance of traditions was maintained, even in homes where knowledgeable and passionately religious women reigned, the infectious effects of secularism and hedonism could not be avoided. After emancipation, Jews in most European countries were granted the rights of citizenship along with participation in public education and the workforce. Once Jewish women could more freely enter secular academies and workplaces they were less likely to adhere to or be satisfied with what has been termed "domestic Judaism."

Doda Rivka would ask me about my studies – especially about my Torah studies. "Tell me what's new," she would open, inquiring about my family and my work. And then she would add, grasping my hand between hers, "Tell me also a *chidush*[17] – you have such a good *piskele*,[18] you can explain it so well, even to an ignoramus like me." And as I would describe an exciting passage in a medieval commentary, or a novel idea which I dared conjecture to resolve an apparent textual enigma, she would smile and her eyes would water, and she would sigh, "If only...."

For further reading:

Zolty, Shoshana Pantel. *And All Your Children Shall Be Learned: Women and the Study of Torah in Jewish Law and History.* Lanham, MD: 1993.

---

[16] Waxman, Chaim I. American Jews in Transition (Philadelphia: 1983), 16.

[17] Literally an item of news; figuratively, Torah novellae.

[18] Yiddish: a little mouth.

David the Psalmist sings:[1] *"From the mouths of babes and suckling infants You have established strength, because of Your enemies, to silence foe and avenger...."*

Rabbi David Kimchi (Radak)[2] *explains that as soon as a baby is born and begins to nurse, the wonders of the Creator are revealed. The milk flows to the nursing baby at just the right tempo, neither gushing nor flowing feebly, so that the baby is not exhausted with sucking. And how many more examples can we mothers bring of the miracle of nursing! Who can forget that moment when the milk suddenly lets down and at the very same instant, the baby begins crying in hunger? And how the flow of milk in the breast ("like a well that springs in time of need"*[3]*) increases as the baby's needs grow and tapers off when as the need dissipates. Likewise, the protection breast milk provides against infection, and the comfort it provides in stormy times.*

The meaning of the verse in Psalms is now clearer: from the mouths of babes and suckling infants the bedrock of faith is secured.

Viva Hammer

What's a Good Jewish Mother like You Doing Alone in Versailles?

Viva Hammer

I hail from a family of legendary breast-feeders. My grandmother was born weighing two pounds and could not suck, so her mother would drip breast milk into her mouth and the mouth of her twin sister until they learned to feed on

---

[1] Psalms 8:3.

[2] 1160–1235. He lived in Provence.

[3] *Hovot Halevavot*, Sha'ar Habechina (Jerusalem: 1964), chapter 5, 161. This book was written by R. Bachya ibn Pakuda in Spain in the early eleventh century.

their own. That milk, and their mother's persistence, nursed them into childhood in an era before incubators or feeding tubes.

This story my grandmother would tell me in her magical dressing room after a bath. "When a baby is born, it needs to nestle close by its mother until it is ready to go out into the world on its own," she taught me. "This way it learns trust, and from there, the beginnings of faith." Just like Hannah, mother of Samuel, we nurse our children until they no longer need us, and then they are ready for a life of service to God. Both my grandmother and mother breast-fed their children for long months, in the 1930s and 1940s and 1960s, decades when it was unfashionable, even unheard of. But they believed that God made the best possible food for babies and that no amount of human research would create a perfect substitute.

At the same time my grandmother told me her tales, my father was telling me others. He grew up in a poor Hungarian village in the 1930s and his family's tailoring business was burned down when he was young. His mother assured him that if he studied hard he might become a teacher and earn a living that couldn't be destroyed in one night. If he studied harder, perhaps he would be admitted to the rabbinical seminary and avoid military conscription.

My father's family was deported by the Nazis in 1944. The Communists confiscated the business they built when they returned to their village after the war, and they fled Hungary during the revolution, coming to Australia in 1957. After each destruction, the family dug themselves out of the rubble and devastation with single-minded brute labor. Work meant that there was money for food and a place to sleep. The discipline of labor provided a rhythm and purpose that helped to heal their minds. There was very little choice in the life of a European Jew, but you could always choose to work harder and so perhaps rise above the degradation. "*Arbeit macht Frei*," my father said to me. "What a shame the Germans stole the expression."

My father did not exempt girls from the general rule: *Arbeit macht Frei* applied to us all. And so, my father drove me mercilessly in study, and I graduated in law and moved to New York City. I found that in the legal profession in that city, my father's attitude was the norm; no amount of toil was ever enough.

Fanaticism can thrive as long as it does not come up against any opposing force. So I managed very well as a New York attorney until I had my first child, a girl. And then my grandmother's voice whispered in my ear about holding a baby until she can hold her own and about feeding her breast milk, the best food God makes. My maternity leave was blissful. I found mothering easy, natural; my milk came effortlessly, and I fed my daughter whenever she desired.

"From the mouths of babes and suckling infants Your strength is established," sang King David, the Psalmist. And for me, faith was affirmed every time my baby cried out for me and I was able to satisfy her.

Then one day, my boss called me at home and suggested it was time for me to end my leave. There was a Derivatives conference in Versailles and since I was the firm expert in the field, attending the conference would be an excellent investment in my career. I cried for days after the call. This wasn't what my grandmother had taught me: she said to hold my baby till she no longer needed me. Would I abandon her for some affair in Versailles? But then my father's demon, too, started his work in my head: my husband would be continuing his studies for as far as we could see; how would we live if I did not go back to work? Would we soon fall into penury? Perhaps, I thought, this was the opportunity to return to work with a bang, showing my commitment to the firm and my job.

The conference in Versailles was scheduled to start soon after my boss contacted me, and ran from a Sunday to a Tuesday. There were multiple problems with that schedule for a Jewishly observant, breast-feeding mother. It was the height of summer, and Shabbat didn't end till late; but if I didn't take a Saturday flight, there was nothing from New York to Paris till Sunday morning, and then I would miss half the conference. What was worse, my rabbi had advised me that if I ceased nursing my daughter from more than seventy-two hours, I would have to stop altogether when she reached the age of two (although divergent views on this matter do exist within Jewish law[4]). There was no way I was going to be forced to give up nursing because of some Derivatives affair in France (even if two years was a long time in the future). There was only one way to do it: fly Concorde! Then I would catch most of the conference and not be away from the baby more than three days, door to door. But the Concorde was absolutely forbidden fruit at our firm.

How do you explain all these things to a non-Jewish, male, manic-workaholic boss? "*My* brother is Jewish and *he* travels on Saturday," was his first reaction. I couldn't even bring myself to mention the nursing; I just assured him I'd take care of the arrangements and planned to attend. But he warned me sternly, "Viva, you are not to spend too much on this trip, or heads will roll."

The firm's policy was to permit attorneys to travel on the Concorde only with the express permission of the CEO. So I gathered up my courage and wrote

---

[4] See Deena Rachel Zimmerman, "The Duration of Breastfeeding in Jewish Law." In *Jewish Legal Writings by Women*, edited by Micah D. Halpern and Chana Safrai, 52–59, especially 58. Jerusalem: 1998. For a practical ruling, consult a competent rabbi.

this man an e-mail, giving all the reasons why I had to travel on the supersonic bird, including all the particulars of Jewish law on nursing and on Shabbat. I reminded him of his recent dictum regarding inclusivist policies regarding women, minorities, and other oddities. I also offered to pay the difference between my proposed travel costs and the next highest travel price.

The CEO wrote back promptly, granting me special permission to fly on the Concorde, wishing me a safe trip, and assuring me I wouldn't have to pay for anything myself.

So at some unearthly hour on Sunday morning, I nursed the baby and then mingled with the rarified crowd at the Concorde terminal before boarding the aircraft. Four miraculous hours after leaving New York, we landed in Paris, and a waiting car drove me straight to the Trianon Palace. What a place for a Derivatives conference! For those not yet enlightened, Derivatives are things like forwards and futures, options and swaps, contracts whose value is *derived* from the value of other things, like stocks and bonds. But there was nothing derivative about this location; it was the real thing. Each participant had a suite the size of my Manhattan apartment; in fact, the *bathroom* was the size of my apartment. The furniture was all period antiques and the view was of the Versailles Palace. It was all so beautiful that my hardened New York eyes almost couldn't bear it.

I came down from my room in time for a five-course dinner, sitting with the European heads of the firm. And for me – a lettuce leaf. (Yes, I assured my mother, I did tell them about kashrut, but who outside of New York knows what that means?)

The next day, the serious part of the program began. It was the brainchild of the Global Head of Capital Markets; he and his henchmen whiz around the world, educating the masses about tax planning opportunities that can be developed using Derivatives. So I sat in the room in which the Armistice agreement was signed after World War I and listened to the dividends of peace. There were firm representatives from fifteen European countries at the conference, from both sides of the 1914–1918 conflict, many of whose home countries were *created* as a result of the conflict. Unfortunately, the multicultural element was the last wondrous piece of the experience. The lecture material was unspeakably boring. I could have recited it in my sleep.

Every few hours, I left the lectures to check my voicemail, call clients, and pump out some milk. Being away from the baby for the first time, I didn't realize how much milk I produced: I was afraid of flooding out the Armistice room! After the second lettuce leaf at lunch, I realized I could skip meals and see Versailles during mealtime. So I slipped out and walked, open-mouthed, around the royal town.

One of the little alleys that pass as roads in Versailles led to a local train station that had some market stalls. And one of those stalls was a kosher butcher shop! Not only were there exclusive cuts of meat, but baked delicacies from Paris as well. I pulled out some francs and wandered back to the Palace with a bag full of kosher French delights.

By lunchtime the following day I had to leave and was comforted in knowing that our Global Tax Leader was leaving at the same time. With us all departing together, I didn't feel so awkward escaping early simply because of my commitment to nursing. On the flight home, I enjoyed quiet time; no e-mails or phone calls, just the opportunity to catch up on the financial literature and collect airplane souvenirs.

Seventy-one hours and seventeen minutes after I had last nursed my daughter, I was back home nursing her again. She had survived those hours with the help of a freezer full of pre-pumped breast milk and a loving father and nanny. I had survived because of those two voices in my head: my grandmother's and my father's. I had been faithful to both.

For further reading:

Abramov, Tehilla. *Straight from the Heart: A Torah Perspective on Mothering through Nursing*. Jerusalem: 1990.

Jacobson, Simon. *Toward a Meaningful Life: The Wisdom of the Rebbe Menachem Mendel Schneerson*. New York, NY: 1995.

There are Good Reasons to Hide the Light

There are good reasons to hide the light:
because our eyes are weak
and would burn out
beneath an unclouded orb,
because when truth is in the thickets
we chase after it more vigorously,
because it astonishes the heart to realize,
later, the gift
that was here all along.

Vera Schwarcz

Reverse Assimilation

Marcia Schwartz

About five years ago my youngest son, then 24, traded in his motorcycle, his ponytail and his ripped-up jeans for a dark suit, a *yarmulke* and *lernen*. Thus he began his new life – a life of this I can't eat, that I can't do, there I can't go. I had a "black hat" where my son used to be.

Somewhere near the start of *Holy Days*, Lis Harris's book about the Lubavitcher *Hasidim* in Crown Heights, she says of her family that "their attitude toward their Jewishness was more or less that of fans whose home team was the Jews." This was the tradition I handed down to my children. Gefilte fish, kosher franks and borscht; staying home from school on the holidays; Hanukkah lights and family Seders.

Now I look back and I wonder: How did this happen, how did my son get here from there? I don't know. He says *bashert*. He also says *gevaldik* and *mamish* and *bli neder* (oh, sweet and loving *zeide* of my long-ago childhood days, are you listening to this?).

Sure there were signs along the way. There was an *erev* Yom Kippur when out of the blue – so it seemed – he ate alone so he'd be finished before sun-down, while we held up dinner for one of his brothers who was late. He began to move in the direction of *kashrut* by no longer mixing dairy with meat, by passing up shrimp and port at the local Chinese restaurant.

Nevertheless he became engaged to a lovely young woman he'd been seeing who was Catholic and they began planning their wedding – they'd keep everybody happy, have a rabbi and a priest. And part of that package was the church's requirement of premarital counseling. Okay, he said, so what if my children are baptized; it's only a little water. We'll celebrate Christmas *and* Hanukkah in our home; we'll let our children decide for themselves. But anyway, he said, I think I'd just like to find out a little something more about where *I* come from.

He started out tentatively – really just wanted to get a little taste. For his first few months he drove to his sessions with his new rabbi, until the day came when he decided he would no longer drive on *Shabbos*. And then he cut his hair. On went a *yarmulke*.

Gradually, the changes in his attitude caused insoluble problems with his bride-to-be, and just a week before the wedding they called it off. It was a sad and painful time but they knew they couldn't make a life together anymore. He spent the next year in Israel.

Oh, yes, things were changing, but not only for my son. I wanted him to be able to eat in my home, so I *kashered* my kitchen, and my other children became resentful. What? I can't have milk with my chicken sandwich? I'm using the wrong plate? I can't feel free in my own mother's house anymore?

For the most part, relatives were patronizing and scornful of his scrupulous adherence to *kashrut*, his stark distinctive dress, his strict Sabbath observance. "What can I talk to him about?" "Just be patient. It'll blow over." "These kids – it never seems to end, does it?" "But at least, thank God, it could have been the Moonies!" My elderly uncle was perplexed – after all, in *his* day you changed your name and said good-bye to all that old country stuff. A close and loving aunt was chagrined: That cute little baby she used to love to kiss and cuddle – now she couldn't hug him anymore?

It was a time of tremendous tension and strain and I was constantly on the verge of tears. My son policed my kitchen, lifting lids from pots, nosing into drawers and cabinets, checking labels. My booklet from the Orthodox Union was falling apart, my *Kosher Calories* was in tatters and I hardly made a move without first checking with Chof-K, Breuers, Lincoln Square Synagogue and anyone who would answer the phone in Monsey.

I color-coded silverware drawers, cabinet shelves and everything that went into them. Sure, I was noddingly familiar with what it means to keep a kosher home, but *this?* There were so many things to remember. Take a *pareve* knife and some newspaper to the fish store. Take out the meat mat and put the milk mat in the sink. Bring the new pot to be *toveled* (dunked in the *mikveh*). Don't forget to disconnect the refrigerator light on Friday afternoon.

We were invited to a Saturday night wedding in Baltimore and drove down early Friday to get settled before sundown. Because we'd been booked into a hotel with the rest of the out-of-town relatives that was in no way within walking distance of a *minyan,* my son would be spending *Shabbos* with an Orthodox family in the area. Which meant he wouldn't be at the prenuptial dinner.

What outrage! "Where's the other son?" "We're not kosher enough for him?" "Was he always a troublemaker?" But they were all understanding about a couple who arrived from Alabama on Saturday afternoon – they couldn't be there Friday night because of business obligations, and *that* already was a *reason.*

My nephew Steven came from Florida to spend a week in New York. We'd enjoyed a lovely *Shabbos* dinner, tomorrow's cholent was simmering away, everyone went to bed. But what a surprise we woke to! Steven had been so worried about the flame being on all night that while the rest of us were sleeping he sneaked out of bed and turned off the light under the *blech.* The cold cholent was not very palatable, so we made it through *Shabbos* on gefilte fish, salads and copious amounts of *halla,* and we had a lovely day. That silly little incident had pulled the plug on a lot of pent-up tension.

But by no means all of it. My son stopped eating grapes. Did this have to do with anything halachic we should know about, or was it just a whim? "What's in this, what's in that?" he asked before every other bite. Were we supposed to *guess* it had to do with *brochos,* the blessings before partaking of food? I was nervous about my kids and they were angry and short-tempered with each other. I thought: if only they would talk, try to understand, but it wasn't happening. I had nightmares that one wouldn't come over when the other one did, that their children would never get to know each other, that my life would be filled with heartache, my days spent running back and forth among them.

Well, you get so tangled in the web you forget about the rock; you're so busy banging your head – what did I do to deserve *this?* – you forget about all the potent forces that went before, the strong bonds, the love right there beneath the surface. So one day I got a call from another son. "Mr. Talmud," as he called his brother, had come up to his office on some business they had together. "He walked in all *yarmulked* up," he said, "and I was really embarrassed. But then I thought, this is my brother. I love him. *He's* the one who's important in my life, so why should I be embarrassed?"

Well, just as he was able to open himself to what he'd thought was his brother's *mishegas,* this son struggled with Yom Kippur and finally decided to observe, maybe for himself, maybe he was doing something nice – who knows? – but it's something he wouldn't have done a short time before. Meanwhile, my eldest son transferred his children from a preschool where there are hardly any other Jewish kids to a school where they have a "Fridays are special" class. My seven-year-old grandson (who taught me how to read the letters on the *dreidel*) was just named "Mensch of the Month" in his Hebrew school; his three-year-old sister waves her little hands over the candles and recites the Shabbos *brocha*.

So our family has something new – and old – going for it these days.

It isn't all roses now and it never will be – but that's life, isn't it? My son is more relaxed and explaining things and this helps all of us. This is major. A *ba'al teshuvah* (returnee to Judaism) can contract a good case of stiff-neckedness; a family can feel defensive. But it's vital to always keep the lines open despite the static.

I'll never be as observant as he is – there's still too much I can't come to grips with. Yet I'm deeply affected by the beautiful spiritual and ethical life – the injunction against *loshon hora* (evil speech), the near-sacredness of hospitality, the morality you can count on every time. Jewishness has become more wonderful to me (I was thrilled when I was finally able to recite the blessings over the candles!) and has brought deep, rich textures into my life.

I've become involved with a wonderful group of other mothers of *baalei teshuva*, a couple of whom are really struggling with the changes in their lives. (I often wonder: where are the fathers? Why don't they come?) We meet, we talk over coffee about our ups and downs and a rabbi discusses Torah with us. (There's inestimable support, comfort and guidance in groups like this. Seek one out, get one going, talk to your rabbi.)

We know our children haven't rejected us because they chose a lifestyle so different from our own. Our generation sought different routes to happiness and fulfillment. I remember that when Herbert Gold asked in *My Last Two Thousand Years* if being American was enough, his poignant answer was touched with irony: "If that's not enough, pleasure will be enough... health, love, money, luck and words surely will suffice. A community could be carved out of all the riches of America without resorting to tribal myths. Those are principles and articles of faith.

"Aren't they?"

Makes you stop and think, just as generation after generation has done down through the ages. Our children were searching for a better life for themselves and their children. And they found their answer in *Yiddishkeit*.

For further reading:

Jaffe, Azriela. *What Do You Mean, You Can't Eat in My Home?: A Guide to How Newly Observant Jews and Their Less Observant Relatives Can Still Get Along.* New York: 2005.

Kaufman, Debra. *Rachel's Daughters: Newly Orthodox Jewish Women.* Piscataway, NJ: 1991.

Thank you Niomi

Thank you for the bath
taken only to share with you...
thank you for the vitality and strength
built especially
to give to you...
thank you for the expansion of heart and mind
opened to love you....

Thank you for the music, the textures, the
awareness of sky and tree
noticed in order to share with you....
Thank you for the humility and the trust
aroused by having you....

Bracha Meshchaninov

A Boy Named Yoni

Minna Hellet

Yonatan Aryeh Hananel (aka: Yoni), my youngest son, descends from the yellow mini-bus that transports him to and from school, his arms akimbo, his gait awkward, his smile illuminating the world around him. As he runs in my direction I wonder at the good fortune that has visited me in this special child who is a constant source of joy and affection, just as I had – for more years than I care to recall – wondered at what I then perceived as the bitterness of my fate. Why me? How different these words sound now, uttered in a voice so greatly altered – for the better – by eleven years of living with a retarded son.

The term *retarded* falls harshly upon ears that are accustomed to the euphemisms that inhabit today's world of political correctness. It seems unfair, unkind, and totally judgmental to employ this antiquated term. And yet, retarded was once the politically correct term for those who had until then been commonly and coarsely referred to as idiots. Those who work closely with the developmentally challenged are well aware that it is not the nomenclature but the reality of a handicapping situation that is painful.

Let me take you back some thirteen years ago, when I was told by the pediatrician that my new son had Down Syndrome. The news altered my life and that of my family forever, in ways that I might never have imagined. The process of acknowledging this reality was lengthy, painful, and uniquely rewarding. I assure you that I am no Pollyanna, and – largely because of the extent to which I am not – the growth that I attained over the next decade was hard-won, and the joy that the experience of raising this very special child – or has he raised me? – came about in spite of the barriers that I consistently set up in my own path. Why me, indeed?

When I was growing up, it seemed as though everyone in school had a special talent, a gift for music, or dancing, or art... everyone, that is, except for me. This is not to say that I was inept. In fact, I could do a number of things reasonably well, but in no one area did I have what one might truly call a "gift." I could carry a tune, but Judy was the musician; I could compose a poem, but Arthur was the real writer. I saw myself as having no special gifts and, therefore, no real identity, except for my ability to do well in school. For this reason, perhaps, I embraced being what the others called "smart" as a vital component of my self image, and I went through a lengthy and particularly obnoxious stage wherein, fortified by massive doses of Ayn Rand, I put down anything I considered unworthy – i.e., anything that I could not understand, accept, or relate to – as "stupid," a term that I would utter with the scathing derision that characterizes so many adolescent utterances. Even now, after that stage has passed – for the most part, that is – much of the joy that I take from life tends to originate from pursuits that some consider cerebral.

I tell you this not to boast of my "intellectual prowess"; I am no longer foolish enough to consider the ability to earn good grades an indication of general superiority. Moreover, experience has taught me only too well that academic success is a very poor predictor of success in any of the most meaningful areas of life. I mention this aspect of my history only because it explains, or at least helps to explain, why I was hit especially hard when I learned that my new baby, my second son, a sweet – if somewhat tiny and flaccid – baby boy, had Down Syndrome and would never learn the way that my others did.

My husband and I could not bring ourselves to discuss the situation with our other children for several months. Our pain and sorrow were an open wound that would not heal for a number of years. Voluminous journal entries testify loudly to this pain while they subtly delineate, for those gifted with hindsight, the concurrent dissolution of my marriage. Well-meaning friends tried to comfort me. I grew weary with their attempts to afford me perspective on suffering by telling me how much worse my situation could be. This was no comfort; one does not live by default, grateful for every tragedy because it was not two or three. Nor was I relieved to think as I was advised to do by one woman – herself the mother of a child with Down Syndrome – that this was "the best possible handicap that you can have." This same woman, who clearly was not trained in counseling, took it upon herself to visit me in the hospital – where she volunteered in the gift shop – and ask me in her best Amway salesperson voice, "So what do you think?" I believe that my baby was three days old at the time. I looked at her with dull, uncomprehending eyes and spoke as only a hardened cynic can to a woman who, while burdened with a child with special needs finds it in her heart and her schedule to volunteer in a hospital – and said, "I think that I hate everything about this. I think that this entire situation will re-define my notion of misery for the rest of my life." She looked at me, and for a moment I saw pain flash through her eyes, and she responded in a somewhat more subdued tone of voice, "Yes, well, I guess you're right."

The distance of time has afforded me the decency to feel shame at having turned away this well-intentioned woman and having possibly created a chink in the armor of optimism that she wore so flamboyantly. In retrospect, I sincerely hope that I did not damage her armor. I realize now, as I could not at the time, that we are all entitled to our coping devices; I had no more right to afflict her with my bitterness than she did to afflict me with her exuberance.

No amount of reading, no amount of talking, no amount of logic could alleviate the pain that I suffered – not for days, or months, but for years. I am not proud of this fact, but feel that I must make the point very clearly nonetheless, so that the reader may better appreciate the end of my story and the fact that even those most confident in their misery may yet derive happiness – in spite of themselves – often from the very situations that had inspired their grief. While Yoni was small, I could not imagine what joy could possibly come from raising "a child like that." Make no mistake; I had no prior experience with special children. No doubt I would have viewed my situation somewhat differently if I had. In truth, I did not know what to expect, and this uncertainty manifested itself as an ache born of fear, an ache that refused to diminish.

I tried, using every ounce of mental energy at my command, to predict the ultimate outcome of my situation. Never – neither through my most logical thought processing nor through my wildest imaginings – could I have foreseen the delight that comes with seeing life through the eyes of a child like Yoni, experiencing simple pleasures in a new way, finding humor and excitement in the most mundane of situations.

I am constantly amazed to discover that those very aspects of personality that I had always considered functions of intellectual development can exist where intellectual development is absent. For a child who says very few words, Yoni communicates eloquently, using his entire body to express a variety of emotions and desires. His excitement in greeting friends and encountering new experiences is contagious. The pride he takes in his accomplishments – a sweet innocent pride, filled with happiness and totally devoid of arrogance – is a pleasure to behold. One wonders why we go through such lengths to teach our children to temper this joy; one wonders why we "civilize out" of our sons and daughters so many delightful displays of excitement. Yoni gives freely of his love, asking nothing more in return than the approval of those around him. He has a talent for knowing how to please and bring joy to those who are sad. This truly unconventional child is by no means without gifts. Had I known Yoni eleven and a half years ago, perhaps I would have learned more readily how to let go of my own pain.

Like all parents, I take great pride in my children's accomplishments, and like many Jewish parents, I cherish most their distinction in the academic arena. My two daughters and my older son are only too well aware of this. While I have always been quick to say that our society places far too high a value on intellectual acumen and that a great many other attributes play a far more prominent role in the make-up of a human being, I did not realize how loudly my actions contradicted this professed belief. Perhaps the best illustration comes from an incident that took place when Yoni was about half a year old and his older brother was seven.

Shai was in his baby brother's room when he asked me, "Mommy, will the baby ever be early for anything?"

I could not really understand what my older son meant. Given my older son's penchant for tardiness I asked, "You mean like for appointments?" (All right, so forget all that other stuff I said about my being smart.)

"No, I mean like how Sarah read when she was three, and I walked early, and Ilana talked early."

I thought for a minute about how I would respond to this question. I realized at that moment how much value I had placed on my children's precocity and wondered about the message that my attitude had communicated. I looked into my older son's eyes and said, "No Honey, he won't be early for anything. But you know what? He'll never say anything to hurt people's feelings and he'll never make anybody cry."

Shai was very quiet. His brown eyes clouded and suddenly became bright again. "You know, Mommy," he told me, with far more wisdom than I had at my command, "that's really a very good thing. I know a lot of people who are very smart, and they use being smart as a way to be mean."

Looking back at that incident I realize how very much my family needed Yoni, that his very being affords us a completion that we would have missed sorely. I think of my four children; they are a study in contrasts. For a moment I focus on my two sons, the one so quick to grasp life's most complicated ideas and the other so quick to grasp its simplest pleasures, dispersing joy indiscriminately to those who are fortunate enough to know him. I ask myself, perhaps for the last time, "Why me? Why my family?"

I don't know. Just lucky, I guess.

For further reading:

Schwartz, Yoel. *Special Child, Special Parent: The Special Child in Jewish Sources*. Jerusalem, Israel: 1998.

> In our generation, one of the most important
> functions of education is to teach the student to
> dignify his humanity: the human being
> distinguishes himself from all other living species in
> that he alone is not enslaved by his instincts, desires,
> and natural inclinations, but has the ability to check
> them and rein them in.
>
> From a letter written by Rabbi Menachem M.
> Schneerson, the Lubavitcher Rebbe, to an
> educator in 1962

Banishing Barbie

Chaya Rivkah Jessel

Recently, one early morning, while sorting out my desk. I came across some old photographs that transported me across time, across continents, and ultimately into another life. In this other life, I was a non-religious university student, fiercely committed to women's rights. The snapshots showed me and several of my friends attending an International Women's Day Rally. The memories of that day came flooding back – banners, speeches, color everywhere, music, drama, camaraderie, sisterhood, ideals worth fighting for, beliefs worth defending, support for women, struggle for women, rights for women, dignity for women....

Later on that same afternoon, a friend brought over a bag of used clothing for me to deliver to one of the neighborhood second-hand stores. Included were four Barbie dolls in excellent condition. Their hair was still shiny, long, and luxuriant. Smiles permanently in place, two sported earrings, another had a pink yo-yo affixed to her hand. The fashions were the typical Barbie fare – backless, sleeveless mini dresses with plunging necklines. The dolls themselves all conformed to the Caucasian, buxom, eighteen-inch waist, leggy standard. I was just about to take the dolls out of the bag (they would make a nice present for my nine-year-old daughter), when something stopped me. The photographs. The memories. The commitment. The ideals. Slowly, as if in a dream, I placed the dolls back into the bag.

Mulling over the incident later that night, I realized that a piece of a puzzle that had been missing for many years, had very smoothly and quietly clicked into place. Even though I had been observant for many years and a mother for nine of those years, it became clear to me that until my encounter with the Barbie dolls, I had not consciously acknowledged just how similar my two lives, past and present, really were. Similar in ways that mattered most to me. My halcyon student days where I lived and breathed feminist theory always seemed so strident, loud, and aggressive compared to my more sedentary existence as a stay-at-home Orthodox Jewish mother. Yet, the image of those photographs reminded me of a long-forgotten truth: both feminism and traditional Judaism share a common goal – upholding and ensuring the dignity of women. How the two ideologies go about expressing and achieving that goal sometimes sets them at loggerheads. But the goal itself is indisputable. Just as I would never have countenanced a Barbie doll in my home when my lifestyle was more overtly feminist, so too, and for exactly the same reasons, I understood that these sorts of dolls are perhaps not suitable in a religious home.

As a left-wing student, Barbie dolls represented to me the most materialistic aspect of American society. I rebelled against the conspicuous consumption they encouraged. More importantly, I fervently disagreed with the stereotyped image of womanhood they depicted. Their standard of beauty was one few women could attain, and those that tried often did so at the risk of becoming anorexic. They looked nothing like any of the real, imperfect yet integrated women I admired. Their beauty was skin-deep, and white-toned at that. My black sister students felt totally alienated by the Barbie ideal – her life of leisure and shopping was insipid and empty compared to the very real issues they and most women of color struggled with. I remember when the manufacturers tried to introduce a talking Barbie. Feminists all over the world reacted wrathfully as the immaculately-dressed icon bleated out mindlessly, "Math sure is hard!"

Is this what we wanted our daughters to emulate? This is what we fought so hard to attain? An image of woman utterly dependent on material products for her happiness, without any social conscience or personal ambition at all? No way would I ever have allowed any of my children, girls or boys, to play with such an ideologically tainted toy.

Not only was my feminist consciousness switched off that day when I almost gave the dolls to my daughter. My Torah awareness was also not up to standard. No self-respecting, thoughtful observant home would play host to a doll that looks more like a Playboy pin-up than a child's playmate. In my current environment, Barbie symbolizes everything that I as a *ba'alas teshuvah* (newly observant woman) rejected about Western culture. She is all body. What you see – and unfortunately this is too much – is what you get. There is nothing about her that even remotely suggests spirituality and internality. She is representative of a culture that views women primarily as sex objects. In this sense, Barbie actually brings together the twin evils of secular culture: the advertising and fashion industries. Neither of these realms are concerned with the betterment of women. Profit and more profit rules the day. Women's bodies are everywhere, adorning cars, computers, dishwashers…. Anything, so long as it sells.

Barbie has always been at the forefront of fashion. Many top designers have succumbed to the lure of designing an outfit for her perfect body. Ostentation, titillation and sexual objectification are the name of the game. Very few of Barbie's outfits are designed with the comfort of the wearer in mind. Too bad if you can't walk properly in such a tight skirt, and who cares if we can see everything when you sit down. Since when have we fashion pundits ever cared what you, our walking mannequins, wanted? As feminist theologian Rosemary Radford Reuther points out, "Women's dress has been continually designed… to make woman's body an object to be displayed rather than a means of her own self-actualization…. Nineteenth century feminists were not off the mark when they insisted that dress reform was fundamental to women's emancipation."[1]

And that's one of the things that attracted me to orthodoxy – the inherent dress reform. I had already been through the "uglification process" necessary to be considered a *serious* feminist. Baggy workers' overalls, cut off at the elbows and knees, ensured that very little of my body appeared curvaceous enough to tempt anyone. No make-up or jewelry allowed, since any form of adornment was viewed as degrading to women in that its sole purpose was to attract men[2]. Granted, I looked so austere that it would take a courageous man indeed to come anywhere near me. I had achieved my goal of being taken seriously as a person, and not viewed solely on the basis of my physical features. But something was missing. My rigid dress code allowed for no individuality, no color, no creativity – in short, no fun! I rebelled every now and again with dangly earrings, but I felt increasingly that I had lost a certain vitality in my dress.

As destiny would have it, it was just at this juncture in my life, when I was feeling stifled by having to toe the party line, that I met a woman who was to shake up my ideas about religion, women, and feminism. Chava had the audacity to call herself a religious feminist, and she answered my questions and attacks with a quiet certainty that unnerved me. Chava was able to show the Torah foundation underlying most of my feminist issues because we shared the same feminist language. For example, I once asked her how she could dress in such a stifling way. It was the height of summer, and she was wearing a skirt that

---

[1]Ruether, R. R. *Sexism and God-Talk: Towards a Feminist Theology.* Norwich, UK: 1983.
[2] Richards, J. R. "The Unadorned Feminist." In *Living with Contradictions: Controversies in Feminist Social Ethics,* edited by A. Jaggar. Boulder: 1994.

reached below her knees, sleeves that covered her elbows, and a high-buttoned shirt. It was obvious to me that her adherence to such a stringent dress code was proof of her subordination to "the rabbis." They were the ones who had formulated the restrictions, and since I understood Jewish law to have been "written by men for men," it was clear to me that the laws of *tznius* (modesty) were not in women's best interests. Her answer shook me to my core. "I am no man's sex object," she said. "I choose to reveal to whom I wish to reveal, *when* I wish to reveal it." Her use of feminist logic shocked me into acknowledging that perhaps the Torah was not so oppressive after all.

She explained that human beings are bidden to emulate their Creator. Just as God "hides" behind the mask of the physical world, so too should we take care not to reveal our essence to all and sundry – only at the right time, in the right place, with the right person. By embracing *tznius*, we acknowledge that spirituality is, in its very essence, private and internal. By flaunting it, we lose it. *Tznius* in this sense refines our self-definition. By projecting ourselves in a less external way, we become aware of our own depth and internality, and are more likely to relate to those around us in a deeper, less superficial manner. Since my feminism was founded upon becoming a more authentic, spiritually aware person, her explanation resonated with me.

What was even more shocking to me was that Chava found no need to de-emphasize her femininity. She dressed well, with a flair for colour, and I yearned to have her sense of security. She knew she was more than just a body, but she also appreciated and enhanced her natural attributes. By way of personal example, she taught me that one may be attrac*tive* but not attrac*ting*. Pretty, not provocative.

Chava went to great pains to teach me that *tznius* is not merely a dress code for women. It is much more than that. Firstly, I learned that the *halachos* of *tznius* are not only for women. Both sexes are required to dress and behave in a dignified way. However, the laws of women's dress are more detailed because women's bodies affect women and men in many more ways. Whether in the personal, reproductive sense (such as menstruation, sexual relations, pregnancy, childbirth, lactation,) or in the more overt sense of women's public sexuality (as evidenced in the music, film, and advertising industries), women's physicality is more palpable and influential. It is precisely because women's bodies are so significant both personally and societally that greater caution needs to be exercised.[3]

---

[3] Manolson, Gila. *Outside/Inside: A Fresh Look at Tzniut.* Jerusalem: 1997.

More significantly, *tznius* is a way of life – how one dresses is simply its most visible application. It encompasses our behavior, our speech, even our thoughts. Whereas in its colloquial sense, "modesty" implies docility, low self-esteem, and a basic lack of "oomph," in Jewish terms, *tznius* is a source of power and self-worth and a prerequisite for spiritual growth. *Tznius* means an awareness of being in God's Presence at all times. This is the reason that *tznius* applies when we are alone as much as it does when we are with others. Always conscious of our Creator, every aspect of our lives assumes a transcendental value far beyond its superficial manifestation.

One of the key words in my feminist vocabulary was "self-esteem." This, I felt, was vital to a woman's sense of achievement and accomplishment. When first learning about *tznius*, I mistakenly associated it with a sense of self-deprecation. As I learned more, it became apparent that, on the contrary, *tznius* is the most significant contributor to a strong sense of self and self-worth.

I was taught this fundamental lesson when reading through the Biblical account of the Garden of Eden. After eating from the forbidden fruit, Adam and Eve made garments for themselves. Prior to their fall, they had been unaware of their primordial nakedness,[4] and had only viewed their bodies as a means of serving God. The traditional commentaries point out that, having internalized the knowledge of Good and Evil, the couple lost their spiritual clarity. Falsehood was no longer an external entity but an intrinsic part of themselves. From that moment on, they were unable to see the spiritual within the physical. For this reason, they had to dim the power of the physical by covering it with garments. Paradoxically, then, the act of covering up enables the spiritual to be revealed. Clothing reminds us that the body is merely the vehicle for the soul and that physical drives and pleasures should not be viewed as ends in themselves. As one Chassidic writer says, "Our physical clothes give us protection *against* the body.... By covering up the body, which no animal does, we affirm the primacy of the soul. Indeed the first parts of the body we cover are those where our strongest physical desires are centered."[5]

Observing the laws of *tznius* makes a statement to ourselves and to the world at large that our self-worth is not reliant upon the approval of others, but rather upon doing what is right in God's eyes. *Tznius* frees people from superficiality. I

---

[4] Rabbi Shraga Silverstein argues that Adam and Eve were not naked. Rather, "at most they were uncovered.... They saw in each other nothing of what is now connoted by the word 'nakedness.' They saw each other as they *were*." (Silverstein, S. *The Antidote: Human Sexuality in a Torah Perspective*. Jerusalem, Israel: 1994.

[5] Greenbaum, A. *Under the Table and How to Get Up: Jewish Pathways of Spiritual Growth*. Jerusalem, Israel: 1991.

am more than my body, and I am no longer ensnared by the current fads of fashion. Tznius frees me to soar to ever greater heights.

By not giving my daughter the Barbies, I was giving her a gift far greater in value. I was giving her the ability to be appreciated for her inner being and not her outer trappings. I was giving her a sense of self-esteem, I was giving her independence. I was giving her dignity and self-control. I was giving her the gift of *tznius*.

For further reading:

Friedman, Manis. *Doesn't Anyone Blush Anymore?* Minneapolis, MN: 1996.
Shalit, Wendy. *A Return to Modesty: Discovering the Lost Virtue.* Southfield, MI: 1999.
Manolson, Gila. *Outside/Inside: A Fresh Look at Tzniut.* New York, NY: 1997.

... Give thanks to the Lord for He is good, for His kindness is everlasting. Give thanks to the Lord for He is good, for His kindness is everlasting. May this little infant (mention his name) become great. Just as he entered the Covenant, so may he enter into Torah, into marriage, and into good deeds.

From the liturgy of the circumcision ceremony

Reflections on a Bris

Lyric W. Winik

I have to confess that among all the joyous things that I was anticipating surrounding the birth of my son, a *brit milah* was not anywhere near the top of the list. After twenty hours of labor, stitches, and all those other things no one tells you until after you've had the baby – including how you will probably feel far more awful the next day – I can't say that I was relishing having to entertain anyone in my home a mere eight days later. About the only thing worse would have been packing up to go someplace else. I remember standing in my kitchen chopping fruits and vegetables to feed guests and wondering: where is it written that a new mother must do this?

Of course it isn't, at least for cubing melon. The Torah and the commentators are quite silent on the finer points of twenty-first century finger-food. Rather, the texts emphasize the sacred act of joining the Covenant. Sometimes, we often find ourselves consumed by the caterer. A bris today can be a far bigger production than a bar or bat mitzvah was when I was growing up – two hundred people, a full buffet or sit-down meal, decorations, videographers, settings like a country club or the Plaza or the Waldorf-Astoria. Yes, it's about the baby, but sometimes it's also about the guest list and the seating chart.

Fortunately or not, I was something of a bris novice when I undertook my son's. I had been to a few of them, but most of our closer friends had more recently given birth to girls. It never occurred to me that it should be a sizeable production. In truth, my biggest worry – and a very real one – was just getting the mohel. Our mohel of choice, Rabbi Henesh, is known as "The Fastest Mohel in Washington," and moments after our son arrived, the obstetrician reminded us to call him. *Right now.* As it was, we were still his last bris of the day. (Rabbi Henesh lived up to his reputation – a good friend of ours who is also a surgeon actually timed him at right under twenty seconds.)

Mohel secured, as it were, my husband called and emailed close friends. And that's exactly who gathered in our family room a little before 7:00 PM on a sunny May early evening. In many instances, they were people whom we had known for five, ten, even fifteen years. Our son's godfather had left a meeting in New York and flown back just to sit as the *sandak.* Another long-time friend, one of whose own sons was still in the hospital after a terrible bicycle crash, came to be with our new son and ended up holding the leash for our much-loved dog. We had the young, the single, the married, the divorced, the widowed. We had Jews and non-Jews. But most of all, we had people who mattered in our lives, and people whom I will be proud to tell stories of, one by one, to my son. People too whom he will know, and who will know him.

Rabbi Henesh offered us a beautiful prayer to read, with the caveat that it might be too sentimental and some parents get weepy. Of course, I said I would be fine. Of course, my nose bunched up and my eyes scrunched in, just as they must have done when I was a baby, and I cried. I remember it all still, two years later, without needing to look at a single photograph. But what I see even more clearly, with the benefit of a little more sleep and some hindsight, is that this moment was the first step on a long journey. When I handed that precious little creature over to two dear friends, who in turn passed him to his godmother, who carried him to the firm hold of his godfather and his momentary perch on a table, and then lifted him up to be cradled by two more friends for the formal recitation of his name, it was his first step on a journey that he will be making for the rest of his life. Our children are part of us, but they also belong to something far larger than we are. They belong to a tradition that reaches back to the writing of the first word, and we hope for them, as the poet Yehuda Amichai once wrote, that they will be written in the book of life until the writing hand hurts.

A bris or a baby naming is, at bottom, a blessing. For those whose child is graced with health, it is nothing short of a moment of thanksgiving. But it is also a moment to remember that ours is a shared joy. We have the pleasure of these little beings, but our purpose is to raise them to be a part of a people and an ethos that extends beyond any one of us. In many ways, Nathaniel took his first step at his bris, away from my arms and tentatively toward this beckoning world. Each new step, each new passage will take him farther away, but will, I hope, also keep leading him back to the people and the traditions that forever lay the foundation of his home. And I hope too that one day he and his wife will taste the same joy, that life will have circled back upon itself, and that they will stand with awe and wonder over the small miracle of a daughter or a son.

For further reading:
Romberg, Henry C. *Bris Milah: A Book about the Jewish Ritual of Circumcision.* Jerusalem: 1982.

Bread Separation: The Lighting of a Candle

Bless the grain dragged free of this bright earth.
Separate from all that burns, or would weigh you down.
Be the one thing that grows as it is consumed.
May your scent to your loved ones be fresh bread.
Know how to be apart, but never lonely.
If tears come, burn them. Pull the bread apart
to bless it. Separate darkness from day;
lead like a flame. Be loving, Chani, be true
to your name.

Liz Rosenberg

Written on the occasion of Chana Slonim's bat mitzvah, Nissan 4, 5759, corresponding to March 21, 1999.

The Woman's Three Mitzvot: Eden Revisited

Sorah Morozow with Chaya Shuchat

Seventeen years ago, I encountered God with the birth of my firstborn child. As the baby emerged sunny side up, I stared back in awe and felt God Himself. For years, I had struggled to integrate my femininity and bodily awareness with the expression of my divine soul. Somehow, I had always felt that my physicality hampered me in my quest to experience Godliness in its purest form. Now, during childbirth, my body experienced the most raw and intense sensations it had ever felt. Yet those sensations in no way eclipsed my awareness of the spiritual – on the contrary, I felt God's creative energy coursing through me like never before. At that decisive moment, a concept I had studied, much expounded on in Jewish mysticism, migrated from the theoretical zone to the realm of my actual experience. Finally, I experienced in my own body how the physical is the ultimate expression of the Unity of God.

The awareness I gained from childbirth spurred me on to take a closer look at some classical Jewish teachings that had often perplexed me. My experiences in childbirth taught me unequivocally that my body was a conduit for the divine, and my femininity an incalculable blessing. So why had I always been under the impression that the function of the female body was somewhat awry, a curse imposed on women as an atonement for the sin of the Biblical Eve, Chava?

According to how I had understood things, my duty as a woman was to remove the blemish Chava had caused; to undo the damage she had inflicted on the universe. I refer to the well-known midrash:

> Why was [the mitzva of candle lighting] given over to the woman? [As a result of Chava eating the forbidden fruit from the Tree of Knowledge and sharing it with Adam,] she extinguished the light of the world [Adam, by causing his death] as is stated, 'The soul of man is a candle of Hashem.' Therefore, women must keep the mitzva of candle-lighting.[1]

> She [Chava] made impure the dough of the world, namely Adam [who is referred to as dough], as it is said: "And a mist rose up from the earth," followed by the verse "And Hashem formed the man" [Hashem mixed the earth with water and then formed man], as a woman who kneads her dough with water and then takes the challah. Therefore, women must guard the mitzvah of challah.[2]

> She caused the spilling of Adam's blood [death], as the verse states, "One who spills human blood, his own blood shall be spilled." Therefore, women must guard the mitzva of nidda[3] [that revolves around her menstrual cycle] through which she shall be forgiven for this sin." (*Yalkut Shimoni* Bereshit 3:32)

---

[1] On Friday evening, eighteen minutes before sunset, Jewish women light candles and recite a blessing to welcome the Shabbat. It is customary that married women light two candles, with a candle added for each member of the family. Many unmarried women and girls light one candle.

[2] While preparing dough, prior to baking it, Jewish women separate a small piece of dough and designate it for God. Before doing so, they recite a blessing. In Temple times, the piece would be donated to the Kohen, the priest. Today, this token piece is set aside and burned.

[3] These laws, elaborated in Leviticus, set parameters for marital union. During menstruation and for seven days afterward, husband and wife may not engage in intercourse or other overt, physical expressions of their love, until the woman immerses herself in the mikvah. For elaboration on this mitzva, see Rivkah Slonim, ed., *Total Immersion: A Mikvah Anthology*.

With motherhood came the realization that my grasp of the story of Chava in the Garden of Eden was incomplete. I knew that my role as a woman encompassed something far broader and more profound than atoning for a sin committed hundreds of generations ago. I was determined to go back to the sources and carefully reread the story of Chava.[4] What had she consumed there in the Garden of Eden that we, her descendants, are still digesting today? What exactly did she do, and what was her motive? I felt that the story of Chava held the key to understanding my role as a woman, as well as the astonishing wave of pure spirituality that had swept over me at the moment of birth.

Chava's Sin

"And God commanded Adam, saying: From all the trees of the garden you may eat. And from the etz ha-da'at, the tree of knowledge of good and evil, do not eat, for on the day you eat from it you shall die." (Bereshit 2:16–17)

"And the woman saw that the tree was good for eating and that it was a delight to the eyes, and that the tree was desirable for comprehension, and she took of its fruit and ate; and she gave also to her husband with her and he ate. And their eyes opened, and they realized that they were naked." (Bereshit 3:6–7)

What unique quality did the fruit of the *etz ha-da'at* have that eating from it could provoke such drastic changes? What went through Chava's mind when she made the decision to disregard the divine commandment and not only eat of the fruit herself but also feed it to her husband?

Chassidic philosophy explains that prior to eating the forbidden fruit, Adam and Chava were not aware of themselves as independent entities, distinct from God.[5] The universe existed in a pristine state because it was an unambiguous reflection of its Divine Master. Each part of creation recognized its unique place in the Divine plan and thus performed its distinct function flawlessly, in complete harmony with every other component. Yes, there was an element of evil, of darkness in the world. However, it existed in its own domain, separate from the rest of creation.[6] There was none of the mingling of good and evil so

---

[4] This article is an outgrowth of my struggle to relate to this midrash and uncover the profound, life-affirming truths embedded within it. Studying this passage in the light of Chassidut, Jewish mysticism, known as the more feminine branch of Torah, enabled me to internalize the message in this midrash despite its stark, masculine tone.

[5] R. Schneur Zalman of Liady, *Torah Ohr*, Bereshit, 10.

[6] Rashi on Bereshit 1:4. See also *Hitvaaduyot* 5743, vol. 1, 354–357.

familiar to our experience – no grappling with conflicting forces within ourselves, no struggle to sort through nuances and shades of grey.

In Chassidic teachings, the form of evil that existed prior to eating of the tree is known as *makif*, or external. When something is external to us, we view it objectively. We have no direct, personal relationship with it; it simply exists outside the boundaries of our experience. After eating of the fruit, Adam and Chava's awareness changed from objective to subjective. This new state is known as *penimi* – they had literally consumed and digested the fruit, internalizing the knowledge that it contained.

God initially warned Adam away from eating from this tree. He knew that Adam, as a human being, would not be able to eat from the fruit and maintain his level of unity with the Divine. Human beings are by nature subjective. It is impossible for us to know evil without being fascinated by it and attracted to it on some level. Eating from the fruit would of necessity change Adam, transforming him from a heavenly being to an earthly creature with base tendencies.

Yet Chava did not accept God's prohibition. As a woman, she sensed the importance of her body's role in serving God.[7] She desired to relate to God with her physical senses – to experience Godliness through touch, taste, smell. In the Garden of Eden, Adam and Chava lived a sublime life, but one that lacked *hergesh* – sensation.[8] The presence of God was so intense that it completely engulfed them and drowned out any possibility of sensing their own being. True, they both experienced an acute awareness of God, but the awareness did not come from within them. It did not have the immediacy and realism of something we connect with through our physical senses. Close your eyes and imagine yourself eating an apple. Now go to the refrigerator, take out an apple and bite in. The difference between the two is analogous to the reality before and after eating the fruit of the *etz ha-da'at*. Chava desired the very physical sensations of tasting, chewing, swallowing – being completely immersed and involved in doing a physical act. In this way, her service of God would belong to her, accomplished through her own efforts and senses.

However, Chava did not realize at the time that her eating from the Tree of Knowledge would cause an entirely new reality to emerge. In Hebrew, the root of the word *da'at* means to join, to merge. Eating from this tree resulted in *da'at* –

---

[7] See R. Menachem M. Schneersohn, *Likutei Sichos*, vol. 20, 40–44. See also *Likutei Sichos*, vol. 19, 210–214.

[8] R. Shalom Dov Ber, *Sefer Maamarim Ateret*, 87–98. See also *Sefer Maamarim Melukat*, vol. II, 145–154.

the merging together of good and evil. Suddenly, the integral perfection of the entire natural world became sullied as each object internalized a bit of the evil contained within the tree. Henceforth, the intrinsic Godliness of every created thing was no longer obvious.[9] Added to this was the element of personal pleasure. This gave rise to the mistaken notion that this physical world is a distinct entity independent of God. In this new reality, our knowledge of earthliness may lead to the belief that physicality is disconnected from God and is an existence of its own. We then perceive God to be within human reach only if we escape our physical trappings and attain true "spirituality."

This dichotomy arose after eating from the fruit because physical pleasure and sensation are of necessity self-centered. In fact, the stronger the physical sensation, the greater our awareness of self. Prior to eating of the tree, Chava had never felt herself as an individual separate from God. Thus, she had no idea how powerful is the desire for physical pleasure or how corrupting and selfish it can become. Eventually, it would lead mankind to forget something that initially was self-evident to Adam and Chava: that God is indeed contained within the physical, and in fact, He expresses His Infinity by being present in the most mundane.[10]

"To the woman He said: I will greatly increase your suffering and your pregnancy; in pain shall you bear children. And your craving shall be for your husband, and he shall rule over you."

God's statement to Chava sounds harsh to our ears. However, in truth God was simply making her aware of the ramifications of her act. He pointed out that by opening the door to experiencing physical sensation, Chava accepted upon herself a full spectrum of sensitivity. Being able to experience pleasure implies also the reverse – to feel anguish, distress and physical pain. Henceforth, every physical act would contain within it dual possibilities: to elevate us or, God forbid, to lead us down a path of ruin and destruction.

This teaching provides context for, and a deeper interpretation of, the following Mishna:

‫על שלש עבירות נשים מתות בשעת לידתן : על שאינן זהירות בנדה ובחלה ובהדלקת הנר:‬

‫(מסכת שבת פרק ב משנה ו)‬

---

[9] *Torah Or,* ibid.

[10] Chassidic teachings explain that God desires a dwelling where He can express Himself and a partner with whom to share it. God's ultimate Infinitude expresses itself in the paradoxical, in the logical inconsistency of a limited, bounded physical world containing God's infinity. See Tanya, Chapter 36.

"For three sins women die in childbirth: for not being scrupulous regarding the laws of niddah, challah, and candle-lighting." (Tractate *Shabbat* 2:6)

During childbirth, the tension between the physical and the spiritual, the blessing of Chava and the curse of Chava, is heightened. The birth of a new human being represents the potential for a new, intense revelation of Godliness in this world. Naturally, the forces that conceal God's presence seek with all their power to impede the birth. Thus, childbirth is a vulnerable time, fraught with hazard. When a woman performs her three mitzvot, symbolizing the elevation of the physical, the mitzvot then become an impetus to ensure that the physical and spiritual will merge seamlessly and strengthen the woman in childbirth. Without the benefit of these three mitzvot, a woman is left susceptible to the natural forces that tend to conceal Godliness and disrupt our efforts to bring holiness into this world.

"*To Adam He said: Because you listened to the voice of your wife and ate of the tree about which I commanded you saying, 'You shall not eat of it,' accursed is the ground because of you; through suffering shall you eat of it all the days of your life.... By the sweat of your brow shall you eat bread until you return to the ground from which you were taken.*" (*Bereishis 3:16–19*)

With her powers of persuasion, Chava convinced Adam to eat from the fruit and join her in a quest to experience Godliness on their own terms, with their physical senses. Having to work the earth to earn their daily bread is just one example of the grittiness to which Adam and Chava *willingly* subjected themselves. "Working the earth" is a metaphor for the task of *berur ha-nitzotzot* – refining the sparks, sifting through the coarse physicality of the world to unearth the divine spark that sustains it.

Sarah Effects *Tikkun*

With her act, Chava unleashed an arduous, sometimes painful process that we have been working on ever since,[11] that of revealing the Godliness hidden within the physical. In truth, though, we can hardly blame this reality on Chava, for her eating of the tree and subsequent banishment was only a continuation of, and

---

[11] The process of exile, dispersion of the Jewish people throughout the nations, was for the sake of *berurim* – finding and elevating the Godly sparks hidden in the physical world. In our time, particularly in the past half-century, the process of dispersal amongst the nations has been completed, as every continent has been settled by Jews who keep Torah and mitzvot. Thus we can say that *avodat ha-berurim* has been done and we await only the final revelation of Moshiach. (See Sefer Hasichot 5752, 176.)

completely consistent with, God's own act of tzimtzum, withdrawing of His light to make possible the existence of worlds.[12] God desired a "dwelling place in the lower worlds," wherein we human beings are given the power and choice to be partners with God and play an active role in reformulating the world as a place where goodness and Godliness reign supreme. The choice God gave Chava, in essence, was either to be an invited, pampered guest in God's palace or to take an active role as hostess.

Chava chose to be a hostess, a partner in creation. Together with her husband, with the work of their own hands, they would invite God into their home and dwell there jointly with Him. However, because she had asserted her own will in defiance of God's, her act created a rift between humankind and God. It was then up to her descendants[13] to undo this schism and restore the unity that had reigned in the universe. Chava's eating from the forbidden fruit resulted in the new world order wherein a perceived dichotomy exists between the spiritual and the physical. Now, all women have the lifelong task of connecting the very physical to the most spiritual, the everyday to the holy, the mundane to the divine.

The chasm between humanity and God continued to widen over the next twenty generations. The first dawn in this saga of heartbreak emerged with the advent of our forebears, Abraham and Sarah. They commenced to restore the breach in the relationship between humankind and God, beginning the process

---

[12] Schneersohn, Menachem Mendel. *Sefer Maamarim Basi L'gani*, vol. II, 31–32.

[13] For ten generations after Chava, humankind descended steadily into idol-worship and depravity until God sent a flood that destroyed the world. Noah, one of the few survivors of the flood, attempted to set things right. His first act after disembarking from the ark was to plant a vineyard. Noah hoped that by drinking wine, he could undo the damage done by Chava's sin and re-establish the unblemished relationship between humanity and God. When we drink wine, we tend to mellow. Social barriers fall; we experience heights of emotion that are inaccessible in a sober state. Thus, Noah thought that he could break down the barrier between man and God erected by Chava's deed. However, Noah's act did not accomplish the desired goal. It led only to a state of drunkenness during which he humiliated himself in his tent.

Noah failed because he tried to reconnect with God through bypassing the normal state of intellect. Losing ourselves in a state of intoxication is not the way to rectify the sin of Chava. Our goal is to achieve the true elevation by keeping our human faculties intact and dedicating them completely to God. (*Sefer Maamarim Ateret*, ibid.)

of luring God's presence back to earth.[14] Sarah in particular, with her special feminine qualities, played the key role in repairing Chava's transgression.[15]

What did Sarah possess that Chava did not? What gave her the ability to rectify Chava's deed? Chava had attempted to serve God through the physical and experience joy in divine service. However, she had not yet learned how to be fully Godly and fully human; i.e., to integrate her feelings of self with the Divine. Sarah's gift lay in achieving unity with the divine without relinquishing any of her own personality in the process. Her name, Sarah, denotes royalty. The quality of *malchut* is humility and receptivity. Sarah internalized Godliness and integrated with it so seamlessly that she never lost her connection to God. Thus, the physical did not serve as a barrier between her and God; on the contrary, she used it in a manner that revealed and reflected Godliness.[16]

The Jewish Home: A Royal Palace

"And Yitzchak brought her into his mother Sarah's tent, and took Rivkah, and she became his wife; and he loved her: And thus was Yitzchak consoled for his mother."(Genesis 24:67)

Rashi[17] cites that three miracles occurred regularly in our Matriarch Sarah's tent. Her Shabbos candles remained lit from Shabbos to Shabbos, her dough stayed fresh the entire week, and a holy cloud continually hovered over her tent. These three supernatural events correspond to the three sacred mitzvot of women and symbolize the Shechinah, God's presence. When our forefather Yitzchak brought his future wife Rivkah into Sarah's tent, the signs reappeared as soon as she entered, for she too excelled in these mitzvot. Thus, he immediately noticed how worthy she was of filling Sarah's place and making their home into a regal dwelling for God.[18]

---

[14] *Midrash Rabba,* Shir Hashirim Chapter 5. This concept is expounded at length in a series of discourses delivered annually by the Lubavitcher Rebbe, based on the final discourse of his father-in-law, Rabbi Joseph I. Schneersohn. See Sefer Hamaamarim Basi L'Gani.

[15] Zohar Vol. I, Chayei Sarah, 122.

[16] *Sefer Maamarim Ateret,* ibid.

[17] Rashi on Bereshit, 24:67.

[18] See *Likutei Sichos* vol. 15. The Lubavitcher Rebbe highlights the fact that according to the progression in the verse, Yitzchok first brought Rivkah into his mother's tent (whereupon the miracles reappeared) and then he married her. We can deduce from this that Rivkah lit candles, etc., even before marriage, and in fact her observance of these mitzvot served as a litmus test for Yitzchok before he married her. This verse thus provides a proof-text for the custom that even young, unmarried girls light Shabbat candles.

Throughout the ages, the Jewish home has been the secret of Jewish survival, a sanctuary against hostile outside elements. While wars raged and enemies vented their fury, the Jewish home remained a bastion of warmth and security. Even in times of poverty and deprivation, the Jewish home, with all its simplicity, glowed more impressively than any palatial estate.

The three mitzvot of Jewish women are the tools through which we transform an ordinary dwelling into a palace for the Divine. The Shabbat candles shed a spiritual radiance over the home. Separating a small piece of dough as challah elevates our daily bread. Finally, observance of the niddah laws ensures that our intimate relationship is imbued with dignity and awe.

Our foremother, Sarah, was the first to introduce these mitzvot. She undertook the rectification of Chava, and understood that her role was to use her feminine, intuitive senses to reveal the Godliness hidden within the physical. Sarah paved the way, and showed generations of Jewish women how to achieve that which Chava had craved – to transform our home into a sanctuary; to reveal the holiness embedded within the physical. Each of these three mitzvot is a potent tool with which to sanctify and exalt our everyday, mundane existence.

Candle-lighting – The Physical Reflecting Godliness

אחד האנשים ואחד הנשים חייבים להיות בבתיהם נר דלוק בשבת אלא שהנשים מוזהרות בו
יותר מפני שמצויות בבית ועוסקת בצרכי הבית (או"ח רסג).

"Both men and women are obligated to have a candle lit in their homes on Shabbos. However, the women are cautioned even more so because they are present in their homes and are occupied with the needs of the home."[19]

What in fact are the "needs of the home"? Our responsibilities reach far beyond cooking, cleaning, or laundry. These tasks we can delegate to a paid worker. Our primary energies are devoted to creating a Godly ambience in our homes, through revealing the Godliness inherent within the physical. When we light Shabbat candles, we illuminate our home and uncover its implicit holiness, thus affirming the unity of God. Every such act restores the bond with God that we have been seeking ever since Chava ate of the Tree of Knowledge.

כי נר מצוה ותורה אור. (משלי ו, כג)

"For a mitzva is a candle and Torah is light."[20]

---

[19] *Ohr Hachaim* 263.
[20] Proverbs 6:23.

Every mitzva offers spiritual illumination; but the mitzva of lighting Shabbat candles has a unique quality in that it also sheds a visible glow over the physical surroundings. The Shabbat candles brighten the home on Friday night "to prevent stumbling over wood and stone."[21] In a deeper sense, the glow of the candles illuminates the physical "wood and stone" with a spiritual radiance. As we sit around our Shabbat table, the candles cast their holiness not only on the Kiddush wine or on the challah loaves, but on everything at the table. The physical act of eating, the furniture, the room itself – all are elevated in the glow of the Shabbat lights. We have transformed something that had previously concealed Godliness into something that reflects the Unity of God.

Challah – Acknowledging God's Presence in the Mundane

The mitzva of challah takes the transformative power of mitzvot one step further. While the Shabbat candles illuminate the atmosphere of our homes, we now focus on exposing Godliness in ways that are more tangible. As we knead the dough, separate challah, and braid the challah loaves, these very tactile acts symbolize the hands-on work we do to elevate the physicality of our homes.

Maimonides codified all 613 precepts of the Torah into fourteen books of law titled the *Mishne Torah* or *Yad Hachazaka*. His book entitled *Sefer Kedusha*, the Book of Holiness, outlines the laws pertaining to forbidden foods and forbidden sexual relationships. What is the link between the two, and why does he title these two subjects "holiness"?

The two functions are essential to the human species: We eat in order to survive and reproduce to ensure the continuation of humankind. Of all human behaviors, these seem most animalistic and thus are perceived as not Godly. As Jewish people, our task is to unveil the holy sparks concealed within these physical activities by performing them according to God's instructions. When we do so, we demonstrate that God is indeed present in every aspect of the physical, that there is no place void of His Presence. This is how the Torah defines holiness.

In the Torah, the law concerning *avoda zara* – idol worship – follows the law of separating challah. The Midrash notes the connection between these two seemingly unrelated mitzvos.

למה נסמכה פרשת חלה לפרשת עבודה זרה? לומר לך שכל המקיים מצות חלה כאילו בטל עבודה זרה וכל המבטל מצות חלה כאילו קיים עבודה זרה. (ויקרא רבה פט״ו, ו)

---

[21] *Shulchan Aruch Admor Hazaken,* Chapter 263, 470.

"Why is the subject of challah followed by the subject of idol worship? To tell us that whoever fulfills the mitzvah of challah is considered to have negated idol worship, and whoever negates the mitzvah of challah is considered to have endorsed idol worship."[22]

How does the seemingly insignificant act of separating dough compare to the fundamental commandment against idol worship, one of the very foundations of Judaism? As explained above, God expresses His infinity through being present in the spiritual as well as in the physical; no place is void of Him. *Avoda Zara*, idol worship, can be translated literally as "worship of *other*" – i.e., the belief that something can exist that is other, independent of God.

When we fulfill mitzvos, we expose the underlying Godly spark hidden in all physical things. What is more physical than bread, produce of the earth, the age-old symbol of sustenance for all mankind? After plowing, planting, harvesting, grinding, and kneading, all with human toil and sweat, we can come to the erroneous conclusion that we produced the bread through our own efforts, aided by "natural means." By separating the challah for Hashem before we even consume the dough, we affirm that Hashem has indeed been involved in every aspect of the preparation of this very physical, seemingly insignificant piece of dough. Separating the challah negates the very notion that anything can exist independent of God – including the laws of nature, e.g. rain and sunshine. Thus, when we take challah, we affirm in the strongest manner possible that *"ain od milvado"* – there indeed is nothing *"other"* – void of God. This act uncovers the Godly spark hidden within the physical, thus restoring the initial state of perfect unity that existed in the Garden of Eden.

The Laws of Niddah, Taharat Hamishpacha – The Physical Transforms Itself into the Godly

The glow of the Shabbat candles brings God into the environment of our homes. The separation of *challa* unveils Godliness in our food and in all our material possessions. Our fulfillment of the *nidda* laws primes us to be a fitting channel to accept God into the most personal, intimate aspects of our being. The act of marital union is the most sensual and pleasurable physical act known to humankind. Symbolic of the mingling of positive and negative caused by eating of the *etz ha-da'at*, this is the area most susceptible to abuse and defilement even as it is a vessel for receiving the most powerful and refined spiritual lights.

When Abraham and Sarah disagreed over which action to take regarding his son Yishmael, God issued this instruction:

---

[22] *Vayikra Rabba*, Chapter 15:6.

כל אשר תאמר לך שרה, שמע בקולה.

"Whatever Sarah may say to you, listen to her voice."[23]

The Zohar explains that Abraham symbolizes the soul and Sarah represents the body.[24] With God's statement to Abraham, He implied that the soul must pay attention to the body's message. We tend to think the reverse: The soul is higher, more spiritually attuned than the body. The body (Sarah) should listen to the soul (Abraham)! Here, God indicates the very opposite: that the body has superiority over the soul and the soul must listen to the body's message.

In truth, the body's superiority over the soul is a fundamental concept in Jewish mysticism.[25] Although the soul has intellectual and emotive faculties with vast potential to experience Godliness, its abilities are nevertheless restricted, as it is impossible to truly comprehend God's Essence. We have the capacity to experience only the part of God that He chooses to make available to us.

The physical stuff, the flesh and blood of the human body, by definition, does not and cannot express Godliness at all. It simply does not possess the tools. Because it is "blind, deaf and mute," so to speak, in its awareness of Godliness, the body connects to God on an existential plane, the level of His very Essence. The body does not become distracted by its comprehension of God's wondrous attributes since it *has* no comprehension to speak of. The only way the body can connect to God is on an essential, absolute level. This level is not accessible to the soul despite, or perhaps because of, its sophisticated God-sensing capabilities.

This is the paradox. The body, which seems to distract from the needs of the soul, in truth contains within it the Essence of God. Furthermore, the body, since it seems to be "lower" and more distant from God, actually epitomizes God's deepest desire to have a "dwelling in the lowest world." The physicality of the body is the most potent manifestation of God, as it expresses infinity within the finite. It follows, then, that the more physical the mitzvah, the more we connect to the Essence of God.

This is the underlying theme of *Taharat Hamishpacha*. When we experience marital intimacy, every physical faculty of the body finds expression. The joy, love, and passion we feel in our union seeps into our every muscle and vein. When we observe the laws of family purity and prepare for intimacy according to the Torah's guidelines, we channel our feminine energy, our passion, our

---

[23] Bereshit 21:12.

[24] See *Likutei Sichot* vol. I, 31.

[25] For elaboration on this concept see Likutei Sichos Vol. 20, 40–44, *Toras Sholom Simchas Torah* 5669, and Levin, Faitel, *Heaven on Earth*.

reproductive capabilities, to connect with the Essence of God. Our intimacy with our husbands then unites God's feminine and masculine energies and restores the three-way, indivisible bond between man, woman and God.[26]

Source of Divine Blessing

כל כבודה בת מלך פנימה. (תהלים מה, יד)

"The entire glory of the King's daughter lies within."[27]

The special quality of a Jewish woman is her ability to work within, to reveal the innermost aspect of every object, namely its connection to the Godly, and assure the integration of the spiritual within the physical. The common thread of these three *mitzvot* is that they express the feminine tendency to transform the mundane, thus unleashing the spiritual sparks hidden within creation, where God appears to be completely absent.

The acronym of the three feminine mitzvot is *ha-chen*,[28] a term meaning *grace*. These mitzvos evoke God's Grace and stir up His Thirteen Attributes of Mercy, issuing forth a plethora of blessings. The woman's role of ensuring that Godliness is absorbed within the recipient causes in turn that God's abundant blessings be absorbed; that is, that they descend as tangible and revealed blessings.[29]

Our sages teach:[30] *"Minhag nashim Torah"* – the traditions and customs of Jewish women are part of Torah. After lighting Shabbat candles on Friday night, while separating challah and before and after immersion in the mikveh, women offer up supplications and silent prayers. These prayers have kept and nurtured

---

[26] In Hebrew, man is called ish and woman is isha. The two words have the same letters, eish, but man has the added letter yud while woman has the letter heh. These two letters make up the Divine name in which the yud represents the divine masculine energy, and the heh the divine feminine energy. When man and woman unite according to the spirit of Torah, they join God's masculine and feminine energies together and thus repair the breach caused by the sin of the etz ha-da'at. For a complete discussion on this, see R. Yitzchok Ginsburg, *The Mystery of Marriage* (2005), Chapter 5.

[27] Psalms 45:14

[28] The three mitzvot are: **Heh** – Hadlakat nerot. **Chet** – Challah. **Nun** – Niddah. See Megale Amukos Parshat Shelach, 17:4.

[29] Jewish tradition is to set aside some coins for charity in connection with each of these mitzvos (prior to candle lighting, food preparation and immersion) to further enhance their impact both on the personal and universal plane. Thus the Lubavitch custom is to keep a tzedaka box in the kitchen, preferably built into the actual wall, to symbolize that the mitzvot have permeated the entire home. See *Sefer Hasichot* 5748, vol. I, 336.

[30] Rabbi Joseph I. Schneerson, *Likutei Diburim*, page 10.

the Jewish people throughout our history, and have drawn down innumerable divine blessings.

תניא ר׳ יוסי בר יהודה אומר : שני מלאכי השרת מלווין לו לאדם בערב שבת מבית הכנסת לביתו, אחד טוב ואחד רע. וכשבא לביתו ומצא נר דלוק ושלחן ערוך ומטתו מוצעת, מלאך טוב אומר : "יהי רצון שתהא לשבת אחרת כך!" ומלאך רע עונה ׳אמן׳ בעל כרחו" (מסכת שבת קיט, ב).

"A baraita[31] teaches: R. Yose bar Yehudah says: Two ministering angels escort a person from the synagogue to his home on the eve of the Sabbath, one a good angel and one a bad angel. And when he comes to his home and finds the lamp burning, the table set and his bed made, the good angel says, "May it be the Will of God that it should be this way the next Sabbath as well," and the bad angel is forced to answer "Amen" against his will...."

The Zohar[32] explains that this passage alludes to three basic human needs: health, sustenance, and children. The woman's three mitzvot are the channel through which these blessings enter our homes.

Lamp burning: Our mitzva of candle-lighting brings blessings in matters of health and life, as a candle represents the soul. When lighting candles, we beseech God to illuminate our homes with the light of true *shelom bayit*[33] and *nachas* from our children. For keeping this mitzva, we merit long life for our families and ourselves, and are worthy to give birth to "children imbued with sanctity who will be a light in the world." The light of our Shabbat candles also adds peace to the world, beginning with our own homes and ultimately radiating outward, until we usher in the era of true peace in the Messianic Age.

Set table: The mitzvah of challah ensures blessing in financial matters. While separating challa, we request that the Almighty grant our families ample livelihood, to provide comfortably for our family and guests, and enable us to support Torah scholars and give *tzedaka* generously.

Bed made: Keeping the *niddah* laws (*the bed made*) draws down blessings in matters of children. Before and after immersion in the *mikveh* we pray for fine, healthy children who will grow up to be Torah-observant, knowledgeable and proud Jews.

Full Circle: Chava and Me

Looking back on my Moment of Truth seventeen or so years ago, I ask myself what made it so powerful. I close my eyes and let my mind wander back to that defining moment; once again I am flooded with feelings of awe and

---

[31] Babylonian Talmud, *Shabbat* 119:2.

[32] Zohar, Bereshit 48b

[33] Domestic harmony.

fulfillment. Now I understand what my body had experienced: I had felt Godliness with my physical sensations. *This* was why Chava ate from the tree – to enable the experience of carrying a baby for nine months, nurturing it within my body, laboring, breathing, and finally birthing a living child from my womb, all with my own concentration and efforts.

Of course, I know that God is behind the entire process. His gift to me is that He allowed me to have a share in it. I am in awe at the overwhelming responsibility that God has entrusted to me. At every waking hour (and even while sleeping) I have a mission of enormous magnitude. I strive to use my body, my possessions, my home, my very being, to reveal the Godliness lurking within. I am gratified that God holds me in such high esteem, giving me the opportunity to share in His creative urge, to build our edifice together.

I feel doubly blessed that God created me as a woman. God gave me myriads of special abilities: the power to spread His Holy light over the world with a feminine touch, to faithfully acknowledge His presence in the mundane, and to appreciate holiness within my physicality every minute, every hour, every day.

I sense that we are at the concluding end of a much-extended process.[34] Throughout history, we have worked to reveal the Godliness within the physical, even though we are unable to behold the full scope of our accomplishment. Very soon, in the Messianic Age, the world will reach its perfection and we will see God with our eyes of flesh.[35] Then, "the woman will envelop the man"[36] and "the soul will be sustained by the body."[37] We will become fully aware of the superiority of the physical forms of divine service as epitomized by the mitzvot of Jewish women.

I think of the work I do, uncovering the Godliness hidden in the mundane, as analogous to the game of Hide and Seek[38] that I play with my children. Sometimes my children find ingenious hiding places, and as I'm a bit less imaginative, I have trouble finding them. Eventually, they get tired of waiting and come running towards me with giggles as I engulf them in a warm hug. God, too, has hidden Himself within this world in some very subtle places. Our

---

[34] In 1991, the Lubavitcher Rebbe, R. Menachem Mendel Schneerson, declared: "Higia zman geulaschem" – the time of your redemption has arrived. We have completed all the preparations, and the only task left is to open our eyes and actually see the redemption. See *Sefer Hasichot* 5751, vol. II, 690, 791–792.

[35] Isaiah 40:5. See also Tanya, Chapter 36.

[36] Jeremiah 31:21.

[37] See *Sefer Hasichot* 5752, vol. 1, 237, and reference 16.

[38] See R. Dov Ber of Lubavitch, Introduction to *Ner Mitzva v'Torah Ohr*, 4–6.

challenge is to search. Sometimes we find Him quickly, but frequently the search tries our patience. Every so often we are blessed and God runs towards us, all smiles, arms outstretched. Thank You, God, for the warm hug that You gave me seventeen years ago.

For further reading:

Freeman, Tzvi. *Men, Women and Kabbalah: Wisdom and Guidance from the Masters.* New York: 2004.

Levin, Feitel. *Heaven on Earth: Reflections on the Theology of Rabbi Menachem M. Schneerson, the Lubavitcher Rebbe.* New York: 2002.

In each journey of your life you must be where you are. You may only be passing through on your way to somewhere else seemingly more important – nevertheless there is purpose in where you are right now.

Meditation No. 28

People want to run away from where they are, to go to find their Jerusalem. Wherever you are, whatever you are doing there, make that a Jerusalem.

Meditation No. 31

If you see what needs to be repaired and how to repair it, then you have found a piece of the world that God has left for you to complete. But if you only see what is wrong and how ugly it is, then it is yourself that needs repair.

Meditation No. 34

From Bringing Heaven Down to Earth: 365 Meditations of the Rebbe *by Tzvi Freeman*

Blessings in India

Wendy Dickstein

Will the Sabbath Queen really come all the way to India?" asks six-year-old Miriam, pausing in mid-flight, her eyes full of questions.

"If we make everything ready for her she will surely come," I answer. We start to make hallah, kneading the dough on the wood-topped table. Miriam wants to make the braids, and she is the one today who remembers to set aside a portion. She rolls it into a tiny doll's hallah and tells me that all the small pieces of dough which were set aside, known as "the taking of hallah," will be made into one big loaf for the angels' Sabbath meal. We carry the braided loaves outside to rise beneath the scorching sun of our prolonged South Indian summer – waiting for the monsoon to break, praying that it will come soon and ward off famine. Everyone is anxious.

Our Sabbath preparations seem strange and solitary here, cut off as we are like the single piece of hallowed bread. The meal is prepared and the table laid with a flowered sheet for a tablecloth. The candlesticks and wineglass stand ready for the fall of the glaring sun, which will be heralded by the *muezzin's* call just at sundown.

Five mosques surround our house and the calls to prayer, which begin at daybreak, remind me of Jews going to pray in their far-flung synagogues around the world at about the same times. These are the Indian Muslims, proudly separate, yet only tolerated by the Hindu majority. They live in their own closed world, busy in their schools and mosques and welfare institutions like the communities of Jews in the Diaspora. Their women remain secluded at home and shadowed when they venture out by their long black burkas, which make them look like nuns slowly moving through the town. They remind me of the observant Jewish women in the streets of Jerusalem who also dress modestly. They seem old-fashioned, yet they succeed in making their more emancipated, modern sisters momentarily thoughtful, even self-conscious, as we hurry past in our casual attire.

Soon it is time to light candles, and the children bend their dark, silky heads towards me to be blessed; first Miriam and then baby Ram, his black hair topped with a white, knitted kippah with strings tied at the back.

"May God make you like Sarah, Rivka, Rachel, and Leah...."

Miriam is thrilled by the magical words, her face shines bright as the candles. We touch each other's fingertips softly in the traditional Indian Jewish Sabbath greeting. We both laugh. It is a precious moment of closeness between us – a harassed mother trying to cope with life in a strange land, and a mischievous, willful child, testing the world and her own power in it. Then it is Ram's turn.

"Bless me, bless me too," he cries, tumbling into my lap, large black eyes and small white teeth sparkling by the flicker of the candles on the table.

Now we go out to the garden to breathe a little of the rare gift of evening's coolness. I open my prayer book and begin to sing *"Lecha dodi,"* the kabbalistic song that welcomes the Sabbath as a bride and a queen. Miriam joins me at the end of each verse.

In our garden little birds jump and call among the bushes and shrubs; and the incense-like smell of jasmine, which flowers only at night and hoards its power in close-fisted buds by day, spreads around us like Sabbath wine.

"Are the birds with no tails also singing for God?" asks Ram, and we all laugh. That morning, the children had torn through the garden, severing heads from flowers and leaves from bushes. Fearing our landlord's displeasure, I had told them a story which I hoped would stop them.

"Once there was a very good man named Rav Kook...."

267

"Was he as good as Mahatma Gandhi?" Miriam asked.

"He was also very good," I answer. "But he lived in Israel and looked after the Jewish people who had come there to live and work. One day, Rav Kook was walking in the fields with a young student who, without thinking, plucked a leaf off a branch. Rav Kook was visibly shaken by this and told the young man that every leaf, every flower, insect and living thing, is constantly singing its own song of praise."

Miriam's silence as she took in the meaning of the story was strong and deep.

"But we don't hear them singing," she said, puzzled.

"You have to listen in a special way. But the angels can always hear it, and if even one leaf stops its song because someone has thoughtlessly destroyed it, the angels hear it stop and they feel sad."

Now Miriam, too, remembers my story from this morning and adds a comment to Ram's. "Yes, and Sabbah too must have those special ears to hear the birds and flowers singing," she reasons.

Now it is time for our meal, and we go inside to wash our hands. Ram's kippah by this time is perilously perched on one ear. We uncover the little warm loaves of hallah, clumsily braided by a child's eager hand and anxiously baked in our battered Israeli Wonder Pot on my infuriating kerosene stove, which spurts black clouds of smoke as it cooks. We recite the blessing over bread. "Blessed are You, Lord, King of the Universe, Who brings forth bread from the earth."

After dinner I feel I must say the Grace after Meals. Often the children will not allow me to sit for so long, but tonight I am determined. Before I came to India, this long prayer had seemed cumbersome and artificial. But now that I live here, eating a filling meal never fails to produce a feeling of guilt, and the idea of raising each meal to a sacrament and the Grace after Meals have taken on a new and urgent significance. Still, the prayer itself is not completely satisfactory, opening as it does with praise to the One who sustains and nourishes all His creatures with the gift of food, and leading to a meditation on the house of Israel and a plea for special care.

As I pray I know that all are not sustained and nourished here where I furtively eat behind closed doors. I know that God's rich abundance remains tightly clutched in the fists of the few, while the rest quietly suffer. I long for the house of my people to reach out and enfold in their prayer the brave, silent children of India who live in misery and despair from birth until death, never with enough to eat. Still, I know that God is not to blame, and there is no reason to refrain from praising Him. I expiate my guilt by prayer and this leads to a new kind of haunting uneasiness.

I have recently begun to give my leftover bread to beggars. I meticulously wrap it in plastic and deposit it in one of the many outstretched hands, which follow me everywhere each day. The chosen beggar is always puzzled, and peers through the plastic wrapper with doubt. I move off quickly, then look back from a distance and watch him break off a piece and eat, first with hesitation and then obvious relish. The joy I feel as I watch a ragged man or woman eat my bread is indescribable. I receive infinitely more than I give, as if I am the beggar and he or she the giver of grace. This is perhaps a tiny step forward. I am learning to be patient here where the endless heat and grimness wastes the flesh and burns the spirit.

The day is closing around us and the children are ready for sleep. Each night Miriam and I recite the night prayer. At six, especially with her father gone, she has occasional bad dreams and nighttime fears and I told her about the four angels who watch through the night around the bed of one who asks for their presence. The first time we had read the prayer together and I had left her room, thinking that this should settle things for the night, a little voice called me back.

"What's wrong, Miriam?"

"I'm afraid."

"Afraid? With four angels to look after you? What exactly are you afraid of?"

"A little bit... of the angels," she admitted in a small, rueful voice.

"Miriam," I said gently, "just think of the angels being like Mother Teresa. Then you will not be afraid of them."

"All right, I will." She was satisfied, remembering our magical meeting with the gentle, wise old nun. Miriam stretched herself out trustingly towards sleep, veiled beneath her pink mosquito net.

Sabbath morning. The sun rises in all its power. The children hop out of their beds early, and the urgency of their small needs breaks through my sleep and binds me once again to the threads of my life.

"Blessed is the Lord when we lie down, and blessed is He when we rise up," we had prayed the night before. The wonder of His continual creation is present in the startling beauty of my children who wake me each morning to a new world.

After breakfast we search for the portion of the week in my big Jerusalem Bible and in Miriam's brightly colored Children's Bible. Today it is Be-Shalah, and I tell Miriam of the miracle of the manna, the heavenly food which magically appeared every day to feed the Children of Israel in their forty years' journey through the desert. She is delighted but slightly puzzled that God has not sent manna for the hungry children of India. I go on reading but the problem of hunger and bread follows me even here. It torments me wherever I turn.

We are told that when the Children of Israel crossed the Red Sea, even the most humble maidservant saw the Divine Presence more clearly than the greatest of the later prophets; and yet we find that a few days' hunger makes them almost forget what they had witnessed, and they begin to complain against Moses. Better to be slaves again in Egypt than to perish in the wilderness for lack of food, they cry out in their hunger. What hope then is there for us? There is no one to help me through this labyrinth of dark thoughts.

"Nature produces enough for our wants from day to day, and if only everybody took enough for himself and nothing more, there would be no pauperism in this world, there would be no man dying of starvation in this world." So writes Gandhi.

Yes, but what of the holy children of Moses's flock who were instructed to take on the sixth day enough manna for two days and yet many of them went out again on the Sabbath, untrusting and unsatisfied?

Perhaps the Exodus from Egypt and the wandering in the desert represent a personal wandering through the barrenness of one's own soul, the small, blind, stubborn burden of the self.

I make an effort to put my puzzled thoughts aside, for today is the Sabbath, a day for joy. Suddenly I laugh as I catch sight of Miriam, followed as always by Ram, jumping up and down like little monkeys, trying to kiss the mezuzah.

The mezuzah is a new addition to our doorpost. The tiny parchment scroll was a gift from a dear friend at the end of our last Sabbath in Safed. At the moment of parting the rabbi's wife had gone inside and come out with the mezuzah scroll as a parting gift. I had accepted it as a piece of protective armor which I hoped was going to make my unknown way to India a little less perilous.

It was meant to be nailed up on the doorpost, but it had been lying in the bottom of my suitcase for many months as I first waited to be settled in a home, and then waited for the right nails to turn up.

My first few attempts to acquire two small nails for the mezuzah ended in frustration. I had gone to several stores which looked as though they might sell them and tried to communicate my need in my rudimentary Hindi and the shopman's non-existent English. My inability to gain what I so much wanted left me feeling lost, as though I were slipping away from my links with my own past and being left empty-handed in a world of incoherent strangeness. Still, I trusted that the proper time would come.

It was a new academic year at the university. The department of philosophy awoke from its summer desolation. Everyone arrived back from the long vacation. The professor of philosophy, full of fresh ideas for the new year, breezed in with an armload of framed, colored pictures. He enthusiastically explained that there had been a small boy hawking these on the pavement outside and he had bought up his entire stock.

"It only cost me twenty rupees for the lot!" he remarked, pleased with his bargain.

What were these treasures he had found, we wondered? They were calendar pictures of saints and gods and goddesses, crudely executed and garishly painted, and encased in cheap plastic frames. I had seen these same pictures in many homes, shops, stalls, eating places, even in buses and taxis, anywhere, everywhere, often with burning sticks of incense and wilting garlands of marigolds arranged around them in reverent devotion. The philosophers were less ecstatic about them than was their professor, and they vied with each other to make joking, disparaging remarks.

"Are they really necessary?" ventured Dr. Subhash. "They only contribute to the glare of the room." He rubbed his plump hands together and winked at me.

"Yes, yes, but they are meant to dazzle you!" responded the professor, unruffled. He sent for two peons from the main office. The two young men arrived, removed their sandals, and began hammering nails all over the departmental walls, climbing onto desks and chairs and window sills, directed by the smiling professor below, while his staff looked on helplessly. As I watched him interacting with the young men, my shocked amusement slowly subsided and I was left with an illuminating impression of the true holiness which lay somewhere beneath the vulgarity of these two-rupee images. For here were the reminders of a higher world which even the poorest could afford. To transport them en masse, from all the religions which flourish here, and give them a place of honor in one of the bastions of privilege was a curious attempt to bridge the gap between rich and poor, between simple piety and educated skepticism. It was an impossible achievement, and yet here it was, gleaming and glaring out of the frames all over the room.

It was a measure of willingness to face life as it is here and now in all its squalor and vulgarity. To search out the sparks of holiness that lie deeply hidden in the world's darkness was a profound Jewish mystical teaching, and this was a most unusual demonstration of it.

But now some of the pictures had slipped into uneven angles on the walls. The young, wispy-bearded peon who was hammering nails, barefoot on one of the desks, decided to put a second nail under each picture to set it straight, and when he had done this he felt that the proper balance was still not yet achieved, and so he asked the professor's permission to put in a third, functionally superfluous, nail to complete the aesthetic balance of the whole.

The professor appreciated his concern and remarked to me that poor children in this country, like this young man had once been, never got a chance to develop their artistic talents. His responsiveness to the young man's suggestions and the young peon's wholehearted involvement in the work made me realize that even the act of placing the nails was meaningful. I thought then of my mezuzah and asked if I could have two nails.

So here at last were the special nails I had been waiting for. Later that day, when I affixed the mezuzah on my doorpost, I proudly sang out the accompanying blessing from my prayer book with Miriam and Ram looking on with delight and waiting to celebrate with cookies and plums.

"Blessed are You, Lord, our God, King of the Universe, Who has sanctified us with His commandments and has commanded us to affix a mezuzah."

This simple act was blessed with new meaning, which never would have been possible had I tried to live out my Jewishness in any place other than this. As I gazed at the mezuzah, I thought of the Shema – that strange and insistent prayer which had always puzzled me. Suddenly it became clear that it was an affirmation that God is with us anywhere in the world we might happen to find ourselves. And the strangeness which appears to surround us outside the walls of our heart's Jerusalem is but a waiting recognition of brotherliness with all things which live out their natures in our shared world. And the oneness – that strongly emphasized *ehad* (meaning "one") of the Shema prayer – is the common longing of all things to draw near to each other. The first words of the Shema – "Hear, O Israel!" – is perhaps an attempt to awaken us to hear this truth with particular acuteness and attention – with " special ears," as Miriam and Ram explained it.

That night, when Miriam came inside to announce that she had found the first three stars in the sky, I performed the Havdalah service. As I slowly chanted the blessing which separates the seventh day from the rest of the days, our Sabbath came quietly to an end. The sweet, precious herbs from the Judean hills, stuffed into my overflowing suitcases, united us with other Jews who were so far away.

The promise of the Messiah was all around us. It rose up with particular urgency like the sandalwood incense which cast its fragrance throughout our little house and drifted out through the open windows.

It merged with the joyous profusion of jasmine and the poignant sadness which settled over our turbulent little town like a tattered starry blanket, carrying us into another week of struggle and of hope.

For further reading:

Freeman, Tzvi. *Bringing Heaven Down to Earth: 365 Meditations from the Wisdom of the Rebbe.* New York: 2002.

Idem. *Be Within, Stay Above: More Meditations from the Wisdom of the Rebbe.* New York: 2000.

When Making My Challah

While sifting the flour, I sing, because joy is the foundation of all spiritual success. Then I add each ingredient consciously: sugar for the sweetness I hope to see in my family's life; yeast so that each member of my family will grow and expand; water represents Torah; when measuring salt, which represents rebuke, I fill two teaspoons, then shake some back into the salt container because we should always give less rebuke than we think we should; and as I slowly pour in the oil, I "anoint" each member of my family by name, praying for his or her specific needs.

Kneading is the time to pray. My teenage daughter and I take turns, each of us thinking of people to pray for by name....

Excerpted from "Dr. Laura, God Loves You" by
Sara Rigler, available at www.aish.com

Eternal Gratitude and a Bissele Nachas

Miriam Luxenberg

I make challah on Friday. But it hasn't always been this way. It all started shortly after my wedding. My cookbook had a few whole wheat recipes, but they all called for five pounds of flour. "Might as well start out on the right foot," I thought. "If I use five pounds, I'll be able to fulfill the mitzva (the Biblical commandment) of taking the challah portion from the dough, and I'll be able to recite the special blessing!"

I mixed and measured, kneaded and punched, and took challah reciting the blessing. The end results were dubious but the die had been cast.

I kept it up, week after week, sometimes Monday, sometimes Wednesday, the challahs lumpy and bulging and not too edible. Often I would forget to remove them from the freezer in time to defrost. Slicing and chewing mightily, my husband continued to praise my efforts, and so I continued trying.

I soon had a baby but he was very sick. He lay quietly in a tiny crib in the hospital for a long time. One night he stopped breathing and slipped into what turned out to be an irreversible coma. My first baby, only three days old, taken from us so suddenly, yet not completely taken, as he lived on in a coma for five more months. I could not imagine how life could continue, how I could continue. I did not know where I would get my strength. It was terrifying, holding my precious baby boy in a sleep from which I already sensed he would never awaken. How long would he live? How would I bear it? The questions were constant, fast and furious, and the answers were known only by the One Above.

My world had turned dark, black, a tunnel from which I was sure I would never emerge.

God surely understood and accepted my limitations, for not long afterwards, He sent me Mrs. Zilberstein, whom I recognized as the woman who had thoughtfully provided a special veil for my wedding. She appeared in the hospital lobby and announced, "You will stay with me until we know what's what here!"

As familiar as we are with her now, that's how unprepared we were when we showed up on her doorstep the following Friday, Sabbath Eve. If you could imagine somebody really being in three rooms at one time, you'd have an idea of what was going on. She greeted us and sat us down immediately for some coffee and kukosh cake fresh from the oven.

"I'm going right now to make your room up," she cried. "I'm giving you big, fluffy pillows so you'll feel good!"

The speaker phone was going full blast as Mrs. Zilberstein simultaneously carried on a lively conversation, rolled out noodle dough on the kitchen counter and got the bedroom ready for us. In the twenty minutes since we had arrived, four people had come and gone already, picking up challahs, puddings, and cakes. A few grandchildren freely roamed the rambling house, and while it wasn't actually noisy, it seemed so because of all the activity. (I asked her one time where she got her strength from. She first thanked the Lord of the Universe profusely and then took a chocolate bar out of the refrigerator).

Somehow in the midst of it all, she found time to sit down with me. I felt like I had been transported to another world, another planet. This, to me, was Torah and lovingkindness in action.

They never told you what it actually looked like. Hectic, for sure, but really marvelous. Even my husband, ever the straight-faced "strongman," was taken in and nurtured in this atmosphere. Weary and distraught from days of holding my baby and receiving no response except from screaming nurses and beeping, screeching monitors, I felt frightened to be there, unworthy of it, but reassured somehow. If all of this kindness was going on somewhere in the world, then I knew God would do kindness with me also.

For four months, almost every Thursday, Friday, Saturday and Sunday night, I sat in a corner of the darkened library next to the kitchen, wrapped in a big blanket, watching and waiting. I couldn't sleep for wondering what would happen with my baby, my family, my life, none of which I felt would ever be the same again. I had never seen anyone like Mrs. Zilberstein. God had "prepared the cure before the blow," I was sure, because I knew my healing was somehow going to be connected to whatever was going on in that kitchen.

One Friday morning at 5 AM, at the end of another sleepless night, I heard Mrs. Zilberstein reciting her prayers in the kitchen. I heard the familiar words of the prayer book... a few minutes of silence and then some strange swishing noises. What was Mrs. Zilberstein doing? I went into the kitchen and saw Mrs. Zilberstein starting to make her challah. The strange noises had been the flour rolling around the sifter, a task I had never taken seriously before. She had her prayer book placed right next to the mixing bowl, and it did not have a speck of flour on it.

"What are you doing?" I asked. "You make your challah on Friday?" She looked up from her prayer book, slightly surprised to see that there was somebody up earlier than she. I guess she was used to having the early morning run of the place.

"Everything fresh for my Sabbath!" Mrs. Zilberstein replied emphatically.

"But... but how? With everything else to do?"

"I didn't always make challah on Friday," said Mrs. Zilberstein, "but it's really the best way."

From then on, every Friday morning at dawn, I watched Mrs. Zilberstein as she sifted the flour into a large metal bowl, prayed, mixed, prayed, kneaded. ("Mimi, what can I tell you? I'm a praying lady. My mother is also a praying lady."). I sat quietly in the corner watching, fascinated.

Despite my suffering I asked her questions on every subject I could think of, and she answered me with her typical straightforward honesty. Occasionally I spoke and not only did she totally understand my mood, but she would predict what I would be feeling next. The phone would ring at 6:00 AM sharp (same person every day), and the quiet spell that Mrs. Zilberstein had woven would begin to fade away. But before it disappeared completely, I would catch some of it and place it in my heart. I didn't even know what it was, but I knew I would be needing it soon. The months passed, the tunnel lengthened, it darkened and at last there was an end. One night the baby passed away as quietly as he had come.

It was, of course, Mrs. Zilberstein we called at 5:00 AM, Mrs. Zilberstein who instructed us, helped to keep us calm and made all the necessary arrangements with the Jewish burial society. For a long time, the memory of those early morning hours in Mrs. Zilberstein's kitchen were all there was to hold on to.

§Ͽ ⳑ

One Friday, not long ago, I was in my kitchen sifting flour. My challas and I have undergone many changes since those cold winter mornings in Mrs. Zilberstein's kitchen. I finally understood a little bit of what she knew so well: God gives us the strength to do whatever we need to do. We only need to ask. Making challah on Shabbos Eves connected me to what I had felt and experienced there.

My husband was observing our little Friday morning challah-making routine with a thoughtful expression on his face. He watched as I carefully separated the handful of dough and held it up, proclaiming "This is the challah."

After I'd recited the blessing and began to shape the loaves, my husband finally put voice to his thoughts. "Your challah is so delicious, Mimi, but that isn't really the main thing, is it?"

"No," I said. "It's the piece I took off for Hashem that's important. The challah we eat is just *oneg Shabbos* (pleasure on the Sabbath)."

He looked at the little ones running all about, and said, "It's kind of like us, no? We brought a sacrifice also. Yet look at all that God has given us to enjoy." I looked at him very surprised. I had never thought about what happened to us that way at all.

"And you know what else, Mimi? You know how we always complain that other people don't appreciate their kids as much as we appreciate ours? I think I know why. I think that because the pain of the loss, our separation from the baby, was so intense, it makes our joy also more intense."

Until that moment, I hadn't realized how much blessing we had received in the aftermath of our sacrifice and how much it had taught us about the ways of God. Our baby is no longer with us, but he has left us a precious gift. As awful as the loss of our baby was, and as against our will and desire, the lessons I learned during that dark time made their way into every single area of my life without exception and, perhaps, made me a better person.

Wait, let me make an amendment. Every area of my life *except* when it came to sifting flour.

"I really don't like sifting flour." It was true. I didn't. Sometimes it took all the energy I had. (Sifting flour in Israel is obligatory because there is the possibility of insect infestation. There is a commandment forbidding the eating of insects.)

As I said this, I had been absent-mindedly staring into my six-year-old's eyes. Never do this. A six-year-old's eyes are serious business.

"But Mommy," she said, in her frank way, "every grain of flour you sift is a mitzva!"

I was shocked. "You're right," I said. "You know, Penina, in the next world there's a big, big scale, where all our mitzvos and all the not such good things we do get weighed up. Do you know about that scale?"

"The scale from Rosh ha-Shana, you mean?"

"Yes, that one. You just made me think of that scale. Do you think if I sift flour and make challah every week that the angels would throw all the flour on my mitzva side if things weren't going so well for me?"

"Of course they would, Mommy!"

℘ ℭ

In the spirit of Mrs. Zilberstein's practical encouragement, here is my challah recipe and some tips on challah making:

1 T dry powdered yeast
2 cups lukewarm water
1/3 to 1/2 cup honey
Caraway seeds or raisins as preferred
3 eggs
1 cup oil
Salt to taste (approx. 3–4t)
10 cups of flour

Putting it all together:

Put the yeast, water and honey into a large bowl. Watch the mixture start to bubble so you know that the yeast is working. Add about 5 cups of flour and mix. Add the eggs, oil, and salt and mix again. Add 3 cups of flour and mix. Then add the rest of the flour.

Mix it up as well as possible with a large spoon. When it gets too thick to mix, turn it out onto the table (it's less sticky if you flour the surface underneath it), and start kneading, 20 minutes by hand. If the dough is sticky at first, don't add anything to it. Wait for it to smooth itself out through your kneading. If after ten minutes the dough still feels very sticky, coat the dough with about two tablespoons of oil. You will be amazed at the immediate transformation of your dough. After you've finished, spread a little oil (about 1 tsp) on it and set it to rise.

Cover it with a damp towel to avoid a draft. Let it rise till double in size, then punch it down. A second rise will really make the challah light, but sometimes there's no time and one rise will have to do.

This is where I separate the challah and make the blessing. This is the main point of this whole project! The bread is the lovely dividend. When we do this, we are harkening back to the high priests in the holy temple. This piece of the dough was given to them as their subsistence. Once this is completed, you can proceed with the preparation of the bread. Divide the dough up into as many loaves as you would like to make. Take each section, cut it into as many strands as you would like (possibilities: three, four, six, twelve) and braid them. Brush egg on them if desired before they start to rise. Cover with poppy or sesame seeds. Place each loaf in an aluminum loaf pan lined with non-stick baking paper (not waxed paper). If you can't find this paper, grease the pan very well. Using the loaf pans will make your challahs very high and they won't stick together in the oven. Let the dough rise again in the pans until they are double in size, about half an hour. (If you are in a hurry, don't leave this step out! The challahs won't rise much in the oven). Be sure to pre-heat the oven to about 350 degrees, and bake the challahs for about one hour. You will know they are done when you tap on the bottom and it sounds firm and hard. Remove them from the pans (otherwise they can get soggy) and let cool. Enjoy!

Some afterthoughts about challah:

- Make a full recipe so that you can take challah and recite the blessing. If this is more challah than your family can eat, freeze it or give challahs away to your neighbors while the challah is still warm. More harmony!
- All white flour challah is delicious, but a small amount of whole wheat flour (about one-third of the total recipe) gives it nice color and texture.
- Put away your mixer. Kneading by hand for at least 20 minutes yields results which are exponentially superior to machine or shorter kneading times. Set the timer, put on some music, or pray. Trying it one time will convince you. Ask the critics (um, I mean, the kids).
- Wash your hands and give a coin to charity in preparation for performing the mitzva of taking challah. Try to concentrate while you're reciting the blessing (see page 163). There are special supplications that may be said at this time, and of course you will want to add prayers of your own. Our Sages taught that this is an especially propitious time for prayers to be answered, so let's make the most of it!
- The priests in the Holy Temple of old performed many seemingly mundane tasks such as removing the ashes, washing the altar, etc. Since the Temple was modeled as an echo of the holiness of our mother Sarah's tent, we can connect the holiness of our tasks with that of the Temple priests and most importantly, the challahs in our Matriarch's Sarah's tent.

- Don't forget to say: "I'm doing this in honor of the holy Sabbath Day." This will guarantee delicious challahs no matter what, and you will have no need for this article whatsoever.
- If you don't already know how, find someone to teach you how to braid with six strands. The results will amaze you. The diagrams in the cookbooks made it seem much more complicated than it really is. One day, my friend Hemla sat me down, tied six long pieces of string together, laid them on the table, looked me in the eye, and said "Aruf, aruf, in de mid. (Up, up and in the middle)." That's all there was to it. After eight years of struggling with cookbook diagrams, one live demonstration set me firmly on the path of six-braid challahs.
- If you find to your dismay that you have baked the challahs a little too long and they have become very hard on top, immediately brush them with oil after you take them out of the oven. This will soften them. It will only work if the challahs are steaming hot. Otherwise you will be left with oily challah.
- Bear in mind that challah dough is one of the most forgiving substances on earth. You can do almost anything to it and it will still present you with delicious tasting challahs. Learn from its forbearance.
- Try to stay in your chair at the Sabbath table after the blessing has been recited on the challah, to begin the Sabbath meal. Don't jump up at once to serve the fish or tend to the baby. Those few moments have the potential to inspire you for the entire week. I have even begun to put everything for the first course on the table before we make the blessing on the Challah so I won't feel rushed. It makes a tremendous difference. Savor the first few bites of your challah, like the queen you are. As Mrs. Zilberstein said, "Everything fresh for my Sabbaths!" It is surely worth a try, and I wish you great success!

For further reading:
Levy, Yamin. *Confronting the Loss of a Baby: A Personal and Jewish Perspective.* Jersey City: 1998.
Kirzner, Yitzchok. *Making Sense of Suffering: A Jewish Approach.* Brooklyn, NY: 2002.
Spice and Spirit: *The Complete Kosher Jewish Cookbook.* Brooklyn, NY: 1990.

*All the souls in the world, which are the fruit of the
handiwork of the Almighty, are all mystically one.
When they descend to this world they separate, each
to its own side, and God brings them together – God
and no other. He alone knows which soul belongs
with which and how to bring them together.*

Zohar I: 85b

Getting a Get and How Life Goes On

Honey Faye Gilbert

The children were sleeping and I sat at the kitchen table trying to catch my
breath after a long day of carpools, meals, homework and the general duties that
four small children require. The newspaper was spread out in front of me. I
actually thought I'd read it, but the words, even the headlines, became blurry. I
was much better bustling around doing something than sitting down and trying
to read, because this was what invariably happened. I would start thinking and
that lead to crying and that lead to my asking myself and God: "How did this
happen?"

I thought I had done everything right and now I was thirty-five years old,
with four children under five, and I was getting divorced. This wasn't supposed
to happen to me. My marriage was going to be a success story. I was going to live
happily ever after.

I had been in my late twenties when I had gotten married and I had thought
long and hard about what my marriage was going to be like: my husband and I
were going to be friends, mutually supportive and understanding of each other's
needs and space. I was really going to work at it.

In general, I was more committed to the institution of marriage than many of
my friends, some of whom felt that getting married was like buying a pair of
shoes at Nordstom's: if they pinched after a while, you just returned them and
got your money back. Anyone can tell you, including scientists who have studied
the "falling in love" phenomenon, that high lasts at most a year and then what? I
had come to truly believe what I had learned in some of the courses that I had
taken: that a marriage is more a union of souls than physical bodies and that the

two people standing under the wedding canopy are there to fulfill the mission of their souls.

It is written in Jewish scripture that forty days before a child is born an angel calls out who its destined mate will be. These souls are meant to be together to help each other accomplish spiritually what each could not do alone. And even now, when my two-year old cried and I went to comfort her, of course, I knew why my soul and my husband's had been meant for each other – we had to bring these four new souls into the world. Would I exchange them if I knew that I wouldn't have to go through the pain of divorce? I smiled sadly at the thought, and just then my daughter smiled a little crooked, half-asleep smile back at me. No. "When there's no way around," a famous rabbi had said, "the only thing to do is go through." Tough it out! Those words are a lot tougher than I am.

I comforted my little girl and went back to the kitchen to make myself a cup of tea. As I held the warm cup, I remembered how clean and whole and right I had felt going to the mikveh and totally immersing myself in the warm water. It certainly wasn't just a bath. I felt reborn and ready for a new life. I remembered the joy I felt when my groom lifted the veil from my face and looked into my eyes as the rabbi blessed us. I thought everyone could hear my heart beating. I especially recalled walking around my husband-to-be seven times and imagining that a host of angels were part of the wedding band, that they were blowing their trumpets to indicate their joy at our union. The singing of the seven benedictions under the wedding canopy by rabbis and friends made me feel safe and accepted into my new state of matrimony.

So what had happened? In the end, I realized that my soul, or my husband's, or both, wasn't strong enough to withstand the pressures intended for its correction and we weren't headed in the right direction to make this work. But I didn't understand this all at once. Whatever knowledge or wisdom I have gained about marriage and divorce was crystallized in the crucible of hard experience. As I understand it now, every soul has its purpose and the people we marry, even just the people we meet in the course of our everyday lives, offer us an opportunity to correct any past wrongs or to climb higher on the soul ladder. This is especially true of our spouses. They offer us the most opportunities to improve our souls, but the two of us did not have the necessary fortitude or insight.

I tried. But things started to fall apart right away and I was very confused. When we were in our apartment (actually his one-room studio) right after the wedding and he handed me the vacuum cleaner, saying: "Clean this place up. My mother is coming over," I felt that I had been hit in the face with a cold, dirty rag, but I didn't want to start a fight, and as I mindlessly pushed the sweeping tool here and there imitating vacuuming, I told myself that he was nervous, that

281

he hadn't really meant to hurt my feelings. Neither one of us had been married before; we were older, we were each used to living alone; we had to get used to one another. I would be kind to him and speak softly and get him to laugh a little; I would bake challas and prepare good healthy meals from scratch and he would relax and come to appreciate me. And soon we would be the kind of team that I thought married partners were supposed to be. This wasn't anything to get upset about. I would have to be more understanding and put more effort into making this work. I would read about how to improve the situation, and read I did. I read *Don't Sweat the Small Stuff* by Richard Carlson and tried to let the disappointment go, just let it go. I tried a women's yoga class to learn to breathe correctly and be less tense. I read *The Path to Love: Spiritual Strategies for Healing* by Deepak Chopra. Nothing would bother me. All beginnings are hard.

That's what I thought when I was thinking clearly, logically, but to tell the truth I cried every day and then I wasn't so logical. Back and forth this went. I would cry and then give myself a pep talk: *you can do this. Why shouldn't you be able to do this?* Then I dissolved in tears again. How can I do this? But I wasn't ready to give up. I just needed a new approach. I would pray harder, longer. I hadn't found the right book. Maybe if I read *The Dance of Connection* by Harriet Lerner, I would be able to connect. I would really focus on what was important.... But it takes two to tango as the old saying goes, but it was always "I would do this, and I would try that." I was dancing alone.

After three months, my husband told me that he wasn't happy either. I wasn't fulfilling his needs. Marriage wasn't what he had expected. I read too many books. He suggested an annulment. I had never cried in front of him, but now the floodgates burst and I wept in big, heaving sobs as I told him that an annulment wouldn't be possible since I was probably pregnant.

We hadn't really talked much during the last month. He had been moody. I wasn't feeling well. I slept a lot, and we were like shadows trying to stay out of each other's way. But I had to try. I would never forgive myself unless I shared some of what I had been thinking. He sat down heavily in his favorite chair, and I sank down to the floor at his feet and tried to explain that there was a reason that God had given us to one another. "Let's spend some time trying to understand why we were put together. To give up now would be a mistake." Pain is the best teacher and I wanted to do it right, to learn what all of this had to teach me, to make him happy, to ensure that my child had a father. If the two of us weren't smart enough to do it on our own, perhaps we needed the help of a counselor, a professional, I suggested. I didn't want to spend the rest of my life thinking, what if I had tried this, what if I had done that, would it have worked? I'm not a quitter.

But after a year of marital counseling and great expense, we weren't any closer. I had just had twins when we decided on a trial separation. He got a small apartment a few blocks away from the house. My other two children were conceived during times when we thought we'd give our marriage another shot. He moved back in for a few months; he moved out for a few months. We still saw the marriage counselor intermittently, and when he told us that there was nothing more he could suggest I felt as if the floor beneath me had given way and I was falling down a mine shaft. If you had asked me then, I would have sworn that I even heard the wind whistling past my ears as I fell. The therapist was shaking my arm. "Are you okay?" she asked. What could I say? How could I tell her the truth – that I had put so much faith in her and in my own efforts to make it right that I couldn't believe there was nowhere else to turn? My youngest child was one year old. Was I now going to be the single mother I had never imagined I would be?

"Yes, I'm fine," I answered as my equilibrium returned. Later that day, when I was thinking more clearly, I had to admit to myself that it was true; I had indeed run out of options and now knew as well as felt that divorce was the only logical next step. But now I felt that I really had tried everything in my power to make this marriage work, and I had failed. That was very hard for me to admit. I felt so empty knowing that there were no more avenues to try, no more books to read with a different approach, no more rabbis to talk to or counselors to see.

Then a famous rabbi came into town, a reputed mystic. Some of my friends suggested that I talk to him. When I was ushered into the library where he was seeing people, a great sense of calm washed over me. I hadn't done so well on my own; I would do whatever this rabbi said. But he didn't really give me any advice. To the one question that had been bothering me, he gave me the only answer that made sense. I wanted to know if my husband was my *basherter*, my destined one, the one the angel called out forty days before my birth and if so, why were we both so unhappy.

"Ah," he said in Yiddish. "You make the mistake of thinking that your *basherter* will make you happy. A person cannot make you happy. If you live your life right, you will be happy… some day." Then he seemed to stare right through me and added, "Raise your children to be good Jews. Be sure to get a Jewish divorce. Go in health." And I knew the interview was over. I backed out of the room in a respectful fashion as I had been instructed but immediately sat down in a chair outside the door. I had to think about this: a person cannot make you happy. That's what all the self-help books had been telling me: happiness comes from within, from doing the right thing.

That night, as I was reading Jacobson's *Toward a Meaningful Life*, after I read the following insight: "Let us decide to acknowledge the need for God in our marriages. Let us commit to making our marriages divine, to making our family's home a place that helps fulfill our Godly mission on earth…. [Marriage] is not just a commitment between you, your spouse – it is a commitment between you, your spouse and God. Such a unity gives off a light that shines throughout the world."

That struck me as being the truest statement to describe the problem in my marriage: the lack of Godliness. I was lighting candles and we were observing Shabbos and the holidays, family purity. Of course I was praying, and of course my mind wandered (but that's another story). But there was very little Godliness between the two of us. We weren't honoring the Godliness in each other's souls. I think I had started out all right, but to be very honest, my outwardly, kindly motions belied the growing distrust and anger I felt inside.

My husband agreed to a divorce. He must have been secretly relieved. He must have felt the same. We had turned into two repelling forces. We were still polite to each other – when we spoke to each other – but we were seething inside. We were not living our lives correctly, this was all wrong, and it got worse every day. Divorce was the only option left to us.

He was now living in his own apartment permanently because when he came home for a while, he couldn't even bear to be in the same room with me. He agreed to the divorce but wanted to wait. He wanted to be very sure that this was the right thing to do. I respected that. We waited.

Although the children were too young to understand what was really going on, they had been very distraught when their father moved out. Yet they were surprisingly calmer when he only saw them on weekends and for dinner on Wednesdays. They were calmer because we were calmer.

But a year went by and I still didn't have a *get*, a Jewish divorce. I talked to my lawyer. I asked if there were anything he could do to speed up the process. There wasn't anything to be done, he said, mumbling something about the separation between church and state. "What's your hurry?" he asked. "You're a good-looking woman. Go out. Have a few drinks. Have a good time." His words struck me like a one-two punch to the solar plexus. How dared he suggest that? He knew nothing about my values, about the world I lived in. To him, I was just another lonely woman waiting for her divorce to be finalized, whose problems could be solved, or rather dissolved, in a dry martini.

But I had always been very particular about the order of things, and I needed to do things right. I understood the magnitude of the situation. Without a *get* I was still a married woman, a woman with a husband. Just as there is a ceremony that binds to people together in marriage, there is a ceremony that dissolves those bonds and separates the two souls. I wasn't about to mess around with supernal forces.

Of course, I immediately agreed when several weeks later my husband called and asked if Tuesday would be a good day for me to receive my *get*. I knew that Tuesday was a good day to get married; in the Bible God says, "It was good" twice on Tuesday. Maybe it was also a fortuitous day to get divorced. The civil divorce would eventually work out, I felt. That was only about money, but the *get* was about my soul, extricating it from this marriage, getting it back. That was more important to me than money, and it was imperative that it be done correctly – by an Orthodox tribunal of three rabbis, so that no one could impugn its validity in the future.

The day came. The three rabbis and the scribe who was going to be writing all this down in Hebrew were very cordial. My soon-to-be ex-husband was there. We were both asked all of our names, that is, our first names in both Hebrew and English and any nicknames that we had. That wasn't bad, I thought. It was funny to think of all the childhood names my father had called me. I could handle this. Then my husband was asked if he was divorcing me of his own free will. The question took me by surprise, and I closed my eyes and prayed that he would give the right answer and not change his mind. When the rabbis asked him if he was divorcing me of his own free will, I could feel his eyes boring into me, although I didn't trust myself to look at him. He hesitated for a moment, took a deep breath (or was it a sigh?) and said, "Yes, of my own free will." It was important that what he was doing had not been coerced because that would have invalidated the whole procedure. I exhaled. I hadn't realized that I had been holding my breath. In fact, it seemed that everyone took a deep breath. And I knew that the worst was over.

It took a while for the scribe to write the *get*. Then it was handed to my husband, who had to drop it in my hands. I had to put it under my arm as a sign of acceptance and walk out of the room, which I did. I had been waiting for this for a long time, so I was very surprised when I started bawling, crying, gulping for air. I went into the ladies' room down the hall and sat down in one of the stalls on top of the commode and cried as if my heart would break. I understand now in retrospect that my soul was crying. It was weeping along with the altar, as it says in the Talmud: "When a person divorces... even the altar sheds tears on his account." I had not been up to the challenge my soul was given, but somewhere deep inside I also knew that I was being given another chance.

When I dried my eyes (there wasn't much I could do about the redness and puffiness), I went back into the rabbis. They were very kind, non-judgmental. One of them asked if I was all right. Another asked if I wanted some water. I was grateful when one of them offered me a chair. I didn't realize how wobbly my knees had become.

They took the *get* that the scribe had written and, interestingly enough, cut it up. They told me that this was for my protection, so that it could never be stolen or invalidated. I was told that I would shortly be receiving a certificate in the mail, and then they all said *mazal tov*, good luck, as if it were a joyous occasion. I appreciated that. They didn't make me feel bad. I had done it right. I had gotten a kosher, Jewish divorce and now they were wishing me luck in my future endeavors. They wished us both luck. It was all very civilized.

I thought I was fine. I thanked them and left the building, but I wasn't fine. It took me twenty minutes to find my way out of the parking lot. I didn't know that the *get* would only take two hours, so I had hired a babysitter for the day; I didn't have to rush back. I drove to a Barnes and Noble and, as usual, reached for a book. This time it was a book on children and divorce, *Surviving the Breakup: How Children Cope with Divorce* by Dr. Judith Wallerstein. I suppose I hadn't done it earlier, because I was still married. My husband wasn't living in the house, but I was still married and that meant that there was still hope. Now I was officially divorced in the eyes of God, and I had to remember that my children would need more of my attention, that they would be experiencing some psychological trauma as well and I had to be sensitive to that.

I was totally numb for a few days after receiving my *get*. I went through all the motions: got the kids up, dressed them, made breakfast, drove carpools. I did whatever a mother of four small children does. My friends actually gave me some breathing room, but after four days the phone calls started coming. "How did it go?" my girlfriends wanted to know. I tried to answer all of their questions. I had thought so long about this whole process and perhaps my answers were more involved than they had wanted to hear right then, but more than one of them said: "You know, I have a girlfriend who has been thinking about divorce for a long time. Could I have her call you?" Naturally, I said yes. If my painful experience could help another human being, of course I wanted to do so. One woman called me and we talked for an hour – that is, I talked while she sniffled, trying not to cry so that her husband wouldn't hear her on the phone. Another woman didn't even want to talk on the phone. She wanted to meet in person. That was nice, actually. I got a babysitter, got to go out for lunch, and made a new friend, Esther, who kept in touch even after she got divorced.

When you're single, it seems that all of your friends are single too. After you get married, you retain some of your single friends, but more and more are young married couples like yourselves. The same is true when you get divorced. One naturally has more in common with friends in similar circumstances.

In addition, the Jewish Family Service had just started a support group for Jewish women who were divorced or in the process of getting divorced. That was really helpful. The ladies were nice and the eight of us clicked. It was someone safe to go to a movie with occasionally or have a cup of coffee with while the wounds healed and I worked on the process of learning to trust my judgment again.

In the process of getting to know these eight new ladies, I also got to know about their ex-husbands. I heard about the good, the bad, and the ugly, but there was one woman who didn't say much. She tried, but she couldn't. She seemed overly-medicated. Someone always picked her up and took her home. We all felt badly for her and protective. She had been in and out of hospitals and was trying hard to cope. It was quite a surprise when I was introduced to her ex-husband at a large shul dinner. He seemed nice, well-spoken, intelligent, not bad-looking. Not for me. I wasn't ready to think about going out yet... but he would be perfect for Esther! I loved the idea and I called her as soon as I had paid the babysitter and checked on the kids.

Esther was grateful that I had thought of her and very excited. They went out. They liked each other. They went out many more times. Call it beginners' luck.

It's funny now, but one could say that my divorce actually led to my becoming a matchmaker. Of course, there are married matchmakers; some couples even work together, but while I was married, I was so wrapped up in my own world – my children, my home, my husband, my own problems, that I had little time to think of the singles in my neighborhood, who wanted desperately to get married. Being divorced and newly single myself had sensitized me in a way that hadn't happened before. And it turned out that I was good at it; I had made my first match.

Soon Esther was telling everyone what a good matchmaker I was, and other people began calling too. I remember picking up the phone one time and a woman began to tell me about herself: I'm 5'5" in my stocking feet. I'm 34, a social worker, never married and so on. It sounded like she was applying for some position. I was nonplussed and she must have sensed it, because she asked, "Isn't this the matchmaker?" "Uh, yes, the matchmaker." Now it was official.

I guess it was meant to be. After the children were asleep, I would look through the list of people that I kept in a notebook and if no one came to mind, I would network. I would call and ask friends if they knew of someone for the person I had in mind at the moment.

Of course, God is always the matchmaker, and I was pleased to be a conduit through which He worked. Actually anyone can do it. All that is necessary is the willingness to try. And I think everyone should try.

One thing led to another and soon I was doing Shabbatonim, large conferences, for Jewish singles. This was a new phenomenon. It was like creating a *tsholent tup*, a stew pot, for singles. We had rabbis there to give talks and answer questions and I was there to facilitate. That was a new thing on the single, social scene.

Wherever I traveled, I met single people and tried to keep them in mind. I soon had a network that included Canada and Australia as well as the United States, and people were traveling to meet one another. A woman from Oregon married a young man from Oklahoma; a divorced man from Denver married a divorced woman with a child from Philadelphia, and so on. Never once did I feel anything less than a messenger in carrying out God's will and grateful to have a part in it.

Now I was really busy; in addition to my family, I was teaching, lecturing about the need for kosher Jewish divorces to end irreconcilable marriages, talking to groups about matchmaking and doing some matchmaking as well. I never charged for my services, although it is certainly permissible for a matchmaker to charge a fee. It is even discussed in the Talmud when the fee should be paid: at the time of engagement or after the wedding ceremony? It also goes on to say that it bodes ill for the future of the marriage if the matchmaker is not paid. I always left it up to the couple's own discretion what the gift would be.

Despite my own experience, I felt with all my heart the veracity of the Talmud's dictum that a man without a wife lives "without joy, blessing, goodness." But it has to be the right match and the two people have to be devoted not only to each other but to the marriage as a God-given institution, and then the whole will be greater than the sum of its parts and Godliness will pervade that union.

Interestingly enough, it was the matchmaking, the selfless doing for others that led me to meeting my second husband. It says in the Talmud that if someone prays on behalf of his friend who has a similar problem, he will be helped first (*Bava Kama* 92a). How much more so, if someone helps his friend with a similar problem. These are more than nice words and pleasant sentiments; it's true.

I was lecturing and facilitating for a Jewish organization having a retreat at one of the kosher hotels in the Catskill mountains. The retreat was mostly for families, but there were about fifty single people there as well, and I was on their program. On Friday night, I was giving a talk entitled, *Jewish Women of Our Heritage: Are They Role Models for Our Time?* and on Sunday afternoon, my topic was *Love and Marriage, Jewish Style.* Both times a very nice man stopped by to ask questions. His questions were intelligent and he listened carefully and appreciatively to my answers. He invited me to sit at his table for dinner on Sunday so that we could continue to talk. He was also divorced. His ex-wife had become a Buddhist. He had given it two years after that, but celibacy was part of her new religion. He also had four children, but they were all out of the house. I liked the fact that he was quite a bit older than I was. I hoped it indicated maturity. He loves children, loves being a father and liked the fact that I still had children at home. When he offered to drive me to the airport after the weekend was over, I felt taken care of, something I hadn't felt in a long time. And the rest, as they say, is history.

Was this man also *bashert*, destined, for me? Of course. One's second mate is also heaven-sent, but in a different way from one's first. The first mate has something to teach your soul, something that only those two souls can accomplish together. The second mate is someone you have earned by merit of your good deeds (Talmud, *Sotah* 2a).

We still have to work on our marriage, like any couple. We can't get so comfortable that we take each other for granted. We have to honor the Godliness in each other, but somehow, this time it is easier to do. We laugh a lot; we talk to each other a lot. We put time aside so that we can spend time together. God was very good to us and gave us a lovely little girl. My other children adore her. I feel very fortunate.

Perhaps this time is better because we are both older. Perhaps this time is better because we are both wiser. I don't know if it would have been this way if I hadn't learned all that I did from my first marriage. Whatever the reason, I'm very grateful to have been given another chance to do it right.

For further reading:

Freeman, Tzvi. *Men, Women and Kabbalah: Wisdom and Guidance from the Masters.* New York, NY: 2004.

Epstein, Mendel. *A Woman's Guide to the Get Process.* New York: 1989.

Manolson, Gila. *Head to Heart: What to Know Before Dating and Marriage.* Jerusalem: 2002.

Lamm, Maurice. *The Jewish Way in Love and Marriage.* New York: 1980.

Kaplan, Aryeh. *Made in Heaven: A Jewish Wedding Guide.* New York: 1983.

The Fifth Commandment

Elizabeth Cohen

To live near a river is a very lucky thing. To live near two is luckier. But to spend the center of your life in a place where two rivers come together feels to me luckiest of all. No matter how exhausted or overwhelmed I am, if I have just lost my glasses or done something spectacularly stupid like drop my laptop, when I am driving to Binghamton and the road sidles up to the Chenango River in a canyon of waterfalls and trees, the river whisks away everything but respect for the very fact of it. Then it joins its sister, the Susquehanna, and becomes a more muscular version of each. It surges with power and something as close to holiness as anything else I can imagine.

Two years ago I tried to hold onto the river's feeling as long as I could after reaching Vestal, New York, where my mother lived in a nursing home. I tried to keep centered, peaceful and directional. But that was hard to do while listening to a "Clifford the Big Red Dog" tape for the hundred and seventeenth time – and if the place one was headed, as I was, was to visit one's mother, who had decided to die.

I was a woman in my early forties. If I shifted the rear view mirror a few inches downward I could see the beginning of crow's feet fan out from my eyes. Behind me was my then two-and-a-half year-old daughter, Ava. And behind her, the busy, blue-black Chenango river.

In a rear view mirror or otherwise, the view from forty-two seemed extraordinary. It was like being in the crow's nest of a ship with a clear, crisp view of all horizons. Beginnings and endings, genesis and exodus – all were familiar places I could see from there. It was breathtaking; sometimes it gave me vertigo.

I'd watched my daughter move from breast to bottle to sippy cup to "big girl" cup at two and a half while simultaneously my father, 82, had traveled from steak and potatoes to pureed steak and potatoes, and my mother from food to softer foods, too.

In the center of my life I had begun to take the Biblical fifth commandment quite literally: I had begun to care for my ailing, elderly parents. First my father, who has Alzheimer's disease, came to live with me in 1999 and my mother, with congestive heart failure, arrived a year and a half afterwards. She lived with me for several months but then announced she could not stand it: I was not clean enough. So after touring local nursing homes and apartments she took up residence in an assisted living facility nearby.

After moving into her new abode my mother became depressed. She dropped weight. She seemed easily confused. On one particular morning she informed me she had decided to give up food entirely. So I drove my car along rivers on that clear, cold morning to her tiny apartment to try to convince her that it would be good to have lunch. In my purse I brought a liverwurst sandwich with fresh green lettuce, her favorite, and a vanilla Ensure. In the back seat of the car my daughter sang along to her "Clifford the Big Red Dog" tape. If only there were something like that to distract my mother from her project of dying, her high and cynical misery. Some tape, food, experience, gift. But there wasn't. Even narcotics, which helped for a time, didn't seem to work anymore. She had married her unhappiness, taken vows. "Till death do us part."

Caring for my mother and father was not something I consciously chose to do. In fact it is something that seems rare in our society. I only have one other friend who has done so. When I did it, it was more like a reflex than a planned-out project. I devoted the center of my life to the ends of my parent's lives, but I was not thinking in particular about the book of Exodus when I took on the task. In that Biblical book it states: "Honor your father and your mother that your days may be long in the land which God gives you."

I had not even thought about my own longevity, nor had I thought about my Jewish faith or keeping true to its commandments. I took in my parents simply because I did not know what else to do.

At the time my mother called me to say she had decided not to eat anymore, my parents were living separately. My father had been transferred to a nursing home in Owego, New York, and she lived in a room the size of a postage stamp in Vestal, New York at Castle Gardens, a fancy and expensive assisted living home.

I would take my mother to visit my father sometimes. They still had conversations then. Their talk was limited to my mother's concern about my father's physical needs. We often came during his meals. She wanted to make sure he was eating right.

"Is the meat good?" my mother would ask my father. He would nod.

"Do you want more juice?"

My parents were married for over forty years and most of that was spent in something very close to, if not exactly, happiness. Then, almost overnight it seems, they fell off a cliff into happiness's opposite. There were only two times in their relationship, bliss and misery. They were beautiful and perfect and then they weren't. No segue, no transition.

Sometimes she would eat lunch with him at his nursing home. She claimed they had better food there than the food in her assisted living facility. I did not tell her that the food was nearly identical. I did not tell her about the cartons I saw in the kitchen, bearing the same labels of pre-prepared foods as they served at her facility. There are many things I did not tell her. If she wanted to think that the food was better there, where he ate his meals, why spoil that? She liked to think she had discovered little secrets to an improved existence. There was better butter in restaurants, better shampoos in hotels. She snatched plastic containers of flavored coffee creams from gas stations because at Castle Gardens they had "non-dairy substitute."

A few days after my father's move to Owego my mother took a fall in the small apartment she lived in. She was taken to the hospital where she was examined, x-rayed, CAT-scanned and prodded. She was dispatched back with her chest taped like a mummy, her right arm blooming with blue-black bruises the size of half dollars and a new silver walker. "Cracked ribs," they said. "Nothing we can do."

She came back, too, with bottles of Darvocet and Oxycontin that she clutched in her hands like winning lottery tickets. An ambulette was supposed to transport her but she'd insisted on me. I drove slowly, avoiding the potholes that made her moan and say "Oh! Oh!" the whole way home. I stopped and got her a hot fudge sundae at Friendly's to improve the situation, as though somehow "sweet and cold" could trump "miserable." She took a bite and dropped the rest on the floor of the car, where it mingled with Ava's favorite stuffed animal, a dog she'd named Angel, that emitted a tired electronic bark.

Once I worried about things like that – spilled ice cream or drinks, food on carpets, food on lapels. But since my parents arrival I'd changed. I had learned how to absorb such occurrences so easily it surprised me. "Don't worry," I said to my mother when she spilled her ice cream, "it's okay." I told her this because she was a woman who kept a spotless house for over forty years. I would say you could eat off her floors, but she would have never allowed such a thing.

The tiny apartment where my mother had chosen to live was so small she could not even open her drawers all the way. Pulled out, they hit the side of the bed. But my mother said she didn't care about the drawers. She didn't care about the view of a parking lot, the cramped feeling, or anything, really. When I took her to see it the first time she surveyed the tiny apartment with a sweep of her eyes and said, "It will do."

But it did not do. Weeks went by and she did not unpack. She never put her toothbrush or bar of soap on the sink. She didn't put her clothes in the drawers or her hairbrush on the dresser top. She never unpacked her Moon Glow night cream or her Mary Kay cosmetics or the tired Vaseline jar she had toted across a continent, all the way from her stately adobe home with cream carpet and brick floors in Albuquerque, New Mexico to a room in Vestal, New York with a view of a parking lot. She didn't plug in her lamps or her television. At night she called me on her cordless phone, the only functional thing she possessed, and said, "The television doesn't work. I can't get any shows."

The first time when I came and plugged it in and showed her how to operate the remote, she looked depressed: "It will stop working as soon as you walk out the door."

She called my sister, Melanie, in Seattle and complained, too. My sister then called me. "Can't you fix her T.V.? It isn't like she has anything else to do," she said.

"It works fine," I said. "She won't plug it in."

"Well, plug it in for her."

"I tried that. She unplugs it."

She called me about the television again that morning, the morning she had decided not to eat, but the complaint was more troublesome. This time she said the shows came on but they were the wrong shows. They seem like the shows she used to watch but they were "all mixed up."

"Sometimes," she told me, "they start yelling at me."

"What do you mean," I asked, "yelling?"

"They tell me to go to sleep, to wake up, to buy things."

"You mean commercials?" I asked.

"Don't get snippy," she said.

When I arrived at Castle Gardens I unbuckled my daughter Ava and she shot like a bottle rocket into the foyer. You are supposed to call the person you are visiting and they buzz you in but my mother had apparently forgotten how to buzz so we banged on the glass door until the annoyed attendant pushed a button that released the lock. Once in, we walked through the lobby past the glazed, smiling eyes of other residents. Ava was a favorite there – the women sitting in the lobby reached out their craggy hands when she flew by as if they wanted to catch her, skim off some of the cream of her energy.

"Say 'hi,' sweetie," I instructed, watching their eyes sorrowfully trail her, like a train they'd missed.

The air in Castle Gardens always seemed heavier than other air. You could feel it the moment you walk in the door, a thickness invaded your lungs. The atoms seemed charged with loneliness. Although it was perfectly pleasant looking, even nice, there was a feeling that something was somehow off, like the neighborhood in *The Stepford Wives*. The neat baskets of large print magazines on the coffee table were always untouched. The grand piano in a corner was stiff and unplayed. The carpet was other-wordly clean. It was a place people came to live right before they died and you could feel it – the waiting.

In the hallway by the mailboxes there was a cage with two mynah birds. Someone once told me that if you caught these birds in the right mood they would whistle the theme song to *The Andy Griffith Show*. This, I had come to suspect, was retirement home legend. I had never heard them say anything but "Caw, okay?" But there they were, and sort of pretty in a caged bird way and provided the needed carrot-on-a-stick to get Ava to go in. Television theme song or no, she was mesmerized, stuck her fingers in between the bars, tempting mynah bird fate. A hand-penned sign taped to the cage says, "No fingers, we bite." Luck was always on her side.

When we arrived at my mother's apartment, she did not answer the door. During that time she had done away with formalities like door and phone answering. Long ago she shucked all greetings, like "Hello" and "Goodbye," and before that she did away with "How are you." On the phone, when she called, she cut right to the chase: "There wasn't any salt on the table at dinner," or "I can't find a station." One by one she discarded the rules of the world.

When she didn't answer the knock we yelled at her. "Mommy? Grandma?" She yelled back. "Come in."

The door was open. We walked through the tiny kitchenette, still full of unopened boxes of things. We wended down the tiny hallway that seemed even tinier because it was blocked by her walker, to an unsettling scene. My mother was lying on the floor, her arms entangled in the television cord. "I fell," she said.

"Mommy! Let me help you," I said, fighting the horror welling in my throat. I had a momentary urge to lie down next to her and pull her close to me, as if I could fix her that way, merge her into me, absorb her whole predicament. She was wearing the same blue nightgown she had on the last time we visited. Her hair was unkempt and her glasses sort of sideways, still I had the same thought I always have when I see her: She was beautiful. She had always been beautiful. She had those kind of cheekbones other women pay to get implanted, and pale green eyes the color of spring leaves. For most of her life she wore silky grey or powder-blue pants with matching shifts or white linen or coffee-colored skirts and "interesting" ethnic shirts that accentuated her svelte frame. She was the sort of woman who could pull off an orange poncho with fringe. An outfit that would make me look like a pumpkin, but on her it was like a page out of *Santa Fe Magazine*.

"What happened?" I asked her, my heart pounding, as I stooped at her side to get a better look.

"I had to stop the television," she said. "It was getting really nasty."

I sat on the ground to examine my mother's position. She was lying next to the bed, legs extending toward the hall. Nothing looked crooked or terribly out of place. I didn't see any blood. "How did you fall?" I asked. "Is anything hurt?"

"I didn't fall, I tripped, not that it matters," she said. "And of course something is hurt. Everything is hurt. I am always hurt. This is what I get with a daughter who lives on top of a mountain who takes two years to get here."

"Let me get you up," I said. "I reached for her arm and tried to gently lift her. But I did it wrong. I always did it wrong. There was no right. She was so thin her shoulders protruded like doorknobs. Her skin and her bones were so close together there was no padding, as she put it. Any touching her hurt. Clothes hurt. Sheets hurt. Air hurt.

Despite cries of pain and protestations I managed to get my mother back on her bed. There I examined her legs, her arms, her fingers, her neck. I cleaned her up and retrieved a pair of clean underwear from a suitcase, combed her limp hair. I got her a glass of juice from the refrigerator, unwrapped the liverwurst sandwich in the kitchenette and served it to her. She took a bite and tosses it back on the plate. "I can't taste anything any more," she said. "Something is wrong with my mouth."

Finally, we lay together on the bed. Ava clambered over me to nestle between us. I plugged in the television and I hunted for a cartoon with the remote.

"Mommy, what are we going to do? You can't live here like this," I said. Her eyes stared at the television screen, as though she, too, was engrossed in the cartoon.

"I can't seem to get it right," she finally said. She took my hand in hers and then she moved her hand to the top of Ava's head where it rested. It was mottled and blue-veined and the nails were too long again. But it was still a beautiful hand. The long-fingered, perfect-nailed sort that you could get paid for in a commercial for a nail-growing product.

My mother definitely could have been a hand model, a lawyer, an investment banker (she saved pennies, she invested), a senator. She could have been a teacher, a baker, a chef, a psychologist, a musicologist, a grant writer, an accountant. She had talents in all these things. But she spent the majority of her life being my mother, my father's wife.

She closed her eyes. "I am trying so hard to die," she said.

We lay there like that for a long time, my daughter occasionally shifting positions and squirming. I was in the middle of them, the way it always felt I was then, straddling their generations, central to their disparate needs. The sun sank down toward the parking lot. The "Clifford the Big Red Dog" cartoon became "Blue's Clues" and "Blue's Clues" became "Dragon Tales" and my mother's head slumped onto her neck. Ava, too, fell fast asleep. She emitted small snores that fell into a rhythm with my mother's larger snores. I lay there with my daughter who was only still when she is sleeping, and my mother, who hardly moved at all. My daughter's face was angelic, her thick lashes tossed twin moons of shadow upon her cheeks. My mother's face was so thin you could see the contours of her skull. Then my own eyelids grew heavy and I fell away toward the sleeping place they had gone.

Ava's was a sleep full of laughing and little grunts. She dreamed, I imagine, of kittens and Popsicles, of people walking on stilts and handing her balloons. My mother's sleep was comprised of tiny, regular snores and moans. I liked to think her dreams started with pain and then took her away from it, to her beautiful before-life, when everything was as she loved it.

My own sleep has always been light. Especially when I was caring for my parents. I would wake in an instant at the slightest noise. But while they were still that day, sleeping on either side of me I slept too. I traveled up and away from my body, across a town and a highway and above a dozen or so small dramas that reached their fingers up to grab me. I escaped, I rose. I floated above them all until I reached a place where broad blue rivers came together, like the letter Y.

This is still the place I go in dreams. I escape to rivers. Maybe rivers remind me of the freedom I had before I took on this responsibility. Maybe it is just a peaceful image my mind gives me to reward me for all the stress of caring for two generations.

Sometimes it seemed to me that my own life had stopped during that time. I felt like I was walking underwater, pulling myself through the days. I told my mother frequently that it would be okay if she died. Not to be cruel, but to reassure her. That I would be okay, she would be okay. That I would somehow see her again someday.

I wasn't sure I really believed that, just as I was never sure how much I believed in anything. I was raised by parents who were very serious about being Jewish but questioning about the existence of an all-knowing creator. My father said that made him even more Jewish: that he questioned, that he asked.

I didn't mean to be a good Jew when I took care of my parents. I didn't do it so that my days would be "long in the land," or for any other reason. But I have come to see that the promise made in the fifth commandment can be more liberally interpreted. Perhaps the words "That your days may be long in the land God gives you," means that someone who loves and cares for their parents, who gives their life over to their parents at a time when they need them most, reaps some more subtle benefits from such an act.

Had you told me at the time my mother was dying that I would someday be happy that I drove each day to see her, slept by her side, spoon-fed her, rationed her medications, held her like an infant, I would have thought you a lunatic. Had you told me I would someday think back fondly on the time my father lived with me, lost his shoes and glasses every day and cried at night out of frustration because he could not remember where he was, or even his own name, I would have told you that you were nuts.

But now it is two years later and it is slowly dawning on me that although this experience was terribly hard, it was one of the best of my life. There is no way to sell this to someone on the outside. There is no brochure for parental caretaking that can make it look like a holiday, or infomercial that sells it like a timeshare. It is no holiday, no picnic, nothing you would daydream about doing one day. But to anyone with a sick parent, or whose parent grows weak or needs them, I can say this: It is time well spent. It will go on your soul's resume. Honor your father and mother and you may like yourself better having done so.

My father lives today in a netherworld between waking and sleep. At a very fine Veteran's Home in Oxford, New York, he drifts through the days, smiling and humming, conducting an invisible symphony with his hands. My mother got what she wanted, too. She contracted pneumonia in October of 2002 and refused all treatment. She bravely strode to her own death, holding the hands of my sister and me.

I went to see a rabbi soon after she died and he gave me a laminated copy of the Kaddish to recite. For a year I said it each morning, at the break of day. Not because she would have wanted me to, not because I was growing more religious, but because it felt right, I needed to do something to mark the end of her life, and the experience I had of walking by her side to that end.

I can say now with conviction that children are also the beneficiaries when parents are honored. The commandment makes a promise I never understood until now. Are my days to be "long in the land"? I think they are. If we think of this as merely a temporal promise it is suspect, seems absurd even. But my days are different now, because I feel the gift of each one so vividly. Explicitly. Each moment seems full of beauty and sanctity, a gift from God.

I know now that each day spent without pain, with a memory of who I am, each day with my daughter, with the sun on my face and a book in my purse, is a giant present from the universe. Every thing I do, skin a carrot, boil a potato, help my daughter put on her socks, seems heaven-sent because it is mine. I own my life in a way I never did before. My parents gave that to me.

First they gave me life. Then they gave me an appreciation for it. And I rest peacefully at night, knowing I honored them and made (in the case of my father, still make) their days as comfortable as possible.

Since the beginning of this calling, this parent-protecting project, I have dreamt of rivers. Now the dream feels less like a place I am headed to as one where I have arrived. Above me, sometimes, I see a flurry of crows. They dip their wings in the water and rise up to the sky. Or fall upon white riverbanks, like ashes.

For further reading:

Cohen, Elizabeth. *The Family on Beartown Road: A Memoir of Love and Courage.* New York, NY: 2004.

Lieber, Moshe. *The Fifth Commandment: Honoring Parents – Laws, Insights, Stories and Ideas.* Brooklyn, NY: 1998.

A Mother's Meditation: Prayerful Thoughts on Raising Children

Sara Lieberman

When God created man and woman and set them down in the Garden of Eden, He directed them to bring down the high heavens to the very bottom of earth and elevate the lowly earth to the very heights of heaven.

When God created man and woman He breathed a soul into the body; He sparked the body with holiness, with the very essence of His inwardness, with the absolute grandeur of infinite potential, with the Godly capacity to conquer the world, to infuse the bitter with the sweet, to transform the dark into light.

From that moment on, God filled the world with challenges and tribulations, multidirectional inclinations, sensory gratifications and intellectual calculations.

Thus it came to pass that man and woman would bear offspring in their likeness, the veritable image of God Himself, and the children from their earliest moments would set out to fulfill their role in creation. Women and men would be heralded into the exercise of parenthood, guiding their young along carefully chosen paths, propelled by love and dedication, fiery devotion, fierce commitment and soulful accomplishment. Women and men would develop into rightful partners in creation bringing forth new life in a threefold union of man, woman and God.

Budding blossoms in the human garden, pretty flowers delectable and fragrant, growing to maturity, adulthood and beyond. How awesome the responsibility, how passionate the love, how tenacious the grip on the hand and the hold on the soul.

Every morning upon awakening I pray, silently but intensely. Every night I pray discreetly and inwardly. And every moment in between I find myself praying, too.

Dear God, help me to be a worthy partner, to do what is right even when I do not know what right is. Help me to be gracious, kind and consistent, to instill in those charges of my blood and flesh values of absolute truth, moral integrity, fear of God, respect for fellow man, refinement, fortitude, uprightness and courage. Help these living gifts to grow to fulfill your very own injunction of doing justice, loving righteousness, and walking humbly before you. Grant us health and sustenance, peace and understanding.

Dear God, thank you for a husband who is wise and kindhearted, benevolent and sensitive, God fearing-and tolerant. Bless him, sustain him, and help me tread the ground of compassion and helpfulness together with him and graciously, as he does, even when I lag behind him as I so often do.

Glorious flowering plants, the little buds blossom into stately trees, veritable forests of human achievement. How formidable the parental venture at this juncture, how seemingly tenuous the impression of the mind, the hold on the heart. Insight turns murky, experience grows limited, resources appear modest.

The memories of one's own childhood loom large on the horizon of the imagination. The uncertainties, defiance, acceptance and yielding with regard to authority, the dreams and wishes of days long gone look us in the eye.

How fine the line between independence and subservience, how much finer the line between letting go and intervention. How easy to identify with these magnificent replicas of our own selfhood manifest in a new adulthood, yet how daunting and dangerous.

The endurance to maintain one's footing upon the inevitable bumps on the intergenerational expressway with grace, the practical wisdom of first hand observation grounded in an inherent faith in an all embracing Father whose stakes in this partnership are no less meaningful than our own, the belief in His infinite goodness, all make for a keenness of sensibility, perception and feeling. Coupled with the joy of living and an unfailing propensity to laugh at oneself and one's shortcomings, these qualities empower a life that is meaningful and rich.

"You are the children of the Lord your God" (Deuteronomy 14:1). Each one of us has been defined by that verse: a child to be molded, guided and loved. "Israel is a youth and I love him" (Hosea 11:1), says the prophet at Godly behest.

I love him because he is a youth, an essential love that has no explanation. And so it is with a parent's love of his or her child: a love that need not be aroused by external elements, a love that can never be vanquished, a love that is selfless and everlasting. A love that is the essence of our very existence, spectacular, unique, a vessel for infinite blessing.

For further reading:

Twerski, Abraham J., MD, and Ursula Schwartz, Ph.D. *Positive Parenting: Developing Your Child's Potential.* Brooklyn, NY: 1996.

Adahan, Miriam. *Raising Children to Care: A Jewish Guide to Childrearing.* Jerusalem, Israel: 1988.

The Last Time

The last time I saw him awake and talking
I tricked my dying father.
...I said, as if casually,
"Dad, do you remember the shema?"

He rattled it off in Hebrew, rapidly.
I nodded as if I didn't know
it is the last prayer one is supposed to say upon this earth.
I did it in the name of Abraham,
his father's name,
in the name of Isaac, and of Jacob,
the latecomer who also tricked
his father, and was blessed.

From the poem by Liz Rosenberg

On the Death of My Father

Liz Rosenberg

Miriam's Well is of great mystical significance to the Jewish people. When the Jews were wandering in the desert, they were given three special miracles. One was the manna which fed them. One was the pillar of light, which led them. And one was the well of water which sprang forth in Miriam's honor. Water is such an essential element that it touches every aspect of our being. It carries the food we need to the organs in our body; it surrounds us, and we are made of it. In this way, Miriam's well is a metaphor for God's presence in our lives, for the transcendent which is always within and around us, often overlooked, yet sustaining us.

When Miriam died, the well stopped giving water for a time and then sprang forth again because the wandering Jews still needed the water. When Miriam's brother Moses died, the well stopped for a second time and did not reappear because the Jewish people had now crossed into the Holy Land. Yet it is said that this Well of Miriam flowed out into the Sea of Galilee, where it still bestows healing powers upon those who visit it.

My father would not have been terribly interested in this story even though his mother's name was Miriam and his own Jewish name was Moishe. He was a man of intellect and culture rather than religion. He was more interested in books and movies, theater and travel, politics and culture. Although he was intrigued by mysticism, he distrusted it. We were ultra-Reform, if there is such a thing. My parents both regarded my increased interest in Hasidic Judaism warily, as if I had entered the realm of a mild but potentially dangerous cult. We were Jews the way most New Yorkers are Yankee fans. We rooted for the Jews because they were our home team. Surprisingly, to me, my father always fasted each year on Yom Kippur, and he drove us dutifully to Hebrew school until one by one my sister and I became disinterested.

The day my father died I was supposed to be giving an honorary doctorate to producer/director Sidney Pollack. It was graduation day at the State University of New York at Binghamton, a Sunday late in May. The evening before, my son and I had gone to an elaborate dinner with Mr. Pollack as our guest. When I had interviewed Mr. Pollack several years earlier he had mentioned to me, almost apologetically, that he had never earned a college degree. The fact that he could feel even briefly ashamed of this fact touched me. Since he had begun his own acting and teaching career in New York State, it seemed fitting that the State University of New York should honor his many contributions to the world of film. Mr. Pollack graciously agreed. My teenage son, an aspiring actor, and I acted as his hosts for the evening.

It was the kind of bright, sophisticated event my father would have loved. My father was outgoing and talkative; he would have gone up to perfect strangers and started conversations, stirred up arguments for the sheer joy of playing out his powerful intellect. But for many years my father had been suffering from increasingly severe senile dementia. I'm not sure he remembered who Sidney Pollack was or that he had made many of the movies that my father used to love – *They Shoot Horses, Don't They?*, *The Way We Were*, and *Out of Africa*.

My brilliant father had done the unthinkable in those last few years: he had stopped reading books. He had turned away, finally, even from the television. Because of his cardiopulmonary disease, he could no longer drink ordinary fluids – everything had to be thickened for him. When I visited him at his nursing home in Philadelphia his coffee was a thick sludge, and even his drinking water had the texture of half-melted gelatin.

I walked back into my house that night, still wearing something long and black and spangled and a pair of too-high-heeled shoes, and found a phone message from my sister on our answering machine. Her voice sounded worried. She wanted me to know that my father had pneumonia and said that perhaps I had better call her right away. I did. Things did not look good, she said. I stood perched on those black high heels, wavering, and asked if I should rush down that night – envisioning waking my mother, who lived a few miles away, driving with her down the long tunnel of route 81 to Philadelphia. No, my sister said, there was no need to come that night. My father was already sleeping. We would not even be allowed to see him till morning.

I made a few hasty calls to my colleagues and arranged for someone else to be present at the graduation ceremony where Mr. Pollack was to give a speech, arranged for someone else to hood my graduate students. Early the next morning, I set off with my mother to Philadelphia. I don't remember anything about the drive or what we spoke about, though I recall passing the various rest stops along the Pennsylvania turnpike, counting them down. And I remember coming into the hospital room. The room was terribly silent, the only noise inside a strong, harsh sucking sound, which came from the machine that allowed my father to keep breathing. As soon as I stepped into that room I understood that everything had changed. My father lay with his eyes closed, his high forehead even higher where my sister had pushed back his hair.

She was standing beside him now, gently stroking his forehead. "He's peaceful," she told us. "He was agitated before, but he's peaceful now." My mother began to cry. It is a strange thing to spend time in a such a room. My father seemed to be floating there, invisible, among us, while we talked about other things, whatever things one finds to talk about. Yet his presence also dominated the room. I felt that he still possessed an enormous life force and exerted an influence over us all. In life, he was devout as a human being. He was scrupulously fair and honest in all his dealings, he was generous and charitable, he was kind, he was dutiful. He had worked for thirty years at a job he disliked intensely, selling screwdrivers in the family business, though he had been trained as a chemical engineer.

Evenings, he'd come home after work, eat dinner with us, help us with our homework, watch TV with us, and then he would read alone late, late into the night – sometimes till three or four in the morning, reading arcane fiction by Thomas Pincheon, his beloved science fiction, or an article in *The New Yorker* that made him grumble or laugh out loud. It seemed as if he lived a second life at night to compensate for the arid one he served all day, week in and week out, year after year, in order to give his family the kind of life he felt we deserved. Even as a child, when I'd go to visit his office, I'd weep. He didn't belong there under the fluorescent lights, among the pink cardboard boxes of Dunkin Donuts, the dry air, tool catalogues and staplers. But he never complained about his job, he never acted as if he were doing anything out of the ordinary.

The doctors had told my sister he was not likely to live through the night. A brutal and succinct diagnosis. It was early afternoon when we arrived at the hospital, my mother and I, and then somehow it became late afternoon, and my mother and sister began talking about dinner. The strain of sitting in that room was beginning to wear on my mother, who had been weakened by years of trying to care for my father's physical and mental illnesses. They had now lived apart for almost two years – my father in a skilled-care nursing home, my mother in an independent living facility. Often my father did not recognize my mother. When she came to visit him on their fifty-first anniversary, he kept turning his face away from her kisses. He seemed distraught at being pulled back to his own past. She had already lost my father once, and now she was losing him a second time in that strangely still hospital room. My father never once moved his eyes or appeared to recognize anyone or anything around him. All he was doing was breathing. His life had now come down to this one, essential, almost impossible thing.

My sister and mother finally stood to go. "I'll stay," I said.

They both looked surprised. "I'm not leaving him," I said. "If it's all right with you, I'd like to stay."

Understand, I am the baby of the family, the protected one. I am the one who was never allowed to see violent movies, who was kept home from family funerals. But my mother and sister seemed to see something stubborn and yearning in my face, and they let me stay on alone. I still think of it as a great gift they gave me, to have the honor of sitting by my father's side, to help him in his journey out of this world, if that was what was about to happen. My sister said she would bring me dinner – maybe Chinese food – sometime later that evening. I wasn't at all hungry, couldn't even imagine eating, but I nodded, because that is what families do. They feed each other. They come when someone is sick. They bury the dead.

I had come woefully unprepared, I thought. All I had was a little paperback book of Psalms. I had read that the Psalms could be strong medicine for the sick. Alone with my father, I opened the book at the very first psalm and began to read aloud. "Blessed is the man that walketh not in the counsel of the ungodly, nor standeth in the way of sinners, nor sitteth in the seat of the scornful." That sounded like my father, so I kept on reading. I plowed through at least a dozen of the psalms, and sometimes I'd stop and look up and talk to my father. I thanked him for being such a good parent. I thanked him for always being there for me, and told him how much we loved him. I stroked his hand or his forehead, I felt the fineness of his thin, gray hair which had once been so curly, black and abundant. When the nurses and aides walked in and found me sitting there reading Psalms, they found a way to work around me. Sometimes I'd wait till they had left the room, sometimes I'd just forge on ahead. I think they all understood that I was there praying in some fashion.

At some point I asked one of the nurses if it was true what we had heard, that my father might not make it through the night. "Don't people sometimes pull back?" I asked. "Don't they ever suddenly get better and turn things around?" "Sometimes they do," she said gently, adjusting the straps around my dad's oxygen mask. "But not usually when it's gone this far. I don't think I've ever seen someone come back when it goes this far."

My father had been suffering from cardiopulmonary disease for years. He had been on oxygen constantly for a year. He had suffered from prostate cancer, and he'd had a sub-catheter snaking down his pants leg for two years. He'd even been diagnosed recently with leukemia, "But," the head nurse at the home had told us, "don't worry, because it's not likely to kill him."

"Why not?" I asked.

"Well…" – at this she lowered her head – "I mean that something else is likely to get him first."

Now he had pneumonia – that disease which is called "the old man's best friend." My father was running a high fever; his skin was hot and dry to my touch, though he showed no apparent discomfort. He would not or could not swallow a sip of water, but I was allowed to moisten his lips with a wet washcloth, and I did this as eagerly as if I were bringing him some great delicacy. I also rubbed his hands and feet with moisturizer, and all of this seemed in some infinitesimal way, in some measure beyond measuring, to ease him. I felt the great, stunning honor of sitting beside my living father. Here he was. Here he still was. That was perhaps my single most persistent consciousness throughout that long night. The pleasure, the gift, and the honor of sitting beside my father while he still lived. It was like being permitted to visit a king. In his absolute silence, even in his struggle for every breath, he was powerful, he was radiant, he was still alive, still my father. I lost count of the hours but I continued to read him Psalms, or sometimes to pray, or sometimes to stop and talk. "Day unto day uttereth speech and night unto night showeth knowledge. Cleanse me from secret faults," I read. "In them he hath set a tabernacle for the sun, which is as a bridegroom coming out of his chamber, and rejoiceth as a strong man to run a race." I was wishing my father strength. I was, it seemed to me, watching his body gather itself for a great leap. "Deliver my soul from the sword, my darling from the power of the dog," I read. "I had fainted, unless I had believed to see the goodness of the Lord in the land of the living." There were moments of terrible depression in that room, and of fear, but I did not altogether feel my own emotions. They seemed to be coming from a long way off. I bent my head and read, or I stopped to moisten my father's lips with fresh water, or I rubbed his hands with hospital moisturizer. Sometimes if his hand looked uncomfortably clenched I would try to loosen it. Sometimes I would stroke his forehead as my sister had done. When I would feel myself begin to panic, I would take deep breaths, I would read on. "For his anger endureth but a moment; in his favor is life: weeping may endure for a night, but joy cometh in the morning."

At some point in the evening my sister, true to her word, brought me dinner. It was after visiting hours now, and the guards downstairs would not allow her up into my father's room. I rode the elevator down to the lobby to get the leaking paper bag of Chinese food, to kiss her and rush back upstairs and thank her again for letting me stay. I could not bear to leave my father alone even for a moment. Neither could I bring myself to eat or drink in his presence, when he could not.

And now – it was very late for me to begin to be thinking about this – I faced the possibility that my father might soon die, and I was not sure what was going to happen to his body. I wanted to bring in a Jewish burial society to perform the rites because I knew that such societies treat the body of the dead with utmost respect and care. I knew they would not leave my father alone for an instant, at a time I imagined of great vulnerability when the soul first leaves the body. I also felt, at some level, that he might even have wanted this.

I thought this partly because of a strange conversation we'd had together the last time I saw my father awake and alert. Granted, he would go on some kick or other, and everything he said or heard or thought related back to that topic. One time it was golf – a game he'd never cared about. Another time he was convinced we were in East Africa together. "For God's sakes if you'd told me, I'd have been ready for the safari," he said. When the aide came into his room to empty his trash he turned to me and announced, "How am I supposed to think when they keep bringing me Ethiopian cherries?"

This last visit we had together, it had to do with Jewishness. He introduced me around proudly as his "Jewish daughter – the very Jewish one."

But his sudden turn toward Jewishness made me think twice. Did it mean anything? Was it like golf, just some notion passing through his brain like a cloud? How could I possibly know? I could only guess. I remembered how strongly he had clung to his own Jewish identity, how fiercely he resisted anti-Semitism, that he had fought in the war against Hitler, his fasting every Yom Kippur. I thought it might be a blessing to call the Jewish Burial Society.

Again, my sister and mother did not object. My sister had already made arrangements with a local funeral home and my mother had chosen the mausoleum where she and my father were both to be interred. I knew that according to Jewish law a Jew should be interred below ground, but I also knew how strongly my mother felt on this subject. If I could work within these parameters, I could call in a Jewish burial society. We could even bury him in a plain pine box.

I asked for a phone book and found the name of a local Jewish funeral home. The man I reached sounded irate, as if I had interrupted him at a dinner party. Very likely I had. "What do you want?" he said. When I tried to explain my situation he brusquely gave me the name of the local Jewish burial society and said he needed more information from my sister. When my sister called him and explained the situation he said, "What are you bothering me for?" If he wasn't doing the whole funeral, the service, the casket, everything, he wasn't interested. It was one of the few bad moments we had. People are extraordinarily gentle in the face of emergencies, I have found, in the face of truly life-altering events.

When I was getting married in a snowstorm, when I was pregnant, strangers had been exquisitely kind. It was true that evening as well. A man from the Jewish Burial Society called me back on my cell phone. He was reassuring. He would try to work with the non-Jewish funeral home, he said. The man from the non-Jewish funeral home agreed to allow the Burial Society to perform all its rites. Both of the men, from different faiths and backgrounds, said the same thing: "I am sorry for your loss."

I called home, to our local rabbi, head of the Chabad House near my university, a man I admire and trust. It was late by now, after nine o'clock at night, but he seemed unruffled, only concerned. He asked me to give him a little time to find someone in the Philadelphia area. I expected him to call back in an hour. He called me back within a few minutes with the name and number of a rabbi nearby. "Call him and he will come."

"But I don't know him," I said. "How can I call him out of the blue?"

"He will come."

I called the rabbi at his home, late on a Sunday evening. He had a gentle voice and asked me which hospital I was in with my father. It seemed a mere matter of minutes before he arrived, prayer book in hand. He was young, he was black-hatted, he was foreign to me and familiar.

"What am I supposed to say?" I asked him. "What am I supposed to do?" I had no guidebook, no map of this strange territory I had entered.

The rabbi was soft-spoken, calming and succinct. He showed me a prayer that I should say if my father did in fact pass away. It would be good, he said, if I were the one to straighten his limbs and close his eyes. It was important that I not leave the body alone, not till the Burial Society arrived. Psalms were good, he said. He suggested Psalms 121, 130, 90, and also, because my father was at that time eighty years old, the psalm with the number one year more than my father's current age, Psalm 81. There were prayers that would need to be said: the *shema* and then *boruch shem kevod* three times and then "The Lord is God" seven times. I sat clutching the little prayer book like a student again as if this were some final exam and by cramming for it, memorizing all its aspects, I might somehow erase the very need to take it. The rabbi handed me the prayer book, wished me well, and left.

I sat alone again in the hospital room with my father. It suddenly occurred to me that the rabbi himself had not said a prayer over my father. I was terrified – it seemed a dreadful oversight. I ran out to the elevators and caught him. "Isn't there some prayer you should say for him?" I asked.

"No," he told me gently. "You are his daughter. You know the right things to say. I will pray for him, but your prayers will have more meaning. Go back inside, and trust yourself."

"The Lord is nigh unto them that are of a broken heart," I read aloud. Sometimes I have joked to friends that I fear I may have bored my father to death. I talked to him about my childhood, about my memories of going into the city with him on the Long Island Railroad, holding his hand. I reminded him about make-believe games we had played, how he and my sister had taught me how to read by writing and illustrating books to serve as my primers. "Let them not say in their hearts: ah, we have swallowed him up."

It was now past eleven at night. The world entirely black outside the hospital window, which had become a mirror, and the night nurses came on their shifts. Two or three women walked in together after midnight, almost one o'clock in the morning, to bathe and turn my father.

"This will make him more comfortable," they assured me. I wanted to leave the room – I was not sure I had the right to stay and watch my father in a moment of nakedness and vulnerability.

I satisfied myself with stepping to the curtain, in the middle of the room, and standing beside it. I noticed that the nurses kept my father covered as they bathed him. They worked around a white hospital sheet deftly, now uncovering a leg, an arm, now wrapping it back around his waist. His body was shining from the basin of water. His old legs, blue-veined, seemed tremendously strong and muscled. His chest was high. He looked incredibly powerful and radiantly beautiful. I wept to see how he shone. I thought of the famous lines of a Rilke poem: "If there weren't light, the curve/of the breast wouldn't blind you.../and the body wouldn't send out light from every edge/as a star does...."

The nurses were gentle with my father, respectful. They spoke in low voices, they seemed to me to be almost unearthly, like angels in their ministrations. I suppose I must have been tired by now but I felt alert. A few minutes after they had left the room I turned to Psalm 81, the psalm the visiting rabbi had recommended I might read to my father. I began, "Sing aloud unto God our strength: make a joyful noise unto the God of Jacob." It was a happy psalm, and my voice was strong and sure. I moved to the second passage. "Take a psalm, and bring hither the timbrel.... And you know, Dad," I added, my head still bent over the book, "It was Miriam who played the timbrel and sang when the Jews had crossed –"

But something made me stop. Something made me look up. At the mention of Miriam, his mother's name, my father's eyes moved for the first time all night. He looked toward the door. In that instant he was gone. It happened that fast. It felt to me as if he flew to her, as if perhaps she had been waiting for him all that long evening. Then Moishe was again with Miriam, and the well of love that is between all mothers and sons, that miraculous well that exists for all Jews, it stopped, as his breath suddenly stopped, and it sprang forth again elsewhere.

For further reading:

Lamm, Maurice. *The Jewish Way in Death and Mourning*. New York, NY: 1969.
Idem. *Consolation: The Spiritual Journey beyond Grief*. Philadelphia, PA: 2004.

Community and Beyond

And God said to Abraham, "In everything that Sarah tells you, listen to her voice."

Genesis 21:12

Introduction

We often think of female activists, philanthropists and communal leaders as a modern-day phenomenon. However, Jewish women have been active in the community and in the larger world for a long, long time – as far back as the first Jewish woman, our Matriarch Sarah who, according to Biblical account, shared equal status with Abraham. As partners they brought the then-radical notion of monotheism to a pagan world, transforming the universal landscape forever. Sarah was followed by illustrious female descendants – women of renown and thousands of unnamed women in each generation who, like Sarah, took responsibility for the spiritual state of our people. Our history is patterned with times of darkness and near-eclipse. In those times it was the women who shed light and hope, pulling our people back from the precipice with their faith and determination. This same devotion manifested itself in less dramatic ways: in the day-to-day – often quiet and behind the scenes – efforts that built, enriched, and guided Jewish communities. It wasn't called "volunteer work." It was what you did if you were Jewish, despite the fact that you had your own home and family to care for – work that, until more recent times, consumed most of a woman's waking hours.

The Torah teaches that when Sarah gave birth to Yitzchak she was ninety, and Abraham was ninety-nine. Many doubted this miracle; more likely, they thought, Abraham and Sarah had found the child in the marketplace and were passing it off as their own! In response, God formed the features of Isaac in the mirror image of his father, thus silencing those who questioned his patriarchal lineage. But how was Sarah to establish her credibility? Rashi teaches that Abraham invited all of the princesses to bring their own children to suckle at Sarah's breast, in effect establishing beyond doubt that Sarah had experienced gestation and birth. In fact, in a remarkable statement the Midrash teaches that all future converts to the Jewish faith are descendants of the children who suckled at Sarah's breast.

Rabbi Menachem M. Schneerson, the Lubavitcher Rebbe, took this teaching even further. The Rebbe taught that a woman has an obligation to the community, to society, to the entire world. It is not enough to feed her own Yitzchak, to care for those within her household. Indeed, as Sarah did, she must give sustenance – offer spiritual and physical guidance and succor – to everyone with whom she comes into contact.

Ours is the most educated generation of Jewish women. Compared to the women of yesteryear we are the most socially integrated, the highest achievers, the most powerful leaders, the most substantial earners. Indeed, women have taken on more formal leadership positions within Jewish organized life and as a people we are the richer for it. Yes, the glass ceiling still looms and must be addressed. But on the essential level we are still Sarah's daughters, working without fanfare to elevate the world.

In this section we follow a physician, a mikveh attendant, teachers of Torah and a doula as they go about their holy works. We find women lovingly preparing the dead for burial and consoling the bereaved, offering hospitality and visiting the sick, helping the needy and mobilizing to save a life, and we share in the journey of one woman's *aliya* to Israel.

These women are not saints, nor are they unencumbered by constraints on their time, money or energy. To give is to receive, these women teach us.

The more we make ourselves a vessel for giving, the more we will have to give. And as the need grows and changes, so will the quality of what we have to offer grow ever richer. To give is to taste of the beneficent flow: to extend oneself is to come closer to the source of all, to find the resources within, even when we feel we can't, is to witness the mystery and majesty of creation within our lives.

Rambam's Ladder of Charity
as rendered by Julie Salamon

8. At the top of the ladder is the gift of self-reliance: to hand someone a gift or a loan, or to enter into a partnership with him, or to find work for him so that he will never have to beg again.

7. To give to someone you don't know, and to do so anonymously.

6. To give to someone you know, but who doesn't know from whom he is receiving help.

5. To give to someone you don't know, but allow your name to be known.

4. To hand money to the poor before being asked, but risk making the recipient feel shame.

3. To hand money to the poor after being asked.

2. To give less to the poor than is proper, but to do so cheerfully.

1. To give begrudgingly.

Rambam's Ladder

Julie Salamon

We spend a lot of time thinking about why people are bad. Just as perplexing, maybe more perplexing, is why they are good. There are some obvious reasons: guilt, remorse, genetic predisposition, familial example, religious instruction, fear of social disapproval or, at the extreme, the terrifying thought of eternal damnation. But why, for some people, does it take a cataclysm to set off a charitable response while others automatically reach into their pockets when they see a homeless person approaching? What kind of giving satisfies the need of a particular giver and where does that need come from? What are the rules?

I once believed it was natural to give. I grew up in one of the poorest counties in Ohio, in a rural town in Appalachia where my father was the only

---

* Edited excerpts from *Rambam's Ladder; A Meditation on Generosity and Why It Is Necessary to Give.*

doctor. As far as I know, he never refused a patient for lack of money and could enumerate whole categories of other people who weren't permitted to pay, including teachers and preachers. I would describe my mother as generous but pragmatic. She likes her giving to be balanced by a tax deduction. My own urge to give has many layers, built on a solid core of contrition. I've felt the need to compensate for being raised without financial stress in a poor community, and for being the daughter of Holocaust survivors who had almost everything taken away from them but made sure I wanted for nothing.

So I've been volunteering at one thing or another most of my life, beginning as a candy-striper in junior high school. I didn't think about the whys too much, being absorbed with my family and work, but I confess to having felt slightly superior to people who were stingy with their money or their time. That cocky self-assurance about my own generosity was probably destined for some sort of comeuppance. I didn't expect, however, that this supposition about who I was – along with so much else – would be tested with a mighty, life-altering blow. But that's what happened when terrorists attacked the World Trade Center about a mile from my home.

On September 11, 2001, I felt no urge to give blood, make sandwiches, or search for the missing. My pervasive, all-consuming desire wasn't altruistic but maternal – to gather my children close and somehow protect them. There wasn't anything wrong with this impulse to protect my own, yet I felt selfish.

Maybe this was because my husband took action – at least tried to. He went to offer blood and decided to go back later because there were too many donors. He showed up at the cavernous Javits Center on a bleak rainy day to sign up for the rescue effort only to realize with grim frustration, as he faced the long line of muscular working men, that his desk job had ill-prepared him for the tasks at hand. He picked up the flyer from a restaurant throwing a fund-raiser for the victims down the block from our home and made sure we gave a check, though we didn't attend the dinner.

Later, struggling to regain my footing, I recalled a story my mother once told me. World War II had just ended. She was twenty-two and living in Prague, having spent the previous year in Auschwitz and in a work camp. Because she spoke several languages and was a hustler, she got a job with a charity that distributed clothing sent from America for the refugees, mainly Jews liberated from the camps. Among the perks she was given were an apartment, which she immediately crammed full of relatives and friends, and first crack at the clothes. In short order she refashioned herself from scraggly waif to chic young woman.

My mother's job required her to visit the refugee camps to find out what was needed. On her first outing, as she looked at the people she was supposed to help, she was overcome with uncharitable thoughts – disgust, actually. Her "clients" were dirty, still in rags, emaciated. She wanted to get away from them as quickly as possible. Later she felt shame, realizing that her disgust mirrored the disgust the Nazi guards must have felt for her at Auschwitz. Then it had been she who was dirty, ragged, pathetic.

All families have their stories, and in my family they became parables – in this case, a way of urging my sister and me to look carefully at people before we judged them as deserving of our praise or condemnation or pity. I always admired my parents for their belief in universal humanity even after they had experienced evil so directly. Growing up with them, I learned first-hand the essence of charity.

How wonderful it sounds, so straightforward and pure. But even before September 11, holding on to those high-minded ideals had never been easy, not with so many charlatans and fanatics warping the benign view. After September 11, while I was glad others were searching for terrorists, for me the quest for goodness became far more compelling and urgent. I wanted proof that Stephen Jay Gould, the late paleontologist and essayist, had been right when he eloquently responded to the World Trade Center attacks.

"The tragedy of human history lies in the enormous potential for destruction in rare acts of evil, not in the high frequency of evil people," wrote Gould. "Complex systems can only be built step by step, whereas destruction requires but an instant. Thus, in what I like to call the Great Asymmetry, every spectacular incident of evil will be balanced by ten thousand acts of kindness, too often unnoted and invisible as the 'ordinary' efforts of a vast majority."

I began talking to people who were seriously engaged in charity and philanthropy – high and low, givers and receivers – finding them via the principle of six degrees of separation. Over time, the ripple effect washed up a tremendous variety of insights, some provided to me by the very rich, some by the very poor. I also relied for sources and wisdom on the staff, board, and clients of the Bowery Residents' Committee, an organization helping the homeless of New York City. I have been involved with the BRC for years.

My touchstone, however, turned out to be someone distant from my time and place – a twelfth-century physician, philosopher, and scholar who spent much of his life trying to reconcile faith and reason. He was Rabbi Moses ben Maimon, known best by his Greek name, Maimonides, and by many as Rambam, an acronym derived from the first letters of his name. Among his most significant works was a treatise on God and metaphysics – the marvelously titled *Guide for the Perplexed.*

What I first liked about Maimonides, especially as the absolutes of my childhood grew murky, was that he offered assurance that reasonableness is always complex. As I read him more, I found myself identifying with him, as unreasonable as that might sound.

How could I not be drawn to someone whose writing and personal narrative resonate with startling relevance and universality? He lived through terrible disruption and exile, and yet carried on, not just to live his life but also to produce philosophical works brimming with humanity and hope. His pursuit of fairness was as dogged as his desire to transcend his own traumatic experiences and to encourage people to find their better selves. What an important message for today, particularly when we remember that he lived in a time when there had been significant philosophical, scientific, and cultural exchange among Jews, Christians, and Muslims.

Born in Cordoba, Spain, in 1135, during an era of peaceful coexistence among these three major religions, Moses ben Maimon and his family fled when Islamic fundamentalists from Morocco invaded Spain in 1147. He wasn't even thirteen years old at the time. After years on the road, stopping in Palestine for a time and then in Morocco, his family ultimately settled in Old Cairo. Maimonides thrived in Egypt. He became physician to the sultan, a leader in his own community, and a significant interpreter of Aristotle's philosophy. His prodigious outpouring of commentary on Jewish law, much of it written in Arabic, remains crucial to modern interpretation of ancient texts.

But make no mistake. Though much of his writing can seem arcane, Maimonides understood how to sell an idea. And perhaps no single idea was more important to his obsessive pursuit of righteousness than considering how to give with compassion and common sense. Tucked into ninety-three pages of exposition on proper treatment of the poor, he provided a handy eight-step program for giving, known as the Ladder of Charity. I think of it as Rambam's Ladder, preferring his almost rock-star nickname to the serious-sounding Maimonides. The more musical Rambam brings him home.

Rambam's Ladder is laid out in rungs of descending order from the most worthy on down. The anonymous giver ranks above the giver who is known. Giving before being asked ranks above giving when asked. The lowest level belongs to the grudging giver; the summit belongs to the person who helps a poor person become self-sufficient. Indeed, Maimonides starts at the top – the highest level of giving – and works his way down, moving from idealism to realism. In this inquiry, reflecting my desire for self-improvement, I suppose, I chose to climb up the ladder, ending with the most exemplary form of giving. But whichever way you look at it, the ladder provides an easy visual metaphor, a way to grasp the idea that there is giving and then there is giving.

… I don't remember when I first noticed him, but it seems to me that he had been panhandling outside the corner grocery for at least a year. He appeared to be in his late thirties, but since he was one of those ageless souls, I could have been off by a dozen years in either direction. He was a pleasant-looking man, African-American, of medium height but thin – too thin. He had a sweet face and a warm smile and favored brightly-colored T-shirts. When I walked by he would say, "How are you doing, sister?" He would make his pitch, almost as an apologetic afterthought. Then he'd say, "Have a nice day," even though I had responded, also apologetically, not with money but with advice.

"Go to the Bowery Residents' Committee," I would tell him. I had been a volunteer at the agency for a long time and had become chairman of its board. I had never questioned the agency's disapproval of panhandling: "Giving money, food or blankets directly to the homeless," its brochures spell out, "encourages them to stay on the street and avoid confronting their needs in a more constructive manner."

In other words, the goal and essential philosophy of the Bowery Residents' Committee (BRC) mirror Rambam's: Aim for that highest rung, where a person becomes self-sufficient.

That was my rationale each time I said to the man on the corner, "You can get help there," and then handed him a card with the BRCs address and phone number on it.

Always polite, he would respond to my unsolicited advice in different ways. He would tell me he wasn't interested in going to a program – guessing correctly that the BRC staff would encourage him to go into detox. Sometimes he would nod and say, "Oh, yes, I'll do that," both of us knowing he was just trying to get me off his back. Each time, he would examine the card and put it in his pocket.

That was the extent of our relationship, if these exchanges could be called that, for several months. I felt a friendly surge of recognition when I saw him, and then my body would tighten, sending warning signals that I shouldn't be supporting his self-destructive habits. It was at those times that I would cross the street to avoid him.

Toward the end of a warm winter came one bitterly cold day. I was walking home and saw David – though I wouldn't learn his name for some months – shuffling toward me. The shuffle was new.

It had taken me a minute to recognize him. He was not in what I thought of as his usual place, but out of context, a few blocks from his post by our corner store. I stopped and asked him what was wrong with his leg. He told me he had taken a fall. He looked miserable, although, as usual, he was neatly dressed.

My earlier reservations about helping him vanished. I asked him if he had had anything to eat yet that day. It was close to one o'clock in the afternoon. He said no. I told him to come with me to the grocery store, where they also made sandwiches, and I would get him some food.

David looked surprised – he hadn't hit me up for money – but adapted deftly to this happy change in circumstance. He limped and I walked slowly up the street, past stores where four-hundred-dollar shoes are readily available; likewise two-hundred-dollar jeans, pre-ripped. He told me, unsolicited, that he had stopped drinking. "Did you go into a program?" I asked him. He waved his hand dismissively. "I don't like programs," he said. "My body told me it was time when I woke up throwing up or everything I had tasted like beer. It's been a month since I had a drink."

I asked him where he slept and he said sometimes in shelters, sometimes in his "lady girlfriend's" apartment in Brooklyn, and often outside. He spoke with some poetry about the pleasures of sleeping outdoors on warm nights up in the Bronx, where he was from, and about how he enjoyed looking at the stars. I considered the possibility that I was being hustled, and suspected – no, knew – that there were grim stories being withheld. But he seemed happy talking about the stars in the Bronx.

Inside the store, the woman behind the register looked disapproving, or so I imagined. Back at the deli counter, David ordered a hearty lunch: a sandwich with meat and cheese, some milk, a banana, some cookies, and chips. The bill came to $6.50.

"That's a good deal," David observed.

He thanked me and then we shook hands and went our separate ways.

I washed my hands when I got home.

I continued to see him on an irregular basis. He thanked me a few times more for the sandwich and then I found myself crossing the street again to avoid the old dilemma of whether to give him money. After about a month of this, on another spirit-chilling day, I saw him standing at his usual corner. This time I crossed the street in his direction, pulled five dollars from my pocket and just handed the money to him. After that I routinely gave him money before he asked, breaking one set of rules but conforming to another. At the time, I didn't know that I had moved up a notch on the ladder, where you give the poor man less than what is proper, but with a smile. Seeing David, reaching into my pocket, handing him money made me feel good. But now another question was left begging: who was giving to whom?

The next time I saw David was back in front of the grocery store. This time I crossed the street to approach him. I had five dollars in my pocket and just handed it to him. He thanked me.

I had been thinking obsessively about Maimonides's admonition against shaming the recipient of charity. Hesitating a minute – had David now become a research project? – l asked him how he felt about taking the money from me.

He didn't hesitate a bit.

"I feel lucky," he said.

I laughed, relieved to hear this honest answer to my earnest question. Still, I pressed on. "Do you feel ashamed at all?"

"Not really," he said. "This is what I do."

That stopped me for a minute. Did he mean begging was his occupation; my gift actually wages?

"You mean, like your job?" I asked.

He looked a little impatient. "No, it's not my job," he said. "I have a business."

I was wishing I hadn't started this conversation. Did I think my handout entitled me to this kind of probing with someone who might be mentally unbalanced?

David continued. "I do feel bad having to ask for money but when my leg is better I'm going to work. This life isn't for me."

I must have looked worried, because he said, "I don't mean I'm going to kill myself or anything like that. I mean I'm going to go into business."

"What kind of work?" I asked him, not seriously. I felt he must be delusional.

"Tube socks," he said.

"Tube socks?" I repeated.

And then he told me how he could buy socks wholesale on Orchard Street and take them around in a cart and sell them. Tube socks! I'd seen plenty of men selling them on the street and his description of how the business worked seemed knowledgeable.

Suddenly my handout felt like seed money, a small business loan. Had it become more virtuous?

David vanished for a couple of months. I thought of him from time to time, fantasizing that he'd set up shop in midtown, where pedestrian traffic was steady and tube sock need was great. Then he reappeared near my house empty handed – no cart, no tube socks. When I saw him back on the corner, unencumbered, I felt disappointed, even though I understood that small businesses tend to fail, and his was most tenuous.

Of course, I'd suspected all along there was another explanation apart from the press of business for his absence. It had been a sweltering summer and he might have been holed up somewhere with air-conditioning. I knew the drop-in center at the Bowery Residents' Committee filled up on hot days.

He was limping a little, wearing a light blue T-shirt and a blue scarf around his head. He seemed even thinner than usual.

"I'm glad to see you," I said and meant it. I confess I have a superstitious streak and felt his reappearance was a good sign, but I was also simply relieved to see him.

"Good to see you, darling," he said, and then told me he'd been sick, some kind of stomach infection.

"I'm ashamed to say it," he said, "but sometimes when I don't get money I do dig around in garbage cans and I must have eaten something that made me sick."

This sounded like a confession. He looked terrible, wasted.

"I was throwing up and couldn't stop," he said. "I ended up in the hospital."

Without him asking, I pulled out my wallet and gave him a five-dollar bill, which had been tucked between some ones and a few twenties. Why didn't I give him a twenty?

He took the money matter-of-factly and said thank you, and then put out his hand, which I shook. His grip was firm – a lot firmer than mine.

... It had been a couple of months since I'd seen David, "my" homeless man, looking thinner even through the camouflage padding of his large parka. He had reappeared in front of the corner store, his usual spot when he was in the neighborhood. I was rushing to the copy shop and then to the post office.

But I stopped to say hello, how are you, any luck starting up again with tube socks?

"I went belly-up," he told me ruefully. "Financial reverses."

Then he told me his boots were killing his feet. I looked down and saw the boots were in bad shape. I remembered the Reeboks in my husband's closet. On more than one occasion he has inexplicably bought shoes that are too small, worn them for a week or two, and then been unable to return them because they'd been used. The Reeboks, the latest such purchase, had been weighing on his conscience.

"What size shoe do you wear?" I asked David, seeing a way to solve two problems.

"Ten."

"Would you like some brand-new Reeboks?"

He lit up. I told him to wait in front of the corner store while I ran over to the copy shop and post office a few blocks away. I'd be back in ten minutes or so, I assured him.

It took me a little longer than I expected at the copy shop, but still just a few minutes. As I turned the corner heading for the post office I saw David coming out of the building.

"I was looking for you," he told me. A policeman had told him to move away from the corner so he had headed toward the post office, knowing that was my destination.

How little I knew of him or his life, the constant dodge.

"Come with me," I said.

As we walked, I realized I didn't want him to come to my home, even though I felt he was trustworthy. I didn't want to subject him to the policeman again, either.

"Go meet me at the little park at the corner, by the benches," I told him. "I'll be there in five minutes – really."

He nodded and walked one way while I ran the other. I quickly found the Reeboks in the closet, making sure to check they were size ten. They looked new. I found a nice shopping bag – this seemed important to me, to offer my gift with proper ceremony – and quickly walked around the corner to the little park. When he saw me coming David looked triumphantly toward a man standing near by. "I told that guy over there you were going to get me sneakers and he told me you wouldn't come back," he said.

Handing him the bag I felt genuinely happy, not superior or even particularly charitable, but rather as though I was giving a present to an appreciative friend. He reached over to hug me. Caught off guard, I hugged him back, knowing full well I had solved nothing for him – or for me – yet feeling no regrets either.

How quickly the ladder can turn into a slide. Or had I finally come to accept the paradox that may be part of any act of giving?

... As for my journey, I realized it might take forever. After all, Maimonides never stopped grappling with these issues, up until his death at age sixty-nine. But I had come to a deeper understanding of Stephen Jay Gould's "great asymmetry." I now agreed with him when he said, "Complex systems can only be built step by step, whereas destruction requires but an instant." Still, I was a little disappointed that I hadn't had an epiphany, the great neon flash of insight that clarified everything. Rambam's Ladder was far more subtle and complicated, like goodness itself.

One day, though, while I was watching a movie on a subject that might seem far removed from this one, I realized that I did understand what Rambam's Ladder has come to mean to me. The movie, a documentary about one of Hitler's secretaries entitled *Blind Spot,* consisted almost entirely of excerpts from interviews with Traudl Junge, conducted fifty-five years after Hitler's death.

As this elderly and articulate woman revisited her experience in the heart of darkness, she didn't seem to be asking for expiation or exoneration, although maybe that was her desire as she confronted her complicity and perplexity: how could she have been in the belly of the beast but seen only Hitler's small kindnesses to her? How had she managed to remain oblivious to the evil taking place all around? Inconsistent as good might be, she implied, evil may be even more paradoxical, more inexplicable. Junge discussed how Hitler created an alternative vision of morality, whose centerpiece was this: "He convinced the German people that they had a task to do. They had to exterminate the Jews because the Jews caused all our problems," she explained. "It wasn't Hitler's own idea. It had been put forth much earlier that they had to make a sacrifice."

She recalls reading an interview with a soldier who had been stationed at a concentration camp. "The journalist asked the guard, 'Didn't you feel any pity at all for the people you treated so badly there?'

"And he replied, 'Yes, I certainly did feel pity for them but I had to overcome it. That was a sacrifice I had to make for the greater cause.'"

As Junge saw it, "That's what happened to conscience. After all, Hitler always used to say: You don't have to worry, any of you. You just have to do whatever I say and I'll take responsibility. As if anyone can take charge of another person's conscience. I do think you can make someone's conscience more sensitive or desensitize it or manipulate it."

The secretary's words chilled me but also made me wonder: if Junge was correct – and history has proven over and over that she might be – could her theory be applied for good? Was it possible to make conscientiousness a national imperative, to make awareness and empathy the dutiful sacrifice for the greater cause?

Probably not. If I'd learned anything from my excursion up and down Rambam's Ladder, it was that empathy couldn't be mandated and that charity shouldn't be thought of as a sacrifice. Goodness can't be willed into being.

But it can be instilled – not by forcing employees to give or by promising children better grades if they do good deeds or by spending too much time analyzing whether the tithe should be taken before or after taxes – but simply by opening your eyes, by paying attention, by not letting those "spectacular incidents of evil," as Gould called them, eclipse the less dramatic but profound acts of goodness that take place every day.

Recalling the World Trade Center attacks again, I remembered the reaction of our local elementary school, where many children had witnessed the destruction from their classroom windows. Within months, after the United States retaliated against the terrorists by bombing Afghanistan, the school organized a dance to raise money for an Afghan school. For my son, this wasn't an act of charity but a logical transfer from richer to poorer that made far more sense to him than the violence that had upended his world.

The hopefulness of those elementary-school children is echoed for me on every rung of Rambam's Ladder. We can't anticipate evil or forestall ordinary difficulty and grief. But we do have a choice in our response to what life throws at us. Maimonides could have survived by meekly succumbing to the people who hated him simply for who he was. He could have spent his days plotting revenge. Instead, he devoted his life to convincing people that they had it in them to do better than those who had come before. Step by step, rung by rung, all of us can improve ourselves – and the world.

That, for me, is the highest level of giving, an antidote to the rhetoric of righteousness invoked so often and fruitlessly to legitimize war and destruction. Giving should not be an afterthought, what nations do to repair the damage they've inflicted on one another, what individuals do to assuage their guilt for their excesses or indifference. But the building material for every step of Rambam's Ladder is conscientiousness – and consciousness. Anonymity, self-sufficiency, absence of reluctance, not inflicting shame: All of these ideas mandate an awareness of our common humanity. They remind us that in the end we are not measured by what we have, but by what we give to one another.

For further reading:

Steinsaltz, Adin. *Simple Words: Thinking about What Really Matters in Life*. New Jersey: 1999.
Taub, Shimon. *The Laws of Tzedaka and Maaser: A Comprehensive Guide*. Brooklyn, NY: 2003.
Twersky, Abraham J. *Do Unto Others: How Good Deeds Can Change Your Life*. Kansas City, MO: 1997.

A person needs a wise physician to endeavor on his behalf. If he can prescribe a remedy for the body, good! If not, he should provide a remedy for his soul. It is on behalf of such a physician that the Holy One, blessed be He, endeavors in this world and in the world to come.

Zohar, *Deuteronomy 299a*

Ask the advice of a doctor who is a friend. Being a friend makes a big difference.

Meditation No. 157 from Bringing Heaven Down to Earth: 365 Meditations from the Rebbe *by Rabbi Tzvi Freeman*

Hand-Washing and Other Rituals

Marjorie Ordene, M.D.

Holding the cup in your left hand, pour the water over your right hand. Then take the cup in your right hand and pour the water over your left. Now dry your hands and recite the blessing. After that return to the table and do not speak until you have said the blessing and eaten the bread. During the meal keep your conversation away from weekday talk or gossip. Stay in the Sabbath mood."

As the rabbi gave instructions to a group of twenty students on Friday night, I couldn't help but recall another group of students receiving similar instructions one weekday morning a decade ago. " Holding the scrub brush in your left hand, scrub your right arm and hand with overlapping strokes until every millimeter of skin is covered. Then place the brush in your left hand and do the same." No mention was made of saying a prayer or observing silence, but ten years later, I found myself thinking that it would have been appropriate if it had. After all, we were about to witness and even participate in the opening up of a human body, the exposure of the fat and blood and nerves and organs, while the patient himself lay asleep, trusting in our expertise and good intentions. At the time, however, it never occurred to me to say a prayer. I was too busy focusing on my assigned task – holding the retractors and cutting the sutures. But looking back on it, I think how different it would have been if the surgeons had prepared themselves mentally and spiritually while scrubbing, observed a solemn silence while being gowned and gloved, and then, after cutting the skin, spoken only in respectful tones, mindful of the gravity of their work.

A year or two ago, an article appeared in the health pages of the *Times*, describing a study by anesthesiologists in which it was found that patients under general anesthesia remembered what was said in the operating room and that those whose surgeons had said they would make a speedy recovery did so. I remember the OR atmosphere as being very macho, even military, full of hierarchical discipline, off-color jokes, and verbal one-upmanship. True, we didn't wish the patients ill, but the term respectful wouldn't apply either. Is it still the same, I wondered, or did that study revolutionize the operating room? What would happen, I wonder, if the patient went under to their favorite music rather than the usual Muzak or pop? Supposing he were to hear inspirational stories about miraculous cures and the power to heal rather than the usual gossip and jokes? Why not seed his dreams with thoughts of healing, after all? That is part of the surgeon's job, too.

A few years ago my parents went on a tour called Jewish Friends of Scandinavia. It was led by a rabbi, and my parents were just about the only non-religious people on the trip. "Everything we did, they said a prayer," my parents told me. "We went on a bus, they said a prayer. We went on a plane, they said a prayer. See? We have the book." They showed me a little book entitled *Prayers for Travel.* "We never felt so safe." I was used to these jokes. My father came from a very religious family. Fanatics, we would say. I imagined they did have a prayer for everything: talking on the phone, doing the laundry, taking a walk. We joked about it, but now I'm beginning to have second thoughts. Perhaps there is a connection between the physical and spiritual. Perhaps the right thoughts and prayers can effect a more satisfying conversation, cleaner laundry, a more refreshing walk.

My Ghanaian friend Dorcas is the most spiritual person I know. Whenever I tell her my problems, she says, "I'll pray for you." I thank her politely. Then one day I was telling her about a very nasty person who came to my medical office demanding care. Dorcas, who counsels patients at a local clinic, told me, "Every day before I open my door, I say a prayer that whoever walks through that door will bring their good energy with them and leave their bad energy outside." Now there's an idea, I thought.

The more I practice medicine the more I am convinced that the unspoken cues – a tone of voice, a smile, a way of being, can either open the patients up to the possibility of healing or shut them tight. Of course, the advice you give is also important but it is most useful in the right medium. So it is with every facet of our lives.

It's Friday night again, and my friend Nancy and Bob have invited me for the Sabbath dinner. As I enter their apartment, the two kids are running around making enough noise for ten. Seth, age four, is demanding a glass of apple juice, and Jed, age seven, wants to know, "When are we going to eat?" Amid the noise and confusion, we manage to get to the table, light the candles, and later, gather round the table to say the Kiddush. Then, Jed jumps up and shouts, "Let's wash our hands!" Finally, the room is still as, one at a time, we pour cold water over first one hand and then the other, recite the blessing, and sit back down in perfect silence, waiting to eat bread.

For further reading:
Remen, Rachel Naomi, MD. *Kitchen Table Wisdom: Stories That Heal.* New York, NY: 1996.

All Things With Their Deficiencies

Sarah Shapiro

In Chaya Rivkah's hospital room in Jerusalem, my awkwardness as I stood waiting for her was bringing back memories.

My sister was massaging my mother's feet in a Los Angeles hospital room, and I... I wasn't really doing anything. Should I fluff my mother's pillow? Fold down the sheet? Smooth the blanket? My big sister had already done all that. Still the baby of the family but well into middle age, I stood there like an idiot, ineffectual and embarrassed, wishing I could do something important. Crank the bed up? Or maybe Mommy needed it down? And was I concerned about all this for her sake or for my self-image? How could I be self-absorbed at a time like this!

Chaya Rivkah appeared, pushing slowly before her the intravenous machine. Then she paused. I stepped nervously to the side, making room for her to pass, and began saying, "Can I do anything?" when I noticed her lips moving. She was reciting *Asher yatzar*, the blessing after using the bathroom. After a moment she resumed the journey.

"Is there anything I can do?" I said, as she made her way across the small room. The dinner tray, with its unappetizing, overcooked fare, appeared to have gotten cold. It looked untouched. "Would you like something to eat? Some fresh fruit, maybe?"

What she probably needs most, I chided myself harshly, is calm companionship. Not these anxious questions.

"Well, first..." Her voice was so faint, I strained to hear. "I just have to get into this bed. If you can help me find a good –" The words faded.

"Oh, of course!"

I pushed aside the twisted-up sheets and blankets, helped her to lower herself to a sitting position on the edge of the bed, then crouched down to take off first the right slipper, then the left. Her bare feet hung limply, just touching the floor. I lifted up one frail leg and stretched it out, then the other, telling myself to no avail: *Relax!*

"Such pretty ankles," I commented inanely. Indeed they were, but compliments of this sort were obviously not what she needed now, or wanted.

"Yeah," she said weakly, with a grin. "Slender ankles. I always liked them." *Oh, Chaya Rivkah! Is this really you?* I still couldn't believe that the jaunty, joking, smiling Chaya Rivkah, the one who was always working on herself minute by minute, the irrepressibly joyous, incessantly creative Chayah Rivkah had been... transformed....

Working together, we arranged her thin self upon the mattress, though there was no successful way to do that. If she lay this way, it was painful that way. That way, and it was painful this way. She wanted to give lying on her back a try, but it made her wince. So, back to lying on her side, the position she'd been in for the last few hours.

"Good," she declared decisively, when her head was in place upon the two pillows. "Thank God." She closed her eyes.

She looked utterly worn out. The trip to the bathroom and back had been too much for her. I didn't know whether to speak. Several minutes went by.

Her eyes opened. My heart jumped up like a puppy.

"You know," she said, "you were saying about fruit." I leaned in close to catch what she was saying. "As a matter of fact, I really... would like a banana."

Off I rushed, out to the nurse's station. No one was there. I trespassed back into the nurses' private area and called out, "Hello?" No one replied. "Hello?" A young American nurse's aide appeared. I told her that the woman in Room 715 hadn't been able to eat anything at all but says she'd like a banana.

"We don't have any up here but they usually have some in the cafeteria. Oh, but it's probably closed. Maybe try the kitchen, on Minus 2."

A child desperate for a mission, down I sailed into the bowels of the hospital. The elevator doors opened to the sight of a long, empty hallway extending in

331

darkness to the left and to the right. Which way? Way down at the end, to the left, there was an open door, and light spilling out. I ran. My heels echoed.

A few minutes later I was back upstairs on 7, the bouquet of over-ripe bananas in hand.

But when I victoriously entered Room 715, she was in what looked like an uneasy, shallow slumber. Her breathing was too fast.

෫෧ ⊂ଋ

There was another hour left on my shift. It was almost ten. All the visitors on the ward seemed to have gone home.

I wanted to go home, too. I knew from previous experience that Chani, the young woman who arranged hospital visitation shifts for all the seminary girls, would come to relieve me on the dot at eleven. Wandering out to the waiting room, whom did I find, sitting over to the side by herself, but a friend from my neighborhood. "What are you doing here?" I exclaimed. I was so glad to see her.

"My mother's been here for a while."

"Your mother?"

"Yes. She's very ill."

I remembered her mother well. A sweet-faced woman. Gentle and soft.

"Yes. Very ill." Chava had an expression of tense uncertainty. She told me how she'd been at the hospital pretty much around the clock for two weeks, coming here directly right after work, staying for a while before rushing home to make dinner and see what was happening with the kids, trying to take care of things before rushing back. I felt a strange kind of jealousy, even for her tension, and the rushing, even for the uncertainty. Her mother was here. Between life and death but here, present. On this side. Alive! And Chava was still able to do things for her, and lose sleep over her, and worry about her, and rush around between hospital and home for her. What mitzvah can compare to that, when you're doing something useful for your mother? The feeling you get from it must be one of the most solid good feelings possible in this world.

My mother's bare feet came to mind. What could have possibly kept me from massaging them for her? My ridiculous insecurities about my sister doing it better? How could I have not seized that once-in-a-lifetime opportunity?

I told Chava that I missed keenly the time of life that she was in right now, and wished I'd done a better job when it had been my turn. I'd have to live with that regret for the rest of my days. The times I boiled her eggs too hard and gave them to her anyway. And the way I'd sit reading when she was too weak to hold a book. I could have read aloud to her. What in the world could have made me so lazy? So blind. So inexplicably selfish. *If I could have her here again for just ten minutes.... Even five! If I could just be with her for one minute.*

"Well, it's hard to know how you're doing when you're in the middle of it," she said. "I know. I always feel I should be doing more."

"I don't know what stopped me, though. If only I had the opportunity now."

"It's hard to be objective. We think we could have been different, but how do we know? If we did have another chance, how do we know we wouldn't do just the same?"

She told me a story she'd just read that Shabbos:

Every year before Succos, a certain Jew sold esrogim, a fruit which is one of the four species upon which one is required to say a blessing during the festival. One of his old customers was a real nudnik. Rarely satisfied, always spotting the blemishes and the flaws, always wanting to get something better, he'd search for an esrog from the time the stall was set up until the last day before the holiday, examining every last esrog again and again. Some years he'd go away without buying. It was annoying.

When the week before Succos arrived, that customer didn't show up. The esrog salesman asked around and someone told him that the man had died.

Over the next few days, the salesman asked himself why he'd always been so irritated by that man. Why had he never made a secret of his impatience? Why had he always been so gruff? Why hadn't he ever expressed appreciation for the man's religious devotion? His remorse grew keen and intensified. If only he had been more kind!

The day before Succos, to the enormous shock of the salesman, the old customer appeared, took a seat, and began checking the esrogim as usual.

"Where have you been?" asked the salesman, concealing his astonishment.

"Sick."

So it had just been a mistaken rumor.

The man remained there going through the esrogim, one after another, meticulously. As one hour passed, and another, the salesman's irritation increased. By the time the man finally came to a decision, the esrog salesman was beside himself.

℘ ℆

Back in 715, Chaya Rivkah was sitting up in bed. Two banana skins were on the tray. I felt like leaping happily into the air and started to say, "You finished the – "

Smiling and nodding, she held up one finger for me to wait a moment.

"*Boruch atoh...*" Her gaze was cast down. "*Hashem Elokeinu, melech ha-olam...*" Her head was moving back and forth slightly in concentration as she pronounced the blessing after having eaten fruit, articulating each word distinctly, deliberately, with a raised voice. "*... Borei nefashos rabos...*" Who creates

333

numerous living things, "*ve-hesronan*," with their deficiencies.... "*Boruch Chai ha-Olamim*." Blessed is He, the life of the worlds.

"I think that's the first time I ever really heard that blessing," I said.

"I do what I can."

"It's as if I never heard the words before."

One eyebrow lifted slyly and she gave a pert little dip of the chin as if to say, *Yup, deficiencies! May God bless us all!*

"Chaya Rivkah, maybe you'd.... Would you like it if I gave you a foot massage?"

"Oh! I'd love one. Yes." She lay back and closed her eyes.

Mine closed too, for a moment.

Mommy.

Her toes were cool to the touch. *Oh, Mommy.*

Let this be for you.

For further reading:

Schur, Tsvi G. *Illness and Crisis: Coping the Jewish Way*. New York: 1993.

Shapiro, Sara, ed. *Our Lives*. Jerusalem: 1992.

Idem. *More of Our Lives*. Jerusalem: 1993.

Idem. *The Mother in Our Lives*. Jerusalem: 2005.

A Door

She asks me what I do with my days
because of all this talk of "the beyond,"
and I tell her, as she raises her forkful of chicken,
that sometimes I wash the dead bodies
and dress them for burial.
She looks away from the food
her own hand hanging in the air.
And I look at her face as I have looked
at the faces of the dead
to see the difference.
And suddenly we have opened a door to the outside,
and we are shivering from the cold that comes in
when death is not beyond
but here like this plate of food and this table
wedged between two people who suddenly know
they are helpless and need God.

Varda Branfman

She Is Pure: The Story of Kathy Engber

Debra B. Darvick

There is always some kind of mystical connection when we close the door to the men outside and I realize once again that we are more than just the sum of the individual women present. Our reader begins the blessings that will be recited throughout the entire process and as I listen to her I feel as I do each time we begin our preparations – that God is in the room, that God is in our hearts, guiding our hands, assuring that our touch is gentle, elevating our work out of the profane into the realm of the sacred.

Master of the Universe! Have compassion on Joyce/Zerel daughter of Lily/Leah Chana, on this deceased one, for she is a descendant of Abraham, Isaac, and Jacob.... May

---

* Excerpted from her book *This Jewish Life: Stories of Discovery, Connection, and Joy.*

her soul and spirit rest with the righteous for You are He who revives the dead and brings death to the living....

Not everyone perceives they are capable of doing the sacred work of a *chevra kadisha*, a Jewish burial society, but when my rabbi asked me if I would consider learning these ancient procedures, I sensed that it was something I could do. I've always chosen things that are a bit outside the lines of tradition. I am a strong feminist, I've worked in what has historically been a male-dominated industry; honoring the rabbi's request just seemed to fit with who I was. And so I became one of five women in the small Wisconsin city where we live who are on call to prepare our community's dead for burial.

We five are from all walks of life, but what unites us is that we are all mothers. It frames our approach to our sacred responsibility – we have all done the intimate hands-on care of children. Preparing the deceased for burial brings us back to that time in our lives when we were involved in the intimate physical care of someone who couldn't care for herself. Someone who couldn't thank us, yet needed our ministrations all the same. I didn't know that is what I would draw on when I first went to Minneapolis to be trained, but I now realize that we all feel quite strongly the link between the care we gave our infants and the care we give the deceased, the *met*. When you care for a newborn you want each touch to be done with love, you want your child exposed to everything soft and gentle. That is also the sensation we want to come to the *met* through our hands.

I am usually the first to go into the room; I want to be sure that nothing will go awry. I make sure we have everything we will need – buckets and pitchers for water; *tachrichim*, the garments we will use to clothe the *met*; strips of linen for washing; natural fiber boards for *tahara*, the ritual purification; earth from Israel to place in the casket.

Then, when we are all assembled we take turns washing our hands – pouring water first on the right hand then on the left, three times until we are ready to begin.

Blessed are You who pardon and forgive the sins and trespasses of the dead of Your people Israel, upon petition. Therefore, may it be Your will, Lord our God and God of our fathers, to bring a circle of angels of mercy before the deceased for she is Your maidservant, daughter of Your maidservant.

The mood in the room is solemn, of course, but it is also filled with love. We are keenly aware that the *met* has a family in mourning and they may be worried about the treatment she is getting; we want it to be the best that it can be. We strive to maintain a high level of modesty for her as we begin our washing. First the entire head, then the neck, the right arm down including the hand.... We often talk as women do to children, "Now we are washing your left arm, now we are washing the upper part of your body... your back."

Our communication focuses on what is happening in the room and often someone has a memory of the *met* or we remember something she particularly loved doing. We are a circle validating this woman's life and we keep that in mind as we clean her and ready her for the ritual immersion.

The first time I worked with the *chevra kadisha* in Minneapolis I was scared, but I really wanted to perform the procedure for this woman I had cared about so much. I found that once you start the process, you put yourself aside and focus on what you are doing and there you go. You forget where you are and just move forward.

... And I will pour upon you pure water and you will be purified of all your defilements and from all of your abominations I will purify you....

The *tahara* that we perform is not done in the traditional sense – standing the *met* upright and pouring the required water over her. Instead we place her on several natural fiber boards that lift her off the table. The boards' absorbency assure she will be surrounded by water. The water has to be poured from our buckets in a continuous stream over the body, and while we are pouring we recite "*tehora hi, tehora hi, tehora hi* – she is pure, she is pure, she is pure." We make sure the water touches every part of her body before we dry her and ready the *tachrichim,* the set of burial shrouds.

When we were first trained there were quite a few deaths in our community all at once. Hopefully we'll never have to prepare another *met* again, but we know we will. I look at Judaism as living in tension between two points. For every issue there are two extremes and you have to find the path between the extremes. We never want to perform another *tahara,* but we are prepared for the moment when we're needed.

The hardest part of all comes after we have dressed the *met,* after we've laced the bonnet over her hair and veiled the face, and put on and tied the white trousers and *kittel,* the long white blouse, winding a white sash once around the waist and twisting its ends four times to represent *dalet,* the fourth letter of the Hebrew alphabet. We've placed the *kittel* on the *met,* wrapped a sash around the *kittel* and tied it with three loops to form the letter *shin.* The *met* herself represents the letter *yod.* In essence, the entire body spells out *shaddai* – shin, dalet, yod, one of the holy names of God. We've recited, "*Ve-El Shaddai yiten lachem rachamim* – and God Almighty give you mercy," and it is time to wrap the *met* in the *sovev* – a sheet that I think of as swaddling – before tucking her into the casket. It is the very last thing we can do for her and it is very hard to let go and close her in. It is a moment of great sadness for all of us. Sometimes, when the *met* is a particularly good friend of one of ours this final act is shadowed by even greater emotion. As we close the casket we ask forgiveness of the *met* for any roughness or inadvertent mistakes we may have committed.

I don't find this distasteful at all. It is meaningful. American culture so alienates us from death; I think this is wrong. You can't begin to understand death when it is so far removed from you. I think it is the genius of Judaism to have developed this ritual to such a degree that it is respectful of both life and death.

Being a part of the *chevra kadisha* has made me appreciate life so much more. We all know that life can end at any time, but you can't live your life fearing death. You square up with death and return to living your life. But I tell you, when there's a *simcha*, I really, really have a good time. In life you get X number of ceremonies. One is definitely a funeral, but there are simchas too. And I enjoy myself when they come around.

The next stage has to happen – that of handing her over to her family and setting the whole painful mourning process in motion. But we know we have laid the *met* to rest in honor; at her most vulnerable time she was not with strangers, but with her own. It is comforting to me to know that when my time comes I will be in the care of my friends. My children will know I was treated with respect and care during the final stage of my existence.

After the *met* is taken from us, we wash a third and final time and hold hands in a circle for a few moments and think once again about this loving act we have just performed. We thank God and thank each other and talk about the emotions we have felt. Sometimes our hands offer consolation as well as the affirmation that we have just completed Judaism's highest mitzvah.

We stand in awe of having witnessed once more Judaism's logic and genius, realizing that those who were created in the image of God will now live on in memory. And then, with one last squeeze of our hands we open the door and depart into that tension between life and death, going our separate ways, until the next time.

… For He will give His angels charge over you to watch you in all your paths… no evil shall befall you nor shall any plague come near your tent. The Lord is a warrior, the Lord is His name. The Lord will fight for you and you shall hold your peace. Amen.

For further reading:

Berman, Rochel U. *Dignity beyond Death: The Jewish Preparation for Burial.* Jerusalem: 2005.

Darvick, Debra B. *This Jewish Life: Stories of Discovery, Connection, and Joy.* Austin, TX: 2003.

Lamm, Maurice. *The Jewish Way in Death and Mourning* (revised and expanded). New York: 2000.

Be Not Far

The consolers come
to the outer courtyard
and stand by the gate that faces
the valley of the shadow of death
with its terror all around.
Standing by the gate is all
they can bear to do.
My soul, too, is miles
from the I of the weeper.
Inevitably.

O Creator of nights and wind,
this terrible weeping is aimed at You –
be not far away.
Let not millions of light-years
stand like a barrier
between You and Job.

Zelda

Translated from the Hebrew by Marcia Falk

Shiva

Sherri Mandell

During the seven days of mourning, the *shiva*, I live in the land of pain. My friends fear I won't return to myself, that I won't have the strength to go on. Seth worries about me because my eyes swing in their sockets; I can't eat. My friends beg me to eat. They rub my shoulders and my back. They try to spoon baby food into my mouth.

The doctor comes and checks my tongue, my blood pressure. He tells me I must eat. But food is for people who are alive, and I am not. I get up and go downstairs and cry out in my pain. I sit on the floor and am cradled by thousands of people who reach out to me. My children join me on the floor; they

---

* Excerpted from her book *The Blessing of a Broken Heart.*

are in their rooms with friends; they play upstairs, I don't know who is taking care of them but I see them eating. I see adults surrounding them. I speak to them and hold them, but they prefer to be with their friends. My pain is a flame that they can feel in my hands, see in my eyes.

Seven days of mourning. The mirrors are covered. Vanity is a luxury in the midst of such pain. One wants to forget the material world, be transformed into a spirit so that one can merge with the dead. This world seems like a world of shadow. The body is insubstantial. I don't want to perform my rituals of vanity – the quick dab of eye makeup, lipstick. I don't bathe. I wear the same ripped shirt all week. Breathing is all I can manage. Most people can't tolerate a mourner's silence and rush to fill it, but Jewish mourning law dictates that a person paying a shiva call should be silent until the mourner speaks. If the mourner says nothing, the person visiting should say nothing as well. Neither should greet each other. The first three days, when the pain is most intense, the mourner is like an egg, without a mouth, dwelling in silence. The point of the shiva is not to comfort a mourner for her loss but to stand with her in the time of her grief. As Rabbi Maurice Lamm notes, the main purpose of the shiva is to relieve the mourner of his loneliness. A person expresses compassion for the mourner through his presence and silence. Job sat with his friends for seven days and none uttered a sound. For only God can comfort. That is why, when, departing a shiva, many traditional Jews state these words: "May God comfort you among the mourners of Zion and Jerusalem." But I am not silent. I need to talk about Koby. I cannot contain the pain of silence.

And there are people who come and offer me words that ease my loneliness. Not formulaic statements like – "He's in a better place" or "Thank God you have your other children," but words that tell me that they can stand with us in this place of sorrow. I need to speak. I need people to talk to me. I ask my friend to put a sign on a door this is a house of shiva and all conversation should be about Koby. I refuse to listen to anything trite, anything mundane. I tell people: only Koby, only Koby.

There are many people who offer me wisdom, and I hold on to their words like a rope that I can climb. The women bend down to me, sitting on the floor, putting their faces to mine. Their faces are so beautiful – their eyes open, their voices soft and strong. Today I know that each person is created in the image of God, because I see and hear God in their faces, the faces of God. I know all of these women are God coming to comfort me, their arms wrapped around me; their eyes looking into mine. They reach into their souls and give me divine pieces of themselves; love and compassion – they feed me with their words. Israeli women are unafraid of suffering; they know death as a companion. They say:

"Your son will not be forgotten. We will not let him be forgotten...."

"We will be with you. You will never be alone, never...."

"He is our son too. We are crying with you...."

"He is with God and he is basking in God's love and you will bask in our love...."

"Your son is like a boat, a beautiful boat sailing and when it goes over the horizon you won't be able to see it, but it's still there, sailing along the open waters...."

And this: "My brother was killed and my mother suffered but after the terrible pain, there were gifts. My mother was a Holocaust survivor, her parents and brothers and sisters were killed in the war. She made a new life here in Israel. Then my brother was killed in a terrorist attack on a bus in 1979." I remember this. I once stayed at this woman's house for Shabbat, and all night, the picture of the handsome young man in the photograph looked down at me, and I felt he had died. In the morning, I asked her, and she told me that her brother had died when he was twenty-six. She says: "My mother had great blessings in her life, even with her misfortune, and so will you. God takes away, but he also gives. You will receive. God will give you bracha."

These words move me, and I want to believe them. But I don't understand them.

The mothers who have lost children to terrorism arrive. One, who lost her teenage son in an attack when he was hiking in Wadi Kelt, says: "You will go on. You will live." She gives me practical advice: "Don't make a shrine for your son. Pack up his things and put them away. Use his room. You don't need to keep out his pictures everywhere."

She is an attractive woman, her hair styled in a fashionable, short cut. She is wearing makeup, earrings. I look at her and realize: You can still be alive after your son is dead.

A woman who lost her nineteen-year-old son in a drive-by shooting says: "He is not gone. He will live inside of you now. We miss their physical bodies but we are still tied to them. You will never forget him."

I reach out for their hands like branches that will pull me across a raging river. One of my friends tells me: "You are all soul, you are letting us see your soul."

The politicians arrive. Israel is a small country with a history of conflict, and them is a custom of politicians attending the funeral or the shiva of each person killed by terror or war, each person killed by a national enemy. I tell the president, Moshe Katzav – I need a father to comfort me. He stares at me without seeing me. The chief rabbi, the ministers, the mayors – none of them have the right words of comfort for me.

"What do we do with the pain?" my husband asks a rabbi who, years ago, lost his eleven-year-old child in a bus accident. The rabbi answers: "You must use it to grow."

Another rabbi says that ours is a heartbreaking test, but we need to turn to God, that only God can give us comfort. Outside the house, my friend Valerie tells me, the rabbis cry like babies.

Because no matter how much we try to intellectualize it or interpret the pain, to will it away, the pain crouches on our heart like a beast waiting to crush us, to chew us to bits until we are nothing, dust that the wind can blow away.

I wake up each morning crying and I go to sleep in tears. My body is a poor companion now. It is too material. I want to peel it away, find the soul inside and merge with my son.

I look at the women who wrap their arms around me, who give me their bodies to cry on. They are my Yemenite and Moroccan and Portuguese and American mothers. There is so much love in that shiva, so much love; the love lifts me up and keeps me afloat like I am a body being carried.

For further reading:

Mandell, Sherri. *The Blessing of a Broken Heart.* New Milford, CT: 2003.

Vorst, Yitzchak. *Why? Reflections on the Loss of a Loved One.* Jerusalem: 1990.

Goldberg, Chaim B. *Mourning in Halacha: The Laws and Customs of the Year of Mourning.* Brooklyn, NY: 1991.

Lamm, Maurice. *The Power of Hope: The One Essential of Life and Love.* New York, NY: 1995

Kirzner, Yitzchok. *Making Sense of Suffering: A Jewish Approach.* Brooklyn, NY: 2002.

The Torah is very clear about the different characteristics and roles imparted by the Creator to man and woman. Man is a "conqueror," charged to confront and transform a resistant, often hostile world. Woman is his diametric opposite. While man battles the demons without, woman cultivates the purity within. She is the mainstay of the home, nurturer and educator of the family, guardian of all that is holy in God's world. "The entire glory of the king's daughter is within."

But "within" does not necessarily mean indoors. The woman too has a role that extends beyond the home. A woman who has been blessed with the aptitude and talents to influence others can and must be an "out-goer."

When she does, she need not, and must not, assume the warrior stance of the man.... There is also a feminine way, a gentle, modest, and compassionate way....

> From the Lubavitcher Rebbe's talks, December 20 and 27, 1986. Extracted from Rabbi Yanki Tauber's rendition in his essay, "Dina: Outgoing Woman" in his book The Inside Story: A Chassidic Perspective on Biblical Events, Encounters and Personalities

Putting Women in the Picture:
A Personal Account of the Lubavitcher Rebbe's Attitude towards Feminism

Susan Handelman

Let me begin with a story I heard from Robert Abrams, formerly the Borough President of the Bronx and District Attorney of the State of New York, and currently a practicing lawyer. As an influential New York politician he had several private audiences with the Lubavitcher Rebbe, Rabbi Menachem Mendel Schneerson, who was often visited by such figures. On one of his visits to the

Rebbe, Mr. Abrams was accompanied by his wife, Dianne, who sat beside him in the Rebbe's office while the two men discussed current political and economic issues. Dianne Abrams is herself an accomplished lawyer and, by her own account, "not a shy person at all." Assuming, however, that the Rebbe was only interested in conversing with her husband, she sat silently as they spoke. After some time, the Rebbe turned to her and said with a smile: "Why aren't you saying anything? These are the days of Women's Liberation."[1]

This little vignette summarizes the essence of what I want to say here, and my study of the Rebbe's writings, talks, activities in relation to women, and my own personal contact with him. I think he discerned the deeper meaning of what was occurring historically in relation to women. He saw within the stirrings of the women's movement a deep spiritual inner dimension and strong redemptive energies. He understood the need to use these energies for the good, and so encouraged women to speak, articulate their yearnings, and achieve their spiritual aspirations. He himself worked very practically to implement all of this, from a global level to encouraging one woman sitting in his office to speak her mind.

While I have written other essays that examine in depth the Rebbe's halachic and theological approaches to the status of women in Torah, this one supplements those with a personal account from the point of view of an outsider/insider or participant/observer. There are many forms of knowledge, and there is a certain dimension of understanding one gains only through an insider's position, and through having known one's subject "face to face."[2] This is particularly true in relation to a rebbe, a figure who functions on many levels – not just as a thinker, writer, teacher, rabbi or public leader, but also as an intimate, personal counselor. So I hope to add a personal perspective to the literature about the Lubavitcher Rebbe's relation to women's issues.

---

[1] See the video interview with Dianne Abrams in which she relates this anecdote.

[2] I have written in depth about this question in my essays, "'Knowledge Has a Face': the Jewish, the Personal, and the Pedagogical" in *Personal Effects: The Social Character of Scholarly Writing*, edited by David Bleich and Deborah Holdstein, 121–144, Logan, Utah: 2002, and "'Stopping the Heart': The Spiritual Search of Students and the Challenge to a Professor in an Undergraduate Literature Class" in *Religion, Scholarship and Higher Education: Perspectives, Models and Future Prospects*, edited by Andrea Sterk, 202–230, Notre Dame, Indiana: 2002.

The Rise of the Feminine Era in Kabbalah and Chassidism

Those familiar with chassidic philosophy recognize the idea that there are "sparks of holiness" (*nitzotzot kedusha*) scattered throughout our lowly physical world, awaiting their redemption through our actions. Concurrently, there is the chassidic-kabbalistic principle that the Rebbe also often cited that "everything that happens below has its source in what happens above." I think he took this principle also to mean that there was a specific historical-theological reason why the women's movement was occurring in our times, and that our task was to infer what it signified for the current generation.

In an oft-quoted passage from a talk on Jewish education for women given in 1990, the Rebbe reinterprets the basic talmudic and halachic sources regarding women's Torah study, draws out the practical implications, exhorts women to increase their study and teaching, and asks for the community at large to support this endeavor. He further asks: why has this increase in Torah learning for women occurred specifically in the recent era? On the one hand, the Rebbe answers, there is the traditional idea that each generation further from the Divine revelation at Sinai is on a "lower" level; and so there is an increasingly greater need to bolster it. Nevertheless, he continues, the result has been a great good, an increase in Torah study; and this increase in Torah study by women he emphatically describes as one of the *"positive innovations* of the later generations."[3]

From another perspective, each generation further away from Sinai is also closer to the final Redemption and Messianic Era. And so, the Rebbe adds, we could say we have merited the increase in Torah study for women precisely because of that proximity: it is part of the preparation for – and already a taste of – redemption. A defining characteristic of the messianic era is a great increase in knowledge and wisdom; and so we now already have a "taste" of it, just as there is a halachah (Torah law) that before Shabbat one is to taste each of the special dishes to be enjoyed at the Shabbat meal.[4] (This also connects to the idea the Rebbe often repeated that different parts of Torah are revealed in the times appropriate for them. Hence, he explained, only in recent generations has the

---

[3] "*Al devar hiyuv neshei Yisrael be-hinukh u-ve-limmud ha-Torah 5750 [1990].*" *Sefer ha-Sichot,* vol. 2. Brooklyn, New York: 1992, 455–459.

[4] See the Rebbe's discourse on the nature of chassidic philosophy and its innovations, entitled *Inyananah shel Torat ha-Chassidut* (and the appendix printed there, a discourse given on the last day of Passover, 1970) on the timing of revealing new insights and aspects of Torah. It is translated into English in the volume *On the Essence of Chassidus* (Brooklyn, New York: 1978).

esoteric "soul" of Torah – kabbalah and chassidism – been revealed and become increasingly accessible to the masses. Even though these latter generations might be on a lower level than previous ones, they also have a greater responsibility, for they are to purify and complete the final *galut* [exile] and open the way to redemption. Hence the most sublime parts and secrets of Torah are revealed in the latter generations and they already begin to "taste" of the Torah of the messianic era.)

Nevertheless – the Rebbe continues – there is an even deeper connection between women and the messianic era. Kabbalistic and chassidic teachings have a special understanding of the role of the feminine in the Era of Redemption and the World to Come. Then, say the classical sources, all the feminine aspects of the world will emerge from their concealment and diminution in the unredeemed world and rise to the highest stature.[5] That is the deeper reason – says the Rebbe – that in our generation the innovations and increase in Torah study connect to and are emphasized in relation to women. The effect of their study is also great, for as the Talmud says in a well-known line: "In the merit of the righteous women of that generation the Jews were redeemed from Egypt."[6] And so, the Rebbe concludes, in the merit of the righteous women of our generation, may the full and complete redemption come.

Many other chassidic leaders and thinkers, including his own predecessors in the Chabad movement, write of the time of the redemption in these kabbalistic terms as the elevation of the feminine side (*Malchut* or *Nukvah*, as it is called in the literature). As far as I know, however, the Rebbe is the only one to connect this long-held and abstract mystical idea to concrete sociological phenomena

---

[5] That is the deeper meaning of the famous verse from Proverbs (12:4), "A woman of valor is the crown of her husband" and from the prophet Jeremiah (31:21), "The woman will encircle the man." The crown, symbolizing the highest kabbalistic sefira (divine attribute) of Keter, sits on top of and encircles the head. Similarly, in the prophecy of Jeremiah, the woman encircling the man signifies the highest level of divine revelation, in the mode of a "circle" (makkif). In a circle, all points are equidistant from the center, as opposed to the hierarchical structure of a line. A circle also symbolizes what encompasses and cannot be contained and delimited. There are hints of this in the wedding ceremony, in which the bride indeed encircles the groom, and in the language of the wedding blessings. See further the chassidic discourse of R. Schneur Zalman of Liady in his Torah Ohr, end of Parshat Vayigash, and his commentary on the siddur and the wedding blessings for the relationship of male and female in the messianic era and the World to Come.

[6] Sotah 11b.

occurring in our time. He did not let it remain a metaphorical depiction of some far-off future era, unrelated to the current realities of women's lives.[7]

This perspective paralleled his reinterpretation of the halachic obligations of women in the mitzvah of Torah study, and within Chabad, his encouragement of their dramatically increased public participation in Chabad outreach activities.[8] He also transformed the role of the *shluchah* – the wife of the *shaliach* or Chabad "emissary." The Rebbe sent thousands of young families to serve as his "emissaries" all over the globe to found Chabad houses and reach out to fellow Jews. He made the women's role independent in its own right. He instituted the *Kinus HaShluchot*, an annual conference in the Chabad Center in New York for these women emissaries, just as the Chabad male *shluchim* had all gathered from all over the world once a year in Crown Heights. The women, who came to New York for a long weekend of workshops and lectures, had special gatherings with the Rebbe in the main synagogue. The men sat upstairs where the women usually sit for prayers, while the women sat downstairs with the Rebbe.

---

[7] However, Naftali Lowenthal adds: "At the same time one cannot quite leave out what R. Yosef Yitzchak [the Rebbe's father-in-law and predecessor] was doing. His presentation (in his Zikhronot) of women secretly studying Talmud in the ancestry of R. Shneur Zalman, his setting up of Achos HaTemimim [a women's study group] in Riga in the 1930s, and his statements about this, are very interesting in terms of a new view of womanhood. The messianic aspect is not stated, but then in general his intense messianism (seen in *Hakeriah veHakedushah*) is not expressed in his discourses and other teachings." (Personal email correspondence with the author, August 19th, 2002.)

[8] See my essay, "Women and the Study of Torah in the Thought of the Lubavitcher Rebbe" in *Jewish Legal Writings by Women,* edited by Micah D. Halpern and Chana Safrai, Jerusalem: 1998, 143–178, for an explication of his technical halachic analysis of the mitzvah of Torah study for women. This analysis was printed in the Rebbe's *Likkutei Sichot,* Vol. 14 (Brooklyn, New York: Kehot, 1978, 37–44) and reprinted in *Chiddushim u-verurim le-Shas,* Vol. 1 (Brooklyn, New York: 1979, 217–223). After a careful analysis of the classical sources and Shulchan Aruch HaRav, the Rebbe concludes that the mitzvah of Torah study for women is not based only on the need she has to know the laws pertaining to her – the classic justification – but acquires its own independent status as Talmud Torah for its own sake, lishmah.

On a sociological level there were also many *"mivtzaim"* – public campaigns initiated by the Rebbe – that involved dramatically increased public participation of women both in their performance and promulgation. Among these were the campaign to have all girls from the age of three upwards light Shabbat candles and to spread and publicize in as many forums as possible public knowledge of the mitzvah of taharat ha-mishpacha, the laws of family purity.

My Personal Experience

My relationship with the Rebbe began when I was a graduate student in English literature in the 1970s and used part of a fellowship I had to research and study for six months in the Chabad world center in Brooklyn, New York, where he had lived since his arrival in America in 1941. Over the years, I developed strong ties to the community and to Chabad Chassidism and had personal contact with the Rebbe in many ways: participating in his *farbrengens* (public gatherings), corresponding and consulting with him, studying his writings intensively, and brief face-to-face encounters. I had ample opportunity to observe him up close and to experience personally his relation to women.

During my time in Crown Heights and afterwards, I wrote several essays about Chabad Chassidism, many of which were based on research into the Rebbe's writings, and several of which he edited personally. In 1978, while completing my Ph.D. work in literature, I also co-translated into English, together with a Chabad rabbi, an important philosophical and hermeneutic discourse of the Rebbe's on the nature of chassidic thought entitled *Inyanah shel Torat ha-Chassidut* (English title, *On the Essense of Chassidus*[9]). The manuscript was given to the Rebbe to be checked prior to its being published in honor of his seventy-fifth birthday. My rabbinical co-translator told me with a smile that it was reported to him that when the Rebbe was shown the manuscript for his comments, he did not question my participation or credentials but instead those of my male colleague, who was well-known as a highly learned Torah scholar: "Since when does Rabbi G. know English so well?" asked the Rebbe.

At the suggestion of one of his secretaries, Rabbi Binyomin Klein, I had also consulted with the Rebbe about my Ph.D. dissertation topic. Of course, I was not the only one to be writing to the Rebbe for advice. The secretary told me that the Rebbe received and answered about four hundred letters a day. This was in addition to the endless phone calls and faxes that deluged his office in the course of any twenty-four hour period, along with the personal audiences he had with his followers and the many different people who came from all over the world to see him, and which lasted late into the night. At the time, I had thought of two possible dissertation topics: one on Shakespeare, and one on literary theory and rabbinic methods of interpretation. I often like to ask people which topic they thought the Rebbe advised me to write about. Many answer, "Shakespeare." When asked why, they surmise he would not like me to mix rabbinic and secular studies, or would not think that as a woman, I had enough knowledge to pursue

---

[9] See note 4 above.

that topic. Those who choose the rabbinics option say they think he would want me to try to bring *Yiddishkeit* into the university as part of the well-known Chabad emphasis on outreach. The answer was neither. The Rebbe's advice, as conveyed to me in the note typed by Rabbi Klein reproduced below, was as follows:

My translation to English:

It depends on what could be surmised about the attitude toward religion and Judaism of those who will be examining her Ph.D. work (that they should not be anti-religious, for then there would be some apprehension that they would disturb her and be opposed, and so forth).

(Parentheses in the original; the Rebbe's answer was also phrased in the third person, in the formal European style of polite respect).

I would say that this response was characteristic of the Rebbe. For as deeply as he was immersed in the mystical traditions of chassidism and kabbalah, as forcefully engaged as he was in a wide variety of campaigns to spread Yiddishkeit to every corner of the world, as idealistic as he was about the "pure spark" in the soul of every Jew and about the ever-present potential of redemption, he was also very grounded and pragmatic to the last detail. The answer reflects an astute awareness of the politics of the university and of academic committees. It was very astute advice which I followed and which I now also give to my own graduate students: choose your academic advisor and dissertation committees very carefully. In the end, I chose to pursue the topic of rabbinic interpretation and its relation to modern literary theory, and my dissertation eventually became my first book, *The Slayers of Moses: The Emergence of Rabbinic Interpretation in Modern Literary Theory*.

The Rebbe Edits My Work

There were other very concrete and pragmatic ways in which the Rebbe assisted me in my writing and encouraged my academic work. One was connected to his active and intense interest in the activities of the Chabad Women's Organization, *N'shei Chabad*. One of the organs of this organization was a journal called *Di Yiddishe Heim*, "The Jewish Home." It is a small bilingual "in-house" magazine, half the articles written in Yiddish and half in English, and directed towards a lay audience of women of the Chabad community. When I came to study in Crown Heights in 1977 as a graduate student in English literature, the feminist movement was in full swing. As a graduate of an Ivy League women's college at the forefront of the movement (Smith College, where my commencement address was given by Gloria Steinem), I was troubled by the issues feminism raised about the role of women in Judaism. As I learned more Chabad philosophy, I found very interesting talks and writings of the Rebbe and sources from previous rebbes which discussed the role of the feminine. In order to help myself deal with these questions, I wrote an article based on these sources for *Di Yiddishe Heim* entitled "The Jewish Woman: Three Steps Behind?"

Articles for the journal were written by both men and women, and the editor was a woman. I wrote the article and handed it in to her and she accepted it for publication. A short while afterwards, long before the article actually appeared in print, I wrote my first personal letter to the Rebbe to consult with him about something. After answering the personal issue he added the following words:

Translation: "I enjoyed her article in the forthcoming *Yiddishe Heim* and may God grant her success in all her other activities."

I was surprised, since I did not know how the Rebbe would have known about the essay before it was published. So I asked the editor, who told me that although few people knew about it, after she had edited all the manuscripts, the Rebbe went over them again, editing them personally himself. He took this time due to his great interest in the activities of women and his desire to support and encourage them. I subsequently wrote several articles for this journal, many based on ideas from his published public talks and discourses, and as a favor to me and as encouragement to write more, the editor gave my original manuscripts back to me with the Rebbe's corrections.

In these corrections, one sees him relating with great care to the efforts of a young academic woman beginning to learn chassidic teaching and trying to relate it to current issues in philosophy, literature and politics. The extraordinary pains he took to read and edit my writing in English – including its typos, punctuation, and grammar as well as phraseology and ideas – astounded me and reminded me of the kind of the detailed, fatiguing reading and commenting I did for my own students when I taught intensive courses in English composition. What follows are some representative examples from these manuscripts.

"One Sentence of Torah"

One essay I wrote was on "The Search for Truth – 'Religion' and 'Secularism,'" discussing the relationships between secular knowledge, Torah, and science, an issue with which I was concerned at the time. In the article, I wrote the following paragraph:

> Scientists, for example, have had to deal with the "uncertainty principle" and the recognition that at a certain level of observation, the observer so interferes with his data that he can't attain any certain conclusions. Philosophers no longer attempt to explain the whys and hows of the

universe, and restrict themselves mostly to analyzying [sic] language and logic – refusing to deal with "metaphysical" questions. Modern literature is extremely bleak, describing in painful detail the emptiness of the mind turning on itself, disconnected from the heart, and incapable of action. [Note: I must add here that this was written before the use of gender inclusive language became prevalent, so all the pronouns refer only to "he."]

The Rebbe edited this paragraph by

- deleting the extra words "so interferes with his data that he"
- changing "any certain conclusions" to "a certain conclusion"
- adding apostrophes to the phrase "why's and how's"
- correcting my typo in the word "analyzying" to "analyzing"
- changing the phrase "language and logic" to "events, phenomena etc."

In this essay, as well as others I wrote in an earlier time of more youthful extremism, he also qualified my large generalizations, as I often find myself now doing with the writing of my own students. Later in the essay, referring to a talk he gave about this subject,[10] I wrote:

… all secular sciences are limited and imperfect. They do not possess anything outside of themselves, or outside of reason – and furthermore, reason itself has its own inner limitations. Nevertheless, the Rebbe points out, it is precisely these limitations that satisfy a person, because he can grasp the entire system and contain it. He feels the satisfaction of mastering a body of knowledge, and hence, secular knowledge leads to arrogance.

In this paragraph, the Rebbe,

- deleted the word "all" in the first line, so it then read instead "secular sciences are limited and imperfect"
- inserted the words "today's human" to the next line, which now read "or outside today's human reason"
- qualified my sweeping generalization in the last line by inserting the adverb "very often" to the phrase "secular knowledge leads to arrogance" to now read "secular knowledge very often leads to arrogance."

The essay continued with my writing in the next paragraph that the opposite was the case with the study of Torah, which is an unlimited, infinite wisdom:

---

[10] *Likkutei Sichot*, Vol. 4, Brooklyn, New York, 1101.

Thus one can never contain Torah, master it. A person always feels how far he is from grasping the whole of it and fathoming its infinite depth. Therefore, he doesn't become arrogant, but on the contrary – humble. And the more he learns, the humbler he becomes, and the greater is his thirst for learning Torah.

Here the Rebbe, in what is my most favorite revision of his, inserted the words "all the content of even one *Dvar* (sentence of)" in the first line. It then read : "Thus one can never contain all the content of even one *Dvar* (sentence of) Torah, master it." Yet he was indeed one of the masters of Torah in our generation. I remember attending his *farbrengens*, the public gatherings that he held. The large synagogue in Brooklyn would be packed with a thousand or more people. If it were a weekday, he would start to speak at around 9:30 P.M. and often give several *sichot* or "talks," each lasting about forty minutes. Without any notes, he would speak into the early hours of the morning, for five or more hours, citing liberally from memory and constructing innovative interpretations intricately woven from of the whole corpus of Jewish literature – Bible, midrash, Talmud, the classic commentaries, Kabbalah, Jewish law, chassidic philosophy.

Women's Unique Power to Elicit Holiness

There was a case, however, in which the Rebbe intensified a large generalization I had made, one specifically about Jewish women.

In an essay I wrote entitled, "Judaism and Feminism: Our God and the God of Our Mothers," I explicated some of his writings on the nature of feminine spiritual power in the light of chassidism and kabbalah. The focus, in particular, was on the relation of the two *sefirot* (the divine attributes in kabbalistic thought which also are the superstructure of the world) *chochmah* and *binah*, "wisdom" and "understanding." These are also called "Father" and "Mother," and he discussed their relation to the "Fathers" and "Mothers," i.e., the Patriarchs and Matriarchs of Israel, and the powers they bequeathed to the Jewish people. To summarize briefly: in commenting on the parashah of *Chayyei Sarah* (Genesis 23:1–25:18)[11], the Rebbe discussed the quality of *binah* and the ability of the feminine attributes to affect the physical world more closely and bring the actual out of the potential both in the kabbalistic schema and on the parallel psychological-physical plane of our mundane world of male and female.

In the essay, I prefaced the idea by explaining a basic premise of chassidic thought: that before the giving of the Torah at Mount Sinai, the physical and

---

[11] *Likkutei Sichot*, Vol. 5, 336–353.

spiritual "realms had been separated from each other and not connected." To this sentence, the Rebbe inserted the adverb "perfectly" – "had not been perfectly connected." He had further elaborated the idea in the *sichah* that the mitzvot performed by the Patriarchs and Matriarchs who lived in the pre-Sinaitic era helped prepare the way for the stronger, more perfect connection that would occur later, but their mitzvot could not affect the physical world as strongly as those we perform after the giving of the Torah.

Here he made a very interesting distinction between the kinds of *kedushah*, "holiness," that the Patriarchs and the Matriarchs respectively brought into the world. He maintained that the Matriarchs of Israel brought a different kind of *kedushah* into the world than did the Patriarchs. The Patriarchs could draw into the world a holiness that would remain in the physical object after the mitzvah they performed was fulfilled – but *only* in that part of the physical that had a connection to the Patriarchs themselves. For example, the mitzvah of circumcision that Abraham was commanded to perform drew *kedusha* into the body that fulfilled the *mitzvah*, but not into the world outside. However, through Sarah, the first Matriarch, *kedusha* was drawn into a part of the world outside herself, and she bequeathed this power to all Jewish women. (For a further analysis of how and why this is so, see the original *sichah* in *Likutei Sichos*, vol. 5 Parashat Chayyei Sarah Hosafot).

In another *sichah*,[12] the Rebbe wrote of another distinctive trait that Jewish women possess more than men do, which is indicated by God's giving Rosh Chodesh (the first day or two of the Jewish month) as a special holiday to Jewish women in all generations and in the World to Come as a reward for their refusal to participate in the sin of the Golden Calf. The Rebbe describes this special female attribute as a certain unshakable attachment to and deep faith in God that helped the Jewish women in the desert resist the trials to which the Jewish men succumbed. Although this feeling of pure faith is rooted in the heart of every Jew, male and female, he says that it can become covered over or concealed due to various difficulties, and its effect on daily life and behavior may no longer be visible. However, he asserts, Jewish women possess a special strength that does not permit the concealment of this feeling and its effect on behavior. As I summed up these ideas in my essay, I wrote:

> The Rebbe points out that the reason why this great reward is given to *all* Jewish women in *all* times, till the coming of the Messiah and after (and not just to the women of that one generation [who left Egypt and contended with

---

[12] *Likkutei Sichot*, vol. 8, 317–319.

the Golden Calf]) is because the power to withstand such a great test which even the men could not endure comes from an innate superior trait that all Jewish women in all ages possess.

In the original version, I myself had twice underlined the word "all" in the first line, but not in the last part of the sentence where this adjective is used again. Here, however, the Rebbe intensified my generalization by underling once again the last two uses of the word "all": *all* Jewish women in *all* ages. And then once more again later on in the essay, where I summed up and wrote, "Every Jewish woman, in every time and every place, has inherited the special powers of the matriarchs," he underlined the first word *"Every."*

"There Must Also Be a Girl in the Picture"

Around 1980, the Rebbe initiated a campaign to encourage children to take more part in the overall public activities and initiatives of Chabad and join Tzivos Hashem, The Army of God. Many pamphlets were produced for this campaign, and the chassidim who were in charge of it founded a journal for children called *The Moshiach Times*. Several highly interesting editorial comments and corrections to this magazine were also made by the Rebbe. One of the later staffers of the journal, Dr. David Sholom Pape, compiled a series of them.[13] He relates that on the cover of the very first issue there was a drawing of two rows of children – one of boys and above it another of girls, each child carrying a banner with a letter on it , which all together spelled the words *Ahavat Yisrael*, "Love of a fellow Jew."

One of the older chassidim on the staff balked, wondering whether it was "modest and *chassidish* for boys and girls to be on the same cover." The younger members of the staff argued that since it was a magazine for both boys and girls, it was indeed appropriate. To resolve the dispute, the cover was sent to the Rebbe for his instructions on the matter. The Rebbe, however, did not instruct the staff to remove the girls from the cover.

The matter arose again when the second issue was prepared for Purim, and the cover had a boy and girl in costume as Mordechai and Esther, blowing bubbles in which were images of the mitzvot of Purim . Again objections were raised that such an image of a boy and girl playing together in proximity was against chassidic ethics; the previous cover had had the boys and girls separated

---

[13] Dr. Pape printed them in the *Souvenir Journal: Celebrating the Wedding of Bentzion and Rochie Pape*, 30 Adar 1, 5760 – a private illustrated gift volume distributed at the wedding of his son. I am grateful to R. Shlomo Gestetner of the Maayanot Institute in Jerusalem for locating this source for me.

in row, but now the boy and girl were next to each other! The cover was again sent to the Rebbe, who simply returned it with a check indicating it was fine to print.

The third issue was designed for Passover and had a cover sketch of a boy looking into a stamp album, each stamp depicting one of the fifteen steps of the Passover seder. The angle of the drawing and size of boy's head and the album left no room for an image of a girl as well. Since the other two covers had been sent in, this cover was also sent to the Rebbe for approval and the answer came back: *Tzarikh lihiyot gam na'arah* – "There also needs to be a girl."

The artist redrew and redesigned the cover to add the head of a girl on the left side and the boy's head on the right side. By then a custom had been established to send the covers in to the Rebbe for all the issues.

A few years later, in 1984, a cover was prepared by a well-known cartoonist for the Elul issue depicting a boy returning home from summer camp to his room, carrying his sports equipment. The room is portrayed as filled with holy objects, equipment for a solider in *Tzivos Hashem* – *chumash, siddur*, charity box, and so forth, and he is wearing a *kippah* and *tzitzit*. The cover was sent to the Rebbe, who returned it with two comments: "The tzitzit should be seen" and "There must also be a girl in another corner."

I conclude with these stories since I think that this directive, "There must also be a girl in the picture," summarizes what I have been saying throughout. On the broadest theological-metaphysical level, the emergence of the aspect of the feminine, of *malchut*, was also the deepest question of Redemption. The Rebbe connected the most abstract speculations and concepts in kabbalah and chassidism to the most practical and detailed endeavors in daily life.

I think this stance was also related to how he saw himself in the role of the seventh Lubavitcher Rebbe. His mission was to continue and expand all the work of the previous rebbes, but especially that of his father-in-law, the sixth Lubavitcher Rebbe, Rabbi Yosef Yitzchak Schneerson – to diffuse, develop and bring the latter's work completely into concrete reality. There is a Chabad chassidic idea that each of the seven Rebbes paralleled a different *sefirah*. In this schema, the sixth rebbe, Rabbi Yosef Yitzchak, paralleled the *sefirah* of *yesod*, and Rabbi Menachem Mendel, the seventh, was *malchut* – the last *sefirah* in the kabbalistic schema, which is on the feminine side of the *sefirot*. Malchut, the last *sefira*, receives and channels all flow from the preceding configurations of *sefirot*, and connects and implements them in the physical world. It is also called "sovereignty" or "kingship," as defined by the notion of a king whose power only comes by virtue of the people and whose life is given over to serve them and implement physical action in the world.

The Rebbe would often end his public discourses with a vigorous recitation of the words *"u-lematah me-assarah tefachim, be-karov mamash!"* ("Below ten handbreadths, soon and really!"). In other words, to bring all the wishes for good for the Jewish people, for redemption, for *tikkun* of the world – to bring this all down from abstract concepts and spiritual ideas to "below ten handbreadths." "Ten handbreadths" is the halachic measurement for a "private domain" on Shabbat, but more to the point, it is a reference to the rabbinic saying that "The *shechinah* (Divine Presence) never descended below ten handbreadths." In other words, bring this all completely down to earth, to the ground, to our collective and individual literal, historical, physical, daily, mundane existence. And this, too, I believe, is what he tried to do in putting women "into the picture" of Jewish life not just in theory, but pragmatically and actually – "soon and really!"

For further reading:

Elper, Ora Wiskind, and Susan Handelman. *Torah of the Mothers: Contemporary Jewish Women Read Classical Jewish Texts.* Jerusalem: 2000.

Schneerson, Menachem M. *A Partner in the Dynamics of Creation: Womanhood in the Teachings of the Lubavitcher Rebbe.* Sichos in English. Brooklyn, NY: 1994.

Schneider, Sarah Yehudit. *Kabbalistic Writings on the Nature of Masculine and Feminine.* Lanham, MD: 2001.

Teaching Mishna in Jerusalem

Karen Kirshenbaum

I grew up in New York in a family of all girls. I actually think that I was lucky I never had a brother. My father is not a feminist; had I had a brother he would have surely spent much of his time studying Torah with him instead of with his five daughters. When my father was often asked: "What's it like to have only girls?" he would answer in a teasing fashion with a smile: "Girls are the best if you can't have a boy!"

I came on aliya after high school and met my husband, a Jerusalemite, and we married young. I studied Talmud at the university and soon began teaching Mishna and Talmud in a religious girls high school. My husband's family respected my love of Torah study even though in Orthodox circles it is not always accepted for women to study Talmud. My husband's grandfather was also born in Jerusalem and was a very active Karliner Chassid. He lived extremely modestly, worked hard and set aside time for daily Torah study. I loved the interpretation of the Tanna Rabbi Eliezer's controversial and much-debated statement that our grandfather liked to quote: "'Rabbi Eliezer said: He who teaches his daughter Torah is as if he teaches her folly.' Notice, it is only 'as if' he is teaching her folly, but he who doesn't teach his daughter Torah is surely teaching her folly!"

For many years I have been teaching in a midrasha, a college for Jewish studies that is geared to teaching Torah studies in depth to young women who have completed high school. They study Torah "lishma," for its own sake, not in order to obtain a degree. The midrasha was originally situated in the Old City of Jerusalem on Chabad Street. In order to reach the midrasha, you had to park outside the Jewish Quarter and then progress on foot. So each day that I taught there I would see the Temple Mount and the Mount of Olives from the parking lot and then walk by the nearly two-thousand-year-old Cardo, the ancient Jerusalem road lined with pillars from the Roman colonnade. As I walked by the Cardo and then through the narrow streets of the Jewish Quarter, I could often hear the voices of young children davening or reciting their studies. I felt that I had fulfilled my dream, teaching Torah in the Old City of Jerusalem, and was able to actually feel the kedushah, the sanctity, all around. I could identify with a Tosafot that I had learned in the Talmud (*Baba Batra* 21a):

כי מציון תצא תורה. לפי שהיה רואה קדושה גדולה וכהנים עוסקים בעבודה היה מכוון לבו יותר ליראת שמים וללמד תורה כדדרשינן בספרי למען תלמד ליראה וגו' גדול מעשר שני שמביא לידי תלמוד לפי שהיה עומד בירושלים עד שיאכל מעשר שני שלו והיה רואה שכולם עוסקים במלאכת שמים ובעבודה היה גם הוא מכוון ליראת שמים ועוסק בתורה.

The Tosafot address the fact that during the Second Temple Period, scholars passed an enactment to open the first elementary school specifically in Jerusalem. The Sages brought the supporting verse from Isaiah to explain why they chose Jerusalem for the location of their first school." כי מציון תצא תורה ודבר ה' מירושלים"

(ישעיהו ב:ג)

"For from Zion shall the Torah go forth and the word of the Lord from Jerusalem" (Isaiah 2:3).

The Tosafot explain that Jerusalem was chosen as the best location because the students who came to study there would see the priests working in the Temple. The atmosphere of sanctity would cause them to devote their hearts to more pious observance and to the study of Torah.[1]

Centuries before education was widespread, Jews made it a priority. This is rooted in the Biblical commandment of "ולמדתם אתם את בניכם לדבר בם" – teach them to your children...." (Deuteronomy 11:19).

---

[1] Similarly, the Sages explained that the second tithe was consumed by the owner in Jerusalem only, so that while he resided in Jerusalem this special atmosphere of kedusha rubbed off on him too. As stated in the verse in Deuteronomy 14:22–23:

"עשר תעשר את כל תבואת זרעך היצא השדה שנה שנה. ואכלת לפני ה' אלקיך במקום אשר יבחר לשכן שמו שם מעשר דגנך תירשך ויצהרך ובכרת בקרך וצאנך **למען תלמד ליראה את ה'** אלקיך כל הימים."

"You shall set aside every year a tenth part of all the yield of your sowing that is brought from the field. You shall consume the tithes of your new grain and wine and oil, and the firstlings of your herds and flocks, in the presence of the Lord your God, in the place where He will choose to establish His name, so that you may learn to revere the Lord your God forever."

Roman historians and Church fathers write about how envious they are of Jewish education. In the ancient Roman world only the aristocracy could afford to educate their children either privately or by sending them to the gymnasium. Clemens, a Church father from Alexandria (second century CE), writes that all Jewish children attend school. Hieronymus, another Church father (fourth and fifth centuries CE), writes that every Jewish child knows the entire Bible. Of course, this is because the Sages required every town in Israel to open and support elementary schools that would teach both Torah and Mishnah to the children.

There is a story in the Talmud (*Avodah Zarah* 19a) about Rabbi Yehuda Hanasi, who taught Torah to his son Rabbi Shimon and to another scholar named Levi. When they had finished the book that they were studying, they had to decide what to study next. Levi asked for Proverbs and Rabbi Shimon Psalms. Rabbi Yehuda Hanasi chose Psalms, as his son had requested. Upon reaching the second verse in Psalms:

"כי אם בתורת ה' חפצו ובתורתו יהגה יומם ולילה."

"But his delight is in the law of the Lord, and in His law he meditates day and night" (Psalms 1:2), Rabbi Yehudah Hanasi cites the following interpretation of the verse:

"אין אדם לומד תורה אלא ממקום שליבו חפץ."

"A person only studies Torah where he delights or his heart desires." To that, Levi replied: You have granted me permission to leave! For Levi wanted to study Proverbs and not Psalms.

This reminds me of a comment that one of my students once made. She had already finished a degree at university and when asked by friends what were her plans for the coming year she replied that she was giving herself a treat. She was going to study Torah *lishma* at a midrasha. When her friend looked at her perplexed she explained: For some people it's a treat to go travel in the Far East for a year. My treat is to go and study Torah!

In the continuation of the passage in the Talmud (*Avodah Zarah* 19a):

"ואמר רבא: לעולם ילמד אדם תורה ואח"כ יהגה.... ואמר רבא, לעולם ליגרס איניש ואע"ג דמשכח ואע"ג דלא ידע מai קאמר שנאמר: 'גרסה נפשי לתאוה.' גרסה כתיב ולא כתיב טחנה."

"Rava states: One should always study Torah first and meditate on it afterwards.... Rava continues: Let one by all means learn even though he is liable to forget, even if he does not fully understand all the words that he studies, as it is said, 'My soul is breaking from longing for Thy Law....' (Ps 119). 'Breaking' is what Scripture says, not 'grinding.'"

According to Rava's methodology one should first obtain a wide range of Torah knowledge, and only then "meditate on it." One should first master a subject before discussing it. Rava's supporting verse uses the verb גרס, "break," which implies coarse crushing or grinding, to connote learning, as opposed to the verb טחן, "grind," which means fine grinding and would imply in-depth learning in order to reach perfect understanding.

Today, when every kind of information is easily accessible and we are able to download entire books from the Internet, there is a danger of not studying enough because you feel that you have the knowledge or information at your fingertips and all you have to do is locate it. Only when you actually learn Torah does it become your own, as Rava explains in the same passage:

"אמר רבא לעולם ילמוד אדם תורה במקום שליבו חפץ שנאמר כי אם בתורת ה' חפצו. ואמר רבא בתחילה נקראת על שמו של הקב"ה ולבסוף נקראת על שמו שנאמר בתורת ה' חפצו ובתורתו יהגה יומם ולילה."

At first the Torah is referred to as belonging to Hashem "בתורת ה'" and only after one studies, it becomes his Torah –"ובתורתו." After diligent study, the subject becomes his own.

It is extremely important to set aside daily time to study Torah; Whatever part of the Torah you choose to study – Chumash, Midrash, Talmud – once you start it is actually addictive! I teach a survey course in Mishna, where the students study up to one chapter of Mishna per day on their own. We are able to cover about two and a half orders per year. A number of students have called me a year or two after they left the midrasha and invited me to a *siyyum* of Shas Mishnayot, a celebration in honor of the completion of all six orders of the Mishna. Once they leave the midrasha they become very busy in the outside world, but as they put it, the time they make for Torah study is precious to them and helps them balance their lives.

About two years before my son's bar mitzvah, my son and I decided to study all of Shas Mishnayot together and make a siyyum in honor of his bar mitzvah. Together we studied approximately one chapter of Mishnah every day (approximately forty-five minutes daily) for two years, and finished studying in time for his bar mitzvah. People often talk about spending quality time with their children. The time we spent studying together was the greatest quality time for us!

I remember going to meet the Lubavitcher Rebbe as a young child with my family. My father told the Rebbe about the Talmud *shiur* that he taught on Shabbat afternoon in our neighborhood in Riverdale. The Rebbe asked what my mother and the other wives of the shiur members did during the shiur. My father explained that the Shiur rotated every week to a different home and the women prepared the seudah shelishit meal for the men. Not satisfied with that, the Rebbe suggested that the women should also have their own study group. After we grew up, my mother started a Mishna study group for women that continued for twenty five years.

Nineteen years ago I started a Mishna study group that meets every Shabbat afternoon. Between fifteen and twenty women attend, and we study Mishna with Rav Ovadia of Bartenura's commentary. The participants in the shiur work in different fields such as medicine, law, education, social work, and ceramics. Each woman contributes her own special knowledge to our class; when we studied Seder *Nezikin* (torts), the lawyer added to the learning with her expertise. When we studied Tractate *Niddah* (the laws concerning the menstruant woman), the neonatologist was especially helpful, and when we studied *Kelim* (the laws concerning the purity of vessels), the ceramicist's knowledge added to our understanding of the material.

I find that women connect to learning in a very special way. We try to visualize the case at hand and understand the material not only theoretically but also practically. For example: Did the explanation that was just given for the purity of the vessel actually work? What exactly did the vessel look like? How was it made? In this way, the material becomes more tangible and perceivable. When we studied Tractate *Mikvaot*, I took my students on a "behind the scenes" tour of the neighborhood mikveh. We got to see how the rainwater enters directly from the roof, filling the reservoirs that are then connected to the pools that are used for purification.

Just recently we completed all the sixty-three tractates of the Mishna and made a festive siyyum (a completion ceremony). As may be imagined, it was a great feeling of accomplishment for all the women in the shiur. The ancient text that we recite at the siyyum begins with the word "hadran," which literally means "repeat once more." We have started learning the Mishna over again from the beginning. For in learning there is no such thing as staying in the same place. You are either actively learning or actively forgetting! As Hillel the Elder says in Tractate *Avot* 1:13: One who does not add to his learning forgets what he has already learned.

One of my goals in teaching is to make the sources come alive for my students. When I teach, I try to imagine the lives of the Tannaim, the Talmudic sages, and their surroundings; I actually picture them in their world discussing, arguing and resolving halachic issues.

It is my hope that in so doing, the learning experience will be made more meaningful and thereby lead to a higher level of fear or awe of God [2] and

---

[2] The sage Rabbi Yannai says (Babylonian Talmud, Shabbat 31b):

חבל על דלית ליה דרתא ותרעא לדרתא עביד.

consequently to a heightened awareness of Hashem's השגחה, Divine providence in our daily lives.

For further reading:

Wiskind Elper, Ora, and Susan Handelman. *Torah of the Mothers: Contemporary Jewish Women Read Classical Jewish Texts.* Jerusalem, Israel: 2002.

Zolty, Shoshana Pantel. *And All Your Children Shall Be Learned: Women and the Study of Torah in Jewish Law and History.* Lanham, MD: 1993.

"Woe to him who has no courtyard yet makes a gate for one." One who studies Torah but does not have יראת שמים – the fear of God – is similar to a man who has no yard but has built a fence. He is lacking the essential part, the essence.

In his book *The Path of the Upright,* Rabbi Moshe Chaim Luzzato (known as the Ramchal, early eighteenth century) instructs the reader how to obtain higher levels of sanctity. He explains that there are different levels of fear of God. The lower level of fear of God is the basic fear of punishment. The higher level is when one feels Hashem's presence at all times and does not sin out of reverence for Hashem. Rabbi Luzzato explains that our world is so materialistic that it is hard to achieve this higher level of fear of Hashem, but through Torah learning it is achievable, as expressed in the verse in Deuteronomy 17:19 והיתה עמו וקרא בו כל ימי חייו למען ילמד ליראה את ה' אלקיך." "And it shall be with him, and he shall read therein all the days of his life; that he may learn to fear the Lord his God."

Is God My Partner or Am I His?

Shoshana S. Cardin

Many times I have been asked how I became so involved in Jewish issues and organizations, as well as civic and communal activities, and I was not able to answer. I would state that I really didn't know - but that I believe that these have been my mission on this earth. I did not come to that conclusion until some years ago.

When I was very young, my father z"l was a teacher in Baltimore at a Talmud Torah community school. He frequently was responsible for teaching the students Hebrew songs and melodies, many from our liturgy as well as from the young Yishuv. These songs were the same ones we sang at home. For my brother and me, they were popular tunes. Although we did not consider ourselves religious and we knew we were not fully observant, we were Jewish to the core. We believed in Klal Yisroel and in the Yishuv that would one day become the State of Israel.

We also believed that *Kol Yisroel arevim zeh la-zeh* – all of Israel are responsible one for another. My parents lived that reality, as did their friends. Students from Yeshivot and the Yishuv were never turned away because there was no money. There was always cake and tea even when finances were very low. All of my parents' friends were the same, concerned about all Jews everywhere. This was to be my mantra – *kol Yisroel* – but I had no idea where that would lead.

There was some doubt as to whether I believed in God, although I did acknowledge that there was a power greater than mankind, certainly greater than I. Yet this power had left a series of needs to be addressed, that we humans would have to struggle with. It was later that I understood the covenant between humankind and God – a covenant that we, as humans, had a responsibility to continue His work on earth. Now I understood my father's and mother's passion for seeking justice in this world, for trying in their own small way to make a difference for good. It was a wonderful heritage to carry on.

Needless to say I had no idea what my personal mission or role would be. My husband and I raised four wonderful Jewish children, kept and still keep a kosher home, still celebrate Shabbat evening, sing Shabbat songs, and discuss issues of Jewish consequence. We all believe in Jewish precepts, with my daughters' homes being more observant than mine, and several grandchildren more observant than I.

My realization that I was religious came when I would pray to God to assist in this illness or that, or when I was addressing a major group of people who needed the inspiration to enjoy and promote Judaism. My confusion was in equating religious with observant. Today I know that at times the words I have spoken from the platform were not mine but were given to me; the strength I have been able to muster has been strength given to me. There is no other explanation. And I confess that while I credit God for the good, I blame only myself for the negative or problematic.

℘ ℭ

When I met the Lubavitcher Rebbe z"l in 1991, it was as if he had been reading my mind. I was truly tired, having put thirty years of work into organized Jewish life. The Rebbe looked at me, asked no question, but said that my work was not over. I could not stop; there was more for me to do. After looking into his penetrating blue eyes I knew this was so, although I was not aware of what that mission would be.

I had held many positions of leadership within the Jewish organizations of my home town and in the mid-1980s had been catapulted into the national sphere, eventually holding the top leadership position in six national Jewish organizations, more than any man or woman had ever held. In all of those positions with the exception of the Jewish Telegraphic Agency, I was the first woman to hold the top volunteer position, and in several have not been succeeded by a woman since my term ended.

At no time did I solicit these positions; rather, they were offered to me even when I had not been a member of the executive or an officer of that organization. At no time did I feel a glass ceiling or discrimination because I was a woman. But then, I was always invited by men to assume the chairmanship, as there were no other women at the top. My mentors were primarily men, chief executives of the national organizations, simply because there were no women professionals at the top either. Each position found me hesitant, uncertain as to whether I was sufficiently qualified, able to perform as the times demanded.

What explanation is there for my strength and resolve to meet with world leaders, presidents, prime ministers either to explain our cause (I did not *plead* our cause) or clarify our request? How was it that I felt that all of those who entrusted me with those missions were with me and supported me?

When I asked "Why me?" the only answer was my husband's. "You have a mission in life. You have been called to serve." Often I remember our teaching, "From whence comes my help? My help comes from God" (Psalms 121:2). Yet I don't really believe in a personal God. There is so much to do in this world of major proportions that my minor requests should not receive any attention. Yet something inside wants me to accept that our covenant requires the acknowledgement that I am a true partner with God as I attempt to use my energies for *tikkun olam*.

May our labors in various fields of Jewish concern merit the blessing of God, and may we be privileged to see our precious State of Israel know peace.

For further reading:

Sacks, Jonathan. *A Letter in the Scroll: Understanding our Identity and Exploring the Legacy of the World's Oldest Religion*. New York: 2000.

Steinsaltz, Adin. *Simple Words: Thinking about What Really Matters in Life*. New York: 1999.

"Our Father, merciful Father who is compassionate, have mercy on us, and grant our heart understanding to comprehend and discern, to perceive, to learn and to teach, to observe, to practice and to fulfill all the teachings of Your Torah with love."

From the daily morning prayers

Thank You, Nehama Leibowitz

Shira Leibowitz Schmidt

In the summer of 1972, I pushed my three infants in one stroller to the post office in Haifa to pick up a magazine and tore off the brown-paper wrapping. My old Stanford University roommate had mailed me the first issue of *Ms. Magazine*. I started to read it on the way back to our apartment and felt a *click!* This was a defining experience for me.

The magazine came out at a time when I had started to attend consciousness-raising sessions where I was prodded into pondering why my graduate research in engineering had ground to a halt while my husband's thesis was proceeding on schedule. I had questions (and accusations) similar to those of my contemporaries about the role of women, and I was ripe to blame a so-called sexist society. As a religious Jew, I began to systematically re-examine many of the religious beliefs and practices that I had taken upon myself over the previous years.

I found myself constantly sparring with my Orthodox in-laws, especially with Nehama Leibowitz, my father-in-law's sister.

Unassuming and unpretentious, Professor Nehama Leibowitz, Israel Prize laureate, insisted that everyone call her simply "Nehama." She was one of the most learned and original expounders of Jewish Biblical commentary in the twentieth century; she was *sui generis*. She taught a more varied spectrum of people Torah over a longer period of time (in Israel and in the Diaspora) than any other scholar, teacher, or rabbi. She passed away in Jerusalem in 1997 at the age of ninety-two. I am forever thankful for her patience in discussing issues related to women's roles in Judaism during the stormy period of my questioning.

Nehama had come on *aliya* to Israel in 1931 after completing her doctorate in Germany. Settling with her husband in Jerusalem, she began teaching Bible, eventually becoming a professor of Biblical studies at Tel Aviv University. But that she did with one hand. With the other hand, and with her head and heart, she responded to repeated requests from students for a correspondence course of thought questions on the weekly Torah portion. She called these study sheets *gilyonot,* and the number of subscribers grew from a dozen to hundreds, spanning the range of the Israeli public – mothers, scientists, infantrymen, blue-collar workers, university students, engineers, nurses, ultra-Orthodox rabbis, ultra-secular kibbutzniks. Eventually they were mailed out by the Ministry of Education over a period of thirty years (one can buy the thirty-year set of some fifteen hundred *gilyonot*) to subscribers who mailed answers to Nehama. On her own time, she laboriously corrected every response she received and mailed it back to the sender. The public demand was so great that she eventually published *Studies on the Weekly Sidra* (in Hebrew, English and other languages) on the five books of the Pentateuch, and a number of additional studies ranging from pedagogy to the Prophets. Nehama traversed Israel teaching teachers, army officers, university students, and new immigrants.[1]

Her impact on two generations of Bible teachers and students was brought home to me when I happened to be in her tiny apartment soon after her brother, Yeshayahu, passed away during the summer of 1994. A package had arrived from Camp Morasha in Pennsylvania. The camp counselors had been using Nehama's material in teaching the weekly Torah portion, and the educational director had suggested to the campers and counselors that they write her condolence letters. As Nehama and I read through over a hundred letters, a picture emerged. "My mother studied with you when she was in Israel for a year"; "My father took a year from his rabbinical studies to study in a yeshiva in Israel and would steal away to go to your classes, which he said was the most valuable thing he did in Israel that year"; "After attending your classes, my aunt became so enthusiastic about Torah studies that she changed her major at college and went into teaching"; "My Jewish day school history teacher said he learned how to really stimulate students' minds by attending your Bible classes." These were the sentiments in letter after letter. Though Nehama had adamantly refused all entreaties to teach outside of Israel once she arrived in 1931, her influence could not be bound by borders.

Jerusalem Rabbi Naftali Rotenberg once remarked that he made a surprising discovery during his years as a roving Israeli emissary to several dozen American

---

[1] See the biography by Leah Abramowitz, *Tales of Nehama* (Jerusalem: Gefen, 2003).

communities. He found two types of rabbis: those who used Nehama's material for their sermons and classes and cited her, and those who used Nehama's material for sermons and classes but did not mention her as the source.

Nehama's influence was not only on the macro level; she affected individuals around her, including myself. During the period when I began to doubt received assumptions about a woman's role in traditional Jewish practice, I pelted Nehama with questions and exhorted her to address these issues. She finally acquiesced to my imploring that she give a lecture on the subject. Or rather, she assented to give a *shiur* since she adamantly distinguished between a *shiur*, which is a text-based study, and a lecture. "I give *shiurim*. I don't lecture," said Israel's premier educator.

I hoped she would take into account some of my concerns on women's issues. That study session was a turning point for me. Before I take you with me to that class, which took place in Beer Sheva in the mid-1980s, let me explain my mindset in those days and how I came to that city in the southern Israeli desert.

I had grown up in a non-observant Jewish home on Long Island, New York, and decided as a teen that I would make my contribution to the Jewish people by desalinating water as a scientist in Israel. To prepare myself for this I was advised to study engineering, and found myself one of five women among two hundred engineering undergraduates at Stanford University. I had one last exam left to take before graduation in sunny California in June 1967, when I decided to go to Israel show my support because the Six-Day War had broken out. When I told my professor that I was leaving to contribute my meager engineering skills to the war effort and would thereby miss the final exam in his thermodynamics course, he grimaced and replied, "I have heard many excuses in my lifetime, but this is the most original. However, if you indeed do go, send me a letter from the war zone. I will count your mid-term as your final exam." I arrived in Israel during the war, decided to stay, and wired my parents not to fly out to graduation in California because, well, I was in Israel. After sending a postcard to my thermodynamics professor, I received my bachelor's degree in absentia.

During my years at Stanford I had met young Orthodox couples and had slowly become religiously observant. In Israel, I went to work briefly for the hydrological services, married (the late Elhanan Leibowitz) and eventually settled in Beer Sheva. The babies were coming thick and fast – by the time the oldest was four, he had three younger siblings. Eventually we had six children. I was an enthusiastic but completely unprepared young mother. The nascent feminist movement thus had an inordinate impact on me – it explained why, with babies crawling underfoot, my work on a doctoral thesis had ground to a near halt; it explained why I had exchanged my ambitions to desalinate water for bathing babies. After reading a few issues of *Ms. Magazine* I went out and ordered disposable dishes by the thousand units; after reading *The Feminine Mystique* I started putting the children to bed with fairy tales from *Free to Be You and Me*. And I argued with Nehama about the place of women in Jewish tradition.

There were many issues I raised with Nehama. It is ironic that Nehama has been presented as a pioneer woman in Jewish scholarship. She had no truck with such formulations; in her own eyes she was simply doing what she loved to do, studying and teaching Torah and sharing her inquisitive mind and vast knowledge of the sources with others. Several scenes remain in my memory from these discussions, and I hope that the passage of time has not distorted them.

I raised socio-political issues. I would protest that there were so few women members of the Knesset, and she would wince and blurt out: Who would want to be a member of the rowdy Israeli Knesset?! Is that progress? I was upset about differences between men and women in Jewish ritual practice and the exemption of women from several *mitzva* obligations such as *tefillin*. "I am happy for every *mitzva* from which I am exempt," asserted Nehama. "If a woman has extra time in the morning, let her use it to visit the sick."

Often I would bring up the differential status between men and women vis-à-vis Torah study (in its broadest sense): men have a fundamental, clear-cut obligation to study, while for women this is not so. Nehama explained that she was not studying and teaching to prove anything. She simply loved studying and teaching. She often lamented that it was only because she and her husband were unfortunately not blessed with children that she had time to pursue her intellectual interests. She gave us to understand that it was the mothers of Israel whom she regarded as the heroines of the Jewish people.

My questions continued for several years, and I persistently importuned her to address them in some way. Exasperated with me, she finally acceded to give a class to a group of women in my neighborhood. She would not lecture on women's issues. She would not discuss contemporary controversies. She would give a serious, analytical, text-based class on prayer.

So it was that we assembled in the living room of a Beer Sheva neighbor one chilly, wet winter night. Ricky Shulman had volunteered her spacious home and had set out a simple collation. The practical furniture had been crammed into a corner to make room for fifty plastic chairs. The announcement for the class had specified that each woman bring a copy of Genesis and most came prepared. Despite the rains, the class was overflowing and Ricky scurried to neighbors to scare up more chairs. Nehama entered, clad in her usual modest attire. Her wardrobe of long woolen dresses in brown or blue with wrist-length sleeves and a dark beret covering her head reflected her utter simplicity and practicality. The women stopped chatting and stood up briefly in respect.

In a short caveat, Nehama said that it was not her wont to talk about "women" in the Torah. "Shira asked me to address women's issues, but I demurred. The Bible has kings, paupers, Pharaohs, shepherds, scoundrels, warriors, mothers, daughters, fathers, sons…. There is no reason to single out any one group." Thereupon she asked us to open to the book of Genesis, *Parashat Vayetze*, chapter 30, and she immersed us in a two-hour study of the first two verses. I had no time to be chagrined that she would not oblige my obsession and would not discuss "women's issues" because I was too preoccupied finding additional seats for the latecomers, locating additional Bibles for those without them, and trying to follow the flow of the class.

That chapter deals with Jacob and his wives, the sisters Rachel and Leah. The verses under study describe the predicament of Rachel, who remains barren while Leah's fecundity (she has just given birth to her fourth son) is an ever-increasing source of distress to Rachel.

> When Rachel saw that she bore Jacob no children, Rachel became envious of her sister and said to Jacob, "Give me children or else I die." Jacob's anger flared up against Rachel and he said, "Can I take the place of God, who has denied you the fruit of your womb?" (Genesis 30:1–2)

Nehama teased out of us an articulation of the main difficulty this passage raised. Why did Jacob get angry? Was his anger justified? She engaged us in the conundrum presented by this dialogue. After she elicited possible explanations of Jacob's anger from the women, she then helped us to compare various explanations suggested by some classic Jewish commentators.

Nehama next handed out copies of the questions and study sheet she had prepared. It juxtaposed several different commentaries on the two verses under study. To help us focus on the essential differences, or similarities, among the explanations for Jacob's (seemingly) disproportionate and angry response, she asked a quintessentially Nehama-like question: What is the difference between the following midrash and Radak (Rabbi David Kimhi, b. 1160, Provence) in their attitude towards Jacob?

Midrash:

> Is this how you answer a woman in distress? By your life, your children [by your other wives] are destined to stand humbly before her son, Joseph, and he will echo your words and say, "Can I take the place of God?" [Genesis 50:19]

Radak:

> Thus Jacob's anger flared up at her because she thought he had
> the power to solve her problem, rather than turning to the All-
> Powerful who alone enables the barren to be fruitful, as it says,
> "And the barren shall give birth to seven." [1 Samuel 2:5]

As we became absorbed in the search for the core differences between such
commentaries, the gears of our minds and hearts became engaged. Many of us
had trouble keeping up with the fast pace of the discussion; I could barely follow
because I would get thrown off course with each additional verse that was
brought to bear as a prooftext. The cross-references in the above passages that the
midrash and Radak cite (Gen. 50:19 and Samuel, respectively) were intended to
anchor and clarify the commentaries; but for those of us unfamiliar with the
context of each new cross-reference, these additional verses would enmesh rather
than enrich us.

Nehama asked us to write down in as few words as possible the difference
between the two commentaries and she walked among us looking at our
scribbling, nodding approvingly at accurate answers, and encouraging those who
were slower to perceive the difference. This is one of the pedagogical techniques
that she favored because often the participants who are faster to answer will
repeatedly respond to a teacher's questions, unintentionally robbing the less agile
students of a chance to think through the problem themselves. In this case, most
of the women eventually were able to formulate an accurate answer: the midrash
criticized Jacob's anger in contrast to Radak, who justified it.

Now it was the commentaries and questions on them that were coming thick
and fast. It was a humbling experience for those of us who had been to leading
universities to be striving to keep up with the pace of the class. One person who
was sailing through the session was a neighbor, Pearl Kagan. Pearl was the only
one who wore a *sheitel* and who had gone through the ultra-Orthodox Bais
Yaakov school system. We had no idea how intellectually demanding that system
could be – not only with respect to familiarity with Biblical verses, but also in
equipping girls with analytical and thinking skills. Pearl was (bewigged) head
and shoulders above the rest of us; while we struggled and straggled, she was
enjoying the fast pace of the questions. What was the context of the quote from
Joseph at the end of Genesis cited by the midrash? Why did Radak choose the

verse from the book of Samuel rather than another similar verse to buttress his support of Jacob? To what theological problem did Radak allude?[2]

As the evening progressed, I became resigned to the fact that Nehama was not going to discuss women qua women, but rather issues such as the underpinnings of prayer and its relation to suffering. But the final question Nehama posed revealed that she had understood some of the questions perplexing me.

Among the commentaries on the *gilayon* were those of the Ramban (Nachmanides, b. 1194, Spain) and R. Yitzhak Arama (b. 1420, Spain). Juxtaposing them, she asked us to ascertain what they had in common, and where they differed.

Ramban:

> Jacob was angry because it is not in the power (even) of the righteous that their prayer must automatically and invariably be granted…. This was why he told her that he could not take the place of God and make fruitful the barren.

Rabbi Yitzhak Arama:

> The two names "Woman" (*isha*) and "Eve" (Chava) indicate two purposes. The first teaches that woman was taken from man (*ish*), stressing that like him, she may understand and advance in the intellectual and moral spheres, just as did the matriarchs and many righteous women and prophetesses and as the literal meaning of Proverbs 31 about the "woman of valor" (*eshet chayil*) indicates. The second name, Eve-Chava, alludes to the power of childbearing and rearing children, as is indicated by the name Chava [which comes from the root *chai*=life] the mother of all living. A woman deprived of the power of childbearing will be deprived of the secondary purpose and will be left with the ability to do evil or good like the man who is barren… since the offspring of the righteous is certainly good deeds.[3] Jacob was therefore angry with Rachel when she said, "Give me children or else I die" in order to reprimand her and make her understand this all-important principle that she was not dead as far as their joint

---

[2] For answers to these questions see Nehama's discussion of this chapter, "Can I take the place of God?" in her *(New) Studies in Bereshit,* trans. A. Newman (Jerusalem: World Zionist Organization, 1972), 331–338.

[3] See Rashi on Gen. 6:9.

purpose in life because she was childless, just the same as would be in his case had he been childless.

While both Ramban and Rabbi Yitzhak Arama justified Jacob's angry rebuke to Rachel, they differed in the way they viewed Rachel's theological mistake. Ramban saw Rachel's error as a misapprehension of the power and purpose of prayer. R. Arama faulted Rachel for misapprehending and minimizing her own role as woman qua human. Nehama went on to discuss in her own words the long quotation of R. Arama, as she does in her chapter on this in *Studies in Genesis*. Rachel had an erroneous view of herself and misunderstood the mutual purpose (*primary* according to Arama) that she and Jacob shared as intellectual and moral beings (*le-havin u-le-haskil*), irregardless of her inability to have children; R. Arama considered the childbearing aspect only *secondary* in purpose.

Keep in mind that R. Arama wrote on the equality of purpose between men and women five centuries ago! A different phrasing of this concept was recently formulated by R. Meyer Twerski[4]. He writes that "the Torah expounds an axiom of dissimilar equality of the two genders." What he means is that they are equal (*ish/isha*) in their primary stance before God; they are dissimilar in that women have the additional secondary Eve/*Chava* capacity. Rabbi Joseph Soloveitchik, of blessed memory, expressed this concept in his posthumously published book *Family Redeemed* and translated it into the halakhic matrix.

> There is no doubt that in the eyes of halakha man and woman enjoy an equal status and have the same worth as far as their *humanitas* is concerned. Both were created in the image of God, both joined the covenantal community at Sinai, both are committed to our meta-historical destiny... and with both He engages in a dialogue. However, Jewish law (*halakha*) has discriminated between axiological equality pertaining to their Divine essence and metaphysical uniformity at the level of the existential personal experience. Man and woman are different personae, endowed with singular qualities and assigned distinct missions in life. Hence axiological equality should not level out the uniqueness of these two sexual personalities.... Man and woman complete, not duplicate, each other.[5]

---

[4] R. Mayer Twerski, "Halakhic Values and Halakhic Decisions," *Tradition* 32:3, (Spring 1998): 16.

[5] R. Joseph B. Soloveitchik, *Family Redeemed: Essays on Family Relationships* (NY: 2000), 71.

This is where I would begin in order to try to answer the challenges that pertain not only to the axiological status of women and men but also to the pragmatic and Jewish legal aspects of these questions: women as witnesses, halakhic obligations of women with respect to comprehensive Torah study, different prayer and ritual obligations, and public vs. private roles of women.

In the weeks following that learning session with Nehama, I refocused. I realized that the answers – and the right questions – were not to be found in modern polemical writings or in gender studies. Indeed, it is not answers that need be sought. Rather the questions must be reformulated as one studies and encounters the sources.

Nehama herself has described the experience of in-depth study:

> If we superficially read, rather than delve into, Biblical verses, then we are like a passenger in a car that is driving through a beautiful landscape: he swiftly travels and takes in the view, but doesn't really see it. In contrast, when we wrestle with the nitty-gritty of a text and its commentaries, we are like the hiker who makes his way struggling to scale a peak, and whose every step higher is at the price of tremendous exertion, but is rewarded tenfold.[6]

I hope that this vicarious learning experience with Nehama may have whetted your appetite to "go study," which in Talmudic parlance is *zil gmor*. This is why I have not directly addressed at length the specifics of the myriad questions about women and traditional Judaism and therefore I may leave the reader somewhat dissatisfied. Dissatisfaction is good: it prompts searching.

For further reading:

Abramowitz, Leah. *Tales of Nehama: Impressions of the Life and Teachings of Nehama Leibowitz*. Jerusalem: 2003.

Leibowitz, Nehama. *New Studies in Bereshit*. Trans. A. Newman. Jerusalem: 1972.

Peerless, Shmuel. *To Study and to Teach: The Methodology of Nechama Leibowitz*. Jerusalem: 2004.

Soloveitchik, Joseph B. *Family Redeemed: Essays on Family Relationships*. New York: 2000.

Hoffman, Ronald, and Shira Leibowitz Schmidt. *Old Wine, New Flasks: Reflections on Science and Jewish Tradition*. New York: 1997.

---

[6]Quoted by R. Koppel Reinitz in *Pirkei Nehama: Nehama Leibowitz Memorial Volume* (Hebrew), edited by M. Arend, Ruth Ben-Meir and G. Cohen, 678. Jerusalem: 2001). Source: Nehama in *Alonim* 1943.

"Fortunate are you, O Israel! Who pronounces you pure? Who ensures your righteousness? Our Father in Heaven!" said Rabbi Akiva.

Just as a mikveh purifies people from their impurity, so does the Almighty purify the Jewish nation.

Talmud, Yoma 85b

Mikveh Appointment

Sheindal G. Muller

In my rear-view mirror, I spot her trailing me. I'm driving home from the mountains speeding, wearily. Tonight I must take a woman to the mikveh. Yet another appointment I would hate to be late for.

The glamour is wearing off. It's starting to feel old and inconvenient. All at once, I feel utterly inadequate, for a job I never considered, never applied for and shouldn't have gotten. If they place an ad in the Cosmic Classifieds it would read: "Sheindal need not apply" at the bottom in polite, fine print.

Too busy, too tired, too shy, too brusque, too clumsy, too secular, too agnostic, too cynical, too self-absorbed.

Why, if the mikveh lady has to be so young; shouldn't she at least be happy reverent, devout, holy, naïve, blushing?

It is right then that I spot her trailing me. I can see her clearly in my rear view mirror. She is flying, attached to the back of my van. Who was it that said women are not witches? For we know even when we try not to know, and yes, we can fly.

She is short, squat, and impossibly old. Wearing layers upon layers of what seems to be woolen sweaters. Actually, it is her arms, tightly folded about her, that are holding her together as she darts silently and purposefully. Then with a fierce jolt I recognize her. She is the mikveh lady of the Warsaw Ghetto. All at once, I feel sure of what it was that she knew. She knew as she supervised each one of the countless immersions, that, she was simultaneously supervising the cleansing of their bodies prior to their passing. "… Went like lambs?" They went like *lions!*

As I speed down the highway I can see that tonight she has company. Another lady, similar era, same matriarchs dotting her lineage. She is flying too, of course. A huge axe is gripped between her hands. A firefighter? Then I recognize her. She swings her axe, repeatedly chopping jagged black holes in to the surface of the thick ice that seems to be suffocating that dark Siberian lake. She is a firefighter! Courageously combating the scorching of Communist Russia in its haste to incinerate all things precious. Her toes may not survive the frigid Gulag. Religion, God even, might not survive Stalin's reign of terror. But she swings again, sinking her axe into my trunk so that she can travel along, too.

Now my rear-view mirror seems more and more to be like a screen projector locked on fast-forward, flashing with images, symbols and icons. A chain is stretching out behind my van, far, far back in time. Lines of powerful women, serenity and defiance magically coexisting.

The valiant women of Masada: no water to drink, yet water in their mikveh.

Two mikveh ladies in their impossibly elegant clothing. The opulence, their patrician, darkly Mediterranean features, their noble bearing, the flames licking at their hemlines seem as perverse as the Inquisition that dragged them there. "The bush is burning, but it is not consumed."

They are flocking, flying, propelling my van all the way down my Highway 26. I see thousands of mikveh ladies. I recognize some of my colleagues, humble folk who quietly and uncomplainingly slip out at night, night after night, interrupting their natural evening rhythm – the bedtime and homework rhythm of their families – to perform an ancient, healing, empowering, feminist service.

There, moving to her rightful place in the front of the line, is Miriam the prophetess, tambourine in hand. She is the Keeper of the Well – the wellspring in the wilderness. She is calling to me: "We were not only archetypes. We were human, too!"

I have arrived. I park the van and hurry in. I don't want to be late for this job I do.

℘ ℭ

My client for this evening is suitably enthralled. I feel briefly like someone out of a study by Margaret Mead. Then came the query.

"Sheindal, you weren't really serious about having to remove my nail polish, were you? I had my manicure this morning."

The question wasn't new and neither was the answer. New, however, was the feeling of something shifting internally in response. I should know by now that one never arrives and you simply cannot get off in the middle of the ride.

I am left alone, as unbidden, my myriad of mikveh women reappear in the steam. I gaze gloomily at the water. Moodily, guiltily, ruminating.

"I think that I was just asked a halachic question," I grumbled. "What would you all have answered? Can you even imagine? What courageous questions were asked of you! What agonizing dilemmas you were asked to solve!"

Images. Halachic Responsa from the Shoah, stories of valor and unbending self-sacrifice are washing over me, threatening to engulf me.

"OK, all you holy ladies, keepers of the faith, transmitters of our heritage. All you ice-breakers and ghetto-dwellers. I live here, where even the twentieth century has quit. It's a tiny community in the South."

It is then that I pause, mid-rebuttal, to look closer at the swirls of mist rising from the small pool. Can it be? My ghosts are standing?

Indeed they are. This is no sweat-lodge trick on my senses. They have come here together to pay tribute to my client. For that which I had assumed to be accusation, judgment and condemnation was, in actuality, incredulous admiration. They are in awe of her. A long-time resident of my own improbable, impossible Columbia, South Carolina.

Like Columbia, I am suspended, as if in a permanent fog of disbelief, between the Upstate's blue mountains and the Lowcountry's golden beaches and brilliant marshlands. We are the Midlands. Jewishly, it would appear to be another demographic disaster, a symptom of the times that we live in. Smaller communities shrinking, larger communities growing.

Yet I am sitting here, in a mikveh. Newly built of imported Jerusalem stone, it is the year 2003 and Jewish Southern women choose to come here. They are still performing mitzvot. They apparently still deeply believe that going to the mikveh, with all that it symbolizes, matters.

Perhaps this evening I flew into Columbia with mikveh attendants trailing in my wake, but it is becoming increasingly clear to me that there are ranks from throughout history of remarkable clients resting on this client's shoulders. The reverence, respect and affection that I feel for so many mikveh attendants is reciprocated by each one of them – for my client!

I have just come from the mountains, and in my mind I keep right on driving south, down to Charleston. Women were using a mikveh there as far back as 1749. Fifty years before that, the ocean, as mikveh, was as available as ever.

Back to Columbia.... I cannot pinpoint the precise moment in time that the grandmothers of the children I sing and dance with at the Jewish day school each Friday stopped riding the train back to Charleston each month. But incredibly, their daughters are back on the train. Some are choosing to use the mikveh again.

My mikveh attendants are applauding the Jewish people because we are achieving the one thing we were quite sure was impossible. Crossing the last frontier, we are starting to survive our own normalization.

I think of my client. How can we be so different? My roots, my childhood – water under the bridge now – a bridge, so we all sang, was falling down. There are records of that very water, from under that very bridge, being drawn to fill a newer mikveh in London in 1664. Are we really so different?

I listen to the familiar sounds coming from the bathroom. The clink-clink, the rustling and muffled clatter, the faucet running. Shower on, shower off, more sounds, feminine sounds of purposeful preparation. Sounds my counterparts across the globe would identify instantly. I smile to myself; How can we be so alike?

The bathroom door opens. Tentatively she steps out, wearing a robe. We are ready to start.

ॐ ᘉ

I still don't have this role down yet. Am I supposed to behave in a confident, efficient, take-charge manner? Or am I supposed to be as unobtrusive as possible? Different women seem to prefer different things. Which type was here this evening? Oh, God, I don't have a prayer. Prayer! The mikveh attendant's Prayer:

> May it be your will, our Father in Heaven, that your Torah and your love be planted in our hearts.
>
> May we stand in awe of you so that we do not sin.
>
> Save us from any stumbling block or mistake in our holy work.
>
> May we merit to increase the number of Jewish women who keep this practice.
>
> Help us to fulfill this holy mission with love and joy
>
> and teach us to do your will with a full heart.
>
> May we merit that the Name of Heaven become beloved through us.
>
> Amen.

I've never been much good at prayer. Covertly, enviously, I have watched friends do it effortlessly, using the familiar words as building blocks to take them on an ascending journey from level to level, up and out of the distractions around them. Like contractions during labor, for prayer is undoubtedly work. That rhythmic opening of the various channels, leaving a gaping, unblocked portal between woman and her God. Permission to speak from deep within their hearts, and knowing what it is that their hearts are saying.

This short prayer, however, seems to sum up the kind of help that I was looking for, seemed to summon up the help that I needed, for a moment later she was standing, heart deep, in the water.

Ready to start, she ducked down, like a mother leaning over her cradle. Her body seemed to fold itself into a fetal position. I love the mikveh. In that briefest of seconds it as if you are transported back into the womb. Back floating, suspended between two worlds in a pool of amniotic fluid. Sometimes it feels to me as if the mikveh's gentle waters are not amniotic; but antibiotic. Healing, soothing, washing away the stubborn residue that persists in clinging to me after yet another month's worth of encounters with the harsh realities, the complexities of our world. I may be an amphibian, but living in this world takes its toll on me. I need to return to the water.

Perhaps my client is herself like a mikveh. Both are metaphors for persistent survival. Both have an elaborate and intricate set of Jewish laws attached to them. Laws that can be upheld or forgotten, incorporated or ignored. Yet both have an inner core that is entirely incapable, entirely above and beyond corruption. It does not matter what a mikveh is used for; it remains a mikveh throughout, and perhaps it does not matter how we choose to identify ourselves, for I believe that there is an inescapable reality called The Jewish People and a transcendental piece that many refer to as "the soul."

If Rabbi Akiva's metaphor for the process of change was dripping water, then his catalyst for change was surely love. Is that what happens to us at forty? Do we finally understand that progress doesn't occur in a straight line? Change is often little more than a trickle. Water, dripping, finding its own way, gradually transforming, penetrating the cold hard surface of the rock. I am watching an unsteady change, the drip, drip, dripping of mikveh water, melting and penetrating the most obstructed of hearts minds and souls across the world.

Once upon a time, not so very long ago, I saw them as "failed test flights" or at best as "practicing." I have tried to learn, however, to see them not as failures but as a real and necessary part of the very process of change itself. Those "false starts," the stopping and starting, the step forward followed by the inexplicable two steps backwards, are absolutely an integral part of the journey itself. Indeed, they are very hardest part of change. It is a lesson I will, no doubt, have to learn over and over again, many, many more times throughout life.

I remember first studying the laws of using the mikveh while engaged to be married, back in London. At the end of the course, my tutor leaned across the dining-room table at which we sat and in a voice barely above a whisper, said:

"And then, the mikveh lady calls out the word 'kosher.'

"'Kosher'?"

"Yes, kosher. And do you know what happens then?"

"What?" I wasn't sure whether to be nervous or afraid.

"The angels hear the pronouncement, and they swoop down and grab that word as it floats past them, and lift it, carrying it up, up, throughout the heavens, through each of the heavenly realms. All the while they are rising, they are echoing the word 'kosher,' singing in unison. All of the heavenly beings hear the word 'kosher' and echo it too. They join the other angels and seraphim, flying up and up until they reach the Heavenly Throne itself. There, they bring this word before God. In that moment, God Himself pronounces your immersion kosher. That is why it is in that split second that one has the opportunity to tell or ask God whatever it is that one wants."

Talk about an open portal! I take it back! I haven't lost the faculty of prayer, for the steps that we take to prepare for and use the mikveh are a sure form of prayer. Why, for all the tears shed in prayer by all the women at the mikveh, it is astonishing that only the ocean waters are salty.

My client recites the blessing. She wants me to say the words with her. I can say the words with her if she is unsure of the Hebrew, but I can never take away, or even fully share this moment with her. It wholly, totally and independently, belongs to her. I watch carefully as she immerses a second time.

I can barely articulate the word "kosher" as in a sudden flash of insight it becomes clear to me that the angels who take the word "kosher" before God have a particularly easy job because they do not fly heavenward alone. They are ably aided by all of the mikveh users and mikveh attendants from throughout our history. All those Jewish women who used the mikveh, many of them under the most harrowing of circumstances, each with at least as many good reasons as we have today not to uphold this extraordinary observance. They all unite now to carry word of yet another immersion upward.

There is a roaring in my ears as loud as the ocean as she immerses for the third and final time.

"Kosher."

Yes, kosher. The physical act of sanctifying time, space and ourselves. An act that is simply right. I am convinced for now, beyond any doubt, that there is something about all of this that will continue to remain "kosher" – fit and right – forever.

She emerges from the water. Each of us feels renewed and refreshed. Each of us is equipped to go back out into the world and start the rest of our lives again.

For further reading:

Slonim, Rivkah. *Total Immersion: A Mikvah Anthology.* Jerusalem, Israel: 2005.

Kaplan, Aryeh. *Waters of Eden: The Mystery of the Mikvah.* New York: 1985.

Abramov, Tehilla. *The Secret of Jewish Femininity.* Jerusalem, Israel: 1988.

For a global mikveh directory, visit www.mikveh.org.

If you offer your compassion to the hungry
And satisfy the famished creature
Then shall your light shine in the darkness
And your gloom shall be like noonday.

Isaiah 58:10

Journey
Iris Rudin

It is hard to imagine that in a country as prosperous as ours an estimated 35 million Americans, mostly children and the elderly, go to bed hungry each night. This is not the same kind of self-imposed hunger we experience when we fast on Yom Kippur, when we know where our next meal will come from, when we know we will have food the next day and the next whenever we are in need.

The problem of hunger is addressed in the Torah. "And when ye reap the harvest of your land, thou shalt not wholly reap the corner of thy field, neither shalt thou gather the gleaning of thy harvest. And thou shalt not glean thy vineyard, neither shalt thou gather the fallen fruit of thy vineyard; thou shalt leave them for the poor and for the stranger:..." (Leviticus 19:9–10)

Here is my interpretation of how this quote applies to our lives today. If we are blessed by God with being able to provide for ourselves, we should share with those who cannot and with those whom we do not know and whose needs we may not know.

This could have all remained academic for me but sometimes our lives change in mysterious ways. Sometimes a simple seemingly insignificant choice we make can lead to an unexpected opportunity for learning or growth or an experience that opens up an entirely new world for us.

Usually I don't watch television during the day but late one cold winter afternoon I turned on the TV and saw something that eventually led me to a website on my computer. What aroused my curiosity was a link called Plant a Row for the Hungry (PAR)[1]. "What could this be?" I wondered. I read with fascination

---

[1] PAR started when Jeff Lowenfels, a garden writer from Anchorage, Alaska, was hesitant about giving money to a panhandler in Washington, D. C. until the man told him, "I'm

and excitement the pages of information I printed out. Plant a Row for the Hungry asks gardeners to plant an extra row in their gardens and donate the produce to help feed the hungry in their own communities.

I was impressed with this grass-roots program that asks not for money but for one's time, energy and compassion. "How could I get it started in my home town of Binghamton? Where could I go with it? How could I set it up here?" were the thoughts that raced through my mind. It seemed like an easy and natural thing to ask gardeners to do what they love and are proud of doing. If they produce only two tomatoes in their garden they would give one away. They always share. I thought if I were able to plant some "seeds of caring" by spreading awareness of the PAR campaign in my hometown, others in the community would nurture these seeds.

And nurture them they did. The seeds grew and spread. In the first year of the campaign in my county, an entire community opened their hearts and hands to donate over a ton of fresh produce from their gardens to CHOW, the local collecting and distributing agency that helps feed the hungry. A marvelous mitzvah!

From childhood, I have always loved the outdoors. I love to dig in the dirt, to plant seeds and nurture a garden. I marvel at and enjoy with wonder the diversity and beauty of God's handiwork, the smell of the damp earth in the woods and the protective feeling of God's presence around me.

Even though we no longer are an agrarian society, many of us still plant gardens. We nurture nature and it nurtures us. Food is tied to most of our holidays. Food and sacrificial offerings, food and symbolism, food and sustenance. On Pesach, Shavuos and Sukkos, the harvest and pilgrimage festivals, we praise and thank God for sustenance, not only for the body, but also for the soul.

---

really hungry." On the flight back home to Anchorage, Lowenfels thought about the hungry in his own community. He conceived the idea that if gardeners in Anchorage would plant an extra row in their gardens and donate the produce to Bean's Café, the local soup kitchen, the hungry could be helped. The response to his idea of Plant A Row for Bean's Café was gratifying.

In 1995 the Garden Writer's Association of America (GWAA) took over this people helping people campaign and renamed it Plant A Row for the Hungry (PAR), asking gardeners to plant an extra row in their gardens and donate the harvest to food banks in their own communities. The campaign grew. Forty-four states in the United States and two provinces in Canada participated in raising a million pounds of food by the millennium. In the year 2000, eight-tenths of a million pounds were raised.

The apples we dipped in honey in our home on Rosh Hashanah came from our own trees and Sukkos was generally a time of preserving the fruits of our labor as well as sharing our harvest. In years past we would bring apples, pears and plums from our trees to decorate the sukkah at our Temple.

During the time I was involved in the Plant a Row for the Hungry campaign, Sukkos was an even more joyous festival because of the response of our community to the campaign. When I recited *shehechiyanu* and when I was in the sukkah I felt God's encompassing love and presence.

At the Passover Seder we recited: "Let all who are hungry come and eat." We opened our doors to our family, to our friends and to the prophet Elijah.

"But," I wondered, "have we really opened all the doors for the hungry to enter and eat?" Then I realized that I was helping to open another door for the hungry with the Plant a Row campaign. I hope their spiritual hunger was also being satisfied.

On Shavuos, the beginning of the summer harvest in Israel, I felt as if it were a new beginning for me as I planted seeds for our fall harvest. I felt I was making a new commitment as we began the second year of the Plant a Row for the Hungry campaign in our community.

My spirit has been fed by the tzedakah of the community, giving when neither the recipient nor the donor knows the other's identity – the second-highest level of tzedakah. In the future I hope that we can give at the highest level: enabling the recipient to become self-sufficient.

In our own lives, we owe a debt of gratitude to all those who have given to us, those who have laid out paths for us to follow and inspired us by their ideas and ideals, those who have helped us along the way with their encouragement, understanding, friendship and love, and those who in spite of our shortcomings, during good times and bad, love unconditionally. My mother, in her Alzheimers days, would repeat to me, "I thank the good Lord for all the good things."

I feel so richly blessed and so thankful to God, who has given me so much. There were dark times in my life when I wondered if God had heard my prayers, but I know now He kept me under His watchful care. He led me step by step, giving me new abilities and strengths I never would have anticipated. I truly feel as if I have been on a pilgrimage.

Anne Frank wrote, "When I end my prayers with the words 'I thank you, God, for all that is good and dear and beautiful,' I am filled with joy."

For further reading:
Salamon, Julie. *Rambam's Ladder: A Meditations on Generosity and Why It Is Necessary to Give*. New York: 2003.

Being Her Guest

Chava Willig Levy

As soon as the glorious news galloped the globe, via telephone and cyberspace, that Michael and I – both nearing forty – had been blessed with a son, the betting began.

During her *mazel tov* phone call, my sister in Israel cut to the chase. "Look, we all know that his first name will be Aharon." (She was right; Michael's dad, Aaron Levy, had left us two years earlier and no one as yet was privileged to carry his name.) "And we all know," she continued, "that his middle name will begin with *El*." (She was right; my mother, Ella, had passed away six month's before Aharon's birth. Given my middle-aged status, the likelihood of having another child was slim. Here was our chance to grace our son with a glimmer of the grandmother who would have loved him so.) "But the mystery is," she concluded, "what letters will follow the first two?"

The votes came pouring in. Elnatan (God gave). Elisha (God will save). Elad (God is forever). Elazar (God helped).

In the end, Michael and I chose the perfect middle name with which to remember my mother, a name that no one had proposed: Elchanan.

Why Elchanan? We had two main reasons for choosing it. First, Elchanan means *God is imbued with grace*, and my mother, Ella Willig, was grace personified. Second, Michael and I had recently read a biography of a saintly leader of European Jewry, murdered by the Nazis, whose name was Rav Elchanan Wasserman. My mother was not a rabbinic scholar, but she and Rav Wasserman shared a love for their holy Jewish heritage in general and a devotion to one of its precepts in particular: hospitality.

Those privileged to visit Rav Elchanan during his occasional fundraising visits to New York were stunned that, when they rose to take their leave, this

Torah giant would rise too and insist upon escorting them to the elevator. Their protests fell on deaf ears. Rav Elchanan would smile and ask, "Did not our father Avraham escort his guests as they continued on their journey?"

Those privileged to visit my mother were treated no less royally. Like Avraham and Sarah, she didn't just wait for guests to arrive at her doorstep; she combed the neighborhood for them.

I will never forget November 9, 1965: A thirteen-year-old high school freshman, I had just finished supper and was settling down to tackle my homework when all our lights began to dim. Seconds later, our home – and the street outside – was engulfed in darkness. Groping clumsily, we finally located our transistor radio and learned that the entire Northeast was in a blackout. My mother immediately put on her coat.

"Imma," I asked in alarm, "where are you going?"

"I'm bringing Shabbos candles to Henrietta," she replied, referring to our wonderful widowed neighbor. "She doesn't keep Shabbos, so she and the kids might need some."

When Imma returned, our dear friend Thea and her daughter were in tow. Imma explained that after dropping off Henrietta's Shabbos candles, she had seen Thea walking up our block, wondering in a panic why her nearsightedness was suddenly deteriorating. And since Thea's husband was away on business, Imma promptly invited mother and daughter to stay the night. Minutes later, Henrietta arrived with her two kids. Joel brought his oboe, Susan played our piano. I vaguely recall melted ice cream capping off the recital. In short, Imma transformed a scary situation into a slumber party.

Even within her own four walls, my mother was always scouting for guests. During our song-filled Shabbos meals, her designated seat gave her a full view of goings-on outside our dining room window. We'd be moments away from dessert when Imma would exclaim, "Look, the Bergers!" She'd instantly rise from the table, open our front door and call out, "You're just in time for tea and cake!" Moments later, the entire Berger family would be seated around our oval table. (Imma was an ardent advocate of round and oval tables. "Somehow," she'd comment, "with a round or oval table, there's always room for one more." And she was right.)

When the Sukkos festival rolled around each autumn, Imma had to give up her ringside guest-detection seat. After all, our tiny sukkah hut was perched on an elevated patio in our backyard. But somehow during Sukkos, my mother didn't have to scout for guests. The moment that she and her brood, often bundled in layers of sweaters and yet surprisingly warm, began to sing Sukkos songs in three-part harmony, neighbors would flock to our outdoor abode. "May we join you for a minute?" they'd ask, adding, "We never heard that song before." Moments later, they'd be singing along and sipping hot tea, practically members of the family.

Every Passover, we would recite the famous seder lines, "All who are hungry, come and eat. All who are needy, come and join the Passover celebration." It never occurred to me that the guests who graced our table were hungry or needy. Weren't they just my parents' friends, somewhat older members of our synagogue? Years later, it dawned on me that many of my mother's friends *were*, in their own way, hungry or needy. Mr. and Mrs. W. were Holocaust survivors whose children lived hundreds of miles away. Mr. and Mrs. T. had no children with whom to share their seder. Mr. and Mrs. J. were both battling debilitating diseases. In short, Imma never confused hospitality with mere entertaining. But her genius was that she never gave her guests – or her family – the impression that she was doing anything *but* entertaining.

Imma even entertained guests who never set foot in her home. She never forgot the invisible ones, people who were hospitalized or homebound, people who deserved her savory chicken soup. So if they couldn't come to the chicken soup, the chicken soup would come to them! Imma would pour her golden elixir into a huge thermos with a bright red cap and off she'd go, and neither rain nor snow nor sleet nor hail would deter her from her appointed rounds.

"Hotel Willig" was the nickname that everyone who knew my mother ascribed to her modest home. She spoke with quiet pride of the day my cousin, activist Rabbi Avi Weiss, phoned her. "Tante Ella, I'm at Kennedy Airport with a special friend who's on her way to Washington and needs a place to freshen up." Minutes later, Imma greeted her nephew at the front door. Behind him stood a demure, dark-haired woman with luminous eyes. "Tante Ella," Avi said nonchalantly, "this is Avital." Imma did a double-take. "Avital? *Avital*?" Eyes downcast, her guest smiled and nodded – and was promptly given Imma's royal treatment of rest and rugelach. Countless American inns display signs boasting, "George Washington Slept Here." Had she been less modest, Imma would have had a banner hanging on her front door declaring, "Avital Sharansky Showered Here."

Other guests were less famous perhaps, but treated no less royally. When a relative was going through a divorce, he and his child moved in with us. When aunts and uncles visited from out of state or abroad, they all came to Hotel Willig and were welcomed with open arms – no matter how long they stayed. Sometimes, as many as four couples were hosted simultaneously in Imma's small house.

On weekends, that house became Grand Central Station. There were always lunch guests, and later in the afternoon, scores of teenagers would visit our home, attracted to Imma's open-door – and open-refrigerator – policy.

Hospitality came so naturally to Imma (as it did to her parents in Poland and later in the tenements of New York) that it confused, even pained her when others found it foreign. "Our house is being painted," a neighbor would explain apologetically. "Otherwise, we would have been happy to put your brother and sister-in-law up for David's bar mitzvah Shabbat." Imma understood that her neighbors' intentions were honorable, but could not accept their logic. "Aren't they living in the house that's being painted?" she'd muse. "Isn't it better to offer a less-than-perfect home than to turn someone down?" "Ella," another friend once said, "we'd love to offer sleeping quarters for the synagogue's scholar-in-residence and his family but we're going away for the weekend." "But an empty house would be perfect.…" she'd murmur in bewilderment, slowly returning the telephone receiver to its cradle. "Why would anyone pass up an easy *mitzvah* like that?"

At Imma's funeral, attended by over one thousand people, many spoke of her legendary dining-room table, the table that continually expanded to accommodate just one more guest. During the week of *shiva* that followed, many visitors – friends of Imma's four grown children, people who had never set foot into her home before – were stunned to discover that Mrs. Willig's dining room table was quite small. One gentleman looked around and whispered in amazement, "*This* is the dining room you spoke of? But it's only a dinette. I was sure you meant something three times as large!" I remember thinking, what was three times as large was my Imma's heart.

These and so many other memories flood my mind when I think of Imma, especially when a visitor rings our doorbell. And when Aharon Elchanan, often the farthest one from the door, calls out eagerly, "I'll get it!," I know that her legacy lives on.

For further reading:

Salamon, Julie. *Rambam's Ladder: A Meditation on Generosity and Why It Is Necessary to Give*. New York: 2003.

Raz, Simcha. *A Tzadik in Our Time: The Life of Rabbi Aryeh Levin*. Jerusalem, Israel: 1976.

Rabbi Yose said: Let all your deeds be for the sake of Heaven.

Ethics of the Fathers 2:12

In all your ways (with all of your talents and strengths) you shall know (serve) Him.

Proverbs 3:6

Avodat Hashem and Community Service

Marian Stoltz-Loike

Although the phrase *avodat Hashem* can be roughly translated into English as "the service of God," the Hebrew phraseology is far more interesting. The word *avodah* derives from the same root as the Hebrew word *eved*, which means slave. So it's easy to translate *avodat Hashem* negatively and see it as a burdensome responsibility of servitude. In fact, the combination of these two words – *avodat Hashem* – actually transforms the phrase so that it has a different meaning than the translation of either word independently would indicate. It's a case of the whole equaling more than the sum of the parts. References from Scripture can help elucidate the meaning of this somewhat intractable phrase.

One reference is from the Talmud. *Avodah* refers to the description of the service performed by the High Priest in the Holy Temple on Yom Kippur in ancient times.

A second reference is from *Ethics of the Fathers* 1:2. We are told: "Shimon ha-Tzadik says: The world has three pillars on which it stands: Torah, *Avodah*, and good deeds." Torah, or the study of Torah, is clearly the pillar that links human beings to God. Good deeds are obviously the links between one person and another – the pillar of society. But then *avodah* – the second pillar mentioned– must link two other elements. Let's come back to the puzzle of this second pillar in a moment.

For many people, *avodat Hashem* at its most basic level represents prayer. In fact, there is a well-known phrase that indicates that in contemporary times, prayer substitutes for the sacrifices in the Holy Temple. To understand prayer, it is necessary to consider why people pray. During a recent lecture, Rabbi Motty Berger of Aish HaTorah asked why, if God is infinite, would He need the prayers of people so intensively that we are commanded to pray three times a day? Furthermore, Rabbi Berger pointed out, each time we pray, we list God's great attributes, "the great, awe-inspiring, Supreme Being." Does God actually need us to praise Him? Imagine that you have given a brilliant lecture to a group of students and a small child who overhears what you say tells you how brilliant you've been. Would that be of any value to you? Probably not. And if none of the students had praised you and only the child had commented, it might in fact be a bit embarrassing or even humiliating. For the child, however, admiring you might be a tremendous motivator. He may spend his life thinking about your great lecture and wanting to be just like you.

Similarly, if you believe in God and pray, it's impossible to believe that an infinite God could possibly need the praise of human beings. But *we* need to pray. Human beings need to pray for themselves – to remind themselves of God's infinite wisdom and greatness so that they can begin to aspire to be great as well. So the first part of the explanation of *avodah* in the statement of Shimon ha-Tzadik in the *Ethics of the Fathers* becomes clearer. *Avodah* relates to what individuals do for their own spiritual benefit within a religious context. This second pillar of *avodah*, then, represents using religion to turn a mirror on oneself – connecting me with myself, so to speak. This second pillar represents all of the various things that I am and the things that I can do to improve who I am. Through hard work (*avodah*), I am capable of spiritual self-reflection and self-knowledge.

Now imagine that the three pillars support the world just as three legs might support a stool. If any of the legs of the stool are removed, the stool will fall over. Similarly, in the conceptualization of Shimon ha-Tzadik, if any of the pillars were removed, the world could not exist. Human beings need to connect to God through Torah, they need to connect to other people through good deeds, and they need to connect to themselves and their spiritual potential. When I connect to myself, I ultimately support the world and reinforce the connection between people and God and the relation between one person and another. My self-knowledge becomes one of the pillars that is required for the continued existence of the world.

Avodat Hashem clearly plays an important role in self-revelation. Prayer, good deeds, mitzvot all are part of *avodat Hashem*. However, unlike daily prayers which are prescribed and circumscribed, *avodat Hashem* has a very personal character. True *avodat Hashem* demands that we hold up a spiritual mirror to ourselves, find out who we are, and then channel our talents toward doing something to benefit the Jewish community and reach the unique potential that

God envisions for us.

For me, *avodat Hashem* and community service are very closely linked. I received a BA in psychology and social relations from Harvard in the mid-1970s and a Ph.D. in psychology from NYU in the early 1980s. I had one child when I began graduate school, gave birth to two children during graduate school and had my fourth child shortly after I received my Ph.D. I wanted to pursue a part-time post-doctoral degree after graduation so that I could be home at least part-time with my children, but in the mid-1980s that was an unheard-of concept even for a professor of developmental psychology, so I pursued other paths. Eventually, I became a vice president at a company called Windham International that focused on cross-cultural understanding and global business. With the support of a very special husband I traveled around the world helping global businesspeople become more effective in their roles by building better understanding of the people with whom they worked.

In each phase of my life, being an Orthodox Jewish woman affected my choices and also made me seem different despite my very pluralistic environments. At college, I kept strictly kosher and observed Shabbat, one of only eight students out of well over one thousand in my entire class. Any temptation to assimilate that I felt would have been fueled by my desire to stop having to explain why virtually the only thing that I ever ate in the university dining halls was plain salad and canned tuna fish.

I married my husband two weeks after graduating from college, and the Orthodox Jewish reproductive imperative for me meant that my life, if I were lucky, would be blessed with children in the near future. My son was born ten months after we were married, and I began graduate school sixteen months later and became pregnant with my second child three months later. And so my graduate school life continued. By the time I graduated, I had three children and was pregnant with my fourth. I did not waver in my commitment to my studies even after my thesis advisor claimed that I was ruining my career and refused to have anything to do with me after I became pregnant with my third child. I was in a Ph.D. program in developmental psychology and only three of us, in the history of the program, had had children during our graduate school career. I excelled in my graduate studies because I was a conscientious student but also because I was a parent of young children and balanced my academic life with my richly religious life involving celebrating holidays and Shabbat with family and friends.

When I began working at Windham, the balance between religious and secular demands became acute and I would routinely travel with extra suitcases filled with kosher food to places such as New Delhi or Jakarta. In the days before e-mail, I would communicate with my husband and children via phone and fax and try to make it home for Shabbat. Jewish holidays were always holy and I made sure never to be away for them.

And through my very demanding personal and professional life, I also learned about turning to God both literally and figuratively when I had done all that was practical for me to do. Several years ago, when my four children were between the ages of about six and thirteen, they had a day off from school so I decided to visit my parents in Brooklyn. The drive from Queens to Brooklyn is an easy one that takes about forty-five minutes but the entire trip is on very busy, continuously-traveled roads. We packed into the car and began our short journey. I pulled on to the always busy Van Wyck Expressway, moved into the center lane, accelerated, and the car just stopped dead. Normally, the Van Wyck is very crowded and cars move at a snail's pace, but on that day cars were zipping along. I had my four children in the car with me, all the cars around me were going sixty miles an hour, and because I was in the center lane there was no way to get my children out of the car safely. I was terrified. I turned on my warning lights, but I was desperately afraid that we would be hit. I tried to start the engine once, twice, three times, but nothing happened. My children kept asking me what we should do, and knowing that technology had failed us, I said in desperation, "Say Shema." And as we said Shema, I looked out of the window and out of nowhere two tow trucks appeared. They realized immediately what had happened. One tow truck stopped behind us, and the other got in front of us and pulled us toward the shoulder. At each step the tow truck behind followed us to be sure that no one hit our car from behind. Once on the shoulder, we all moved to the tow truck and the driver towed the car to a gas station so we could get the car fixed.

Would the tow trucks have come had we not said Shema? For me the question is irrelevant. Instead the event was an epiphany. I finally understood that my role was to do whatever was humanly possible and then turn to God and ask for the rest. That became a defining perspective for me in my personal life, my professional life, and in my community service.

In the late 1980s and the early 1990s I was very active politically in organizations such as AIPAC and the OU's Institute for Public Affairs. I met with members of Congress, and was one of the hundred Jewish leaders for Clinton during the 1992 Presidential campaign. From the late 1990s through the present time, I have served as the Chair of Diplomatic Outreach for the American Jewish Committee. Together with members of my committee, we meet with consuls general and UN ambassadors to discuss issues related to Israel and the Jewish community both in the US and in the diplomats' home countries. We conduct two large events a year – a diplomatic tour of Jewish New York and a diplomatic Seder.

For me, each of these different political and diplomatic roles represents a unique way of expressing my *avodat Hashem*. My training as a psychologist made me sensitive to nuances of discussions and interactions. It enabled me to realize how often what is not said is as critical as what is. Similarly, my work in cross-cultural communication enabled me to build broad awareness of differences in communication, values, interactions, and perspectives across cultures. It taught me how to listen and learn what cultural keys are important in different countries. My training as a psychologist has been important for me in working with politicians and diplomats. Nothing is more important in working with diplomats than understanding the value of nuanced comments and statements. For example, the discussion about the OSCE's Berlin Declaration against anti-Semitism is very different with countries whose Jewish populations were decimated during the Holocaust than with those who have a different history and view themselves as supporting Israel since the 1948 vote for partition.

Although I have always worked in the business world, I am an intellectual at heart. Therefore, I view a strong part of my *avodat Hashem* in my work with diplomats as enabling them to understand issues of critical importance to the Jewish community. They know that we have a connection to Israel, but part of what I try to do is to explain why Israel is so important by discussing what Israel means to me. By discussing my personal feelings when I have heard of a terrorist attack in Israel when one of my children is over there, or my memories of listening to my father's description of gathering around the radio to hear the UN vote on partition, or correcting some subtle or more profound historical misunderstanding, I can link my community service and my *avodat Hashem*.

Diplomatic visits are very interesting. They provide an opportunity to speak with representatives of foreign governments about issues of key importance to the Jewish community. For me personally, I recognize that while saying the wrong thing is a risk, saying the right thing to the right person at the right time can have tremendous impact. For example, after a recent UN vote against the separation fence, where the vote was strongly against Israel, it was essential for friends of Israel to weigh in with their disappointment and frustration with the vote. Silence on the issue might have been taken as tacit acceptance of the vote. We knew, however, that our perspective would be shared after the fact and could have no retroactive impact on this terribly negative vote. In this case, as in others, I was faced with doing my community service – my act of *avodat Hashem* – and feeling desperately afraid that I would not nuance my comments correctly. I needed to express outrage and respect in a single message that could not be misconstrued and at the same time preserve our relationship with the diplomat. Before each diplomatic visit, I thought about what I would say and reviewed our team strategy. But before each meeting, I also prayed to God using a simple formula to ask Him for insight so that I would be quick to respond intelligently and diplomatically in these visits with foreign diplomats. I would repeat the passage from the *Shemona Esrei* that says, "You have generously given people intelligence and taught humankind how to understand. Favor us now with knowledge and deep understanding." This was my *avodah she-ba-lev* – my intellectual and emotional work – commonly referred to as prayer before each diplomatic visit. My prayers left me feeling more centered, confident, and prepared so that during some particularly difficult and challenging discussions I was able to construct cogent, creative, effective responses. And so many times, I recognized that my success did not come from my hard work alone. I had done the legwork and then God enabled my performance to move up to the next level.

For me, being able to express my *avodat Hashem* through community service as an advocate for Israel and the Jewish community in Congress or at the UN has been a unique privilege. In the *Shema*, we are commanded to love God with all "our hearts, all of our souls, and all of our money" (*me-odecha* in Hebrew). Rashi, the great Biblical commentator explains that *me-odecha* can mean money or it can be looked at as a derivative of the Hebrew word *midot*, which means personality characteristics. Thus, Rashi is suggesting that we love God with all the elements of our unique personality or individuality. For me, being able to express my *avodat Hashem* using my knowledge and experience within the context of my personality, represent the most critical capital that I possess, and ensures that for me *avodat Hashem* is transformed from servitude to love. But it has to be within a religious context. True *avodat Hashem* requires consideration of spirituality, of Mitzvot, and the potential that God says we can reach.

The Talmud says that when Moses went up to Mount Sinai, Moses approached God's presence and was silent. God turned to Moses and asked: Don't people in your city greet one another when they see each other? Do they just remain silent? Moses responded by asking whether it were possible that the servant (*eved* from the same root as *avodah*) should greet the king? In his comment on the story, Rabbi Hillel David said that God wanted to teach Moses the way of the just: that even the servant should greet the King. It is fundamental to human interaction to acknowledge the presence of others. I might even suggest that when each person takes an active role and engages in *avodat Hashem*, it elevates them so that the *eved* – servant – may be transformed to a member of the King's court with the right to greet the King himself. I challenge each person to discover a way to use their unique talents to serve God and to reach their God-given potential so that by doing *avodat Hashem* they will be able discover who they really can be.

For further reading:
Twerski, Abraham J. *Twerski on Spirituality.* New York: 1998.

R'shimon Bar Yochai said: The Holy One, blessed is He, gave three good gifts to Israel, and He gave all of them only through suffering. They are: Torah, the Land of Israel and the World to Come.

Talmud, Brachot 5a

Hello from Jerusalem

Susan Elster

Preface: March 2004

It is mid-morning, erev Shabbat. I am sitting in our small garden for the first time since winter began to recede, amidst a cacophony of birdsong, and trying to retrace the intentions and steps that launched this journey. Just over a year ago our family – my husband Steve and I and our children, Kayla, fourteen, and Arieh, ten – made aliya to Jerusalem from Pittsburgh. Our oldest daughter Chana, seventeen, arrived to study in the Old City of Jerusalem five months before the rest of us. Yesterday hundreds were murdered in Madrid in what, at this moment, appears to be another attack emerging from the culture of death that has become fundamentalist Islam. We greet the news with a kind of grim recognition. We have much practice receiving bad tidings. Four of the last five major terror attacks in Israel occurred along streets surrounding our small neighborhood. Kayla, upon hearing the news, quietly commented that somehow the news makes her feel less alone.

Kayla, at fifteen, indicates no apparent interest in understanding the anatomy of the conflict in which we find ourselves immersed – either in Israel or in the world at large. When the sounds of sirens multiply beyond a few undulating wails, indicating mass casualties, she simply calls to confirm that we are all safe – and then moves on with her studies and friends, visits to cafes and video stores. She rarely chooses to discuss it later.

Some call it the second intifada ("to throw out or off" in Arabic), others the Al Aksa (a reference to the mosque on Temple Mount) intifada. Whatever its name, after three and a half years of bloodshed, we cannot escape the fact that we have chosen to make our lives not only in a country at war but at its heart, here in the City of Jerusalem.

Kayla told us a few months ago that she feels strong and sure of herself, able to address most of the threats she can imagine. Then she softly added, "But then I think back on a dream I once had of swimming in the sea. A wave crested over my head and pulled me under and away from the shore. I realized that my strength was no match at all for this wave. I had no control over what would become of me. Sometimes I think that this is the truth of what we face here."

As our first year comes to a close, I confront the question that haunts every American-born parent living in Israel. It is the question that catches us by the throat and heart, sudden as a nightmare: Do we have the right to make choices that at best profoundly affect the way our children view their reality and at worst threaten their lives? We who have come from the land of unbounded material comfort and personal safety – are we permitted to place our children in harm's way?

ℰℷ ℭℛ

Years ago, before our children were born, Steve and I dreamed of making aliyah. As we saw it, the most incredible events in the past two thousand years of the Jewish drama were unfolding in our lifetimes.

Steve studied in Jerusalem for a year in college, bicycling alone around the perimeter of the country, getting to know the land most intimately, never imagining that he would live anywhere else. In 1984, two years after we married, we led a summer tour of twenty-nine sixteen-year-olds from America. It was my first trip to Israel and I fell deeply in love, especially with Jerusalem. As a convert to Judaism, I marveled that an "outsider" could feel such an intense and immediate attachment.

Late one afternoon we walked along rooftops of the Old City along a seam between the Muslim, Jewish and Christian Quarters. At almost the same moments, we heard church bells chime, the muezzin over loudspeakers calling Muslims to prayer, and Jews hurrying towards synagogues for the mincha, or afternoon, prayers. The intellect knows that three major religious traditions arose in Jerusalem. But that afternoon I knew that there could have been no other place on earth in which this was possible. In those moments, in the blur of twilight and multiple forms of prayer, I understood that the layers between heaven and earth were somehow thinner in Jerusalem, as though conversation with the Almighty is just within reach.

I absorbed as well the knowledge that the "broadcasts" from the Heavens, despite their intensity, are only as clear as our capacity to hear without distortion

– the nearness acutely magnifying our imperfections as receivers. Paradoxically, because the broadcast is so loud, we become convinced with absolute certainty that we have really heard the One True Voice. God broadcasts a message of profound love and too many of us, because we are still far from what we could be, receive it in a way that has caused much suffering over thousands of years.

Years later, as life kept us rooted in America, I found myself aching for Jerusalem. But our Chana was the first grandchild born in both of our families. We could not imagine taking her, or the two children that followed, so far from grandparents. I worked on a doctorate for fully ten years while raising our children, receiving my diploma while in labor with Arieh. And the finances of a young family made even visits a fantasy.

Then, in the autumn of 2000, a new Arab uprising in Israel began and a dormant anti-Semitism, now in the guise of hatred of Israel – resurfaced in many places around the world. The new vitriol called into question not *where* to draw the borders of the modern state of Israel but *whether* to draw borders at all. We began to imagine a world in which Israel might not exist.

Later that spring, with the intifada raging, Chana announced that she wanted to study in Jerusalem over the summer. We were frankly terrified. On the one hand, her request seemed the most natural extension of everything we had taught her. Here was tangible demonstration of her support for Israel – and of ours. On the other hand, the threat to her safety felt palpable. There are times when one's convictions are put to the test. We asked ourselves: Did we really believe that we control the timing or manner of our death?

As we gave her permission to go, something opened in us as well and we began to plan our own visit to Israel after nearly fifteen years away. Steve, Kayla, Ari and I departed at the end of July 2001, not admitting our fears even to one another.

℘ ℭ

August 2001

In a late-night, cool Jerusalem breeze, surrounded by bougainvillea, Chana and I sat together in an outdoor café catching up on her summer experiences. Citing the writings of an eighteenth-century kabbalist, Chana told me that one of her teachers argued that the Torah provides us with the tools to strip away the barriers separating us from our Creator. This description evoked for me an image of the sculptor's art: skilled hands, working in stone or wood, do not create the sculpted form but rather "release" it. This shedding of layers to reveal a truer form – layers of comfort creating the illusion of "safety" in America – is the subtext of our summer visit to Israel.

The land we returned to after far too many years is full of hard edges amidst unimaginable beauty. The sun is fierce, the scent of jasmine, eucalyptus and rosemary pervasive. We hiked the Golan, the precipices at once gorgeous and life-threatening. We crawled through the tunnels of caves in which Bar Kochba and his followers hid in their desperate attempt to prevail against Roman occupation sixty years after the destruction of the Second Temple: the small, dark passages both safe and terrifyingly confining. Without effort, time dissolved, revealing the unspeakable glory and agony beneath the barely concealed layers of the Land's more than three-thousand-year-relationship with the Jewish people.

Not only the current security situation (the *matzav* in Hebrew), not only millennia of Jewish history, but also the harshness and majesty of the Land itself seems to conspire to force a recognition of our utter dependence on our Creator. And we knew without the smallest doubt that any generation in the past two thousand years would have given anything to trade their danger for ours – that true, gut-wrenching danger is not having this postage stamp land as our return address. It was an awareness as strong as memory.

I am reminded of the words to a well-known song, "Gesher Tzar Me'od": "The whole world is a very narrow bridge. The important thing is not to be afraid at all." The "bridge" formed by this land is indeed very narrow; there is no room for fear – no room for lulling the self into believing that life is easy or free from pain... or "safe." There is no room for the illusion that we are actually in control of our destiny, of any destiny. The main thing is not to be afraid at all.

September 11, 2001

As soon as Chana returned to America, she announced that she could not possibly remain in America for two more years of high school. She pleaded with us to help her find a way for her to complete her studies a year early so that she could return to Israel on aliyah.

My mother and I spoke early this morning. She is terribly worried about Chana's safety in returning to Israel and wondered how we could allow her to take such risks. I spoke about a newfound awareness that safety is a feeling we talk ourselves into, that it has no independent, objective reality.

As we spoke, Steve, looking pale and tense, rushed upstairs: "Do you know what is going on? All hell is breaking loose!" We were overwhelmed by the enormity of the losses taking place before our eyes. The World Trade Center Towers collapsed and three thousand worlds came to an end. For a time, Pittsburgh's airspace was threatened until one of the four hijacked planes, apparently bound for Washington, D.C., crashed about forty-five minutes east of the city, midway between my mother's home and mine. We were unable to reach my sister, who works in Washington, D.C., until late in the evening. From her office window, she described seeing the Pentagon in flames. The state of alert and evacuations from the District meant that she abandoned her car and walked the six miles home to Virginia.

The cancerous culture of death attacking Israel was spreading. Calculations of risk necessarily changed. Maybe running from it was not possible. Many questions followed: Were we sitting out the drama of the return of the Jewish people to the land of Israel because we could not justify putting our children at risk? Was there not now risk in living in America? And how good was a decision based solely on an impossible risk assessment? Was there work that we could do in Israel that would help in some small way in moving Israel – and perhaps all of the world – towards some kind of healing?

ℴ ℭ

We did not decide to make aliyah then. Instead we began cleaning the house – beginning to lighten the considerable load of our material possessions. Each morning, I prayed that we would find a way to return "home." At the same time, I prayed that if my desire was not in the best interest of our children, that barriers would be placed in our path. We agreed that we would take very small steps – a single phone contact, filling out a form, reading about aliyah – and try to be alert to signs both of welcome and of rejection.

August 1, 2002

Dear friends,

Yesterday, in the same moments that I was on the phone speaking with someone about a job possibility in Israel, there was a terror attack at the cafeteria on the Mount Scopus campus of Hebrew University in Jerusalem. Towards the end of the day, friends called to tell us that Ben Blutstein, z"l, the son of mutual friends from Harrisburg, was murdered in this attack.

August 4, 2002

We paid a shiva call to the Blutsteins today. Shock and boundless sadness fill all of the spaces. We listened for a long time, trying just by our presence to share some of their pain, and silently hoping to hear what we most needed to hear. Without prompting, Kathryn said, "Ben was the happiest he had ever been in Jerusalem. Even now, I would not have wanted to take this time from him."

October 2, 2002

Steve and I are leaving on a pilot trip to Israel – we will be focusing on job contacts. I still feel as though I am at the apex of a fulcrum – no, that I *am* the fulcrum, but that, I suspect, is more a description of reality than a reflection of confusion.

Thanks for all of your support – whatever happens will be for the best. There are no options that I do not love.

October 30, 2002

Our job contacts went very well, but we are terrified that we won't have written offers in hand before we leave. We have to decide how much we are willing to risk financially. We are in daily contact with representatives of the Israeli government here and in Israel; continuing the process of cleaning house for a major move; putting together information necessary to rent our house; looking for rental housing in Jerusalem, and trying to confirm schools for Ari and Kayla. An ulpan in the neighborhood in which we want to live begins on January 15. It is strange that everything has to move ahead even though we have not put the final seal on the decision.

November 18, 2002

This morning we were officially recognized as Jews by the State of Israel, which is now prepared to issue us visas. The "proclamation" is unexpectedly heart-stopping – for both Steve and me. There is something very private about considering oneself to be Jewish or being recognized as Jewish by a single community. This feels entirely different. How strange and somehow how wonderful this all is. I feel as if in a dream, sleep-walking into the unknown. Filled with both dread and anticipation, hoping beyond hope that we have made the right decision for our children.

16 January 2003

Our journey to Israel began with a nine-hour drive to JFK through non-stop snow and sleet. We tried to maintain a reasonable speed, but slowed our two-vehicle caravan down after we saw an overturned Budget rental truck (like the one Steve was driving) in the oncoming lane and, in the medial strip, a damaged blue Subaru Outback (a clone of our Pittsburgh car). I cried on and off throughout the drive, although I straightened myself out when I realized that my visibility was further impaired. It was wrenching to leave all of you, no matter how frequently we will be in touch. It helped also when Kayla shared her conviction that, while there is a spiritual assistant guiding every aliyah, she believes that ours is being aided directly by the Almighty. May she only be right! In any case, if wild emotions, sadness, doubt and worry can conjure storms – I figured we bore some responsibility for this particular snowstorm.

We were quite a sight unloading the truck at the airport – thirteen very large boxes and bags, an enormous dog crate, a cat crate, carry-on luggage and of course the four of us. Most of the passengers on El Al were Americans, so it felt odd to enter the line with the few Israelis and proceed to the immigrant absorption center. The world being as it is these days, it was not exactly crowded. In perhaps thirty minutes we became citizens of Israel.

A very small vehicle pulled up to take us to Jerusalem (this ride is also courtesy of the Israeli government). He looked only amused when it became clear that the enormous pile of "stuff" on the curb was ours. We figured that fitting it into his cab was not even an option, so we ignored him as he patiently tried to convince us to let him try. After struggling unsuccessfully to find an alternative vehicle, we finally conceded. Using his roof and our ropes, we squeezed everything in or on.

As we drove through the night under the new moon of Tevet towards Jerusalem, Yitzhak, the driver, asked Steve what he would be doing for work. Steve responded that he had good job contacts and that he hoped all would work out. Our driver responded, "Ba'aretz, ein lanu tikvah; yesh lanu bitachon" – roughly, in Israel we don't have hope, we have trust. Then this somewhat grizzled sixty-plus-year-old man, who works as an auto mechanic by day and a taxicab driver by night, told us that he studies kabbalah so that he can remain optimistic about the world. He dropped us off at our new home after giving us a gift of a small book by Rabbi Shimon – for our protection, he said.

We are living in Baka, a Jerusalem neighborhood just south of the Old City. The week we arrived, winter took a few days' break from previous days of rain and cold. While we lived out of our boxes, slept four in one room and ate too many restaurant meals, we enjoyed hours of walking to and from appointments through the neighborhood's beautiful streets in bright sunshine. It is difficult to describe the light here – an incredible depth of blue in the sky and a clarity seen nowhere else.

Our lift arrived Friday morning and by sunset on our first Shabbat, the dining room table was set with china and beautiful meals from the kids' day school and the room filled with flowers from friends at shul. Chana joined us and the five of us celebrated Shabbat together for the first time in many months.

Kayla and Arieh began school this week and while both will struggle mightily with the Hebrew in the coming months, we are off to a good start. Kayla is attending a school that is a five-minute walk from the apartment. While we waited for her interview, one of the administrators told Kayla that some students wanted to meet her. We turned around to find ourselves amidst a crowd of beautiful ninth-grade girls, all welcoming her.

We visited a public religious school for Arieh, located in the Jewish Quarter of the Old City, around the corner from Chana's dorm. There are perhaps five small schools surrounding a central two-thousand-year-old courtyard. Ari's school is actually built into a wall of the Old City. The classroom doors open onto a wide walkway – a hallway with no roof, edged by a stone rail that overlooks the courtyard. It is completely magical.

At the end of our one-hour interview, Ari asked if he could just stay at school for the rest of the day. He will be one of only thirteen children – an extremely small class by Israeli standards. He proudly arrived home with a notebook filled with Hebrew translations of Arabic from his Arabic class and Hebrew translations of Aramaic from his Talmud class! Perhaps most unique to this school is its focus on the Old City. By the time the children finish the sixth grade, they are so knowledgeable about the history of the Old City that they are able to serve as guides. After school Ari grabbed his soccer ball and headed for a local park to practice for a game. With so few boys in his class, he informed us, every player counts. We could not have summarized this whole experience better: Yes, Arieh, every player does indeed count.

February 25, 2003

We awoke this morning at 5:00 a.m. to a pervasive silence. Perhaps eight inches of snow blanketed Jerusalem overnight, bringing the city to a nearly Yom Kippur-like quiet. The schools are closed; there are no public buses and children burst outside with more vigor than on any school day, engaging in intense snowball battles while making their way through the small rivers running through the deep trenches that crisscross the streets. Among the frightening undercurrents rocking the world, this storm, at least, was anticipated – a problem of recognizable dimensions. There was a run on milk and bread yesterday and the Jerusalem Post ran photos of snowplows lined up like tanks under captions assuring preparedness. Apparently, this is the biggest snowstorm to hit Jerusalem in fifty years!

We are aware that the Israel Defense Forces are fully mobilized in anticipation of an American attack on Iraq. Fighter jets patrol the skies at regular intervals; the sound is strangely comforting. I easily imagine the young men piloting these aircraft, guarding a land so small that most of the borders would be visible to them as they fly. In a true citizen's army, everyone can say, "Those are my sons, my brothers and my fathers." The sound makes me feel protective of them even as they protect me.

We read the daily news about terror alerts in America and are struck by what the media describe as high levels of public fear. By contrast, people in Israel – who are clearly much closer to the eye of this storm – are quite calm. A week or so ago, the huge supermarkets were packed with shoppers stocking up on staples, water and plastic sheeting, as we have been instructed to do. Schools conducted drills to prepare for the possibility of air strikes. A week later, preparations completed, most people have returned to their routines. We read an interview with a young American immigrant in the Jerusalem Post this past Friday. She recalled hearing the news about a terrorist attack on a bus in Israel last November while waiting at a bus stop. Confused about what to do, she asked the man next to her, "What now?" He replied, "What now? Now, we get on the bus."

Steve and I continue to attend 25 hours of Hebrew Ulpan a week. We are the "parents" in classes with young people from all over the world. Our vocabulary words and textbook sentences, our dialogues and lectures, are all shaped by an Israeli experience: Fill in the correct word: "The UN inspector _____ Israel in his report." Correct choice: "denounced."

I began work at a research job a couple of weeks ago that has given me the chance to take a bird's-eye view of the Jewish world. How about this for an amazing fact: in all of the years since the founding of the State in 1948, only 100,000 Jews from North America made aliyah. I guess we make 100,005.

March 2003, Purim 5763

If Purim is the holiday where everything is "hafooch" – upside down and inside out – then this year's celebration of Purim in Jerusalem was a "perfect" Purim.

Preparations began weeks before the holiday actually arrived. The City of Jerusalem posted colorful "Purim Sameach" signs weeks ago along all of the boulevards. The shops began to stock items for mishloach manot. Even with limited Hebrew, the radio advertisements for Purim-related items were unmistakable. Children and adults alike began planning costumes.

I pass the Jerusalem Theatre on my way to and from work every day. Last week, on the return trip, there were traffic barriers lining the street in both directions in front of the theater, making it impossible to park anywhere nearby. Police vehicles and several ambulances surrounded the building. Security guards and soldiers were posted everywhere. While security is evident everywhere here, I had never seen anything like this. I figured that maybe the theater was hosting a meeting of top political figures or perhaps even a police convention. Once again,

I felt so frustrated that I could not understand the radio news – since surely this must be news.

Upon arriving home, I was delighted to learn that Ari's elementary school began celebrating Purim with a special concert, along with schools from around Jerusalem. Having him feel a sense of national celebration is part of the reason we are here. Later, when I asked Steve if he knew anything about what had been going on at the theater that day, he responded that Ari's Purim concert had been there. For a moment, I could not breathe. *Children* were in the building? *Children* were the potential target the intensive security was meant to protect?

There are moments like these when the nature of what we confront here is unbearable. Rationally, I can understand that there are two peoples who can both make a claim to this land and I can even feel sadness at the terrible human loss in both communities. But there is no way I can wrap my mind around the possibility that children could be intentionally targeted. More than half of the world's Jewish children live in Israel. And yet, less than sixty years after the Holocaust, we find it sad but inevitable that they are again surrounded by guns and barbed wire and soldiers. Must I find it somehow inspirational that they are *our* guns and *our* barbed wire and *our* soldiers?

Because Jerusalem, like Shushan of old, is a walled city, we celebrate Purim a day later than the rest of the country. Hearing the megillah read in a community that understands the Hebrew was magnificent. The reader modulated his voice to sound feminine when Esther spoke and haughty when it was the king's turn. The melancholy Eichah trope stood out so strongly because the sadness of the words was apparent to everyone. People hissed when the name of Zeresh, Haman's wife, was mentioned and made a ruckus towards the end of the reading when we read that "King Achashverosh levied taxes on both the mainland and the islands." Taxes are a sore subject here.

There is no dust on this story. It is strikingly alive, perhaps because its themes are often the subject of the morning news. It felt good to realize that despite what feels like painfully slow Hebrew language progress, I understood so much more. On the other hand, this was not so difficult: much of the megilla's central vocabulary – to destroy, to kill – is sadly still today's vocabulary.

So much of our celebration this year felt surreal. Steve watched a parade of kids in costume from a couple of neighborhood elementary schools – all smiling, happy faces while military escorts poured out of army vehicles and distributed guns to the teachers to provide additional protection while the children paraded down the street. We enjoyed the megillah while two volunteer congregants remained posted outside the shul with weapons to guard us.

We laughed watching a juggler at a party after the megillah and then danced home through the rain to seal Kayla's bedroom for a possible Iraqi chemical attack. We celebrated a brit at the restaurant on the Tayelet after the morning megillah reading, enjoyed a hearty Purim seudah in the afternoon and then returned home in the evening (again through the rain!) to open and fit our gas masks. Still in the Purim spirit, we ate hamantaschen and Steve took our pictures while we adjusted the head straps, practiced not feeling claustrophobic and made lots of Darth Vader jokes. Ha-kol hafooch – everything is mixed up, inside out and upside down. Like Purim.

May 2003

We have been in Israel for about four months. Other immigrants – both to Israel and to the States – have told us that this period marks one of many benchmarks on the way to absorption. One achieves just a modicum of stability, fragments of "normalcy." The road to and from the office is no longer new and challenging. The office emails in Hebrew and the notes sent home from teachers don't engender the same panic.

One friend, now in Israel some twenty years, recalls the comfort at seeing the beautiful red wild flowers bloom in Jerusalem's fields and parks during her second spring here. It was the first time that she remembers seeing anything significant for the second time.

May 18, 2003

Even a short while ago it wasn't hard to wake up to the news because, no matter how terrible, I really did not understand it. This morning at 6:00 a.m. it was different. I realized exactly what had happened – a bus had been blown up at an intersection in the Jerusalem neighborhood of French Hill. I understood how many had been injured, how many injured seriously, and how many killed. At one point the broadcaster called someone to interview him "on location." The man being interviewed began his little part with the perfunctory greeting, "Boker tov" – "Good morning." The broadcaster immediately corrected him with "Ein boker tov" – "It is *not* a good morning."

Later this morning I learned about a Lebanese man who had been a paid spy for the Israel Defense Force and whose information had led to the capture of forty members of Hizbullah. Apparently he now wants to immigrate to Canada and is being denied entrance for (if we have the story straight) "crimes against humanity."

Abu Mazen, who denies that the Holocaust was a conflagration that destroyed six million Jews, becomes the Palestinian Authority's prime minister and a world leader. Major American newspapers report on IDF incursions into

Gaza to stop the firing of rockets into the city of Sderot – and fail to mention the seventy-plus rockets that have fallen on Israeli population centers in the past several months.

Why is simple truth becoming increasingly difficult to identify? Why and of what are people so afraid that they are willing to believe the baldest lies?

I love to watch baseball pitchers. I love the lull before he releases the ball.

The lulls are not unlike the spaces between attacks here. For most of us, however, the lulls in this war are filled with stupefied relief, without intention, without preparation, and I am sure I am wasting time. Worse, I am afraid that I am becoming deadened, that I risk shutting down and approaching this life with a closed hand and heart.

I am acquainted with a lovely twenty-five-year-old woman who remarked last week that it has been a long time since a bus has been bombed in Jerusalem. Thank God, she said. When I reminded her that a "long time" meant only six months, she was surprised. And then she told me that her father, during this terrible past year, told her that if she was suspicious of someone while traveling on the bus, she should throw herself to the floor between the seats. There would be no time to get out, but she could perhaps protect herself a little by dropping to the floor.

She told me that she was traveling by bus one day near Machane Yehuda, the sprawling Jewish market, when an Arab youth with lots of packages got on the bus. He seemed suspicious to her and as he walked down the aisle, he caught her eye and seemed to glare. She panicked and threw herself to the floor in the small space between the seats, hurting and embarrassing herself terribly, as there was no danger from this particular young man. She seems so unaffected by everything, confident, aggressively pursuing a career; but inside there is terror.

There are helicopters circling overhead now, as they have been all morning. There is never a lull in the sound.

September 2003

We continue to experience both highs and lows as we make our way through this first year. Take the meeting last week in which I sat in utter silence. I understood only that my colleagues were engaged in a heated discussion of a survey sampling issue related to a recent study on food security in Israel. I actually know something about survey sampling and so it was frustrating not to be able to participate.

Or take my decision that the one small contribution I could make despite my less-than-adequate language skills is to drive with extraordinary courtesy, yielding right-of-way to pedestrians with a smile. So guess who got a ticket for gliding through a stop sign?

And then there are the unbelievable highs. At a nearby shul this past Friday night, we were immersed in song of such beauty and such power, that, with tears in my eyes, I laughed out loud. Yet, as we reached the recitation of the Shema, I reflected on what it means to declare that God is One. This unity must also somehow encompass the horror in which we find ourselves immersed. Accounts of the bombing of the No. 2 bus on the way from the Kotel filled the media. Twenty-three people were killed, including many children, and over 130 wounded. In the days that followed, few people even wanted to mention it. This was something too terrible for words. We wanted to run from the images, from the families torn forever. When I recognized the impulse to flee, I forced myself to read the personal accounts – of a hall filled with weeping men, including the police officers posted to provide security at the funeral of an eleven-month-old child.

And so, as I read the Shema last Friday night and considered the mounting losses, I cried again. Tears instead of laughter? Tears with laughter? Someone once told me that a Jew must be able to laugh and cry and at the same time. I am beginning to understand.

Against this backdrop, the children are so full of life. They move rapidly towards a comfort and an integration that remain more distant goals for us, particularly because they acquire the ability to communicate so much faster.

Kayla just completed reading the short story "Tehilla" by Shmuel Yosef Agnon. Her tutor explained that there are three kinds of Hebrew: the Hebrew of the Bible, modern spoken Hebrew, and Agnon's Hebrew. We wondered why her first book of literature could not have been a translation of *Winnie the Pooh*. She took it all in stride and compared Agnon to Dickens, saying both use too many words.

Arieh has been working with his tutor to begin the long process of bringing his Tanach and Talmud skills up to the level of his Israeli peers. In order to help him learn the Hebrew calendar – the number and names of the months and all of the special days within each, he drilled, while doing push-ups, barking out like a boot-camp recruit: "Tishrei: Rosh Hashana, Yom Kippur, Sukkot!... Shevat: Tu bi-Shevat... Iyar: Yom ha-Shoah, Yom ha-Zikaron, Yom ha-Atzma'ut, yom huledet sheli (my birthday)!"

Chana is attending Hebrew University's Mechina Program, an intensive Hebrew-language ulpan followed by a year of classes related to her intended major (environmental science), taught in Hebrew. She is also dating a very special young man; it is hard to describe how happy and at home she is. Chana asked the only other English speaker in her class, an Israeli Arab, to translate the five-times-daily Muslim call to prayer for her. Apparently it is a declaration of the oneness of God, as well as a call to prayer. Perhaps it is more than bad luck that we struggle over this land with our cousins.

Next week my parents are scheduled to arrive for a visit. Some may remember that my parents are not Jewish. I am amazed and, if you will permit me, terribly proud that they are willing to travel here – especially my father, who watches television news far too often. I guess this is what family is all about.

Today, September 5, 2003, 8th Elul 5763, it rained in Jerusalem! We are still praying for dew and instead we were granted rain.

October 2003/Tishrei 5764, Erev Sukkot

At dawn one morning, when I was a little girl growing up in Chicago, my sister and I awoke to stormy, sickly yellow skies. As my parents gathered us into the safety of our basement, we heard a roar like a freight engine as an enormous tornado passed overhead. Our home was spared, but adjoining neighborhoods fared less well.

We drove around the next day to survey the aftermath of that very powerful storm. In the next subdivision stood a house from which the walls of a second-floor bedroom had been torn away, exposing the pink flowered wallpaper of a child's room. Nearly forty years later, I can still recall the scene in detail. The bedroom could have been my sister's and mine.

Yehuda Amichai wrote a beautiful poem, which is included in his collection *Poems of Jerusalem* (1988), that evokes this memory for me and gives me some language to express what it feels like to live here. He describes finding himself suddenly, and at too young an age, like the inner walls of a house exposed by war or destruction. He writes that he almost forgot what living on the "inside" feels like and yet, while pain is dulled, colors on the inside are not as brilliant, nor smells as sweet, nor love as strong. Living here in Jerusalem, I relate to these images of exposure – frightening and life-affirming at the same time. After only nine months, I too, am beginning to forget what living on the "inside" feels like.

For months, my parents said they were coming to visit on September 9th. Only after a cursory check of their itinerary, about an hour before leaving for the airport, did I realize that I had forgotten to add a day for travel time. And so it was that they arrived the day after, rather than the day of, the bombing of Café Hillel.

The explosion was loud enough to be heard even in relatively distant neighborhoods. We live only a five-minute walk away. After the blast, there were perhaps ninety seconds of utter silence, during which I prayed: *Please let it be something else....* And then the blare of sirens and the overhead staccato of helicopters filled every space. Hours after the crisis had ended and the grieving began, I still heard the echoes of sirens.

These recent attacks have been particularly difficult. They seem to form a pattern designed to systematically rip down our emotional walls – to expose the inner walls of our collective home. First a bus filled with children on its way from the Kotel and then, at Café Hillel, the death of a beloved physician and his daughter on the eve of her wedding. Among the twenty dead from the bombing of the Maxim restaurant in Haifa three weeks later were ten people from just two families.

Managing the illusion of safety gets us through the day. But there are times when we are forced to confront the reality that we really control so little – the sudden loss of a job, the diagnosis of a terrible illness, a tragic accident, a terror attack. And we are forced to admit that no matter where we live, every day we walk the razor edge between life and death. We control only what we do with our fear or our grief, or our joy. I wonder: if we lived anywhere else, would we remember so viscerally to appreciate our children and each other, to remind ourselves how much we love and are loved? Would we offer and receive as readily the small daily kindnesses that are part of the fabric of living here? Would we feel so grateful to have been given the opportunity to play a small part in these remarkable times (or wish so hard to do the right thing with that opportunity)? Despite the very real difficulties, I think I would have to conclude that anything else would be like living on the inside again, and a choice we could no longer make.

November 2003

So many friends told us that we are so lucky – that nothing can compare to celebrating the High Holidays in Israel. In many ways, they were right. It was beautiful to walk to synagogue for Kol Nidre and see literally hundreds of people strolling, dressed in white, to the dozens and dozens of synagogues in the neighborhood. With the exception of occasional police cruisers, there were *no* cars on the street. Teenagers gathered by night and day in small groups, sitting in the middle of normally busy roads. I actually thought that there must be a law prohibiting driving in the country on Yom Kippur – otherwise, why would secular Israelis refrain from driving? When I asked a non-religious friend about this, she was surprised that I found it strange not to see cars. There are no laws, but even in completely secular cities in this country, she said, nobody thinks to drive.

The country was on high alert over Yom Kippur and holiday leaves were cancelled for Jerusalem's police force. As we walked home along Emek Refaim

Street to break our fast, we saw a couple of police officers eating a small meal, spread out on the trunk of their cruiser. The sound of hammers rang throughout the neighborhood that evening as our neighbors began constructing their sukkot in the dark. And for the first time in our experience, it did not rain on Sukkot. The first rains fell only after Shemini Atzeret, during which we actually recite the prayer for rain. The children are off from school and offices are closed for the entire week of Sukkot. Together with the kids we sailed in the Mediterranean and spent every possible moment reading, eating, and talking in the sukkah in our garden.

And yet despite the wonder of all of this, I was not "in the moment" for most of the holidays.

Seemingly extraneous details – like where to purchase a lulav, in which synagogue to pray, whether to invite friends for meals – all require information-gathering and decision-making. We are so new that none of these details can be attended to automatically, making some of the preparations exhausting and crowding the space for contemplation.

I am learning enough Hebrew to have had my davening continually interrupted as I came upon words in the prayers whose meaning I now recognized – completely distracting me from the meditative aspects of prayer. At one point, during Neilah, the final Yom Kippur service, I simply closed my machzor, exhausted by the uninvited intrusions, and began to pray in my own words.

Perhaps this is somewhat like the years during which we first began to observe Shabbat. Paradoxically, it initially took enormous effort and intention to refrain from working. And it took a long time to engage in the physical preparations for Shabbat (shopping, inviting, cooking, and cleaning) in ways that permitted reflection on why the physical preparations were important.

The whole experience also reminds me of what it is like to travel to a destination that requires following a set of complicated directions. One has to be alert for every sign and landmark along the way. Time seems to stretch out endlessly, although the same distance traveled on the return trip seems to pass quickly.

Once we know where we are going, it is possible to focus on the beauty of the passing fields or to become engrossed in conversation without worrying about missing the exit. True, once we "know the way," we lose a certain sensitivity, a heightened attention to our surroundings. On the other hand, being able to take some of the details for granted makes it possible to engage in dialogue, to reflect and to imagine.

March 2004

Our oldest daughter married on February 17th in Jerusalem, overlooking Bet Lechem, the birthplace of King David. Chana married very early, but to a young man for whom we feel instinctively and strongly she was destined to join. There was urgency in their desire to marry – to not wait and linger; one never knows what the future brings here. In some ways their marriage was an act of defiance in the midst of great suffering. Both have been touched by losses related to this war. As a declaration of intense love, theirs may be the only rational response to the intense hatred surrounding all of us.

At the wedding people crowded around (or in the case of little children, under) the chupah – holding hands, crying, singing to the heavens with joy. Our children danced until nearly two a.m. We worried last year that we would not have a community with whom to celebrate Ari's bar mitzvah in 2005; a year later nearly 400 people helped us to celebrate this wedding.

℘ ☙

I will always be haunted by the questions regarding our children's personal safety. I worry about them without interruption – a background hum of ever-present anxiety. All of my instincts as their mother are to circle around them and protect them. And all of my instincts as a Jew are to circle around my people and protect them. Sometimes these feel like contradictory urges, although the Torah teaches us that they are one and the same.

We read in Parashat Matot-Masei that, as the tribes approach the borders of Israel, about to enter and conquer the land, Reuven, Gad and half the tribe of Menashe ask whether they might leave their children, wives and herds on the eastern side of the Jordan, where they hope to settle. They are willing to be warriors on behalf of the other tribes, but at the same time they wish to protect their children, their wives and their animals. Moshe responds that everyone must join in the conquest of the land and share in its risks. Only after all of the other tribes can live in safety can Reuven, Gad and half of Menashe return to their land east of the Jordan.

This is one of the sources for the Jewish assertion that "All Israel is responsible one for the other." These cannot just be words. There are just over five million Jews living in Israel – fewer than those who perished in the Holocaust. Despite chronic embattlement, they insist on living – raising children, making weddings and funerals, and grappling with the demands of building of a new country informed by an ancient faith. They are trying to ensure that there is a place of safety for our collective children and grandchildren, and perhaps also helping to bring a new kind of light to the rest of the world. We are no more able to claim an exemption than were our ancestors.

Postscript

In this remarkable year, we have learned to recognize the extent to which we defined ourselves by an accumulation of externally-generated "facts." In so many ways, we constructed our identity from the outside-in, using as our building blocks the multiple ways in which others perceive us. And at forty-something years old, we have had many years to accumulate a well-padded definition of "self." We are the valued colleague, working at a high level and well paid. We are the respected volunteer, the caring mother, the trusted adviser, the bright student and so on.

And then we make aliyah at mid-life, moving to a place where none of our personal narrative means anything or matters to anybody. We conduct ourselves like children because we have no capacity in Hebrew to convey complex thought. We punch a time clock for the first time in our lives, bridling and bucking at the implications. We confront our most painful limitation – our inability to protect our children and even to successfully advocate for them in a new language. There is no way to describe this experience except as a kind of ego death. We stand as if empty – beginning the process of "becoming" all over again.

In a beautiful passage, the Maharal suggests that *lechem oni* – the bread of the poor to which *matzah* is compared – is not what we eat as slaves in Egypt. Instead, *lechem oni* is the bread we eat in freedom, only *after* leaving Egypt. It is bread eaten without adornments – bread that the Maharal likens to "a poor man who stands with nothing but himself."* Freedom then is bound up with our capacity to stand alone, without adornments. That capacity seems to be at once the source of suffering and of salvation.

Perhaps this contraction of ego, and the redefinition of self that becomes necessary in its wake, is a gift. It is a state of being that is filled with uncertainty but also with possibility. Maybe the humility that comes from seeing oneself as a child again – not knowing all of the answers – is the gift we most need to navigate the frightening and wondrous times in which we now find ourselves. We have more room to receive, to grow – perhaps to hear the still small voice of God in a world in which we can no longer even agree that the intentional murder of innocents is contemptible.

---

* With thanks to Dr. Avivah Gottlieb Zornberg for sharing this in her Pesach 5764 shiur.

Would we have chosen this path had we known how difficult and at times how painful it would be? Without a doubt, yes, although in retrospect, the difficulty of this journey should not have come as a surprise. Rabbi Shimon bar Yochai, as recorded in the Talmud in Tractate *Berachot* 5a, said, "The Holy One, Blessed be He, gave three good gifts to Israel, and he gave all of them only through suffering. They are Torah, the Land of Israel and the World to Come."

I am years, perhaps lifetimes, from being able to say that I have acquired any of these gifts. Instead, I simply hope to merit enough time in this new life to try.

For further reading:

Coopersmith, Nechemia, and Shraga Simmons, eds. *Israel: Life in the Shadow of Terror.* Jerusalem: 2004.

Blank Paper

Devorah Leah Rosenfeld

There's nothing in the world that thrills me like a fresh sheet of paper and a new box of crayons. The blinding whiteness of the paper and the intoxicating aroma of wax crayons hold the promise of every new beginning. It's like cradling a newborn baby in my arms and knowing that for this child, I have yet to raise my voice, issue a time-out, make a mistake. It's like facing a class of preschoolers on their first day of Hebrew day school and realizing that we are embarking on a familiar but momentous journey.

These feelings are intensely personal, but hardly original. Thousands of years ago, the Sages expressed it this way: He who studies Torah as a child, to what can he be compared? To ink written on fresh paper.

What I couldn't have known is how deeply my time with children, teaching them, writing stories for them, and raising my own, would affect my own spiritual growth. I have always loved young children, but never considered a teaching career for that age group. All the preschool teachers I knew radiated that syrupy sweet quality that I knew I didn't have and couldn't fake. I'm too impatient, too uptight, the anti-*Romper Room* lady. When I did find myself in a classroom with a bright bunch of four-year-olds, my lessons were structured minute by minute, much the same way I prepared for my high-school students.

Surprisingly, it worked. And I felt a connection to those little ones that gave energy and meaning to my day in a way nothing else could.

The power lay in the raw honesty and intensity required for every interaction. As I prepared the material, I was conscious of my own inner struggle with issues like faith, the purpose of life, the imperfection of the world. How could I articulate all these existential, spiritual truths to people who still needed help zipping their jackets?

Without any previous misconceptions about Judaism, or the angst and ambivalence of world-weary adults, children are open to spirituality completely and enthusiastically. It is like writing on fresh, clean paper! And in telling them about Divine Providence, the power of prayer, the holiness of Shabbat, I was reinforcing all this for myself as well.

"Who wants to give charity?" I asked.

"I do," they'd yell.

And at that moment, more than anything else, they really did.

"How fast did the Jews have to leave Egypt?"

Bright-eyed, they dashed around the classroom, reliving history.

"What should we do if a friend is sick?"

"Go and visit… call him up."

Can goodness and kindness be so obvious, so simple?

I found myself getting back to basics…becoming more careful with mitzvot, more aware of God's presence. Taking my own preschool lessons to heart meant writing on the fresh, clean tablet hidden within my soul.

Of course there were times when I envied the secular teacher, especially at story time. Why did I have to discuss the burial of Sarah when all she had to do was read "The Gingerbread Man?" Not fair. I recoiled at the thought of bringing up such a somber subject. But it was the Torah portion that week and I was obligated to present it. The ensuing introduction went something like this:

"Do you children remember when Hashem (God) created the very first person?"

"Yes," they chorused.

"What was he made of?" I asked, doubting they'd recall.

"Mud," they answered correctly.

"That's right," I beamed, "His body was made out of earth."

"And a piece of Hashem inside," one added. I took a deep breath.

"Well, after a long life, when the piece of Hashem in every person goes back up where it came from, what part is left?"

"The body," they said, as if this were child's play rather than a deep philosophical discussion.

"And if the piece of Hashem flies back up where it came from, then where should the body be put?" I asked.

"In the earth," they answered, as if it were the most natural thing in the world.

I was staggered. We had just tackled the topic of death according to Judaism's teachings. We discussed it quite matter-of-factly, with absolute clarity, in a way I had rarely heard adults address anything that important. There was nothing morbid about anything we said. And as we toddled off to drink our apple juice, I wondered at the capacity of children to understand.

Twenty years have passed since that moment in the classroom when we deconstructed death. During that time, I have seen more than one waxy newborn gulp his first breath of air and unfold into a squalling pink person. Yet only recently was I present as a warm, living human being breathed his last.

My father took his final small breaths at dusk, and the long night and day that followed became a confusing jumble of disbelief, numbness and the crushing heaviness of loss. But one slice of time stood out from the rest. As my father's casket was laid gently in the earth, and those who loved him best covered it with shovel after shovel of dry rocky soil, I stood dry-eyed, reassured, calmly watching.

Just then, like those four-year-olds had patiently explained to me, it really was the most natural thing in the world.

For further reading:

Orlowek, Noach. *My Disciple, My Child.* Jerusalem: 1999.

Hodakov, Chaim Mordechai Isaac. *The Educator's Handbook: Principles, Reflections, Directives of a Master Pedagogue.* Brooklyn, NY: 1998.

*All the world is a very narrow bridge but the main
thing is not to fear at all.*

Rabbi Nachman of Breslov

Birthing Lives

Tamara Edell-Gottstein

You are fully dilated. You can push your baby out now," the midwife beams.

"No, I won't. I've had enough. I'm going home," Dana hisses through teeth clenched in determination. We all burst into compassionate laughter. Clearly, stopping is not an option.

In many life situations, we can decide when enough is enough. We can take a break, then continue when our thoughts are clearer and we are more rested. Birth and parenthood dispel this luxurious illusion of control. Birth cannot be planned or predicted. One birth may progress slowly; another may begin with the splash of broken waters and develop quickly into unrelenting contractions. A labor in full swing rarely stops until the squiggly newborn cries its first cry and nestles into its parents' arms. Despite Dana's experience, we usually don't really want to stop our births. We want our children to come forth. The hours riding contraction after contraction, through uncertainty, exhaustion, pain, fear, faith, and joy, embody every kind of human drama. The birth context differs from other life situations that feature pain. It is easier to keep in mind that our effort and struggle are clearly for something good. We know that the challenge is temporary and produces life. This allows us to approach birth with simplicity, admit our vulnerability, and do whatever works to help us get through. The times that we "lose it" are inevitable, and we accept them for what they are – a rite of passage.

We can learn a lot from how we live the intense hours at our breaking edge. How can we harvest the profound lessons learned from our contractions? These lessons apply to all life's challenges and particularly to times when we are overwhelmed. Assisting at hundreds of births and meeting their intensity with pragmatic optimism has slowly transformed my attitude to other areas of life. I am much more accepting of myself, of others, and of the mysterious unfolding of life.

Beginnings

My fascination with birth started with our first birth. After years of difficulty conceiving, our pregnancy was at risk right from the start. Thankfully, with good care, I held the pregnancy. Labor began with a splash in the middle of the night. The contractions came fast, strong, and close together. The entire event was exceptionally easy for a first birth. Those two and a half hours were the most exhilarating of my life. We entered the hospital just in time for me to dilate from two to ten centimeters in one short hour.

Between contractions, we sang a song that a group of spiritually vibrant ultra-Orthodox Jews, the Lubavitcher Hassidim, sings on the Jewish New Year. The words are, "Our Father, our King, we have no other God, only You." The melody has penetrating strength. During contractions, I anchored deep in my husband's elated gaze. The peaks of the contractions only lasted for two long breaths. It was intense, but something I would not really label as pain. Between contractions, waves of energy seemed to move up and down my spine. Our first son, Elisha, entered the world exactly at sunrise. The first sound he heard was his father's awestruck voice, fervently reciting the prayer, "Hear, O Israel, the Lord our God, the Lord is One." This experience turned me into a woman who enjoys giving birth. I wanted to do it again.

After our second son's gentle delivery, my gratitude to our doctor and the hospital staff eventually led me to volunteer at the hospital. I trained as a labor companion, a doula, and have since accompanied hundreds of couples in their journey to parenthood.

One particular birth inspired a deeper understanding. I was helping the granddaughter of a Rebbe with her first birth. Bracha came prepared, not by Lamaze, but with her list, written carefully on three pages of lined yellow paper. These sheets contained the names of all the couples in their community who were yearning for children. Bracha settled into the hospital, donned her gown, and started to pray. Over and over she read this list, closing her eyes to concentrate, focusing her prayer on one couple at a time. When the contractions intensified and it was harder for Bracha to read, she handed the list to her mother who continued to whisper each name in her ear, then paused to allow her time to pray before giving her the next name.

As Bracha neared transition, the external fetal monitor signaled that the baby was in distress. The staff came in and began to prepare her for a Caesarean section. Bracha cooperated with whatever was needed, but during every window of time she had, she kept peacefully returning to her list and to her prayers. Suddenly the monitor cleared, the baby's distress passed, surgery was averted, and the birth proceeded beautifully. Her son entered the world surrounded by prayers of gratitude.

The Divine Presence

Our sages said regarding the birthing woman that "the key of birth is only in God's hand and is not given to any messenger," as it says, "and God opened her womb." At every birth there is the indwelling of supreme Godly holiness.

Those close to the birthing woman often notice this sacred presence as they come close to their time to deliver. It is also nothing short of miraculous to see the newborn take its first breath. And as the bluish newborn transforms, flushes with rosy hue, opens his/her eyes and looks around, the words from Genesis come alive, "*And HaShem God formed man of the dust of the ground, and* **He blew into his nostrils the soul of life and man became a living being.**"

The strength of this divine connection can empower a woman in birth. She may know exactly what she needs to do and when she needs to do it. Bracha modeled a lovely new possibility for me. As a woman completely opens and a new soul is about to enter the world, the gates of heaven may also be open to receive our prayers.

Traditionally a Jewish woman prays for others when she stands under her wedding canopy, so why not at birth? It is difficult to feel sorry for oneself when praying for families that would do anything to experience labor. What better time is there to pray for one's family and for a better world? I was so moved by Bracha's use of labor as a time to pray for others that I started to research our traditions and teachings about childbirth. We formed a group of couples who wanted to learn religious texts as a spiritual preparation for their births.

We focused our learning on the metaphor of the birth of Israel from the womb of Egypt. Among the many themes that emerged was the parallel between contractions and the rhythmic appearance of plagues and the pauses between them. The intensity of these events led to the expulsion of the people of Israel. We touched on how much anticipation and effort went toward the Exodus from Egypt yet when the moment to leave arrived it happened suddenly, as a surprise, *be-hipazon*. The climax of the class occurred on the seventh day of Passover, the day that we celebrate the miraculous splitting of the Red Sea and Israel's final redemption from Egyptian slavery. Much to our surprise, three of the four babies expected by class members were born that day.

The excitement generated by this group inspired me to convene a group of midwives, doulas and mothers. We started the group by exploring the unique role of the midwives mentioned in the book of Exodus, both as preservers of life and as social activists, courageous fighters against the corrupt and destructive regime of

Pharaoh. We looked at the character traits that are needed to facilitate birth. We spoke about how we handle the complex emotional reality when a child is born with a birth defect. We studied the midrash regarding the power of the midwife's prayer, looked at some texts of *tehinnot* and wrote our own prayers. Basing ourselves on a text that states, "Who is wise? The one who sees the *nolad* (that which will be born)," we explored the traditional commentary that defines this wisdom as the ability to see from the inception of an event what will come to pass. I posed the question to the group, "How has facilitating birth increased your wisdom?"

Who Controls Birth?

During one session of the midwives' group a spirited discussion ensued when a midwife who promotes natural birth shocked us all by saying that she mentally throws women's birth plans "in the garbage." Many women of our generation enter their births with carefully-thought-out, written plans for their care and that of their newborns. They dutifully deliver these to the labor ward staff.

The question arose, who is served by birth plans? They have helped put consumer pressure on hospitals to change policies and recognize patients' rights. This has led to the development of some new, more flexible birth centers, but do these plans work psychologically against the birthing mothers by fostering the illusion that every aspect of birth can be planned and controlled?

When I challenged the midwife to clarify why she discards birth plans, she spoke of the pain that accompanies any deviation from "the plan." The obvious goal is to have both mother and baby come through the birth in optimal health, but many women feel profound disappointment if their dream birth does not materialize. Rigid attitudes, however, can lead to scenarios that are truly dangerous. In one case, the mother refused an episiotomy even though the monitor showed serious fetal distress. Although we will never be sure whether this infant's subsequent brain damage was a result of oxygen deprivation during those critical moments of the birth, the story reminds us to maintain balance and flexibility. For birth plans to be a truly useful tool, they need to be discussed, and unrealistic expectations challenged. They are useful in helping chose a medical environment harmonious with one's ideals. Yet for the birth itself, one needs genuine flexibility.

"From the Narrow Straits I called to God. God answered me with expansiveness."

In Hebrew, contractions are called *tzirim*. This word has the same root as *Mitzraim*, Egypt. A *metzar* is literally a narrow, contracted place. A *tzir* is also a hinge, that which allows a door to open, an axis, a turning point. It is precisely from the place that we contract that we are enjoined to call out and allow an opening.

Most women face birth with trepidation. We fear the unknown. Often women have heard stories of difficult deliveries or had previous traumatic deliveries. In modern Hebrew, *mashber* means "crisis." The root *shever* means to break. For new life to come forth something must yield, just as a seed coat decomposes as the seed germinates. Just how controllable is birth? Tova Leah Nachmani, one of the mothers in the learning group, eloquently furthered the discussion as follows:

Do you know what the birthing stool is called in the Talmud? *Mashber*, crisis. There is no birth without crises. Not only birth brings crises; an approaching marriage or a divorce does as well. Crises exist in our daily lives…. Each crisis we go through brings us to a new level of growth. It brings us to something that we were not before, something that we didn't understand before. It **brings us to some new strength**.

This question of why HaShem wants us to have crises seems very important. The redemption is not just going to fall out of the sky. *Hevlei Mashiach*, the birth pangs of the Messiah, will be a time of crises. There will be birth pangs – you can't have birth without them…. This crisis has a purpose.

Faith in the Face of the Unknown

The Slonimer Rebbe teaches that there are three levels of faith.

First is *emunat ha-moach*: mental faith (i.e., we intellectually believe in God). Higher than this is the faith of the heart, *emunat ha-lev*…. The distance between faith of the mind and faith of the heart is greater than the distance between heaven and earth. There is another level that is higher than both – the faith of the limbs, *emunat ha-evarim*, in which faith in God penetrates every limb and organ, as it is written, "All my bones will praise you, God…" meaning that every organ, even one's bones, knows that there is nothing else but God.

According to the Slonimer Rebbe, the people of Israel achieved this level of total faith through crossing the Red Sea. This was the birth of the people of Israel. A woman needs the same faith to bring forth life. Birth invites her to live her faith in every limb and organ of her body.

There are fascinating physiological correlations between fear and faithful surrender during the birth process. When a woman is fearful she is in the physiological state described as "fight-or-flight syndrome." Most of her blood leaves her internal organs, including her womb, and is diverted to her muscles, enabling her to run or fight. This compromises oxygen flow to the baby and may weaken the contractions. The chronic fearful clenching of her muscular system produces a metabolic byproduct called lactic acid. The presence of lactic acid causes fatigue and lowers her pain threshold.

In contrast, when a woman relaxes deeply between contractions and works with her labor, her body releases endorphins. Endorphins are chemically similar to morphine. They cause a euphoric sense of well-being and actually provide natural pain relief. We may know that relaxation in labor is good for us, yet to maintain faithful surrender we need reminders.

The Slonimer Rebbe further elaborates that it is from the faith of the limbs (*emunat ha-evarim*) that new songs spring forth. Song releases us and carries us to our faith. The words of the Psalms focus our hearts and thoughts on God's loving presence. I often encourage women to find one line from the Psalms or prayers that speaks especially to them. They keep this as a constant companion throughout the birth. Singing makes one breathe. Singing has another unexpected side benefit: it creates a special atmosphere on the labor ward. Midwives often hover near our door to enjoy the melodies. Thus, it becomes easier to invite their help.

Sandra chose a line from Psalm 32: "Lovingkindness surrounds the one who trusts in God." During contractions, she swayed in big round circles, as if she were using a hula-hoop in slow motion. When the baby came out, we watched amazed as the midwife unwound the umbilical cord from around the baby. It was wrapped four times around the neck, and across the chest. Lovingkindness surrounded her new daughter. Normally one sees dips in the monitor when there are cord problems, yet her daughter was fine throughout the labor.

At one point during Jenny's birth she froze in fear. Her gaze became distant, her face rigid and listless. I brought her to the window. Together, arm in arm, we began to sway as we gazed at the view. Spontaneously, I started to pray aloud for her. Eventually she was able to pray as well. She regained her focus and equanimity through her prayer.

Sometimes the husband is the one who creates the atmosphere of prayer. Many Jewish men recite psalms at their wives' sides. One memorable birth began on Friday. As the Sabbath approached, the husband began to recite the traditional evening prayers. The couple knew that they were expecting their fourth daughter. As the husband earnestly sang, "Come, O bride; come, O bride, O Sabbath Queen," all of our hearts were inviting their daughter. The moment he finished his prayers his wife began to push their daughter out. The midwife handed his daughter to him and he began to sing *Shalom Aleichem*, the greeting we sing to the angels on Friday night when we return from the synagogue. He sat at his wife's side and sang *Eshet Chayil*, "Woman of Valor," for both his wife and new daughter. They made a blessing over the wine and had a little Sabbath meal as if they were in their own home.

The births described above were lovely. Not all women labor so peacefully.

The Experience that Heals

Some women begin their birth experience weighted by difficult past births or other past traumas. For example, Elisheva had a difficult and lengthy recovery from spleen surgery only one year before she conceived her twins. She was terrified that she would not be able to take care of her babies if the birth became a Caesarean section. This fear haunted her. One day I came over for a pre-birth session. Elisheva met me shining. She announced, "Enough worry! I've decided that no matter what happens it will be a *havaya metakenet*, a healing experience. The final stage of her birth was anything but ideal. The first baby came out with the help of a big episiotomy. The midwife tried to turn the second baby into a better delivery position, and he went into distress. Twin number two was delivered by emergency C-section. Even though she had some post-surgical complications, she stayed firm in her good humor, thrilled with her boys, cheerfully conveying her faith that this was a rectifying and healing experience. Her husband was infused with her optimism. One day I walked into the hospital and there was a new complication, this time with the breast-feeding, that necessitated the use of a breast pump. Jeremy cheerfully expressed his confidence in handling the pump. He felt right at home after years of managing a dairy farm.

Perhaps more than any other idea, Elisheva's "experience that heals" positively challenges me when I try to resist the opportunities that life brings.

Is it possible to rectify everything, or are some situations so traumatic that there is no way to heal?

Sara's delicate beauty gave no hint of her desperately painful past. She had been raped repeatedly as a child. When she was in her teens, she ran away from her difficult family into an equally impossible marriage. Her first child was taken away from her. In her late teens, she was violently raped and her uterus injured with a sharp object. The doctors felt the only way to save her life was to do a hysterectomy. With every last ounce of strength, she insisted that they save her womb and refused general anesthesia for the surgery to ensure that they left her intact. She desperately wanted children that she could keep. She remarried, this time a patient and devoted man, and they had several children together. At her previous birth, the staff was rough with her. She suddenly felt abused again, and responded by defending herself, attacking the staff with her teeth and nails. We did a lot of work together before the birth of her daughter to establish a language of trust and to understand what triggered her violent reaction.

More than from any other birth, I learned from Sara's what a profound role the medical staff plays in determining if the experience re-wounds or heals. In Sara's case we made it a cooperative project. I did the sensitive pre-work and stayed at her side throughout the labor and initial nursing. The midwives that cared for her were careful how they touched her. They did a minimal number of vaginal exams. During exams, they were careful to let her guide their hands, entering only with her permission, going deeper only when she was composed and could handle it. In early labor, she actually dozed in my arms, and later she participated actively in the delivery. Once her newborn's head and shoulders cleared, the midwife guided Sara's hands to grasp her daughter under her arms and onto her waiting breast. The pediatric staff conducted bedside exams and made sure never to separate this baby from her mother. The birth was an extraordinary victory over her previous births.

Many of us have wounds. Thankfully, most of them are not as devastating as Sara's. Some wounds we can heal via prayer and profound shifts in our attitudes. Others, especially those inflicted by violent touch, seem to need a counter-touch that cares.

What makes the difference between those who are able to heal through life's challenges and those who fall into re-injury? This is a question that I will carry in my heart for the rest of my life. Our choices and determination certainly play a key role. Sometimes it is the grace of a loving person who reaches and catches us, refusing to let us fall. This is not control, but rather containment – safe holding which allows one to let go of old survival patterns and reorganize in a healthier way.

Acceptance

The Slonimer Rebbe teaches:

Every day God gives us exactly what we need for the life purpose we have entered this world to live. No two people are alike and no one else can fix for another that special thing that he/she was brought into this world to repair. A person does not know what their special mission is, but it is written, "Look, I am placing before you today life (blessing) and death (curse)." Look and contemplate all the conditions that surround you, because God, Who is good and bestows goodness, gives these life conditions precisely so that through them you can fulfill your special work in this world. When we accept these life conditions and work with them then it is the greatest blessing. Only if we do not listen is it a curse.

It is crucial to accept that real change often occurs at our breaking edge, precisely where we are wounded or frightened.

When I prepare women for birth, I encourage them to see their contractions as allies and welcome them. It helps to cheer them on. Take a deep breath and relax deeply as you feel the contraction rise, soften your jaw, drop your shoulders, sway with it, breathe through it for as long as you can. If you "lose it" and tighten against it, don't worry. It will continue to work for you anyway, but as soon as the intensity of the peak passes, begin to relax, say, "Yes, it is passing," shake off any fear and tension. Now you can let go totally, get comfortable, breathe deeply, and gather your strength for what will come next.

Sometimes ten minutes pass between contractions. In transition, it can be barely one. Sometimes we think that we don't have any pause at all. Even a one-minute break can create a sense of well-being, and one minute can be stretched to two by greeting the contraction in relaxed openness and releasing the tension as soon as the contraction hints at easing.

Making the most of the pauses sustains me through the hardest periods of my life. Somehow, I learn to accept the tears, anger, fear, or weakness, and the moment it begins to ease, I really let it go and draw new inspiration. Since God "renews the work of creation" every day, then every breath and every moment we and the world have another chance. I can relax into the extraordinary range of new possibilities.

I marvel daily at the Israeli ability to go on through war and the current terror attacks while living as normally as possible. Our spirits are frequently sustained by humor about the very things that weigh so heavily on us. When trouble strikes, we have to respond; constant worry only causes fatigue. Only a relaxed mind and a buoyant spirit can respond quickly to danger.

Birth transforms the birthing couple and their caretakers. Meeting the danger with awe, stepping out of our normal realms of control into God's vast and magnificent dance, can renew all involved. Birth's rhythmic sway, from crisis to relief, from pain to pause, from cries to laughter and ultimately to celebration provides a training ground for facing life with optimistic pragmatism.

Not only does childbirth afford us this golden opportunity, but each day finds us birthing ourselves to maturity as well. We seem to return to our broken edges, drawn as if by some invisible magnet. From the far reaches of the universe, a whisper of faith tells us: "You can heal it this time." This is your moment to birth a better self and a healthier world. May God in his infinite kindness fill our hearts with the faith to meet these precious opportunities with courage. May today's challenge truly be a *havaya metakenet*, a taste of redemption.

For further reading:

Weisberg, Chana. *Expecting Miracles: Finding Meaning and Spirituality in Pregnancy through Judaism*. Jerusalem: 2004.

This is what the Holy One said to Israel: My children, what do I seek from you? I seek no more than that you love one another and honor one another.

Tanna de-Vei Eliyahu

Friends Can Hear

Leah Golumb

Have you ever wondered how friends hear each others' silent whispers? How the cry of one woman can touch the entire universe? "Kol Yisroel chaverim" – all Israel are friends. We are one soul, one family – all connected. The word *chaver* in Hebrew has the same root as *chibur* – a connection. A mother is tied to her child with an umbilical cord of love and care; a husband and wife are connected to each other through holiness and purity in ways no one else may touch or even witness or really understand; and friends are tied to one another with bonds of love and respect and concern and faith. One person suffering – a family in crisis and then a transatlantic network opens up to help. One person crying and soul sisters hear that cry and come forward.

This is my story.

My father, *olav hashalom* – may he rest in peace – died at a very early age (I was sixteen) from an internal illness called polycystic disease. At nineteen, I was diagnosed and began to come to terms with this disease and was determined not to let it rule me. I pushed myself, sometimes relentlessly, to *davka* be the opposite of conservative, healthwise. I tried to prove in every way possible that I would not be limited by my fate or controlled by it. The arrogance of my youth, I guess. Marathon swimming, trick diving, biking down the West Coast – pushing, always pushing to go the extra mile.

Eventually Hashem sent me to Eretz Yisroel and I married and began a family with my husband, Michael. A daughter, a son, another son. Already I was beginning to show the effects of my disease but I wouldn't let it rule me. After being advised by every doctor and/or healer not to get pregnant, either right now or possibly ever, I got pregnant again. Hashem had listened to my inner prayer to have triplets. I carried my babies full term and delivered three healthy, fully mature baby boys. Triplets! Yeah, even I was stunned!

After their birth I was in a car accident and was injured and laid up again. But nothing could hold me down for long. By now I discovered my disease had spread to my liver, not just my kidneys. But I kept on and worked hard raising six children with very little livelihood, but managed to maintain a cheerful and warm home and was happy with my blessings. As the years went by my health slowly and insidiously deteriorated, but my attitude was that I should just keep on trucking and therefore would be able to continue. As long as I didn't let myself lie down or get down for long, I could stay up and keep doing. I worked as the mikveh lady of my yishuv (settlement), I taught classes in Torah and chassidut, I was a certified swim teacher and lifeguard and worked for the Board of Education and privately. I ran my home – baking bread, making noodles from scratch, washing floors and dishes and doing homework with some of my kids while trying to spend lots of time with my other kids and well, I was one busy woman. But it was good. As the pain became stronger and stronger so did my will. "I will not give in. I will not stop. I will not ask for help." It went against my grain to think that I would need someone else's help. That would be a defeat. Eventually my body just couldn't keep on functioning and I knew I was wearing down. It was time for dialysis and I knew that was not the way I wanted to go. I still could conjure up the images of my father after being on dialysis. I had felt as though I had already lost him. Every time I walked in the dialysis unit at my hospital I would have a panic attack – no breath, tunnel vision and an ever clearer vision that this was not my way. So many heartbreaking stories, so much exhaustion connected to dialysis and also I had heard that the chances for a successful transplant were much greater in those who had not done dialysis at all. I began in earnest to look for a donor. Hashem sent us messages in many ways. We had heard of different agents dealing in this vista of transplants abroad. There were people who knew how to find donors, people who wanted to be donors but nothing panned out. My son went to a doctor for his problem with his kidneys and his doctor mentioned an agent he knew of and we decided it was time to go with it. But I needed to raise one hundred thousand dollars for the transplant which was going to happen in South Africa and I needed to raise enough money to live on while recovering before I could work again. But now I was really in a dilemma – I couldn't ask for help, could I? It went against my nature. I had an anxiety attack if I had to ask someone the time. And time was ticking away. I didn't want my donor to change her mind or give her kidney to someone else. My first call was to my dearest friend Breindi – next-door neighbor, friend in need and in deed, soul sister and confidante. I squeaked out my idea that I needed to raise an enormous sum of money. And so began an

427

incredible odyssey of chesed and determination. One friend called another and soon a network was up and running. Miriam thought to use the email. She and her mom, Naomi, wrote the first letter that eventually circled the globe many times over in many variations. Then my cousin Yossi told me that rather than think of trying to raise so much money so quickly I should think to raise little sums of money from lots of people. And so it went for the most part. Abby put out a poster and got her community in Riverdale involved. Neshama put a letter and an appeal on her email list – in three minutes she raised two thousand dollars. My cousin Dori in Karnei Shomron raised money in her yishuv where no one even knows me. My cousins Moishie and Penina raised money in Efrat. Laya in New Jersey began to contact high school alumni from my class of 1971 – some of whom I haven't seen or heard from since then! The circle was ever-broadening and widening. On and on until the circles began to overlap and people were sending letters to people who had themselves sent out a letter. My *mechutanim* in LA appealed to their community. Many people worked through their shuls to ask for and raise money for me. Esther helped me arrange a nonprofit fund in Israel and Eric helped to set one up in Great Neck, NY. The secretary there, Shoshana, worked non-stop for over a month opening letters and dealing with the money and receipts and so on. Zelda mobilized her already up-and-running chessed committee and had kids knocking on doors all over the place. Family in California reached out and helped.

I called out to Hashem and I whispered to my friend and a circle of friends surrounded me with their loving concern, their prayers and their hopes for me and a willingness to put themselves out over and over – phoning, writing, asking, recording and most of all loving me and helping me the most in my time of need. I have never felt so cherished in my life and I wish I could reach out to everyone who helped in any way to bless them with everything they need to continue serving Hashem in the sweetest way. When I returned home after my operation I found my home surrounded by flowers and plants that the ladies of my moshav had planted in my garden to cheer me up and welcome me as I walked in. My boys and their friends had straightened my yard and prepared it for my lady friends to make it beautiful. My sons planted grass out in my backyard so all through the winter as I rested in my bed I could look out on the beautiful lawn and new trees they had planted for me. Most people knew that after a transplant you cannot be exposed to other people's germs – I was on very high doses of immunosuppressant drugs which meant no visitors. But everyday Dina came and brought some bread she had made or some soup or a challah for Shabbat for my family. Shayna came and cooked a few times a week. Niffi came and cleaned and now Aliza still helps me around the house. Rachel Bryna brought me books to read and Sara lent me more books to read. My daughter

Bacall and Josh, my son-in-law, and Yedid, my grandson, came all the time to spend time with me and just be there. My son Ohev and Mayaan, my daughter-in-law shlepped from Tsfat to visit for Shabbatot. My son Maoz cooked and cleaned and fixed things all over the house and my triplets, Yehudah, Elnatan and Elishama, showered me with their loving presence constantly dovening for me always. Michael was always there, holding me up physically and spiritually, ever cheerful, ever positive. So much chessed, so much kindness. When I was so afraid of asking for help in a way it was saying I needed to be in control. I can take care of everything. I don't need anyone or anything. More and more I am learning we all need each other, we all need to learn from each other. If you are in charge of everything there might not be room for all the wonderful things that happen when you are open to other people.

I still don't like to ask what time it is; I still don't like to ask from someone else a favor; but I am learning that my friends do love me and want to help and want to feel they are a part of my recovery also. What a blessing to be surrounded by love.

I am preparing for the next operation to remove the remaining enormous and very sick kidney. I will be down for a while, I know, but I am praying Hashem will bless me to recover quickly to be there for my family, for my community and for that someone who may come knocking on my door asking for help. I pray I will have the courage to step outside myself to do what needs to be done. Actually, if we are all connected on the most inside level then I need to have the courage to step within myself to that place where we are all one and then do what needs to be done. I pray I can also become a part of the circle of chesed to which Yidden everywhere belong. The late Slonimer Rebbe of blessed memory says the other word in Hebrew for friend is *yedid* – *yad be-yad* – hand in hand. (My grandson's name is Yedid.) May we walk hand in hand to not just greet Mashiach but to bring it on already. May we be truly blessed to be friends with all of Israel.

For further reading:

Salamon, Julie. *Rambam's Ladder: A Meditation on Generosity and Why It Is Necessary to Give*. New York, NY: 2003.

Raz, Simcha. *A Tzadik in Our Time: The Life of Rabbi Aryeh Levin*. Jerusalem, Israel: 1976.

Twersky, Abraham J. *Do Unto Others: How Good Deeds Can Change Your Life*. Kansas City, MO: 1997.

"May it be Your will, Lord my God and God of my forebears, that you provide nourishment for your humble creation, this tiny child, plenty of milk, as much as he needs.

"Give me the disposition and inclination to find the time to nurse him patiently until he is satisfied.

"Cause me to sleep lightly so that the moment he cries I will hear and respond...."

By an anonymous author of tkhines, or women's supplications, written in the Middle Ages

His sister said to Pharaoh's daughter, "Shall I go and summon for you a wet nurse from the Hebrew women, who will nurse the boy for you?"... So the woman took the boy and nursed him.

Exodus 2:7–9

Nursing at the Dawning of Day

Ruth Seligman

Each year at *Pesach*, we are asked to experience the *seder*'s recounting of the Exodus as a time when we ourselves are leaving Egypt. Throughout the years during which I sat at my parents' *seder* table I imagined the scene joyfully, picturing my family and our invited friends able to leap from bondage toward freedom. Those were the young years for all of us, when to imagine myself leaving Egypt was to imagine someone untethered to belongings or responsibilities. In my youthful vision, I left Egypt in an age-appropriate way, alongside my able-bodied parents.

When I became a mother I realized how generations themselves have internal ages. It was as a mom who pushed a double stroller down a city street, often leaving such essential items as an Elmo toy in my wake, that I understood what it must have meant to rush away from one home to journey toward another home as yet unknown, with children straggling behind. Not until I became a daughter-in-law trying to negotiate my father-in-law's wheelchair toward a leveled corner crossing did I fully comprehend what it meant to keep up with the throng headed toward the miracle of the splitting sea. Seeing one's own self as a seeker of freedom came to mean a release not only from physical slavery, but from spiritual slavery. The idea of pursuing freedom anew in each generation represented an appreciation for the guideposts that tradition and *halacha* provided along life's journeys, no matter how challenging. Indeed, such lessons of maturing experience harkened back to one I had learned earlier, when I sat *shiva* for my own father. Amid the sorrow, we bereaved acquired a respect for the psychological acuity our sages demonstrated in laying down the laws of mourning, dividing this time from *aninut* (the period of time immediately after death before burial) to burial, to the first three days of loss, to thirty days, and to a year of progressive comfort and ascendance for both the soul of the deceased and the heart of the mourner.

This learning was to be reinforced for me once and for all, and perhaps more tellingly than ever before, in a most unlikely circumstance – through an assignment I had as a writer for the United Nations. Among the most suspect of institutions in the eyes of observant Jews, the UN was the focus of my professional life when I worked there and at several of its related agencies for nearly fifteen years. During that time I often faced or dodged the question of how a committed Jew could work for an organization so apparently anti-Israel. There were times I had to rationalize the answer, particularly on days when every Security Council vote turned against Israel. Yet, there were also times when I took pride in the real *kiddush Hashem,* the sanctification of God's name, I believe occurred whenever a lunchtime Torah-learning group convened among fellow Jewish staffers on UN premises or when Israel itself partnered with UN-related aid agencies to supply irrigation technology or social-service training to a developing country. But, mainly and selfishly, I loved the job of writing about the needs of people throughout the world, of traveling to remote countries in order to report their stories, and of believing I was fulfilling a mitzvah of *tikkun olam..*

Just before December, one decade ago, I was asked to write an article for the *BFHI News*, a newsletter published by the nutrition section of the United Nations Children's Fund (UNICEF). *BFHI News* was the print voice of the Baby Friendly Hospital Initiative, an internationally-endorsed and, in some countries, legislatively-promoted, agenda to encourage women to breastfeed their babies. Recommended throughout the developed world for reasons ranging from the health benefits that breastfeeding provides to the psychological support of newborns these societies have the luxury of citing, in many developing countries breastfeeding is on the political map because it is absolutely critical to the well-being of infants living in poverty. Where food is scarce and balanced diets are compromised, substituting expensive formula for natural breast milk can deprive the rest of a baby's family of costly food. In places where water quality is so poor that mixing it with formula can actually be lethal, breastfeeding is seen as a nutritional necessity. Thus, in order to promote its work in spreading the BFHI concept in developing countries, this newsletter was packed with information about breastfeeding practice and related legislation and distributed to individual women and to government policy-makers through UN offices around the world.

For this December 1994 issue, the *BFHI News* editor sought to depart from the publication's usual articles on medical research or legal directives supporting breastfeeding and take advantage of winter's Judeo-Christian "holiday season" by offering an account of what the world's religions say about breastfeeding. No doubt because of my reputation as a religiously observant person, the assignment came to me. Yet in the process of researching my piece I was to learn more than any other reader, for the assignment launched me on a continuing pursuit of references to the act of nursing in Jewish tradition. I found them everywhere – not only in Jewish law but also in the Biblical writings, psalms, and in the special prayers of penitence said before the High Holidays. Their wisdom also offered insights into the human soul and enabled me to take pride in sharing the wisdom of our tradition and our sages, while introducing its groundedness in natural law and human consciousness as liberating and uplifting, and as a guidepost on the path of a just society. At the same time, like the *seders* and *shiva* of years before, my research and writing strengthened my own observance and personal resolve to steer our children along its path.

These many years later I continue to find references – to nursing, still, but also to all the other progressions of life to which I had not been as attuned as I might have been had I not been experiencing them personally. I became alert to all the goings out of Egypt that are physically and spiritually within the realm of life experience. When my nursing years subsided, I became acutely aware of our Sages' writings about the inner life of children, about childrearing, and about children's education. Today, as my age advances, related verses leap from the page.

The assignment for *BFHI News* came to me after I had completed nursing one child, was still nursing a two-year-old, and was pregnant with a third. Nursing came naturally and easily. I had observed my sister share this experience with her babies in the years before I had children of my own, and was fortunate to be able to fashion a freelance writing career that allowed me the luxury of breastfeeding nearly any time the babies requested as long as I was not out of the house reporting. My husband, writer Jonathan Mark, gave all his support to my career adjustment.

I nursed because I knew it was healthy for the child. But, again, I had an underlying selfish reason. All the nursing literature describes breastfeeding as an act that can strengthen the bond between mother and child. Though I never discussed my choice to nurse well past infancy with friends who chose not to breastfeed or who were unable to, physically or financially, because of job restrictions, because they were adoptive parents, or because the practice did not seize them emotionally, I saw my action selfishly as some kind of insurance. To me nursing offered a subconscious connection for anticipated times when I knew I would be a less-than-patient mother to a toddler, when teenage arguments would erupt, when battles over homework would ensue. But mainly I nursed because the feeling of my babies' cheeks, the sound of their lips smacking in search of their food, and the satisfied sighs that indicated their bellies were full – to say nothing of the joy of holding tight each child I fed… well, that was pure delirium.

Still, it was not until I began writing that I learned that Jewish tradition validated my personal yearning for a deep tie to cushion my future relationship with my children during times of upheaval that my anticipated failings as a mom would render inevitable. In the Talmud's Tractate *Kethuboth* (60a), Rav Ashi says that a blind child knows its mother's breasts by smell and taste. An infant who already knows its mother may not be given to another woman to suckle because of danger to the baby's life if the baby refuses to feed (*Tosefta Niddah 2:5*). Numerous laws provide for wet-nursing should the baby's natural mother die, be unable to breastfeed, or choose not to, but, the law prevents a mother who desires to breastfeed from being deprived of that right.

It was also as if I had not yet left Egypt that I discovered the liturgical and historical connotations of nursing in verses of *Torah* I had heard hundreds of times before. Each verse I was capable of finding for my *BFHI News* article resonated to me with a sense of private privilege that elevated the simply-accomplished and physically natural act of nursing my children to the link I had often sought to connect me with the heritage of our Matriarchs and Patriarchs. Transmitting my study to others afforded me great pride in a heritage of later generations of mothers who recited *tkhinot*, or supplications, that they wrote themselves, for enough milk to nourish their offspring and enough wisdom to raise them.

In my article I was able to share the stories of Sarah, Chanah, and Ruth, and the prescriptions of a tradition based upon their life experiences. In one instance I wrote these thoughts:

> Through Sarah's joyful nursing of Isaac we learn that breast milk should never be considered impossible for a mother to provide once she has given birth, and that a nursing mother is able to supply milk to a child for at least two full years. In Sarah's incredulous appreciation of having given birth to a son in her old age and of her ability to nurture him herself, she asks:

Mi millel le-Avraham henikah banim Sarah? Ki yaladeti ben le-zekunav. "Who is the One Who said Sarah would nurse children? For I have borne a son in his [Abraham's] old age!" (Genesis 21:7) Nearly nine hundred years ago the great Jewish sage Rashi interpreted these lines to mean that Abraham and Sarah had to prove that Isaac was their child and not a baby the couple adopted in order to establish a line of inheritance for Abraham's great wealth and preeminent position as a leader. Thus, Sarah invited all the families of the princes of the community, as well as of other nations as well, to give her their babies to nurse, and she fed them. Others have noted that using the plural in the context of Sarah's nursing referred to the generations of Jewish people who would descend from this matriarch – the sucklings who were as numerous as stars in the sky or sand along the seashore.

The act of nursing was so auspicious a first step in the life of a child and, in this case, a future Patriarch, that Avraham hosted a grand celebration upon the weaning of his son Yitzchak. The first feast noted in the Bible, the commentator Rashi interprets it to have taken place when the baby was twenty-four months old as Abraham marked Isaac's transition toward independence, to the confident walking, talking, and acquisition of understanding that takes place when a child is two.

The first book of Samuel begins with the story of Chanah, who so desired a child that her earnest prayers for a baby have been cited as the basis for all prayer. She wanted a baby so badly that she promised Eli, the High Priest of the sanctuary at Shiloh, that if she had a boy she would give him over in service to God and the sanctuary. When Chanah gave birth she told her husband Elkanah that she would not join the family's annual pilgrimage to the sanctuary in Shiloh but rather would remain at home to nurse the long-awaited child until he was weaned (Shmuel 1:1–2:10). This period of nursing and weaning has been set at two years of age, causing commentators to name this as an appropriate length of time to nurse. Some commentators even allow for nursing up to five years if it is of necessary benefit to the health of the child.

The injunction in the last will and testament of R' Yehudah HeChasid that a mother should nurse her offspring for the first time from her left breast because it is closest to the heart was a pleasure for me to pass along. The heart was believed to be the place in a human's physiology where wisdom originated – an "intelligent place," as we read in *Tehillim* 103:3. Indeed, a current source from a humanitarian aid agency that instructs uninitiated women in third world countries on how to breastfeed suggests feeding first from the left side, a more comfortable and natural place. And, in another Talmudic source, the very fact of a woman's anatomy renders her feeding to be holy, separating human life from animal life, where teats are near the genitals, rather than further above. Yet, uttering respect for all of God's creations, numerous animal images are assigned to the very natural instinct of any mother, human or animal, to nurse. *Pesachim* 112a states: "More than a calve wishes to suck does a cow desire to suckle."

The article, and subsequent speeches I was asked to give, also addressed the widespread influence of Sarah's story through its dissemination in the Five Books of Moses, a source for both the New Testament and the Koran. I described the weaning ceremonies of the Hindus and presented literature on Alexander of Greece following a Biblically-inspired two-year course of feeding by wet-nurses. I recounted ancient images of breastfeeding in iconographic Asian art, and Confucian writing that harks back to historic interpretations of three years being the proper time for nursing before weaning takes place. I recounted the *tkhines* composed and recited by Jewish women throughout the ages asking for both the physical ability to provide enough milk and the psychological ability to have the patience to do so, and traced similar supplications in other traditions. I told the story of Ruth handing her baby to her mother-in-law Naomi to nurse, and noted that this story has been cited as a source in some cultures to prove medically – and for economic reasons, where wet-nursing is a profession – that once a woman has nursed, she is capable of doing so again even if the child is not her own.

Yet perhaps most important to the audience of impoverished women in developing countries whom this article was meant to support and inspire was the way that Jewish law, codified so very long ago, considers the nursing mother an important contributor to her household, both to its financial security and to the important task of child-rearing and education – and, by extension, to the well being of future society. Jewish law prescribes special considerations in recognition of a mother's nursing status. *Mishnah Ketubbot* 5:9 enjoins: "And if she were nursing, they (the Sages) reduce for her from the work of her hands, and they add for her onto her food."

In many parts of the world a woman's work, to this very day, has been calculated to extend over an eighteen-hour continuous period. Rising before dawn to walk miles past dried-up wells to fetch clean water for a family's drinking, bathing, washing, and cooking needs, returning home in the still-early hours to light a fire and grind grain for the day's meals, getting children off to school where opportunities for education exist, and then heading out to the fields, gardens or artisan shops to grow the family's food, sell the village produce, or work in income-providing crafts, the ability to fit breastfeeding into a woman's overwhelming schedule is a luxury. The practice is replaced by handing a newborn to a sibling, most certainly a girl if the baby has a sister, who props up the infant with a bottle of formula mixed with poor water. Not a few cases of disease and death result, and many a young girl-child in the caregiver's role is deprived of the chance for an education by the demands of the household. Thus, the cycle of illness, poverty, and lost opportunity continues. These scenarios are not exaggerations. I have walked alongside women in Africa on such a typical day.

I am not a scholar either of Torah or of much else. I'm not even all that great a mother. My nights before one of my children's fifth-grade building project is due at school, when one sibling has to be driven to a tutor, another to play practice, and I have a work deadline to meet, could easily be factored into my qualifications in a mother-of-the-year competition: I'd get the award for "worst." But in June 1995 I enjoyed a tiny bit of celebrity as both a nursing mother and someone knowledgeable about religion. I was by then working as an editor at *BFHI News* and covering the preparatory conference before the Third United Nations International Conference on Women scheduled to take place in Beijing in the fall. Breastfeeding, as a health and economic issue and as a woman's right, was on the agenda of the document to be voted upon at that final conference. Nursing lobbyists from around the world had gathered at the "Prep-Com" in New York to make sure their point of view was represented.

My third child was due in three months. The women in the constituency to this conference were the most encouraging of partners, offering me their chairs in crowded meeting rooms or suggesting natural remedies from their own cultures to alleviate the small discomforts of the final term of pregnancy. They applauded the topic I was writing on, as well as my efforts to mix family and work life, with a warm geniality I had rarely experienced in Western society. These women included distinguished physicians and professors from India in colorful, sweeping saris, and activists from the Philippines who told me how important *BFHI News* was to the women for whom they advocated. They commented specifically on the inclusion in the newsletter of the article on religion, and on how the ideas they learned from the writings of the Jewish sages helped them with their advocacy work. Some shared stories of nursing and weaning rituals in their own cultures and religions. Others praised my citations of Talmud concerning a man's economic obligation to his wife during the time she is either nursing or securing a wet nurse for a couple's child as beneficial to society. They also offered me studies and findings on the health and economic benefits of nursing that would help me in my future writing on behalf of BFHI.

Although my nursing days are now over, if with grave humility I may accept this honor, my role as an educator to my children continues. If the words of both our sages and more recent commentators – Rav Klonymus Kalman among them

– are to be acknowledged, this is a role a parent partakes of in partnership with *Hashem*. Thus, in my days of continual discovery of the depths of wisdom of our heritage, in my continuing going forth from Egypt, in the *shivas* we observe and the *britot* and *simchat bat* ceremonies we celebrate, in the cycles of ritual renewal of each year, each season, and each week that our *chagim* and *Shabbatot* provide, I see again and again the physical and economic privilege that I had to nurse my children as the one thing I was able to do without struggle, without impatience, without ignorance, without question, to fulfill a fraction of my role in participating in the holy partnership of raising a child.

Today I am struck not only by the historical experience of nursing as recorded in *Tanach*, not only by the Sarahs, the Batyas, the Chanahs, the Ruths and Naomis who nursed their children, but by the way in which the language referring to breastfeeding a baby occurs at essential moments in the Jewish people's relationship with God.

What is the most basic acknowledgement of that relationship that we have? It is the recitation of the *Shema*. It is the *Shema* we utter upon waking, and upon our deathbeds. In generations deprived of beds for their death, it was the *Shema* that was recited as those Jews became martyrs. The *Shema* is the prayer we teach our children before any other. When do we say *Shema*? The Talmud in *Berakhot* (9:14d) tells this story concerning the time for reciting *Shema* in the evening and in the morning. In the evening, it is:

"Until the end of the first watch," said R. Eliezer.

The Sages say: "Until midnight."

Rabban Gamliel says, "Until the break of dawn."

Rabbi Eliezer takes the view that the night is divided into three watches.

> And [in heaven] over each watch the Holy One, blessed be he, sits and roars like a lion, as it is said, "The Lord roars from on high and raises his voice from his holy habitation, he roars mightily because of his fold" (Jer. 25:30). The indication of each watch is as follows: at the first watch, an ass brays, at the second, dogs yelp, at the third, an infant sucks at its mother's breast or a woman whispers to her husband.

The Talmud asks: if he is reckoning from the end of the several watches, then what need is there to give a sign for the end of the third watch? The third watch is marked by the coming of the day. The answer is this: It is important for the recitation of the *Shema* in the case of someone who sleeps in a darkened room and does not know when it is time for reciting the *Shema*. When a woman whispers to her husband or an infant sucks from the breast of its mother, it is time for him to get up and to recite the *Shema*. This division of watches is also cited as the time when we are to be engaged in pursuit of Torah... and that is at all hours of the day.

Telling, too, are at which places in the Jewish lexicon references to nursing appear. They are found in the stories of our greatest historic figures: Avraham and Sarah, our first founding father and mother, in the story of Yaakov, patriarch of the twelve sons from which the twelve tribes of Israel would emerge, in the biography of Moshe, who delivered the Jewish people from slavery, from extinction, and crafted us into a nation, and in the narrative of Shmuel, whose life work continued that of Moshe's as he stood at the precipice of our history in our land overseeing the succession of prophets and kings who would guide our further development as a historically identified people.

Sarah and Avraham established the very legitimacy of their line and heritage through the act of nursing their one child, by having Sarah nurse many children to prove that she was a mother capable of bearing a son and, subsequently, a nation. On his deathbed Yaakov blessed his son, the great leader Yosef, with blessings of breast and womb (*Bereshit* 49:25). This blessing, according to the midrash (*Bereshit Rabbah* 98:20), refers to the love of the wife of his heart, Rachel, "Blessed be the breasts that suckled thee and the womb that gave birth to thee." In so doing, Yaakov elevated Rachel's natural act of physical nurturing into one deserving of eternal reward both for this mother of Yosef and for mothers throughout Jewish history.

Moshe was returned from the hands of an Egyptian surrogate mother to be nursed by a Hebrew woman who, unbeknownst to Pharoah's daughter, was Yocheved, Moshe's very own mother. As the midrash teaches, it was at her breast that Moshe received his first education, an education so powerful that words whispered to him in infancy transcended years of education as an Egyptian noble and enabled Moshe to emerge as deliverer of the Jewish people rather than grow up to become a prince of Egypt and an oppressor of the Jews. Shmuel became the prophet to anoint kings – the kings of Israel who would settle the land and build a dwelling for God. Where did Shmuel's relationship with Hashem and the Jewish people begin? In the arms of his breastfeeding mother, who did not give her son over to the sanctuary until he was fully nursed and weaned and, presumably, launched on his first phase of education as a Jew and a Jewish leader.

When are these stories read? The nursing done by Sarah and Chanah are both recounted on the first day of Rosh HaShanah, when we observe the birthday of the world and commit ourselves anew to lives dedicated to pursuing holiness. The tale of Moshe, Batya, and the intervention of Moshe's sister, the prophetess Miriam, is told during the Pesach *seder*, when we celebrate becoming a nation and embark on the road toward God's granting of the Torah. The story of Ruth and Naomi is read on the holiday of Shavuot, when we commemorate the giving of the Torah itself and our acceptance of its guidance. The Book of Ruth concludes with the birth and nursing of a child who is to become the ancestor of King David and the progenitor of the line of descendents who will lead to the birth of our Redeemer.

Moshe, the greatest prophet of all of Jewish history, himself compares his role of leader to that of a nursing mother. Having brought the Jews from slavery, he beseeches God: "Did I conceive this people or give birth to it that You say to me, 'Carry them in your bosom, as a nursing mother carries a suckling, to the Land that You swore to its forefathers?'" (Numbers 11:12) Moshe, having birthed the Hebrew nation, finds raising its people a challenge. Even after the Children of Israel are free and have been granted the light of Torah they complain as they journey toward the Holy Land. Like small children, they think only of the moment. Unable to visualize their future, they look back on their days of slavery, when they recall only the good, only the sweets of the land of Egypt. For Moshe, the burden is at long last too much. He cries out to God for help, using the analogy of suckling to convince the One Moshe has served for so long. Apparently convinced by this potent analogy God steps in to help, offering Moshe a complement of seventy elders to assist in dealing with the peoples' complaints. This august panel will eventually become the basis for the Sanhedrin, the Jewish High Court, and the rules of the Sanhedrin, the basis for all of *halachic* authority that develops subsequent to the divinely written laws of Torah. The Sanhedrin becomes the precedent for Talmudic authority of old and for rabbinic authority to this day.

Each Jewish person who ever lived, and each Jewish child of the future, has a relationship with God that continues those established by the lofty founders and prophets of the Jewish people. We express that relationship most often through prayer, particularly prayer uttered at critical times in our lives. One such time is during the observance of Tisha be-Av, the day that commemorates the destruction of the Temples in Jerusalem and the Jewish peoples' expulsion from that Holy City. On that day, we read from *Eicha*, the Book of Lamentations, a powerful text that drives us to recall not only the negative actions that set into motion this darkest period of our long history but also the continuing missed opportunities to pursue holiness. In recounting the woes and wrongdoings that led to the destruction of God's dwelling place on earth, the people of Israel are compared unfavorably to jackals. So dire has been the behavior of the Children of Israel become, even at the most essential level of human conduct, that we hear that the jackal – at least – still nurses its young, while the mothers of Israel have turned their breasts away. (Eicha 4:3). So deep is the sadness we experience on Tisha be-Av, that the Torah comes to our rescue a week later, when we observe

Shabbat Nachamu, the Sabbath of Comfort. The *haftarah,* or prophetic reading following the Torah portion of that Shabbos, asks us to take comfort: We will one day return to our Holy city as a complete people under God's care, when Hashem's willingness to take us back is likened to the feeling of "a shepherd, who brings close to his breast the one who suckles." (Isaiah 40:11)

In the days before Rosh HaShanah we are given an opportunity to focus our thoughts for the coming Holy Days, and the time of repentance before Hashem metes out each year's judgment. The process starts the week before the New Year with *selichot* services, or prayers for forgiveness of our transgressions. The *selichot* prayers recited before Rosh HaShanah and Yom Kippur contain lines in which we beseech God in the name of His own grandeur to listen to our thoughts. We also ask him to forgive us in the name of the tiny "nursing infant." In this liturgy even a nursing baby is empowered with the status of a supplicant able to represent us before the Almighty.

Then there is the Book of Psalms to which we turn daily, and specifically during special holidays, services, and celebrations. We also turn to them to for a diverse set of personal reasons – to heal the sick, to express great joy, or simply to comfort our souls. King David, the sweet singer of Israel and the author of these Psalms, derived comfort in their very writing, saying to *Hashem* in *Tehillim* 131:2 "Surely I have stilled and quieted my soul like a suckling upon its mother; like a suckling was my soul within me." *Im lo shiviti ve-domamti nafshi ke-gamul alei imo, ka-gamul alai nafshi.*

Rashi writes that a *"gamul"* is one who sucks at the breast. This definition is a curious one because *"gamul"* appears in many places in the Scriptures and refers to an infant who has been weaned from his mother's milk. As the commentator Radak explains it (*Parshandatha, Yerushalmi* Sanhedrin 2:4), this means: "Like a suckling was my soul with me. My soul was with me before you as an infant sucking at its mother's breast." Radak explains further that David asserts that he calmed and quieted his soul like a weaned child on its mother, suggesting, "Just as a child, when weaned from its mother's breasts, begins to develop and walk little by little, supporting itself on its mother, so did I conduct my soul. I quieted it so that it would not rely on its own intellect in such matters but rather on teachers and tradition, which can be compared to the mother, 'so did I wean my soul and not rely on my understanding.'" The Radak adds that David emphasizes the importance of the mother in this growth process by repeating: "like a suckling was my soul with me."

My research and writing of this article a decade ago brought me at last to this Psalm. I wondered then – hoped – that it was not too far a stretch to believe that such a comparison sanctifies the mother's role in the hour of nursing as one that complements Jewish teachings without which even a King would not be complete.

I have lost my temper with my children. I have been late to pick them up from school and misplaced a homework assignment in the disarray of my own papers. I have failed my family in many ways. Most of all, I have been negligent in failing to educate myself enough in the ways of Torah to teach my children all that I wish I had been able to in our home, in my kitchen, or at my Shabbos table.

Yet I have had the great privilege of nursing my children at the hour when it is proper to say *Shema*, at the hour when this prayer was whispered over centuries by our Jewish ancestors at the moment they ascended to Heaven or in the waking hours of affirming *Hashem*'s eternity and our unity with His name. Mine was the privilege of nursing at dawn, at the hour when each person on earth regains the opportunity for a bright new beginning at the start of each day, indeed, for a bright new future. For the future is, after all, the very essence of every child's life.

For this God-given privilege I feel forever blessed.

Dedicated to my sister Susan Seligman Mandel, who inspired my nursing experience, to Jonathan Mark, who supported my efforts to juggle my work so I could nurse, and to Sara Noa, Rivka Yona, and Zev Mordechai Mark.

For further reading:

Abramov, Tehilla. *Straight from the Heart: A Torah Perspective on Mothering through Nursing*. New York/Jerusalem: 1990.

ABOUT THE CONTRIBUTORS

Emily Benedek is the author of *The Wind Won't Know Me: A History of the Navajo-Hopi Land Dispute; Beyond the Four Corners of the World: A Navajo Woman's Journey* and *Through the Unknown, Remembered Gate: A Spiritual Journey*. She lives in New York City with her husband and two daughters.

Gila Berkowitz is a medical journalist and the author of the forthcoming novels, *The Devil's Diet* and *The Ugly Sister: A Novel of the Holocaust*.

Varda Branfman wrote station breaks for public television, was a copywriter for a major drug company in New York City, and taught poetry in rural New England public schools, nursing homes, and prisons, before landing in Israel. For the past twenty years she has been busy raising her family in Jerusalem, as well as continuing to write and teach. She is the author of *I Remembered in the Night Your Name* and the co-author, with her husband, of a book on the phenomenon of free loans in the worldwide Orthodox community, *The Hidden World*.

Shoshana S. Cardin is currently the Chairman of the Shoshana S. Cardin School, Baltimore's Independent Jewish High School. She is also the Chairman of the Press Ambassadors, The Israel Project and the Jewish In-Marriage Initiative as well as the Vice President of the Jewish National Fund and the Wilstein Institute. Cardin also serves on the Executive Committee of more than a half dozen national organizations.

In addition to holding countless posts in her home town of Baltimore, Shoshana Cardin was President of the Council of Jewish Federations (1984–1987); Chairman of the National Conference of Soviet Jewry (1988–1992); Chairman, Conference of Presidents of Major American Jewish Organizations (1991–1992); Chairman, CLAL, National Center for Learning and Leadership (1992–1994); Chairman, United Israel Appeal (1994–1998); and the President of JTA, the Global News Agency of the Jewish People. She has won numerous awards for her efforts on behalf of the Jewish people and was twice named among Maryland's Top 100 women. Cardin has been awarded an honorary Doctor of Humane Letters from Boston Hebrew College, Baltimore Hebrew University, Bar-Ilan University, The Jewish Theological Seminary, Touro College, Syracuse University and Western Maryland College.

Bella Chagall (1895–1944) is the author of *Burning Lights: A Unique Double Portrait of Russia* (1946). She was the wife of the artist Marc Chagall.

Elizabeth Cohen is the author of *The Family on Beartown Road: A Memoir of Love and Courage* (2004), a memoir about caring for her father and daughter, and co-author of

The Silver Bear and the Scalpel: A Biography of the First Navajo Woman Surgeon (1998). She is a newspaper reporter in Broome County, New York.

Debra B. Darvick's work has appeared in numerous Jewish presses including *Moment, The Forward, Hadassah* and *The Detroit Jewish News,* as well as in *The Chicago Tribune, The Dallas Morning News, The Detroit Free Press* and *The Detroit News.* Her column, "Life in the Jewish Lane," was a monthly fixture on jewishfamily.com. Ms. Darvick's book *This Jewish Life: Stories of Discovery, Connection, and Joy* is now in its third printing. She may be contacted at debradarvick.com.

Wendy Dickstein was born in New Haven, Connecticut and grew up in Australia, where she received an MA in English literature. Wendy lived for several years in England and in India, where her Indian husband was teaching philosophy at Hyderabad University. After living for several years in Los Angeles, Wendy made aliyah with her children in 1986 and now lives in Jerusalem.

Wendy is the literary editor of *B'Or HaTorah.* Her writing has been published there, in *Moment Magazine, The Jerusalem Post* and in other publications both in the US and in Israel. She was a technical writer for a hi-tech company and the editor of *Holyland Magazine,* a monthly journal for tourists, before it ceased publication. She has also edited some thirty books for various Jewish scholars, including thirteen books in the Commentators' series of Torah literature for Rabbi Isaac Sender, a Rosh Yeshiva in Skokie Illinois.

Wendy is married with a son, a daughter and a granddaughter.

Elizabeth Ehrlich lives with her family in Westchester County, New York. She is the author of the award-winning book *Miriam's Kitchen: A Memoir.*

Susan Elster, Ph.D., is a researcher from Carnegie Mellon University's Heinz School of Public Policy and Management. As a consultant to nonprofit organizations and foundations, she designs and implements research aimed at addressing health, education, and employment challenges. Susan and her family arrived in Israel in 2003 and reside in Jerusalem.

Tzivia Emmer is a writer and editor living in Sacramento, California, after having lived for several years in Crown Heights. A mother of five, she grew up in Brooklyn as Iris Siegal. Her work has appeared in *Wellsprings; Feeding among the Lilies: The Wellsprings Anthology,* and other Jewish publications including *Body and Soul: A Kashrus Handbook; Spice and Spirit: The Complete Kosher Jewish Cookbook* and *The Jewish Press.*

Dr. Tamar Frankiel holds a Ph.D. in history of religions from the University of Chicago. She is the Assistant Dean of Students and a professor of Hasidic thought and Jewish spirituality at the Academy of Jewish Religion, Los Angeles.

Dr. Frankiel, who is known as a scholar of American religious history, has published many works on the history of Christianity and American religious history, including studies of religion in California. She has taught at major universities including Stanford, Princeton, the University of California at Berkeley and at Riverside, and the Claremont School of Theology.

She first became internationally known for her work in Jewish spirituality with the 1990 publication of *The Voice of Sarah: Feminine Spirituality and Traditional Judaism*, which highlighted the importance of women in Jewish tradition. Later, she co-authored with Judy Greenfeld two books on prayer: *Minding the Temple of the Soul* (1997) and *Entering the Temple of Dreams* (2000). These books teach ways of enriching our spiritual life through prayer, meditation, movement, and dreams.

Her most recent book is an introduction to Jewish mysticism entitled *The Gift of Kabbalah: Discovering the Secrets of Heaven, Renewing Your Life on Earth* (2001).

Dr. Frankiel lives in Los Angeles with her husband Hershel; they have five children, aged fourteen to twenty-four years.

Jan Feldman received her B.A. from Swarthmore College and her M.A. and Ph.D. in government from Cornell University. She has been an Associate Professor of Political Science at the University of Vermont since 1982 and is currently a visiting professor in the Social Studies Program of Harvard University.

She has published extensively in the area of collaborative weapons production within NATO, Soviet legal theory and ideology. Her recent book, *Lubavitchers as Citizens: A Paradox of Liberal Democracy*, is an exploration of multicultural accommodation. Feldman currently resides in Newton, MA with her four children.

Ruchama King Feuerman lived for ten years in Israel, where she studied and taught Torah to college-age women. Upon returning to the U.S., she received her M.F.A. in fiction writing from Brooklyn College. She has published many works of fiction for adults, young adults and children. Her acclaimed novel, *Seven Blessings* (2003), tells the story of men and women seeking romantic and spiritual connections in Jerusalem. She gives creative writing workshops, ghost writes, and works with budding writers one-on-one. She now lives in New Jersey with her husband, Yisrael Feuerman, and their four children. Ruchama can be contacted at: e-mail: ruchamakingfeuerman@msn.com.

Elana Freidman lives in Jerusalem and, among other activities, writes and teaches. She became religious in the early seventies and has a penchant for Hassidut of all types. She can be contacted at treebird@actcom.co.il.

444

Honey Faye Gilbert earned her Ph.D. in Hebrew language and literature from Columbia University in New York. She continues her matchmaking efforts in addition to teaching Hebrew, translating and lecturing widely on women's issues. She has five children and lives with her husband in Akron, Ohio.

Ellen Golub (Elkele@aol.com) was trained as a psychoanalytic literary critic at the State University of New York at Buffalo and taught Jewish literature for several years at the University of Pennsylvania. After the births of her four children, she began a second career as a columnist in the Jewish press. She is currently professor of communications at Salem State College. She wrote this piece while a scholar in residence at the Hadassah-Brandeis Institute and would like to thank HBI for its generous support of her work.

Leah Golumb originally hails from New Jersey. She attended religious day schools through high school and then went to a variety of universities without receiving a degree. In 1977 she moved to Israel, where she married and raised a family of six children on the moshav of Rabbi Shlomo Carlebach, zt"l. Leah is a certified swim instructor and lifeguard who has worked in the Israeli Board of Education for many years as a supervisor of learn to swim programs. She has been a mikveh lady for over twenty years and teaches Torah and Chassidut in many venues.

Tamara Edell-Gottstein holds a bachelor's degree in education and administration. She is currently a graduate student at the Interdisciplinary Center in Herzliyyah, studying Jewish leadership and not-for-profit management. She serves on the executive committee of the Forum to Address Food Insecurity and Poverty in Israel. A certified childbirth assistant, Tamara has worked as a childbirth companion since 1991. She studied at the Yakar center in Jerusalem and went on to teach Jewish texts related to fertility, midwifery and birth both to the women's bet midrash at Yakar and to a group of midwives.

Shulamis Yehudis Gutfreund teaches Judaic studies and writing in Boston. She is the former founding editor of *The Jewish Women's Journal.*

Viva Hammer (vivahammer@aol.com) is Attorney-Advisor in the Office of Tax Policy at the U.S. Department of the Treasury. She has written for *The Washingtonian, Lilith, Jewish Action, Los Angeles Jewish Journal, The Potomac Review,* and many other publications.

Susan Handelman, Ph.D., is a professor of English literature at Bar-Ilan University. She taught literature and Jewish studies at the University of Maryland for many years before making aliyah to Israel. Her books include *The Slayers of Moses: The Emergence of Rabbinic Interpretation in Modern Literary Theory* and *Fragments of Redemption: Jewish*

Thought and Literary Theory in Scholem, Benjamin, and Levinas. She also co-edited *Torah of the Mothers: Contemporary Jewish Women Read Classical Jewish Texts* and *Wisdom from All My Teachers: Challenge and Initiatives in Contemporary Torah Education.* She is also the co-translator of the discourse of the Lubavitcher Rebbe, Rabbi Menachem M. Schneerson, "On the Essence of Chassidus."

Minna Hellet is the mother of four children and has worked in Jewish education throughout her adult life. She also freelances as a writer and editor.

Chaya Rivkah Jessel, of blessed memory, was born in Johannesburg and lived in Australia and Canada before settling in Israel. An idealist with a passion for learning, she attended university in Sydney, and became an expert in feminist theory and practice, while immersing herself in women's struggles. Providentially, she became exposed to traditional Judaism and came to appreciate the Torah's well-developed, enduring concept of the feminine.

A writer and lecturer, she considered it vital to describe the woman's role in Judaism in ways that would neither be condescending nor apologetic. In one ambitious project, she interviewed women who had formerly been very involved in the women's movement but who, like her, had now become uncompromisingly loyal to Torah and *halacha*. Their responses formed the basis of her unfinished book, which was aimed at the well-educated secular woman.

When Chaya Rivkah was diagnosed with a serious, debilitating illness, she faced the obstacles with strength, courage and conviction and became greatly excited over the new insights she acquired in the midst of her trying experience. She was especially struck by the love, dedication and support that her friends afforded her throughout her illness. She was awed by the quiet greatness of womankind, by their ability to stretch so far beyond themselves for the other, and derived intense pleasure from seeing the bonds between women that were created and deepened in the process.

A pillar of integrity, Chaya Rivkah pursued truth in interpersonal relationships just as she did in her writings. She would seek forgiveness and make amends even when she found it very difficult to do so, and even if she had had no contact with the other person for years. She was also a woman of indomitable spirit with true *joie de vivre*. She was so genuinely caring, so instinctively capable of seeing and bringing out the good in people, that just one conversation with her was enough to cement a friendship.

Chaya Rivkah left this world on 12 Teves 5764 (January 6, 2004), leaving a mother, a brother, a husband and four young children. They can be contacted at Jessel@softhome.net.

Karen Kirshenbaum teaches Mishna and Talmud at Midreshet Lindenbaum (formerly Michlelet Bruria) and Nishmat, women's colleges for advanced Jewish studies in Jerusalem, and lectures widely. She received her B.A. and M.A. in Talmud from Hebrew University and is now working on her doctorate in Talmud at Bar Ilan University. She lives in Jerusalem with her husband and six children.

Francesca Lunzer Kritz lives in Silver Spring, Maryland with her husband Neil and their two children, Dina and Matthew, who attend the Melvin J. Berman Hebrew Academy in Aspen Hill, Maryland. The Kritz family belongs to the Kemp Mill Synagogue in Silver Spring.

Fran currently covers consumer drug issues for the *Washington Post* Health Section and has been a staff reporter for *Forbes Magazine* and *U.S. News & World Report*. Her work has also appeared in *The Forward, The Jewish Week, Redbook, Good Housekeeping, Self, Newsweek, Woman's Day, Family Circle, Parenting* and on MSNBC.com.

Chava Willig Levy is a New York-based writer, editor and lecturer who zips around in a motorized wheelchair and communicates with uncommon clarity about the quality and meaning of life. A collection of her essays and speeches, *Deeper by the Dozen*, is soon to be published. With humor, passion and compassion, Chava's lectures have captivated audiences the world over. She is available for speaking engagements and can be reached at primerib@chavawilliglevy.com.

Sara Lieberman is a teacher of Judaic Studies at the Bais Rivkah High School and Teacher's Seminary, a much-sought-after lecturer and the editor of the English section of the journal *Di Yiddishe Heim*. She and her husband are the proud parents of seventeen children.

Dr. Marian Stoltz-Loike is the Chief Executive Officer of SeniorThinking, a human resources consulting company that builds organizational effectiveness across generations by providing products and services customized to the concerns of mature employees and their organizations. In the late 1980s, Marian built Stoltz-Loike Associates, one of the first consulting firms to focus specifically on work/family issues. Marian is the author of two books: *Managing a Global Work Force: A Cross-Cultural Guide* and *Dual Career Couples: New Perspectives in Counseling*, and numerous articles relating to the maturing work force, generational diversity, women's careers, and work/life issues. She has been a frequent speaker at professional conferences, such as NEHRA, NEWFA, HRPS, Work/Life Congress, and SHRM, and delivered webinars for Working Mother Media and Linkage. Marian received a BA from Harvard University and a Ph.D. in Developmental Psychology from New York University.

Marian is involved in a wide array of Jewish community activities. She is the Chair of Diplomatic Outreach and Vice President for the NY Chapter of the American Jewish Committee and a member of the Board of Governors of the National organization. She is a member of the Board of Directors of the Union of Orthodox Jewish Congregations of America. She has participated for the last eight years in a dialogue among Orthodox, Conservative, Reform, and Reconstructionist women through the American Jewish Committee. She is the Chair of the Committee for Israel Action at the Young Israel of Jamaica Estates and a former member of the Board of Education of Yeshiva of Central Queens. She served as the Chair of the OU's Institute of Political Affairs Internship Program for many years. She is a former member of the 100 Jewish Leaders for Clinton that was organized during the 1992 Clinton/Gore campaign and a former Queens Committee Chair of AIPAC.

Marian has been married to John Loike for twenty-eight years. They are parents and parents-in-law to Chaim, Gila, Devora, Ashira, Pesha, and Danny.

Miriam Luxenberg is a forty-year-old happy lady fulfilling her dream of living and raising a family in Eretz Yisrael. She is living proof that one should never, ever give up hope and that everything in life is subject to change, so often for the better!

Sherri Mandell is a graduate of Cornell University and received an MA in Creative Writing from Colorado State University. She taught writing at the University of Maryland and Penn State University. She is the author of *The Blessing of a Broken Heart* (2003) and *Writers of the Holocaust* (2000), and has published articles in *The Washington Post, The Denver Post, The New York Post, The Forward, Hadassah Magazine,* and *The Jerusalem Post.* She worked as senior writer for Wholefamily.com, an award-winning site for family wellness.

Ms. Mandell is currently co-president of The Koby Mandell Foundation, which creates, initiates and funds programs that promote healing for victims of terrorism and other human-rights abuses. The key programs are Camp Koby and Yosef for children aged 9–17, the Mothers' Healing Retreat for bereaved mothers and widows and Family Healing Retreats. For more information about the work of the foundation visit www. kobymandell.org.

Sara Morozow is lecturer on topics related to Jewish women, a teacher of Chassidic philosophy and counselor to brides and women of all ages in the Brooklyn community of Crown Heights where she lives with her husband and their ten children.

Sheindal Goldblatt-Muller has served as an emissary of the late Lubavitcher Rebbe in South Carolina for the past thirteen years. She and her husband Meir founded and continue to run the Columbia Jewish Day School, where she teaches Judaic studies to students ranging in age from preschool through high school. Sheindal also lectures on a wide range of topics.

Marjorie Ordene, a holistic physician, lives in Brooklyn with her husband and son. Her short stories, poetry and essays have appeared in small presses and alternative health magazines.

Debbie Perlman (1951–2002) was an occupational therapist who spent many years on the other side of the bed, applying her training to her own life. A twenty-year cancer survivor disabled by the side effects of treatment, she possessed an indomitable spirit and hope. She was the author of *Flames to Heaven: New Psalms for Healing and Praise* (1998), a collection that was an outgrowth of the psalm-poems she wrote for friends and acquaintances, many of whom were undergoing crises. From 1996 until her death, Debbie was the resident psalmist at Beth Emet, The Free Synagogue in Evanston, Illinois.

Roxane Peyser lives in Atlanta, Georgia with her husband Ted and six children. Ms. Peyser, who is general counsel for Environmental Planning Specialists, Inc., is currently working on her doctorate, specializing in Middle Eastern and Security studies

Yocheved Reich finds self-expression as an at-home mother, raising her family in Lakewood, NJ.

Rachel Naomi Remen, MD has been counseling those with chronic and terminal illness for more than twenty years. She is co-founder and medical director of the Commonweal Cancer Help Program in Bolinas, CA and is currently clinical professor of family and community medicine at the University of California at S. Francisco School of Medicine. She is the author of *Kitchen Table Wisdom; Stories That Heal* (1997) and *My Grandfather's Blessings: Stories of Strength, Refuge and Belonging* (2000).

Liz Rosenberg is the author and editor of more than thirty books including two novels, two books of poems, a volume of prose poetry and numerous books for young readers, including four prize-winning anthologies of poetry. She teaches English and creative writing at the State University of New York at Binghamton, where she lives with her husband, son, daughter, and two dogs.

Devorah Leah (Dina) Rosenfeld is the editor in chief of Hachai Publishing, where she shepherds manuscripts all the way from first to final draft, chooses artists to illustrate the work and oversees each book's layout and design. A former preschool teacher from Pittsburgh, Pennsylvania, she is now the author of eighteen Jewish children's titles of her own. Devorah Leah lives in the Crown Heights section of Brooklyn with her family.

Iris Rudin (1928–2004) wrote from Binghamton, NY. Of all her accomplishments, she was most proud that she started a Plant A Row for the Hungry program in her community so that garden surplus could be supplied to food distribution centers to feed the hungry.

Julie Salamon, a culture writer for *The New York Times*, is the author of the bestselling novella, *The Christmas Tree*. Her other books include the novel *White Lies; The Devil's Candy* (about the making of *The Bonfire of the Vanities*), *The Net of Dreams*, a family memoir, and *Facing the Wind*. Previously a reporter and critic for *The Wall Street Journal*, she has also written for *The New Yorker*, *Vanity Fair*, *Vogue*, and *The New Republic*. She lives with her family in New York City.

Chaya Rivkah Schiloni is a writer, artist, and the Director of the Mid East Education Team, she may be contacted at chai36@msn.com.

Shira Leibowitz Schmidt earned a B.Sc. in engineering from Stanford University, an M.Sc. in urban studies from the Technion in Israel and an M.Sc. in civil engineering from the University of Waterloo, Canada. She has taught at Ben-Gurion University and at Netanya Academic College and is currently connected with the Haredi College in Jerusalem. Together with Nobel chemistry laureate Roald Hoffman, Shira is the author of *Old Wine, New Flasks: Reflections on Science and Jewish Tradition*. A professional translator, Shira is a widely published freelance writer on popular Jewish issues.

Sarah Yehudit (Susan) Schneider is the founding director of A Still Small Voice, a correspondence school that provides weekly teachings in classic Jewish wisdom to subscribers around the world. Susan is the author of *Kabbalistic Writings on the Nature of Masculine and Feminine* (2001). In addition, she has published two booklets, *Eating as Tikun* and *Purim Bursts*. She has also published journal articles in *B'Or HaTorah* entitled "Evolution, Form and Consciousness," "The Underside of Creative Expression," and "The Daughters of Tslafchad: Toward a Methodology of Attitude around Women's Issues." An expanded version of the latter article appears in the anthology *Torah of the Mothers: Contemporary Jewish Women Read Classical Jewish Texts*.

Sarah Yehudit has a bachelor's degree in molecular, cellular and developmental biology from the University of Colorado in Boulder. Before immigrating to Israel she worked as a laboratory researcher for the Celestial Seasonings Herb Tea Company. She can be contacted through her Still Small Voice website at www.amyisrael.co.il/smallvoice/ or by email at smlvoice@netvision.net.il.

Marcia Schwartz is a writer/editor living in New York. She gets lots of nachas from her three children and twelve grandchildren.

Ruth Seligman is an Ohio journalist living in New York. She is the author of *Mommy, When Will the Lord Be Two?* and *A Child's-Eye View of Being Jewish Today* with co-author Jonathan Mark. The couple are the parents of Sara Noa, Rivka Yona, and Zev Mordechai Mark.

Wendy Shalit was born in Milwaukee, Wisconsin, and received her B.A. in philosophy from Williams College. Her essays on literary and cultural topics appear in The Wall Street Journal, Commentary, and other publications. Her book, *A Return to Modesty: Discovering the Lost Virtue*, was published by the Free Press in January of 1999 and won a Barnes & Noble "Most Original Thinker" award. She has been invited to speak at educational institutions around the world, and has appeared as a commentator on *Good Morning America, The Today Show* and other programs.

Sarah Shapiro is the author of *Growing with My Children: A Jewish Mother's Diary*, the *Our Lives* anthology series, *Don't You Know It's a Perfect World?* and, most recently, *A Gift Passed Along: A Woman Looks at the World around Her*. The fourth volume of *Our Lives, The Mother in Our Lives*, was published in 2005. She writes regularly in a number of publications in America and Israel and lives with her family in Jerusalem.

Dr. Esther Shkop is Dean of the Blitstein Institute for Women of Hebrew Theological College in Chicago, where she also serves as Associate Professor of Bible. Dr. Shkop earned a Ph.D. in public policy analysis from the University of Illinois, a MHL in Biblical studies from Shapell College for Women in Jerusalem, and a B.A. in English literature and philosophy from the University of Denver. She has published in a variety of academic journals, and is a renowned speaker on topics related to Jewish Education and Biblical Studies. Dr. Shkop is a mother of seven and grandmother of a growing clan.

Shira Leibowitz Schmidt earned a B.Sc. in engineering from Stanford University, an M.Sc. in urban studies from the Technion in Israel and an M.Sc. in civil engineering from the University of Waterloo, Canada. She has taught at Ben-Gurion University and at Netanya Academic College and is currently connected with the Haredi College in Jerusalem. Together with Nobel chemistry laureate Roald Hoffman, Shira is the author of *Old Wine, New Flasks: Reflections on Science and Jewish Tradition*. A professional translator, Shira is a widely published freelance writer on popular Jewish issues.

Leah Perl Shollar hails from Palo Alto, CA. She is a graduate of Beth Jacob High School in Denver and Machon Devorah Seminary in Jerusalem. For the past decade

Shollar has lived in Pittsburgh, Pennsylvania with her husband and six children, where she teaches high-school Bible and Jewish history studies at yeshiva schools. Shollar is the author of several children's books, including the award-winning title *A Thread of Kindness*, which was a finalist for the National Jewish Book Award. Shollar lectures extensively on Women in the Bible and related subjects.

Chaya Shuchat is a mother of four lively boys and a teacher in Bais Chaya Mushka High School in Brooklyn. She enjoys writing commentary on issues relating to Jewish women and contemporary life. She is currently working on adapting a series of classic Chassidic works for children.

Chana (Jenny) Weisberg, also known as the Jewish Pregnancy Lady, is the founder of the popular website JewishPregnancy.org. Originally from Baltimore, Maryland, she is a graduate of Bowdoin College and Hebrew University's Graduate School of Social Work, and devoted several years to intensive study at institutions for Jewish learning. Chana is the mother of five and lives in Jerusalem.

Lyric W. Winik is an award-winning writer and the Washington correspondent for *Parade Magazine*. She is the author of *Run East: Flight from the Holocaust*.

Alys R. Yablon was formerly an editor at The Free Press, Simon and Schuster. She now lives in Jerusalem, Israel and works as a freelance writer, editor and book reviewer.

Deena Yellin is a journalist who has written for *The New York Times, Newsday, The Jerusalem Post* and *The New York Jewish Week*. She is currently a reporter at *The Record of Hackensack* and is the mother of three children.

Side Bar Contributors

Mindy Aber Barad, who moved to Israel in 1977, has a BA from Washington University (St. Louis), and an LLB from Hebrew University. She practiced law, but writing is her first career choice. In 1997 Ms. Barad won second prize in the Jewish Librarians' Choice competition for a children's story, "Hannah's Succah" (published in a Pitspopany anthology, *Jewish Humor Stories for Kids*). Her poetry, stories, book reviews and essays have been published in *The Jerusalem Post, The Jewish Press* and other publications both on- and offline.

Judy Belsky is a writer, artist and psychologist in private practice in Jerusalem and in Ramat Bet Shemesh. She is the author of a memoir entitled *Thread of Blue* (2002). She has published many poems and several children's books, and has just completed a memoir about her Sephardic childhood.

Varda Branfman wrote station breaks for public television, was a copywriter for a major drug company in New York City, and taught poetry in rural New England public schools, nursing homes, and prisons, before landing in Israel. For the past twenty years, she's been busy raising her family in Jerusalem, as well as continuing to write and teach. She is the author of *I Remembered in the Night Your Name* and the co-author, with her husband, of a book on the phenomenon of free loans in the world-wide Orthodox community, *The Hidden World.*

Marcia Falk is the author of *The Spectacular Difference*, a collection of poems by Zelda that she translated from the Hebrew; *The Book of Blessings*; a translation of *The Song of Songs; With Teeth in the Earth,* a volume of translations from the Yiddish of Malka Heifetz Tussman's poems; and two books of poems, *This Year in Jerusalem* and *It Is July in Virginia,* which won the Claytor Award of the Poetry Society of America. She holds a Ph.D. in comparative literature from Stanford University and was a professor of Hebrew and English literature and creative writing for two decades.

Rabbi Tzvi Freeman is a father, teacher and writer currently residing in Toronto, Canada. He is author of several popular books on meditation and Jewish thought, including *Bringing Heaven Down to Earth: 365 Meditations from the Rebbe*. Much of his writing can be found at chabad.org and TheRebbe.com. Rabbi Freeman's books are available by contacting him at TzviFreeman@sympatico.ca.

Bracha Meshchaninov lives in upstate New York with her husband and five children. When she's not writing, taking photographs and tending the home fires, she gives classes in Jewish women's spirituality.

Zelda Schneurson Mishkovsky – known to her Hebrew readers simply as Zelda – was the daughter and granddaughter of prominent Chassidic rabbis from the Lubavitch dynasty. Born in Russia in 1914, she immigrated to Palestine in 1926, studied in religious girls' schools, and became a schoolteacher. She began writing poetry early in life and when her first book was published in 1967 it was an overwhelming success, appealing to the diverse Israeli public. Five more volumes followed, winning the poet numerous literary awards including the prestigious Bialik and Brenner prizes. Zelda died in Jerusalem in 1984. *The Spectacular Difference* by Marcia Falk is the first full-length book of her poems to appear in English translation.

Linda Paston, poet laureate of Maryland from 1991 to 1995, is the author of ten collections of poetry. She lives in Potomac, Maryland.

Rabbi Menachem M. Schneerson (1902–1994) is still considered "the Rebbe" by Jews worldwide even more than a decade after his passing. He has been described by Rabbi Dr. Jonathan Sacks, chief rabbi of the U.K., as "a personality of biblical proportions in modern times." His public talks, letters and other writings have been collected and edited in close to a hundred volumes, touching on every aspect of Jewish wisdom and human life. A one-of-a-kind social activist, he trail-blazed the Jewish outreach movement and initiated a set of "mitzvah campaigns" to revitalize and reunite the Jewish people.

Vera Schwarcz holds the Freeman Chair of History and East Asian Studies at Wesleyan University in Connecticut. She is the author of five books, including *Bridge across Broken Time: Chinese and Jewish Cultural Memory* (1998) and a finalist for the National Jewish Book Award. Schwarcz is also a published poet whose most recent collection of poems, *In the Garden of Memory*, is based on a collaborative exhibit with Israeli artist Chava Pressburger. This exhibit was shown in Connecticut and in Prague. Vera Schwarcz lives in West Hartford with her husband and two children.

Esther Sheldon was born in New York, where she married and raised her three children, two of whom live in Israel. She made aliya in her later years and lived in Jerusalem. An avid reader of Torah, she attended many shiurim and made a great contribution to many organizations by her volunteer work and fundraising.

Arlene Geist Sidelsky is an American living in London, England with her husband and two teenage children. She obtained a master's degree in mathematics from the University of Michigan in 1966, became religiously observant in 1973 and in 1986 returned to the University of Michigan, where her husband earned an advanced dental degree. She then took poetry classes in order to fulfill the directive of the Lubavitcher Rebbe, who had given her a blessing to write and spread Chassidus. Her book, *Quest*, is available by contacting her at Agsidelsky@aol.com.

RIGHTS AND PERMISSIONS

Rivkah Slonim, an internationally known lecturer and activist, addresses the intersection of traditional Jewish observance and contemporary life with a special focus on Jewish women in Jewish law and life. Over the past two decades, she has appeared before audiences in hundreds of locations across the United States and abroad and served as a consultant to educators and outreach professionals. Slonim is the editor of *Total Immersion: A Mikvah Anthology* (Jason Aronson, 1996; Urim, 2006). Slonim and her husband, Rabbi Aaron Slonim, have been the shluchim of the Lubavitcher Rebbe, of blessed memory, to Binghamton, NY since 1985. Together they founded and direct the Chabad House Jewish Student Center at Binghamton University. Rivkah and Aaron Slonim are the parents of nine children.

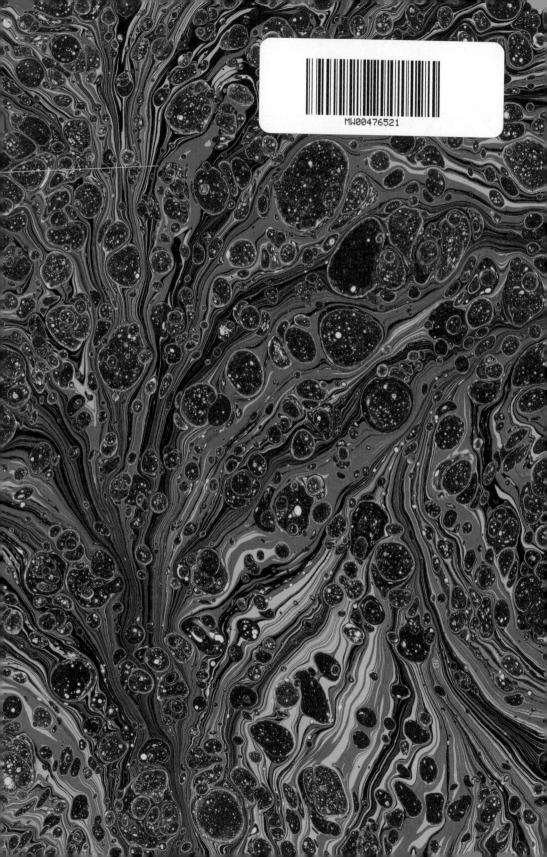

GLORY DAYS

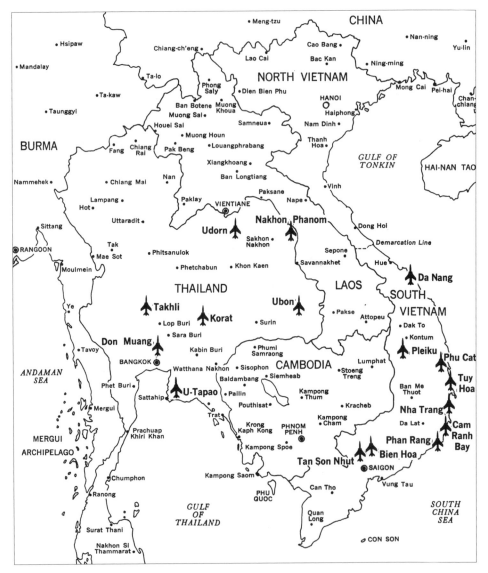

Principal USAF bases in Southeast Asia. From Aces & Aerial Victories: The United States Air Force in Southeast Asia 1965-1973. Air University and Office of Air Force History, AF/HO, Headquarters USAF, Washington DC, 1976, p. 23.

GLORY DAYS

The Untold Story of the Men who Flew the B-66 Destroyer into the Face of Fear

Wolfgang W.E. Samuel

Colonel, U.S. Air Force (Ret)

To Pete with best wishes — may your dreams carry you above and beyond — [signature] W.E. Samuel 7/09/2023

Schiffer Military History
Atglen, PA

Published by Schiffer Publishing Ltd.
4880 Lower Valley Road
Atglen, PA 19310
Phone: (610) 593-1777
FAX: (610) 593-2002
E-mail: Info@schifferbooks.com.
Visit our web site at: www.schifferbooks.com
Please write for a free catalog.
This book may be purchased from the publisher.
Try your bookstore first.

PREFACE AND ACKNOWLEDGMENTS

Some years ago my daughter Shelley returned home over spring-break from Virginia Technical Institute in Blacksburg, better known as Virginia Tech, a university openly proud of the honorable military service many of its graduates rendered to the nation. Shelley said to me, "Dad, you flew the B-66 in Vietnam, didn't you? My cadet friends at Virginia Tech say there never was such an airplane." I never forgot my daughter's comment. Never forgot the twinge of pain I felt when she told me that my service and the sacrifices of so many of my friends had not only been forgotten, but had never even been remembered. In the years that followed I looked in vain for a book that told the story of the B-66 and the men who flew and maintained it. I began to do some research into the airplane's history, a plane in which I have less than 500 flying hours and of which I knew all too little. I came away from my research humbled by the bravery of those who flew their unarmed aircraft into the missile tainted skies of North Vietnam so that others might live. I decided it was time to write the story of this Cold War warrior, the story of the *B-66 Destroyer* and the men who flew it into the face of fear.

The B-66 was an interim medium jet bomber and reconnaissance aircraft to be retired as soon as the ultimate medium bomber came along. Like so many things in life, the interim became the ultimate. Its name *Destroyer* was a misnomer from the start since for the briefest period of its nearly twenty years of service it carried guns and bombs. Rather than being a destroyer, the B-66 for many years served as the eyes and ears of the tactical air forces as a day and night photo and electronic reconnaissance platform. The *Destroyer's* claim to fame, however, came in the early years of the Vietnam War when the United States Air Force found itself confronted by a sophisticated North Vietnamese radar guided anti-aircraft and surface-to-air missile defense network for which it was ill prepared. The only aircraft in being to effectively counter the North Vietnamese radar threat was a small number of aging and often neglected electronic countermeasure (ECM) equipped EB-66 aircraft. These few 'whited out' the screens of North Vietnamese radars trying to direct anti-aircraft guns and surface to air missiles against bomb-laden F-105 and F-4 fighters. The men flying the unarmed EB-66s saved many a fighter pilot's life, and as a result they were hunted by North Vietnamese MiGs and surface to air missile battalions charged to gun them down. The EB-66 flyers took their losses, yet prevailed. They were there in the beginning, and they were there to the end, the very last combat planes to leave the field of battle. *Glory Days* is the untold story of an airplane and its brave flyers who deserve to be remembered like all others who valiantly served our nation in time of war. The two EB-66 combat squadrons which flew from bases in Thailand from 1965 to the end of the air war in 1973 earned the Presidential Unit Citation for valor in combat, as well as numerous Outstanding Unit Awards with V-device for valor in combat, and the equivalent U.S. Navy citation. EB-66 flyers earned Silver Stars and Distinguished Flying Crosses for heroism, Air Medals galore, and all too many Purple Hearts, attesting to their courage and sacrifice.

In *Glory Days* I tell the B-66 story the way men experienced and lived it, and as much as possible in their own words. Interviews and correspondence if needed were edited for clarity, brevity and word choice. Although I tried to minimize the use of Air Force jargon, that wasn't totally possible nor desirable. After all, *Glory Days* is a story about Air Force flyers and their flying machines, so feel free to make good use of Appendix 1 - Terms and Abbreviations. I also set the story within the context of its time, a time when the Soviet military juggernaut came close to taking our world into nuclear war. The Cold War, including major confrontations between East and West over Berlin (1948 to 1949), Korea (1950 to 1953), Cuba (1962) and Vietnam (1962 to 1973), was at times rather hot incurring the loss of nearly 100,000 American lives, and many more wounded. The B-66 and its flyers played a significant role in the outcome of this long-lasting struggle. In the end, we, the free world, prevailed over darkness and oppression, and the Soviet threat collapsed and vanished. *Glory Days* is one story of how it was done.

I would not have been able to put together this tale of courage and dedication without the support and cooperation of many organizations and individuals, including Dr. James O. Young, Chief Historian at the Air Force Flight Test Center at legendary Edwards Air Force Base in California. Dr. Young provided essential pictures and test data of the B-66 as it went through flight test at Edwards and

Wright-Patterson Air Force Bases. Ms. Yvonne Kinkaid at AF/HO at Bolling AFB, Washington, DC., was equally helpful in supporting my research efforts to retrieve historical records of B-66 units and operations from a vast Air Force historical data base, as was Mr. Louie Alley, Freedom of Information Act Manager at Kirtland Air Force Base. Mr Alley's enthusiastic support provided accident reports without which it would have been impossible to accurately reconstruct the history of the airplane and how it was flown. In the process of doing my research I met Mr. Clifford Parrott, better known in the B-66 community as 'the B-66 Doctor.' As the senior Douglas Aircraft Corporation technical representative at Shaw Air Force Base, South Carolina, Cliff Parrott shepherded the B-66 through its early growing pains, and more than any other individual helped make the B-66 a safe combat plane to fly. Fortunately Cliff was in the habit of never throwing anything away and generously provided me access to his files. I extend my appreciation and thanks to Colonel James Milam for his and the B-66 Association's support, to Colonel Paul Duplessis for developing and maintaining an extensive interactive B-66 website, to Colonel Paul Moore for supporting my research efforts at the Museum of the United States Air Force, and to Lieutenant Colonel Robert Mendonca, one of the last commanders of the 42nd Tactical Electronic Warfare Squadron at Korat, Thailand, for providing historical data of the last years of the squadron's operation in Southeast Asia. Mr Robert Kempel of Lancaster, California, a long time aerospace engineer at the NASA Dryden Flight Research Center, generously provided engineering advice and valuable suggestions.

I also want to express my appreciation and thanks to the many who consented to be interviewed for the B-66 story, who shared personal experiences through letters and emails, as well as pictures dating back to the earliest days of the aircraft as it was undergoing flight test. Lieutenant Colonel Robert Stamm was a most generous contributor of written and pictorial material, as were William Starnes, David Frankenberg, William McDonald, Joseph Snoy, Toni Tambini, Ted Pruss, Robert Webster, Vern Luke, John Norden, Ken Hintz, David Cooper, Joe Yeater, Lloyd Neutz, Stan Tippin, Bob Welch, Tom Taylor, Gayle Johnson, Edward Monger and many others mentioned in the book. David Holland, Kermit Helmke and Donald Harding were more than generous in providing critical insights into the shoot-down of an RB-66 over East Germany in 1964, and about the role of the B-66 in the 47th Bombardment Wing at RAF Sculthorpe, England. My thanks go to Major General Harrison Lobdell, USAF (Retired), for allowing me to quote from his interview, and to Lieutenant Colonel Gerald Reponen for sharing his extensive unpublished autobiography which covered much of the period when the B-66 first deployed to Germany, France and England. My thanks go to everyone who contributed in any fashion and made this long overdue book possible – a story of American courage, dedication to and love of country. I regret that I could not mention everyone by name, there were so many of you who reached out and contributed. I thank you all.

Wolfgang W.E. Samuel
Colonel, U.S. Air Force (Ret.)
Fairfax Station, Virginia

CONTENTS

DEDICATION

**DEDICATED TO THE MEN WHO PERISHED
IN SERVICE TO THEIR COUNTRY**

1956
CAPTAIN GEORGE MORRIS

1957
1/LT RICHARD J DINGER
A/2C ARTHUR J DUFRESNE JR
1/LT DAN K HENDERSON
T/SGT STANLEY P KLATZ
CAPT ARTHUR J MANZO
CAPT JOHN A RUNION
2/LT GLEN D WATSON

1958
1/LT THOMAS C BRYCE
CAPT WILFRED E CATHER
CAPT DONN F CHANDLER
1/LT ROBERT A CHASE
1/LT SMITH DAVIS JR
1/LT ROBERT B HANDCOCK
CAPT ROBIN W GRAY
1/LT HELMUT HEIMANN
S/SGT HOWARD M HICKS
CAPT RICHARD W HUGHES
CAPT JOSEPH D LOEFFLER
MR BLAINE L MAINS
1/LT LAWTON D MUELLER

A/1C JULIUS J RAUSCH
MR GEORGE E SARABALE
CAPT JAMES M STITZEL
CAPT HOWARD E STRANDBERG
CAPT GEORGE A TAYLOR
CAPT ROGER E TAYLOR
T/SGT BERNARD M VALENCIA

1959
1/LT CHARLES L BOONE
1/LT GARY R COAD
CAPT ALLEN H DAY
1/LT HAROLD W GLANDON
CAPT JAMES L JUNGE
A/2C MICHAEL J KEMP
1/LT WILLIM H MCCASLAND
A/2C RALPH L NOELL
CAPT JAMES T POWELL JR
CAPT JULIAN T STEWART JR

1961
CAPT HARRY V ARMANI
MAJ PAUL BROOKS
CAPT RALPH DAVENPORT
CAPT DANIEL HARVEY
CAPT JESSE KENDLER

CAPT PAUL J SAVAGE
1/LT FRANK L WHITLEY JR

1962
1/LT WILLIAM R BECRAFT
S/SGT LEROY DAUGHENBAUGH JR
1/LT REYNOLDS W MCCAABE
1/LT JAMES T WEYMARK

1963
CAPT WILLIAM H COX JR

1965
CAPT ROBERT L MANN
1/LT JAMES A MCEWEN
CAPT JOHN WEGER

1966
T/SGT CHARLES BORDELON
CAPT JOHN B CAUSEY
1/LT DONALD E LAIRD
CAPT DWIGHT A LINDLEY
1/LT CRAIG R NORBERT

1967
LT/COL HERBERT DOBY
CAPT REY L DUFFIN
CAPT KARL D HEZEL
1/LT THEODORE W JOHNSON

1/LT PAUL S KRZYNOWEK
MAJ WILLIAM E MCDONALD
CAPT LARRY A MOORE
MAJ MAX E NICHOLS
LT/COL RUSSELL A POOR
COL WOODROW H WILBURN
LT/COL JACK M YOUNGS

1968
MAJ POLLARD H MERCER JR

1969
LT/COL EDWIN P ANDERSON JR
CAPT JOHN A HOLLEY
MAJ KENNETH H KELLY
CAPT JOSEPH M ORLOWSKI
LT/COL JAMES E RICKETTS JR
MAJ EDWIN B WELCH

1972
CAPT WILLIAM R BALDWIN
COL WAYNE L BOLTE
CAPT ROBIN F GATWOOD
COL ANTHONY R GIANNANGELI
COL CHARLES A LEVIS
MAJ HENRY J REPETA
MAJ GEORGE F SASSER
LT/COL HENRY M SEREX

CHAPTER ONE

THE PRICE OF VICTORY

World War II was a rude awakening for an America that thought itself safely isolated from the wars and conflicts of a historically strife ridden Europe. Two oceans, benign neighbors, and a large fleet to defend its shores, provided an illusionary sense of security few other nations on earth enjoyed. That insularity of thought and ill-founded sense of security was shattered when Imperial Japan surprised America's fleet at Pearl Harbor on a sunny Sunday morning in December 1941. Days later, an arrogant Nazi Germany declared war on the United States, not because of any belligerent acts committed by the United States against Germany, but solely because Germany was allied with Japan. Germany, Japan and Italy, the Axis powers, pledged mutual support to each other in case of war, no matter the reason. With its fleet sorely wounded, faced by aggressive enemies, the nation took inventory and discovered that its armies and air forces were in terrible shape: too small for the task at hand, poorly trained and equipped with obsolete arms – from the rifles soldiers carried, to the helmets they wore, to the tanks they drove, to the airplanes they flew. Less than three years later America not only had recovered from the initial shock of finding itself at war, but had Imperial Japan and Nazi Germany on the proverbial ropes. American industry was producing so much war related equipment that the materiel losses incurred in battle were nearly irrelevant. In 1944 alone the United States produced 96,318 war planes of all types, more than any other nation, friend or foe.[1] Not only did America's awakened industrial might and ingenuity produce the planes to overwhelm its enemies, but the hundreds of thousands of reciprocating engines needed to power them, the bombs, bullets and

A hastily assembled group of 3rd Bombardment Wing B-26s awaits take-off instructions at Ashiya Air Base, Japan, late June 1950. As the Korean War began, America's tactical air force was still largely of World War II vintage.

guns to arm them, and the pilots, navigators, bombardiers, radio operators, and gunners to fly them into harm's way. When war ended in Europe on May 8, 1945, the United States Strategic Air Forces in Europe, USSTAF, was deployed on 152 air bases and 226 lesser installations manned by 450,000 airmen who flew or supported an armada of over 17,000 aircraft of all types.[2]

War came to America in December 1941 in the form of 400 Japanese combat planes launched from six aircraft carriers off the Hawaiian Islands, inflicting damage that was soon repaired. That war was effectively terminated on August 9, 1945, when a single B-29, named *Bock's Car,* of the 20th Air Force, dropped on the city of Nagasaki the second of two atomic bombs dropped on Japan. The Japanese surrender was officially signed on September 2 onboard the *USS Missouri* anchored in Tokyo Bay. The flimsy airplane of an earlier day had matured, determining the very outcome of battle, and ending World War II in favor of the United States and its allies. In August 1945 it appeared to many Americans that the world was finally at peace, able to go ahead and rebuild itself. The most optimistic thought that the rest of the world might just be ready for the ultimate human experience – democracy. In 1945 the United States of America was the undisputed military and economic power in the world, the sole possessor of the awe inspiring and feared atomic bomb, with its territory and people largely unscathed by the war it entered so reluctantly less than four years earlier.

At war's end the 'boys' clamored to come home, to go on with their lives, take advantage of the innovative GI Bill of Rights to gain an education, perhaps have a family and participate in the building of a vibrant and exciting new America. With over sixteen million men and women under arms at the height of the war, America's forces soon shrank to less than two-million. The U.S. Navy's battle fleet of 6,768 ships declined to a mere 634.[3] Disarmament was the very first postwar task politicians threw themselves into with a vigor difficult to imagine unless you were there to see it happen for yourself. Colonel Marion C. Mixson vividly remembers his own experience. Born in 1918, a South Carolina boy, he, like so many of his generation always wanted to fly, and soloed in a little 45-horse power *Aeronca* in 1939 at the age of twenty-one. "What a thrill it was to soar above Charleston on my very own," he recalls. "I'll never forget that first flight." By 1944 he found himself piloting a B-24 bomber out of Italy against targets in Germany, Austria, Hungary and Czechoslovakia. Hack, as his friends called him, flew 35 combat missions, some so brutal, he still wonders how he survived. After the war ended he remained in Italy for another year and sadly recalls, "All those B-25 and B-17 bombers in Italy were destroyed. None were sent home. For a while I flew a brand-new B-25. German prisoners took the armor out of it, stripped the paint, and polished the airplane to a high gloss. Although I had orders to turn the plane in to be destroyed like all the other bombers, I kept stalling for about two months. Finally, I got a message that if I didn't turn in the plane I was going to be courts-martialed. I flew it down to the Pomigliano Depot. My buddy came in a C-47 to take me back. By the time we finished filing our clearance for our return trip, they had drained the gas out of that beautiful B-25, cut the engines off, cut holes in the crankcase and into the propeller blades. That airplane was completely smashed in about an hour."[4]

At Landsberg-am-Lech in bucolic Bavaria, a former Luftwaffe airfield was filled with B-26 bombers of the 1st Tactical Air Force (Provisional). The planes were lined up wing tip to wing tip by the hundreds to be burned and turned into scrap by Germans who only weeks earlier tried hard to shoot them down. Most of the 1st TAF's P-47 Thunderbolts were simply stripped of their instruments and destroyed, smashed, buried in place. John Hay, who lives in Tulsa, Oklahoma, remembers while stationed at Holzkirchen, Bavaria, in 1945, helping to remove the radios and batteries from 186 brand-new B-17 bombers never flown in combat, then placing one-and-a-half-pound TNT charges in their cockpits and blowing them up.[5] The 12th Air Force inactivated on 31 August 1945. The 15th Air Force followed suit on September 15. And the fabled 9th Tactical Air Force inactivated on 2 December. The process of inactivation continued into 1946. At the end of that year a force of a mere 33,000 airmen remained in Europe, scattered across 33 airfields and miscellaneous installations, with less than 2,300 airplanes of all types, mostly transports, trainers and liaison aircraft.[6]

In 1948, when the first open confrontation between East and West occurred over access to occupied Berlin, then Lieutenant General Curtis E. LeMay, commander of the United States Air Forces in Europe, USAFE, the former USSTAF, recalled, "When they [the Soviets] clamped down on all surface traffic and transportation, we in the Occupation needed suddenly to consider something beyond the demolition or housekeeping duties which had concerned us during previous months. It looked like we might have to fight at any moment, and we weren't self-assured about what we had to fight with ... At a cursory glance it looked like USAFE would be stupid to get mixed up in anything bigger than a cat-fight at a pet show. We had one Fighter group, and some transports, and some radar people, and that was about the story."[7] By 1948, United States military power had been stripped by an over exuberant Congress beyond what was needed for a prudent defense of homeland and national interests abroad. The Air Force boasted of few jet aircraft, and the U.S. Army had been largely reduced to a constabulary force in Germany and Japan. Clearly, American military power deployed in occupied Germany was no match for the artillery heavy Soviet armored divisions across the inner German border, the future boundary between East and West.

Fortunately, not all politicians saw the world through rose-colored glasses. None other than the former Prime Minister of wartime England, Winston Churchill, warned on March 5, 1946, in an address at Westminster College in Fulton, Missouri, that "From Stettin in the Baltic to Triest in the Adriatic, an Iron Curtain has descended across the Continent." Even before Churchill's address, George Kennan, serving in Moscow, wrote a lengthy telegram on February 22, 1946, to his State Department colleagues, giving his considered professional assessment of the Soviets, and providing rules of how to deal with them: "A. Don't act chummy with them. B. Don't assume a community of aims with them which does not really exist. C. Don't make fatuous gestures of good will," and so on. Although "The Long Telegram," a real eye-opener for many, was read widely in political Washington, it was an article published in the July 1947 issue of *Foreign Affairs* which firmly set America on its course for the coming Cold War. Entitled "The Sources of Soviet Conduct," commonly referred to as The Article X because Kennan just put an X where his signature would have been, spoke of the *containment of the Soviet Union* and its territorial ambitions. Although Kennan insisted that his article "was not intended as a doctrine," that is precisely what it became.[8] The "doctrine of containment" became the intellectual foundation for the future United States military posture vis-a-vis the Soviet Union. With a clear national strategy at hand, our military structure began to adjust ever so slowly to the evolving postwar world, a world of the atomic bomb, the jet plane, the ballistic missile, and the Soviet Union, a former ally turned adversary.

Even before the Army Air Forces became the United States Air Force, USAF, and a co-equal partner of the Army and Navy as the result of the National Security Act of 1947, on March 21, 1946, SAC (Strategic Air Command), TAC (Tactical Air Command) and ADC (Air Defense Command) were formed as major combatant commands. This was a long overdue action sorting out the roles and missions previously carried out by a multitude of numbered air forces. The creation of the three commands was also a clear indication of the maturation of airpower doctrine and concepts, and recognition of its three principal functions – strategic, tactical, and homeland defense. The *Strategic Air Command* task was clearly stated and unambiguous: "To be prepared to conduct long range offensive operations in any part of the world ... conduct maximum range reconnaissance over land or sea" and "provide combat units capable of intense and sustained combat operations employing the latest and most advanced weapons," meaning the atomic bomb.[9]

The *Tactical Air Command* was given the mission to provide the necessary trained forces to provide close air support for Army operations, interdict enemy forces and supplies moving toward the battle area, conduct essential aerial reconnaissance to satisfy its own needs and those of the U.S. Army, and to achieve and maintain air superiority over the field of battle. Not only was TAC required to work closely with the Army to effectively perform its mission, it found itself with the responsibility to train the combat squadrons for its two sister commands, USAFE (the United States Air Forces in Europe) and FEAF (the Far Eastern Air Forces), headquartered in Germany and Japan respectively. While SAC tightly controlled all of its combat squadrons regardless of location from one centralized headquarters – at first Andrews AFB in Maryland, later Offutt AFB at Omaha, Nebraska – the tactical air forces responded to three separate headquarters, all with their own planning staffs, unique geographically dictated requirements, and parochial interests. Unity of command, a cherished principle of successful warfare, was solidly imbedded in the SAC architecture, but hard to find in the tactical air forces organizational structure. Tactical Air Command, headquartered at Langley Air Force Base, Virginia, found its principal mission to be training rather than war fighting – training combat ready fighter and bomber squadrons for USAFE and FEAF (redesignated Pacific Air Forces, PACAF, on July 1, 1957). Who was going to train and who was going to fly and fight became a contentious and divisive issue, symptomatic of the lack of unity of command within the tactical air forces. The fractured tactical air force structure was to have consequences in terms of aircraft and weapons procurement and aircrew training, consequences which would not become apparent until a distant war in Southeast Asia.

Air Defense Command was left with the mission of providing the necessary radar network to detect enemy intruders, to provide ample warning time for SAC and its bombers to get airborne, and to intercept and destroy enemy bombers before they reached the United States. In contrast to the strategic and tactical air forces, ADC had a strictly defensive mission of homeland protection. However, it was a mission still less clear than SAC's, requiring coordination not only with the other military services, but a foreign country as well – Canada. Still, ADC like SAC, was organized around a single unifying command structure, unlike the three tactical air forces which largely retained their World War II derived relationships. Roles and missions arguments among the services and among the newly created Air Force commands were endemic. Who should own and control long-range surface to air missiles was an early issue to be resolved between the Army and Air Force. Other technology driven issues soon followed and required resolution, among them ballistic missiles and cruise missiles, then referred to as unmanned aircraft. Who would own and operate them? Who would receive the funding, and with that the political clout that came with budgets and force structure. Once the Army Air Forces gained independence the question arose if the Army should surrender all of its aircraft to the fledgling Air Force, or did the Army have a right to retain an air component of its own? If so, where was the line to be drawn?

Helicopters versus fixed wing aircraft? Large, long-range versus small, short-range aircraft? If so, what type? Transports, liaison, close air support? The issue was never cleanly resolved and is still with us today. Issues needing resolution within and among the military services seemed endless. Answers came slowly, and often only after contentious and acrimonious debate. It was all about money and power, and of course national defense.

It was one thing to create new combat commands – SAC, TAC and ADC – and to assign them missions to execute, it was quite another to translate noble words into combat power. On October 16, 1948, when Lieutenant General LeMay, soon to be promoted to four-star rank, took over the Strategic Air Command, there wasn't much substance there for him to actually execute the mission SAC had been given. None of SAC's airplanes could reach Moscow. Of the 837 diverse aircraft assigned to SAC in 1948, 515 were B/RB-29s – World War II vintage airplanes. Only 35 long-range Convair B-36 bombers had joined the command. But even the B-36 was a World War II design, developed when it appeared that England might not survive the Nazi onslaught. Aside from two heavy bomber groups of B-36s, SAC had 12 medium bombardment groups, and two fighter groups equipped with F-51s and F-82s to escort the bombers. LeMay observed on taking command, "There's not a single realistic mission being flown. Practically nothing in the way of training. Sorry shape? You can say that again." So he directed "the whole damn command. By radar," to attack Wright Field. "So we ran a Maximum Effort mission against Wright Field at Dayton, Ohio. Oh, I'll admit the weather was bad. There were a lot of thunderstorms in the area; that certainly was a factor. But on top of this, our crews were not accustomed to flying at altitude. Neither were the airplanes ... Most of the pressurization wouldn't work, and the oxygen wouldn't work. Nobody seemed to know what life was like upstairs ... Not one airplane finished that mission as briefed. *Not one*."[10] Over the years SAC grew into the most powerful air force in the world, an air force within an air force, with thousands of bombers and aerial refueling tankers under its control. In its early days, however, SAC had little combat power to point to.

LeMay, with his mission clearly defined and unity of command assured through a centralized headquarters organization, decided early on what kind of an air force he wanted to create, and what kind of men he wanted to have fly his airplanes. LeMay's approach to training and mission execution shaped SAC, and was to fundamentally differentiate SAC flyers from those in the tactical air forces. "No longer did we stress cross-training. We did not dissipate our energies. We made every man concentrate on being as nearly perfect as possible in his own specific enterprise. Hell, we made every man concentrate on being *perfect*."[11] That meant flying by a checklist, making on-time take-offs within plus or minus five-seconds at any time of day or night, in any kind of weather – sunshine, rain, snow and ice. When given an order to launch, the message was, you will launch or die trying. SAC would have a checklist and procedure for everything, and mistakes were not tolerated. The Commander-in-Chief of the Strategic Air Command, CINCSAC, was in no need of innovative thinking over the battlefield. He wanted men to execute their assigned missions without fail, wanted men who could be counted on to be where they were told to be and deliver their weapons – or perish trying. In time, this iron clad concept of controlling the delivery of nuclear weapons on specified targets in the Soviet Union evolved into the Single Integrated Operations Plan, the SIOP, which controlled the delivery of nuclear weapons by bombers, land based intercontinental missiles, and those launched from nuclear submarines – the 'boomers.' The focus for SAC was nuclear war, an all or nothing type of conflict, soon to be emulated by the tactical air forces – because that's where the money was. Conventional capabilities atrophied. Limited war was not a phrase in the vocabulary of planners or strategic thinkers.

Colonel Kevin Gilroy earned the Air Force Cross as an Electronic Warfare Officer, EWO, in the backseat of an F-105F *Weasel*, killing SAM sites in North Vietnam. Earlier in his career Mike flew in SAC B-52s. Mike experienced SAC and TAC in peace and war. In an interview he described the differences between SAC and TAC flyers this way: "SAC probably never made the same mistake twice. Once you made a mistake, there was a procedure put in place to keep that from happening again. In TAC you were supposed to be a free thinker. 'We are not going to give you any unnecessary restrictions,' was the message. 'Go do it.'"[12] SAC flyers and TAC flyers – two different breeds.

Lieutenant Harrison Lobdell Jr., who rose to the rank of major general, provides another perspective of a flyer's life in the tactical air forces. Lobdell graduated from one of the accelerated West Point classes in 1946. He didn't go into the Army, instead chose the Army Air Forces. "I think I just wanted to fly," he recalls. "I was a gymnast in college at West Point and I just thought I could handle that and thought it would be fun. I applied for Air Cadet status. I had wanted to be a fighter pilot and actually went through fighter transition, but they sent me to RB-26s at Brooks. We were there just a short time and I thought my career had come to an end, because I was sent away for a three-day TDY to Langley. It lasted six weeks. I had just gotten married, and when I got back, my wife had the car all packed with our belongings, which was just one suitcase. She said, 'You're going to Supply School at Keesler.' And again I thought my career was done. While I was at Keesler, my squadron moved to Langley Field. My wing, the 363rd Tactical Reconnaissance Wing, 363TRW, consisted of two RF-80 squadrons, they were just coming into the inventory, and one RB-26 squadron. I can't recall more than three or four times when I ever dropped a flash bomb during the time I was in the unit. My reconnaissance squadron, the 162nd, did lots of interesting things. I remember going to McChord Field with the RB-26s. We mapped Seattle. My wife's family has a dude ranch in Montana. Up the Blackfoot River Valley from Missoula. My friend, Whitey Yeoman, and I flew out there in formation and buzzed the ranch. Of course, I was very proud of myself, and called back to my wife's cousin and said, 'Well, did you see us?' She was just beside herself. All the dudes were out on horseback having a treasure hunt, and my wife's uncle, on horseback, was putting a clue on a rock in the middle of the river. Of course he was dumped in the river when we flew over. Guys would be doing acrobatics over their girl friends houses, do all sorts of crazy things. And you just never did hear much about it. If somebody got caught, or if there was some damage, well, they'd get chastised. You could fly almost anywhere you wanted to in the United States. You could take your wife up once a year, and I did. It's an era that's long gone. It will never come back, obviously. The air force then, compared to today's air force, was almost unprofessional."[13]

While disarmament dominated the immediate postwar years, and defense budgets became exceedingly tight, the Army Air Forces and private industry managed to continue the development of a new type of airplane – the jet powered swept wing fighter and bomber which could fly faster, higher and farther than any other type of plane before. While World War II was still on-going, the engineers at Wright Field had turned to industry and asked them to participate in a design competition for a futuristic jet bomber. Then Colonel Donald Putt, a member of the Wright Field evaluation board and future three-star general and commander of Air Materiel Command, AMC, recalled, "The jet aircraft was pooh-poohed by a lot of people that were authorities in their day ... My one big job just before I went overseas in December 1944 was the running of the competition that had the B-45, B-46, B-47 and B-48 in it. All of them were straight-wing aircraft, very conventional looking except for hanging some engines on the wings that had no propellers on them."[14] Things changed quickly once captured German technology became available. We built a few of the quite conventional looking B-45 jet bombers, but the all-jet *Wundervogel* of its day was the Boeing B-47 with its six jets slung under 35 degree swept-back wings. The B-47, of which a total of 2,032 were produced, put SAC on the map, and led to the even more capable B-52 bomber. North American Aviation, like Boeing, took advantage of German aeronautical test data and dropped what it was doing on the XP-86. The once straight-wing XP-86 was redesigned and featured 35 degree swept-back wings, automatic leading edge slats, a moveable tailplane, and other advanced design features which allowed the F-86 *Sabrejet* to best the Soviet designed and German inspired MiG-15 in a war yet to come.[15]

Jets, however, were still a rarity when the newly independent Air Force found itself caught up in an epic roles and missions battle with the U.S. Navy. Always adept at correctly fathoming the future implications of new technology, the Navy had responded admirably when the airplane threatened the viability of the battleship. The aircraft carrier fit nicely into the fleet of the future, an appropriate follow-on to the one time queen of the seas, the battleship. The Navy understood that in the postwar world the atomic bomb was the weapon of the future and felt challenged by the newly established Strategic Air Command. Who did those SAC folks think they were anyway? Their bombers couldn't get anywhere without first landing on foreign bases to refuel. We, the United States Navy, have a much more practical and elegant approach. We will build a super-carrier, the *USS United States*, of 80,000 tons displacement, the largest aircraft carrier the world has ever seen, allowing us to launch our equally new, twin-jet, atom-bomb carrying A3D *Skywarrior* against any belligerent from off their shores. This was going to be an ugly fight – it was about the future, about money, about flag and general officer positions, about who was going to wield the most influence in the soon to be formed Department of Defense. SAC responded to the Navy challenge by slapping four J-47 jet engines under its lumbering B-36 strategic bomber to give the 360,000 pound behemoth additional speed and range. On December 8, 1948, a B-36 flew nonstop from Fort Worth, Texas, to Hawaii and back – 9,400 miles, a distance great enough to reach most targets in the Soviet Union from the United States. The U.S. Navy took note.[16]

Even before LeMay took command of SAC, the Air Staff in the Pentagon got serious about aerial refueling, realizing the implications behind the lack of range of its bombers and fighters. Eighty B-29 bombers were converted at Boeing to KB-29M refueling tankers and B-29MR receivers. On June 30, 1948, the 43rd Air Refueling Squadron was established at Davis-Monthan AFB, Arizona, and the 509th at Walker AFB, Roswell, New Mexico. Although the looped-hose refueling system developed by the Royal Air Force had its limitations – soon to be replaced by a more practical probe and drogue concept – it allowed the Air Force to stage a spectacular around the world flight in February 1949. In great secrecy KB-29Ms were positioned at Lajes in the Azores; Dharan, Saudi Arabia; Clark Air Base in the Philippines, and at Hickam AFB, Hawaii. On February 26, 1949, *Lucky Lady II*, a modified B-50 bomber, took off from Carswell AFB in Fort Worth, Texas, and flew nonstop around the world, again landing at Carswell on March 2.[17] This was not only a message from SAC to the Soviet Union, but to the U.S. Navy as well: Take note, we can do our job anywhere, anytime. Defense spending was extremely tight, and when Secretary of Defense Louis Johnson, on April 23, 1949, canceled the *USS United States* five days after its keel laying, the admirals revolted.[18] As anticipated, the struggle between the services was intense and impassioned, but the choice had been made who would carry war to the heartland of the Soviet Union should that become necessary. The U.S. Navy, as always, recovered from its setback. On January 21, 1954, the nuclear powered submarine *USS Nautilus* was launched at Groton, Connecticut. And on June 9, 1959, the first ballistic missile carrying submarine, the *USS George Washington*, slipped into Atlantic waters.

Limited defense budgets and roles and missions struggles continued to divert attention from threatening developments in other parts of the world. The infighting between the three military services got so bad that in March 1948, only six months after the Air Force gained its independence, President Truman, while vacationing at Key West, Florida, agreed to settle some of the thorniest disputes. The informal Key West Agreement, or Functions Papers, was formalized in August 1949 in an amendment to the National Security Act, which also established the Department of Defense. That same August the North Atlantic Treaty was signed and NATO came into being, the result of the Berlin blockade and continued Soviet intransigence. And on August 29, 1949, the Soviet Union exploded its first atomic bomb. The Soviets finally had our full and undivided attention. War, if it came, would of course be nuclear, and we scrambled to get ready. But seldom do things go the way of the planners. On June 25, 1950, on a warm Sunday morning, the North Korean Peoples Army crossed the 38th parallel with the aim of unifying the country on its own terms. There was nothing nuclear about the invasion, it was conventional in every sense of the word.

CHAPTER TWO

AN AIRPLANE WITH
ONE-WAY ENGINES

"We were, in short, in a state of shameful unreadiness when the Korean War broke out, and there was absolutely no excuse for it," wrote General Ridgway. "The state of our Army in Japan at the outbreak of the Korean War was inexcusable. The outbreak of that war came to me as a complete surprise, as it did to all our military men – from Seoul to Washington."[1] The North Korean invasion was indeed a total intelligence failure, comparable to the disaster that befell America one December morning in 1941; and another yet to come in the far distant future, on September 11, 2001. General Matthew B. Ridgway's surprise was shared by many Americans. Captain Charles E. Schreffler, an F-51 pilot in the 18th Fighter Bomber Group at Clark Air Base in the Philippines had just transitioned from the F-51 to the F-80 jet. He received orders to return to the United States. "Our household goods were picked up as scheduled. That evening my wife mentioned a curious thing. The household goods people had contacted her and asked if she wanted to change the destination of our shipment. When she asked them why she would want to do that, they told her that her husband wouldn't be accompanying her. 'Is that true?' she asked me. That's how I learned about the invasion of South Korea. My wife took the ship home to San Francisco, while I left for Johnson Air Base, near Tokyo, Japan, to pick up an old and familiar F-51. By the time her ship docked in San Francisco harbor, some of the returning wives learned that their husbands had died in South Korea, in a war of which they knew nothing."[2] Schreffler's F-51, and hundreds like it, decimated the North Koreans' onslaught in daylight hours. B-26s took over searching for enemy columns at night. In

Douglas Aircraft Corporation test pilots and support personnel celebrate the 100th flight of RB-66B 53-441 on April 10, 1957, at Edwards Air Force Base, California. The first operational RB-66B, 53-442, had been delivered to the 363rd Tactical Reconnaissance Group at Shaw AFB, South Carolina, on January 31, 1956.

self-sacrificing attacks, flying their aging and vulnerable fighters and bombers, these airmen slowed the enemy's advance, then brought it to a halt at the Pusan perimeter. An F-51 pilot, Major Louis J. Sebille, and a B-26 pilot, Captain John S. Walmsley, earned the Medal of Honor posthumously flying close air support for beleaguered Army troops. Their sacrifice is representative of the fierceness of combat and with what valor it was waged.[3]

Two years earlier, in 1948, young Lieutenant Lobdell had received an assignment from the RB-26s at Langley Field to the 8th Tactical Photo Reconnaissance Squadron at Johnson Air Base, Japan. Lobdell flew the RF-61, the photo reconnaissance version of the *Black Widow* night fighter. "My wife joined me about eleven months later. Then the 8th Squadron was deactivated and I moved over to the 13th Bomb Squadron, the *Grim Reapers*, of the 3rd Bomb Group at Yokota," flying B-26s. It was June 1950, and "we were scheduled to go on this mobility exercise to Matsushima where we flew against the air defenses on Okinawa. Then the war began and the North Koreans came down [the peninsula]. We were immediately sent to Ashiya. We had two squadrons, the 8th and the 13th, and we could muster, I guess, 12 airplanes among us. We sat around the briefing room for about three hours, they had canceled the mission and told us to standby. So we were standing by. Our group commander was supposed to lead the mission, and the squadron commanders the flights. Then they came and took the group commander's name off the board and made me the group lead. Took the squadron commanders off and put captains up as flight leads. I was a lieutenant at the time. Then they came out and briefed the mission – you're going to Pyongyang. I remember everyone writing their will and handing it to the guy next to him to sign, and we turned them in to the intelligence officer.

"'OK,' the briefer said, 'you are going to use fragmentation bombs.' People were looking around. We didn't have any bomb tables. So Frank Bullis who was my bombardier and a guy by the name of Barnett went off in the corner and did some trigonometric calculations and figured out the bomb tables. There were only two bombardiers in the whole outfit. We took off late in the afternoon on June 28 with 12 airplanes. Our target was the airfield at Pyongyang. We went in at about ten to twelve-thousand feet. A lovely evening I remember, it was just beautiful. We droned on and of course thought, 'Holy smoke, when we get to Pyongyang things are really going to happen.' There was some flack way off in the distance. I think I dropped a bomb on an airplane taking off and that was about it. And we turned around and came home. I concluded if I ever go to war again, I'm going on the first day because nobody knows what they are doing.

"We moved from Ashiya to Iwakuni and set up operations. I became the armament officer and didn't know anything about armaments. We had both the glass nosed airplanes, the bombers, with Norden bomb sights and six forward firing guns in the wings, and some hard-nosed airplanes that had eight forward firing guns in each wing [and in the nose] for a total of 16. None of the guns had ever been bore-sighted. Nobody knew how to do that. We finally found a kit and figured out how to bore-sight these things. It took us a long time. When you'd attack with one of those airplanes it would scare everybody to death, I'm sure. We went to the night intruder mission in July or August, and you'd fire those things off. They'd blind you immediately. So we'd root around in the dark and see lights coming down the road and would hope to get to them before they turned off their lights. We tried various techniques. We finally would fly out of Iwakuni, then cycle back to Taegu to refuel and rearm, then fly another mission and go back to Iwakuni. I flew a total of sixty combat missions."[4]

The Korean War, a total surprise to an unprepared military, should have been anything but that. After all, the military's business is to be vigilant and ready to defend the country, not let itself be surprised by a third rate military power. It also quickly became apparent that the old World War II airplanes carrying the brunt of the fighting in Korea were wearing out. The Air Staff in Washington and TAC at Langley, Virginia, were searching for a quick replacement for the aging fleet of fighters and bombers. It was not that TAC's staff officers had fallen asleep at the wheel as the saying goes, instead they were aiming too high, looking for the ultimate tactical fighter, bomber and reconnaissance aircraft. This ultimate tactical airplane they were looking for was to fly high above the reach of enemy air defenses, perform equally well at very low altitudes, have a range of at least 1,000 miles, carry a big pay-load, be able to operate from airfields with short runways, and fly supersonic. Such unrealistic and often mutually exclusive requirements ensured that nothing truly useful evolved. The airplane TAC put its faith in for years was the Martin XB-51, an innovative design resulting from a light bomber competition in February 1946. Air Force and TAC continued to change requirements as the XB-51 evolved. On October 28, 1949 the XB-51 made its maiden flight. Testing continued and a second airplane was built. In May 1952, during a low level demonstration at Edwards AFB, California, one of the two XB-51s crashed, killing its pilot. The second aircraft soon crashed as well. The contract, for what once was thought of as TAC's ultimate tactical bomber, was canceled.[5] The XB-51 was a true disappointment to the TAC staff, but plenty of studies, concepts and starry eyed alternatives emerged and were vigorously pursued. It was clear, however, that what was needed in the summer of 1950 were airplanes on the ramp, rather than more studies.

About this time the term 'weapons system' began to creep into the tactical requirements vocabulary. The weapons system approach was a SAC concept introduced with the B-47 jet bomber. Using this approach meant designing essential mission related equipment directly into an airplane, rather than, as was the practice in World War II, acquire an airframe first, then fill it with whatever equipment was needed to make it a bomber, photo-reconnaissance aircraft, or what have you. The SAC B-47, first flown on the very day the Korean War began, had its K-5 radar bomb system designed directly into the airframe. TAC became enthusiastic about the weapons system approach as well. It made sense, and promised substantial savings. But it didn't seem to work for the multiplicity of missions TAC aircraft had to fulfill. "One of the reasons why the weapons system method was not succeeding," lamented the author of the 1954 TAC Headquarters Aircraft Requirements History "was the policy of incorporating the capability of more than one mission into the design of any weapons system."[6] Yet the basic approach remained valid in a budget constrained environment, and helped rationalize conflicting demands to a scrutinizing Congress.

Within weeks of the outbreak of the war in Korea the USAF Board of Senior Officers began looking at options to replace the aging Douglas B/RB-26 *Invader*. The board agreed that what was needed was a light jet bomber that could operate from short runways and unimproved airfields, one with a ceiling of 40,000 feet, a range of about 1,000 miles, and a maximum speed of around 550 knots. The board looked at what was available, including foreign aircraft. The Martin XB-51 was the first choice of course, but it was still undergoing flight testing and probably would not be available for a number of years. The North American B-45 was looked at but found unsuitable for the tactical bomber role, limited by a conventional airframe with little growth potential. The Canadair CF-100 failed on many counts, as did the British Vickers Valiant and SAC's B-47 medium bomber. The one aircraft that looked as close to an off-the-shelf combat airplane as one could hope for was the English Electric *Canberra*. Air Force technical intelligence officers attached to the London embassy were impressed when witnessing its first flight at RAF Wharton in 1949. The Air Staff tasked Brigadier General Albert Boyd, the Air Force chief of test and evaluation at Edwards Air Force Base, to take a look. Boyd generally liked what he saw. But he wanted the *Canberra* to undergo rigorous tests and evaluation. Two British *Canberras* were purchased and flown to the Martin Company in Baltimore. Although the British aircraft exhibited many shortcomings as they underwent detailed examination and tests, the *Canberra* gained more friends than enemies and became a serious contender to replace the B-26 as an *interim* night intruder and reconnaissance aircraft for employment in Korea. On February 26, 1951, the Senior Officer and USAF Weapons Board each chose the *Canberra* as the best interim aircraft available for service in Korea. General Hoyt Vandenberg, the Air Force Chief of Staff, signed off on the recommendation. It was a done deal.[7]

The Martin Company, testing the XB-51, seemed the logical choice to build the American copy of the *Canberra* and was selected to build what eventually became a buy of 403 B-57 aircraft of all types. The plane was never given an American name, instead becoming and remaining the B-57. The immediate need was for a bomber in the role of night intruder, and an equally night capable RB-57 reconnaissance aircraft. Eight B-57A bombers were built before it was realized that this really was not an off the shelf airplane. It showed numerous shortcomings which had to be fixed, not the least of which was the J65 engines which took the place of the British Rolls Royce turbojets. The B-57 program stalled. The first flight of a production B-57 did not take place until July 20, 1953. The Korean Armistice was signed on July 27. The RB-57A was much the same airplane as the bomber, but instead of bombs it carried cameras. The entire program was nearly killed by a string of spectacular accidents. By July 1954, the first of 67 RB-57s were assigned to the 345th Bomb Wing at Langley AFB, Virginia, and the 363rd Tactical Reconnaissance Group at Shaw AFB, South Carolina. Several of the B-57As trickle down to the 17th Bomb Wing at Hurlburt Field, Florida, and still others to squadrons of the 66th Tactical Reconnaissance Group based at Sembach Air Base, Germany, and Laon Air Base, France. However, the B/RB-57A accident rate remained high, groundings for one reason or another frequent. Structural problems soon arose and required modification. Then, in 1955, the entire B-57 fleet was grounded for engine compressor stalls.

Yet, with all its limitations, it was the B/RB-57A which was to serve as the principal aircraft for pilots to transition from the conventionally powered B-26 into the twin-jet B/RB-66B *Destroyer*, another *interim* aircraft selected by TAC and the Air Staff. The RB-57As were withdrawn as the RB-66 began to arrive on the scene in numbers, and were subsequently modified to serve in special Cold War reconnaissance programs and as electronic countermeasure training aircraft for ADC radar sites. With the overall failure of the B/RB-57A program one might expect that the B-57 would have been canceled, and there were efforts underway to do just that. However, prudence prevailed, and the needed time and funding was invested in the airplane to make it work. In years to come, in another war, the B-57B bomber, of which 202 were built, would many times over justify its initial high development cost.

In her book *Post-World War II Bombers*, Marcelle Size Knaack writes, "The Air Force accepted a grand total of 403 B-57s. Production ended in 1957, but at the close of the year USAF records showed that 47 of the 403 aircraft had been destroyed in major accidents. The B-57 was not easy to fly. Prior to modification of its longitudinal control and stabilizer systems, the B-57 was uncontrollable if one of its two engines failed on take-off or landing. Fifty percent of the major accidents resulted from pilot error, with 38 percent occurring on landing. Yet, while the number of accidents was high – 129 major and minor accidents as of 1958, the rate compared with that of the B-47 and other jet powered aircraft."[8]

While the B-57 selection appeared to be a knee-jerk response by the Air Staff and TAC to a pressing need forced by the unexpected war in Korea, a follow-on aircraft was being considered even before the B-57 made its maiden flight. In June 1951 the Air Staff initiated action to select a B-57 replacement, to be delivered to operational units in 1954. Pretty much the same palette of existing aircraft was considered as had been looked at during the initial B/RB-57 selection process, with the addition of the Navy XA3D-1. When the Navy had its supercarrier, the *USS United States,* canceled during the B-36 controversy in 1949, it chose to continue with the design and development of the A3 nuclear bomber – the largest and heaviest carrier based aircraft ever built. The B-47, which was entering squadron service with SAC in 1951, was recommended by the Air Research and Development Command, ARDC, as an option, but its high support requirements and questionable availability eliminated it as a viable contender. The B-57 itself was too small to carry existing *special* weapons, a euphemism for nuclear bombs, and a principal reason why another interim follow-on aircraft was required until the XB-51 became available. The Navy A3D looked attractive although it had yet to be built. Again, the promise of an off-the-shelf aircraft had great appeal and entertained visions of cost savings and quick delivery.

The Douglas Aircraft Company, designer and future builder of the A3D, and long time provider of U.S. Navy aircraft under the able tutelage of Edward H. Heinemann (Mr. Attack Aircraft), quickly put together a proposal and submitted it to the Air Staff for consideration. Changes proposed by Douglas didn't seem all that major: deletion of carrier provisions such as folding wings, catapult equipment, and arresting gear; addition of ejection seats and anti-icing provisions to give the aircraft an all-weather capability; increasing the airframe load factor to handle up to 3.67Gs at 70,000 pounds gross weight to compensate for the stresses of low altitude high speed operations; and an enlarged search radar antenna to increase radar capability. On 29 November 1951 the USAF Aircraft Weapons Board accepted the Douglas proposal and recommended the aircraft, designated B-66, for both the bomber and reconnaissance roles. Two months later, in January 1952, the Air Force issued a GOR, a General Operational Requirement document, for RB-66A, RB-66B and RB-66C aircraft.

The original RB-66A buy was for five pre-production aircraft to be used for test purposes. It was decided that no X-coded test aircraft were required. It was after all an off the shelf aircraft, and time was of the essence. The logic was flawed since the Navy A3D had yet to be built and flown. The RB-66B, of which a total of

145 aircraft were eventually procured, was a day and night photo reconnaissance jet designed to use both flash bombs and cartridges. The RB-66C, a surprise addition, was a tactical electronic reconnaissance aircraft similarly equipped to SAC's RB-47H strategic reconnaissance bomber which began flying with the 55th Strategic Reconnaissance Wing, 55SRW, out of Forbes AFB, Topeka, Kansas, in 1954. Eventually, 36 RB-66C electronic reconnaissance airplanes were acquired. Three months later, in April of 1952, the Air Staff issued the expected GOR for the procurement of B-66B bombers. The bombers were to be configured with the sophisticated state of the art K-5 radar bombing system designed for use on the SAC B-47. Seventy-two B-66B bombers would eventually be produced to serve with the 47th Bombardment Wing at RAF Sculthorpe, England, replacing the North American B-45A, America's first all jet bomber. Not until three years later, in August 1955, did the Air Staff issue a final procurement directive for 36 WB-66D weather reconnaissance aircraft in lieu of an equal number of RB-66C electronic reconnaissance aircraft. The total B-66 buy when production ceased in January 1958 was 294 aircraft; a small quantity compared to the huge World War II bomber and fighter buys. Aircraft costs had increased dramatically along with capabilities, and buys of quantities of less than 1,000 combat aircraft of a particular type became the rule rather than the exception. (See Appendix 2)

The production schedule Douglas signed up to would have been achievable had no further changes been required than those initially anticipated, and if the engine selected by the Air Force to power their new jet had been available. Neither was the case. In addition, there was a significant shortage of grinders, planers, and milling machines. These had to be imported from Germany.[9] It is actually remarkable that the Douglas Aircraft Corporation managed to design a practically new aircraft and build four distinct versions with only a two year schedule slip. As a result of flight test and Air Force and TAC initiatives, additional changes to the B-66 continued to accumulate. Wouldn't it be nice to have larger tires to permit landing on runways built for lighter fighter aircraft? Done. Rudder pedal nose wheel steering certainly made sense, but the Navy designed hydraulic system had too many potential single points of failure to accommodate that change, so it had to be redesigned. Of course Air Force electronics had to be substituted for Navy electronics, and an in-flight refueling capability certainly made sense and was quickly added. The landing gear had to be beefed-up to accommodate all the extra weight. Other design changes were not optional. When flight testing revealed significant wing-flutter problems, the solution was to put 250 pound weights in the wing tips, changing the center of gravity for the aircraft. Every change induced more change. Excessive landing roll was dealt with by incorporating anti-skid breaking and a brake chute. And so it went.

Then the TAC staff insisted that the airplane needed a pair of guns to defend itself. Quickly a General Electric A-5 fire control system with two 20mm tail guns was added, requiring a gunner, ejection seat and life support system, and 500 rounds of 20mm ammunition for each gun – adding extra weight which reduced speed, range, and increased take-off roll. When at a later date the gun-system was removed from the aircraft and replaced with an electronic countermeasure, ECM, tail cone, the weight reduction resulted in a measurable increase in air speed, reduced take-off roll, increased altitude and a 113 mile range improvement.[10] Even the 20mm guns seemed inadequate to some, and proposals were circulated around TAC and the Air Staff to replace them with 30mm guns. TAC Operations Analysis, TAC/OA, took a dim view of that proposal and quickly shot it down. "The take-off ground roll on a standard day at sea level is increased from about 6,400 feet to 6,800 feet," cautioned TAC/OA, and "on a hot day the increase is much more. The take-off distance over a 50 foot obstacle is increased from 9100 to 9750 feet," and cruise altitude and maximum speed will be reduced. Most important though, the center of gravity of the aircraft will shift backwards with significant consequences in a breakaway maneuver for special weapons delivery.[11] The 30mm gun proposal died. Even while the 20mm gun system was being installed, forward thinking staff officers at the Air Staff were planning to do away with the guns all together and substitute ECM equipment.

Changes to the aircraft continued into the production cycle, including modifications to the spoilers, a revised fuel management system, increased cockpit pressurization, and modifications to the leading edge slats to deal with a pitch-up problem. A seemingly endless parade of smaller modifications materialized such as the addition of an external AC/DC power receptacle to eliminate the use of aircraft power when performing ground electrical maintenance. Provisions for a periscopic sextant seemed necessary should the aircraft be operated in the polar region.[12] For aircraft which had already gone through the production line it meant they had to be recycled through the Douglas Long Beach or Tulsa facilities for modification, or be modified in the field by Douglas and Air Force maintenance teams. When all was said and done, the B-66 was a new airplane and bore little resemblance to its Navy A3D counterpart other than an external likeness. Karl Schroder, a Douglas design engineer responsible for flight and mechanical control systems on the B-66 lamented, "While the TAC types are reported to have liked the bird, the Wright-Patterson Weapon System Project Office almost killed it with add-ons and alterations via the Engineering Change Proposal, ECP, route."[13]

The B-66 aircraft TAC asked for in the beginning to perform the tactical bomber and day and night photographic and electronic reconnaissance missions was supposed to have a 1,000 nautical mile radius, be able to use short runways, maintain commonality among models to keep logistics and maintenance simple, be fast, highly maneuverable, and able to operate equally well at high and low altitudes in all kinds of weather. Even without the additional weight added to the aircraft as a result of the many modifications, it would have been difficult to achieve many of the stated requirements. At 80,000 pounds gross weight and with the less powerful J71 engine, rather than the J57, neither short landing or short take-off distances nor other flight parameters once deemed essential were achievable. Although the airplane would perform well as a bomber, photo- and electronic reconnaissance aircraft, and in a role none of the earlier planners ever envisioned, as the principal electronic warfare aircraft of the Vietnam War, the one decision that would limit the B-66 throughout its twenty years of service in every role it was assigned was the choice of the J71 Allison engine.

In the early '50s jet turbines were still a work in progress. Only ten years earlier the German Me 262 jet fighter made its appearance. Its engines had to be replaced and overhauled after only ten hours of combat flying.[14] Although Kelly Johnson designed the P-80 for General 'Hap' Arnold in 185 days in 1943 to counter the Me 262 threat, the P-80 never saw combat in World War II. It wasn't Kelly's fault: we couldn't come up with a reliable engine. Our ace of aces in World War II, Major Richard I. Bong, was killed in a P-80 jet taking off from Burbank, California, on August 6, 1945. His loss was only the latest of many pilots to perish in the P-80 due to engine failure.[15] By 1948, as the Soviets put the squeeze on Berlin, there were no F-80 jet fighters sitting on a tarmac somewhere in Germany. They were all at home getting modified once again. Early engines, such as the J47 in the B-47, or the J65 in the F-84F and B/RB-57A, had too little thrust to be considered viable candidates for the B-66. (See Appendix 2) The engine of choice at the time was the Pratt & Whitney J57, and the engine recommended for the B-66 by the Douglas Aircraft Corporation.

SAC's B-52 heavy bomber, which first flew in 1952, was powered by eight J57s, each providing 13,750 pounds of thrust with water injection. In the early '50s, that much thrust from an engine was viewed as phenomenal. The KC-135A *Stratotanker*, a private Boeing initiative based on its 707 commercial jet liner, was slated to have J57s as well. TAC's F-100 *Super Saber*, which first flew in 1953, was powered by the J57, as was the F/RF-101 *Voodoo*, ADC's F-102 *Delta Dagger*, and the Navy's F4D *Skyray*. Although every aircraft flew different versions of the J57, every J57 produced a static thrust rating without after burner or water injection of over 10,000 pounds, soon to reach 15,000 pounds. The May 31, 1954, issue of *Aviation Week* notes, "Power is the Key – The 10,000-lb thrust Pratt & Whitney Aircaft J57 split-compressor axial turbojet is the most powerful American engine now flying in production aircraft ... New Air Force contracts for

F-101s and F-102s were disclosed last week in a Commerce Department summary of government contract awards ... Both the F-101 and F-102 are powered by Pratt & Whitney J57 jet engines."[16]

As early as May 1952 Air Materiel Command, AMC, initiated an engine competition for the B-66 considering the General Motors Allison J71, the General Electric J73, the Westinghouse J40, and the Pratt & Whitney J57. The J40 and J73 were quickly eliminated for technical reasons. The favored Pratt & Whitney J57 engine was dropped from consideration. The official reason for selecting the unproven 9,570 pound thrust J71 was: it was available and the B-66 had a lower priority than other weapons systems. "It was felt there would not be enough engines to go around," was AMC's position.[17] SAC of course received the blame for taking every J57 it could lay its hands on for the B-52 *Stratofortress* program. Its soon to appear companion aircraft, the KC-135 *Stratotanker*, was to be powered by four J57 turbines; the B-52 used eight. SAC's J57 requirements were indeed enormous. But the J57 availability issue for the B-66 wasn't solely a SAC creation, it was really a TAC and AMC issue. TAC in effect let the Materiel Command dictate the engine choice for the B-66 and by so doing willingly compromised aircraft operational requirements for payload and its ability to "use makeshift or short runways."[18] It didn't help that the B-66, primarily a reconnaissance aircraft, was represented by action officers from the TAC Bomber Branch whose interests lay elsewhere. In effect, there was no one at TAC to stand up for the airplane and argue its requirements, much less have the courage to point out to senior officers the long term consequences of selecting a marginal power plant. As for re-engining an aircraft at some future date, that was rarely ever done. And who knew how long an airplane would really be around, what missions it might be required to fly? The best and only responsible course of action at the time would have been to give the B-66 the best power plant available – the J57.

TAC's commander, General John K. Cannon, whose career dated back to the 6th Pursuit Squadron at Luke Field in 1925, was focused on the F-100 *Super Sabre*, not the B/RB-66 program. The F-100 made its first flight on May 25, 1953, at Edwards AFB, and was of course powered by a J57. It was the kind of airplane that made a fighter general's heart beat faster, unlike the twin-engine subsonic B-66. "What an airplane," swooned one TAC staff officer about an F-100 demonstration at Palmdale, California. Its "appearance was made spectacular by the aircraft's achieving a speed of approximately 750 miles per hour, shattering windows and splitting door frames."[19] In fairness to General Cannon, he had genuine concerns that the F-100 could be delayed by a diversion of J57 engines to higher priority programs. The F-100 was at the heart of giving TAC a credible nuclear strike force, turn TAC into a 'mini-SAC,' and make TAC a contender in the bitter budget battles on the 'Hill' for scarce defense dollars. To the neglect of conventional precision bombing capabilities TAC commanders, from John Cannon to Gabriel Disosway, pursued the nuclear option, and succeeded all too well. It is ironic to note, that when then Lieutenant Colonel Kenneth Chilstrom, in July 1957, presented the nuclear delivery capability of TAC's new F-105 fighter to the recently appointed vice chief of staff of the Air Force, General Curtis E. LeMay, the general's terse comment to Chilstrom was, "Sending a boy to do a man's job."[20]

On July 23, 1953, General Cannon sent a letter to the Air Staff requesting light weight J57 engines for his new F-100A jet fighter on a first priority basis. Colonel Bruce K. Holloway, the same Holloway who 15 years later would become commander of SAC, then serving as deputy director of requirements at the Air Staff, responded by explaining that a program was underway to substitute titanium alloy for steel in the J57, and that "AMC was directed by this headquarters to allocate titanium J57 engines in the following order of priority: a. B/RB-52 b. F-101 c. F-100 d. F-102. The latest aircraft production schedule indicates that B-52 and F-101 production is such that it will absorb completely the initial quantity of 250 titanium engines. No estimate can be made at this time when such engines will be available for F-100 aircraft."[21] The F-101, like the B-52, was of course a SAC airplane, intended as an escort fighter. The priorities were clear – SAC was number one with the Air Staff and the Congress. With the Korean War over, money was drying up quickly for everything but the strategic forces. "There was a real fear that the development and production of the F-100 might be impeded by plans for the allocation of the J57 engine to other programs."[22]

Lieutenant Lobdell, the same young airman who flew the first raid of the Korean War against Pyongyang airfield in a Douglas B-26 light bomber, finished his combat tour in late 1950 and was assigned to headquarters USAF in Washington DC. "One of the interesting things," he recalls, "I was in the Pentagon at the time the B-66 was started. Both the RB-57 and the RB-66 work came out of the shop that I was in. My tactical division was very much a part of all that and the configuration of those airplanes. What I didn't realize at the time was that we had a reconnaissance branch, a bomber branch and a fighter branch. The bomber guys handled all the B-66 stuff."[23] The B-66 was of course principally a reconnaissance aircraft, only 72 bombers were built out of a total aircraft buy of 294. The fighter boys were pushing J57s for the F-100, and the bomber boys were busy focusing on the *ultimate* tactical bomber, the XB-51, not the *interim* B-66.[24] Not having an advocate on the Air Staff or at Headquarters TAC was a fatal flaw for the B-66. There was no one willing to take on AMC when it selected the inferior J71.

The Allison people had significant problems with the engine even after AMC made its choice. They had difficulty passing a 50-hour qualification test, leading the AMC program office at Wright-Patterson AFB to actually have second thoughts and start looking for an alternative engine. Allison suddenly managed to complete the 50-hour qualification test by October 1953, causing, yet surviving, a production slippage of four months for the B-66 program. Certainly, it would have been prudent at this time for the AMC program office to take a hard look at what might be going on at Allison. Unfortunately AMC was already behind the proverbial power-curve – a slipping B-66 production schedule and pressure from above to get the airplane to fly all combined to move on with the program. It was the last opportunity for AMC to right a wrong for good and valid reasons. Instead, nothing was done. Allison continued to experience problems meeting its 150 hour qualification test. Production J71-9 engines were slow to accelerate, surged, flamed out and stalled even while taxiing. On October 8, 1955, test pilots at the Air Force Flight Test Center at Edwards Air Force Base flying RB-66B aircraft filed an unsatisfactory report against the J71-9 and -11 engines: "Several pilots, while flying the RB-66B aircraft have experienced compressor stalls. The stall condition has occurred at different RPM settings and at times when the throttle is being advanced and other times when the throttle is being retarded ... Some pilots have experienced compressor stalls during ground taxiing operations ... Pilots are of the opinion that this is a very hazardous flight condition. The cause for the compressor stall cannot be determined. However, it is believed that the J71-9 and -11 engines may not have been completely developed prior to acceptance by the Air Force. It is recommended that consideration be given to provisioning a different engine for the B-66 type aircraft."[25] In spite of all its documented flaws and short-comings, the General Motors Allison J71 remained the engine choice for the B-66 aircraft. Lieutenant Colonel Clifford T. Manlove in 1955 was assigned to the AMC B-66 Weapons System Program Office. "I immediately was briefed and became aware of the B-66 problems. Believe me they had them. Douglas was on hold and 18 months behind production schedule. The A3D had 15,000 pound thrust engines; the B-66 9,500 pound thrust engines. With TAC adding numerous engineering changes, the B-66 was rapidly becoming a heavy bomber with not enough power. Word was that on a hot day in Denver the B-66 would not get off the ground with a combat load."[26]

Surely other than technical factors played a role in the selection and retention of the J71 jet turbine for the B-66 aircraft. Charles E. Wilson was Secretary of Defense from January 1953 to October 1957. Wilson came to the Defense Department from General Motors, and Allison, the maker of the J71, was a division of General Motors. The loss of the J71 contract at the time would have been a severe blow to Allison, possibly forcing the division out of the jet turbine business at a time when demand was high. Also, the Air Staff certainly wanted to maintain more than just one viable production line for jet turbines, especially after both General Electric with its J73 engine and Westinghouse with its fatally flawed J40 experienced severe technical difficulties resulting in their quick elimination as a source of power plants for the B-66 program. The Allison J71-11 engine was installed on production aircraft "starting with the 18th B-66B and the 21st RB-66B. Thirty-seven earlier airplanes received the -11 engine by retrofit."[27] The changes Allison made to come up with the -11 did not entirely solve the stall and surge problems encountered under conditions of high acceleration, so there evolved the J71-13. The -13 had a dry thrust rating of 10,200 pounds vice 9,700 pounds for the -11, and largely dealt with the problems of the -9 and -11, but not entirely. Over the years the Allison J71-13 provided reasonable performance, having no more than the usual problems for engines of that generation – until the Vietnam War came along. In 1965 the B-66 was suddenly the only tactical airplane available to provide ECM support to both Air Force and Navy strike forces going after targets in North Vietnam defended by radar controlled anti-aircraft, AAA, guns, and SA-2 surface to air, SAM, missile batteries. The airplane, never enjoying more than minimum support for maintenance and spare parts, was practically 'flown into the ground.' High sortie rates in a high temperature, high humidity environment, with engines which often had more than 10,000 hours flying time on them, resulted in a spectacular crash of an EB-66B ECM aircraft on April 8, 1969. The aircraft, 53-498, one of the original *Brown Cradle* airplanes, was on its take-off roll from Takhli Royal Thai Air Force Base when its number one, left engine, failed at about the 5,200 foot point of the runway. The B-66 never did attain single engine speed until well after climb out. The crew of three perished in the ensuing crash. A lengthy grounding of EB-66 aircraft followed. I was at Takhli at the time flying with the 41st Tactical Electronic Warfare Squadron and remember many engines being flown back to the United States for re-certification. It was at this time in the life of an aging airplane when younger aircrew learned that the J71 had also powered the *Snark* cruise missile, and began to refer to the B-66 as the airplane with the one-way engines.

As for the issue of J57 availability. It turned out that Pratt & Whitney had a good thing going, knew it, and ramped up J57 production to provide engines to anyone willing and able to buy them. The Navy A3D, which we in the Air Force referred to in gallows-humor as the All Three Dead airplane – since it didn't have ejection seats but only a rudimentary escape chute – was configured with J57s. So was the Navy's F-8E Crusader which first flew in 1955. There was a Navy seaplane under development, the *Seamaster*, that was powered by J57s. A spectacular crash and lack of a clear mission assured that the *Seamaster* never went anywhere. Both the Boeing 707 and the Douglas DC-8 airliners, then in development, were of course powered by J57s, the most powerful and reliable jet engine of its time. In view of the J71's inadequacies, and the B-66's significant increase in gross weight, it was a tragic oversight not to have reinstalled the arresting gear provisions into the B-66 airframe – a capability which would have saved many lives and aircraft. Ironically, in the summer of 1956, the Northrop *Snark* cruise missile, which gave the J71 the *one-way engine* nickname, swapped its J71 for a J57. The *Snark* was an unmanned aircraft built to intentionally crash into a target – no one but enemy combatants would die in the process. When a B/RB-66 crashed because of J71 engine failure, up to seven aircrew were at risk. One can only presume that no one in authority sitting behind a mahogany desk in a leather swivel chair ever gave that simple fact a second thought.

CHAPTER THREE

FLIGHT TESTING THE DESTROYER

Since the inception of the B-66 program in 1952 the Cold War assumed form and substance. On April 17, 1952, three RB-45C reconnaissance aircraft of the 322nd Strategic Reconnaissance Squadron, based at Lockbourne AFB, Ohio, manned by British aircrews, flew deep into the Soviet Union on a provocative spy-mission. The flights emanated from RAF Sculthorpe in County Norfolk, England, home of the 47th Bombardment Wing (Light) equipped with 50 nuclear armed B-45 bombers.[1] The Soviet response to the overflight was mute. The war in Korea ended in July 1953, six months after General Dwight D. Eisenhower replaced Harry Truman as president. The workers' uprising in East Berlin on June 17, 1953, gave an early indication that not all was well in the 'peoples paradise.' Perhaps Communism was not as homogeneous as politicians and strategists thought it to be. Nor was it necessarily the wave of the future, as President Eisenhower made it appear ten months later when he spoke of 'dominoes falling' at a news conference on April 7. The war in Korea may have ended, but relations between the United States and the Soviet Union could not have been frostier. To emphasize the point, in January 1954, Secretary of State John Foster Dulles spoke of 'massive nuclear retaliation' as a viable defense strategy for the United States and its allies against any type of Soviet aggression. SAC underlined that point by rolling out its first eight-jet B-52 bomber on March 18 to much fanfare at the Boeing plant in Seattle. In a mere six years since General LeMay assumed command, the Strategic Air Command had grown from puny beginnings to a force of 2,640 aircraft, including 342 B/RB-36 heavy bombers, 1,060 B/RB-47 all-jet medium bombers, and 597 KC-97 tankers deployed at home and on bases in England, Spain and North Africa.[2]

Acceleration tests revealed a seriously flawed canopy design. A number of B-66B and RB-66B aircraft had to be returned to the Douglas Long Beach production line for modification.

SAC flexed its muscle in other ways as well. On March 5, 1954, the entire 22nd Bombardment Wing flew 6,000 miles from England to March AFB near Riverside, California. Reported *Aviation Week*, "By this *nonstop* mass B-47 flight the Strategic Air Command has underscored global air power. Congratulations to the United States Air Force! Your triumph over time and space gives new security to the free world. Colonel John B. Henry, pilot of the lead aircraft in the record smashing flight" was shown in an accompanying photo flanked by Major General Walter C. Sweeney, Jr., 15th Air Force Commander.[3] General Sweeney believed in leadership by example and on June 21, 1954, led a flight of three B-47s on a non-stop flight from March AFB to Yokota Air Base near Tokyo, Japan – 6,700 miles in less than 15 hours. And on November 17 Colonel David A. Burchinal flew a distance and endurance record in a B-47 bomber when after taking off from Sidi Slimane, French Morocco, weather kept him from landing in England. He flew back to Sidi Slimane, only to find the base socked in. Colonel Burchinal remained airborne for over 47 hours, flying 21,163 miles, with the help of nine aerial refuelings. The message was clear: SAC could reach any target anywhere in the world.[4] SAC, however, was not only flexing its muscle with show-case flights of its B-47 bombers. Although the RB-45C had been transferred to TAC as SAC's force of RB-47E reconnaissance squadrons increased to four wings, General LeMay nevertheless arranged for a second overflight of the Soviet Union by three of TAC's recently acquired RB-45Cs. The aircraft were assigned to the 19th Tactical Reconnaissance Squadron, 19TRS, at Shaw AFB, South Carolina. Colonel Marion C. Mixson, mission coordinator for earlier RB-45C overflights, had been reassigned to the RB-47E equipped 91st SRW which had deployed to Nouasseur AB, Morocco. Mixson was summoned to Offutt AFB to meet with General LeMay – immediately. "Once I got to Offutt, LeMay told me to get down to Shaw, pick up four RB-45s and take them to Wright-Patterson for modifications to their radars. Then fly them over to Sculthorpe. TAC crews flew the aircraft to Wright-Patterson. The radars were peaked by British engineers until the picture was crisp and clear. When the aircraft arrived at Sculthorpe in early April, Squadron Leader Crampton and his bunch were waiting for the airplanes. They were repainted in RAF colors, and the night of April 28 the Brits flew them on routes nearly identical to those flown in 1952." All returned safely, not that the Russians didn't try to shoot them down. The "Ruskies frightened the life out of me over Kiev when they finally got our height right and sent up a highway of predicted flak, fantastic it was, but by the grace of God they got our speed wrong and chucked the stuff just ahead of us," recalled Squadron Leader Crampton.[5] Ten days later, General LeMay sent Captain Harold R. Austin in an RB-47E photo-reconnaissance aircraft on a daring daylight flight over the Kola Peninsula to photograph Soviet air bases and determine if the Russians had moved any of their strategic *Bison* bombers, shown-off at the May Day Parade days earlier, onto airfields where their presence posed a threat to the United States. Austin returned to RAF Fairford, England, after surviving the attacks of scores of Soviet fighters and nearly having his flying career terminated by a MiG-17 firing a 30mm cannon shell into the innards of his RB-47E.[6] The Soviets were furious at the brazen Brits and Americans, and not the least at their own impotence.

While LeMay was making life miserable for the Soviets, General Nathan Twining, the Air Force chief of staff, did the same type of work at home. He warned Congress and the nation that "the Russians have thousands more combat planes than the U.S. military combined."[7] The 'bomber gap' arose. The Air Force rhetoric of escalation was all about budgets and funding to continue the expansion of SAC strike forces and their supporting tankers, fighter escort and transport elements. ADC and TAC were hard pressed to get funds for even their most essential programs. The Eisenhower administration was aiming for reduced defense budgets at a time when the Air Force and SAC were painting a picture of strategic weakness. Other troubling events occurred in the fateful year of 1954, events which were noted but deemed not sufficiently important to figure in the greater national security picture. Dien Bien Phu fell to the Viet Minh on May 7, the day before Hal Austin flew his RB-47E over the Kola Peninsula. The French pleaded with President Eisenhower for intervention in Indochina. Eisenhower replied, "I can conceive of no greater tragedy then for the U.S. to become involved in an all-out war in Indochina."[8] Prescient words indeed. On July 21 Vietnam was partitioned into North and South at the Geneva peace conference, and divided by a Demilitarized Zone similar to one on the Korean peninsula. It was the very beginning of a tragedy.

The B-66 program in 1954 found itself in a precarious position – behind schedule and its funding threatened by expanding strategic bomber programs. Program cancellation was a distinct possibility.[9] The Douglas Company was very much attuned to the political situation. When Douglas staged a Contractor Technical Compliance, CTC, Inspection for the RB-66A at its Long Beach plant on March 22, 1954, Douglas made sure that it was done right. The CTC Inspection was attended by Air Force representatives from any and all offices that had anything remotely to do with the RB-66. The CTC inspection was an important 'do or die' affair in the evolution of the RB-66. No detail was too small not to be gone over with a fine tooth comb. A fancy, hard-cover folder outlining the four day agenda was provided to every attendee. There were live indoor demonstrations on the first RB-66A built to convince the customer that Douglas had complied with directions and was providing the expected product. It was a meticulously organized and executed event. On Tuesday, 23 March, the schedule called for:

8:30: Demonstrate actuation of camera doors and flash cartridge doors.

9:00: Demonstrate operation and removal of cameras and mounts.

10:00: Demonstrate operation of driftmeter fairing. Demonstrate operation of horizontal stabilizer.

10:30: Turret operation – no ammunition will be fed, however, loaded ammunition box will be loaded and removed.

11:00: Demonstrate operation of surface lock and power control interlock. Demonstrate release of 1 JATO bottle, each side of airplane. Demonstrate installation of 12 JATO bottles.

12:00: Demonstrate actuation of bomb bay doors. Demonstrate operation of aileron, rudder, and elevator surface boost systems. Demonstrate operation of speed brakes.

Other demonstrations were equally detailed in execution and the company passed its customer's close scrutiny. A similar demonstration was held for the B-66B bomber in August 1954.[10] The first flight of an RB-66A occurred on June 24, three months after the CTC Inspection. Problems arose almost immediately and were addressed energetically by Douglas engineers and test pilots. The B-66B bomber made its first flight on January 4, 1955. A substantial number of bombers then became part of the test program, not only because of the various special weapons test requirements, but also to assure the effective integration of the B-47 K-5 bomb/navigation system into the aircraft. It turned out that the K-5 system had to undergo significant adaptation to fit into the B-66 airframe. Nothing seemed to come easy and no money was saved by adapting a Navy aircraft to Air Force needs. The RB-66B, incorporating the many changes required as a result of flight tests in the A-model, flew for the first time on October 29, 1955, the same day the RB-66C, built at the Douglas Tulsa plant, made its maiden flight. Only three months later, on January 31, 1956, the first RB-66B photo-reconnaissance aircraft was delivered to Shaw AFB, flown by Captain Thomas Whitlock and his navigator First Lieutenant Griffin. Whitlock, along with Captain Click D. Smith, who later rose to the rank of major general, had been sent to Edwards AFB to become familiar with the RB-66B and participate in flight tests. Whitlock and Smith would subsequently check out other pilots on the new twin-jet aircraft in the 16th Tactical Reconnaissance Squadron. Shaw AFB was the tactical reconnaissance base of the U.S. Air Force and host to the 363rd Tactical Reconnaissance Group, soon to become a Wing.

The Air Force committed a total of 25 B-66s to the flight test program, including the five A-models which were not to be delivered to combat units.[11] The test pilots were the best available, having gone through a rigorous Air Force selection and training process. In the abbreviated two year period allotted for flight testing, Captains Charles C. Bock, as lead test pilot, and John C. Carlson and John E. Allavie, wrung out the airplane and made it what Tom Whitlock later spoke of as "a very stable airplane with good control response which gave you plenty of stall warning. A pleasure to fly."[12] The purpose of the tests was two-fold: to determine the flight characteristics and performance parameters of the aircraft and to discover any defects and deficiencies. If categorized as affecting safety of flight such defects would be fixed; other defects flyers would be made aware of and had to cope with as best they could. For instance, the pilot's ability to see anything aft of the 35 degree swept back wings of the B-66 was zero – a condition duly noted by the test pilots, but there was nothing that could be done short of designing a new airplane. The flight performance and stability tests were principally flown at Edwards AFB, while adverse weather testing was done at Wright-Patterson AFB, Ohio, by Captains Ralph W. Lusk and John A. Porter. Test piloting in the early postwar years was a precarious profession requiring the utmost skill and depth of system knowledge. Taking an airplane to its limits, at times beyond, and surviving to fly another day was all part of a day's work. All too often pilots did not survive the idiosyncrasies of the aircraft they were testing.[13]

The five RB-66A aircraft committed to the test program turned out to have a number of serious flaws, one of which was canopy design. While most subsequent aircraft were configured with individual escape hatches for the pilot, navigator and gunner, the A-models featured a single canopy that covered the entire flight deck. If the crew elected to eject and an ejection handle was pulled by one of the three crew members, it activated a set of rocket thrusters mounted on each side at the rear of the canopy which then jettisoned the cockpit canopy. If the aircraft was moving at 425 knots, a violent blast of air would hit the crew with the most likely result that no one would survive the ejection sequence. Why this design seemed attractive to engineers at one point in time is not known. Captain Bock's group, however, found the design wanting even before taking off in the aircraft for the first time. It was decided to do some realistic testing. Chimpanzees were strapped into the ejection seats of a B-66 cockpit mounted on a sled. When the sled was fired and the canopy ejected, the air blast was so great it bent the ejection seat rails backward when the seat was near the end of its travel. The navigator's instrument panel broke free and came back into the navigator's seat.

Rocket thrusters used to jettison the canopy and to eject the seats burned seat occupants. Cliff Parrott, who would spent much of his professional career as the lead Douglas RB-66 technical representative to the 363TRW at Shaw wrote "About 15-20 aircraft were manufactured with the canopy system and had to be put back through a modification program. The flight deck had to be taken apart and the revised three hatch cockpit configuration installed. Anytime you have to re-do something during production you are asking for trouble, and these airplanes would give me plenty of trouble at Shaw."[14]

Captains Lusk and Porter had two RB-66B aircraft assigned for flight testing at Wright-Patterson AFB – 53-416 and 53-419. To learn how the aircraft behaved in a thunderstorm they had to go out and find one to fly into. "Take-offs were made at gross weights ranging from 49,000 to 73,000 pounds. Directional control was satisfactory during the entire take-off roll," they noted in their reports. "To provide adequate control immediately after take-off in gusty surface winds and when the 90 degree crosswind component exceeded 15 knots, the take-off airspeed was increased by 10 knots. Handling characteristics were satisfactory with bank angles as high as 45 degrees using normal VFR climb schedule." The test pilots wrote of how the aircraft behaved in a holding pattern, in descents, and during instrument approaches, missed-approaches and on landings – noting every possible flight parameter for subsequent evaluation. Pilots of course are warned not to enter thunderstorms – but if they do how will the airplane behave? How should the pilot behave?

"The recommended penetration speed in turbulence is 250KIAS," knots indicated airspeed, their report noted. "The power setting and pitch attitude for this airspeed should be established before entering the thunderstorm and, if maintained throughout the storm, will result in approximately a constant average airspeed regardless of any false reading of the airspeed indicator." To paraphrase what they were so calmly reporting: Once you enter a thunderstorm all hell will break loose. You can't trust your instruments, so stay with what you have until you get through the worst of it. "Prepare the aircraft prior to entering a zone of turbulent air," and make certain "all safety belts are fastened." I've never forgot to do that one. "Do not chase the airspeed indication, since doing so will result in extreme aircraft attitudes." What they are saying is that you will probably crash if you insist on doing so. And "use as little elevator control as possible in order to minimize the stresses imposed on the aircraft." You don't want to have to pick up the pieces once you get on the ground. By the way "the altimeter may be unreliable because of differential barometric pressure within the storm. A gain of several thousand feet may be expected."[15]

Flying in adverse weather conditions is not all that unusual in a military environment and therefore tests, as flown by Captains Lusk and Porter, were essential. Our two test pilots did the same sort of thing to learn what it was like when the airplane iced up. Their report again notes calmly that "the aircraft is capable of maintaining flight in icing conditions with as much as two inches of ice accumulated on the wing and empennage leading edges with an airspeed loss of 8 to 10 knots. With the operation of both engine and surface ice removal systems, a loss of five percent rpm and 8 to 10 knots in airspeed will occur. Advance throttles to recover these penalties."[16] In the 21st century flight testing is much safer and more comprehensive as a result of computer assisted simulation. In the '50s the computer was the slide rule, and a test pilot did the rest.

In 1962 I reported to my first operational duty assignment as a First Lieutenant with the 55SRW at Forbes AFB, Topeka, Kansas, after two years of flight training. The 55th flew top of the line six-jet RB-47H/K reconnaissance aircraft. Within two-months of my arrival we lost three airplanes – eleven men died. It was a shocking experience for a young officer just entering the military flying profession. Two-thousand flying hours later in the B-47 I didn't give such things a second thought, it was a part of the career choice I had made. Military flyers often perished when their airplanes were involved in catastrophic events, all too many of which occurred in realistic combat training. But the first B-66 related death was not caused in flight, but by an aircraft parked on the tarmac after returning from a test flight.

On April 3, 1956, Captain Edward Kayworth of the 3245th Test Group, Eglin AFB, Florida, was involved in engine suitability tests for high elevation take-offs at Kirtland AFB, New Mexico. He performed two take-offs and landings in one of the early production RB-66Bs, serial number 53-418. After his second landing, Captain Kayworth turned off the runway and returned to the parking area. He did not use excessive braking during either landing nor while taxiing, although some smoke was observed from tires and wheels during the final portion of the landing roll. That smoke was ascribed to the anti-skid cycling device which tended to cause smoke under normal conditions. Sitting on the ramp the right wheel assembly began to smoke and an airman applied CO_2 from a fire extinguisher. About six minutes later white smoke was observed coming from the same wheel assembly. The crew chief, Technical Sergeant Richards, determined it had to be a magnesium fire. Based on his training and experience Sergeant Richards cautioned everyone in the vicinity of the aircraft to move away from the wheel, expecting an explosion. Just then the base provost marshal, Captain George Morris, drove up and parked his car about 80 feet from the RB-66, got out, and began walking toward the airplane when the wheel assembly exploded. Parts of the wheel assembly struck Captain Morris. He died instantly.[17]

CHAPTER FOUR

THE BLACK KNIGHTS OF HURLBURT FIELD

If not beautiful, I always thought the B-66 elegant. Its 35 degree wing sweep making it look as if it could conquer the sound barrier. It couldn't. In contrast to the two-pilot bombers and tankers populating the SAC inventory, all versions of the B-66 required only one pilot. One pilot, as in a fighter, makes for a different kind of flying. There are no shared functions, no shared responsibilities, no opportunities to rest or daydream while another flew the aircraft. Flying the B-66 required a fighter pilot mentality, and those who possessed that independence of spirit and judgment were clearly the men who flew it best. Although many TAC generals with a bomber background tried, they never succeeded in changing the Tactical Air Command flyer into the rigid, response type aircraft operator General LeMay required for his SAC bombers. By 1956, both bomber and reconnaissance versions of the B-66 began flowing into their designated squadrons in the United States, England, Germany and Japan.(See Appendix 3) On March 16, 1956, Colonel Howard F. Bronson, commander of the 17th Bomb Wing, the *Black Knights*, based at Eglin Auxiliary Field #9, adjacent to the sugar-white beaches of the Florida panhandle, flew the first B-66 bomber from Norton AFB, California, to Hurlburt Field in four hours and forty-five minutes at an average ground speed of 580 knots. Bronson was pleased with the way the aircraft flew and handled. He also knew that the days ahead would be filled with daunting challenges.[1]

The Black Knights had returned from duty in Japan and Korea in April 1955, flying war-weary B-26 twin-engine Douglas *Invader*s. Within days of their arrival at Hurlburt they learned that they were slated to convert to the new B-57B twin-

Aircraft 53-483, the second B-66B bomber to come off the production line at the Douglas Long Beach plant, is shown using JATO, jet/rocket assisted take-off, from Long Beach, California, on March 18, 1957. JATO was used in the '50s to get B-66 aircraft off short runways such as at Midway Island and Clark Air Base in the Philippines. JATO fell into disuse as air-refueling became routinely available to tactical aircraft crossing the Pacific and Atlantic.

jet bomber. Hurlburt Field began to undergo a major make-over to get ready for the new jets. Everything from the main runway to the hangars, field lighting, taxiways, refueling systems, to the workshops and administrative buildings was refurbished, renovated or rebuilt. Conversion plans were proceeding on schedule when, in September, Colonel Bronson was informed that there had been a change in plans: the 17th Wing was slated to receive the even newer B-66 twin-jet bomber, rather than the B-57. It was enough work for any organization to convert from one type of aircraft to another, converting from *prop-jobs* to jets was a horse of a different color. Yet no one at higher headquarters thought of it as anything but routine. It certainly appeared that way when the 17th Bomb Wing was directed to maintain its three squadrons combat ready in the B-26 while at the same time transitioning into the new B-66 jet.

Not only did TAC headquarters require every pilot to have at least 150 hours jet time before stepping into the cockpit of a B-66, but 50 of the 150 hours were to be flown in twin-jet aircraft. Other than SAC's six jet B-47 and USAFE's obsolescent and few in number B-45, there were hardly any multi-jet aircraft in the Air Force inventory available to nascent B-66 flyers. The first of 50 twin-jet F-101A *Voodoos* did not arrive in TAC until May 1957, and the trouble-plagued F-89 *Scorpion* was an ADC bird not available to TAC. Several single-engine T-33 jet trainers were provided to the 17th Bomb Wing to allow its pilots to gain their initial jet flying experience; and six B-57B twin-jet bombers, which arrived at Hurlburt before the decision to convert to the B-66 was announced, remained behind to provide multi-engine jet training. Six B-57s were hardly enough to satisfy the 50 hour multi-jet flying requirement for three squadrons of 17th Bomb Wing pilots. More often than not these six airplanes were unavailable because of frequent groundings. When not grounded, the B-57s were restricted in flight altitude, speed and maneuvers in which they could be flown. So the *Black Knights* were forced to look for a home-grown solution. They turned to SAC's 3245th Test Group at nearby Eglin AFB, and worked out an arrangement allowing 17BW pilots to acquire multi-jet flying time in the group's B-47 aircraft.[2] It's not the way an air force should be run, but that's how it was done.

The disjointed 17th Bomb Wing transition from conventional aircraft to jets was unfortunately representative of the Air Force as a whole. In an article in the Winter 2005 issue of *Air Power History*, Dr. Kenneth P. Werrell, a 1960 Air Academy graduate and professor emeritus at Radford University, writes about flying safety in the 1950s. "The new powerplant and greater performance of jets brought a new set of difficulties unappreciated by the system. The early jet engines were unreliable and required different techniques and skills in both maintenance and flying. The service may have recognized, but certainly did not adequately respond to the fact that jets were fundamentally different than prop-powered aircraft requiring different training and procedures. The Air Force did not provide an adequate program for transitioning prop-trained pilots into jets or preparing new pilots for operational service flying jets."[3] Not until General LeMay's training regime was implemented in SAC, and accidents were not shrugged off but viewed as unprofessional, did the other part of good flying training receive adequate attention – flying safety. At Hurlburt Field, the B-26 to B-66 transition experience was one of on-the-job training, with a disturbing lack of attention, direction and positive support from higher headquarters, explaining many of the accidents and incidents experienced by the 17th Bomb Wing. *Pilot error* was all too frequently the label attached to aircraft accidents, when in fact it should have read *training error*.

In addition to the pressures of transitioning from prop to jet aircraft, the 17th Bomb Wing was burdened with flying and maintaining eight different types of airplanes, a maintenance nightmare under the best of circumstances. There were the jets – the B-57, B-66 and T-33. The conventional aircraft included the B-26 bomber, C-47 and C-119 transports, and one each T-29 and B-50 trainers. The C-47 and C-119 were essential to keep the Wing flying, hauling spare parts from depots and manufacturers. There were never enough qualified maintenance personnel around, so the out of commission rates for parts and maintenance were high. Under these troubling circumstances the Wing found it necessary to go to TAC headquarters and ask for a waiver to reduce the number of hours required in multi-engine jet aircraft before its pilots could move into B-66 training. The waiver was granted.

Navigators had to train in the sophisticated K-5 radar bomb system. The Air Force Armament Center at Eglin accommodated the Wing and installed a K-5 system in a B-50 bomber to allow the navigators to at least obtain a minimum of in-flight training until sufficient numbers of B-66 aircraft became available. Nothing came easy for the Wing. By November 1956 the Wing had received 40 B-66s, and many of the aging B-26 twin-engine bombers were finally flown to Arizona for desert storage. But things did not get any easier for the stressed unit. With the arrival of the new aircraft, and before the Wing became combat ready, numerous requests came in from politicians and civic leaders to participate in static displays and air shows. TAC could hardly say no. There was a fly-over of three B-66s at MacDill AFB near Tampa on November 10 in conjunction with the first annual convention of the newly formed Medal of Honor Society. To insure a successful fly-over two airborne spares were provided – five aircraft days were expended on this exercise. A firepower demonstration at Eglin required three B-66 bombers to drop 14 750 pound bombs each. Requests for static displays were numerous – the

National Air Show at Oklahoma City required a B-66 with a typical conventional bomb load of 14 inert 500 pound bombs, and the U.S. Military Academy air indoctrination course wanted a B-66 as part of its curriculum. The requests for static display aircraft were as diverse as they were numerous. All this had to be accommodated while acquiring proficiency in the new aircraft and getting three bomb squadrons ready to fight.[4]

Training began in an organized fashion in November 1956 when sufficient numbers of the new B-66 became available to dedicate aircraft both to aircrew and maintenance training. Four pilots and two navigators had been sent to Edwards AFB to participate in the flight test program of the B-66 to acquire the necessary skills to teach others in the 17th Bomb Wing. Lieutenant Colonel James B. Story was one of those pilots. "For six months I and the others flew the B and RB-66, checked out its air refueling capability, and drafted a training syllabus for a flight simulator we had never seen. Upon completion of our training we ferried aircraft back to Hurlburt and began transition training for our pilots. Since no provisions had been made to accommodate instructor pilots in the aircraft, we improvised a jump-seat which we called the 'MA-1 Milk Stool.' It consisted of an empty ammunition box and an attached lap-belt for use in our checkout program. Later we used the same rudimentary set-up to give instrument training and flight checks."[5] The issue of a dual-control B-66, like the dual control B-57C, had been raised by Air Force with TAC as early as 1953. TAC agreed that sufficient numbers of B/RB-66 dual-control aircraft should be built to provide each wing with several aircraft of the type to use for training purposes. In the ever more difficult budgetary environment of the post Korean War years, coupled with the insatiable appetite of SAC to acquire ever more bombers, the B-66 dual control trainer dropped through the proverbial cracks.[6] Instructor pilots, IPs, were required to get out of the gunner's seat, which they occupied on take-off and landing, and sit on a home-made stool or ammunition box behind the pilot to instruct and observe. It was not a safe set-up and should have never been allowed. There simply was no one at either TAC headquarters or the Air Staff to stand up for the B-66 and its requirements when program cuts were made.

General Otto P. Weyland took the reigns of the Tactical Air Command from John Cannon on April 1, 1954, and remained around as one of the longest serving TAC commanders, until July 31, 1959. 'Opie' Weyland was a former commander of FEAF, the Far Eastern Air Forces, the predecessor organization to the Pacific Air Forces, PACAF, and came to TAC to shake things up. In his eyes SAC was the organizational model to emulate. To start with, he was going to instill in his aircrews a greater sense of discipline by establishing command and control centers at Wing level, ala Strategic Air Command. Such centers were to be manned 24-

hours a day and tasked to track all aircraft and crew movements. The TAC flight crews hated this heavy handed approach and never quite took to it. Then Weyland implemented his dream, a rapid reaction force, which went by the name of CASF – Composite Air Strike Force. CASF envisioned tailored tactical strike forces, including fighters, bombers and reconnaissance aircraft, deploying on short notice to world trouble spots. To go along with the CASF concept, Opie made a subtle but important change in the mission statements of his wings. Before July 1, 1956, the primary mission of the 363rd TRW, for instance, was "to train replacement reconnaissance crews" while the secondary mission was "to prepare for and maintain combat effectiveness of assigned or attached tactical reconnaissance units."[7] General Weyland reversed the order and put war-fighting first, training second.

The mission realignment fit right in with Weyland's CASF concept, as well as an ongoing NATO reorganization which stripped USAFE, TAC's sister command in Europe, of its unique specified command status. That authority, the employment of special weapons, was transferred to the U.S. Commander-in-Chief Europe, USCINCEUR, who also became the Supreme Allied Commander Europe, SACEUR. USCINCEUR, headquartered at Patch Barracks in Vaihingen, Germany, commanded both U.S. Army and Air Force divisions, wings, armies and air forces, while SACEUR commanded all NATO forces from his headquarters in Paris, later Brussels. Not being able to be in two places at once, SACEUR's deputy largely took care of the national USCINCEUR functions at Vaihingen. The arrangement worked most of the time, and assured national control over America's nuclear arsenal. The fact that the NATO Supreme Commander was always going to be an American was the issue that soon was to cause President Charles de Gaulle of France to withdraw his forces from the military component of NATO. While USAFE became just another component of the USCINCEUR/SACEUR force structure, the Strategic Air Command remained a specified command, reporting directly to the Joint Chiefs of Staff, the JCS, in the Pentagon, on war-fighting matters – not the Air Force chief of staff.

General Weyland decided the time was right to put his new CASF concept to the test. Supreme Headquarters Allied Powers Europe, SHAPE, in Paris, scheduled an atomic joint forces – Army, Air Force – exercise code-named *Operation Whipsaw*. The 17th Bomb Wing, still in the process of converting from B-26 to B-66 aircraft and not yet combat ready, was directed to support a task force, *Mobile Baker*, with four B-66B bombers. The call came in late August for the four aircraft and their supporting elements to deploy in September. There was little time to get ready for this important first employment of the B-66 in an operational exercise. With no aerial tanker support available the four aircraft needed to carry pylon mounted fuel tanks for additional fuel. A problem quickly arose. The mounting lugs for the tanks did not match the aircraft installation. The sway braces had been reversed during installation at Douglas. Of course the fuel feed lines from the pylons to the tanks did not match either. The on-site Douglas support team and Air Force maintenance men installed the drop tanks and got the aircraft ready. On September 18 the four B-66s departed for Loring AFB, Maine. From there they flew in loose trail formation to Lajes Field in the Azores, then to Sidi Slimaine, French Morocco, and on to Spangdahlem Air Base in Germany.

The USAFE Air Operations Center, AOC, controlled all air tasking for the exercise. It turned out that the USAFE people had expected RB-66Bs and didn't know what to do with the bombers. There were no target materials available, and the targets that were assigned within 150 miles of Spangdahlem did not take advantage of the capabilities of the B-66, namely its sophisticated K-5 bomb system. States a 17th Bomb Wing report, "It is doubtful if the AOC was aware of the capability and performance of the B-66 or the navigational and bombing equipment installed in the aircraft." However, as far as the CASF concept went, it was considered "sound and workable," by the participating aircrews.[8] The four aircraft returned along nearly the same route as the one flown from Hurlburt to Spangdahlem, substituting Harmon Air Base, Newfoundland, in place of Loring, Maine. B-66B 54-497 was piloted by Captain Zacheus W. Ryall, Captain Darrell E. Selby served as navigator, and Airman First Class Callix J. Perusse was the gunner. Approaching Harmon on October 5, 1956, Captain Ryall experienced fluctuating fuel flow on his number one engine about 50 miles out of Harmon at an altitude of 37,000 feet. Shortly thereafter the right, number two engine began to lose power. Both engines ran at low power, flaming out on occasion. Ryall broke through a 1,500 foot overcast and established a pattern for a no power landing. While turning on base-leg both engines regained full power and Captain Ryall made an uneventful landing. The maintenance officer and Douglas techrep (technical representative) who were in place at Harmon checked the fuel tanks for water, presuming the most likely cause to be icing in the fuel system. The engines operated normally on the ground. The following day, October 6, all went well until the aircraft, again cruising at 37,000 feet, came near Front Royal, Virginia, when both engines began to lose power. It was a cloudy day. Captain Ryall contacted a nearby Ground Control Intercept, GCI, radar site and requested a vector to a suitable airfield. The radar site gave him a heading to Blackstone. The weather at Blackstone: a 300 foot ceiling, 3/4th of a mile visibility. Ryall was at 13,000 feet, between cloud layers, and realized there was no way he could take the aircraft down safely. He asked for a vector to an unoccupied area. Gunner, navigator and pilot ejected in that order. The crew survived without sustaining injuries. The loss of the first B-66 aircraft was an unfortunate end to an otherwise flawless overseas deployment.[9] (See Appendix 5)

Many problems are discovered during flight-test of a new aircraft. Some, however, do not surface until aircraft enter operational service. Examination of the wreckage revealed that a combination of flat and very fine mesh fuel screen was to blame for the loss of engine power. At altitude, in sub-freezing temperatures, JP-4 jet fuel thickened and became jelly like. The jelled fuel could not pass through the fine mesh of the screens designed to keep out impurities. The screens collapsed, blocking the flow of fuel to the engines. A cone-shaped filter with a larger mesh was substituted and solved the problem. The ill-designed fuel screens were to be removed from the supply system to preclude the same thing from happening again. Someone, somewhere, rather than removing the filters, pushed them to the back of the shelf, or something on that order. On September 5, 1961, Captain Jesse B. Kendler flew a WB-66D weather reconnaissance aircraft on a standard weather track out of Kindley Air Base, Bermuda. On the return leg to Kindley both engines flamed out. They restarted when Captain Kendler got to a lower altitude, then failed again. Captain Kendler gave the signal to eject. The two weather personnel in the back of the aircraft ejected downward. Then the navigator and an observer on a familiarization ride ejected. All were rescued. Captain Kendler perished in the crash of the aircraft, to the last moment trying to restart the on-again-off-again jets. The suspected cause of the flame-out was the previously condemned fuel filter. Negligence had now caused the loss of a life.[10]

Only five months later, on February 7, 1962, an RB-66C electronic reconnaissance aircraft with a crew of seven crashed at RAF Chelveston, England, when the engines faltered on landing, killing four of the crew. The cause of the crash: fuel filter icing caused by a flat, fine mesh filter, the same filter that killed Captain Kendler.[11] This time the old filters were purged for good from the supply system. The obvious thought comes to mind that if somewhere some nameless supply sergeant or supply officer had done his job lives would have been saved. And what about the airman who replaced the filters during maintenance? Shouldn't he and his supervisor have become at least a bit suspicious when a flat, fine mesh fuel filter suddenly replaced a cone shaped filter with a coarser mesh? Fuel filter design was to be only the first of several problems to beset the B-66 in its early years, an experience not all that different from its sister aircraft, the B-57.

Wile TAC was struggling to integrate the B-57 and B-66 into its inventory, SAC continued to expand in both size and influence. Tasked to "conduct long range offensive reconnaissance operations in any part of the world" General LeMay aggressively employed his resources to do just that. Between March 21 and May 10, 1956, 20 RB-47E/H photo and electronic reconnaissance aircraft, flying out of Thule AB, Greenland, photographed the length and breadth of Siberia from 'Banana Island,' as aircrews referred to banana shaped Novaya Zemla, to the Bering Strait. *Operation Homerun* was only part of an extensive and top secret war of reconnaissance waged by the Strategic Air Command and other military services and agencies to gain the Soviet Union's military secrets, a war about which the American public knew next to nothing. On the 4th of July 1956, only eight weeks after *Operation Homerun*, the Central Intelligence Agency launched the first high flying U-2 photo surveillance aircraft from Wiesbaden Air Base, Germany, over the Soviet Union. That first flight was quickly followed by others on July 5, July 8, and many more thereafter. Overflights of the Soviet Union became nearly routine by the apparently 'untouchable' U-2.[12] Not one to let himself be outdone by the CIA, on June 11, 1957, General LeMay took delivery of the first U-2 at Laughlin AFB, Texas, equipping his 4080th Strategic Wing.[13] If LeMay was a thorn in the side of the Russians, he was equally ruthless in the pursuit of his assigned mission toward the Eisenhower administration, putting them on the defensive in public statements and testimony before congressional committees. "The Russians are building the comparable Bison at a higher rate than the B-52," LeMay pointedly remarked to the press in May 1956. Eisenhower and his Secretary of Defense, Charles Wilson, fired back that LeMay was parochial and only focused on SAC. To LeMay's credit, that was in fact his task.[14] Before the Senate Air Power Investigating Committee in May 1956 LeMay stated that "within three years the USSR will have the capability to deliver a knock-out blow which would destroy the U.S ... There is grave doubt that SAC would present an effective deterrence in the 1958-1960 period." He cautioned against reliance on defensive forces, "and it is one of the principles of war" he lectured, "that the advantage lies with the offense."[15] Whatever the case, no one, military or politician, dared to seriously oppose the general – nor touch his budget. B-52s continued to roll off the production lines at an increasing rate, while ADC and TAC aircraft buys and operating budgets were reduced.

Plagued by manpower shortages, parts shortages and training deficiencies for nearly every aspect of the conversion from the B-26 to the B-66B jet bomber, the 17th Bomb Wing struggled on during the remainder of 1956. Accidents continued to plague the Wing. After the loss of Captain Ryall's aircraft over Virginia on October 6, an aircraft returning from an instrument training flight in November had to make a gear up landing when its right gear would not extend. No one was injured, but damage to the aircraft was extensive. In December a B-66 ran off the end of the runway in an attempt to abort its take-off. The nose wheel collapsed, again resulting in substantial damage to the aircraft. Losing airplanes in peacetime is not what commanders are rewarded for. Early in 1957 Colonel Reginald J.

Clizbe assumed command, a highly decorated World War II veteran who made full colonel at age 25, attesting to the high losses of his bomb group. Clizbe went by RJ, never allowing the use of his first name if he could help it. The hectic pace at Hurlburt continued. Training began for ground crews to learn to load and handle special weapons, and aircrews were certified in the Bomb Commander's Course. Nothing was left to chance when it came to atomic bombs.

The remainder of 1957 was marked by the tragic loss of two more aircraft, both from the 95th Bomb Squadron. On April 1, 1957, Lieutenant Richard Dinger launched early in the morning into light rain and thunderstorms, losing an escape hatch soon after lift-off. As he entered a turn to return to base, the ground control approach, GCA, radar operator watched the aircraft disappear from his scope, hitting trees and crashing into a swamp one mile short of the runway. The crew of three was killed. They were the first aircrew fatalities experienced by the 95th Bomb Squadron, by the 17th Bomb Wing, and by the B-66 community at large.[16] Early in September a routine practice radar bombing mission against a radar bomb scoring, RBS, site near Houston, Texas, turned into tragedy. Caught up in a violent thunderstorm, the pilot lost control of the aircraft and the crew ejected. Captain Arthur Manzo, the navigator, was killed.[17]

In November 1957, soon after becoming combat ready, the 17th BW was tasked to participate in *Operation Mobile Zebra*. *Mobile Zebra* was another short notice deployment similar to *Mobile Baker* the previous year. Two B-66s, one flown by Colonel Clizbe, the other by Captain Jack McClenny, deployed in just 17 hours non-stop from California to Clark Air Base near Manila in the Philippines. They then flew simulated bombing missions out of Clark – at least that's what the Air Force public relations machine cranked out for the press. What really happened was much less glamorous. A CASF was a composite force of fighters, light bombers, reconnaissance and support aircraft as dictated by the situation that was to be dealt with. Within short notice the force was supposed to be deployable anywhere in the world. It did two things for Weyland's Tactical Air Command: it put the emphasis on combat rather than training replacements for the overseas tactical air forces, and it was an imaginative, if ultimately unsuccessful, first attempt to diminish reliance on overseas bases. The CASF was pulled together from various flying units as needed and commanded by Brigadier General Henry Viccelio. Secretary of Defense Charles Wilson, of 'What's good for General Motors is good for the country' fame, was thinking of reducing U.S. forces in the Pacific region. To reassure a doubtful Philippine government, Wilson called on General Weyland to exercise his Composite Air Strike Force.

"Our flight surgeon saw a wonderful opportunity to experiment a bit," recalls Ken High, then a young 17th Bomb Wing lieutenant. "He started designing low residue meals the crews would be fed prior to the 17 hour flight from George AFB, California, to Clark Field. Wing operations set up a training program that included 17 hour flights in the simulator. That didn't last long because simulator flying consisted of take off, level off at altitude and going on autopilot, playing bridge with your pals, and every four hours descending to 15,000 feet and saying: Refuel. Then climbing back to cruising altitude until the 17 hours were up. The crews and planes assembled at George AFB in California for a week of preparation. Each day we rose at 5 a.m., ate our low residue meals, and retired at 9 p.m. There was absolutely no alcohol allowed and no snacks between meals. One of my best friends, Charlie Gravat, met a waitress in the Officers' Club who recognized him from when she worked at a club in Fort Walton Beach, Florida. Charlie, being a quick thinker, gave her some money and told her he wanted her to substitute martinis for water in his and my glass at dinner time. This went well until Thursday night, her day off. She had briefed her replacement, who showed up with our martinis in water glasses served with an olive. Colonel Clizbe, our wing commander, and Lieutenant Colonel Fulton, the 37th squadron commander, sat across from us at our table. Charlie and I had to look like the cat that ate the canary with our hands wrapped around our glasses – not daring to take a sip.

"The KB-50 tanker squadron that was to give us our first load of gas as we headed for Hawaii had formed only six weeks earlier. All were inexperienced at refueling. On the morning of the flight we got word that the KB-50 tankers that were to meet us over the Pacific had big-time problems. Only three were at the refueling point, the others either aborted or couldn't find their way. Colonel Clizbe was lead of the first flight – three primary aircraft and one spare. We were to take off in ten second intervals. Our flight consisted of Colonel Clizbe, Jack McClenny, and I was number 3. Warren Gould was number 4, the designated spare. When I got up to about 120 knots, Colonel Fulton, who was sitting in a plane of the second flight started transmitting over the radio, 'Number three,' that was me, 'your flaps are up.' A B-66 trying to take off with its flaps up will roll all the way to China before it will fly. Other pilots joined in telling me my flaps were up. I checked the flap indicator, it showed 60 percent. I checked the hydraulic pressures, they read 3,000psi. By this time I was well over lift-off speed and decided to hold the airplane on the ground for a bit longer. I put the flap handle all the way down, and when I did the airplane popped nearly straight up for about 100 feet. I slowly milked the flaps up and everything seemed to be working fine. What I didn't know was that Warren Gould, our spare, had forgotten to put his flaps down, and they were yelling at the wrong aircraft. Warren went off the end of the runway. Luckily he made it.

"By the time we got to the coast we learned that only two tankers had made it to the refueling area. I became the spare. We found the tankers and Colonel Clizbe hooked up, then backed off, saying he wasn't receiving fuel. The airplane had an IFR, inflight refueling, switch that dumped the pressure in the tanks so the fuel from the tanker could flow in. I told my navigator, Ralph Davenport, 'He forgot to flip the IFR switch.' Jack McClenny then came on the air and said, 'Colonel, check your IFR switch.' The next time Clizbe tried he was getting gas. I was not too pleased with my friend Jack knocking me out of the trip. The 12 bombers and 4 reconnaissance aircraft that started from Hurlburt for Clark ended up a two airplane flight. I don't know how Colonel Clizbe explained all that, but he had 17 hours to think of something."[18]

In 1953 TAC planned on two wings of B-66 bombers. In May 1955 that plan was changed by the Air Staff to one wing. Instead of the 345th Bomb Group at Langley AFB, Virginia, getting the B-66, it was the 17th Bomb Wing at Hurlburt Field. Langley converted to the B-57B instead. Budget pressures after the end of the Korean War, and the subsequent build-up of SAC forced the Air Staff to continually reevaluate its objectives. Instead of 143 wings, the Air Staff downsized to 120 wings in 1954.[19] By 1956, the number was back up to 137 wings – 51 for SAC, 41 for TAC, 34 for ADC and 11 for airlift.[20] That number remained in flux as budgets shrank and the pressures for strategic superiority over the Soviets continued to mount. In November 1956, while two of its B-66 bombers were flying across the Pacific to the Philippines, the 17th Bomb Wing was notified by Headquarters TAC that it would be inactivated. Its bombers were to "replace the B-45s assigned to the 47th Bombardment Wing and serve as USAF's all-weather Atomic Strike Force in Europe," stated the operations plan that implemented the movement of aircraft and personnel. Rather than a unit move, it became a transfer of aircraft, equipment and supplies peculiar to the B-66 from the 17th Bomb Wing to the 47th Bomb Wing in England, and every "effort was to be made to insure maximum utilization of personnel assigned to the 47th BW to insure that minimum numbers are deployed with the 17th Bomb Wing."[21] Money, or the lack of it, was the driving force behind the instructions. The three squadrons transferred to the United Kingdom. Through a paper exercise they were returned in name only to Hurlburt Field where they and their parent wing were stricken from the rolls of active Air Force units on June 25, 1958.(Appendix 3) However, the 17th Bomb Wing designation was not yet ready to die, it was after all the group to which *Doolittle's Raiders* belonged when they launched their epic attack against Imperial Japan off the *USS Hornet* on April 18, 1942. The 17th was to come to life again in 1963, this time flying SAC B-52B bombers out of Wright-Patterson AFB, Ohio. One of its young bombardier/navigators was a Captain 'Pete' Pedroli.

CHAPTER FIVE

THE RED DEVILS
OF RAF SCULTHORPE

"I was born in 1929 in Tulsa, Oklahoma. Went to high school there, then attended the Spartan School of Aeronautics. When I turned 15 I began taking flying lessons and soloed on my 16th birthday. On my 17th birthday I got my private pilot's license. Once I had my license I flew anything I could lay my hands on. Then I joined the Air Force," Donald Harding recalled wistfully when I interviewed him in October 2006 at a B-66 Destroyer Association reunion in San Antonio, Texas. Don and I had flown together in the EB-66 years earlier. He was by far one of the best pilots I had the privilege to share an airplane with in my Air Force career. "I went through the first jet engine mechanics course at Chanute AFB, Illinois," Don continued. "While there I qualified for aviation cadets. It was 1948 and I was 19 years old. One day the instructor handed out assignment forms and told us to sign up for either the 1st Fighter Wing in Alaska, or the 51st Fighter Wing on Okinawa, the first F-80 equipped fighter wings overseas. I told the sergeant, 'I'm going to air cadets. I don't want to fill out this form.'

"'Well,' he said, 'you have to put down something.' I put down South Pacific, and that's where they sent me. I was very unhappy. All I ever wanted to do was fly airplanes. I went to Okinawa as a crew chief on the F-80 in the 51st Fighter Wing, 26th Fighter Squadron. I played basketball on the squadron team with Jimmy Jabara. In Korea Jimmy would become a triple-ace. Nobody could out-shoot Jimmy in the squadron. The ground target we used for practice was a large sheet, like an oversized bedsheet. Jimmy put more bullet holes in the thing than anybody else. He was very good and had excellent eye sight. When I returned

53-506 was one of 72 B-66B bombers built. First flown by the 17th Bomb Wing at Hurlburt Field, Florida, then transferred to the 47th Bomb Wing at RAF Sculthorpe, Norfolk, England. The bombers had only a UHF radio capability. An HF antenna was built into the vertical stabilizer of the RB and WB series of aircraft.

from Okinawa I became an instructor at Sheppard AFB in Wichita Falls, Texas. I never heard anything more about my cadet application, so I applied for OCS, Officer Candidate School, and I was accepted. They sent me to pilot training at Grant Aviation in Florida, a civilian contract school, where I flew the PA-18, which I had flown before, and the T-6, which I dearly loved. I aced the program because I already had a lot of flying time. The flight commander had many other duties besides teaching, so he'd say to me, 'Harding, go fly.' I got more solo time than anyone else in the class. Then I went to Laredo AFB, Texas, for basic in the T-28 and T-33. After I got my wings I remained at Laredo as an instructor pilot.

"I loved flight training, loved taking students and making good pilots out of them. The time came when I had to move on. It was early 1959. A friend of mine had applied for RF-101s at Shaw, so I did the same. When we got there they shunted us into the B-66 program. I was very unhappy, didn't even know what a B-66 looked like. We then went out on the flight line and looked at one. It looked like a fast machine, and I began to feel better about my new assignment. We went through the photo-reconnaissance course at Shaw, learned to take pictures, then they assigned us to the 47th Bombardment Wing at RAF Sculthorpe in England. They flew bombers, not reconnaissance aircraft."[1]

Royal Air Force Station Sculthorpe, some 100 miles northeast of London, was one of many World War II bases dotting the eastern part of England. At war's end the base was moth-balled. In 1948 the Berlin Airlift brought it back to life. B-29 *Superfortresses* and B-36 *Peacemakers* made Sculthorpe their home for a while. In May 1952 the 47th Bomb Wing arrived with three squadrons of B-45 jet bombers. I personally remember RAF Sculthorpe, my first overseas assignment as an airman from 1955 to 1956, having a temporary look about it; made up mostly of flimsy barracks-like structures with corrugated metal roofs and Quonset huts. Major Mengel's chapel was a Quonset hut, the large cross above the door the only feature identifying its purpose. The shopping center, including the base exchange and numerous vendor shops carrying everything from Harris tweed to fine English bone china and lead crystal, was a sorry-looking assemblage of small concrete buildings with corrugated metal roofs. The wing headquarters, officers' and noncommissioned officers' clubs were not much more than barracks, differentiated from each other only by the signs above their doors. The hospital, where I gave up my four wisdom teeth, was a refurbished World War II barracks, primitive to the extreme. If any money was spent on this barren airfield it was on the concrete of its runways and ramps, and on the aircraft hangars, certainly not on the facilities which served the men and their families. I was assigned a very small room, more like a large walk-in closet, in one of the few permanent looking structures on base; a room I shared with another airman. He had squatter's rights because he arrived before me, so I got to sleep in the upper bunk. We shared a small closet, a tiny table and a lamp; no room for anything else. Toilets, showers and washbasins were down the hall in one large unheated concrete floored room. I remember the quaint villages with their squat little houses built of stone, and the incessant rain and cold wind. The 47th Bomb Wing's three squadrons – 84th, 85th, and 86th – had a nuclear mission. Only the 84th and the 85th squadrons were initially at Sculthorpe; the 86th was bedded down at nearby RAF Alconbury. The 47th was at the time the most powerful American combat unit in Europe facing the Soviet colossus across the inner German border. I left Sculthorpe before the Wing turned in its B-45 bombers for the newer and more capable B-66 in 1958, which Don Harding came to fly.

A significant change was made to the wing's combat posture almost immediately after the B-66 bombers arrived. "Higher headquarters decided to emulate the Strategic Air Command by having strip alerts," recalls retired Major General David V. Miller, then a colonel and Director of Operations for the 47th Bomb Wing. "We had four aircraft, two from each of the Sculthorpe squadrons, on five minute alert with weapons on board and crews at their duty stations. We were not manned nor organized for strip alerts. It was a real chore to comply with the orders, but of course we did."[2] When the 86th Bomb Squadron moved to Sculthorpe in 1959 the number of aircraft on alert increased to six.

"It was May 1959 when I arrived in the 84th Bomb Squadron," Don Harding remembers. "I checked out right away and before I knew it I was sitting *Victor Alert*. The planes on *Victor Alert* were ready to go, loaded with A-bombs, two planes from each squadron, a total of six. The first eight months I was there we had the Mark V weapon – essentially the same bomb that was used against Japan, known as Fat Man. The thing filled the whole bomb-bay. There was a place up front, near the crawlway, for a canister they would bring out with the bomb, it held a ball of uranium we referred to as the 'nukki.' It had a threaded hole, and with special clamps, wearing a hood and rubber gloves, we'd screw this big, shiny, threaded rod into the nukki. You never lifted anything so heavy in your life. There was a rack in front of the bomb. It would slide down and we'd pop the top half back and then clunk this thing into a holder, clamp it off, and push it into the center of the bomb and lock it. The bomb worked on the implosion principle. All these 'sticks' of TNT were molded around it, and everyone had a detonator attached, a gillion wires ran here, there and everywhere. To make it work they all had to go off at once, the way I learned it in Bomb Commander's School. Our plans called for us to fly in at 38,500 feet. After I dropped the bomb it armed at 14,000 feet, and it was set for a 3,000 foot above ground-level air burst. In the cockpit there was an instrument panel with a number of dial-like gauges, they all had to read right or we were instructed to abort our mission. Lots of switchology was involved. It about drove me nuts. We had a checklist, but you really had to have it all in your head. Every six months we had to take the Bomb Commander's Test – me and my radar navigator, Chester Burnett.

"We operated under a two-man concept, meaning nobody could approach the airplane by himself once the bomb had been loaded. The guards, with live ammunition chambered in their carbines, couldn't come closer to the plane than 50 feet. Later, hallelujah, we got the Mark 28 weapon. It was two feet in diameter, 18 feet long, and you just uploaded it and plugged it in. Then I'd go to the tail of the bomb and open a little flip- door and punch in the Y-settings, one through four, which determined the yield. If it called for Y-1, that was the greatest yield, 1.1 megatons, I'd punch in a one, and zeroes on the other settings. The target would call for a certain yield level, and we'd program the weapon accordingly. At that setting there was no safe fly-over of the target. At 38,000 feet, the bomb would blow us out of the sky. So the procedure was to drop, break hard left or right into a 135 degree turn, and go as fast as you could to get away from the bomb blast. In our squadron we were limited to Mach .98. If you flew faster than that the plane started to do strange things. We had white, beaded, reflective blast curtains which wrapped around the inside of the cockpit. Going into the target I would zip the blast curtain. The chances of us getting away were small. We carried one of the older *Big Boy* type, and two of the new Mark 28 H-bombs. We never flew with the weapons over England.

"We pulled *Victor Alert* for seven days at a time. It was a self-contained compound. There were a lot of bridge games going on, and a lot of reading and studying. I'd take a couple of my golf clubs with me and hit wedge shots on a grassy area near the fence. *Victor Alert* got to be a real drag. Our Wing command post just loved to ring the bell in the middle of the night to test us. We'd all pile out of bed, jump into our boots and flying suit and head for the airplanes. The power unit was already connected to the alert planes, so we'd do everything but start the engines. Every time there was a guard change someone would get me and introduce me to the new guard – within the compound everything was based on personal recognition. Security was very tight. The gunner on my crew was a staff sergeant. Bill would stay outside, pull the pins on the landing gear, and if we had to go he would disconnect the power unit, then jump on board, and off we'd go. We'd practice that on alert days. The squadron would have a simulated alert, bring the bombs out, upload the bombs, we'd go through our cockpit checks, then they would download the bombs, and we would race as fast as we could to the end of the runway and take off.

"For practice we dropped *Blue Beetles*, inert cement practice bombs. They had the same trajectory as the Mark 28, and we'd drop them from the same altitude at the Jurby Bombing Range, between Ireland and the British west coast. A 60 by 90 foot metal covered raft was our target. It was easy for the bombardiers to put their cross hairs on that target. The Brits who ran the range had three bomb scoring radars on shore and would get a triangulation fix on the geyser that came up when the bomb hit the water to determined where the bomb hit in relation to the raft. We had a top secret additive by which they communicated to us how we did. It was a string of numbers, only some of them were valid. The Brits would read us our score using the additive. I'd subtract one from the other to learn that I had a 200 footer, for example, at 90 degrees from the raft, or something like that. Captain Ken High was a pilot in StanEval, the Wing Standardization and Evaluation section, and he gave me my first tactical evaluation ride. We went up and I dropped the *Blue Beetle*. Ken was sitting in the gunner's seat and came up behind me to watch. Within 45 seconds of dropping the practice bomb the Brits would usually say, 'Bomb's out.' Then one waited for the score. When the Brit was ready he'd call 'Ready to copy?' Then you would copy your additive numbers to get your score. That day we waited and waited. There was no call that a bomb had been observed. After well over a minute I called in, 'Any bombs?' The Brit replied, 'Stand-by, sir. We are checking.'

"I wondered what the hell could they possibly be checking? A couple of minutes later he came back on the radio with his string of numbers and said, 'You hit the bloody raft, sir.' A 'shack' in our language. In telling me so he compromised our top secret code. After we dropped a *Blue Beetle* we'd go down below 20,000 feet, the gunner would get out of his seat and visually check that the bomb left the bomb-bay. That done, we'd climb back up to altitude and fly to a radar bomb scoring site and make RBS-runs. They had those sites all over England and Scotland. We'd call Edinburgh Control, a radar site, and simulate bombing power plants, factories, that sort of thing. Again, we would get scored on how we did. When we ran against London, we'd pick Buckingham Palace for our target. The Serpentine made a marvelous radar return.

"My actual target was a Russian naval headquarters in one of the Baltic states. The damn thing sat about a quarter of a mile up in the city. We would have killed everybody just to get the Russian naval headquarters. Then I would have broken away and headed for Katowicz airfield to drop my second bomb. We had a look-alike radar target on the Riviera in southern France. It was almost the identical radar return of my assigned targets, and we'd fly all the way down there and 'bomb' it and fly back toward Chateauroux, France, meet a KB-50 tanker, get some fuel and go home, or land a Chateauroux. I kept the same targets for three years. Chester, my bombardier, got very familiar with them. Chester was the best bombardier in the Wing. He had the lowest CEP, circular error probable, of any bombardier in the squadron. CEP was averaged over the last 11 practice bombs we dropped at Jurby Range. A crew was removed from combat ready status if their CEP average dropped below 1,500 feet. Our squadron commander, Big Jim Morrow, demanded 1,000 feet. He would make a crew go through remedial training if their CEP was above 1,000 feet. I really enjoyed my years at Sculthorpe. Didn't like the seven days on *Victor Alert* away from the family, but it came around only about every six weeks.

"Big Jim Morrow didn't make things easy for his air and ground crews. He was so dedicated to the mission, so demanding, he expected everyone else to be like him. One couldn't go to the base exchange in the middle of the day to run an errand. When you came to work, you stayed at your place of work until five o'clock or whatever your schedule called for. The word DUTY was written in capital letters for him."[3] John Davis summarizes the times from the perspective of a B-66 crew chief at Alconbury and Sculthorpe: "It was a time of no recognition for us, and lots of very hard work with extremely long hours on the flight line."[4]

"We had a monthly competition," Harding recalls, "between the three bomb squadrons called *Operation Gift*. This competition rotated among the squadrons and went off rain or shine. My squadron, the 84th, had won *Gift* for the month. We launched ten out of twelve airplanes at ten minute intervals. If you launched less than the ten airplanes, you were down a bunch of points before the competition ever got underway. Each airplane in the competition dropped a *Blue Beetle*, then you flew three RBS runs, came back and hit a KB-50 tanker. We had a tanker squadron at Sculthorpe, the 420th Air Refueling Squadron. You had to spot the tanker at the prearranged orbit without making radio contact, chase him down, pull up on his wing, then the tanker pilot visually cleared you in for the refueling. You'd plug in, get your 5,000 pounds of fuel, a token amount, then we'd fly down to the Leman Banks Gunnery Range, get down really low, like 500 feet, and I'd authorize the gunner to fire 50 rounds from each gun – brrrrrrrrrrr. It was a reliability check, we didn't shoot at anything. Finally, we'd get to go home. Two airplanes out of the ten would be designated for extra points. I got tagged this time around. Ken High came over and yelled, 'Bring your chutes and seat-packs with you.' The seat pack was hooked to the chute and contained the survival kit, life raft, and all that other good stuff that keeps you alive when you need it most. We three crawled out of our airplane with chutes and seat packs. Ken High said, 'I have a letter signed by the wing commander, Colonel Kenneth C. Dempster, authorizing you to dump your chutes and packs on the ramp. Go do it.' Fortunately it was a sunny day. We pulled the ripcords on the chutes, opened the survival packs, inflated our life rafts, then we had to demonstrate how to use our survival equipment. We won that competition. Big Jim Morrow was so happy, he threw a beer, beans and hamburger party outside the squadron. The *Red Devils,* the 84th Squadron, won the majority of the competitions.

"The 20mm tail guns we carried were quite reliable. On occasion I flew in the gunner's seat when we gave check rides and I'd turn on the gun-laying radar. The guns could be locked, but I could still use the tracking handle and run the cross hairs around. We frequently had F-100s and Brits in their fighters come up and play with us. I'd put the cross hairs on them, and the radar would show how close they were. You were not supposed to point the guns at anyone. They were always loaded. All you had to do is hit the charging switch and they were ready to fire. One time a couple of F-100s came up and decided to play with us. They'd dive in and come up right under us, uncomfortably close. They did this about five times. When they came again I said to my gunner, 'Bill, unlock the guns and point them at them – but make sure the charging button is off.'

"'OK, sir. You really want me to do that?'

"'Yea, Bill. Do it.' Bill aimed the guns at them, and off they went. They didn't come back.

"We had very few problems with the airplanes. They were new and flew well. I did have one experience though which scared me half to death. I was getting a check ride from my flight commander, Major Jack McClenny, who was the first pilot to get 1,000 hours in the airplane. Jack was one of the early guys who started with the 17th Bomb Wing at Hurlburt. He was riding in the gunner's seat when I started to smell fuel. Jack said, 'We better check the back.' I let down to about 1,000 feet above ground level and depressurized. Jack unstrapped from his chute and went down in the crawlspace and looked in the bomb bay. He came back, buckled back in, and said on the intercom, 'There is fuel nearly a foot deep in the bomb bay.' He turned to the navigator, 'Turn your manual handle RIGHT NOW. DO NOT hit the electrical switch.' The nav pulled the manual bomb bay door handle and dumped the fuel. Both the navigator and I could open the bomb bay doors electrically, but he also had an emergency manual handle he could pull to open the doors hydraulicly. Jack said, 'We better fly it this way. There is a pipe running from the front tank to the back tank through the CG, center of gravity, valve that is leaking.' Normally we never flew with the bomb bay doors open. 'Just add a few extra knots Harding, and you'll be OK.'

"The worst thing in England was the weather. We flew in some horrendous conditions. Big Jim Morrow was a lieutenant colonel, later made full colonel. He liked to show up the other squadron commanders. He would launch ten airplanes into the weather. We often blasted off betting on the come that when we returned the weather was good enough to land. The runways were painted beautifully – big white stripes along the edges, line check marks so you could cross check your speed on take-off. You could see them flash by and you'd say to yourself 2,000 foot check – OK; 4,000 foot check – OK, and after that you knew you had the speed and lifted right off. I taxied in conditions when I couldn't see the lines – after all, ours was a nuclear mission, and we were to respond regardless of weather. Once the weather didn't cooperate. It was February 1960. We were sitting over London Bomb Plot, going back and forth, waiting for things to improve at Sculthorpe. Big Jim checked in with the squadron on the radio and said, 'Let's go home boys.' Everybody gets in line and heads for Sculthorpe. One lands, then the bottom dropped out again. By then we were running low on fuel, below bingo fuel for our nearest alternate at Chateauroux, France. Everything in Britain was down. We high tailed it to Chateauroux. There was this big snow storm obliterating Europe and we were right in the middle of it. I was last in line to come down, really getting low on fuel. The snow was banging against the windshield. Jack McClenny, my flight commander, was with me again flying in the gunner's seat. I said to him, 'You want to take over?'

"'Nah,' he said, 'you'll be alright.'

"Guy Bumpas, a Virginia boy with a deep southern drawl, broke in on GCA final and said, 'Don, you better hurry, it's really bad down here.' We had what we called a bug on the K-5 bomb radar. The navigator/bombardier could set the altitude on his radar, and it was tied into the altimeter. I told him to set it at 50 feet. On my altimeter a red light would come on when we hit 50 feet AGL, above ground level. I wanted to concentrate on my descent, keep the wings level and fly my instruments. The red light came on and I couldn't see the runway. I told the guys, 'We don't have enough fuel to go around. It's do or die.' Suddenly I saw concrete. I rounded out, pulled the power back, pulled the brake chute, didn't hit hard, just kinda skipped a little, then I couldn't see anything. I let the nose down, and it was going pum, pum, pum, pum. I looked over, and the center line was to my left. I was running over the runway lights. Fortunately the concrete extended way past the lights. That was a landing to remember. I earned my flight pay that day. I got behind a Follow-Me jeep. Its driver couldn't see the taxiway, so we just sat there for a while. We remained at Chateauroux for five days, snowed in. Big Jim flew us hard, but we had one helluva combat ready squadron. You either knew how to fly that airplane in all kinds of weather, or you died trying.

"We experimented with LABS, low altitude bomb system, maneuvers in the B-66, a low-level toss bombing technique. The airplane wasn't built for that. There were only a few among us who could get the airplane across the top, that's where you had to release the bomb. In 1962, when we got the news that the 47th Bomb Wing would disband it was a sad day for us all. I flew one of the planes to the boneyard at Davis-Monthan AFB, in Tucson, Arizona. I taxied off the runway, up a dirt road and parked it. In less than two years they sold all 54 bombers for scrap."[5]

The B-66B had an excellent safety record at Sculthorpe, losing only two aircraft. On March 30, 1958, soon after the 84th Squadron transitioned from the B-45 to the B-66, Lieutenant William H. Fulton was caught in a bad weather situation. Only the short 6,000 foot runway was open. Fulton wanted to divert to his alternate, Chateauroux, but was directed by the wing commander, Colonel John G. Glover, to land even though the 10,000 foot runway was closed. Fulton could not bring the aircraft to a full stop before running off the end. There was damage, but the airplane was repairable. Instead, it was used for spare parts and eventually written off.[6] Major General Miller recalls Colonel Glover's penchant for declaring Sculthorpe at or above landing minimums when in fact the field was well below minimums, as in the case of Lieutenant Fulton's experience. "I was returning from a photo mission over Germany," General Miller wrote me. "The ceiling was about 500 feet, quite high for Sculthorpe. So I decided to make a touch-and-go landing. As I went around and entered the base leg to land, the tower called and said the field was below minimums and closed. The exhaust from my first touch-and-go had generated a dense fog closing the field. About that time I heard John Glover come on the radio, he was in his car at the end of the runway, telling me that he had a 200 foot ceiling and one-half mile visibility – our weather minimums. From the sound of his voice I knew that conditions were zero-zero. I landed with the able assistance of the GCA controller. After landing I proceeded straight to the bar."[7] The next and final accident occurred on a night training mission soon after take-off on October 26, 1961. The 85th Bomb Squadron aircraft entered an uncontrollable spin when attempting to avoid a collision with a passing DC-8 KLM airliner bound for New York. The two pilots and the navigator perished.[8]

There were lighter moments as well, not driven by unrelenting training requirements, when it was fun just to fly the friendly skies. In December 1959 President Eisenhower went on an eleven nation goodwill tour dubbed by the Air Force *Operation Monsoon*. The President was flying in his new Boeing 707 jet, redesignated VC-137, leased from Continental Airlines. The 707 replaced *Columbine,* a four-engine Lockheed *Constellation*. Unfortunately the new jet had virtually no navigation equipment for travel outside the United States. A navigator's seat was squeezed in behind the pilot's seat, but the radar, according to Major Ken High who toured the airplane with its navigator, "was lucky to pick up Long Island when they flew over."[9]

In 1958 the Russians lured a U.S. Air Force C-130 intelligence plane across the border from Turkey into Armenia, then shot it down, killing its seventeen man crew. The President's scheduled trip was to take him to Athens, Greece. From there to Ankara, Turkey, and then to Karachi, Pakistan, passing near the Soviet border region where the C-130 had been lured into Armenia. New Delhi, India; Kabul, Afghanistan, and Tehran, Iran, were on the President's schedule as well. The Air Staff directed two B-66s from the 47th Bomb Wing to escort Air Force One from Ankara, Turkey, on December 7, to Tehran, Iran, and again from Tehran to Ankara on December 14. Headquarters USAFE in Wiesbaden upped the number from two to four B-66 bombers. The stated purpose of the escort was to "support *Operation Monsoon* with airborne radar as a navigation aid to Air Force One." Crews selected to perform the honor of escorting the President's plane were identified to Colonel Draper, the President's Air Force aide and pilot, by name, as were the aircraft tail numbers. Captain Kenneth High, pilot, Lieutenant Bobby H. Lynn, navigator, and SSGT Paul O. Morris, crew chief, were to crew B-66B 53-499. 54-481 was crewed by Captains Robert C. Hanson, Vincente Rodriguez-Mattei, and SSGT Charles P. Manor; 54-550 by Major Donald E. Orr, Captain William Thomas, and A/2C William R. Cox. And the fourth aircraft, 54-479, was manned by Captains George J. Parkhurst, Robert A. Gould and Frederick W. Carter, another pilot. Parkhurst was to transfer to Air Force 1 in Turkey and serve as 47BW liaison officer. Major Orr, the operations officer for the 84th Bomb Squadron, was to lead the four-ship Presidential escort. By direction from the Secret Service the B-66s were to come "at no time nearer than 5,000 feet vertically or horizontally" to Air Force 1, and they were to be unarmed.

"On 5 December 1959," recalls retired Lieutenant Colonel Donald Orr, "two C-130 transports carrying our support team departed from RAF Sculthorpe, followed by two KB-50 tankers from the 420th Air Refueling Squadron. We rendezvoused with the tankers over Elba, refueled, and continued on to Incirlik at Adana, Turkey. The two KB-50s and two C-130s arrived later in the day. On the 7th of December, two of our B-66s intercepted Air Force One as it was departing Ankara. The other two proceeded to a prearranged refueling area, and we assumed the prescribed escort formation through Turkey into Iran. We overflew Tehran, and proceeded on to the Pakistan border where our escort duties terminated and Air Force 1 continued on its own to Karachi, Pakistan. We recovered at Tehran Mehrabad airport and remained there until the 14th of December. On the 14th only I took off from Mehrabad and intercepted Air Force 1 at first light as it came over the Afghanistan border east of Birjand, Iran. Air Force One then landed at Mehrabad where the President met with the Shah."[10] "The Iranians laid a red carpet from the airport to the gate of the Shah's palace, and the road was lined by a flower throwing throng of people," recalls Ken High.[11]

Between 1956, when the B-66 bombers first arrived at Hurlburt Field, and their final departure from RAF Sculthorpe in June 1962, the world changed in ways few had foreseen. The launch of *Sputnik I*, the first artificial satellite to orbit earth on October 4, 1957, and the subsequent launch of *Sputnik II* by the Soviet Union on November 3, carrying a little dog named Laika, announced that the space age had arrived. As an airman stationed at South Ruislip Air Station, 3rd Air Force Headquarters, on the outskirts of London, I recall the shock on the faces of officers. They couldn't believe what the Russians had done. Everyone knew it was a turning point: the space age had arrived, but not the way we had envisioned it. On January 31, 1958, the U.S. finally launched *Explorer I* as an answer to the Soviet challenge, an answer that was significantly diminished by five spectacular launch failures of the Navy *Vanguard* rocket, Eisenhower's choice, between February and September 1958. Finally, in February 1959, the first *Titan* ICBM lifted off a launch pad, restoring America's prestige, followed on June 9 by the launch of the U.S. Navy's first ballistic missile carrying submarine, the *USS George Washington* armed with *Polaris* missiles. Bombers were to share more and more of their strategic nuclear role with intercontinental ballistic missiles launched from silos on land and submarines at sea. The demise of the small B-66 nuclear bomber force was hastened by the shoot down of Gary Francis Powers' U-2 by a salvo of SA-2 surface to air missiles over the Soviet Union. To survive, bombers had to change tactics – fly low instead of high, and deliver their weapons using the preferred LABS toss-bombing maneuver, something the B-66 was not built to execute. Then there were of course the incessant budgetary pressures to put more money into the strategic forces, especially missiles. One way to do that was to stop funding the old, such as the B-66B bombers.

Within the NATO alliance relationships changed as well. As early as July 1959 President Charles DeGaul ordered U.S. nuclear forces out of France, resulting in the total withdrawal of U.S. combat units from France by 1966. The only thing that never seemed to change was change itself. And then there was a book published in 1961 by Bernard Fall, *Street Without Joy*, which presented a vivid portrait of the French debacle in Indochina in the 1950s. Fall would die in 1967 alongside U.S. Marines on the road north of Hue, the street without joy. It was a book that should have been read by every senior American government official, but especially the President and his secretary of defense.

Colonel Harris B. Hull from Headquarters PACAF in Hawaii wrote his long-time friend, retired General Ira Eaker, on February 3, 1958, "Everyone here is pepped up that we finally got a satellite in orbit. I have the feeling that we have a lot to learn about running a real good Cold War. As I feel that a Cold War is a war that can be won, in contrast with a general war, which I think both sides will lose ... I expect I am not telling you anything very new. But I do feel it is a war that can be won, and probably will be won by someone. Sincerely, Harris."[12] Colonel Hull was right, but it was to be a close thing – cold war versus hot war.

CHAPTER SIX

THE 19TH TACTICAL RECONNAISSANCE SQUADRON

The 10th Tactical Reconnaissance Group, 10TRG, at Spangdahlem Air Base, Germany, received its first B-66 aircraft in November 1956, an electronic reconnaissance C-model – aircraft number 54-459. Other squadrons based in Germany and Japan assigned to the 66th and 67th Tactical Reconnaissance Wings completed their conversion from the RB-26 and the problem plagued RB-57A in 1957; as did the 9th, 16th, 41st and 43rd Reconnaissance Squadrons at Shaw AFB. The last aircraft delivered by the Douglas Corporation were 36 WB-66D weather reconnaissance models, arriving at their squadrons at Yokota, Spangdahlem and Shaw in 1957 and 1958.(See Appendix 3)

Among the squadrons converting to the new RB-66B in January 1957 was the 19th Tactical Reconnaissance Squadron (Night Photographic) commanded by Major John B. Anderson. Major Anderson assumed command of the 19th on July 20, 1953, when the squadron was activated at Shaw AFB and equipped with RB-45C spy-planes released by the Strategic Air Command. At Shaw the squadron was *attached* to the 363TRG for administrative and logistic purposes, but remained operationally *assigned* to 9th Air Force, also located at Shaw. The reason for a higher headquarters retaining operational control of the 19th was its unique mission – flying secretive spy flights over the Soviet Union. Few assigned to Shaw AFB in those days ever recalled seeing an RB-45C sitting on the ramp or flying overhead. The aircraft were kept out of sight, and while at Shaw had their tail guns reinstalled which SAC had chosen to remove. Then four of its aircraft were flown to Wright-Patterson AFB, Ohio, for extensive modifications to their

The 19th TRS, formed at Shaw AFB, SC, and was initially equipped with RB-45C photo-reconnaissance aircraft released by SAC. The squadron soon transferred to RAF Sculthorpe, England. In March 1955, three 19TRS RB-45Cs flew deep into the Soviet Union on a daring reconnaissance mission. RB-66B 53-453 is shown after the 19th TRS, having converted to RB-66B aircraft, transferred to the 10th Tactical Reconnaissance Wing at Spangdahlem Air Base, Germany. The vertical stabilizer is decorated with the 10th Wing emblem, a falling star. The black stripe in the vertical stabilizer is the HF antenna isolation strip.

ground mapping radar before participating in yet another top secret spy mission over the Soviet Union on April 28, 1954. It was a night reconnaissance mission flown out of RAF Sculthorpe along routes similar to an April 1952 overflight. The aircrews on both flights were British. Three weeks later, on May 7, 1954, Major Anderson led the remaining 19TRS aircraft from Shaw AFB via Newfoundland and Iceland to RAF Sculthorpe. At Sculthorpe the 19th was again *attached* to the 47th Bomb Wing for administrative and support purposes, but the 3rd Air Force, headquartered at South Ruislip Air Station, a London suburb, retained operational control over the squadron, just as the 9th Air Force had at Shaw. Ten months after the 19th arrived at Sculthorpe, on the night of March 27, 1955, Major Anderson led three of its RB-45C aircraft on a deep penetration over the Soviet Union, Anderson flying the longest and most exposed route taking him beyond Moscow. They all returned safely and the three aircrews were awarded the Distinguished Flying Cross for obtaining essential radar photography needed by the *Fat Man* type bomb carrying B-45 bombers at RAF Sculthorpe.

The 19th TRS, attached to the 47th Bomb Wing upon arrival at RAF Sculthorpe and assigned to the 3rd Air Force in London, England, underwent a number of re-attachments and reassignments without ever leaving Sculthorpe, until finally, in January 1958, the squadron was attached to the 10th Reconnaissance Wing at Spangdahlem Air Base, Germany. Two months later, on March 8, 1958, the squadron was officially *assigned* to the 10th Wing. There would be no more overflights of the Soviet Union for the 19th TRS. The squadron became just another of several ordinary photo reconnaissance squadrons based in Europe. Lieutenant Colonel Lewis J. 'Doc' Partridge assumed command of the 19th on October 4, 1958, a position Doc held longer than any other 19TRS commander, until February 1962. One of Doc's first tasks was to move the 19TRS from RAF Sculthorpe to Spangdahlem. With the arrival of the 19th at Spangdahlem in January of 1959, the base hosted four 24-aircraft reconnaissance squadrons – 1st, 19th, 30th and 42nd. The 10th TRW was the largest Air Force combat wing in Europe.

The families of 19TRS flyers had barely settled at Spangdahlem when President Charles De Gaulle had second thoughts about French sovereignty and ordered American atom bomb carrying aircraft out of France. The F-100D fighters based in France were moved to Spangdahlem, and the 10th Wing relocated to England – including, of course, the hapless 19th TRS. On August 25, 1959, seven months after moving from Sculthorpe to Spangdahlem, the 19th opened shop at an old World War II bomber training base with the barest of accommodations and facilities, RAF Bruntingthorpe. The battle lines, should war come, would of course be drawn in central Germany. England was a bit far removed for its reconnaissance squadrons to be of much use to Army and Air Force commanders battling an enemy in Germany. So the 19th, along with other reconnaissance squadrons moved again in 1962, this time back to our reluctant ally France. The squadron bedded down at Toul-Rosieres Air Base, then, in October 1965, it moved for the last time to nearby Chambley.

Major General David V. Miller, then a colonel and the Director of Operations for the 47th Bomb Wing in 1957 when the 19th TRS transitioned from the RB-45C to the RB-66B recalls being sent to Sembach, Germany "to go through the B-66 simulator. This was a 15-hour course and included more emergency situations than one would encounter in flying the aircraft for years. Once back at Sculthorpe I was briefed by a recently qualified B-66 pilot and took off with a navigator and a flight engineer. I felt very comfortable making my first take-off because I thought I could handle nearly any emergency that might arise. The only thing I needed was to get the feel of the airplane. It turned out flying the B-66 was very different from 'flying' the simulator. The aileron boost for instance was 20 to 1; the rudder boost 10 to 1; and the elevator boost about 8 to 1. I climbed out at mach .78. The RB-66 flew like a jet fighter. I loved it."[1]

All went well for the 19th TRS the first year of operation. Then on April 14, 1958, Captain Roger Taylor and his crew, Lieutenant Robert Handcock, navigator, and TSGT Bernard Valencia, gunner, took off on what they referred to as a round-robin flight – a training mission originating at Sculthorpe and returning to Sculthorpe. The weather was about as good as it got in rain soaked County Norfolk with a 500 foot ceiling and several layers of broken and solid cloud. Three and one-half hours later, their mission complete, Captain Taylor began his approach to Sculthorpe. Visibility was one mile. "The traffic pattern was normal and the aircraft was handed to the final controller on the base leg approximately eight miles out. Final approach was normal." Then the aircraft drifted above, below and to the left of the glide slope. The GCA controller told Captain Taylor "to go around because he was high and to the right" of the glide slope. The aircraft vanished from view of the GCA radar controller and did not respond to instructions. Two minutes later a crash was reported by the village of Fakenham police.[2]

The crash of 54-422 and the accompanying loss of life was a shock to a squadron with an excellent flight safety record. What happened? The weather was fine. The aircraft was new. It was just a routine training flight. Sergeant Ken Weiand, a gunner in the 19th TRS remembers, "they were about three miles out from touchdown when an explosion occurred within the aircraft. Then it apparently nosed down and exploded on contact. There wasn't much left of anything."[3] Sergeant Weiand did not know that less than three months later he would be involved in an accident himself, although not with the tragic consequences of Captain Taylor's flight. His was a round robin out of Sculthorpe as well. A training mission, on July 2, 1958, for Lieutenant Harvey, the navigator. Ken Weiand flew as gunner and acted as crew chief when necessary. The weather 'tanked' on them and they decided to divert to their alternate – Chateauroux, France. Lieutenant Van Young, the pilot, and Sergeant Weiand helped the alert crew at Chateauroux refuel the aircraft. A spare drag chute was installed, and Sergeant Weiand assisted in replenishing the liquid oxygen on the aircraft. Lieutenant Young went to base operations, checked on the Sculthorpe weather and decided to chance it. While over Calais Lieutenant Young checked with Anglia Center on the Sculthorpe weather and learned that conditions had actually improved from what he had been given at Chateauroux. When arriving over the Sculthorpe beacon the visibility was two miles in light rain and ground fog. He initiated his approach to runway 06 – which was 9,000 feet long and 300 feet wide. Over the landing threshold Lt. Young reported his airspeed at 150 knots, it may have been a bit higher, pulled the throttles to idle, deployed the brake chute, which billowed, then collapsed but remained attached to the aircraft. The Tower Officer on duty reported touch down 1,200 feet from the approach end of the runway. The GCA operator, located at the 4,500 foot point of runway 06 looked out of his unit noting that the aircraft passed at a speed he estimated "as very fast. The aircraft continued past the end of the runway, rolled on the sod for a distance of 991 feet, went through a security fence, and 250 feet farther into a field of growing barley where it came to rest with the nose gear collapsed." There was no fire. The crew jettisoned their hatches and escaped without injury. The aircraft suffered minor damage and was quickly returned to duty. But surely it was an exciting landing for all. Young lieutenants learned by doing. One lesson learned: keep the runway ahead of you when landing, not behind you.[4]

Airmen are a superstitious lot, and even if they deny it, they believe and are absolutely certain that misfortune always comes in lots of three. The 19TRS flyers didn't have to wait long for the third accident to materialize. On July 3, one day after Lieutenant Young ran his airplane into a field of growing barley, Captain Bill Maroum and his crew encountered a more serious problem. Captain Willis Gray, the instructor navigator flying in the gunner's seat, was giving Lieutenant Constantin Costen a navigation check. The check completed, with plenty of fuel remaining, Captain Maroum decided to shoot some missed approaches. On a go-around the left gear did not fully retract and lock. He recycled the gear and all gears went where they were supposed to go. Maroum then decided to burn off some fuel. Because of a high power setting he extended his speed brakes to slow the aircraft. The crew heard a loud thumping noise in the crawlway when the speed brakes extended – never a good sign. Captain Maroum then noticed his hydraulic pressure dropping to zero. Captain Gray unstrapped, looked in the crawlway, and their worst fears were confirmed – the hydraulic reservoirs were empty. Gray proceeded to lower the gear using the emergency system. The nose and right main gear came down and locked – the left gear did not. One cannot land an airplane in such a configuration, so all three were forced to eject. Before ejecting Captain Maroum engaged the automatic pilot, trimmed the aircraft for straight and level flight and headed it toward the North Sea. Maroum estimated they had about 20 minutes of fuel remaining when they ejected. "After the crew abandoned the aircraft it entered a turn to the left and made four circles about five miles wide north of Sculthorpe. It then flew over the base and crashed 27 miles from Sculthorpe after flying for 26 minutes. Both engines flamed out prior to impact.[5] It was to be a somber 4th of July celebration for the 19th.(See Appendix 5)

Lewis J. 'Doc' Partridge was commander of the 43rd TRS at Shaw in 1958 when he was tapped to take over the 19th at RAF Sculthorpe. He packed his things and arrived with his family that October. "I had no sooner settled in at Sculthorpe when I received orders to move the squadron to Spangdahlem in early January 1959. All went well. It is the 3rd of July, I remember, when Colonel James D. Kemp assumed command of the 10th Tactical Reconnaissance Wing at Spangdahlem from Colonel Kenneth R. Powell. The change of command ceremony was going to be a first rate affair, including a huge 48 ship fly-by, 12 aircraft from each of the four B-66 squadrons at Spangdahlem. The F-100s at Bitburg Air Base, just down the road, added another 12 of their aircraft. I had the honor of leading this huge formation of 60 aircraft. I lined up my 12 aircraft on the taxiway. We performed our preflight checks, including running the fuel selector switch through its positions to check all the tanks – forward, aft, and the wing fuel tanks. I guess one of my crews got too interested in a ball game near our taxiway and left the fuel selector switch in the Emergency Forward Tank position. Flight time for that tank is about 30 minutes. We got off OK and were at our join-up point over the Buechel beacon at 2,000 feet above the terrain, when Captain Jim Wells called a double flame out. He was attempting an air start, then informed me that he intended to make a power out landing at Spangdahlem if he couldn't get the engines started. He was at a very low altitude and I couldn't afford to have him close the runway with this many airplanes in the sky, so I ordered him and his navigator to eject. Best decision I ever made. I then got everyone back together and we flew across the field in a fairly good looking formation, minus one aircraft."[6]

The fly-by proceeded as scheduled, although A/2C Pete West, standing tall on the ramp watching and counting the planes wondered how it was that he had helped launch 48 airplanes, but only 47, by his count, passed overhead in formation.[7] Not only were there only 47 aircraft in the formation, but Captain 'Swede' Jensen decided to do a slow roll while the formation passed over the reviewing stand. Swede was grounded for ten days, Colonel Kemp's first official act as commander of the 10th Wing.[8] Colonel Kemp and Lieutenant Colonel Doc Partridge, wing and squadron commander respectively, soon found themselves standing in front of the 4th Allied Tactical Air Force, 4ATAF, commander at nearby Ramstein Air Base, Major General Gabriel Disosway, explaining the loss of one of their aircraft. It was a fairly cordial meeting, Colonel Partridge recalls, until General Disosway's vice commander, Brigadier General Benjamin O. Davis Jr., asked why the crew – Captain James Wells and Lieutenant Edward Mullarkey – was wearing low quarter shoes instead of flight boots. "The rest of the time that we were at Spangdahlem," Colonel Partridge recalls, "either the commander, that was me, or the operations officer, had to run a boot check on all crews before they were allowed to fly."[9]

Before ejecting from a perfectly good airplane that sunny July day in 1959, Captain Wells put it on a heading where it would not endanger life or property once it crashed. "The aircraft contacted the ground in a wings level attitude, skipped through a wheat field for 480 feet, flew across a 150 foot wide ravine, then smashed into the face of the ravine and exploded."[10] The crew was picked up by a Spangdahlem rescue helicopter, no worse for wear, but a little apprehensive about what was going to happen next. Fortunately for the two young flyers it was a much more forgiving Air Force than today's. The men had little time left on their overseas tours and soon departed for other assignments without career impact, other than their damaged egos.

The 10th Wing frequently was called upon for fly-bys on Memorial Day and similar occasions. Their 48 aircraft formation passing over American military cemeteries in Belgium, Luxembourg and France was a sight that brought out huge crowds. The small village of Ettelbruck remembered General George Patton and his tanks liberating them from Nazi occupation in 1945. Every year the villagers put on a big celebration in honor of their beloved general who lay buried in the nearby American cemetery. On the occasion of the 14th anniversary of their liberation in June 1959, 48 Spangdahlem based RB-66s passed over the celebrants at Ettelbruck, followed by 12 F-100C fighters from Bitburg Air Base. Such fly-bys and accompanying open houses made Americans good and wanted neighbors.[11]

Airman Robert Ganci was a gunner in the 19th squadron. His perspective of squadron life was of course a bit different from that of the officers. Ganci joined the Air Force right out of high school. In 1958 he found himself at Lowry AFB, Denver, Colorado, going through gunnery school. "Just about my entire class was sent to RAF Sculthorpe. I went to the 19th TRS which at that time was a part of the 66th Wing at Sembach, Germany. My first regular assignment was on the crew of our squadron commander, 'Doc' Partridge. Doc was a great pilot, but he flew the RB-66 like it was a passenger plane. Everything was done very gently. It was a night flight out of Sculthorpe I remember most. We were cleared for landing when the famous Norfolk fog set in. Doc continued our descent following the GCA operator's instructions. After we landed I still could not see the ground, it was that foggy. Then Doc asked me to unstrap, get out of my seat and walk in front of the aircraft shining my flashlight, he was going to follow. I had this vision of being run over by a jet bomber. The navigator saved me by suggesting to Doc that we just leave the airplane on the runway, which we did. The field was closed for the night anyway.

"Flying at Sculthorpe was fun, but the real fun was the night life off base," Ganci recalls. "I was 19 years old, and between my base pay, overseas pay, flight pay, separate rations, and TDY money, I was making much more money than the average Brit my age, and more than I ever had before in my life. During the week we gunners would go into Kings Lynn to the infamous Palm Court pub which attracted beautiful young English girls from all the small towns and villages nearby. On weekends we went to Great Yarmouth, a seaside resort on the east coast. Yarmouth was one of the few towns that would not allow the Air Police to enforce the law, as they did in Kings Lynn. So the town was a great place to have fun. When the 19th transferred to Germany in January 1959 we were told it was a scheduled move, but the rumor among us enlisted men was that we were kicked out of the United Kingdom because we were having too much fun."[12] Bob Ganci made the Air Force a career. Most of his fellow gunners got out after their four year enlistments ended.

Captain Lester Alumbaugh was an F-86 and F-102 pilot who considered himself lucky to get a B-66 flying assignment in 1960, a time when the Air Force was shrinking and many pilots found themselves assigned to remote radar sites watching airplanes on flickering radar screens, rather than flying one themselves. Lester came from a small town, Robinson, in east-central Illinois, eight miles from the Indiana state line. "My father worked in the pottery. They made plumbing fixtures – toilets, sinks and bidets. At age 16, which was the minimum hiring age then, I went to work after school in the pottery sweeping floors and boxing things for shipment. What I really wanted to do was fly. A couple of my high school chums decided to enlist in the Air Force and asked me if I wanted to come along. I enlisted on July 6, 1948. I was 19. After basic training I became an aircraft mechanic at Chanute AFB, Illinois, close to my home. At Chanute I applied for aviation cadets. You had to be 20 years old, had to have good eye sight, and didn't need a college degree. I took the test and failed it by one question. The sergeant looked at me and decided to give me credit for that one question. In June 1949 I went to James Connally AFB in Waco, Texas. I was selected for jet training, but I wanted to fly the F-51. I had an instructor who had flown the F-80. He told me 'F-51s are the past. Go into jets.' I went to Williams AFB near Tempe, Arizona, and graduated in June 1950. My first take-off in the F-80 fighter by myself was an experience beyond words. It was the thrill of a lifetime! I checked out in the F-86A with the 81st Fighter Wing at Moses Lake AFB in Washington state, then went on to the F-86D at Truax Field in Wisconsin, staying long enough to transition into the F-102. Life was as good as it could get for a kid from a small town in rural Illinois.

"In 1960 the handwriting was on the wall, ADC was downsizing. An awful lot of guys were being selected to go to GCI sites. My group received a levy to provide a pilot for a B-66 assignment. I jumped at it. I went through RB-66 training at Shaw. The course was 21 weeks long. The instructor pilot sat in the gunner's seat on take-off and landing and moved to the aisle behind the throttles after level off. He sat on some kind of a box with no belt or chute. Not a very safe situation. Obviously, going into the B-66 required adjustments. The first thing I had to adjust to was the size of the airplane and my position in the cockpit. I was now sitting on the left side, and I am used to having a stick in my right hand, the throttle in my left. This airplane did not have a stick, it had a yoke. And the throttles were in the center. To move a throttle I had to do it with my right hand, fly the airplane left-handed. The airplane seemed a little heavy on landing compared to the fighters I had been flying, required a little more arm effort to move the wheel and of course you controlled the aileron with the wheel not a stick.

"After training at Shaw I was assigned to the 19th TRS at RAF Bruntingthorpe. The 10th Wing headquarters was at Alconbury, along with two of our squadrons, the 1st and the 30th TRS. The 42nd was at Chelveston, they flew RB-66Cs and Ds, and we were at Bruntingthorpe. Our wing was scattered over three airbases in England, not an ideal situation. I found the B-66 a nice airplane to fly and became quite attached to it. I don't recall any problems, just routine stuff. As far as take-off distance, it took about 5,500 to 6,000 feet with a full internal fuel load. Only occasionally did we practice in-flight refueling from a KB-50. It wasn't too bad on the tail drogue, but the wing drogues were hell to refuel off. We mastered it, but didn't like it. It took me about 300 hours flying time to learn to grease the airplane in, make a really smooth landing. I did that every time after that. Now and then I'd get another pilot's navigator flying with me and I get complimented on my landings. They'd say, 'John doesn't land like that.' I became an IP, then a flight commander. Our wartime mission was bomb-damage- assessment, BDA, as well as pre-strike reconnaissance. We practiced those missions and had an annual reconnaissance competition called *Royal Flush*. Our squadron lost a crew practicing for that competition in 1961. One of those unexplained mysteries."[13]

On the evening of March 16, 1961, Captain Harry Armani, pilot, with Captain Daniel Harvey and First Lieutenant Frank Whitley, both navigators, launched in aircraft number 54-430 on a practice *Royal Flush* mission from RAF Alconbury along with two other RB-66 photo-reconnaissance aircraft. Armani, Harvey and Whitley were from the 19th TRS at Bruntingthorpe. Doc Partridge had chosen them precisely because they were his best. Every NATO country with an airborne reconnaissance capability sent crews to this annual competition. Armani had flown 54-430 for his last 20 sorties, logging nearly 55 hours of flying time. He thought he knew this airplane inside out. The three RB-66s proceeded to their practice area in a loose trail formation. The target area was clear, a dark night with stars, no moon. Their two targets were located on the West Frisian Islands of Vlieland and Terschelling. Armani contacted 'Cornfield' the airborne range controller and was cleared for his first practice run on the Vlieland target. Subsequent runs were live runs using flare cartridges. The procedure called for the first run on Vlieland, then a turn into the target on Terschelling. A left hand race-track pattern was flown. While one plane was dropping flare cartridges over Vlieland, another would be dropping over Terschelling, and the third aircraft would be on a cross-wind leg near the Dutch coast. Ten runs were made, five against each target. Each pilot flew the same run at the same altitude on the same target. After the last run, aircraft one and two reported in to the airborne range controller – Armani did not. After six to seven minutes the range controller attempted to contact 54-430. There was no response. A search was immediately initiated. "Bits of wreckage and one crewmember's helmet was later found which definitely established that the aircraft crashed into the North Sea in the vicinity of the range. The area where the aircraft was determined to have crashed was a WW-II mined area which was subsequently swept by Royal Navy mine sweepers. The Royal Netherlands Navy conducted an extended search of the area," but found nothing. The tragic loss hit hard in a close knit community of flyers.[14] Over the years that the 19th TRS flew the RB-66B the squadron lost seven aircraft to non-combat related causes, more than any of its sister squadrons.

"The guns came out of the airplanes soon after I got to Bruntingthorpe in 1960," Lester Alumbaugh remembers. "ECM tail cones replaced the guns. We then flew with a flight engineer instead of a gunner. In August 1962 the 10th Wing moved again. The 19th and 42nd TRS went to Toul-Rosieres, France. After we left, Bruntingthorpe and Chelveston closed. Toul was a pretty plush base compared to Bruntingthorpe with the necessary support facilities for families, which was nice to have for a change. It was also nice being on the Continent. It wasn't far to Germany and the big air bases at Ramstein and Wiesbaden with their large base exchanges. Our relations with the French were good I thought, although we did not talk to each other much. We didn't learn much French, and they didn't speak English, even if they knew it.

The Wing had a fair weather base at Moron Air Base, Spain, near Seville. It was always a treat to go there. We also used Nouasseur in Morocco, just outside Casablanca. My navigator was Bill Robinson. Bill and I got crewed up at Bruntingthorpe and stayed together until we rotated home in 1963. Like many navigators, Bill had wanted to be a pilot. One day Bill said to me, 'Les, will you let me fly?' So I said, 'Why not. I'll scoot my seat back and you come up here and sit on my lap and we'll see how it goes.' Bill unstrapped, came up front and actually did quite well. We were flying low level, at about 1,000 feet. So we did that a few times while flying out of Nouasseur. When it came time to go back to Toul, Bill asked if he could fly us home. I told him I would take us off, climb to altitude and get everything set, then he could take over. He wanted to hand fly, while I would have been on autopilot. I told Bill not to strap in. If anything came up we would change positions quickly. I had another navigator in the third seat. Bill and I changed seats. After Bill got settled down he said, 'I'm all set, Les. Can I kick it off autopilot?'

"I said, 'Sure, go ahead.' We were above the clouds, in the clear. Bill kicked her off autopilot. I noticed he was moving things around. Then he said, 'Hey, Les. How do I stop this?' He was in a dutch roll. I told him 'just hold the wheel in one place, then level the wings.' He tried. The next thing I know we are doing a barrel roll. Of course I came out of my seat, pulled the power to idle, and took the wheel and completed the roll. I was off the intercom when I moved forward and I told Bill to tell Ed, the second navigator, not to punch out, that all was OK. Recovering the airplane was a piece of cake, but I didn't know Ed very well, and didn't want him punching out on me – things like that happened. After that experience Bill didn't ask to fly anymore.

"At Toul-Rosieres we stood alert with the 42nd TRS, our sister squadron. We flew the photo-birds and pulled *Whiskey Alert*, while the 42nd flew B-66B bombers converted to the ECM role, known as *Brown Cradles*. Their alert posture was known as *Echo Alert*. They would accompany the F-100s if war broke out and jam Soviet radars to help the 100s get through to their targets. I rotated back to Shaw in 1963 and was assigned to the 9th TRS flying C and D models. I got just over 1,000 hours in the B-66. It was a good airplane to fly. They always said the engine was a weak link, but I never had any difficulties. My experience in the airplane was very positive."[15]

CHAPTER SEVEN

THE B-66 DOCTOR
OF SHAW AIR FORCE BASE

In 1940 Sumter, South Carolina, was just another small town in the deep south, nestled among forests of pine and fields of cotton. Mule drawn wagons were a common sight on its streets. Yet, some of its citizens were looking toward a future filled with airplanes, not mules. A war was raging in Europe and the United States might very well become involved. Leading citizens put their heads together and set off for Washington D.C., to meet with their powerful senator, the Honorable James F. Byrnes, a future Secretary of State in the cabinet of President Harry Truman. Evidently Byrnes chatted with Major General 'Hap' Arnold, the Army Air Corps' chief, and by May of 1941 Sumter had acquired an Army Air Corps training base. The good citizens of Sumter knew it was a beginning. If they could hold on to their good fortune, and hold on they did, it meant good jobs for years to come. The citizens of Sumter did not have to think very hard about a name for their new airfield: Shaw Field. Lieutenant David Shaw, a Sumter County native, lost his life on a reconnaissance mission behind German lines on July 9, 1918. Piston powered training planes at Shaw Field gave way to jets in the early postwar years and Shaw Field was renamed Shaw Air Force Base, becoming the tactical reconnaissance center for the United States Air Force.[1] In 1956 it was once again time for change as the swept wing RB-66 made its appearance. The four squadrons of the 363rd Tactical Reconnaissance Group, the 9th, 16th, 41st and 43rd, shed their old aircraft and transitioned to the jet powered, swept wing newcomer.

The first RB-66B photo reconnaissance jet was flown into Shaw AFB on January 31, 1956, by Captain Tom Whitlock. Perhaps Tom arrived too early in the

The occasion is the delivery of an RB-66B to the 10th TRW at RAF Alconbury in August 1962. Colonel Victor N. Cabas, 10TRW commander, is standing on the left next to the senior Douglas technical representative to the 10th TRW, Clifford Wilcott. Third from right is Major Richard Miller who piloted the plane from Tulsa, Oklahoma, to RAF Alconbury. Major John Conlon, navigator, third from left. Cliff Parrott, the 'B-66 Doctor of Shaw Air Force Base,' second from right, accompanied the delivery crew to Alconbury. Far right is Lawrence Gunderson, Director of Service Engineering of the Douglas Tulsa Division.

year for a proper welcome. Instead, the first RB-66C electronic reconnaissance model, flown into Shaw from the Douglas plant at Tulsa by the 363rd Group commander, Colonel Paul A. Pettigrew, on May 11, 1956, received the welcoming ceremony Tom Whitlock did not get. The sun shone bright, the press was out in force, and a quick thinking Air Force public relations team took advantage of the opportunity to christen the RB-66C, tail number 54-452, *City of Sumter*. The mayor, Ms. Priscilla Shaw, beamed and spoke kind words. Sandra Jernigan, Miss Sumter of 1956, planted a big kiss on Colonel Pettigrew's cheek. Everybody was happy.[2]

In December of 1955 a young Douglas Aircraft Corporation technical representative and his family had arrived in Sumter. Clifford 'Cliff' Parrott's job as the senior Douglas representative at Shaw Air Force Base was to take care of all the little and large glitches that inevitably accompanied the introduction of new technology. Cliff was a strapping six-foot-two young man with the optimism of an Alaska gold rush miner. He would need every bit of that inner strength in the years to come. Cliff Parrott was born in November 1927 in San Diego, California. His mother died before he reached the age of one, and he was raised by a compassionate aunt and uncle in Kansas City. The family moved to Pasadena, California, where Cliff graduated from the Christian Brothers High School. At age seventeen he joined the United States Marines. "I completed airborne radar training, and before I knew it I was sitting in the back seat of a Grumman F-7F *Tigercat* night fighter. I served with a night fighter squadron in the Pacific and in 1948 was discharged at Marine Corps Air Station El Toro with the rank of sergeant. While in the Marine Corps I discovered that I liked airplanes and electronics, so I entered the National Engineering School in Los Angeles. I was looking for a job after graduation when a friend from San Diego said, 'We can use you down here. They are looking for someone with an electronic background. You could hire into the Air Force plant representative's office, AFPRO, at the Convair Division.'

"What are they doing down there?' I asked.

"'Modifying B-36s.' So I went down to San Diego, filled out an employment form, and they hired me within the week. I ended up in the Quality Assurance Office of AFPRO, inspecting B-36Bs which were being converted to D-models. They took the B-models and put two J47 jet engines on each wing, then upgraded the radar bombing system from K-1 to K-3. I got checked out in all that stuff and really enjoyed my work. Soon I was asked to go along on some Air Force acceptance tests. I remember my first flight in the B-36D. It was like a house, compared to what I had been flying in. You could go from the front of the airplane through the bomb-bay to the back through a tunnel using a contraption like an auto mechanic's roll-around with a rope to pull you along. I thought the experience incredible. They served hot meals. It was like being in a flying restaurant. I flew with these people, saw what the problems were, then tried to figure out how to fix things. I remember the flight engineer on the B-36, he had his hands full with six reciprocating and four jet engines.

"Later in the year I was called to the front office and told that they would like to transfer me to the Douglas plant in Long Beach. So I went there in 1952, about the time Douglas was awarded the B-66 contract. Right away AFPRO picked me out to attend all sorts of schools. I thought they had a quota to fill and I was the new guy, that's why they were sending me. Most were electronics schools, but they even sent me to a metallurgical school in Pittsburgh in the summer of '53. They would take us from the school right down to the factories and show us how steel was made, how they made iron and copper. This experience helped me later in the B-66 program when we began to experience corrosion problems. At least I knew what the engineer was talking about when he said we are having structural fatigue. The school was completely out of the field of electronics, but it would fit in just right for me.

"When the B-66 started coming along there was a lot of emphasis on the bomber and the K-5 bomb system. So they sent me off to school again. Many parts of the K-5 system I already knew, like the APS-23 radar. They sent me back to APS-23 radar school even though I protested because I already knew the system. I went to Johnson City, Tennessee, to Western Electric, the maker of the K-5 system. Once back at Long Beach I was there the night the first two pieces of metal were riveted together for the first B-66. I watched intently, not knowing the impact that airplane was going to have on my life. I watched the assembly process, looked down into where the fuel tanks would fit, saw what the wings looked like before they put the skin on. I could picture in my mind for years exactly how the airplane was made. That was a great experience. After they put the wiring in, I did the inspection.

"I think it was 1954 when I was told they were doing a structural test on the aircraft. It had been going on for some time. They'd hooked all these tension gauges to the wings to simulate flight hours, trying to find out what would go wrong after 2,000 hours, and so on. This day, I was told, was going to be the final test. Usually the aircraft would have to fail 150 percent above what the engineers said it should fail at. I went into the hangar, and there were all these firemen hanging around holding hoses hooked up to a tank of fire suppression foam. They kept bending the wings up, up, up – the plane looked like a bird getting ready to land where the wings are way high. One of the firemen said to me, 'Parrott, you better stand back!' Pretty soon the right wing spar broke between the number two engine and the fuselage. That spar caught fire, there was that much tension in there. It sounded like a cannon going off inside the closed hangar when the spar broke. I knew this airplane was never going to lose a wing – and it never did.

"It was February 1955. A friend of mine from my Marine Corps days came to see me. He worked for Douglas. I was up on the wing of an airplane doing something. He came up on the wing and said, 'Cliff, did you ever think of coming to work for Douglas?'

"'No,' I replied.

"'You'd find it very satisfying work with all you know about the B-66. They are looking for people to go into the field with the airplane. Service engineering they call it.' I talked to my wife about it and decided to give it a try. The Air Force was a little more than disappointed after all the training they had invested in me. Soon after I went to work at Douglas I was sent to Edwards AFB, to the Douglas flight test facility. They had five A-models and one B-66B bomber. In those days test data had to be reduced with a slide rule. They'd fly one day, and before they could get the data reduced it would be a week before they knew the results and fly again. That's where I first met Captains Tom Whitlock and Click Smith, pilots sent up from Shaw AFB to become familiar with the RB-66. Tom Whitlock was the first Air Force pilot to fly the airplane, Click Smith the second. We got along really well, and it was about September of '55, I think, when they put in a request to have me go to Shaw. I should have gone to the 17th Bomb Wing at Hurlburt, I'd been trained on the K-5 system, but instead I was sent to Shaw in December, and we were going to get 100 RB-66s.

"Once at Shaw we started giving classes to supply people who were trying to get the Air Force supply system working for the B-66. My team worked with the electronic warfare officers, EWOs, of the 9th Squadron on their ECM systems, and the electronics people on autopilot issues. I had a technical representative in each of the four squadrons. The Air Force maintenance people were outstanding. They knew airplanes. This one was just a little different. Guys would be out on the ramp at two o'clock in the morning working on their airplane. No time clock to punch there, nobody haranguing them 'do this, do that.' They did what needed to be done, and more. Tom Whitlock and Click Smith got all the pilots together and briefed them on everything they knew about the airplane. We had no simulators, only procedure trainers that had a seat, control column, and switches. You learned the switch to throw to put your boost pumps on, and you'd have to reach over and throw or turn the switch. It was all very basic. Whitlock and Smith taught others to fly, who in turn taught still others. All of the pilots had some jet time. We had several RB-57C dual control trainers and T-33 trainers, so it was relatively easy for most to transition into the B-66. I began flying with them after a pilot came to me and said 'I was flying around and all of a sudden

I heard a strange noise. It goes like this,' and he made a sound I couldn't figure out. As we were climbing through 15,000 feet, all of a sudden there was a bang that sounded exactly like a door slamming shut. 'That's it,' he said. 'What do you think it is?' It was two dissimilar metals expanding and contracting at different rates. Every morning at Shaw I would meet with the maintenance people starting with the 9th Squadron, which was at the end of the parking area. Then I'd go to the other three squadrons, that's about a mile, and I'd ask the crew chief of every airplane about his problems. Every morning I would do that and it proved to be a sound approach. The maintenance people knew I was interested. At times I was able to short-cut the supply system, which I didn't like doing, to get a part quicker through Douglas. I liked the system to work. If it doesn't work when I am not there, that's no good. But sometimes I had to intervene to keep things moving. The first big problem I ran into had to do with windshields delaminating."[3]

During acceptance inspections of the RB-66s in the 16th Squadron windshield glass was found to be delaminating. Eight aircraft were grounded pending repair. The probable cause was over-heating caused by the deicing system. The deicing control switch, near the pilot's left arm, could be accidentally tripped to the on position leading to excessive heating of the glass. Corrective action involved the replacement of the defective panels and constructing a guard to place over the offending switch.[4]

"Well, we changed the windows," Cliff Parrott recalled with a wry smile. "A sergeant came over to me carrying some window panels.

"'You know how to do it?' he asked.

"'I changed one at Edwards once,' I replied honestly.

"'Oh,' he said, 'I'm going to learn a lot, because I've never tackled one of these new canopies before.' My experience was on the A-model, not the B-model, which had a completely different canopy. We had an awful time changing that window panel. It was installed with a sealant that looked like black tar. Putting it in was bad, but if you ever wanted to take one of those windshields out you had to destroy it. It was bonded in there. Once removed, we had to take chisels to remove the sealant. It was horrible. The glass problem was one of the biggest problems in terms of cost – buying spares, the man hours involved in replacing a windshield, and the time the airplane was down.

"Early on the engines were giving us problems as well. The first thing to go wrong was a shroud around the alternator, fastened with screws that were not safety wired. The screws came loose, went through the engine and damaged the engine to the point where it had to be changed. Things like that I called 'horse shoe nails.' Remember the fairy tale of the king who lost his kingdom because of a horse shoe nail? I'd see some of these problems and I'd say to the maintenance people, we have a horse shoe nail working here, pretty soon we are going to lose the kingdom."[5]

On October 31, 1957, First Lieutenant Robert Webster, a former B-57 pilot with the 66th TRW at Sembach AB, Germany, took RB-66B 53-451 out on a routine training flight. Of course all flights are routine until things go wrong. "We made several RBS runs," Bob Webster recalled. "On the last run I made a large loop, went down low to burn a little more fuel, aiming to fly low over the house of a gal I was dating. It was a starry night, no moon. I could see well. I went by this gal's house, pushed up the power to climb out when the number two engine blew. I closed the fuel valve to the engine. It turned out that when the engine broke up it ripped off the valve and fuel kept pouring into the dead engine, something I didn't know at the time. There was fire, but after ten minutes or so it blew itself out. I had the navigator look out his window and tell me how the fire was progressing. I didn't want it to get into the pylon and up into the wing. The airplane was flying fine, so I headed for home. Avoiding to overfly towns. My navigator was saying that pieces were kind of hanging out of the engine cowling here and there. The engine had less than 200 hours on it."[6]

"We went out to the airplane first thing in the morning," Cliff Parrott remembers. "Bob Webster had landed late that night. We lowered the engine cowling and the entire engine fell out just as though it had never been assembled – all the rotors, all the blades. I looked at the mess and wondered how in the world this could ever have happened? How could an engine blow up to this extent and not cause a big fire? But this happened more than once. I can remember the people responsible for the engine, a depot in Pennsylvania, coming down to talk to us about engine failures. This man from the depot was talking. He said, 'Gentlemen, we have to take a calculated risk. We are going to fly the engine until it has 100 flight hours on it. Then we'll pull it off and inspect it.' One of the navigators present stood up and said, 'Sir, have you got a mouse in your pocket? What's this WE stuff? What's this WE have to take a calculated risk?' That shut him up." Lieutenant Colonel Donald MacClellan, the 16th Squadron commander, knew great airmanship when he saw it and put Bob Webster in for an Air Medal. In time the medal was presented to Bob at a 363rd Wing parade and awards ceremony.[7]

"We finally got to the point where every hundred hours we'd pull the engines – a lot of manhours. Have another one ready to put on in its place, take the old one and check all the blades, the entire engine. We finally found out the reason the blades failed, then wiped out the compressor and the rest of the engine. The 5th stage compressor produced a resonant frequency at cruise speed which caused the blades to grow and hit the compressor case. The blades would fail at the base of the blade where it dovetailed into the rotor, and the results were what Bob Webster experienced on his flight in October. The length and weight of the blades was changed and that solved the problem. That was one big horseshoe nail.

"The good thing we had going at Douglas was, if I had a problem at Shaw, like these engines, I'd call the Douglas techrep at the 17th Bomb Wing and tell him about things to look out for. We overcame the windshield problem and the 5th stage problem with the engine. Then we started having trouble with the tailcone of the engine nacelle. It had a titanium ring around it, and all of a sudden after about a year pieces of the tailcone were missing, pieces as big as a hand. It turned out to be a fatigue crack caused by the noise level of the engine. As soon as we fixed that problem we started having problems with the control surfaces – flaps, ailerons, elevators. They began showing cracks, usually rivet to rivet. All the control surfaces were hollow on the inside, like a drum. When the engines were operating, the exhaust flexed the aluminum skin causing the cracks. Someone at Douglas came up with the idea to drill a hole between every rib, then fill the void with stuff they called stafoam – some kind of plastic foam that when injected expanded and filled the void. A good idea that quickly went bad.

"About a year later I got a call from a maintenance supervisor. 'I've got a little problem on one of my flaps, Polly,' that's what they called me because of my last name. We went out to the aircraft. There was a green colored residue oozing from the flap. I looked at other airplanes and saw the same thing. What happened was that when the airplane went up to 40,000 feet with these stafoam filled control surfaces it cold soaked to minus 50 degrees Fahrenheit. Then the airplane came down and sat out on the hot and humid Shaw tarmac. The moisture within the control surfaces condensed, then became infested with algae. The foam within deteriorated and reacted with the aluminum skin. It was a nasty looking mess. Not only that, but the control surfaces became unbalanced because of varied amounts of water within them. The one-time fix proved to be worse than the problem it was supposed to fix. This was a railroad spike, not a horseshoe nail."[8]

The 363rd TRW history of January through June 1958 reflects that, "during this reporting period the operational capability of the RB-66 aircraft suffered due to a maintenance remodification program pertaining to the removal of all Stafoam from aircraft control surfaces."[9] The Air Force depot at Norton AFB fixed the problem in coordination with Douglas by sending teams to the various B-66 bases and replacing all of the control surfaces. The cause for many of the failures – skin cracking, shroud rings failing – was acoustic fatigue caused by the more powerful J71-13 engines which replaced the earlier failure prone -9 and -11 versions.[10] Over time Cliff Parrott became known as 'Polly Parrott the B-66 doctor.' If there was a problem with an airplane, Polly was the one maintainers and flyers alike turned to for help. Sometimes small things, like a washer, could bring an airplane down.

On 18 September 1957, Captain Jay Spaulding of the 9th TRS flew a brand new WB-66D, a weather bird, up to Westover AFB, Massachusetts, to participate in an airshow over the fairgrounds at Springfield. "Half of our squadron was equipped with weather ships, the other half with ECM birds," Jay Spaulding recalls. "We were briefed on the program schedule and given an orbit area in which to hold until it was our time for the fly-by. With just the navigator on board I took off using fuel from the forward tank. When in my assigned orbit I switched to the rear fuel tank and suddenly both engines flamed out. I tried air starts, selected another fuel tank – nothing happened. When the engines had nearly spooled down I lost my alternators, and with them went my AC power and hydraulics. Our orbit was within 20 miles of Westover. With the field in sight I decided on a belly landing. Without hydraulics I couldn't get my gear down. Knowing that after the fly-by numerous aircraft would be short on fuel and would have to come in and land, I landed on the extreme side of the runway and slid to a stop. The accident investigation revealed that a small washer on the fuel selector switch failed, and when I rotated the switch, nothing happened. I only had access to the forward tank, which was empty, and had a full load of fuel in the other tanks. The washer design was changed and that solved the problem. The airplane, 55-391, which only had 45 hours flying time on it, was repaired and returned to flying status."[11]

"There was an airplane out of Lajes in the Azores in 1959, and as he came in for a landing, he lost hydraulic pressure, lost nose wheel steering, and once you lose nose wheel steering you become a passenger in your own airplane. There is a steep bank running adjacent to the runway. This WB-66D, 55-400, returning from a weather reconnaissance mission over the Atlantic, ran right up on that earthen bank. Colonel Ford, the 363rd Wing commander, called me into his office and in a firm voice said, 'Polly, I want you to head out to Lajes right away, and I better not hear that it was pilot error.' I caught a B-29 out of Langley AFB, Virginia, and flew up to Argentia, Newfoundland. From there we were going to go straight to Lajes. At Argentia there is a lot of talk by the flight engineer about the number three engine. He puts a ladder up the side of the engine and shortly tells the pilot that someone put plugs in that were too long and when the pistons came up they hit the plugs. The pilot said, 'What do you think?' The engineer replied, 'We can do it on three.' They caged number three engine and off we went, down the runway lined by burned wrecks of airplanes, reminding you to get your airspeed up. As we got down the runway there was further banging, so we aborted. We aborted three more times. The fourth time we finally made it off and made it to Lajes. After landing, the pilot came over to me and said somewhat apologetically, 'Well, I got you here, didn't I.' That he did. We shook hands.

"The people at Lajes were C-124 transport types, and they figured right away the pilot of 55-400 had caused the crash. 'He landed wrong and couldn't control his airplane,' they said. So I went out to the airplane. The pilot who accompanied me was very nervous. He didn't know what was going to happen to him. The first thing I did was drop the cowling on the engine, took the hydraulic pump off, took it to the hydraulic shop and pressurized it. It was cracked. The accident had nothing to do with the pilot. Now I had to convince the accident investigation board at Lajes, which I did. I saved the pilot's career and felt good about what I had done. He never came by to say thank you."[12] The airplane belonged to the 9th TRS, as had the one that bellied in at Westover in 1957. Its ECM tail cone had broken off and both wings were badly damaged. The Air Force decided the damage to the airplane did not justify its repair and scrapped it.[13]

"Fixing problems was my business, and in time we got to a point where things were running pretty smoothly. We had a number of accidents, but then we also had a large number of airplanes. Some accidents were of the foolish variety," Cliff Parrott recalls. The first happened on April 11, 1957, at Eglin. Captain John McLain flew an instrument training mission, then was supposed to pick up his squadron commander, Lieutenant Colonel Paul Vanderhock, and take him back to Shaw. The weather at Eglin was 1,000 feet visibility in light rain. On his first approach, McLain broke out 1,000 feet to the right of the runway and was instructed by GCA to go around. On his second approach, as his commander was watching, McLain again was to the right of the runway, corrected, came in hot, landed long and deployed his brake chute prematurely, which immediately separated from the aircraft. Then the aircraft continued to bounce down the runway, onto the overrun, down an embankment, and nosed into a swamp. The aircraft was destroyed, but fortunately no-one was hurt.[14]

If this accident was due to a lack of basic piloting skills, the crash of 53-473, an RB-66B photo plane assigned to the 16th TRS, was due to bad judgement and had tragic consequences. Three aircraft returned from a photo mission over Virginia. Flying in formation the pilot of 473 climbed above the other two to take a picture, but lost sight of the two aircraft he was trying to photograph. The navigator bent over his driftmeter, located the aircraft and gave the pilot a heading correction. Then a slight bump was felt as one of the two aircraft flying below 473 made contact. 473 went out of control. The navigator was killed instantly as the eye piece of the driftmeter punctured his skull. The pilot and a second instructor navigator ejected. The other two aircraft landed safely. The wing commander's wrath was understandable and had severe consequences for many in the 16th Squadron. These were accidents beyond the skills of a Polly Parrott, having nothing to do with aircraft hardware or electronics, fuel pumps or hydraulic systems. They simply were accidents caused by human failure.[15]

Overall the B-66 accident rate for the 363rd Tactical Reconnaissance Wing in 1959 was 40.92 for 100,000 flying hours, the worst year for the Wing, losing a total of four aircraft.[16] Yet that rate was not excessive when compared to other aircraft such as the RF-84, RB-57 or B-47. In other years B-66 squadrons had substantially lower accident rates than B-47 or B-57 bombers or reconnaissance aircraft. In 1953 for example the accident rate for jet fighters was 71 per 100,000 flying hours. The early jet engines were unreliable, and neither trainers nor realistic simulators were available. It did not help the situation that the Air Force attitude toward conversion to jets from propeller driven aircraft was one of 'an airplane is an airplane.' It was not until the Strategic Air Command introduced checklists and rigid procedures expected to be followed by aircrew that the Air Force attitude toward flight safety and accidents began to change. In the early years, an accident or incident was often considered part of doing business. The Spangdahlem accident of July 3, 1959, is a prime example of this attitude. On that occasion the pilot failed to properly set his fuel selector, flamed out and lost his aircraft. In later years commanders were judged harshly on flight safety, and such pilot-caused losses ended promising careers for many wing commanders.[17]

Polly Parrott's days at Shaw were filled with diverse challenges. He met most of them and became part of the furniture, so to speak. No-one could imagine doing without Polly and his incisive instincts. Cliff Parrott was transferred from Shaw to the Brookley Air Materiel Area at Mobile, Alabama, in the summer of 1961. "By that time we didn't have too many day to day problems anymore. The major issues had all been worked out. I still had responsibility for the Shaw airplanes while I was at Brookley, so I found myself frequently back at Shaw. I was on a business trip to Long Beach when I got a call from an Air Force captain who said, 'We have an award we want to present to you at the Douglas corporate offices. Major General Osmond Ritland is going to do the honors.' People were always calling me from Shaw and teasing, so I said to the captain, 'Yea, sure. I'll see you later,' and hung up. Then one of our directors came into my office and said, 'Cliff, there is an Air Force captain on the line who wants to talk to you. He told me he works for General Ritland. They got something planned for you. Talk to the guy.' So I picked up the phone and the captain said, 'We have an award for you. General Horace Aynesworth, the commander of the 837th Air Division at Shaw has been working on it for some time. He got this thing pushed all the way up to the top. Since the general cannot be here personally, General Ritland will present the award at your corporate headquarters. We want to make sure the date and time is alright with you.' I had the call on the squak-box, so my director got the vice president involved, and they decided they were all going with me to Santa Monica. When I arrived at Santa Monica there was Mr Douglas and a slew of vice presidents, and anyone else who thought he was important. The general came over and shook my hand like we've known each other for ever and presented me with a certificate signed by the Chief of Staff of the Air Force, General Curtis E. LeMay. General LeMay and I had met years earlier. I was told when they took the certificate into the general's office for him to sign he said, 'I know this man. They call him Polly.'

"I was in Washington with General Aynesworth. We were at a reception when Aynesworth went over to General LeMay, he was vice chief of staff at the time, and brought him over to introduce me to him. 'He is our Douglas representative at Shaw on the B-66,' Aynesworth said, 'Mr. Clifford Parrott. The men call him Polly.'

"'Glad to know you,' General LeMay replied, holding out his hand. 'What are you famous for?'

"'Well, nothing up to this time. But now I can say that I met you and I can tell my grand-kids about it.' It was a cordial meeting, and the general didn't forget it anymore than I did.

"Late in 1962 at Brookley I met a pilot and navigator from the 16th Squadron. 'What are you guys doing here?' I asked them. One was Captain Jerry Campaigne, a navigator, the other Andrew Mitchell, a pilot. Andy was from Mobile. 'Oh, we're over at Hurlburt, Eglin number 9, we're checking out in the B-26. We are going to Vietnam.'

"'Why?'

"'As instructors. To teach them how to fly B-26s.'

"'Kind of strange, isn't it? You guys are checked out in the B-66, not the B-26.' In April of 1963 I picked up the Mobile newspaper and here is a big headline – Local Boy Killed in Vietnam. Their B-26 had crashed. According to the newspaper they were number 98 and 99 killed in a war that would claim nearly sixty-thousand American lives; a war that at the time none of us knew anything about. The whole point of the story was, isn't it horrible, almost 100 people have been killed over there? A month later I was at Douglas engineering. As I was talking to someone on a technical matter, an Air Force officer entered and said to the engineer I was talking to, 'I want to see you. Was tech order so-and-so complied with on the B-26s?'

"'That tech order came out in 1945,' the guy I was talking to replied. 'You need to look at an access plate on the wing to see if the order was complied with. It dealt with corrosion.' Then the engineer dug out some old files and found the technical order number for the officer. This was the proverbial guy in tennis shoes with green eye shades who never threw anything away and remembered all. There was a company by the name of On-Mark over at Van Nuys Airport which converted Douglas B-26s into VIP airplanes. So the Air Force officer and the guy in 'tennis shoes' went over there to look at access plates. They pulled the plate off one airplane and found a crack in the spar. The tech order had never been complied with. What we think happened to Mitchell and Campaigne was, while on a strafing run, as they pulled off the target, a wing came off the airplane. This is how I was introduced to the Vietnam War.

"When I was first assigned to Edwards AFB in 1955, I would travel from the Douglas Long Beach plant to Edwards on Monday and return on Friday evening. This travel was done in a Douglas Aircraft Company owned DC-3. It flew daily from Long Beach to El Segundo to Santo Monica and on to Edwards. I was returning home one Friday evening when Mr. Donald W. Douglas came on board, going back to Santa Monica from a meeting at Edwards. He came over and sat next to me and asked my name and 'What are you doing for me?' I explained that I was on the B-66 program and wanted to learn all I could about the airplane, and how it performed in the air.

"'How do you manage to do that?'

"Well, sir, it probably isn't company policy, but I have been going to the Douglas Test Division where they are flying various company required tests and bumming rides. How can I tell the military about the aircraft unless I have actually been in it?' He thought that was a great idea and gave me his blessing. At Edwards I logged 25 hours in the RB-66A preproduction aircraft, the first five produced – 52-2828 through 52-2832. These airplanes never went into the Air Force active inventory, instead they were used in various R&D programs. I finished my career in 1972 with 2,025 hours flying time in the B-66."[18]

CHAPTER EIGHT

OPERATIONS RED BERRY AND DOUBLE TROUBLE

By 1958 the four squadrons assigned to the 363rd TRW at Shaw AFB had become pretty familiar with their new airplane and its peculiarities. The B-66, all in all, was an honest plane. It responded well to control inputs, and once settled down, it pretty much flew itself. Bob Webster, of a generation fascinated by airplanes, says "I've been nuts about airplanes since I was a kid." Bob was born in 1931 in Lauderville, Maine. By the time he turned 16 he soloed in a J-3 Cub, obtained his private pilot's license on his 17th birthday, and was working on his commercial license when he ran out of money. His fascination with flying uncannily paralleled that of another young flyer, Don Harding.

Robert Webster was accepted into aviation cadets and trained in the T-6, T-28 and B-25. In 1954 he found himself flying the RB-57A out of Spangdahlem, the trouble plagued predecessor of the RB-66B. "The only airplane we couldn't beat in turns was the Canadian F-86. But at 40,000 feet and up, I could fly rings around them as well. We were supposed to stay below 43,000 feet. That order was pretty much ignored, cruising routinely up to 45,000 feet. We didn't have pressure suits. I remember doing some tests on a new MSQ radar system, and the test started at 35,000 feet. They kept asking me to go higher, and higher, and I finally got to 55,000 feet and the thing was still climbing at 500 feet per minute. I knew it would have gotten to 60,000, but I quit there. Refused to go higher. It sure looked like a long way down from there. I was used to that kind of flying when I got into the B-66 program. On one of my early solo flights in the B-66 out of Shaw, cruising at about 37,000 feet, this old National Guard F-80 tried to fly a pursuit curve on me.

First Lieutenant Frank W. Bloomcamp, left, checks maps with his crew, Major Hecht, navigator, and Technical Sergeant Ring, gunner, before take-off on a photo-reconnaissance mission over Lebanon from Incirlik Air Base, Turkey. RB-66Bs and RF-101s from Shaw's 363TRW deployed on July 15, 1958, in support of Operation Double Trouble. Several RB-66B aircraft were hit by small arms fire while flying over Lebanon and Syria.

I put my speed boards out to help him along. We flew formation for a while, then he turned back. I went into a 50 degree hard bank, something I'd done in the B-57 many times, and went by him like he was parked. I recovered at about 27,000 feet, fell another 10,000 feet before I had the airplane under control again. I learned not to do sharp turns in the B-66."[1]

In the '50s pilots either lived and learned, or died flying their new jets. Training was still pretty much a seat of the pants affair, at best an evolving art. Although the B-57 was used as a transition airplane into the B-66 because it was powered by two jets, their flying characteristics were so dissimilar that in retrospect one must wonder if it was really a good idea. Bob Webster chuckled when recalling that "the RB-57A had a very different wing from the B-66. I was used to making high angle landings, using the large wing surface to slow me down rather than riding my brakes. I was coming back from refueling practice with some KB-50s. They had three drogues and wing tanks, but no jets. I got my 12 hook ups, but it was a struggle working with those tankers. On the way back we went to a gunnery range off the Carolina coast. The gunner fired out our 20mm tail guns. He then stowed the guns and locked them in the full down position, rather than full up. I came into Shaw making a B-57 type high angle landing and ground those gun barrels down to stumps. My timing couldn't have been worse. Ken Thomas was my squadron's operations officer and he was in the Wing headquarter's building in conversation with the head man. When they looked out the window, there I was with my nose high and, according to Ken, putting on a veritable fireworks display, sparks trailing me down the runway. Needless to say, a new set of gun barrels was required. In spite of that performance in front of the Wing commander, I was soon upgraded to instructor pilot. As an IP I would sit behind the student on a box with no chute or harness. The Air Force and TAC never got around to buying a dual-control B-66 trainer like we had in the B-57C.

"It was January 1958, and I was checking out Captain Heath who had a bunch of B-57 time. You didn't make single engine go-arounds in the B-57 if you wanted to live. I made the take-off. When I leveled out Heath got out of the gunner's seat and took his place behind me on that 'salt box' – no chute, no harness, no ejection seat. I demonstrated a number of things, then I nearly gave him heart failure when I pushed the power up on one engine, pulled the other to idle, and went around the pattern. The B-66 had terrific single engine control, but he had never been told that. He figured he was a goner. He was so terrified when he saw me pull the power on that second engine, he shot off the box in the aisle and bolted back to his ejection seat to strap in. I thought the B-66 was about the best handling airplane I flew in the Air Force. I am partial to the B-57, that was one heck of an airplane for its day, but it was heavy on the controls. It had no boost except on the rudder on the E-models."[2]

War planes, unlike their civilian counterparts, are made to fly and fight. Fortunately, war is the exception rather than the rule. But to keep the crews sharp and the airplanes in flying condition both are exercised regularly and put through their paces. Any experienced military flyer knows that the best airplane is the one that's flown a lot. If given a choice, never take the shiny plane, always choose the one that looks dirty, just landed, and most likely has only minor write-ups. Training aircrews, however, is quite another matter. Training for what? Well, one has to fly a minimum number of hours each month to collect flight pay. But those few hours in the cockpit don't make anyone a good pilot or navigator. Attaining and maintaining the level of proficiency to survive in war means lots and lots of flying under varied, often extreme conditions stressing the airplane and one's flying skills to the maximum. Making a successful take-off under varied field conditions is of course fundamental; as is the skill to make a successful and if possible smooth landing – a skill, unfortunately, some pilots never seem to acquire. One must be as comfortable flying at night and in adverse weather as on a sunny, blue-sky day, if a flyer longs for long life and the joys of experiencing his grandchildren. Above all, a pilot needs to be proficient in instrument flying. When flying in the polar regions, for instance, under total whiteout conditions, or over water at night, there are no horizons, and many a novice pilot has paid the ultimate price flying by the seat of his pants rather than his instruments. With the advent of the aerial refueling tanker came a requirement to be able to refuel in flight. Flying a combat aircraft and maintaining proficiency, for pilot and navigator alike, was and is demanding and a never ending task. On top of all that come unique mission related skills – firing guns and missiles and hitting one's target, air to air or air to ground; dropping bombs, taking photos. Whatever the mission, it meant training and more training. It is what military flying is all about.

For the SAC flyers in their B-47 and B-52 bombers it was a pretty straight forward matter of finding their target and dropping their nuclear devices. Their training was fairly uncomplicated compared to that of a TAC flyer. For the TAC boys, the mission was never clearly focused. Although supporting the Army was written in large letters in the mission statement of the tactical air forces, the money in the '50s went to those who carried special weapons. Recalls General Lobdell who then was a staff officer at Headquarters Tactical Air Command, "SAC was making all this hay out of the nuclear delivery mission. And if we were going to get any money, that's the only way we were going to get it ... So the F-105 was a nuclear delivery [aircraft] and the B-45 was. The B-66 was. All these airplanes were designed as nuclear, sort of one-mission, one-bomb kind" of airplanes. "After the Korean War was over, the only money was in nuclear delivery ... Nobody thought we'd go through another Korea again ... We were going to drop nukes."[3]

General 'Opie' Weyland's rapid reaction Composite Air Strike Force was conventional in nature and all about getting somewhere fast. TAC's money however went principally to the nuclear delivery mission for the B-66, the F-100, and of course into the development of the exciting and new supersonic F-105. With an internal bomb bay, highly unusual for a fighter, the F-105 was principally designed for all-weather nuclear weapons delivery. Special weapons, that's where the money went, and the rest of the force was kept on a very tight budget. "They were repairing the runway at Shaw in the summer of 1957 and we were sent to Hurlburt Field," Dave Eby recalls, "that's where the 17th Bomb Wing was bedded down. Colonel Clizbe was the 17th Bomb Wing commander and didn't like us reconnaissance types mucking around his base. He parked our planes on the east side of the field in the brush. I was number two for take off, watching Jimmy Junge, he had about 30 hours in the 66, come in for a landing. A voice said, 'Mobile. That aircraft landed short.' Jimmy replied, 'No, I didn't,' and he didn't, I was right there watching him come in. The next radio transmission was 'This is Clizbe. That aircraft landed short.' Silence. Clizbe didn't like having us around and made life difficult for us at every turn. That summer Shaw ran out of TDY money, called us back from Hurlburt and parked our aircraft on a ramp. Another pilot and I along with five crew chiefs baby-sat about 20 airplanes. I flew two per day to keep them operating properly." There was little money allocated for anything other than the nuclear mission.[4]

As an instructor pilot Bob Webster trained others in the RB-66B. When not doing so he found himself sitting on flight lines showing off his airplane to throngs of eager lookers, or doing fly-bys on the 4th of July or on Armed Forces Day, in addition to flying photo recce sorties in support of Army exercises or whatever the flying schedule called for. "May 19, 1957, Armed Forces Day, was the day I nearly died. I remember it as killer day. I was number three in a flight of three. We pulled up as scheduled over the crowd, and number two rolled to the right – he was supposed to roll to the left. I had a whole windshield full of airplane. People watching, seeing me fall out of my roll, probably thought I didn't know what I was doing. I was just trying to save my life. Killer day.

"I flew numerous sorties out of England AFB, near Alexandria, Louisiana, supporting Army maneuvers. One maneuver was called *Sledge Hammer*. I was flying at 1,500 feet and popping out my photo cartridges when all of a sudden everything in front of me disappeared. It was like a curtain had come down. I thought the windshield had probably cracked. I pulled the power back and pulled up. It was two o'clock in the morning and I had run into a flock of small birds which had splattered all across the windshield, dented the leading edges of the wings and the engine cowlings, went through the engines, it was a mess. I don't know what kind of birds flock at that time of the morning, but after I figured out that nothing drastic had happened, we went back and finished our photo run." Bob Webster flew the B-66 for three years from 1956 to 1959 when the B-66 experienced most of its teething problems. He accumulating 550 frequently challenging flying hours. Then he transferred into SAC KC-97 refueling tankers at Pease AFB, near Portsmouth, New Hampshire. "The Boeing KC-97 had a gross weight of 153,000 pounds, with a 2,000 pound overload limit. We sat alert and regularly flew the airplane at 175,000 pounds. That made it a horrible airplane to fly."[5]

Other big tasks laid on the 363TRW in support of the Army were *Operations Red Berry* and *Cold Bay,* both operations were flown out of Eielson AFB, a few gravelly road miles outside Fairbanks, Alaska. I flew out of Fairbanks in the early sixties in an RB-47H reconnaissance plane. Conditions in that part of the world in mid-winter are grim. The cold and very low humidity has to be experienced to be appreciated. The 43rd TRS sent seven RB-66Bs to Eielson on October 15, 1957. They returned on March 29, 1958, and were replaced by another B-66 contingent. The Wing history for that period reflects that "Despite the extreme cold, all work was accomplished. The maintenance section performed the majority of its maintenance work out of doors to prevent aircraft damage due to temperature changes."[6] If I had not been at Eielson for a four months TDY in the Winter of 1963, this simple sentence would have meant little to me. But I know very well the extreme conditions the B-66 maintenance crews endured to keep their planes flying.

While *Cold Bay* supported Army winter maneuvers, *Red Berry* supported an Army mapping project to photograph approximately 2,301 square miles of the Alaskan peninsula. The specifications for photography were stringent: minimum snow cover, no clouds, fly at 21,000 to 24,000 feet, with a minimum sun angle of 30 degrees. The weather, not aircraft maintenance, turned out to be the greatest problem for *Red Berry*. A secondary problem was the distance of Eielson AFB from the target area which limited the time available to make photo runs once the aircraft arrived. Tankers were not available to support this project, and Elmendorf AFB, near Anchorage, turned out to be unsuitable as a base because of its changeable weather and lack of nearby alternates. In April 1958 75 hours were scheduled to support *Red Berry* requirements. Weather canceled 13 missions, and three more aborted due to mechanical difficulties. In May the RB-66s flew 92 hours, canceling only six sorties due to weather. Dave Eby, a retired colonel, then a young lieutenant, participated in *Operation Red Berry*. "Coping with the cold and the weather was a challenge. We sent an aircraft to Cold Bay every day the weather permitted. I remember Art Smith flying our T-33 to the target area and calling back, 'It's all clear – come on out.' So off we went. On my first pass I laid a contrail that spread in a short time obscuring the entire area. I never got any pictures that day."[7]

While committed to Operation *Red Berry* the B-66s also flew intruder missions against Alaskan Air Command radar sites, participated in fly-bys on Armed Forces Day at Elmendorf and nearby Ladd AFB, and provided the usual static display aircraft for such events. Flight proficiency checks were administered, training continued. In the last half of 1958, with nearly 100 assigned aircraft, the 363rd TRW flew 1,100 hours in July, 1,200 in August, and a mere 1,000 hours in September, the end of the fiscal year. As the new fiscal year made new money available the number of flying hours jumped back up dramatically to 1,450 for October, 1,550 for November, and 1,350 for December, even though December was a short month because of the holidays.[8] The planes flew on JP-4 jet fuel, but what really kept them flying was money and budget allocations.

• • •

"The only shade is in the shadows cast by our Shaw aircraft drowned in a sweltering, unrelenting sun. The area is flat and barren. It is a vast ocean of monotonous brown: thirsty sand and dry, dust-drenched grass, its dullness broken only in spots by small sparse patches of green fighting vainly for life in the parched earth. Ropes hang limply from the neatly-arranged canvas tents. They sway slightly and lazily – the only hint of a breeze in the still air. It is the flight-line of Shaw's 363rd Composite Reconnaissance Squadron of TAC's Composite Air Strike Force. Soon our jets will roar overhead on another sortie," wrote Major Art Frank in the *Shaw Recon Record*, the base paper, on September 12, 1958, after returning from Turkey. RB-66B and RF-101 photo reconnaissance planes from the 363TRW had deployed as part of a CASF from Shaw AFB to Incirlik Air Base near Adana, Turkey, in support of *Operation Double Trouble*.[9]

On July 15, 1958, President Eisenhower announced that he had given orders for United States Marines to deploy to Lebanon at the request of President Camille Chamoun. Chamoun feared for his government's survival because of threats from rebelling Muslims supported by Nasser's Egypt and the Soviet Union. The previous day, King Faisal II of neighboring Iraq had been killed by his own army officers. Within a day of the coup Iraq joined Gamel Abdel Nasser's United Arab Republic. Militarily and politically the situation continued to deteriorate. Lebanon was not the first Cold War crisis faced by the United States, but it was the first in which General Weyland's Tactical Composite Air Strike Force became a major player. Most of the Air Force budget went into special weapons and the planes and missiles that carried them. Yet, they were of little use on occasions when the need was for the swift application of small, carefully tailored elements of conventional military force. The JCS acted promptly on President Eisenhower's direction, dusted off Middle East contingency plans, and within 72 hours "5,000 Marines, 1,700 Army paratroops, 70 Navy warships, 270 carrier-based Navy aircraft and 150 Air Force land-based aircraft" moved into Lebanon, or were on their way to the Middle-East.[10] Major General Henry Viccellio, commander of the 19th Air Force and nominal CASF director, received a call from General Weyland to activate Task Force Bravo and move the CASF immediately to Incirlik Air Base, Turkey. Within hours B-57 bombers from the 345th Bomb Wing at Langley AFB, Virginia, F-100Ds of the 355th Fighter Squadron from Myrtle Beach AFB in South Carolina, and RF-101 and RB/WB-66 reconnaissance aircraft from the 363rd TRW at Shaw, were on their way east across the Atlantic – none of the crews knowing their final destination which was to be announced enroute. Everything was very, very hush-hush and not a little confused. Only weeks earlier the first of TAC's KB-50 aerial refueling tankers had arrived on Bermuda and in the Azores. So this deployment was not only the first real-life test for Opie Weyland's composite strike force, but also for TAC's newly acquired tankers to support a large scale movement of aircraft across the Atlantic. It was a night time deployment, the weather over the Atlantic was lousy, and neither tankers nor receivers had much experience with each other. In spite of such difficulties and the refusal of Greece and Morocco to grant overflight rights, within 24-hours of 'Opie' Weyland's deployment order the first F-100s arrived at the sleepy Turkish airport of Incirlik. Two days later, the entire task force of over 100 aircraft was in place. Ten RB-66B and WB-66D photo and weather reconnaissance aircraft were part of *Operation Double Trouble*.[11]

On July 15, 1958, the same day President Eisenhower made his Lebanon decision, four aircrews of the 43rd TRS at Shaw AFB were alerted for a *High Flight* ferry mission. All aircraft deliveries across the Atlantic, other than operational deployments, were executed under the auspices of the 4440th Aircraft Delivery Group at Langley AFB, Virginia, and code named *High Flight*. Most aircraft were flown from the United States to Chateauroux Air Base, France, then moved to their final destinations in Europe. A similar delivery procedure for Pacific based squadrons was code named *Flying Fish*.[12] One of the designated B-66 *High Flight* crews was that of Captain Clyde Trent, pilot, and his gunner, A/1C Julius Rausch, both from the 43TRS. Lieutenant Roth Owen was borrowed from the 41TRS, since Trent's navigator was on emergency leave. The remaining 43TRS crews were committed to *Operation Red Berry*. The *High Flight* mission was suddenly changed to one of a classified nature, with the final destination to be announced enroute. The crews and planes were destined to be part of *Operation Double Trouble*, but were not told that. They were to proceed to a tanker rendezvous near Bermuda, then land at Lajes, in the Azores, and await further instructions. Two of the crews had their departure delayed because of crew rest limitations. The remaining two aircraft, including RB-66B 53-459 piloted by Captain Trent, proceeded with their pre-flight preparations. Lieutenant Owen noted during preflight that the aircraft's N–1 compass system was overdue calibration. It had not been swung in a year. Since the gyroscopically controlled compass system was the primary means of navigation across the Atlantic, failure could spell disaster.

Both aircraft taxied to the end of the runway ready to take off. Trent's partner suddenly experienced a malfunction requiring a maintenance delay. Instructions received with the classified mission directive dictated that the abort of one aircraft would not be cause for delay of another. Disasters never happen because of only one isolated incident, but nearly always are a confluence of a string of often seemingly unrelated events. The tragedy in the making was to be no exception. Captain Trent took off, coasting out over the Atlantic over Myrtle Beach, South Carolina. Before take-off he checked the N–1 compass and noted that its reading coincided with the runway heading. Enroute to their refueling area near Bermuda they were notified by radio that they would not land at Lajes, but instead refuel from another KB-29 tanker and continue on to a destination to be announced. They made their tanker rendezvous near Bermuda and continued into the night. Lieutenant Owen plotted dead reckoning fixes, then noted that his navigation system indicated they were 60 miles north of the course he had plotted. As day dawned Owen tried to get some wind readings from his driftmeter, but the sea was too calm. About 30 minutes from Lajes Owen put his radar on its maximum 200 mile range looking for the Azores. There was no sign of land. At their estimated time of arrival, still seeing no land, the crew knew they were in trouble. At 40,000 feet, with 5,000 pounds of fuel remaining, they had about an hour's flying time left.

Crossing the Atlantic in the '50s and '60s was fraught with danger. To insure the safe arrival of aircraft ferried in either direction, two ocean going ships were located along the northern and southern *High Flight* routes. They remained largely 'in place' to assist passing aircraft with navigation and weather data. In addition, every time *High Flight* aircraft were scheduled to cross the Atlantic the Air Rescue Service launched *Duckbutt* aircraft – SA-16 *Albatross* and longer range C-54 transports equipped with sea survival equipment. Their mission was to assure the survival of downed aircrew. The *Duckbutt* aircraft also carried extensive radio and radar equipment allowing them to provide radar tracking, homing and steering, to aircraft in need. If an aircraft ever needed *Duckbutt* assistance it was RB-66B 53-459. Unfortunately there were no *Duckbutt* aircraft airborne. The scheduled *High*

Flight had been canceled. Captain Trent's lone aircraft was on an unannounced, classified mission.[13]

The APN-82 navigation system indicated they were twelve miles south of Lajes, but there was no land in sight. Captain Trent began to broadcast Mayday, the international distress call, on UHF. He decided to look for shipping lanes because he knew that they would have to abandon their aircraft soon. With about 15 minutes of fuel remaining they spotted a Norwegian ship, the *Vespasian*, and decided this was the place. Trent descended to 10,000 feet, approaching the ship on a parallel heading. The gunner, Airman Rausch, was to eject first, the navigator, Lieutenant Owen, next, then Captain Trent. Before ejecting Rausch asked Trent when to deploy his life raft. "In the air, before you hit the water," Trent replied. Parallel to the *Vespasian*, at 10,000 feet, Trent slowed the aircraft to 200 knots, lowered the flaps to 60 degrees and jettisoned the escape hatches. Rausch ejected first, then Owen, and finally Trent. Seven hours and 15 minutes had elapsed since they left Shaw AFB. Trent and Owen were picked up by the crew of the *Vespasian*. Rausch vanished, never to be found. The loss was tragic. Even more so because the ultimate cause, the failure of the C-2 remote compass transmitter, could not be identified because the aircraft wreckage was not available for examination.

The C-2 transmitter was located in the extreme left wing which, along with another sensor in the vertical stabilizer, provided magnetic direction and drift errors to the N–1 compass and the APN-82 navigation system. Later, it turned out that the access panel over the C-2 sensor in the wing tended to leak if maintenance did not carefully apply a sealer. Moisture, once inside, corroded the sensor terminals. As the saying goes, little things mean a lot. In this case these little things, as a chain of seemingly unrelated coincidences, brought down an airplane and cost one man his life. When 53-459's navigation system failed, providing erroneous data to the navigator over the vastness of the Atlantic Ocean, Trent and his crew became as lost as many a storm tossed sailor before them.[14] A tragedy within the tragedy: Airman First Class Julius J. Rausch was scheduled to be discharged from the Air Force within a week of his death.

Ten RB-66 and WB-66 aircraft followed 53-459, arriving safely at Incirlik Air Base. They flew low altitude photographic and visual reconnaissance over portions of Lebanon, Syria and Iraq. During the July 17 to September 8, 1958, deployment to Turkey in support of the Lebanon Crisis, the aircraft encountered frequent 30 and 50 caliber small arms fire. Three of the RB-66 aircraft were hit in rudders, wings, and fuselages. The damage was repairable and no crew members were wounded. Lebanon was not a milk run. Somebody was mad enough to want to shoot down our airplanes. Four of the deployed aircraft returned to Shaw on August 30, and the remaining six returned on September 8, accompanied by one lone RF-101.[15] General 'Opie' Weyland's Composite Air Strike Force concept passed its first actual test with flying colors. He called the operation "A prompt and most successful one to the Middle East under the most difficult conditions." Lieutenant Colonel Allan Webb, the commander of the 363TRS Composite Reconnaissance Squadron, cobbled together from 10 different Shaw squadrons, called all the men together on their return to praise their skill, ingenuity and dedication under difficult circumstances. They flew a record number of sorties without incident. The maintenance guys beamed. For once they too got a pat on the back.[16]

Ronald Darrah was an A/2C crew chief from the 16th TRS. He and his friend A/2C Jim Aspel, also an RB-66 crew chief, slept in squad tents on folding canvas cots. "I don't know what the aircrews did," writes Ron Darrah, "but we enlisted men stayed in a tent city set up alongside the Incirlik flight line. We had left Shaw AFB on a C-130, refueled and ate lunch at Kindley Air Base, Bermuda, then pressed on to Lajes in the Azores. There we stayed overnight before continuing on to Chateauroux, France, then Wheelus Air Base in Libya. We finally arrived exhausted at Incirlik. The temperatures got to over 100 degrees Fahrenheit every day, then dropped at night into the thirties. You could not touch the bare metal B-66s during the day without blistering your skin. We had to leave all the hatches and access doors open to keep from cooking the electronics. Yet nothing really went wrong and the airplanes flew just fine. The RB-66s flew over Lebanon nearly every day. Some came back with bullet holes in them. The holes in the wet-wings we patched with bolts and sealant. The worst thing for us was that there was little drinking water. We had to drink reconstituted milk, and it tasted awful. We dug a hole next to our tent and buried a 55 gallon fuel drum. We then went to town and bought big slabs of ice to fill the drum. A couple of cases of soft drinks went in last. It turned out to be a pretty good refrigerator, even on blistering hot days. We spent our spare time watching U-2s take off and land. We didn't know their missions were Top Secret. When we got home we told everybody."[17]

CHAPTER NINE

RAVENS, CROWS, AND EWOS

1957 was a year of change for the Strategic Air Command. Its visionary creator, General Curtis E. LeMay, left for Washington in June to assume the office of Vice Chief of Staff. It meant no change for SAC. General LeMay's disciple, General Thomas S. Power, was to continue SAC's preeminence and growth in the spirit of his mentor. The brand new 9-million dollar SAC headquarters building at Offutt Air Force Base was finally ready for occupancy, and the all-jet nuclear strike force was coming close to reality. The B/RB-36, a cumbersome leviathan, was about to leave the inventory, replaced by 1,285 sleek B-47 medium jet bombers and 243 eight-jet B-52 heavy bombers, with more on the way. The first KC-135 refueling squadron had been formed, and four more squadrons were in the process of formation allowing SAC to phase out its KB-50 tankers. By 1958 SAC began to augment its bomber force with nuclear armed inter-continental ballistic missiles – *Atlas* and *Titan* missiles flowed quickly into the SAC inventory, augmented by the *Snark* cruise missile, then referred to as a pilotless plane.[1]

If bombers and ICBMs and their special weapons received most of the attention of the press and Congress, LeMay had not ignored the eyes and ears needed to gain essential target information. He was after all a combat veteran of World War II, a battle-tested flyer who knew all too well that up-to-date intelligence was essential to mission success. So LeMay built a sizeable reconnaissance force right along with his strike force. The first high altitude U-2 spy plane joined the 4080th Strategic Wing on June 11, 1957, at Laughlin AFB. Laughlin, a remote and dusty Texas airfield near the legendary Rio Grande River, was the ideal place to hide

Midway Island served as a staging base for RB-66 deployments to and from Yokota Air Base, Japan. Yokota was the home of the 67th Tactical Reconnaissance Wing and the 11th and 12th Tactical Reconnaissance Squadrons, equipped with RB-66B/C/D aircraft.

a plane that was to define the clandestine nature of the Cold War in the years to come. 216 less exotic but essential RB-47E/H/K photographic and electronic reconnaissance jets, augmented by 20 high altitude RB-57Ds, assigned to 13 squadrons, rounded out the SAC reconnaissance force. Everything about SAC was new and plentiful, from the planes it flew, to the air bases they launched from, to the housing and mess halls the men slept and dined in. There were ample spare parts and supplies to sustain the strategic force, and its flyers never wanted for boots, suits, helmets, watches, and what ever else it took to outfit the men of the Strategic Air Command. Even its promotion system was unique and special, providing 'spot-promotions' to those who qualified as 'select' air crews. Spot-promotions, over and above those normally earned, provided recipients extra money and prestige. SAC was America's first, and deemed by many its only, line of defense in the Cold War years. It was an air force within the Air Force, the needs of which were carefully tended to on the Hill.[2]

In contrast to SAC, TAC was much less focused in defining its needs and in convincing those who allocated budgets that as a force it was still relevant to the defense of the country. TAC didn't help itself by pursuing unrealistic and ill defined medium bomber projects such as the ill fated XB-51 and the equally flawed B-68. TAC did little better in the fighter field, its bread and butter aircraft. The acquisition of large numbers of the underpowered and straight wing F-84, earning it the sarcastic moniker of 'lead sled,' went against all logic. While the swept wing defined the jet aircraft of the strategic forces, TAC continued to cling to dated straight wing fighters. The North American F-100 *Super Sabre*, a supersonic derivative of the supremely successful F-86 with a 45 degree wing sweep, finally put TAC on the right track. And recognizing that budgets were mostly allocated to nuclear forces, TAC vigorously pursued the design and development of the supersonic and nuclear bomb carrying Republic F-105. Both the F-100 and the F-105 were company designs, not TAC generated initiatives. This trend of being unable to define its own aircraft requirements continued in future years, forcing TAC to acquire Navy developed aircraft to stay up to date, such as the A-7 and the ubiquitous F-4.

To find needed funds within its own limited budget every program was repeatedly scrutinized and reviewed by both TAC Headquarters staffers and the Air Staff, especially squeezing the *interim* B-57 and B-66 medium bomber force. Spot promotions were not a part of the TAC flyer's lingo, nor was there sufficient funding for essential TDY, temporary duty, travel, flight gear, aircraft fuel, spare parts for its combat aircraft, or anything else that mattered. The tactical forces operated on a shoe string to make the SAC build-up possible, and to pay for its own follies. As a result of the frequent program reviews the initial B-66 bomber buy was cut nearly in half to 72 aircraft. The RB-66B night photo reconnaissance aircraft numbers were reduced and a one-time planned purchase of 72 RB-66C electronic reconnaissance aircraft was cut back to 36. Instead, 36 weather reconnaissance aircraft were substituted, aircraft which never received the required sensors, such as dropsonds and real-time communications gear, to make them anything other than visual reconnaissance aircraft – a task that could have been performed by nearly any other airplane. The J71 Allison engine had to do for the *interim* B-66, rather than the more powerful and vastly more reliable J57. Money for a dual-control B-66 trainer vanished as well. Although TAC certainly was fumbling and unfocused in its efforts to stay relevant, the tactical air forces were clearly neglected by powerful members of Congress who considered the SAC nuclear force as the ultimate answer to war. Such skewed notions prevailed not withstanding the fact that neither the Berlin crisis of 1948, nor the Korean police action, as it was initially referred to, nor the French struggle in Indochina, nor many other conflicts around the globe, were anything but conventional in nature and not remotely resolvable by the employment of nuclear weapons.

The squeeze on the B-66 force extended not only to the basic air frames but also to the development and acquisition of equipment to make the RB-66C the tactical electronic collection platform it was intended to be. The C-model, when first fielded in May 1956, had the same reconnaissance suit as SAC's RB-47H strategic reconnaissance aircraft – ALA-6 direction finders, ALA-5 pulse analyzers, APR-9/14 search receivers, APD-4 automatic collection system, as well as wire recorders which were obsolescent even then. The equipment to configure the C-models came from SAC resources and was initially slow to arrive. Once installed, TAC didn't have the money, interest, nor initiative to continue an upgrade program of its own. The greatest need was for improved recording and direction finding equipment. TAC was a fighter pilot's Air Force, and anything that didn't relate to firing bullets, launching rockets, dropping napalm or bombs, wasn't of particular interest nor deemed deserving of scarce funds. It is hardly surprising that while SAC's electronic reconnaissance capability continued to improve, nothing similar was undertaken on the tactical side. The RB-66C would largely continue to fly with its dated electronic suite into the Vietnam War years.

In 1960, 32 of an initial buy of 35 RB-47H electronic reconnaissance aircraft assigned to the 55th SRW underwent the *Silverking* modification at Douglas-Tulsa. That update provided the three Ravens flying in a capsule in the rear of the aircraft with state of the art audio and video recorders – the ALH-2 and ALH-4 – and APR-17 search receivers, a significant improvement over the older APR-9. More importantly, every aircraft was modified to carry an externally mounted ALD-4 pod developed by the E-Systems Corporation, now a part of Raytheon, which provided a far superior automatic collection capability than the APD-4. This was the opportune time for the RB-66Cs to have received a similar upgrade, but they continued to fly with what they had.

The mission of the RB-66C and the RB-47H was as different as their airframes. The B-47 collected radar information in peace time for inclusion in a master radar data base known as the Electronic Order of Battle, EOB, to support SAC strike force planning. That data base was fairly static and not suited to a fluid Vietnam War style situation where *Fansong* SAM radars and their associated SA-2 missiles relocated on a daily basis to hundreds of prepared launch sites. Information collected by the RB-66C in contrast was designed to benefit the battlefield commander to be able to respond to such a fluid combat situation. The RB-47H mission for all practical purposes ended once war began. The opposite was true of the RB-66C mission. The RB-47H differed in other respects from the RB-66C. It carried three Ravens, while the RB-66C had four. The RB-66 could climb with ease beyond 40,000 feet, while the RB-47H was too heavy and underpowered to even reach 40,000 feet. While the RB-47H could fly twice as far as the B-66, it was not survivable in a tactical battlefield situation. Nor did it have any electronic counter measure, ECM, capability against enemy ground based radars as did the RB-66C.

The men who manned these spy planes were Electronic Warfare Officers, EWOs, trained in my time at Keesler AFB, Biloxi, Mississippi. Starting in the mid-60s such training moved to Mather AFB, near Sacramento, California. Those who manned the electronic countermeasure and defensive systems of the EB-66 and SAC B-52s were referred to as Crows, while those involved in the collection of radar parameters referred to themselves as Ravens. Crows and Ravens – smart and clever birds. The 36 RB-66C models came off the Douglas production line in Tulsa, Oklahoma, in early 1956. Twelve of the aircraft were delivered to the 9th TRS at Shaw; 12 to the 42nd TRS at Spangdahlem, Germany; and the last 12 RB-66C aircraft went to the 11th TRS at Yokota AB, Japan. Each of the three RB-66C squadrons also received 12 WB-66D weather reconnaissance aircraft manned by the usual front end crew of pilot, navigator and gunner, and two weather observers in the rear compartment, vice the four Ravens in the electronic reconnaissance C-models.

Yokota was a long time reconnaissance base for USAF operations, flying aircraft over and along the periphery of China, North Korea, and Russian territory abutting the Sea of Japan. The 67th Tactical Reconnaissance Wing was the parent wing of the 11th TRS with its RB-66C and D-models, as well as the 12th TRS, an RB-66B photo reconnaissance squadron. The 67th TRW was the only remaining reconnaissance wing in the Far East as of July 1957. In addition to the RB-66 squadrons the 67TRW also had RB-57 and RB-50 aircraft assigned. Recalls Bob Stamm "As a green second lieutenant stationed at Itami AB in 1955, those were heady times. Just out of aviation cadets and B-26 transition training into the left seat of a black, glass-nosed Douglas WB-26C assigned to the weather flight of the 11th TRS, life could hardly get any better. After a year or so I began hearing rumors that we might get new airplanes. Before I knew it the 12th was headed north to Yokota, while we in the 11th continued to fly our weather missions in the Yellow Sea around Korea. Soon it was our turn to head north, up the still unpaved road to Tokyo. It was February 1957 when the first RB-66Bs arrived, we didn't get our first C-models until June."[3]

Robert Stern, then an A/2C, retired as an FSO-1 Foreign Service Officer, fondly remembers the delivery of some of the RB-66Bs to Yokota. "Back in early 1957 the Douglas 'Ironworks' in Long Beach, California, released a number of RB-66B aircraft to go to the 12th TRS at Yokota. It was decided to island hop them across the Pacific. The aircraft would fly from Long Beach to McClellan AFB, then to Hickam AFB, Hawaii, with one aerial refueling, and on to Midway Island, Guam, and finally to Yokota. As very few people had even heard of a B-66, let alone seen one, a couple of small detachments of nominally competent troops were sent forward to await their coming on each island. I was one of the lucky souls to go to that Pacific paradise of Midway Island. Our small contingent consisted of a second lieutenant, a staff sergeant and two A/2Cs, of which I was one. Only we two airmen had ever laid eyes on a B-66 before. At age nineteen I was the old pro in the bunch. Ignorant of the Pacific as I was, I assumed that Midway would be like Hawaii, and packed lightweight clothes in February. Big mistake. Midway is cold, and there is always a wind blowing. That wasn't the biggest mistake. Someone seemed to have failed to check the length of the runway, because a fully loaded B-66 on take-off would possibly have gone over the edge into the reef and the shark kingdom without JATO. As it was, their landings were interesting enough, stopping with very little room to spare.

"Luckily, there were JATO bottles on Midway, which the Navy used with their P2V patrol aircraft and they turned out to be compatible with the RB-66. Of course none of us had ever installed a JATO bottle, and the pilots had never used JATO. So we had to put a lot of faith in the technical manuals. We got the first aircraft off without a hitch, and I must say, with quite an audience of 'swabbies' watching to see if the Air Force would screw this one up. We backed the planes to the very edge of the runway with their tails hanging over the edge and with six JATO bottles on each side. Away they went in a real cloud of smoke when they cut those bottles in. I am confident that these were the shortest and fastest takeoffs of B-66s in history. In due course all 24 RB-66Bs got to the 12th TRS. I was transferred to the 11th TRS when they received their RB-66Cs in June 1957, and it was my privilege as a 19 year old A/2C to be the crew chief on the first RB-66C in PACAF. The Air Force was both shrinking in size in 1957 and slowly converting to the jet age. Virtually all the NCOs and officers were coming out of reciprocating aircraft units and only us kids had been school-trained on the B-66. All of us crew chiefs were A/2Cs. Unfortunately, we would all stay that way as our specialty codes were frozen and there was quite literally no promotion this side of the ocean, or on the other side for that matter as well. After four years service I separated in 1960, still an A/2C."[4]

Jet Assisted Take-Off, JATO, was a World War II innovation. The B-47, B-66 and F-100 were all JATO qualified, however, JATO was rarely used. Robert Walker states that "JATO was used by the Douglas pilots when flying newly manufactured B-66s from Long Beach to the Douglas facility in Tucson for final flight test before acceptance. Fred Borman and I were the Air Force flight test acceptance pilots there." In the Pacific region short runways and great distances between airfields frequently required JATO use in the early years of B-66 deployments. Once sufficient air-refueling tankers became available, allowing B-66s to take off with lighter fuel loads, JATO fell into disuse. The B-66 could carry a maximum of 12 JATO bottles, six on each side. Each bottle provided 1,000 pounds of thrust during the critical take-off phase. Usually only six bottles were used, three on each side. The bottles didn't always fire. "We used JATO once at Spangdahlem while I was assigned to the 1st TRS," recalls Peter West. "One of the bottles didn't fire. Lieutenant Dick Wilson jettisoned the bottles as he was passing the tower. The failed bottle then ignited and went spiraling through the air causing plenty of excitement." Frank Doyle and Bob Green recall a similar incident at RAF Alconbury. "The bottles on one side of the aircraft fired, the others didn't, causing the plane to spin around on the runway." John Parson remembers practicing JATO take-offs at Wheelus Air Base in Libya. "We dropped the empties in the Mediterranean. This was for training only." As for using JATO in the Pacific region, recalls Dick Miles, "We used it every time we flew out of Clark Air Base in the late '50s. The runway was only 8,000 feet long at the time, and it was very hot. We needed all the help we could get."[5]

Lieutenant Robert Stamm, the one-time B-26 pilot, eventually found himself checking out in the new RB-66C jet. After many classroom sessions and studying the -1, the B-66 flight manual "I found myself jammed into the gunners seat and watched my instructor pilot make the take-off. The flight didn't last long. Just as we lifted off the exhaust nozzle on the left engine failed. The IP showed little concern and made a quick recovery. The next day that brave soul got to watch me make the take-off. Probably no one who flew those wonderful planes in the early years ever forgot his first flight. Once airborne the outcome for me was never in doubt, I loved that airplane. Training and integration into seven man crews was a major part of my life at Yokota. Early on things didn't go too well for the aircraft as its engine, the Allison J71-11, was still experiencing growing pains. We had to overhaul the engines every 200 hours, at times that interval was reduced to 100 hours. Eventually we got the -13 which had a few hundred pounds more thrust with most of the bugs worked out of it.

"Other exciting events were also taking place. The 67th Wing had its own tanker squadron of KB-50s, the 421st ARS, and we soon got more than our share of refueling practice. This was an interesting mating between incompatible aircraft. The B-66 moved right along once airborne, and it was not particularly happy hanging on the end of a slow flying tanker's hose while getting heavy with fuel. Most of the tankers had a J47 jet engine mounted on the outboard station of each wing to give them a little more airspeed during refuelings. We normally used the tail drogue, but had to practice occasionally on the wings. It was not unusual to have a fighter on a wing drogue while a B-66 was using the tail drogue. We soon added more excitement by putting drop tanks on the C-models. The extra fuel gave us another hour of flying time on long reconnaissance missions."[6]

The transition in the 67th TRW from conventionally powered aircraft to jets went relatively smoothly, although some pilots took to jet flying better than others. Although the 11th TRS by December 1957 had all of its 12 RB-66C aircraft, only three back-end crews of Ravens, four EWOs for each crew, were combat ready, and eight pilots. EWOs were slow to arrive in the squadron from units and schools in the States, and there was a lack of authorized ECM equipment. "In October the austerity program cut down available RB-66 flying time to less than the amount required. This discouraged any additional checkout of pilots and crews because of the time required to maintain the checked-out crews proficiency. Unforeseen maintenance problems occurred and the training program was impacted" even more, reads the 67th Tactical Reconnaissance Wing history from July to December 1957. The repair, replacement and maintenance of the 20mm guns on the RB-66C aircraft was yet another issue. Lack of maintenance personnel made it necessary to have "the gunners pull the weapons from the aircraft, transport them to the Weapons Section, then reinstall the guns in the aircraft."[7]

On the positive side, in November 1957, the 11th TRS was awarded the 5th Air Force Flying Safety Award for six months of accident free flying from January through June 1957. Since October 1955, the 11th had flown 13,684 accident free hours in the RB-26 and RB-66C. Its sister squadron, the 12th TRS, wasn't quite that lucky. "The squadron experienced in July its first major aircraft accident in forty-five months and 23,303 hours of accident free flying." On July 18 Captain George

Slover was on a navigational training flight in RB-66B 54-428, accompanied by Captain Ruderman, navigator, and his gunner TSGT South. There was a rumble in the left engine, the tachometer dropped to zero, the elevator would not function, "unable to force the column forward to nose the aircraft down," Captain Slover alerted the crew. "When the aircraft assumed a nose high attitude," they ejected. The aircraft dove into a hillside and exploded. "All three crew members ejected safely with the pilot landing in a tree, the navigator landing in a rice paddy, and the gunner touching down on a river bank. The only injury, broken ribs, was suffered by the pilot" when he fell out of the tree.[8] On September 6, 54-417 landed in an extreme nose-high attitude striking the aft fuselage on the runway, resulting in the loss of the brake chute, hot brakes, and considerable damage to the aircraft. Then on the 16th, 53-439, returning from a photo mission landed 100 feet short of the runway, skidding 2,000 feet before coming to rest. No one was injured in the latter two accidents.[9]

On November 15, 1957, the 11TRS flew its first classified reconnaissance mission over the Sea of Japan along the Russian, Chinese and North Korean coastlines. The aircraft was piloted by Captain Jack Furneaux. First Lieutenant Dave Frankenberg was the navigator, and SSGT Townsend the gunner. The four Ravens in back were Captain Collier and First Lieutenants Tharp, Kay and Vititow. Like its soul-mate, the RB-47H, the RB-66C flew in radio silence from take-off to landing. At a prearranged time they met a KB-50 tanker flying a racetrack pattern. Using his search radar Dave Frankenberg picked up the KB-50 and talked Jack Furneaux into refueling position. At no time during the flight was the aircraft allowed to be more than ten miles either side of its planned track. After recovering at Yokota the crew debriefed with the local intelligence section, handing in their logs, recordings and film. Two rotational RB-47H aircraft from the 55th SRW in Topeka, Kansas, were attached to the 67th TRW, flying complementary missions. All data collected was forwarded to the 544th Technical Reconnaissance Squadron at Headquarters SAC, Offutt AFB, Nebraska, where it was used to update the master radar order of battle.[10]

Captain Arthur Kibby Taylor arrived at Yokota in the summer of 1957, soon after the first RB-66C models arrived to replace RB-26s in the 11th TRS. "I am named for two of my father's old World War I buddies – Arthur Hall and John Kibby. I've gone by Kibby for as long as I can remember. I was born in Butler County, Kentucky. My brother being two years older got to drive the tractor on our farm. I had to plow the fields walking behind a team of mules. When I graduated from high school in 1948 I decided 'I didn't want to walk behind mules no more.' I attended Western Kentucky University in Bowling Green and joined Air Force ROTC. I really wanted to fly. I majored in mathematics and physics, got married by the time I graduated, and was sent to Greenville, Mississippi, for T-6 training. Then I moved on to Reese AFB in Lubbock, Texas, where I flew the T-28 and the B-25, before ending up at Barksdale AFB, in the 376th Bomb Wing (SAC), flying as a copilot in KC-97 tankers. I spent three years as a KC-97 copilot. When the chance came to get out of that outfit I took it. When Joy and I got off the boat in Japan, Bob Stamm was there to meet us. He was my sponsor from the 11th TRS. Bob told me that I had made captain while I was on the ship. We quickly found a place to live off base. I got kerosene heaters from the nearby Army post, and we were in business. When I signed in at the 11th I found that I was the last on a long list of pilots to check out in the RB-66C. So it was about six months before I got to step into the cockpit of a B-66. In the mean time I flew the T-bird, the T-33 trainer, and did any number of make-work jobs. Three of our aircraft deployed to Misawa AB in northern Japan. They were picking up a strange radar flying the Soviet coast line in the Sea of Japan and they wanted to nail it down. While they were up there I would fly their mission materials back to Yokota in a T-33 to the reconnaissance technical evaluation unit.

"When I checked out in the airplane I had Bob White as my instructor. The first time up I was on my knees in the aisle behind him watching. When I looked at the instruments turning on final, he was at 120 knots when he should have been at no less than 140. That scared the daylights out of me. I scrambled back to my ejection seat and strapped in. I was certainly glad when we landed, and even happier to fly the airplane on my own from then on. On my air-refueling check I had a little trouble with that KB-50. I finally stuck the probe through the slats of the refueling basket, ripped the little bastard off, and carried it back to Yokota with me on my fuel probe. In the 11th TRS we flew Cs and Ds, we were compartmentalized, so I never knew what the Ds were doing, and they didn't know what we did. We were teamed up as crews – pilot, navigator, and four Ravens. We'd fly together and get certified together. By the time I got checked out the 55SRW with their RB-47H aircraft had pretty well taken over the Sea of Japan missions, and we were only infrequently called upon to fly that area. Occasionally we were intercepted by MiGs – Russian and Chinese.

"At times we'd launch out of Kunsan Air Base, South Korea, and fly up to the DMZ, go across Korea, then follow the coast line down to Taiwan and cut over to Kadena AB on Okinawa. At other times we'd launch out of Yokota and refuel over Korea, then fly the same route. I used to laugh," Kibby Taylor noted when I interviewed him, a generous smile spreading across his face "I was a captain then and the rest of my crew were first lieutenants and a staff sergeant gunner. We would meet the SAC RB-47H crew from the 55th Wing going into or coming out of recce tech for their briefings. They were all 'spot' majors and lieutenant colonels.

"I got so good at refueling that one day I decided I was tired of the tail drogue and wanted to try refueling off one of the wing drogues. I called the tanker pilot during our briefing and told him when I came up I wanted to try the left drogue. We refueled over Korea. I hooked up, got my gas, then flew down through the Taiwan Straits toward Hong Kong. About the time I came out of the Taiwan Straight I got the damndest headache. The checklist then didn't call for us to be on 100 percent oxygen during refueling. We sucked in the fumes from the J47 auxiliary jet engine the tanker had mounted on his wing and I got carbon monoxide poisoning. I was feeling so bad I declared an emergency. We were wearing *poopy suits*, it was winter and really cold up north. I made my approach to Clark Air Base in the Philippines. In the turn that hummer started mushing on me. I looked at my flaps and noticed I didn't have any. They had crept up on me. I applied full power and started easing out of the turn, heading straight for the control tower. They abandoned the tower. The navigator gave me hydraulic override to lower the flaps as we came around the second time. We landed and taxied in. By then they had fire trucks and ambulances waiting. We must have been a weird sight, seven people climbing out of the airplane in poopy suits," winterized water resistant flying suits. "I went to the hospital. They gave me some medication and I got a good night's sleep and got over it. Within days they issued an emergency change to the refueling checklist – 100 percent oxygen. On the way back we went up into the Gulf of Tonkin, a quiet place. We flew around Hainan Island off the China coast and then back to Kadena and Yokota.

"At Clark Air Base they only had an 8,000 foot runway at the time. We used eight JATO bottles, four on each side, to get us off the ground. When the JATO bottles fired it gave us a pretty good kick. About five seconds after they fired I was airborne, and it felt like I lost an engine when they quit. There was a dry riverbed near Clark where we dumped the empty bottles on a clear day. If it was undercast, we'd dump them over water. I was flying out of Clark one day, thunderstorms out the ears. We were bouncing around and St. Elmo fire was dancing all over my windshield and on the refueling probe. It was a bit unnerving, the sort of flight you don't easily forget. Most of the flights were pretty routine. It was a great plane to fly."[11]

CHAPTER TEN

HOURS OF BOREDOM -
MOMENTS OF STARK TERROR

Kibby Taylor, a seasoned RB-66C reconnaissance pilot by November 1958, had been detailed to Kadena AB, Okinawa, as RB-66C project officer. It was his responsibility to get the air crews debriefed once they landed, take care of their classified mission material, and make certain they were adequately housed and fed. Captain George Taylor and his crew were tasked to fly a standard reconnaissance mission from Yokota to Kadena. A couple days later the crew was to fly the same route in reverse. "George was supposed to hit the tanker over Korea," Kibby Taylor recalls, "then recover at Yokota. But the tanker was having trouble getting off, and we knew that, so we delayed our take-off. We had a two-hour window to get off, after that our coordination would run out with the air defense controllers and everyone else we had to coordinate these missions with. George told me before he took off, 'I want the GCA on the air at Kunsan.' After he took off I called 5th Air Force and they relayed the message to Kunsan. An extensive effort was made to get the GCA up and running, but it was a weekend, and the guys were in town and could not be located."[1]

Aircraft number 54-476, an RB-66C piloted by Captain George Taylor with over 300 flying hours in the C-model, departed Kadena AB at 0815 in the evening. The weather at Kunsan was forecast to be good with a ceiling of better than 3,000 feet and five-miles-plus visibility. Three hours later Captain Taylor contacted Kunsan approach control reporting that he was at 38,000 feet over the Kilo Sierra Beacon. "54-476, you are cleared for a normal jet penetration," replied Kunsan Control. George Taylor aligned on runway 17 flying a right hand traffic pattern.

A flight of three WB-66D aircrews – pilots, navigators, gunners and weather personnel – assigned to the 11th TRS, 67th TRW, stand morning inspection in front of one of their aircraft at Yokota AB, Japan, sometime in 1959. Captain D.J. Hegland, standing at attention to the left of the formation, is the flight commander. The 11TRS hangar is in the background.

He was cleared to land and reported his gear down. While on short final Captain Taylor notified the tower that he was going around and passed the control tower at about 100 feet altitude. Approximately one mile beyond the end of the runway he was observed to enter a gentle descending turn.[2] "When banking a plane," Kibby Taylor noted, "it tends to lose altitude because the wings no longer provide sufficient lift and you have to increase your power to make up for it. Water and sky look alike at night as well, and Captain Taylor apparently didn't realize his plane was losing altitude. A wing tip touched the water and the aircraft cartwheeled. There was no explosion or fire, and no survivors. By the time I returned to Yokota the following day, the squadron intelligence officer had already contacted my wife to let her know that it wasn't I who had crashed. My name was Taylor as well, and friends had come by the house to offer my wife their condolences."[3] The loss of seven men was a crushing blow to the small RB-66C reconnaissance community at Yokota. No one could figure out why the aircraft went down. Once retrieved, nothing was found among the wreckage to cause such a disaster. Neither could anyone explain why Captain Taylor went around rather than land on his initial approach to the runway. The brutal fact remained that George Taylor's aircraft lost airspeed in a low level turn and seven men died. It was the first RB-66C to be lost by the three squadrons flying the C-model. For the 11th TRS, worse was yet to come.

First Lieutenant David Cooper was assigned to the 11th TRS on graduating from navigator training at Harlingen AFB, Texas, in March 1957. "I and Second Lieutenant Edwin Vokes arrived at Tokyo International Airport in April, Good Friday, in a Pan American Stratocruiser – the much more comfortable civilian version of the austere Air Force C-97 transport or KC-97 aerial refueling tanker. We were processed through Yamata Air Station for assignment and approval by 5th Air Force Headquarters. Within days Ed and I were assigned to the 11th Special Activities Squadron at Yokota, awaiting the arrival of the 11th TRS from Itami and the new RB-66C aircraft which were to replace their aging RB-26s. Several 11TRS pilots were at Yokota already transitioning to jets in the T-33 trainer. Ed and I had to scrounge flying time wherever we could find it. I was fortunate to get on Captain Benjamin Maloney's crew. He was a senior pilot with World War II experience. Our permanently assigned call sign was *Outbreak* which we used on training missions. On classified reconnaissance missions, our first on January 30, 1958, we maintained total radio silence and there was no need for a call sign. We were just an aircraft type and number in someone's log tracking us while we were airborne. Between January 1958 and February 1959 I flew fifty classified reconnaissance missions – many of them at night. Most of our missions were routine, including the presence of Russian MiGs off our wings.

"One of the most interesting missions I flew was out of Misawa. The Russian Navy was having an exercise and we were put on alert. On this particular morning we were scrambled, and after becoming airborne we were turned over to one of our GCI sites. We were directed to climb to flight level 320. Shortly after reaching our altitude we were directed by a rather excited sounding controller to reverse course and begin an immediate descent to 10,000 feet to make an identification of an unknown target. Ben Maloney put out the speed brakes and went into a port turn, descending rapidly. I looked out the little side window at my navigator station and saw two MiGs go screaming by. Apparently the MiGs had approached us visually and neither the GCI site nor we knew of their approach. The MiGs never returned. We continued our descent and made contact with the unknown aircraft. It turned out to be an RB-50, most likely on a mission similar to our own and probably from the 6091st Reconnaissance Squadron at Yokota. We then flew our mission against the Russian fleet. I am grateful to say that the balance of the missions I flew were never that spontaneous and uncoordinated.

"In early February 1959 we were scheduled on a four mission package from Yokota to Kadena, with an aerial refueling enroute. Then from Kadena along the China coast to Clark AB in the Philippines. After two days in the Philippines we were to fly the same route in reverse. On the first refueling out of Yokota the KB-50 tanker had to feather the number two engine. Normally the refueling would have been canceled, but since it was a classified operational mission the tanker crew decided to stay with us. We got our fuel and recovered as scheduled at Kadena. The following day we flew the next leg of our mission to Clark. As we were nearing Clark Air Base we had to shut down one engine, making an uneventful single engine landing. We remained at Clark until February 15 when a replacement engine had finally been installed in our aircraft. While our aircraft was down for maintenance another crew commanded by Captain Robert White was tasked to fly that portion of our mission that we were unable to fly."[4]

First Lieutenant Leon Kirk arrived in Japan in May 1958 and was assigned to the 11th TRS. "I generally flew as Raven 3 after I checked out in the aircraft. Our missions were largely canned, meaning that we flew the same route at the same altitude over and over. Our flights were tracked by Russian and Chinese radar and we were frequently intercepted by pairs of fighters. We had a seven man crew – pilot, navigator and gunner up front, and four Ravens in the rear. The B-66 pilot had to perform all the functions shared with a copilot in other reconnaissance aircraft such as the RB-47H. For many pilots this worked, but for pilots with marginal skills, or who had hot and cold days, take-off and landing became a challenge. Captain Robert W. White piloting our plane on February 9, 1959, was a West Point graduate. Sometimes he was very good, and at other times he 'couldn't hit the runway with both hands' to use an Air Force expression. February 9 was not one of his good days. Our navigator was Lieutenant Dunn, the gunner A/2C Jolly, Raven 1 Lieutenant Powell, Raven 2 Lieutenant Glandon, I was the Raven 3, and Captain Day was the Raven 4. The Raven 4 was the designated officer in charge of the back-end crew. We Ravens were totally dependent on the intercom for all flight information coming from the front end.

"We wore poopy suits, suits made of rubberized material. Since most of our trips were over long stretches of very cold ocean we flew our missions in these cumbersome survival suits. We sat on dinghy packs with parachutes on our backs. Our planes had ejection seats – upward firing for the front end, downward firing for the back end crew. We were told that we could eject from as low as 600 feet off the ground with the zero second lanyard connected, opening the chute the second we cleared the plane. But most of us believed that at that low altitude we would just make holes in the ground.

"We were to fly from Okinawa up the China Coast, one of our canned routes, across Korea below the DMZ, refuel from a KB-50 tanker over the Sea of Japan and recover at Yokota. We taxied out for take off, but it soon became apparent that we had a hydraulics problem. We taxied back to have the rudder/elevator hydraulic boost pump on the number two engine replaced. Although the pump was replaced, the hydraulic lines were apparently not properly bled. Air remained in the system. Because of the coordinated take-off time and the need to arrive at the tanker at a prearranged time, the pilot elected to take-off. We climbed to our assigned flight altitude of 39,000 feet and flew along the China coast, crossed near the Korean DMZ and rendezvoused with our tanker on schedule. The tanker went into a shallow dive to gain speed and our pilot tried to hook up. Captain White tried three times while the aircraft went through wild gyrations caused by the air in the hydraulic system. Then he broke off his attempt to refuel and informed us that he had only taken on as much fuel as he burned off during the refueling. We couldn't make it to Japan. We reversed course and began a rather slow, low level flight across Korea. We could have landed at a base on the east coast, but continued on toward Kunsan on the west coast. It was early evening when we began our descent into Kunsan Air Base, K-8. We did a normal pitch-out over the base, turned back, about five miles out, at 1,200 feet it suddenly became very quiet. There was no more engine noise. I asked the pilot over the intercom if we were going to make it to base. He responded, 'I have idle power.' What he had were two wind-milling engines. We heard nothing more from him during the brief ride from 1,200 feet into the sea.

"Apparently our aircraft hit the water nose high and the panels below our ejection seats in the rear of the aircraft came off on impact. The cabin filled with water instantly. I have no recollection of the water rushing in. I was simply suddenly looking up through water toward the escape hatch on top of the plane. It had been jarred loose by the impact of our aircraft with the water. I swam for the escape hatch opening, pulled myself about half way through, when I realized that the dinghy attached to my chute was too big to make it through the hatch opening. Frantically I unfastened one side and pulled the dinghy through side-ways. While I was occupied with my dinghy, I felt someone clawing at my legs. It was Captain Allen Day, our Raven 4. I helped him through the hatch, but it was evident that he was in deep shock. I had inflated my water wings, but couldn't get him to do the same. He was unresponsive. I pulled the knobs on his water wings, got them inflated, then fastened the straps in front and back so he wouldn't slip out. I then turned to inflate my dinghy. I had a tear in my flight suit and the water was very cold. All this was very difficult and exhausting and it took me several minutes to climb into the dinghy. When I was finally inside, I collapsed and lay there for a few minutes to get myself together. When I looked outside again I noticed that Captain Day was still floating on his water wings, but had taken no action to inflate his dinghy. He had drifted away from me while I was busy getting into my dinghy. I yelled at him to inflate his dinghy and to climb in, but I got no response. Twilight set in and it was hard to see. As I floated along I could see Captain Day rise on a wave and disappear on the other side, but there was no evidence of life.

"I was aware that the front-end crew had climbed out the top hatches, but lost track of them as I floated over the top of waves and into the troughs between waves. About an hour and a half passed without any rescue attempts. Then I heard the sound of a helicopter in the distance and since it was nearly dark, I popped a flare and the helicopter came in overhead and dropped a horse collar rescue device on a cable and I put my arms through the collar and they began to hoist me up. A short distance below the helicopter they stopped and the crew chief yelled something. I couldn't make out what he was saying. After several more unsuccessful attempts at communication they resumed hoisting me up. My dinghy was tied to me by a strap, something we were taught to do in survival school and it was dangling below me. The crew chief was trying to tell me to untie it and let it go. He was afraid it could be sucked into the rotors. As soon as I arrived at the door he cut the strap, the dinghy dropped away and they hauled me in. I later learned that the helicopter was flown by South Korean student pilots who had been diverted from their flying training somewhere in Korea for the rescue. They couldn't speak English, but they did visit me in the hospital. Apparently no other rescue capability was available at Kunsan. Captain White, Lieutenant Dunn, and A/2C Jolly were rescued along with me and hospitalized. Captain Day was not found until daylight the next morning. He was still floating on his water wings.

Lieutenants Glandon and Powell, the other two Ravens, were found strapped in their seats with broken legs."[5]

The *Stars & Stripes* military newspaper reported the story of the Monday evening crash the next day, quoting an Air Force spokesman who portrayed the crash as a routine training accident. "The twin-jet aircraft was on a training flight from Yokota AB, Japan, to Kunsan. It crash-landed two miles short of the Kunsan runway after the pilot reported he was low on fuel. The aircraft was visible on the mud-flats early Tuesday, the Air Force spokesman said. However, at high tide it was submerged under water."[6]

Captain Kibby Taylor was appointed Summary Courts Officer for the deceased Captain Allen Day. Taylor put Captain Day's affairs in order at Yokota, transferred his belongings to his family and assisted them in every way possible. The subsequent investigation of the wreckage revealed that the aircraft still had 1,500 pounds of fuel in the forward tank. Evidently it all began on Monday when the rudder/elevator hydraulic pump failed at Kadena prior to take-off. It was a 'Red X' system failure which normally would have grounded the aircraft. The mission, although of an operational and high priority nature, should have been aborted by the pilot who unfortunately decided otherwise. A pump replacement was attempted by harried maintenance men within the time constraints dictated by the mission. The replacement may not have been accomplished precisely in accordance with the maintenance technical order which required bleeding of the hydraulic lines to preclude the presence of air bubbles. The pilot assumed that when maintenance signed off the Red X that all was in order. The crew was still within the two-hour launch window, so they took off from Kadena. With air in the hydraulic lines and a resultant erratic rudder/elevator system, an aerial refueling was a near impossibility. The aircraft carried 450 gallon wing tanks in addition to its standard fuel load in two internal wing tanks and the main fore and aft fuselage tanks.

The engines normally were fed from the aft fuel tank, which in turn was fed by transferred fuel from the forward tank or the internal wing tanks. The Center of Gravity, CG, valve regulated the flow of fuel to the aft tank to keep the aircraft weight distribution in balance. In normal operations, wing fuel transfer was not initiated until the forward fuel tank was down to 3,900 pounds. At that point the wing fuel transfer switch was turned to the ON position to transfer fuel from the internal wing fuel tanks to the aft tank. In turn, the external wing tanks fed the internal wing tanks. The CG valve between the forward and aft tanks was closed when the wing fuel transfer switch was on. When the aft fuel tank quantity began decreasing one knew that the wing tanks were empty and the wing fuel transfer switch must be moved to the OFF position. If not, one will flame out even though there is fuel in the forward tank, since the CG valve allowing transfer from forward to aft tank is closed. The pilot could also monitor his fuel quantity by flipping a switch between wing and fuselage tanks. The switch was normally left in the fuselage tank position. Captain White very likely forgot that he had the wing fuel transfer switch in the ON position, glanced at his fuel quantity indicator – which gave him fuselage tank fuel readings and figured he had enough fuel to make it to Kunsan. When the engines flamed out at 1,200 feet it was undoubtably a shock to him. He should have immediately given the order to eject – having earlier prepared the crew prior to this to be ready for just such an emergency. Sadly, the November 1958 and the February 1959 crashes were both attributable to human error.

The 11th TRS flew its twelve WB-66D aircraft on standard weather reconnaissance tracks known as *Wild Goose* missions. Similar missions were flown by WB-66D aircraft of the 9th TRS at Shaw and the 42nd TRS at Spangdahlem. The WB-66s of the 11th TRS at Yokota frequently turned into typhoon hunters, in addition to flying their standard Pacific weather routes. Lieutenant Lloyd L. Neutz flew the D-model in the 11th TRS, and frequently found himself playing typhoon hunter – always a memorable experience for the crew, especially the two weather observers in the rear of the aircraft. "It was our job to fly into the storm's eye and report on its diameter, speed, direction of movement, and the position of wall-clouds. We passed our findings to the Guam Weather Central using HF radio. We would fly directly through the eye of the storm at 40,000 feet. Because the air was very warm in the center, providing less lift, it was necessary to increase my power setting to 100 percent. Even at full power we still lost 5,000 feet of altitude by the time we reached the eye's far wall-clouds. Returning from one typhoon hunting mission we nearly didn't make it. I was low on fuel, and approached Kadena AB on Okinawa in heavy rain. The field was below landing minimums. The GCA controller led us down in zero visibility in heavy rain and severe turbulence. By the time I saw the runway it was too late for me to round out and I hit nose wheel first and started porpoising. Every bounce I took became more severe. I felt I was losing control over the aircraft, so I deployed the drag chute at a higher than recommended speed and pulled back on the control column, hoping for the best. Thank God it worked!"[7]

In the first half of 1960 the 11th and 12th Tactical Reconnaissance Squadrons and the 67th Tactical Reconnaissance Wing at Yokota Air Base were deactivated. With the region largely at peace there appeared to be no need to maintain this costly reconnaissance capability in the Far East. The Air Force, under continuing pressure to meet strategic force structure requirements decided not only to deactivated the 67th TRW, but to go ahead and retire the aircraft of the 11th and

12th squadrons although they were barely three years old. The RB-47H aircraft from the 55th SRW extended their surveillance missions to include the routes previously flown by the RB-66Cs of the 11th TRS. It was not only a time of low military budgets, but also a time when technology was changing the world as never before. On April 1, 1960, the first television/infrared satellite was launched to provide instant and broad-based meteorological data, diminishing the need for the WB-66D aircraft. And on June 22, 1960, the U.S. Navy, in great secrecy, launched the GRAB (Galactic Radiation and Background) signals intelligence satellite to collect Soviet radar emissions. That August a super-secret Corona satellite launched from Vandenberg AFB, California, and began transmitting high resolution pictures of the Soviet Union from space, foreshadowing more change to come.[8]

"We flew the airplanes back to the States in January 1960," Kibby Taylor remembers. "We landed at Wake Island. Then we went on to Hawaii and McClellan AFB in California. Two C-models, including mine, were diverted to Hickam AFB, Hawaii, where we were to assist in locating the film package dropped from one of our secret photo-reconnaissance satellites to be retrieved by a specially configured C-119 transport. We were to help locate the film capsule's beacon as it was descending, then guide the C-119 toward it. We picked up the beacon and passed the information to the controllers, then we saw the parachute and hung around long enough to see the C-119 catch the capsule."[9]

The 12TRS RB-66B photo reconnaissance aircraft were sent directly into storage in the Arizona desert. The ten C-models, however, because of their low number of flying hours, were flown to Shaw AFB in Sumter, South Carolina. Ten of Shaw's older C-models were sent instead to the aircraft boneyard in the Arizona desert where they were scrapped. RB-66C 54-452, the *City of Sumter*, feted and celebrated upon its arrival at Shaw a scant four years earlier, was quietly flown to Davis-Monthan AFB near Tucson, Arizona, and along with nine other Shaw RB-66Cs stripped of its equipment and sold for scrap. Clearly, it wasn't one of the best decisions the Air Staff ever made. The Japan based aircraft of the 11th TRS had flown in a much more severe environment from those at Shaw, soon showing signs of salt water corrosion which had to be dealt with. Only five years later, as a growing war in far off Vietnam came to the public's attention, these ten C-models, so quickly disposed of in 1960, were desperately needed. Their quick sale and destruction gained the Air Force little. For some strange reason there was no room to store them in the vast Arizona desert for possible future contingencies.

CHAPTER ELEVEN

THE MISSILES OF OCTOBER

The 42nd TRS at Spangdahlem AB, Germany – moved to RAF Chelveston, England, in 1959, then in 1962 to Toul-Rosieres, France, and to nearby Chambley Air Base in 1965 – flew the same type of reconnaissance missions along the Warsaw Pact periphery as did the 11th TRS out of Yokota. Captain Arthur Roehling and his crew departed Spangdahlem on March 12, 1958, and headed for Wheelus AB, near Tripoli, Libya. They then proceeded across the Mediterranean to Incirlik AB, near Adana, Turkey, where they remained for ten days flying Black Sea reconnaissance. Similar missions were flown directly out of Spangdahlem Air Base along the East German and Czechoslovakian borders. The Soviet Group of Forces in the GDR, the German Democratic Republic which was neither democratic nor a republic, was nearly always the first of Soviet groups of forces to receive new equipment – especially air defense related radar and missile systems. After the shoot-down of Francis Gary Powers' U-2 spy plane near Sverdlovsk on May 1, 1960, by a salvo of 14 SA-2 surface to air missiles, interest in intercepting the associated *Fruit Set* radar, later renamed by NATO *Fansong*, became the highest radar intercept priority for U.S. collectors. The RB-66Cs of the 42nd TRS, along with many other airborne and ground based collectors, were actively involved in searching for the *Fansong* SAM radar – to determine its parameters (pulse width, pulse recurrence frequency, tracking-, guidance- and fusing frequencies, pulse modulation, and whatever else might reveal itself) and thereby its capabilities. By 1960, RB-66C crews from Shaw's 9th TRS augmented the RB-66Cs of the 42nd TRS in *Operation Swamp Fox*. *Swamp Fox* was a rotational deployment, sending

President John F. Kennedy ties an Air Force Outstanding Unit Award streamer to the colors of the 363rd Tactical Reconnaissance Wing at Homestead AFB, FL. The honor was bestowed upon the Wing for its performance during the 1962 Cuban Missile Crisis. Colonel Arthur A. McCartan, commander of the 363TRW, stands facing the President. President Kennedy personally thanked the Wing and its members for their outstanding work.

two of Shaw's C-models and associated air and ground crews to RAF Chelveston to give their Ravens experience with Soviet radars. The rotations usually lasted about three months, then another group of ground and air crews would replace those who had come before.[1]

In September 1961 three RB-66C aircraft from the 9th TRS were tasked to participate in an operation to monitor a suspected Russian satellite launch from their customary launch site at Tyuratam, Kazakhstan. The pilots were Major Paul Bjork and Captains Alvin Bobbitt and Jim Byram. They were to fly from Shaw AFB to RAF Chelveston, with air refuelings near Bermuda and again near the Azores. The second leg of the deployment was to take them to Naval Air Station Sigonella, near Catania, Sicily, and then onward to their final destination at Incirlik AB, Turkey. "Major Bjork, as the senior officer, was designated mission commander," recalled retired Lieutenant Colonel Ned Colburn, then a Raven on Bjork's crew. "Bjork began the crew briefing at Shaw by saying that we would fly in a loose three ship formation, remaining within radio range of each other, with Captain Bobbitt as number two, and Captain Byram flying as tail-end Charlie. The flight to Chelveston was uneventful, aside from the never ending give and take between Major Bjork, as our aircraft helmsman, and Captain Carl Covey, Bjork's Magellan, our navigator. We departed Chelveston on September 11 heading for Sigonella. As we neared Sigonella, while watching smoke rising from the crater of Mount Etna, Carl Covey announced on the interphone that he had Sigonella on his radar scope off the right side of the aircraft. "Paul Bjork responded, 'I've got the field in sight,' then went ahead and canceled our IFR clearance with Catania Control and called Sigonella tower.

"'Air Force 389, flight of three RB-66s. Request VFR approach and landing. 360 degree overhead pattern.'

"'Air Force 389,' Sigonella tower responded, 'understand a flight of 3 RB-66s. Report five miles initial. Left break.' At this point Carl Covey, our navigator, questioned whether or not Bjork had the correct airfield in sight. He was summarily chastised and told to shut up, with further instructions for everyone else to stay off the ship's intercom. Paul Bjork then called Bobbitt and Byram and told them, 'OK guys, tuck it in real tight. We're going to show these U.S. Navy and Italian types how to fly close formation and put on a real air show.' Bobbitt and Byram got as close as possible to the other's aircraft and the show began.

"Bjork: 'Sigonella tower, Air Force 389, flight of three, five miles initial.'

"Sigonella: 'Roger 389. Not in sight. Continue approach. Report one mile initial.

"Bjork: 'Sigonella, 389 one mile initial.'

"Sigonella: 'Roger 389. Not in sight. Continue approach. Report left break.'

"Bjork: 'Sigonella 389 left break for landing.'

"Sigonella: 'Not in sight. Discontinue approach and re-enter pattern. Report five miles initial.' A go-around was made, and we again entered initial for a 360 degree, full circle, overhead pattern and subsequent landing.

"Bjork: 'Sigonella tower. Air Force 389. Flight of three. Five miles initial.'

"Sigonella: 'Roger 389, not in sight. Continue approach. Report one mile.'

"Bjork: 'Sigonella, 389 one mile initial.'

"Sigonella: 'Roger 389, not in sight. Continue approach. Report left break.'

"Bjork: '389 left break for landing.'

"Sigonella: 'Not in sight. Are you sure you are at the right airfield?'

"Bjork: 'Roger, we are directly overhead.' Sigonella then asked if he could see a fishing village off to the left side of the airport with a long jetty and boats anchored on both sides.

"Bjork: 'Roger, I see the village.'

"Sigonella: 'You, sir, are at the wrong airfield. You are over Catania, not Sigonella.' We landed red faced at Sigonella where the U.S. Navy and the Italian Air Force let us cool our heels sitting on the bare floor of base operations for about four hours before refueling our aircraft. Bjork in the meantime was walking around muttering unintelligibles. We took off from Sigonella and landed at Incirlik about midnight. As we pulled off the runway onto the taxiway to jettison our brake chute, Bjork pulled the throttles back to idle, with number one throttle slipping past the detent into the off position. Realizing what happened, Paul Bjork, our dear senior pilot, threw the number one throttle forward whereupon the pooled fuel ignited in the engine and torched fore and aft, creating a fireworks display against the dark Turkish sky. The gunner got out of the airplane, opened the fuel drains and we shut down on the taxiway. After an engine change, we finally got to fly our first ELINT (electronic intelligence) mission over the Black Sea.

"The RB-47Hs and RB-47E Tell-Two telemetry collectors from Forbes AFB in Kansas were there, as well as the Navy A3Ds, and Willie Victors, Navy EC-121s from their base at Rota, Spain. The SAC types from Forbes didn't wear any name tags or wings on their flight suits, and wouldn't talk about why they were at Incirlik. We had gone through flight training with many of the SAC crew members and had fun asking them who they really were and what they were doing in Turkey. In contrast we took the Navy types through the RB-66C, and they in turn gave us a tour of the A3D and their EC-121. On September 21 we left Turkey on our scheduled redeployment back to Shaw via Wheelus AB, Libya; Moron AB, Spain, and the usual refuelings near the Azores and Bermuda. Paul Bjork announced that he had flown fighters out of Wheelus and knew the base like the back of his hand. 'Wheelus has a long runway,' he said 'so do not deploy your brake chutes.' Bjork called Wheelus tower for a straight-in VFR approach, and as we came in over the water he had to add power three times to rescue the aircraft from mushing into the sea. Ed Breck in position two became a little bit nervous having survived the crash of RB-66C 54-471 at Donaldson AFB in South Carolina six months earlier. Bjork made a good landing on the runway numbers, but during roll out he forgot that the runway at Wheelus had a hump in the middle. Seeing the runway disappear in front of him at the high point, he mistakenly thought he was nearing the end, stood on the pedals and 389 ended up with hot brakes. After the mandatory brake-cooling period the aircraft was towed to the ramp for refueling and instead of a minimum time quick turn-around we spent nearly four hours on the ground before heading to Moron Air Base in Spain. At Moron we lost elevator trim and instead of the scheduled non-stop flight back to Shaw we island hopped to Lajes, Azores, then Harmon Air Base, Newfoundland, before arriving back at Shaw on September 23, 1961. But there were small compensations such as the 57-cent *All You Can Eat Steak Night* at the Lajes Officers' Club; the 5-cent shoe shines; 15-cent haircuts, and 25-cent sauna – all well worth stocking up on."[2]

Whether Air Force, Navy, Marine or Army – flyers are the furthest any human being could possibly be from being robots. They have to cope with the vicissitudes of nature, coax often recalcitrant flying machines into doing things they were never built to do, and fly into harms way whenever and wherever told to do so. They are men, today women as well, with needs and wants and ambitions, having learned early on not to suppress their fears, but to use the rush of adrenalin to their advantage. At times, they just want to be foolish and free, letting off steam, relieving the stresses of the world they live in and cope with twenty-four hours a day. They fly, sleep, eat and drink together, all too often spending more time with one another than with their families. They know each others strengths and weaknesses, survive each others annoying little quirks by maintaining a forgiving, if at times sarcastic sense of humor. In time of war and emergency when teamwork is essential and reliance on one another is absolute, it is precisely then that these carefully cultivated bonds enable men to accomplish the seemingly impossible. And so our three RB-66C aircrews were quite typical.

On May 4, 1962, the 16th TRS and the 29th TRS at Shaw deployed nine RB-66B and eight RF-101 aircraft to Eglin AFB, to participate in a firepower demonstration for President John F. Kennedy. It was to be the biggest demonstration of its kind ever put on by the Air Force. It was also a subtle yet unheeded warning to the island nation gone Communist 90 miles south of Florida. Captain Gerry Reponen was one of the pilots from the 16TRS selected to go to Eglin. "I was chosen to fly the low level aerial refueling demonstration behind a KB-50 tanker flying past the President. We deployed to Eglin on April 13 to practice. The final practice was flown on April 27 before the vice president, Lyndon B. Johnson, the secretary of defense, Robert S. McNamara, and too many generals to recall. This was quite a show. There were a total of 164 aircraft, and 126 of them were from TAC – 63 F-100s, eight RF-101s, seven F-104s, 31 of the new F-105s, two L-28s, four KB-50s, nine RB-66s, and three C-130s. The practice on the 27th began with the RB-66 aircraft flying at 3,000 feet and 250 knots, with the lead aircraft dropping twenty-one time release flash cartridges with a two second delay in a twenty-one gun aerial salute to the President, with the cartridges set to burst at 1,500 feet in front of the reviewing stand."[3]

Gayle Johnson, also from the 16TRS, flew the lead aircraft and was to drop the 21 flash cartridges. "General LeMay, the Air Force Chief of Staff, and the TAC commander, General Walter C. Sweeney, were in the audience. Only 20 cartridges came out – and LeMay did the counting. We learned all about the 20-count versus the 21-salute immediately after landing when we dropped the entrance door to our aircraft. Our remedy was to have the number two aircraft have its cartridge door open to pick up any misses. The armament people filed and shined those firing pins on the cartridge shells. Came the real thing – 21 cartridges went off on schedule for the President. Our demonstration was preceded by a pair of F-104s doing a supersonic run past the reviewing stand. President Kennedy sat in his famous rocking chair on the platform, and word had it that he nearly got knocked off his chair by the sonic boom."[4]

Three RF-101s from the 363rd TRW followed the RB-66s, demonstrating the latest side-looking photo technology, flying 100 feet off the ground at 350 knots. Photographs taken by the RF-101s of the presidential party were developed immediately upon landing and presented to Vice President Lyndon B. Johnson two hours after the fly-by. This was the same technology that was to bring home the pictures of the Soviet SA-2 missile sites four months later on the Island of Cuba. There were various fighter aircraft making passes at maximum speed and minimum altitude, some firing guns and rockets. Other aircraft performed maximum rate of climb demonstrations, aiming to intercept B-57s cruising at 20,000 feet. The new F-105 TAC fighter demonstrated nuclear weapons delivery tactics, other fighters shot down a QF-80 drone aircraft with a missile. All this was followed by a B-52G launching a simulated nuclear weapon at low altitude. "Finally, my turn came," recalls Captain Reponen, "Mission #11 – a mass in-flight refueling demonstrating TAC's global reach and ability to move its aircraft to any part of the world using aerial refueling. The first flight had an F-100 refueling from one wing-drogue of a KB-50 tanker, and an RF-101 on the other. The second flight had an F-104 and F-105 refueling off the wings of a KB-50, and the third KB-50 had one RB-66B with me as the pilot refueling from the tail drogue. Following me were two C-130s.

"We had been flying in orbit just off shore over the Gulf at 2,000 feet. It was extremely hot in the aircraft and we were bouncing all over the sky with low puffy cumulus clouds in the area. As we fell in line to make our pass, all of us were to make our connection to the tanker as we descended to 1,000 feet. I was bouncing all over the place in the descent as I made my connection and pushed the refueling hose in to about twenty-five feet. Passing the grandstand, I was told later, the fighters were all over the sky and the only aircraft hooked up and close to the tanker was the RB-66. Was I ever proud to hear that. The 3rd of May was a stand-down day for maintenance to insure all aircraft would be ready the following day for the real thing. We had a squadron softball game with the officers against the enlisted men, to be followed by a barbecue. During the game I got hit by a line drive on the end of my right index finger. It hurt terribly. The following day my hand was swollen twice its size and I could only move my thumb and little finger. I pretended everything was fine and hid my hand as best I could. I was not going to miss flying past the President, a once in a lifetime opportunity. I told Neil, my squadron commander who was flying in the gunner's seat, that he would have to get out of his seat and turn the fuel selector and radio switches for me. I could push the throttles back and forth with my right hand but that was all I could use it for. We were briefed that no one was going to connect to the KB-50s so it would all look uniform.

"We flew the same orbit pattern, the weather was just as ugly, turbulent and hot as before. As we descended to 1,000 feet I flew up to the drogue of the tanker and put the basket up against the right windshield so it was hidden and it looked like I was connected. In that position we flew past President Kennedy. Neil got out of his seat and tuned the radio for me so I could get landing instructions. After we taxied in and shut the engines down I found our flight surgeon who was stunned when I told him that I had just flown a low level refueling. I had a broken joint where the finger joins the hand and it was too late for a cast. So I ran around with a splint for a couple of weeks. The range demonstrations were extensive with all the fighters doing various types of weapons deliveries. The C-130s made an assault landing, unloaded a bunch of troops and then took off again. Probably the most impressive demonstration was a flight of F-100s making a napalm and strafing run, followed by another flight of four doing a bomb and strafing attack, who were followed by yet four more F-100s firing rockets and strafing as well. The very last mission showed off SAC's newest bomber, the B-58, making a minimum altitude high speed fly-by. The entire show took 45 minutes and was a constant flow of aircraft demonstrating one thing or another. In my Air Force career I was never to see anything like it again."[5]

In October 1962 the Cuban Missile Crisis erupted, putting the nation and the world at the edge of Armageddon. I remember those days well. I was a young first lieutenant, flying as a Raven in one of SAC's RB-47H reconnaissance aircraft. Suspicions were rampant for some time that the Soviets were up to something in Cuba. U-2 and RF-101 aircraft had photographed tell-tale SA-2 Star-of-David missile sites. And we in the 55th SRW had picked up, recorded and located some of the SA-2 associated SAM tracking radars. But it was Major Richard Heyser, flying his U-2 spy plane over Cuba on the morning of October 14, 1962, who photographed and brought back the first pictures of Soviet SS-4 Medium Range Ballistic Missiles mounted on trailers. SAC took its time verifying what it had, coordinating with the CIA and other intelligence agencies before confronting the President with the news on Tuesday morning, October 16. "President John F. Kennedy was still in his pajamas when his national security advisor, McGeorge Bundy, delivered the news. Kennedy was stunned – Soviet leader Nikita Khrushchev had given him a personal pledge not to deploy offensive weapons in Cuba. 'He can't do that to me!' Kennedy exclaimed. Summoned to the White House to look at Heyser's pictures, the President's brother Robert pounded his fist in his palm and moaned, 'Oh shit! Shit! Those sons a'bitches Russians.'"[6]

On Monday, October 22, President Kennedy, in a televised speech to the nation, announced that the Soviet Union was in the process of installing nuclear-tipped missiles ninety miles off America's shores. A naval quarantine was to be imposed on the island of Cuba until all missiles were removed. Missile-carrying ships were to be intercepted and not allowed to proceed. By presidential directive the Strategic Air Command went from Defense Condition 5 to Defense Condition 3 – from a routine alert posture for the nuclear strike forces to a readiness posture where all aircraft were loaded with nuclear weapons and ready for launch. On the day the quarantine went into effect, on Wednesday, October 24, the SAC commander, General Thomas S. Power, unilaterally ordered SAC forces from Defcon 3 to Defcon 2, making an already touchy situation worse. Over 1,000 SAC bombers sat on their dispersal bases crewed, loaded and ready to strike the Soviet Union. Others were on airborne alert flying racetrack patterns high in the sky above the Arctic Circle. Polaris nuclear submarines assumed their final launch positions. It seemed that General LeMay's carefully crafted strategy of nuclear deterrence was about to fail. As a child in wartime Germany I survived 1,000-bomber raids on Berlin. I knew that neither I nor my young family would survive a nuclear exchange with the Soviet Union. While the bombers sat alert or flew their elliptical racetrack patterns high in the sky, we in the 55th flew our RB-47H reconnaissance aircraft twenty-four hours a day around Cuba, maintaining electronic surveillance and searching for an elusive missile-carrying Russian ship

– the *Groznyy*. High altitude U-2 photographic spy planes of the 4080th Strategic Wing and low flying RF-101 photographic reconnaissance aircraft of the 363rd TRW brought home the pictures needed to prove and monitor the Missiles of October.

Black Saturday, October 27, proved to be a watershed day. A 55th Wing RB-47H involved in the search for the Soviet ship carrying additional SS-4 missiles crashed on take-off from Kindley Air Base, Bermuda. Its crew of four perished. Another RB-47H located the *Groznyy*, crates of missiles crowding her deck. Navy destroyers quickly challenged the Russians, putting the quarantine to the test. A U-2 piloted by Major Rudolph Anderson from the 4080th Strategic Wing was downed by an SA-2 missile while on a high altitude photographic run over Cuba, killing Anderson. The fat was in the fire, as the saying goes. The *Groznyy* stopped at the quarantine line, sat there for a while, then turned back. The following day, Sunday, October 28, Russia agreed to remove its offensive missiles from Cuba. The crisis was over.[7]

While the focus throughout those fateful October days was on the Strategic Air Command, its bombers and high flying U-2 spy planes, the men of the 363rd Tactical Reconnaissance Wing flying RF-101 and RB-66 reconnaissance aircraft did what light, tactical aircraft did best. The RF-101s, relocated from Shaw to Homestead AFB on the east coast of Florida, flew photo reconnaissance over Cuba at treetop level with their sensitive optical and infra-red cameras. They picked up the residual heat-generated silhouettes of missiles on trailers parked on concrete aprons, after they were hastily moved and hidden from their all-seeing eyes. The RB-66Cs flying out of MacDill AFB, on Tampa Bay, picked up SA-2 radar emissions, but it took Major Heyser's undeniable high altitude U-2 photographs to leave no doubt of what the Russians were up to. RB-66B aircraft flew the film from returning RF-101s to Headquarters Tactical Air Command at Langley AFB, Virginia, where it was processed before being passed on to the Pentagon and the White House. RB-66Cs from the 9th TRS at Shaw continued to fly electronic surveillance missions around Cuba out of MacDill until 1965, when another more urgent war required their services.

On November 26, 1962, after the quarantine of Cuba was lifted, and the last IL-28 *Beagle* bomber had been removed from the island, President Kennedy met face to face with the men of the 363rd Tactical Reconnaissance Wing and the 4080th Strategic Wing at Homestead AFB. While pinning the Outstanding Unit Award streamer onto Wing flags he recognized their sacrifices: "May I say gentlemen, that you take excellent pictures, and I have seen a great many of them, beginning with the photos which were taken on the weekend in the middle of October which first gave us conclusive proof of the build-up of offensive weapons in Cuba ... You gentlemen have contributed as much to the security of the United States as any group of men in our history. We are much indebted to you."[8] And the entire nation was indeed indebted to these men, as well as to the visceral courage of a young President who rose to a mortal challenge to the nation, coolly focused on a peaceful solution until one was found.

Captain Eldon Canady was a Raven in the 9th TRS at Shaw and flew numerous *Red Lemon*, later called *Potato Chip*, missions in RB-66C aircraft out of MacDill around Cuba. This was good training that would stand him in good stead in 1965 when he deployed to Takhli Royal Thai Air Force Base, RTAFB, in Thailand, about 100 miles north of Bangkok, at the beginning of the Vietnam War. "During those electronic reconnaissance missions the Cuban/Russian operators often locked onto us with their *Firecan* anti-aircraft radars. We were under orders not to jam them or drop chaff unless we were under attack. On one mission my curiosity got the better of me. I wanted to find out how effective our jammers and chaff would be against them. I knew that any chaff I released could be tracked by our own radars in Florida, but jamming might not be detected. A *Firecan* radar I had been DF-ing (direction finding) and analyzing locked on to us. I decided to drop several bundles of chaff. Within moments after the chaff deployed the lock was broken and the signal got weaker as it followed the false target. Once the operator realized that lock had been broken, he went back into acquisition mode and once again locked on to us. I again dropped some chaff and broke his lock. After we passed out of range I wondered how I was going to explain all this once we landed, because I was sure our own radars had tracked and reported this activity. I saw myself getting grounded, or receiving some other punishment. But I never heard a word about it. On another mission in the same area we again were tracked by an anti-aircraft, AAA, fire control radar, this time I decided to use one of our noise jammers. As before, I broke his lock. He tried to come back. I broke his lock again with jamming. Then a rare thing happened. An SA-2 missile tracking radar, a *Fansong*, came on the air. It was a really strong signal. I would not see a *Fansong* again until I got to Vietnam. The purpose of our missions of course was to pick up these signals, record their parameters, so they could be analyzed. I got a really good recording of this particular *Fansong* radar, but I didn't try to jam him or drop chaff. These Cuban surveillance missions gave me great confidence when I deployed to Vietnam that we could successfully suppress their fire control radars."[9]

The Cuban Missile crisis was not only a good training ground for the Ravens of the 9th TRS, but also a wake-up call for Air Force planners of the lethality of the SA-2. The loss of Major Anderson's U-2 over Cuba was preceded by the loss over China of a U-2C to an SA-2 missile a month earlier, on September 9, 1962.

That aircraft was flown by a Taiwanese pilot. Still another Chinese Nationalist U-2C was shot down on November 1, 1963, to be followed by another on July 7, 1964, and a fourth U-2C on January 10, 1965.[10] It became obvious that the day of the high flying bomber was a thing of the past. SAC's XB-70 high altitude bomber, destined to be the follow-on aircraft to the B-52, was one of the first major weapons system programs to become a casualty of advancing technology. B-47s and B-52s began practicing on low level *oil burner* routes, flying 500 feet above the terrain, hoping to under-fly and evade enemy missile radars. Nuclear weapon carrying fighters such as the F-100D and the new F-105 would have to penetrate enemy territory low level as well and get expert at toss-bombing. The full impact of the SA-2 SAM system on Air Force weapons systems and tactics would not reveal itself until well into the air war against North Vietnam, but then it changed the U.S. Air Force in ways few could imagine at the time.

CHAPTER TWELVE

ONE MAN's STORY

Gerry Reponen turned six in 1935. "It was the year when my cousin Marvin told me about a Pure Oil station on 6th Street in Duluth, Minnesota, where I lived, giving away Jimmie Mattern books called *Cloud Country*. There were three books in the series giving a pictorial history of famous flights up to 1935. Jimmie Mattern also had a radio program and his first twenty episodes made up Book One, titled *Wings of Youth*. The Book Two episodes were titled *Hawaii to Hollywood*, followed by Book Three, *Lost in Siberia*. I picked up the books at the Pure Oil station when they came out and intently listened to Jimmie's radio program. There was another radio program I listened to as well, *Captain Midnight*. By age ten I was hooked on airplanes and flying and I thought about becoming a pilot. I attended college and in 1952 was commissioned a second lieutenant in the United States Air Force. I reported for duty with a hundred other newly commissioned officers at McChord Air Force Base in Washington state. I applied for pilot training, passed the physical and was selected, but didn't get a class assignment until February 1954. I starting with the PA-18 Piper Cub and ended up flying the twin-engine B-25 of World War II fame. After getting my wings, I chose a T-29D assignment at Mather AFB, near Sacramento. We trained navigator/bombardiers for the Strategic Air Command. After two years there I had 2,000 flying hours. I would have had more, but the Air Force only allowed us to fly a maximum of 320 hours a quarter. It was at this time when I received a call from personnel. They offered me the choice of a B-47 or a KC-97 assignment. I was getting ready to pack up my family to move to Plattsburg AFB, in New York

An RB-66C from the 42nd TRS, 10TRW, approaches a KB-50 aerial refueling tanker from the 420th Air Refueling Squadron, of the 47th BW, over the North Sea.

state, when I got a call canceling my SAC assignment and sending me to the 66th Tactical Reconnaissance Wing, at Sembach Air Base, Germany. I was thrilled. First though I had to report to Craig Air Force Base, near Selma, Alabama, to qualify in the T-33 jet trainer. I was to report to Sembach in September.

"It was my last flight in the T-33 after 42 hours, a solo night mission. I flew over Selma and marveled at the bright lights below. I decided to see what the city looked like upside down, rolled over and flew again across Selma. Once I passed the lights I rolled right side up and I found myself in total blackness – there were no lights, no horizon. I couldn't tell which way was up. It took a lot of concentration staring at the attitude indicator and convincing myself that I was flying straight and level, while the seat of my pants was telling me I was flying into the ground. I had a severe case of vertigo, and the many hours of instrument training in the T-29D at Mather probably saved my life. On Wednesday, September 25, 1957, I turned in my car for shipment to Germany and boarded a C-118 at McGuire Air Force Base, New Jersey, to Frankfurt, Germany."[1]

When Germany was divided up at Yalta in February 1945, the American zone of occupation was in the south and the British in the north. The French zone was subsequently carved out of the British and American zones. American air bases were clustered around Munich, Bavaria, such as Erding, Fuerstenfeldbruck and Oberpfaffenhofen. Not exactly ideal locations for combat squadrons. The most promising sites for alternative air base locations were in the remote Eifel Mountains in the French zone of occupation. The French granted basing rights to American forces in France in 1951, and acceded to the construction of three new airfields and the expansion of two others in their zone of occupation as well. Construction of Spangdahlem, Bitburg, and Hahn Air Bases began in 1951. Sembach and Ramstein/Landstuhl, former Luftwaffe bases, were expanded to accommodate jet aircraft and the families of American servicemen. The cost of building the bases was born by a defeated Germany in the form of reparations. By late 1952 the new air bases in the Eifel Mountains were mostly ready and the 36th Fighter Bomber Wing moved its F-84Es from Fuerstenfeldbruck to Bitburg. The 10th Tactical Reconnaissance Wing moved to Spangdahlem Air Base, within sight of Bitburg, and the 50th Fighter Bomber Wing moved into Hahn Air Base. Construction at Sembach was slowed down by opposition from local farmers who did not want to give up their land, but by late 1952 Sembach Air Base was mostly completed as well and became the headquarters of the 66th Tactical Reconnaissance Wing, 66TRW, and two of its squadrons. The Air Force's post World War II base realignment in Europe was pretty much completed by late 1952, and American air power was facing its new adversary to the east from new and well positioned air bases. First Lieutenant Gerald Reponen, on his way to Sembach via Frankfurt Air Base, the port of entry for troops and dependents traveling to Germany by air, arrived on September 26.

"After collecting my bags I went to the Officers' Club and had a German beer. If I had been smart I would have gotten a room in the Bachelor Officers Quarters, BOQ, but I chose instead to take a bus to Sembach and arrived there well after dark. It turned out that Sembach had no quarters available and I ended up staying in the Ramstein Visiting Officers Quarters, VOQ, getting to bed well after midnight. Within days I was shunted off to a BOQ in Vogelweh, a huge Army installation down the road from Ramstein and Landstuhl Air Bases. Although only September, it was cold. All I had with me was my Class-A blue uniform. Clearing into the 66th TRW was a paperwork nightmare. Every office seemed to have its own form and special requirements. When I went to the finance office to collect the travel money due me, about $900, I didn't get paid in American dollars, but was handed a stack one-half inch thick of script money, issued by the military in lieu of dollars. When I reported to the 30th TRS, my squadron, there were more surprises in store for me. They had too many pilots and not enough flying hours nor airplanes to go around. The 30th had six RB-57As in its inventory, and only twelve of its authorized twenty-four RB-66Bs had arrived so far. I was assigned to Headquarters Squadron to fly a desk. When I went to the personal equipment section I was able to check out one flight suit. They didn't know when they would have a helmet for me, nor any of the other flying gear I was authorized and needed. There was a lot of make-work for newcomers – taking the military and European drivers tests, and briefings on European flying conditions and Air Defense Identification Zones and procedures. Getting settled in seemed a never ending process. I needed a transformer for my electric razor, was looking for a cheap used car, spent endless hours trying to get my family's travel arrangements straightened out, and put in for military housing. Using the military telephone system and trying to call from one base to another was another riddle wrapped in an enigma. Every evening I felt like I had gone through a meat grinder, yet I hadn't touched nor seen an airplane since I arrived at Sembach.

"On October 7 I was finally notified that I would be the pilot of the 18th crew in our squadron. This news got me only one thing, a room in the BOQ at Sembach. Other than getting assigned to a squadron, going to ground school, reading regulations, and moving ten miles, nothing changed. The following day I learned that our squadron was scheduled to move to Spangdahlem in March. We were supposed to move in December I heard, but the runways weren't ready. The runway at Sembach couldn't take the weight of the B-66, so the airplanes which had arrived from the factory sat at Landstuhl and Ramstein. A couple days later I was informed that I finally would be able to get a T-33 flight. I still only had one flight suit and a clip board, no boots and no helmet. Then I was supposed to go to Laon AB, France, for two weeks to get 50 hours in the B-57 before I could even think about checking out in the B-66. Germany was pretty I discovered. I found the villages interesting – the houses closely spaced, the roads paved with cobblestones, a manure heap in every farmyard, close to the road and next to the main house. I presumed the larger the pile the more prosperous the farmer."[2]

The mission of the 66th TRW at Sembach was to provide day and night reconnaissance information to the commanders of what the Wing's history referred to as, 'air-ground teams.' Its squadrons and aircraft were scattered and diverse. The 19th TRS was assigned to the 66TRW in January 1957 and located at RAF Sculthorpe in far away England, flying the RB-45C Tornado. The 19th converted to the RB-66B Destroyer in February 1957. Another of its squadrons, the 30th TRS, flew World War II vintage RB-26Cs, T-33 jet trainers, and trouble prone RB-57A jets, while the 302nd and 303rd reconnaissance squadrons flew single engine RF-84Fs. The 302nd and 303rd squadrons' RF-84s sat at Sembach and Laon, France, as did the B and RB-57As. Once the RB-66Bs arrived in July 1957 (Appendix 3), they were parked at Landstuhl and Ramstein, because the runway at Sembach could not support their weight. The 66 Wing's diversity of aircraft and far spread locations was a nightmare for any commander to manage and control. Not surprisingly, Headquarters USAFE, located in an old German Kaserne in the spa-town of Wiesbaden, Lindsey Air Station, late in 1957 decided to reorganize. In January 1958, the RB-66B, C and D equipped squadrons were all put under the 10th Wing at Spangdahlem. The 1st TRS and 42nd TRS, already there, were augmented by the 30th TRS from Sembach in early 1958 and by the 19th TRS from RAF Sculthorpe in January 1959. Finally, all the 10th Wing squadrons would be under one roof so to speak. All RF-84F squadrons were placed under the 66TRW at Sembach with aircraft at both Sembach and Laon, France. In late 1957 Lieutenant Reponen found himself thrown into what one might call a dynamic situation. His unit of assignment was in the process of aircraft conversion, anticipated physical relocation and organizational change.[3]

"October was a period of turmoil for me just trying to understand what I had become a part of," Gerry Reponen wrote. "I hadn't flown since I left the States and I needed four hours flying time desperately to get my flying pay, or lose it. So on the 21st of October I managed to get on an SA-16 *Albatross* rescue plane as a copilot and flew to Belgium and back. I was thrilled when I finally got an RB-66 orientation flight. I rode in the gunner's seat behind the pilot. Money seemed to be very tight. They were deactivating squadrons and cutting down on the number of people. There was very little flying time available for us because of cutbacks in flying hours. Nevertheless, being in a combat squadron gave me an elite feeling.

We were always joking back and forth between the RF-84 pilots and those who flew the B-57 and the B-66. Such camaraderie I had never experienced before.

"To qualify in the RB-66 I had to have 50 hours twin-engine jet time. To get that I had to go to Laon where the Wing had some B-57B bombers. Crossing the border was an ordeal, but once on the other side driving was easier than in Germany. The roads were wider, straighter and paved with black top, not cobble stones. The fields were larger as well, not broken up into little strips as in Germany. The villages were similar, but there were few people about nor cars on the roads. Laon Air Base was spread all over the place and had a temporary look about it. There were no trees on the base, house trailers instead of base housing, the BOQ looked thrown together, with walls so thin that sound carried throughout the building. I started flying in the B-57B on November 16. The weather was bad throughout my stay and I never was able to get a VFR check ride. They finally signed me off and I returned to Sembach and got a couple of flights in the RB-57A. The RB-57A was very different from the bomber. The pilot sat in a bubble not seeing any part of the airplane, otherwise the view was excellent. It was a strange feeling sitting in this cockpit, like being at the head of a pin. To see the instrument panel I had to duck down – not very safe. The second person rode in a compartment below, to the right and back of the pilot. To change seats, the instructor pilot got out of his seat and parachute and then kneeled down facing backwards holding the yoke of the plane to control it as there was no autopilot. Then the other pilot would crawl up beside him and step up into the bubble and sit down. This was not the safest way of doing things, but the only way to get checked out in the A-model. Then they grounded the planes because of flight control problems. I still didn't have 50 hours multi-engine jet time which I needed to fly the RB-66.

"Ruth and the children finally arrived at Frankfurt on December 23. We drove to Vogelweh where I had two BOQ rooms waiting for us. There we celebrated Christmas. We left for Spangdahlem Air Base on January 2, 1958. Finding a house on the economy was difficult, base housing was not available. We moved in on January 5, a small apartment on the main road to the nearby town of Bitburg. The apartment was heated with a coal stove. We had an electric range in the kitchen, and hot water came from a small electric appliance over the washbasin. The bathroom was small and cold. At one end of the bathtub was a coal fired hot water heater. If we wanted to take a bath we first had to make a fire to heat the water. We had a lot of learning to do about life in a foreign country.

"My squadron, the 30th TRS, moved into a small cement building in the forest near the east end of the runway at Spangdahlem. The main base was more than a mile from our location. A Field Training Detachment, FTD, from Shaw AFB ran an RB-66B aircraft familiarization course for us, going into the details of every aircraft system to the point where after a few days I thought my head would explode. I didn't actually get to fly the RB-66 until March, and not at Spangdahlem, but at Nouasseur Air Base, French Morocco, where the skies were nearly always clear. After sixteen hours with an instructor I finally flew my first solo mission on March 22, and within the week I was certified as a qualified RB-66 combat pilot."[4]

The RB-66B assigned to Lieutenant Reponen was the last aircraft to be transferred from the 66TRW to Spangdahlem – 54-528, a hangar queen. The 10th Wing just had an Operational Readiness Inspection, ORI, and had been severely criticized for the number of non-operational planes. The principal reason for the groundings and cannibalization was that the Stafoam filled control surfaces, ailerons and elevators, accumulated water inside and became too heavy to function.[5] "Captain Fred Flanders flew the aircraft to Spangdahlem, making the flight with the gear down," Gerry Reponen writes. "When Dan McGreevy, my navigator, and I took it up, the landing gear would not retract. Trying to remember my FTD lectures, I actuated the JATO jettison button. Suddenly I had hydraulic pressure to the gear and it retracted. Dan said, 'Now that we have the gear up, how do we get it down?' Placing the gear handle in either the up or down position had no effect. Making my descent I hit the speed brake switch, and the gear came down. Maintenance found a problem with the way the hydraulic lines had been hooked up. It was the first of many challenges I encountered flying the RB-66.

"In April I pinned on captain's bars, a welcome raise came along with that promotion. In addition we got the good news that an apartment had become available in base housing at Bitburg. Ruth was excited – finally hot water again when you turned the faucet, a washing machine in the basement laundry room with plenty of lines to hang your wash, a small balcony to sit on, and central heating, no more coal to mess with. At work I was appointed squadron flying safety officer, and within days we had a puzzle to deal with. It was early summer and that morning one of our aircraft taking off to the east knocked the arresting barrier down. After much back and forth we recalculated our take-off data. Runway 05 was slightly up hill, and for the weight of our aircraft with the current weather conditions and field elevation at Spangdahlem we found to our surprise that we needed 8,300 feet to make a take-off. No wonder the barrier was knocked down, because we only had an 8,000 foot runway. From then on we all learned how to use the performance charts in our flight manual, and computed every take-off roll. During the summer months we couldn't take off with a full fuel load from Spangdahlem.

"The Lebanon Crisis blew up that summer and we were put on alert and restricted to the base. After a couple of weeks things calmed down again and I was allowed to go on a long planned two-week family vacation. Wherever we went on our travels we found the Germans to be friendly and kind. That year I flew my first mission at Wheelus AB, Tripoli, in support of *Matador* missile tests. We chased the missile down range and recorded its impact point in relationship to its assigned target. In October the weather took a turn for the worse. And on December 9, 1958, the 30th TRS had its first aircraft accident."[6]

Aircraft 54-535 was on a practice radar bomb scoring flight from Spangdahlem to Nancy, France, then to Cologne, Germany, and back to Spangdahlem. Captain Howard Strandberg, the pilot, intended to make a straight in GCA approach to runway 23. It was near midnight as the aircraft approached. Captain Strandberg requested to level off above the undercast, reporting that his engine anti-icing system seemed to be inoperative. The aircraft descended from 7,000 to 4,000 feet, then continued to descend to 2,700 feet. Nine miles from the end of the runway the final GCA radar controller took over. The aircraft responded to his directions up to the two mile point. At 1.8 miles from the runway the aircraft disappeared from the radar scope and crashed, killing its crew of three. The subsequent investigation did not reveal aircraft malfunction. It appeared to be pilot error.[7]

"Acrobatics in the B-66 were a no-no. The wing fuel-bladders were hung in such a way that unless positive G-forces were maintained they could come off their hangars and bend the fuel probes inside the bladders. Acrobatics may have been against the rules, but we all violated the rules – it was such an exhilarating feeling no jet pilot could resist. In early 1959 our planes were finally equipped with refueling probes and soon thereafter my flight commander, Captain Don McKeon and I took off for our first try at aerial refueling from a KB-50 tanker. Little did they know that we had no experience. The tanker was in a 30-mile orbit over Germany. I stayed off to the left to watch Don try to make a connect with the tanker's drogue. For the best closure with the drogue we had been briefed to fly five knots faster than the tanker, after connecting we would continue to push forward until about 25 feet of hose remained before reducing speed. Refueling was not easy at the slow 180 knots flown by the tanker, compared to our normal cruise speed of 300 to 360 knots. I discovered quickly that a closure speed closer to ten knots faster worked better. When coming in to the drogue too slow the air pressure would build up in front of the drogue and deflect it away in one direction or another. With a little faster closure speed I found things beginning to fall into place. The biggest problem was reaching the IFR switch, (Inflight Refueling Switch) located just above the floor and to the right, a difficult place to reach. Reaching for the switch tended to give me vertigo. When transferring fuel the added weight required additional power and created a nose high attitude. When this happened I asked the tanker to tobaggon, and he would go into a slow descent. Air refueling with the KB-50 tanker was work and it took lots of practice to get good at it.

"In 1959 I participated in three 48-aircraft fligh-bys, a practice the 10th Wing had become known for. During Armed Forces Day, and on two other occasions. The 19th squadron had finally arrived from RAF Sculthorpe, and each of the four squadrons put up 12 aircraft carefully assembled in one gigantic diamond formation. It took work to get that done. I felt like I was just barely clearing the trees and getting bounced around in the jet wash of other planes in the formation above me. On August 13, 1959, my squadron, the 30th TRS, published orders for us to move from Spangdahlem to RAF Alconbury. This came as a complete surprise. We knew that relations between the U.S. and France had deteriorated, but none of us expected it to have such an immediate impact."[8]

President Charles de Gaulle ordered all American nuclear armed aircraft off French soil in July 1959. Headquarters of the 10th TRW moved to RAF Alconbury along with two of its squadrons, the 1st and 30th TRS. The 42nd TRS with its RB-66C and D aircraft relocated to RAF Chelveston, and the 19th TRS, which had arrived at Spangdahlem only in January, was sent to RAF Bruntingthorpe. All of the British locations were old World War II bases with minimum facilities. "I was told I would have to move my family to England within three weeks," Gerry Reponen notes "or they would be shipped back to the States and I would be put in an unaccompanied tour status. On September 15 I finally found a house in Cambridge, and was granted ten days permissive TDY to make arrangements to move my family from Germany to England. Our English house was in a workingman's neighborhood, a long row of narrow tenement houses with small backyards. The house was cold and drafty. The weather in Germany had been warm and pleasant compared to England where for some reason it seemed colder. From October on almost every flight out of Alconbury was in weather. As a result we did much of our flying out of Moron Air Base, near Seville, Spain. For our night photo missions we used nearby bombing ranges where we could drop our photo cartridges, and most of our day photo missions were of our own choosing.

"On January 4, 1960, I was not scheduled to fly and reported to my squadron wearing Air Force blues, our Class-A dress uniform. Wearing a flight suit when you were not scheduled to fly was prohibited. My flight suit and boots were at home, twenty-five miles away. Because of the persistent inclement weather my squadron was behind in its flying, and I was only one of two pilots in the 30th squadron with a green instrument card, which permitted me to fly in weather conditions others were not qualified to fly in. Before I knew it I found myself taxiing an aircraft from the ramp to the runway, wearing my blue uniform and low quarter shoes. I could see maybe 30 feet ahead, the fog was dense. As I passed 80 knots on my take-off roll, I suddenly could no longer see the runway. Switching to instruments I continued the take-off, all the while hoping I wouldn't veer off to the side. The fog bank that covered the base hugged the ground and was not very deep. I could see the tops of buildings protruding through the fog as I climbed out. I flew the mission as briefed and on my return to Alconbury the base was still fogged in, forcing me to recover at Chelveston. Finally, on the 8th, the weather improved and I was able to get back. After five days without any change of clothing nor proper flight gear I had flown a total of five missions for 18 hours in my Class-A uniform. I took a lot of ribbing from my squadron mates who referred to me as the *gentleman pilot*."[9]

In early 1960 the 42nd TRS at Chelveston phased out its WB-66D weather planes and replaced them with 13 modified B-66B bombers, *Brown Cradles*, originally based at RAF Sculthorpe. The 13 aircraft had their bomb bays filled with 22 noise jammers designed to jam Soviet anti-aircraft, missile guidance, acquisition and height finding radars. In late 1959 three *Brown Cradles* were flown in a very successful ECM exercise against U.S. Navy ships off the east coast of the United States, *WEXVAL II*. The *Brown Cradle* aircraft were now ready to assume alert duties like other B-66 aircraft in support of various war plans. Although the *Brown Cradles* were assigned to the 42nd TRS at Chelveston, they pulled *Echo Alert* at other 10th Wing bases as well, using crews from the various squadrons. "Several *Brown Cradle* B-66s arrived at Alconbury," Gerry Reponen remembers. "With their bomb bays filled with electronic jammers it changed the airplane's center of gravity. More of the weight was forward which required that we taxi very slowly around corners or else it would shear the tread off the nose wheel tire. A new alert facility was built for the *Brown Cradles*. *Echo Alert* was a seven day affair. There were never more than four of the *Brown Cradles* at Alconbury, two on *Echo Alert* while the other two were being flown and their ECM equipment calibrated. We weren't too crazy about this new mission nor the airplane.

"The only English neighbors I got to know at all were Jack and Margaret Hunter who lived directly across the street from us in Cambridge. The English were very reserved, not exactly fond of Americans either, other than our money, except for Jack, who was outgoing and liked Yanks. Jack would take my two young boys into his garden with him and muck around in the dirt. The only vegetable I remember him raising was brussels sprouts, which he seemed to have an unending supply of. Jack would have me over for a drink on occasion. He would go into his dining room, lift up a floor board, where he hid a bottle of scotch whiskey presented to him on some memorable occasion during World War II. He would pour a teaspoon of it into a small shot glass for each of us, then I would sit there listening to his war stories.

"My squadron building at Alconbury was an old Quonset hut. In the center of the hut we had two oil-fired stoves. In the winter of '59 to '60 those stoves were always going full blast. The heat didn't radiate very far. We stood around the stoves, all too often burning holes into our padded winter flying suits. Early that summer I received a new assignment to Shaw AFB in South Carolina. During my nearly three years in Europe I had flown the RB-66 for over 600 hours. It had been a good airplane and I encountered few problems. The best places to fly out of I thought were Spangdahlem and Moron. The German countryside was so beautiful to look at from the air, and in Spain the weather was always warm and sunny. There we stayed in a hotel in Seville, mingled with the Spanish people, and ate our meals in the city where they didn't start serving dinner until after nine in the evening. I looked forward to going home, taking back with me many fond memories."[10]

CHAPTER THIRTEEN

THE BLACK SHEEP SQUADRON OF TOUL-ROSIÈRES

In the summer of 1960 the Air Force was at the beginning of significant structural change. While SAC's generals still believed in the primacy of the bomber, the bomber had already reached its zenith and was in decline. After 1962, when the last B-52 rolled off Boeing's production lines, the total bomber force continued to shrink and its importance diminish as the intercontinental ballistic missile, ICBM, grew in numbers and lethality. The missiles in SAC's inventory were not only ascendent, but soon were to replace, then modify the role of the few remaining bombers. The last of four *Atlas-D* ICBM squadrons was activated in 1960. Three *Thor* IRBM squadrons manned by British crews and based in the United Kingdom became operational that same year, as did the J71 powered *Snark* cruise missile at Presque Isle Air Base, Maine. The nuclear-tipped missiles of the future – *Titan* and *Minuteman* – were just around the corner. In 1960 the Strategic Air Command had in its inventory 538 B-52s, 1,291 B-47s, and 58 B-58s, a total force of 1,887 bombers, not including squadrons of reconnaissance and *Blue Cradle* ECM aircraft, as well as numerous spare bombers not included in the operational count. SAC's missile force was at its very beginnings, consisting of 30 *Snark* pilotless aircraft and 12 *Atlas* ICBMs. By 1965 SAC's bomber inventory had declined to 825 aircraft – 600 B-52s, 132 B-47s and 93 B-58s, while the missile force had grown to 59 *Titan IIs* and 821 *Minuteman*. *Snark*, *Atlas-D*, E and F, and *Titan I* had come and gone. Obsolescence came rapidly in a fast moving technological field under the assertive leadership of General Bernard A. Schriever.[1]

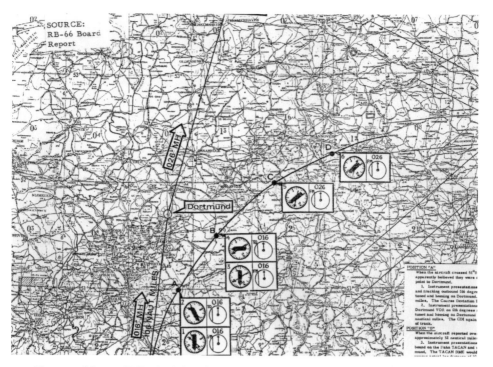

The route of Captain Holland's ill-fated flight into East Germany. The planned route is shown on the left, passing over Dortmund, heading for Nordholz. The actual route shown on the right leads the aircraft into the central Berlin air corridor and a fateful encounter with two Soviet MiG-19 fighters.

As SAC changed so did the rest of the Air Force. With the buildup of the strategic missile force, the deployment of shorter range *Matador* and *Mace* missiles in Europe, and the introduction of the nuclear capable Republic F-105 *Thunderchief* into the USAFE inventory, the rationale to retain nuclear armed medium bombers not capable of low level special weapons delivery disappeared. In 1962 the 47th Bomb Wing at RAF Sculthorpe shut its doors and sent its aircraft to the bone-yard in the Arizona desert. The reconnaissance world was undergoing major changes as well. The shoot-down of a U-2 over the Soviet Union on May 1, 1960, by SA-2 surface-to-air missiles ended the Eisenhower sanctioned overflights of the Soviet Union and Iron Curtain countries. Again it was missiles which provided a safer alternative to spy-planes, lifting reconnaissance satellites, euphemistically referred to as National Technical Means, into near-earth orbits. The RB-66 photo reconnaissance force in the Pacific region along with the B-66B USAFE bombers were among the first to feel the impact of new technologies. The two PACAF reconnaissance squadrons inactivating in 1960, and the USAFE B-66 bombers in 1962. The USAFE RB-66 reconnaissance squadrons were undergoing change as well. Although the numbers remained fairly constant at less than 100 aircraft, the force composition changed. By 1962 the WB-66D weather reconnaissance aircraft of the 42nd TRS were retired. And by 1965 the RB-66B photo reconnaissance force was largely in the process of being replaced by the newer and more capable RF-4C *Phantom*. The remaining B-66 aircraft in the USAFE inventory were withdrawn from Europe by late 1965 and committed to war in Southeast Asia. There, in the steamy world of triple-canopy jungles, in a totally unanticipated environment and field of air combat, the B-66 along with the B-57 justified an Air Force investment made many years earlier.[2]

Colonel James D. Kemp, the innovative commander of the 10th Tactical Reconnaissance Wing from July 1959 to June 1962, was less than thrilled with the move of his command in 1960 from Spangdahlem to Alconbury. Not only were his squadrons scattered across several air bases, but the facilities were minimal and the English flying weather terrible. He also felt that his aircraft were too far removed from the potential battlefield. When the *Brown Cradles* arrived in 1960 and began to assume an alert posture at Alconbury and Bruntingthorpe, Kemp felt something had to be done to make this important asset more relevant. He moved the alert aircraft to a forward operating location at Toul-Rosieres Air Base in France. The RB-66Cs of the 42nd TRS at Chelveston had a similar problem. They conducted tactical electronic reconnaissance along the East German and Czech borders and had to spend much too much time flying to and from the area of interest. In August 1962, just before the Cuban Missile Crisis, both the 19th TRS from Bruntingthorpe, flying RB-66B photo-birds, and the 42nd TRS from Chelveston, with its *Brown Cradles* and RB-66C electronic reconnaissance aircraft, relocated to Toul-Rosieres. Bruntingthorpe and Chelveston closed. The 10th Wing headquarters, however, along with the 1st and 30th TRS, remained at Alconbury.

Captain Earl McClintock came up through the Aviation Cadet program. Flew F-86Fs in Korea, F-86Ds in Air Defense Command, then transitioned into the F-102. Then the bottom fell out of Earl's world. ADC began cutting back in 1960 and sending surplus pilots to remote radar sites. "This was like a death sentence to me. It was about this time when a bulletin came down from Air Force looking for volunteers for the RB-66. The assignment was to England, including concurrent travel for my family. I knew nothing about the B-66, but the chance to take my family with me to England and to continue flying was hard to pass up. I volunteered and got the assignment. I checked out at Shaw, then went to RAF Bruntingthorpe, to the 19th TRS. After two years there we transferred to Toul-Rosieres. It was here at Toul-Rosieres, on April 5, 1963, that I was asked to check out another pilot in aerial refueling, Captain Bill Lawson.

"Bill Lawson worked in the command post and didn't get all that much flying time. My responsibility was to teach Bill how to refuel from a KB-50 tanker. Since the B-66 only had one pilot seat, I flew in the old gunner's seat. Once he was behind the tanker, I'd get out of my seat, kneel behind him, and from that awkward position grasped the right side of the flight control with my left hand and the throttles with my right to demonstrate a refueling hook-up. Bill Lawson went through the normal start up procedures. We pulled the pins from our ejection seats and prepared for take-off. From my position I could not see any of Bill's instruments, but I could see Captain Douglas Grafflin's altimeter, Doug was our navigator. The weather was IFR with a low overcast. We entered the clouds shortly after gear up. Almost immediately I felt the airplane go into a rapid rolling motion accompanied by the onset of a stall. Bill began to swear in an excited voice and my eyes were on Grafflin's altimeter, which was unwinding at an alarming rate. It seemed to me that Bill had lost control of the plane. Having flown fighters, I was very much aware of how it felt to be in an accelerated stall. The last thing I saw in the cockpit was the navigator reaching for the ejection handles on his seat, and I followed suit immediately, not knowing if a recovery was possible. My chute opened, and I was in the open air below the clouds not far from the ground. I heard the engine noise of the airplane and looked in that direction to see it dish out of a rolling dive well below the clouds, just above the terrain, then pull back up. The navigator and I were quickly picked up. There were no injuries. It all happened very fast."[3]

Captain Kermit Helmke was in the control tower at Toul-Rosieres the day Earl McClintock and Douglas Grafflin ejected from Bill Lawson's aircraft. "One of the ejection seats fell into a transformer field and caused some power outages. The weather at Toul-Rosieres was barely above landing minimums while the weather at Alconbury, only a short flight away, was clear. Another B-66 piloted by Joe Wagner was ready to take-off. Wagner was directed by the 10th Wing command post to accompany Bill Lawson's sick bird to Alconbury where they landed without further incident."[4] The 19th squadron was well on its way to becoming the 'Black Sheep Squadron' of the B-66 force. Only two months earlier, on February 4, 1963, a 19TRS aircraft coming out of IRAN (Inspect and Repair as Necessary) at the Douglas Tulsa plant in Oklahoma, caught fire soon after take-off, killing its pilot, Captain William Cox.[5] Captain Lawson came awfully close to becoming yet another statistic.

When President Eisenhower ended the U-2 overflights of the Soviet Union in 1960, he in no way limited the Peacetime Aerial Reconnaissance Program. The RB-47s of the 55th Strategic Reconnaissance Wing continued to fly the borders and coast lines of the Soviet Union and its satellites, monitored Soviet missile launches at Tyuratam, and conducted other specialized operations to ferret out the secrets of Soviet combat aircraft, missiles and radars. It was in the peripheral reconnaissance role, flying over international waters, where Soviet fighters were most prone to lash out at American aircraft. On July 1, 1960, only two months after the shoot down of a Central Intelligence Agency U-2 aircraft near Sverdlovsk, an RB-47H of the 55th SRW was downed over the Barents Sea by MiG-19 interceptors. As early as April 8, 1950, the Soviets downed an American aircraft in the Baltic Sea off the coast of Latvia, a Navy PB4Y2 with a crew of ten. Over the years American reconnaissance aircraft of all types had been downed by Soviet fighters over the Sea of Japan, Baltic Sea, Sea of Okhotsk, off the Kamchatka Peninsula, over the Bering Strait, and Black Sea.[6] Ben R. Rich, the director of Lockheed's legendary *Skunk Works* wrote, "Had the American public known about the ongoing secret air war between the two super-powers they would have been even more in despair than many already were about the state of the world."[7] By 1964, little had changed. Soviet military commanders of PVO Strany, their air defense command, remained paranoid about intrusions into Soviet territory. On January 28, 1964, a T-39 *Sabreliner* from Wiesbaden Air Base on a routine flight through the southern Berlin corridor strayed beyond the 20 mile limit and was shot down by Russian fighters. The crew of three perished.[8]

Captain David I. Holland reported for duty with the 19th TRS at Toul-Rosieres in 1963. "After flying a number of training missions I was declared combat ready. I was assigned a brand new navigator straight out of navigator training, Second

Lieutenant Harold Welch. Hal Welch was eager, alert, and a pleasure to work with. After flying a dozen training missions together, I was pleased to have him as my partner. The time for Hal's combat qualification check arrived – March 10, 1964. Captain Melvin J. Kessler was the instructor navigator who would monitor and evaluated Lieutenant Welch. A few minutes after noon on March 10 the three of us pre-flighted the aircraft, taking off at 1300. We proceeded to fly the mission as briefed – a high-low-high profile to include a low level photo run of several bridges in northwest Germany near Osnabrueck. The flight was scheduled to last about two hours and twenty minutes. It was our practice on a check ride to leave radio navigation aids tuned to Toul-Rosieres, because the navigator was being evaluated and he could see the pilot's instruments from his position. When we were about 100 or so miles from Toul, the VOR/TACAN was out of range of the Toul VORTAC. We leveled off at 33,000 feet. I engaged the autopilot and reported my position to the Frankfurt air traffic controller. We were flying in clear skies above an undercast. Captain Kessler sitting to the left of Lieutenant Welch could read the doppler latitude and longitude, showing that we were on course. In reality, we were flying into the central Berlin corridor. Lieutenant Welch gave me a new heading and time to descend for our low altitude photo target. I made the turn, began the descent, and extended my speed brakes. We had gone down about 2,000 feet when I felt a slight jolt and heard what sounded like a 'crump.' I looked outside and saw at ten o'clock a fighter streaking away and jettisoning his external tanks. At first I thought it was a NATO fighter that had jumped us and come a little too close. When my airspeed began to increase and my hydraulic pressure was going to zero I realized that the aircraft was seriously damaged and this was no ordinary event.

"I was on a westerly heading, I thought, with a standard penetration angle and speed brakes extended. With the loss of hydraulic pressure the speed brakes retracted, and elevator and aileron response was zero. I attempted to raise the nose of the aircraft and the left wing, applying 100 percent power to the left engine, but if there was a response it was negligible. When I heard Captain Kessler tell me that we were passing through 15,000 feet and I had no control over the aircraft I ordered the crew to eject. I heard two loud bangs, saw the airspeed indicator passing through 400 knots, and then went through the ejection sequence myself – left pre-ejection lever up, right pre-ejection lever up, squeeze trigger in right pre-ejection lever. I believe I went out at about 10,000 feet as the plane cartwheeled downward in flames. I then blacked out and didn't wake until I felt a terrible pain in the groin from my parachute straps. I tried to unbuckle my chute, then realized I was still several thousand feet above the ground. One thing I remember clearly, how quiet it was as I was floating to the ground. It turned out to be a very soft landing with the tree branches catching the chute just right to allow me to touch down gently on my feet. My first thought after touching ground was, 'Oh shit, what have I done.'"[9]

On March 10, 1964, senior pilot Captain Ivannikov, at Wittstock airfield, was on alert duty at readiness level two. "At 1646 Moscow time I was given orders by my fighter division command post to assume readiness level one. I started my engines, took the runway and took off at 1649, assuming a heading of 330 degrees. As I was climbing to 15,000 feet the controller informed me that my target was on a heading of 090 degrees at 30,000 feet. Four minutes later, to the left and about 6,000 feet above me, at an approximate range of about six miles, I spotted the intruder, pulling contrails for about 1,500 to 2,000 feet behind him. I also saw the aircraft of Captain Zinoviev. Without losing sight of either aircraft I completed a hard left turn into the target. I saw there were no guns in the back of the B-66 – otherwise we would have been immediately destroyed. Captain Zinoviev fired his guns as a warning signal for the intruder to land. After Zinoviev fired, the target turned left to a heading of 270 degrees, and while he was turning Captain Zinoviev fired again, but I couldn't tell if he hit anything. Half-way through the turn I assumed an attack position behind the violator at a distance of about 1,000 feet, he extended his speed brakes, and my distance decreased to 600 feet. At 1657, after Captain Zinoviev finished his attack he turned left and away from the target, I received a command from the controller to fire my C-5 rockets from a distance of less than 500 feet. The rockets were programmed to fire singly. I saw the rocket leave my plane, hit the target, its left engine began to smoke. I fired no more rockets, because I was too close and the rocket's proximity fuse would not have armed in time, so I used my 23mm cannons from a distance of about 300 feet. I observed hits in the vertical stabilizer and lower part of the fuselage and speed brakes. I reported the results to the command post of my fighter division. I broke off my attack and climbed away to the right. I inadvertently flew past the aircraft, into the debris zone, and as a result punctured one of my wing fuel tanks, something I didn't know until after landing. The target rolled to the left, entered a steep spiral, and I saw three red and white parachutes, which I reported to the command post. I was then ordered to land at Altes Lager airfield, because Wittstock was below minimums. The entire flight from beginning to end lasted about 25 minutes."[10]

"It seemed only minutes after I had disconnected from my chute and taken off my helmet that a jeep-like vehicle appeared with three people. Two in uniform, one in civilian clothes. They indicated through gestures that I should get in and accompany them. I didn't think I had a choice. Where I touched down was near the small town of Gardelegen in East Germany. I later learned that there were

6,000 Soviet troops in the area on maneuvers. I inquired about my crew, but no one talked to me – this being the way things remained for the next 17 days. We arrived at a hospital where I was made to disrobe, put in a bed, and examined by medical personnel. I indicated to them that I had pain in my left arm and they X-rayed it. I was frightened. I remembered the U-2 shoot-down in 1960 of Gary Powers. I also thought about the three USAF officers on the T-39 from Wiesbaden who had been shot down and died on January 28, just a little over a month ago. One of the nurses whispered, 'I so wish you were not here,' adding to the drama. Sometime during the middle of the night I was put in an ambulance and taken for a bumpy ride to a Russian hospital in Magdeburg. My private room was small, a guard was at the door, and the food was far from gourmet. I enjoyed pickled herring, but what I thought was a piece of delicatessen fish turned out to be just raw fish. The borscht wasn't too bad.

"Interrogation began the following day. The Russians clearly believed we were on a spy mission, and tried hard to have me admit it. I was worried about Hal and Mel, but the Russian interrogators wouldn't give me any information about them. I had no idea whether the Air Force really knew what happened, whether my family knew of my plight. I was kept in total ignorance. Although I knew nothing about what was going on in the outside world, my relatives were notified of our missing status, and the incident became a media event in Time, Newsweek and all the dailies. Headlines continued until the Alaska earthquake overshadowed our predicament. There was of course no way for me to know that my government – President Lyndon B. Johnson, former Ambassador to the Soviet Union Llewellyn Thompson, and Secretary of State Dean Rusk, were making every effort to secure our release.

"During the 17-days of detention and isolation there were five interrogations, some threats of a trial in Moscow, and questions about 'Madrid Control.' The Russians had salvaged the wire recorder from the RB-66 which evidently still contained recordings of a pilot talking to Madrid Air Traffic Control when proceeding to or from our fair weather base near Tripoli, Libya. Standard procedure became being awakened at three or four in the morning to sign a paper, which I of course refused to do. The days passed slowly, no radio, no newspaper, no one to talk to. I had attended survival training at Stead Air Force Base near Reno, Nevada, prior to reporting to Shaw. The training I received was effective in preparing me mentally for this period of detention. I have the greatest admiration for those who survived long periods of imprisonment as prisoners of war. The one thing that sustained me during that relatively short detainment was my faith in my government making every attempt to obtain my release.

"After the 16th day I was led to a bathroom and allowed to take a shower. The next morning, to my great surprise, I received a breakfast of scrambled eggs with bacon. Something was up, but I didn't know what. After breakfast a Russian officer entered my room with what he called a 'clothing list' and asked me to sign it. It was in Russian and I refused to do so. He argued, but finally left. Another person arrived later with my flight suit, underwear, socks, and boots. I began to get my hopes up not to be going to Moscow, but back to my Air Force. What happened next was puzzling. A Russian major escorted me to a room on the first floor. There we sat and waited for a time. Then he escorted me to a waiting car with a driver. When I asked where we were going, he put his index finger to his lips. I got the message. We drove into Magdeburg, it was about noon. I was struck by the lack of traffic and people in the streets. The Russian said something to the driver, who pulled over to the side of the street and parked. It seemed that whatever we were involved in had something to do with timing. Apparently we were ahead of schedule. Then the major turned to me and asked me if I believed in God. I said, 'Yes.' Answering his own question he said, 'Nyet.' We arrived at the Helmstedt border crossing the same time as another car with Captain Kessler. Prior to getting out of the car the Russian major told me not to shake his hand when he turned me over to a U.S. Army officer.

"Kessler and I boarded an Army staff car which took us to Hannover. The media was relentless, attempting to get newsreels and photographs of two U.S. Air Force officers being released from Soviet captivity. In Hannover Kessler and I boarded a C-54. A flight surgeon gave us a cursory physical examination, then we flew to Wiesbaden Air Base. We were driven to the large Air Force hospital in Wiesbaden. When I entered my room I was met by General Gabriel Disosway, the commander of the United States Air Forces in Europe. 'I'm glad you're back,' he said, shaking my hand. He cautioned me not to talk to anyone about my experience except the OSI, Office of Special Investigations, officer assigned to me. And added that this was ordered by President Johnson. I was also told by General Disosway not to speak with Lieutenant Welch, who had the room next to mine, or to Captain Kessler. While the general was giving me instructions an airman ripped the telephone out of the wall.

"I was allowed to say hello to my crew mates, learning for the first time of the extensive injuries suffered by Lieutenant Welch during his ejection. His left leg was broken in two places, and his right arm was broken as well. He had a neck fracture, which was not discovered until he was X-rayed at the Wiesbaden hospital. While in the East German hospital, Hal Welch had been allowed a visit by an Air Force flight surgeon, who, after examining him, asked for his immediate release so he could get proper care. Lieutenant Welch was released after ten days of captivity. The next five days I spent almost entirely with the OSI – daily interrogations, a polygraph test, a visit to a psychiatrist who questioned me and then administered a Rorschach test. Finally, it was over, and I boarded a T-29 for Toul-Rosieres to meet the inevitable Flying Evaluation Board."[11]

The shoot-down by a Russian MiG-19 fighter on March 10, 1964, of the straying RB-66B 53-451, piloted by Captain David Holland reverberated through the 19th Squadron, the 10th Wing, Headquarters USAFE in Wiesbaden, the State Department, right up to the White House. It was one of the notable Cold War incidents ranking right up there with the 1960 shootdown of Francis Gary Powers U-2, and the downing of the RB-47H electronic reconnaissance aircraft over the Barents Sea that same year. Within four days of the B-66 shoot-down Headquarters USAFE established an Air Defense Identification Zone, ADIZ, and *Brass Monkey* procedures for flights along the inner German and Czech borders to preclude any further such incidents from happening. Any aircraft entering this identification zone without authorization was contacted on Guard channel, monitored by all aircraft at all times, and directed to immediately reverse course.

The *Stars and Stripes* military newspaper, *Newsweek* and *Time* magazines, among many others, carried lengthy articles about the loss of the RB-66. "One of the trickiest games of the cold war is a sort of airborne electronic 'chicken,'" speculated *Time Magazine*, "in which a high-speed aircraft without warning dashes headlong for the enemy's border, turning away just in time. The game is played both by East and West, and not just for fun. From such phony forays has come a wealth of crucial information about one another's defense capabilities ... In the past two years, according to one unofficial source, Soviet jets have poked their noses into Western airspace 95 times – mostly on just such sniffing missions. But when a Western plane goes into Communist territory, innocently or not, the Russians do not hesitate to shoot. Since 1950, 108 U.S. airmen have died or disappeared within Communist airspace, the last three only seven weeks ago when an unarmed – and demonstrably innocent – T-39 jet trainer was blasted from the leaden skies over Vogelsberg," *Time Magazine* wrote. "Last week," the weekly magazine continued its story, "a U.S. Air Force RB-66B reconnaissance bomber bellowed off the runway at Toul-Rosieres Air Base in France, then sloped east by northeast on a routine, 2 1/2 hour 'navigational training mission.' The flight plan called for the 700 m.p.h., twin-jet bomber to swing over Germany's beautiful Mosel Valley to Hahn Air Base, then bank north to Bremerhaven before returning with zigzags and altitude changes to Hahn and home ... The big swept-wing Douglas jet crossed into Communist East Germany in the vicinity of the central Berlin air corridor. Moments later, two swift blips rose on the radar screens – Soviet MiGs in deadly pursuit. The slower-moving blip that marked the RB-66 leaped suddenly into wrenching, zigzag evasive maneuvers, four minutes later disappeared from the screen well within East German territory. On the ground a German schoolboy watched the last moments of the flight: 'The fighter closed on the bomber from behind and fired on it. The American plane burst into flames. I saw a fireball on one wing. The crew of three came out by parachute. The first two came out together. The third one came a bit later.' ... Whatever the nature of the RB-66's mission, the Russians had all the ingredients for a fat, propaganda-loaded 'show trial' like that of U-2 pilot Francis Gary Powers."[12] Although East and West played games aplenty as the *Time* magazine article chose to speculate, the RB-66 was clearly a victim of circumstance and an overly aggressive Soviet regime.

• • •

Kermit Helmke, one of the more experienced navigators at Toul-Rosieres, remembers that day well. "I was about to start a top secret briefing concerning a change to our war plans. It was about one o'clock or so on the 10th of March. The command post called the briefing room and asked for Lieutenant Colonel McCormack, my boss and the chief of plans. We waited for about ten minutes. Then I got a call to scrub the briefing and come down to the CP. When I got there I learned that a border violation had occurred, and that a 19th Squadron airplane was suspected. We called Bill Schrimsher, who was flying one of the *Brown Cradles* in the same area where Dave Holland was supposed to be, to see if he had heard from Dave. Nothing. In the next hour or so we learned that Holland had been shot down. Then things got quiet for awhile. Colonel McCormack obtained a radar plot of the track of Holland's aircraft and asked me what I made of it. It's a compass malfunction I told him.

"'How do you know that?' The track is a very smooth curve leading me to believe that a gyro was steering the aircraft. An open rotor or stator lead in the system would cause a precession of this nature. My answer was based on experience with selsyns as a remote control turret mechanic on the B-29. Vern Gardina was listening to our conversation. Vern was the 19th Squadron senior navigator."[13] Early that evening the Wing commander, Colonel Arthur Small, arrived from Alconbury and had dinner with Major Gardina. "We discussed the possible causes," wrote Major Gardina. "I told him that something happened to me seven years earlier that may have also happened to Dave Holland. In 1957, Captain Hainley and I flew from Shaw to the Douglas plant in Long Beach, California, test hopped an RB-66, then flew it back to Shaw. We were on auto pilot. Halfway to Shaw I gave Hainley the heading and ETA, estimated time of arrival, to the next check point, then slid my seat back and went to sleep. It had been a long day. I woke up about 30 minutes later and looked at the radar scope and couldn't believe what I saw. I checked the N–1 compass immediately and it was reading as it should, 90 degrees, but there was the Mississippi River running east and west, directly under the radar heading marker which was on 90 degrees. We flew into Shaw using the standby whiskey compass. I described the symptoms to maintenance. The next day they told me that one leg of a delta-wound coil had failed and caused the compass to precess at a rate of two to three degrees per minute to maintain the 90 degree heading.

"Colonel Small then instructed me to select the people I needed to pursue this possibility. By day-break I was in the compass mock-up area in the Armaments & Electronics shop. I told the maintenance men that I wanted to fail each leg of the delta wound coil of the N–1 compass alternatively. There were three 120 degree legs in the coil located in the left wing of the aircraft. I wanted to check the precession rate and duration especially on headings between 000 degrees and 010 degrees, the heading from Hahn air base to Nordholz. We found the compass mock-up too crude for a convincing test. So I had an RB-66 ground test run with maintenance failing one, then another of the coil legs with all equipment operating. We timed the precession and the effects on all associated equipment that directly used the N–1 inputs. This test showed that if the B-phase of the coil failed when the aircraft was trying to maintain a northerly heading, it would cause the aircraft to turn toward 090 degrees in order to maintain a 360 degree heading on the compass."[14]

The N–1 gyro stabilized magnetic compass system in the B-66 aircraft was its primary directional reference. The navigator and pilot alike relied on it. The N–1 had a high level of reliability, so much so that few ever questioned the system. The whiskey compass in the pilot station, installed as an emergency backup, was notoriously unreliable as a meaningful cross-check reference. Not only because of the distorted magnetic field in the cockpit, but also because of a serious problem with a magnetized nosewheel in many of the B-66 aircraft. The N–1 was the only directional input to the Doppler-driven ground position indicator, GPI, system. The GPI provided continuously updated latitude and longitude to the navigator station, and stabilized the navigation radar display to true north. Colonel Don Adee taught the N–1 compass system to basic navigator-bombardier students at Mather AFB, California. Adee remembers teaching his students that the power failure warning light on the N–1 would illuminate whenever alternating current was lost on the system. Only after Dave Holland's shoot-down was it discovered that the warning light measured only one phase of the three-phase AC power. The phase lost on aircraft number 53-451 flown by Dave Holland was not the one being monitored, so Lieutenant Welch, Holland's navigator, had no warning of the N–1 compass failure. "In tactical radar navigation the navigator was required to obtain periodic radar fixes. The beginning of the fix process was to obtain an initial position, in this case Hahn Air Base, which would routinely have been obtained from the GPI counters or by manually taking time, speed and direction from a last known position. Next, the navigator would have looked at his navigation map using the initial position he established as his starting point, then tried to determine the radar return pattern for his next fix. In the German environment where there are so many cultural radar returns it is quite easy to find a similar pattern of returns that matches those expected from your next position. Starting from an erroneous position, then checking an incorrectly oriented radar display, the consequences were predictable. The crew, flying over a total undercast, however, thought everything was alright."[15]

After running a test on a squadron aircraft to prove his N–1 precession theory, Major Gardina "hurriedly drew charts and graphs of all equipment affected by the N–1 – autopilot, radar, APN-82 Doppler system, and the RMI – and briefed Colonel Small. We also drew a prediction of the track from Hahn to Nordholz if the compass failed. At a precession rate of two and one-half degrees per minute, the prediction led the aircraft from Hahn into the central Berlin corridor. We had no previous word on where the aircraft crossed the border, only our prediction. Colonel Small in the meantime was under unbelievable pressure to find the cause of what happened. He sent me and a standardization and evaluation pilot to brief the Headquarters USAFE staff on what I had come up with on Wednesday evening, the 11th of March. USAFE accepted us and my briefing like we were raw meat in a lion's den. They were totally negative to anything technical and spent their time berating and condemning us and the entire 10th Wing.

"We picked up our briefing charts and tattered remains, and returned to Toul late Wednesday night. I proposed to Colonel Small that we fly a test with the B-phase disconnected and photograph and record the instruments and the ground to establish our actual track, using checkpoints to simulate Hahn Air Base and Nordholz. We soon learned that our test had to be approved by the Edwards Flight Test Center. We spent hours on the phone with them. Since we were the world's center of attention at this time they gave their approval. The Headquarters USAFE staff was totally negative to our doing the test, so we by-passed them and went directly to friends in the Pentagon."[16] Major Gardina, flying in the gunner's seat of an RB-66B photo-reconnaissance aircraft exactly like the one flown by Dave Holland, jury-rigged a cut-off switch on the N–1 compass leads in the C-2 compass transmitter housed in the left wing of the aircraft. That allowed him to interrupt AC current flow, inducing the same error that led 451 into East Germany. Norm Goldberg flew as navigator. "We headed north out of France toward the UK," recalls Norm Goldberg. "Verne disconnected the C-2 sensor lead when we got over the English channel. After about 25 minutes of flight we were heading due east toward the Dutch coast. The picture on my radar scope was photographed with an 0-15 camera, standard equipment to record B-47 and B-66 radar presentations."[17]

"When we landed," Major Gardina states "the film was immediately processed. The test proved that the entire navigation suit of the aircraft, including the RMI, range measuring equipment, gave false indications. Even an experienced navigator wouldn't have been able to recognize the misplaced returns encountered by young Lieutenant Welch in a heavy industrial environment. We took this information, the photographs and a better prepared set of charts and graphs, back to Wiesbaden. Again, we were received like the plague. They condemned our reasoning and discredited our test flight. We returned to Toul in the wee-hours of Friday morning, March 13. Reflew the test Friday morning to overcome some of the USAFE objections. Again hurriedly put the data together and Colonel Small and I returned to Wiesbaden. When we arrived in Wiesbaden the situation was worse than before. There was pressure from the very top for an explanation – the very top being President Johnson and Secretary of Defense McNamara, the Air Force Chief of Staff General Curtis LeMay, and too many others to mention. Scores of general officers were inbound to Wiesbaden to join in the melee. Before the big meeting between Generals LeMay, McConnell, Disosway, and a jillion other nervous generals, I briefed Major General Thorn, the USAFE Director of Operations, and Lieutenant General Edmundson, the 17th Air Force commander. Then Colonel Small and I tried to brief Major General Puryear, the 3rd Air Force Commander, to make certain he was knowledgeable (the 10TRW fell under the 3rd Air Force at South Ruislip Air Station, England) since Colonel Small and I were not permitted to be present in the General officer meeting – we were *persona non grata* so to speak. I began to brief Puryear. He threw Small, me and all of our charts out of his office and told us he wouldn't brief that bull-shit, and wished he was 1,000 miles away.

"General Edmunson then got us two sharp generals who would be in the briefing and I brought them up to speed and gave them my charts so that the two could at least make a half-assed presentation. They were very nervous, not technically oriented, and not convinced we knew what we were talking about. While the meeting was going on Small and I were in a large room outside the briefing room with a score of others. I was a major, everyone else was either a bird-colonel or a general. Every damn one of them was giving me and Colonel Small hell. Small was getting most of it. About 2100 hours that evening Small was called to a command post telephone. Major Miller, from the 10th Wing Headquarters detachment at Toul, was on the line. 'Colonel,' he said, 'I have the best news you ever heard.' Poor Small was under so much pressure that his first thought was 'They found out that Holland was a defector.' Instead, Major Miller informed him that they had located the film from the GCI radar site. It, and Gardina's plot, was no more than two or three miles off the whole way into East Germany. Small came back and handed me the coordinates he had taken down from Miller. I had gotten up at five o'clock on Wednesday morning, flew two test flights, made numerous ground tests, prepared and gave briefings, and had made three trips to Wiesbaden. I was exhausted. Flying back, wouldn't you know it, the weather was bad at Toul, and we had to divert to Laon. I finally got to bed on Saturday morning."[18]

Colonel Arthur Small was relieved of command effective March 24, 1964, by General Disosway, the USAFE commander. As always, there had to be a scapegoat. Colonel Small, as the 10th TRW commander, fit the bill. As General LeMay was quoted when responding to the firing of several B-47 bomb wing commanders when they failed to properly execute a no-notice Cocoa alert – practicing their assigned wartime mission – "I cannot differentiate between the incompetent and the unfortunate." The border violation was due to a technical malfunction, and Colonel Small was indeed unfortunate, and anything but incompetent. Yet he was the wing commander, the man at the head of a combat wing who usually paid the price for failure, no matter the cause. Major Dave Holland attributes his exoneration by the Flying Evaluation Board to the extraordinary efforts of Major Verne Gardina. Holland continued to fly and serve his country in Southeast Asia, flying 146 combat missions. He was awarded five Air Medals and retired in the rank of major. Major Gardina suffered no ill effects from his courageous investigation to save one of his own. In 1976 he retired from the United States Air Force in the rank of colonel. His last duty assignment was as Vice Commander of Langley Air Force Base, Virginia, the location of TAC Headquarters.

As a patriotic teenager in 1942, wanting to serve his country, Verne Gardina carried a letter of commendation from his high school principal to the Army enlistment center. His principal described Vern as "a young man of good character, manly bearing, and excellent poise. He is sincere and straight forward, and in my judgement he possesses the qualities of leadership necessary in military service." He served in the Pacific, was shot down, but survived. Colonel Gardina served in the best traditions of the United States Air Force and certainly was all his high school principal said of him, and more. He passed away on January 24, 1995. Lieutenant Harold Welch, upon his return from Soviet detention, was unable to recall any events after take-off from Toul-Rosieres. Welch did not return to the 19th TRS.[19]

Things didn't end with that star-studded meeting of March 13, 1964, at Headquarters USAFE in Wiesbaden. American overflights of the Soviet Union, and the occasional shoot-down by Soviet fighters or surface-to-air missiles, was an ongoing topic of discussion and formal exchanges between East and West. The March 10 shoot down of the RB-66, soon after the shoot down of the errant T-39 over the GDR, was obviously grist for the Soviet propaganda mill. At an April 4, 1964, meeting between Ambassador at Large Llewellyn E. Thompson and the Soviet Ambassador to the United States, Anatoliy F. Dobrynin, Dobrynin handed Ambassador Thompson the Russian-language text of a letter from Chairman Khrushchev to President Johnson. As expected, the letter was long winded and self-serving, stating "The fundamental position of the Soviet Union is the improvement of Soviet-American relations and strengthening peace, and we would prefer of course, not to engage in demonstrations of force, of hard firmness, and in the elimination of the consequences of incidents provoked by the acts of American military forces, but to concentrate, with you, our efforts toward guaranteeing for the peoples of our two countries a durable peace." Such verbiage came from a man who only eighteen months earlier tried to put nuclear tipped missiles on the island of Cuba aimed at the United States.

Chairman Khrushchev continued, referring to the T-39 shoot-down, "In spite of the warning and the order to land, the aircraft continued to fly deep into the GDR until it was shot down. The American side stated that this violation was unintentional, that this was not a military plane but a training plane which had lost its bearings. It is difficult to agree that even a training plane could stray off course in such clear weather and over territory which is quite familiar to flying personnel ... But hardly six weeks had gone by and on March 10 there occurred a new violation of the frontiers of the German Democratic Republic. This violation was committed by a military aircraft, a reconnaissance-bomber equipped with air cameras as well as radio reconnaissance facilities which were in operation at the time of the flight ... Can we fail to reach the conclusion, Mr. President, that the RB-66 intentionally violated the air space of the GDR and did so in order to engage in air reconnaissance? ... I believe that the flight of the RB-66 was arranged without instructions from the President of the United States of America. But I declare to you that I do not accept the idea that this was an accidental border violation." The letter continued at length in the same spirit, counseling President Johnson that he had a run-away military on his hands.[20]

Khrushchev chose not to take the route of a show-trial. On April 17, 1964, the President responded in a direct and brief letter, "I can quite well understand your concern that within a short period of time two American airplanes crossed the demarcation line. There is little I can say about the incident involving a training plane, since the crew were killed and we are unable to ascertain what actually happened. I am disturbed that in both cases, however, there does not appear to have been justification for the rapidity with which there was a resort to force by Soviet planes. The American planes should not have been there, but I believe that this fast and violent reaction is quite unjustified ... I recognize that this is an astonishing series of errors, and upon my instructions the American military authorities have established the most rigorous procedure possible in order to prevent any repetition of such an incident."[21] Chairman Khrushchev had less than six months left in power when he received President Johnson's reply.

Don Adee, who in later years taught young aspiring Air Force officers the intricacies of aerial navigation at Mather AFB, wrote, "I arrived at Toul-Rosieres in April 1964 and was assigned to the 42nd TRS. I became a navigator flight examiner at Toul before we moved to Chambley in 1965. After the two shoot-downs over East Germany, all of us new guys had briefings running out our ears before we were allowed close to an airplane."[22]

General LeMay who flew into Wiesbaden after Captain Holland's shootdown on March 10 to whip his generals into line, had less than a year remaining as chief of staff before retiring. With his departure an era in American military aviation ended. In early August 1964 a fateful meeting between the destroyer *USS Maddox* and North Vietnamese torpedo boats changed the American political and military landscape. A rallying Congress passed the *Gulf of Tonkin Resolution* on August 7. The once secret war in Southeast Asia was out in the open. Few understood what the United States was letting itself in for. Even fewer understood how unprepared we were to fight a conventional air war half way around the world. We neither had the iron bombs on hand to sustain an air campaign nor aircrews trained for anything other than nuclear weapons delivery. Air-to-air combat of the World War II and Korean War variety had been literally declared obsolete, and our newest fighter, the F-4C *Phantom*, came armed only with air-to-air missiles. The technologies necessary to further the development of conventional weapons had long ago been put on the back burner by senior Air Force leaders focused on nuclear conflict. Although precision guided munitions achieved a high level of development and success toward the end of World War II – such as the U.S. Navy's *Pelican* and *Bat* bombs, the Army Air Forces *Azon* and *Razon* glide bombs, and the German *Fritz-X* and *Henschel 293* – such weapons and their continued development was deemed irrelevant in the nuclear age.[23] In 1964 the U.S. Air Force had little more than old fashioned general purpose bombs, and not enough of them, to take out a bridge the way it was done in World War II. If an aircraft didn't break the sound barrier or was unable to carry a nuclear device it apparently wasn't needed in a world of absolutes defined by mega-tonnage. As a nation and an Air Force we were about to be given a costly lesson.

CHAPTER FOURTEEN

OF BROWN AND BLUE CRADLES

Once the 47th Bomb Wing disbanded in June 1962 Captain Donald Harding was reassigned to George AFB, an obscure base in the California desert on the road to Las Vegas. Here the 355th Tactical Fighter Wing was forming and equipping with the new supersonic F-105. "It was my job to check out pilots in the T-33 dual control trainer," Harding said "before they were allowed to transition into the F-105. Every day I made two or three flights. It was all very boring. After all, I had 4,000 hours in the T-33 already. I stayed at George for a little over two years. One evening my wife was waiting up for me. 'Mark called,' she said. Mark Blizzard was a long time friend from Sculthorpe who had the same kind of job I had at McConnell AFB in Wichita, Kansas. 'Mark got a message sending him back to B-66s in France.'

"Really? Then she smiled, 'He also said your name was in the message.' Was I ever happy to get that news. I went to personnel the next morning. A sergeant looked and couldn't find anything on me. Shook his head and said laughing, 'You aren't going anywhere, sir. We need you here.' I called Mark and got the message number and gave it to the sergeant. About an hour later he called me back, 'You are going to France, sir.' This is about the time when things in Vietnam began to pick up; they stopped the retirement of the RB-66 and found themselves short of qualified B-66 pilots. I went to McGuire AFB in New Jersey to catch a plane to France. When I arrived at Chambley there were no airplanes there, they were still at Toul-Rosieres. Several of us then were sent TDY to Toul-Rosieres, about 20 miles south of Chambley, to check out in the RB-66B. But the weather was so

In 1966 the United States Air Force withdrew its combat aircraft from bases in France at the request of President Charles de Gaulle. RB-66 squadrons lowered the American flag for the last time at Chambley Air Base on August 22, and Toul-Rosieres on October 5. The Brown Cradle ECM aircraft, shown above, which stood Echo Alert first in England then on bases in France, departed NATO under a shroud of secrecy for a war building in Southeast Asia.

bad, they couldn't generate any training flights. Off we went to Moron Air Base in Spain with two airplanes and instructor pilots. We stayed there for about three weeks. I never felt like I've been out of the airplane at all. When I got back to Toul I was put in StanEval to help check out other incoming pilots. We had 13 *Brown Cradles* in the squadron, and two C-models, the electronic reconnaissance version of the RB-66. The RB-66B photo birds were still being prepared in the States for return to France."[1]

The *Brown Cradle* ECM aircraft was a take-off on the SAC B-47 *Blue Cradle*, a creation of General Curtis E. LeMay. LeMay was the bomber general of all bomber generals, a product of the bloody air battles over Europe in World War II. As that war approached its end, radar countermeasures were routinely employed by 8th and 15th Air Force bombers against German radars. Writes Dr. Alfred Price in the April 2006 issue of *The Journal of Electronic Defense*, "In return for this investment in jammers, plus some $5 million spent on chaff, an estimated 400-450 heavy bombers of the 8th Air Force and 100 of the 15th Air Force were saved from destruction by enemy flak."[2] LeMay knew that for his SAC bombers to survive over the Soviet Union, a world of radar directed guns and missiles, he had to give them a decent chance and provide the necessary electronic countermeasure equipment to defeat the Soviet radar threat. The B-47 six-jet bomber, the mainstay of the SAC bomber force in the 1950s, did not have enough space to carry its own ECM self-protection equipment. Since SAC had an abundance of B-47s, two wings, totaling 90 aircraft, were equipped with electronic noise jammers and assigned a bomber escort mission.

The *Blue Cradles*, as these bombers were called, came in two versions. One version carried 14 slow-sweeping jammers in its bomb bay, preset to specific Soviet radar frequencies. The co-pilot would turn on the jammers at a designated time and place, but had no controls to make adjustment of any kind. The other version, the *Phase V Capsule,* had a pressurized capsule in the bomb bay manned by a crew of two, who had receivers to monitor the Soviet radar environment allowing them to make frequency and sweep rate adjustments to their jammers if that was required. The conversion of the B-47 to an ECM jamming platform was not a 'weapons system' approach, unlike the K-5 bomb/navigation system which was designed into the airplane from the start. The noise jammers were stuffed into the B-47's bomb bay as in the good old days, when you bought an airplane and then figured out what to use it for. When the concept first was introduced to the Air Staff, the B-47 *Blue Cradle/Phase V Capsule* conversion was viewed like so many other things as a simple, low cost effort. As in the case of the Canberra to B-57 and A3D to B-66 conversions, the *Blue Cradle effort* again was anything but simple, nor low cost. SAC made the *Blue Cradles* and the *Phase V capsules* work, but it cost a bundle of money the Air Staff had earmarked for other projects. If it had not been for General LeMay's dogged insistence on ECM for his strike forces, regardless of cost, the effort would probably have died and there would not have been further meaningful ECM development. Electronic warfare would have atrophied both for lack of money and interest by other major air commands. In spite of many obstacles, money being the greatest, SAC continued to develop both active and passive countermeasure and reconnaissance equipment for its fleet of B-47 and B-52 bombers. With the arrival of the spacious eight-engine B-52, however, there no longer was a need for escort jammers, and the EB-47E *Blue Cradle* force was retired. The B-52 carried its own receivers and suit of tuneable jammers operated by a dedicated electronic warfare officer. In the end, the tactical air forces who watched passively, benefitted greatly from SAC's investment in ECM.

As early as 1952, as the B-47 *Blue Cradle* conversion was running into cost problems, the Air Staff insisted on electronic countermeasures for the *interim* B-66 bomber force using an orderly weapons system approach. In a February 20, 1953, letter to the Commanding General of Air Research and Development Command, ARDC, the Deputy Director of Research and Development at the Air Staff, Brigadier General Kelsey, wrote, "On 26 August 1952, this headquarters requested that your Command study the installation of jamming equipment on the B/RB-66. The decision was made at that time to install the APS-54 Radar Warning Receiver and the external chaff dispenser. The presentation on the installation of electronic jamming equipment, however, was unsatisfactory. In view of the tremendous problems that have been encountered in the B-47 electronic countermeasures installation, every effort must be made to install all required provisions for countermeasures in future aircraft before they are built."[3] On March 18, 1953, ARDC replied, "Since the effective utilization of the extensive electronic countermeasures capabilities listed as a requirement for Tactical Air Operations is dependent upon a continuous and thorough electronic reconnaissance capability, it is the opinion of this Command that the endeavors to fulfill both the electronic countermeasures and electronic reconnaissance requirements must be concurrent as a single program." ARDC then recommended "That approval be given of the proposed plan of action for incorporation of an electronic countermeasures capability into the B and RB-66, and for the proposed configuration of the electronic reconnaissance version of the RB-66."[4]

The dialogue between the Air Staff and ARDC, summarized in the above two letters, in effect bore fruit and resulted in a cost effective weapons system approach for the installation of self-protection ECM equipment in all types of B-66 aircraft. It also resulted in a requirement for the RB-66C, the electronic reconnaissance version of this *interim* bomber then under consideration. About this time staffers at Headquarters TAC began to show at least a lukewarm interest in the B-66 ECM program, calling a conference for March 25, 1953. It was at this conference where the *Brown Cradle* concept first surfaced. The ARDC representatives recommended a "jamming installation to afford jamming protection for other than the ECM equipped aircraft." In other words, they wanted an escort jammer similar to the B-47 *Blue Cradle* in addition to self-protection ECM equipment carried by B/RB-66 aircraft. The TAC representative expressed his doubts and requested ARDC to determine if the proposal would actually work. "If it does not," he noted, "TAC requires that packaged inserts (a bomb bay pod) for the tactical bomber be provided to be used on special missions where area jamming is needed." The idea was to have some sort of ECM pallet available that could be inserted in any B-66 bomber if there appeared a need for it. If not, the ECM pallet would remain in storage. TAC stated its position but remained reluctant to commit itself. The conference conclusions were presented as *suggestions not representing TAC requirements*. But the train had left the station, the Air Staff was not to be denied, wanting an ECM equipped B-66 force, and in a cost effective manner.[5]

On December 16, 1954, Major General Irvine opened the meeting at Headquarters TAC to present the findings and conclusions of the ARDC ECM Weapons Phasing Group that had been sanctioned by the Air Staff. A production, cost, and installation breakdown was provided for APS-54 warning receivers and ECM tail cones to replace tail guns in all but 30 flight test aircraft. "ECM tail cones and ECM *Brown Cradles* (bomb bay ECM inserts similar to the SAC B-47 *Blue Cradles*) will be provided as optional features. They will be available as accessories for operational use by TAC commanders." The plan was to pre-wire B and RB-66 aircraft and allow commanders the option to replace guns with ECM tail cones, and to wire all B-66B bombers as potential *Brown Cradle* jammers. Initial planning called for 50 ECM cradles, a number that was soon reduced to 35, and one ECM tail cone for three B-66Bs. "Headquarters USAF arranges to expedite this modification program without formal AFR 57-4 action by Tactical Air Command. A typical operational concept using the above configurations would permit a bomb carrying B-66B using an ECM tail cone to employ four jammers and two internal chaff dispensers enroute to the target. A companion B-66B carrying the *Brown Cradle* could supply ECM support," configured with "ten electronic jammers and eight chaff dispensers, and is likely to totally disrupt enemy GCI radar and ground to air links."[6]

In the end, 113 ECM tail cones were procured replacing the 20mm guns on selected RB-66B, C and D model aircraft. The *Brown Cradle* wiring on bombers was to provide the option to quickly reconfigure a fleet of them as ECM support aircraft. Like the *Blue Cradle* development effort, the *Brown Cradle* conversion, envisioned as low risk and low cost, turned out to be complex and costly. Instead of an easily installable and/or removable pallet, it became a permanent installation in only 13 B-66B bombers. The *Brown Cradle* aircraft that finally evolved replaced twin-20mm guns and 1,000 rounds of ammunition with a much lighter tail cone, housing two ALE-1 chaff dispensers. Its jammer configuration of initially ten active ECM jammers would in time grow to as many as 22. For its day, the B-66 *Brown Cradle* became the best escort jamming aircraft in existence anywhere in the world. But if it had not been for an air defense exercise that TAC was forced to participate in, these 13 Brown Cradles might never have materialized. Although the Air Staff was enthusiastic and supportive of escort jamming, the TAC senior leadership remained unconvinced and viewed the entire concept as a diversion of funds that could be spent in more productive ways.

"In 1958 the Institute for Defense Analysis [IDA] formulated a series of elaborate tests to evaluate the effectiveness of various parts of the U.S. Armed Forces. The purpose of the first Weapons Evaluation Test, WEXVAL, starting in August 1958, was to evaluate the ability of the Air Defense Command to defend the metropolitan USA against bomber attacks supported by electronic countermeasures. Although the purpose of the tests was to evaluate" ADC, SAC saw itself on trial. "The Nike missile batteries belonged to the Army, which was anxious to demonstrate that the day of the manned bomber was nearing its end." SAC, of course wanted to prove just the opposite.[7] "When the jamming EB-47s came in I expected to see the radar screens suddenly to go white with jamming," recalls Major Ingwald 'Inky' Haugen, an Air Force observer from the 801st Air Division Tactics Branch at Lockbourne AFB, Ohio. "Instead, there was hardly a flicker of jamming. We SAC people could hardly believe our eyes."[8] The WEXVAL exercise proved that the SAC concept of slowly sweeping noise jammers across a given frequency band was flawed. It also proved that ADC and the Nike air defense missile system could operate effectively under degraded conditions. In the fall of 1959, IDA decided to run another series of tests, this time against the U.S. Navy – WEXVAL II. Air Force planes supported by ECM aircraft were to attack Navy vessels. Interservice rivalry doesn't get any bigger than that. IDA did not pass the task to SAC, as expected, but to the Tactical Air Command. "TAC's level of interest in jamming was commensurate with the amount of jamming equipment it had available – hardly anything. The Command was populated mainly by fighter and fighter-bomber pilots who relied on surprise, speed, maneuverability and skillful low level flying to survive in the target area."[9]

WEXVAL II gave TAC the incentive to actually configure several of its B-66 bombers with electronic countermeasure equipment. Three aircraft were equipped with Hallicrafter noise jammers tuned to Navy radar frequencies. The jammers were procured under a special Air Force Quick Reaction Capability, QRC, program which dispensed with multiple bids and various tests required for standard acquisition programs. QRC filled an immediate, and at times transient, operational need. The three *Brown Cradle* aircraft were sent to Griffiss AFB, near Rome, New York, for testing. William Starnes, a retired Air Force lieutenant colonel now residing in Knoxville, Tennessee, was one of a few TAC long time EWOs in a period when TAC hardly knew how to spell electronic warfare. Starnes was selected to participate in the *Brown Cradle* tests and served as the Air Force and TAC project officer. "They were configured at the Douglas plant in Long Beach where that airplane was originally built. I was there for the roll-out and test-hop of the first aircraft. Then we flew the modified aircraft to Wright-Patterson AFB, Ohio, where the lab guys tweaked the jammers for the *Green Dragon* tests at Griffiss AFB, New York. The aircraft did very well flying against the instrumented Verona test site and the Rome Air Defense Sector." In his usual direct way Colonel Starnes said, "The *Brown Cradle* B-66B just blew out all the radars, something the SAC boys never were able to do."[10] As a result of these tests and WEXVAL II tasking an additional ten aircraft were diverted from the 47th Bomb Wing at Sculthorpe and configured as *Brown Cradle* ECM platforms.

Captain Jerry Sensabaugh, an electronic warfare staff officer at Shaw AFB, participated in WEXVAL II as an Air Force observer and evaluator. "TAC flew F-100s out of Myrtle Beach AFB against the Navy task force off the East Coast. The *Brown Cradle* B-66s flew jamming escort missions in support of the fighter bombers, while RB-66Cs kept a check on the frequencies the ship radars were using. I spent three days on the *USS Forestal* watching the exercises from the Navy side. I saw our jamming on their radar screens; it was effective and prevented several interceptions."[11] Cliff Parrott, the hands-on 'show me I'm from Missouri' Douglas senior technical representative at Shaw AFB had yet a different perspective of the exercise. Cliff decided to go along on some of the WEXVAL B-66 missions. "As the jammers came over," Cliff recalls, "they bloomed the scopes on the Navy ships. Those Navy guys wanted to intercept our aircraft at any cost, and so, as we were flying along, it was a cloudy day, these damn interceptors kept popping through the cloud deck like SA-2 surface to air missiles. The Navy had no idea where our planes were, but I knew there was someone down there telling the pilots 'You better get up there and find them.' So, they sent up their Douglas interceptors, F4D Skyrays, and stuff like that. Seeing them punch through the clouds I thought 'Hell, this is really dangerous.'[12] The results of WEXVAL II fell out positively for the TAC *Brown Cradles*, vindicating the Air Staff push for ECM capability in TAC. After WEXVAL II the 13 *Brown Cradles* were configured with standard ALT-6B noise jammers and returned to the 47th Bomb Wing at RAF Sculthorpe.

The *Brown Cradles* soon began sitting *Echo Alert* at RAF Alconbury, later Toul-Rosieres in France, in support of F-100s sitting *Victor Alert* with H-bombs strapped to their bellies. In 1960 three *Brown Cradles* participated in an air defense exercise in the British Isles. August 'Gus' Seefluth, then the 10th TRW Wing EWO observed the exercise from a British GCI site near Newcastle. "The standard RB-66B photo airplanes with their load of four tail-cone jammers each, were assigned to penetrate English air defenses from the east, coming in over the North Sea. Though all of their jammers were operating, ground based radar burned through the jamming and detected the planes, tracking them for interception by British fighters. Then came the *Brown Cradles*. They never appeared on the radar screen until they reached Scotland, and London air traffic control requested termination of all jamming so it could resume commercial operations."[13] Lieutenant Bill Sears was one of the pilots on the B-66B *Brown Cradles* on another occasion. "We flew 12 aircraft to the Norwegian coast and returned to the United Kingdom line abreast. The *Brown Cradles* wiped out most if not all the radar and communications in the United Kingdom."[14] For the first time USAFE and NATO had an escort jammer that really worked.

Gus Seefluth was one of the officers in the middle who made things happen. It was Gus who convinced the 10th Wing commander, Colonel James D. Kemp, to remove the guns from the RB-66Bs and install the ECM tail cones. Their principal mission was night reconnaissance. Enemy fighters if encountered would be guided by GCI radar and use their airborne radars to locate the RB-66s. In such a situation ECM noise jamming, combined with chaff, provided much more protection to the RB-66 than a pair of 20mm tail guns. In addition, the reduction in weight resulted in decreased take-off distance and increased the airspeed by 35 knots. That clinched it for Colonel Kemp. Then Gus persuaded Colonel Kemp to request the transfer of the *Brown Cradles* from the 47th Bomb Wing to the 10th TRW. The 10th was losing its WB-66D weather reconnaissance mission anyway, so there wasn't a problem integrating the *Brown Cradles* into the 42nd TRS at RAF Chelveston. Although the WB-66D weather mission went away, several D-models were retained by the 10th Wing until 1965 for pilot and navigator training. Finally, Gus tightened up the RB-66C electronic reconnaissance operation, pulling them out of Black Sea flights which were not related to their tactical mission, and focused them instead on the Group of Soviet Forces in East Germany and nearby Warsaw Pact countries.[15]

The *Brown Cradles* moved with the 42nd TRS to Toul-Rosieres in 1962. By the time Don Harding arrived at Chambley in early 1965 they were standing

Echo Alert. The photo birds were gone and the conversion to the RF-4C was in full swing. The 1st and 30th TRS at RAF Alconbury, Headquarters of the 10th Reconnaissance Wing, began converting to the RF-4C in early 1965. The 10th Wing became an RF-4C wing. The 42nd TRS with its RB-66C and B-66B *Brown Cradle* aircraft was reassigned effective July 1, 1965, to the newly activated 25th Tactical Reconnaissance Group at the one-time dispersal base of Chambley. Although the 25th activated, the planes were still at Toul-Rosieres as Don Harding found out when he arrived at Chambley. The 25th was a group with one squadron. Toul-Rosieres transferred to the newly formed 26th Tactical Reconnaissance Wing, its two RF-101 squadrons from Laon Air Base converted to the RF-4C once they arrived at Toul. Reconnaissance wings and groups proliferated in USAFE. One had to wonder if the USAFE headquarters staffers really knew what they were doing. It was at this time of the 'great reconnaissance rodeo' when two things were discovered by the busy bees at Headquarters USAFE in Wiesbaden. First, the runway at Chambley did not support the 83,000 pound gross weight of a B-66 *Brown Cradle* – the runway needed reenforcement before the 42nd TRS could move to Chambley from Toul-Rosieres. Second, the RF-4Cs arriving at Toul-Rosieres and Alconbury suddenly developed camera problems and USAFE found itself with no night and little day photographic capability. So the RB-66Bs of the 19th TRS were returned from Davis-Monthan and Shaw AFB to France – and that was the reason Don Harding and his friends got to come back into the RB-66 program. The 19th TRS was put under the 25th Reconnaissance Group at Chambley effective October 1, giving the 25th Group two squadrons, the 19th and the 42nd TRS, and allowing the planners in Wiesbaden to re-designate the 25th a reconnaissance wing.

"The RB-66B photo birds had already been sent home," recalls Don Harding, "so they ended up bringing them back. Once the RB-66s left Toul they had turned in all their support equipment including the all important film processing trailers. None of the photo and intelligence specialists were there either. All that equipment and personnel had to be returned to make the squadron combat ready. We had a terrible time putting humpty-dumpty back together again. To make matters worse, the 25th Reconnaissance Group was scheduled for a Headquarters USAFE directed Operational Readiness Inspection, ORI. I kept telling the Director of Operations, 'We are not ready for an ORI, colonel.' His reply, 'Oh, we'll do alright.' He had connections. I guess they weren't good enough. We did poorly. We busted that first ORI, and I had never busted an ORI before in my life. It made me feel pretty bad. The first ORI was in September, the second 60 days later. We passed by the skin of our teeth the second time around. I flew photo missions and was happy doing so. It came back to me easily how to operate the cameras, and all else.

Before I was sent to Sculthorpe they had sent me through the photo-recce course at Shaw. Finally, I was able to put all that knowledge to use."[16]

In a letter to President Johnson, dated March 7, 1966, President Charles de Gaulle informed the United States of France's withdrawal from NATO's integrated military structure, and directed the United States to remove all military forces from French soil by April 2, 1967. "From our headquarters building, my office was on the second floor, I could look down across the security fence at the squadron area where all the airplanes were parked," Don Harding recalls. "Base operations was at the other end of the field. Here came this French tanker, making low approaches. We had sold the French twelve C-135Fs, their version of our KC-135. This tanker came by every day for a week, making low approaches. They had never done that before. I got a set of binoculars and discovered that in back of the wing a porthole had been cut that was not normal for the KC-135. So I went over to the squadron to watch him make his low approaches, and I could clearly see the camera inside the porthole. They were keeping track of us. They had gotten wind that we had sent some *Brown Cradle* aircraft to Moron AB, Spain, then to Takhli in Thailand. It was a sensitive political issue and the United States had not told NATO that we had flown those airplanes out. Anyway, our French friends were here counting our airplanes. We only had one hangar that could hold two airplanes, so they could make a daily headcount. We had a top secret 'bug-out' plan which called for us to blast off for Germany at low level should that be necessary. We just didn't know what de Gaulle might have in store for us. All the birds went back to the States – some to Shaw, others to Takhli, Thailand, not to sit alert, but to fight a real war."[17]

Chambley may have been the worst base in France, with few amenities. Family housing consisted of 8x30 foot trailers, French economy housing wasn't much better. Captain Ned Colburn, the 25TRG ECM officer claims there wasn't a tree to be seen anywhere. When first activated, the 25th Tactical Reconnaissance Group may have had only one squadron, but it had generally good leadership and a fair number of seasoned B-66 flyers. Colonel *Black* Jack Fancher was the Group commander, and well liked by his men. Captain Don Harding with thousands of flying hours to his credit teaching men how to fly ran the pilot standardization program, while Captain Bob Stamm, who had flown RB-66Cs in the Pacific, was assigned to quality control in the maintenance shop, which included flight testing aircraft after they'd gone through maintenance. Writes Bob Stamm, "My flight test engineer was Technical Sergeant John Kelly. John was a natural for the job and he and I did all the flight checks together. In 1966 the Lear-Siegler company received a contract to perform an IRAN program on Chambley RB-66s. I don't know how much experience Lear-Siegler had with B-66s, I don't think very much.

They set up shop at Etain Air Base, a few miles northwest of Chambley. When the first aircraft was ready for pickup Sergeant Kelly and I went to Etain to test hop the aircraft. The profile called for a climb to 38,000 feet, followed by a descent to flight level 300 while the fuel selector switch was checked. Suddenly both engines flamed out – first the right, then the left. The sound of silence was deafening. I selected Emergency Forward Tank to Both Engines – nothing. For about 10,000 feet we were a glider. I switched the fuel selector switch back to Flight Normal and at 25,000 feet tried an air start on the right engine – no joy. The book says 18,000 feet or below, so I was pushing things. I tried the left engine at 22,000 feet, and it started – what a sweet sound that was – followed by a good start on the right engine. Then, as they say, an uneventful landing was made. It turned out that the Forward Tank to Both Engines position had been miswired causing the flame out. This wouldn't show up on the ground check of the fuel selector switch because the forward tank boost pump was only required above 14,000 feet altitude."[18]

The 25th TRW was not to be around for long, serving more as a parking place for men and planes destined for the war that was ramping up in Southeast Asia. Both the 19th and 42nd TRS were inactivated in 1966, only to rise again at Shaw AFB for the 19th, becoming the 19th Tactical Electronic Warfare Squadron, and Takhli, Thailand, for the 42nd, which became the 42nd TEWS on December 15, 1966. The 25th Tactical Reconnaissance Wing officially struck its colors on August 22, 1966. With that act, Chambley Air Base went back to the French. The 26th TRW at Toul-Rosieres relocated with its two RF-4C squadrons to Ramstein Air Base on October 5, 1966. On April 1, 1967, the American flag was lowered at Toul-Rosieres for the last time and the base reverted to French control. NATO headquarters moved from Paris to Brussels. The NATO alliance adjusted and survived.

CHAPTER FIFTEEN

MOONGLOW

"During the spring of 1965 I was part of a *High Flight* delivering two RB-66Bs from RAF Alconbury to Davis-Monthan AFB in Arizona," recalls Lieutenant Frank Oldis, a navigator on one of the planes. "The RF-4Cs had been arriving at Alconbury steadily for several months and our 66s were headed for the 'bone yard.' My pilot was Major Delbert C. Hainley, commander of the 30th TRS. Lieutenant Ira Kroses was the navigator on the other crew in our two-ship formation. I can't remember the other pilot's name, although I can still picture him, even hear his voice, having shared many hours of *Whiskey Alert*. We were on our way to Zaragoza Air Base in northern Spain, our fair weather base for a couple of years after the U.S. military pulled out of Nouasseur, French Morocco, in 1963. We had an agreement with the Spanish Air Force to give their F-86 pilots some intercept practice when we crossed into Spain. We would try to jam their radar which in their particular model of the F-86 provided range information only. Since the weather was generally fair over Spain, especially above 30,000 feet, they usually eyeballed us about 50 miles out. On this occasion as we watched the intercept unfold, the pair of approaching F-86 fighters collided about the time they began to convert from a frontal to a stern attack. We watched as one F-86 spiraled down and ended in a fireball. I saw no chute. At our post-flight debriefing at Zaragoza a Spanish air force officer questioned us briefly, then stated that the F-86s had probably been flying too close to each other. The other F-86, we learned from him, had limped to a nearby airfield and landed safely. Rumor had it that Franco had taken away their parachutes since too many pilots were bailing out. That was

The B-57B, like the B-66, was an interim aircraft selection by the Tactical Air Command. Both the B-57 and B-66 more than paid for themselves during the Vietnam War years. Two squadrons of B-57B bombers based at Clark Air Base, the 8th Bomb Squadron Yellow Birds and the 13th Bomb Squadron Red Birds, deployed to Bien Hoa AB, SVN, in early August 1964. Tragedy struck immediately.

possibly the reason why we didn't see a chute on the one that crashed. A couple of days later, after many briefings and flight planning, followed by many boring hours crossing the Atlantic, while approaching the east coast of the United States we received word to divert to Shaw Air Force Base. Once at Shaw we learned that many RB-66Bs were to undergo a transformation from photo-reconnaissance to electronic warfare. It seemed that the tough old gal was needed in Southeast Asia to live and fly another day."[1]

Although war had been going on overtly in Vietnam and Laos since August 1964, the Air Force was slow to respond to the situation. The phase out of the RB-66B photo reconnaissance force continued as if nothing had changed. Little money had been spent in years past on the limited electronic warfare capability available to TAC. As a result the RB-66C electronic reconnaissance aircraft were still flying with the same equipment they received when they first came off the Douglas production line at Tulsa in 1956 and 1957. And the 13 *Brown Cradle* aircraft were the only aircraft of its type in the TAC inventory. SAC was just as slow, and reluctant, to emerge from its Cold War nuclear mantle, and divert B-52 bombers from nuclear strike to the mundane business of dropping conventional bombs. Not until February 1965 did the first contingent of B-52 bombers arrive at Andersen Air Base, Guam, and the first B-52 strike was not flown until June 18. Yet B-57 tactical bombers and F-100 fighters had been waging war in South Vietnam and Laos since August 1964. On their first *Arc Light* mission on June 18, 1965, against a target in South Vietnam, two B-52s collided and crashed at sea. Eight flyers died. It was not an auspicious beginning. By April 1965 the big shift from European and mainland U.S. bases to the Far East began in earnest. Aircraft parking spaces at Clark AB in the Philippines, Kadena on Okinawa, Andersen on Guam and any number of bases in South Vietnam suddenly became hard to come by. American airpower may have been slow in its shift from a Cold War to a hot war posture, but once the shift began it was a mass movement of steel, aluminum, explosives, men and machines reminiscent of World War II.

The first Air Force jet, a B-57 bomber, had been downed by ground fire in South Vietnam on August 6, 1964. The following day an F-100 was downed by ground fire over Laos. And on the 9th of August F-105Ds flew their first combat missions out of officially secret air bases in Thailand. By November 1 the war became ugly when Viet Cong guerillas mortared Bien Hoa Air Base outside Saigon, destroying five B-57s armed and lined up for take-off, damaging 15 more. On February 7, 1965, President Johnson authorized *Operation Flaming Dart*. The following day American aircraft attacked their first targets in the Democratic Republic of Vietnam, the DRV. On March 2, three F-105s and two F-100s were lost over the DRV flying the first *Rolling Thunder* missions of many thousands yet to come. Captain Hayden J. Lockhart, flying an F-100D out of Da Nang Air Base, was among those lost that day, becoming the first American prisoner of war. On April 4, two F-105s were downed by MiGs as they struck targets near Hanoi. Suddenly the need for real-time tactical electronic reconnaissance and ECM support to suppress enemy radar controlled anti-aircraft artillery, AAA, became obvious.[2]

According to the 41st Tactical Electronic Warfare Squadron history, DRV air defenses in early 1964 were rudimentary, consisting of approximately 1,500 guns, a mere 22 early warning radars, some of Japanese vintage, and four *Whiff* AAA fire control radars. There were no jet fighters, nor surface to air missile sites.[3] But as early as November 17, 1964, the Soviet Politburo approved the dispatch of military aid to the DRV, including military advisors and SA-2 SAM missiles, the same missiles which in earlier years had claimed several of the high flying U-2 spy planes. In January 1965 the DRV formed its first SAM regiment, the 236th.[4] The situation in the DRV was changing rapidly – guns, jet fighters, SA-2 missiles and Russian advisors flowed into the DRV inventory. The U.S. Air Force at last realized that "modern military forces, let alone tactical air forces, could not survive in South East Asia, SEA, without effective ECM support."[5] The only tactical EW assets available, both jamming and passive reconnaissance, were in the process of being phased out of the Air Force inventory. That ill-advised process was finally stopped, and in April 1965 two things started in a hurry: the movement of available EW assets to Southeast Asia, and the augmentation of the limited B-66 *Brown Cradle* force through the conversion of RB-66Bs to EB-66Es.

Captain Frank Oldis's RB-66B photo reconnaissance aircraft originally destined for the scrap heap was diverted to Shaw AFB to be used as a trainer. An additional 51 RB-66B aircraft were withdrawn from desert storage to have their camera provisions removed and their bellies stuffed with 27 jammers covering the entire radio frequency spectrum actively used by DRV air defense radars. Obviously there is nothing like war to focus planners away from studies and dream scenarios onto the compelling needs of the moment. Funding suddenly became available as well from a willing Congress wanting to support the President and the troops in harm's way.

On April 5, 1965, Major Bob Long was briefing officer for the 9th TRS at Shaw AFB, South Carolina. "I was giving the final update for *Exercise Banyan Tree*," remembers Bob. "We were to deploy to Puerto Rico. Colonel Cabas, the 363TRW commander, walked in and said, 'Stop the briefing.' You can imagine my feelings. I was trembling. He was a stickler for perfection. I thought I had really screwed up. Lieutenant Colonel Kuhlman, the 9th TRS commander, appeared equally shocked. Colonel Cabas came on the stage, both RB-66B and RB-66C crews were assembled in the briefing room, and announced that buses were lined up in front of the building and everyone except Colonel Kuhlman, Majors Bill Madsen, Jim Estes, and I was to leave, board the buses, and go to the Officers' Club and have coffee. Then Cabas said to us, 'Break out the deployment packages for SEA.' Our instructions were to quarantine the aircrews and maintenance support personnel and plan on leaving the next morning, April 6. There were four RB-66B infrared equipped photo birds, and six RB-66C models involved. RF-101s from the 363rd Wing had departed earlier for Udorn Air Base in Thailand and Tan Son Nhut near Saigon. No one was allowed to call home. For some, their families lived on base only three blocks away. We stayed in a dorm across the street from the dining hall. Monday morning we all launched for George AFB with an enroute refueling. The RBs were first in line for take-off with Bill Kuhlman, Jack Seech, Bob Mann and Gerry Reponen as pilots. The C-models were piloted by Jim Estes, Dick Wilson, Bob Long, Ralph Lashbrook, Adrian Cordoni and Vern Johnson. Other crews were sent after us by commercial air. We flew from Shaw to George. Short tanker support on Tuesday, Wilson and Long were left behind. The first group then proceeded to Hickam AFB, Hawaii, then flew on to Andersen AFB, Guam, and into Tan Son Nhut near Saigon – arriving Friday, after four days of flying, losing a day in the 'time-zone thing.' The two stragglers followed a day behind, but were diverted to Clark Air Base, because there was no more parking space at Tan Son Nhut or Bien Hoa. We stayed in a rented hotel in town that night."[6]

Tom Taylor, an EWO, left Shaw on April 5 as well on a C-130 transport, leading an advance party to prepare for the arrival of the RB-66s at Tan Son Nhut. "We departed Shaw on three C-130Bs on April 5 and arrived at Tan Son Nhut around 1:30 in the morning on April 8. Total flying time: 36 hours and 25 minutes. We only stopped to refuel. We had all been issued M-16s with lots of ammunition at Shaw. At Tan Son Nhut all of us and our equipment were unloaded from the 130s at a rapid pace onto the parking ramp in an unlit area. The C-130s departed immediately, leaving us sitting in the dark in a strange place with no-one to meet us. After about 45 minutes a gaggle of military police showed up, confiscated our M-16s and ammunition, and left us there in the dark. At daylight the RF-101 guys from Shaw and RB-57G crews helped us get somewhat organized. There were no quarters on base for us. We had to fend for ourselves and stayed in a rented house in Saigon. The RB-66Cs arrived soon afterward. The rush was on to get the birds over to protect the F-105s from DRV radar guided AAA. After all that hurry up, the C-models were not tasked to fly their first missions until May 4."[7]

In 1963 four RB-66Bs were flown to Greenville, Texas, to have the latest infrared equipment installed by Texas Instrument engineers. One of the aircraft also was scheduled to receive a powerful strobe light system. "This was to be an operational test with the strobe lights. We had no idea if the theory would work in practice," recalls Gerry Reponen, one of the test pilots for the system. "The lights filled the entire bomb bay, like a giant photo-flash camera. In April and May 1964 we took the four airplanes to Luke AFB, near Phoenix, Arizona, for operational testing and to participate in *Exercise Desert Strike*. The flights were almost all at night. I flew one mission between Phoenix and Tucson using the strobe lights, flying close to the main road. This is 'flying saucer country' and sure enough, one lady reported that a flying saucer had chased her down the highway, she doing 90 miles per hour to escape, the whining saucer in hot pursuit. She couldn't shake it, she said, feeling intense heat from it. It must have been a strange sight having the strobe lights flash on and off as we were taking pictures from as low as 500 feet above the terrain. But the system didn't work out and we never used it operationally. That was not the case with the IR-system. After we worked out the initial bugs the infrared photo system worked just fine."[8]

"The IR equipment on the RB-66 was the same as that installed by General Dynamics Corporation on a limited number of RB-57Es, the AAS-18. It had a germanium iodide detector cooled by liquid nitrogen. We tested it on a remote set of railroad track," Tomayasu 'Kaz' Kazuto recalled "that ran from Sumter to Myrtle Beach, flying at 500 feet at 350 knots. The initial images were very clear, but rapidly deteriorated as the detector warmed up, being exposed to ambient air. The engineers went back to the drawing board and came up with a fix that kept the detector temperature at minus 250 degrees. Jerry Reponen and I were eventually able to photograph the entire length of the 20 mile section of railroad track."[9]

"By early 1965 I had passed the 2,000 hour mark in the RB-66, been promoted to major, and was assigned to a test squadron at Eglin Air Force Base," Jerry Reponen recalls. "The morning of April 5 my navigator, Neil Woollen, and I were doing some testing down at Homestead when we were notified to pack our bags and get on a waiting C-54 that would take us to Shaw. The crew said they had no other information, just to get us back to Shaw as quickly as possible. They stopped at Eglin allowing Neil and me to go home and pack a B-4 bag and bid our families good-bye. My wife returned from a doctor's visit as I was walking out the door. She inquired what I was doing home? I explained that I knew nothing, only that I was to get myself to Shaw as quickly as possible. 'You are going to Vietnam,' she said. As soon as we landed at Shaw a car drove up and took us to a briefing room where we learned that we were to take four IR equipped RB-66s to Saigon. It was day time and hard to go to sleep. Early in the wee-hours of the morning someone came around and banged on our door in the VOQ. After breakfast we were taken to a briefing room filled with other aircrews and told of our destination. The first stop was George AFB in California. It was a five hour flight to George. I landed first. On the roll-out I blew the right tire. I called the aircraft behind me and told them that I would remain on the right margin of the runway and for them to stay to the left, there was plenty of clearance. As I was shutting down the engines a staff car with a single star flag flying on the front fender pulled alongside. As I got out of the plane, there was Brigadier General James Kemp, my old 10th Wing commander at Spangdahlem and Alconbury. He recognized me and said, 'Reponen, what do you mean closing my runway?' I saluted and we had a pleasant chat. It had been over five years since I saw him last, but he remembered my name.

"We flew to Hawaii, passing Midway and Wake Islands on our way to Andersen AFB on Guam. It was a 3,500 mile leg, took two air refuelings, and over eight hours. We passed the international date line and doing that – lost a day. Now it was the 9th, not the 8th of April. Our departure from Andersen was delayed because of a lack of tankers. I had never seen so many fighter aircraft as there were on the ramp at Andersen. Between 100 and 150 F-4s, F-105s, F-104s and F-100s were parked in whatever open spot was available when they arrived. We finally got out of Andersen and made it to Tan Son Nhut. Once we landed our problem was to find a place to stay. There was no advance party to set things up like on a normal deployment, although later I learned that there was and that they encountered problems similar to our own finding a place to hang their hats. Neil and I finally managed to get a bed for the night in the Majestic Hotel in downtown Saigon. The night of our arrival Major Clyde Trent and Lieutenant Marvin Sproston flew the first RB-66B IR sortie. They arrived earlier and waited for our planes to land so they could fly their first mission.

"The Majestic was located at the foot of Tu Do Street, across from the Saigon River. At the hotel they assigned rooms according to rank. I was assigned a room with two Navy lieutenant commanders, equivalent in rank to Air Force majors. Neil was on the floor above with other Air Force captains. The best part of it was the room was air-conditioned. Dr. Hursey was our flight surgeon. He arrived before us and found a villa which was supposed to be available in a few days. Flight crews were allowed to live in private houses if they could find them. All others had to live in hotels. Living in a villa had advantages, not the least being that we would receive a much higher per diem rate to compensate us for paying rent. By several of us living together it worked out in our favor. The RB-57 crews lived in apartments around the city and paid about $80 in rent a month. Their night missions were similar to ours, to locate Viet Cong charcoal fires. They had the same IR equipment as we did."[10]

Kaz Tomayasu was there, flying RB-57Es. "We used the IR-gear to detect 'Charlie' preparing his evening meal around nine in the evening. They carried small tin cans in which they put charcoal to cook their meal of rice and vegetables. We could detect individual cooking stoves and on landing, intelligence would read the still wet film and immediately call in the find to an artillery base. The Viet Cong would deploy along the trail rather than coming together in a large group. One of our technicians, from the University of Illinois I believe, was the IR-system expert. He fine tuned the imagery to enhance only the cooking fires."[11]

"Our first flights were in the vicinity of the base and not up country until we were fully familiar with the area," Gerry Reponen explains. "We used the same call-sign as the RB-57s – *Moonglow*. On each flight when we were ready to taxi we would call the control tower and say, *'Moonglow 235'* or whatever our number was, 'ready to taxi tactical.' The tower would respond with the active runway number in use. We would taxi out to the end of the runway and call again with our call sign, '*Moonglow* ready for take-off tactical.' Using the word 'tactical' meant you were flying a combat sortie and no one was advised where it might go. The day after our arrival we were aiming to launch all four aircraft within a two hour period. We had problems. I didn't get my first sortie until the following evening. The next day I flew a third sortie at twilight which was the norm for night missions. It was best to take-off in daylight and fly to the target area getting there just as it got dark. At that time the Viet Cong were doing most of their cooking. We carried no personal items on us, just our dog tags. The only other thing we carried was an escape and evasion kit stuffed with various items, including plastic maps, pointy-talky sheets in Vietnamese, a wire saw, gold coins and medicine. We carried loaded .38 caliber revolvers in a shoulder holster over our left arm plus lots of ammunition.

"The IR-missions we flew at 2,000 feet above the ground, while the RB-57s flew down to 1,000 feet. At the altitude we flew we were safe from small-arms fire. The first month or so no one was fired at. The Viet Cong obviously weren't sure what we did and were trying to figure us out. The RB-57Es looked like the bombers, but didn't carry forward firing guns. Our tail guns had been removed long ago. Each flight was a combat mission, and if we flew six or more within a month we collected combat pay. For each 25 missions we were awarded an Air Medal. The RB-57 top mission pilot had 188 missions when he finished his tour. It looked like I would get about 50 or 60 before I rotated home. On April 25 Neil and I moved into a villa I had located for us. The next day Al Kunkel and Jack Seech moved in with us. For our villa we had to buy linens, pillows, towels, pots and pans and dishes. The house had recently been built for a district police chief, so we felt reasonably secure. It came with a 24-hour maid which was good, someone to guard our things while we were gone. Language was a barrier. The house, unlike the hotel, had no airconditioning. The outside temperature was near 100 degrees every day.

"I was the first to fly six missions, so I had to sit around for ten days until everyone else had their six missions to qualify for combat pay. Normally we only had two aircraft ready, the other two undergoing maintenance. Life became relaxed and easy. We went to work at two in the afternoon and finished night flying around ten, then went to the Officers' Club for dinner, and got to bed around midnight. Chuck Fox came to see me when he heard the B-66s were at Tan Son Nhut. The last time we were together was in England. He was flying out of Bien Hoa for two weeks TDY, then was scheduled to return to Clark Air Base in the Philippines where his squadron was based. He had just two months left on his overseas tour before rotating home. At Bien Hoa they were under fire every night from Viet Cong lobbing mortar rounds into the base, which was only 15 miles north of Saigon. He spoke of his missions, sometimes two or three a day, each dangerous, especially those flown outside South Vietnam. When I think of dedicated airmen, Chuck Fox was one."[12]

"At 08:15 on Sunday morning, May 16, 1965, Captain Fox and his navigator, Captain Haynes, were sitting in their B-57B at Bien Hoa about to start engines to lead a flight of four aircraft on a strike. Fox's Canberra was loaded with four 750lb bombs under the wings and nine 500lb bombs in the bomb bay. Fox's aircraft exploded and debris hit other aircraft on the flight line causing further explosions in what seemed to be a chain reaction. When the smoke cleared the scene was one of utter devastation, with dead, dying and wounded airmen and wrecked aircraft everywhere. A complete B-57 J65 engine was hurled half a mile, and smaller fragments were found at twice that distance from the flight line. The only man of Captain Fox's flight of four aircraft to survive was a navigator, Lieutenant Barry Knowles ... The cause of the explosion was thought to have been a malfunction on a time-delay fuse on one of the bombs carried by Captain Fox's aircraft."[13]

Gerry Reponen wrote his wife Ruth "I am writing this letter with tears in my eyes. Chuck was among those who died instantly. I flew over the base taking pictures at 1730 hours that evening and the flight line was a shambles. The next morning some of the bombs were still exploding among the wreckage. We were not using the strobe light at all, it would have been too dangerous to get low enough, 500 feet, to have it work. At night we used either the photoflash cartridges, which produced 265 million candlepower of illumination, flying at 5,000 feet, or infrared at 2,000 feet. All of our flying was in-country, but we did fly to Da Nang and north as far as the DMZ. Another friend of mine was Captain Vern Johnson, he wore a hearing aid. Vern flew with the RB-66C spooks. They went North, but I had no idea where they went. The best source of information for us was the local Saigon English newspaper. It would list all of the air strikes, special forces operations and casualties on a daily basis – and it was very accurate.

"I got a mission up to Da Nang where the biggest VC build up was. We were flying a lot of missions in that area trying to detect where the VC were concentrating their forces. It was a pretty mountainous area, as was most of the countryside north of Saigon. South of Saigon and west it was all flat, flooded rice paddies. The mountains were covered with dense jungle with trees up to 100 feet with three layers of canopies. The jungle was burned in many areas, and there were always fires from air strikes in the area we were photographing. In May we were told that we would stay until the RF-4Cs came to take our place. The RB-66Cs were leaving for Thailand. There were several times when all four of our aircraft were out of commission for various reasons. We had two down at one time for broken windshields. Eating so often in the club and drinking soft drinks with ice gave us stomach cramps and diarrhea. There were pills we could try, but they did little. I decided to try a bottle of Vietnamese 33 beer. We were told that it was aged with formaldehyde. I thought it might work on my stomach cramps. Lo and behold my stomach cramps disappeared and I had no further trouble. The one after effect of drinking 33 beer though was a headache as big as if someone hit me on the head with a hammer. Every night I could hear mortars going boom, boom in the distance."[14]

Captain Jack Seech flew with Gerry Reponen. They lived in the same villa. Jack's navigator was 'Spanky' McFarland. They were flying an IR mission in the Delta, but carrying a full load of 80 M-123 flash cartridges. Jack was flying his briefed racetrack pattern, assuring a certain amount of overlap. Suddenly a 50-caliber machine gun opened up. "He kept getting better every pass I made until a tracer came between the fuselage and the engine," Jack wrote, describing the scenario. "I needed to do something. I came over the bend in the river where he was, at about 200 feet and salvoed my full load of flash cartridges on top of him. That was the end of him. I flew back the next day to do an unofficial BDA. But early that June morning was the first B-52 *Arc Light* bombing of the Vietnam war, and my target of the night before was right in the middle of their strike zone. There was nothing left to look at other than lots of bomb craters. That river bend was totally obliterated." The *Saigon Post* carried the news of the first B-52 strike of the war, even giving names of crew members that perished when two aircraft collided enroute.[15]

"I flew my 41st and last mission on July 8. I enjoyed my stay in Saigon. It was a pretty city. In the downtown district people were relaxed and moved slowly. They were friendly toward Americans and would try to speak English, which many of them did quite well. The thing that always amazed me was the clothing the women wore – white, neat and clean. Some wore very thin silk dresses with pretty colored patterns over silk slacks. With the dirt all around the city I could never understand how they could look so neat and clean. I read somewhere that there were only 45,000 cars in the country, ninety-five percent of them must have been taxis. The streets were always jammed with taxis, pedicabs, motor bikes and bicycles. There were few buses, and those I saw were always jam packed with people. Saigon changed a lot during the three months that I was there. On July 16 Neil and I caught a Pan American flight out of Saigon for Hong Kong. Four days later I was back home in Florida."[16]

John T. Madrishin retired from the United States Air Force as a Chief Master Sergeant, the highest enlisted rank. John was a gunner on RB-66s, and in September 1965 flew as the third man in one of the IR equipped RB-66Bs out of Tan Son Nhut on Captain Robert L. Mann's crew from the 9th TRS. Mann and his navigator, James S. McEwen, arrived on the 27th and flew their first mission two days later on September 29, 1965. Bob Mann had been at Tan Son Nhut in the first deployment from Shaw in April with Gerry Reponen, Jack Seech and others. Bob returned to Shaw in July, and was on his second deployment to Tan Son Nhut. "We were in TDY status, flying two missions a day," John Madrishin recalls, "photo and infrared. I was flying in the third seat tending to the infra-red equipment. We found Viet Cong cooking fires every night. One of the enlisted crew chiefs broke his leg and was sent back to Shaw for treatment, so Lieutenant Colonel Mattson had me train Lieutenant Weger, a navigator, to operate the camera and infrared systems. On October 22 I reported to Operations for a night mission. Colonel Mattson felt I was in need of rest and decided Lieutenant Weger would take my place. That night we flew two missions piloted by Captains Mann and Puckett. After Colonel Mattson and I returned from dinner that evening we went by Operations, only to learn that Captain Mann's aircraft was missing. We called all the bases to see if a B-66 had made an emergency landing, but without success. Captain Puckett reported that they were flying in an area with a lot of fighter action when he lost contact with Captain Mann. He tried to raise him on the radio, but received no response. He recalled seeing a large fireball in the area where Mann was working. At first light Colonel Mattson took one of our 66s, along with an RF-101, to the area Captain Mann had been working the night before. We saw wreckage on top of a mountain and we knew it was 53-452. This plane had large red stripes painted on the wings and around the rear fuselage near the speed brakes. The red showed in the photos we took and was proof we had lost our crew. It was a year later when a chopper finally lowered a man down to the crash site to determine that the crew was killed in action." The aircraft went down in very rugged terrain west of Pleiku near the Laos border. "Not a day goes by that I do not think of those three officers," Sergeant Madrishin writes.[17] 53-452 was the first B-66 lost in the war in Southeast Asia. It was not to be the last.

CHAPTER SIXTEEN

NOT FOR THE TIMID

Tan Son Nhut Air Base on the outskirts of Saigon was a sprawling, teaming city that never went to sleep. In April 1965, Tan Son Nhut was a place filled to overflowing with men, materiel and airplanes, reflective of the hurried confusion that accompanied the sudden escalation of the war. Its ramps were filled with aircraft of every variety and type, except for the big bombers and tankers, which soon were to trickle, then deluge, Andersen on Guam, Kadena on Okinawa, and U-Tapao Air Base in the southern panhandle of Thailand. The four RB-66B infrared equipped aircraft went into action within hours of their arrival at Tan Son Nhut on April 9. After the rush to deploy, the C-models did not fly their first mission until the 4th of May. Their task would be to build the electronic order of battle, the EOB, for North Vietnam, and to support RF-101 and F-105 missions over the DRV. The B-66s trickled into Tan Son Nhut, some having been diverted to Clark in the Philippines because of a lack of parking space. Many of the air and maintenance crews arrived by commercial air, others on military transports. Finding a place to stay once they arrived was no small problem. There were few military quarters at Tan Son Nhut, and many of the Saigon hotels rented by the military were filled beyond capacity. Frequently the solution was finding friends who had rented a villa in Saigon and were willing to share their quarters – a rather unusual way to run a war. Perhaps a tent city would have been appropriate for the men in blue, as it was done in World War II by airmen deployed in the Pacific region. But this was another war, another time. Still, it was not a good omen. No way to run a war.

An EB-66E, returning from a combat mission over the North, pitching out for a high-speed, low level, 100 mission end-of-tour pass over Takhli RTAFB. A view of an EB-66 North Vietnamese SA-2 SAM crews coveted, but seldom got.

Captain Clarence Reuben Autery, known as Rube to his fellow flyers, was the pilot of the first RB-66C mission flown into the DRV on May 4, 1965. Rube had flown the RB-66C for many years out of England and France. He was no newcomer to the game of electronic reconnaissance. Rube would climb to his assigned altitude, then tried to give his four Ravens a stable platform to do their work. The navigator on this mission was First Lieutenant Joe Sapere. Joe, young and spirited, was a top of the line navigator and would prove his mettle many times in the difficult days ahead. The back end crew was led by Lieutenant Joe Canady flying in position four, with Ravens Larry Becker, Ken Sexton, and Curt Nelson. Captain Tom Taylor, who arrived earlier in April on a C-130B, was the staff EW briefing officer for this and subsequent RB-66C missions flown out of Tan Son Nhut. The instructions provided by Tom Taylor to the aircrews were both brief and non-revealing. According to Joe Canady Tom told them "'Provide ECM for the fighter strikes.' In other words – go do your jobs. We decided we would figure things out." Little guidance or direction was given aircrews. Little information was available to briefers like Tom Taylor as to the existing ROB or the deployment of DRV anti-aircraft guns.[1]

The SAC ROB maintained at distant Offutt Air Force Base in Omaha, Nebraska, was of little use in Vietnam. It was relatively static and not reflective of the current situation. Since North Vietnam had not been a strategic target for SAC bombers in a general war, little effort had been expended by the 55th SRW to fly reconnaissance in this region. Even if they had, the SAC process of validating and integrating information into the ROB was slow and ponderous, not useful for a tactical situation which changed on a daily basis. The reason the RB-66Cs were here in the first place was to develop and maintain that dynamic, ever changing ROB; then accompany the strike force and provide protection by jamming the enemy's threat radars. "I got the route of the fighters," Joe Canady wrote, "then laid out our route to provide the best possible ECM support to the F-105s. We decided we would fly a zig zag pattern, back and forth, along the path of the fighters up to their target at about 25,000 feet, then do a 180 and zig zag outbound. We planned to do this several times, arriving about twenty minutes ahead of the fighters, seeding in some chaff every three miles while jamming the *Whiff* and *Firecan* AAA radars.

"One problem I had as the senior raven were the newly installed ALT-28 jammers. I had never seen them before. Our checklist called for leaving all ECM equipment off until after take-off. I cheated and turned my equipment on during taxi. By the time we were airborne the jammers were warmed up and operating. I familiarized myself with the dials on the jammers, then tried them out, watching the jammer output on my receivers. By the time we reached the DRV I had things figured out. With our chaff and the new jammers we took out all the AAA radars, at least that's what I was led to believe. The mission went smooth as glass and it was the first time I later learned from the fighter pilots that they had not seen lots of AAA as they were inbound at higher altitudes. They were really impressed that all the AAA radar controlled stuff had suddenly left town. We were an instant hit with the fighter boys."[2]

Joe Canady was a dedicated Air Force officer and anxious to put his skills to use in a wartime environment. He had gained experience during the Cuban Missile Crisis in October '62 with Soviet deployed radars in Cuba, thinking about what tactics he might employ against them if he ever had to. A saying firmly believed in the electronic warfare community is that 'The best electronic counter-measure is a well trained operator.' Joe Canady applied that philosophy skillfully when planning the employment of the means available to him. He flew several more missions out of Tan Son Nhut, then transferred to Takhli, Thailand, on May 25, when the runway construction there was completed and the B-66s were able to move out of Tan Son Nhut. Joe flew his 100th combat mission over North Vietnam on December 13, 1965. Not only was he the first RB-66C Raven to fly 100 missions over the North, but he was the first airman regardless of rank and aircraft to do so.[3]

Of the first six C-models deployed to Southeast Asia, only five were at Tan Son Nhut at any one time. One aircraft was always at Clark undergoing heavy maintenance. This was only the first contingent of a total of 23 RB-66Cs still in the Air Force inventory. Others from the 9th TRS at Shaw were undergoing equipment upgrades and modifications before deployment to Takhli. For a time no C-models were left at Shaw for training of follow-on aircrews. "The RB-66Cs were modified over several weeks with ALT-28 S-band jammers" recalls Tom Taylor, "with the controls located on a fold-down table between Raven 3 and Raven 4. The four ALT-28s allowed us to spot jam the *Firecan* radar which controlled the AAA guns. Our mission was simple: Fly up north and keep the *Firecan*s from being a threat to the RF-101s and the F-105s. The guidance from up top was next to nil. We were on our own to plan the way we were going to fight. It was common knowledge that with an RB-66C present, there were no losses to radar directed AAA fire. Our type of mission was a first for the Air Force, it hadn't been done before. The Marines beat us to being the first ECM aircraft over the DRV by four weeks. They deployed a few old Douglas F3D *Skynights* of Korean War vintage, redesignated EF-10B, to Da Nang in April 1965. They were slow, underpowered aircraft, and had short range, but they were there going in with the strike force."[4] The *Skynight* crew of two, seated side by side, had no ejection seats. They used a chute to escape the aircraft in an emergency. Not having an ejection seat saved on weight and production costs, but was not conducive to saving lives in combat. VMCJ-1 operated its *Skynights* out of Da Nang until 1968, losing five of its ten aircraft in combat. All ten crew members were killed in action.[5]

Keeping high performance aircraft flying in an inhospitable climate is no easy task either. Sergeant Jerry Mosby recalls that "no real maintenance facilities were available at Tan Son Nhut when we got there. We set up in a Quonset hut style tent. Since our test equipment for the ECM equipment on the airplanes required temperature stability we were the only place on the flight line with air conditioning. That didn't last long. Arriving for work one morning I discovered the air conditioners gone, along with the generator that provided the power. There was a note scrawled on the wall that read 'Thanks for the cooler. Your U.S. Army.' We did get a replacement airconditioner and continued to work in the canvas shop until we deployed to Takhli. When it came time to leave we loaded everything on the C-130s using a small Army fork lift. After the equipment was loaded, we loaded the fork lift on the last plane and took it with us. Turn-around is fair play."[6]

After additional C-models from Shaw had been outfitted with the new ALT-28 jammers and the jamming patterns tested on the Eglin range, the remaining aircrews were sent to Takhli, Thailand. Maurice Turcotte, then a first lieutenant remembers that move well. "The pilots and navigators accompanied by a crew chief flew the aircraft to Thailand. The Ravens went commercial." The back-ends of the C-models were filled with spare parts and test equipment, as was the case in the initial deployment to Tan Son Nhut. "We left San Francisco on Continental Airlines. Shortly after arriving in Bangkok we boarded a train for Takhli about 130 miles north-west of Bangkok. That was the ride of a lifetime. Sweltering heat and more flies and bugs than one could stand. They came through the open windows which didn't provide much relief from the heat. If one dared open his mouth, a delicacy of one sort or another was sure to fly in. The train seemed to stop at every crossing, never picking up enough speed to provide relief from the heat. What I remember most is the dining car. Food was prepared over an open pit fire on the floor of the car where rice was boiled and fried. Some five or six hours later we arrived at the Takhli train station. We couldn't wait to get to the base to sample American life once again. Big surprise. We were escorted to our hooch – a teakwood open air barracks-like building where some 14 metal beds were lined up, seven on each side, three feet apart. Of course we had the same airconditioning system we had on the train, only this time the hooch was stationary. We did have fans which helped when the electricity was on. After a brief introduction to our hooch we were shown our communal showers and stall toilets – privacy at last.

"On August 8, 1965, we newcomers flew our first combat mission over North Vietnam, trying to electronically pinpoint the locations of SAM sites. Missions came fast and furious during this time. On three separate occasions my crew flew three missions in one day. As a result most of us had amassed some 80 combat missions over the DRV by late November 1965. At this time a rumor made the rounds that a mission limit was to be imposed – 100 or 150, no one knew for sure. We were given the option of going home, we were there on temporary duty, or PCSing (Permanent Change of Station) in place. All but two of us chose to PCS in place. The 100 mission rule prevailed, and once you had 100 missions over the North or 12 month on station, you could go home."[7]

100 missions always arrived first, and with that there suddenly appeared a shortage of aircrews – pilots, navigators and electronic warfare officers. Before the arrival of Maurice Turcotte's group of additional aircraft and crews from Shaw, the six 'early birds' from Tan Son Nhut kept a busy schedule. They were the ones who carved out the tactics for escort and stand-off jamming which others would follow. Not until 1968 would an EB-66 Tactics Manual be written. Until then, word of mouth tactics were passed down from Rube Autery, Joe Sapere, Paul Duplessis, Joe Canady, and others to the newly arrived. In 1965, before the introduction of SAMs and MiGs, the RB-66Cs went where the strike forces went. The only difference being that they operated at higher altitudes than the fighters. There were certain restricted areas neither bombers nor ECM support aircraft were allowed to enter – principally around Hanoi and Haiphong, and along the Chinese border. DRV airfields also were off limits. It was frustrating once the MiGs showed up. Aircrews could look down and see the MiGs sitting in their revetments below, but were not allowed to touch them.

On July 24 Rube Autery's crew flew two missions up North in support of F-105 strikes near Hanoi. They positioned themselves across the ingress and egress routes of the F-105s, to provide maximum jamming support for the fighters as they went in and came out again. The area became known as 'the pocket' running from northeast to southwest of Hanoi, outside the restricted Hanoi area and up against the 20 mile Chinese border restricted zone. Joe Sapere was the navigator on both missions. On each sortie a second C-model accompanied Autery and his crew. One was flown by Captain Vernon A. Johnson, the other by Lieutenant Colonel Willard G. Mattson. It was to be a watershed day in the air war against the North. The morning mission was anything but routine, recalls Larry Bullock, one of the Ravens on Autery's crew. The *Firecans* came up and we drowned them out with clouds of chaff and intense noise jamming. The radar directed AAA was as usual impotent and forced to rely on optics. Then the unexpected happened. Two strong *Fansong* signals came on the air from the Hanoi area. Their track-while-scan radars appeared to be following the egressing fighters. No missiles were fired, at least no launch was detected by the RB-66C Ravens. The Ravens did their thing – recording the *Fansong* signals, taking down the signal parameters for subsequent analysis and confirmation: Pulse Width, Pulse Recurring Frequency, Radar Frequencies, and most important, determining the location of the two surface to air missile sites. Joe Sapere remembers "logging fixes every minute to try to get an accurate plot of our location versus the SAM sites. Intelligence until then had the misguided belief that SAMs could only be installed into hardened, fixed sites. All the SAM sites being built were tracked by Intelligence, and there were none in the corridor we flew northwest of Hanoi. Guess at our surprise when we picked up not only one, but two sites."[8] Both aircraft passed their electrifying discovery to 7th Air Force headquarters at Tan Son Nhut while still in flight.

John Norden, the navigator on Captain Vern Johnson's crew recalls, "First Lieutenant Howie Shorr was the first Raven on our aircraft to get cuts on the *Fansong* radar, Captain Jim Wolpert was a close second. Howie was a shining star for about a week until he reported a Kresta class cruiser well up the Mekong River. As the navigator I remember Howie's excitement and plotting the bearings to the SAM site. We had the location of that SAM within three miles, which is very good considering that we were using ONC charts where the size of a pencil point was about a mile. Of course 7th Air Force didn't believe us, until a flight of F-4Cs was nearly obliterated by the very SAM batteries we had discovered. Then they had us flying around the clock. Of course the bad guys didn't turn their radars on until they needed to. So it was a week of wasting JP-4 jet fuel." To be fair to Lieutenant Howie Shorr, the North Vietnamese actually used several Soviet naval radars normally deployed on Kresta class cruisers. Howie was right – only this time the radars were not mounted on cruisers.

"The afternoon mission for the RB-66Cs was in the Dien Bien Phu area," recalls Larry Bullock, "in Route Pack 6, away from the SAM sites we discovered earlier that morning. A flight of F-4s providing MiG cap for our strike apparently did not get the word from 7th, or maybe 7th had not distributed the information about the two SAM sites discovered by us that morning. Whatever the case, the F-4s were trolling through the danger area. The SAMs came up, we called out a SAM warning, they launched and shot down one F-4 – it blew up, and the others in the flight of four were damaged. Captains Roscoe Fobair and Richard Keirn managed to eject from their stricken aircraft, but were listed as missing in action."[9] Keirn was released as a POW on February 12, 1973. Fobair, a former 55SRW RB-47H pilot, was not among the POWs who came home.[10] The three RB-66 crews involved in the 24 July 1965 operation were awarded the Distinguished Flying Cross by Headquarters Seventh Air Force for extraordinary achievement.

The North Vietnamese 236th SAM Regiment formed in January 1965. It was staffed with the best and brightest technical talent the small country had to offer. Equipment and missiles arrived in April 1965 aboard a Soviet ship accompanied by 70 Soviet advisors. The training program was intense. "On 24 July 1965 the regiment fought its first engagement, shooting down one U.S. Air Force F-4C *Phantom* and damaging three others. Because there had not been enough time to train the Vietnamese missile crews, Soviet advisors personally took part in this missile launch ... The Vietnamese admit it was one full month before the first all Vietnamese missile crew conducted a combat missile launch."[11]

The events of the 24th of July grabbed the attention of an at times all-knowing and forever sceptical 7th Air Force staff. For the next two days the RB-66Cs stood down – planning retaliation along with Takhli's and Korat's F-105s. They were going to go in and take out those SAM sites with conventional bombs, unguided rockets and napalm. Joe Sapere switched to Major Richard Wilson's crew for the mission on the 27th. They asked Intelligence for anything they had on SA-2 missile sites in the area. "The photography of the sites was given to us," recalls Joe, "and the date [on the photos] was July 15. Just another case of having the intelligence, but not getting it out to the people who need it."[12] Distribution of perishable intelligence information by headquarters organizations like 7th Air Force to the combat units that desperately needed it was a recurring problem not solved by Air Force Intelligence for many years.

The mission on the 27th was the first coordinated Air Force operation against the seemingly emboldened North Vietnamese 236th SAM Regiment. The SAM sites were taken out but at the cost of six F-105s and five pilots. Only one pilot was rescued by a recently established *Jolly Green Giant* helicopter squadron which didn't even have maps of that area of North Vietnam when they went in to pull out Captain Frank Tullo. It was the first of many dramatic rescues performed by that courageous and self-sacrificing unit. "It was also becoming obvious that the greatest danger posed by the SA-2 was not the kill capability of the missile but the fact that its mere presence forced U.S. aircraft to fly at lower altitudes where AAA and small arms fire became more deadly." The air war had taken a decisive turn.[13]

Aircraft and crews continued to arrive at Takhli from Shaw to join the recently reactivated 41st TEWS and the 6460th TEWS – the latter deriving its designation from the fact that it was the 6th squadron of the 460th Tactical Reconnaissance Wing to which both the 41st and 6460th were briefly assigned. They were at Takhli, Thailand; the 460th TRW was at Tan Son Nhut Air Base, South Vietnam. Apparently composite wings were not yet acceptable to the Air Force leadership or both squadrons should have been assigned to the 355th TFW at Takhli, as they later were. The only type of EW aircraft at the time at Takhli were RB-66Cs. Surprisingly, none of the *Brown Cradle* aircraft had yet been moved from Europe to support an ongoing war. They continued to sit Cold War *Echo Alert* at Toul-Rosieres in France, facing east. The rapid build up of tactical forces in Southeast Asia was accompanied by organizational chaos. No one seemed to have a rational idea how to organize the arriving B-66 contingent. Should they have their own Group or Wing? Maybe, maybe not. The 25th Tactical Reconnaissance Group at Chambley was established effective 1 October 1965 with only one squadron. Apparently such a solution was not deemed appropriate for the two electronic warfare squadrons at Takhli. Instead, the RB-66s were reassigned in September 1966 from the 460th TRW to the 432nd TRW at Udorn – while they continued to be based at Takhli with the F-105s of the 355th Tactical Fighter Wing. Finally, in August 1967, the by then redesignated EB-66 squadrons were attached to the 355th TFW – the obvious solution came to pass after two long years. The best solution would have been to establish a tactical electronic warfare group at the very beginning – but being part of a fighter wing was better than being managed from afar by a commander who had little feel for nor understanding of EB-66 operations. The 355th Wing Commander managed his diverse combat squadrons, F-105 and EB-66, by appointing deputies for EB-66 and F-105 operations. The first Deputy Commander for EB-66 operations was Colonel Harrison Lobdell, a long-time RB-66 flyer, having served in the 10th TRW at Spangdahlem in 1959, then at RAF Chelveston and Alconbury. He retired in September 1978 as Deputy Chief of Staff for Plans at Headquarters U.S. Air Forces in Europe, Ramstein Air Base, Germany, in the rank of Major General. Colonel Lobdell ran a tight ship at Takhli, but with a velvet hand. He was greatly admired by the air crews he sent into daily combat, flying some of the most dangerous missions himself. Unfortunately that was a practice few if any general officers in the Vietnam War were known for. Had they done so, maybe the air war would have been fought a bit differently.

"On September 30, 1965, an F-105 lit its afterburner at Takhli and began its take-off roll down the 3,000 meter long concrete runway. It was about three o'clock in the afternoon," recalls Ken Coolidge, an RB-66C navigator. "I was walking to the squadron from the hootch area. The F-105 was part of a multi-aircraft raid and had been rolling down the runway for about 15 to 20 seconds when all of a sudden the afterburner roar stopped. So did my heart. I started running for the flight line, and about that time the sirens went off. There was a plume of smoke rising from near the end of the runway and a bunch of fire trucks were headed in that direction. Suddenly they stopped and turned around. Someone told them about the bombs. An ambulance, however, continued to head toward a lone figure standing near the end of the runway. When the F-105 aborted its take-off roll it went off the runway, wiped out its gear, and caught fire as it went bouncing over the ground into the swamp. The pilot managed to get out with a broken arm and injured back and now was standing about 200 yards from his burning aircraft. The ambulance crew scooped up the pilot and sped away from the burning plane toward the hospital.

"The wreckage burned and burned. The bombs did not go off. Since it was the departure end of the runway the field was closed to air traffic. No take-offs or landings over the burning wreckage until the bombs were disposed of. We had planes all over the place looking for a place to land and spend the night. The next morning at 2 a.m. our crew – Bernie Russell, pilot; myself as the navigator; Joe Canady our chief Raven, and Larry Becker, Ken Sexton and Bob Rein, the other three Ravens on the crew, were awakened and told to report for a 3 a.m. briefing. Seems we were to take off from the departure end of the runway for an ELINT sweep up north and to recover at Da Nang. We flew our mission as briefed and landed at Da Nang where we had a late breakfast. Off we went again on another ELINT mission north and west of Haiphong. After returning from our second mission to Da Nang 7th Air Force fragged (tasked) us to fly a third ELINT sweep up north. There were numerous thunderstorms and the Ravens in back were having a field day with all sorts of new and unusual signals to work. Seems the bad guys didn't know we were there as they were transmitting up a storm. Usually, as soon as we got within a hundred miles they shut down and only came up for a sweep or two to verify our track. This night they must have been training. We were picking up St. Elmo's fire on the windscreen and heading for a really big thunder-bumper when Bernie, our pilot, wanted to turn. The Ravens wanted us to go on just a little further. A SAM site locked on to us. The Ravens wanted to keep on going. I figured we'd turn when the main bang on the Radar Warning Receiver (APR-25/26) hit the 20 mile ring – then I told Bernie to turn. He rolled into a standard 30 degree bank, I had my head in the scope keeping an eye on the thunderstorms. All of a sudden there was a bright flash of light and the hair on my arms stood straight up where I had rolled up my sleeves. The Ravens shouted something about a ball of fire rolling down the aisle of their compartment. We'd been hit by lightning – not a SAM. Bernie was looking at the refueling boom when we got hit. He was blinded by the flash and hit the second station button for me to take over and continue the turn and roll out. About five minutes later Bernie had his night vision back. The rest of the flight was uneventful. We landed back at Takhli at 2200 hours. We'd been up for 20 hours, flown three 'counters' over North Vietnam, experienced a lightning strike, and had a chance to write and mail free letters home from Da Nang. October 1, 1965, was the first day of free mail from Vietnam – the reason I remember the date and those missions. I checked with maintenance the next day. They found a burn mark on the fuselage, but no damage. Oh, yes. A young captain took an explosive charge out to the wreck of the F-105 and wired it up for a blast on site. All the bombs went off and we were back in business. Sure gave the snakes something to think about!"[14] Life at Takhli was never dull.

CHAPTER SEVENTEEN

THE BROWN CRADLE PATHFINDERS

The Air Staff was slow in moving the remaining *Brown Cradle* and RB-66C aircraft from France to Southeast Asia. Part of the reason may have been a lack of appreciation for their need. After the July 24, 1965, shoot-down of an F-4C by an SA-2 surface to air missile, coupled with the heavy losses sustained by F-105s from Takhli and Korat on July 27, it became clear to even the most ardent 'fly 'em low and fast and damn the guns' advocates that the world had changed. It was high time to bring to Southeast Asia the never quite understood, often neglected, EW assets sitting on Cold War nuclear alert in France. In great secrecy preparations were made to move a small number of the *Brown Cradles* out of France. They had a NATO commitment, but NATO was not informed of the impending move. Orders issued by the 25th Tactical Reconnaissance Wing on October 10, 1965, read "The following individuals, unit indicated, USAFE, this station, will proceed on or about 12 October 65 from Chambley AB, France, to Moron AB, Spain, with variations authorized on TDY for approximately 179 days, in support of operation unnamed."[1]

A/1C Alexander Underwood was a *Brown Cradle* crew member. He turned on the 18 jammers in the RB-66's belly when there was a need to do so, dropped chaff, refueled the airplane at strange bases, took care of small discrepancies, performed preflight and postflight inspections. In other words, Underwood, and others like him, were every pilot's dream of the proverbial 'man Friday' who would and could do nearly everything to keep an airplane flying. "In October 1965 some of our crews were asked by personnel if they would like to go TDY

198

During the Monsoon season EB-66B Brown Cradle Pathfinders equipped with the sophisticated K-5 bomb/navigation radar provided a means of guiding F-105, F-4 and B-57 aircraft to cloud obscured targets.

to a tropical climate," Underwood recalls. "My crew volunteered to escape the cold French winter. Before we knew it we had orders in hand sending us and four other crews on a top secret mission for 179 days to Moron Air Base, Spain, for air refueling training. Nobody knew where we were going."[2]

USAFE's one KB-50 air refueling squadron, the 420th ARS at RAF Sculthorpe, was disbanded in May 1964. The last KB-50 was scrapped at Yokota Air Base in 1965. In December 1965 the last SAC KC-97 air refueling tanker was sent into storage. SAC became an all jet air force and the single manager of Air Force air refueling assets. The new tanker aircraft replacing the KB-50s and KC-97s was the four-jet, J57 powered, KC-135. No more trailing hoses or triple refueling stations on wings and fuselage. On the new KC-135 there was one boom lowered from the aft section of the tanker and flown by a boom operator directly into the receiving aircraft's fuel port. The hard-boom method transferred fuel faster and at higher pressure than the old probe and drogue method. Although SAC aircraft such as the B-47, B-52 and B-58 were refuelable in that manner, many of TAC's older aircraft, such as the F-100 and the B-66, were not. They had been designed for the probe and drogue refueling method. To refuel the older planes required the KC-135 to have a flexible hose and a refueling basket, a drogue, attached to its boom. Once so configured the KC-135 could refuel only probe equipped aircraft. The F-105 and the older F-101 fighters were unique in that they were capable of using either system.

The pressures emanating from Southeast Asia affected the Strategic Air Command in numerous ways. For one, air refueling requirements sky-rocketed. Since the other combat commands, USAFE and PACAF, no longer owned tankers, SAC was under immense pressure to provide tanker support for both its nuclear strike force sitting or flying alert, and the tactical air forces with their ever increasing demands. Budget restrictions forced Secretary of Defense McNamara to look in-house for resources. He found them of course in SAC. McNamara phased out the last B-47 bomb wings. A pilot shortage arose as well due to accelerated hiring by commercial airlines. SAC pilots coming out of B-47s or other discontinued bomber programs found themselves heading straight to TAC and Southeast Asia. In December 1965, B-52Bs and B-58s were added to McNamara's list of aircraft headed for desert storage. Base closures followed to save money for the insatiable demands of the growing war in the Pacific. A contentious SAC promotion program was given the boot as well by Air Force Chief of Staff General John P. McConnell. There would be no more 'spot promotions,' the very successful incentive promotion program instituted by General LeMay in 1949.[3] Under the pressures of the Johnson administration, the Vietnam War and the continued march of technology, SAC, the premier nuclear strike force of the

United States, was undergoing dramatic change, finding itself being drawn ever more deeply into a conventional war.

When the five *Brown Cradle* crews arrived at Moron Air Base they received two days of air refueling practice with the new KC-135. Airman Underwood's pilot and navigator were Captains Art Smith and Ed Presto. Notes Ed Presto, "The 12th and 13th of October were spent flying local practice refueling sorties, as some of the pilots had to become current. We departed on the 14th for Brookley."[4] "Once at Brookley," notes Airman Underwood, "we were told not to call home. We took off for McClellan in California, but shortly after take-off lost thrust on one engine and headed back to Brookley. The B-66 had no fuel dump capability" something that was added later in Southeast Asia, "so we had to make a heavy-weight landing. Maintenance found a broken potentiometer cable which adjusted the movement of the exhaust nozzle and regulated engine thrust. Because we missed our tanker we proceeded to Amarillo, a SAC base, to refuel. The transient alert sergeant asked me what base I was from. I told him that I couldn't give him that information. 'Well,' he said, 'then I can't give you any fuel.' So I gave him the Chambley APO number and he filled us up. We joined up with the other four aircraft at McClellan, then followed a pair of tankers to Hawaii. Hickam AFB was a good place to crew rest. On the 18th of October we headed across the Pacific for Andersen Air Base on Guam. Some things we had to do differently refueling from a KC-135. We no longer lowered our wing flaps to reduce airspeed. It was the KC-135 which reduced its power settings on their inboard engines instead. They also started a slow descent so that by the time we had a full fuel load we could keep up with the tanker. That night at Andersen I didn't get much sleep. B-52s were taking off. The noise level was deafening. I decided to do my laundry at two o'clock in the morning. Later I headed for the SAC mess hall to have breakfast. I grabbed a metal tray and started loading up on all kinds of good breakfast food. When I arrived at the grill the cook asked me if I was in SAC. I said, 'No.'

"'Then you must be on that *High Flight* crew. Give me your tray, we already have your breakfast ready. How do you want your steak?'

"I said, 'Keep your steak and leave me with the bacon.'

"The cook replied, 'I have my orders, steak and eggs for you guys. Some of our guys here haven't had a good steak in six months. Take what's coming your way.' I did. It was a long take-off roll from Andersen's hot and sloping runway. The KC-135s took off before us. We had our last in-flight refueling just past the Philippines. Somewhere over the South China Sea Captain Smith opened an envelope and handed a map to Captain Presto. We finally had our destination – Takhli Royal Thai Air Force Base, Thailand." Smith, Presto and Underwood logged a total of 38.7 hours flying time from Moron Air Base to Takhli.[5] The five

Brown Cradles to arrive at Takhli on the 19th of October were 53-482, -491, -495, -497, and -498. 491 and 498 would not survive the war.

The newly arrived *Brown Cradle* contingent at Takhli became Detachment 1 of the 25th TRW. They remained in TDY status at Takhli until January 1966 when they were replaced by another group from the 25th TRW. The second group became known as Detachment 2. Once Detachment 2 returned to Chambley in June 1966, they promptly were turned around and returned to Takhli. This time it was a permanent change of station move, a PCS. They were assigned to the newly activated 6460th TRS which fell under the 460th Reconnaissance Wing at Udorn. The 6460th assignment was for flyers only – the maintenance men were assigned to the 355th Tactical Fighter Wing at Takhli. None of it made much sense, but that's the way it was.[6]

The remaining eight *Brown Cradles* of the 42nd TRS flew from Chambley to Takhli in late May and early June 1966. The squadron's C-models did not depart for Southeast Asia until August. That same month the RB-66B photo reconnaissance aircraft of the 19th TRS were flown to the 363rd TRW at Shaw, and the 42nd and 19th Tactical Reconnaissance Squadrons along with the 25th TRW inactivated. The 19th reformed at Shaw on September 1. The 42nd reappeared at Takhli in December, absorbing the assets of the 6460th TRS, which ceased to exist. (Appendix 3) Captain Charles Schaufler, who was part of the October '65 deployment from Chambley to Takhli notes, "For quite awhile our families were not told where we were. Even the finance office at Toul-Rosieres asked if we were at war with Spain, since that was where our orders said we were, and we were drawing combat pay."[7]

The arrival of the *Brown Cradles* was a welcome addition to the over utilized C-models at Takhli. Within a week of their arrival the *Cradles* were flying their first combat missions in the company of the more versatile Cs. Routine problems arose in a new environment and had to be tended to. Recalls then Staff Sergeant Robert Mansperger "We suddenly had maintenance problems we never experienced before. I remember watching one of our *Brown Cradles* on its take-off roll. Just as it lifted off two overhead escape hatches blew off. The crew turned around and landed. We adjusted the hatch release mechanisms in every one of our aircraft for a tighter fit."[8] Hatch blowing was an old problem, one which the 'B-66 Doctor at Shaw' thought he had fixed permanently. Yet it came up once again in a different climate.

Alexander Underwood was promoted to Staff Sergeant while at Takhli. He flew 100 combat missions over North Vietnam with the 6460th TRS. Alex reenlisted on his 100th mission on September 21, 1966, over North Vietnam. He earned several Air Medals and the Distinguished Flying Cross for a mission he flew on

June 29, 1966. The flight he remembers most though is the one he didn't go on. "I went to the squadron to check when I was flying again. When I got there I was told that my pilot and navigator, Captain Dwight Lindley, a former 55SRW RB-47H pilot, and First Lieutenant Donald Laird, were taking an aircraft back to the States for modification. They were going to install a receiver in my position and replace me with an electronic warfare officer. It looked like the flying engineer's job was coming to an end for me. I did some quick figuring and thought I would at best get a day or two while in the States to visit my folks in Philadelphia. I asked our squadron commander, Lieutenant Colonel Noble McSwane, if maybe one of the married engineer's would like to go in my place. 'I'd rather stay and fly missions over the North than go home,' I told him. So I stayed and Technical Sergeant Charles Bordelon went with my crew island-hopping back to the States. They had been gone for a little over a week. As I walked into the squadron I was called into the intelligence briefing room and told that they had gone down somewhere near the Hawaiian Islands and were missing."[9]

Wreck 22, the call sign of Captain Lindley's RB-66C, 54-475, had completed IRAN at the Tulsa-Douglas plant and was functionally test flown on August 18. That same day Captain Lindley, Lieutenant Laird and Sergeant Bordelon flew the aircraft to McClellan AFB. A number of discrepancies were quickly cleared up and the aircraft was prepared for overseas delivery. It was a *Flying Fish* mission, under the control of the 4440th Aircraft Delivery Group at McClellan. No significant enroute weather was forecast. Estimated time from McClellan to Hickam AFB was five hours. Wreck 22 was accompanied by another RB-66C, Wreck 21. Each aircraft completed two refuelings. After four hours of flight, Wreck 22 was flying a close right wing formation with the tanker. The aircraft suddenly dropped down to the left, passing under and behind the KC-135.

"Wreck 21: 'What's the trouble 22?'

"Wreck 22: 'I've got control problems.'

"Wreck 21: 'What's the matter?'

"Wreck 22: 'I've lost my boost.'

"Wreck 21: 'Which one?'

"Wreck 22: 'All three.' (Apparently speaking of flight control surfaces rather than boost systems.)

"Wreck 21: 'Well, did you lose it or is it intermittent?'

"Wreck 22: 'I lost it. All boost pressures are zero. No, I'm getting it intermittently now.'

Wreck 22 kept falling behind. The conversation between Wreck 21, Wreck 22 and the tanker continued. Wreck 22 managed to get back behind the tanker, hooked up once more, and started taking on fuel. Then "Wreck 22 was observed by the boom operator to move forward and under the tanker and out of sight. This was the last time Wreck 22 was seen ... Shortly after turning around, Wreck 21 spotted an oil slick." The aircraft and crew were lost 300 miles northeast of the Hawaiian Islands. There were no survivors and no wreckage was recovered.[10] The loss of Wreck 22 and its crew was a sad day for Sergeant Underwood; a sad day for many, including myself when I learned of Dwight's death. Dwight Lindley and I flew together in the 55th SRW out of Forbes. The war took its grim harvest in strange and different ways.

There was one unique thing about the RB-66B *Brown Cradle*s. They were former bombers converted to the ECM role and as a result had the K-5 bomb/navigation system, far superior to the standard run of the mill navigation radar carried by other B-66 aircraft. When the *Brown Cradles* arrived at Takhli in October of 1965 it was the beginning of the Monsoon season. Visibility in the target areas of North Vietnam was a major problem for the F-105s. If you can't see the target, you can't deliver your bombs. Captain Charles Schaufler, a *Brown Cradle* pilot, his navigator, Captain Bill Mahaffey, and an F-105 pilot, Captain Bob Green, "were sitting in the club one night," Schaufler noted, and "Bob was explaining all the problems they had with dive bombing. If a 3,000 pounder didn't release, more than likely the F-105 would mush into the target with the bomb. If all 750 pounders did not release, it caused the aircraft to roll due to the asymmetrical loading. Then there was the problem of finding the target in marginal weather. They were short of bombs and required to retain the bombs on aborted missions and land with them. Bill then jokingly said to Bob that we could do a better job with our K-5 radar in the RB-66B. Bob rose to the challenge and said, 'OK, prove it.' We didn't have bomb tables to use to figure when to tell him to release his bombs because they never dropped their bombs from straight and level flight. The wing commander approved a test using the range at Sattaheep in Thailand. On the day of the test we went in at 23,000 feet and released three bombs – the first hit 50 feet short, the second was on target, and the third was 50 feet long. When the results were reported to 7th Air Force in Saigon, the B-66s were back in the bombing business."[11]

Pathfinder bombing was a common practice in World War II. The Royal Air Force Bomber Command routinely employed Mosquito fighters during night bombing raids to pinpoint targets for the following bomber stream. In NATO, F-100s of the 36th and 49th Fighter Bomber Wings teamed up with RB-66Bs of the 1st TRS at Spangdahlem in 1958 to form a combat team. The idea was for the RB-66B to lead the F-100s to their target during inclement weather. Once a bombing run was completed, the RB-66B would return to the target and take pictures for bomb damage assessment purposes. The *Pathfinder* mission was briefly implemented, but discontinued when the 10th Tactical Reconnaissance Wing was forced to move from Spangdahlem to the United Kingdom in the summer of 1959. In 1965 the *Pathfinder* mission was back for real. The way it worked, a *Brown Cradle* aircraft would lead several flights of F-105, F-4 or B-57 aircraft to the target. Near the target the aircraft would fly straight and level in a tight formation. The bomb run was under the control of the B-66 navigator, Jerry Grimes recalls, "his skill was the primary factor in mission success." Captain Jerry Grimes led numerous *Pathfinder* missions in early 1966. Jerry alerted the accompanying fighters over the radio just before he broadcast a tone. When the tone stopped, the fighters dropped their bombs. If by chance anyone had an inoperable radio, he dropped when the others did. The system worked.

The *Pathfinder* B-66 gave Air Force a bad weather and night capability which none of the Air Force fighters possessed on their own. The U.S. Navy introduced the all-weather A-6A *Intruder* in February 1966. At the time it was the only all weather tactical aircraft operational over North Vietnam. General John D. Ryan as commander of PACAF pushed hard to obtain a limited night and bad weather bombing capability, but until the arrival of the F-111 'all-weather and night' bombing was mostly a patchwork of unsuccessful fixes. *Ryan's Raiders* was the best known effort along those lines, flying F-105s on night missions out of Korat. Their impact, however, was minimal.[12] The most consistently successful effort remained the B-66 *Pathfinder* mission. The tragedy is that the B-66B bombers so hastily retired in 1962, and all too quickly scrapped, would have provided Ryan the night intruder and bad weather capability over the North he so desperately wanted and needed. The B-66B, with its sophisticated K-5 bomb navigation system, could operate down to 500 feet AGL at night and in bad weather. To fulfill the role of the night intruder was one of the reasons why these aircraft were procured in the first place. In its spacious belly the B-66B could carry 14 750-pound general purpose bombs, 14 960-pound cluster bombs, or four 3,000 pounders. Enough ordnance to have done the Doumer Bridge on a rainy night.[13]

"13th Air Force was apparently quite happy with some of the early bombing results, but soon began targeting smaller and smaller targets on the Ho Chi Minh Trail," recalls then Captain Bill McDonald. "Lieutenant Colonel Webb, Monty Givens and I finally made a trip to Clark to convince the staff that a wooden bridge over a small stream under two layers of jungle canopy did not make a good radar return from 20,000 feet up. I guess they believed us, because the targeting after that became a bit more realistic. The *Pathfinder* role was the one I was the most proud of. It vindicated my three years of unrequited bombardiering without bombing, endless practicing for WW-III, and interminable periods of *Victor Alert* in the 47th Bomb Wing at Sculthorpe. My satisfaction was not even slightly diminished by the fact that instead of a Mark-6 A-bomb or a couple of Mark-28 H-bombs, the *Brown Cradles* were filled with electronic gear and our bombs were transported under the wings of our entourage of F-105, F-4 or B-57 aircraft."[14]

On 25 December 1965 President Johnson and Secretary McNamara announced their second bombing halt, a crucial part of their ill considered strategy of gradual escalation. That pause lasted until January 31, 1966. The day after, Captain Jerry Grimes led 20 F-105s from the 355th TFW at Takhli "on the first official *Pathfinder* bombing raid over North Vietnam." On his initial run Jerry had two flights of eight F-105s on his wings. On the second run he led an additional 12 aircraft over the target, dropping a total of 60 750-pound bombs on the harbor installations of Vinh in the southern panhandle of North Vietnam.[15]

Captain Don Harding, who arrived at Chambley Air Base, France, in 1965 to reconstitute the dismembered 19th RB-66B photo reconnaissance squadron, found himself at Takhli RTAFB in Thailand by April of 1966. "I went through Jungle Survival at Clark before I reported for duty at Takhli. That school was very good training. There weren't many crews at Takhli yet, so we'd fly around the clock. We were supposed to have eight hours rest after a flight. We weren't getting that. I didn't care, I loved to fly. When I arrived at Takhli it was during the Monsoon and they were flying *Pathfinder* missions. I got ten of those under my belt before they axed the program. We dropped a lot of iron on Mu Gia Pass, mostly night missions, when we thought they were putting trucks and people through there. I don't know how effective we were. I never saw anything through the thick cloud cover. But there was one memorable mission. Intelligence got word of some barges coming down the coast. Just north of the DMZ they pulled into an inlet where we caught them. I had a flight of four B-57s on my wings, and a good bombardier on board. It was a moonlit night. I pulled them in real tight and we made our bomb run. We emitted a ten second tone, the bombardier turned it on the last ten seconds of the run, beeeeeeeeeeeeeep. When the tone stopped, the B-57s dropped their bombs. The barges must have been loaded with ammunition, because when they blew they lit up the sky like it was the 4th of July on the Mall in Washington. We got all seven. The B-57 guys congratulated us, 'Good run, guys,' and went home. I made about eight circles for 20 minutes watching the fireworks."[16]

The B-66 *Pathfinder* mission was stopped in May 1966 and replaced by *Combat Sky Spot* – former SAC MSQ-77 RBS, Radar Bomb Scoring, ground based radars installed in both South Vietnam and Laos to guide aircraft to their targets. The most famous of these sites was Lima Site 85, installed on top of a 5,200 foot karst mountain just inside Laos, on the very border of North Vietnam, and 160 miles west of Hanoi. The site was nearly impossible to reach from the ground. It was manned by Air Force enlisted men wearing civilian clothes under the tutelage of the CIA and protected by Meo tribesmen. To flyers the site was known as Channel 97, a thorn in the DRV's side. The North Vietnamese tried to take out Lima Site 85 by using three Russian built AN-2 *Colt* bi-planes armed with unguided rockets and 250mm mortar rounds set in vertical tubes. The attack was launched on January 12, 1968. It failed. A CIA helicopter, piloted by Ted Moore, was in the air over Lima Site 85 as the attack began. Moore pursued the fleeing AN-2s. His crew chief, Glenn Woods, shot one AN-2 out of the sky with an AK-47. Another crashed trying to escape. The third *Colt*, chased by the persistent *Air America* helicopter, came down 18 miles north of Lima Site 85, inside Laos. The downing of the three DRV *Colt* bi-planes by an *Air America* helicopter was indeed one of the strangest aerial victories in the annals of aerial warfare. The North Vietnamese, however, were not deterred; intent on getting rid of Lima Site 85. On March 11, 1968, a sizeable North Vietnamese force supported by artillery climbed the mountain and routed some 100 Meo defenders. They destroyed the radar equipment and everything else of value. Twelve of the nineteen U.S. Air Force personnel manning Lima Site 85 escaped, the other seven perished.[17]

The July 15, 1966, edition of the *Klong Times*, published at Don Muang Royal Thai Air Force Base in Bangkok, Thailand, ran a large front page photo of a silver colored RB-66 leading a flight of four F-105s on a bomb run. Just like the B-66, one of the 105s was still unpainted. It was obviously early in the war when the picture was taken. "Radar Bombing" read the by-line, "SAIGON – Flying under radar control with a B-66 *Destroyer*, Air Force F-105 Thunderchief pilots bomb a military target through low clouds over the southern panhandle of North Vietnam." The presence of U.S. combat forces in Thailand, although obvious to everyone, was still officially a secret. B-66s had operated out of Tan Son Nhut AB in South Vietnam in 1965, the obvious reason for mentioning SAIGON in the by-line, but by July of 1966 they were long gone and the *Pathfinder* mission had ended for the B-66 a few weeks earlier.[18]

CHAPTER EIGHTEEN

DODGING SAMs AND MiGs

At the end of 1966 the DRV had a total of 114 combat aircraft: 99 MiG-15/17s and 15 of the advanced MiG-21s. 28 of their aircraft had been lost in aerial combat – five MiG-21s and 14 MiG-17s succumbed to Air Force missiles, the others met their demise courtesy of the U.S. Navy.[1] Their tactics were straight out of the Soviet playbook – guided by GCI controllers they made quick hit and run attacks. When they were forced or trapped into dog fights, their losses rose steeply. The most famous of such staged kill scenarios was *Operation Bolo* on January 2, 1967, planned by Colonel Robin Olds. Olds' F-4C *Phantoms* appeared to the North Vietnamese as bomb laden F-105s. The F-4s wiped out seven of the MiG-21s that morning, two more four days later. The small DRV fighter cadre was severely mauled and intimidated, requiring political re-indoctrination and augmentation by North Korean and Russian pilots. Later in 1967 the DRV moved many of its combat aircraft into China.[2]

By the end of 1966 the DRV AAA count had more than doubled over 1965. There were an estimated 4,435 20mm through 57mm guns, and 4,435 guns of calibers greater than 57mm with a reach up to 30,000 plus feet. The large caliber guns were directed by *Firecan* or *Whiff* radars, easily defeated by the electronic countermeasures employed by the RB-66 crews.[3] The F-105s faced thousands of optically controlled guns of lesser calibers when they went into their low level bomb runs, which took a heavy toll, and there was nothing the B-66s could do to help. The obvious solution was to attack from up high. Unfortunately, the World War II experienced fighter jocks who ran the war wouldn't hear of that obvious

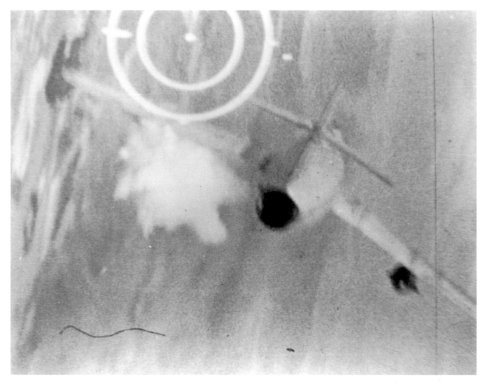

This MiG-17 was downed by Colonel, then Major, Ralph Kuster flying an F-105D from the 388TFW/ 13TFS, based at Korat RTAFB, Thailand, on June 3, 1967. Both MiG-17s and MiG-21s frequently attempted to intercept EB-66 aircraft, but with little success.

solution and continued to taunt fate by having the pilots practically fly their bombs into their targets. During the *Rolling Thunder* air campaign, 85 percent of Air Force, Navy, and Marine Corps aircraft shot down over the North fell to the smaller caliber guns.[4] When supporting B-52 air strikes in an EB-66E across from Mu Gia and other passes leading into Laos, we frequently had 100mm rounds lobbed at us. None ever hit anything. They were just fireworks in the sky. To have an impact the heavy AAA required guidance from their fire control radars, which we jammed effectively, or be applied in much greater numbers than the North Vietnamese appeared capable of doing. Their heavy guns proved noteworthy for their lack of effectiveness throughout the war.

The SA-2 SAM system consisted of six *Guideline* missile launchers and a radar guidance and control center built around the *Fansong* track while scan radar. The SA-2 SAM was the critical factor that forced tactical air operations to lower altitudes. Yet neither B-66s nor fighters especially feared the SA-2. If one could see the missile coming it was easily avoided. Throughout the war the SA-2 claimed less than 100 of the nearly 1,000 aircraft lost over North Vietnam during *Rolling Thunder*.[5] By the end of 1966, the DRV had 137 prepared SA-2 sites, a number that continued to grow until it reached 320 by the time of the *Linebacker II* campaign in 1972. Unlike other users of the SA-2 SAM system, the North Vietnamese turned their missile battalions into a rapid deployment force. If not truly a mobile system, by being able to break down an SA-2 site's components and moving to another site within less than a 24-hour period, the SA-2 in fact came pretty close to being just that.[6]

One way the Air Force responded to the F-4C shoot-down on July 24, 1965, was the formation of a SAM Task Force. Out of it grew the *Iron Hand Wild Weasel* hunter killer concept, first flying two-seat F-100Fs, but soon converting to more capable and survivable F-105Gs. "During the first years of the war, long-range jamming by electronic warfare aircraft, primarily RB-66s, flying just outside the battle area, and *Iron Hand* strikes gave North Vietnamese missile crews the most problems. The North Vietnamese immediately began targeting the RB-66s during 1966."[7] The RB-66 electronic warfare crews would never forget 1966. They flew unwavering into the face of fear, armed with neither guns nor bombs, trusting in the electronics at their finger tips. The initial RB-66C and B-66B *Brown Cradle* aircraft deployed largely with active jamming and passive search systems first installed in the aircraft in the 1950s. The Air Staff and tactical commands spent little money on upgrading their electronic warfare systems until 1965. Over the next several years the B-66s received a large number of upgrades from recorders to receivers to active jammers and steerable antenna systems, all provided through the Quick Reaction Capability program. QRC allowed managers to put money against an immediate need in support of combat operations. The conversion of 51 former photo reconnaissance planes to EB-66E active jamming aircraft was a major jump in electronic warfare capability. Although the EB-66E had many more jamming systems than the *Brown Cradle* aircraft, it still didn't have a directional jamming capability.

Major Robert Walker was a long time RB-66 pilot. He flew with the 10th TRW out of Spangdahlem in the late '50s, then transferred to RAF Alconbury with the 30th TRS in 1959. Bob served at Shaw with the 363rd TRW, and in early 1965 accompanied the four RB-66B infrared equipped aircraft to Tan Son Nhut Air Base as their maintenance officer. Major Walker had lots of experience flying and maintaining the B-66, ending up at Clark as chief of maintenance for B-66 operations. Clark was where the heavy maintenance for the B-66 was done, work that couldn't be accomplished at Takhli or anywhere else in Southeast Asia. But he wanted to get back into the flying business, so he wangled an assignment to the 6460th TRS at Takhli. On February 25, 1966, Major Walker and his crew were assigned RB-66C 54-457 to fly a surveillance mission over the Gulf of Tonkin, crossing over to the other side near Vinh, in Route Package 3. Their call sign was Gull 1.[8]

"This was my 13th combat mission," recalls Captain Wayne Smith, the Raven 2 on the mission. "I was stationed at March AFB, California in B-52s and didn't have the opportunity to go to any transitional training before reporting to Takhli. Shaw had not set up a training program yet. Another Captain and I were the first replacements for the original RB-66 crews sent to SEA, rotating home after completing their 100 combat missions over the North. This day all missions were canceled except ours. The weather was terrible. It was the height of the Monsoon season. They told us to go anyway and do a little reconnaissance. In SAC I had extensive signal recognition training, therefore I was intimately familiar with the sound of the SA-2 *Fansong* radar. I was amazed when I got to Takhli that the RB-66 crews turned off the APS-54 warning receiver. It was wired into the intercom on the B-66 and the crews didn't want to listen to all the noise it generated. I convinced them to keep it on at a reduced volume. This way I was able to listen to the electronic environment we were passing through. Our flight took us over Vinh and I heard what I thought was the faint sound of a *Fansong* radar on the APS-54. I told Captain John Causey about it, the chief Raven flying in position four. He looked for it on his receiver but the signal must have gone down. On our return down the coast I heard the *Fansong* come up again, and I called Causey's attention to it. When he intercepted the signal it was very strong, and he told the pilot to turn. Then the Raven one said that he intercepted a strong missile guidance signal," the BGO6 "and the chief Raven told the pilot to start a steep SAM break. I heard a loud pop. When Major Walker was finally able to level off he discovered he had little control over the aircraft."[9]

Major Walker recalls that the plane wanted to pitch up. He had no rudder, but seemed to have enough aileron to keep the wings level, and controlled the plane with the engines which were still running fine. "The control column wheel came back into my stomach and I had both knees on the wheel trying to keep it forward, but with little success." It was time to leave and he gave the order to eject. The seat gave him problems and didn't eject the first three times he tried. "The plane was going very much out of control. One last squeeze of the trigger, this time it worked."[10] First Captain John Kodlick, the navigator, ejected, then Major Walker. Ravens one, two and three ejected. For some unknown reason Captain John Causey didn't make it out, and crashed into the sea along with the plane. Wayne Smith remembers that after the Raven one went, it was his turn. He became confused. The B-52 ejection seat was different from the one in the B-66. "I pulled that lever and then everything blacked out or redded out, and the next thing I remember, I was dangling in my parachute. I do not know whether those extra couple of seconds could have been the cause of Captain Causey not making it. It haunts me to this day."[11]

Gull 1's Mayday call was heard and the Air Force launched a recovery effort. But the precise location of the crash was unknown. "A Navy A-1H Skyraider from the *USS Ranger* was participating in a practice search and rescue exercise when its pilot picked up several emergency beepers from an area where none were supposed to be. He was able to establish voice contact and vectored two Navy helicopters to make the pickup before the two Air Force *Jolly Green*s arrived."[12] Captain Causey was never found. Major Walker injured both feet during the ejection from the crippled aircraft. The other men suffered no injuries. Captain Smith completed 100 combat missions over the North, the only one of his crew to do so. This first loss of an RB-66C to an SA-2 was not publicized by the Air Force, announcing a subsequent loss on July 20 as being the first aircraft of its type to be lost over North Vietnam. The first kill of an EB-66, however, was credited to the SA-2 site near Vinh, then manned by Russian advisors. A/1C Richard Evans, assigned to Detachment 2 of the 42nd TRS, 25TRW, at Takhli, remembers the loss of 54-457 for other reasons. "I was an ECM technician and 54-457 was the first RB-66 to have the new APR-25/26 Radar Homing and Warning receiver installed. This system was a real step forward in electronic detection technology. Two technical representatives from Applied Technology were waiting for the return of the aircraft to get the reaction of the crew. I was in the ECM shop when the tech reps came in and told us that the aircraft may have been shot down. It was a sad day in maintenance."[13]

"I was flying a *Brown Cradle* over the Gulf of Tonkin, off Haiphong. It was a clear day," Don Harding remembers. "We got a strobe on the APR-25/26 warning receiver at about 2 o'clock, and my EWO said over the intercom 'I think they are locked on to us.' All of a sudden I saw this contrail coming up toward us. I did a hard break to the left and dove to force the missile into a turn it couldn't execute, but the darn thing went off right in front of our airplane. We ingested a lot of scrap metal into the right engine and it started running a little rough. I shut it down, went back into orbit, and finished our mission. When we got back to Takhli we found a few shrapnel punctures in the engine cowling, but most of the stuff went right into the engine. On another occasion the consequences were more severe. A piece of metal went into the side of one engine when the missile exploded near us. The engine began to run rough, but at a certain RPM setting it would smooth out. So I kept it there and we finished our orbit. But instead of returning to Takhli I decided to land at Udorn. I didn't feel right about that engine, and decided we needed to get down quick. After inspecting the engine after landing, I think it would have blown off the plane in a few more minutes. It was in really bad shape. My crew and I went home on a C-47. Two weeks later I came back to pick up the plane after they changed the engine. It was night. I began my take-off roll when I saw a truckload of Thai workers on one of their big fancy painted trucks on the runway. Oh my God!!! I didn't think I could clear the truck, but I couldn't afford to just plow into it either. At the last possible moment I yanked the wheel into my stomach and went right across the top of the truck. I stalled over the truck and came back down on the other side and continued my take-off. I heard later that some of the workers were badly hurt. The tower apologized profusely. It could have been worse.

"Many times we flew in overcast conditions and that was scary. You couldn't see anything and had to totally rely on your equipment to give you warning of a missile launch. On July 20, 1966, I was flying a *Brown Cradle* directly behind a C-model piloted by Captain William Means. We were near Dien Bien Phu when the missile came up through the clouds and hit him. Bob Hubbard was in France with me, the navigator, and a good friend. The missile came out of nowhere and smacked him square where it hurts. I was five miles in back of him, could see his exhaust trail. It was sort of a broken cloud environment. He'd disappear from view every few minutes, and all of a sudden all I heard was beepers going off. I heard no transmission, it happened that quick. I got the hell out of there. They snuck a missile site way out of their normal deployment area west of Hanoi and caught us by surprise. We let our guard down, were on the way home, in a place where no SAMs were supposed to be. They wanted us, and they came after us."[14] Devil 01 was the EB-66C shot down that day, serial number 54-464. Five of the crew of six were captured. First Lieutenant Craig Norbert, one of the four Ravens, was killed in action.[15]

Getting 'nailed' by an SA-2 surface to air missile was not the only problem facing B-66 aircrews. Oftentimes they ran afoul of whatever restrictions Washington imposed on their operations, and the slimmest of violations could see their careers heading south at the whim of any number of people at different levels of authority – from the wing commander to the all mighty secretary of defense, Robert S. McNamara. An ECM mission was to cover a strike force of F-105 fighters going into the Hanoi area on June 29, 1966. "We normally would have been a flight of two, one *Brown Cradle* and a C-model," Captain Vaughn Wells remembers. "This day we were three. Two B-66Bs and a C-model. I had an extra RB-66B, Devil 33, on my wing for the express purpose of keeping my new navigator Alexander Birgerson out of trouble. Our call sign was Devil 32, and the C was Devil 31 – the lead. The Cs always led. Birgie had never seen North Vietnam, this was his first trip. Ed Presto, the radar navigator in Devil 33, was experienced and proficient to see any mistakes Birgie might make, and was to prevent what actually happened. Birgie never said a word the entire mission. As it turned out he was lost the whole time, but didn't know it.

"The C-model went to a point just southwest of Hanoi to hold over the Thuds ingress route. We went to a point directly west to hold over the egress route. A flight of F-4s providing high cover had lost one member to a maintenance abort, so there were only three of them. The three stayed together, as fighters never work in less than pairs. They stayed with us, Devil 32 and 33, thereby protecting two aircraft instead of just one – leaving the C-model to tool around MiG country without an escort. The F-4 guys were thinking of me as Devil lead, a critical mistake. The C-model was Devil lead. I told Birgie to mix up our headings in the holding pattern so as not to fly a totally predictable pattern. Birgie would give me headings to fly, and I had no way of knowing if they were right or wrong. It was a solid undercast. No sweat, I thought, Mike Schurig, the other pilot in Devil 33 with Ed Presto, the experienced navigator, was tucked in on my right and surely would never let Birgie take us into no-no land. Birgie would interpret those weird little green blobs of light on his scope and give me a new heading every couple of minutes, flying what we thought was a clever figure-eight modified racetrack pattern. He took us into no-no land, also known as the Peoples Republic of China, not once but four times, flying his nonstandard pattern and drifting with the high altitude winds. Every time we approached the Chinese border the F-4 flight lead with his up-to-date inertial navigation system would call, 'Devil lead' and give the border violation code. I said to Birgie, 'Do you think he might be talking to us by mistake?' Silence. The real Devil lead was of course the C-model, and if I had used my brain properly I could have – should have – called the F-4 lead and said, 'F-4 lead, this is Devil 32 rocking wings. Are you calling me?' As it was, those extra brain molecules weren't there that day and Birgie and I trusted Presto, the old head navigator, to closely watch Birgie's progress and prevent the very thing that happened. Not a word from Ed Presto. After the final crossing into China the strike was over and we all started south. Birgie had us heading directly toward Udorn, he thought. Long after the time when Udorn TACAN (Tactical Air Navigation aid) should have come alive on my instruments, I was still without any navigation aids – and getting concerned. As I was about to ask my trusted navigator about this discrepancy the F-4 flight lead said that we were out of MiG danger and he was going to peel off and RTB (Return to Base). I gave him a salute of thanks and he turned his flight 90 degrees to port. I did not like the looks of that, so I said to Lieutenant Birgerson, 'Do you know where the hell we are?' Birgie came up from behind his scope with the most forlorn look in his eyes I had ever seen and said, 'I'm in the weeds, man.' I asked Mike Schurig if he was picking up Udorn TACAN and he answered, 'Affirmative.' I said, 'You have the lead.' He too turned 90 degrees left. We were about to enter Burma." They landed at Udorn, short on fuel. Then returned to Takhli.

"The next day," Captain Wells recalls "I left for Bangkok on R&R (Rest & Recreation) only to be recalled on an urgent requirement to go and visit with Colonel Daniel 'Chappie' James in Saigon. Schurig, Presto, and 'Birgie' had preceded me on a C-47 out of Takhli to Saigon to meet with the 432nd staff. I reported as ordered to then Colonel James, a legend in his own time. When he stood up from behind his desk he went to about nine feet before he stopped rising – glaring down on me. The man wanted to flay the hide from my bones, but I was one of only two guys of five aircraft who truly had no way of knowing where we were. The F-4s had their inertial navigation systems, and Birgie and I had Ed Presto, a supervisory navigator, on our wing. James wanted to kill me, that was certain. But being a fair man and understanding of the circumstances, in great frustration and disappointment, he just threw me out of his office.[16]

The 'intrusion' into Communist China ended with that meeting between Colonel James and Captain Vaughn Wells. Unlike an earlier intrusion on May 12, 1966, which only violated the 20-mile buffer zone along the Chinese border. That one gained the attention of President Johnson and ended up before Secretary of Defense McNamara. McNamara seemed to relish harassing the very airmen who on a daily basis put their lives on the line to implement his flawed strategy of gradual escalation. Captain Stanley L. Tippin was a Raven on the crew of Lieutenant Colonel Allen 'Spider' S. Webb, commander of the 41st TRS at Takhli. On May 12 they were assigned aircraft number 54-387 to fly an ECM mission northwest of Hanoi in support of an F-105 strike. Their tasks were to jam *Firecan* AAA and SA-2 *Fansong* radars and to provide missile warnings to the strike force if that became necessary. Captain Verla O. Eary was the navigator, getting a flight check from 1/Lt William H. Hill, an instructor navigator. The rest of the back-end crew of Ravens consisted of Captains Dave Gingery, Jim Barkley and 1/Lt Norman Kasch. "We were flying a northeast to southwest orbit," Stan recalls, "only to come face to face with a flight of MiG-17s which had approached from the rear to make a visual attack with their 23mm cannons." Norm Kasch adds, "We completed our mission a little early. The 105s were running a bit ahead of schedule so we called in RTB and initiated our turn to a southwesterly heading. As soon as we rolled out on our new heading, that's when we encountered the MiGs." Stan continues, "Colonel Webb had World War II combat experience flying P-40s against the Japanese at Guadalcanal, and instead of avoiding the MiGs he turned directly into them, causing them to break formation and fire wild. He then executed a split-S and dove for the deck. Meanwhile we Ravens in the back were cleaning up our stations and getting ready to eject. One of the MiGs recovered and followed in hot pursuit. We had a three ship F-4C MiG-cap. Major Wilbur R. Dudley and his backseater 1/Lt Imants Kringelis, flying one of the three F-4s, saw the single MiG-17 on our tail. He kicked in his afterburner and in short order was trailing the MiG bent on shooting us down. Kringelis got a lock-on with his radar. Dudley worried that if he fired a *Sidewinder* it might take out the B-66, but if he didn't do something the MiG-17 was going to do the job for him. They fired an AIM-9 heat seeking *Sidewinder* missile which failed to track. They immediately set-up for a second shot. That missile went straight up the MiG's tail, the aircraft exploded and rolled into a spin and crashed. No parachute was sighted, nor did the F-4 crew see the markings on the aircraft. Upon landing at Takhli we were met by Colonel William Holt, the 355th Wing Commander and escorted to the wing command post. Here Colonel Holt informed us that the Chinese government had lodged a protest with Washington that an F-4 and RB-66 had violated Chinese territory and shot down one of their aircraft. Within hours Secretary of Defense McNamara called for an investigation and all seven of us were flown to 7th Air Force Headquarters in Saigon where we spent a grueling eight days documenting our flight. The F-4 crew was already there when we got there. The press was all over the story. I have clippings from the Bangkok Times, the Saigon English language paper, the Los Angeles Times, and of course the *Fort Lauderdale News*, my home town paper."[17]

That engagement started when two of the F-4s protecting the RB-66 were jumped by three MiG-17s firing their 23mm cannons. As his wingman took evasive action, Major Dudley saw a fourth MiG line up behind the RB-66. "The

MiG pilot apparently had a case of tunnel vision (target fixation) when he bore in on the RB-66 and never knew we were behind him. That was his mistake, and one mistake is all you are allowed in this game." Dudley and Kringelis, the F-4 back-seater, both said that the MiG-17 was firing on the RB-66 when they launched their missiles. "I guess I was a little excited and fired the first *Sidewinder* before the MiG was in firing range. Anyhow, it whipped off past him and missed," causing Dudley to fear that "their own heat-seeking *Sidewinder* missile would hit the RB-66." By then Kringelis had obtained a radar lock-on and was yelling at Dudley, "Go radar! Go radar!" to fire one of their radar guided missiles instead of a *Sidewinder*. "But I had that MiG in my sights dead on, and I let loose with another *Sidewinder*. I watched the missile, a little red ball with smoke spiraling out, wind right into the MiG's tail. The next thing we saw was smoke and debris. We were through it almost before it happened. There was no chance the MiG pilot could have ejected." Dudley's wingman saw the MiG spinning to the ground out of control. The other MiGs fled. "I never got close enough to see his markings," said Dudley.[18]

"The Joint Chiefs of Staff, at the request of the President, sent a board of officers headed by Marine [Corps] Brigadier General Robert G. Owens to gather evidence on the incident," reported the Los Angeles Times, adding, "The instructor navigator, Lt William H. Hill, was flown to Washington and is slated to testify before a board of high ranking officers today, according to Lt. Gen. Joseph H. Moore, U.S. Air Force Commander in Vietnam." All hands put in a week of long hours in Saigon compiling information from a myriad of sources into a detailed 5-inch report. It was Lieutenant Norm Kasch, the Raven 2, who had worked early warning and GCI radars during the mission and plotted their locations along with the navigator's position reports which verified the position of the RB-66 as being over DRV territory, but within the 20 mile buffer zone established by McNamara along the Chinese border. The Marine Corps general returned to Washington with his report, which apparently the Secretary didn't like."[19]

The MiG-17 downed by Dudley and Kringelis from the 390TFS, 35TFW, was the 12th MiG kill of the war, the 9th kill for Air Force pilots.[20] Many more were to follow as the North Vietnamese, with the help of Chinese, Russian and North Korean pilots, continued to attempt to shoot down RB-66 aircraft. There was no better testimony to the effectiveness of B-66 jamming against DRV AAA and SAM operations than the DRV's continued efforts to destroy the B-66s, or at least force them into more distant orbits to diminish the impact of their jamming. As for the RB-66 crew, they returned to Takhli to fly their 100 missions over the North, nauseated at having their Secretary of Defense side with the Chinese Communist. Aircraft number 54-387 was not to survive the war. It was downed by an SA-2 surface to air missile on February 4, 1967, while supporting an air strike against the Thai Nguyen industrial complex near Hanoi. Three of the Ravens were killed in action – Major Woodrow Wilburn and Captains Herbert Doby and Russell Poor. Three others became prisoners of war – Major Jack Bomar, Captain John Fer, and 1/Lt John Davies.

A *Wild Weasel* F-105F SAM killer, piloted by Captain Edward Larson with Captain Kevin 'Mike' Gilroy in the back seat as the electronic warfare officer, was hit by AAA fire north of Hanoi on August 7, 1966, and barely made it to the Gulf of Tonkin where the two flyers ejected. They came down among a group of islands occupied by North Vietnamese forces. Air Force and Navy jets were in the area to keep the North Vietnamese at bay while an SA-16 was called in to make a rescue attempt to get the two flyers out.[21] An RB-66C, 54-470, piloted by Major Rex Deaton, was in orbit off Hanoi during the strike and ready to return to base. His escorting F-4 fighters called bingo fuel and left. Regulations called for B-66s to depart a threat area once they lost their fighter escort. An accompanying *Brown Cradle* aircraft did just that. As the drama of the downed F-105F Weasel crew began to unfold below, Major Deaton's crew decided to stay on and continue to suppress AAA radars which were providing guidance to guns firing at the F-105s and F-4s trying to keep the North Vietnamese away from their downed buddies. They turned all of their jammers on the *Firecan* radars. With the AAA radars rendered ineffective, the F-105s and F-4s were able to roll in on repeated strafing runs to suppress the ground fire. The SA-16 piloted by Captains Ralph Angstadt and Bob Morita was now able to land on the water and rescue Larson and Gilroy. (On a subsequent mission Mike Gilroy earned the Air Force Cross, his pilot, Merlyn H. Dethlefsen, the Medal of Honor).[22] The RB-66C crew, including Captain Stan Tippin and First Lieutenant Norman Kasch, was awarded the Distinguished Flying Cross for heroism. The *Brown Cradle* crew that departed the area, although following instructions, received "a royal tongue-lashing from their Wing commander." One has to do the right thing, rules or no rules. Rex Deaton and his crew did the right thing.[23]

CHAPTER NINETEEN

KIBBY TAYLOR FINDS A CLOUD

As 1966 drew to a close there were no signs that the DRV was responding to either the increased pace of the *Rolling Thunder* campaign or to bombing pauses. To the contrary, the North Vietnamese used every opportunity to repair and, if possible, strengthen their air defense network, and exploit the sanctuaries provided by Washington's politicians. Supplies of every kind poured into the port of Haiphong, untouched by the fleet of American warships in the Gulf of Tonkin or by Air Force jets roaring overhead. Although the build-up of American military force continued in the South, the Viet Cong, contrary to Washington's expectations, wouldn't go away. Bien Hoa Air Base, Da Nang, and any number of other American airfields continued to be targets of mortar and daring sapper attacks. The McNamara strategy of gradual escalation seemed to work precisely opposite of the way it was intended. Gradual escalation, in fact, gave the enemy the opportunity to gain experience, to adjust to its powerful adversary and, in time, cope and prevail.

Not only did politicians in Washington have a false and distorted picture of the realities in the former French Indochina, the military response implemented by Secretary McNamara was equally unimaginative and ponderous. The Commander-in-Chief Pacific, CINCPAC, a Navy admiral, sat in a plush headquarters in Hawaii, thousands of miles from the theater of war that he was directing. It is doubtful Generals MacArthur or Eisenhower would have ever thought of fighting Imperial Japan and Nazi Germany that way. CINCPACAF, the Commander-in-Chief United States Air Forces in the Pacific, also had his headquarters in the Hawaiian Islands. Occasional trips to Thailand or Vietnam air bases presumably

L to R standing – Lieutenants Klaus Klause and Wilbur Latham, Major James Tuck and Lieutenant Rabini. A/2C Williams and A/1C Klodgo are their crew chiefs. In three minutes, on November 5, 1966, the two F-4C crews from the 366TFW/480TFS from Da Nang Air Base, downed two MiG-21s attempting to shoot down an EB-66C electronic warfare aircraft near Hanoi.

made up for the lack of actual first hand experience for himself and his generals. None of the generals and admirals directing the war in Vietnam had the smell of gun powder in their nostrils, instead delegating responsibilities to a convoluted and often over staffed headquarters conglomerate which would have done Rube Goldberg proud. The 13th Air Force thought itself close to the war at Clark Air Base in the Philippine Islands to make sound and timely decisions. Actually, only the 2nd Air Division, redesignated 7th Air Force in April 1966 at Tan Son Nhut Air Base could hear the sounds of war. But its commanders and deputies largely ran the air war like their peers, sitting in leather covered high back swivel chairs from behind mahogany desks, rather than being field commanders – a concept that seemed to have gone out of vogue with the end of the Korean War. These multiple headquarters were, of course, staffed by thousands of men. General Spaatz, who at one time ran the strategic air war in Europe, and the first Air Force chief of staff, was known for his disdain of intermediate headquarters. Spaatz would not have believed what the men he once led into combat had wrought. On top of it all, SAC continued to run its own Vietnam air show from Offutt AFB in frigid Omaha, and Andersen Air Base on Guam.

The policies that flowed from this convoluted political and military effort were clearly suspect. Evidently war was to be run on a nonintrusive basis, meaning that the people at home should be inconvenienced by it as little as possible. Nothing like the World War II approach when the nation pulled together and in short order defeated two mighty adversaries in less than four years. On the Air Force side this part-time war mentality expressed itself by making only limited use of reserve and air guard elements. Within the active force the transition from peace to war was slow, even lethargic at times. The 363rd Tactical Reconnaissance Wing at Shaw Air Force Base, in Sumter, South Carolina, was the school house for all RB-66, RF-101 and RF-4C tactical reconnaissance training. By December of 1966 Shaw had yet to establish a viable RTU, Replacement Training Unit, for the combat squadrons in the field. Those squadrons in Vietnam and Thailand would not only experience losses from enemy action or accident, but with the implementation of the 100 mission rule, large numbers of flyers would return home in less than a year's time. Everyone else, from airman to general, would rotate once their 12-month tours were up. If World War II or Korea had been fought on such a part-time basis, the outcomes of those conflicts would have been decidedly different.

On December 31, 1966, the 363rd TRW had all of three RB-66C aircraft to train the replacement electronic warfare officers for the two combat squadrons deployed in Thailand. It had no simulator for the Ravens to train on. When one was finally procured it turned out to be a former SAC RB-47H simulator from the 55th SRW with only minor modifications to accommodate RB-66C differences. I trained on that simulator when I flew with the 55th SRW; trained on it again at Shaw before being sent to Takhli. It provided little that could be referred to as simulation of an actual signal environment or an aircraft configuration representative of the EB-66C.¹ The result: when the first replacement EWOs arrived at Takhli they received little more than academic training. Their first combat missions provided the flying training they should have received at Shaw. The initial RB-66 force that arrived at Takhli, regardless if pilot, navigator, or electronic warfare officer, was highly trained and experienced. Most having flown in the aircraft for many years. As they departed the combat zone, they took with them an irreplaceable level of experience and insight into an aircraft not all that common in the Air Force inventory. They were replaced by SAC flyers who came from a very different weapon system environment, and by young lieutenants just out of flying school. Both combat effectiveness and flying safety suffered as a result.

John Matlock was a 'green EWO,' in his words; a young lieutenant undergoing electronic warfare training at Mather AFB. "Our instructor said that he needed three volunteers for SEA, and that we single guys should go ahead and volunteer as all sorts of benefits would accrue, including choice of assignment after we finished our Southeast Asia tour of duty. Three of us volunteered and were short circuited straight to Takhli in January 1967. We did not even go to Shaw. My first ride in an Air Force jet was a combat mission over North Vietnam. This was just a couple of days after the John Fer shoot down [John Fer was the pilot of EB-66C 55-387 which was downed on February 4, 1967, by an SA-2 missile]. I completed 100 missions in August and put in for my choice of assignment as promised. SAC wasn't even my hundredth choice, but that's where I went. At least I got to marry the girl I left behind. I signed into my new unit at Fairchild AFB, Washington. They were so glad to see me as they were about to deploy to SEA. I explained that I had my tour of duty in SEA and they couldn't send me back until all other EWOs had gone over. I wound up with two *Arc Light* tours in B-52s."²

Frank Widic came from a little town on the eastern shore of Maryland named after a big namesake – Berlin. Tobacco and chickens were the products of choice. Frank was looking for something more than that. He joined the aviation cadet program, graduating in December 1964 from navigator training at James Connally AFB in Waco, Texas. Frank then completed electronic warfare officer training at Mather AFB. "I applied for B-66s and was the only one in my class selected. My next assignment was the 9th TRS at Shaw. When I arrived in September 1965 there was hardly anyone there. They were all in Southeast Asia. There was no formal training program, there was nothing. A friend had an assignment to Takhli, his wife was eight months pregnant, so I volunteered to take his place. Just before I left Shaw I flew on an RB-66B for nearly three hours. That was my first flight in a B-66 and my first flight in an Air Force jet. My second flight was on December 14 in position number 1 on an RB-66C. I remember that flight vividly because one of the Thuds we were protecting got hit. His wing man was screaming 'Get out. Get out.' He never punched out."[3]

The Air Staff and TAC had been so busy phasing the B-66 out of the inventory that when war came in earnest and the situation changed, no one at the Pentagon or at TAC headquarters took a hard look at future requirements. As a result young second lieutenants straight out of flight training learned by doing over North Vietnam. To their credit, and to the credit of the Air Force instructors who prepared them at Mather, they performed well. On November 1, 1967, Air Force finally bit the bullet and came out with a formal replacement policy. "The personnel situation resulting from the USAF commitment in SEA," wrote Lieutenant General Horace M. Wade, Deputy Chief of Staff for Personnel, "demands urgent action by commanders and personnel managers at all levels. The Air Force has reached the point where it must soon join the other services in returning some personnel to SEA involuntarily to support combat operations and to preclude mission degradation. It is Air Force policy to prevent the involuntary return of any member to that area until other similarly qualified personnel have served a tour there ... The Chief of Staff further directed that policies governing deferrals of personnel selected for SEA be reviewed in an effort to reduce the number of personnel excused or deferred from assignment."[4]

The assignment policy, however, like the draft, had plenty of loopholes. Special security clearances were a sure way for many to avoid a combat assignment. The Air Force Chief's letter directed close scrutiny of such deferments. The result was that as time went on older and older staff personnel appeared in aircraft cockpits, many not always well suited for the type of aircraft they were assigned to fly. While the B-66 crews in the early days of the war were principally lieutenants and captains, by 1970, majors and lieutenant colonels proliferated. Our adversaries in the meantime manning radars, anti-aircraft guns and surface to air missile sites had no 100 mission rule or one-year tour limits. They served for the duration of the war or until they died, which ever came first. As a result, they developed a very high level of expertise, in time learning to cope even with all but the most severe EB-66 jamming.

In late 1965 the Navy introduced the ALQ-51 deception jammer which "rather than trying to overpower radar receivers, created a number of false returns on the SA-2 radar screens. The ALQ-51s initially gave the Vietnamese problems. For a three month period in the summer of 1966 the Navy aircraft loss rate in SAM-defended areas dropped precipitously ... By 1967 the Vietnamese became so proficient against the Navy's deception jamming that during an engagement on 13

August 1967, two SA-2 missiles hit and destroyed three Navy A-4s."[5] Thereafter, EB-66E aircraft which came into the inventory about that time, flew a significant number of missions in support of Navy strike aircraft on the Gulf of Tonkin side of the DRV.

Major Kibby Taylor last flew the B-66 in 1960 when still assigned to the 11th TRS at Yokota. After the RB-66s were retired in 1960, he spent the remainder of his tour at 5th Air Force Headquarters at Yokota. Then he volunteered for KC-135 tankers, and was given an assignment to C-124 transports at Dover AFB, Delaware. That unwelcome assignment came to an end when he was selected to attend Air Command and Staff College at Maxwell AFB, Montgomery, Alabama. "Out of Air Command and Staff I had an assignment to B-66s at Chambley, France, but that was cancelled and I was sent directly to Takhli. Lieutenant Colonel Dick Keller was with me and we went through Snake School together at Clark before reporting to Takhli. When we arrived at Takhli they told Dick he was the commander of the 41st TEWS. The previous commander left after flying his 100th mission, and the operations officer was leaving the next day. I became the operations officer for the squadron. There went the much prized continuity of command. Dick and I knew nothing of anything about the operation. It was to be a busy time for us.

"Two tactical electronic warfare squadrons were at Takhli, the 41TEWS and the 6460TEWS, which later became the 42nd TEWS. It was in 1966 that Air Force changed our squadron designations from Tactical Reconnaissance to Tactical Electronic Warfare. The aircraft were re-designated from RB-66 to EB-66. Nothing ever stays the same. Both of the squadrons were assigned to the 432nd Tactical Reconnaissance Wing at Udorn, with maintenance and other support provided by the 355th Tactical Fighter Wing, the host organization at Takhli. We were under the operational control of 7th Air Force in Saigon, and assigned to 13th Air Force at Clark Air Base in the Philippines. 7/13th Air Force at Udorn was the on-site coordinator of things. In administrative and personnel matters we were controlled by Headquarters USAF. Such was the way our Air Force was organized to train, fly and fight. Many of the EB-66Cs assigned to the 41TEWS were the same aircraft I flew in Japan. Then they had a pair of radar controlled 20mm guns in the tail, but the guns had been replaced with a tail-cone housing chaff dispensers and some jammers, giving us in the C-model a total of nine. Fortunately I had been qualified as an instructor pilot in the B-66 and had operational experience with the passive electronic surveillance mission and the larger crew of the C-model. I had confidence in the aircraft in spite of it being under-powered, resulting in long take-off rolls. We were operating at maximum gross weights of 83,000 pounds or heavier. Most new pilots had no experience

The B-66B bomber version of the Destroyer, of which 72 were built, could carry 14 750 pound. 4 3,000 pound or 3 5,000 pound conventional bombs. When assigned to the 47th BW the aircraft initially carried one Mark V (Fat Man) nuclear bomb, later two Mark 28 hydrogen bombs.

The day/night photo RB-66B carried either 48 flash bombs in a chain driven rack or 104 M112 flash cartridges. Its APN-82 doppler navigation system was the first to be installed in a production aircraft providing automatic position, ground speed, drift angle and heading data.

The RB-66C was the tactical equivalent of the SAC RB-47H strategic reconnaissance aircraft. Its four Ravens, seated in the bomb-bay area of the aircraft, were tasked to detect and locate hostile radars. Over time the RB-66C acquired a substantial jamming capability which the RB-47H did not posses. The C-model is easily identifiable by the wing-tip APD-4 antenna pods.

The WB-66D weather reconnaissance aircraft was built in lieu of 36 RB-66C aircraft. It housed two weather observers in the aft compartment. The WB-66D never reached its potential because the atmospheric sensor and necessary in-flight communication equipment was never procured. As a result the D-model was the first aircraft in the series to be retired from active service.

The MD-1 fire control system, initially installed in all versions of the B-66, consisted of a gun-laying radar and two 20mm tail guns with 500 rounds of ammunition each. The guns were replaced starting in the late '50s with ECM tail cones consisting of ALE-2 chaff dispensers and ECM jammers. With the loss of the gunner and his radar the pilot lost the only means of observing the aft quadrant of the aircraft.

Cockpit of a B-66B Brown Cradle, a former B-66B bomber, 13 of which were converted in the late '50s into ECM support aircraft. Their NATO role was to accompany B-66 and F-100D strike aircraft in time of war and jam enemy AAA and SAM associated radars.

The first RB-66C, 54-459, was delivered to the 42nd TRS of the 10th TRW at Spangdahlem AB, Germany, on November 28, 1956. In the Spring of 1957 459 was the star of an open house attended by over 30,000 Germans. Named the City of Wittlich by its mayor, the city's coat of arms was ceremoniously painted on the nose section of 459, barely visible in the picture.

An RB-66B on final approach to Spangdahlem AB, Germany, on a not so common blue sky day. RB-66Bs, assigned to the 10th TRW, arrived in numbers in 1957, replacing trouble plagued RB-57As and aging RB-26s.

A 1st TRS/10TRW RB-66B turning off the active runway at Spangdahlem AB, ready to release its billowing brake chute. The B-66's landing roll was nearly as long as its take-off roll, 7,000+ feet, using speed brakes, brake chute and anti-skid brakes.

The 10th TRW became famous for its mass fly-bys on ceremonial occasions, launching 12 aircraft from each of its four squadrons. In the foreground is an RB-66B of the 19th TRS, three RB-66Cs from the 42nd TRS, with ECM tail cones rather than guns fly in the background. 1958.

An RB-66B of the 363TRW from Shaw AFB, SC, piloted by Randy Johnston over the Atlantic, July 1958, enroute to Incirlik AB, Turkey, in Operation Double Trouble – the 1958 Lebanon Crisis. It was the first employment of TAC's Composite Air Strike Force, CASF, concept instituted by TAC's commander General Otto P. Weyland.

L to R – Lieutenants Johnson and Jefferson, and A/1C Spotts, the gunner, in front of their aircraft at Incirlik. Maintenance crew tents along the flight line are visible in the background. 1958.

Maintenance crews at Incirlik inspecting bullet holes in an RB-66B after returning from a low level reconnaissance mission over Lebanon and Syria. 1958.

Three 30-caliber automatic weapon bullet holes are circled in red on RB-66B 53-470. Several RB-66B aircraft were hit by 30 and 50-caliber bullets while flying over Lebanon and Syria during Operation Double Trouble.

The seven 363TRW RB-66B aircrews which participated in Operation Double Trouble in front of one of their aircraft at Shaw AFB, SC, in September 1958. Pilots in front, navigators in row two, and gunners in last row standing. They called themselves the 'Turkey Trotters.'

A widely circulated 1958 photo of TAC's first line combat aircraft taken over Shaw AFB, SC. A KB-50 tanker, only released by SAC to TAC weeks earlier, with an RF-101C photo reconnaissance aircraft on the left wing drogue, an F-100D fighter bomber on the right wing drogue, and an RB-66B photo reconnaissance aircraft on the tail drogue, followed by two C-130As. The picture represented 'Opie' Weylands Composite Air Strike Force concept – 'Have airplanes, will travel anywhere in the world.'

Lieutenant Bob Webster's aircraft at England AFB, LA. Assigned to the 16th TRS at Shaw, Bob was flying in support of US Army maneuvers. On a low level night run he ran into a flock of birds, an occasion he would never forget. May 7, 1957.

In August of 1957 Bob Webster and the 16th TRS moved to North AFB, SC, a satellite of Shaw AFB, during runway repairs at Shaw.

Lieutenant Webster while at England AFB in May 1957 admires the names of his crew and crew chief freshly painted on the wheel-well door of his aircraft.

Captain Vern Johnson in front of his aircraft. The left windshield has been removed after cracking in flight, one of many problems that bedeviled the RB-66 in its early years.

Four 16th TRS/363TRW RB-66Bs at England AFB, LA, May 1957.

RB-66Bs from Shaw AFB passing through Chateroux AB, France, in September 1958.

RB-66C 54-470 of the 42TRS/10TRW at RAF Chelveston, England, in 1959. The 10TRW moved from Spangdahlem AB in August 1959 to bases in England when France insisted on the removal of American nuclear armed aircraft, which were moved to bases in Germany.

54-459, the City of Wittlich, taking off from RAF Chelveston, its new home, after leaving Germany. 459 would fly for nearly 20 years out of bases in England, France, Thailand and return to Germany before being retired. I flew 459 many times, and it always brought me home.

An RB-66B from the 16th TRS/363TRW at Shaw, flown by Bob Webster, is refueling from a Langley AFB, VA, based KB-50 tanker. Refueling from a slow KB-50 was a challenge for B-66 pilots, especially if they had to refuel from wing drogues. Once the B-66 became heavy with fuel it was a 'bear' hanging on to the tanker.

Lieutenant Bob Stamm, 11TRS, behind a KB-50 refueling tanker. Both aircraft were based at Yokota AB, Japan, and assigned to the 67th TRW. The KB-50s released by SAC to TAC only in 1958, were forced into retirement in 1964 because of severe airframe corrosion. Those based at Yokota were in such bad shape that they were not flown home, but dismantled in place.

Once the KB-50s retired, SAC became the single manager for air refueling assets. The KC-97 tanker was a great improvement over the KB-50, but still too slow. 53-441 was used extensively at Edwards AFB, CA, for test and evaluation purposes by both Douglas and Air Force test pilots.

The KC-135 jet tanker revolutionized aerial refueling. While newer aircraft used the high-pressure boom refueling method, older aircraft such as the B-66 and the F-100 required a basket, a drogue, be attached to the boom to allow them to get their fuel. The F-105 was the only tactical aircraft configured to use either boom or drogue and probe refueling.

An EB-66E piloted by Captain Bob Welch, 42TEWS/388TFW, Korat RTAFB, in Vietnam era camouflage coming in to get its fuel from a KC-135. 1972.

What a perfect hook-up between tanker and receiver looks like.

In 1960 Shaw based RB-66C electronic reconnaissance crews and aircraft from the 9th TRS began regular deployments to RAF Chelveston to gain operational experience flying along Warsaw Pact borders – Operation Swamp Fox. Two aircrews and staff personnel are shown posing before one of their aircraft at Shaw AFB before departing for the UK.

A B-66B bomber, 54-418, of the 84th Bomb Squadron at RAF Sculthorpe is receiving a post flight inspection by a maintenance team led by SSGT James Lord.

RB-66Bs of the 1st TRS/10TRW at RAF Alconbury in September 1959 soon after their move from Spangdahlem AB.

A 1st TRS RB-66B, 4-520, taking off on a rare clear day from RAF Alconbury, Sept 1959.

4-520 about to suck up its gear after taking off from RAF Alconbury. The 10th Wing falling star is clearly visible on the vertical stabilizer.

RB-66B formation, 19TRS, TRAB, France, 1963. Crew of aircraft from which picture was taken: Capt Kellum, pilot; Capt Colosimo, nav; A/1C Phillips, flight engineer.

In 1962 the 19th and 42nd TRS moved to Toul-Rosieres AB, France, TRAB. TRAB had the typical layout for a French air base, a runway flanked by two daisy-like parking areas on one end, and a third at the other, to accommodate three aircraft squadrons. The picture shows the 42nd TRS parking and dispersal area at TRAB.

A 2008 overhead satellite shot of TRAB shows that little has changed over the intervening years. (Google)

19TRS RB-66B formation, TRAB, 1963.

Chambley AB, France. 42TRS aircraft are shown on their hardstands, lower left, while deployed to Chambley AB during TRAB runway construction from May to October 1963. Picture was taken from a 19TRS aircraft.

RB-66Cs from the 9th TRS, Shaw AFB, SC, after initially deploying to Tan Son Nhut, SVN, arrived at Tahkli, RTAFB, Thailand, in May 1965. R-L – Dick Wilson, a fabled RB-66 flyer who acquired over 5,000 hours in the RB-66 and Adrian 'Hoss' Cordoni. Bill Keels on left.

1/Lt John 'Jack' Norden, 9TRS/363TRW, posing in home-made survival vest before his aircraft after arriving at Takhli from Tan Son Nhut AB, SVN. May 1965.

Airman Richard Erbe, left, unknown crew chief, right. By October 1965 the first B-66B Brown Cradles arrived at Takhli from Europe. Erbe was an enlisted ECM operator. Once the Cradles were modified with receivers and tunable jammers, the enlisted men were replaced by EWOs.

Takhli village as seen from the air.

Takhli's 10,000 foot runway. On hot days with a full fuel load, EB-66s used every foot of it.

This Japanese-built structure served as the 355TFW hospital. The signs in front give direction and mileage to diverse cities in the world, mostly American.

Crew quarters 'hooches' built of teakwood. These are airconditioned, many were open air.

F-105 fighter bombers – the planes we were there to protect from radar guided AAA and SAMs.

Takhli flight line 1968. RC coded aircraft belonged to the 41st TEWS; RH to the 42nd.

Heading north to the 'pocket' above Hanoi.

Two back-end EB-66C Ravens – Hank Shimabakuro and Jim Handschumacher.

Joe Snoy and Bob Sherman, two Ravens, in front of the 41st TEWS squadron building at Takhli.

Last mission for Joe Snoy, second from right – mission #123, July 1968. A time for a champagne toasts and a subsequent dunking in the swimming pool.

EB-66 noses and F-105 tails and open canopies on the Takhli flight line.

Bob Hope was accompanied by Raquel Welch, Dianna Carol – Miss USA – and Art Buchwald. 1967.

Colonel Heath Bottomly, 355TFW commander in 1969 on the right, his vice commander on the left.

In October 1969 the 41st TEWS was inactivated, its aircraft transferred to Kadena and Spangdahlem – the Brown Cradles went to the bone-yard. 54-459, here shown after returning from a combat mission, returned to its old home of Spangdahlem, Germany.

A year later the 42nd TEWS transferred from Takhli to Korat and to the 388th TFW. 42nd TEWS aircraft are shown taking off in support of Linebacker II operations – the bombing of Hanoi/Haiphong that brought the NVN to the negotiating table.

The Air Force frowned on pictorial art on its airplanes, but the day Bob Welch, the 42nd TEWS maintenance officer had sharks teeth painted on his aircraft General John Ryan, the Air Force Chief of Staff, came to visit and loved what he saw. The wing commander felt differently, let Bob keep the teeth on his airplane, but allowed no others to be decorated.

Party suits – 42nd TEWS crews at Korat RTAFB, Thailand. L-R Captain Welch, Lt Broadaway Welch's navigator sitting next to him; Lt/Col Giannangeli, center, standing, and Lt Savilago.

The 19th TEWS formed at Kadena AB, Okinawa, in October 1969. An EB-66E of the 19TEWS on the Kadena ramp.

The 39th TEWS activated at Spangdahlem AB in April 1969, a longtime RB-66 base. Spangdahlem was a satellite to Bitburg AB and the 36TFW. In January 1972 Spangdahlem became home of the 52nd TFW.

EB-66E of the 39th TEWS at Spangdahlem AB, Germany.

The fate of old airplanes – 54-465, a C-model, is displayed at Shaw AFB, SC, the one-time 'reconnaissance school house' of the United States Air Force.

The author and son, Lt/Col Charles Samuel, who flew into Wright-Patterson AFB, Ohio, in an A-10 to be present for the dedication ceremonies of the B-66 memorial at the Museum of the United States Air Force in 2004. Charles served in the 52nd TFW at Spangdahlem in the 1990s.

operating the B-66 at such heavy weights. I recall one pilot who came in when I did, as he neared lift-off he retracted his gear on the first skip, and as the gear was coming up he was settling. He got airborne but only after grinding two inches off the ECM antennas on the belly of the aircraft. We thought he'd belly in, but he made it off.

"The take-off roll was a very critical phase of flight for the B-66 in a high temperature environment. It may have been a 'lead sled' and could not outmaneuver a fighter, but it was a stable platform and responded well if you flew it with authority. Pilot visibility was limited making it difficult to see threats approaching from below and within a 90 degree cone from the rear. That's one thing I liked about having a tail gunner. He could see that rear quadrant on his radar. We were essentially defenseless against fighters and very limited in our ability to see and evade strikes from surface to air missiles. If attacked by either, our best defense was high G turns, which could only be sustained by applying full power in a rapid descent. Adding to our dilemma was the fact that we frequently could not tell which direction to turn in. We believed our jammers were very effective against AAA radars, and we were not scheduled to fly without fighter cover in areas where the threat from MiGs was high.

"Our job was to protect our strike forces by degrading the capability of enemy radar controlled weapons. In the heavily defended Route Packs 6A and 6B, the Hanoi/Haiphong area, we usually flew an EB-66C and an EB-66B or E. We flew in trail formation in the threat area to always have one aircraft in level flight, since jamming effectiveness was reduced in a turn. To do the job my squadron had about twenty crews assigned at any one time, with one pilot, one navigator and four Ravens per crew. When I arrived at Takhli some of our navigators had come directly out of navigation training at Mather AFB, others had been withdrawn from non-flying jobs, and only a few had recent operational experience. Three quarters of our EWOs came directly out of electronic warfare training into a combat assignment. The experience level had really declined. Most of the missions we flew were over North Vietnam.

"The policy at the time was that for every 20 missions flown, a month was taken off your one year tour. So after seven or eight months most of the guys were rotating out of the squadron which resulted in a near total drain of experience. We had a five mission checkout procedure. You'd start out flying in the lower Route Packs – one, two, three and four. An instructor pilot would sit in the gunners seat in the C-model and observe you. The first three flights must have been routine for me because I can't recall anything spectacular, other than the intense activity on the flight line during mission launch. My fourth mission was in the lower two Route Packs on the east side over the Gulf of Tonkin requiring air refueling. I was a little apprehensive, this was my first night refueling from a KC-135. I wanted to set a good example as the squadron operations officer. The flight did not get off to a good start. Someone set off his survival beacon and we had to listen to that eerie sound through take-off. The beacon did not fade with distance, so it was one of my guys. We had to listen to it for the next six hours. They do not put the beacons where you can easily get to them in flight. Once we landed, it turned out that the beeper noise came from my own survival pack.

"The last of five missions was my flight check – up North in the Hanoi area, November 5, 1966. The instructor pilot sat in the gunner's seat. I was lead, Newark 1, and an EB-66B, Newark 2, was to follow in trail. We were to cover a large strike near Hanoi. Newark 2 aborted while climbing out and it was too late to launch a spare, so we went on as a single ship to do the best we could with our nine jammers instead of thirty. We rendezvoused with Opal flight, four F-4Cs out of Da Nang Air Base. When I told Opal 1 lead that Newark 2 had aborted, he advised Opal 3 and 4 to climb to a higher altitude to conserve fuel because they didn't get topped off by their tanker. We started jamming the longer range acquisition radars to degrade their ability to acquire the in-bound strike force. Entering North Vietnam Opal 1 and 2 took up defensive positions behind and above us. We went into the pocket northwest of Hanoi, just on the edge of the known SAM rings and the 20 mile buffer zone along the Chinese border. The entry point into the pocket was only about 12 miles wide and it took some maneuvering to get in there.

"About the time our time on target was up, I was listening to the 105s coming off their strike, *Red Crown* called me by call sign, 'Newark 1, bandits 290 radial, 50 miles Bulls Eye.' Bulls Eye was Hanoi. *Red Crown*, a radar picket ship in the Gulf of Tonkin, usually didn't do that. As a rule they gave an area warning. My Ravens picked up the call and immediately began tracking the MiGs IFF, Identification Friend or Foe. So I alerted Major James 'Friar' Tuck flying Opal 1 to watch for MiGs at 12 o'clock. Things began to happen fast. The Ravens picked up the IFF of one MiG in our six o'clock position. I advised Opal 1. Then all hell broke loose. From a position to my right rear Opal 1's guy in back called, 'MiG!' and Opal 2 also saw the MiG coming between the two F-4Cs headed straight for us. The F-4Cs dropped their wing tanks to clean up their airplanes and get ready for a fight when the second MiG-21 came in between them. Listening to the Ravens tape at debriefing it sounded like the first MiG was locked on to us and ready to fire. The MiG pilot fired a missile, and I heard Friar calling, 'Break right, B-66. Break right.' That wasn't my call-sign. It took me a microsecond to register, but about the second time he called he didn't have to call a third. I went full power, hard right bank, full right rudder to start the nose down, followed by a hard pull to haul that mother around. About that time I heard my navigator, Jack

McGinn, repeat, 'Break right and all the way down.' I could not see the MiG and was totally dependent on Opal lead for guidance. The missile came screaming by us to my left. I was going down rapidly in a tight spiral at above .92 Mach, redline speed, into a hard shudder, near a high speed stall, pulling all the Gs I could. Then I let up a little, banking, continuing my tight spiral. I was right up against Mach 1. Friar later told me that he lit his afterburners and went through the Mach going after the MiG. I was going down, the MiG was on me, and Opal lead, Friar Tuck, was on the MiG. A second MiG was on Friar's tail, and Opal 2 was behind that MiG. Opal 2 called, 'Lead, you've got a MiG on your tail.'

"Friar coolly replied, 'How are you doing on him?' We had five aircraft following in trail down a steep spiral. Friar Tuck told me later that he flew his F-4C very close to the MiG-21 to try to drive him off us, and that we were pulling too many Gs for him or the MiG to get off a missile. The MiG did pull off and swung out to the left for a better position to get off a missile. We were down below 20,000 feet, and Friar called, 'He's doing a whifferdill on you. Take it back under him.' So I broke left. When I reversed the spiral, I cut under the MiG and denied him a shot at us. By this time we were down to 15,000 feet and I was about to run out of ideas, altitude and airspeed. Then I saw a little white cloud in an otherwise clear sky to my right. I pulled over to the right and flew into that cloud. As soon as I hit that cloud I did a real tight turn to the left, heading down to 10,000 feet, and continuing to turn. I could not sustain the high turn rate, and rapidly lost airspeed at full power. I had to ease off and look for a new solution. The MiG pursuing me went right on through the cloud, and Friar did too. While the MiG was distracted looking for me, Friar got a missile off, exploding up the MiG's tail pipe. Friar watched the MiG pilot eject from his aircraft. In the meantime Opal 2 fired a *Sidewinder* up the tail of the second MiG as it was positioning itself to fire on Opal 1. I heard Opal 2's call as I was fighting for our lives, 'MiG splash into the ground.'

"I was down to 10,000 feet and all the jammers were off line because of the Gs we pulled. I wanted altitude. Get back up there and away from the AAA. The Ravens were warning me that *Firecan* AAA radars were locked on to us as well as a *Fansong* SAM radar. Then they picked up a missile launch signal, but we did not see the missile. I had to do a little trade off between airspeed and altitude, and I climbed back up to 15,000 feet. The F-4 guys were shouting with joy, debriefing while they were flying. I said to them, 'Hey guys, cool it. I want to get out of here.' So we headed out of there and went home, escorted out of the area by two of the four F-4s of Opal flight. They flew the airplane the next day. All they found was a cracked aileron bracket as a result of me pulling all the high Gs.

"When I was in Japan in the late '50s with the 11th TRS I used to go out in the local training area and fly that thing around doing engine stalls, pulling hard turns, just wring the crap out of the airplane. I'd feel that 'Douglas rock' rattle and shake, but never had any qualms that I couldn't make that airplane do anything I wanted. Douglas put those airplanes together rock solid. Doing that stuff back then is what saved my life that day near Hanoi. God must have put that cloud there. Things like that make a believer out of you. The entire encounter took place between 30,000 and 9,000 feet altitude and lasted 90 seconds.

"Later in the evening I talked to Major James E. Tuck, we all called him Friar, and his back-seater, First Lieutenant John J. Rabini, and the crew of Opal 2, Lieutenants Wilbur J. Latham and Klaus J. Klause. I thanked them for saving us from the MiGs and congratulated them on their kills. I had a friend stationed at Da Nang act as my proxy, buying the Opal flight crews a well deserved dinner and drinks. I elected not to tell my wife, who was living at Shaw. About ten days later I received a letter from her including a news clipping about two F-4C crews shooting down two MiGs and saving a B-66. 'Maybe you know someone,' she wrote 'on that plane. Please give them this clipping.' She had no idea it was me."[6]

First Lieutenant Klaus Klause was flying the back seat of Opal 2 trying to kill the MiG on Opal 1's tail. The MiG "reversed his turn and started a vertical pull to the left. I looked at the radar and it showed 200 knots overtake and we were inside a mile. The next thing I heard was the whoosh of a missile leaving our jet. I looked over Joe's right shoulder and saw the corkscrew path of our *Sidewinder* fly directly toward the tail of the MiG-21. It hit the aft section and a red fireball followed. At this time we were smoking by the right side of the MiG. As if in slow motion we watched it snap roll and start a downward spiral, getting a glance at an open cockpit. Of course we were excited and made one more 360 over the trundling airplane – proclaiming our aerial victory. 'We got one, we got one,' Joe and I shouted over the radio, when the calm voice of the EB-66 pilot brought us back to our senses, informing us 'I'm OK. Now watch for other MiGs.' We checked our fuel and looked for the rest of the flight – no joy. We had 4,000 pounds left in our tanks, not the ideal fuel quantity sixty miles from Hanoi. We started a climb into the ionosphere and got vectors to the nearest tanker, when two more MiG-21s passed above us, heading toward the Chinese border. On the way home we learned that Friar and Rabini also got their MiG, and Opal 3 and 4 found the EB-66 and escorted it to safety. There was a hell of a celebration at the DOOM (Da Nang Officers' Open Mess) club that night as our two MiGs gave the 480th TFS its fourth and fifth MiG kill."[7] It was the 22nd and 23rd MiG kill of the war over North Vietnam.

Captain Roland Valentine was the Raven two on Kibby Taylor's aircraft and had a uniquely different perspective of the entire engagement. He saw and heard the world around him on the electronic receivers he operated at his position. "I intercepted the MiGs radio transmissions which were getting stronger, and from the directional strobes I was getting from my ALA-6 direction finder it seemed they were moving from abeam to aft. I relayed this information to our pilot, who relayed it to the F-4s. The MiGs flew right through the F-4s and attacked us. Upon seeing the MiGs, Friar Tuck then called out, 'Break right 66, break right.' Kibby, apparently unsure of what he heard then said something like 'What did he say?' Our very cool navigator, Jack McGinn, said in a calm and firm voice, 'Break right NOW, all the way down,' which Kibby did with great skill and determination. About this time the lead MiG fired a missile. As the left engine went up from Kibby's right break I saw the missile pass underneath harmlessly. We continued to trade G-forces for altitude until what I thought was about ground level in the Red River valley. There were many *Fansong* and BG06 missile guidance radars up, but none fired, probably because they were told to stand down for fear of hitting their own aircraft," they had shot down one of their own MiG-21s on another occasion. "I recorded the MiG conversations with their GCI controllers while all this was going on. When we got back to Takhli our electronic analysis center passed the tape to 7th Air Force in Saigon. I was rousted out of bed early the next morning by a very angry colonel who chewed me out for recording politically sensitive information. Apparently the pilot of the lead MiG was not Vietnamese, but Chinese."[8]

Later on in the war the North Koreans would send an entire squadron to bolster a depleted DRV fighter force. The Chinese stuck their noses into the DRV on other occasions as well. Frank Widic was lead Raven on an RB-66C on June 29, 1966, part of the force that conducted the first strike against the Hanoi petroleum storage sites. "One of our Ravens, Jim Osborne, spoke fluent Mandarin Chinese. Jim would sit in position 1 or 2 and pick up the GCI controllers. When the intelligence people debriefed him they would tell him that under no circumstances would he mention this to anyone."[9] Political Washington was extremely nervous, paranoid is probably a better word, about anything Chinese. A see nothing, hear nothing kind of mentality prevailed.

Don Harding remembers Friar Tuck. "Larry Wensil was one of the Ravens on the C-model that got jumped by the MiGs. Larry made a recording of the intercept and the shoot-down of the MiGs. Friar was a Virginian with a deep southern drawl. The tape opens up with Friar Tuck calling out, 'B-66 break right, break right ... ' in that deep southern drawl of his. Made for a good laugh after it was all over. We called him Friar because he was pear shaped. Great guy and an even greater pilot."[10]

"In late November 1966 7th Air Force scheduled a tactics symposium," Kibby Taylor recalls, "to discuss operational tactics for Air Force units involved with strike missions over North Vietnam. The symposium was hosted by Colonels Robin Olds and Chappy James, commander and vice commander of the 8th Tactical Fighter Wing at Ubon. I attended along with two of our EWOs. The importance of electronic support for air strikes was given emphasis when Colonel Robin Olds chose to chair the ECM discussion panel and displayed good knowledge of the technical aspects of electronic warfare. On Christmas day I flew a single EB-66C to support strikes in the lower Route Packs. Occasionally I could see the ground near Mu Gia Pass. The area was covered with bomb craters and looked like a different planet. As we departed our orbit I contacted a radar site for clearance. The operator's response was 'Roger Nelson,' followed by clearance to Channel 49, Takhli TACAN. This routine response was like a personal Christmas greeting – my navigator's name was Roger Nelson. Small things mean a lot and lightened our spirits as we returned that Christmas day from a combat mission. We all rejoiced over the MiG sweep Robin Olds led the first of January 1967, bagging 7 MiG-21s. I envied the men who flew the EB-66C in support of that mission."[11]

CHAPTER TWENTY

TO CHANGE AN AIR FORCE

The Tactical Air Command and its sister overseas commands, USAFE and PACAF, always had been a 'Kick the tires, light the fires, first off is the leader,' kind of operation. Some bomber generals ran the show for a while, but they didn't change the hearts and minds of their pilots. The arrival of the nuclear bomb constrained the long cherished, free-wheeling approach of taking the fight to the enemy ala *Zemke's Wolf Pack*. Vietnam looked like it was an opportunity to get back to the good old days. It turned out it wasn't. By 1965 TAC and USAFE combined had all of 22 RB-66C tactical electronic reconnaissance aircraft remaining in their inventories. They were augmented by 13 aging B-66B *Brown Cradles*, former bombers with their bellies stuffed with 22 noise jammers. That was pretty much all there was when it came to electronic countermeasure capabilities in the tactical air forces. When the North Vietnamese changed the rules of air warfare by introducing not only radar guided AAA, but the SA-2 SAM system as well, our strike fighters were in trouble. On the afternoon of July 24, 1965, the SA-2 missile made its spectacular entry into the air war over North Vietnam when it blew an F-4C out of the sky and severely damaged three others. It was a shock to the planners in Saigon, Clark Air Base in the Philippines, Hawaii and Washington. Yet the response to the DRVs introduction of SA-2 SAMs was slow, even lethargic.

Not until October did the Air Staff come around to releasing six *Brown Cradles* from their USAFE Cold War commitment, well after the SA-2 entered the fray in the North. The remaining seven *Brown Cradles* didn't arrive at Takhli until late May 1966. Additional C-models arrived at an equally glacial pace. By

EB-66 noise jamming on radar scopes, such as that shown above, deprived North Vietnamese radar operators of the target information they desperately needed to aim their AAA guns and surface to air missiles against attacking F-105 and F-4 strike aircraft. The effectiveness of EB-66 jamming is attested to by the frequent NVA attempts to intercept and down EB-66 aircraft, and the creation of special MiG-21 and SAM units whose sole task it was to take down these hated American planes.

the time the last *Brown Cradle* aircraft arrived at Takhli, *Rolling Thunder Phase IV* was being implemented, and the North Vietnamese integrated air defenses had grown quantitatively and improved significantly in performance. Air losses rose correspondingly. The RB-66 aircraft and crews, their value obviously initially not well understood, suddenly were in high demand to suppress the growing DRV air defense threat. Although the RB-66Cs and the *Brown Cradles* were well equipped to handle the DRVs AAA and missile acquisition radars, the SA-2s *Fansong* track-while-scan radar was a challenge for the B-66 crews to defeat. Even the most ardent 'kick the tires and light the fires' TAC flyer saw the writing on the wall – they needed help, and soon. When the air war against the North first began it may have been viewed as *a piece of cake*, but by "mid-1967 it became necessary to cover strike forces in Laos with EB-66 ECM aircraft and *Wild Weasel* F-105s. The air war had changed dramatically in our disfavor from what it had been in early 1966."[1]

Unlike TAC, the Air Force R&D community had taken a somewhat more measured approach to ECM and its development. After the loss of two U-2 aircraft over the Soviet Union and Cuba to SA-2 missiles, and several more over Communist China, Air Force Systems Command initiated efforts to develop self-protection countermeasures for individual aircraft. Several approaches were tried. Some of the new countermeasures were dismal failures, acting more like beacons for the SA-2 missile crews who were tracking overflying U-2s.[2] August Seefluth, a World War II flyer whose B-24 had been shot down late in the war over Hungary, served as a Raven in the 10th TRS in Germany and England. In 1962 he found himself at Wright-Patterson AFB as a project engineer on a new and exciting project – the QRC-160-1 ECM self-protection ECM pod. "When I got there, General Electric at Utica, New York, had just received a contract to develop a podded barrage self-protection noise jamming system to be carried by fighter aircraft. It was supposed to go on the RF-110, which became the RF-4C. We tried to get the pod development into normal production channels, but TAC gave us little encouragement, so we stuck with the QRC approach. Quick reaction meant that anything we produced would be contractor supported and not enjoy the conventional in-house support of a normal weapon system. Our flight test airplane was an F-100 and our pilot was Captain Ed White, the first Astronaut to venture outside the capsule. He later died in the Apollo fire. By the time I left the office we had 200 ECM pods on order with GE."[3]

The QRC-160 was the first instance where equipment of that nature was pod configured for external mounting on a fighter. The pod took up a weapon's station, something TAC didn't like. The QRC-160 was optimized against AAA radars such as the *Whiff* and *Firecan*, and the *Fansong* SAM radar. It was a system specifically designed to provide self-protection for a single aircraft, complementary to the EB-66 jamming which provided protection for many aircraft. Testing was hurried and done under combat conditions. The initial buy was for 58 QRC-160-1 pods allocated to Misawa and Kadena Air Bases in Japan, then hurriedly sent to Tan Son Nhut beginning in April 1965. The initial deployment of the pods proved to be a disaster under a less than competent project management team. The RF-101C was flying some of the toughest missions early on in the war and needed all the self-protection it could get. The airplane was not designed to carry ECM pods on its wings. It had no hard points to mount external stores. All that had to be developed, including the pylon on which the QRC-160 was to be hung. Tactically the pod was designed to be carried on each wing of an aircraft. Seventh Air Force project managers decided that four pods, two on each wing, would probably be even better and make the RF-101 something of a mini EB-66. In addition to a lack of understanding of how to properly employ the new QRC-160 system, the pods received rough handling. As a result reliability plummeted. Then the pods were incorrectly tuned, mounted and maintained and acted more like beacons when used, rather than providing protection for the vulnerable RF-101s. General Hunter Harris, the PACAF commander, became utterly disgusted with what was going on and got rid of both the pods and the people who brought them in.[4]

David R. Zook was an electronic warfare officer who loved his profession. In 1963 Dave was assigned to Eglin AFB in Florida. "I tested a variety of ECM equipments while at Eglin, but by far the most important turned out to be the QRC-160-1 jamming pod. These pods had been given a combat test during 1965 at Ubon in Thailand. The RF-101 was selected for the test because their losses were high. If anything could be done wrong it was done wrong at Ubon. As a result ECM got a black eye. I was assigned a project named *Problem Child*, which was to retest the QRC-160-1 pods. By virtue of my tests I became involved with the Anti-SAM Task Force established by General McConnell in August 1965. There was a lot to learn about the SA-2. The Foreign Technology Division at Wright-Patterson AFB had gathered the available intelligence on the *Fansong* radar and contracted for the building of a surrogate model on the Eglin test range – SADS-1 (Soviet Air Defense System -1). At the heart of the system were three operator positions. Each had a B-scope that was higher than it was wide. One displayed azimuth and range, the other elevation and range. A master operator operated an expanded range scope. It was the job of the master operator to match azimuth, elevation, and range information when more than one target appeared on the scope at the same time. When the operator had isolated a target and it was between 6 and 30 miles away, he could initiate a simulated missile launch.

"We calculated from the data we collected that the probability of getting a missile within 200 feet of a target where the missile's proximity fuse would work was 97 percent if the airplane was not jamming. Four percent if four airplanes in the correct formation were all jamming the radar. The formation tactic was the original idea of retired Lieutenant Colonel Ingwald Haugen. Inky Haugen knew more about ECM than any other person I've ever met. Working with Inky was like getting a graduate degree in ECM. Inky's tactic required four QRC-160-1 pod equipped airplanes to fly in formation at altitude straight and level. The operators on the ground saw their entire radar scopes filled with noise jamming. There was no way for them to pick a single target. Firing a salvo of missiles into the mass of airplanes only had a four percent probability of getting a missile close enough to an airplane to trigger its proximity fuse. We flew the missions over and over against the SADS-1 radar. The tactic defeated the radar. I hardly had written the first draft of the test report when I was reassigned to the 41TRS at Takhli to fly the RB-66C ECM aircraft.

"I arrived at Takhli in May 1966. Whenever I had the opportunity I would engage someone in conversation about the high loss rate of the F-105s and the lack of self protection jamming. I told them about the success I had with the QRC-160 pods at Eglin. One day Lieutenant Colonel Danny Salmon approached me and asked me to accompany him to his mission planning room. Danny was the commander of one of the three F-105 squadrons at Takhli. Several of his pilots had gathered to hear what I had to say. There was an EWO present whom I hadn't met before. As it turned out he had been responsible for the first combat test of the pods at Ubon. I explained the *Fansong* radar and the importance of Inky Haugen's formation tactic. Within a few days I was talking to Colonel Robert R. Scott, the 355th Wing commander. Colonel Scott had me develop a flip chart briefing, cautioning me to 'Keep it in fighter pilot jargon. Don't sound like an engineer.' He arranged for me to give the briefing at 7th Air Force Headquarters in Saigon. At Tan Son Nhut I briefed the director of operations and his staff. He asked what I needed – people who know how to maintain the pods, and pilots willing to fly straight and level into their target. Seventh Air Force passed its desire to run a combat test to PACAF. PACAF was still adamantly opposed, but by this time the *Problem Child* test report had made its way into distribution and was gaining interest at the Air Staff. With strong reservations PACAF finally gave in. I recall the captain who conducted the first test saying to me, 'Good, this test will bury those pods once and for all.'

"Our plan was to load a QRC-160 pod on each wing of the F-105s and to start with a mission into a low threat area. The four Thuds flew the formation at an altitude above most of the AAA fire. I was in an RB-66C monitoring and recording the mission. I could see the jamming on my ECM receiver and all pods checked out. No missiles were fired. After each mission I went to the fighter pilots' debriefing to gather the details and then went to the command post to call my contact at 7th Air Force with the results. The day came for the final combat flight test. The 'frag order' came in from 7th as it did every day, assigned the number of aircraft and their targets. That day the frag specified 8 F-105s carrying the QRC 160-1 pods to be flown as two four-ship formations. Their target, the Nguyen Khe fuel storage tanks in the most heavily defended area in North Vietnam, Hanoi/Haiphong. My RB-66C crew and I went into an orbit northwest of Hanoi to provide stand-off jamming for the strike force. It was a savage mission. As the last of the Thuds passed through the target area we all headed back to Takhli. As soon as we parked our RB-66C I jumped out and headed over to the fighter pilot debriefing. None of our pod carrying F-105s received any damage. I ran all the way to the command post to make my report to 7th. From that day forth every Thud pilot wanted pods on his airplane. The jamming pod formation was accepted by 7th Air Force that October. In the preceding six months 72 F-105s were lost over North Vietnam to radar guided AAA and SAMs. In the six months following, losses fell sharply to 23. Every available pod, at that time 140, was sent to Thailand."[5]

A Headquarters PACAF operations analysis paper reported in March 1967 that "Since their initial combat use on 26 September 1966, QRC-160-1 ECM pods have been carried on an increasing number of sorties into North Vietnam and Laos. In concept and in practice the QRC-160-1 pods complement the electronic warfare capabilities of the EB-66 and other EW equipment. Pilots' reaction to the pods and their effectiveness has been enthusiastic, and a lower percentage of SA-2 missiles was reported to track or guide."[6] Carrying anything other than ordnance and fuel on the wings of its fighters was something new to the tactical fighter community in 1967. Today, every Air Force combat aircraft routinely not only carries ECM pods into combat, but also flares and chaff. The SA-2 and subsequent even more deadly SAM systems changed everything in the way air warfare was conducted. The EB-66 proved itself as a tenacious and essential strike force element, was followed by the EF-111 *Raven*, and today's EA-6B Navy/Air Force jointly manned ECM aircaft. Change didn't come easy.

In time the North Vietnamese SAM crews discovered a weak spot in the QRC-160-1. "On 15 January 1967 USAF bombers attacked a bridge near Hanoi. The jamming patterns on the radar screens of the 236th Missile Regiment covering Hanoi's inner defensive perimeter were unlike anything the radar operators had ever seen. Only one of the regiment's four battalions was able to launch missiles, and no U.S. aircraft were hit." North Vietnam's most experienced SAM regiment, the 236th, "had been immobilized." Little changed for the DRVs SAM and AAA radar operators over the next several months. "On 5 May 1967, after a lull of almost one week, USAF aircraft again attacked targets around Hanoi. Intense jamming from QRC-160-1 jamming pods, combined with long-range jamming from EB-66s northwest of Hanoi, covered the screens of the SAM units and blinded the radars controlling Vietnamese 57mm and 100mm guns. Every missile launched by the 274th Regiment either self-destructed or crashed back to earth. The AAA guns were forced to use optical fire control equipment or iron sights on the guns to engage the attackers. While several aircraft were shot down, the situation was desperate ... The 5 May battle produced a bright spot. The 63rd Missile Battalion, located southwest of Hanoi, fired at USAF aircraft from the rear as they exited the area, destroying one F-105." The SAM crews had found a possible weakness and a solution to their dilemma. They perfected the three-point and track-on-jam method which relied on keeping the *Fansong* radar in a receive mode for much of the time and relying on data inputs from *Spoonrest* acquisition radars. They also began to launch SA-2 missiles in massed barrages. "Brutal interrogations of newly captured pilots aimed at gaining tactical and technical information increased significantly," as well. Losses to the SA-2 began to rise again.[7]

Otis McCain got into the ECM business in the early days, just after World War II. He flew in the few B-25 and B-26 aircraft TAC chose to convert to that role. Those aircraft were too small in number to pose a threat to a potential adversary, but provided excellent training for GCI, AAA and missile radar sites. After serving in the 363TRW at Shaw flying RB-66Cs, in July 1967, McCain found himself assigned to an ASCAT team, an Anti-SAM Combat Assistance Team. His assignment was to the 8th Tactical Fighter Wing at Ubon Air Base in Thailand. The wing was awaiting its first QRC-160-1 jamming pods, and the installation of APR-25/26 radar homing and warning receivers. Few of the pilots showed any enthusiasm for the new gadgets. It was Otis's job to change attitudes. Reports kept coming in of a sudden increase in losses of ECM pod equipped aircraft. "It occurred to me that one method to defeat the SAM missiles after launch was to jam the missile guidance signal, the BGO6. I was told in no uncertain terms that this could not be done since the receiving antenna was in the missile's tail. I was not convinced that pod jamming of the critical beacon signal could not be accomplished. The difficult part was to get the necessary information from the intelligence community of the precise frequencies."[8]

Although Otis did not know it, that information had been obtained on February 13, 1966, by a Ryan Firebee target drone guided and monitored by a specially equipped *Firefly* RB-47H of the 55th SRW flying out of Bien Hoa Air Base. I myself flew on the *Firefly* aircraft after the Cuban Missile Crisis of October 1962. By the time the aircraft modification was completed the crisis was over. The Cubans did not oblige us to fire any of their SA-2s so we could pick up fusing and terminal phase guidance signals. The RB-47H crew that flew that critical February mission in 1966 was awarded the Distinguished Flying Cross for heroism. The SA-2 missile had a 286 pound warhead that exploded in a fan shaped pattern ahead of the missile. After initial launch it achieved a speed in excess of Mach 3 and had a maximum range of about 25 miles, reaching targets at heights in excess of 80,000 feet. Below 1,000 feet the missile was not a threat.[9] When Otis McCain received the information he needed he had several ALQ-160-1 pods retuned from just jamming the *Fansong*'s track-while-scan radar to also jam the missile beacon frequency. What evolved was that in a flight of four F-105s, QRC-160 pods carried on the right wings were set to counter the SA-2s 'beacon mode.' Pods carried on the left wing of aircraft one and three were set to counter the azimuth beam of the *Fansong* radar, while left wing pods on aircraft two and four were set to counter the *Fansong* elevation beam. Losses to SAMs dropped dramatically. "My greatest reward was not the Bronze Star I was awarded for this effort, but the thanks I received from pilots and weapons systems officers returning from their missions."[10] On December 14, 1967, targets in the Hanoi area came under heavy air attack, "almost every missile launched crashed back to earth as soon as it left its launcher ... On 15 December the 236th and 275th Missile Regiments launched a total of eleven missiles. Every missile crashed back to earth shortly after launch. Once again the 236th Regiment took the lead in identifying the cause of the problem. In August one of its battalions first detected a new jamming signal directed at the missile guidance data-link frequency. The DRV Air Defense Command, which was still congratulating itself for finding a solution to the QRC-160-1 jammers, was in a state of shock."[11] Not only had -1 pods been retuned to cope with the missile guidance, but Air Force had also moved on to a new version of the pod, the -8, which later became the ALQ-87. ECM always has been and always will be a game of one-upmanship. By late 1967, before the fifth bombing pause, a Christmas cease fire, we were getting quite good at the ECM game, and few remembered ever being opposed to carrying ECM pods.

When the war against the North ended in 1972, 83 percent of the 1,726 USAF aircraft lost in combat over the North had been lost to ground fire ranging from small arms to 100mm AAA guns. Of the 17 percent, or 289 aircraft, lost to other combat causes, 37 percent, only 107 aircraft, were lost to the SA-2 surface to air missile. The combat loss rate peaked in late 1965 and early 1966. Thereafter it declined sharply, from 5.53 aircraft lost per 1,000 combat sorties flown in 1965, to 3.16 aircraft lost per 1,000 sorties in 1966, reflecting the impact of the increased presence of EB-66 ECM aircraft, to a rate of 2.60 aircraft lost per 1,000 sorties, reflecting the increased reduction in losses due to the introduction of the QRC-160

ECM pod. Although some of the toughest missions were flown during this period, the pods, combined with support jamming, saved the day. By 1968 the loss rate dropped to a low of 1.32 aircraft per thousand combat sorties. North Vietnamese missile sites during that same period increased from a low of 65 in 1965 to a high of 320 at the end of the *Linebacker II* campaign in 1972. In contrast, their AAA showed a steady decline in numbers from a peak of 6,452 pieces in 1967 to a low of 1,203 guns deployed in North Vietnam in 1971. Much of the shift in AAA numbers reflected movement into Laos and South Vietnam. The SAM sites, of course, were not all occupied. As the war wore on, the 32 SA-2 SAM battalions, with 192 launchers, reached a high level of proficiency in relocating from one site to another within less than 24-hours. Their success rate, however, remained low.[12]

By the time President Johnson called a bombing halt against targets above the 20th parallel, on April 1, 1968, American fighters could again cruise at high altitudes unmolested by SAM missiles and radar guided AAA, just as they had when B-66s guided them in 1966 on *Pathfinder* missions. "The QRC-160-8 jamming pods could be used by small flights of four to eight aircraft to attack areas such as Hanoi with powerful air defenses without having to worry about our surface-to-air missiles," reflects the official Air Defense Command history of the Democratic Republic of North Vietnam.[13] At this juncture of the air war, American political will to continue the fray faltered and the Secretary of State began to look for a graceful exit. The air war over North Vietnam once and for all put World War II and its brute force employment concepts behind us. A changed and battle wise Air Force emerged from the skies over the DRV, once again equipping its fighters with guns as well as air to air missiles, using 'smart' bombs to do what dumb bombs couldn't, and routinely carrying ECM pods for self-protection to defeat the electronic challenges posed by a wily enemy. We learned the hard way to fight brawn with brain. Unfortunately, we paid an unnecessarily high price to learn such simple and timeless lessons.

CHAPTER TWENTY-ONE

THE 41ST TACTICAL ELECTRONIC WARFARE SQUADRON

1967 began with a bang. On January 2 Robin Olds and Chappie James led the fighter boys from the 8th Tactical Fighter Wing on an elaborately designed ruse into North Vietnam, shooting down 7 MiG-21s. Two more MiG-21s were claimed by F-4Cs of the 8th two days later. Maybe the politicians in Washington did not know what it was they wanted out of the war, but the flyers from the 8th TFW were totally focused on what they did best – kill MiGs. The MiGs were baffled by their losses. North Vietnam's "Air Defense Command issued new orders: 'MiG-21s will temporarily suspend combat operations to derive lessons learned, to study and refine MiG-21 tactics, and to conduct further training to improve technical and tactical skills.'"[1]

War, of course, is arbitrary and cuts both ways. Major Arthur Kibby Taylor, the operations officer of the 41st TEWS, on his fifth flight on November 5, 1966, literally had two MiG-21s shot off his tail by his F-4C escort. Taylor remembers "As 1967 began we had a change of commanders at 13th Air Force in the Philippines. The old commander had grounded one of our pilots, Captain John Fer, an Air Force Academy graduate and experienced flyer who ran his C-model off the runway while landing in an intense rainstorm in the fall of 1966. You had to experience the downpours we had at Takhli during the rainy season to understand a pilot's problems when caught up in one of them. Our efforts to return him to flying status resulted in his misfortune. On February 4 Captain Fer and his crew were scheduled to support strikes in the lower Route Packs. Then 7th Air Force directed a change and sent them up north to support a strike near Hanoi. Without

The loss of EB-66C 54-473 on November 17, 1967, was one of the darkest days for the men of the 41st Tactical Electronic Warfare Squadron. The picture shows the desperate attempt of the pilot to eject, the seat and pilot falling back into the flames of the burning aircraft.

hesitation the crew launched on that mission. In the pocket northwest of Hanoi they were hit by an SA-2 missile and went down, too deep in enemy territory for a search and rescue attempt. Three of the Ravens were killed in action. Captain Fer, his navigator Major Jack Bomar, and a young Raven, First Lieutenant John Davies were captured. They spent six long years behind the infamous prison walls of what we aircrew dubbed the *Hanoi Hilton*, a prison from French colonial days turned into a rudimentary prisoner of war camp.

"In March, one of our returning aircraft couldn't get its left gear down. When they burned off extra fuel we ran out of ideas and they had to set up for a gear-up landing. The four Ravens in back of the aircraft had to escape through a single, narrow hatch opening. The pilot and navigator could exit through their own individual hatches. It was essential to repress fire to get them out. Crash crews were positioned along the runway, an HH-43 fire suppression helicopter was in place, cranes, anything we could think of to get our flyers out if the worst happened. The aircraft landed, sparks flew, the crew exited successfully. April 30 was a black letter day for our brave F-105 flyers. The raid that day was led by Colonel Jack Broughton, the vice commander of the 355th. Three 105s went down, including one *Weasel* aircraft. I wore a Leo Thorsness POW/MIA bracelet until his return in 1973. In June the new arrivals came in, including my replacement. I flew my last combat mission on the first of July in 54-459. Two days later Colonel Keller, our squadron commander and I departed for Bangkok."[2]

Like many other Ravens, I myself flew many missions in 54-459 after Kibby Taylor left the 41st, both at Takhli and later at Spangdahlem Air Base in Germany. 459 was one airplane that never let us down – always brought us home. Perhaps airplanes have no souls and are just pieces of metal, plastic, glass and rubber – but don't say that to anyone who flew a particular airplane into combat that brought him back over and over again to live another day. That plane became more than just a piece of metal, and was viewed with the sort of affection normally reserved for human beings. The late General Robin Olds, a man I greatly admire, late in World War II along with five fellow P-51 flyers attacked a German airfield. The other five perished. Robin's P-51 was badly damaged but he would not abandon the plane which had taken him through many a scrape with the Luftwaffe. Said he, "Scat VI had taken me through a lot and I was damned if I was going to give her up." With his determination to survive and her resilience both Robin and Scat VI made it home in one piece. Such are airmen's sentiments about the machines they fly into mortal combat.[3]

Air Force planners had a eureka moment in August 1967, finally assigning the two B-66 squadrons at Takhli to the 355th Tactical Fighter Wing, their host wing ever since they arrived in May 1965. For reasons only planners are privy to, the squadrons had been assigned as detachments to remotely located reconnaissance wings. Colonel John C. Giraudo, later to become major general, assumed command of the five squadron wing on August 2, 1967. Giraudo, on his third combat tour, embraced the B-66s like no other commander before or after. The B-66s were part of his team and he would make sure they knew how he felt about them. In an interview soon after he took command Giraudo said "The EB-66s are fragged for 500 to 600 combat sorties a month, flying between 70 to 80 hours each. This morning we had 16 EB-66s up working for the Navy, for the other F-105 and F-4 wings, for everybody. Virtually no major air strikes are conducted into the heavily defended airspace of North Vietnam without radar-jamming support." At his change of command ceremony Giraudo turned to Colonel Harrison Lobdell, his deputy for B-66 operations, and said "You now fly the F-66." Giraudo never again referred to the 66 as a bomber. He was a fighter wing commander and all of his airplanes were fighters. End of story. "I must confess I wasn't eager to find out about these twin-engined electronic jammers," Giraudo said. "They were old, ugly, underpowered relics from the past and they did things fighter pilots usually were not interested in. In good conscience they were part of my Wing and I had to show an interest. How fortunate that I did. Ace (Colonel Harrison Lobdell) had a crew standing by to show me their aircraft. I came away from this meeting thinking what great soldiers these crews were, to operate unarmed and unescorted in a war zone under such dismal conditions. Back inside I gathered with Ace and his top people and we discussed their problems and ours. I was curious what they detected and recorded during their missions. And obviously how long it took for their mission data to be processed and new information to be disseminated to the fighter wings. I figured that from detection time to re-tuning our jamming pods usually took two days. I was afraid to believe what I had heard. I called the DO (director of operations), DM (director of maintenance), and told them to bring their pod experts and meet me ASAP. When they arrived I asked them 'Why can't procedures in the F-66 and the F-105 units be streamlined so that our pod people can be informed that night about new frequencies and our people can then retune the pods that same night in time to be used on tomorrow's mission? There ensued a considerable technical discussion. In fact, they did accomplish it to our great defensive benefit.

"Next came a discussion about the F-66 jamming capabilities. Ace and his people showed us the fan-shaped beam pattern his aircraft transmitted and how the jamming strength and effectiveness was proportional to their distance from the ingress and egress route right down and up the F-66 jamming fan. In this manner the radars had to look directly into the very powerful F-66 jamming, which, in addition to the F-105 pod jamming made radar tracking near impossible. I directed that our F-105 mission leaders would have at their elbow while mission planning the F-66 leader for that mission to coordinate jamming orbit locations with ingress and egress routes, and adjusting them as necessary."[4]

Giraudo was a compassionate, thinking, hands-on leader, the kind of commander people followed to hell and back. He became suspicious that the North Vietnamese were tracking their IFF over North Vietnam. I had no backup for my gut feeling," Giraudo recalls. "That night I called Gordy Blood at 7th. The next day I jumped into the *Big Kahuna* (his trusty F-105) and headed for Saigon to meet with General Momyer. Momyer agreed to let the Takhli 105s turn off their IFF over North Vietnam. General Blood argued against it. Momyer ended the meeting saying, 'Gordy, send out a wire to the three wings involved approving the 355th to leave IFFs off over enemy territory.'

"When I returned to my office after visiting with General Momyer I was met by an irate SAC general. He had come down to inspect the KC-135 detachment, had been looking for me, and sounded mad. In strode this medium-sized, fit, burr-haircut one-star who introduced himself as 'General Selmon Wells, commander, 322d Air Division, SAC,' and proceeded to inform me that the KC-135s were not my aircraft but his and he would have no signs over their building saying they were F-135s. He had ordered the sign taken down. I couldn't help but smile, and said to him, 'General, no problem, that sign will be down every time you visit. I must tell you that we couldn't do our job without your great people and their fuel and, in fact, our people consider them part of our family.' The sign went back up when he left."[5]

The Takhli flyers and maintainers, no matter the aircraft, were working their proverbial asses off. The 41st was authorized 15 EB-66C aircraft, but at any one time only had ten or eleven available. In July 1967 they flew 288 sorties, 262 in August, and 272 in September. In 822 sorties they had only one abort. The B-66s were always where they were supposed to be. Aircraft utilization averaged nearly 93 percent – an astounding statistic for an old airplane and a credit to the legion of maintenance men who worked day and night to keep the airplanes flying. Others noticed. Colonel Robin Olds sent a certificate of appreciation for the support provided by the 41st's EB-66Cs. The 7th Fleet commander, Admiral John J. Hyland, did the same.[6] The history of the 41st TEWS reflects "During this period four additional Hearts and Flowers memos were received from other Navy and Air Force units relative to specific missions supported by the squadron." It was also the time when the old wire recorders finally came out of the airplanes and Leach 14-track audio and video recorders were installed. High gain omni directional antennas were provided for the APR-14 receivers in Raven positions 1 and 2. The BGO6 missile guidance signal amplifier was modified to preclude failure, and long overdue improvements were finally made to EB-66C collection and jamming systems.[7]

Alexander 'Alex' J. Kersis was typical of the Ravens who manned the back-ends of the EB-66Cs at the time. Born in 1943 in Elizabeth, New Jersey, Alex attended Virginia Technical Institute in Blacksburg, majoring in metallurgical engineering. "When I went to VPI (Virginia Polytechnical Institute) I didn't realize that it was a military college, sort of like VMI, the Virginia Military Institute. Every freshman had to join the corps of cadets. We had a plebe system. The freshmen were called rats, and we had hazing. We would march to breakfast, lunch and dinner. It was a regimented experience and if you were in the corps of cadets it was expected of you to join ROTC. I signed up for Air Force ROTC, thinking I wanted to be a pilot. My eyes weren't good enough, so I took the next best thing, navigator. I was commissioned in 1965 and assigned to Mather AFB. When I graduated the following year I chose to continue training as an electronic warfare officer. Of course the war was going on and I heard from others that if I went into B-52s I would spend a lot of time on Guam. Not only that, it didn't count toward a SEA combat tour. I'd fly my B-52 missions, then I would end up at Takhli in the B-66 anyway.

"The B-66 was a twin-jet tactical airplane and that sounded exotic to me. So I, and a couple of my classmates, chose the EB-66 when we graduated in February 1967. The three of us got into a car and drove across the country to Shaw AFB in South Carolina. We finished our training in May and received orders to Takhli, Thailand. First though we went to Homestead AFB, Florida, for sea survival training, then on the way we stopped at Clark Air Base in the Philippines for jungle survival. We were ready to head for the jungle at Clark when they canceled our class. The class ahead of us was in the jungle and got caught in a massive rainstorm. A cliff below which they had made their camp collapsed and buried many. I learned later that one of the people killed was a classmate from VPI who lived across the hall from me. When we arrived in Bangkok we caught a C-47 *Gooney Bird* to Takhli – door wide open, flying at 6,000 feet, with the clouds rushing in. The rule then was 100 missions over the North and you got to go home. They were knocking off *counters* every day, every third day at the most. So the experienced guys didn't stay around long.

"The accommodations at Takhli weren't anything like what was there several months later. There were muddy ditches, wooden plank sidewalks, open hooches with blankets strung on ropes to separate beds. The lights never went on because someone was always coming off or going on a mission and they had to sleep. I show up at my assigned hooch, open the door – and there is this musty smelling black cavern. I had to get a flashlight to find my bed. Blankets everywhere. When

I first got there most of the people were the old B-66 flyers from France, England and Shaw. As they moved out over the next couple months they were replaced by a mix of lieutenants from Mather straight out of school, like myself, and majors and lieutenant colonels who had just graduated from service schools and AFIT (Air Force Institute of Technology). And later yet SAC B-58 and B-52 people began showing up. They were also dredging up former SAC EB-47 *Blue Cradle* people who had wandered off into staff positions. The Military Personnel Center at Randolph AFB in San Antonio, Texas, was combing through its personnel records – there was no place for an EWO to hide. The same was true for pilots and navigators. As time went on the rank structure rose to where there were more field grade than company grade officers on our crews. I was at Takhli three months when a massive modernization of base facilities began. Bulldozers and Thai workers were everywhere digging holes, planting plants, pouring concrete. They were gutting the hooches, putting in air-conditioners, paving roads.

"My first flight out of Takhli was on June 21, 1967, up in the pocket northwest of Hanoi. There was no local checkout. It was get in the back of the airplane and go. I flew 133 missions over the North. Many of our missions were in support of the Navy which lacked a good jammer until the EA-6A came along. It was on a mission up north in the pocket northwest of Hanoi where I got my Distinguished Flying Cross. It was on July 7, flying tail number 55-388. I was flying position 2, covering the lower frequency bands. Suddenly all the acquisition radars started to come up, it was almost like in a simulator. I had a *Spoonrest* stop its scan and point right at us. The next thing we knew a *Fansong* SA-2 radar popped up, and an F-4C flying cover for us called out a SAM launch. By then the *Fansong* radar signal was off the scale on our receivers. The acquisition radars were off the scale – they meant to get us. We made a SAM break into the missile and the thing went right by us. After the SAM passed we discussed what to do next – move our orbit further out or stay where we were and support the 105s. We stayed in that orbit until the strike force returned. A couple of years later I was assigned to Ramstein Air Base in Germany. We were telling war stories and I mentioned that I flew the B-66. A major said, 'I had an occasion to save a B-66.' Then he told me where and when. I shook his hand: 'You saved me!' A small Air Force it was at times. It seems they only launched one missile to get us to move as the strike force was approaching, but didn't work.

"Unlike the E-model, which was set-up like a B-52 with good jammer optimization against the *Fansong* missile radar with the ability to modulate its jamming output, the C-model had no modulators. But we had the advantage of being able to concentrate our jamming on a targeted radar with our steerable antennas. We had lots of chaff and dropped that as soon as the pilot went into a

SAM break. If we flew the C in the Gulf of Tonkin for the Navy, we would see the *Fansong*s out of Hanoi and Haiphong. As we flew up the coast we would pick up their *Flat Face* acquisition radars, see the ground picture evolve. One radar would pick us up then pass us on to another and another. Once in a while we'd do fun things like take a heading of 270 degrees and drive straight for the coast, dropping chaff along the way. All of a sudden the entire radar network would come up. Anything unusual they reacted to. I was on a frag team when I wasn't flying, it's called an Air Tasking Order today. We would have people come over from the F-105 squadrons and the *Wild Weasel* crews and we'd coordinate our locations, times and tactics. Many of our orbits were assigned by 7th Air Force in Saigon, but they gave us the latitude to shape our missions. This collaboration was not always there. You do your thing, we do our thing was fostered by higher headquarters by laying out every aspect of our missions. Coordination between the 105s and us usually occurred when they were going *downtown* and knew they needed all the insurance they could lay their hands on."[8]

Major Chris Divich who ended his Air Force career as a major general, was assigned to the 41st TEWS. Chris was the kind of guy people remembered – tall, handsome, a ready smile, always willing to help. Chris hailed from a little town in South Dakota, Durham. "My dad was a Yugoslavian immigrant. Came through Ellis Island in 1911 and worked for the railroad and the WPA. I grew up in Durham and was offered a basketball scholarship at the University of Kansas. I went down there to play and joined Air Force ROTC for the ninety-dollars a month. Upon graduation I completed flight training and ended up in the 40th Air Refueling Squadron of the 40th Bomb Wing at Schilling AFB, Salina, Kansas. Then I was sent to Squadron Officer School at Maxwell AFB, Montgomery, Alabama. I really got into trouble there. There were 1,000 in the class, sixteen students in each seminar – and there was one black kid named Jimmy Smith. This was in September 1960. One of the first things our seminar leader said, right in front of Jimmy, 'We can't have any parties off base, and you really can't go anywhere downtown with Jimmy, and you probably shouldn't have him to your house.' And I just went ballistic. 'This is absolute bull-shit, pardon my expression, nobody is going to tell me that. I went through this stuff at the University of Kansas, and I'd be goddamned if I am going to go through this again. If I want Jimmy to my house for dinner, I'll have him over for dinner. I'm going to do whatever I want to do. If the Air Force doesn't like it, they can tell me to go home.' Well, the Air Force didn't like it. When I got back to Kansas my squadron commander said, 'I tell you Chris, you probably ought to get out.' I looked for a flying job but had too little time for any of the airlines to show any interest. So I kept flying KC-97s.

"In 1959 we deployed 22 KC-97s to Thule Air Base in Greenland for three months. At Thule we supported two RB-47H reconnaissance aircraft from the 55th Wing. Our job was to provide fuel. They needed 108,000 pounds of fuel to go out and do their job and come home. It took three KC-97s to do that. We'd drop them off near the Russian coast. The first time we launched three airplanes, one aborted; launched four the next time and two aborted. It was so cold that we had to take off with such high power settings, it diluted the oil and the engines failed. Before we knew it we were doing eight ship MITO (minimum interval) take-offs, 15 seconds apart to support one RB-47H reconnaissance aircraft. And because of that everybody got fired – the squadron commander, the operations officer, the wing commander. Whoever they were at SAC headquarters finally realized that KC-97s couldn't operate in 50 below zero temperatures. They replaced us with KC-135 tankers out of MacDill. They came up and did the job with no problems.

"It was 1966 when my squadron commander told me that I was on the list to go to Air Command and Staff College, also at Maxwell. I told him, 'That has to be an error. I never told you this, but in my personnel records it says Not Recommended for Air Force training.' He said, 'No Chris, you are on the list.' So I went to Maxwell. One-hundred percent of my class received Vietnam assignments. My initial assignment was to RF-4s in Saigon. That was a one year assignment because they only flew over the South and Laos. Walt Sticher, a real good friend, had a B-66 assignment. B-66s flew over the North and after completing 100 missions you went home. So Walt and I switched. I went to B-66 training at Shaw, then over to Takhli. The irony, my friend Walt was shot down on his first mission over Laos and became a POW until 1973. Once I started flying out of Takhli they changed the rules. They were really short on people and kept us there for a year, 100 missions or not. I ended up with 565 hours in the airplane.

"I loved the B-66. I didn't have any problems flying night, weather, turns in the clouds, refueling, pulling Gs, what have you. We had tons of people who couldn't do that. They'd fly straight and level and refuel, but they couldn't refuel in a turn. When the B-52s started bombing the passes from North Vietnam into Laos, we got a lot more night flying. I flew every single night I could. Sometime I'd fly ten nights in a row because we didn't have enough people who could refuel at night. The only scary thing was flight checks with people who couldn't fly very well – on my hands and knees out of my seat with no chute on can scare the crap out of you.

"I got crewed up with Bill McDonald at Shaw. He was in my seminar in Air Command and Staff, a SAC navigator. Bill McDonald and I flew every flight together at Shaw, and we played tennis every afternoon. We got to Takhli in October. They were so short of crews at Takhli that half of our bunch never went through Jungle Survival School at Clark. I got my 'dollar' ride, and Bill got his 'dollar' ride. The next day he was killed. That was the worst day of my life and really put a damper on things for me. Bill was flying with Major Max Nichols. On his very first combat mission, on November 17, 1967, they took off and lost the number two engine on climb out. They were heavy with fuel. Nick elected to go around and come right back in for a landing. Just before reaching the runway the aircraft dropped and hit the ground, maybe 150 yards from the runway, slid up to the runway and caught fire. A very minor fire at first that quickly spread. Nick didn't jettison the escape hatches, he was probably too busy flying the airplane with both hands. He tried when on the ground, but his hatch only went up an inch or two. The fire trucks were there when the aircraft stopped sliding. I can still see the guy on the ladder with this great big crash axe, I am standing ten yards from him, hacking away at that goddamn hatch. He couldn't break it. Nick is in there screaming, can't get out, and in desperation ejects – his seat went through the partially closed hatch and fell right back into the burning aircraft. Sitting behind Nick is Bill McDonald and young Lieutenant Ted Johnson, the instructor navigator. Both navigators broke their legs in the crash landing. They couldn't have gotten out on their own. The Ravens in back got their escape hatch open, but only two of them made it out in time, severely injured. After Bill was killed I never played tennis again. My wife had bought me the most expensive tennis racket in the world, and I thought I would have a good time over there – I am going to fly in the morning and play tennis every afternoon with Bill. I was so sick when Bill was killed, I took my racket and smashed it to pieces. I never played a game of tennis again."[9]

The loss of aircraft number 54-473, including the loss of five of their squadron mates, may well have been the darkest day for the 41st TEWS. The aft fuselage section "was immediately engulfed in flame. The fire suppression and rescue helicopter set down the fire suppression kit and fire fighting and rescue team of three men." One of those men was SSGT Joseph A. Vultagio of the 355th Air Force Dispensary. "This team was in action in less than 30 seconds. The rescue craft by this time was again airborne in a hover position to deflect fire and smoke. The first vehicular fire fighting unit was in position within the first minute. Captains Robert Peffley and James Stamm evacuated the aft crew compartment within this time period. Approximately 3 or 4 minutes later, as an attempt to reach the pilot was in progress, the pilot's seat ejected, catapulting him to the top of the fuselage. Further attempts to rescue crew members were unsuccessful."[10] Staff Sergeant Vultaggio "with complete disregard for his own safety, rushed to the burning aircraft and dragged one of the collapsed crew members to safety. In spite of intense heat and grave danger of exploding fuel cells he remained at the burning aircraft and persevered in his life saving efforts until ordered to withdraw when the fire was declared out of control."[11] Sergeant Vultaggio was awarded the Airman's Medal for his heroism, pinned on his chest by Lieutenant General Albert Clark, the vice commander of Tactical Air Command.

Then came the always depressing task of assembling the personal belongings of the deceased and returning them to their loved ones. Chris Divich was appointed Summary Courts Officer "to make disposition of personal effects of Major William E. McDonald."[12] Al Kersis says "After that accident I looked at life differently. How precious it was. It wasn't just flying over North Vietnam that could cost you your life, but it was flying the airplane too. Then on December 6, another EB-66C, 54-462, encountered sudden windshear on its final approach returning from a combat mission. Once again it was an aircraft from the 41st TEWS. Three more men died. One of the Ravens ejected, got out of his parachute, walked across the field to his hootch and lay down on his bed. The lights were out and nobody knew he was there. Someone finally found him – in shock. Jack Youngs was the pilot, he worked in Wing headquarters and was attached to us for flying. It appears he wasn't strapped into his chute when he punched out. It was probably fatigue, utter exhaustion. He had worked so many hours. I was in the club at the time when the word reached us that another B-66 had crashed at the end of the runway. The club was across the street from the hospital built by the Japanese in World War II. Two hours later we were walking out of the club, by the hospital, and there lay three body bags on the sidewalk – the guys I had breakfast with, the guys I was at the pool with. It was very hard.[13]

"What happened shortly after this," recalls Chris Divich, "six or seven young SAC EWOs got together and said they were not going to fly the C-model anymore. The operations officer came over to see me and said, 'Chris, you have better rapport with any of these guys than anyone else here. You need to get together with them and explain that this won't fly. They will be courts martialed. They will be out of the Air Force, could go to jail, but their lives will never be the same again. I got together with Pete Pedroli, Pete and I were Air Command and Staff College class-mates. I told Pete about the situation. So Pedroli and I got these kids in a room and we closed the door and sat down. We must have talked for three hours. The rules – you can say anything, nothing will leave this room, nobody else will ever know that you refused to fly, but you have to get your asses back out there and fly. And everyone did. They were really young kids, all lieutenants, not a captain in the bunch."[14]

November 17 and December 6, 1967, left a deep scar in the psyche of the 41st Tactical Electronic Warfare Squadron.

CHAPTER TWENTY-TWO

PETE PEDROLI AND THE MiG-21

In early January 1967 the DRV Air Defense Command sent four SA-2 battalions to an area northwest of Hanoi to ambush the EB-66s and drive them out of effective jamming range. On 4 February 274th Missile Regiment's 89th Battalion shot down an EB-66C over Bac Can province. Three crewmen from the downed aircraft were captured. In the words of an official Vietnamese history, "The wreckage of this EB-66C yielded numerous documents and provided extensive information on enemy electronic warfare to the Air Defense Command's research and analysis components, to the Military Technical Institute, and to the General Staff." The Air Defense Command proclaimed the EB-66 shootdown as the Command's most important achievement during the first three months of 1967 and awarded 89th Battalion the Military Achievement Medal First Class, North Vietnam's highest unit citation.[1] Maybe there were doubts in the minds of senior staff officers at 7th and 13th Air Forces, and all the way up at Headquarters PACAF and on the Air Staff, about the effectiveness of the EB-66, but there were no doubts in the minds of the North Vietnamese decision makers. No other weapon employed by the hated Americans caused them more grief, confusion and failure to intercept their bombers than the EB-66. Combined with the newly introduced ECM pods, the EB-66 severely diminished the effectiveness of the DRV's radar network. No matter what the North Vietnamese did, the hated EB-66s kept coming back.

MiG-21 interceptors tried several times to get an EB-66, but every attempt resulted in one failure after another. Either their aircraft were shot down by vigilant F-4C fighters, or the B-66 skillfully evaded its attackers. Pushing them

A happy group of EB-66 flyers at Takhli RTAFB, Thailand, in 1968. Among the six of them they had flown 739 combat missions over the North. Major Chris Divich, second from right, stands next to Pete Pedroli, first on right, who was shot down on an earlier mission by a MiG-21, was recovered, and chose to remain with his squadron to complete his 100 missions over the North. Such was the courage of these men.

into more distant orbits provided only temporary relief. They kept coming back. "Vu Ngoc Dinh claimed six kills in the skies over North Vietnam with only six K-13 *Atoll* air to air missiles. Born in Thanh Hoa province Dinh had witnessed the first dogfight of the war. Dinh's first claim was an F-105 ... several victories followed, after which Dinh was given command of a special anti EB-66 unit. The North Vietnamese had been continually frustrated by these aging bombers crammed with electronic countermeasures equipment. Dinh's task was to devise tactics to counter this thorny problem. The unit's only [successful] action [against the EB-66] took place over Thanh Hoa province when GCI directed Dinh and Nguyen Dang Kinh onto a strike force protected by EB-66s. The two MiG-21s bore in and Dinh quickly claimed a kill and a probable."[2] It was not the unit's only action against the EB-66 aircraft, but it was the only action crowned by success during the entire war. The Vietnam Peoples Air Force, however, claimed not one, but three aerial victories against EB-66 aircraft – on November 19, 1967, another on January 14, 1968, and a third EB-66 on March 3, 1968.[3]

"I have a very clear image in my mind of events related to November 19, 1967," says Joseph Snoy, an EB-66C Raven. "While flying a mission 50 miles southwest of Hanoi, my aircraft was attacked by two MiG-21s. We were providing electronic reconnaissance and countermeasure support to a strike force of F-105 and F-4 aircraft. We had established our orbit at 30,000 feet when over the radio we heard calls that MiGs were airborne and headed south from Hanoi. The radio calls continued to broadcast the progress of the enemy aircraft as 50 miles south, then 90 miles south, then 120 miles southwest of Bull's Eye. Since we were 50 miles southwest of Hanoi it was obvious that we were in a vulnerable position. A minute later we were called by call sign that the MiGs were at our 6 o'clock position at a distance of 10 miles. Then followed the longest sixty seconds of my life. The MiGs made a single high speed pass and fired their missiles. My pilot reported seeing the missiles explode below us as the MiGs flew past, back toward Hanoi. I have never been so scared in my life. We were awarded the Distinguished Flying Cross for that mission."[4]

The North Vietnamese MiG-21 squadron kept pushing hard. On January 4, 1968, two EB-66C and E aircraft were covering air strikes in the Hanoi area. Lieutenant Colonel Jess Allen, flight leader of the F-4C MiG cap reported "We put two aircraft on each of the B-66s. The two aircraft flying on the lead ship flew one to three miles in trail and approximately 1,000 feet high. The two F-4s on the rear B-66 would fly approximately 1,000 feet low. Our primary mission was not to shoot down MiGs, but to protect the B-66. In our pre-brief we stressed the importance of radar and visual search at all times, particularly as we crossed the Black River in Route Package 5, and of course the Red River into Route Package

6. It was our intent not to ask the B-66 to maneuver unless the MiGs became a real threat, because frequently there would be MiGs in the area but they would not approach the flight nor attempt to engage. Shortly after we crossed the Red River we picked up two blips on the radar at 35 miles. We assumed they were MiGs. We were on the radio with the B-66. He too had picked them up. We acquired the bogies visually climbing in our direction. I directed the B-66 to turn to port 180 degrees. The B-66 broke to the left. We got a lock-on at 15 miles and in-range light somewhere around six miles and they continued to press. We were still unable to determine the type aircraft because they were coming at us head-on. I was thinking of probably positioning myself off to the right to follow around in their six o'clock position because they were still headed for the B-66, when suddenly they broke to the right. At that time they were easily identifiable as MiG-21s, heading back toward Phuc Yen. I started an immediate hard left turn, went into three-quarters afterburner, and proceeded back toward the B-66. This could have been a feint of two aircraft coming in high and at the same time they could have been sending in two low from the opposite side. I rendezvoused with the B-66 as rapidly as possible."[5] Positive visual MiG identification was difficult for escorting F-4 crews early in the war, especially when the enemy aircraft approached head-on and appeared as no more than rapidly approaching blips. As the war progressed F-4 aircraft were modified to enable them to identify MiG IFF transmissions. This largely solved the friend versus foe identification problem. The next day, January 5, the MiGs returned for another try. Wildcat 1, an EB-66C, and Wildcat 2, an EB-66E, were providing ECM support northwest of Hanoi. The two EB-66s had a four ship F-4 MiG cap. "Two MiG-21s appeared to be on a quartering head-on visual attack, closing to one to two miles of Wildcat 1. Vegas 1 and 2 dropped their centerline tanks and attempted a chase, as did Vegas 3 and 4. The MiGs turned east. There was no IFF signal or *Fansong* radar activity at the time of the sighting. Wildcat 1 intercepted an AI radar, *High Fix*, which would possibly indicate a MiG-21C. The MiGs were silver and no markings were observed."[6]

"Ron Lebert and I had been on R&R together," recalls Al Kersis. "We spent New Year's in Hong Kong. Once back at Takhli we were waiting to get back on the schedule. On the 14th of January, 1968, I flew tail number 388 in the morning. We received MiG warnings from *Red Crown* while in orbit. We were on the border of Laos and North Vietnam. The interesting thing was that the MiGs came out of North Vietnam, went south into Laos, then turned around and came back heading north toward us. Everyone on the crew was saying 'What's going on? Why are these guys going so far south?' I believe they were making a practice run. Once they were headed toward us they peeled off and went back into North Vietnam. That afternoon, same orbit, same mission, same aircraft, different crew, and they get hit. A rescue chopper went down as well and 7th Air Force went berserk. General Momyer had good reason to ask, 'What the hell is going on? It's eleven o'clock at night and I have 12 people down in North Vietnam. How can this happen?'[7]

"I began my Air Force career as an enlisted man," Attilio 'Pete' Pedroli told me during his interview. "After being commissioned I spent the next 11 years in SAC, much of it in the 17th Bomb Wing at Wright-Patterson AFB, Ohio, flying B-52B models. I was a radar navigator. From there I went to Command and Staff College at Maxwell AFB in Montgomery, Alabama. Chris Divich and I were classmates. I guess when they looked at my records they thought the B-66 was a good fit for me. I had no choice in selecting my assignment. Here came this piece of paper instructing me to report to Shaw AFB in South Carolina. I think I had a week between graduation from Command and Staff before I had to report to Shaw. I probably had about 4,500 hours flying time at this time. At Shaw I went through the same training everyone else did. About three months later I was headed to Takhli. I liked the B-66. It was a good, reliable airplane. I'll be brutally frank, I didn't know much about its mission until I got there and we started flying. I enjoyed the crew atmosphere, and at the time we had the 100 mission rule and people were rotating every 7 to 8 months. So they needed replacements in the worst way. On the way to Takhli I stopped at Clark in the Philippines to go through jungle survival training. I had the dubious distinction to arrive when a typhoon was moving through, so I never got to go. I flew to Bangkok, then caught a C-47 shuttle out of Don Muong Airport for Takhli. Everybody who came in about the same time as I did was either from the Staff or War College. In terms of age we were a pretty senior group to be doing this kind of thing, a lot of majors and lieutenant colonels.

"At Takhli the checkout procedure was quick and dirty. I had experience with the K-system which we had in the B-36, but not the specific system installed in the B-models. But a radar is a radar and I was a radar navigator. You turn it on and it all works pretty much the same after that. The only difference in the B-models was that it was a bombing radar, while the C-models had a much simpler navigation radar. I had plenty of experience with that, so we just started flying. I guess I was on my 29th or 30th mission when we got jumped by MiGs. We were flying a C-model trying to pick up their AAA and missile radars and jam them before the strike aircraft arrived. We were in our orbit about fifteen minutes when we got jumped. I don't know what happened because we had little warning. I thought I heard one of the Ravens call 'MiG, MiG,' and then the next thing I knew there was an explosion and we lost the right wing. It was a heat seeking missile and it caught us in the right engine. Best I can remember we were about 65 miles southwest of Hanoi. Ours was a crew of seven. I was flying as an instructor with a new navigator. It was the 14th of January, 1968, a Sunday.

"All the morning missions had gone well. I was working on the desk that day. The guy who was supposed to be flying as the instructor came down with dysentery and we couldn't find a replacement. So I went. I had my flight suit on and was ready to go. We were at 28,000 feet when we got hit. The winter monsoon was on. The airplane went into a tight spin. Sonny Mercer was the pilot. I heard him saying, 'I can't control it.' I was watching the altimeter spinning. I think I punched out at 21,000 feet. The chute opened. I came down in heavy rain and wind. I was going through undercast, overcast, more cloud layers than I can remember, all the way down I never saw the ground. I ended up in some trees, and I still couldn't see the ground. Clouds were below me. The next thing I tried was to figure out how the hell I was going to get out of that tree. I had a tree-lowering device attached to my chute, it had a friction lock so I could stop myself. Then I thought, wait a minute. If I go down and there isn't anything there I can't go back up. So I changed my mind. I guess it was about four o'clock in the afternoon when we got hit. I hung in the tree for a while to think things over. Looking around I noticed some giant bamboo, and my chute was draped over it, two stalks about ten to twelve inches thick. They had split and turned 90 degrees, like they were hanging over the edge of a karst mountain, but they were right next to me. I figured if I can get over to that bamboo, maybe I can get down. So I played Tarzan, pretending that I was on a swing and started pumping to get over far enough where I could grab one of the bamboo stalks and pull myself up in a sitting position in-between the two stalks. I got in position. When I felt comfortable I released my chute. Then I sat there for a while. When I had assembled enough courage I swung around one of the trunks and started sliding down. Then all of a sudden it was straight down, and there were these little knurls every 18 inches or so. I thought I'm glad I had my kids, because there won't be anymore.

"When I hit the ground at the foot of the bamboo tree I noticed there was a steep drop-off. I had landed on top of a big karst mountain. By then it was getting dark. I was wet and cold with all that rain. I took my dinghy and opened it and buttoned it around me to get warm. Then I opened my survival kit. I had taken some shrapnel in my left arm, and banged up my right arm going out of the plane. I decided to do something about the cuts. Ripped off pieces of adhesive tape and put them across the cuts. Then I put some gauze over the cuts and taped it all down. By then I was exhausted and fell asleep. The next morning when I awoke I was scared to death. When the animals started feeding at first light their noise was unbelievable. I thought the entire NVN army was out looking for me. It just turned out to be birds and what have you that I don't know about lives in jungles.

I figured out that I was above a village. I heard them banging a gong. I could only assume it was the morning call for breakfast, or to go out in the rice paddies or the fields or the forests. I had no idea where I was, because as I was coming down the wind blew me all over the place.

"I didn't see or hear any member of my crew. That day I heard F-4s and F-105s coming over. I got out my survival radio and made contact. One of those flyers said that he took a bearing on me. Of course my chute was still up in the trees and my beeper was still beeping. They said, 'Stand-by.' I only had one radio and was worried about the batteries. I actually had two radios, but the other one was up in the tree with my chute. They asked me what my condition was and I told them that I had minor problems. Later that day I heard people out in the jungle. They had dogs with them. That scared the hell out of me. But I was obviously above the trails and I assumed because of all the heavy rain the dogs couldn't pick up a scent. Whatever the reason, they made no effort to climb the mountain. Then they started shooting into the brush, probably just trying to get me to run. I thought, what the heck, and dug in deeper, playing the hand I had been dealt. The next day they came out again. When I didn't hear anyone I talked to passing aircraft. Otherwise I kept my mouth shut. I moved up the hill a bit more. When it was quiet again I moved back down to my position. It was Tuesday now. On Monday I had heard a number of people from my crew talking on the radio. On Tuesday I only heard a couple. I assumed that some of the guys had already been captured. Then a *Jolly Green*, an HH-53 helicopter, tried to rescue us and crashed. I don't know why, but he went down."[8]

Howard Sochurek, a reporter for the *National Geographic Magazine*, wrote about Pete Pedroli's rescue from the perspective of the guys whose job it was to retrieve downed airmen from enemy territory. "Captain Gregory Etzel," wrote Sochurek, "from Albany, Georgia, who wears the Air Force Cross among his decorations, got the call on January 15, 1968. An Air Force plane with seven men aboard had gone down, hit by an air-to-air missile from a MiG-21 about 80 miles west of Hanoi. Captain Etzel with a crew of four took off in a *Jolly Green* for the crash site. 'Visibility was 50 feet,' he said, 'and clouds were poring like milk over the edge of the cliff. We had one more ridge to cross when we hit the mountainside. The rotor blades broke on impact, the right front section of the cockpit fell off, and I was thrown clear of the ship still strapped in my seat.' Etzel suffered a broken leg. Captain David Holt, the copilot, had a broken foot. Sergeant Angus Sowell broke both a leg and an arm. Two others on the crew escaped injury. The Five men," like Pete Pedroli, "found themselves on a rock face that dropped at a 45-degree angle. Clouds and mist swirled over them, making prompt rescue impossible. The rock they were on was black and slippery with wet vegetation and moss. They tied stretchers to the ruins of the helicopter to keep the injured men level and waited in the fog. Now there were two planes with a total of 12 men down in North Vietnam. The weather cleared on the morning of the 17th. The pickup of the plane crew came first. The jungle was so thick, they passed right over the pilot of the downed B-66 at 50 yards. When he popped his smoke, it took three minutes to drift up through the foliage. The B-66 pilot had a broken leg, and Airman Michael Dodd went down on a penetrator to get him. They located two other survivors, Lieutenant Colonel 'Pete' Pedroli and Lieutenant Colonel Jim Thompson. When they got Pete, he went to the back of the cabin where the pilot, [Major Pollard 'Sonny' Mercer] was lying on a stretcher, and they just hugged each other for a long time out of relief at being saved. No trace was found of the other four crew members, who presumably were captured. A second Udorn 'Buff' rescue helicopter was searching for their comrades lost on the mountainside ... recovering the five" and barely making it back to Udorn.[9]

"They came on Wednesday afternoon," Pete Pedroli remembered. "First I heard a bunch of *Sandys* flying overhead." Douglas A1 *Skyraiders* flown by the Air Force out of NKP, Nhakom Phanom Air Base, Thailand, in support of rescue operations, had the call sign *Sandy*. "I called them. They told me to get the hell off the radio, they were working a rescue. So I did. They had two different teams going. I think they were working with Sonny Mercer. Sonny broke his legs when he ejected. I don't know if the column didn't stow properly. Something didn't happen. He caught his legs ejecting, and he had compound fractures in his legs and one of his arms. He was a mess. He hung in a tree for almost four days. A PJ, pararescue man, had to go down and get him. Then they came over and got me. I could hear them coming up the valley next to the karst mountain I was on. There was this huge umbrella shaped tree. I asked them if they could see it. They said, 'Yea.' I said, 'Come over to the tree, make a left turn, come down about 1,500 feet and you'll see my smoke.' When I heard them coming I popped some red smoke. They dropped the tree penetrator almost on my toes, perfect, with about 200 feet of cable. I got on the penetrator and they pulled me up. At that point they decided to get out of there, peeled off, dragging me behind. When they leveled off they pulled me up the rest of the way and a PJ grabbed me and pulled me in. Of course they dropped me on my bad arm, and I kind of let out a groan. The PJ said, 'Sorry, colonel.'

"I said, 'No, that felt good. That was a groan of happiness.' We picked up a Raven, Lieutenant Colonel Jim Thompson. Jim had left his survival kit and was just wandering around down in the valley, disoriented, in shock. They went down and got him. So Thompson, Sonny and I were on the chopper. They had given Sonny some morphine. He asked me for a cigarette, so I bummed a cigarette.

I had never smoked in my life. I lit it for him, trying to make him comfortable. Of course they had ambulances waiting for us when we got to Udorn. They took Sonny first and whisked him off to the hospital. I went on the other ambulance. I had a hospital corpsman helping me. He said, 'You look like you could use a boost.' So he handed me a bottle of *Old Overholz*, or whatever it was called. I had one swig, then I had another. At the hospital they offered me more whiskey. I said, 'No, but I want something cold.' They gave me a beer. I hadn't had anything to eat for four days. Two drinks and a beer – that was it. Then the intelligence people showed up and wanted to sit down and write down everything that happened. I said, 'You got to be kidding me. Get out of here.' It was a young captain just doing his job. 'I'll get with you later,' I told him.

"They cleaned up Sonny and flew him to the main hospital at Clark in the Philippines. H. Lobdell, we all called him 'H,' our B-66 deputy commander, flew up in a C-47 and came to the hospital to see me. He asked me if I wanted to stay. I said, 'Hell no, I don't want to stay here.' I walked out with him and got on his C-47 and we flew back to Takhli. At the dispensary they let me shower and clean up, gave me a straight razor so I could shave. I got one Purple Heart for getting shot down. I should have gotten eight or ten for shaving. I was bleeding like the proverbial stuck pig, never having used a straight razor before. John Giraudo, our wing commander, then came to see me. We talked. Actually, they had me under guard in the hospital. I asked him, 'Why do you have a security policeman at the door of my room?'

"'What do you mean?'

"'Look, isn't that a security policeman? Why do you have me under guard?'

"'I don't know.' He called in the doctor, a young captain. A helluva funny guy and a super doctor.

"He said, 'General,' Giraudo was a colonel, 'I'm only a doctor. What do I know about these things? He showed up. That's why he is there.'

"Giraudo said, 'Does he have to stay in the hospital?'

"'I guess not,' replied the doctor. 'Exposure, dehydration, contusions, abrasions, some cuts. Other than that I can't think of any reason to keep him here.' So I walked out of the hospital with Colonel Giraudo. We got in his car, me in slippers and a seersucker robe and pajamas, and we went to the Officers' Club and spent the rest of the night in the bar. Later on they just carried me to my bed. After that I flew to Clark for a thorough examination. While there, I was invited to spend some time with the jungle survival school people. We talked about the situation, what I did and didn't do, and how I was able to find all the water I needed by cutting down small bamboo shoots. There was a lot of water in the bamboo. About four o'clock that afternoon they decided we needed to have a beer.

So we sat around and drank and talked some more. Then they presented me with a certificate – a master's degree in jungle survival. They had checked my records and found that I had not completed their program.

"There was very little to eat in the survival kit. I drank a lot of water. I really wasn't hungry. You can last a long time without eating as long as you get plenty of water. I carried baby bottles of water in the lower pockets of my flight suit, everyone did. They were still there when I landed in the trees. That was my first water. Then, after I got on the ground, I used a little knife I carried to make a small hole in the bamboo and pored the water in my mouth or the empty baby bottles. It took a lot of time, but I had little else to do. When I ejected my straps were tight, but I lost my helmet in the wind and the rain. I was bleeding. I couldn't steer my chute, so I just relaxed. I used to tell my kids when they climbed in trees, if you get in a situation, don't just jump, sit and think about it a little. Sometimes doing nothing is the best thing. I stayed in the trees about four hours before I got down on the ground.

"Everybody got out of the airplane. Sonny died in the hospital at Clark from an embolism. I got there on a Saturday afternoon, and I believe he died that morning, just before I arrived. When I asked to see him the nurses gave me no real answers, kept evading my question. I finally said, 'Just tell me what room he is in.' The head nurse then came over and said, 'You better talk to the doctor.' I found the doctor who told me that Sonny had just passed away. I then returned home on 30 days convalescent leave. Everyone was telling my wife I didn't have to go back. John Giraudo had said to me, 'Pete, please come back.' I went back and finished my year, flew 119 combat missions, and left for home in October 1968.

"The others on my crew were captured. Lieutenant Ronald Lebert, a Raven, came straight out of EWO school at Mather to Takhli. My next assignment was to Mather, initially as an instructor, then as executive officer to the wing commander, vice commander, and base commander. At that point in time the POW wives organized and became active. The wives in the area came in and it was my job to meet with them. I met Ron Lebert's wife and we had her over to the house for dinner a number of times. I got to know her quite well. I heard from a friend in Intelligence, who swore me to secrecy, that Ron was OK. He said, 'Don't tell her anything. Just say he is OK.' So I did.

"She said, 'How do you know?'

"'Don't ask, please,' I told her, 'just take my word for it.' She did. In 1973 Ron was released along with the other POWs. In the meantime I had been assigned to Europe and returned to Mather as wing vice commander, later I became wing commander. When Ron returned, he was an engineer, they put him in a civil engineering job. Ron wanted to get back to flying. So I set up a special program for Ron and got him re-qualified allowing him to return to crew duty. Major Thomas Sumpter and Captain Hubert Walker were the other two Ravens onboard the aircraft. Major Irby Terrell was the navigator whom I was giving a flight check that day. All three were captured and spent five years as POWs of the North Vietnamese.

"As for my tour at Takhli. I think if you have to be in a combat environment, you couldn't ask for a better place. Probably the most professional group of people I associated with. Even though we had the constant rotation, people coming and going, the quality of the people remained high. Unfortunately we didn't fly as crews. I would show up and walk in and there were a couple of other people there, or five or six depending on the aircraft. Many times I wouldn't even know who they were. We got on the airplane and flew the mission. I believe the Ravens had a crew system among themselves, and we pilots and navigators would try to fly as a team, but there were no integrated crews as I was used to in SAC. It just wasn't possible with the constant turn-over. When I became the 41st squadron navigator, I would wait for a day when I didn't have much going on and jump on an airplane and fly. There were not many I didn't want to fly with, not many. We had one pilot we shipped to Saigon because he aborted every mission.

"As far as maintenance went, it was a reliable airplane. Extremely reliable. We lost one C-model, November 17, 1967. He lost an engine on take-off. A young major, Max Nichols, he was a good pilot, an instructor pilot. I remember him the night before it happened talking with others at the club. They were discussing what not to do when you lose an engine right after take-off – 'Don't try to land the damn airplane, because it can't. When you get down low, you are heavy with fuel, and it will stall out on you.' The next day it happened to him. He lost an engine right after take-off. I am sitting at the end of the runway when he decided to come in and land. I could see when he was about a couple thousand feet off the end of the runway that he was settling. He hit short and the damn airplane burst into flames. The pilot, two navigators and two Ravens didn't make it. Nick ejected on the ground and came down in the flames.

"Occasionally Chris Divich and I would go to Bangkok for two or three days. Go out and have a good Kobe steak. I loved the old Erawan Hotel. They had fabulous lobster soup."[10]

The war went on. There was no end in sight. Dedicated Air Force people kept flying North, and kept on dying.

CHAPTER TWENTY-THREE

POETS, PRIESTS,
AND FLIGHT SURGEONS

Takhli Royal Thai Air Force Base, Thailand, was home to five squadrons of F-105 and EB-66 aircraft. There wasn't a time of day or night when aircraft didn't roar down the 10,000 foot runway headed towards North Vietnam. Aircraft were lost, men died, were wounded, or psychologically shattered after seeing friends perish. It all became very routine. Not that anyone got used to it. Chris Divich remembers one of his Air Command and Staff College classmates. "He was a Thud pilot, so fat when he first arrived at Takhli I didn't know how he fit into the cockpit, much less stay in the Air Force. He went up every day in the hot, hot afternoon, sometimes early in the morning, wearing big combat boots, shorts, and a T-shirt. He said to me, 'Chris, when I get home my wife isn't going to recognize me.' He slimmed down the way he wanted and got killed on his 98th combat mission. That really had an impact. Everyone knew him, monitored his weight, joked with him about how fantastic he was doing."[1] 350 out of 733 F-105s built were lost in combat over Laos and North Vietnam – 31 to SAMs, 23 to MiGs, and the rest to AAA.[2]

In many ways it was a war like no other. The strategic bombers, the B-52s, flew interdiction in Laos, and close air support in the South. The tactical aircraft flew the strategic missions against the heavily defended heartland of the North. The flyers chafed under the restrictions imposed by Washington politicians who didn't seem to have the slightest idea of what real war was like – a place where men died. At times it appeared that the men at the highest levels of the Johnson administration couldn't care less about what happened to those they sent into

Father McMullen in June 1965 on the flight line at Takhli RTAFB, Thailand. The indefatigable 'combat' Priest flew enough missions to earn an Air Medal – and the displeasure of the Air Force chief of chaplains.

battle. A feeling of abandonment and resentment, particularly against Johnson and McNamara, found expression in the bawdy songs they sang at the bars at the Takhli and Korat Officers' Clubs. This also was a world of men without women and it showed. Recalls Major General John Giraudo, "A special all-time best fighter pilot's song book had been proposed to me, and I approved. I signed a welcoming letter which would become the Foreword for the book ... The guys had really done a great job," Giraudo thought. "Fighter pilot songs from World War I onward were included. But also included were some songs unimaginable, one's I'd forbidden them to sing at the club. I got red-faced just flipping through the book. Even more embarrassed and mad when I saw my stupidly innocent welcoming letter at the front. To this day I cringe when I think of some nice people running across one of those songbooks in an attic or museum."[3] Yet there were many other sentiments expressed in poetry and lyric by men somewhat more introspective and creative, reflecting on the burdens they carried, trying to cope with death.

Captain William Rothas, an EB-66 EWO, reflected his pain in these touching words while up high in the 'pocket' northwest of Hanoi, as he listened to his friend Dick, down below, die in his F-105:

Different Missions
by William Rothas

The land appears so peaceful from thirty-thousand feet,
Though pockmarked by bombs and simmering in the heat.
You're aloft, and aloof, and thinking of the States,
While down below the Thuds are due, about to keep their dates.

Guard channel crackles and comes alive, Mayday, I'm going down,
Off eighty-nine, sixty east, do you read, *Red Crown*?
A pause, and then a calm, sure voice, Roger Scotch 2, we do.
We're on our way, balls to the wall, we've got three Sandys, too!

So I sit there in my orbit, five miles above the ground.
Sun in my face, warfare below, nice and safe and sound,
While Scotch 2, my buddy Dick, is scrambling to be free.
But there's little time, too many Gs – the rest is history.

My mission's over, successful again, it's time to RTB.
Red Crown calls on Guard, Scotch 2 come up! Silence.
The Officers Club's like death tonight, all eyes are filled with sorrow.
Dick is gone, forever now, and I fly again tomorrow.

• • •

The Red River Valley reflects both on the futility of the air war as experienced by the combat crews and the disconnect between those doing the fighting and those directing the war from comfortable headquarters environments:

The Red River Valley
by George Thatcher

Down this valley we're jinkin' and weavin' in our bomb loaded, over-grossed Thuds,
Soon the air cover fighters are leavin', and somehow we're not feelin' like studs.

Come and fly on my wing in the moonlight, do not hasten to call 'bingo fuel',
There are SAMs torching bright in the June night, you're in Nam, not graduate school,

There's a bridge that they say we must take out, it's the same one we've bombed before,
Through the clouds it's not easy to make out, with our bomb sights from some other war.

But the frag, it was deadly specific, said the bad guys had made some repairs.
Mission count makes the staff look terrific, as they lead from their large swivel chairs.

So press on, count the scalps, just like Custer, your rewards are so easy to see,
Twenty missions earn you an Air Medal cluster, every hundred a new DFC.

• • •

Major Eugene Cirillo, assigned to the 355th Tactical Fighter Wing at Takhli, Thailand, wrote the unforgettable and heart touching lines of *The Wingmen From Takhli*. None of us who were there will ever forget them – the wingmen from Takhli:

The Wingmen From Takhli
by Eugene Cirillo

When time passes on, and we have reached the twilight of our lives,
I shall harken back to over a hundred flights in these war-torn Asian skies and,
Once again, I'll hear that roar of burner, blast of cannon and screech of tires.
Through weak and misty eyes in vain will I look and search the skies for those wingmen no longer here.
And always, my heart, my soul, and my memory will take me back, Perhaps to Quang Khe, or maybe Dong Hoi, but always
to those wingmen from Takhli.

These three poem are representative of many more written by men who faced death every day in hostile skies. Unlike their fathers in World War II, theirs was not a war understood or supported by the people back home. Upon their return they received no parades or welcome home receptions, and their sacrifices were not recognized for the longest time. Yet, they knew they served their nation well, and believed in each other.

• • •

Captain Frank McMullen, known to flyers at Takhli as Father McMullen, relieved the stresses of combat in a different way. He was at the end of the runway waving us off, day or night. He was there when we returned. He was there for everyone. To this day he is remembered for the calming inspiration he brought to the flight line. Father McMullen was a flying priest. Born in Newark, New Jersey, in 1927, Frank attended Brooklyn Catholic School after his parents moved there. "As a youngster I admired the local priests, looked up to them, found them to be good role models, real men and leaders. Our parish was very large and had six priests. One of the priests told me that he lost a friend at Pearl Harbor, and immediately volunteered to join the military. They put him in the Army Air Corps. He was killed in action. A second priest joined the military as well. I thought if I'd ever become a priest I'd want to be a military chaplain. I attended the seminary in Huntingdon, Long Island, and was ordained to the diocese of Brooklyn. I asked my bishop several times for permission to join the military, but the response always was, 'We are too short-handed. I can't let you go.' Then Vietnam built up and I received permission. The bishop asked me, 'How long is this going to be?'

"I replied, 'Three years.' I retired as an Air Force colonel twenty years later.

"My first assignment in October 1963 was to March AFB, California. I was there a little over a year when one morning I received a telephone call and was informed that I was going to Southeast Asia. Here I am, a brand new chaplain, just finding my way around, and going to war. It was a bit intimidating. I got my shots and in due course ended up at Takhli Air Base in Thailand. Things were rather basic at Takhli in April 1965, they were just beginning to build hooches, few people were there. We had a couple old Japanese buildings from the Second War, not much else. This was a new world for me – the military, a tropical environment, and the poisonous snakes. There were cobras everywhere. We had F-105s, two squadrons, on temporary duty. I remember them flying missions over the North every day, the newspapers denying anything like that happened. I got close to the pilots. I'd go out to the flight line to bless them, see them on their way, and be there for them again when they returned.

"Soon the B-66s came in. At first there were only a few planes, then more arrived. I never forget the day when one of the B-66 pilots, Dick Wilson, said to me, "You want to come along on a mission?' I had never gone through an altitude chamber or survival school, flying was not in my job description. He said, 'You'll be alright, Father.' So they put me in the spare front seat of the C-model, the one-time gunner's seat, checked me out on the parachute and the ejection seat, and off we went. Before take-off Dick added my name to the AF Form 1. In the column where it read Crew Position he penciled in: DGS. Dick was a PLT. The navigator a NAV. The four Ravens in back were identified as EWs. I asked Dick, 'What does DGS stand for?' He gave me a sheepish look and said, 'Father, that should be obvious. It stands for what you are – Divine Guidance System.' So that's what I was from then on, a DGS. I don't know exactly where we went that day, but it was up North, just west of Hanoi somewhere. It was a day mission, the F-105s were coming in below us. I remember looking out the window on my side and seeing the F-105s. My next mission I flew with the Ravens in back where all the black boxes are and you had to eject downward. So I came to know all the flyers well.

"When the fighter pilots were getting into their cockpits I would go down the flight line and climb up the ladders and bless them, 'God bring you home safely.' I said that many, many times. I remember one day going down the line of F-105s preparing for a strike when one of the pilots said to me, 'My wife is expecting any day now. This is going to be a tough mission. If I don't come back, will you contact her and tell her that my last thoughts would have been about her. Tell her I love her.' Well, it was a bad mission. We lost a number of planes that day. Marty Case came back. In 1984 the *River Rats* had their convention in Washington DC, and of course I attended, being a proud *River Rat* myself. I looked around for

Marty, and there he was with his wife. I went over to her and said, 'I want to deliver a message to you Mrs Case,' and I told her what Marty had tasked me to say so long ago when he thought he might not return.

"I remember the times at the end of the day when the guys came back and they had lost one or two of their own. There were no smiles, only sadness. One day one of the pilots came back and he was in tears. They had been up North and his closest friend had gone in. He cried, 'He's gone. He's gone. There's no way he could have gotten out. No way.' He was inconsolable, deeply distraught. He had stayed over the crash site as long as he could and circled around. He was soaking wet, tears running down his face. He put his arm around my shoulders and walked back to the debriefing room with me – a visibly broken man. Several months later we learned that his friend had gotten out after all, and become a POW. He was so pleased, but couldn't figure out how he got out of that plane. I'll never forget that day when this F-105 pilot put his arm around my shoulders crying, 'He's gone. He's gone.' Such are the things that touch your heart. I knew all these men. Saw them the night before in the club. Blessed them just before they took off on their dangerous missions.

"I was on the mission on July 24, 1965, when the Ravens in back of our aircraft intercepted the first operational *Fansong* radar near Hanoi. The crew received the Distinguished Flying Cross for that mission. When we returned to Takhli the squadron commander came out to meet our plane. He congratulated each member of the crew personally, saying 'You earned your DFC today.' I said to him, 'If anybody should get a cross, it should be me.' He smiled, 'Sorry Father, I can't do that,' was his reply. I flew with the B-66s because they allowed me to do so, invited me to go along and share their life. The reason why I wanted to fly with them was to better understand what they were facing. Army chaplains go into combat with their troops, they stay near them at the front lines, they want to be there if they are wounded. Navy chaplains go on board ship. And those with the Marines are right up there with them. In the Air Force the best I could do was to share the life of the flyers, experience what they experienced. I remember a night mission. We were coming back over Laos when a ground radar site contacted us that we had an unknown ten miles behind us. I remember our pilot saying, 'Brigham, where is he now?' We never learned who that unknown aircraft was, but that was life in the air. A little scary at times.

"One day a crew chief said to me, 'Father, you should have a chapel out here on the flight line where we are most of the time.' They had little tents near the flight line where they stayed while their planes were off on a combat mission. So they built me a tent chapel, and over the entrance they put a sign reading: *Spiritual Maintenance – Flight Line Chapel*. I had Mass out there every Sunday morning, usually around seven or eight. The early morning strikes had gone out and things were kind of quiet then. The other days of the week I had Mass at six in the morning in a little library section in the Wing administration building.

"I flew sixteen missions with the B-66s, day and night missions. I remember seeing the lights of Hanoi. Dick Wilson put me in for an Air Medal when I left that September for March AFB, in Riverside, California. Six months later, in April '66, I got orders to go to Goose Bay, Newfoundland. There were six radar sites I visited regularly. We had a little *Otter* plane equipped with floats in summer, skis in winter. That's how I got around. I spent the next 18 months up there. Then I was transferred to Wichita Falls, Texas, a training base. One day I was notified to attend the noon parade. All the students would march out before going to their afternoon classes. This particular day Colonel McNabb, the commander, was on the reviewing stand as well and he read the citation that accompanied the award of the Air Medal. I remember him saying as he pinned the medal on me, 'How does a chaplain get an Air Medal?' I just smiled."[4]

The B-66 crews fondly remember Father McMullen. John Norden, one of the B-66 navigators at Takhli says "Father McMullen got along with everyone, airman and officer alike. He was a fixture at the bar, glad to buy anyone a drink – and he was always ready to listen. The first time I really took notice of him was when the airmen erected a tent along the flight line with a sign above the entrance that read, 'Spiritual Maintenance.' Dick Wilson was the first to put him in the gunner's seat for a mission. Father McMullen would get out of the aircraft when we passed the arming area to bring canteens of water to the Thud jocks as they waited to get their bombs and guns armed. Then he would get back in his seat. While we were in orbit near Hanoi I could see him sitting next to me, doing laps on his rosary while watching the air strikes below. Dick Wilson had our Awards and Decorations guy, Sergeant Schantze, put Father McMullen in for an Air Medal. The medal came through, and that's when the stuffing hit the fan. The Air Force Chief of Chaplains reassigned Father McMullen to Newfoundland, and we received orders never to do that again. Four years later, I'm sitting in the bar at Bien Hoa on my way to the 1st Cavalry Division to fly OV-10s. I look at the next bar stool, and if it isn't Father McMullen. He got himself another Southeast Asia assignment."[5]

Vernon Johnson, gently kidded by his fellow flyers for being the only Air Force pilot with a hearing aid, recalls that night mission with Father McMullen when a MiG tried to have a go at them. "We arrived in our working area over the North. We never had fighter cover in the early days. GCI, Brigham, advised us that a bandit was headed in our direction. I put the aircraft in a high-speed descent toward the deck, figuring if the bandit had radar guided missiles he would have to pick us out of the ground clutter, making it more difficult to achieve lock-on. On the way down I hit Mach .92, and the B-66 buffets considerably when it gets close to the speed of sound, making for a rough ride. I queried Brigham on occasion about the position of the bandit who was closing on us. At one point Brigham informed us that the radar return of the bandit and ours had merged on his scope. I continued on down to ground level, leveled off and took up a heading for Ubon. GCI then notified us that the bandit had broken off and was heading north. I climbed back to altitude and returned to Takhli. I believe Father McMullen and the rest of the crew earned their Air Medal that night."[6]

Maybe Larry Bullock tells it best how the air crews felt about Father McMullen, "Following one of our missions we were all standing around the B-66 operations hooch having a cold beer. Father McMullen came up. One in our group remarked, 'It is Sunday Father, and we missed church.' Without missing a beat, Father McMullen dipped his finger in his beer and proceeded to bless each of us. I don't think they came any better than Father McMullen."[7] Amen.

• • •

Combat and the stresses it imposes can be fully appreciated only by those who have been there and done it. No flyer can share with anyone else his fears of what he has faced and what the future might bring. Everyone in his own way tries to find release from burdens and pressures at times seemingly unbearable. Some find release at the bar singing loudly, others reading scripture, writing poetry, or in any number of other ways. There are real physical maintenance issues to be addressed as well by those injured in body and mind. It is the flight surgeon's task, a familiar figure to every airman, to deal with injury and sickness, real or imagined. It is one thing to do annual flying physicals at a well equipped Stateside air base, quite another to operate under rudimentary conditions in a combat zone. Doctor Kenneth G. Gould, a retired Air Force colonel, then a Major, was no more ordinary as a flight surgeon than Father McMullen was as a priest. He was assigned to Takhli Air Base in July 1966 as Director of Professional Services at the 355th TFW dispensary, becoming its commander in March 1967. For flying he was assigned to the 6460th TRS, the squadron that flew the *Brown Cradles*. Before Dr. Gould knew it he was operating ECM equipment, flew 24 combat missions, and helped alleviate a critical shortage of electronic warfare officers. Colonel Gould earned two Air Medals in his part-time job as a B-66 combat flyer.

Doc Gould was born in 1929 to a physician father who in 1943 became the chief flight surgeon for the 3rd Air Force in Tampa, Florida. Like his father he too wanted to be a medical doctor. "My mother made me go to Duke in 1946 because the University of Florida was too much of a party school and she wanted me to be a doctor like dad. I loved Duke. Became an SAE and learned to drink beer." Ken Gould interned at the Ohio State Medical Center and joined the Air Force in the summer of 1955. "In June 1966 I found out that I was to be assigned to Takhli RTAFB, about 100 miles north of Bangkok, Thailand. On the north end of the base the Thais had a squadron of F-86 jet fighters, on the southside the USAF had about 5,000 men, no women, supporting three squadrons of F-105s and EB-66 electronic warfare aircraft, a detachment of KC-135 tankers, and one ancient *Gooney Bird*, a C-47. The headquarters of the 355th Tactical Fighter Wing and the base hospital were in a two story wooden building built by the Japanese during the Second World War. Many of the enlisted men lived in tents, the lucky ones lived in screened in hootches on stilts, as did most of the officers. There were a few trailers housing senior officers. Construction was going on everywhere. About the time I came the rains came as well. The wooden walkways between hootches and other buildings floated in the water that was often a foot deep. The cobras, kraits and other snakes sought refuge in the hootches, although no one was bitten in the year I was there.

"Officers took their meals in the Officers' Club where young Thai girls waited tables. We knew no Thai. They knew no English. The menu consisted of a dozen numbered items, so meals were by the numbers. Early in my year only one menu item was available. It made no difference what you ordered, you always got the same thing. Somehow there was always beer in the bar. There were only a few things to do – fly, drink, eat, drink, go to town to visit the ladies in the bars, and drink some more. None of the pilots wanted to fly the missions they had to fly, but they did. Not to fly meant courts martial and discharge from the service they loved, all they ever considered doing. They were asked to bomb the same targets three days running. Johnson and McNamara called targets from the White House for three days – because they were too busy to do it every day. On the first day the target was destroyed and there was only light opposition. On the second day the target was still destroyed but the North Vietnamese had moved in antiaircraft guns that occasionally shot down an aircraft. On the third day the target was still destroyed but had now sprouted surface to air missiles as well. On that day we always lost one or more planes. Pilots were killed or ejected and were captured or occasionally rescued in dramatic fashion. They had to operate under the rules promulgated by the White House, ridiculous in the extreme.

"I cared for many good men who were physically ill on that third morning. They could not eat or if they did, they went out behind the club and threw up. They had difficulty sleeping. They lost weight and smoked too much. Their hands shook and their vision blurred. They cried in my office, but never in front of other aircrew. They were frightened beyond all measure and still they flew as they were ordered to. My role was to provide care for these dedicated men who deserved better leadership from the White House, and better understanding from their fellow citizens in the USA. They were vilified daily in the press and by demonstrations and did their duty at the direction of their president. They did not want the war they fought and yet they could not quit. They were sworn to do as ordered. They were wonderful heroes – all of them.

"When I was sent to Takhli as a flight surgeon I was to oversee the health of one of the squadrons on base – the 6460th Tactical Reconnaissance Squadron. While in Southeast Asia flight surgeons were excused from a monthly four-hour flying requirement. Most flight surgeons, however, flew whenever possible. When I reported to my squadron, I was astonished to learn there was a shortage of EWOs, and they offered to teach me to fly that seat in a *Brown Cradle* aircraft if I wished. I did! I read through a stack of manuals about electronic warfare and the EB-66B. Then one day I found my name on the 'frag' or schedule. Later on I learned, after several flights, that I was mostly sent on low threat missions outside of Route Packs 5 and 6. These low threat missions didn't count toward 100 missions required of aircrew to rotate back home and were therefore not popular – give it to Doc. One day though, I was snookered into a mission by an EWO who didn't want to fly this one. I showed up late for the briefing, it was 4 a.m. This EWO came over to me and said 'My pilot is drunk.' I went over and talked to his pilot who seemed perfectly normal to me. 'He's not drunk,' I told the EWO. 'Well,' he replied, 'if you are so sure Doc, why don't you go.' So I went. Not until we were airborne did I learn the nature of our mission, that we would fly in the red circles where the SAMs were without turning on our jammers so the Thuds could evaluate the effectiveness of their new QRC-160 ECM pods. Only if they ran into trouble were we to turn on our jammers. We had a couple of SAMs fired at us, but jinked well enough. The commander of the 6460th put us in for the Distinguished Flying Cross.

"Each of us had a small locker assigned in which we placed our personal belongings before a flight – wallets, money, rings, bracelets and even our squadron patches. We wore our rank, but no ratings," such as pilot, navigator, or flight surgeon wings. "Each of us had our own helmet, parachute, and survival vest. Mine was a little different than all others. When I had my first fitting, I had a business-like 38 caliber pistol in a holster with extra clips of ammunition. I asked the personal equipment specialist to remove the pistol and give me an additional radio instead. 'But Doc,' he protested, 'what are you going to do if you get shot down? How are you going to protect yourself?'

"'I want search and rescue to come and get me. I don't want to shoot the village chief's son and then have his father run me through with a pitchfork,'

I told him. Everyone laughed because the vests already had two radios plus an automatic radio beeper in the parachute. I was the only one as far as I knew who flew with four radios – and for that I took a fair amount of ribbing.

"The dispensary in the old Japanese built wooden building was painted a puke green. The paint on the door frames and walls was dirty and worn. Inside the dispensary there was a waiting area. Along one wall of the hallway stood about ten chairs of variable parentage. Around the corner was a bottled water dispenser. The turbidity and color of the water did not give a feeling of confidence. In places the floor had more than a slight slant. We didn't complain, this was one of the few air-conditioned buildings on base. Downstairs were tiny offices for three of the eight physicians assigned. The other doctors had offices in the buildings of the various squadrons to which they were assigned. The pharmacy had few medicines and the more frequently used items seemed often to be in short supply. In the spring they had been down to their last bottle of Kaopectate, affectionately known as *cork*. Diarrhea was something hard to avoid, it was only a matter of time for each arrival until the symptoms set in. Fortunately there was an adequate supply of penicillin to treat the almost epidemic gonorrhea that 5,000 airmen 12,000 miles from home managed to find on an almost daily basis in the little town of Takhli. When I arrived on base I spent some time trying to figure out who could authorize shipment of medical supplies we so desperately needed. One day I discussed the matter with one of our senior NCOs. He came up with a solution. He thought the answer was to send men on 3-day R&Rs to Clark Air Base in the Philippines with its well stocked and large hospital. They would meet with their friends and 'liberate' what we needed most. Miracles were produced. We set up one of the best labs in all of Southeast Asia. We were never again short of *cork*.

"One morning the sergeant in charge of the lab called out, 'Hey major. Come look at this, indicating the microscope. This summons was part of the usual game between the lab techs and the doctors to see if the doctors really knew their stuff. Peering through the lenses, I saw an ascaris egg typical of the intestinal parasitic roundworm endemic in the local population. 'Who's ill?'

"'No one.

"'Well then? Where did this ascaris egg come from?'

"I was astounded by the answer. 'The water bottle in the hallway.' The water came from supplies processed on the Thai side of the base. Water was drawn from the nearby dirty brown canals, or klongs, that were used for every imaginable purpose by the local population. The water was drawn into huge tanks and treated with barium to flocculate the solids. Chlorine in large amounts was added to kill anything alive. After the solids settled the clear clean water could be drawn off the top and safely consumed. The trouble was that the system was inadequate to supply the needs of the 5,000 Americans and the several thousand Thai airmen and their families on the north side of the runway. Water was being drawn out of the tanks before flocculation was complete. Actually the amount of chlorine used was so great that nothing living survived in the water. It always choked me a little to drink the water."[8]

Doc Gould, like everyone else, rotated home after a year or so and was replaced by other dedicated flight surgeons. The war developed a life of its own and kept going on and on. In 1970, as part of a draw down of forces in Thailand, the EB-66s moved from Takhli to Korat. Gerald Hanner, a navigator in the 42nd TEWS remembers it was "just another sortie in the EB-66C. We had the flight surgeon with us in addition to the four Ravens in back. Things were moving smoothly, until at about 18,000 feet there was this soft 'P-toom' coming from somewhere. The aircraft shook just a little. I scanned the number two engine, the pilot scanned number one – we looked at each other. Everything seemed to be fine. The flight surgeon sitting next to me in the gunner's seat looked just a bit uncomfortable, probably wishing he had tagged along with someone else. Then the lead Raven called to say that we had to return to Korat. 'Why?' the pilot asked. Because we lost the escape hatch on climb out. They routinely had the hatch open on the ground for ventilation, and unfortunately, this particular hatch on this occasion did not latch properly, and poof, off it went when the Ravens pressurized their cabin. We went back to Korat, changed aircraft, and off we went again sans our good flight surgeon. Apparently, he had enough excitement for one day."[9]

CHAPTER TWENTY-FOUR

THE ASQ-96 FIASCO AND THE BIRTH OF THE EB-66E

The first RB-66Cs arrived in South Vietnam in April 1965 when the war was beginning to assume substance. The first five *Brown Cradle* jamming aircraft followed six months later. By late summer of 1966 nearly all RB-66C and all *Brown Cradle* aircraft had been moved from France and Shaw AFB to Takhli RTAFB in Thailand. Few aircraft of the type remained at Shaw, forcing replacements to report for duty at Takhli with little or no training in the aircraft they were to fly into war. In the war zone, especially north of 20 degrees latitude, survival without ECM support pushed the odds in the enemy's favor. Unarmed, trusting in their technical skills, holding a deep seated belief that the *fighter boys* depended on them for survival, made the EB-66 crews go out day after day, night after night.

The RB-66C, with its crew of four Ravens, was flown nearly around the clock. Only in the lower, less defended Route Packages could the *Brown Cradles* operate on their own. Without the presence of a C-model the *Cradles* were practically blind to the radar environment around them and would have been easy victims to an SA-2 attack. The location of the SAM associated *Fansong* radars was monitored by the RB-66C aircrews on a daily basis. If a *Fansong* radar came up, its presence and location was passed to F-105 and F-4 strike fighters. If within range of the SA-2, the B-66 would move just far enough to preclude the missiles from reaching – and continue its critical jamming support of the strike force. Joe Sapere was the navigator on the first RB-66C to fly into the DRV and is representative of the caliber of aircrew manning these planes. Frank Widic, the lead Raven in position 4 in the back notes "With Joe we were flying with the APS-

A KC-135 tanker over Laos refueling two EB-66C electronic reconnaissance aircraft from the 42nd TEWS bound for a combat mission near Hanoi. The C-model, the most versatile of the EB-66 aircraft series, was flown more than any other model, and suffered the highest losses.

54 radar warning receiver in the ON position. We were picking up a *Fansong* radar. The whole crew could hear it tracking our aircraft. The *Fansong* was about 15 miles off to our right, we were within easy range of its *Guideline* missiles. Joe called over the intercom in his usual calm, smile filled voice, 'Raven 4.'

"'Yea.'

"'How about if we slide over to the left five miles? Would that be alright with you?' The Raven 3 was jamming the upper beam of the *Fansong*. I was D/Fing the lower beam. The Raven in position one was searching for the BGO6 missile guidance signal which wasn't up yet, so they hadn't launched a missile. I replied, 'Joe, do it.' I remember that exchange because I thought it was so cool the way Joe handled the situation – as if it was the most routine thing in the world to ask of me. After all, it was just a surface to air missile site trying to kill us. When the BGO6 missile tracker came up and the signal jumped in intensity it meant the missile had been launched. Only then, and if we were within range, would we execute a SAM break. A SAM break was a modified split S for about 110 degrees away from the SAM site, all the while descending and maintaining positive G-loading. After that we'd execute a maximum performance climb in the opposite direction. The *Guideline* missile could not follow steep turns and eventually self-destructed. All the scrap from the exploding missiles fell on someone down below. SAM breaks were not made unless absolutely necessary to survive, because while in the break the B-66 was not providing protection to the strike force below. Crews learned to cope with SAMs on instinct. If you flew often enough you knew just by what you heard how close you could get to the site," Frank Widic asserted. "The closer we got to the strike target, the harder it was for the SAM operators to deal with the jamming. We pushed the envelope whenever we could."[1]

The task of the RB-66C and the accompanying *Brown Cradle* aircraft was to warn the strike force and to handle threat radars. Two jammers were put on the horizontally polarized upper beam of the *Fansong* radar, and two vertically polarized jammers on the lower beam at a predetermined sweep setting. In addition, barrage jammers were put on the missile's tracking beacon frequency, and random bundles of aluminum chaff were dropped to present false targets. Chaff, a World War II technique of dropping aluminum strips cut to a radar's resonant frequency, continued to be a powerful countermeasure. The North Vietnamese radar operators, assisted by their Russian tutors, in time acquired their own techniques. A favorite of theirs was to keep their *Fansong* tracking radars off the air as long as possible while tracking potential targets from information provided by acquisition and early warning radars such as *Flat Face*, *Spoon Rest* and the powerful, multibeam *Barlock*. They attempted to launch on RB-66 generated jamming strobes, but that technique proved to be much more difficult to implement in practice then in theory. The Ravens of 1965 and 1966 had lots of experience in the B-66 and were not easily succored into traps by North Vietnamese radar operators.

The B-66s changed their tactics when the radar environment in North Vietnam expanded and the number of SAM missile battalions grew. A break came about the time Captain David Zook perfected the QRC-160-1 ECM self-protection jamming pod for installation on the Takhli F-105s. In three test missions flown in quick succession by ECM pod equipped F-105s the pods proved their value. With the strike fighters carrying their own self-protection devices it was now possible for the RB-66s to jam not only SAM and AAA threat radars, but also the equally dangerous SAM acquisition radars. Nothing remains static in war, even less so in the battle of the beams, where seemingly small electronic innovations often made a big difference. Constantly operating in a high threat SAM and MiG environment, the B-66s took their lumps. The first C-model was downed by a SAM near Vinh in February 1966. Six RB-66Cs had been lost by January 1968 after flying thousands of missions in support of their F-105 and F-4 strike buddies. Consequently, there was an urgent need for additional aircraft of this type. For once the Air Staff moved swiftly. In late 1966 permission was received from Secretary McNamara to pull 9 WB-66Ds out of storage and reconfigure them as RB-66C electronic reconnaissance aircraft using the latest technology available. Then everything went wrong on that promising and essential project.[2]

The ASQ-96 was a semi-automatic reconnaissance system designed to perform many of the functions accomplished manually by four Ravens in the RB-66C. The prototype system was installed in RB-66C 54-467. The aircraft had a history of being used for purposes other than what it was originally intended for. When assigned to the 42nd TRS at Spangdahlem in the late 1950s, and later at RAF Chelveston and Toul-Rosieres, 54-467 was modified to serve as a flying command post. It was a very early version of much more sophisticated aircraft with the same type of mission developed and flown in later years by the Strategic Air Command. The aircraft received an ARC-65 single sideband HF radio and seven additional UHF radios which served as radio relays. RB-66C 54-467 served in an airborne command post capacity for the United States Air Forces in Europe for many years. In time, 467 ended up at Eglin AFB, Florida, as a test aircraft with the Armament and Development Test Center, ADTC.

Captain Stan Tippin led a small group of electronic warfare officers from ADTC to a facility of the TRW Corporation at Los Angeles International Airport – LAX. There, Stan and his group of Ravens was to become familiar with the ASQ-96, fly test missions out of LAX, then return with the aircraft to Eglin for final flight testing and evaluation before the system was installed in the former WB-66D weather reconnaissance aircraft and the remainder of the RB-66C fleet.

The officers finished their familiarization course for the ASQ-96. Then they spent a considerable period of time waiting for TRW to get the system installed and ready. "They just could never get the ASQ-96 to work," said Stan Tippin.[3] TRW remained optimistic. The Air Force continued to prepare for the much needed upgrade to its EB-66C tactical electronic reconnaissance fleet.

Lieutenant Al Kersis completed B-66 training at Shaw in May 1967, then went to Homestead AFB, Florida, for ten days of sea survival training. Enroute to Takhli his orders directed him and two other Ravens to stop for two weeks at Redondo Beach, California, for ASQ-96 training. The idea was for Lieutenant Kersis and others to train on the new equipment, and in turn they would train Takhli aircrews once the ASQ-96 configured aircraft arrived. "It was gee-whizz stuff back then," Al Kersis recalls, "but nothing ever came of it. At Takhli we continued to fly the old C-models and the upgrades consisted of QRC-fixes to our old equipment."[4] Finally the Air Force decided to test-fly only the automatic direction finding portion of the ASQ-96. "We took 54-467 back to Eglin," notes Stan Tippin, "and flew it for several months. The airplane was so over-grossed that everyone was a little afraid of it. Taking off south out of Eglin AFB, we feared to get salt water on our belly from the surf as we struggled to get airborne. The DF-system was a flop. Nothing worked. We finally flew 467 to Davis-Monthan in October 1970 and parked her in the desert. On August 25, 1975, 54-467 was sold to Southwest Alloys Company for scrap.[5]

A second much more successful effort initiated by the Air Staff quickly bore fruit, providing a significant upgrade in active ECM support capability for the tactical forces in Southeast Asia. Beginning in mid 1967 the 13 aging *Brown Cradle* jamming aircraft at Takhli were augmented by the much more capable EB-66E. The EB-66Es were 51 former RB-66B photo reconnaissance planes withdrawn from desert storage, reconditioned at the Douglas Tulsa facility, then configured with a very capable and up-to-date ECM suit of receivers, modulators and 28 noise jammers. The E-model was a significant improvement over the *Brown Cradle*, in fact it was close to being a new airplane. However, the E-model proved to be significantly heavier than the RB-66B photo airplane that it once was, with a reconfigured cockpit which put the electronic warfare officer on the right and the navigator on the left. Installation and integration of various electronic systems was accomplished by Dynalectron at their Cheyenne facility under the direction of the Sacramento Air Materiel Area, SAMA. The delivery of the new E-models to the user organizations was not without problems. For instance, no new documentation was provided to the flyers or maintenance crews to reflect the aircraft's increased gross weight and higher fuel consumption. Such things the good folks at Takhli and at Shaw had to figure out for themselves. There was a formal OT&E, Operational Test and Evaluation, of the E-model conducted by the 4416th Test Squadron at Eglin AFB. Captain Norman Kasch who survived several surface to air missile attacks while flying over the North, as well as an attack by two MiG-17s, ran the OT&E for the EB-66E. The aircraft was flown against the SADS-1 system at Eglin using various jammer configurations and settings before delivery to the field.[6]

Don Harding had returned from Takhli to Shaw in late 1966 and was assigned to the 4417th Combat Crew Training Squadron where he flew mostly RB-66B photo reconnaissance aircraft as an instructor pilot, training pilot replacements for Southeast Asia. "It was April 1968 when I flew the *High Flight* from hell," Harding recalls. "It was a *Flying Fish* delivery flight, the code name for aircraft being ferried across the Pacific. Flights to and from Europe were coded *High Flights*, but we referred to all aircraft deliveries as *High Flights*. I believe it was aircraft number 54-446, a former photo plane that had been converted to an E-model configuration. I was to pick it up in Cheyenne, Wyoming, where the Dynalectron Company had worked on it for the past six months. Any airplane that isn't flown for that long will give you problems. The airplane had 39 external antennas, I counted them, including several big sail antennas on the side and top of the fuselage. When I first laid eyes on the plane it was leaking hydraulic fluid. I started the engines, exercised all the control surfaces and taxied out to the 10,000 foot runway. The tower controller said, 'The runway has just been closed for construction.' There isn't anything on the runway, and I have a full fuel load. I tell them about my situation, but they remain adamant. I taxied back, downloaded all my fuel except 8,000 pounds to get off a 7,000 foot runway at an elevation of 5,000 feet. I thought I'd fly to Buckley Air National Guard base near Denver, they had a 12,000 foot runway. There was a housing development off the end of the short runway in Cheyenne. I said to the tower controller, 'Those people are going to get their dishes broken when I come over.' Still they wouldn't budge. So I took off and headed for Buckley.

"At Buckley I got a full fuel load to get me to McClellan AFB in California. After an uneventful take-off I set the power to 96 percent, the cruise speed setting I've always used when I flew the RB. That should have given me about 450 knots. Well, this heavy beast only gave me 420 knots and each engine was gobbling 3,000 pounds of fuel each hour. As soon as I got to McClellan I had to call the 4440th Aircraft Delivery Group at Langley AFB in Virginia to tell them about my problem. They arranged for the SAC tankers to meet me over the Pacific, and the tankers would only give me the fuel quantity called for in their charts for my airplane. So I started cruising at 94 and one-half percent, that gave me 420 knots, but only used 2,800 pounds of fuel per hour. Coming into McClellan my N–1 compass failed and without that I couldn't go anywhere. I knew nothing about the navigator they put on board the aircraft, so I wanted to make doubly sure that we didn't vanish somewhere over the Pacific. They had civilian workers at McClellan, good guys, and I told them my problem. They said they knew what it was – the amplifier. They got another amplifier, installed it, I flew the aircraft – same problem. Now I knew what the problem was – the C-2 Compass sensor in the left wing. They didn't believe me. After two more amplifier changes they did. That fixed the compass problem and I was ready to go.

"I waited a week before I could get a tanker to get me to Hawaii. It was a perfect rendezvous. That's when the navigator's oxygen regulator blew its diaphragm. We had eight liters of liquid oxygen on board, and the leak was slowly depleting our oxygen supply. I had no choice but to turn back. They changed the oxygen regulator, and another week went by before I got a tanker. Everything went well on our flight to Hickam. Out of there we headed for Guam. The tanker was going to take me and two F-100 fighters all the way. There was a Typhoon between us and Guam. We got into it near Wake Island. I'd never seen so much water in the sky in all my life. I was sitting on the tanker's wing tip, not more than 10 feet away from him, and if I got any further out I lost sight of him. The water was just gushing against the airplane. I wondered why the engines were still running. I'd look at the instruments, they weren't even flickering. It was amazing. We landed at Andersen Air Base on Guam. I was supposed to take off the next morning with the same tanker. We did. About 90 miles out the KC-135 lost its number two engine. We turned back. After landing I went through the checklist with the crew chief. We were sitting on an incline on the taxiway and it was raining. The chief said to me, 'Sir, I see hydraulic fluid running down the ramp.' Sure enough my pressure was dropping. The main utility system had failed. I couldn't taxi and had to get a tug to pull me to a parking place. There was only one thing that could cause a total loss of hydraulic fluid, a broken pump casing. Andersen was a SAC base filled with B-52 bombers and KC-135 tankers. The good SAC folks were totally uncooperative. I didn't think we were in the same Air Force. I finally got them to order the part I needed, which was flown in from Takhli.

"My sergeant and I changed the hydraulic pump on that engine. He looked at me skeptically. 'Sarge, I used to be an aircraft mechanic,' I said to him. 'I know how to do this. Don't worry.' He smiled, 'Let's go for it, sir,' he said. So we did. No help from our SAC friends. A major came by, looked us over, I was a captain, and said, 'What are you doing captain?'

"'Changing the goddam hydraulic pump, sir. I got to get it into the war, you know!'

"'Can't you get any help?'

"'Nothing from that bunch in transient alert.'

"'I'll look into it,' he promised. Nothing happened. After my crew chief and I changed the pump I flew about an hour's test hop. Then we waited for a tanker again. Finally a tanker became available and we headed toward the Philippines, across the South China Sea. We came upon a magical line that my tanker friend would not cross. It was at the point where I had scheduled my refueling. I slid over in back of him, and all of a sudden he turned. 'Where are you going?' I asked the tanker pilot.

"'I can't cross this line,' the copilot replied, 'because then they have to pay us combat pay, and they ain't going to do that. I have to turn.'

"'Can't your navigator doctor his charts? It's easy.'

"'We don't do things like that,' he replied. I ended up going the wrong way for the next ten minutes to get my gas. His little trick cost me 20 minutes of precious flying time. We finally made it to Takhli without further incident. It was the *High Flight* from hell and took me nearly three weeks to fly an airplane from Cheyenne, Wyoming, to the war zone."[7] Although we all wore the same color flight suits, SAC ran its war from Offutt AFB, Nebraska, and Andersen Air Base in Guam. The tactical forces ran their war from 7th Air Force in Saigon, if it wasn't being run by the generals at 13th Air Force in the Philippines, or by CINCPACAF from far off Hickam AFB in the totally unwarlike setting of the Hawaiian Islands. Hawaii also was the headquarters of CINCPAC, an admiral, who ran the whole show when it wasn't being run out of Washington. To be totally fair to our SAC tanker friends, there were few like the rigidly bureaucratic aircrew Don Harding ran into. Many of them did in fact fly into North Vietnam or high up in the Gulf of Tonkin, disregarding instructions, to save a fighter running short on fuel, knowingly putting their own Air Force careers on the line. The SAC tanker crews received all too few rewards for the service they provided and the many lives and aircraft they saved. As a result, if a tanker crew entered a bar in Southeast Asia and TAC flyers were present, no fighter pilot worth his salt would let them pay for their drinks. Maybe the tanker crews did not receive the medals they deserved, but they earned our gratitude and respect.

Colonel Paul Maul, operations officer for the 41st TEWS at Takhli in 1968 to 1969, was as capable a pilot as I ever flew with. The B-66, whatever model, was a new airplane to him, having come from a long string of assignments in the Strategic Air Command flying everything from KB-29 tankers with the old English style trailing hose refueling system to B-47 and B-52 bombers. "By the summer of 1968, my EB-66 class of new guys was filled with folks whose last flying was in SAC or some other command," recalls Paul. "I have no idea what the training costs were during the Vietnam War to assure that no one was involuntarily reassigned to a second Southeast Asia combat tour until all other Air Force flyers had a first tour there. Under *Palace Cobra* a program was implemented whereby the large pool of pilots, navigators and electronic warfare officers assigned to SAC, TAC, MAC, ATC, and other commands and operating agencies, was tapped to replace those finishing their initial combat tours. Every month the major air commands had to provide the Military Personnel Center at Randolph AFB in San Antonio, Texas, with a list of names for air crew replacement training. It caused a great amount of turbulence among flyers not to mention the high cost of training. Fairness was the goal, if not always the result.

"In 1968 I graduated from the Air War College and found myself on my way to Shaw AFB to become a TAC pilot. I considered myself an experienced and skilled pilot. The probe and drogue refueling system, however, used in the B-66 was a new challenge. It was in this mixed environment of flyers from different commands with very different backgrounds that we suddenly had the opportunity to learn from each other. The rendezvous with the tanker flying the EB-66 was very similar to my previous experience in SAC, with one significant exception. TAC taught its flyers to approach the tanker not from directly behind, but to chase the tanker slightly offset to the right. Also, the EB-66 had a very effective speed brake for deceleration which allowed us to use significantly higher closure speeds than what I had been used to flying B-47s or B-52s. After using the new procedure I was amazed at how much less time was consumed in the chase before taking on fuel. How many tanker overruns had I witnessed in tail chases through the years in SAC. So many could have been avoided by that simple offset change. The tail chase gave the receiver a single image on his windscreen of the rear of the tanker growing slowly larger in size. The offset approach gave a three-dimensional view of overtake speed, and it made it a safe overrun should that occur. The move over to the pre-contact position was an easy sideways slide and the use of power to move forward just short of the drogue.

"Once the sun set and it got really dark, even the simple could become complex. There is that basket in front of you, moving, as a result of the bow wave created by the EB-66. To have a successful connect the probe must be inserted in the center of the basket, push the basket slightly forward so there is a curve in the hose attached to the boom, and keep it that way. Sometimes the basket is moving about, don't rush, settle down, move forward, don't push against the side of the basket, reduce power. If I'd persist in applying power, the basket would tip over and the airstream would push the drogue off the probe, then it would begin to spin and hit the EB-66's probe. So it is essential to move slowly into the drogue and hit he center of the basket – connect and take on fuel." The technique to ensure a good refueling sounds all too simple, but add a bit of air turbulence and erratic movement of the throttles and many EB-66 flyers returned to base with a refueling basket on their probes or, in some cases, with bent probes. "Part of the problem was that the EB-66 refueling lights did not work well. As a result some pilots never got good at night refuelings. A few months after I left for Southeast Asia, a former SAC pilot pointed out the problem: 'For crying out loud you guys need better light to see what you are doing at night' or something like that must have been said. So the EB-66 got new refueling lights so the pilot could finally see what he was doing. The positive side of this turnover of the crew force was that for once there was an opportunity to learn from each other.[8]

"When I arrived at Shaw in the summer of 1968 and looked around, I found that in my class there was only one captain. The rest of us, both pilots and navigators, were majors or lieutenant colonels. Almost all of us had never flown the B-66 before. Instruction in the bird was not easy, lacking dual controls. The first time around the instructor sat in the pilot's seat and demonstrated, from then on he sat on a home-made box of sorts behind the new pilot and taught air refueling, formation flying and rejoins, tactical overhead approaches and landings that most of us had never done flying heavies. The formation rejoins, while both aircraft were turning, were dangerous. For the instructor pilot not to have access to flight controls and out of his seat required courage and communication skills. My instructor was 'Smiley' Pomeroy. Smiley was one of the best" a legend in the B-66 community. "Absolutely fearless. Sitting on his box without a chute, he demanded me to bank steeply and pull on the stick hard enough until the airplane shook as we dropped the gear and flaps. The speed bled off as I pulled a 360 degree turn around to a short final approach. During a particularly steep turn and hard shake Smiley flashed a big grin and gave a thumbs up to my navigator Clark Aamodt, we trained as a team. When Clark later told me what Smiley had done I was pleased. Smiley was a major and I was a lieutenant colonel.

"Many of the instructors at Shaw were outranked by their students, and it didn't take long for some of the students to start being testy with their instructors. My class soon had a tarnished reputation. We decided to throw a cocktail party to make things right. Some of the instructors we had were the best pilots in the world – Smiley Pomeroy had over 3,000 hours in the B-66, Don Harding had flown the airplane as a bomber pilot at Sculthorpe, and Ike Espe had close to 3,000 hours. These guys were good and deserved our thanks. I was the project officer for the party. I sat down with the staff at the Shaw Officers' Club and decided to have an open bar and heavy *hors d'oeuvres*. We looked at other recent parties and came up with a cost. We couldn't have done anything that would have enhanced our image more with the instructors than have them and their wives as our guest at a cocktail party. Everyone had a good time. When the bill was presented the next day, my mouth dropped open. I couldn't believe it. We had sixty guests at the party and estimated 240 shots – we had consumed 610. Every student had to pay double. Those B-66 instructor pilots and navigators were not only good flyers, they could hold their liquor as well. We had a lot of parties at Takhli, and at every one of those parties I had to endure the retelling of the Shaw Goodwill Party."[9]

CHAPTER TWENTY-FIVE

WINDING DOWN
A FAILING WAR

January 1968 was a turning point in the Vietnam War. It began with the resumption of the *Rolling Thunder* campaign against the North, was followed by the shoot-down of the first EB-66C ECM aircraft by a MiG-21, and ended with the start of the bloody Tet Offensive by the Viet Cong in South Vietnam. Responding quickly to the new threat, B-52 *Arc Light* missions increased from 800 to 1,200 a month. Two weeks later the B-52 mission total rose to 1,800. The Viet Cong managed to sustain their offensive until the end of February when it collapsed as a result of heavy losses. The greatest loser, however, was the United States. Bodycount – a measure of combat success implemented by Secretary of Defense McNamara was, in fact, not a good indicator of success or failure. It turned out that perceptions of war were what counted at home, and those perceptions were nearly all negative. Gradual escalation as a strategy had failed. President Johnson, in recognition of that fact, and in agreement with the position taken by his former Secretary of Defense McNamara who resigned the previous November, limited bombing of the DRV to targets south of the 20th parallel. In a nationally televised address Johnson revealed his intention not to run for a second term. He called for Hanoi to come to the negotiating table for peace talks. It was all backwards from the way it was supposed to happen. By November 1, 1968, Johnson halted all air and naval attacks against the North. The final outcome of the war was now just a matter of time and circumstances. War always has been an all or nothing affair requiring a nation's total commitment – a lesson neither McNamara nor Johnson understood.

Itazuke Air Base, Japan, of Korean War fame, was reopened for Operation Combat Fox in response to the capture of the USS Pueblo by North Korean gunboats on January 23, 1968. EB-66 and RF-101 aircraft from the 363TRW at Shaw AFB were quickly dispatched, first to Kunsan AB, Korea, then to Itazuke. 54-510 is parked serenely below Itazuke Tower, made famous in a similarly named Korean War vintage song.

Six days before the beginning of the Tet Offensive in South Vietnam, on January 23, 1968, the *USS Pueblo*, a small 350 ton electronic intelligence gathering ship was seized by North Korean torpedo boat crews and towed into Wonsan harbor. Calls for help by the doomed ship resulted in no response from U.S. forces, a situation that had not changed since an RB-47H of the 55th SRW was attacked by North Korean MiG-17 fighters on April 28, 1965. The severely damaged aircraft managed to shoot down one of the attacking MiGs, then made a miraculous landing at Yokota Air Base. The lack of a timely response by either Air Force or Navy aircraft doomed both the RB-47 and the *Pueblo*. A Navy EC-121 was to fall prey to aggressive North Korean fighters a year later, on April 15, 1969, with heavy loss of life. Fighter caps were never put in place to protect vulnerable reconnaissance aircraft and ships from North Korean attacks, known to be highly probable.[1]

A week after the capture of the *USS Pueblo* the 363rd TRW was tasked to provide a reconnaissance and electronic warfare element, including RF-101 and EB-66 aircraft, for a strike force headed to Korea – *Operation Combat Fox*. Two EB-66Cs and four EB- 66Es were tasked to deploy withing 48 hours. Major Carwin 'Smiley' Pomeroy wrote, "Crews were formed immediately from instructor personnel, all of which had already completed a combat tour in Southeast Asia. Maintenance personnel were selected, and essential parts kits were created. The catch was that no-one knew anything at all about the new EB-66Es which had just arrived and been put in flyable storage. We had no technical data on the new aircraft, no maintenance manuals, no Dash-1, nor aircrew checklists" – none of that was apparently included in the contract. "Most of us had never been inside an E-model, but all of us knew that the aircraft had been highly modified. On Monday morning, February 5, we took off from Shaw for Hickam AFB, Hawaii. I was flying a C-model with Harry Allison as my navigator. Ike Espe was flying the other C with Stan Soszka navigating. Lieutenant Colonel Gere Martini was the B-66 group commander, flying in the gunner's seat on Ike Espe's aircraft. Bob Murdoch, Al Salisbury, Dick Miller and Dan Christian flew the four E-models. None of them had ever flown the E-model before nor seen a scrap of paper describing the airplane. I remember one of them coming over to me on Sunday afternoon as we were laying out our mission saying, 'Smiley, I'm not refueling qualified on the KC-135.'

"'You will be tomorrow,' I told him. He walked away chastened, knowing what was expected of him. This was the first computer scheduled 'receiver consumption and tanker off-load' deployment. Tankers would give us, the receivers, a specified amount of fuel based on the past history refueling the B-66. We quickly discovered that the fuel-burn on the E-model was higher than on the other models, so we had a little problem. Things went fairly well crossing the U.S. The original tanker cell dropped us off at the California coast and was replaced by another group of tankers. As we proceeded toward Hawaii I tried to find out how much fuel they were going to give us. I didn't get a straight answer. I was going to get a certain quantity of fuel from one tanker, then a little more from another, and the same went for the other B-66s. My navigator computed how much fuel we would need to reach Hickam. After I continued to push the tanker-lead for a straight answer he finally came across with a number – which would flame me out about 200 miles short of Hawaii. A spirited discussion followed between the tanker cell commander and Gere Martini. Martini told the tanker lead that we were going to abort and return to California. Well, that wouldn't look so good. After all, this was an operational deployment ordered by the Joint Chiefs of Staff. So the tanker cell commander agreed to give us the required fuel off-load and in addition stay with us all the way to Hawaii.

"We arrived at Hickam, spent the night, and launched the next morning for Guam. At Andersen we split into three flights – two EB-66s to a KC-135 tanker. The first flight made it into K-8, Kunsan Air Base, with no problems. One of the Es in the second flight had to return to Guam thirty minutes out, and Dick Miller flying the remaining EB-66E joined Ike Espe and me. We arrived at K-8 with my aircraft having an inoperative TACAN, ADF, VOR and radar, so we made a formation penetration in a raging snow storm. It turned out to be way less than minimums and a hell of an interesting experience and test of my formation flying ability. We went through the normal penetration from 32,000 feet down to 25,000 feet and into intense weather. We got down to 200 feet when the ground controller announced 'minimums' and ceased providing further instructions. Here we were, three aircraft, 200 feet off the ground unable to see anything. I had difficulty seeing Ike Espe's aircraft with about one-half of a wing overlap, who initiated a missed approach with no radio call."[2]

Smiley, busy concentrating on not losing sight of Espe's aircraft, did not know that Dick Miller had decided to go it alone. So they were a two ship formation. Espe clearly remembers calling over the radio, "'Gear up. Flaps up.' I'd been stationed at Kunsan in the mid-50s so I knew there was a small hill immediately to the west of the runway and I was not about to tangle with it. Smiley admitted to me later that he had already sucked up his flaps before my call, and that caused him to come under my right wing and almost overshoot me, and also lose some lift. So he was wobbling a bit, stuff I thankfully didn't know about."[3]

"Espe initiated his missed approach," writes Smiley Pomeroy. "When he applied power and retracted his speed brakes and gear he disappeared in the snow. I poured the power to my plane, retracted the gear and the speed brakes, and set sail to find Ike. I was completely blind without him. I found him in that snow storm and rejoined without colliding. Then I heard him calling for a vector to K-55, Osan, and the minimum enroute altitude. I frantically told him to take us to 20,000 feet, I was running out of fuel. He did, and as we leveled off at flight level 200 I checked my fuel gauges and realized I was not going to make it. My first thought was that the Air Force did not accept pilots running out of fuel and losing their aircraft. Here I was in such a situation on a deployment that had attention at the highest levels. I told Harry Allison, my navigator, to zip his pockets and get ready to eject."[4]

"We got close to Osan," Espe continues, "and broke out of the weather into a nearly clear sky. Smiley pulled his throttles back and started down. My fuel situation was bad, but not desperate as Smiley's was. So I stayed high until I got a visual on the runway. Smiley sneaked in on a short final, but I thought, 'Hell, I'll let them know who's coming.' So I did a low approach to show off the EB-66 and landed with 1,200 pounds of fuel. We walked into the Officers' Club a little later. A bunch of RF-101 jocks from Shaw were already there as well as crews for about every other airplane in the USAF tactical air force inventory, all veterans of Vietnam."[5]

With the Korea deployment the Shaw training establishment was again unable to train electronic warfare officers, since most of the instructors and all but one of the aircraft had deployed. Shaw had only three C-models, and two of them were in Korea. In late January and early February 1968, about 30 EW Officers reported to Shaw for combat crew training in the EB-66, with subsequent assignments to Takhli, Thailand. Gerald McBride was one of those lieutenants. "I got to Shaw in early January and discovered that the fully equipped E-models and the instructors had left for Osan Air Base, Korea. Later they moved to Itazuke Air Base in Japan. Our trainers were staff officers hurriedly drafted from Ninth Air Force Headquarters, also located at Shaw. My Takhli assignment was eventually canceled. I became an instructor. Then I was sent along with three other EWs to Itazuke in early July. Itazuke had been closed after the Korean War, but hastily reactivated to accommodate aircraft pulled together for the Pueblo crisis. We stayed busy flying training missions for Japanese Air Force F-86 and F-104 interceptors, and flew jamming missions against their *Nike Hercules* missile sites."[6] The deployment simply petered out. The *Pueblo* issue was low-keyed by the Johnson administration with its plate filled to overflowing with Vietnam related events. On December 23, 1968, the *Pueblo* crew was released. The men crossed the DMZ from north to south over the 'bridge of no return.'

On 5 August 1967 the 41st and 42nd Tactical Electronic Warfare Squadrons were reassigned from the 432nd Tactical Reconnaissance Wing at Udorn to the 355th Tactical Fighter Wing at Takhli. Common sense finally prevailed. At the time of reassignment the 41st had 15 EB-66s assigned, flying 60 hours per aircraft per month, and the 42nd had 13 EB-66 aircraft. The Secretary of Defense increased the number of aircraft by 13 EB-66Es and raised the flying hour program to 72 hours per aircraft per month.[7] That action increased the two squadrons' unit equipment from 28 to 41 aircraft. Through March of 1968 the 41st squadron lost three C-models and one of the new EB-66Es. Two of the lost aircraft were replaced, bringing the total count down to 39. On any given day the squadrons had no more than 24 aircraft available to fly combat missions. That limited number of aircraft flew 2,950 hours per month in April, May and June of 1968.[8]

On April 8, 1968, five EB-66B/E models supported 14 Air Force strike aircraft in Route Pack 1. The 57/85mm AAA fire was inaccurate as a result of the EB-66 jamming, and no aircraft were lost. On April 15 six EB-66B/C aircraft supported strikes by Air Force and Navy fighters in Route Packages 1,2 and 3. No aircraft were lost to AAA while the EB-66s were on station. On 31 May, 9 EB-66B/C/E aircraft supported 24 strike aircraft hitting targets in Route Packs 1 and 2. On June 9, 6 EB-66Es supported 14 strike aircraft in the same Route Packs without experiencing losses. The fighters, however, took losses during that period from non-radar directed guns while operating at altitudes between 2,000 and 6,000 feet. While support of tactical strike aircraft was a bread and butter mission for the EB-66s, support increasingly went to B-52 *Arc Light* missions attacking the passes leading from North Vietnam into Laos. It was during this time period that it was discovered that when the EB-66 entered into a bank of 10 degrees or more, jamming effectiveness was considerably reduced. All crews were briefed to fly straight and level for a period of two minutes before to three minutes after the B-52 drop-times. That allowed the full power of EB-66 jamming to be directed against the target area.[9]

From October to December 1968 the EB-66 aircraft of the 355th TFW flew 2,044 combat sorties for a total of 7,258 flying hours. An older *Brown Cradle* aircraft was lost in July, bringing the total number of aircraft possessed by the two EB-66 squadrons down to 38. For the entire year of 1968 the sortie rate for the EB-66s remained high. The low was 577 combat sorties flown in January, and the high was 831 in August.[10] The total bombing halt of the North, effective November 1, diverted fighter and bomber strikes to interdiction points in Laos. Reconnaissance missions, however, continued to be flown over the North by Air Force RF-4s, Navy aircraft, and drones controlled from C-130 aircraft. The bombing halt's immediate effect on EB-66 operations was that active jamming shifted to support reconnaissance operations over the North, and to increased electronic intelligence gathering.

Lieutenant Tom Copler arrived at Takhli in April 1968. Tom, a Ball State University graduate, took Air Force ROTC and finished up in February 1966. He went to Mather AFB for navigator training. While his classmates decided to go into electronic warfare, Tom wanted 'bomb school.' When he arrived at Shaw for his B-66 training they only had one EB-66E. Most of the aircraft and instructors were deployed to Korea. "The pilot I was training with," Tom Copler recalls, "was Dave Eby. Dave didn't want to be there. He had flown the B-66 in earlier times, the bomber version, and then the RB-66B in France, and had close to 2,000 hours in the aircraft. The Air Force was in desperate need of B-66 flyers and his name popped up during a records check. So here he was, a reluctant warrior. At Shaw I got six missions with a pilot instructor sitting on a box behind the student pilot. The next six missions were with a navigator instructor to get me checked out – airborne radar approaches, how to pick up a tanker at night, find the beacon and making sure it was MY tanker, because we were going to wind up with three or four tankers in a cell refueling a number of aircraft. Then you had to call the pilot into the picture so he could visually acquire the tanker. In the dark in marginal weather that was a tricky thing at times. I was lucky being paired with a pilot with previous B-66 experience. Most of the pilots that came into the B-66 about this time flew KC-135s, C-141s, every type of airplane you can think of other than fighters. Most had never flown a fighter or a one pilot aircraft, hadn't had air refueling training either. It was a hard go for many of them. Some never got good at night refueling. There was a lot of ground training as well – hydraulics, engines, and other critical aircraft systems. Then Dave and I went to water survival training at Homestead, jungle survival at Clark, and on to Takhli. When I checked out at Takhli the first six months was really rough. We flew missions every 12 hours between debriefing one mission until the start of briefing for another. After the bombing halt in November things slowed down.

"On May 23, 1968, we were flying off Vinh supporting a Navy strike. We were supposed to sit in an orbit just out of range of the AAA and SA-2s, at 25,000 feet, and prohibited from going north of the 16th parallel unless we had MiG cap. We called *Red Crown* and were cleared into our jamming area. We forgot to confirm our MiG cap with *Red Crown*, and *Red Crown* forgot to ask. We could see the Navy A-7 strike aircraft coming in below. There was weather over the Gulf, but it was clear over land. Our jamming was apparently doing a great job. We saw little AAA, nothing close to the A-7s, and only two SAMs which didn't go anywhere. Then all of a sudden *Red Crown* called, 'Bandits approaching south of Bulls Eye.' They kept getting closer and closer. When they got within 20 miles, less than three minutes flying time, I asked *Red Crown* about our MiG cap. There was a pause. Then the controller said, 'The cap is on the cat,' meaning they were just launching from the carrier and wouldn't do us any good. About that time *Red Crown* called 'Bandits at your 5.' I could see two of them screaming toward us. Two little dots on the horizon. I wasn't flying with Dave Eby for some reason. My pilot said to me over the intercom, 'My mama told me to bring no medals home,' and he ripped the airplane over and maneuvered it down into the cloud deck. I kept up with our position because I had to know based on the calls we were getting from *Red Crown* where the MiGs were and where we were trying to top out again. At that point our MiG cap was on station. It was about time for the A-7s to come back out, so we popped back up, watched them cross the coast line. We got jumped by two MiGs right away again. They were at five miles, six o'clock position. What confused *Red Crown*, and us, was that they had two MiGs coming toward us, and the original two attackers were heading north. The MiG cap saw the attack unfold and called to us – left turn, right turn. While we were evading the MiGs the Navy F-4s shot one down and got a possible on the other. When we returned to Takhli we thought we had done pretty good for one day. The intelligence officer sent our debriefing up the chain. The result: the operations folks at 7th Air Force were madder than hell that we had put ourselves and an aircraft in danger and not paid attention to the rules of engagement. We wondered what kind of a reprimand we were going to get. I mean they were hostile and had nothing good in mind for us. Well, the admiral whose A-7s we supported and who had launched the MiG cap that got the two MiGs got on the phone and called our wing commander, commending the EB-66 crew that had supported his A-7 strike force and ensured the guys got back safe and assisted with the kill of two MiGs. Three or four weeks later we were put in for the Distinguished Flying Cross rather than a reprimand.

"Some of our missions, especially when we got into the post *Rolling Thunder* period, after November 1, 1968, were, to say the least, unusual. One was called *Gray Creeper*, the code name was later changed to *Frantic Goat*. It was a C-130, grey in color, dropping leaflets over the Ho Chi Minh trail. We had to put our flaps down, speed brakes out, gear down, even fly a scissors maneuver, back and forth, just to be able to stay with the C-130. It was a real mismatch. I don't know how much jamming support we were really providing because of our constant maneuvering, we were raising our wings up and as a result our jamming effectiveness had to be less than optimum. Then there was the *Busy Bee* mission – a Navy C-130 launching reconnaissance drones over North Vietnam. The drones would fly into the Vinh area, and when they returned they were let down by parachute and recovered. It was always interesting to watch that thing being launched, go in, then we'd sit there in our orbit waiting for the drone to come back out. Most of the time they did."[11]

The Air Force began launching unmanned reconnaissance drones beginning in 1967. A total of 1,976 drones were launched with the highest number of launches, 500, in 1972. A total of 364 Air Force launched drones were lost over the years. The worst year being 1969 with the loss of 97. The North Vietnamese AAA gun crews, SAM missile launch crews, and fighter regiments continued to receive plenty of opportunities to exercise their systems even after the *Rolling Thunder* campaign came to an end. Most of the drone launches were supported by EB-66 aircraft, providing jamming support at the entry and exit points. Although the drone had a smaller radar cross section than most strike aircraft, it did not carry an ECM self-protection pod. The overall loss rate for the drones was 18.4 percent. Of those losses, 110 were due to system malfunctions of one kind or another, bringing the actual loss rate due to enemy action and unknown causes down to an acceptable 12.8 percent. The loss rate from all causes steadily declined from a high of 38 percent in 1967 to a consistent 10 percent level in 1971 and 1972. The North Vietnamese success rate for all of their defensive systems declined drastically to a mere six drones killed in 1971, and a truly diminutive total of only five for 1972. The greatest cause of drone losses in those two years was a lack of reliability.[12]

"One night we had gone in at dusk supporting a drone mission," Tom Copler continues. "We noticed as we came out of our orbit that our wing tanks were not feeding. We didn't have enough gas to get back to Takhli and called for a tanker. *Red Crown* came up and said 'We got a tanker for you at twenty miles.' I looked into my radar and couldn't pick up a beacon. Then *Red Crown* called 'fifteen miles.' I still couldn't pick up a beacon. Dave Eby couldn't see anything either. Then they called 'five miles.' I looked hard and finally picked up some skin paint. I had the antenna pointed all the way up and was picking up something out there. I said to Dave, 'Dead ahead at four miles.' He looked, finally came back and said, 'I can see something up there, but it doesn't look right.' We got behind that 'something,' and it turned out *Red Crown* had vectored us to a Navy A3D tanker. The tanker pilot said, 'I got five to six-thousand pounds to give you. Will that do you any good?' It was enough. The Navy does everything visual. No electronic beacon like I was used to on the KC-135. It was a real shock to come up behind that A3D. There was just a length of hose whipping around. It was sporty getting our fuel, but much appreciated.

"The second time we ran into a fuel problem *Red Crown* couldn't come up with a tanker and we headed to Da Nang. The GCA radar operator vectored us in on a short final. We didn't see any runway lights. Just keep going the controller said, we'll bring the lights up as you get closer. Just as we are coming down the glide slope they turned on the lights, he had us dead center on the runway. We flared, touched down, and the lights went out again. We had a totally dark runway, no lights on the edge, no reference marks, it was exciting in a strange way. As we slowed we could see just the dimmest of lights of a Follow Me truck. The lights on the truck turned out to be two flashlights held by an airman. Evidently there were constant mortar attacks from the hills outside Da Nang. We got our fuel and got out of 'Dodge' as quickly as possible.

"When I finished my tour at Takhli in '69 I had flown 150 combat missions. I volunteered for a consecutive overseas assignment to get into the F-4 program at Spangdahlem, Germany. My wife and I were looking forward to that assignment. I received my orders to report to Holloman AFB, New Mexico, for F-4 training. Everything was looking good. Suddenly my orders were canceled and instead I was assigned to the 19th Tactical Electronic Warfare Squadron at Kadena Air Base, Okinawa. In April I left for Kadena to fly the EB-66 again. I wondered about what had happened and why. Then I learned that my good friend Dave Eby, my pilot since our training days at Shaw, had called a friend at the Military Personnel Center in San Antonio. Dave was going to Kadena to be the staneval pilot in the 19th TEWS, and he wanted me as his staneval navigator.

"I never had a real emergency in the B-66, much less an accident. The closest I came to punching out was one of those things you didn't talk about for years because you might get caught up in a courts martial. We were coming off our orbit. I wasn't flying with Dave Eby, and we had lots of fuel remaining. So my pilot decided to climb the airplane to well over 40,000 feet, then dove to pass through the sound barrier. We found out the reason why you can't do it in the B-66. The airflow and the engine nacelles are not compatible. We passed through 10,000 feet in total silence. My pilot yelled at me, 'Don't punch out. Don't punch out. I'll get them back.' And at 5,000 feet above the terrain he began to level off and started up the left engine, then got the right one going. That was a sweet sound to my ears."[13]

CHAPTER TWENTY-SIX

THE TRAGEDY OF 53-498

The bombing halt of November 1, 1968, and the accompanying termination of *Operation Rolling Thunder*, was one of the last major actions of the outgoing Johnson administration to affect the conduct of the Vietnam war. The incoming Nixon administration was under immense pressure to get United States military forces out of Southeast Asia, and end a war that cost the country more than just money and the lives of tens of thousands of its servicemen. Although combat operations over North Vietnam had been terminated, the bloody war in South Vietnam and the secret war in Laos continued while peace negotiations in Paris were under way. The draw-down of American military forces in South Vietnam began within months after Nixon assumed the presidency. A more modest reduction of Air Force units was initiated in Thailand as well. In contrast the DRV moved in the opposite direction, expanding its fighter inventory from a low of 80 at the beginning of 1968 to 254, including 86 MiG-21s, 32 MiG-19s, and the remainder older, yet still very capable, MiG-17s. Launch capable surface to air missile sites remained steady at around 200. AAA units, however, declined and began to move south from the Hanoi area, and west into Laos, soon to be followed by SAM fire units. Immediately following the bombing halt the number of DRV early warning and *Firecan* AAA and *Fansong* SAM radars increased by nearly 50 percent. None of that had the sound, smell or look of peace about it.[1]

While the Takhli based EB-66 squadrons continued to provide support for B-52 *Arc Light* raids, bombing the passes leading from North Vietnam into Laos, and to an ever increasing number of reconnaissance missions over the North,

The tragic crash of 53-498, an EB-66B Brown Cradle, on April 8, 1969, at Takhli RTAFB, Thailand, resulted in the loss of its crew and was a reminder of how grossly underpowered the B-66 was. The picture shows a J71 engine of RB-66B 53-451, years earlier at Shaw AFB, that fell in pieces to the tarmac after maintenance opened the engine cowling. Bob Webster, the pilot, received the Air Medal for bringing the aircraft back to Shaw. Although catastrophic failures of that scope were rare, the General Motors Allison J71 engine remained the greatest single limiting factor throughout the life of the B-66.

there remained enough slack capacity to augment the still ongoing *Combat Fox* commitment at Itazuke Air Base, Japan. Although the *Pueblo* episode was long over and the ship's crew had returned in December 1968, a tactical strike force continued to be maintained in Japan. The 355th TFW provided crews and aircraft to the *Combat Fox* force. The commitment began with three EB-66 crews rotating to Itazuki, Japan, in December 1968. Then in January 1969 the Air Staff announced a more permanent arrangement, activating the 19th TEWS at Kadena as part of the 18th TFW. The 19th would take over the *Combat Fox* commitment, as well as the aircraft and crews at Itazuke, then move to Kadena. It would remain a small squadron, consisting of only four EB-66E aircraft and two EB-66Cs. The squadron's focus was Korea, and for that task the 19th was about the right size. Concomitant with the creation of the 19th, the Takhli based squadrons were reduced from 41 to 38 aircraft. Additionally, a new EB-66 squadron was activated at Spangdahlem, Germany, the 39th TEWS, to satisfy a NATO requirement that had been inadequately supported since the withdrawal of the EB-66 force from France in 1966. The 39th TEWS officially came into being on April 1, 1969. A cadre of personnel from Takhli was reassigned to Spangdahlem to get the squadron off the ground. Finding volunteers for this assignment was not difficult.[2]

There obviously were no EB-66 aircraft sitting around idly to allow the Pentagon to open up new squadrons at will. The only source was the Southeast Asia force at Takhli. The creation of the 39th TEWS in Germany portended other organizational changes. With the war in the doldrums, the hard core requirement for ECM support had vanished. It came as no surprise then when the news was announced that the *Brown Cradles* were going to be retired. The one-time bombers converted to ECM duties in the late '50s had just too many hours on their airframes. Of the original 13, 11 remained. I only flew a few missions in the B-model and hated everyone. The B was a low-tech ECM aircraft compared to the E-model, and the chance of surviving an ejection by the EWO was dim, unless he was a very small person. Tom Copler recalls sitting in a B-model at Takhli when he first arrived in early '68. "I was sitting in the right seat. I looked over, and the EWO across from me was about six feet. I looked at the panel above him and said to him, 'You are not going to make it.' I looked at the angle of the seat and knew it would not pull him back far enough for him to make it out without losing his knees. Scheduling made an effort to schedule only EWOs who were 5 foot nine inches or less, a not always achievable task."[3] The 11 surviving *Brown Cradles* were flown to Davis-Monthan AFB in Arizona in three flights on October 27, 29 and 31. No tears were shed when those long-serving aircraft took the runway at Takhli for the last time.[4] The biggest change, however, came on October 31, 1969, with the deactivation of the 41TEWS. "This decision, a part of the overall reduction of U.S. forces in SEA was evidently a part of an economy move by the Department of Defense to trim three billion dollars from the defense budget. On October 29, 1969, the *Stars & Stripes* military newspaper announced that over 300 military installations in the U.S. and abroad were to be deactivated."[5]

The remaining Takhli squadron, the 42nd TEWS, retained 21 EB-66C and E-models. In early March 1969 the new ALA-32 steerable antenna was used for the first time on an EB-66C in support of a *Bumpy Action* reconnaissance drone flying over North Vietnam. Developed by the U.S. Navy for use in its EA-3B ECM aircraft, the ALA-32, in combination with the QRC-279 transmitter control coupled to ALT-27 jammers allowed the EB-66C to focus its jamming on a specific radar, rather than jamming in a 360 degree omni-directional pattern and wasting much of the radiated energy. Within one day Air Force Security Service in San Antonio indicated that the ALA-32/QRC-279 combination was highly effective. That assessment was further documented on subsequent missions by *Comfy Coat* evaluations issued by the Security Service. The EB-66s were given credit for saving drones from SAMs in the Hanoi/Haiphong area, with the ALA-32 given as the probable reason for the increased jamming effectiveness. Three EB-66Cs had been modified with five ALA-32 steerable antennas each coupled to QRC-279 transmitter control boxes. The integrated tactical antenna system proved to be an important step forward in the application of electronic countermeasures. For the first time it gave the EB-66C the ability to simultaneously provide effective jamming support and conduct electronic reconnaissance.[6]

About the same time the Navy fielded its version of the EB-66, the EA-3B *Skywarrior*. The *Skywarrior*, the one time Navy strategic bomber that played a part in the acrimonious B-36 controversy in the 50s, briefly flew as a bomber in the early days of the Vietnam war, then metamorphed into several roles, including electronic warfare. The EA-3B had two state of the art J57 Pratt & Whitney engines producing 12,400 pounds of thrust with water injection and supporting a gross weight of only 70,000 pounds. The EB-66E flew the dated J71 Allison engines with a thrust of 10,200 pounds with no water injection, supporting a gross weight in excess of 83,000 pounds. The EA-3B was equipped with 20 steerable antenna systems, vice five for the EB-66C, and soon took over many of the *Bumpy Action* drone support missions launched from the Gulf of Tonkin side into the Hanoi/Haiphong area. It was a logical step. The Navy was closer to the areas over the Gulf where the drones were launched, and it eliminated the requirement for aerial refueling essential for EB-66 operations over the Gulf of Tonkin. In addition, the EA-3B with its many steerable antennas proved more effective than the EB-66E. Although equipped with 23 jammers, the omni-directional radiation patterns of the E-model made it less effective than the very directional jamming of the Navy aircraft.[7]

Such changes were not viewed favorably by the men in blue who wore the stars in Saigon, at 13th Air Force headquarters in the Philippines, and at Headquarters PACAF in lush and tranquil Hawaii. Statistics ran this war, and combat mission count and hours flown were only two of many statistics by which the military services defined success or failure for themselves, made claims on the defense budget, and used often spurious data for any other number of purposes beneficial to themselves. Major Kenneth High, a long time B-66 flyer noted, "In January 1967 I flew a mission in support of a flight of F-4s in the Haiphong area. As I was departing my orbit I was contacted by the Navy and asked if I could support a flight of A-6 *Intruders* because their ECM aircraft had aborted. I told them I would have to have a tanker, and in an instant a KA-3D tanker appeared. I refueled and remained on station until the strike aircraft had cleared the area. When I returned to Takhli I learned 7th Air Force was seething. I was spoken to strongly by the 355th TFW commander, who told me that, 'The Navy got six sorties out of that.' Headquarters 7th Air Force then followed up with a message saying that the B-66 was incompatible with Navy fuel and that refuelings with Navy aircraft would not occur again. Since I was the squadron standardization and evaluation officer, I replied that the B-66 manual lists JP-5 as an unrestricted substitute. That was quickly responded to with another message that read: 'Repeat, the B-66 will not refuel from Navy aircraft.' We got the message."[8] Unfortunately it was that kind of a war.

The 42nd TEWS found itself rather busy after the departure of its sister squadron, supporting a substantial number of B-52 *Arc Light* and *Bumpy Action* drone missions. Equally important, its EB-66C reconnaissance missions revealed an alarming spread of North Vietnamese SAM and AAA fire units into both Laos and the lower Route Packs of North Vietnam. In the three month period from October through December 1969, EB-66s on two occasions had SA-2 missiles launched at them in the Ban Karai and Mu Gia Pass areas. On December 19 the B-52 *Arc Light* and EB-66 support force came under SA-2 attack, but all missiles succumbed to the effects of the combined EB-66 and B-52 jamming and went wild. EB-66C intercepts and aerial photography indicated that four to five SA-2 missile battalions had deployed into the Vinh-Ban Karai-Mu Gia Pass areas. An equally worrisome picture emerged for the deployment of medium and heavy anti-aircraft guns.[9] The war might be in the doldrums, but it was far from over.

The one event towering over all others in 1969 was the loss of aircraft number 53-498, on April 8, 1969, one of the original *Brown Cradles*. Lieutenant Colonels James E. Ricketts and Edwin P. Anderson were the pilot and navigator, and young First Lieutenant Joseph Orlowski was the electronic warfare officer. The day before Joe and I ate lunch together in the Officers' Club, ordering from the standard menu labeled from 1 through 12. We'd just point at the number, and the shy, always smiling young Thai woman would take our order. We were in flight suits, talked about our families and our plans for the future; not about the war or the airplanes we flew. War takes an arbitrary toll, and Joe and I did not know that he had less than 24-hours to live. I remember the morning of April 8, a clear, nearly cloudless sky, no wind. The temperature was a bearable 80 degrees, the humidity always high. The huge geckos in the big tree near the Thai BX sounded as if they could swallow a man whole, unlike the little beasts on the ceiling of our shower. Thailand, Vietnam, Asia were so different from anything any of us ever experienced before. It happened as I walked to the Thai BX: the abrupt sound of engines terminating, the black cloud at the end of the runway. I thought another bomb laden F-105 had crashed. I was wrong. It was my friend Joe. When I learned of his death I wanted to cry.

Colonel Ricketts aircraft, Hydra 9, was scheduled for a routine ECM support mission with a 7:50 local take-off time. The aircraft had been serviced with 27,400 pounds of fuel. During the take-off roll at approximately 5,200 feet from brake release, the tower controller called, 'Hydra 9, Takhli, you have white smoke coming from your left engine ... your engine is on fire.' Hydra 9 did not acknowledge and continued the take-off, becoming airborne just before the overrun. The runway at Takhli was 9,855 feet in length with a 1,000 foot overrun. The landing gear retracted immediately after lift off. The aircraft was observed to climb, veer gradually to the left and impact nearly 5,000 feet from the end of the runway, where it exploded.[10]

Colonel Paul Maul, at that time the operations officer in the 41st TEWS writes, "I was always happy to achieve Minimum Single Engine Control Speed, MSECS, after take-off." So was everyone else who flew the EB-66. "There was this interval between S-1 – the speed on take-off beyond which an abort due to engine failure would result in running off the end of the runway – and MSECS, which was well beyond take-off speed, where an engine loss would result in a certain accident. Sometimes this time interval between S-1 and reaching single engine flying speed was as much as 40 seconds. The safest course of action when an engine failed within this 'coffin corner' was to pull the good engine to idle and crash-land straight ahead while still in control of the airplane. It is one of the conditions all aircrew flying the EB-66 in Southeast Asia faced on a daily basis and speaks volumes as to their dedication and courage. Jim Ricketts lost an engine in 'coffin corner' and may have reverted to his B-52 experience which called for the take-off to be continued after S-1 speed was reached. Whatever course of action a pilot chose in such a desperate situation, the outcome was most likely the same.[11]

Tom Mangan remembers the tragic loss that day. "I lost two good friends. The active runway was 22, so they took off in the direction of the road leading to Takhli town. I know that Jim Ricketts was between a rock and a hard place. If he tried to abort the take-off, the plane would overshoot the runway and the crew would probably all die in the resultant crash and fire. If he chose to fly the airplane in an attempt to reach the critical airspeed needed to eject, the airplane would crash just beyond the runway and the crew would probably die as well. Jim had been a B-52 pilot before he came to the B-66, so he did what any B-52 pilot would do, he tried to fly the airplane. The plane came down in a bone-dry rice paddy on the other side of the road. Jim Ricketts was a big man with a big smile, and an uncanny ability to make his subordinates feel at ease. I met him at Shaw when we both trained in the B-66. I was a first lieutenant, a brand new navigator headed for my first operational assignment. He was a lieutenant colonel and an experienced B-52 pilot. When we were off duty he called me Tom. I called him Jim. That's the way he wanted it. When we arrived at Takhli Jim became the commander of the 42nd TEWS. I was assigned to the 41st. I distinctly remember a party we had in one of the junior officer hooches one night. Jim was standing in the small common area surrounded by lieutenants from our Shaw class. He made us feel good about ourselves.

"Captain Joseph M. Orlowski, Joe, was a quiet, dignified man, an Air Force Academy graduate, and a classmate of mine in navigator training. When we graduated, Joe and I with our wives took a trip to Hawaii. He then entered electronic warfare officer training. I went into navigator bombardier training. From there we went to Shaw together. We were in different squadrons at Takhli, so we didn't fly together anymore. There was a memorial service for them the next day, but I couldn't go. Jim was a father figure to me, a friend. We were all getting short. I had to bury things I didn't quite know how to cope with in some far corner of my brain and get on with my life. In another 49 days Jim's tour would have been over and he would have flown back to the States. Like Jim and Joe, many of the men I knew who died in the war had been stationed outside Vietnam – in Guam and Thailand. When the Vietnam Veterans Memorial was dedicated in 1982, I honestly didn't know if their names would be on the Wall. That Memorial Day I sat in my living room watching NBC's television coverage of the dedication. At the end of the program, as the credits scrolled across the screen, the camera panned across the black granite panels and I saw Jim Ricketts name etched on the Wall. It was the first time I realized that somebody cared about what we had done. Until that moment I didn't even know if anybody considered us Vietnam veterans. Both my sister and sister-in-law told me that I was not a Vietnam veteran. It's strange how people who were never there view those of us who were. When I went to visit the Wall I found Joe's name. Andy Anderson's was three lines above Joe's. Jim's name was two panels away, as if the government hadn't gotten the word that they all died in the same airplane."[12]

It appears highly likely that Colonel Ricketts had no cockpit indication of engine failure. A few days after the crash a maintenance crew running up an engine observed flames and molten metal come out of the tail pipe. There were no indications of problems on the cockpit instruments. Several days after that a crew getting ready to go on a night mission was running up the engines when the tower called that flames came from the tailpipe of one of the engines. Again, no indication of engine failure in the cockpit. It was the old-timers who remembered that the 13th stage of the engine was prone to fail after 12,000 hours.[13] The crash of 53-498 curtailed EB-66 operations at Takhli for about three months. The accident again focused attention on the fact that the EB-66 at high gross weights was underpowered during take-off. "The accident also revealed the cause of the crash to be failure of engine components. This led to an examination of all EB-66 engines and a complete overhaul and replacement program. The result was a virtual stand-down during May."[14] As executive officer of the 41TEWS I recall getting together with our first sergeant, Master Sergeant Joseph Kupiek. Joe and I hitch-hiked our way home on SAC KC-135 tankers on a quick unscheduled R&R. The SAC schedulers couldn't have been more accommodating to hurry us home and back again when the time came. The MAC C-141 types laughed in our faces, 'Can't take you along guys. We carry dangerous cargo,' I remember one MAC scheduler telling me. 'I bet you do,' I responded in frustration, 'a can of paint?' He shrugged his shoulders and left me standing. I wondered who the hell he thought he was talking to. MAC, SAC, TAC – three air forces rather than one.

Don Christman arrived at Takhli in August of 1969 and remembers one immediate change as a result of the April 8 crash – the take-off fuel load was reduced. "We took off from Takhli, and later Korat, with only 15,000 pounds of fuel, 28,000 pounds was a full load without external wing-tanks. Then we refueled soon thereafter somewhere over central Thailand in an orbit that didn't cross the Mekong River into Laos."[15] The accident had more far reaching implications than the temporary curtailment of mission activity and a reduced take-off fuel load. The Air Staff pushed one more time for a new engine for the EB-66. There were plenty of used and new J57s available, as well as 15,000 pound thrust TF41 Allison/Rolls Royce turbofan engines from the A-7D program.[16] But the Defense Department turned the proposal down, a proposal that had many opponents within the Air Force who viewed the B-66 as an old airframe not worthy of re-engining. Aircrew safety never seemed to have been an issue that was considered, nor the state of the J71 engine inventory, which was well past its prime.

In May 1969, soon after the crash of 53-498, General John P. McConnell, the Air Force Chief of Staff, stopped EB-66 modernization as part of the cost reduction efforts then under way. "The Air Staff made it known that remaining EB-66s would have to be maintained through normal processes for perhaps five more years."[17] What that statement meant was that the Air Staff had abdicated its responsibility to deal with the extant problems plaguing the B-66, specifically its aging and underpowered power plant. In time, not even the absolutely essential B-66 IRAN – inspect and repair as necessary – program was funded. B-66 maintenance fell upon truly hard times. Shortages were everywhere. Parts were scavenged from static display aircraft. The aircraft storage center at Davis-Monthan AFB in Arizona was running out of fuel bladder replacements, or for that matter anything else that was B-66 related. By early 1973 the EB-66 fleet in PACAF was maintained on a shoe string. "The heavy frag of December [1972] had put a strain on maintenance just keeping the aircraft marginally combat capable (code II). There was simply no time or parts to put the planes in code I shape. After months of continuous heavy combat requirements, aircraft OR/MR rates began to drop. On 2 January [1973] the frag load was 11 lines with 5 spares. Maintenance supplied all but 2 spares; however, most of the planes came back Code III – non-combat ready. 3 January was indeed grim. The frag load was 12 lines and 5 spares. 7 lines were not flown because maintenance could not supply any aircraft. There were no spares. The problems were engines, hydraulics, flight controls, fuel cell leaks, you name the part and it was wearing out."[18]

Lieutenant Colonel Terry Buettner, then a captain, was the flight safety officer in the 42nd TEWS at Korat. "Most of the flying during the last few years was from hot runways," Terry wrote. "The engines had lots of hours on them, and parts were always a problem at Korat. There were times when we had only two or three aircraft flyable out of a squadron of 24. They would fly those three airplanes for three or four days, and one would break. By then they would have another one working to replace it. It was like that for most of my tour. Many times I remember waiting for an aircraft to return so I could fly the next mission. Several times I went out to an airplane that was on jacks with no engines in the pods. This was so that the mission could be called a 'ground abort' and not a 'maintenance non-delivery.' Ahh, the games we played. We got a new maintenance officer who promised the wing commander a 12-ship fly-by. We actually started 14 airplanes, got 12 into the air, and did the fly-by. When it was over, only five of the planes were capable of flying again. Korat had the last operational B-66 squadron. The supply lines were long and slow. I don't feel there were any unsafe airplanes sent out, but they were getting old in 1973, and it took hundreds of hours of maintenance for every hour of flying time."[19]

CHAPTER TWENTY-SEVEN

THE PEACE THAT
WOULD NOT COME

General John D. Ryan, once the commander of Pacific Air Forces, took the reins from General McConnell as Air Force chief of staff on August 1, 1969. A few days earlier, on July 20, Neil Armstrong set foot on the Moon, declaring "One small step for a man, one giant leap for mankind," capturing our imagination. President Kennedy's dream, articulated in more peaceful days in the early '60s had become reality. A rare bright moment for our nation, torn by ever more frequent, at times violent, anti-Vietnam demonstrations. On November 15, 1969, 250,000 anti-war protesters gathered in Washington. More anti-war demonstrations followed in San Francisco, in other large American cities, and on college campuses. By 1970 there was little doubt that the United States was getting out of Vietnam. U.S. military personnel in South Vietnam peaked at 536,000 in 1968, of which 58,000 were Air Force. By 1970 the numbers were 334,000/43,000, and by 1971 157,000/29,000. South Vietnamese combat squadrons increased impressively in number, flying everything from C-119 gunships to F-5 jet fighters. Their flying skills and staying power was another issue. USAF strength in Thailand declined as well. In November of '69 all F-105 aircraft were moved from Korat to Takhli. And in October of 1970, this combat veteran of the *Rolling Thunder* campaigns, was finally told to call it quits. The 355th Tactical Fighter Wing folded its colors, along with the 333rd and 357th Tactical Fighter Squadrons. Their 66 aircraft were transferred to air national guard units in the United States. An era ended with the departure of the F-105 from the scene in Southeast Asia. Takhli Royal Thai Air Force Base closed its doors, at least the American side. For a year or so the geckoes

The 41st Tactical Electronic Warfare Squadron at Takhli RTAFB, Thailand, in October 1969. Lt/Colonel John C. Reed, Squadron Commander, standing front center. Colonel Heath Bottomly, 355TFW Commander standing to the left. Lt/Colonel Robert Childs, B-66 Deputy Commander, on the right. Lt/Col Paul Maul, operations officer, far left front standing at attention. Author, in summer 505s, sixth from left, standing behind row of men seated on tarmac.

and cobras had the run of the base. The 42nd TEWS preceded the departure of the F-105s by moving to Korat on September 22. B-52 *Arc Light* missions followed the same declining trend, being reduced in March 1970 from 1,800 to 1,400, to 1,000 missions in August. B-52 operations were then closed out at Andersen and Kadena and consolidated at U-Tapao in southern Thailand.[1]

While American force reductions were ongoing and peace negotiations in Paris were progressing at a languid pace, there was no corresponding let up in North Vietnamese supplies passing down the Ho Chi Minh trail. North Vietnamese AAA and SAM units continued to expand into areas they had never been seen in before. Even the MiG interceptor force, at 257 combat planes, had never been larger and was showing its muscle. On January 28, 1970, an HH-53 helicopter on its way to rescue an F-105 pilot down in Route Pack 1, was attacked and shot down by a MiG-21 while still over Laos. This was the first combat action with a MiG since the 1968 bombing halt. On March 28 a Navy F-4J shot down an aggressive MiG-21 over the Gulf of Tonkin. SA-2 missile sites, long suspected to be present in the Mu Gia and Ban Karai Pass areas were photographed and confirmed on November 3, 1970. It wasn't long before a SAM site was confirmed on the Laos side of Ban Karai Pass.

On January 1, 1971, Tom Leeper was the EWO on an EB-66E flying a B-52 support mission. "In the vicinity of Ban Karai we were engaged by a *Fansong* radar. The site launched one or two missiles at us, and we went into a standard SAM-break. Our jammers had been modified so they no longer went off line as soon as you initiated a violent maneuver. I had a TWS (Track While Scan) function on some jammers. I turned it on and realigned my jammers on the *Fansong* radar. We pulled out of the SAM-break at 18,000 feet, and the missile went off behind us."[2] An F-4D flying near Dong Hoi on March 22 was not that lucky. Nor was an O-2 observation plane, blasted out of the sky by an SA-2 missile on April 26, fired from the same site that engaged Tom Leeper's plane two months earlier.

Air Staff intentions were to phase out the EB-66 force in 1970. As things were shaping up that plan no longer looked like a good idea. In April 1970 Colonel Heath Bottomly, the commander of the 355th Tactical Fighter Wing at Takhli, wrote the commander of 13th Air Force at Clark, "Request the EB-66 flying hour allocation for Fiscal Year 4/70 be reduced from 4,000 hours to 3,426 hours." Plainly speaking, Bottomly no longer had the resources to maintain the aging aircraft, after a hefty slice of his maintenance force had been taken from him in an earlier force reduction. The 42TEWS was programmed for a reduction from 20 to 18 aircraft effective April 1, 1970. While personnel strength was reduced in accordance with the Thailand Force Reduction directives issued on March 12, a reduction in aircraft was not implemented. "Maintenance capabilities have been exceeded this past quarter," wrote Bottomly, "a projected net loss of 150 aircraft mechanics has placed maintenance in a position where sustained overflying could jeopardize flying safety and decrease mission effectiveness."[3]

That September, in accordance with the downsizing directions received under *Operation Banner Sun*, the EB-66 force at Korat was reduced to 15 aircraft – five C-models and 10 E-models. The small EB-66 squadron at Kadena, the 19TEWS, was inactivated on October 1, its four E-models were flown to Clark Air Base and scrapped. The two precious EB-66C reconnaissance aircraft were returned to Shaw to provide training for replacement crews. About that time the projected phase out plans for the EB-66 came to a halt. In October, CINCPAC, Admiral John S. McCain, directed his component commanders to initiate a "concentrated ELINT program to provide increased tactical intelligence on threat radars in the areas of the Mugia and Ban Karai passes."[4] General George S. Brown, the 7th Air Force commander in Saigon found that he did not have the resources to mount a 24-hour ELINT collection program. He turned to PACAF and the Air Staff for augmentation, requesting 11 additional EB-66 aircraft. CINCPAC reduced General Brown's request from 11 to six, and the Joint Chiefs of Staff agreed to "deploy six EB-66 aircraft and 158 personnel to Thailand for six months."[5] By November 26 the 2nd Aircraft Delivery Group reported that the initial deployment of additional EB-66 aircraft to Thailand under the nickname *Coronet West* was under way. The 42TEWS aircraft inventory would in fact rise to a total of 22 by May 1971.[6]

Admiral McCain's staff then went back to the JCS and expressed concern over General Ryan's plan to phase the EB-66 force out of the Air Force inventory by July 1971.[7] The Air Staff responded that actions to retain the force were already underway, extending the 42TEWS with 13 aircraft to FY 4/72.[8] It actually became 15 aircraft, with an additional two NOA (Nonoperational Active) aircraft provided without corresponding manpower support. Ryan's staff then extended the entire remaining EB-66 force world-wide. The 39TEWS at Spangdahlem with 16 aircraft was rescheduled for inactivation in FY 1/73, instead of 1/72. The 39TEWTS at Shaw, with 10 aircraft, was to inactivate in FY 2/72, instead of FY 3/71. Ryan's plans to inactivate the EB-66 force bowed to CINCPAC and JCS pressure, but didn't do anything to alleviate the ever-increasing maintenance requirements of aging aircraft which continued to be flown beyond their limits.[9]

Commando Hunt V, directed by Admiral McCain, provided for 24-hour ELINT coverage in October 1970, and illustrated how thinly the EB-66 force was spread. "Daily 24-hour electronic reconnaissance coverage of Route Pack 1 was considered vital because of the threat posed by enemy SAMs and radar-controlled AAA. Poor weather during the first weeks of the campaign limited effective photo reconnaissance, making electronic reconnaissance even more important to fix the location of enemy missiles and AAA guns. To compound the problem, the enemy practiced excellent transmission security, keeping his radars turned off until ready to fire. The broadest possible coverage was required to enhance the probability of intercepting enemy radar emissions during times when he was performing maintenance and calibration tests on his equipment. The five EB-66Cs of the 42TEWS constituted the primary ESM force available to 7AF for *Commando Hunt V*. The aircraft were capable of providing approximately eight hours of coverage each day." A coordinated schedule was then developed with the U.S. Navy's Carrier Task Force 77 by which EA-3Bs began covering periods between EB-66 missions augmented by EA-6As from the 1st Marine Air Wing. Combat Apple EC-135M aircraft out of Kadena filled in the slack by covering "RP-1 for 12 hours on two consecutive days each week." The data collected was sent to 7AF and the PACOM ELINT processing center in Hawaii which produced the enemy electronic order of battle. In some cases the process took up to 24 hours before mission data reached field commanders, much too slow for a tactically fluid situation but the best that could be done with the resources available.

"The effective interface of USAF, Navy and Marine resources gave *Commando Hunt V* the 24 hour ELINT coverage it required. But the experience underscored the critical nature of the USAF's diminished ELINT force." In addition to aircraft shortages, "the Air Force badly needed a new tactical electronic warfare support platform, while the time delays in data processing pointed out the need for a near real-time in-flight relay capability. Even more serious was the fact that the EB-66 was itself antiquated and that many of its sensors reflected the 'state of the art' of the late 1940s. A critical shortcoming was the inability of the EB-66s direction finding equipment to accurately locate enemy radar sites. At best the DF and navigation equipment was capable of placing a radar within a radius of approximately 10 miles. The inherent inaccuracy of the equipment was compounded by the enemy's transmission discipline, frequently permitting only a single line bearing on the transmitter location." Efforts by 7th Air Force to increase the 42TEWS to a 20 plane force, which it was back in April 1970, were unsuccessful. Like it or not, "the aging EB-66 continued as the backbone of the USAF ESM force in SEA."[10]

The EB-66s patrolled Laos, looking for fire control radars, and flew ELINT missions on the Gulf side of North Vietnam. Laos had never been a benign area to operate in and with the increased introduction of larger caliber guns and fire control radars by the North, it continued to be a very dangerous place. Reconnaissance aircraft losses alone over Laos from January 1970 to May 1971 included three O-2, eight OV-10, six RF-4C and one EC-47 aircraft. The EB-66 aircrews and staff continued to strive to provide the best possible support with the aircraft they had.

The primary mission for the E-models was to protect the B-52 bombers on their daily raids against the passes leading into Laos from North Vietnam, and along the DMZ, which was anything but demilitarized. The EB-66 squadron planners held regular tactics meetings and were suspicious of their *Arc Light* support orbits, which in the estimation of the EB-66 planning staff were too predictable. The EB-66s were required to be in their orbits 15 minutes prior to the B-52s arrival time over target. In their estimation, the position of the orbits relative to the bomber ingress and egress headings provided tracking information to the enemy. They wanted the flexibility to eliminate the orbits (designed and tasked by 7th Air Force in Saigon) and insert themselves between the bombers and the enemy threat. They felt the same about predictable orbits supporting drone and RF-4C missions. Seventh Air Force gave a little, but essentially stuck to what they had been doing for years past. Headquarters staffs and men on the line rarely view things the same way.[11]

EB-66 effectiveness continued to resurface as a topic of discussion at various staff levels whenever the pace of combat operations declined – a discussion as predictable as the monsoon rains. Not only EB-66 effectiveness, but electronic countermeasures in general continued to be viewed in some quarters of the tactical fighter community with scepticism. For some unknown reason, SAC never discounted ECM, wouldn't fly into an area without adequate ECM protection, and considered its onboard jammers more valuable than the guns they carried on their planes. The Navy, although initially lagging behind the Air Force in tactical ECM aircraft, in a short time had remedied that situation and introduced the EA-3B, then the newer and much more capable EA-6B tactical jamming and reconnaissance aircraft. Little had been done for the EB-66 fleet, yet it continued to be the major source of protection for *Arc Light* operations, as well as manned and unmanned reconnaissance operations over the North.

The Security Service in San Antonio, Texas, had various means to monitor enemy responses to jamming and issued *Comfy Coat* evaluations. Refined over the years, they proved remarkably accurate, were highly respected in the intelligence community, and provided the only means to assess an effort that did not leave behind bomb craters or bullet holes. Electronic countermeasures are comparable to the efforts of a successful police department. As crime rates diminish, or major crimes no longer occur because of police effectiveness, the department frequently finds itself on the defensive in budget battles or when asking for new equipment and additional manpower. Success frequently equals cutbacks and reductions. It is indeed difficult to measure that which has been prevented. The EB-66 force had found itself in such a position for years. How many aircraft did it save from destruction? How many air crews owed their lives to the silent warriors? How many fighter bomber and reconnaissance missions were completed because the EB-66s were there? The North Vietnamese air defense organization recalled the EB-66s more vividly than its own detractors. In the words of Ho Si Huu, writing in the *History of the Air Defense Service*, he recalls the "jamming pods, combined with long-range jamming from EB-66s northwest of Hanoi, covered the screens of the SAM units and blinded the radars controlling Vietnamese 57mm and 100mm guns. Every missile launched by 274 Regiment either self-destructed or crashed back to earth. The AAA guns were forced to use optical fire control equipment or iron sights on the guns to engage the attackers."[12]

In a January 2, 1971, evaluation, the Air Force Special Communications Center (AFSCC) noted in one of its periodic reports that "The EB-66 is effective against low frequency early warning and acquisition radars which provide data to the SA-2 system. During *Arc Light* operations it adds a confusion factor to the enemy's air defense system. The effectiveness of EB-66 jamming vs *Fansong* is dependent upon optimum positioning relative to the threat radar and target aircraft. The combined efforts of the B-52 jamming, *Iron Hand* suppression, F-105 *Wild Weasel* aircraft, and EB-66 jamming have contributed to aircraft survival in the threat environment ... In view of the EB-66 effectiveness against the enemy's low frequency early warning and acquisition radars, it is recommended that EB-66 support not be withdrawn from current *Arc Light* operations."[13] That, of course, was a sound suggestion. No B-52 was ever lost to 100mm gun fire, or to SA-2 missiles while flying *Arc Light* missions supported by the EB-66. Even more revealing is the fact that no MiG-21 intercepts were attempted against the B-52 force when EB-66s were present.

Seventh Air Force position papers echoed the AFSCC assessment of the EB-66 and recommended retention, along with the selective use of ECM pods. ECM pods, they pointed out correctly, will not prevent tracking by low frequency acquisition and early warning radars.[14] Colonel Joseph E. Thome, the director of electronic warfare at Headquarters Pacific Air Forces in a message to 7th Air Force wrote, "The jamming provided by the EB-66 must not be considered alone, but as an integral part of the overall protection effort. It complements and enhances the protection provided by *Wild Weasel* aircraft and the B-52 on-board jammers. In presenting the role of the EB-66 I believe the term stand off jammer is inappropriate and should be avoided. Escort or support jamming is a much better choice of terminology."[15] Not only was effectiveness evaluation of the EB-66 jamming support a continuing issue, labeling was as well. The leadership of the tactical air forces was long overdue providing a viable support jamming and tactical electronic reconnaissance capability. In the absence of that, the EB-66 force at a minimum needed to receive whatever technical support it required to remain effective. Little was done. While generals and colonels argued about EB-66 effectiveness, whether to retain them or not, how many aircraft to employ where, when and for how long – the men who flew and maintained the airplanes kept doing their jobs, largely unaware of the bureaucratic battles waged from behind polished mahogany and scratched and dented grey Air Force issue metal desks. Their problems were of a more immediate nature – eat, drink, sleep, fly, survive another day. A cycle that repeated itself day after day, week after week. Rumors came and went but little changed on the flight line or in the maintenance docks.

"The C-model missions were solitary flights conducting passive reconnaissance," recalls Don Christman, who flew as navigator. "We flew a late night mission most nights up the Laos side of North Vietnam to the Fish's Mouth, west to what used to be Burma, and back and forth until we had to go home for fuel. The Ravens in back would usually only catch an early warning radar up for one sweep, making sure we were doing what they expected us to be doing. They knew our routes as well as we did. On one of these long and boring missions I suggested to the pilot that we overshoot our turning point on the east bound leg back toward the Fish's Mouth, the most northern of the natural passes coming out of the North and feeding into the Ho Chi Minh trail in Laos. The pass was heavily defended by AAA and SA-2 SAMs. He said, 'OK, but keep us out of North Vietnam.' We weren't a minute past that planned turning point before the Ravens in back hollered with joy over the intercom because of all the radars that suddenly appeared on their scopes. They woke up in a hurry when we deviated from our flight plan. Maybe we got a little too close, because one of the Ravens called 'station passage on a *Firecan* radar.' Which means we flew directly over him. I flew several C-model missions in the Gulf of Tonkin supporting drone missions. A C-130 would launch a drone out over the Gulf. The drone would descend to around 500 feet, fly at about 400 knots as far as I could tell, and penetrate the coast north of Haiphong, making for Hanoi, overflying the airfields, then head south. The North Vietnamese expended a lot of AAA ammunition and SA-2 missiles trying to knock down these small birds. It was one of these drones that got the picture of our POWs waving from the Hanoi Hilton prison. The Ravens loved these missions because of all the radars that would suddenly come up trying to track the drones."[16]

Although most of the flying was war related, there were many routine flights, such as functional check flights (FCF) after an aircraft had gone through maintenance and required to be certified as operationally ready. Other aircraft were flown to Clark Air Base in the Philippines for heavy maintenance that could not be accomplished at Takhli or Korat. Others yet had to be flown back to the

Douglas factory at Tulsa for periodic inspections and repair. On April 21, 1970, with the 42TEWS still at Takhli, Wring 69, an EB-66E, was getting ready to take off from Hickam AFB, Hawaii, to McClellan in California, enroute to the Douglas plant at Tulsa, Oklahoma. Major William Fletcher was the pilot, Major Charles Quinn the navigator, and Sergeant George Stevens served as crew chief. At 0930 in the morning Major Fletcher started engines and taxied out to a position short of the runway. He was cleared to take the runway by Honolulu Tower. When Major Fletcher advanced the power an explosion occurred followed by severe vibrations. Fletcher shut down the number one engine. Seeing flames shooting up from the right side he ordered the aircraft abandoned. Fire trucks arrived within less than two minutes blanketing the right wing and number two engine with foam.[17]

Major Thomas Boyle, flying safety officer at Hickam, was talking to the base operations officer when the secretary came up to him and calmly announced, "A B-66 is burning on the runway." Recalls Boyle, "I ran out to my car in front of base operations and rushed to the airplane just short of the runway. The entry door was lying on the ground, the crew of three was about 1,000 feet to the left of the aircraft, running away. The crew must have assumed the plane with a full fuel load was going to explode. I pulled myself up into the cockpit, sat down in the pilot's seat, pulled both throttles to idle, turned off both master switches, and pulled the engine fire control handles. The fire went out. The damage to the right wing, however, was so extensive that the airplane was declared Class 26 – not repairable."[18]

Furl, an EB-66C with tail number 54-384, was scheduled to fly an *Arc Light* support and reconnaissance mission, accompanied by Tint, an EB-66E. The mission, on October 26, 1970, barely four weeks after the 42TEWS moved to Korat, was scheduled for nearly seven hours with two in-flight refuelings. Furl was delayed because its oxygen system had not been adequately replenished. Tint took off without Furl to provide coverage for the *Arc Light* B-52s. Upon returning to Korat, Furl descended to flight level 180, 55 miles east of the base in weather. Major Donald Eversole, the pilot, and Major John O'Malley, the navigator, were advised that the precision approach radar was down for repair and they should expect a surveillance approach to runway 06. Should the approach fail they were to proceed to Takhli where the weather was more favorable. The official Air Force accident report notes, "Two items aboard the aircraft were not used: the TACAN and the radar altimeter. All was going well down to the six mile point where the aircraft was cleared to the published Minimum Descent Altitude. MDA is defined in the Enroute Supplement as 'An altitude specified in feet above mean sea level, below which descent will not be made until visual reference has been established with the runway and the aircraft is in a position to execute a normal landing.'

Based on an intercom transmission from the navigator, 'I have the field and it looks clear,' the Raven monitoring the altimeter did not think it unusual when the pilot descended below the MDA. However, the navigator was referring to a radar presentation rather than a visual reference. The descent below MDA was continued by the pilot, even though neither he nor the navigator had the field in sight. The aircraft struck the ground three miles short of the runway, more than 360 feet below the MDA. Initial impact was light and the aircraft became airborne again. It finally came to rest two miles short of the runway." Miraculously no one was killed, although several of the crew suffered serious back injuries.[19] Everyone involved regretted the omissions that led to this accident. Crew coordination, the accident investigation board found, was lacking, and "the use of the radar altimeter would have warned of proximity of terrain."[20]

Captain Merlyn Luke retired as a colonel and was one of the Ravens onboard the aircraft. "We managed to extricate ourselves from the downward firing ejection seats, get the overhead escape hatch open and assist one another out to the top of the plane. The rain had let up somewhat and we could see the flashing approach lights off in the distance. I went forward on top of the plane to check on the pilot and navigator. The navigator was in a daze and I coaxed him into consciousness and helped him exit the aircraft. Fuel was everywhere, floating on top of all the water, running downhill toward the cockpit. The pilot's seat had ripped loose and was jammed into the instrument panel. He was conscious and busy trying to get out of his harness. About this time the fuel from the leaking aft tank ignited in a large explosion. The navigator jumped over the side and broke his ankle. I went next. The pilot followed. We gathered near a tree, well clear of the aircraft and watched it burn. A rescue helicopter picked us up and flew us to the airfield. Except for me, all others were injured and flown home via a medical evacuation flight. I had a sore back and a lacerated tongue. I remember thinking of my new wife and our nine month old daughter. After a couple of visits to the flight surgeon I was scheduled on my next C-model flight. The scheduler took pity on me and decided I should fly the E-model instead for a few sorties."[21]

On January 18, 1971, Captain Robert Mead departed Korat, completed his air refueling, and climbed to flight level 270 on his way to support an *Arc Light* strike. Oil pressure on number 1 dropped rapidly to zero, the alternator failed, and the ECM equipment and radar began to malfunction. Captain Mead shut down number one engine, declared an emergency and headed for NKP, Nakom Phanom. NKP could not locate them on their radar because their IFF was inoperable. The oil pressure on number two engine began to drop. Captain Mead restarted number one and left it in idle as a precautionary measure. At five miles the aircraft was cleared to land, when at the one mile point a C-47 pulls onto the active runway and the tower cancels the landing. Going around acceleration was marginal. The aircraft climbed with difficulty to about 300 feet at 160 knots indicated airspeed. Rolling out on the downwind leg, number one engine began to vibrate, then seized. The oil pressure on number two decreased to zero. The final turn and landing was accomplished using the number two engine.[22] A nightmare of an accident was barely avoided.

On March 11, 1971, a C-model suffered a runaway trim condition soon after take-off, precluding the pilot from controlling the aircraft. The crew of seven ejected successfully from the stricken aircraft. Later in the year the 42TEWS temporarily moved operations to Udorn while the Korat runway was being repaired. On November 17, Mascot 22, an E-model, took the runway, "completed its line up and before take-off checklist. The throttles were advanced to military power with both engines responding normally. Within a few seconds an explosion occurred in the number two engine, causing the engine to disintegrate." All three crew members evacuated the aircraft. "Captain Ardis, the EWO, had initially attempted to egress through his escape hatch, but when he opened it flames entered the cockpit causing slight burns to his right ear and neck. He closed the hatch and egressed through the navigator's hatch opening. Then the navigator's ejection seat cooked off." The aircraft was a total loss.[23]

1970 and 1971 provided more than enough excitement for the flyers of the 42nd Tactical Electronic Warfare Squadron.

CHAPTER TWENTY-EIGHT

THE 39TH TACTICAL ELECTRONIC WARFARE SQUADRON

The 39TEWS became an active Air Force squadron on April 1, 1969. By October 1969 all of its aircraft and personnel were in place at Spangdahlem Air Base, Germany. Spangdahlem was a satellite base of nearby Bitburg Air Base, the home of the 36th Tactical Fighter Wing. Two of the Wing's squadrons of F-4E aircraft were based at Bitburg, while the other two, the F-4E equipped 23rd TFS, and the 39th TEWS with its 16 EB-66C and E aircraft, were bedded down at Spangdahlem. Three years later, on December 31, 1972, the dual-base relationship for the 36th TFW would end. Spang, as aircrews from the earliest days of its existence referred to Spangdahlem, became the home of the 52nd Tactical Fighter Wing, and still is to this day. Surrounded by thick pine, oak and beech forests, green meadows and well tended fields, Spangdahlem was everything Takhli and Korat was not. It was a permanent assignment for the new arrivals, as permanent as any military tour of duty can be – usually about three years in duration. Airmen were once again accompanied by their families, lived in well cared for on-base housing which, as the base itself, was built in the early '50s as the Cold War began to take shape. The three story apartment buildings had two or three stairwells, six apartments to a stairwell, with American style kitchens, living and dining rooms. The number of bedrooms varied from three to four. The basement of each apartment house provided room for storage and the communal washer/dryer area, with every family assigned its own laundry day. There was an amply stocked Base Exchange, BX, and commissary at both Spangdahlem and Bitburg, providing all the amenities of home-town USA, and the schools were within walking distance for the children.

Three 39TEWS EB-66E crews at Aviano AB, Italy, 1970. L to R standing – Captains Siders, Johnson, Grazier, Wensil and Lieutenant Colonel Brammer. L to R sitting – Captain Allison, Majors Samuel (author) and Harding.//Lower picture – Armed Forces Day at Spangdahlem AB, Germany, 1957. RB-66C 54-459 is the third aircraft from the left.

After the snakes and geckos of Thailand, the torrential downpours during the monsoon season, and the oppressive heat and high humidity, Germany was the ultimate good overseas assignment. Here the weather had four seasons, Santa Claus came on Christmas day, the Weihnachtsmann on Christmas eve, and the church bells rang loudly on Sundays across the quiet land. There was no flying permitted on Sundays. War was but a memory for Americans and Germans alike, although each remembered different wars.

Although many of the new arrivals were lucky enough to be assigned on-base housing, there was not enough room for all. Villages and small towns surrounding Spangdahlem such as Hereforst, Binsfeld, Trier, Dudeldorf, Speicher and others became home to another generation of American servicemen and their families. No longer here as occupiers, as in the early '50s, but as partners in the North Atlantic Alliance formed in opposition to the threat posed by the mass armies of the Soviet Union to the east. The nearby villages and towns were quaint with their cobblestone streets, still a manure pile here and there attesting to an agricultural heritage. The villages nestled in narrow river valleys around steepled churches, houses built close together like chicks around a mother hen. Fairytale castles, such as nearby Burg Elz, beckoned for Sunday visits. When there was time, the more distant military recreation centers in Berchtesgaden, Garmisch-Partenkirchen and Chiemsee provided vacation opportunities in a splendid setting. *The Berchtesgadener Hof* in Berchtesgaden, a one time Nazi era elite hotel with a spectacular view of the Watzmann Mountain, excellent restaurants, and a large swimming pool, was my own family's favorite. From here we could explore the Obersalzberg where Hitler once had his Eagle Nest perched high up on a mountain top, or experience the joy of riding mining cars through narrow tunnels in a one-time salt mine, sliding down steep wooden chutes into remote chambers beneath the mountain, or visit Salzburg in nearby Austria, a city of light and music, or any number of other cultural treasures dotting the Bavarian and Austrian countryside.

The Eifel mountains surrounding Bitburg and Spangdahlem Air Bases were not high like the Alps, but more like the White Mountains of Vermont, or New York State's Adirondacks. Here the cuckoo called in April and May, and at night the calls of screech owls added an eery quality to life in a foreign land that somehow felt to many like home. Spangdahlem and Bitburg were near one of Germany's great wine regions as well. On take-off we would turn over the winding Mosel Valley with mile after mile of fabled vineyards decorating steep slopes. Each fall there were winefests aplenty. Not only that, Bitburg was home to one of Germany's most renown breweries as well. 'Ein Bit' Bitte,' as the jingle went, a Bitburger Beer please, was a phrase that became as familiar to Americans as to Germans.

I finished my combat tour at Takhli in October 1969 flying with the 41st TEWS, which deactivated days after my departure. My follow-on assignment was at Headquarters United States Air Forces in Europe, USAFE, in the beautiful spa town of Wiesbaden. I had left Germany in January 1951 as a refugee boy, leaving behind a war torn land where people were hungry, ill clad, and living in house ruins and rotting former military barracks. This time I arrived at Frankfurt International Airport accompanied by my wife and two children, Charles seven and Shelley four. Admittedly I was a bit anxious to return to a land I had left behind 18 years earlier under very differing circumstances. My sponsor met us at the airport and had rooms reserved for us in the *American Arms*, a military hotel in downtown Wiesbaden. Base housing would take a while. When housing did become available we moved into a standard 3-bedroom apartment in Aukamm, one of several American housing areas built along a ridge line above Wiesbaden. Charles entered school, Shelley Kindergarten, and I reported for duty at Lindsey Air Station, a former German army Kaserne dating back to the Kaiser's days, which served as the headquarters of American airpower in Europe since 1945.

As the headquarters manager for the newly arrived EB-66 squadron at Spangdahlem I would fly with the squadron, and anything that had to do with the 39TEWS and its B-66 aircraft came across my desk. It was admittedly one of the best assignments I ever had in my Air Force career. My second task dealt with the F-111Es slated to come into the 20th Tactical Fighter Wing at RAF Upper Heyford, replacing aging 'Huns'. The F-100 was about the same vintage as the B-66 and on its way out of the inventory. CINCUSAFE's highest priority at the time was to bed-down the F-111Es at Upper Heyford and get them combat ready. My own task was to deal with the electronic warfare aspects of the F-111E – its ALQ-94 jamming system, flares, chaff, and the aircraft simulator. I had no idea what tricks and subterfuge I would have to use in the weeks to come to obtain things which I thought, as a novice headquarter's manager and junior major, should be accompanying a new aircraft as a matter of course. Finding stocks of flares, re-certifying them for use, and flying them into Upper Heyford was the least of my problems. The ALQ-94 internal ECM system of the F-111E, touted by the Sanders Corporation as the ultimate automatic deception jammer, was anything but ultimate nor automatic, and was already in need of being updated. The F-111E simulator was in little better shape. I had my hands full and spent about as much time at Upper Heyford and Wright-Patterson AFB in Ohio on F-111 business as I did at home.

In early December 1969 I set out for Spangdahlem to get some needed flying time. We had a heavy snow fall the night before and I got as far as the Rhine River bridge which was totally blocked by deep drifts. I waited two days, then tried again. This time I got as far as the little town of Simmern in the Hunsrueck Mountains. Again I had to turn around. The winter of '69 to '70 was very cold with lots and lots of snow. The children in the American housing areas loved it, building huge snow forts, or riding their American Flyer sleds down nearby hillsides from morning to night. I finally made it to Spang in early January. It was good to smell kerosene again, to strap on a parachute, get into the confines of an ejection seat, and go somewhere, anywhere where the sun shone, like sunny Spain, Greece or Italy. If it was a NATO country, the 39TEWS went there and provided air defense fighters and ground radar controllers realistic electronic warfare training.

When I arrived at Spang there was a surprise waiting for me. On the ramp nearest the fence sat 54-459 – my favorite C-model. On seeing that plane I felt I had come home. 54-459 arrived at Spangdahlem for the first time on November 28, 1956, then brand new with less than 100 flying hours on it. The plane was promptly christened *Kreis Wittlich*, then the county seat, in the presence of local dignitaries at an elaborately staged ceremony during Armed Forces Day attended by over 30,000 Germans. Then the aircraft was part of the 42nd TRS, assigned to the 10th Tactical Reconnaissance Wing, the same wing which routinely put on 48-ship fly-bys on Memorial or Armed Forces Day. I had flown many missions in 459 out of Takhli, and the plane had always brought me home. This plane was special to me. Everyone assigned to the 39th squadron had at least one combat tour in Southeast Asia. Many had flown 100 missions or more over the North in Route Packs V and VI where the missiles and the MiGs came out to play. The experience level of pilots, navigators and EWOs in the 39th TEWS was very high. Many of the aircrew had thousands of hours of flying time in the B-66 – Bill Puckett, 'Smiley' Pomeroy, Don Harding, Ike Espe, Jim Weir, Joe Sapere, and many others were part of that elite group of flyers. Many had been among the first to go to Tan Son Nhut and Takhli in 1965. These men had trained me when I went through Shaw in '68. They were the very best our Air Force had to offer. My first flight at Spangdahlem was in 54-459.

In April 1970 I scheduled three of our E-models to participate in *Exercise National Week*. *National Week* was fun. We flew against the Navy, the 6th Fleet, and only at night. First we had to find the Fleet though. To our surprise we learned that the Mediterranean wasn't all that small, it was large enough to hide a powerful American fleet, its aircraft carrier, cruisers and destroyers. Usually a careless radar or radio transmission would lead us to them. We played the enemy, flying combat profiles of Soviet Badger bombers. It was good training for everyone and Sigonella Naval Air Station on Sicily wasn't a bad place to operate out of. On that April deployment I met Don Harding. He was my pilot. We took off from Spangdahlem heading for the French border, climbing out slowly to 38,000 feet.

We coasted out over the Mediterranean passing over Nice, then headed southwest toward the U.S. Naval Air Facility Sigonella, near Catania, Sicily. From there we flew several missions against the Navy, then returned to Spangdahlem via Aviano, the main USAF air base in Italy. Don and I hit it off and became friends. When our conversations turned to Vietnam we talked about things that made us laugh. "You won't believe this," I recall Don saying to me. "I was above Hanoi, near the Chinese buffer zone. The mountains start there, high mountains, wooded, beautiful scenery." We were in a Catania restaurant bar, after dinner, talking. "I looked down and there was this beautiful mountain lake surrounded by spacious looking houses. There was a boat cruising the lake and a guy behind it water skiing. I got my navigator/bombardier, Bill Crofoot, on the intercom. I called him Willi. I said 'Willi, you've got to see this. Look out your window,' and I rolled the airplane on its side so he could see. Neither one of us could believe what we saw. F-105s were dropping bombs a few miles south, and here was this guy water skiing. Another time we were in an orbit outside Haiphong. We flew right up to the edge of the SAM site. He had a slant range of 20 miles and locked his radar on us, but he couldn't touch us, we were just out of his range. As I looked down to my left there appeared this beautiful four-masted schooner painted solid white. Everything was white – masts, sails, everything. It headed straight for Haiphong harbor. Our time was up and I said to my navigator, 'I have to take a closer look. This is so unreal, so bizarre. I went down to 18,000 feet but couldn't see any people on board. There was a flag, but it just hung there. If I hadn't been short on fuel I would have gone down and buzzed that thing." Then Don said to me, "You know about Kelly, don't you?

"'Yea. I flew with him at Takhli. Great guy. Funny. Loved his beer. What about him? I haven't run into him yet.'

"You won't," Don said. "He's dead. So is John Holley." My mouth must have dropped open. "I thought you knew. It was in early October. He aborted his take-off, ran off the end of the runway and burst into flames.'[1] I was devastated to hear the news. I didn't know Holley that well, but Ken Kelly and I had been close. Before he left Takhli he came by to see me to 'pull my chain' and tell me how much he was going to enjoy bratwurst and beer at Spang. And he assured me that he would be thinking of me while he was enjoying himself.

"Cern 34, an EB-66E, was scheduled for a 'routine training mission,' the accident report states matter of factly. Take-off appeared normal up to the computed take-off point at 6,550 feet. At approximately 8,000 feet down the runway Cern 34 was heard to retard engines, the drag chute deployed, and Captain Kelly called on departure frequency 'Abort, abort, abort.' The aircraft continued straight ahead for the remaining 1,700 feet of runway, continued on the 800 feet of PSP (perforated steel planking) overrun, then made a slight left turn to the boundary fence, went through the fence 'and immediately became engulfed in flames. There was no apparent attempt at ejection by the crew members. The surviving crew member, Lt/Colonel Fucich, was found approximately 20 feet forward of the aircraft with a broken leg and extensive burns and was evacuated by helicopter to the 36TFW hospital at Bitburg."[2]

Major Donald Harding and Lieutenant Colonel Carwin 'Smiley' Pomeroy, the 39TEWS operations officer, participated in the accident investigation. At first they could not figure out what could possibly have gone so very wrong. It wasn't the engines. Harding recalls "When I looked at the aircraft, there was little left of Kelly, he had been thrown over the side under the left engine. The airplane came to rest down a steep slope, up against the tree line of a dense forest. There was a slight breeze coming down the canyon, and the left wing flap was swinging freely in the breeze. I looked at that thing and called to Smiley, 'Come over here.' I pointed out to him that the flaps were up when we first came down here. There was no smoke residue on the remaining flap surface dangling in the breeze. It was clean. Everything else was covered with soot. If the flaps had been down when Kelly made his take-off, they would have been black and torn. The other wing was burned too much to check that flap. Those flaps were up. He miss-set them. If you take the flaps to 60 percent, then 80, while performing your pre-take-off check, then, if you come back up to 60 percent and stop, what you've done is push the hydraulic fluid to the other side of the cylinder. You've pushed that fluid right out of there, and the flaps will blow up on take-off. We questioned the crew chief and he saw Kelly reset the flaps in the parking area.

"When the aircraft came down the runway and went over the hill it hit several concrete approach light stanchions. One came up into the cockpit and cut off Kelly's legs, then the cockpit turned sideways and he rolled under the engine. A large splinter from one of the poles caught Holly square in the chest, like a spear. And poor old Frank Fucich, the navigator, was sitting up there, going down the hill with no one around him as the fuselage hit two big oak trees. His ejection seat fired, then 'I went tumbling down that hill, got out of my seat, looked back up and thought I'll crawl toward the sun,' he told me in the hospital. Well, there was no sun, just a burning forward fuel tank that had been thrown out of the airplane and was burning fiercely. Frank, in shock, crawled up toward 'the sun' and that's how he got his burns. Otherwise he would have gotten out of that accident nearly unscathed. His hands and face were burned."[3] Al Kersis will never forget that day either. "I was watching this fire truck come racing up on the runway, then following in the path of the EB-66E that had just roared down that same runway moments before. I was supposed to be on this airplane. I arrived in the morning at the squadron. I looked up at the scheduling board and my name was up there as the EWO. About five minutes later the scheduler wiped my name off the board and wrote in another's name – Holley. Holley was new and needed a flight."[4]

Black Eagle was another exercise we participated in regularly, it took place up north, involving air defense sites in Denmark and northern Germany. At times the effect of EB-66 jamming was traumatic for inexperienced radar operators not trained to cope with whitened out radar scopes. They activated their countermeasure circuitry, but in the process also lost sensitivity and target information. The Shah of Iran requested that his GCI sites be evaluated. We promptly sent a flight of EB-66Es to Tehran. Ground observers were stationed at the radar sites. They reported in their formal report seeing the Iranian controllers going into near shock when their scopes whited out with jamming from the EB-66 aircraft. At Lindsey Air Station the branch I worked in was located next door to the RF-4C reconnaissance branch. We all thought it a good idea to team up the RF-4s with the EB-66s to monitor the Soviet Mediterranean fleet, which often was at anchor off the island of Crete. We then flew day and night reconnaissance against the Russians out of Athens Airport – the RF-4s taking pictures after the EBs led them to the Kresta cruisers whose radar emissions gave them away. The crews loved the variety of deployments, taking them all over Europe from the North Cape to Turkey, and at times beyond.

We routinely provided training for NATO interceptors. It was an early morning mission I was on. The aircraft I flew had returned the night before from a *Black Eagle* exercise and been turned around quickly. We flew an orbit over the Black Forest at 28,000 feet. It was a beautiful day, little wind, and the Alps in the distance rose in all their splendor. The first flight of German F-104s came up and I dropped chaff with the usual effect. The second and succeeding flights of interceptors, however, reported no effect on their radars. I was puzzled. Then Frankfurt Control came on the air and demanded, 'Cease ECM.' We did. When we landed at Spang, two blue Air Force staff cars followed us into our parking area. The Wing commander accompanied by several of his deputies, all colonels, was not in a good mood. "Samuel, did you check your chaff load before take-off?" I still had no idea what all the fuss was about, or why the wing commander was involved. I took out the Form 781 and showed them the chaff load that maintenance supposedly had loaded on the aircraft – high frequency chaff for use against fighter radars. "Damn, Samuel. You took the Munich airport radar off the air with your stuff. The Germans are really upset. They had to divert air traffic to Frankfurt and Paris. How the hell did you do it? Did you drop some bundles of chaff before take-off to verify that the proper stuff was loaded?" I had, and signed off on the Form 781 accordingly. By then maintenance had opened the two ALE-1 chaff dispensers in the tail of the aircraft, and low and behold, the remaining chaff in the hoppers was not high frequency stuff that we used against fighter radars, but the low frequency chaff we used against GCI and early warning radars up north during *Exercise Black Eagle*. The maintenance crew that regenerated the aircraft after it returned from the *Black Eagle* exercise did not empty the chaff hoppers, just topped them off with a few bundles of high frequency chaff.

Come late autumn through winter into early spring, weather frequently posed a challenge to flying at Spangdahlem and Bitburg. More than once I sat in the squadron building cooling my heels waiting for the fog to lift. Sometimes we made it out to the end of the runway, then had to turn around, that's how quickly the situation changed on us. The Eifel Mountains were notorious for their marginal weather conditions. Of the four American fighter bases in the Eifel – Spangdahlem, Bitburg, Ramstein and Hahn – Hahn had by far the worst weather and the fewest flying days. Major Bill Rothas, pilot, and Captains George Ciz and Gil Cooley, EWO and navigator, launched from Spangdahlem on a routine training mission in an EB-66E into a typical Eifel sky – grey, nearly touching the runway, but not quite, ready to spit snow at any moment. "We took off, barely got to altitude," recalls George Ciz, "when we received a call from our command post directing us to return to base ASAP, before the weather closed the base. We flew back to Spangdahlem and were on final approach when we were diverted to Bitburg. Off we go to Bitburg. Do the same thing all over again. Get on final approach and the base closes on us for weather and we are diverted to Hahn of all places. At this point we were getting a bit low on fuel, so Hahn was going to be it. We lined up for our final approach, the weather and snow closing in on us. Bill could barely make out the runway. It gets dark early in the northern latitudes in winter, and twilight was turning into darkness. Finally Bill saw the runway lights, and as the wheels touched the runway the lights went out on us. We still had our aircraft lights, the chute deployed properly, the brakes worked and Bill stopped the aircraft. Where to next? The tower called us and directed us to shut down our engines and to remain where we were – on the runway. The runway was closed until further notice. We put the pins in our ejection seats, closed up the aircraft, and since no one could come out to pick us up because of the snow and no lights, the three of us walked through the driving snow to base operations. We then went to the Officers' Club, ate dinner, stayed in the VOQ over night and took off the next morning on another training mission."[5]

In addition to flying ECM training missions and participating in numerous exercises, the squadron's C-models routinely flew electronic reconnaissance along the East German and Czech borders as the 42nd TRS had done before them in the 50s and early 60s. They were the first to pick up the SA-6 SAM radar when it first deployed with the Group of Soviet Forces in the former GDR. They were good at what they were doing. I had scheduled myself on a C-model on August 28, 1972. The 39TEWS schedulers always put us 'staff weenies,' as they referred to me and Major Gerry Bailey, my counterpart at 17th Air Force at Ramstein Air Base, into positions one or two – keeping the more interesting work in positions 3 and 4 for themselves. That day I was supposed to fly position one. The afternoon of the preceding day, as I got ready to drive to Spangdahlem, my boss caught me in the parking lot and told me that I had to cancel my flight. "General Jones wants a briefing tomorrow morning on EB-66 operations in the Mediterranean. Forget about flying and build your briefing." Jones, our four star, was the Commander in Chief, United States Air Forces in Europe. I called the 39th and they got Captain Bob Sherman to fly in my place. Bob was one of the Ravens to deploy to Takhli from Shaw in April 1965, flew the pocket and had 100 missions over bad guy country.

Major Don Harding was the chief of stan/eval for the 39th TEWS. "I had no assistant, so I administered all pilot flight checks. I had a navigator and an electronic warfare officer assigned to me. Larry Wensil, my EWO, was in the rear compartment on August 28, evaluating the three Ravens, while I was up front. This was to be a pilot proficiency and standardization flight check for the crew on a standard electronic reconnaissance mission along the East German border. Captain Dan Craven, a former SAC KC-135 tanker pilot, had proven himself to be a steady pilot in the squadron. I did not anticipate any problems. Dan Craven was a straight and level type of flyer, while I flew the airplane more like a fighter. Dan and I made the preflight walk-around. I paid particular attention to the elevator boost hook engagement above the drag chute compartment. Start up and taxi went well. The quick-check team checked us over before taking the active runway and found nothing out of the ordinary. We began our take-off roll. Dan made the elevator boost engagement check at 80 knots. The check was made by pulling back the control column to see if the boost was working. The pilot could feel if there was a problem in the elevator control and be able to abort the take-off safely if that was necessary. At the 145 knot check I looked for rotation to take-off attitude, and take-off at 155 knots, when Dan exclaimed 'The elevator's locked.'

"I saw Dan shaking the yoke, but the control column was solidly locked in the neutral position. We were accelerating now, and the airplane really wanted to fly, beginning to porpoise. I saw 170 knots on the navigator's airspeed indicator and yelled at Dan, 'Trim it off Dan. Trim it off!!!' That thing would have flown off just using the trim control. Then you adjust the trim and establish climb, or you bank and drop the nose and then trim it out. But Dan wasn't used to that sort of flying, fighter pilot type of flying. Instead, Dan chopped the throttles. My heart jumped into my throat. I knew what was coming next. We were in the same boat Ken Kelly found himself in in '69. There was a delay after the throttles were cut, the drag chute was not deployed, so I yelled, 'Pull the gear up, pull the f ... gear up!!' Dan finally reacted.

"Of course the way the gear comes up – nose first, then right followed by the left gear – the right wing went down. We went on our belly with a slight right hand skid. We hit an arresting gear unit at the end of the runway with the left engine – blaaammmm. It ripped the arresting gear right out of the ground, but it jarred the left side so badly that it ruptured the wing tank and it soon caught fire. I immediately released my escape hatch, at the same time telling the Ravens in the rear to jettison their hatch. The navigator, Major Harry Wilkerson, jettisoned his hatch. Dan didn't. It was an extremely rough ride. The aircraft bumped and banged along, finally it slid to a stop, just short of the airfield perimeter road. I unstrapped and saw the fuel fire fed by the ruptured left wing tank boiling up around the left side of the cockpit. We were on a slight downhill grade and I elected to jump into the edge of the fire, hitting hard in a football type roll and came up running.

"I still had my helmet on, didn't get burned, and felt as if God had his hand around me all this time. I ran to the other side and saw that Dan was still sitting in the pilot's seat. He had cut his arm on something, looked dazed. I hollered at him and he gave me a thumbs up sign and started throwing his shoulder straps off. Wilkerson was letting himself down easy from his hatch position. I didn't realize how badly he was hurt, he suffered compression fractures of the spine, making his way to an open area near the left wing tip. Dan was emerging through the navigator's hatch. I was standing near the right engine and it was still turning, making an awful clattering sound. The first Raven came running down the wing, then Captain Wensil followed, hobbling along with a broken right ankle. Things that followed are hazy, but I do remember pulling myself up on the wing. The third Raven was standing on top of the fuselage close to the raging fire, looking dazed and confused. I gave him a shove toward the right wing tip and said, 'Thatta way.'

"The last Raven was Captain Bob Sherman who somehow had managed to get up the aft compartment ladder and had his arms on top of the fuselage. I grabbed his right hand and pulled his 175 pounds out of there, over to the leading edge of the right wing. My adrenalin was really pumping. The fire was coming over the top of the fuselage and it was very hot. Then one of these strange little things your mind records in a situation like this occurred. I saw a stream of fuel shooting into the air from the aft fuel tank vent. The fuel cell bladder had probably collapsed and was forcing fuel out the vent. It looked like the stream from a high pressure garden hose, and I thought that aft tank filled with 12,500 pounds of fuel was going to go up in flames any minute now.

"I jumped to the ground and will never forget Bob Sherman swinging his leg in front of my face exclaiming, 'Don, I think my leg is broken.' I said, 'Yeah, Bob,' and slid him off the wing onto my shoulders. His shinbone was sticking out through his flight suit and his foot was swinging free. I carried Bob 40 yards past the wing tip, and sensing we were safe my legs turned to rubber and I collapsed. Bob was in great pain and thrashing around. I got his chin under my elbow, arm across his chest, and I grabbed the left leg of his flying suit and pulled his leg up. I didn't want him to stab the bone into the dirt. I was holding Bob, seeing the rescue chopper approaching with a fire bottle attached. It was then that the aft tank exploded and engulfed the entire fuselage in fire. The forward tank caught fire next. It was one of those old fashioned Kaman HH-43 rescue choppers. We put Bob on board and they flew him to the Bitburg hospital. JP-4 had gotten into everything and I soon came down with a severe rash on my feet. So I went to supply and got a new pair of boots and wore plastic bags over my feet until they healed. A few days later I gave Captain Craven his pilot proficiency check in an E-model."[6]

Major Harding was awarded the Airman's Medal for his heroic rescue of Captain Robert Sherman. Bob Sherman was evacuated to the larger Wiesbaden hospital, then sent to Fitzimmons Army Hospital in Denver, Colorado, for recuperation and treatment. One day Bob was sitting in his doctor's waiting room at Fitzimmons Army Hospital. He was in his Class-A blue uniform. The elderly gentleman sitting next to him glanced at Bob's cast, then asked, "May I ask what happened to you? My son is in the Air Force."

Bob, in his usual jovial manner introduced himself, "Captain Bob Sherman. I was in an aircraft accident. Lucky to get out alive."

"What kind of Airplane did you fly?"

"I am not a pilot," Bob said. "I am an electronic warfare officer and I fly in B-66s at Spangdahlem Air Base in Germany." The elderly gentleman could hardly contain himself. "So does my stepson," he said. "His name is Wolfgang Samuel. Do you know him?" Bob didn't tell my dear stepfather, Leo Ferguson, that it was I who should have been in that aircraft that day, and that he had taken my place when I was pulled off that flight. Fate.

In the spring of 1972 the North Vietnamese began their invasion of the South and *Operations Freedom Train* and *Linebacker I* got underway, unleashing American air power against an over confident invader. Crews from the 39TEWS were sent to Korat, Thailand, in order to augment the 42nd TEWS. *Linebacker I* ended in October, and on December 18 *Linebacker II* was launched – a massive B-52 led assault against the Hanoi and Haiphong areas. By that time the former 39TEWS aircraft had either returned to the United States or to the war zone to augment the 42nd TEWS at Korat Air Base. On January 1, 1973, the 39TEWS was officially inactivated. Fittingly, Colonel Karwin 'Smiley' Pomeroy was the squadron's last commander.

And what happened to good old 54-459 – the C-model that in November 1957 arrived at Spangdahlem Air Base to much fanfare? For years, as part of the 42nd TRS, 459 flew out of bases in Germany, England and France, went to war in 1965 in Southeast Asia, returned from Takhli to Spangdahlem in 1969, and in the summer of 1972 was flown once more back to Korat Air Base in Thailand to support Linebacker I and II operations. In March of 1973 the old war horse, for one last time, went through corrosion control at Kadena Air Base on Okinawa, receiving a new paint job in the process. Then in January 1974, after thousands of hours of flying time in both peace and war, 54-459 was flown to Clark Air Base, Philippine Islands. There the plane was parked on an unused ramp along with 23 other B-66s, stripped of its electronics, and months later cut up for scrap.[7]

CHAPTER TWENTY-NINE

BAT-21

1972 began the way 1971 left off, with the North Vietnamese continuing to push SAMs and AAA into Laos and South Vietnam. President Nixon continued his efforts to get the United States out of a war which had little support at home – a fact the enemy was well aware of and counted on to prevail. The demonstrations of May 4, 1970, on the campus of Kent State University in Ohio resulted in the death of four students, indicative of the deep divisions within American society and the dissatisfaction of a large segment of the American public with the war in Southeast Asia. The American troop level in South Vietnam continued to decline from 139,000 at the start of the year to 69,000 by May 1. Most Air Force combat squadrons had already redeployed to the United States, or turned their aircraft over to the South Vietnamese. Negotiations in Paris were at a near stalemate. The Secretary of State, Henry Kissinger, was getting nowhere with stone-faced North Vietnamese negotiators sitting across the table waiting for the final departure of American military forces from the South. When that happened, obviously, there no longer was a need to negotiate. The situation was about to change.

At Korat the 42nd TEWS continued to struggle to meet its tasking from 7th Air Force. In late November three additional aircraft arrived to replace 54-427, lost on November 17 due to an engine fire on runup. Two more aircraft were pulled because of wing cracks. February 2 was not a good day at Korat. An F-105G from the 17th *Wild Weasel* Squadron crashed on take-off, killing the pilot Major Charles Stone.[1] Two EB-66s, one C-model, Cobra 24, and one E-model, Cobra 25, were delayed for two hours, waiting for the F-105 wreckage to be

Jungle Survival School at Clark Air Base, PI, provided the best possible preparation for downed aircrew in a difficult environment.

cleared from the runway. Master Sergeant Steve Hock, a combat photographer at Korat, was tasked to fly on the C-model, but was pulled off the mission to photograph the remains of the crashed F-105. Cobra 24, the flight lead, rolled at 1236. Cobra 25, EB-66E 54-540, followed at 1237. All line checks were normal. At 140 knots Captain Neil Henn rotated, placing the gear handle in the up position at 150 knots. The Korat runway had a dip in its middle. When Captain Henn rotated he was on the upward sloping portion of the runway. The aircraft's tail skid made contact, broke contact for about 100 feet, then made contact again, this time breaking from the aircraft. Then the lower antennas contacted the runway and the rest of the airplane followed, coming to rest 656 feet beyond the overrun. All three of the crew escaped unharmed.[2] Another airplane gone. The 42nd was running out of spare parts and airplanes. Headquarters PACAF went to the Air Staff and requested an additional four aircraft and crews. In response to that request six EB-66E/C aircraft were sent from Shaw AFB to Korat, along with experienced aircrews from both Shaw and the 39th TEWS at Spangdahlem.

The North Vietnamese, counting on South Vietnamese weakness and the fast disappearing American presence, launched their offensive in the early morning hours of March 30, 1972. Three regular NVA divisions supported by T-34 and T-55 tanks, 105mm artillery, and a formidable air defense capability including SA-2 SAMs, and for the first time, hand-held SA-7 anti-aircraft missiles, rolled across the DMZ into Quang Tri province. NVA attacks were also launched in the highlands to the west of Quang Tri and to the northwest of Saigon. This was a conventional attack, a reflection of how certain the NVA was of success. Thousands of trucks supporting a conventional army moved from north to south. It was the type of military operation American airpower was built to defeat.[3] In response to this overt challenge, American combat squadrons returned in a massive movement of aircraft from the United States to bases in Thailand. Under *Operation Constant Guard* the 49th TFW moved its 72 F-4Ds from Holloman AFB in New Mexico to Takhli, the onetime F-105 and EB-66 base. F-105G *Wild Weasels* from McConnell AFB in Wichita, Kansas, deployed to Korat, and more F-4Es followed. B-52s returned to Andersen Air Base on Guam in February. By May of 1972, 161 additional B-52Ds and Gs brought the total number of B-52 aircraft in the western Pacific to 206.[4]

On April 2 two OV-10 observation planes flying over the Ben Hai River in the DMZ dividing North from South Vietnam, looking for survivors of a downed EB-66C aircraft, Bat 21, had a surprise waiting for them. As they broke into the clear one of the FAC's called out to the other, "My God, you should see the people down here – all over the place – people, tanks, trucks, the whole nine yards. And everybody is shooting."[5] Bat 21, an EB-66C, and Bat 22, an EB-66E, both from the 42nd TEWS at Korat, were flying ECM support for a B-52 *Arc Light* strike against NVA units crossing the DMZ into South Vietnam. The EB-66s were heading east along the DMZ. "As the B-52s drew close to their target at least ten missiles were fired in salvoes. All missed. When the EB-66s turned northwest to clear the target area a SAM site to the north of the DMZ launched three more missiles, one of which hit Bat 21 at 24,000 feet" while initiating a SAM break.[6] The missile struck the aircraft in the belly where the four Ravens sat. The Ravens did not have a chance. Only the navigator, Lieutenant Colonel Iceal 'Gene' Hambleton, was able to eject.[7] The rescue of Gene Hambleton would turn into a harrowing and deadly experience for many, in later years chronicled in two books and a movie starring Gene Hackman. Not only would the mobile SA-2s accompanying the invading North Vietnamese Army divisions take a toll of F-4s flying air strikes, but the slower moving conventionally powered A-1E *Sandies*, OV-10 observation planes and helicopters were to suffer heavy losses from the handheld SA-7 *Strela* missile.

After many years in the ICBM field, Lieutenant Colonel Gene Hambleton's turn came to return to the cockpit and pull a Vietnam tour. Gerald Hanner, an EB-66 navigator, recalls going through training at Shaw with Gene. "He was one of three Lieutenant Colonels who were rather long in the tooth, but they all took the assignment because they wanted to retire with thirty years. Gene seemed to glide through training with little effort. He made it look easy. Then we were all off to Korat via one or more survival schools."[8] Hambleton went to Turkey Point in Florida for water survival, then headed to Clark for snake school – jungle survival. At Korat he soon became squadron navigator and began flying combat missions. The area adjacent to Route Pack 1 was considered a milk run throughout the war when compared to missions further north in and around Route Packs V and VI, in the Hanoi/Haiphong area. "Part of the EB-66s role was trolling for SAMs at an altitude seven to eight-thousand feet below the B-52 formation, putting themselves between the bombers and the SAM sites. If electronic countermeasures did not defeat a SAM, they would insure it was locked on their aircraft and not the B-52s. Count to ten after a launch to allow the missile to get up to 25,000 feet, then go into a SAM break. The EB-66 could get into a five-G break in a hurry while the SAM's gyroscopes tumbled at just over two-Gs as it tried to follow. 'We'd giggle and laugh and drop down to about 10,000 feet, then come up and let them shoot another one at us'" Hambleton said in an interview after his rescue.[9]

The NVA air defense build-up which started in January 1972 progressed to the point where aircrews reported that the intensity of fire near the DMZ was equal to that encountered during raids in the Hanoi area. The fact that SAMs had been forward deployed was not news to Hambleton or his crew. "The SAM site that shot us down we had been plotting for about two months. I kept telling people there's a missile site there and nobody would believe us, because they never launched. You'd fly one mission and there wouldn't be any signal there. Somebody else would come back and say, 'Hey, I plotted this guy right there,' and that was south of the DMZ.'" The 42nd TEWS had good intelligence on where the active SAM sites were, but did not connect their presence with the NVA's spring invasion. Nor did 7th Air Force intelligence in Saigon put much credence in their reported SAM intercepts. After all, the EB-66C's direction finding equipment was not state of the art. They just didn't DF it right. Such is the stuff of tragedies.[10]

As the squadron navigator Hambleton had the ironic opportunity to schedule himself for his last mission. When the SAMs came up south of the DMZ they fired two salvos of at least ten missiles at the B-52s and the EB-66s protecting them. All ten missiles went wild, attesting to the effectiveness of the electronic countermeasures employed. The *Fansong* radar signal did not come up as usual though. The APR-25/26 radar warning receiver gave no low and high power indication. The SAM site was probably using a *Spoonrest* or *Flatface* acquisition radar for its target inputs. The first indication of a launch came when the BGO6 missile guidance signal popped up. Then the crew of Bat 21 and 22 got launch lights, but the missile was already on its way. "The timing count was started for a right hand break, but the Ravens shouted, 'Negative, negative,' believing the SAM was tracking from the south, not the north. The pilot, Major Wayne Bolte, tried to correct the SAM break, the missile got there first, they were hit in mid-break. The crew of Bat 21 had been caught five seconds late, looking in the wrong direction. The North Vietnamese stole a five second lead on Bat 21 by launching the missile at the EB-66 without the use of the *Fansong* track-while-scan radar. Hambleton knew the guys in back were lost when the SAM detonated, and he ran through his ejection sequence on the pilot's signal. He fully expected to see the aircraft commander [Major Bolte] to follow. Almost immediately after he ejected a second explosion rocked the air, disintegrating the aircraft and putting Hambleton in a spin. He opened his parachute manually to stop the spin at somewhere below 28,000 feet. 'I didn't realize it was going to take me 16 minutes to hit the ground. But opening the parachute when I did was probably the smartest thing I did. There was a fog bank starting to roll in, and it gave the bank time to move in completely. When I came down, I came right through it. If I'd waited for the barometric opener [to open the chute at 14,000 feet] I'd have been out in the clear with 30,000 enemy troops around me, and I wouldn't be here today. I got down about half-way, probably at 16 or 17-thousand feet when I saw this little O-2 orbiting. So I unzipped the survival vest and took one of the radios out and cranked up Guard Channel. I called, 'O-2, O-2, do you hear me?'

"He came back, 'Yes, where are you?'

"'I'm in a parachute hanging about four or five thousand feet above you.'

"'You gotta be kidding me.'

"'No, I'm not.' So, he poured the power to that little thing and he came up and orbited with me right down to the ground. While he's orbiting with me, he calls in other aircraft, *Sandies* and F-4s who 'sterilized' the area. When I hit the ground I had a pretty clear area and there weren't too many people too close, if you know what I mean.

"This all happened about twilight, it was five o'clock in the afternoon. I landed in a rice paddy, so I got up against this mound of dirt and lay there for two or three hours. As soon as it got dark I took off, got up in the jungle, and dug in for the night. The third day I went out and got some food, corn, four little ears of corn about as big around as your thumb. It's not too tasty unless you are very hungry. I didn't have any water with me. I think it was the third night, it started to rain and I had one of these rubberized escape and evasion maps that I laid on top of a bush. I got my plastic bottle out and filled it with water." On the fourth day the OV-10 got shot down and Hambledon was ready to give up. But a FAC, a first lieutenant, wouldn't let the colonel entertain the thought. "He called me every name in the book and he told me what he was going to do to me if I gave up. He wouldn't let me quit." The second low point came when the *Jolly Green* got shot down, about two days later. "They were within two minutes of picking me up and all at once that thing goes up in a ball of fire. I thought, this thing isn't worth it. I was a 53 year old lieutenant colonel and I cried. The people that shot the chopper down were in this village and the Air Force decided to neutralize it. The day before I started to walk, they came in with two or three F-4s with smart bombs and they did a pretty good job on the village. I didn't think there was anyone left." But Hambleton did run into someone as he passed through the village. He was stabbed in the back, then ran for the river where he was supposed to be picked up. "I got down to the river and got lost in a banana grove. Around four o'clock in the morning, about daylight, I saw the river. I was so damn excited, I stepped off into nothing – and fifteen or twenty feet later I am laying up against a tree. I fractured my arm."[11] Hambleton had been told to get across the river as quickly as possible. "I hadn't been on the other side thirty minutes when twenty or so of these guys walked right up to where I'd been sitting. They beat the bushes for a while and then they took off, they never came across the river. There were two or three nights early on when patrols walked within 20 feet of my hiding place. They stopped, sat down, lit cigarettes and talked. Finally they just put out their cigarettes and walked away. That happened twice. And there's a little word in the English language – pray. I did. You sit there and pray that everything will work out right." Then a sampan appeared on the river and it had a Navy SEAL team on it. Tom Norris, a Navy Seal received the Medal of Honor for his part in the rescue. Lieutenant Colonel Hambleton was awarded the Silver Star, the Distinguished Flying Cross, the Air Medal, and the Purple Heart.[12]

EB-66C 54-466 was one of Shaw's electronic reconnaissance training aircraft flown over to Korat to augment the strained resources of the 42nd TEWS. I had flown training missions in 466 back in 1968 before reporting for duty with the 41st TEWS at Takhli. When 466 was shot down that first Sunday in April 1972, five men died. A UH-1H Huey helicopter was shot down attempting a rescue with the loss of four lives. Two OV-10 FACs were downed by SA-7s – two men were killed, a third became a prisoner of war, and a fourth made good his escape. Six more lost their lives when a *Jolly Green* rescue helicopter was shot down. *That Others May Live* is the motto of those who risk their lives rescuing airmen in distress – no truer words were ever spoken in the rescue of Gene Hambleton. Nearly 1,000 air strikes were flown in support of Hambleton's rescue at the cost of eight aircraft and four seriously damaged. Bat 21 was the most extensive and costly rescue effort ever undertaken by the U.S. Air Force.[13] The Marines take pride in never leaving any of their own behind, so does the Air Force – if it is at all possible. Says Gerald Hanner "One quote I do recall Hambleton making to us once he returned to Korat, 'It was a hell of a price to pay for one life. I'm very sorry.'"[14]

Hambleton's rescue, although massive in scale, was just one of many such rescues between 1964 and 1972. Only six weeks later, as air battles raged over the North, and the North Vietnamese air force was being decimated as never before by well trained and missile and gun equipped F-4Ds and Es, Captains Lodge and Locher in an F-4D on May 10 downed their third MiG-21. Moments later, with another MiG-21 in their sights, their aircraft was riddled by 30mm gun fire from a MiG-19 coming in from behind and below. Captain Lodge, the pilot, died. Locher ejected and survived 21 days northwest of Hanoi, a few miles from a large MiG base. "On June 2, we went back," said Dale Stovall the HH-53C *Jolly Green* pilot, who retired as a brigadier general. "We shut down the war to go get Roger Locher. There were 119 aircraft over North Vietnam supporting us," among them EB-66s from Korat. Stovall's HH-53 crew hoisted Locher into the helicopter from a steep, 1,200-foot slope while crew members blazed away at North Vietnamese troops with mini guns. Stovall was awarded the Air Force Cross. The men of the Aerospace Rescue and Recovery Service saved 1,298 aircrew members in Southeast Asia, many, like Hambleton and Locher, from deep inside enemy controlled territory – almost always at great risk to themselves.[15]

The NVA spring invasion of Quang Tri province did not sit well with President Nixon and his cabinet in Washington. He promptly authorized air attacks against targets in North Vietnam up to 20 degrees latitude – *Operation Freedom Train*. That restriction was soon lifted and targets further north were authorized. On April 9, 12 B-52s struck a POL storage area and rail yard near Vinh. On the 12th 18 B-52s from U-Tapao attacked Bai Thuong Air Base south of Hanoi. On April 15, 17 B-52s, again coming from U-Tapao in Thailand, received the go-ahead to attack a POL site near Haiphong. *Time Magazine* in an article entitled, *The Harrowing War in the Air*, posted Monday, May 1, 1972, described the effect of that raid on the surprised North Vietnamese. "It was slightly before 2 a.m. of what was to be the first warm and sunny Sunday of the year in North Vietnam. Suddenly, inside the big Soviet-built area surveillance radar stations near Haiphong and Hanoi, the radar scopes exploded into life with the blips of approaching aircraft – more than the technicians had seen at any one time in years. After a moment, the images smeared and the blips disappeared, as if overtaken by some evil magic. The radar scopes filled with impenetrable 'snow' – or simply went dark. As U.S. intelligence experts later reconstructed what had probably happened, the Communists worked furiously to switch their jammed equipment to alternate frequencies and different antenna systems, but with no success. They knew what the electronic symptoms meant: for the first time in the war, the U.S. was sending its eight-jet B-52s to bomb targets in North Vietnam's Red River heartland. The tip-off was the havoc created by the electronic 'pilot fish' that, as the North Vietnamese know by now, often precede the B-52s: EB-66 *Destroyers* and EA-6B *Intruders*, designed to confuse ground radar, as well as needle-nosed F-105 *'Wild Weasels,'* whose special radiation-seeking missiles lock onto and streak toward active enemy radar installations. Then, after the pilot fish, came the sharks: 17 B-52s. The B-52s dropped their 30-ton bomb loads into the darkness over Haiphong from 30,000 feet. The explosions destroyed a petroleum tank farm near the Haiphong harbor quay, provoking a fireball so large that it was seen from the bridge of the aircraft carrier *Kitty Hawk* 110 miles out at sea in the Gulf of Tonkin. At 2:30 Sunday afternoon, the sirens wailed again in Haiphong. For more than an hour, 40 Navy jets from carriers wheeled around the city, pummeling warehouses, a huge truck park and nearby Kien An Airfield, where three MiG-17 fighters were destroyed on the ground. By the time the third attack had ended the sky over Haiphong was streaked by the vapor trails of SAM missiles. In all, the North Vietnamese gunners fired an astonishing 242 missiles at the American warplanes ... Thanks largely to the new sophistication of U.S. electronic wizardry, the Communists had managed to score only two hits ... Only four of the 88 MiG-21s known to be based in the Hanoi-Haiphong area rose to meet the invading U.S. planes: three were shot down ... The rapid air buildup continues. Within the past three weeks, more than 150 warplanes – F-4 Phantoms, all-weather F-105s, stubby EB-66s, B-52s – have been flown to the theater from Japan, the Philippines and even the U.S."[16]

Captain Tom Copler, who returned to Shaw AFB in November 1970 after the inactivation of the 19th TEWS at Kadena, Japan, was one of those experienced EB-66 flyers returned to Korat. Tom had flown over the North on an earlier tour of duty. He was going to get a chance to do so again. "I went over in April for 120 days. It was pretty exciting. The war was different from before, the tempo higher than when I first got to Takhli in '68. We were going North all the time. We actually flew the airplanes over there. I remember asking how long we had at McClellan before we launched for Hawaii, and I was told that we had dedicated tankers and we were going straight from Shaw to Hickam AFB. It was a brutal flight. We took off from Shaw about eight in the morning in two flights of three, taking six airplanes to Korat. Joe Sapere had come over from Spangdahlem and was a navigator in my flight. Joe had flown the first B-66 mission over the North back in '65. From Hickam we went to Clark, then straight to Korat. We arrived in less than 72 hours. We immediately started flying combat.

"The guys in the 42nd at Korat wanted to keep their crews together. We agreed. Then they complained that we were getting all the easy missions. So we went to the operations officer, we were all experienced crews, and proposed to take all the night missions. Then they thought we had gone crazy. At night, can you see the SA-2s coming up? You bet you can. Also, there were hardly any MiGs to worry about. We thought the new arrangement was great. Almost all of our orbits were either off Haiphong harbor supporting the Navy, or in Route pack VI, probably 30 miles west of Hanoi, wherever we could find a hole between the 20 mile circles of the SA-2s. This happened on one of my early missions, a day mission. I always liked to do a figure eight and change the end points of my orbit by about three or four miles right or left. Never do the same thing twice. We had three aircraft in three separate orbits backed up against one another at different altitudes with some overlap. The guy in the center kept flying the same way, back and forth. My pilot said to me, 'Look at him. What is he doing?' About that time the 85mm got his range and started coming up. When we got home we had a big discussion – don't ever be predictable." It was predictability that would cost the B-52s dearly in *Operation Linebacker II*.[17]

The entire war assumed a different character after the POL strike by the B-52s on April 15 near Haiphong. The following day F-4Ds from the 432nd Tactical Reconnaissance Wing at Udorn, a composite wing with a variety of aircraft types, downed three MiG-21s. It was the beginning of a long death spiral for North Vietnamese fighter pilots, or whoever was manning their cockpits, Russians and

North Koreans. Between April 16 and October 15, F-4s from Takhli and Udorn downed 42 MiG-19s and MiG-21s. On April 21, the B-52s struck again at a target near Than Hoa. For the first time a B-52 was damaged by a surface to air missile and had to make an emergency landing at Da Nang. Six days later, on the 27th of April the Than Hoa bridge was severely damaged by 2,000-pound electro-optically guided *Paveway* smart bombs released by four F-4 fighters, even though the weather was bad. And on May 13, with the weather improved, 14 F-4s returned and put the bridge into the river, without loss to themselves.[18] Earlier in the war, that same bridge had withstood the concerted attack of 871 F-105 sorties with superficial damage. The Paul Doumer bridge soon joined the fate of the Than Hoa bridge, probably the two most important bridges of North Vietnam's transportation network. On May 10 and 11 Mk-84 laser guided bombs dropped several spans of the Doumer bridge into the river. "All flights encountered heavy AAA ground fire and it was later estimated that more than 160 SAMs were fired at the strike force. It seems hard to believe that not a single aircraft was lost ... A great deal of credit for this remarkable record went to the support crews whose job it was to protect the strike force," including four EB-66 aircraft.[19] "It was an outstanding display of the effectiveness of the EB-66s."[20] It was a different air force the North was facing. The F-4s were armed not only with air to air missiles, but again carried guns for the close-in kill. 'Knife fighting' as Navy flyers referred to it, was back in style in the Air Force. Smart bombs had taken the place of unguided conventional bombs. Missing its target was as rare for a smart bomb as a hit was for dumb bombs in days gone by. Not only had the American tactical fighter force changed, but the B-52 strategic bombers were finally employed in the manner intended: pounding the strategic targets up North once reserved for more vulnerable tactical fighters.

By May 8 the North Vietnamese began to understand that their hasty invasion of the South and their continued stalling tactics in Paris had produced a painful backlash. President Nixon not only authorized the resumption of air strikes throughout North Vietnam, but authorized the mining of its ports and harbors as well – a tactic that should have been used early on in the war now proved eminently successful. There were no threats of nuclear retaliation from Communist China or the Soviet Union as President Johnson and his advisor McNamara once feared. The North Vietnamese had finally committed a cardinal sin, a sin which for many years had been the sole province of American politicians in Washington: underestimating their enemy.

Major Gerald P. Hanner flew a night mission south of the DMZ after the loss of Bat 21 and the Doumer Bridge attack. They were no longer certain if any of the SA-2s the NVA had dragged south into Quang Tri province were still operational.

"An hour or so passed. We were flying an E-model in the Hue vicinity, supporting an *Arc Light* strike, looking for SAMs. Below we could see lots of flares and fires burning as the South Vietnamese army was battling the NVA. My pilot, a relatively new guy, was puffing away on his pipe and watching the show below. Then something caught his attention. We were heading north-northeast, and out in the distance he could see two or three bright yellow-white lights. The lights were getting bigger. He was about to ask me what those lights were in front of us, when it suddenly dawned on him what he was seeing. 'I've got SAMs,' he said. At that time our EWO called over the intercom, 'I've got uplink.' Our pilot executed a SAM break to the right, and directed me to make a SAM call on guard channel. I hesitated, not knowing where the SAMs were coming from. Finally I went out over UHF guard channel with 'SAM, SAM, vicinity of Hue.' Immediately an F-105G *Wild Weasel* patrolling closer to the DMZ, and at the moment engaged in a duel with a SAM site, called, 'SAM, SAM, DMZ.' That cleared things up.

"We recovered from our first SAM break, when two more missiles came off a launcher, and we went into another. As we recovered from the second break I saw that we were about 20 miles off shore, and considerably lower than when all the excitement had started. I told my pilot we were clearly out of range of any SAMs and to stay wings level if they fired again. Sure enough, another missile came off a launcher, but this time our jamming was effective and the missile went ballistic. We were bingo fuel and headed for home. I worked in the 388th TFW frag shop where we processed the daily tasking that came in from 7th Air Force. The next day I read a report on the previous night's action and learned that the SAM site that engaged us had been involved in a fight with some F-4s, shooting one down. Then my boss, an F-4 pilot, came back from a mission that afternoon extolling the courage of a KC-135 tanker crew. 'They crossed the DMZ into Route Pack I with me on their boom to rescue another F-4 that had been shot up and was badly in need of fuel.' He showed me where the tanker took him – right across the area of last night's SAM firings."[21] Dumb luck is better than no luck at all.

CHAPTER THIRTY

OPERATION LINEBACKER II

The air war over the North continued and Captains Ritchie, DeBellevue and Feinstein became aces. *Operation Linebacker I* began the day the Doumer Bridge fell to smart bombs. B-52s routinely began to strike targets in the lower Route Packages again. By early June 1972 the Strategic Air Command had assembled 206 of its B-52 bombers at Andersen on Guam and at U-Tapaoh in Thailand. It was the largest SAC bomber force ever assembled in the western Pacific, aimed to strike at the North. As impressive as that assembly of conventional striking power was, it also reflected the changed role of the strategic forces. Originally designed to overpower the Soviet Union in a massive nuclear confrontation, the force now was largely supporting a conventional war scenario. The nuclear role was to a great extent carried by *Minuteman* and *Titan II* ICBMs, and submarine launched *Polaris* missiles. The vaunted TRIAD of air, land and sea based nuclear deterrence still existed, but the air component had definitely become a reduced player.

General John C. Meyer assumed command of SAC on May 1, 1972, from General Bruce Holloway. He, as his counterpart at TAC, General William W. Momyer, had risen quickly in World War II to the rank of colonel. Momyer was credited with eight aerial victories and Meyer with 26, two of which he added in Korea. Their principal training ground had been World War II and its massed employment of air power against Nazi Germany. Their past experience clearly left its imprint on how American air power was employed in Vietnam. General Meyer's SAC, however, was a pale shadow of the force once commanded by

A B-52G SAC bomber in pre-Vietnam colors refueling from a KC-135 tanker over the Cascade Mountains. The D-model, not the G, was the workhorse of the Vietnam war. The G proved to be significantly more vulnerable to enemy missiles because of its wet-wings and a less sophisticated ECM suit than that carried by the B-52D.

General LeMay. The 206 B-52s assembled in the Pacific region in June 1972 represented fifty percent of the total B-52 force of 402 combat aircraft. Nearly 2,000 B-47 bombers had retired a number of years earlier, along with the early models of the B-52. Sixty FB-111s added little extra striking power to SAC. The FB-111s were viewed by SAC old timers as tactical aircraft playing a strategic role. At best, the FB-111s were an interim aircraft choice again, like the B-47, B-57 and B-66 before them. They would do until the next ultimate strategic bomber came along.[1]

SAC had changed in ways other than the types and numbers of aircraft it flew. No longer did a homogeneous SAC-trained and SAC-for-life crew man its bomber force. The aircrews were riddled with 'outsiders' as a result of the Air Force policy not to return crew members to Vietnam for a second time until all others had their turn. Men like Captains David Zook and Nutter Wimbrow, former EB-66 electronic warfare officers with 100 combat missions over the North, found themselves flying SAC's giant bombers and pulling *Bullet Shot* tours of duty on Guam flying *Arc Light* and *Tiny Tim* missions. Once assigned to a Stateside strategic bomber unit, however, the Vietnam combat tour exception no longer applied. Dave Zook would go to war again over the North in a B-52G during Operation *Linebacker II*, the 11 day air campaign against the North intended to bring the North Vietnamese delegates back to the Paris negotiating table. *Linebacker II* achieved its objective, although things started off pretty shakily. The late Captain David S. Zook, who retired as a lieutenant colonel, tells the story of the 11-day air campaign against the North as part of his unpublished manuscript *Seven Years of Vietnam: A Raven Goes To War*. I chose excerpts from Dave Zook's manuscript to portray the *Linebacker II* air campaign. Although *Linebacker II* involved many types of tactical aircraft, from aging EB-66s to the newest F-4E and F-111, it is a bomber story – the B-52 story, and at that their finest hour.

"I arrived in Los Angeles on New Year's Day of 1967," wrote then Captain David Zook, "after a long flight from Bangkok. I was glad my tour in Southeast Asia was at an end and that I had made a contribution. I didn't know then that my time in SEA had not ended, but was to continue for six more years. I was assigned to the 5th Bomb Wing at Travis AFB, California. Within the year we moved our B-52Gs to Mather. The only downside of it was a lot of TDY – both *Bullet Shot Arc Light* tours and ground alert at remote bases. The *Bullet Shot* tours would start at Andersen Air Base on Guam, then rotate to Kadena on Okinawa, and finally to U-Tapao, Thailand. Flying a few hundred missions from these three bases comprised the most boring segment of my adult life. However, on my last *Bullet Shot* tour there was to be an exciting conclusion – four missions during *Linebacker II*.

"I was on a thrown-together crew flying B-52Gs out of Guam. We carried a smaller bomb load than the B-52Ds and had a much inferior ECM suite to work with. Also, because the B-52G had a wet wing, it was far less survivable than the D, E and F models. Only one B-52G ever made it back to an American base after suffering battle damage. Our crew was a strange blend. The radar navigator/ bombardier was Lieutenant Colonel Walt Nickerson. The two of us had been crewed up for a long time and had been on a senior standardization and evaluation crew at Mather AFB. Our pilot had a helicopter background, and the new co-pilot had flown light observation planes as a Forward Air Controller. Our navigator came from a desk job and had been getting his flying time in KC-135 tankers. We had been on Guam for a few weeks flying routine iron bomb missions over the South. Even though these were real bombing missions they also served as crew training. Except for Walt and me, none of the other crew members had flown on a regular SAC combat crew. A lot of mistakes were made, and Walt and I tried as best we could to train our new crew members. The co-pilot was trying hard to learn, but the pilot took our suggestions as challenges to his authority as aircraft commander. It was a touchy situation for all of us.

"We weren't expecting what we found when we went to the briefing room on the 18th of December 1972. There were a lot more than the normal number of crews at the briefing, the room was packed. First the briefing officer took the stage and announced, 'Standby for time hack.' Then he called for the curtains to be drawn back from the screen. As the screen was coming into view he said, 'Gentlemen, tonight's targets.' There, before us, was a map of North Vietnam. And the targets were all in the Hanoi area. The silence was deafening. After several seconds the briefer continued, '129 B-52s from Guam and U-Tapao are going to join in three waves to bomb the Hanoi area.' My only thought then was, 'Well, it's about bloody time ... we've had this war dragging on for seven years of my life and we've wasted too damn many fine airmen bombing some pretty meaningless targets. After the primary briefing we separated for our specialized briefings. I could hardly believe some of the things I was told we could and could not do during the mission. No chaff was to be dispensed unless we were under attack by a fighter. Even with the Phase III ECM suit I would have on my B-52G, I was to allocate one jammer to jam the missile downlink signal. That was more than wasted jamming power, it would also take a jammer away from the more important role of jamming a threat radar. We went over the known threat radars in our target areas and there were lots of them. The SA-2 SAM sites overlapped so there was solid coverage from before the Initial Point, IP, to the Egress Point. The boundary was called the Lethal SAM Line, LSL.

"After the briefing our crew reformed outside the alert facility awaiting transportation to our aircraft. Our pilot didn't seem to know how he was to act or feel. He only had a couple of hundred hours in the B-52 and still felt awkward trying to manage a six man crew. When we reached the plane he ordered us to line up for a pre-mission personal inspection. He wanted our helmets lined up and us standing behind them. Walt and I hadn't done anything like that since the Bombing Competition a year and a half earlier. Walt looked at our pilot and said, 'Captain, do you want to take a group picture?' No, he wanted to conduct an inspection. I had a small 35mm camera in my helmet bag and I handed it to the crew chief and asked him if he would take our picture. Three shots. One close in of just the crew, one with the crew and the nose of the airplane, and one further away to include most of the airplane. When the pictures were taken the chief returned the camera and I turned to our pilot, 'You were just kidding about the inspection, right?' I patted him on the back and we started loading our gear on the plane. The bombers had already been pre-flighted by crews not scheduled to fly. The mission was to be 16 hours long, plus briefings before, and debriefings after, would make for a very long day. All we had to do was climb into the airplane, start engines, and we were ready to take off.

"Finally it was time to start engines for the first wave. The noise level rose as the eight-engine bombers came to life. KC-135 tankers were already airborne and heading for the rendezvous points to top us off. We were scheduled for three airborne refuelings. The bombers taxied to the active runway and began a minimum interval takeoff, MITO. Bomber takeoffs continued for 87 minutes. The noise level rose to an ear splitting crescendo. All over the field people stopped to watch as one after another of the big bombers lumbered down the Andersen runway. At about the midpoint the wing tips would rise and then slowly the bomber would separate itself from the concrete and begin to fly. The end of Andersen's runway went almost to the cliff at the edge of the island. As each bomber came to the edge, it dropped down slightly, picking up speed before starting to climb. About a mile from the end of the runway the plane and its black exhaust would reappear and climb from view. Our call sign was Charcoal 02. We were next for takeoff. We swung onto the active, the pilots advanced the throttles to maximum power and the big bomber began its roll, everyone watching time and airspeed as we became committed to our takeoff.

"I heard the landing gear retract and I knew that put us over the cliff. A few seconds passed when I heard the radar navigator tell the pilots, 'Get the nose down!' We were almost at stall speed. The pilot tried to climb the aircraft too fast, and the plane began to shudder as it entered the beginning of a stall. Again Walt called over the intercom, 'Get that nose down!' The co-pilot acknowledged the call, pushed forward on his control column to start a shallow descent and pick up some airspeed. I am eternally grateful that Walt had been monitoring our airspeed and altitude. It was reassuring to have a veteran B-52 crew member pull our butts out of the fire. At our first refueling it became increasingly clear to me how nervous our pilot was. He made several attempts before finally getting hooked up to the tanker. We continued on to Thailand and entered a timing pattern so we could join up with the planes from U-Tapao. After the first attack wave had formed we continued north across Thailand and Laos. We had been preceded by chaff laying F-4s, but high winds at our altitude had blown most of the chaff cloud away before we arrived.

"The night sky over North Vietnam was filled with a variety of aircraft, there to support the B-52s. While still over Laos I began to see the North Vietnamese air defense radars appear on my receiver. By the time we reached the North Vietnamese border it was clear they knew we were coming as they must have had every radar they owned turned on. The first of our planes were over the target and released their bombs. On my scope I saw clusters of strong *Fansong* signals as well as missile launch indications. I notified the crew over the intercom of the greatest threats. The radio chatter increased as crews broadcast SAM sightings. Occasionally one of our two pilots would describe what they were seeing. I wasn't hearing anything from our navigators. I went on private intercom and called Walt, our radar navigator and bombardier. 'Walt, what's happening down there?' He replied, 'The navigator has folded his hands and bowed his head and has been praying from the time we turned inbound.'

"Walt was getting ready for the bomb run and returned to his task. Shortly afterwards he announced we were at the IP and told the pilot to center the PDI. I was calling out missile launches, and the pilots occasionally described the battle scene. The radio chatter continued to mount, and now there were also distress signals. Only moments before our bomb release the copilot announced that Charcoal 01, our cell leader, had been hit and was going down in flames. He mentioned that he was seeing missiles coming up at us. We were too close to bombs away to do anything but press on. I had covered the strongest *Fansong* radar signals with my jammers and I knew we were probably being tracked. Walt announced bomb release, then called for the post-target turn. We were at a point of maximum vulnerability. As a B-52 banks, it doesn't send its jamming energy down toward the radar and we could be more easily tracked. Since the bomber in front of us was gone we had lost any mutual jamming support we may have gotten from him, so I decided to put out three bundles of chaff as we began our turn. I figured *Fansong* operators were only human beings. My dispensing chaff added one new element to their tracking problem. It might just help us survive. It was at that time that we began to hear the emergency beepers of crews that ejected from their aircraft."[2]

Tom Copler arrived at Korat on December 16. "On the 17th," Tom recounts, "one of the permanent party guys came over to me and asked, 'Have you been North?' I said, 'Probably 40 to 50 times in early '68.' He pulled out a map, showed me where the B-52s were going and where we were supposed to be 15 minutes in front of them at 25,000 feet. They were coming in at 35,000 feet. We had three orbits lined up to cover them coming in. They did a 180 degree turn over the target, changed altitudes and came back on the same track they had come in on. Why wouldn't you go out over the Gulf? The B-52s became predictable, and that cost them dearly a couple of nights later. The planes came in on the same exact corridor, 15 minutes apart, giving the bad guys just enough time to reload and fire again. We were jamming, and they were lobbing SAMs up blind. They lobbed 200 and some missiles up the first night on the 18th of December. I saw a B-52 fall out of the sky, it made you want to cry. We did this every night until Christmas, then for a couple days more.

"The number of tankers over the Plain des Jars to refuel bombers, fighters and ECM aircraft was unbelievable. One night the wing tanks stopped feeding on one of our planes in orbit near Hanoi. He called for a tanker, but knew he wasn't going to make it. One of our radar sites put him on a frequency with a tanker over northern Laos. The tanker pilot said to our guy, 'Just keep coming at me.' He flew that KC-135 right into North Vietnam and picked him up. Then he said, 'For God's sake, don't tell anybody that I refueled you here.' He came right into North Vietnam and saved one of our EB-66s. In the end, the guys on the hot end of the stick are the ones who have to make things work.[3]

"We had a strong tailwind going into the target," Dave Zook continues, "and as we turned around it became a headwind slowing our egress. The turn seemed to last forever and the SAM radar signals were saturating my receivers. I was still receiving missile guidance signals, but the pilots couldn't see anymore missiles coming our way. Finally we were wings level and departing the target area. Walt and our navigator were having a conversation and the navigator had finally gone back to work. I then did something I had never planned on doing, send a missing aircraft report to SAC via HF radio. I pulled out the book with report formats and filled in the blanks for the loss of Charcoal 01 with grease pencil. We were now well out of SAM range, so I sent the report – a chilling moment for me. The flight back to Guam was long and quiet. By the time we landed the second day wave was getting ready for takeoff.

"We learned that we were scheduled to fly again on day three. We had a pretty intense crew meeting. The experience of the first night motivated everyone to work as a team, both to accomplish the mission and to survive. We were given a special breakfast on day three – steak and eggs, and just about everything else you could imagine seeing in an Air Force mess hall. I thought maybe it was our last meal, like the condemned get in prison before being executed. As always we started our briefing with a time hack and then the route and targets were shown. Same route, same general target areas. I found it difficult to believe that for three nights in a row massive B-52 strikes would so closely follow the same routes and use the same tactics. It seemed Air Force planners were violating the rules of war and becoming predictable. I felt better about the airplane we were to fly on night three. It had an improved ECM suite to give us better protection. We had the call sign Tan 02 and our target was the Kinh No military complex on the northwest side of Hanoi. We would be even closer to downtown Hanoi then on night one.

"The crew seemed more together than on any of our previous missions. The air refueling went well and we settled down and got ready to do our jobs. Ninety-nine B-52s were to make up the strike force. Our wave consisted of 12 B-52Gs and 9 B-52Ds from Andersen, plus 18 additional Ds from U-Tapao. We formed up and headed north. I was monitoring the radios and I could hear on the HF radio that the first wave had lost three planes with others damaged. As we approached Hanoi I could hear the battle activity and our pilots could see it. Later I learned that 220 SA-2 missiles were fired at our strike force that night. There was a mass of *Fansong* signals on my receiver. The little screen on the APR-25 warning receiver showed SAM strobes from the 9 o'clock position to the 3 o'clock position. This was an electronic war. Our wave leader was over his target, the Hanoi rail yards. One plane was hit, but the crew managed to fly to a safe area where they could eject. The cell directly in front of us with the call sign Olive had gotten out of formation, taking evasive action. Olive 03 ended up about two miles ahead of Olive 02 at the target. Olive 01 was hit by a SAM. Olive cell had been bracketed by seven SA-2 sites and they reported 38 SA-2 missiles during their time over Hanoi. We were next. Less than ten minutes after Olive cell had released its bombs we were in the target area. A missile hit Tan 03 and the plane blew up. Only one crew member was able to eject. The toll for the night – four B-52Gs and two B-52Ds.

"The SAC planners were finally seeing the light. The B-52Gs were pulled out of the lineup for the time being, and only the more survivable and better ECM equipped B-52Ds were to carry on. The single line of bomber tactic was discarded, instead, we were to tighten up the time between cells and waves to give the NVA less time to reload their missiles. The high banking turn coming off the target was also discarded. In addition we would attack from different directions to make the North Vietnamese air defense problem more difficult. This was beginning to make some sense to me. 120 bombers were going to bomb ten targets in the Hanoi and Haiphong area with a common time over target on the eighth night, December 26, of *Linebacker II* operations. Seventy-eight bombers came from Andersen, including 45 B-52Gs and 33 B-52Ds. The other B-52Ds came from U-Tapao. The better ECM equipped D-models were to attack in the heavily defended Hanoi area. We would be in a force of 15 G-models and three D-models targeting the Thai Nguyen rail yards north of Hanoi. Our cell of 18 planes took no hits. There were strong *Fansong* and launch signals and the pilots could see missiles in flight, but they caused no harm. Our after release turn was to the left out over the Gulf of Tonkin. The new tactics produced good results and the NVA defenders couldn't meet the challenge. I flew only one more mission on night ten. There were no losses for us that night."[4]

Operation Linebacker II ended on December 29, 1972. The North Vietnamese delegation returned to the Paris negotiations chastened, but not defeated. Air Force losses over 11 days of around the clock air operations against North Vietnamese targets included 15 B-52 bombers, two F-4 fighters, two F-111s and one HH-53 search and rescue helicopter. The U.S. Navy lost two A-7s and A-6s each, one RA-5A and one F-4B. Seventeen of these losses were attributed to SA-2 missiles, three to MiGs, three to AAA, and three to unknown causes.[5] The NVA's showing was dismal. During those 11 days the MiGs were pretty much a no show force. Five that chose to come up were shot down, two by vigilant B-52 gunners, the only occasion the B-52 bombers used their defensive armament in a combat situation. Anti-aircraft defenses were largely nullified by having their tracking radars, *Whiff* and *Firecan*, jammed. Over 1,000 SA-2 missiles were fired at the attacking force. Again, electronic countermeasures applied by B-52s, EB-66s and EA-6Bs largely rendered the SA-2 surface to air missile system ineffective. "By 28 December, the North Vietnamese air defenses had been practically neutralized, and on the last two days of *Linebacker II*, the B-52s were able to fly over Hanoi and Haiphong without suffering damage." While SAC entered the battle using dated World War II bomber tactics. Its staff quickly learned a critical lesson: to survive in the electronic age you adapt or perish. They adapted. "Of the 92 crew members aboard the downed bombers, 26 were recovered by rescue teams, 33 bailed out over North Vietnam and were captured, 29 were listed as missing, and four perished in a bomber that crash landed."[6] Among the dead was Captain Nutter Wimbrow, an electronic warfare officer on Ebony 02, a B-52D out of U-Tapao, shot down over Hanoi on the night of the 120 bomber raid. Captain David Zook may not have known that his one-time EB-66C crew mate from Takhli was in the air that night, in a B-52 cell just ahead or behind him.

There were other operational losses as well, not reflected in the official Air Force listing of combat losses. The EB-66s of the 42nd TEWS from Korat were there every night to help protect the vulnerable B-52 bombers. They flew their defensive orbits, arriving fifteen minutes before the B-52s, and staying until the last bomber exited the target area. The EB-66s flew lower than the bombers to provide optimum ECM support, and were frequently within easy reach of the SA-2 missile systems. Yet surprisingly none of the EB-66s or Navy EA-6Bs were lost or damaged. On December 23, the sixth night of *Linebacker II* operations, the 42nd TEWS was tasked to provide ECM support for 30 B-52s attacking targets in the Haiphong area. Their orbits were to be east of Haiphong. Seventh Air Force tasking called for a minimum of two aircraft, three if possible. Hunt 01, 02 and 03, three EB-66Es, took off on time and proceeded to their refueling track over the Gulf of Tonkin. After 30 minutes of flight, Hunt 02 returned to Korat when his canopy cracked and pressurization was lost. *Blue Chip*, the 7th Air Force command post, requested a relaunch, based on a 45-minute time over target slip for the B-52s. Another aircraft was available, 54-529. The crew switched planes and took off to rejoin the other two EB-66Es. Again, they experienced pressurization problems and had to return to Korat.

Hunt 02 was eight miles from touchdown. Major Sasser was advised by the final controller, 'Wheels should be down. Begin descent.' At four miles Hunt 02 was on glide path, then turned left, was on course at three miles, continued on glide path. At decision height, Hunt 02 was 'On course, on glide path, over the approach lights.' It was then that Major Sasser called 'Going around.' The GCA controller continued, 'Over landing threshold. Understand you are going around?' Sasser replied 'I just lost an engine.'[7] The aircraft was over the landing threshold. Could have and should have touched down. Instead, Major George Sasser elected to go around, experienced engine failure, made a gentle, descending 90 degree turn off the end of the runway – and crashed.

Captain Terry Buettner arrived at Korat in October 1972. As the squadron flying safety officer Terry was tasked to lead the accident investigation. "It was a clear night, with no wind to speak of," Terry recalls. "Major Sasser flew a precision radar approach, and the tapes from the tower indicated that he was pretty much on course, on glide slope all the way. The left engine flamed out, and he started a go-around. We never knew why he initiated the go-around. At about 500 feet above the ground, and three-fourth of the way down the runway, people reported seeing the aircraft enter a gentle left turn, the aircraft was descending slightly, and continued to descend until it was lost from sight. The aircraft impacted in a Royal Thai Air Force housing area. The crew of three perished in the crash. I conducted flight tests with a similar aircraft at the computed gross weight of the accident aircraft, and it was completely controllable. It would climb on one engine, even with the landing gear extended. All members of the accident board kept asking 'Why would he go around when the landing was assured?' We never found an answer."[8]

CHAPTER THIRTY-ONE

A TIME FOR WAR
AND A TIME FOR PEACE

The last MiG-21 of the war was downed on January 7, 1973, by an F-4D from the 4th Tactical Fighter Squadron, 432nd Tactical Reconnaissance Wing, at Udorn RTAFB, Thailand. *Linebacker II* had ended on December 29, a week earlier. On January 15, offensive operations against North Vietnam were officially suspended and the Paris negotiated cease fire became effective on January 28. On February 12 *Operation Homecoming* was initiated, the return of 591 American prisoners of war from North Vietnamese captivity – men incarcerated under utterly degrading circumstances, having experienced both torture and deprivation. On April 17 the last B-52 *Arc Light* mission of the war was flown against targets in Laos, and the last Air Force combat missions of the war were flown by A-7D and F-111F aircraft against targets in Cambodia. The shooting war in Southeast Asia was over. No 'dominoes' fell as a result of the war's outcome. In years to come a black marble monument would arise on the Mall in Washington D.C., commemorating the ultimate sacrifice of over 50,000 American fighting men. On April 30, 1975, Saigon was captured by the North Vietnamese Army and renamed Ho Chi Minh City – the final irony of a strange war.

The 42nd TEWS at Korat entered an operational twilight zone in 1973. In early January EB-66Es supported 192 B-52 *Arc Light* missions over the North Vietnamese panhandle and Laos. By February *Arc Light* support dwindled to 116 missions, then 41 missions in March. When on April 17 the last B-52 *Arc Light* mission was flown, the EB-66E jamming aircraft was out of a job. Since the E-model was considered an offensive aircraft, 7th Air Force decided that their

Going home. Lieutenant Al Kersis, second from left, celebrates completing 100 missions over North Vietnam in 1968. He later flew with the 39th TEWS at Spangdahlem, then transferred to the backseat of an RF-4C at Ramstein Air Base, Germany.

jammers could not be turned on even for training purposes. The EB-66C moved to the fore, flying ELINT missions against North Vietnam in the Gulf of Tonkin and along routes over Laos. Cambodia was added as a potential location for SA-2 SAM systems. Searches by EB-66C aircraft turned up no *Fansong* radars, nor any other radars in Cambodia. Even these limited training opportunities dwindled as the Cambodian cease fire on August 15, and the earlier Laotian peace agreement, restricted reconnaissance flights to routes within the borders of Thailand.

In spite of the war's end, the 42nd TEWS, only authorized a total of 13 aircraft, maintained a strength of 25 E and C-models. Pilots, navigators and electronic warfare officers from the 39th TEWTS at Shaw AFB continued to augment a squadron which did not have enough work for the men it had assigned. In the draw-down of forces someone at Headquarters Tactical Air Command at Langley Air Force Base, Virginia, forgot about them. Captain Tom Copler, on his third temporary duty tour at Korat, did not. "I went over in April '72 for 120 days, then again in December '72 for 90 days, and back again in May of '73 for my last TDY. The war was over, and we weren't flying at all. The general commanding 13th Air Force at Clark had one of his budget officers get suggestions on how to save money. I submitted a suggestion on how much it was costing to keep us on TDY over here, not flying airplanes, when we could be back home, and if necessary return within 72 hours. What was the sense of us sitting at Korat? Evidently TAC headquarters had forgotten us, and the folks at Shaw weren't saying anything. I put this thing together and sent it to 13th Air Force. The next thing I know I get a phone call from Shaw raising holy hell with me for getting them into trouble. Phone call or not, we were out of there within 48 hours." By February of 1974, after the 39th TEWTS at Shaw closed its doors, Tom Copler, Joe Sapere and several other EB-66 navigators received assignments to F-111s at Mountain Home AFB, Idaho. Tom retired in the rank of colonel.[1]

Colonel Robert K. Crouch was the commander of the 388th Tactical Fighter Wing at Korat. It had become a composite wing including F-4E, A-7D, EB-66, F-105G and C-130 aircraft. It no longer bothered anyone that a fighter wing accommodated different aircraft types. "On assuming command in July 1973 my primary task was to continue supporting the Cambodian and Laotian war efforts," wrote Colonel Crouch in his end of tour report. "On average we launched 18 F-4Es a day and 14 A-7Ds, three or four EB-66s, and five C-130s. The F-105G *Wild Weasel* aircraft were withdrawn when it was determined that a SAM threat did not exist in Cambodia. We also had three EC-121s from the *College Eye* task force as a tenant unit. On August 15, the day of the Cambodian cease fire, the war in Southeast Asia officially ended." A-7Ds from the 388th TFW flew the last bombing mission that afternoon, and the honor of flying the last combat mission of the war went to an EC-121 aircraft which landed at Korat after the A-7Ds had already returned. "On 15 August an era of combat ended and we entered a period of training. The 388TFW continued to fly 7AF directed missions over unfriendly territory in C-130 and EB-66C aircraft. These were electronic surveillance missions of Laos, Cambodia, South and North Vietnam, but only overflew Laos and Cambodia. To provide training for our crews we developed an exercise with the Navy, WEASELEX. In this exercise the EB-66Es flew together with the F-105G *Wild Weasels* against the radars of the U.S. Navy ships in the Gulf of Tonkin. This training was ended in November 1973 because of the war in the Middle East and the ensuing fuel shortage."[2] One war ended. Another began.

Keeping its 25 aging EB-66 aircraft in flying condition continued to be a problem for the commanders of the 42TEWS. On February 4, EB-66E 54-442 developed low oil pressure which led to the engine being shut down. On shutting down the engine, complete electrical failure was experienced and the back-up systems were not operating as they should have. A night blackout single engine landing was made at Nakom Phanom Royal Thai Air Force Base – no panel lights, no cabin lights, no interphone nor radio. The EWO used his flashlight to illuminate the flight instruments for the pilot. The aircraft landed long, the drag chute failed, and the right tire blew when brakes were applied. The aircraft ran off the end of the runway. Reflects the squadron history, "The crew escaped safely with minimal damage to the aircraft." On February 23, 54-523 on a local training sortie had number two engine flame out – complete electrical failure was the immediate result. The engine restarted and an uneventful landing was made. The aircraft was grounded until all electrical systems were thoroughly checked. On another occasion an aircraft experienced an engine fire while taxiing. A major fuel leak in an engine occurred on yet another aircraft as it was passing through 10,000 feet. Rudder trim mechanisms jammed. The throttle on an aircraft jammed so power could not be reduced. There seemed to be no end to the number and type of problems these worn out aircraft began to experience. Engines, flight controls, landing gear, hydraulics, flaps – all had multiple failures in the first quarter of 1973.[3]

With a reduced flying schedule in the second quarter of 1973, maintenance was able to substantially improve the in-commission rate of their airplanes. Then on May 3 the routine turned into tragedy. EB-66E 54-445 was at the maintenance dock undergoing a Phase VI inspection, which included up and down jacking of the aircraft, trimming the engine, and hot jet calibration. The engine trim and hot jet calibration were scheduled for the morning hours, with Staff Sergeant Clarence Lords as the A-man, the man in the cockpit. Lords's assistant, called the B-man, was Technical Sergeant William E. Tompkins who would do the outside work.

Technical Sergeant Larry A. Kelly was with Lords to receive instructions. The crew chief for the engine trimming and calibration work was Sergeant Vauriece D. Maddox. Sergeant Lords began his walk-around with Kelly by his side. They noted that the aircraft chocks were in place and snug. In the cockpit, Kelly sat down in the pilot's seat. Lords stood to his rear instructing him on circuit breakers, panels and switches. Somehow the anti-skid switch was overlooked – it should have been in the off position. Immediately after the accident the switch was found to be in the on position.

The engine start-up continued in accordance with established procedures. The parking brakes were set before the right engine was started and brought to 80 percent power. Then the left engine was started. Both engines were stabilized in idle at which time the parking brakes were reset. The next step was to bring the engines to military power, allow them to run for three minutes, and then start the calibration check. After two minutes of running the engines at full military power, the aircraft suddenly lurched forward. Maddox, sensing motion, tried to run, then threw himself to the ground. Tompkins, not perceiving aircraft movement, was knocked down. The right tire of the plane virtually severed his left leg six inches below the hip joint. In the cockpit, Kelly tried to reapply the brakes by hitting the brake pedals, but got no braking response. He cut off the engines. The aircraft traveled about 170 feet, knocked down a concrete electric pole and a wooden outside latrine before coming to a stop off the trim pad. Lords ran over to Tompkins and stopped the bleeding by pinching off a severed artery to the leg. He continued to do that until the doctor arrived. Lords quick thinking saved the life of Sergeant Tompkins. Sergeant Tompkins was evacuated to the U-Tapao hospital where his leg was amputated.[4] Damage to the airplane was minor. However, the decision was made to take Class 26 action and write the airplane off as a loss.

Aircrew proficiency began to decline as flying was reduced to a minimum. Ninety-five percent of the new crews had little B-66 experience. Their first experience with the aircraft was at Shaw AFB. It is hardly surprising that the average for EB-66 flying time for all aircrews was between 150 and 175 hours. Lieutenant Colonel Robert R. Mendonca, who took command of the squadron in July, had his job cut out for him to keep his inexperienced aircrews flying safely and responding to inflight emergencies in an appropriate manner. To Mendonca's credit, he did just that. Although the aircraft continued to experience a variety of in-flight emergency situations, his pilots always brought the aging aircraft back. In September a number of squadron personnel had their tours curtailed and were reassigned to other duties. By October all training flights were suspended for the EB-66E. EB-66C training missions were canceled effective November 5 as a fuel conservation measure. On December 24, the last combat coded mission was flown by an EB-66C. A message received the following day from 13th Air Force at Clark directed the deployment of all aircraft to Clark Air Base where 'reclamation would be accomplished.' All 24 aircraft were to be ferried to Clark in two, two-ship formations every third day. On 2 January 1974 the first four aircraft departed Korat for Clark Air Base near Manila in the Philippine Islands, a frequent stop for B-66s since 1957. The last group of four aircraft departed Korat on January 17, arriving without mishap at their final destination. There the aircraft were stripped of all useable equipment. For a long time their fading hulks sat on an unused ramp at Clark reminding arriving aircraft of the eventual fate of all combat planes. For nearly nine years these airplanes, manned by truly courageous aircrews, had flown into the face of fear so that others might live. MiGs and SAMs tried hard to knock them from the skies, few succeeded. Time eventually did what a determined enemy failed to accomplish.[5] The remaining members of the 42nd TEWS departed Thailand in early February 1974, and the squadron was formally inactivated on March 15. While involved in combat operations in the Vietnam War the 42nd Tactical Electronic Warfare Squadron was awarded the Presidential Unit Citation; the Air Force Outstanding Unit Award with combat V device for valor on four different occasions; the Navy Meritorious Unit Citation, and the Republic of Vietnam Gallantry Cross with Palm. The men, those who flew and those who maintained, earned everyone of those scant recognitions for their years of challenging and difficult service to their nation.[6]

With the demise of the last EB-66 combat squadron, there was no further need for the 39th Tactical Electronic Warfare Training Squadron at Shaw AFB at Sumter, South Carolina. The squadron, like the 42nd TEWS at Korat, began transferring its remaining aircraft early in the year to the Aircraft Storage and Disposition Center at Davis-Monthan AFB, in Tucson, Arizona, better known as the boneyard. Al Kersis, a Raven assigned to the 39th TEWTS recalls "Jim Milam and I took a C-model from Shaw to Nellis AFB on January 4, 1974. We stayed there until February 2nd, flying the Nellis air combat ranges doing signal measurements. That was the last operational mission flown by a B-66 aircraft."[7] The formal squadron inactivation ceremony was presided over by the 363rd TRW commander, Colonel William J. Bally. All that remained to be done was to mount 54-465 at Shaw's front gate. 54-465 became a symbol of memories and accomplishments spanning twenty years of service to the nation in peace and war – a reminder for the men who flew and maintained these aircraft, for their families and friends, and all visitors to Shaw Air Force Base, of a proud and stellar past.

NOTES

Notes Chapter 1

1. Samuel, Wolfgang, W. *American Raiders: The Race to Capture the Luftwaffe's Secrets*, University Press of Mississippi, Jackson, MS, 2004, p. 63.

2. James, Martin E. *Historical Highlights, United States Air Force in Europe, 1945-1979*, Office of History, Headquarters USAFE, APO New York 09012, 28 November 1980, p. 4.

3. Hooper, Craig. *Going Down With the Ships*, The Washington Post, March 5, 2007, p. A15.

4. Samuel, Wolfgang W.E. *I Always Wanted to Fly: America's Cold War Airmen*, University Press of Mississippi, Jackson, MS, 2001, p. 182.

5. Samuel, Wolfgang W. E. *American Raiders: The Race to Capture the Luftwaffe's Secrets*, University Press of Mississippi, Jackson, MS, 2004, p. 429.

6. James, Martin E. p. 9.

7. LeMay, Curtis E. *Mission With LeMay*, Doubleday & Company, Garden City, New York, 1965, p. 411.

8. Kennan, George F. *Memoirs 1925-1950*, The Atlantic Monthly Press, Boston, MA, 1967, pp. 291-292, 364.

9. Bohn, John T. *Development of Strategic Air Command 1946-1976*, Office of the Historian, Headquarters, Strategic Air Command, Offutt AFB, Omaha, NE, 21 March 1976, p. 2.

10. LeMay, Curtis E. pp. 432-433.

11. Ibid, p. 441.

12. Samuel, Wolfgang W.E. *I Always Wanted to Fly,* p. 305.

13. Lobdell, Harrison, Jr., Interview by Hugh N. Ahmann, 15 March 1991, Maxwell AFB, AL.

14. Samuel, Wolfgang W. E. *American Raiders*, p. 152.

15. Ibid, p. 434.

16. Bohn, p. 13.

17. Smith, Richard K. 75 Years of Inflight Refueling, Highlights, 1923-1998, Air Force History and Museums Program, Washington DC, 1998, pp. 29-31.

18. Tilford, Earl, H. *Setup: What the Air Force did in Vietnam and Why*, Air University Press, Maxwell AFB, AL, June 1991, pp. 11-15.

Notes Chapter 2

1. Ridgway, Matthew B. *Soldier: The Memoirs of Matthew B.* Ridgway, Greenwood Press, Westport, CN, 1956, p. 191.

2. Samuel, Wolfgang W. E. *I Always Wanted to Fly*, p. 99.

3. Summers, Harry G. Jr., Korean War Almanac, Facts on File, Inc., New York, 1990, p. 117.

4. Lobdell, Harrison, Interview.

5. Knaack, Marcelle S. *Post-World War II Bombers 1945-1973*, Office of AF History, Washington DC, 1988, pp. 546-551.

6. *History of the Tactical Air Command*, Volume IV, Jan-Jun 1953, Langley AFB, VA, p. 54.

7. Ibid, pp. 297-303.

8. Ibid, p. 343.

9. *B-RB-66 Tactical Support Airplane*, Memorandum, HQ AMC, Wright Patterson AFB, OH, 5/22/53, to CC/TAC, Langley AFB, VA, p. 9

10. Wagner, Reginald W. *Report of TDY*, HQ AMC, ECM Weapons Phasing Group, Wright-Patterson AFB, OH, 16 Dec 1954, p. 3.

11. *Improved Turret for B-66*, Memorandum, HQ TAC/OA, to DO/DM/RQ, 9 March 1954.

12. *Aircraft Equipment (B/RB-66)*, Ltr from HQ TAC, Langley AFB, VA, to Director Requirements, HQ USAF, Washington DC, 2 April 1953.

13. Schroder, Karl H. *Readers Forum, Letter to the Editor*, Air Classics, January 1974, p. 61.

14. Samuel, Wolfgang W. E. *American Raiders*, p. 218.

15. Ibid, p. 131.

16. Hotz, Robert, Moscow's May Day Air Review. Reds' Surprise: 15,000-lb-Thrust Jets, Aviation Week, 5/31/54, pp. 11-12.

17. Alling, Frederick A., *History of the B/RB-66 Weapon System 1952-1959, Vol I, Historical Study No. 324*, Air Materiel Command, Wright-Patterson AFB, OH, 1960, p. 10.

18. Ibid, Knaack p. 407.

19. *History of the Tactical Air Command, Aircraft Requirements*, Jan-Jun 1954, Langley AFB, VA, p. 1.

20. Interview with Colonel Kenneth Chilstrom, USAF (Ret.), June 19, 2007.

21. *Lightweight J-57 Engine for F-100 Aircraft*, Ltr HQ USAF, Washington DC, to CC/TAC, Langley AFB, VA, 10 Sep 1953.

22. *History of the Tactical Air Command*, Jan-Jun 1954, p. 2.

23. Lobdell, Harrison, Interview.

24. Knaack, Marcelle S. Post-World War II Bombers, pp. 546-551.

25. *Unsatisfactory Report*, RB-66 J-71-9/11, AFTO Form 29, #55-1690, AF Flight Test Center, Edwards AFB, CA, 8 Oct 1955.

26. Manlove, Cliff, The Early Years, The Destroyer, Summer 2005.

27. Ibid, Alling p. 11.

Notes Chapter 3

1. Samuel, Wolfgang W. E. *I Always Wanted to Fly*, p. 183.

2. Bohn, John T. *Development of Strategic Air Command*, p. 43.

3. *Destination Freedom*, Aviation Week, April 26, 1954, p. 44.

4. Bohn, John T. *Development of Strategic Air Command*, pp. 44-45.

5. Samuel, Wolfgang W. E. *I Always Wanted to Fly*, pp. 188-189.

6. Ibid, pp. 198-214.

7. *News at Deadline – Newsletter*, American Aviation, May 24, 1954, p. 3.

8. Ferrel, Robert H. ed. *The Twentieth Century: An Almanac*, World Almanac Publications, New York, 1985, p. 331.

9. Knaack, Marcelle S. *Post-World War II Bombers*, p. 415.

10. RB-66A CTC Inspection, Douglas Aircraft Company, Long Beach, CA, March 22, 1954, pp. 1-71.

11. B-RB-66 Tactical Support Plane, Memorandum, HQ AMC, Wright-Patterson AFB, OH, 22 May 1953, to CC/TAC, Langley AFB, VA, p. 6.

12. Email June 20,2006, from Colonel Tom Whitlock to Cliff Parrott, former Douglas Company Senior Technical Representative at Shaw AFB, SC, Subject: B-66.

13. Chilstrom, Kenneth and Leary, Penn, ed., Test Flying at Old Wright Field, Westchester House Publishers, Omaha, NE, 1993.

14. Email Nov 30, 2006, from Cliff Parrott to Colonel Wolfgang Samuel, Subject: Ejection Questions.

15. Lusk, Ralph W. & Porter John A. *Phase V (Adverse Weather) Flight Test of RB-66B Aircraft*, Wright-Air Development Center, Wright-Patterson AFB, OH, July 1956, pp. 1-9,17.

16. Ibid, pp. 11-16.

17. Aircraft Crash, Fire and Rescue Report, AF Form 282, Explosion of Right Wheel Assembly, B-66B 53-418, Kirtland AFB, NM, 3 Apr 56.

Notes Chapter 4

1. *Operations and Air Training Activity and Status Report*, from HQ 17Bombardment Wing, Hurlburt Field, FL, to CC/9AF, Shaw AFB, SC, 5 April 1956, p. 2.

2. Ibid, p. 32.

3. Werrell, Kenneth P. *Those Were the Days: Flying Safety during the Transition to Jets, 1944-53*, Air Power History, Winter 2005, pp. 49-51.

4. Ibid, *Operations and Air Training Activity and Status Report*, p. 2.

5. Email, James B. Story, Lt/Colonel, USAF (Ret.), January 31, 2007, to Colonel Wolfgang Samuel, USAF (Ret.), Subject: B-66.

6. *History of the Tactical Air Command, Aircraft Requirements*, Langley AFB, VA, Jan-Jun 1954, p. 20.

7. *History of the 363D Tactical Reconnaissance Wing*, Shaw AFB, SC, Jan-Jun 1956, p. 1.

8. *Operations and Air Training Activity and Status Report*, p. 27.

9. *Report of Aircraft Accident*, AF Form 14, 34BS/17BW, Hurlburt Field, FL, B-66B 54-497, Fuel Filter Design, 6 October 1956.

10. *Report of Aircraft Accident*, AF Form 14, 9TRS/363TRW Shaw AFB, SC, WB-66D 55-394, Fuel Filter Design, 5 September 1961.

11. *Report of Aircraft Accident*, AF Form 14, 42TRS/10TRW, RAF Chelveston, RB-66C 54-460, Fuel Filter Design, 7 February 1962.

12. Ibid, Samuel, Wolfgang, I Always Wanted to Fly, pp. 215-229.

13. Ibid, Bohn, John T., *Development of Strategic Air Command*, p. 60.

14. Witze, Claude O., Administration Hits Airpower Opponents, Aviation Week, May 14, 1956, pp. 26-27.

15. Johnson, Katherine, USSR Will Have Knock-Out Punch in '59, Aviation Week, May 28, 1956, p. 27.

16. *Report of Aircraft Accident*, AF Form 14, 95BS/17BW Hurlburt Field, FL, B-66B 54-493, April 1, 1957.

17. *Report of Aircraft Accident*, AF Form 14, 95BS/17BW Hurlburt Field, FL, B-66B 54-495, Sept 3, 1957.

18. High, Kenneth Lt/Colonel, USAF (Ret.), Memorandum, *'Mobile Zebra,'* April 13, 2007.

19. *History of the Tactical Air Command, Aircraft Requirements*, Langley AFB, VA, Jan-Jun 1954, p. 16.

20. *Air Force to Use Fiscal '57 Funds to Build Successor to B-52*, Industry News Digest, American Aviation, May 7, 1956, p. 10.

21. 17BW Supplement to USAF Operations Plan 57-2, *Deployment of B-66Bs*, and Operations Order 79-57, HQ 17BW, 20 December 1957, *Air Operations*.

Notes Chapter 5

1. Interview with Lt/Colonel Donald Harding, USAF (Ret.), October 2006, San Antonio, Texas.

2. Memorandum from Major General David V. Miller, July 2007.

3. Harding interview.

4. Email from John Davis, June 27, 2006, Subject: B-66.

5. Harding interview.

6. *Report of Aircraft Accident*, AF Form 14, 84BS/47BW RAF Sculthorpe, B-66B 55-314, March 30, 1958.

7. Miller memorandum.

8. *Report of Aircraft Accident*, AF Form 14, 85BS/47BW RAF Sculthorpe, B-66B 54-499, October 26, 1961.

9. Memorandum from Major Kenneth High, USAF (Ret.) to author re presidential escort mission in 1959.

10. Ltr from Lt/Col Donald Orr to 89 Airlift Wing, Andrews AFB, MD, dated April 21, 2004. Subject: Escort of Air Force One by B-66B Aircraft on 7/14 December 1959 over Turkey and Iran. HQ/USAF msg, 4 Dec 1959. Subject: Jet Fighter Escort for Monsoon. HQ/USAFE msg, 2 Dec 1959. Subject: Jet Fighter Escort for Monsoon. HQ/USAF msg, 4 Dec 59, same subject.

11. High memorandum.

12. Ltr from Colonel Harris B. Hull, HQ PACAF, to Lt/General Ira Eaker, February 3, 1958.

Notes Chapter 6

1. Major General Miller interview.

2. *Report of Aircraft Accident*, AF Form 14, RB-66B 54-422, 19TRS/10TRW, RAF Sculthorpe, April 14, 1958.

3. Email, August 7, 2006, Sgt Ken L. Weiand, USAF (Ret.), Subject: *B-66 Incidents*.

4. *Report of Aircraft Accident*, AF Form 14, RB-66B 54-437, 19TRS/10TRW, RAF Sculthorpe, July 2, 1958.

5. *Report of Aircraft Accident*, AF Form 14, RB-66B 54-433, 19TRS/10TRW, RAF Sculthorpe, July 3, 1958.

6. Email, July 26, 2006, Colonel Lewis J. Partridge, USAF (Ret.), Subject: *19TRS*.

7. Email, Aug 10, 2006, Pete West, Subject: *June 59 Crash at Spangdahlem*.

8. Email, Aug 16, 2006, Thomas Fitzgerald, Subject: *And Now the Rest of the Story*.

9. Email, Aug, 2006, Colonel Lewis Partridge, USAF (Ret.)

10. *Report of Aircraft Accident*, AF Form 14, RB-66B 54-432, 19TRS/10TRW, Spangdahlem, July 3 1959.

11. *Village Plans for Annual Patton Tribute*, Cackle, Paul, Skyblazer, Spangdahlem Air Base weekly paper, June 1959.

12. Email, July 24, 2006, Robert J. Ganci, Subject: *A B-66 Gunner's Life*.

13. Interview with Lt/Colonel Lester Almbaugh, USAF (Ret.), Vienna, VA, July 7, 2006.

14. *Report of Aircraft Accident*, AF Form 14, RB-66B 54-430, 19TRS/10TRW, RAF Alconbury, March 16, 1961.

15. Almbaugh interview.

Notes Chapter 7

1. Hrivnak, Michael J. *50th Anniversary Shaw Air Force Base, S.C. 1941-1991*, Office of History, 363 Tactical Reconnaissance Wing, Shaw AFB, SC, 1991, pp. 2-35.

2. Ibid, p. 64.

3. Interview with Cliff Parrott, Senior Douglas Aircraft Corporation Representative (Ret.), at Shaw AFB, SC, June 6, 2006, Knoxville, TN.

4. History of the 363d Tactical Reconnaissance Wing, Shaw AFB, SC, Jan-Jun 1956, p.52.

5. Cliff Parrott interview.

6. Interview with Robert R. Webster, USAF (Ret.), October 2006, San Antonio, TX.

7. Cliff Parrott interview.

8. Cliff Parrott interview.

9. History of the 363d Tactical Reconnaissance Wing, Shaw AFB, SC, Jan-Jun 1958, p. 15.

10. Cliff Parrott interview.

11. Email from Jay Spaulding, USAF (Ret.), July 29, 2006, Subject: RB-66 Accident.

12. Cliff Parrott interview.

13. Report of Aircraft Accident, AF Form 14, May 29, 1959, 9TRS/363TRW Shaw AFB, SC, WB-66D 55-400.

14. Report of Aircraft Accident, AF Form 14, April 11, 1957, 43TRS/363TRW Shaw AFB, SC, RB-66B 53-410.

15. Report of Aircraft Accident, AF Form 14, May 8, 1959, 16TRS/363TRW Shaw AFB, SC, RB-66B 53-473.

16. History of the 363d Tactical Reconnaissance Wing, Shaw AFB, SC, Jan-Jun 1959, p. 7.

17. Werrell, Kenneth B., Those Were the Days: Flying Safety during the Transition to Jets, 1944-53, Air Power History, Winter 2005, p. 51.

18. Cliff Parrott interview.

Notes Chapter 8

1. Email from Robert R. Webster, USAF (Ret.), February 7, 2007, Subject: B-66.

2. Email from Robert Webster, USAF (Ret.), February 26, 2007, Subject: Interview Tape.

3. Interview with Harrison Lobdell, Jr. Major General, USAF (Ret.), by Hugh N. Ahmann, 15 March 1991, Maxwell AFB, AL.

4. Email from Dave Eby, Colonel, USAF (Ret.), January 27, 2007, Subject: B-66 Book.

5. Interview Robert R. Webster, USAF (Ret.), February, 2007, Hardin, KY.

6. History of the 363d Tactical Reconnaissance Wing, Shaw AFB, SC, Jan-Jun 1958, p.48.

7. Email from Dave Eby, Colonel, USAF (Ret.), January 27, 2007, Subject: B-66 Book.

8. Ibid, History of the 363d, Flying Hour Allocation.

9. Frank, Art, *Report from Adana*, RECON Record, 12 September 1958, 363d TRW, Shaw AFB, SC.

10. Out of Briefcases & Red Folders, a Classic Show of Power & Speed, Jul 28, 1958, National Affairs, Time Magazine (www.time.com).

11. Richards, Leveret G., John Day Co. Inc., 1961, *TAC: The Story of the Tactical Air Command*, pp. 159-173.

12. History of the 4440th Aircraft Delivery Group (TAC), 15 January – 30 June 1958, Langley AFB, VA, pp. 124-128.

13. Report of Aircraft Accident, AF Form 14, 17 July 1958, RB-66B 53-459, 41TRS/363TRW, Shaw AFB, SC.

14. Ibid.

15. Memo from Cliff A. Parrott, Douglas Service Representative, Shaw AFB, SC, to R.F. Killingsworth, C213, 11 September 1958, Subject: Battle Damage of RB-66B Aircraft.

16. Shaw Contingent Commended, RECON Record, September 1958, 363d TRW, Shaw AFB, SC.

17. Letter from Ronald Darrah, recollections of deployment to Adana, Turkey, during 1958 Lebanon crisis.

Notes Chapter 9

1. Bohn, John T. Development of Strategic Air Command 1946-1947, Office of the Historian, Headquarters SAC, Offutt AFB, Omaha, NE, March 1976, pp. 65-74.

2. Ibid.

3. Stamm, Robert Lt/Colonel, USAF (Ret.), Reflections on the 11th and 12th TAC Recon Squadrons, 67TRW, Yokota Air Base, Japan, The Destroyer, Summer 2002, p. 3.

4. Stern, Robert FSO-1 (Ret.), The Very Old Corps, The Destroyer, Summer 2005, pp. 9-10.

5. Emails from Dick Miles, John Parsons, Peter West, Dave Henby, Ken High and Leon Kirk, June 27, 2007, subject: JATO.

6. Email from Robert Stamm February 8, 2007, re KB-50 aerial tanker and RB-66 refueling.

7. History of the 67th Tactical Reconnaissance Wing, Yokota Air Base, Japan, 1 July – 31 December 1957, p. 32.

8. Report of Aircraft Accident, AF Form 14, 18 July 1957, RB-66B 54-428, 12TRS/67TRW, Yokota Air Base, Japan.

9. Ibid, History of the 67TRW, pp. 12-13.

10. Ibid, History of the 67TRW, pp. 142-143.

11. Interview with Arthur K. Taylor, Colonel, USAF (Ret.), October 2006, San Antonio, Texas.

Notes Chapter 10

1. Interview with Arthur K. Taylor.

2. Report of Aircraft Accident, AF Form 14, 15 November 1958, RB-66C 54-476, 11TRS/67TRW Yokota Air Base, Japan.

3. Ibid, Interview with Arthur K. Taylor.

4. Memorandum from David D. Cooper, USAF (Ret.) and emails dated June 27, 28 and July 9, 2006 re reconnaissance operations of 11TRS and crash of RB-66C November 15, 1959.

5. Email from Leon Kirk, USAF (Ret.), May 12, 2006, Subject: B-66, relating to events surrounding crash of RB-66C on February 9, 1959; and Report of Aircraft Accident, AF Form 14, 9 February 1959, RB-66C 54-472, 11TRS/67TRW Yokota Air Base, Japan.

6. *AF Jet Crashes In Korea; 4 Safe, 1 Dead, 2 Missing*, The Stars & Stripes, Pacific Edition, date unknown.

7. Email from Major Lloyd Neutz to author, January 31, 2007, Subject: B-66 DFC Flight.

8. Air Force Magazine, 2007 Space Almanac, Mehuron, Tamar A. ed., pp. 74-91, August 2007.

9. Ibid, Interview with Arthur K. Taylor.

Notes Chapter 11

1. Email Jerry Mosby, December 28, 2006, Subject: More RB-66 Info.

2. Email Ned Colburn, July 18, 2002, Subject: Paul Bjork & Carl Covey Remembered.

3. Reponen, Gerald Lt/Colonel, USAF (Ret.), unpublished memoir, p. 8-26.

4. Email Gayle P. Johnson, April 12, 2007, Subject: Eglin Firepower Demo.

5. Ibid, Reponen, pp. 8-26 – 8-27.

6. The Washington Post Magazine, story about The Missiles of October and the role of Major Richard Heyser, October 26, 2003, Michael Dobbs, pp. 15-21.

7. *The Missiles of Cuba – 1962*, Part I, Sanders A. Laubenthal, Klaxon, Vol 7, Spring 2000, pp. 1-2; Part II, Fall 2000, pp. 36-39. *The Naval Quarantine of Cuba, 1962*, January 2001, Naval Historical Center, Washington DC.

8. Hrivnak, Michael J., 50th Anniversary Shaw Air Force Base, S.C. 1941-1991, pp. 83-84.

9. Email Joe Canady, December 18, 2006, Subject: B-66. Addresses reconnaissance operations against Cuba.

10. Ibid, Samuel, Wolfgang W. E., *I Always Wanted to Fly*, pp. 150-151.

Notes Chapter 12

1. Reponen, Gerald Lt/Colonel, USAF (Ret.), unpublished memoir.

2. Ibid.

3. History of the 66th Tactical Reconnaissance Wing, 1 July 1956 – 31 December 1956, pages not numbered.

4. Ibid Reponen.

5. Emails Steve Wooden, May 7, and May 11, 2006, Subject: B-66.

6. Ibid Reponen.

7. AF Form 14, Report of Aircraft Accident, 9 December 1958, RB-66B 54-535, 30TRS, 10TRW, Spangdahlem AB, Germany.

8. Ibid Reponen.

9. Ibid Reponen.

10. Ibid Reponen.

Notes Chapter 13

1. Bohn, John T. pp. 57-60.

2. James, Martin E. pp. 29-31.

3. Letter, April 22, 2007, from Earl McClintock, USAF (Ret.), describing the events surrounding the ejection from an RB-66B on April 5, 1963, Toul-Rosieres AB, France.

4. Email from Kermit W. Helmke, April 28, 20007, Subject: RB-66B Ejection.

5. AF Form 14, Report of Aircraft Accident, February 4, 1963, RB-66B 54-530, 19TRS, 10TRW, Tulsa, OK.

6. Ibid, Samuel, Wolfgang W.E. I Always Wanted to Fly, pp. 148-151.

7. Rich, Ben R. Skunk Works, Little Brown & Company, New York, 1994, p. 123.

8. Ibid, Samuel, Wolfgang W. E. I Always Wanted to Fly, p. 150.

9. Letter from Major David I. Holland, USAF, (Ret.), October 10, 2006, with attachment: 'Check Ride to Soviet Detention.'

10. Fighter Regiment of Strategic Containment, from the History of the 35th Fighter Air Regiment, The world of Aviation, February 2002, pp. 44-50, as translated by N. Connors, June 2, 2004.

11. Ibid, David E. Holland.

12. *The 120-Mile Error*, The World, Time Magazine, March 20, 1964, Time Archive 1923 to the Present.

13. Email Kermit W. Helmke, October 17, 2004, Subject: RB-66B.

14. *Check Ride to Soviet Detention*, Major David I. Holland, USAF (Ret.), Daedalus Flyer, Spring 1990, p. 23.

15. Email Don Adee, August 10, 2006, Subject: RB-66 Shootdown 1964.

16. Ibid, *Check Ride to Soviet Detention*, letter from Colonel Gardina, USAF (Ret.) reflecting on the events after the shoot-down of Major Holland, pp. 23-24.

17. Email Norm Goldberg, September 18, 2006, Subject: B-66 Shootdown.

18. Ibid, *Check Ride to Soviet Detention*, letter from Colonel Gardina, USAF (Ret.) reflecting on the events after the shoot-down of Major Holland, pp. 23-24.

19. Handwritten note from Mrs. Rosemary Gardina to Kermit Helmke, January 9, 1996, including an unidentified newspaper clipping of the obituary of Colonel Verne Gardina. Colonel Gardina was laid to rest in Arlington National Cemetery on January 30, 1995.

20. U.S. Department of State, Foreign Relations of the United States 1964-1968, Volume XIV, Office of the Historian, Document 20, Message from Chairman Khrushchev to President Johnson, Moscow, April 2, 1964.

21. Ibid, Document 21, Letter from President Johnson to Chairman Khrushchev, Washington, April 17, 1964.

22. Ibid, email Don Adee.

23. Baxter, James P., Scientists Against Time, The M.I.T. Press, Cambridge, MA, pp. 187-200.

Notes Chapter 14

1. Harding, Donald E. Major USAF (Ret.), interview, October 2006, San Antonio, Texas.

2. *Magic Carpet to Survival*, Dr. Alfred Price, The Journal of Electronic Defense, April 2006, pp. 31-33.

3. Letter from Headquarters USAF/R&D, Washington DC, February 20, 1953, to Commanding General, ARDC, Baltimore, MD, Subject: Electronic Countermeasures in the B/RB-66.

4. Ibid, HQ ARDC response to HQ USAF ltr of February 20, 3/18/53.

5. Memorandum on *Conference on ECM Configuration of B/RB-66 Aircraft*, HQ Tactical Air Command, Langley AFB, VA, 3/26/53.

6. Report of TDY by Major Reginald W. Wagner, HQ/TAC, at HQ/AMC, HQ/AMC – WADC ECM Weapons Phasing Group, dated 12/16/1954.

7. Price, Alfred, *The History of U.S. Electronic Warfare, Vol II*, Association of Old Crows, Washington DC, 1989, pp. 211-212.

8. Ibid, pp. 213-214.

9. Ibid, pp. 248-250.

10. Email William Starnes Lt/Colonel USAF (Ret.), July 7, 2006, Subject: B-66B *Brown Cradle* Operation WEXVAL.

11. Ibid, Price, Alfred, pp. 250-253.

12. Parrott, Cliff, Interview, June 6, 2006, Knoxville, TN.

13. *The Other Jammer*, August R. Seefluth, Air Force Magazine, March 1992, pp. 74-77; also letter from August R. Seefluth, undated, Subject: *Preparing for Electronic Combat*.

14. Email Rex L. Davis, 11/22/2006, Subject: Operation Shabaz Nov 62, details *Brown Cradle* ECM exercise over the UK.

15. Ibid, August R. Seefluth.

16. Harding interview.

17. Ibid.

18. Emails Robert W. Stamm, Lt/Colonel, USAF (Ret.), Feb 5, Mar 30, Oct 2, 2007, Subject: Chambley AB/First Etain Test Flight.

Notes Chapter 15

1. *She Lived to Fly Another Day*, Frank Oldis, The Destroyer, Summer 2005, p. 10.

2. USAF Management Summary, *Southeast Asia Review, Calendar Years 1961-1972*, As of 31 December 1972, Headquarters USAF, Washington DC, 1973, pp. 1-2.

3. History 355TFW/41TEWS, Takhli RTAFB, Thailand, October – December 1969, War in Vietnam – Background, p. 59.

4. *The -Ology War: Technology and Ideology in the Vietnamese Defense of Hanoi, 1967*, Merle L. Pribbenow II, Journal of Military History, Vol. 67, No. 1, January 2003, p. 177.

5. Ibid, History 355TFW/41TEWS, October – December 1969, p. 60.
6. Email Robert Long to Jim Milam, April 5, 2001, Subject: B-66 in SEA.
7. Email Tom Taylor December 3, 2006, Subject: B-66 Information, initial deployment aspects.
8. Reponen, Gerald, unpublished memoir.
9. Email Kazuto Tomayasu November 23, 2006, Subject: EB-66C with B-57s Dropping Bombs. Infrared equipment and tests on RB-66 and RB-57 aircraft.
10. Reponen, Gerald, unpublished memoir.
11. Ibid, email Kazuto Tomayasu.
12. Ibid, Reponen, unpublished memoir.
13. Hobson, Chris, *Vietnam Air Losses*, Midland Publishing, Hinckley, England, 2001, p. 20.
14. Ibid, Reponen, unpublished memoir.
15. Email Jack Seech November 26, 2006, Subject: Early Days in SEA. Deals with photo recon mission in the Delta region.
16. Ibid, Reponen, unpublished Memoir.
17. Madrishin, John T. CMSGT, USAF (Ret.), on B-66 web site// ltr from Captain William R. Puckett, Operations Officer, Det 1, 6250 CSG/9TRS Task Force, Tan Son Nhut AB, SVN, to Commander 9TRS, Shaw AFB, SC, Subject: Letter of Commendation for SSGT J. T. Madrishin.

Notes Chapter 16
1. Email Eldon J. Canady, Major USAF (Ret.), December 18, 2006, Subject: RB-66 Operations – Cuba and 100 Missions Over North Vietnam.
2. Ibid.
3. Ibid.
4. Email Tom Taylor, USAF (Ret.), January 5, 2007, Subject: RB-66C Operations.
5. Hobson, *Vietnam Air Losses*, p. 270.
6. Email Jerry Mosby, USAF (Ret.), January 10, 2007 Subject: B-66 Operations Tan Son Nhut AB, SVN.
7. Turcotte, Maurice E. *Memoirs of 1st RB-66C Deployment to Takhli Royal Thai Air Base*, November 10, 2001, B-66 Website.
8. Sapere, Joseph, Lt/Colonel USAF (Ret.) Interview November 21, 2006. Email November 23, 2006, Subject: Early Days in SEA.
9. Emails John Norden USAF (Ret.), November 23 and 24, 2006, subject: Early Days in SEA. DAF, HQ7AF, SO-G-529, dtd 1 July 1966, "Each of the following is awarded the Distinguished Flying Cross for extraordinary achievement while participating in aerial flight on 24 July 1965," includes Lt/Colonel Willard G. Mattson; Captains Clarence R. Autery, Vernon A. Johnson, Frank A. Noble, Edwin R. Payne, David F. Schnelker, Thomas J. Taylor, James H. Wollpert. First Lieutenants James K. Beaty, Lawrence J. Bullock, Lowell D. Girod, James R. Maury, Curtis V. Nelson, John A. Norden, Joseph R. Sapere, Howard L. Shorr, Richard A. Utzke.
10. Hobson, *Vietnam Air Losses*, p. 26.
11. Ibid, *The -Ology War: Technology and Ideology in the Vietnamese Defense of Hanoi, 1967*, Merle L. Pribbenow II, p. 177.
12. Ibid, Sapere, interview and email.
13. Ibid, Hobson, *Vietnam Air Losses*, p. 27.
14. Email Kenneth Coolidge, USAF (Ret.), March 6, 2007, Subject: When the F-105s Aborted.

Notes Chapter 17
1. DAF/HQ 25TRW (USAFE), APO New York 09247, Special Order T-375, dtd 10 October 1965, directed named individuals to deploy "from Chambley AB, France to Moron AB, Spain, with variations authorized on TDY for approximately 179 days, in support of operation unnamed."
2. Memorandum, *B-66 Story – Pins, Canopy, Lanyard*, undated, Underwood, Alexander, MSGT USAF (Ret.).
3. Bohn, John T. Development of Strategic Air Command, pp. 119-125.
4. Letter, *The B-66B Brown Cradle Deployment to SEA in October 1965*, February 20, 2007, Edward J. Presto, USAF (Ret.).
5. Ibid, Underwood.
6. DAF/HQ 25TRW (USAFE), APO New York 09247, Special Order A-468, dtd 4 May 1966, relating to assignment of individuals to 355TFW, APO San Francisco 96273 – Takhli, Thailand.

7. Schaufler, Charles H. USAF (Ret.), *Deployment of the EB-66Bs From Europe to Thailand*, undated, B-66 website.

8. Email to author, Robert Mansperger, SMSGT USAF (Ret.) March 13, 2007, Subject: EB-66s at Takhli.

9. Ibid, Underwood.

10. AF Form 711, USAF Accident/Incident Report, August 20, 1966, EB-66C 54-475, 460TRW/41TRS, Takhli RTAFB, Thailand.

11. How the EB-66B *Brown Cradles* Got in the Vietnam Bombing Business (*Pathfinder*), Charles Schaufler, The Destroyer, Issue V, 2002, p. 2.

12. *Radar Bombing During Rolling Thunder – Part 1: Ryan's Raiders*, W. Howard Plunkett, Air Power History, Spring 2006, pp. 11-19.

13. B-66 General Information Report No. LB-22387, Douglas AC Corp., 1 March 1956.

14. Email to author, William McDonald USAF (Ret.), Subject: B-66 *Pathfinder* Missions in SEA.

15. Ibid, W. Howard Plunkett, Radar Bombing ... , p. 7.

16. Harding, Donald, interview.

17. Berger, Carl, ed., The U.S. Air Force in Southeast Asia, 1961-1973, Office of AF History, Washington DC, 1977, pp. 126-127.

18. *Radar Bombing*, Klong Times, Don Muang RTAFB, Thailand, July 15, 1966, p. 1.

Notes Chapter 18

1. USAF Management Summary, Southeast Asia Review, p. 38.

2. *Aces & Aerial Victories, The United States Air Force in Southeast Asia 1965-1973*, multiple authors, Office of Air Force History, Headquarters USAF, Washington DC, 1976, pp. 38-42.

3. Ibid, USAF Management Summary, p. 40.

4. Tilford, Earl, H. Jr., *Setup – What the Air Force Did in Vietnam and Why*, Air University Press, Maxwell AFB, AL, 1991, p. 123.

5. Ibid, pp. 123-125.

6. Ibid, USAF Management Summary, p. 39.

7. *The -Ology War*, Merle L. Pribbenow II, p. 178.

8. Email Major Robert P. Walker, USAF (Ret.) to Cliff Parrott, November 30, 2006, Subject: Shoot Down of RB-66C February 25, 1966.

9. Smith, Wayne H. USAF (Ret.), First EB-66C Shot Down in Vietnam February 25, 1966, B-66 website. Smith is a survivor of the shootdown; and email from Paul Duplessis to author, November 27, 2006, Subject: First RB-66C Shotdown in SEA.

10. Emails Major Robert P. Walker to Cliff Parrott, December 2 and 16, 2006, Subject: Shootdown of RB-66C February 25, 1966, Elevator Slab.

11. Ibid, Wayne H. Smith.

12. Lopez, John Jr., Major USA (Ret.), Postscript on loss of Gull 1 on February 25, 1966, and recovery of crew by Navy helicopters. B-66 website and email to author by Paul Duplessis, November 27, 2006.

13. Email Richard A. Evans, USAF (Ret.) to author, January 10, 2007, Subject: APR 25/26 installation in EB-66C aircraft lost on February 25, 1966.

14. Harding, Donald interview.

15. Hobson, Vietnam Air Losses, p. 67.

16. Emails Vaughan Wells, USAF (Ret.) to author, February 2, 15 and 16, 2007, Subject: China incursion; Edward Presto, USAF (Ret.) to author, same subject, April 7 and 11, 2007.

17. Memorandum from Stanley L. Tippin on events relating to the shoot-down of MiG-17 fighter on May 12, 1966, making an intercept on an EB-66C reconnaissance aircraft.//Email Norman Kasch to author, January 16, 2007, Subject: May 12, 1966 Events. Kasch and Tippin were Ravens on the EB-66C aircraft.//DAF/355CSG (PACAF), APO San Francisco 96273, Special Order T-511, 24 May 1966 – order extends TDY of EB-66C aircrew being interrogated at HQ/7AF, Tan Son Nhut Air Base, SVN, re May 12 events.

18. Various newspaper clippings quoted Major Dudley and Lieutenant Kringelis including the Fort Lauderdale News, May 13, 1966, *U.S. Downs MIG, Ponders Raiding N. Viet Jet Fields* and *Stepped-Up Air Fighting Looms Over North Vietnam. AF Bags MIG No. 12*, Stars & Stripes Asia

edition, 13 May 1966, p. 1. Air Force News, Tan Son Nhut AB, Vietnam, Vol 2, No 19, May 20, 1966, *Phantom Crew Scores 12th MiG Jet Kill*.

19. Ibid Stanley L. Tippin memorandum.//Los Angeles Times, May 30, 1966, by Jack Folsie, *U.S. Navigators Deny Craft Crossed China*.

20. *U.S. Air Force Combat Victory Credits Southeast Asia*, Office of AF History, Headquarters USAF, Washington DC, 1974.

21. Samuel, *I Always Wanted to Fly*, Lincoln Flight, pp. 300-322.

22. Schneider, Donald K., *Air Force Heroes in Vietnam*, Air University, Maxwell AFB, AL, 1979, pp. 22-31.

23. Memorandum, undated, from Stanley L. Tippin re RB-66C mission over the Gulf of Tonkin, August 7, 1966.//DAF/HQ7AF (PACAF), Special Order G-869, 10/18/1966, awarding the DFC for heroism on 8/07/1966 to Major Deaton; Captains Alexander, Lundberg and Tippin; First Lieutenants Kasch and Niemoller.

Notes Chapter 19

1. History of the 363rd Tactical Reconnaissance Wing, Shaw AFB, SC, July – December 1966, pp. 37-66.

2. Email John Matlock to William Starnes, September 13, 2002, Subject: Takhli and lack of training at Shaw AFB.

3. Interview with Lt/Colonel Frank Widic USAF (Ret.), February 16, 2007, Fredericksburg, Virginia.

4. Letter from Headquarters USAF/AFPM, Washington DC, 1 November 1967, to all major air commands and operating agencies. Subject: Personnel Rotation Programs for Southeast Asia. Signed – Lt/General Horace M. Wade.

5. *The -Ology War*, Merle L. Pribbenow II, p. 179.

6. Interview with Lt/Colonel Arthur K. Taylor, USAF (Ret.), October 2006, San Antonio, TX.// Autobiographical sketch by A. K. Taylor, March 2002, B-66 website.

7. Email Klaus Klause to author, January 28, 2007, Subject: MiG Kill Summary.

8. Email from Roland Valentine to author, April 12, 2007, Subject: MiG attack; recorded NVN GCI controller/pilot conversation.

9. Widic, Frank interview.

10. Harding, Donald interview.

11. Taylor interview.

Notes Chapter 20

1. Momyer, William W. General USAF (Ret.), *Airpower in Three Wars*, Department of the Air Force, Washington DC, 1978, pp. 204-205.

2. Rich, Ben R., *Skunk Works*, Little Brown & Company, New York, 1994, pp. 162-163.

3. Commentary, *The Nature of ECM Types*, August Seefluth, undated, B-66 website.

4. QRC 160-1 Assistance Team Trip Report, Visit to SEA, DAF/Warner Robins Air Materiel Area (AFLC), Robins AFB, GA, 6 December 1966, pp. 1-8.

5. Autobiography, unpublished, *Seven Years of Vietnam – A Raven Goes to War*, Lt/Colonel David S. Zook USAF (Ret.), p. 8.

6. Headquarters, Pacific Air Forces, Operations Analysis Working Paper No. 31, QRC 160-1 Effectiveness, Samuel J. Scott and James J. Donaghy, 16 March 1967.

7. *The -Ology War*, Merle L. Pribbenow II, p. 183.

8. Memorandum to author, undated, Lt/Colonel Otis E. McCain USAF (Ret.), Anti-SAM Combat Assistance Team member, 8TFW, Udorn RTAFB, Thailand. Observations on QRC-160 employment and effectiveness.

9. Bailey, Bruce, Lt/Colonel USAF (Ret.), *The RB-47 and the RC-135 in Vietnam*, 55SRW Website.

10. Ibid, McCain memorandum.

11. Ibid, Pribbenow, p. 196.

12. USAF Management Summary, Southeast Asia Review, p. 30.

13. Ibid, Pribbenow, p. 199.

Notes Chapter 21

1. *The -Ology War*, Merle L. Pribbenow II, p. 182.

2. Taylor, Arthur K., interview.

3. Email, Bob Hipps, June 29, 2007, Subject: Warrior. A tribute to General Robin Olds.

4. Giraudo, John C., Major General, USAF (Ret.), Oral History Interview 8-12 January 1985 by Lt/Colonel Charles M. Heltsley, Treasure Island, FL.

5. Giraudo interview.

6. Citation from Commander Seventh Fleet, Vice Admiral John J. Hyland, to the 6460th TEWS for combat operations over North Vietnam from 8 January to 15 May 1967 for providing 'outstandingly effective electronic countermeasures support for strike aircraft from the Seventh Fleet attack carrier striking force.'

7. History of 355 Tactical Fighter Wing, 41 Tactical Electronic Warfare Squadron 1 July – 30 September 1967, Operations, unnumbered pages.

8. Alex Kersis, Lt/Colonel USAF (Ret.), interview July 21, 2006, Alexandria, VA.

9. Chris Divich, Major General USAF (Ret.), interview October 4, 2006, San Antonio, TX.

10. AF Form 711B Aircraft Accident/Incident Report, November 17, 1967, EB-66C 54-473.

11. News clipping w/o date from the local 355TFW, Takhli RTAFB, base paper including picture of General Albert P. Clark, TAC vice commander, awarding the Airman's medal to SSGT Vultaggio.

12. DAF/HQ 355TFW (PACAF), APO San Francisco 96273, Special Order A-98, para 6, "Major Chris O Divich, FR57944, 41 TAC Elect Warfare Sq, PACAF, this stn, is appointed as Summary Courts Officer to make disposition of personal effects of MAJOR WILLIAM E MCDONALD ... "

13. Kersis interview.

14. Divich interview.

Notes Chapter 22

1. *The -Ology War*, Merle L. Pribbenow II, p. 182.

2. *Aces of the Yellow Star – The Little-Known Story of North Vietnam's Aerial Aces*, Michael O'Connor, Air Combat, September 1978, pp. 77-82.

3. Toperczer, Istvan, *Air War Over North Vietnam: The Vietnamese Peoples' Air Force 1949-1977*, Squadron Signal Publications, Carrolton, TX, 1998, pp. 23-26 and 63.

4. Email Joseph Snoy, USAF (Ret.) to author with attachments, October 29, 2006, Subject: EB-66 Info (Attachment: My Air Force Career 1965-1985).

5. Debrief of Lt/Colonel Jess Allen, MiG-cap F-4C lead pilot providing protection to two EB-66 aircraft in the Yen Bai area of North Vietnam.

6. Message from 432TRW, Takhli RTAFB, Thailand to CINCPAC/PACAF CC/7AF, Subject: MiG Sighting.

7. Kersis interview.

8. Interview with Attilio Pedroli, Brigadier General USAF (Ret.), July 12, 2006, Richmond, VA.

9. *Air Rescue Behind Enemy Lines*, Howard Sochurek, National Geographic, September 1968, pp. 346-369.

10. Pedroli interview.

Notes Chapter 23

1. Divich interview.

2. Hobson, Vietnam Air Losses, pp. 270-271.

3. Giraudo interview.

4. Interview with Father Frank McMullen, January 26, 2007, Accokeek, MD.

5. Email from John Norden USAF (Ret.) to author, January 27, 2007, Subject: Father McMullen.

6. Email from Vernon Johnson USAF (Ret.) to author, February 16, 2007, Subject: Father McMullen.

7. Email from Larry Bullock USAF (Ret.) to author, January 27, 2007, Subject: Father McMullen.

8. Memoranda from Dr. Kenneth G. Gould Jr., MD PHD, Colonel USAF (MC) Retired, provided to author: Doctor We Have a Problem; How To Go To War; My Sometime Role As An EWO.

9. *What the Hell was That?* Gerald P. Hanner, Destroyer, Summer 2006, p. 13.

Notes Chapter 24

1. Widic interview.
2. Knaack, Marcelle Size, *Post-World War II Bombers*, p. 455.
3. Memorandum from Lt/Colonel Stan Tippin USAF (Ret.), undated, Subject: RB-66C 54-467 and the ASQ-97 installation and test. Lt/Colonel Tippin led the team of four EWOs who were to test the system.
4. Kersis interview.
5. Email from Stan Tippin to author, December 21, 2006 Subject: EB-66C 54-467.
6. Email from Norman Kasch Lt/Colonel USAF (Ret.), February 15, 2007, Subject: EB-66E OT&E.
7. Harding interview.
8. Email from Paul Maul, Colonel USAF (Ret.) to author February 9, 2007, with attachments, Subject: Cross Fertilization of Cultures: Palace Cobra and New Guys in TAC Aircraft.
9. Email from Paul Maul to author December 5, 2006, with attachment, Subject: B-66 Training at Shaw – a Tribute to Smiley Pomeroy.

Notes Chapter 25

1. Samuel, Wolfgang W. E., I Always Wanted to Fly, The Last Flight of 3-4290, pp. 230-254.
2. Hand-written notes written by Colonel 'Smiley' Pomeroy shortly before his death September 5, 2003, and provided to his friend Colonel 'Ike' Espe by Mrs Louise Pomeroy.
3. Email from Colonel Espe to Colonel Milam May 22, 2006, and forwarded to the author, Subject: Comments on Smiley's Notes.
4. Pomeroy notes.
5. Espe email.
6. Email from Gerald McBride USAF (Ret.) to Colonel Espe and provided to author, November 5, 2005, Subject: Deployment to Itazuke after Pueblo capture.
7. Message from CINCPACAF to CSAF/AFOMO, 17 April 1968, Subject: EB-66 Organization Takhli.
8. History of 355TFW, April – June 1968, Volume III, Electronic Warfare, Aircraft Maintenance Data, EB-66 Aircraft, no page number.
9. History of 355TFW, 41TEWS, April – June 1968, Volume I, Operations, unnumbered.
10. History of 355TFW, October – December 1968, Volume II, Appendices 1-4, Sorties Flown EB-66B/C/E January to December.
11. Copler interview.
12. USAF Management Summary, Southeast Asia Review, USAF Drone Activity – Launches and Losses, p. 24.
13. Copler interview.

Notes Chapter 26

1. USAF Management Summary, Southeast Asia Review, pp. 36-40.
2. History of the 355TFW, January – March 1969, Vol 1, p. 16-17. "Twelve officers, four with projected assignments and eight who were June returnees, received directed orders to the 39 TEWS scheduled for activation April 1, 1969."
3. Copler interview.
4. 355TFW message to 7/13AF, 29 October 1969, Subject: 41TEWS Deactivation. Outlines deactivation of squadron and scheduled aircraft and personnel reductions.
5. History of 355TFW, 41TEWS, October – December 1969, Vol II, p. 89.
6. History of 355TFW, 41TEWS, January – March 1969, Vol I, pp. 64-65.
7. History of 42TEWS, 1 October – 31 December 1969, p. 9.
8. Letter to the editor by Major Kenneth H. High, USAF (Ret.), Air Force Magazine, May 1992, p. 10.
9. History of 42TEWS, 1 October – 31 December 1969, p. 15.
10. AF Form 711 USAF Accident/Incident Report, April 8, 1969, EB-66B 53-498, 42TEWS, Takhli RTAFB, Thailand.
11. Memorandum Colonel Paul Maul, USAF (Ret.) to author, June 28, 2007, Subject: Minimum Single Engine Control Speed.

12. Email Thomas J. Mangan, USAF (Ret.) to author, August 13, 2006, Subject: EB-66 Crash on April 8, 1969.

13. Email Lee Walters, USAF (Ret.) To author, August 10, 2006, Subject: EB-66B 53-491.

14. History 355TFW, 41TEWS, October – December 1969, Condensed History 13 November 1917 to 31 October 1969, The 41st TEWS is beset with engine problems, p. 82.

15. Email Don Christman USAF (Ret.) to author, July 1, 2006, Subject: B-66 Operations 1969-1970.

16. B-66 Destroyer Association Newsletter, *RB-66B Engine Test Bed*, Bill Keels, Fall 2007, p. 12.

17. Knaack, Marcelle Size, Post-World War II Bombers, p. 429.

18. History of the 388TFW, 42TEWS, January – March 1973, Vol 2, p. 22.

19. Emails Terry Buettner, Lt/Colonel USAF (Ret.) to author, August 3,4,6 and 7, 2006, Subject: RB-66 Accidents.

Notes Chapter 27

1. Southeast Asia Review 1961-1972, HQ USAF, Washington DC, Jan 31, 1973.

2. Email Tom Leeper USAF (Ret.) to author, January 29, 2007, Subject: EB-66 Story. SA-2 encounter near Ban Karai Pass.

3. Letter Colonel H. Bottomly, CC/355TFW, to CC/13AF, 17 April 1970, Subject: Reduction of EB-66 Flying Hour Allocation.

4. CINCPAC msg to component commanders, 112037Z Oct 70, directed initiation of ELINT program to provide increased tactical intel of threat radars in Mugia/Ban Karai Pass areas.

5. 7AF/IN message 151135Z Oct 70 to MACV/PACAF requests ELINT aircraft augmentation.// 7AF/CV message 191300Z Oct 70 to MACV/PACAF affirms requirement for 24 hour ELINT coverage, however, lacking assets to provide such.//PACAF message 040300Z Nov 70 requests 7AF submit requirement for additional EB-66 aircraft.//7AF/DO in message 061145Z Nov 70 states a requirement for 11 additional EB-66 aircraft.//CINCPAC message to JCS 131042Z Nov 70 recommends six.//JCS message 162039Z Nov 70 directs CSAF to deploy six EB-66 aircraft and 158 personnel to Thailand.

6. Project CHECO Report, USAF Tactical Reconnaissance in SEA, July 69 – June 1971, 23 Nov 1971, HQ PACAF/DOA.

7. CINCPAC message 230035 Dec 70.

8. CSAF message 232015Z Dec 70.

9. CINCPACAF message 310045Z Dec 70 to 7AF and 13AF, Subject: Changed inactivation dates for EB-66 squadrons.

10. Ibid, Project CHECO Report, pp. 43-44.

11. Letter from 355TFW/DOE, 23 March 1970, to PACAF/DOEW, Subject: EB-66 Support Tactics. Attachment: Minutes of EB-66 Tactics Meeting, *Arc Light* Support Tactics, 7 Feb 1970.

12. The -Ology War, Merle L. Pribbenow II, p. 186.

13. Staff Summary Sheet, 7AF/DOPR, 2 January 1971, Subject: EB-66 Evaluation. Recommends retention of EB-66 force.

14. 7AF Position Paper on Removal of EB-66 ECM Support for Photo Reconnaissance in RP-1, undated. Recommends retention of support jamming; that RF-4C carry QRC-335 pods; that F-4D escorts give up their Mark 82 bombs and carry two ECM pods.

15. Message January 5, 1971, from Colonel Thome to Lt/Colonel Shortt at 7AF, Subject: Force Plans.

16. Email Don Christman USAF (Ret.) July 1, 2006, to author. Subject: EB-66 Operations 69 to 70.

17. AF Form 711 USAF Accident/Incident Report, April 21, 1970, EB-66E 54-439, 42TEWS/355TFW, Takhli RTAFB, Thailand.

18. Emails Thomas Boyle USAF (Ret.) to author August 2 and December 14, 2006. Subject: April 21, 1970 EB-66E fire at Hickam AFB.

19. AF Form 711 USAF Accident/Incident Report, October 26, 1970, EB-66C 55-384, 42TEWS/388TFW, Korat RTAFB, Thailand.

20. B-66 Flight Safety Officer Study Kit, Feb/Mar 1971, 42TEWS, Korat RTAFB, Thailand, written by Lt/Colonel Gerald A. Kutz'

21. Memorandum on the events surrounding the crash of EB-66C 55-384 on October 26, 1970, from Colonel Vernon Luke to author.

22. Message 231110Z Jan 71, from 388TFW to various orgs, Subject: USAF Aircraft Incident Message Report.

23. AF Form 711 USAF Accident/Incident Report 17 November 1971, EB-66E 54-427, 42TEWS/388TFW, Korat RTAFB, Thailand.//Emails from David G. Ardis USAF (Ret.) August 6,7 and 10, 2006, to author. Subject: EB-66E fire at Udorn.

Notes Chapter 28

1. Harding interview.

2. AF Form 711 USAF Accident/Incident Report, October 9, 1969, EB-66E 54-536, 39TEWS/ 36TFW, Spangdahlem Air Base, Germany.

3. Harding interview.

4. Kersis interview.

5. Email from George Ciz USAF (Ret.) to author, May 3, 2007. Subject: B-66 Operations in Germany.

6. Harding interview.

7. History 388TFW/42TEWS, January – March 1973, Vol 2, p. 24.

Notes Chapter 29

1. Hobson, Chris, Vietnam Air Losses, p. 218.

2. AF Form 711 USAF Accident/Incident Report, February 2, 1972, EB-66E, 54-540, 42TEWS/ 388TFW, Korat RTAFB, Thailand.

3. Lavalle, A. J. C., ed. Airpower And The 1972 Spring Invasion, U.S. Government Printing Office, Washington DC, 1976, pp4-9.

4. Ibid, pp. 20-27.

5. Ibid, pp. 31.

6. Ibid, Hobson p. 220.

7. Ibid, Lavalle pp. 36-37.

8. *Remembering Gene Hambleton*, Gerald P. Hanner, The Destroyer, Winter 2005, pp. 10-12.

9. U.S. Army War College Military Studies Program Paper, Bat 21: A Case Study, An Individual Study Project by Lt/Colonel Stanley L. Busboom, USAF, Carlisle Barracks, PA, 1990, pp. 6-14.

10. Ibid.

11. Ibid, 15-19.

12. Ibid, 73-81.

13. Ibid, Lavalle, pp. 34-43.

14. Ibid, Hanner, p. 13.

15. *Emblems of Courage*, Fred L. Borch and Robert F. Dorr, Military Officer, May 2007, p. 73.

16. *The Harrowing War in the* Air, The Nation, Time Magazine, May 1, 1972, Time website.

17. Copler interview.

18. Lavalle, A. J. C., ed. *The Tale of Two Bridges and The Battle for the Skies over North Vietnam*, Government Printing Officer, Washington DC, 1976, pp. 79-86.

19. Ibid, pp. 90-92.

20. The USAF's Destroyer, Richard K. Schrader, Air Classics, April 1988, p. 78.

21. *SAMs on the DMZ*, Gerald P. Hanner, The Destroyer, Spring 2006, pp. 12-13.

Notes Chapter 30

1. Bohn, John T. *Development of Strategic Air Command 1946-1976*, pp. 160-163.

2. Autobiography, unpublished, *Seven Years of Vietnam: A Raven Goes to War*, Lt/Colonel David S. Zook, USAF (Ret.)

3. Copler interview.

4. Ibid, Zook.

5. *Operation Linebacker II*, Air Force Historical Studies Office, AF/HO, Washington DC. An operational summary.

6. Ibid, Bohn, p. 164.

7. AF Form 711 USAF Accident/Incident Report, 21 December 1972, EB-66E 54-529, 42TEWS/ 388TFW, Korat RTAFB, Thailand.

8. Email Terry Buettner, Lt/Colonel USAF (Ret.) to author, August 4, 2006. Subject: B-66 Accident 54-529. Colonel Buettner was a member of the accident investigation board.

Notes Chapter 31

1. Copler interview.

2. Crouch, Robert K. Colonel, Commander, 388TFW, Korat RTAFB, Thailand, End of Tour Report, 1 July 1973 to 3 January 1974.

3. History of the 388TFW/42TEWS, January – March 1973, Vol 2, Flight Safety, pp. 14-15.

4. AF Form 711 USAF Accident/Incident Report, 3 May 1973, EB-66E 54-445, 42TEWS/388TFW, Korat RTAFB, Thailand.

5. History of the 388TFW/42TEWS, 1 October 1973 – 31 January 1974, pp. iv-v.

6. History and Lineage of the 42nd Squadron, USAF Historical Research Center, Maxwell AFB, AL.

7. Kersis interview.

APPENDICES

Appendix 1
Terms and Abbreviations

AAA - Antiaircraft artillery.

A/1C - Airman first class.

A/2C - Airman second class.

A/3C - Airman third class.

AB - Air Base

Acquisition Radars - Medium range radars which acquire target aircraft for AAA or SAM terminal defense radars and feed the information to gun laying/terminal defense radars prior to target engagement. *Flat Face* and *Spoonrest* were Soviet designed acquisition radars used by the North Vietnamese.

ADC - Air Defense Command.

ADIZ - Air Defense Identification Zone.

AFB - Air Force Base.

AFPRO - Air Force Plant Representative Office.

AGL - Above Ground Level.

AOB - Air order of battle.

AR - Air refueling.

Arc Light - Code name for B-52 bomber strikes in Vietnam and Laos.

ARCP - Air refueling control point.

ARDC - Air Research and Development Command, USAF.

Bandit - Enemy aircraft.

Barlock - Powerful Soviet multi-beam early warning radar.

BDA - Bomb damage assessment.

Barrel Roll - Laos

Bingo Fuel - The minimum fuel needed to arrive at home base with 5,000 pounds of fuel remaining.

Bogey - Unknown aircraft presumed hostile.

Brown Cradle - B-66B bomber aircraft modified for ECM operations.

BS - Bomb/Bombardment Squadron.

Bullseye - Hanoi, used as a reference point for MiG warnings.
Burnthrough - Point at which the enemy can read through jamming.
BW - Bomb Wing.
BX - Base exchange - an Air Force on-base dry-goods store for military personnel.

CAP - Combat Air Patrol.
CASF - Composite Air Strike Force.
CCTS - Combat Crew Training Squadron.
CEP - Central Error Probable; a calculation of bombing accuracy integrating past and present results.
CG - Center of gravity.
Chaff - Strips of aluminum foil used to jam enemy radar.
CIA - Central Intelligence Agency.
CINCPAC - Commander-in-Chief-Pacific
Combat Sky Spot - MSQ-77 radar controlled bombing missions
Constant Guard - Aircraft deployment code to SEA in 1972 in response to NVN spring invasion
Counter - Mission over Route Packs III to VI, counting toward 100 missions to be flown to complete a tour of duty.
CSAF - Chief of Staff United States Air Force.

DDR - Deutsche Demokratische Republic Germany (Communist East Germany)
DF - Direction finding.
DFC - Distinguished Flying Cross.
DME - Distance measuring equipment.
DMZ - Demilitarized Zone established between North and South Vietnam at the Geneva Peace Treaty of 1954. It was demilitarized in name only.
DRV - Democratic Republic of Vietnam (North Vietnam).

Echo Alert - NATO alert status code for *Brown Cradle* B-66 ECM aircraft.
ECM - Electronic countermeasures such as noise or deception jamming, the dropping of chaff, anything that will prevent or reduce the effective use of the electromagnetic spectrum by enemy radar.
EOB - Electronic Order of Battle.
ELINT - Electronic Intelligence (Radar).
EGT - Engine Exhaust Temperature.
ELINT - Electronic intelligence.
EOB - Electronic order of battle. The disposition of enemy radars throughout an area.
ETA - Estimated time of arrival.
EW - Early warning radar; or a term used to refer to an electronic warfare officer; or the art and science of electronic warfare.
EWO - Electronic warfare officer.

FAC - Forward Air Controller.
Fansong - The track while scan radar that acquires a target and through uplink guidance controls the Guideline missile's flight path.
FCF - Functional Test Flight.
FEAF - Far East Air Forces.
Fence - The Mekong River that divides Thailand from Laos.
Firecan - Soviet AAA radar.
Flaming Dart - US air raids against North Vietnam in February 1965.
Flatface - Soviet intermediate range target acquisition radar.
Frag - Fragmentary Operations Order. The daily listing of 7th Air Force directed combat sorties.
Freedom Train - Air campaign against lower route packs in North Vietnam in response to the spring invasion of South Vietnam.

G - Unit of acceleration exerted upon a body at rest equal to the force of gravity.
GCA - Ground control approach radar. The radar that leads an aircraft to a runway.
GCI - Ground control intercept radar. The radar that leads a fighter to a target aircraft.
Guard - A UHF radio frequency monitored by all air and ground receivers.

HF - High frequency.
Ho Chi Minh Trail - The routes taken by NVN forces through Laos and Cambodia into South Vietnam.

IAS - Indicated airspeed.
IDA - Institute for Defense Analysis.
IFR - Instrument flight rules.
IFF - Identification friend or foe. A coded transmission transmitted by a transponder from an aircraft in response to an interrogating device at a ground radar station. In the Vietnam War many aircrews believed that the enemy could read their IFF.
IFR - Instrument Flight Rules.
IMC - Instrument Meteorological Conditions.
IP - Initial point from which a bomb run is initiated. Also, Instructor Pilot.
IR - Infrared.
IRBM - Intermediate Range Ballistic Missile.
Iron Hand - The mission flown by F-105F/G aircraft used for suppression of anti-aircraft and surface to air missile sites.

JATO - Jet/Rocket assisted take-off.
JCS - Joint Chiefs of Staff
Jolly Green Giant - Nickname for USAF rescue helicopters, specifically the HH-53.

KIA - Killed in action.
Knot - One nautical mile per hour.

LABS - Low Altitude Bomb System - a high G low altitude nuclear weapons delivery looping maneuver.
Linebacker I - Air campaign against North Vietnam April to October 1972.
Linebacker II - Air campaign against North Vietnam December 1972.

MAC - Military Airlift Command.
MACV - Military Assistance Command Vietnam.
MHZ - Megaherz, referring to radio frequencies.
MIA - Missing in action.
MiG - Soviet fighter aircraft designed by the Mikoyan and Gurovich design bureau, such as the MiG-15, MiG-17 and MiG-21 used by the North Vietnamese air force.
MSL - Mean Sea Level.
MSGT - Master sergeant.

NCO - Noncommissioned officer; a sergeant.
NIKE - Army surface to air anti-aircraft missile.
NKP - Nakhon Phanom RTAFB.
NRO - National Reconnaissance Office (During Vietnam War even its name was classified; organization responsible for high altitude reconnaissance operations such as the U-2/SR-71 aircraft and satellites).
NVA - North Vietnamese Army.

ORI - Operational Readiness Inspection.

PACAF - Pacific Air Forces.
PARPRO - Peacetime Aerial Reconnaissance Program.

PCS - Permanent change of station
POW - Prisoner of war
PRF - Pulse recurrence frequency.
PSP - Perforated steel planking.
PW - Pulse width.

QRC - Quick reaction capability referring to the rapid acquisition of electronic warfare related equipments or modifications outside the normal acquisition cycle.

RAF - Royal Air Force.
Raven - An electronic warfare officer on an ELINT collecting reconnaissance aircraft.
RBS - Radar Bomb Scoring site, used especially by SAC bombers for training/evaluation purposes.
Red Crown - A GCI capability on-board the naval vessel *USS Long Beach*, a cruiser in the Gulf of Tonkin, which controlled air traffic in its positive radar identification zone, the PIRAZ, issuing MiG warnings to friendly aircraft.
ROB - Radar Order of Battle.
ROC - Required Operational Capability.
Rolling Thunder - US air campaign against North Vietnam 1965 to 1968.
Route Packages - North Vietnam was divided for targeting purposes into 6 route packages, referred to as route packs. Route pack 1 started in the lower southern panhandle of NVN; Route pack 6 was divided into 6a and 6b covering the Hanoi/Haiphong area.
RHAW - Radar homing and warning equipment such as the APR-25/26, later the APR 36/37.
RTAFB - Royal Thai Air Force Base.
R&R - Rest and Recreation.

SAC - Strategic Air Command.
SAM - Surface to air missile, in the context of the Vietnam War it refers to the Soviet designed SA-2 air defense missile system.
SEA - Southeast Asia
SEAL - Navy special operations group - Sea/Air/Land.
SIF - An electronic device with variable codes for identification purposes of airborne aircraft.
SIGINT - Signals intelligence.
SIOP - Single Integrated Operations Plan (nuclear).
SLAR - Sidelooking radar.
SMSGT - Senior master sergeant.
Spoonrest - Soviet acquisition radar used by North Vietnamese.
SRS - Strategic Reconnaissance Squadron.
SRW - Strategic Reconnaissance Wing.
SSGT - Staff sergeant
Stall - The point where the wing no longer produces lift.
Staneval - Standardization and Evaluation Section of a squadron or a wing that ascertains that aircrews fly according to established directives.
SVN - South Vietnam.
SW - Strategic Wing,(SRW - Strategic Reconnaissance Wing).

TAC - Tactical Air Command.
TACAN - Tactical air navigation system using a ground-based UHF transmitter providing bearing and distance information to the ground station from an aircraft.
TARC - Tactical Air Reconnaissance Center at Eglin AFB, FL.
TDY - Temporary Duty. TDY duty is normally limited to 179 continuous days, or it becomes a permanent change of station assignment, a PCS.
TEWS - Tactical Electronic Warfare Squadron.
Tet - Vietnamese lunar new year.
TFW - Tactical Fighter Wing.
Thud - Nickname for the F-105.

Tiny Tim - B-52 raids into North Vietnam and Laos.
TRS - Tactical Reconnaissance Squadron.
TRW - Tactical Reconnaissance Wing.
TSGT - Technical sergeant.
TWS - Track While Scan - a radar tracking technique used by the SA-2 Fansong radar.

UE - Unit equipment from a table of authorization.
UHF - Ultra High Frequency.
UK - United Kingdom.
USAF - United States Air Force
USAFE - United States Air Forces in Europe.
USCINCEUR - United States Commander in Chief Europe.
USMC - United States Marine Corps
USN - United States Navy
USNS - United States Naval Ship (transports/non-combatants)
USS - United States Ship (combatants)

VC - Viet Cong (North Korean led guerilla group operating in South Vietnam)
VFR - Visual flight rules.
Victor Alert - NATO Alert status code for nuclear armed fighters/bombers.
VOR/VORTAC - Radio ranging and directional aid.

WEXVAL - A series of weapons evaluation tests run by the Institute for Defense Analysis to determine ECM readiness of national air defense assets.
Whiff - Soviet AAA radar based on the US WW-II SCR-584.
Whifferdill - To change direction 180 degrees - raising the nose 30 to 60 degrees, then applaying 90 degrees of bank to reverse direction and pulling the nose down below the horizon.
Whiskey Alert - NATO Alert status code for RB-66C electronic reconnaissance aircraft.
Wild Weasel - Aircraft modified to locate and destroy SAM sites or any other ground based radar guided system used for aircraft targeting.

Zulu - Z time; Greenwhich mean time.

Appendix 2
Selected U.S. Post WW-II Jet Aircraft Developments

Aircraft	# Engines	Type & Thrust Rating	1ST Flight (Proto)	T.O. WT (Lbs)	T.O. Run	Total Built
Strategic						
B-47E Stratojet Boeing	6	J47-GE-25A 6,000lbs s.t. dry 7,200lbs wet	1947	206,700	10,000'+	2,032
B-52F Stratofortress Boeing	8	J57-PW-43W 11,200lbs s.t. dry 13,750lbs wet	1952	420,000	7,000'+	744
B-58A Hustler Convair	4	J79-GE-5B 10,000lbs s.t. 15,600lbs with a.b.	1956	163,000	8,000'	116
KC-135A Stratotanker	4	J57-PW-59 13,700lbs s.t.	1954/56 Civ/Mil	316,000		732
Tactical						
F/RF-84F Thunderstreak Republic	1	J65-W-3/7 7,220lbs s.t.	1950	28,000	5,000'	3,063
F-100D Super Saber North American	1	J57-PW-21A 11,700lbs s.t. 16,950lbs with a.b.	1953	34,800	5,000'+	2,294
F/RF-101A/C Voodoo McDonnell	2	J57-PW-13 10,100lbs s.t. 14,880lbs with a.b	1954	48,100	4,000'	327
F-105D Thunderchief Republic	1	J75-PW-19W 17,200lbs s.t. 24,500lbs with a.b. 26,500 wet	1955	52,500	6,000'+	833
B/RB-57B Martin	2	J65-W-5 7,200lbs s.t.	1953	57,000	5,000'	383

RB-57D Martin	2	J57-PW-9 11,000lbs s.t.	1955			20
B/RB-66 Destroyer Douglas	2	J71-A-13 10,200lbs s.t.	1954	83,000	7,000'+	294
Air Defense F-101B/F Voodoo McDonnell	2	J57-PW-55 10,700lbs s.t. 16,900lbs with a.b.	1957	45,664	3,000'	480
F-102A Delta Dagger Convair	1	J57-PW-23 11,700lbs s.t 17,200lbs with a.b.	1953	31,500	3,000'	906
F-104C Starfighter Lockheed	1	J79-GE-7 10,000lbs s.t. 15,800lbs with a.b.	1954	27,853	6,000'	663
F-106A Delta Dart Convair	1	J75-PW-17 17,200lbs s.t. 24,500lbs with a.b.	1956	38,250	3,000'	340
U.S. Navy F3H Demon McDonnell	1	J71-A-2E 9,500lbs s.t. 14,250 with a.b.	1951	39,000		522
F4D Skyray Douglas	1	J57-P-8B 10,200lbs s.t. 16,000 with a.b.	1951	30,000		422
A3D Skywarrior Douglas	2	J57-PW-10 10,500lbs s.t. 12,400lbs wet	1952	82,000		282
A4E Skyhawk Douglas	1	J52-PW-6A 8,500lbs s.t.	1954	24,500		2,960
F-8E Crusader Chance Vought	1	J57-PW-20A 10,700lbs s.t. 18,000lbs with a.b.	1955	34,000		925

Abbreviations
s.t. = Static Thrust
with a.b. = with after burner
wet = using water/alcohol injection to increase thrust
T.O. Weight with bomb load if applicable
A - Allison
GE - General Electric
PW - Pratt & Whitney
W- Wright

Notes
Production quantities shown are for all models, including test aircraft and Military Assistance Programs.

First flight is for the initial prototype.

The J71 engine powered the A/B/C models of the Snark (SM-62) cruise missile. Was replaced with the J57 engine in the SM-62D model.

Take-off ground runs for air force aircraft are at sea level. Distance is longer if aircraft is to clear 50' obstacle off end of runway. T.O. runs increase with altitude and temperature, requiring download of weapons and/or fuel. N/A for Navy aircraft which are catapult launched from carriers.

RB-57D production quantity of 20 is part of total production run of 403 B-57 aircraft.

It is worth noting that the J40 Westinghouse turbojet failure had a significant cascade effect on several other aircraft programs at the time, including the B-66 aircraft.

Sources
The World's Fighting Planes, William Green, Doubleday, NY, 1965; Post-World War II Bombers, Marcelle Size Knaack, Office of Air Force History, Washington, D.C., 1988; Post-World War II Fighters 1945-1973, Marcelle Size Knaack, Office of Air Force History, Washington, D.C., 1986; American Military Aircraft, Barnes&Noble Books, New York, 2005. Combat Aircraft of the World, John W. R. Taylor, Putnam, New York, 1969.

Appendix 3
B-66 Squadrons 1956 - 1974

B-66 Squadrons

1954-55

Test and evaluation was principally conducted at Edwards AFB, CA, Wright-Patterson AFB, OH, and Eglin AFB, FL. First flight of an RB-66A - June 28,1954. Two RB-66Bs flew in March 1956 from Tucson, AZ, to Crestview, FL, at an average ground speed of 700mph. Placard restrictions limit the aircraft to mach .95 at altitudes above 5,000 feet. The B-66 was not designed to be a supersonic aircraft.

1956

9TRS (E&W)	363TRW	RB-66C	Shaw AFB, SC	From RB-26
First RB-66C, 54-0452, delivered to Shaw AFB, SC, May 11 (*City of Sumter*)				
16TRS (NP)	363TRW	RB-66B	Shaw AFB, SC	From RB-57A
First RB-66B, 53-0442, delivered to Shaw AFB, SC, January 31				
34BS (T)	17BG	B-66B	Hurlburt Field, FL	From B-57A
37BS (T)	17BG	B-66B	Hurlburt Field, FL	From B-26
First B-66B delivered to Hurlburt Field, FL, March 16				
41TRS (NP)	432TRW	RB-66B	Shaw AFB, SC	From RB-26
42TRS (E&W)	10TRG	RB-66C	Spangdahlem AB, GE	From RB-26
First RB-66C, 54-0459, delivered to Spangdahlem AB, Ger, Nov 28 (*Kreis Wittlich*)				
43TRS (NP)	432TRW	RB-66B	Shaw AFB, SC	From RB-57A
95BS (T)	17BG	B-66B	Hurlburt Field, FL	From B-26

1957

1TRS (NP)	10TRW	RB-66B	Spangdahlem AB, GE	From RB-57A
9TRS (E&W)	363TRW	R/WB-66C/D	Shaw AFB, SC	From WT-33A
First WB-66D, 55-0391, delivered to Shaw AFB, SC, June 26				
11TRS (E&W)	67TRW	R/WB-66C/D	Yokota AB, JP	
Five RB-66Cs delivered in June, last of 12 delivered Aug 10				
12TRS (NP)	67TRW	RB-66B	Yokota AB, JP	
First RB-66Bs delivered in February				
16TRS (NP)	363TRG	RB-66B	Shaw AFB, SC	
19TRS	66TRW	RB-66B	RAF Sculthorpe, UK	From RB-45C
First RB-66B arrives at RAF Sculthorpe Feb 3/to 66TRW as of Jan 1				
30TRS (NP)	66TRW	RB-66B	Sembach AB, GE	From RB-57A
First RB-66B delivered to 66TRW, Landstuhl AB, Ger, July 7				

Squadron	Aircraft	Wing	Location	Notes
34BS (T)	B-66B	17BW	Hurlburt Field, FL	
37BS (T)	B-66B	17BW	Hurlburt Field, FL	
41TRS (NP)	RB-66B	432TRW	Shaw AFB, SC	RN Dec 8
42TRS (E&W)	R/WB-66C/D	*10TRW*	Spangdahlem AB, GE	
43TRS (NP)	RB-66B	432TRW	Shaw AFB, SC	
95BS (T)	B-66B	17BW	Hurlburt Field, FL	

1958

Squadron	Aircraft	Wing	Location	Notes
1TRS (NP)	RB-66B	10TRW	Spangdahlem AB, GE	From RB-57A
9TRS (E&W)	R/WB-66C/D	363TRW*	Shaw AFB, SC	Jan 8 to 10TRW
11TRS (E&W)	R/WB-66C/D	67TRW	Yokota AB, JP	Jan 8 to 10TRW
12TRS (NP)	RB-66B	67TRW	Yokota AB, JP	Jan–Mar/IA Jun 25
16TRS (NP)	RB-66B	363TRW*	Shaw AFB, SC	May/IA Jun 25
19TRS	RB-66B	10TRW	RAF Sculthorpe, UK	
30TRS (NP)	RB-66B	10TRW	Spangdahlem AB, GE	
34BS (T)	B-66B	17BW	RAF Sculthorpe, UK	
37BS (T)	B-66B	17BW	RAF Alconbury, UK	
41TRS (NP)	RB-66B	363TRW*	Shaw AFB, SC	
42TRS (E&W)	R/WB-66C/D	10TRW	Spangdahlem AB, GE	
43TRS (NP)	RB-66B	363TRW*	Shaw AFB, SC	
84BS (T)	B-66B	47BW	RAF Sculthorpe, UK	From B-45

First B-66B delivered to 47BW, RAF Sculthorpe, Jan 18

Squadron	Aircraft	Wing	Location	Notes
85BS (T)	B-66B	47BW	RAF Sculthorpe, UK	From B-45
86BS (T)	B-66B	47BW	RAF Alconbury, UK	From B-45
95BS (T)	B-66B	17BW	RAF Sculthorpe, UK	

IA Jun 25

*837 Air Division activated Feb 8 with 363TRW (RB-66) and 432TRW (RF-101)

1959

Squadron	Aircraft	Wing	Location	Notes
1TRS (NP)	RB-66B	10TRS	Spangdahlem AB, GE	As of Aug 25
9TRS (E&W)	R/WB-66C/D	363TRW*	RAF Alconbury, UK	
11TRS (E&W)	R/WB-66C/D	67TRW	Shaw AFB, SC	
12TRS (NP)	RB-66B	67TRW	Yokota AB, JP	
16TRS (NP)	RB-66B	363TRW*	Yokota AB, JP	As of Jan 10
19TRS	RB-66B	10TRW	Shaw AFB, SC	As of Aug 25
			Spangdahlem AB, GE	
			RAF Bruntingthorpe, UK	

Squadron	Wing/AD	Aircraft	Location	Status
30TRS (NP)	10TRW	RB-66B	Spangdahlem AB, GE	As of Aug 25
41TRS (NP)	363TRW*	RB-66B	RAF Alconbury, UK	IA May 18
			Shaw AFB, SC	becomes 4415CCTG
42TRS (E&W)	10TRW	R/WB-66C/D	Spangdahlem AB, GE	As of Aug 25
			RAF Chelveston, UK	IA May 18
43TRS (NP)	363TRW*	RB-66B	Shaw AFB, SC	
84BS (T)**	47BW	B-66B	RAF Sculthorpe, UK	
85BS (T)**	47BW	B-66B	RAF Sculthorpe, UK	
86BS (T)**	47BW	B-66B	*RAF Sculthorpe, UK*	As of Aug 5
4411CCTG	837AD*	RB-66B	Shaw AFB, SC	AC April 8
4415CCTG	*837AD**	*RB-66B*	Shaw AFB, SC	AC April 8

*837AD reorganizes - 432TRW and 41TRS/43TRS inactivate May 18.

20TRS/29TRS (RF-101) transfer to 363TRW. 4411CCTG/4415CCTG activate April 8 directly under 837AD.

**13 B-66B ECM-configured bombers (*Brown Cradle*), return to 47BW in November after participating in Exercise Wexval II against U.S. Navy.

1960

Squadron	Wing/AD	Aircraft	Location	Status
1TRS (NP)	10TRW	RB-66B	RAF Alconbury, UK	
9TRS (E&W)	363TRW	R/WB-66C/D	Shaw AFB, SC	
11TRS (E&W)	67TRW	R/WB-66C/D	Yokota AB, JP	IA Mar 8
12TRS (NP)	67TRW	RB-66B	Yokota AB, JP	IA Mar 8
16TRS (NP)	363TRW	RB-66B	Shaw AFB, SC	
19TRS	10TRW	RB-66B	RAF Bruntingthorpe, UK	
30TRS (NP)	10TRW	RB-66B	RAF Alconbury, UK	
42TRS (E&W)	10TRW	RB-66B/C*	RAF Chelveston, UK	
84BS (T)	47BW	B-66B	RAF Sculthorpe, UK	
85BS (T)	47BW	B-66B	RAF Sculthorpe, UK	
86BS (T)	47BW	B-66B	RAF Sculthorpe, UK	
4411CCTG	837AD	RB-66B	Shaw AFB, SC	
4415CCTG	837AD	RB-66B	Shaw AFB, SC	

*13 B-66B Brown Cradle ECM aircraft from 47BW replace 12 WB-66Ds.

1961

Squadron	Wing/AD	Aircraft	Location	Status
1TRS (NP)	10TRW	RB-66B	RAF Alconbury, UK	
9TRS (E&W)	363TRW	R/WB-66C/D	Shaw AFB, SC	
16TRS (NP)	363TRW	RB-66B	Shaw AFB, SC	

Unit	Wing/Cmd	Aircraft	Location	Notes
19TRS	10TRW	RB-66B	RAF Bruntingthorpe, UK	
30TRS (NP)	10TRW	RB-66B	RAF Alconbury, UK	
42TRS (E&W)	10TRW	RB-66B/C	RAF Chelveston, UK	
84BS (T)	47BW	B-66B	RAF Sculthorpe, UK	
85BS (T)	47BW	B-66B	RAF Sculthorpe, UK	
86BS (T)	47BW	B-66B	RAF Sculthorpe, UK	
4411CCTG	837AD	RB-66B	Shaw AFB, SC	
4415CCTG	837AD	RB-66B	Shaw AFB, SC	

1962

Unit	Wing/Cmd	Aircraft	Location	Notes
1TRS (NP)	10TRW	RB-66B	RAF Alconbury, UK	
9TRS (E&W)	363TRW	R/WB-66C/D	Shaw AFB, SC	
16TRS (NP)	363TRW	RB-66B	Shaw AFB, SC	
Deployed to MacDill AFB 10/22 to 11/30 during Cuban Missile Crisis				
19TRS	10TRW	RB-66B	RAF Bruntingthorpe, UK	To Aug 1
			Toul-Rosieres AB, FR	To Aug 1
30TRS (NP)	10TRW	RB-66B	RAF Alconbury, UK	
42TRS (E&W)	10TRW	RB-66B/C	RAF Chelveston, UK	
			Toul-Rosieres AB, FR	
84BS (T)	47BW	B-66B	RAF Sculthorpe, UK	IA Jun 22
85BS (T)	47BW	B-66B	RAF Sculthorpe, UK	IA Jun 22
86BS (T)	47BW	B-66B	RAF Sculthorpe, UK	IA Jun 22
4411CCTG	837AD	RB-66B	Shaw AFB, SC	IA Jan 31, 1963
4415CCTG	837AD	RB-66B	Shaw AFB, SC	IA Jan 31, 1963

1963

Unit	Wing/Cmd	Aircraft	Location	Notes
1TRS (NP)	10TRW	RB-66B	RAF Alconbury, UK	
9TRS (E&W)	363TRW	R/WB-66C/D	Shaw AFB, SC	
16TRS (NP)	363TRW	RB-66B	Shaw AFB, SC	
19TRS	10TRW	RB-66B	Toul-Rosieres AB, FR	
30TRS (NP)	10TRW	RB-66B	RAF Alconbury, UK	
42TRS (E&W)	10TRW	RB-66B/C	Toul-Rosieres AB, FR	
4411CCTG	*TARC*	RB-66B	Shaw AFB, SC	May-Oct at Chambley AC Feb 1/was 837AD
4415CCTG	*TARC*	RB-66B	Shaw AFB, SC	AC Feb 1
4416TS	*TARC*	RB-66B	Shaw AFB, SC	AC Feb 1

1964

Unit	Wing	Aircraft	Location	Notes
1TRS (NP)	10TRW	RB-66B	RAF Alconbury, UK	
9TRS (E&W)	363TRW	R/WB-66C/D	Shaw AFB, SC	To RF-4C
16TRS (NP)	363TRW	RB-66B	Shaw AFB, SC	
19TRS	10TRW	RB-66B	Toul-Rosieres AB, FR	
30TRS (NP)	10TRW	RB-66B	RAF Alconbury, UK	
42TRS (E&W)	10TRW	RB-66B/C	Toul-Rosieres AB, FR	
4487TS	4485TW	RB-66B/C	Eglin AFB, FL	AC Aug 4
4411CCTG	TARC	RB-66B	Shaw AFB, SC	
4415CCTG	TARC	RB-66B	Shaw AFB, SC	To RF-4C
4416TS	TARC	RB-66B/Other	Shaw AFB, SC	

1965

Unit	Wing	Aircraft	Location	Notes
1TRS (NP)	10TRW	RB-66B	RAF Alconbury, UK	To RF-4C May
9TRS	363TRW	RB-66B/C	Shaw AFB, SC	WB-66D to DM
19TRS	10TRW	RB-66B	Toul-Rosieres AB, FR	As of Oct 1
	25TRG/W	RB-66B	Chambley AB, FR	To RF-4C
30TRS (NP)	10TRW	RB-66B	RAF Alconbury, UK	AC Jun 30
41TRS	363TRW	No AC	Hq TAC/Langley AFB	Nov 8 to Feb 66
	3557FW	RB-66C	Takhli RTAFB, TH	RN Jul 1, 65
42TRS (E)	10TRW	RB-66B/C	Toul-Rosieres AB, FR	As of Jul 1
	25TRG/W	RB-66B/C	Chambley AB, FR	
4411CCTG	TARC	RB-66B	Shaw AFB, SC	
4416TS	TARC	RB-66B/RF4	Shaw AFB, SC	
4487TS	4485TW	RB-66B/C	Eglin AFB, FL	IA 1965
Det 1/41TRS	33TACGP/6250CSG	RB-66B(4a/c)	Tan Son Nhut AB, SVN	As of April
Det 1/9TRS	363TRW	RB-66C(9a/c)	Tan Son Nhut AB, SVN	As of Apr 13

To Takhli RTAFB May 25

Unit	Wing	Aircraft	Location	Notes
6460TRS	*460TRW*		*Takhli RTAFB, TH*	As of Jul29 (was Det1, 9TRS)
Det 1/42TRS	*4327TRW*			AsofSep 18/IA Oct 25
	25TRW	RB-66B(5a/c)	Takhli RTAFB, TH	Brown Cradle

October 18, 1965 to January 1966

1966

Unit	Wing	Aircraft	Location	Notes
9TRS	363TRW	RB-66C	Shaw AFB, SC	To RF-4C
19TRS	25TRW	RB-66B	Chambley AB, FR	IA Aug 22
19TEWS*	363TRW	E/RB-66B/C	Shaw AFB, SC	As of Sep 1
41TRS	460TRW	EB-66C	Takhli RTAFB, TH	Feb 18
41TEWS*	432TRW			Sep 18 to 432TRW
42TRS (E)	25TRW	EB-66B/C	Chambley AB, FR	IA Aug 22
42TEWS	432TRW	EB-66B/C	Takhli RTAFB, TH	AC Dec 15
4411CCTG	TARC	RB-66B	Shaw AFB, SC	IA July 1
4411CCTG	363TRW			July 1 to 363TRW
4416TS	363TRW	RB-66B/F4	Shaw AFB, SC	AC Feb 1
4417CCTS	363TRW	E/RB-66B/C	Shaw AFB, SC	AC Jun 8
6460TRS**	460TRW	EB-66B	Takhli, RTAFB, TH	Sep 18 to 432TRW
	432TRW			IA Apr
Det 1/41TRS		RB-66B	Tan Son Nhut AB, SVN	Jan to Jun 1966
Det 2/42TRS	25TRW	RB-66B	Takhli RTAFB, TH	

*Redesignation from TRS to TEWS October 8. **IA Dec 15

1967

Unit	Wing	Aircraft	Location	Notes
19TEWS	363TRW	EB-66B/C	Shaw AFB, SC	
41TEWS	355TFW	EB-66B/C	Takhli RTAFB, TH	5 Aug to 355TFW
42TEWS*	355TFW	EB-66B/C	Takhli RTAFB, TH	5 Aug to 355TFW
4416CCTS	363TRW	E/RB-66B/C	Shaw AFB, SC	RN Jul 67
4417CCTS	363TRW	E/RB-66B/C	Shaw AFB, SC	

*Was 6460TRS

1968

Unit	Wing	Aircraft	Location	Notes
19TEWS*	363TRW	EB-66B/C	Shaw AFB, SC	
41TEWS**	355TFW	EB-66B/C/E	Takhli RTAFB, TH	
42TEWS***	355TFW	EB-66B/C/E	Takhli RTAFB, TH	
4416CCTS	363TRW	E/RB-66B/E	Shaw AFB, SC	
4417CCTS	363TRW	E/RB-66B/C	Shaw AFB, SC	

*Six EB-66C/E aircraft deployed Feb 68 to Osan, then Itazuke, JP, *Operation Combat Fox*, in response to the capture of *USS Pueblo* by North Korea.
**Effective 17 April 41/42TEWS UE aircraft increased from 28 to 41.

Year / Squadron	Wing	Aircraft	Base	Notes
1969				
19TEWS	*18TFW*	EB-66C/E	Itazuke AB, JP	As of Dec 31, 68
			Kadena AB, JP	As of May 15
39TEWS	36TFW	EB-66C/E	Spangdahlem AB, GE	AC Apr 1
39TRTS	363TRW	R/EB-66B/C/E	Shaw AFB, SC	AC Oct 15/was 4417
41TEWS	355TFW	EB-66C/E	Takhli RTAFB, TH	IA Oct 31
42TEWS	355TFW	EB-66C/E	Takhli RTAFB, TH	IA Oct 31
4416CCTS	363TRW	E/RB-66B/C	Shaw AFB, SC	IA Oct 15
4417CCTS	363TRW	E/RB-66B/C	Shaw AFB, SC	
1970				
19TEWS	18TFW	EB-66C/E	Kadena AB, JP	IA Oct 31
39TEWS	36TFW	BE-66C/E	Spangdahlem AB, GE	AC
39TEWTS	363TRW	BE-66E	Shaw AFB, SC	RN Feb 15 was 39TRTS
355TFW	355TFW	BE-66C/E	Takhli RTAFB, TH	To Sep 22
42TEWS	*388TFW*	EB-66C/E	*Korat RTAFB, TH*	As of Sep 21
1971				
39TEWS	36TFW	EB-66C/E	Spangdahlem AB, GE	
39TEWTS	363TRW	EB-66C/E	Shaw AFB, SC	
42TEWS	388TFW	EB-66C/E	Korat RTAFB, TH	
1972				
39TEWS	*527FW*	EB-66C/E	Spangdahlem AB, GE	Effective Jan 1
39TEWTS	363TRW	EB-66C/E	Shaw AFB, SC	
42TEWS	388TFW	EB-66C/E	Korat RTAFB, TH	
1973				
39TEWS	52TFW	EB-66C/E	Spangdahlem AB, GE	IA Jan 1
39TEWTS	363TRW	EB-66C/E	Shaw AFB, SC	
42TEWS	388TFW	EB-66E/C	Korat RTAFB, TH	Dec 24 final mission
1974				
39TEWTS	363TRW	EB-66C/E	Shaw AFB, SC	IA Mar 15
42TEWS	388TFW	EB-66E/C	Korat RTAFB, TH	IA Mar 15

Abbreviations:

AD = Air Division
RN = Renamed
AC = Activated
IA = Inactivated
BW = Bombardment Wing
E&W = Electronics & Weather
NP = Night Photo
TFW = Tactical Fighter Wing
TS = Test Squadron
TAC = Tactical Air Command
TARC = Tactical Air Reconnaissance Center
RD = Redeployed
TRW = Tactical Reconnaissance Wing
TRS = Tactical Reconnaissance Squadron
TRG = Tactical Reconnaissance Group
TEWS = Tactical Electronic Warfare Squadron
TEWTS = Tactical Electronic Warfare Training Squadron
TRTS = Tactical Replacement Training Squadron
CCTS = Combat Crew Training Squadron
CCTG = Combat Crew Training Group

Sources:

Wing/Squadron Histories; air crew orders; *50th Anniversary, Shaw AFB, SC, 1941-1991*, 363TFW, Office of History, Shaw AFB, SC, 1991. Active Air Force Bases Within the United States, Volume I, Robert Mueller, Office of Air Force History, Washington DC, 1989. Historical Highlights: US Air Forces in Europe, 1945-1979, Office of History, USAFE, APO 09012, November 28, 1980. USAF Management Summary, Southeast Asia Review, 1961-1972, 31 Jan 1973. CINCPAC msg 170415Z Apr 68.

Appendix 4
Significant Events of the Vietnam War

1945

08 May: VE Day.

02 Sep: Ho Chi Minh and the Viet Minh proclaim the independent Republic of Vietnam, the day the Japanese sign surrender documents on the USS Missouri. When the French attempt to reestablish colonial rule the Viet Minh begin guerilla warfare.

1946

06 Mar: France recognizes Vietnam as an independent republic within the French union however, Ho Chi Minh and the Viet Minh insist on independence.

23 Nov: French bomb Haiphong killing 6,000 - the war begins in earnest for both the French and the Viet Minh.

1950

00 Jan: Viet Minh recognized by Communist China and the Soviet Union.

1954

10 Feb: President Eisenhower warns of U.S. involvement in Vietnam, rejecting requests by the French to intervene.

07 Apr: President Eisenhower speaks of 'dominoes falling' at a news conference.

07 May: Dien Bien Phu falls to Viet Minh. Decisive defeat. Battle began on Nov 20, 1953. Over 95,000 French soldiers died in the struggle for Vietnam.

21 Jul: Vietnam partitioned in Geneva into North and South at the 17th parallel. Cambodia and Laos recognized as independent states. US provides economic and military aid to the South, accepts but does not sign accords.

11 Oct: Viet Minh take control of North Vietnam.

1955

12 Feb: First U.S. military advisors sent to SVN. North supports continues insurrection by Viet Cong in the South from 1955 to 1961.

1961

00 000: Bernard Fall publishes *Street Without Joy.*

10 Mar: National Front for Liberation of South Vietnam announces guerilla offensive against SVN to prevent elections scheduled for 9 April.

00 May: U.S. Army deploys radio direction finding teams to SVN.

20 Oct: Four RF-101C reconnaissance aircraft from 363TRW arrive at Tan Son Nhut Air Base, SVN.

14 Nov: Operation Farmgate - Det 2A, 4400CCTS, arrives at Tan Son Nhut and Bien Hoa Air Bases with 16 T-28/C-47/B-26 aircraft.

1962

02 Feb: First American fixed wing aircraft, C-123, lost in SVN. (Air Force combat and operational losses between 1962-1972 total 2,236 aircraft)

08 Oct: 2nd Air Division established at Tan Son Nhut Air Base.

1963

08 Apr*: Captains Mitchell and Campaigne, former RB-66 flyers from Shaw AFB, KIA when their Bien Hoa based B-26 lost a wing on a strafing run.*

01 Nov: President Diem assassinated.

1964

08 June: Six F-100s arrive TDY at Takhli RTAFB, Thailand.

02 Aug: Destroyer USS Maddox engages NVN torpedo boats in Gulf of Tonkin.

04 Aug: USS Turner Joy and USS Maddox report engagement with NVN vessels; attack disputed; no evidence it ever took place.

05 Aug: Operation Pierce Arrow - 7th Fleet aircraft from USS Ticonderoga and USS Constellation bomb NVN torpedo boat bases.

20 B-57 aircraft from 8BS (Yellow Birds) and 13BS (Red Birds) deploy from Clark, PI, to Bien Hoa. Two a/c collide on landing. Others land at Tan Son Nhut, one crashes.

One squadron of 18 F-105s deploys from Japan to Korat RTAFB, Thailand.

07 Aug: Congress passes Gulf of Tonkin Resolution.

01 Nov: Vietcong mortar attack at Bien Hoa destroys 5 B-57 aircraft.

1965

20 Jan: Lyndon B. Johnson is sworn in as president of the United States.

07 Jan: NVN forms first SAM unit - 236th SAM Regiment.

07 Feb: President Johnson approves Operation Flaming Dart, air strikes by Navy aircraft against targets in the Dong Hoi area of North Vietnam.

12 Feb: B-52Fs arrive at Andersen Air Base, Guam.

02 Mar: Beginning of Operation Rolling Thunder. Limited to targets in NVN below 20 degrees North Latitude.

First air force aircraft downed over NVN (3 F-105s/2 F-100s); first Air Force pilot captured - Captain Hayden J. Lockhart.

08 Mar: 3,500 Marines arrive at Da Nang - 1st US ground forces in Vietnam.

04 Apr: First loss of U.S. aircraft to MiGs over NVN (2 F-105s downed by MiG-17s attacking the Than Hoa bridge).

25 Apr: *Four IR equipped RB-66Bs arrive at Tan Son Nhut Air Base, SVN.*

03 May: First Army troops arrive - 3,500 men of the 173rd Airborne Brigade.

12 May: **First bombing pause**.

16 May: B-57B explodes at Bien Hoa. Secondary explosions destroy 10 B-57Bs, 11 VNAF Skyraiders and one F-8 Crusader.

18 May: Rolling Thunder Phase II begins. Targets gradually expanded north - except for 30 mile buffer along Chinese border and 30/10 mile Hanoi/Haiphong buffer.

17 Jun: 2 MiG-17s downed by Navy F-4Bs.

18 Jun: 27 B-52Fs carrying 51 750-lb bombs each fly the 1st *Arc Light* mission against a target near Saigon, SVN. 2 B-52s collide enroute and crash.

30 Jun: *41TRS activated at Takhli, Thailand.*

00 Jun: B-57Bs move to Da Nang, assigned to 35TFW.

10 Jul: 2 MiG-17s downed by F-4Cs from 45TFS/2Air Div - first Air Force MiG kills of war. (Holcombe/Clark & Roberts/Andersen)

24 Jul: *RB-66C intercepts first Fan Song SA-2 radar NW of Hanoi in a morning mission.*
First Air Force aircraft (F-4C) downed that afternoon by same SA-2 battery.

27 Jul: First attack on SA-2 site by F-105s; flack trap; six F-105s lost.

13 Aug: General John P. McConnell, USAF Chief of Staff, forms Anti-SAM task force.

31 Aug: President Johnson signs law outlawing draft card burning.

22 Oct: *RB-66B lost on low level IR mission out of Tan Son Nhut. First combat loss of B-66 aircraft.*

07 Nov: 236 SAM regiment nearly destroyed with loss of 2 of its 4 SA-2 fire battalions and its technical support battalion.

28 Nov: *4 F-100F Wild Weasels from Korat fly orientation flights with EB-66C.*

20 Dec: First F-100F Wild Weasel aircraft lost to AAA. Two additional F-100Fs arrive.

22 Dec: Wild Weasels kill first SAM site.

25 Dec: **Second bombing pause** lasting 37 days, to January 31.

1966

08 Jan: U.S. troop level in SVN - 190,000.

31 Jan: Rolling Thunder Phase III - limited to 300 strikes a day below 20 degrees North Latitude. US aircraft attack after 37 day bombing pause.

00 Jan: *NVN moves 4 SA-2 battalions, 24 launchers, NW of Hanoi to ambush RB-66C.*

25 Feb: *RB-66C 54-457 damaged by SA-2 near Vinh. Crashes in Gulf of Tonkin - 1 fatality.*

31 Mar: Rolling Thunder Phase IV - all of NVN released except for certain sanctuaries.

00 Mar: *RB-66Bs begin Pathfinder missions.*

01 Apr: 7th Air Force established at Tan Son Nhut; 2nd Air Division inactivated.

12 Apr: First B-52D Arc Light strike against NVN, Mu Gia Pass. The B-52D, modified in 1965 to carry 108 500lb bombs or 66 750lb bombs, replaced the B-52F.

26 Apr: *MiG-21s launch attacks against EB-66 aircraft. First MiG-21 downed by F-4C.*
480TFS/35TFW (Gilmore/Smith)

29 Apr: US troop level in SVN - 250,000.

12 May: *EB-66C attacked by MiG-17s; one MiG downed by F-4C escort.*
390TFS/35TFW (Dudley/Kringelis)

29 Jun: *Attacks on Hanoi/Haiphong authorized. EB-66Bs supporting strike force violate China buffer zone.*

20 July: *EB-66C 54-464 shot down by two SA-2 Guideline missiles near Thai Nguyen. One fatality.*

20 Aug: *EB-66C 54-475 from 41TRS, Takhli, crashes near Hawaii, 3 fatalities.*

00 Sep: QRC-160 ECM pods tested successfully at Eglin.

26 Sep: First use of QRC-160 by Takhli F-105s.

00 Oct: 8 and 13BS, B-57, move to Phan Rang, SVN.
Soviet Union announces it will provide military assistance to North Vietnam.

01 Nov: SAC authorizes 600 B-52 Arc Light sorties per month.

05 Nov: *EB-66C attacked by MiG-21s - both MiGs shot down by F-4C escorts.*
480TFS/366TFW (Tuck/Rabeni & Latham/Klause)

14 Dec: First loss of Air Force aircraft, F-105, to Mig-21.

24-25 Dec**: Third bombing pause**.

1967

02 Jan: Operation Bolo, led by Colonel Robin Olds of 8th TFW. 7 MiG-21s shot down.

05 Jan: *2 MiG-21s attack 2 EB-66s. Driven off by F-4C fighter escort.*

06 Jan: F-4Cs from 8TFW down 2 more MiG-21s.

01 Feb: SAC increases B-52 Arc Light sorties to 800 per month.

04 Feb: *EB-66C 55-387 downed by SA-2 SAM north of Thai Nguyen. 3 fatalities.*

08-15 Feb**: Fourth bombing pause** - Lunar New Year; TET.

19 Feb: Bernard Fall, author of *Street Without Joy* dies on the road he wrote about.

26 Apr: *NVN unable to cope with EB-66 ECM - shoot down own MiG-21; N. Korean pilots arrive to augment NVN air force.*

13 May: F-4Cs of 8TFW shoot down 2 MiG-17s.
F-105s of 355/388TFW shoot down 5 MiG-17s.

14 May: F-4Cs of 366TFW shoot down 3 MiG-17s.

20 May: F-4Cs of 366/8TFW shoot down 2 MiG-21s/4 MiG-17s.

07 Jul: Two B-52Ds collide over South China Sea. Six aircrew killed including MG William Crumm, 3AD/CC.

08 Jul: B-52D crashes attempting emergency landing at Da Nang. 5 KIA.

30 Sep: U.S. casualties exceed 100,000 (killed and wounded).

19 Oct: Air Force loses 1,000th fixed wing aircraft in SEA operations.

27 Oct: NVN moves most of its jet combat aircraft into southern China.

17 Nov: *EB-66C 54-473 crashes at Takhli. 5 fatalities.*

20 Nov: *MiGs attack EB-66 unsuccessfully.*

29 Nov: SecDef Robert McNamara resigns.

06 Dec: *EB-66C 54-462 crashes at Takhli. 3 fatalities.*

24-25 Dec**: Fifth bombing pause** - Christmas cease fire.

1968

01-02 Jan**: Sixth bombing pause**.

03 Jan: Rolling Thunder Phase V.

14 Jan: *EB-66C 55-388 shot down by MiG-21 west of Hanoi. 1 fatality.*

31 Jan: Beginning of Tet offensive in SVN by Viet Cong; lasts until 29 Feb.

00 Jan: 13BS, B-57, deactivated.

01 Feb: B-52 Arc Light missions increase from 800 to 1,200 a month.

15 Feb: B-52 Arc Light missions increase from 1,200 to 1,800 a month.

06 Mar: *EB-66E 54-524 crashes during refueling.*

31 Mar: President Johnson announces he will not seek a second term.

01 Apr**: President Johnson limits bombing** of NVN to area south of 19th parallel (Route Packs 1,2 & part of 3).

10 May: Peace talks begin in Paris.

23 May: *EB-66 attacked by MiG-21s over Gulf of Tonkin. Navy MiG-cap downs two.*

25 May: EA-6B EW aircraft makes first flight at Long Island.

01 Jul: General Creighton Abrams replaces General Westmoreland.

19 Jul: *EB-66B 53-491 crashes on landing at Takhli.*

01 Nov**: President Johnson halts air and naval attacks against NVN.** End of Operation Rolling Thunder.

1969

20 Jan: Richard Nixon becomes president of the United States.

08 Apr: *EB-66B 53-498 crashes on take-off at Takhli. 3 fatalities.*

08 May: National Liberation Front offers peace proposal in Paris.

24 Jun: *RB-66B 53-415 363TRW, Shaw AFB, loses engine during refueling. 1 fatality.*

02 Sep: Ho Chi Minh dies.

08 Jul: Redeployment of U.S. military personnel from SVN & Thailand begins.

00 Sep: 8BS, B-57, down to 9 aircraft; returned to DM. Of 94 B-57s assigned to SEA, 51 were lost in combat including 15 destroyed on the ground.

31 Oct: *41TEWS (EB-66C/E), Takhli RTAFB, Thailand, inactivated.*

24 Nov: F-105 tactical fighter squadrons (4) consolidated at Takhli.

00 Dec: Total US military deaths in SEA due to hostile action exceed 40,000.

1970

28 Jan: HH-53 helicopter attempting pick up of F-105 pilot is shot down over Laos by MiG-21 using air to air missiles. 1st MiG encounter since Nov '68 bombing halt.

20 Mar: B-52 Arc Light missions reduced to 1,400 a month.

28 Mar: Navy F-4J shoots down first MiG-21 since 1968 bombing halt.

21 Apr: *EB-66E 54-439 burns at Hickam AFB, HI.*

17 Aug: B-52 Arc Light missions reduced to 1,000 a month.

19 Sep: B-52 Arc Light operations consolidated at U-Tapao, Thailand.

22 Sep: *42TEWS moved to Korat from Takhli.*

00 Oct: F-105 squadrons redeploy from Takhli RTAFB, Thailand. 355TFW and its three squadrons inactivate;66 aircraft transferred to air national guard.

26 Oct: *EB-66C 54-384 crashes on landing at Korat.*

03 Nov: SA-2 sites photographed in vicinity of Mu Gia and Ban Karai Passes.

00 Nov: *Six EB-66 aircraft deploy from Shaw AFB to Korat to counter expanding threat to B-52s over Laos. (Total EB-66 count at Korat: 26)*

21 Nov: USAF and Army helicopters raid Son Tay POW camp near Hanoi - unsuccessful.

21 Nov: USAF and Navy aircraft strike suspected SAM and AAA sites in NVN south of 18 degrees North.

00 Nov: 6010TFS F-105 Wild Weasel activated at Korat.

1971

04 Mar: First SAM site confirmed in Laos, 2.5 miles west of Ban Karai Pass.

11 Mar: *EB-66C 55-389 crashes after take-off from Korat. Crew ejects.*

15 Mar: *Four additional EB-66s deploy from Shaw to Korat in support of B-52 operations. Total EB-66 aircraft at Korat: 30.*

22 Mar: F-4D shot down by SAM near Dong Hoi, NVN. First since Feb 68.

26 Apr: O-2 shot down by SA-2 over Laos, near Ban Karai Pass.

01 Jun: Arc Light sortie rate returns to 33/day. U-Tapao beddown decreases to 42 B-52s.

00 Jun: *Ten EB-66 aircraft deployed from TAC in support of B-52 ops return to CONUS. Number of EB-66s at Korat: 20.*

12 Nov: USAF strength in SVN 26,898.

17 Nov: *EB-66E 54-427 engine failure on run-up - a/c lost.*

22 Nov: *Three EB-66s arrive at Korat from Shaw AFB to replace 2 aircraft with wing cracks, and another destroyed when an engine exploded.*

1972

00 Jan: President announces military strength reduction in Vietnam from 139K to 69K by May 1.

02 Feb: *EB-66E 54-540 crashes on take-off.*

16 Feb: B-52 Arc Light strikes increase from 33 per day to 51 sorties per day.

  SA-2 sites move into DMZ - fire 81 missiles. F-4D shot down by SAM..

21 Feb: MiG-21 downed by F-4D, 555TFS/432TRW.

00 Mar: Contingency package of ALQ-101-4 ECM pods arrive at Udorn to counter possible introduction of SA-3 SAM.

01 Mar: MiG-21 downed by F-4D, 555TFS/432TRW.

28 Mar: AC-130A gunship downed by SA-2 over Laos - 14KIA.

30 Mar: MiG-21 downed by F-4D, 13TFS/432TRW

  NVN troops and armor cross DMZ into Quang Tri province (Spring Invasion).

31 Mar: AC-130E Pave Specter gunship downed by AAA over Laos. Crew of 15 recovered.

02 Apr: *EB-66C 54-466 shot down by SAM while supporting B-52 air strike near DMZ. 5 fatalities, one survivor.*

06 Apr: US aircraft authorized to strike targets in NVN to 20 degrees North Latitude (Operation Freedom Train).

09 Apr: 12 B-52s strike POL storage area and railyard in Vinh area, NVN.

12 Apr: 18 B-52s (Freedom Dawn) from U-Tapao, strike Bai Thuong AB, NVN.

15 Apr: 17 B-52s (Freedom Porch Bravo) from U-Tapao, strike POL area at Haiphong.

  F-105G shot down by SAM - 250 SA-2 missiles fired during raid.

16 Apr: Two MiG-21s downed by F-4Ds from 13TFS/432TRW

  One MiG-21 downed by F-4D, 523TFS/432TRW:

21 Apr: 18 B-52s (Freighter Captain) from U-Tapao, strike transshipment point near Than Hoa. One B-52 hit by SAM makes emergency landing at Da Nang. One F-4D lost to SAM.

23 Apr: F-4E downed by SAM near Dong Hoi.

27 Apr: 4 AF fighters releasing Paveway smart bombs knock down Than Hoa Bridge - previously 871 sorties using dumb bombs resulted in only superficial damage.

00 Apr: *PACAF requests 4 EB-66 replacement aircraft as additional EB-66 aircraft, crews and instructors from Shaw and Spangdahlem move to Korat for 90 days TDY (Constant Guard).*

  President announces reduction of military strength in SVN from 69,000 to 49,000 by 1 July.

08 May: Pres. Nixon authorizes mining of NVN ports and resumptions of air strikes throughout NVN; Navy A-6 Intruders mine Haiphong harbor May 9.

  MiG-19 downed by F-4D, 13TFS/432TRW

  MiG-21 downed by F-4D, 555TFS/432TRW

10 May: **Start of *Linebacker I*** - 8TFW F-4s put Paul Doumer Bridge out of action using smart bombs.

3 MiG-21s downed by F-4Ds, 555TFS/432TRW.

  F-4D and F-4E shot down by MiG-19s.

10 May: Lt Randy Cunningham and Lt(jg) Willie Driscoll, USN, shoot down three MiG-17s, then eject after being hit by SA-2, becoming 1st aces of war with two earlier kills on Jan 19 & May 8 (USS Constellation).

11 May: MiG-21 downed by F-4D - 555TFS/432TRW

  F-4D shot down by MiG-21.

12 May: MiG-19 downed by F-4D, 555TFS/432 TRW

18 May: F-4D shot down by MiG-19.

20 May: F-4D shot down by MiG-21.

23 May: MiG-19 downed by F-4E, 35TFS/366TFW

  MiG-21 downed by F-4E, 35TFS/366TFW

31 May: MiG-21 downed by F-4E, 13TFS/432TRW

  MiG-21 downed by F-4D, 555TFS/432TRW

02 Jun: MiG-19 downed by F-4E, 58TFS/432TRW

08 Jun: B-52s total 206 - largest SAC bomber force ever assembled in Western Pacific.

08-21 Jun: B-52s routinely strike targets in Route Pack 1, NVN.

13 Jun: F-4E shot down by MiG-21.

18 Jun: Third AC-130A gunship downed over Laos by SA-7 - 12KIA/3 survivors.

21 Jun: MiG-21 downed by F-4E, 469TFS/388TFW.
    F-4E shot down by MiG-21.

22 Jun: B-52s fly all time daily high of 111 sorties against 37 targets.

24 Jun: F-4E/F-4D shot down by MiG-21s.

27 June: Two F-4Es shot down by MiG-21s.

05 Jul: Two F-4Es shot down by MiG-21s.

08 Jul: MiG-21 downed by F-4E, 4TFS/366TFW.
    2 MiG-21s downed by F-4Es, 555TFS/432TRW
    F-4E downed by MiG-21.

18 Jul: MiG-21 downed by F-4D, 13TFS/432TRW.

24 Jul: F-4E shot down by MiG-21.

29 Jul: MiG-21 downed by F-4D, 13TFS/432TRW.
    MiG-21 downed by F-4E, 4TFS/366TFW
    F-4E shot down by MiG-21.

30 Jul: F-4D shot down by MiG-21.

00 Aug: ALQ-119 ECM pods shipped to SEA to counter possible SA-4 SAM threat.

12 Aug: MiG-21 downed by F-4E 58FS/432TRW (Richard/Ettel - USM/USN).

15 Aug: MiG-21 downed by F-4E 336TFS/8TFW

19 Aug: MiG-21 downed by F-4E 4TFS/366TFW

28 Aug: MiG-21 downed by F-4D 555TFS/432TRW

02 Sep: MiG-19 downed by F-4E 34/34TFS/388TFW

09 Sep: MiG-21 downed by F-4D 555TFS/432TRW
    2 MiG-19s downed by F-4Ds 555TFS/432TRW

11 Sep: MiG-21 downed by F-4J (Cummings/Lasseter); only USMC MiG kill.
    F-4E shot down by MiG-21.

12 Sep: 2 MiG-21s downed by F-4Es 35TFS/388TFW
    MiG-21 downed by F-4D 469TFS/388TFW
    F-4E shot down by MiG-21.

16 Sep: MiG-21 downed by F-4E 555TFS/432TRW

05 Oct: MiG-21 downed by F-4E 34TFS/388TFW
    F-4D shot down by MiG-21.

06 Oct: MiG-19 downed by F-4E 34TFS/388TFW
    F-4E shot down by MiG-21.

08 Oct: MiG-21 downed by F-4E 35TFS/388TFW

12 Oct: MiG-21 downed by F-4D 555TFS/432TRW
    F-4E shot down by MiG-21.

13 Oct: MiG-21 downed by F-4D 13TFS/432TRW

15 Oct: MiG-21 downed by F-4E 307TFS/432TRW
    MiG-21 downed by F-4E 34TFS/388TFW
    MiG-21 downed by F-4D 523TFS/432TRW

22 Oct: *Linebacker I* **ends - USAF flew 9,315 sorties over North Vietnam; 2,750 SA-2 missiles were fired resulting in loss of 46 aircraft (60 SA-2/aircraft vs 18 SA-2/aircraft in 1965)**

11 Nov: CINCSAC personally designates missions scheduled into high threat areas of NVN Route Packages 2, 3 and 4.

22 Nov: First B-52 lost to SAM near Vinh, crew ejects successfully over Thailand.

18 Dec: Paris peace negotiations stall.
    Linebacker II begins - 129 B-52s attack targets in Hanoi area - 3 B-52s lost to SAMs. One B-52 reaches Thailand where crew ejects successfully.

MiG-21 downed by B-52D 307SW

19 Dec: 93 B-52s hit targets in Hanoi area - 1 B-52 hit by SAM, recovers at Nam Phong, Thailand.

20 Dec: 99 B-52s attack targets in Hanoi area - 6 B-52s lost to SAMs. Crews of two eject over Laos and Thailand.

21 Dec: 30 B-52s attack Hanoi - 2 B-52s lost to SAMs.

MiG-21 downed by F-4D 555TFS/432TRW
22 Dec: 30 B-52s attack Haiphong - no losses.
    MiG-21 downed by F-4D 555TFS/432TRW.
23 Dec: 30 B-52s attack Haiphong - no losses.
    EB-66E 54-529 crashes on returning from a Linebacker support mission. 3 fatalities.
24 Dec: 30 B-52s attack Hanoi - no losses.
    MiG-21 downed by B-52D 307SW
26 Dec: 120 B-52s attack Hanoi/Haiphong - 2 B-52s lost to SAMs
27 Dec: 60 B-52s attack Hanoi - 2 B-52s lost to SAMs
    F-4E shot down by MiG-21.
28 Dec: 60 B-52s attack Hanoi/Haiphong - no losses.
    MiG-21 downed by F-4D 555TFS/432TRW
    F-4E shot down by MiG-21 - last US aircraft lost to MiGs.
29 Dec*: **Linebacker II ends**.* Paris negotiations resume on January 8, 1973. (Total of 27 USAF aircraft lost in Linebacker II; 15 B-52s).

1973
03 Jan: B-52D hit by SA-2 near Vinh, abandoned over water near Da Nang.
07 Jan: MiG-21 downed by F-4D 4TFS/432TRW (Howman/Kullman) - last of 137 confirmed USAF aerial victories.
13 Jan: B-52D damaged by SA-2 during Arc Light raid lands at Da Nang. Scrapped.
15 Jan: **Suspension of offensive operations against NVN.**
28 Jan: Paris negotiated cease fire becomes effective.
29 Jan: Last combat missions flown in South Vietnam.
12 Feb: Start of Operation Homecoming - return of 591 POWs.
21 Feb: Laotion cease fire signed.
17 Apr: Last B-52 Arc Light strikes into Laos.
03 May*: EB-66E 54-445 ground accident, Class 26 - last B-66 loss.*
16 Jun: Last American aircraft lost to enemy action, F-4E, while flying over Cambodia.
15 Aug: Last Air Force bombing mission flown by A-7Ds attacking targets in Cambodia.
    Cambodian cease fire agreement signed. War in Southeast Asia ends.
15 Sep: Laotion peace agreement signed. Overflight of Laos by US aircraft prohibited.
24 Dec: EB-66C of 42TEWS, 388TFW, Korat RTAFB, Thailand, flies last operational ELINT mission of Vietnam War.

1974
02 Jan: First four EB-66 aircraft flown to Clark Air Base, PI, for 'operational salvage.'
17 Jan: Last four of 20 EB-66 aircraft flown from Korat RTAFB to Clark Air Base.
15 Mar: 42TEWS and 39TEWTS, last two EB-66 squadrons, formally inactivated.

1975
30 Apr: Saigon captured by NVN forces.

Note: USAF airmen were given official credit for the downing of 137 enemy aircraft (MiG-17/19/21) between 1965 and 1973. There were many more kills claimed but disallowed due to insufficient data to positively confirm such claims. 73 Air Force fixed wing aircraft were lost to MiGs, including one EB-66C; 99 fixed wing Air Force aircraft were lost to SA-2 surface to air missiles, including 17 B-52 heavy bombers and four EB-66C electronic warfare aircraft.

Sources: USAF Management Summary - Southeast Asia in Review 1961 - 1972, Headquarters USAF, Washington, D.C. January 1973. U.S. Air Force Combat Victory Credits Southeast Asia, Office of Air Force History, Hq USAF, March 1974. Aces & Aerial Victories, The United States Air Force in Southeast Asia 1965-1973, Office of Air Force History, Hq USAF, 1976. Air Force Magazine, December 2003, Up From Kitty Hawk; and September 2005 issue, The Air Force and the Cold War: A Chronology, 1945-91. Vietnam Air Losses by Chris Hobson, Midland Publishing, 2001. Development of Strategic Air Command 1946-1976, Office of the SAC Historian, 1976. The Encyclopedia of Military History, Ernest & Trevor Dupuy, 1970.

Appendix 5
B-66 Combat Losses and Major Accidents

Over the span of the aircraft's service life from 1954 to 1974 a total of 51 aircraft were downed by enemy action, crashed from a variety of causes, or were so severely damaged that they were written off by the Air Force as total losses (Class 26). This is the complete listing of losses experienced by all versions of the 294 B/RB/WB-66A/B/C/D aircraft built by the Douglas Aircraft Corporation. The prefix EB took the place of RB in October 1966 for aircraft with a SIGINT/ELINT/ESM/ECM function.

Summary of Aircraft Losses

S/N	Type	Date	Org	Base
54-0497	B-66B	10/06/56	17BW/34BS	Hurlburt Field, FL
54-0493	B-66B	04/01/57	17BW/95BS	Hurlburt Field, FL
53-0410	RB-66B	04/11/57	363TRW/43TRS	Shaw AFB, SC
54-0428	RB-66B	07/18/57	67TRW/12TRS	Yokota AB, Jap
54-0495	B-66B	09/03/57	17BW/95BS	Hurlburt Field, FL
54-0517	RB-66B	12/16/57	10TRW/1TRS	Spangdahlem AB, Ger
55-0314	B-66B	03/30/58	47BW/84BS	RAF Sculthorpe, UK
54-0422	RB-66B	04/14/58	10TRW/19TRS	RAF Sculthorpe, UK
54-0433	RB-66B	07/03/58	10TRW/19TRS	RAF Sculthorpe, UK
54-0444	RB-66B	07/08/58	10TRW/1TRS	Spangdahlem AB, Ger
53-0459	RB-66B	07/17/58	363TRW/41TRS	Shaw AFB, SC
53-0411	RB-66B	10/07/58	363TRW/41TRS	Shaw AFB, SC
54-0476	RB-66C	11/15/58	67TRW/11TRS	Yokota AB, Jap
54-0535	RB-66B	12/09/58	10TRW/30TRS	Spangdahlem AB, Ger
54-0472	RB-66C	02/09/59	67TRW/11TRS	Yokota AB, Jap
54-0547	RB-66B	04/01/59	363TRW/16TRS	Shaw AFB, SC
53-0473	RB-66B	05/08/59	363TRW/16TRS	Shaw AFB, SC
55-0400	WB-66D	05/29/59	363TRW/9TRS	Shaw AFB, SC
54-0544	RB-66B	06/26/59	363TRW/16TRS	Shaw AFB, SC
54-0432	RB-66B	07/03/59	10TRW/19TRS	Spangdahlem AB, Ger
54-0421	RB-66B	12/14/59	10TRW/19TRS	RAF Bruntingthorpe, UK
53-0409	RB-66B	11/01/60	10TRW/1TRS	RAF Alconbury, UK
54-0430	RB-66B	03/16/61	10TRW/19TRS	RAF Bruntingthorpe, UK
54-0471	RB-66C	03/31/61	363TRW/9TRS	Shaw AFB, SC
55-0394	WB-66D	09/05/61	363TRW/9TRS	Shaw AFB, SC
54-0499	B-66B	10/26/61	47BW/85BS	RAF Sculthorpe, UK
54-0460	RB-66C	02/07/62	10TRW/42TRS	RAF Chelveston, UK
54-0530	RB-66B	02/04/63	10TRW/19TRS	Toul-Rosieres AB, Fr
54-0541	RB-66B	03/10/64	10TRW/19TRS	Toul-Rosieres AB, Fr
53-0452	RB-66B	10/22/65	4485TW/4487TS	Eglin AFB, FL-TSN AB, SVN
54-0457	EB-66C	02/25/66	460TRW/6460TEWS	Takhli RTAFB, Thai
54-0464	EB-66C	07/20/66	432TRW/6460TEWS	Takhli RTAFB, Thai
54-0475	EB-66C	08/20/66	460TRW/41TEWS	Takhli RTAFB, Thai
55-0387	EB-66C	02/04/67	432TRW/41TEWS	Takhli RTAFB, Thai
54-0473	EB-66C	11/17/67	355TFW/41TEWS	Takhli RTAFB, Thai
54-0462	EB-66C	12/06/67	355TFW/41TEWS	Takhli RTAFB, Thai
55-0388	EB-66C	01/14/68	355TFW/41TEWS	Takhli RTAFB, Thai
54-0524	EB-66E	03/06/68	355TFW/41TEWS	Takhli RTAFB, Thai
53-0491	EB-66B	07/19/68	355TFW/41TEWS	Takhli RTAFB, Thai
53-0498	EB-66B	04/08/69	355TFW/42TEWS	Takhli RTAFB, Thai
53-0415	RB-66B	06/24/69	363TRW/4417CCTS	Shaw AFB, SC
54-0536	EB-66E	10/09/69	36TFW/39TEWS	Spangdahlem AB, Ger
54-0439	EB-66E	04/21/70	355TFW/42TEWS	Takhli RTAFB, Thai

54-0384	EB-66C	10/26/70	388TFW/42TEWS	Korat RTAFB, Thai
55-0389	EB-66C	03/11/71	388TFW/42TEWS	Korat RTAFB, Thai
54-0427	EB-66E	11/17/71	388TFW/42TEWS	Korat RTAFB, Thai
54-0540	EB-66E	02/02/72	388TFW/42TEWS	Korat RTAFB, Thai
54-0466	EB-66C	04/02/72	388TFW/42TEWS	Korat RTAFB, Thai
54-0386	EB-66C	08/28/72	52TFW/39TEWS	Spangdahlem AB, Ger
54-0529	EB-66E	12/23/72	388TFW/42TEWS	Korat RTAFB, Thai
54-0445	EB-66E	05/03/73	388TFW/42TEWS	Korat RTAFB, Thai

October 6, 1956   B-66B 54-0497   34BS/17BW, Hurlburt Field, FL

Returning from *Exercise Whipsaw* in Europe, accompanied by three other B-66s, via Lajes Field, Azores, to Harmon AB, Newfoundland, aircraft number 54-0497 experienced fluctuating fuel flow about 50 miles out of Harmon. Then, both engines flamed out. Captain Zacheus W. Ryall prepared to make an engine out landing, when on the base leg both engines regained full power. Fuel system icing was suspected. On the following day, October 6, Captain Ryall intended to fly from Harmon to Hurlburt Field, FL, his home station. While over Virginia, at flight level 370, both engines flamed out again, and Captain Ryall prepared to make an engine out landing at the Blackstone, VA, airport. Unfavorable weather prevented an engine out landing, and the crew of three ejected eight miles from Blackstone, after directing the aircraft toward an unoccupied area. First Lieutenant Darrell E. Selby, navigator, and A/2C Callix J. Perusse, gunner, as well as Captain Ryall ejected without injury to themselves. It was later determined that at altitude the fuel thickened and the fine mesh fuel filters became barriers to fuel flow. Redesigned filters solved this problem. However, two more B-66 aircraft would crash, with loss of life, because not all old filters were purged from the supply system. Source: Air Force Safety Center, Kirtland AFB, NM, (AFSC); Cliff Parrott, Douglas Aircraft Corporation B-66 Technical Advisor.

April 1, 1957   B-66B   54-0493 95BS/17BW, Hurlburt Field, FL

The aircraft was one of three scheduled to participate in *Exercise King Cole,* launching at 0015 hours into light rain and thunderstorms. Immediately after take-off the pilot reported the loss of his escape hatch. The tower gave Lieutenant Dinger clearance for a requested visual approach; GCA monitoring the aircraft throughout the remaining portion of flight. Three miles from the runway the aircraft was observed by GCA to be going dangerous low. The aircraft entered ground clutter, hitting a tree and shearing off the leading edge slat on one wing, briefly reappeared on the radar scope, then crashed into a swamp one mile short of the field. Flight time: 7 minutes. Aircraft and crew perished. 1/Lieutenant Richard J. Dinger, pilot. Captain John A. Runion, navigator. TSGT Stanley P. Klatz, gunner. Source: AFSC.

April 11, 1957   RB-66B   53-0410 43TRS/363TRW, Shaw AFB, SC

Aircraft departed Shaw AFB, SC, at 1045. on an instrument training flight, with the secondary mission of picking up the 43TRS commander, Lt/Colonel Paul Vanderhock, from Eglin AFB, Florida, and fly him to Shaw AFB, SC. The weather at Eglin was 1,000 feet in light rain. After the pilot was turned over to Eglin GCA for a precision approach, he broke out at 1,000 feet to the right of the runway and was instructed to go around. On his second approach he was again to the right of the runway, pulling the throttles to idle when he realized he was going to land long. The drag chute was deployed prematurely, and immediately separated from the aircraft (Speed limit for chute deployment was 170 knots). The aircraft bounced, continued down the runway centerline onto the overrun, went over a 40 foot embankment, became airborne again for 175 feet, then struck a swampy area in a left wing low, nose down attitude, breaking up on contact. The navigator, Captain George F. Duncan, was not injured, and assisted the injured pilot, Captain John T. McLain, to safety. There was no fire. The aircraft was destroyed. Source: AFSC.

July 18, 1957   RB-66B   54-428   12TRS/67TRW, Yokota AB, Japan

Less than an hour into their round robin navigational flight from Yokota Air Base, the navigator, Captain Max Ruderman, called the pilot, Captain George H. Slover, and asked, "What is making the aircraft shake so much?" They were flying IFR at flight level 350. Captain Slover ascribed the shaking to turbulence from nearby thunderstorms. Then he noticed that the left engine alternator was carrying a heavy load, and the right alternator was near zero. A sudden loud rumble was followed by the tachometer on the number 1 engine dropping to zero and the off flag popping up on the flight indicator. Captain Slover immediately took the aircraft off autopilot. When he did, the plane entered a nose high attitude. Pushing the control column forward to nose the aircraft down he realized that his elevator control was frozen, and he alerted the crew to prepare for ejection. The airspeed was falling off rapidly, at 170 knots the aircraft began to buffet, at 120 knots it stalled and entered a steep spiral to the left. Captain Slover attempted to blow the escape hatches, but due to the high G-loads he had to get both hands on the Emergency Canopy Release to pull it out. The gunner, T/Sgt Wilburn G. South, ejected first, followed by the navigator. As the aircraft accelerated past 200 knots Captain Slover extended the speed brakes, ejecting at 17,000 feet at 300 knots. The aircraft dove into a hillside and was totally demolished. All three crew members landed safely and were unhurt. Source: AFSC.

September 3, 1957   B-66B   54-0495   95BS/17BW, Hurlburt Field, FL

The aircrew was scheduled to fly a practice radar bombing mission against the Houston radar bombing range. Bomb plot altitude was flight level 370. The weather was clear, except in the Houston area where layers of cloud and thunderstorms were expected. Shortly after the bomb run two explosions were heard from the #2 engine. Instruments became erratic, and while the pilot was trying to assess the situation, he entered a thunderstorm, encountering moderate turbulence. The altimeter was descending, airspeed was past 'the barber pole', with no immediate effect noticed when power on #1 engine was reduced to idle. The pilot felt he could not regain control of the aircraft and ordered the crew to eject - the navigator, then the pilot, and finally the gunner ejected, in that order. The three crew members and the aircraft landed near Alvin, Texas. The pilot, 1/Lt David E. Moore and the gunner, S/Sgt R.J. Newland, suffered major injuries. The navigator, Captain Arthur J. Manzo, was killed. Source: AFSC.

December 16, 1957   RB-66B   54-0517   1TRS/10TRW, Spangdahlem AB, Germany

Aircraft departed Spangdahlem Friday, 13 December, for a photo mission to Chateauroux AB, France, Nouasseur AB, Morocco, and return. Weather delayed the crew at Chateauroux until December 16 when an early morning take-off was scheduled. The right engine torched on run-up due to excessive fuel accumulation and late ignition. At the end of runway 04 the pilot was observed to run-up his engines several times, switching landing lights on and off before taking the active. As he rolled down the runway the landing lights went off after 150 feet. The aircraft became airborne at the computed take-off distance of 5,000 feet, the take-off appearing normal to observers, seeing a continuous red glow from both engines. The aircraft leveled off at 200 feet, began a shallow descent, disappearing beyond the horizon, where next an explosion was observed. All observers heard the sound of the engines until the explosion and thought they sounded normal. Aircraft and crew perished. 1/Lieutenant Dan K. Henderson, pilot. 2/Lieutenant Glen D. Watson, navigator. A/2C Arthur J. Dufresne, Jr., gunner. Source: AFSC.

March 30, 1958   B-66B   55-0314   84BS/47BW, RAF Sculthorpe, UK

The crew of 55-0314 along with two other 84BS aircrews briefed at 1300 hours on Friday, 28 March, for a weekend mission to Landstuhl Air Base, Germany, practicing radar bombing on London bomb plot on the outbound leg. Take-off was scheduled for Saturday morning before 0900 local, after which the 9,000 foot runway was to be closed. Take off was made and the mission proceeded uneventfully. Sunday early afternoon the three B-66s were cleared IFR on top direct to Sculthorpe. Upon arrival at Sculthorpe visibility was reported as 1.8 miles in light rain and dropping. The landing was to be made on the short, 6,000 foot runway, the primary runway was still closed for repairs. First Lieutenant William H. Fulton, the pilot of 314 was the last of the three B-66s to attempt a landing. By the time he was inbound to the homer beacon at 5,000 feet visibility had dropped to 1.2 miles or less, braking action though was reported as good by the preceding B-66. Fulton touched down 500 feet from the runway threshold at a flare speed of 141 knots, deployed the brake chute, which blossomed, then immediately released. Fulton applied maximum braking with anti-skid. With approximately 2,000 feet of runway remaining the B-66 was still traveling at 80 knots. He informed GCA that he would go onto the overrun, then shut down the right engine. The aircraft proceeded onto the runway overrun, onto the grass beyond, then tore into the perimeter fence, collapsing the nose gear, and came to rest in a plowed field where a small electrical fire started below the crew compartment. The gunner, A/1C Earl

W. Churchill, opened his escape hatch manually and exited the aircraft, followed by Captain George T. Dugan, the navigator. Lieutenant Fulton exited the aircraft last, after turning off all switches. The aircraft was deemed repairable at an estimated cost of $400,000 and 3,500 man hours. Lieutenant Colonel Fulton, USAF (Ret.), stated in an interview in October 2006 that because of the short runway and the deteriorating weather he had requested to divert to his alternate, a French base. His request was denied by the Wing Commander, Colonel Glover. The accident, according to Colonel Fulton, was subsequently classified as 'supervisory error,' by the accident investigation board. The aircraft was placed in a hangar, where it remained, being used for spare parts. It was eventually taken off the active rolls and disposed of through Class 26 action. Source: AFSC/Lt/Col William Fulton.

April 14, 1958   RB-66B   54-0422   19TRS/10TRW, RAF Sculthorpe, UK
Aircraft departed Sculthorpe at 1051 local for a three hour round-robin training flight. Weather was changeable. At 14:06 weather was 600 feet overcast, two miles in fog and haze, with fog increasing rapidly. The aircraft was handed over to the final controller on the base leg 8 miles out. The final approach appeared normal, then the aircraft started to go high on the glide slope, drifting left, then right. At 14:22 the GCA controller suggested a go-around, "turn to a heading of 300 degrees and climb to 1,500 feet." The pilot responded that he was on a missed approach, heading 060 degrees. He was advised to turn to 100 degrees and climb to 5,000 feet, or 1,000 feet on top. The pilot did not respond. At 14:25 the Fakenham police received a report of an airplane crash. Aircraft and crew perished. Captain Roger E. Taylor, pilot. 1/Lieutenant Robert B. Handcock, navigator. TSGT Bernard M. Valencia, gunner. Source: AFSC

July 3, 1958   RB-66B   54-0433   19TRS/10TRW, RAF Sculthorpe, UK
The aircraft departed Spangdahlem Air Base, Germany, for its home station of RAF Sculthorpe in the United Kingdom. En route the aircraft experienced a total loss of utility and main emergency hydraulic pressure. Arriving over RAF Sculthorpe, Captain William A. Marcum, pilot, attempted to lower the landing gear. The nose and right main gear extended and locked; the left main gear stayed in the wheel well and would not move. Captain Marcum then put the aircraft on autopilot and ordered Captains Willis B. Gray, instructor navigator, and Constantin Costen, Jr., navigator, to eject. The crew ejected successfully. After the crew abandoned the aircraft, it flew for another 20 minutes, doing several large circles near the base, once flying over RAF Sculthorpe, before crashing in a field after both engines flamed out. Source: AFSC.

July 8, 1958   RB-66B   54-0444   1TRS/10TRW, Spangdahlem AB, Germany
"Carrot Blue One" was on a training mission to take aerial photos in the LeHavre area of France. Departure was normal and all photo runs were accomplished as scheduled at 10,000' with a ground speed of 325 knots. The aircraft began its penetration to Spangdahlem at 1656Z, crashing at 1711Z, 7,200 feet short of the runway. The crew of three ejected at a low altitude and were killed on impact, with chutes not fully deployed. Aircraft and crew perished. Captain Donn F. Chandler, pilot. Captain Robin W. Gray, navigator. 1/Lieutenant Helmut Heimann, navigator. Source: AFSC.

July 17, 1958   RB-66B   53-0459   41TRS/363TRW, Shaw AFB, SC
Four RB/WB-66 crews in the 43rd TRS were placed on alert status on July 15 and briefed to proceed on a classified mission (1958 Lebanon crisis) from Shaw AFB to Lajes AFB, with air refueling near Bermuda. The pilot and gunner of the crew involved in the accident were from the 43rd TRS, the navigator from the 41st TRS, because Captain Trent's regular navigator was on emergency leave and no spare 43rd TRS navigators were available. Two of the crews were delayed in their departure because of aircraft maintenance problems. The crews of 'Smokestack Delta 1 and 2' proceeded to their aircraft for preflight. SD1, the lead aircraft, aborted temporarily for maintenance. SD2, having been briefed that because of the seriousness of the mission to proceed, continued with its preflight. The Form 781 reflected that the N–1 compass was overdue a swing. SD2 lined up for take-off, the pilot checked the N–1 compass with the runway heading noting no difference. A normal take-off was made at 0720 on July 17. Near Bermuda they refueled from a KB-50 tanker, and were given instructions to refuel over Lajes, instead of landing, and await further instructions as to where to proceed to next. About 30 minutes out of Lajes the navigator began to concentrate on his radar using its full range of 200 miles. There was no sign of land. Five minutes before ETA the pilot turned to UHF

Guard and began to broadcast his difficulty in the blind. The crew realized that they were lost with a malfunctioning N1 compass (The APN-82 indicated that they were within 12 miles of Lajes, but they could see no land). SD2 then turned north toward active shipping lanes searching for the islands, with the navigator keeping his radar on maximum range. They sighted no land. The pilot then got out his Dash-1 and reviewed bailout procedures with the crew. Spotting the Norwegian freighter *Vespasian* they descended to 10,000 feet and approached the ship on a parallel heading. The pilot reduced speed to 200 knots, lowered flaps to 60 degrees, jettisoned the hatches, then they ejected - the gunner first, the navigator second, and the pilot last. The pilot, Captain Clyde B. Trent, and the navigator, 1/Lt Roth O. Owen, were rescued by the *Vespasian*. The gunner, A/1C Julius J. Rausch, was lost at sea. Source: AFSC.

October 7, 1958   RB-66B   53-0411   41TRS/363TRW, Shaw AFB, SC
Aircraft was on a routine cross-country flight from Shaw AFB, SC. Captain Richard Wilson, the pilot, wrote up the #2 engine as being 'soft,' not maintaining normal thrust, and decided to land at McClellan AFB, CA. Maintenance at McClellan (Sacramento Air Materiel Area - SMAMA) decided to replace the engine. Captain Wilson and his navigator returned to Shaw, intending to return for a FCF when the aircraft was ready. The Functional Check Flight was flown instead by a SMAMA pilot, accompanied by two SMAMA civilians. Shortly after takeoff #2 engine failed and the aircraft crashed and burned. Apparently nuts/bolts (FOD) was left in the cowling of #2 engine and ingested when the inlet screens retracted on lift-off. Aircraft and crew perished. The Shaw Douglas technical representative had planned to accompany Captain Wilson to McClellan AFB for the functional check flight of the aircraft, once notified by the depot that the aircraft was ready. The inlet screen FOD inspection was a regular part of the walk-around checklist, and may have been overlooked. Captain Richard W. Hughes, pilot. Mr Blaine L. Mains, SMAMA. Mr George E. Sarabale, SMAMA. Source: C. Parrott/AFSC.

November 15, 1958 RB-66C   54-0476   11TRS/67TRW, Yokota Air Base, Japan
476 was returning from a night reconnaissance mission to Kunsan AB, Korea. Due to the classified nature of the mission, no flight plan had been filed, and radio silence was maintained until the aircraft was within 100 miles of Kunsan. Approaching Kunsan, the pilot was cleared for a normal jet penetration. Two miles out of Kunsan the pilot reported VFR conditions and was cleared by the Kunsan tower for a visual landing pattern. He reported gear down on long final, and was cleared to land. On short final, the pilot advised that he was going around. He executed his go-around and passed the tower at an altitude of approximately 100 feet. He continued until about 1 mile beyond the end of the runway when he was observed to enter a gentle right descending turn, crashing into the water off the end of the runway with no explosion or fire resulting from the crash. The aircraft was destroyed, the crew of seven perished. Captain George A. Taylor, pilot. 1/Lieutenant Robert A. Chase, navigator. Staff Sergeant Howard M. Hicks, gunner. Captain James M. Stitzel, Electronic Warfare Officer. 1/Lieutenant Thomas C. Bryce, Electronic Warfare Officer. 1/Lieutenant Smith Davis, Jr., Electronic Warfare Officer. 1/Lieutenant Lawton D. Mueller, Electronic Warfare Officer. .Source: AFSC.

December 9, 1958   RB-66B   54-0535   30TRS/10TRW, Spangdahlem AB, Germany
Returning from a practice RBS training flight from Spangdahlem to Nancy to Cologne, back to Spangdahlem, 'Research 19' was contacted by Rhein-Control and accepted a radar letdown and GCA approach to Spangdahlem air base. At 16 miles from the runway the aircraft was handed from Spangdahlem approach control to GCA for a straight in approach to runway 23. The aircraft descended from 7,000 to 2,700 feet. At 9 miles from the end of the runway the GCA final controller took over. The aircraft was reacting to heading instructions up to the 2 mile point, after which there was no response from the pilot. The aircraft crashed 1.8 miles from the runway. The aircraft was destroyed and the crew perished.   Captain Howard E. Strandberg, pilot. Captain Wilfred E. Cather, navigator. Captain Joseph D. Loefler, navigator. Source: AFSC.

February 9, 1959   RB-66C   54-0472   11TRS/67TRW, Yokota Air Base, Japan
EB-66C reconnaissance aircraft of the 11th TRS routinely flew missions from Yokota air base, to Kadena on Okinawa, then to Clark air base in the Philippine Islands, and back. On February 9, 472 with a crew of seven, was to refuel over the Sea of Japan before proceeding on its final leg to its home at Yokota air base. As usual the take-off from Kadena was under radio silence. While taxiing the

pilot noted a hydraulic discrepancy, taxied back to the parking area and had the rudder and elevator boost pump replaced. Apparently the pump replacement was hurried, and the hydraulic lines were not properly bled, leaving air in the system which would cause erratic rudder and elevator operation. As a result the pilot was unable to obtain sufficient fuel from a KB-50 tanker, and decided to divert to Kunsan AB, South Korea. At about 5 miles from the runway, at about 1,200 feet, the engines flamed out, the aircraft ditching in the water in a nose high attitude. Captain Robert W. White, pilot; 1/Lt Marcell J. Dunn, navigator; A/2C Forrest E. Jolly, gunner; and 2/Lt Leon S. Kirk, electronic warfare officer, survived the crash. Three electronic warfare officers in the rear compartment of the aircraft perished. An accident investigation board subsequently determined that at flame out the aircraft still had 1,500 pounds of fuel remaining in the forward tank, suggesting insufficient knowledge of fuel management procedures on the part of the pilot. Captain Allen H. Day, Electronic Warfare Officer. 1/Lieutenant Harold W. Glandon, Electronic Warfare Officer. 2/Lieutenant James T. Powell, Jr., Electronic Warfare Officer. Source: AFSC/survivor.

April 1, 1959   RB-66B   54-0547   16TRS/363TRW, Shaw AFB, SC
Captain James H. Moore and crew were assigned aircraft 54-547 for a night photo reconnaissance training mission over the Avon Park Bombing Range. He was assigned the number two position in a flight of three. All three aircraft were assembled on runway 22. The lead aircraft started a normal take-off roll and thirty seconds later number two released brakes and began his take-off. Acceleration was normal and computed line speeds were met at the proper distances. At 140 knots IAS the pilot began to exert pressure on the flight controls to rotate the aircraft to take-off position. The control column moved only slightly and resisted all further efforts of the pilot to exert back-pressure. By this time lift-off speed and take-off distance were exceeded. Realizing the ineffectiveness of the flight controls, the pilot actuated high speed AC trim to the nose up position, but noticing no effect, he elected to abort the take-off, moved the throttles to the cut-off position, deployed the drag chute, then alerted the control tower and prepared to engage the arresting barrier. At approximately 400 feet from the end of the runway, Captain Moore realized he would not stop on the runway, so he deliberately retracted the landing gear and pulled the emergency jettison handle for all escape hatches. The aircraft crashed through the arresting barrier, the right main gear door engaging the barrier cable and bringing the aircraft to a stop. Fire developed in both engines and along the left central fuselage. The crew of three - Captain Moore, pilot; Captain John A. Reinsmith, navigator; Technical Sergeant Kenneth H. Latzka, gunner - escaped without harm. Extensive damage was done to both engine nacelles, underside of the fuselage, nose and main gears, as well as fire damage to the fuselage, resulting in the aircraft being classified as a loss to the aircraft inventory and to be reclaimed for the spare parts program. Source: AFSC.

May 8, 1959   RB-66B   53-0473   16TRS/363TRW, Shaw AFB, SC
Three RB-66B aircraft (53-0418, 53-0473, 53-0413) were to fly a photographic mission in Virginia, and upon their return take a photograph of the formation above the city of Sumter, SC. After completing the Virginia mission, the lead aircraft, 473, assumed the #3 position to take the required photo; 413 assumed the lead, with 418 in the #2 position. The formation descended VFR to 11,500 feet and leveled off. Captain Woodworth in 473 dropped back and climbed to 12,100 feet to make a pass above the formation and take the picture. As he approached in this position, the formation disappeared from sight below the nose of his aircraft. After receiving a heading correction from his navigator by use of the driftmeter, a jolt was felt, then 473 began to tumble. Captain Roy E. Woodworth, pilot, and James F. Young, instructor navigator ejected successfully. Captain Julian T. Stewart, the navigator, was thrown from the aircraft upon impact (and may have been already killed during initial contact as he was looking through his driftmeter). 473 crashed and burned 5 miles east of Sumter. The pilot of 418, after feeling the initial contact, maintained control of his aircraft, reported the incident to the Shaw AFB tower, and landed successfully. "The primary cause of the accident was supervisory error in that the briefing officer prepared, briefed and flew a mission which was not authorized and in violation of Air Force Regulation." Source: AFSC/363TRW History.

May 29, 1959   WB-66D   55-0400   9TRS/363TRW, Shaw AFB, SC
On landing at Lajes, Azores, the pilot made one application of brakes, then lost all braking action and nosewheel steering. Attempts to arm the emergency air brake failed. Apparently the hydraulic pump

on engine #2 failed, which affected nosewheel steering and braking. The aircraft veered off the runway and hit an adjacent embankment. The crew of two weather observers (1/Lt A. L. Kellerstrass and M/Sgt E. R. Iverson), gunner (A/2C W. E. Ross), navigator (Major V. R. Morris), and Captain Willard G. Mattson, the pilot, survived without injury to themselves. The aircraft was declared Class 26 and scrapped. Source: C. Parrott/AFSC.

June 26, 1959   RB-66B   54-0544   16TRS/363TRW, Shaw AFB, SC
'Ridge Fox Blue' departed Langley AFB, VA, at 0000Z on June 26 for San Antonio, Texas, with an enroute refueling from a KB-50 tanker. The tanker rendezvous was uneventful, off-loading 10,000 pounds of fuel. At 0410Z approaching Kelly AFB, Ridge Fox Blue was cleared to descend to flight level 200. Upon reaching 20,000 feet RFB was cleared for an ILS approach, straight in from the Kelly OMNI beacon to runway 15. It was a clear night with visibility reported at 7 miles. At 0423Z Ridge Fox Blue was observed by San Antonio approach control radar to be 11 miles WNW of the Kelly OMNI at 7,000 feet. He was given Kelly winds and current NOTAMS on lighting condition at Kelly (only _ of the runway was lit). The pilot reported leaving 7,000 feet. At 0427Z radar contact was lost. The aircraft crashed and burned near the top of the hill 5 miles northwest of the Kelly OMNI. The aircrew perished. "The most probable cause was pilot error in that the pilot descended below the minimum published altitude during a jet penetration." Captain James L. Junge, pilot. 1/Lieutenant William H. McCasland, navigator. A/2C Michael J. Kemp, gunner. Source: AFSC/363TRW History.

July 3, 1959   RB-66B   54-0432   19TRS/10TRW, Spangdahlem AB, Germany
On July 3, 1959, the 10th TRW launched 48 W/RB-66 aircraft for a formation fly-by at a wing change-of-command ceremony. The formation was to be led by 12 19th TRS aircraft, Alpha Flight, commanded and led by Lt/Colonel 'Doc' Partridge. Each Alpha Flight aircraft received a full fuel load of 27,000 pounds. The crew of Alpha 10, RB-66B 432, was element lead of the slot element of Alpha Flight, and while going through their pre-takeoff checklist, left the fuel selector switch in the AUXILIARY position. The flight assembled and held in an orbit over the Buechel beacon while Bravo Flight, 30TRS, Coco Flight, 42TRS, and Delta Flight, from the 1st Tactical Reconnaissance Squadron, took off from Spangdahlem Air Base and assembled in their respective holding areas. Flight level was between 3,000 and 4,000 feet AGL over the Buechel beacon. After all the formations had assembled and the fly-by was about to begin Colonel Partridge ordered his 12 aircraft to initiate a 'transfer of wing tank fuel' from the wing tanks to the main tanks. About 2 minutes after starting the fuel transfer Alpha 11 and 12, flying off the wings of Alpha 10, noted flame coming from Alpha 10's exhaust cones, and momentarily Alpha 10 reported a double flame out and intention to attempt a crash landing in an open field. Colonel Partridge ordered the crew of two - Captain James A. Wells, the pilot, and 1/Lt Edward J. Mullarkey, the navigator - to eject from their aircraft, which they promptly did. The aircraft landed on the ground wings level, skipped through a field, and only after smashing into a ravine did it burst into flames. Colonel Partridge continued the fly-by, now flying a missing man formation. Neither pilot nor navigator were injured. Source: AFSC/Colonel Partridge.

December 14, 1959   RB-66B   54-0421   19TRS/10TRW, RAF Bruntingthorpe, UK
Crew delivered RB-66B 54-0430 to RAF Alconbury to undergo periodic maintenance; then picked up aircraft #421 which had completed scheduled maintenance and been released after a functional check flight for return to RAF Bruntingthorpe. 'Puff Zero Five' was airborne at 1732Z, climbing to flight level 370, and entered a holding pattern upon arrival over Bruntingthorpe. At 1948Z Puff 05 reported penetration turn to Bruntingthorpe tower, which requested Puff 05 report field in sight. Puff 05 acknowledged transmission, stating that they were trying to find the field. At 1950Z Puff 05 crashed into the ground at a point 11 miles from the BT beacon, three miles short of Bruntingthorpe, with flaps and gear down. The aircraft was destroyed and the crew perished. 1/Lieutenant Gary R. Coad, pilot. 1/Lieutenant Charles L. Boone, navigator. A/2C Ralph L. Noell, gunner. Source: AFSC.

November 1, 1960   RB-66B   53-0409   1TRS/10TRW, RAF Alconbury, UK
Aircraft launched on a routine photographic training flight in the Laon-Toul area of France. After starting engines the pilot experienced alternator and oil pressure problems which were apparently resolved by maintenance before take-off. After about five minutes of flight, in IFR conditions, at 10,000 feet, the #2 engine flamed out, both left and right alternator warning lights came on - which

resulted in the loss of AC power. An attempt to obtain AC power from the emergency inverter was unsuccessful. Still in IFR conditions, with all instruments inoperative, the pilot experienced vertigo, but broke out of the clouds in a wing level, nose down attitude just before ordering ejection. The pilot then felt extreme heat emanating from near the control column, the control column initiator fired, stowing the column without warning. The pilot pulled the control wheel from the stowed position and regained partial control, attempting to join up with a 2nd B-66 which had come up to render assistance and guide him to a straight in landing. Before the rendezvous was made 409 yawed to the left, which the pilot interpreted as a loss of engine power, and he ordered the crew to eject. The aircraft impacted the ground in a near vertical descent. 1st Lieutenant Larry N. Fealy, pilot; 1st Lieutenant Peter J. Hollitscher, navigator; and SSGT John R. Gaskill, flight engineer, ejected without serious injury to themselves. The aircraft crashed near RAF Bruntingthorpe. Source: AFSC.

March 16, 1961   RB-66B   54-0430   19TRS/10TRW, RAF Bruntingthorpe, UK
On the evening of 16 March 1961, three photo-reconnaissance aircraft, comprising the Royal Flush competition team, were scheduled to participate in a night photography training exercise off the Dutch coast in preparation for the annual NATO photographic reconnaissance competition. An IFR clearance was filed - the weather was clear, a dark, starlit night, no moon. The targets were located in a danger area on the West Frisian islands of Vlieland and Terschelling. After ten runs were made, in a left hand racetrack pattern starting with the Vlieland target, then the Terschelling target, turn, and repeat the same procedure, 430 was observed to pass overhead of the other two aircraft. The pilot stated to the range controller that he had a radar problem, had the other two aircraft in sight, and would resume his position behind the second aircraft at 1,000 feet as they exited the range. The pilots of the other two aircraft reported to the range controller as they exited the range; 430 was not seen or heard from again. Bits of wreckage and one helmet were later found in the vicinity of the range. Attempts by the Royal Navy to locate the aircraft were unsuccessful. A Dutch fishing vessel reported an oil slick the following day near the Terschelling Islands, and several ships reported seeing a sudden brilliant glare in the same area Thursday night; although all three of the aircraft dropped numerous photo flash cartridges during their respective runs. The aircrew, initially listed as missing, was subsequently declared deceased Captain Harry V. Armani, pilot. Captain Daniel Harvey, navigator. 1/Lieutenant Frank L. Whitley, Jr., navigator. Source: 10TRW History/AFSC.

March 31, 1961   RB-66C   54-0471   9TRS/363TRW, Shaw AFB, SC
'Tasty One Five' an RB-66C electronic reconnaissance aircraft, piloted by Major Henry Gibbia, was scheduled to fly weather reconnaissance from Shaw AFB to Minot AFB, North Dakota. A weather officer, 1/Lt David Gurkin, flew in the gunner's/flight engineer's seat. The weather at Shaw on take-off was 300 feet overcast, 1 mile in rain and light fog. Tasty 15 reported to Atlanta Center arriving at flight level 310, losing #2 engine and requested a let down to Donaldson AFB, SC. Weather at Donaldson was similar to the weather at Shaw on take-off. Donaldson GCA picked up Tasty 15 on guard channel and proceeded to direct the aircraft. Tasty 15 descended to 2,500 feet, GCA had good radar and radio contact at this time and directed 15 into position for an approach to runway 040. Then Tasty 15 asked, "Do I have open country under me?" The controller did not understand the question - Tasty 15 dropped its two wing fuel tanks (one impacting harmlessly in a field, the other near a small shopping area causing no injury or damage). Despite full left rudder and trim, according to the pilot, the aircraft yawed to the right, and when GCA called the aircraft too far off centerline to land, Major Gibia initiated a one-engine go-around. On the second attempt the aircraft again ended up 1,500 feet right of the runway. GCA called for a missed approach, the pilot lost altitude, then struck the ground 50 feet too the right and 1,700 feet short of the runway. Fire damaged the aircraft beyond economical repair. The crew of 7 suffered no noteworthy injuries. A claim of backward wired rudder trim was not substantiated by the Douglas technical representative. Source: AFSC/other.

September 5, 1961   WB-66D   55-0394   9TRS/363TRW, Shaw AFB, SC
The aircraft was scheduled for a routine weather reconnaissance mission from Kindley AFB, Bermuda, returning to Kindley, with an estimated time enroute of 2:15 hours. The flight progressed normally until turning point #2 when an electrical power surge affected radios and navigation equipment. On the return leg to Kindley both engines flamed out. The aircraft descended from flight level 200 to 90; both engines restarted, then failed again. While the pilot attempted several engine restarts, the two weather

observers, Captain Kenneth F. Gordon and M/Sgt Ercell R. Iverson, ejected when they received a warning bell. Simultaneously with the ejections, one engine restarted, and the aircraft leveled at 2,500 feet. When the remaining engine flamed out abruptly, the pilot said, "Let's get out of here," and 2/Lt Donald R. Fritz, the navigator, and Lt/Colonel William K. Bush, on a familiarization flight riding in the gunner's seat, ejected in that order. As Lieutenant Fritz ejected he saw the pilot still at the controls attempting to restart the engines. Bush, Fritz, Gordon and Iverson were rescued the following day. The pilot, Captain Jesse B. Kendler, was killed in the crash. The suspected cause of the flame-out was installation of previously condemned fuel filters, which resulted in filter icing and fuel starvation. Source: AFSC.

October 26, 1961   B-66B   54-0499   85BS/47BW, RAF Sculthorpe, UK
The aircrew was scheduled for a normal round robin training flight of 3 _ hour duration. Fuel on board the aircraft was for 4 hours and 15 minutes. Major Brooks, the instructor pilot, was sitting on a 'bucket' in the aisle adjacent to the pilot's seat observing Captain 'Doc' Savage during engine start, taxi and presumably throughout the flight. The bucket is a can the IP sits on; not a part of the aircraft configuration, nor secured in any way. Take-off at 1846Z was normal. At 1848Z 499 contacted Anglia Control (USAF Radar Air Traffic Control Center) and advised of being airborne and proceeding to the departure fix. Anglia instructed the pilot to continue climbing to flight level 300. At 1856Z 499 reported "just passing FL 200" and requested permission to reverse course and continue climb. With 499 halfway through its turn Anglia advised, "499, traffic in your one o'clock position, direction of movement unknown, range three miles." "499 is IMC" was the reply (Instrument Meteorological Conditions - they couldn't see a thing). "499 tighten your turn, you should miss him." There was no response from 499. The two blips merged on the radar screen. Between 1859Z and 1900Z the pilot transmitted, "Eject, eject, 499, 499" followed by some garbled utterings. Subsequent evaluation of the tape from Anglia control center revealed the garbled uttering as "Help" and "It's alright Doc." Doc was the nickname of Captain Savage. One of the two blips emerged on the radar scope, the other target return varied in intensity (picked up by British GCI sites and photographed), possibly due to rotation, spinning and tumbling of 499 until it disappeared from observation. The other aircraft, a KLM DC-8 from Schiphol Airport, Amsterdam, Holland, on a flight to New York, was on top of the clouds at FL 285, and didn't know anything happened. Anglia control had no knowledge of the KLM flight. The crew perished and was never found. Aircraft wreckage was not located until 15 November 1961. Major Paul W. Brooks, instructor pilot. Captain Ralph L. Davenport, Jr., navigator. Captain Paul J. Savage, pilot. Source: AFSC.

February 7, 1962   RB-66C   54-0460   42TRS/10TRW, RAF Chelveston, UK
Aircraft departed Chelveston for a tactical reconnaissance mission along the East German border with a scheduled landing at Toul-Rosieres, France. The tactical mission was aborted due to a failing navigation radar, and after 2:30 hours local flying at flight level 340, a standard approach/landing at RAF Chelveston was initiated. The approach configuration for the aircraft was gear down, flaps down, speed brakes extended. On the glide path the pilot experienced gusty winds and turbulence. While still maintaining near level flight, he detected a slight surge in engine power. Then the surging intensified, leading to a loss of thrust - RPM and EGT decreasing. While near the end of the runway, at about 700 feet altitude, the pilot alerted the crew to prepare for ejection, attempting to gain additional altitude while the engines continued surging. Flameout of both engines seemed imminent when he advised the crew to eject. The navigator ejected successfully. The pilot's right ejection lever malfunctioned and forced him to ride the aircraft to the ground, where it slid for 540 feet before coming to a stop. No fire ensued. He evacuated the aircraft through the overhead escape hatch, noting that one of the electronic warfare officers, whose seat also malfunctioned, was making an escape through the aft escape hatch. The cause of the crash was determined to be fuel filter icing, caused by a flat, fine mesh screen design. The fuel filters had been redesigned as a result of a 6 October 1956 crash of a B-66B flown by Captain Ryall of the 17th Bomb Wing. Obviously not all old filters had been removed from inventory - costing four men their lives. There was insufficient altitude for the three electronic warfare officers in the rear compartment, with their downward firing ejection seats, to survive. The pilot, Captain Charles E. 'Skip' Jones, suffered minor injuries. 1/Lt Norbert J. Maier, the electronic warfare officer whose ejection seat malfunctioned and 1/Lt Richard A. Morris, the navigator, suffered no injuries. The remainder of the crew perished. 1/Lieutenant William R. Becraft, Electronic Warfare Officer. 1/Lieutenant Reynolds

W. McCabe, Electronic Warfare Officer. 1/Lieutenant James T. Weymark, Electronic Warfare Officer. SSGT Leroy Dauphenbaugh, Jr., Flight Engineer. Source: AFSC.

February 4, 1963   RB-66B   54-0530   19TRS/10TRW, Toul-Rosieres AB, France
Aircraft 54-530 was based at Toul-Rosiere, had completed IRAN (inspect and repair as necessary) at the Douglas-Tulsa plant, and was on its way back to T-R via Langley AFB, VA. On February 4, Captain William Cox, Jr., assigned to the 10TRW at RAF Alconbury, filed a flight plan from the Tulsa VOR, at flight level 330, direct to Langley AFB, VA. 'Alive 71' departed the Douglas ramp at 1505 local, climbed out to FL 330 and reported a malfunctioning APN-82. In conversation with Douglas representatives it was decided that the malfunction could not be fixed in the air and Alive 71 was to return to the Douglas plant after burning off fuel. The aircraft made several overhead approaches to Tulsa Municipal. On the final approach Captain Lynwood Odom, the navigator, detected popped circuit breakers which would not reset, subsequently radio and intercom was lost, and he detected the reflection of fire on the right engine nacelle. Captain Cox, losing response from the control column, motioned for Captain Odom to eject, which he did without injury. Ground witnesses reported seeing the aircraft on fire and shedding parts, impacting at 1700 local time 16 miles east of the Tulsa VORTAC. Captain Cox perished in the aircraft. Subsequent analysis determined that a fire broke out in the crawl way under the forward fuel tank. Source: AFSC.

March 10, 1964   RB-66B   54-0541   19TRS/10TRW, Toul-Rosieres AB, France
On a navigation check flight a precessing N1 compass put the aircraft in the central Berlin air corridor over East Germany where it was shot down by Soviet MiG 19 fighters. The aircraft crashed near Gardelegen. The crew of three - pilot, Captain David Holland, and two navigators, Captain Melvin J. Kessler and 1st Lieutenant Harold Welch - successfully ejected, were captured by Soviet troops, then released to US authorities. Source: Various.

October 22, 1965   RB-66B   53-0452   4487TS/4485TW, Eglin AFB, FLwith duty assign-
                                          ment Det 1/33TAC GP, Tan Son Nhut AB
The first B-66 aircraft lost in Southeast Asia, 53-0452 was deployed on temporary duty to Tan Son Nhut Air Base, Vietnam. During a night, low level, IR reconnaissance mission while in a turn the aircraft flew into an adjacent mountain 25 miles west of Pleiku. The crew perished. Cause: Combat loss. Captain Robert L. Mann, pilot. Captain John Weger, Jr., navigator. 1/Lieutenant James A. McEwen, navigator. Source: Hobson/other.

February 25, 1966   EB-66C   54-0457   6460TEWS/460TRW, Takhli RTAFB, Thailand
'Gull 01' was damaged by an SA-2 surface to air missile north of Vinh. Major Robert P. Walker, pilot, managed to get the aircraft out over the Gulf of Tonkin where the crew of six ejected. All but one crew member was rescued by US Navy helicopter. Killed in action was: Captain John B. Causey, electronic warfare officer. Source: Hobson/other.

July 20, 1966   EB-66C   54-0464   6460TEWS/432TRW, Takhli RTAFB, Thailand
'Devil 01' was providing ECM/ESM support to F-105 strike aircraft near Thai Nguyen when it was hit by up to two SA-2 surface to air missiles. Captain William H. Means, pilot, managed to fly the aircraft 55 miles toward friendly territory, but then had to give the order to eject. Five of the crew of six were captured and became POWs - Captain William H. Means; 1/Lt Edward L. Hubbard; Captain Lawrence Barbay; Captain Norman A. McDaniel, and Captain Glendon W. Perkins. 1/Lt Craig R. Norbert, electronic warfare officer, was KIA. Source: Hobson/other.

August 20, 1966   EB-66C   54-0475   41TRS/460TRW, Takhli RTAFB, Thailand
'Wreck 22' completed IRAN at the Tulsa-Douglas facility and was functionally test flown on 18 August. Captain Lindley and his crew accepted the aircraft and flew Wreck 22 to McClellan AFB, California. Wreck 22 then paired up with another EB-66C, Wreck 21, and a KC-135 tanker, 'Brim 68', and on August 20 proceeded on a standard aircraft delivery route (Flying Fish) to Hickam AFB, Hawaii. Less than an hour out of Hickam Wreck 22 suddenly dropped down and to the left, passing under the tanker and out of sight. Wreck 21 called Wreck 22 trying to determine what the problem was. Wreck 22 responded, "I've lost my boost." Wreck 22 then fell about four miles behind the tanker

and Wreck 21. 21 was running short on fuel and hooked up to the KC-135 to obtain 2,000 pounds of additional fuel. During the refueling Wreck 22 moved under the tanker and the refueling B-66, and out of sight of the boom operator. That was the last time Wreck 22 was seen. After disconnect the two aircraft searched for Wreck 22 - spotting an oil slick and possibly a life preserver. None of the search aircraft or vessels ever found the oil slick or any wreckage or survivors. Search and rescue operations were terminated at sundown of the 4th day. The crew was eventually declared dead. Captain Dwight A. Lindley, pilot. 1/Lieutenant Donald E. Laird, navigator. TSGT Charles Bordelon, crew chief. Source: AFSC.

February 4, 1967   EB-66C   55-0387   41TEWS/432TRW, Takhli RTAFB, Thailand
'Harpoon 01' was providing ECM/ESM support to F-105 strike aircraft when it was hit and downed by an SA-2 surface to air missile north of Thai Nguyen, North Vietnam. Of the crew of six, three were captured (Captain John Fer, pilot; Major Jack W. Bomar, navigator; and 1/Lt John O. Davies), three perished. Major Woodrow H. Wilburn, electronic warfare officer.   Captain Herbert Doby, electronic warfare officer. Captain Russell A. Poor, electronic warfare officer. Source: Hobson/other.

November 17, 1967 EB-66C 54-0473   41TEWS/355TFW, Takhli RTAFB, Thailand
"Elmo 1" followed "Elmo 2" on take-off at 20 second interval at 1255 hours. Take-off and initial climb were normal. After a right turn for enroute climb the pilot advised of #2 engine failure and requested vectors to return for immediate landing, requesting a ten mile final approach, appearing to have full control of the aircraft. At 6 nautical miles from touch down the pilot advised that he was unable to maintain altitude and losing it slowly. The aircraft continued settling, wings level, nose high, trailing a heavy exhaust trail indicative of a high power setting for #1 engine. Just prior to impact the EW overhead escape hatch was jettisoned; the three hatches for the forward compartment were not. A controlled, wings level, gear up touchdown was accomplished on level terrain 1195 feet short and 205 feet right of an extension to the runway centerline. The aircraft was engulfed in flames immediately after coming to rest, and destroyed by fire. A rescue helicopter set down a rescue team within 30 seconds of the crash. An attempt by the pilot to open his escape hatch was unsuccessful, he then ejected, the seat dropping into the burning fuselage. Further rescue attempts were unsuccessful. Two crew members, Captain James D. Stamm and Captain Robert D. Peffley, both with serious injuries, escaped the aft crew compartment. Five crew members perished. Major Max E. Nichols, pilot. 1/Lieutenant Theodore W. Johnson, instructor navigator. Major William E. McDonald, navigator. Captain Rey L. Duffin, electronic warfare officer. Captain Karl D. Hetzel, electronic warfare officer. Source: AFSC.

December 6, 1967   EB-66C   54-0462   41TEWS/355TFW, Takhli RTAFB, Thailand
On December 6, 462 flew an uneventful reconnaissance mission on the Laos side of the North Vietnamese border. On returning to base the pilot began his GCA controlled final approach at 1,500 feet AGL with landing gear down and locked, flaps 100%, and speed brakes extended. The aircraft gross weight was computed at 57,000 pounds giving an approach speed of 150 knots, and a stall warning speed of 117 knots IAS. The approach was excellent to 400 feet AGL when the aircraft descended 40 feet below the glide path, then the aircraft rose rapidly above the glide path and GCA asked if the pilot wanted to go-around. The response, "Roger, got a control problem." At this time the pilot had full throttle on both engines, was holding the yoke full forward and was attempting to keep the wings level as the aircraft first rolled to the right, then to the left. The next and final transmission: "Eject! Eject!" Thirty seconds later the aircraft crashed and burned 1,800 feet right of the overrun. Cause of the accident may have been sudden wind shear, also experienced by other aircraft, some crashing on final, others experiencing hard landings. All crew members ejected, but only three survived - 1/Lt Ronald A. McBride, navigator; Captain Alvin Taylor, Jr. and 1/Lt Arvid O. Peterson, both electronic warfare officers. Three perished. Lieutenant Colonel Jack M. Youngs, pilot. Captain Larry A. Moore, electronic warfare officer. 1/Lieutenant Paul S. Krzynowek, electronic warfare officer. Source: AFSC/other.

January 14, 1968   EB-66C   55-0388   41TEWS/355TFW, Takhli RTAFB, Thailand
Aircraft was shot down by a MiG-21 over North Vietnam, west of Hanoi. MiG-17 and MiG-21 aircraft made several attempts to down B-66 aircraft which were causing severe degradation to their

air defense radar network. 'Preview 01' would be their only success. Of a crew of seven, three were rescued (Lt/Col Attilio 'Pete' Pedroli, Lt/Col Jim Thompson, and Major Pollard H. 'Sonny' Mercer, Jr., pilot. Major Mercer later died, on January 20, from injuries received during ejection from the aircraft. Four crew members were captured and became POWs: Major Thomas W. Sumpter, Captain Hubert C. Walker and 1/Lt Ronald M. Lebert, all electronic warfare officers, and Major Irby Terrell, navigator. Source: Hobson/other.

March 6, 1968   EB-66E   54-0524   41TEWS/355TFW, Takhli RTAFB, Thailand
'Baffle 2' was fragged for a 6+ hour night, classified ECM support mission, with an air refueling scheduled 2+35 hours after take-off. The flight progressed normally. Viking Control vectored Baffle 2 to the scheduled refueling rendezvous with a KC-135 tanker; Call sign: Blue Anchor 35 Papa. Baffle 2 made several brief contacts, but was unable to take on sufficient fuel. At about 2+50 after take-off Baffle 2 experienced a rumble in #2 engine; the engine flamed out. Momentarily the other engine flamed out as well, came back on line, then flamed out for the final time. As the aircraft descended through flight level 120 the pilot made the decision to abandon aircraft. The ejection occurred in the prescribed sequence, with the pilot, Captain William H. Lewark, Jr., ejecting last. Major Alfred S. Benziger's, navigator, automatic chute device failed. While clawing for the D-ring Major Benziger ripped off a portion of a finger on his right hand. Captain Warren K. Marler was the electronic warfare officer. Blue Anchor 35 Papa then observed a huge explosion as Baffle 2 impacted the ground. The tanker circled the area for the next three hours, initiated the rescue effort, stayed in continuous contact with the downed aircrew, and provided essential navigation fixes for rescue aircraft. Source: AFSC.

July 19, 1968   EB-66B   53-0491   41TEWS/355TFW, Takhli RTAFB, Thailand
'Hokum 4' flew a standard night tactical ECM support mission, experiencing IFF/SIF failure about 100 miles out of Takhli. Approach control, using skin paint, positively identified Hokum 4 by having the aircraft make a 30 degree identification turn. The pilot reported good visual contact with the airfield and the runway 20 miles out from the base. When handed over to the final controller Hokum 4 flew a reportedly satisfactory precision approach, never more than 30 feet off the glide path. At three-quarters of a mile from touchdown the controller informed Hokum 4 of being 30 feet below glide path, when the aircraft entered a sudden heavy rain shower, obscuring the pilots view of the runway. Captain David M. Bentley decided to initiate a go-around when the aircraft struck the ground 2,473 feet short of the GCA touchdown point. The aircraft skidded along the ground for a considerable distance, a small fire developing under the left wing, and heavy rain continuing to fall. The crew jettisoned their escape hatches and assembled about 100 yards in front of the wrecked aircraft. The fire was rapidly extinguished. There were no injuries. Captain Wesley R. Hill was the navigator and Captain Robert B. Huey, Jr., the electronic warfare officer. Source: AFSC.

April 8, 1969   EB-66B   53-0498   42TEWS/355TFW, Takhli RTAFB, Thailand
'Hydra 9' was scheduled for a standard 2+50 hours ECM support mission near the MuGia Pass, a standard target for B-52 bombers. The crew had sufficient time for a thorough preflight, taxied, maintaining communication with the tower through clearance for take-off. Local procedures called for a change to departure control and to monitor guard frequency just before take-off. The pilot "Rogered" his intent to do so. Weather was clear, temperature 79F. During the take-off roll, at approximately the 5,200 foot point from brake-release, the tower controller called on UHF guard channel, "Hydra 9, Takhli, you have white smoke coming from your left engine...your engine is on fire." Hydra 9 did not acknowledge, continuing its take-off roll, lifting off, climbing very little before crashing left wing slightly low, tumbling and bursting into flame. (It is suspected that the pilot may have been talking on the interphone while the tower tried to contact him). The navigator and electronic warfare officer ejected too late, and landed in the burning aircraft. As a result of this accident and two other similar incidents, all engines with 12,000 hours were pulled to replace the 13th stage, prone to failure. Rescue arrived within 5 minutes of the crash, across the highway from the base, in Takhli township. All three crew members perished. Lieutenant Colonel James E. Ricketts, Jr., pilot (Commander 42TEWS). Lieutenant Colonel Edwin P. Anderson, Jr., squadron navigator. Captain Joseph M. Orlowski, electronic warfare officer. Source: AFSC/other.

June 24, 1969   RB-66B   53-0415   4417CCTS/363TRW, Shaw AFB, SC
We were flying out of Myrtle Beach AFB, because Shaw's runways were undergoing repair, training replacement crews for Southeast Asia. The night of June 24 Major Edwin B. Welch was the IP on 'Flaw 61', an RB-66B model we used for aerial refueling training. This night refueling was the final sortie for Majors Jimmy L. Cornwell, pilot, and Rudolph H. Hentschel, navigator, before certifying them as combat ready. The squadron commander, Lt/Colonel Delbert Hainley, was in another airplane, on the 'perch', behind Welch, when the accident happened. Hainley saw 415 get its fuel, back off from the KC-135 tanker, and immediately after clearing the refueling basket (drogue) the airplane snap to the left and disappear into the darkness of night. I was 5 miles back in the stream of aircraft awaiting my turn to refuel when I heard the commotion, and almost immediately heard beepers. I knew they had gone in. Hainley flying behind the stricken aircraft on guard frequency canceled all further refueling and ordered his aircraft to return to Myrtle Beach. By the time we landed the two student survivors of 415 had already called in and were being picked up. When we assembled the wreckage on the floor of a hangar at Seymour Johnson AFB, this is what we found. After getting his fuel and disconnecting from the tanker's drogue, the student pilot yawed his airplane just a little and allowed the #2 engine to ingest 20-40 gallons of fuel spray (normal). This engine had a 10-inch crack in the compressor case (we were allowed to fly with up to an 8-inch crack). The ingested fuel was forced out of the crack around the hot section of the engine nacelle and exploded. The explosion took out the front engine mount, the engine dropped to a 20-30 degree angle, the slip stream ripped it off, pulling the pylon off with it. The loss of the right engine caused the airplane to roll violently to the left. As the airplane rolled, the engine hit a tail fin and tore off the aft section of the airplane. The airplane ended up in an inverted spin until hitting the ground. Major Edwin B. Welch, the instructor pilot, who was out of his seat observing the student pilot, managed to get back to his seat and eject. He incurred fatal injuries upon releasing himself from his parachute harness, caught in a 40-foot high tree, falling head first to the ground. The fact that the aircraft was allowed to fly with a known crack in the engine compressor is a controversial decision with dire consequences. All aircraft at Takhli were grounded for a period while engines were inspected for cracks in compressor casings. Source: Maj D. Osborne/Accident Inv. Off./AFSC.

October 9, 1969   EB-66E   54-0536   39TEWS/36TFW, Spangdahlem AB, Germany
'Cern 34' was scheduled for a standard USAFE Reg 51-66 training mission with a take off time of 1200Z. All preflight and take-off preparations were normal. The computed take-off distance was 6,550 feet. The aircraft did not break ground, instead, at the 8,000 foot point the engines were heard being retarded, the drag chute was deployed, and the pilot broadcast 'Abort. Abort.' Cern 34 continued down the centerline of the runway and overrun, its final resting place being 950 feet from the end of the overrun. The aircraft immediate burst into flames. The navigator, Lt/Colonel Frank W. Fucich, managed to escape with serious burns and a broken leg. Major Kenneth H. Kelly, pilot, and Captain John A. Holley, electronic warfare officer, perished. Aircraft apparently did not achieve take-off speed, suspected flap-blowback. Source: AFSC/other.

April 21, 1970   EB-66E   54-0439   42TEWS/355TFW, Takhli RTAFB, Thailand
At 1000 Local, 21 April 1970, 'Wring 69' was on its way from Takhli AB, Thailand, via Hickam AFB, Hawaii, to Tulsa, Oklahoma, for IRAN - inspect and repair as necessary. The aircrew, from the 42nd TEWS at Takhli was Major William A. Fletcher, pilot; Major Charles D. Quinn, navigator; and Sergeant George W. Stevens, crew chief. At 0930 the pilot started engines and followed his accompanying KC-135 tanker toward the active runway. At 0959 Wring 69 advanced power to take the active, when number 2 engine experienced explosions and severe vibrations, and began to burn. The pilot seeing only flames shut down number 1 and ordered the crew to abandon the aircraft. The navigator and the crew chief escaped through the crew entrance door; the pilot released his escape hatch and escaped down the fuselage and over the left wing. The crash-net was activated at 1000, the first fire trucks arrived at 1002 and blanketed the right wing and #2 engine with foam and CO2; the fire was under control at 1002:40. Source: AFSC.

October 26, 1970   EB-66C   54-0384   42TEWS/388TFW, Korat RTAFB, Thailand
"Furl" was returning from a night combat mission the morning of 26 October 1970. The aircraft was cleared for an airborne surveillance radar approach; weather was 3 miles in rain. The penetration was

normal. On final approach the aircraft was cleared to a minimum descent altitude of 1,140 feet to runway 06. The pilot, Major Donald L. Eversole, continued descent below the MDA although neither he nor the navigator, Major John F. O'Malley, had the field in sight visually. The aircraft then passed through small trees and bushes, struck the ground about 3 miles short of the runway, became airborne again, and several seconds later reimpacted the ground, finally coming to rest two miles short of the runway. The aircraft was destroyed by fire. All crew members survived, although several with severe injuries. The electronic warfare officers on board were Lt/Colonel Alton B. Duke, Jr., Majors Alva E. Driscoll and Richard L. Bartholomew, and Captain Merlyn L. Luke. Source: Ltr from 42TEWS/CC to Sq Personnel/AFSC.

March 11, 1971   EB-66C   55-0389   42TEWS/388TFW, Korat RTAFB, Thailand

'Rick 31' was scheduled for an electronic search mission of North Vietnam. Takeoff and climb were routine until departure control requested Rick 31 to level off at 7,000 feet MSL. When the autopilot pitch trim knob was rotated to initiate the level off, the aircraft pitched up violently. Lieutenant Colonel Melvin L. Jackson, pilot, pushed the control column full forward, disengaged the autopilot, and initiated forward A/C trim, in an attempt to counteract the pitch-up condition. The aircraft continued to climb but the airspeed had dropped by 130 knots, causing Colonel Jackson to roll the aircraft to the right to decrease lift and lower the nose so that flying airspeed could again be regained. As the aircraft rolled right it pitched up and entered a heavy buffet. Colonel Jackson gave the order to eject. Lt/Colonel Robert W. Curry navigator, and Majors George K. Klump and Albert R. Bernard, Jr., and Captain Robert J. Osterloh and 1/Lieutenant Darryl J. Bullock, electronic warfare officers, all ejected from the disabled aircraft, some suffering minor to severe injuries. Source: AFSC.

November 17, 1971   EB-66E   54-0427   42TEWS/388TFW, Udorn RTAFB, Thailand

The runway at Korat was being resurfaced at night. Missions scheduled to land during runway downtime recovered at Udorn Air Base, and after crew rest, flew another combat mission, then recovered at Korat. Captain Robert C. Helt was the pilot, 1/Lt George W. Cantrell the navigator, and Captain David G. 'Butch' Ardis served as electronic warfare officer. 'Mascot 22' took the active runway 30, completed the before take-off checklist, then advanced the throttles to military power with the brakes set, as was the procedure, when the right engine disintegrated, sending turbine blades through the main body fuel tank, just aft of the crew compartment. Captain Helt pulled engine power to idle and ordered the evacuation of the aircraft. All three crew members egressed through canopy escape hatches. The navigator and EW through the navigator's hatch, and the pilot through the pilot's hatch. Captain Ardis had initially attempted to open his escape hatch, but when flames entered the cockpit, slightly burning his right ear and neck, he had taken off his helmet, he quickly lowered the hatch again. After the crew had evacuated the aircraft the navigator's ejection seat "cooked off." The fire was under control within 10 minutes of occurrence. Source: David Ardis/George Cantrell/AFSC.

February 2, 1972   EB-66E   54-0540   42TEWS/388TFW, Korat RTAFB, Thailand

Captain Neil F. Henn, the pilot of 'Cobra 25,' led the standard pre-takeoff mission briefing for his crew of Major Merlin H. Thompson, the navigator and 1/Lt Colin D. Greany, the electronic warfare officer. It was to be a two-ship joint mission. Cobra 24 would be the lead aircraft for take-off and the duration of the mission. Engine start, taxi and quick check were all normal for both aircraft. Cobra 24 initiated take-off at 12:36. Cobra 25 followed one minute later. The take-off roll appeared normal to the crew with all systems operating normally and the computed acceleration line speeds met or exceeded at the 7, 6 and 5,000 foot runway markers. Captain Henn rotated for take-off at 140K IAS, placing the gear handle in the up position at 150K IAS. The aircraft tail made contact with the runway, then the lower ECM antennas contacted the runway, followed by fuselage contact. The aircraft slid for over 5,000 feet, coming to rest beyond the runway overrun. The crew evacuated through the pilot's and navigator's escape hatches. The aircraft was written off; there were no injuries. Source: AFSC.

April 2, 1972   EB-66C   54-0466   42TEWS/388TFW, Korat RTAFB, Thailand

'Bat 21 and 22, both EB-66C ECM/ESM support aircraft, were providing support to three B-52s striking targets just south of the DMZ. The North Vietnamese had moved SA-2 surface to air missile batteries to the area and fired two salvos of at least 10 missiles at the B-52s and B-66s. All missiles missed. A SAM site north of the DMZ then entered the fray firing three missiles, one of which hit Bat

21. The only member of the crew of six to eject safely was Lt/Colonel Iceal E. Hambleton, navigator. The remainder of the crew was killed in action. Major Wayne L. Bolte, pilot. Lieutenant Colonel Charles A. Levis, electronic warfare officer. Lieutenant Colonel Anthony R. Giannangeli, electronic warfare officer. Major Henry M. Serex, electronic warfare officer. 1/Lieutenant Robin F. Gatwood, electronic warfare officer. The rescue of Lt/Colonel Hambleton became a major SAR effort resulting in additional loss of life and aircraft. A feature movie was made of the incident in 1988. Source: Hobson/other.

August 28, 1972   EB-66C   54-0386   39TEWS/52TFW, Spangdahlem AB, Germany
'Yate 71' was scheduled for an annual tactical proficiency check, and a Creek Mule reconnaissance mission along the East German border. All aspects of the take-off were normal until reaching 6,000' of roll and 145KIAS. At this time the pilot was unable to move the yoke far enough to rotate the aircraft to a take-off attitude. A second attempt, using both hands on the yoke, failed, and the pilot initiated the abort. After the crew evacuated the aircraft it was destroyed by fire. Major Daniel H. Craven was the pilot; Major Donald E. Harding, flight-examiner pilot; Major Harry C. Wilkerson, navigator; Majors Roland M. Valentine and Larry E. Wensil, and Captains Robert S. Sherman and Kenneth L. Lykosh, electronic warfare officers. All but Craven and Harding sustained some injuries. Source: AFSC.

December 23, 1972   EB-66E   54-0529   42TEWS/388TFW, Korat RTAFB, Thailand
'Hunt 02' was one of three EB-66E aircraft launched to support Linebacker operations with ECM orbits east of Haiphong harbor. The aircraft was returning to Korat after aborting its mission due to pressurization problems. Hunt 02s approach to Korat was normal in every respect. At 2 miles the aircraft was on glide path; at decision height, Hunt 02 was on course. The final GCA controller then called "on course, on glide path, over the approach lights, on glide path" when Hunt 02 responded "Going around." The controller continued, "over landing threshold" and gave the pilot of Hunt 02 the tower frequency. Hunt 02 responded, "I just lost an engine." The landing light was observed from six miles on final until the go-around was initiated, indicating that the gear was down and locked. All available information indicated that the aircraft was in a favorable position to land when the go-around was initiated. The aircraft climbed to about 500 feet, approximately 3/4th down the runway it entered a gentle left turn to the north, descending slightly until lost from sight. The aircraft impacted in a Royal Thai Air Force housing area. Major Sasser ejected just before impact, but struck the ground before his parachute could inflate. Captain Baldwin ejected, striking a house, and the electronic warfare officer, Major Repeta, was found in the wreckage. The accident board was unable to determine the reason for the go-around when the landing was assured. This was the last B-66 to be lost in Southeast Asia. Major George F. Sasser, pilot. Captain William R. Baldwin, navigator. Major Henry J. Repeta, electronic warfare officer. Source: Lt/Col T. Buettner/Member accident inv. board/ AFSC.

May 3, 1973   EB-66E   54-0445   42TEWS/388TFW, Korat RTAFB, Thailand
The aircraft was sent to the dock for Phase VI work which included a jacking phase. When the aircraft was down-jacked, the struts were left in the extended position, which was in violation of maintenance directives. Being in the extended position meant that the landing gear safety switches were in the inflight, struts extended, position. The next action was engine trim and hot jet calibration, both required as part of Phase VI work. SSGT Lords was in the cockpit, while TSGT William E. Tompkins worked on the outside. Because of their familiarity with the procedure they did not use a checklist, and the struts remained in the extended position. Also it was later noted that the anti-skid switch was in the on position; it should have been in the off position. Both men noted that the chocks were in place and snug. The engine start-up proceeded normally. Once the engines were stabilized in idle, the parking brake was reset. Then the engines were run at full military power. After approximately two minutes running time at military power, the aircraft lurched forward, the right tire running over TSGT Tompkins left leg, virtually severing it six inches below the hip joint. The aircraft continued to travel about 70 feet before coming to a stop, colliding with and knocking down a concrete electric pole. Sergeant Lords ran to TSGT Tompkins aid and stopped the bleeding by pinching off an artery to the leg, which he continued to do until a doctor arrived. Lords' action most probably saved Sergeant Tompkins life. Although the aircraft was repairable, the phase-out of the EB-66 was expected in the near future, therefore, the aircraft was declared Class 26 and released for fire fighting practice. A number of small oversights led to a tragic end. Source: AFSC.

A Sobering Statistic
Out of a production run of 36 R/EB-66C electronic reconnaissance aircraft, 15 were lost in combat or crashed due to other causes.

Where Did All The Airplanes Go?
11TRS Yokota AB, JP - deactivated 8 March 1960
10 RB-66Cs flown to Shaw AFB, SC, and 10 363TRW C-models were flown to MASDC,
  Davis-Monthan AFB, Tucson, AZ, and scrapped.

12TRS Yokota AB, JP - deactivated 8 March 1960
  22 RB-66B aircraft put in storage at MASDC, Tucson, AZ

19TEWS Kadena Air Base, Okinawa - deactivated 31 October 1970
  4 EB-66E aircraft flown to Clark Air Base, PI, and scrapped.

39TEWS Spangdahlem Air Base, Germany - deactivated 1 January 1973
  Aircraft distributed to 42TEWS/363TRW.

39TEWTS Shaw AFB, SC - deactivated 15 March 1974
  Aircraft flown to MASDC, Tucson, AZ and scrapped.

41TEWS Takhli RTAFB, Thailand - deactivated 31 October 1969
  EB-66C/E aircraft to 39/42TEWS
  11 EB-66B aircraft stored/scrapped at MASDC, Tucson, AZ.

42TEWS Korat RTAFB, Thailand - deactivated 15 March 1974
  24 aircraft flown to Clark AB, PI, in January 1974, scrapped.

84/85/86BS RAF Sculthorpe, UK - deactivated 22 June 1962
  50 aircraft flown to MASDC, Tucson, AZ, scrapped.

RB-66Bs of units converting to the RF-4C were put in storage at MASDC, 51 of which were refurbished in 1966-67 by the Douglas Aircraft Corporation and converted to EB-66Es. The surviving 34 WB-66Ds were transferred to MASDC between 1960 and 1965 and either scrapped, or used as test beds or display aircraft.

Last Flights
EB-66C 54-0465, in January 1974, flew calibration missions against radar equipment on the Nellis Air Force Base ranges, then returned to Shaw AFB, SC, on 2 February. That was the last Air Force EB-66 mission flown. Upon deactivation of the 39th TEWTS, on March 15, 53-0465 was mounted on a pedestal in front of the Shaw Air Force Base main gate. WB-66D 55-390 was used by the Westinghouse Corporation of Baltimore, MD, as an EW test bed until 1976. It made its final flight to Kelly AFB, TX, that year, then was towed to Lackland AFB, adjacent to Kelly, for display.

B-66 Aircraft on Display
EB 54-0465C Shaw Air Force Base, SC
RB 53-0412B Chanute Aerospace Museum, Rantoul, IL
RB 53-0466B Dyess Air Force Base, TX
RB 53-0475B Museum of the United States Air Force, Wright-Patterson AFB, OH
WB 55-0390D Lackland Air Force Base, TX
WB 55-0392D Warner Robins Air Museum, GA
WB 55-0395D Pima Air & Space Museum, Tucson, AZ

B-66 Aircraft Losses by Year
(Non-combat/combat and operational)

1955	1956	1957	1958	1959	1960	1961	1962	1963	1964	1965	1966	1967
00	01	05	08	07	01	04	01	01	00/01	00/01	01/02	00/03

1968	1969	1970	1971	1972	1973	1974
00/03	02/01	01/01	00/02	02/02	01/00	00/00

*The 1964 shoot-down of an **RB-66B** over East Germany is classified as an operational loss.

B-66 Aircraft Losses by Squadron

34BS - 1	1TRS - 3	16TRS - 3	39TEWS - 2
84BS - 1	9TRS - 3	19TRS - 7	41TRS/TEWS - 9
85BS - 1	11TRS - 2	30TRS - 1	42TRS/TEWS - 10
95BS - 2	12TRS - 1	43TRS - 1	4417CCTS - 1
			448TS - 1
			6460CCTS - 2

Principal Causes of B-66 Losses

Fuel filter design - 3	FOD - 1
Pilot error - 8	Fire (broken fuel line/brakes) - 2
Supervisory error - 2	Combat (SA-2/MiG-21) - 6
Engine failure - 9	Weather - 2
Hydraulics/Mechanical/Electrical - 7	Ground accident - 1
N1 Compass failure - 2	Unknown - 8

Frequently more than one factor played a role in the loss of an aircraft.

B-66 Losses by Type
(# Built/# Lost to Combat or Accident)

RB-66A   005/00   Preproduction aircraft were used for test purposes only.

B-66B   072/05   Bombers served with 17BW; then 47BW, were equipped with B-47 K-5 radar bomb system. Retired in 1962 and scrapped. 13 airframes were converted to EB-66B Brown Cradle tactical ECM aircraft in 1959; 4 were used by ASD to conduct load bearing, gear, brake and other endurance tests.

RB-66B   145/20   Photo reconnaissance aircraft replaced by RF-4C starting in 1965. 4 aircraft equipped with IR sensors and SLAR in 1963; employed in Vietnam in 1965. 51 RB/B-66B airframes removed from storage and converted to EB-66E ECM configuration

RB/EB-66C   036/15   Electronic reconnaissance version flew from 1956 to 1974

WB-66D   036/02   Entered service in 1956. Retired between 1960 and 1965.

EB-66B   000/02   Converted B-66Bs to Brown Cradle ECM aircraft (13)

EB-66E   000/07   Converted RB-66Bs to EB-66E ECM aircraft (51)

B-66 production/losses of all types: 294/51

B-66 Aircraft Serial Numbers

RB-66A	Pre-production aircraft - 5	52-2828 to 52-2832
B-66B	Bombers - 72	53-0482 to 53-0507, 54-0477 to 54-0505,
		54-0548 to 54-0551 and 55-0302 to 55-0314
RB-66B	Photo reconnaissance aircraft - 145	53-0409 to 53-0481, 54-0417 to 54-0446
		and 54-0506 to 54-0547
RB-66C	Electronic reconnaissance aircraft - 36	54-0447 to 54-0476 and 55-0384 to 55-0389
WB-66D	Weather reconnaissance aircraft - 36	55-0390 to 55-0425

RB-66C and WB-66D models were produced at the Douglas-Tulsa plant. B-66B and RB-66B aircraft were produced at the Douglas-Long Beach plant. The 'EB' prefix replaced 'RB' in 1966 in recognition of the aircraft's primary function being electronic warfare rather than reconnaissance.

BIBLIOGRAPHY

Remembering the planes we flew, the places we saw, the men with whom we served, and that freedom is not free, never has been free, and will be ours as long as there are men and women willing to serve and die for their country.

Books, Monographs and Technical Documentation

Alling, Frederick A. History of the B/RB-66 Weapon System (1952-1959). Wright-Patterson AFB, OH: Historical Division, Office of Information, Air Materiel Command, U.S. Air Force, 1960.

Baxter, James P., Scientists Against Time, The M.I.T. Press, Cambridge, MA, 1946.

Berger, Carl, ed. The United States Air Force in Southeast Asia, 1961-1973. Washington, D.C.: Office of Air Force History, U.S. Air Force, 1977.

Bohn, John T. Development of Strategic Air Command, 1946-1976. [Omaha]: Office of the Historian, Headquarters Strategic Air Command, 1976.

Chilstrom, Kenneth and Leary, Penn, Test Flying at Old Wright Field, Westchester House Publishers, Omaha, NE, 1993.

Craven, Wesley F., and James L. Cate. The Army Air Forces in World War II. Vol. 6, Men and Planes. Washington DC: Office of Air force History, 1983.

Cunningham, Randall, Fox Two, Champlin Fighter Museum, Mesa, AZ, 1984.

Douglas Aircraft Corporation, Douglas B-66 Report No. LB-22387. Long Beach, CA, 1956.

Douglas Aircraft Corporation, RB-66A Contractor Technical Compliance Inspection. Long Beach, CA, March 22, 1954.

Dupuy, Ernest and Trevor, The Encyclopedia of Military History, Harper & Row, New York, 1970.

Eden, Paul. ed. The Encyclopedia of Modern Military Aircraft. Aerospace Publishing Ltd, London, England, 2006.

Ferrell, Robert H. ed. The Twentieth Century An Almanac. New York: World Almanac Publications, 1985.

Fletcher, Harry R. Air Force Bases: Air Bases Outside the United States of America, Vol. II. Washington, D.C.: Center for Air Force History, U.S. Air Force, 1993.

Gianutsos, Peter E. The Black Knights of the 17th Bomb Wing, Yearbook 1957, 17BW, Hurlburt Field, FL, 1967.

Green, William. The World's Fighting Planes. Doubleday and Company, Garden City, NY, 1965.

Gordon, Doug. Tactical Reconnaissance in the Cold War: 1945 to Korea, Cuba, Vietnam and the Iron Curtain. Barnsley, Great Britain: Pen & Sword Books Ltd, 2006.

Hall, Cargill R. NRO History - Early Cold War Strategic Reconnaissance. The NRO History Office, Washington DC, no date.

Hall, Cargill R. ed. Early Cold War Overflights - Symposium Proceedings. Volume I: Memoirs. Office of the Historian, National Reconnaissance Office, Washington DC, 2003.

Hall, Cargill R. Military Space and National Policy: Record and Interpretation, The George C. Marshall Institute, Washington DC, 2006.

Hanak, Walter, ed., Aces and Aerial Victories: The U.S. Air Force in Southeast Asia, 1965-1973. AF/HO/U.S. Air Force, Washington DC., 1976.

Haulman, Daniel L. One Hundred Years of Flight. Air Force History and Museums Program. Air University Press, Maxwell AFB, AL, 2003.

Hobson, Christopher M. Vietnam Air Losses: United States Air Force, Navy and Marine Corps Fixed-Wing Aircraft Losses in Southeast Asia 1961-1973. Hinkley, England: Midland Publishing, 2001.

Holzapple, Joseph R. The 47th Bombardment Wing in England 1955, Yearbook, 47BW, RAF Sculthorpe, UK, 1955

Hrivnak, Michael J. 50th Anniversary Shaw Air Force Base, S.C. 1941-1991. Sumter, SC: Office of History, 363 Tactical Fighter Wing, 1991.

James, Martin E. Historical Highlights, United States Air Forces in Europe 1945-1979. APO New York 09012: Office of History, Headquarters USAFE, 1980.

Jones, Vincent C., Manhattan: The Army and the Atomic Bomb, U.S. Army, Washington, D.C., 1985 pp. 530-540.

Kennan, George F. Memoirs, 1925-1950, Boston: Little, Brown, 1967.

Knaack, Marcelle S. Post-World War II Bombers 1945-1973. Vol II. Washington, D.C.: Office of Air Force History, U.S. Air Force, 1988.

Knaack, Marcelle S. Post-World War II Fighters 1945-1973. Washington, D.C.: Office of Air Force History, U.S. Air Force, 1986.

Lavalle, A.J.C. ed. The Tale of Two Bridges and The Battle for the Skies over North Vietnam, Vol I. Washington, D.C.: Office of Air Force History, U.S. Air Force, 1976.

Lavalle, A.J.C. ed. Airpower and the 1972 Spring Invasion, Vol II. Washington, D.C.: Office of Air Force History, U.S. Air Force, 1976.

Lavalle, A.J.C. ed. Last Flight From Saigon, Vol IV, Washington D.C.: Office of Air Force History, U.S. Air Force, 1978.

LeMay, Curtis E. Mission with LeMay. New York: Doubleday, 1965.

Lorell, Mark A. Bomber R&D Since 1945: The Role of Experience. Santa Monica, CA: RAND Corporation, 1995.

Lyon, Peter. Eisenhower: Portrait of the Hero. Boston: Little, Brown, 1974.

Manchester, William. The Glory and the Dream: A Narrative History of America, 1932-1972. Boston: Little, Brown, 1973.

McCullough, David. Truman. New York: Simon and Schuster, 1992.

McDaniel, Norman A. Yet Another Voice, Hawthorne Books, New York, 1975.

McVeigh, W. B. ed. RB/B-66B Familiarization Manual, Douglas Aircraft Corporation, Long Beach, CA, 1956.

Mack, Stephen B. Shaw Air Force Base, South Carolina, 1956, Army & Navy Publishing Co., Baton Rouge, LA, 1956.

Momyer, William W., Air Power in Three Wars (WWII, Korea, Vietnam). Washington, D.C.: Department of Defense, Department of the Air Force, 1978

Mueller, Robert. Air Force Bases: Active Air Force Bases Within the United States of America on 17 September 1982, Vol I. Washington, D.C.: Office of Air Force History, U.S. Air Force, 1989.

Nalty, Bernard C. Air Power and the Fight for Khe Sanh, Office of Air Force History, U.S. Air Force, Washington D.C., 1973.

Palmer, Bruce, Jr. The Twenty-five-Year War: America's Military Role in Vietnam. Lexington: University Press of Kentucky, 1984.

Pribbenow, Merle L. II. The -Ology War: Technology and Ideology in the Vietnamese Defense of Hanoi, 1967. The Journal of Military History, Vol 67, January 2003.

Price, Alfred. The History of US Electronic Warfare: The Years of Innovation-Beginnings to 1946, Vol I. Westford, MA: The Murray Printing Company, 1984. Vol II: The Renaissance Years, 1946 to 1964, 1989. Vol III: Rolling Thunder Through Allied Force, 1964 to 2000, 2000.

RB/B-66B Familiarization Manual. Long Beach, CA: Douglas Aircraft Company, 1956.

Rich, Ben R. Skunk Works. New York: Little, Brown, 1994.

Richards, Leverett, G. TAC: The Story of the Tactical Air Command.

Ridgway, Matthew B. Soldier: The Memoirs of Matthew B. Ridgway. Westport, CT: Greenwood Press, 1956.

Roth, Mick & Francillon, Rene. Aerofax Minigraph 19: Douglas B-66 Destroyer. Arlington, TX: Aerofax Inc., 1988.

Samuel, Wolfgang W. E. American Raiders: The Race to Capture the Luftwaffe's Secrets. Jackson: University Press of Mississippi, 2004.

Samuel, Wolfgang W. E. I Always Wanted to Fly: America's Cold War Airmen. Jackson: University Press of Mississippi, 2001.

Schlight, John. A War Too Long: The History of the USAF in Southeast Asia. Washington, D.C.: Air Force History and Museums Program, U.S. Air Force, 1996.

Schneider, Donald K. Air Force Heroes in Vietnam. Maxwell Air Force Base, AL: Airpower Research Institute, 1979.

Smith, Richard K. 75 Years of Inflight Refueling: Highlights, 1923-1998. Washington, D.C.: Air Force History and Museums Program, Department of the Air Force, 1998.

Stroop, Paul D. Chief of Bureau of Naval Weapons, Aircraft Recognition Manual NavWeaps 00-80T-75, Department of Defense, Washington DC, 1962.

Summers, Harry G. Jr., Korean War Almanac, New York, Facts On File, Inc., 1990.

Summers, Harry G. Jr., The Vietnam War Almanac, Novato, CA, Presidio Press, 1999.

Tilford, Earl H. Jr. Setup: What the Air Force did in Vietnam and Why. Maxwell AFB, AL: Air University Press, 1991.

Toperczer, Istvan, Air War Over North Vietnam: The Vietnamese People's Air Force 1949-1975, Squadron/Signal Publications, 1998.

Truman, Harry S. Memoirs. 2 Vols. Garden City, NY: Doubleday, 1955.

United States Air Force Combat Victory Credits Southeast Asia. Washington, D.C.: Office of Air Force History, U.S. Air Force, 1974.

Winchester, Jim. Ed. American Military Aircraft. Barnes&Noble Books, New York, 2005.

Periodical Articles

A Good Thought to Sleep On, John L. Frisbee, Air Force Magazine, March 1992.

Birds of a Feather, Steve Pace, Airpower, July 1988, pp 10-37.

Ceaseless Watch, Warren E. Thompson, Fly Past, pp 62-67.

Cold War: The Douglas RB-66 Story, Warren E. Thompson, Airpower, May 2006, pp 29-41.

Destination Freedom, Fletcher Aviation Corporation, Aviation Week, April 26, 1954.

Douglas EB-66/EKA-3B, Allin R. Scholin, Air Progress, October 1968, pp 46-48.

EB-66 Training, Kenneth B. Coolidge, Tactical Air Reconnaissance Digest, November 1967, pp 6-9.

Emblems of Courage, Fred L. Borch & Robert F. Dorr, Military Officer, May 2007, pp 70-73.

Going Down With the Ships, Craig Hooper, The Washington Post, March 5, 2007, p A15.

Hostile Radar Location Gear Pushed, Barry Miller, Aviation Week & Space Technology, September 1, 1969.

Letter to the Editor, Major Kenneth H. High, USAF (Ret.), Air Force Magazine, May 1991, p 10.

Letter to the Editor, Karl H. Schroder, Air Classics, January 1974, p 61.

Magic Carpet to Survival, Dr. Alfred Price, The Journal of Electronic Defense, April 2006, pp 31-33.

Missiles of October, Michael Dobbs, The Washington Post Magazine, October 23, 2003, pp 15-18.

Missions Accomplished: The Incredible Story of the USS Indianapolis, Stephen White, Solano Historian, Vol. 19-2, Winter/Spring 2003-2004, pp. 8-25.

Radar Bombing, Klong Times, Don Muang RTAFB, Thailand, July 15, 1966.

Radar Bombing during Rolling Thunder - Part 1: Ryan's Raiders, W. Howard Plunkett, Air Power History, Spring 2006, pp 4-21.

Radar Bombing during Rolling Thunder - Part 2: Combat Lancer and Commando Club, W. Howard Plunkett, Air Power History, Summer 2006, pp 4-19.

Reds' Surprise: 15,000-Lb-Thrust Jets, Robert Hotz, Aviation Week, May 31, 1954.

The ADC Story, Richard F. McMullen, Interceptor, September 1972, pp 10-15.

The Air Force and the Cold War: A Chronology, 1945-91, John T. Correll, Air Force Magazine, September 2005, pp 70-75.

The Other Jammer, August R. Seefluth, Air Force Magazine, March 1992, pp 74-77.
The Periscope, Newsweek, November 23, 1955, p 23.
The USAF's Destroyer, Richard K. Schrader, Air Classics, April 1988, pp 20-22.
Those Were the Days: Flying Safety during the Transition to Jets, 1944-53, Kenneth P. Werrell, Air Power History, Winter 2005, pp 39-53
USAF Simulates Soviet Defense System, Barry Miller, Aviation Week & Space Technology, May 30, 1970..
Various, American Aviation, May 24, 1954, pp 1-66.
Veteran Aircraft Returns to Spang, Skyblazer, 36TFW, Bitburg and Spangdahlem air bases, Germany, March 20, 1970.
Vietnam TAC-RECCE, Part I, Doug Gordon, Air Enthusiast, July/August 2004, pp 66-75.
Vietnam TAC-RECCE, Part II, Doug Gordon, Air Enthusiast, Sept/October 2004, pp 58-68.
War of the Wizards, Loren B. Leonberger, Airman, November 1970, pp 17-19.
Yesteryear...The Douglas B/RB/WB-66 Destroyer, R.E. Williams, Douglas Service, June 1982.

Internet Sites
Air Force Historical Studies Office, Operation Linebacker II, www.airforcehistory.hq.af.mil
Air Force Historical Research Agency, www.afhra.maxwell.af.mil
Answers.com, USS Pueblo, www.answers.com
Army, Navy & Air Power, Time Magazine, July 12, 1954, www.time.com
B52 Combat Losses/Operational Losses in Vietnam, www.nampows.org/B-52.html
B-66 internet site, www.b66.info.com
1958 & Beyond, Time Magazine, Feb 25, 1957, www.time.com
Rushden.Org, RAF Chelveston, www.rushden.org
The Harrowing War in the Air, Time Magazine, May 1, 1972, www.time.com
Out of Briefcases & Red Folders: A Classic Show of Power & Speed, Time Magazine, July 28, 1958, www.time.com
USAF Historical Research Center, Maxwell AFB, AL. History and Lineage of the 42nd Squadron www.au.af.mil
Zook, David S. Lt/Colonel, USAF (Ret.), Seven Years of Vietnam - A Raven Goes to War. www.ocs60c.com/zookraven.htm

United States Air Force Documentation/Correspondence
Active Passive ECM Spt of Commando Club on MSN, msg, 355TFW to 7AF, 11 Feb 1968.
Aircraft Equipment (B/RB-66), Ltr from HQ TAC, Langley AFB, VA, to HQ AF/Director of Requirements, Washington DC, 2 April 1953.
B-47 vs Aircraft Now Programmed for Tactical and Light Bomb Units, Memorandum from HQ TAC/ OA to TAC/RQ, Langley AFB, VA, 1 December 1954.
Conference on ECM Configuration of B-RB-66 Aircraft, HQ Tactical Air Command, Langley AFB, VA, memorandum, 26 March 1953.
Control Evaluation RB-66B, AF Flight Test Center, Edwards AFB, CA, 2/Lt Jerome B. Reed, Project Engineer, Lt/Colonel Harold G. Russell, Project Pilot, October 1955.
Cooper, Larry T. Colonel, USAF, 388TFW/DO, Korat RTAFB, Thailand, End of Tour Report, 2 June 1973 - 2 June 1974.
Crouch, Robert K. Colonel, USAF, Commander 388TFW, Korat RTAFB, Thailand, End of Tour Report, 1 July 1973 to 3 January 1974.
EB-66 Effectiveness Evaluations, Comfy Coat, USAFSS, San Antonio, TX, undated.
EB-66 Assistance Team Recap, msg from 355TFW to WRAMA Robins AFB, GA, 26 Feb 68.
EB-66 Evaluation, Summary Report, USAFSS, 2 January 1971, 7AF/DOPR.
EB-66 Organization, Ltr, CSAF/John D. Ryan, to CINCPACAF, 4 Sep 1969.
EB-66 Organization Takhli, msg, CINCPACAF to CSAF, 17 April 1968.
EB-66 Support Tactics, Ltr from 7AF/DOE to PACAF/DO, 23 March 1970.
Electronic Countermeasures in the B/RB-66, Ltr from HQ/USAF to Commanding General, Air Research and Development Command, Baltimore, MD, 20 Feb 1953.
Forty-two TEWS Crew Manning, 7AF Recon/EW Division, 31 December 1970.
History of the Tactical Air Command, 1 January - 30 June 1953.

History of the Tactical Air Command, 1 January - 30 June 1954.

History of the Tactical Air Command, Vols I, II, III, 1 July - 31 December 1954.

History of the AF Plant Representative, Douglas Aircraft Co, Long Beach, CA, Jan - Jun 1955.

History of the AF Plant Representative, Douglas Aircraft Co, Long Beach, CA, Jul - Dec 1955.

History of the 17th Bombardment Wing, 1 July - 31 December 1955.

History of the 66th TRW, 1 July - 31 December 1956.

History of the 363rd Tactical Reconnaissance Wing, Vol I, III, 1 January - 30 June 1956.

History of the AMC Liaison Office, San Bernardino AMA, Edwards AFB, CA, 1 July - 31 December 1956.

History of the 363rd Tactical Reconnaissance Wing, July 1 - 31 December 1956.

History of the AF Plant Representative Office, Douglas Aircraft Co, Long Beach, CA, 1 Jan - 30 Jun 1957.

History of the 67th TRW, 1 July - 31 December 1957.

History of the 47th Bomb Wing, 1 January - 30 June 1958.

History of the 363rd Tactical Reconnaissance Wing, 1 January - 30 June 1958.

History of the 4440th Aircraft Delivery Group (TAC), 15 January - 30 June 1958.

History of the 363rd Tactical Reconnaissance Wing, 1 January - 30 June 1959.

History of the 4440th Aircraft Delivery Group, Langley AFB, VA, 1 Jan 62 - 30 Jun 62.

History of the 363rd TRW, 1 July - 31 December 1966.

History of the 41st TEWS, 355TFW, Takhli RTAFB, Thailand, 1 July - 30 September 1967.

History of the 355th TFW, Takhli RTAFB, Thailand, January - March 1968.

History of the 41st TEWS, Takhli RTAFB, Thailand, 1 April - 30 June 1968.

History of the 355th TFW, Vol I, Takhli RTAFB, Thailand, April - June 1968.

History of the 355th TFW, Vol II, Takhli RTAFB, Thailand, October - December 1968.

History of the 355TFW, Vol 1, Takhli RTAFB, Thailand, January - March 1969.

History of the 2nd Aircraft Delivery Group, Langley AFB, VA, 1 October - 31 December 1969.

History of the 355TFW, Vol III, Takhli RTAFB, Thailand, October - December 1969.

History of the 41TRS/TEWS, (condensed), June 1965 - 31 October 1969.

History of the 42nd TEWS, 355TFW, Takhli RTAFB, Thailand, 1 October - 31 December 1969.

History of the 388TFW, Vol 2, Korat RTAFB, Thailand, January-March 1973.

History of the 42nd Tactical Electronic Warfare Squadron, Korat RTAFB, Thailand, 1 April - 30 June 1973.

History of the 42nd Tactical Electronic Warfare Squadron, Korat RTAFB, Thailand, 1 July - 30 September 1973.

History of the 42nd Tactical Electronic Warfare Squadron, Korat RTAFB, Thailand, 1 October 1973 - 31 January 1974.

Improved Turret for B-66, Memoranda, from TAC/OA to DO, 9 March 1954.

Increasing Electronic Warfare Officer Training, Ltr, AFMPC, Randolph AFB, TX, to ATC/SR, Randolph AFB, TX, 31 August 1967.

Letter Order 10CAG (3-451), HQ 10TRW, Spangdahlem Air Base, Germany, 11 March 1958.

Letter Order 10ADM (4-696), HQ 10TRW, Spangdahlem Air Base, Germany, 11 April 1958.

Lightweight J-57 Engine for F-100 Aircraft, Ltr HQ AF, Washington DC, to Commander, TAC, Langley AFB, VA, September 10, 1953.

Limited Phase IV Performance and Stability RB-66C, AF Flight Test Center, Edwards AFB, CA, Harry W. Berkowitz, Project Engineer; Captain John E. Allavie, Project Pilot, Jan 1958.

Minutes of EB-66 Tactics Meeting, 42TEWS/355TFW, Takhli RTAFB, Thailand, 7 Feb 1970.

North American Report No. NA-53-955, Memorandum HQ TAC/OA to OT/RQ, Langley AFB, VA, 11 Jan 1954.

Operations Plan 66-56, Annex B, Logistics, 17BW, Hurlburt Field, FL, 28 October 1955.

Operations Proposal IX, from 41/42TEWS Tactics Team to DCO/66, 20 Feb 68.

Operations Order 79-57, 17BW, Annex B, Air Operations (47BS deployment to RAF Sculthorpe), 20 December 1957.

Personnel Rotation Program for Southeast Asia, Ltr, AF/MPC, Randolph AFB, TX to all Commands, 1 November 1967.

Phase IV Performance Test RB-66B, AF Flight Test Center, Edwards AFB, CA, Eldon J. Snawder (Engineer), Captain Charles C. Bock, Project Pilot, 25 April 1956.

Phase IV Stability and Limited Performance Test, AF Flight Test Center, Edwards AFB, CA, 1/Lt
Jerome B. Reed, Project Engineer; Captain John M. Carlson, Project Pilot, Sep 1957.

Phase V (Adverse Weather) Flight Test of RB-66B Aircraft, Wright-Patterson AFB, OH, Edward A.
Vincent, July 1956.

Position Paper on Removal of EB-66 ECM Support for Photo Reconnaissance in RP-1, 7 AF,
undated.

Preparation for Conversion to B-66B Aircraft - 345BG, from HQ TAC, Langley AFB, VA, to
Commander, 405FBW, Langley AFB, VA, 29 July 1954.

Program Changes, msg from CSAF to CINCPACAF, 23 Dec 70.

RB-66 Tactical Support Airplane (Description of airplane and requirements), Report provided by HQ
AMC, Wright-Patterson AFB, OH, to Commanding General, TAC, Langley AFB, VA, May 22,
1953.

Reconnaissance in SEASIA, July 1966-June 1969, Project CHECO Report, HQ PACAF, Directorate,
Tactical Evaluation, 15 July 1969.

Reduction of EB-66 Flying Hour Allocation, Ltr from 355TFW/CC to 13AF/CC, 17 Apr 1970.

Reports of Aircraft Accidents, B/RB/WB/EB-66A/B/C/D, AF Forms 14.

Report of TDY - Major Reginald W. Wagner; HQ AMC - WADC, ECM Weapons Phasing Group, re
Ground Rules Governing the B/RB-66 ECM Modification Program, 16 Dec 1954.

Report of TDY - Major E.T. Eden, to 26th Meeting of B/RB-66 Weapons Phasing Group, HQ AMC,
Wright-Patterson AFB, OH, 10 December 1954.

Retention of EB-66 in SEA, Ltr Colonel Joseph E. Thome, HQ PACAF, to Lt/Colonel Gilbert E.
Shortt, HQ 7AF/DO, 28 Dec 1970.

Retention of EB-66 in SEA, Response from Lt/Colonel Shortt to 28 Dec 57 ltr from Colonel Thome,
Jan 1971.

Special Orders 25TRG P-6, 8 July 1965; 25TRW T-375 10 Oct 1965; T-457 20 Oct 1965; T-44 12
January 1966; A- 468 4 may 1966.

Special Orders 363TRW TB-172 4 May 1965; TB-200 29 June 1965.

Special Order HQ 7AF, G-529, 1 July 1966.

Status Report, Operations and Air Training Activity 1956, HQ 17BW, Hurlburt Field, FL, to
Commander 9th Air Force, 5 April 1956.

Status Report, Operations and Air Training Activity 1959, HQ 17BW, Hurlburt Field, FL, to
Commander 9th Air Force, re transfer of B-66 to 47BW.

Support Forces for Arc Light, Talking Paper, undated.

Syllabus of Instruction for Tactical Reconnaissance Crew RB-66, 4411CCTG, Shaw AFB, SC, 1959.

Tactical Electronic Warfare in SEA (EB-66), 355TFW/DCO-66, 28 Sep 1969.

Technical Order 1B-66{E}B-1 Flight Manual EB-66B, RB-66B & EB-66C Aircraft. U.S. Air Force,
1967.

Trip Report, QRC-160 Assistance Team, Visit to SEA, 6 Dec 1966; Warner Robins Air Materiel Area,
Robins AFB, Georgia, to HQ PACAF, 6 December 1966.

Unsatisfactory Reports, AFTO 29, Serial Numbers: 55-1016; 55-1123-25; 55-1155-56; 55-1629-30;
55-1678-80; 55-1688-94; 55-1703(1-4); 55-1719-21; 55-1744, AF Flight Test Center, Edwards
AFB, CA, 1955.

USAF Electronic Warfare in SEA, Talking Paper, 7AF/DOE, Colonel Wack, 12 Nov 1969.

USAF Tactical Reconnaissance in Southeast Asia, July 69 - June 71, Project CHECO Report, HQ
PACAF, Directorate of Operations Analysis, 23 November 1971.

United States Air Force Management Summary: Southeast Asia Review, Calendar Years 1961-1972.
Washington, D.C.: Headquarters United States Air Force, 1972.

Interviews
Alumbaugh, Lester Lieutenant Colonel, USAF (Ret.)
Belli, Robert E. Lieutenant Colonel, USAF.
Bloomkamp, Frank Colonel, USAF (Ret.)
Chilstrom, Kenneth Colonel, USAF (Ret.)
Copler, Thomas Colonel, USAF (Ret.)
Divich, Chris Major General, USAF (Ret.)
Eby, David Colonel, USAF (Ret.)

Giraudo, John C. Major General, USAF (Ret.)
Harding, Donald E. Lieutenant Colonel, USAF (Ret.)
Kaehn, Albert Brigadier General, USAF (Ret.)
Kersis, Alexander J. Lieutenant Colonel, USAF (Ret.)
Lobdell, Harrison Major General, USAF (Ret.)
Martin, Francis T. Lieutenant Colonel, USAF (Ret.)
McMullen, Francis R. Father, Colonel, USAF (Ret.)
Milam, James R. Colonel, USAF (Ret.)
Parrott, Cliff Douglas Aircraft Corporation (Ret.)
Pedroli, Attilio Bridgadier General, USAF (Ret.)
Reponen, Gerald Lieutenant Colonel, USAF (Ret.)
Sapere, Joseph R. Lieutenant Colonel, USAF (Ret.)
Starnes, William Lieutenant Colonel, USAF (Ret.)
Taylor, Arthur K. Colonel, USAF (Ret.)
Webster, Robert Lieutenant Colonel, USAF (Ret.)
Widic, Frank Lieutenant Colonel, USAF (Ret.)

Pictures
Pictures used in the book came from various sources including the author, the Air Force Flight Test Center, Frank Bloomkamp, David Cooper, Thomas Copler, David Eby, Robert Ganci, Scott Hegland, Alexander Kersis, Guenther Klassen, Francis McMullen, John Norden, Cliff Parrott, 'Pete' Pedroli, Theodore Pruss, Joseph Snoy, Robert Stamm, Anthony Tambini, Thomas Taylor, Robert Webster, Robert Welch, Alec Bailey, Richard Anderson, James Phillips.

Letters/ Other Written Communications
B-66 Destroyer Association Newsletters, quarterly 2002-2007
Bruenner, Willi, Colonel, USAF (Ret.) - Emails re RB-66 operations in Germany/SEA.
Buettner, Terry Lt/Colonel, USAF (Ret.) - emails B-66 operations at Korat 1972-1973.
Bullock, Lawrence - emails re RB-66C operations in 1965, SEA.
Canady, Joe Major, USAF (Ret.) - email: Brief History of Joe Canady's 1st 100 Missions over North Vietnam 1965 to 1966.
Ciz, George C. Lt/Colonel, USAF (Ret.) - email Flying with the 39th TEWS.
Christman, Don Lt/Colonel, USAF (Ret.) - email Pilot perspective of flying the B-66 out of Takhli, Thailand.
Colburn, Ned Lt/Colonel, USAF (Ret.) - Memorandum: A perspective on his AF career. Emails: Remembering old friends - Paul Bjork & Carl Covey; Black Sea operations;
Coolidge, Kenneth - email re early Vietnam combat missions.
Cooper, David D. - Ltr, B-66 operations out of Yokota AB, Japan.
Douglas Aircraft Company, Douglas-Navy A3D Skywarrior Background Release, El Segundo Division, CA, undated.
Darrah, Ronald L. - Memoranda re Lebanon Deployment 1958.
Davis, John MSGT, USAF (Ret.) - email 17BW/37BS, Victor Alert at Sculthorpe.
Davis, Rex L. - email re Royal Flush and Brown Cradle employment in England.
Eaker, Ira C. Lt/General, USAF (Ret.) - Ltr to Colonel Harris B. Hull, HQ PACAF, re lack of spares for B-66 aircraft.
Erbe, Richard MSGT, USAF (Ret.) - emails: deployment from Toul-Rosieres to Tan Son Nhut.
Espe, Ira K. Colonel, USAF (Ret.) - email Comments on B-66 deployment to Korea , Feb 68.
Everson, Dale Lt/Colonel, USAF (Ret.) - email Blue Cradle operations at Lockbourne AFB, OH.
Fitzgerald, Tom - re R/EB-66C 54-459.
Frankenberg, Dave Colonel, USAF (Ret.) - ltr re RB-66 operations out of Yokota AB, Japan.
Ganci, Robert J. MSGT, USAF (Ret.) - emails re life of a gunner 47BW/10TRW.
Gould, Kenneth G. Dr. MD PhD, Colonel, USAF (Ret.) - Memoranda: A flight surgeon's perspective on war in Southeast Asia, Takhli RTAFB, Thailand.
Hegland, Scott - Emails re RB-66 operations out of Yokota AB, Japan.
Helmke, Kermit W. Lt/Colonel, USAF (Ret.) - Emails relating to B-66 operations.
High, Kenneth Lt/Colonel, USAF (Ret.) - Memos re Mobile Zebra and Presidential Escort.

Holland, David I. Major, USAF (Ret.) - Memorandum 'Check-ride to Soviet Detention.'

Hull, Harris B. Colonel, USAF - Ltr dtd Feb 3, 1958 to Lt/General, USAF (Ret.) Ira C. Eaker, re Sputnik and Cold War.

Johnson, Gayle P. - Email re firepower demo at Eglin AFB, FL.

Kash, Norman Lt/Colonel, USAF (Ret.) - emails re EB-66E OT&E at Eglin.

Leeper, Tom - email re SA-2 launch near Ban Karai Pass, NVN, 1971.

Long, Robert - email re initial deployment from Shaw to Tan Son Nhut.

Mansperger, Robert SMSGT, USAF (Ret.) - email re failing escape hatch seals on RB-66.

Maul, Paul Colonel, USAF (Ret.) - Memo re Palace Cobra, New Guys in TAC, Air Refueling Challenges.

McCain, Otis E. Lt/Colonel, USAF (Ret.) - emails re testing and introduction of ECM pods.

McClintock, Earl - Ltr, Ejecting from a B-66 at Toul-Rosiers AB, France.

McDonald, William Major, USAF (Ret.) - Email re B-66B and Pathfinder operations.

Mendonca, Robert Lt/Colonel, USAF (Ret.) - 17/47BW documentation; 42TEWS reports.

Milam, Jim Colonel, USAF (Ret.) - email EW training.

Mosby, Jerry MSGT, USAF (Ret.) - emails Deployment Shaw to Tan Son Nhut; Swamp Fox, Cuban Missile Crisis.

Neutz, Lloyd Major, USAF (Ret.) - emails re RB-66 operations out of Yokota/SEA.

Norden, John A. Lt/Colonel, USAF (Ret.) - email re 1965 combat missions SEA.

Orr, Donald E. Lt/Colonel, USAF (Ret.) - Documentation relating to 1959 escort of Air Force One by B-66B bombers from 47BW.

Parrott, Cliff - Emails re B-66 design, build, delivery to Shaw AFB, SC; operations at Shaw.

Pase, Roy - Email re Victor Alert at 47BW.

Presto, Edward - Email re deployment from France to SEA; B-66 intrusion into China while under MiG attack.

Pruss, Ted - Ltr, re Itazuke operations.

Roland, Valentine - email re MiG attack on RB-66C; shoot down of 2 MiGs by F-4Cs.

Seech, Jack - email re IR equipped RB-66Bs flying out of Tan Son Nhut.

Stamm, Robert W. Lt/Colonel, USAF (Ret.) - emails re B-66 operations Yokota to Toul-Rosieres; RB-66 air refuelings. Memorandum: Reflections on the 11th and 12th Tactical Reconnaissance Squadrons, 67TRW.

Starke, Richard Major, USAF (Ret.) - emails: Black Sea operations.

Story, James B. Lt/Colonel, USAF (Ret.) - email re B-66 operations in Europe.

Taylor, Tom - Email re RB-66C mods, ALQ-87/QRC-160 testing, pods on RF-101s, SEA deployment 1965.

Tippin, Stanley Lt/Colonel, USAF (Ret.) - Flight logs/emails & related documentation re ASQ-96 testing at LAX/Eglin AFB, FL.

Underwood, Alexander, MSGT, USAF (Ret.) - B-66 Story: Pins, Canopy, Lanyard - reflections on flying the B-66B Brown Cradle in France and Vietnam.

Welch, Robert, Lt/Colonel, USAF (Ret.) - emails re initial deployment of RB-66C to Vietnam.

Wells, Vaughn - email re B-66 intrusion into China while under MiG attack.

Whitlock, Thomas, Colonel, USAF (Ret.) - Emails re wheel explosion at Kirtland AFB, NM; aircraft stability.

Wooden, Steve - email re Hangar Queen at Spangdahlem, 10TRW; problems with control surfaces.

Ziegler, Robert - email re Victor Alert at 47BW.

INDEX

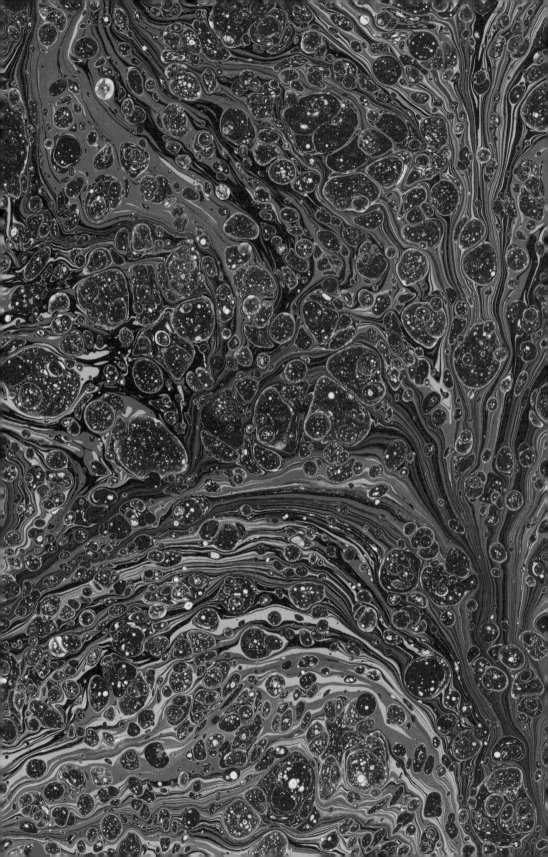